W9-CDE-013

ons
ndon

Chris Baty &
Karla Zimmerman

Chicago

The Top Five

1 Lincoln Park Zoo
It would be a must-see even if it weren't free (p83)

2 Sears Tower
Sky-high views from Chicago's tallest tower (p70)

3 Millennium Park
The arty new kid on the block (p69)

4 Navy Pier
A playground for Chicago kids and young-at-heart adults (p75)

5 Field Museum of Natural History
Where dinosaurs still roam the earth (p108)

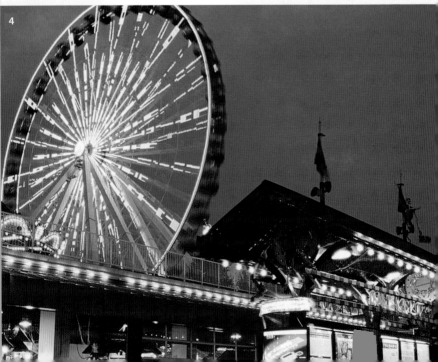

Published by Lonely Planet Publications Pty Ltd
ABN 36 005 607 983

Australia Head Office, Locked Bag 1, Footscray, Victoria 3011, ☎ 03 8379 8000, fax 03 8379 8111, talk2us@lonelyplanet.com.au

USA 150 Linden St, Oakland, CA 94607, ☎ 510 893 8555, toll free 800 275 8555, fax 510 893 8572, info@lonelyplanet.com

UK 72–82 Rosebery Ave, Clerkenwell, London, EC1R 4RW, ☎ 020 7841 9000, fax 020 7841 9001, go@lonelyplanet.co.uk

© Lonely Planet Publications Pty Ltd 2006
Photographs © Ray Laskowitz and as listed (p284) 2006

All rights reserved. No part of this publication may be copied, stored in a retrieval system, or transmitted in any form by any means, electronic, mechanical, recording or otherwise, except brief extracts for the purpose of review, and no part of this publication may be sold or hired, without the written permission of the publisher.

Printed through SNP Security Printing Pte Ltd, Singapore

Lonely Planet and the Lonely Planet logo are trademarks of Lonely Planet and are registered in the US Patent and Trademark Office and in other countries.

Lonely Planet does not allow its name or logo to be appropriated by commercial establishments, such as retailers, restaurants or hotels. Please let us know of any misuses: www.lonelyplanet.com/ip.

Although the authors and Lonely Planet have taken all reasonable care in preparing this book, we make no warranty about the accuracy or completeness of its content and, to the maximum extent permitted, disclaim all liability arising from its use.

Contents

The Authors

Chris Baty

Chris got his start in freelance writing while in grad school at the University of Chicago, penning record reviews for the student newspaper. Having made the discovery that he liked writing about Jonathan Richman's dance moves much more than the anthropological phenomena he was allegedly there to document, Chris swerved from his academic path and ended up in Oakland, California, where he now makes a living writing about everything from travel to country music to professional wrestling. Chicago remains his true love, though, and Chris spends an inordinate amount of time poring over gapersblock.com and carefully planning his next swim in Millennium Park's Crown Fountain.

Karla Zimmerman

Karla lives in Chicago, where she has been testing bar stools and cheering on the hopeless Cubs for the past 16 years. She writes travel features for newspapers, books, magazines and radio, and has contributed to *National Geographic Traveler,* National Public Radio, the *Chicago Tribune* and *Time Out Chicago*, among many others. She has authored or coauthored several of Lonely Planet's US and Canadian titles; she wrote the Shopping and Excursions chapters for this book.

LONELY PLANET AUTHORS

Why is our travel information the best in the world? It's simple: our authors are independent, dedicated travelers. They don't research using just the Internet or phone, and they don't take freebies in exchange for positive coverage. They travel widely, to all the popular spots and off the beaten track. They personally visit thousands of hotels, restaurants, cafés, bars, galleries, palaces, museums and more – and they take pride in getting all the details right, and telling it how it is. For more, see the authors section on **www.lonelyplanet.com**.

PHOTOGRAPHER

Ray Laskowitz

For photographer Ray Laskowitz, photographing Chicago was a break from the heat and humidity of his hometown of New Orleans. Although he had passed through Chicago on many occasions, he had never really spent much time there. He was delighted to find a wealth of cultural diversity, very friendly people and great food. He has been photographing all manner of subjects for almost 30 years, and lists making travel images among his favorite work.

CHRIS' TOP CHICAGO DAY

Wake up at the crack of 10am with a cup of locally roasted Intelligentsia coffee and a pre-breakfast slice of leftover Giordano's pizza. Properly caffeinated, I ride my bike down to the Gold Coast's Original Pancake House for my *real* breakfast. From there, it's an easy pedal northwards through Lincoln Park to the free zoo, dropping in on the unbearably cute meerkat and the irresistibly creepy Wall of Cockroaches. If there's a Cubs game I catch the Clark St bus up to Wrigley Field; if not, it's down to the Loop on the Brown Line to check out the Joseph Cornell boxes at the Art Institute. My lunch is a Chicago-style hot dog devoured by the Cloud Gate sculpture in Millennium Park. Then it's all about the Blue Line as I head to Wicker Park's Rodan for electronic music, videos and a heaping plate of wasabi tempura fries. Capped off, of course, with a late-night hot fudge sundae at Margie's.

Introducing Chicago

You're standing in the cool waters of Millennium Park fountain. It's late afternoon, and warm embers of sunlight glint across the windows and spires of the Loop skyline. Your thoughts are right where they should be: on dinner. Deep-dish pizza? Or Lake View Thai? Suddenly, a mouth opens on the fountain above you. The crowd gasps and you fumble for your camera as a long jet of water arcs out from the fountain's lips. Children shriek and surge toward the waterfall, and you scramble right after them. Dinner can wait until after a quick dip.

Welcome to Chicago, a city brimming with immersive experiences. Like the new Crown Fountain in Millennium Park – built as high art but known far and wide as the city's best water ride – Chicago has a way of providing much more than you bargained for. Though it ranks third behind Los Angeles and New York size-wise, the Windy City is a vast and vibrant metropolis – a place where running shoes and a good train map are a must if you even hope to make a dent in the city's copious and unique attractions.

Unique? You bet. This is the city that invented both Twinkies and house music, after all. The Chicago spirit is one of unlikely improvisations and delicious discoveries. You can taste the restless adventuring in its weird, pan-everything restaurants, see it in the myriad of groundbreaking, rib-tickling theater companies, and feel it in the Blue Line train that roars along ancient tracks, depositing today's crop of computer programmers and next-wave filmmakers among the towering forests of ancient skyscrapers.

LOWDOWN

Population 2.9 million

Time zone Central (GMT minus six hours)

Nicknames Second City, Windy City, Chi-town (pronounced *shy*-town), City of Big Shoulders

Downtown hotel room $125

Chicago-style hot dog $2.50

Cup of coffee $1.50

El fare $1.75 (transfer 25¢)

Essential drink Old Style beer ($2)

No-no Unflattering comparisons to New York

And there's something else unique about Chicago: people are downright friendly to tourists here. It's kind of creepy for those accustomed to big-city brusqueness. If you ever find yourself lost along Lake Michigan, or disoriented in Daley Plaza, you can count on Midwestern hospitality to help get you out of the jam. Just pantomime distress and a Good Samaritan will be along shortly. (Note: this kindliness does not apply to Chicago's bloodthirsty population of taxicab drivers, who help maintain the city's urban credibility by honking and yelling at anything that moves.)

The quintessential Midwesternness of the natives – cheerful, hardworking and a little conservative – acts as a steadying anchor for the city's more adventuresome impulses. For all its eagerness to embrace the new, Chicago is still a place where steak wins out over soy, and where a half-pound of crème-filled doughnuts is considered a legitimate breakfast.

There is something, though, that Chicago's artsy, reckless yin and no-nonsense yang both agree on: drinking. True to its long-established reputation as a bootlegger's paradise, Chicago is a place that knows how to throw a party. The best times to come to Chicago are when the scores of city-sponsored music and food festivals transform the lakefront Grant Park into a boogying, carousing mass of humanity. June, with its Gospel and Blues Festivals, is especially prime, as are September and October. Summers are deadly hot and miserably humid, and winters…sheesh. If you come in the snowy season, plan on spending *a lot* of time getting to know the area's museums and drinking establishments (not such a bad fate, really).

The other best time to come to Chicago is between conventions. During the larger trade shows, power-suited attendees will snap up most of the city's available rooms. Even if you're lucky enough to find a room, you'll end up paying twice or three times what you should. If your arrival date happens to coincide with a major convention, plan on reserving far, far in advance.

Not that you're going to end up spending much time in your room, no matter how much you had to pay for it. From the bustling energy of the Loop to the pageantry of the Magnificent Mile, Chicago has a way of pulling visitors out of their shell and into the surging melee of the friendly, expansive city. Bring a towel and a change of clothes. When you come to Chicago, you're bound to get wet.

ESSENTIAL CHICAGO

- **Art Institute of Chicago** (p67) Miraculous finds in every room.
- **John Hancock Center Signature Lounge** (p79) At dusk, you'll cry into your beer, it's so beautiful up here.
- **The lakefront on a bicycle** (p120) The wind in your hair, the Loop in your sights.
- **Wicker Park & Bucktown** (p90) Quirky shopping + live music + food = love.
- **Wrigley Field** (p85) The Cubs' defeat and a great time are both guaranteed.

City Life

City Life

CHICAGO TODAY

Whether or not you make it out to Second City for some comedy while you're in Chicago, you're going to see acts of tremendous improv. Much of the dynamism on the streets of Chicago today comes from the city's bullheaded determination to invent its own cultural trends and lifestyle niches, regardless of the winds blowing in from New York or California.

That energetic, maverick spirit is most visible in the city's creative realms. Between the Pilsen artists creating canvases from the innards of taxidermized animals to the Andersonville thespians whose stock-in-trade is staging 30 hilarious plays in 60 minutes, Chicago is a city that marches to the beat of its own drummer. A desperately overworked drummer who waits tables in the Ukrainian Village during the day and plays in five different indie rock bands at night.

But Chicago is not all song and dance. The city's steely business engine is firing on all cylinders these days. The Chicago area is home to industry titans such as Boeing, McDonald's and Motorola, and it's in Chicago boardrooms and brainstorming sessions that the future of American products and popular culture is born.

Or reborn, we should say. After a nervous economic slowdown in the early 2000s, Chicago is dusting itself off, both socially and culturally. Now there's a craving for kicks; a hunger for the new. In 2003 the culinary trend was upscale comfort foods. Now sushi prevails, and Indian *chaat* houses – with their array of exotic chutneys and spices – are packed.

It's a time of marvels in the city. Millennium Park is a beaming source of pride for the city, and the park is just one tiny portion of an overall citywide makeover currently underway. The pace of change in Chicago at this moment feels faster and grander than it has in a decade. When developers announced in 2005 that they hoped to build the tallest building in the United States on Chicago's skyline, the declaration seemed almost self-evident. And the fact that the planned structure would be filled with condos, rather than office spaces, seemed even more obvious. Every walk-in closet and cramped parking garage in the city seems to be undergoing condo-fication, as decrepit old buildings get renamed things like 'the Loftarium,' and a younger generation looks to settle down somewhere closer to the action.

The lofts in the Loop also help the new residents avoid the hellish commutes that have only been growing more grueling each year. In 2005 Chicago moved up a spot in the 'most clogged freeways' list. Only Los Angeles can top Chicago's gridlock now, and the average Windy City resident spends a week and a half every year stuck in traffic.

HOT CONVERSATION TOPICS

So you're in a bar in Wrigleyville and you want to strike up a conversation with the native sitting next to you. Here are some opening salvos that are guaranteed to get Chicagoans talking:

- What they should really do with the former Meigs Field is put some affordable housing on it.
- The money spent on creating a downtown Theater District for big traveling productions is an insult to Chicago's history of innovative theater.
- Enforcing the cell-phone ban for drivers has been a worthwhile use of the police department's time.
- Rechristening Marshall Field's as 'Macy's' is exactly the fresh start the old mercantile dinosaur needs.
- Roger Ebert is a tool for the liberal elite.
- A corrupt local government that gets stuff done is better than an honest one that doesn't.
- Logan Sq is the new Wicker Park. And Humbolt Park is the new Logan Sq.
- All the kids flopping around in the Crown Fountain have ruined the sanctity of Millennium Park.
- Steve Bartman did something every one of us would have done in the same situation.
- The man to end the Daley reign will be Jesse Jackson Jr.

The traffic is a downside of the city's rising profile; one of several urban planning conundrums that Chicago faces as it grows into the 21st century. From the ongoing loss of historic neighborhoods to a long legacy of public-housing mismanagement and racial segregation, Chicago still has some tough problems ahead of it to solve.

But ultimately, the unifying forces in Chicago outnumber the divisive ones. Sports in Chicago are a perfect example. Regardless of their age, ethnicity or annual income, Chicagoans come together in the city's stadiums and sports bars to share the experience of watching their home team get trounced. Despite the constant losses of Chicago teams, locals keep the faith and keep each other's spirits high, buying tickets and reading the sports pages to stay up-to-date on the latest games.

It's not the most realistic behavior for the fans, perhaps, but it's perfectly in keeping with a city fanatically dedicated to doing things its own way. And they must be doing something right, because 2005 marked the first baseball World Series championship since 1917 for the White Sox.

CITY CALENDAR

Chicago stages an exhausting array of festivals, concerts and events. The moment the thermometer registers a single degree above freezing, you can count on some group lugging out a stage and speakers to Grant Park to celebrate the good news. We've listed some of the major events here, but a complete listing would likely provoke hernias in anyone who tried to pick it up: between March and September alone, Chicago throws over 200 free day- or weekend-long shindigs. And that's not counting the events that last all summer, like the **Grant Park Music Festival** (www.grantparkmusicfestival.com), which presents top-notch free pop and classical concerts in Millennium Park's Pritzker Pavilion most Wednesdays, Fridays and Saturdays.

The biggest events of the summer – Blues Fest, the Jazz Fest and Taste of Chicago – all go down in Grant Park, and many of the major parades take place along S Columbus Dr nearby. But even if you can't make it to Grant Park during festival time, you're still likely to get caught up in some local celebration. Check the **Mayor's Office of Special Events** (www.cityofchicago.org/specialevents) website for details.

A word on holidays: public holidays in Chicago will likely affect business hours and transit schedules. And while holidays have little impact on shopping, eating and entertainment opportunities, things like banks, post offices and government offices will be shuttered for the day. Plan your important mail runs and bank deposits around the holidays listed below to ensure you don't get shut out in the cold (or the heat, as the case may be).

JANUARY & FEBRUARY

Ah, January. The city wakes to another year with a lampshade on its head and fuzzy memories of the night before. These are the months with the most snowfall in Chicago,

TOP FIVE QUIRKY CHICAGO EVENTS

- **Carol to the Animals** (Lincoln Park Zoo) Hordes of people sing Christmas tunes to perplexed zoo critters.
- **Fast Forward Film Festival** (Around Chicago) Every two months, the organization sponsors a weekend movie-making binge in which teams shoot and edit a three-minute movie overnight, then screen their work to a packed house the next day. Sleep is not included.
- **Mike Royko Memorial 16in Softball Tournament** (Grant Park) The World Series for a uniquely Chicago brand of softball is named for the late, great Chicago writer who loved the sport. The ball's bigger, the games are shorter and no one wears mitts (ouch). Held on the last weekend in July.
- **Polapalooza** (Congress Theater) In June, this Polish and Czech music blowout features a dozen bands, lots of beer and, of course, sausage.
- **Smelt Season** (Chicago beaches) When the tiny fish swarming into Chicago harbors to spawn are met by amateur anglers, nets and deep-fat fryers from April 1 to April 30.

the coldest temperatures – average 24°F (–4°C) – and the fewest festivals. Sigh. New Year's Day is celebrated on January 1. Martin Luther King Jr Day is celebrated on the third Monday of January. President's Day falls on the third Monday of February.

CHINATOWN'S CHINESE NEW YEAR

☎ 312-225-6198
A massive celebration with millions of little firecrackers, a parade and more takes place in Chinatown. Exact date varies according to the ancient Chinese calendar.

BLACK HISTORY MONTH

☎ 877-244-2246
Events and exhibits all around the city celebrate African-American history in February.

CHICAGO AUTO SHOW

☎ 630-495-2282; www.chicagoautoshow.com
Detroit, Tokyo and Bavaria all introduce their latest and finest vehicles to all the excited gear-heads in a huge show mid-February at McCormick Place.

SPRING FLOWER SHOW

☎ 312-742-7529; www.garfield-conservatory.org
Zillions of blooms are at their best at the Garfield Park Conservatory and Lincoln Park Conservatory, just north of the zoo, from mid-February to mid-May.

MARCH

Is that the sun making a long-awaited reappearance? It is! Hope reappears on the horizon, as the daily high moves up to 45°F (7°C) and Chicagoans can feel their toes and noses for the first time in weeks. Easter Sunday brings out tentative forays to backyards for egg-hunts.

CHICAGO FLOWER & GARDEN SHOW

☎ 312-222-5086; www.chicagoflower.com
It may be sleeting outside, but this mid-March garden event on Navy Pier puts a little spring into everyone's step.

ST PATRICK'S DAY PARADE

☎ 312-942-9188; www.chicagostpatsparade.com
This city institution includes dyeing the Chicago River green near the N Michigan Ave bridge, and a parade along S Columbus Dr by the Buckingham Fountain.

HELLENIC HERITAGE GREEK PARADE

☎ 773-994-2222; Halsted St, from Randolph St to Van Buren St
The streets of Greektown come alive in this celebration and parade, held the last Sunday of the month.

APRIL

The windiest month in the Windy City. The temperatures are rising, and can break 60°F (16°C) during the day, but freak snowstorms still threaten all those cute little blooms and buds appearing throughout the city.

EARTH DAY

☎ 312-742-7726; www.naturemuseum.org
The Peggy Notebaert Nature Museum and the Chicago Park District sponsor an annual Earth Day with lots of activities and exhibits, and even a little ecothemed comedy. Held on the fourth Saturday of the month.

MAY

The average temperatures are hovering around 70°F (21°C), and Chicagoans are starting to mow their lawns in earnest. Memorial Day falls on the last Monday.

POLISH CONSTITUTION DAY PARADE

☎ 773-282-6700

Chicago's Polish community comes out to party at this annual parade, held on the first Saturday in May on S Columbus Dr.

CINCO DE MAYO FESTIVAL & PARADE

☎ 773-843-9738

This annual bash celebrating the Mexican army routing the French in 1862 draws more than 350,000 people to Pilsen with food, music and rides on the first Saturday in May.

ART CHICAGO

☎ 312-587-3300; www.artchicago.com

This massive midmonth festival in Grant Park is a Very Big Deal in Chicago's art world. Over 3000 artists are featured, and citywide events are held at museums and galleries.

GREAT CHICAGO PLACES & SPACES FESTIVAL

☎ 312-744-3370

This architectural festival includes boat, bike and walking tours of some Chicago treasures on the third Saturday in May.

JUNE

Highs are over 80°F (27°C), lows down to 50°F (10°C). Grant Park is packed most weekends with festivalgoers glad to be outdoors. Summer – and the festival season has arrived. This is a great time to be here.

CHICAGO TRIBUNE PRINTERS ROW BOOK FAIR

☎ 312-222-3986; www.printersrowbookfair.org

This event features thousands of rare and not-so-rare books on sale, plus author readings, at the beginning of the month on the 500–700 blocks of S Dearborn St.

CHICAGO BLUES FESTIVAL

☎ 312-744-3370

This highly regarded three-day festival features more than 70 performers on six Grant Park stages on the first June weekend.

CHICAGO GOSPEL FESTIVAL

☎ 312-744-3370

Hear soulful gospel music on the second weekend of the month in Grant Park.

ANDERSONVILLE MIDSOMMARFEST

☎ 773-664-4682; www.andersonville.org

The Swedes go nuts at this Andersonville event, featuring plenty of Swedish dances, songs and maypole activities. Held midmonth.

CHICAGO COUNTRY MUSIC FESTIVAL

☎ 312-744-3370

A hoedown takes over Grant Park on the third weekend of the month, with music spanning the gamut from slick new artists to old-school favorites like Loretta Lynn.

GAY & LESBIAN PRIDE PARADE

☎ 773-348-8243

Held the last Sunday in June along Halsted St, the Pride Parade is packed with colorful floats and revelers.

TASTE OF CHICAGO FESTIVAL

☎ 312-744-3370

This enormous festival closes Grant Park for the 10 days leading up to Independence Day on July 4. More than 60 local eateries serve some of the greasiest food you've ever tried to rub off your fingers. Live music features on several stages.

JULY

The weather takes a turn for the hot and humid, with average highs around 85°F (29°C). Block parties take over the streets and flip-flops become the city's official footware. Independence Day is celebrated on July 4.

FOURTH OF JULY FIREWORKS

Though it really happens on July 3, the day before Independence Day, the city pulls out all the stops for this spectacular concert, which features a long fireworks show bursting out over Lake Michigan and a stirring rendition of Tchaikovsky's 1812 Overture, played with gusto by the Grant Park Symphony Orchestra. For the best view, try the embankment east of Randolph St and Lake Shore Dr.

CHICAGO FOLK & ROOTS FESTIVAL

☎ 773-728-6000; www.oldtownschool.org
Midmonth, one of Chicago's coolest organizations throws this two-day party that features everything from alt-country to Zimbabwean vocalists.

CHICAGO OUTDOOR FILM FESTIVAL

☎ 312-744-3315
Running from mid-July to the end of August, this Grant Park festival is like a drive-in but without all the obnoxious cars. Screened on Tuesdays at sundown, the films are all classics, and are preceded by Chicago shorts.

TALL SHIPS CHICAGO

☎ 312-744-3370
The 30 or so wind-powered ships that show up for this celebration at month's end travel through the St Lawrence Seaway on their way to Navy Pier. Shipboarding encouraged.

VENETIAN NIGHT

☎ 312-744-3315
Late in the month, yacht owners decorate their boats with lights and parade them at night in Monroe Harbor to the adulation of the rabble. Fireworks follow.

AUGUST

The bad news: you're most likely to get rained on in August. The good news: it's so hot, you probably won't care. Temperatures range from 72°F (22°C) to 84°F (29°C), and the beaches are crowded.

BUD BILLIKEN PARADE

☎ 877-244-2246; www.budbillikenparade.com
Held on the second Saturday of the month, this huge parade features drill teams, dancers and floats; it runs along Martin Luther King Dr, from 39th St to 51st St, and features a picnic in Washington Park afterwards.

NORTH HALSTED MARKET DAYS

☎ 773-883-0500
The costumes and booths get wild at this gay neighborhood street festival, held in mid-August.

CHICAGO AIR & WATER SHOW

☎ 312-744-3370
The latest military hardware flies past the lakefront from Diversey Pkwy south to Oak St Beach. Acrobatic planes and teams perform both afternoons on the third weekend in August. North Ave Beach is the best place for viewing.

VIVA! CHICAGO LATIN MUSIC FESTIVAL

☎ 312-744-3370
This festival, held the third weekend in August in Grant Park, features *cumbias,* merengue, salsa and ranchero music delivered by some of the biggest names in the industry.

CHICAGO JAZZ FEST

☎ 312-744-3370
Usually held at the very end of August in Grant Park, the 25-year-old Chicago Jazz Fest features national and international acts.

SEPTEMBER

Fall colors begin to strut their stuff towards the end of the month, and the mild weather makes this an excellent time for a visit. Labor Day is on the first Monday.

MEXICAN INDEPENDENCE DAY PARADE

☎ 773-328-8538
You'll see lots of cute kids dressed to the nines at this colorful and loud event, held in early September along Columbus Dr.

AROUND THE COYOTE ARTS FESTIVAL

☎ 773-342-6777; www.aroundthecoyote.org
A great introduction to the alternative world of the Wicker Park and Bucktown arts community, this series of gallery open houses and performances features hundreds of local artists in and around the Flat Iron Building at 1579 N Milwaukee Ave. It is typically held on the second weekend in September.

CELTIC FEST CHICAGO

☎ 312-744-3370
Bagpipers, storytellers and Celtic culture abound at this midmonth festival.

BERGHOFF OKTOBERFEST

☎ 312-427-3170
The Berghoff restaurant's Oktoberfest holds true to the traditional German dates

in mid-September. Huge crowds cram Adams St at the Berghoff during the week.

GERMAN-AMERICAN FESTIVAL

This much more enjoyable Oktoberfest happens on the third weekend of the month in the heart of the old German neighborhood at Lincoln Sq, 4700 N Lincoln Ave.

WORLD MUSIC FESTIVAL

☎ 312-742-1938

Musicians and bands from around the world come to Chicago late in the month to perform and take classes with the masters.

AUTUMN GARDEN SHOW

☎ 312-746-5100; www.garfield-conservatory.org

Beginning in late September, the Garfield Park Conservatory shows off its autumn finery in a wonderful display.

DAY OF THE DEAD CELEBRATIONS

☎ 312-738-1503

The Mexican Fine Arts Center Museum in Pilsen puts on exciting Day of the Dead events over two months, running from late September to mid-December.

OCTOBER

Temperatures have dropped substantially from the previous month – lows around 42°F (6°C) and highs of 63°F (17°C). Halloween is one of the mayor's favorite holidays and the city pulls out all the stops for it. Columbus Day is on the second Monday.

CHICAGO BOOK FESTIVAL

☎ 312-747-4999

The Chicago Public Library organizes this month's worth of readings, lectures and book events, held throughout the city.

CHICAGO INTERNATIONAL FILM FESTIVAL

☎ 312-425-9400; www.chicagofilmfestival.org

Early in the month, scores of films compete during this weeklong event.

LASALLE BANK CHICAGO MARATHON

☎ 312-904-9800; www.chicagomarathon.com

On the third Sunday of the month, runners from all over the world compete on the 26-mile course, cheered on by a million spectators.

CHICAGOWEEN

☎ 312-744-3370

From mid-October through Halloween, the city transforms Daley Plaza into Pumpkin Plaza and sets up a Haunted Village for kids.

NOVEMBER

The first wee snowflakes have begun to fall over the city. The thermometer registers a cold 40°F (4°C). Late in the month, Michigan Ave takes on a cheery glow. Veteran's Day is celebrated on the 11th and Thanksgiving falls on the fourth Thursday.

MAGNIFICENT MILE LIGHTS FESTIVAL

☎ 312-642-3570

The lighting of all 600,000 tree lights takes place midmonth, after which the little fellas continue to twinkle sweetly on Michigan Ave north of the river through January.

TREE LIGHTING CEREMONY

☎ 312-744-3370

The mayor flips the switch to light up Chicago's Christmas tree in Daley Plaza on Thanksgiving Day.

CHICAGO'S THANKSGIVING PARADE

☎ 312-781-5681

The annual turkey day parade runs along State St from Congress St to Randolph St.

DECEMBER

Everyone loves Chicago's museums, and this is a perfect opportunity to get to know some of them (not to mention the underground walkways connecting some parts of the Loop). Lows are around 20°F (-6°C). Christmas falls on the 25th.

KWANZAA

☎ 312-744-2400

The increasingly popular African-American holiday celebration adds new events and locations each year. It is celebrated from December 26 through January 1.

NEW YEAR'S EVE FIREWORKS AT BUCKINGHAM FOUNTAIN

☎ 312-744-3370

Ring in the New Year with fireworks at Chicago's famous fountain.

CULTURE

The cultures of some big cities – Berlin, say, or New York – can be tough nuts to crack. Visits to these hectic, polished places are invariably exciting, but can also be frustrating for those looking to move beyond the tourist-customer role and dive into the social fabric of the city. No matter how many times you go back to the same store or eat at the same restaurant, it seems, the cities' cultures remain tucked politely out of view.

Not so with Chicago, a city that wears its passions, beliefs and lifestyles on its sleeve. You'll find that almost everywhere you go in the Windy City – bars, stadiums, museums, El stops – you'll have a chance to get to know real Chicagoans and gain insight on what makes them tick. What follows is an overview of Chicago culture, a bare-bones guide to help launch your own explorations of this open and friendly city.

IDENTITY

When actor (and *Friends* star) David Schwimmer's Lookingglass Theatre Company opened its sparkling, renovated digs in the Water Tower Water Works building, its choice for an inaugural play seemed odd – an adaptation of Studs Terkel's nonfiction book *Race: How Blacks and Whites Think and Feel about the American Obsession*. However unusual, the play was perfect for Chicago, where a decidedly heterogeneous population grapples with racial understanding and misunderstanding on a daily basis.

The latest census tells the story pretty clearly. Chicago's 'diversity index' – a percentage likelihood that two randomly chosen people in an area will be of different races – is 74%, a full 25% higher than the US as a whole. Blacks actually outnumber Whites in Chicago, with Latinos running a close third.

Despite the high diversity, integrated neighborhoods are rare in Chicago, with Blacks tending to live on the city's south and west sides, Latinos showing a strong presence in Pilsen and many areas on the North Side, and Asians in Chinatown and along Argyle St in Uptown. Whites tend to make up the bulk of the population in areas visited by tourists (which is why visitors who don't venture off the beaten path will get a mistakenly monochromatic – and much less interesting – view of the city).

The paucity of mixed-race neighborhoods has its roots in Chicago's history, including the 'White Flight' of the 1950s, '60s and '70s, where Whites on the South, West and Southwest Sides engaged in panic selling at the first sight of Black families moving onto the block.

Whatever its many causes, segregation is a fact of life in Chicago. Locals tend to socialize with others of their race and class and live in areas where most of their neighbors look and talk like they do. This makes visiting Chicago's distinct neighborhoods sometimes feel a little like globetrotting – it's not uncommon to find stretches of the city where stores advertise their specials only in Polish, or where understanding the difference between *damas* and *caballeros* is essential in avoiding some serious bathroom embarrassment. (Hint: the *damas* door is for women.)

Segregation among Chicago Whites falls along ideological and political lines, with artists and alternative types living and socializing in out-of-the-way neighborhoods like Logan Sq and Humboldt Park, carefully avoiding wealthier neighborhoods like Lincoln Park, where postcollegiate, career-oriented conservatives tend to roam.

Though Chicago sometimes feels like a series of homogenous enclaves, there are plenty of places where the lines between groups are blurred. Music – especially dance clubs – has helped bring young Chicagoans

TOP FIVE PEOPLE-WATCHING SPOTS

- **Art Institute of Chicago** (p67) See tourists and locals posing in front of some of the country's greatest artworks.
- **Cloud Gate** (p69) Sit on the steps by this shiny Millennium Park sculpture and watch the city stroll by.
- **Damen Avenue Blue Line El stop** (p128) The disembarkation point for Chicago's coolest shopping corridor.
- **Murphy's Bleachers** (p125) On a game day, the Cubs mania here reaches dangerous levels.
- **Navy Pier Ferris wheel** (p76) Okay, so the people are very small from up here, but you sure can watch a lot of them at once.

together, giving them a chance to forget about skin color and class, and address the *real* problem of the day: how to get the phone number of the hottie by the bar.

Religion-wise, Catholicism is running strong in the Windy City. How strong? Consider the tale of 'Our Lady of the Underpass,' where an outline of the Virgin Mary appeared near the on-ramp for the Kennedy Expressway at Fullerton in 2005. The sighting prompted candles, vigils and weeping from the city's believers (and a lot of eye-rolling from everyone else). Chicago has the largest Catholic archdiocese in the country, and ongoing immigration from Catholic countries like Mexico and Poland ensures that those pews will stay full for decades to come. In Black neighborhoods, Baptist churches are the mainstay, and Chicago has a sizable Jewish population as well. As with most major cities in the US, though, church attendance in the under-40 set is declining, and faith often takes a back seat to issues of friendship, recreation and family.

Old St Patrick's Church (p94)

For younger folks, hashing out what it means to be a Chicagoan requires its own sort of devotional intensity. Chicagoans have a zealous faith in their city, but also nurse a deep-seated insecurity that comes from being regularly discounted by coastal tastemakers. Chicago's 'Second City' nickname once proudly proclaimed the town's powerhouse size and status in the country – from 1890 to 1990, only New York could give the headstrong city a run for its money. When Los Angeles supplanted Chicago in 1990, it confirmed the worst fears of Chicago's backers – that Chicago had become a flyover city. The drop from second to third, however insignificant to outsiders, threw the city's civic identity into a muddle, sparking an ongoing debate on what, exactly, it meant to be a Chicagoan.

It's a question that local scholars and philosophers have taken to heart. One of Chicago's best-known writers, Studs Terkel, has made a celebrated career out of collecting vivid oral histories that often feature Chicagoans puzzling out issues of personal and national identity. Terkel's humanistic torch has been carried on by the radio program *This American Life,* broadcast by Chicago's WBEZ. Hosted by Ira Glass, the program draws heavily on the stories of ordinary Chicagoans to help illuminate the truths and fictions of an uncertain age.

Even lofty academics here love to roll up their sleeves and wrangle with issues of Chicago identity. The University of Chicago – best known for ivory-tower philosophizing and its phone book's worth of Nobel Prize winners in economics – regularly uses its massive brain trust to help understand what makes locals tick. To wit: the popular U of C professor Richard Epstein wrote a high-level economics paper about 'Dibs in the Snow,' a quirky Chicago tradition of squatters' rights for winter parking spaces. Another U of C prof published a groundbreaking ethnography called *Slim's Table* on the Black regulars at a Hyde Park cafeteria.

All of the civic and academic navel-gazing has yet to produce an acceptable answer explaining what it means to be a Chicagoan in the 21st century. And in some ways, Chicago's insecurity about its identity has become a vital part of its self-conception. It's an ongoing issue that will come up in a myriad of guises when you talk to locals. Here's hoping they never figure it out; watching the debate unfold is one of the great joys of a visit to this ever-changing city.

LIFESTYLE

The pace of life in Chicago has two speeds: driving and not. When behind the wheel – which they are frequently – Chicagoans move at a velocity that would make jet pilots nervous. Pause for a fraction of a second too long at a stop sign or slow down at a yellow light, and you can be sure you'll hear about it from the car behind you. The vibe on the streets is bossy, loud and more than a little chaotic. Witness the famed 'Chicago Left' – as soon

ONLY IN CHICAGO

Ever since the world witnessed the first majestic Oscar Mayer 'Wienermobile' rolling through the city streets of Chicago in 1936, the city has wowed the world with a series of inventions and discoveries made in the city. Along with the Wienermobile, you can thank Chicago for bringing you:

- roller skates (1884)
- softball (1887)
- the cafeteria (1895)
- malted milkshakes (1922)
- Hostess Twinkies (1930)
- pinball (1930)
- controlled atomic reaction (1942)
- Peter Cetera (1944)
- first baseball curse involving a goat (1945)
- daytime TV soap operas (1949)
- Weber Grill (1951)
- Lava Lite 'Lava Lamps' (1965)
- house music (1977)

as the light turns red, rows of cars 10 deep gleefully fling themselves into the intersection, blocking oncoming cars to a chorus of honks as the left-turners slowly push their way through the clogged crossing.

This ire-raising Chicago Left is indicative of the city's go-go pace in the mornings. Once Chicagoans have made it safely to work, they move at a less breakneck speed. That's not to say people loaf – jobs and working are taken seriously here, and questions about occupation are usually one of the first bits of information strangers will exchange. Accountant or auto mechanic, the workers in Chicago tend to clock in early and eat lunch on the go. Unlike New Yorkers, Chicagoans leave work at sane hours: the Loop empties around 5:30pm on weeknights, as commuters pile into outbound trains and hit the traffic-clogged highways for the journey home.

Home – be it an apartment, condo or Astor St mansion – is a sanctuary for Chicagoans. Even in more modest neighborhoods, lawns are kept tidy and weed-free, and fixing up the house on weekends is a time-honored creative outlet for older Chicago males. The typical pied-à-terre for 20- and 30-somethings, though, is an apartment.

The flats in Chicago tend to be large and long, and often shared by a friend or two. Backyards and back porches are common, and in warm weather these outside areas serve as staging grounds for regular barbecues and impromptu get-togethers. A gas grill and a collection of mismatched lawn chairs are must-have accoutrements for young Chicagoans.

For those without the space to entertain, the city's copious neighborhood parks serve as much-loved areas for cookouts and picnics. In spring and summer the parks are overrun with parents keeping one eye on the cooking and the other on gleefully screaming offspring.

At the fall of night (or the onset of winter), though, Chicago hits the bars. Free of California's niggling health concerns and New York's antismoking laws, Chicago is a bar-based bacchanal. The anything-goes philosophy, coupled with late bar hours on weekends and easy availability of cabs and public transportation, makes Chicago a place where having a beer or two is often just a warm-up for a long evening of merriment.

The city's bars are also the choice hunting grounds for Chicago singles. Online dating, while growing in popularity, still carries a stigma that a drunken hookup in a Wrigleyville

SMOKE ALL YOU WANT, BUT, HEY, CAREFUL WITH THAT PHONE

Visitors to Chicago may be surprised by the smell of something old and familiar in restaurants: cigarette smoke. Yep, you can still smoke in restaurants and bars here, though the subject is currently a hot-button issue in the city. Smoking supporters – restaurateur and former Bears coach Mike Ditka foremost among them – have managed to keep a ban at bay by predicting a total collapse of the restaurant and bar industry in the city should it happen. Aldermen are shy about pushing the issue because the mayor refuses to say which side of the debate he's on. It may seem like a typical politician's dodge, but Mayor Daley isn't a man afraid to take unpopular stands. In 2005 he backed a movement that successfully made it illegal to drive and use a hand-held cell phone in the Chicagoland area. The move was heralded as visionary by some and idiotic by others, who point out that Chicagoans can still talk themselves into distraction while driving, they just need to use a headset while doing so. Regardless, Chicago police have begun issuing $50 tickets to drivers they see yakking without the hands-free headsets. So if you're cruising Lake Shore Drive and want to use your phone to share the moment with a long-distance friend, be sure you pull over lest it become a *very* expensive call.

sports bar apparently does not. Make no mistake, the majority of Chicago watering holes are friendly but not *that* friendly, and table-hopping and number-exchanges aren't an integral part of most pubs' scenes. But if you are looking to get to know Chicago on a more, ahem, intimate level, you'll find a plethora of establishments to suit your needs.

Chicagoans also make plenty of time for diversions that don't involve beer coasters. With so many musicians in Chicago, almost everyone knows someone in a band, and getting out to see the friend's group is a common Saturday activity. Heading out to a serious play is a beloved pastime for older Chicagoans; the younger audiences spend their money at the raucous improv and comedy houses like Second City and IO.

FOOD

Though the city's foodies would kill us for saying so, the Weber Grill restaurant at the corner of State and Grand says a lot about Chicago's food scene. Only the Windy City could make an unequivocal success out of a theme restaurant based on backyard cookouts.

Chicagoans simply love meat. And not in that fussy 'nouvelle cuisine' way, where a sliver of steak tartare lists artfully against a single asparagus tip. In the Chicago restaurant world, you'd better serve heaping portions with plentiful sides or you're not going to last long. You can see the city's populist tastes writ large on *Check, Please!*, the local TV show on channel 11 that allows everyday citizens to play restaurant critic and bring down the hammer on Chicago eateries whose serving sizes are found lacking.

It's fitting, then, that Chicago's best-known culinary contributions are ones that will never show up on a Weight Watchers plan. If you really want to sample the culinary delights of the city, seek out a Chicago hot dog (see the boxed text, p160). Or try some ribs, another Chicago speciality. Ribs have their roots in African-American culture on the South Side. The preferred variation, slabs of pork baby back ribs, get the long, slow treatment in an oven, usually with lots of smoke. The sauce is sweet, tangy and copious. Another popular variation is rib tips, the cheap bits of pork chopped away near the ribs. These meaty pieces can be a real mess to eat but are usually excellent.

Chicago-style pizza is absolutely nothing like any pizza that was ever tossed in Italy; lofting one of these deep-dish leviathans in the air could actually hurt someone. To prepare their mammoth pies, pizza chefs line a special pan – not unlike a frying pan without a handle – with dough and then pile on the toppings. These must include a red sauce, chopped plum tomatoes and a mountain of shredded American-style mozzarella cheese. Optional extras include Italian-style herb sausage (actually almost mandatory), onions, mushrooms, green bell peppers, pepperoni, black olives and more. Although Pizzeria Uno (p144) likes to claim that it invented Chicago-style pizza in the 1940s, some of its rivals also vie for credit.

You'll find a good representation of regional American cuisine throughout the city, but it's in purely ethnic cuisine where Chicago excels. The waves of immigrants who populated the city have created restaurants devoted to scores of cultures. Italian remains the most common variety by far, with pasta joints in every corner of the city. The breadth of cuisine served in these places ranges from northern Italian to Sicilian, as well as plenty of local interpretations. Chicago's improvised 'Italian' dishes include garlicky chicken Vesuvio (sautéed chicken with potatoes and peas) and Italian beef sandwiches.

Mexican food and flavors also shine in Chicago. Gringo kitchens like Topolobampo (p142) and Flo (p161) play with Mexican spices and staples, and real-deal *taquerias* stay open all night throughout the city, giving carousing Chicagoans a place to go after the bars close. And in the bars themselves, the tamale has become as common as Pabst Blue Ribbon, thanks to enterprising Mexican heroes who lug cooler-loads of homemade pork and chicken delights though the smoky pubs after midnight.

Don't get us wrong, Chicagoans do not subsist entirely on barbecue, 5lb pizzas and Mexican fast food. The fine-dining scene here is world class, spurred on by the millions of business travelers who come here and are every night in need of a setting that will impress a client or colleague. As Spiaggia chef Tony Mantuano did in 2005, the heads of Chicago's kitchens regularly pull in James Beard awards for culinary excellence, and some of the country's most innovative dishes can be found on Chicago menus.

Regardless of whether Chicagoans are doing it in a Kentucky Fried Chicken or Charlie Trotter's (p146), dining out is a key setting for socializing. The 'dinner and a movie' outing is still very much alive in the city, and weekend brunch is similarly beloved. For 20- and 30-somethings especially, a late breakfast outing to the nearest upscale diner is an ideal way to start a Saturday (not to mention an efficient way to get the scoop on any scandal from the bar-hopping the night before).

FASHION

Chicago is a casual town. The apex of fashion for most men is a pair of khakis and a Gap button-down shirt. Women's dress is similarly low-key, valuing comfort over high fashion. In the scorching summer, much of the population looks like they're heading off for a lifeguard shift at the local pool – flip-flops, shorts and T-shirts are acceptable attire most everywhere in the city. (Though arctic-cold air-conditioning in shops and movie theaters can sometimes make tank tops a regrettable choice.)

In winter, fashion disappears entirely beneath layers of Thinsulate, Gore-Tex and North Face merchandise. Even when summer is a distant memory, though, a surprising number of Chicago residents have the bronzed look of someone who commutes in from the Bahamas, courtesy of discreet visits to Chicago's 100-plus tanning salons.

These tanned and fashion-forward locals are often horrified by the lack of attention their peers pay to appearance. Happily for the fashionistas, things are changing. A quick tour of Wicker Park boutiques turns up a wealth of hip, international labels mixed in with high-concept, high-priced outfits from local designers. These sleek little stores have virtually eliminated the lag between Milan runways and Chicago shop displays, allowing Chicagoans to spend $200 on a belt just like they do in New York.

Chicago even boasts its own underground fashion scene. Hipsters proudly sport the latest creations from local button-maker Busy Beaver, and attend ramshackle, box-wine fashion shows where works by XNX Designs and fashion artist Cat Chow debut before making their way to Ukrainian Village resale shops.

If you plan on hitting the clubs while you're in town, tight black clothing is the rule for both men and women. Some clubs don't allow blue jeans, tennis shoes or baseball caps; if you only brought Levi's and Adidas and still want to go dancing, do yourself a favor and call ahead to make sure there won't be a problem.

SPORTS

Chicago doesn't exactly have a recent reputation for domination in the sporting arena. While its teams aren't laughingstocks of their leagues, they haven't been the subject of ticker-tape parades along State St either.

Despite it all, almost every Chicagoan will declare a firm allegiance to at least one of the city's teams, and going to a game is a great way to bond with Windy City natives. For details on venues and getting to games, see Watching Sports (p200).

Baseball

Winning is not a tradition in Chicago baseball. The Cubs, one of Chicago's two baseball teams, last hoisted the World Series trophy four generations (yes, that's *generations*) ago. In 2003 they hoped to turn things around with a new manager, Dusty Baker. After the team's fourth-place finish in its division (of six teams) in 2005, Cubs' fans love for Baker had soured, and there were widespread calls for his resignation.

The disappointment had as much to do with lingering feelings about the season the year before, when the Cubs nearly made it to the World Series. The team's momentum was stopped during a particularly heartbreaking (and now legendary) event, when a die-hard fan named Steve Bartman tried to catch a foul ball, inadvertently preventing fielder Moises Alou from making a crucial out. Alou missed it, and the opposing team rallied and won the game, turning the tide of the series and putting the Cubs out of contention for the billionth year in a row.

With little to celebrate on the field, fans have instead celebrated the field itself. Known as 'the Friendly Confines,' Wrigley Field dates from 1914. Although often changed through the years, it retains its historic charm and remains the smallest and most intimate field in major-league baseball. Popular new stadiums in other cities, such as Baltimore and Denver, have borrowed heavily from its charm.

Cubs fan at Wrigley Field (left)

Few experiences in Chicago can equal an afternoon at Wrigley: the clatter of the El, the closeness of the seats, the spectators on the rooftops, the derisive return of the opposing team's home-run balls, the often-friendly folks around you and, yes, the green leaves of the ivy glistening in the sun. Whether it's riding the El to the Addison stop, grabbing a pre-game beer on the patio at Bernie's or going a little nuts in the bleachers, each Cubs fan has his or her own rituals that make a day at Wrigley not a spectator sport but an almost religious experience.

Chicago's other baseball team, the White Sox, plays in less charming surroundings. US Cellular Field (shortened to 'the Cell' by many) was one of the last large, antiseptic stadiums to be built before trends began favoring smaller designs like Wrigley. The team itself labors under one of the least popular owners in baseball, Jerry Reinsdorf (who also owns the Bulls), a perplexing man who makes no effort to win any popularity contests.

Like the Cubs, the White Sox hadn't seen a championship win in a long, long time. But the 2005 team changed that, with talented Sox pitcher Mark Buehrle being named as a starter for the American League All-Star game, and the Sox celebrated as the World Series champions at last.

As is the case with many ballparks, the best reason to go to the Cell is the fans. They love the team despite the stadium and owner, and they direct many creatively profane slogans toward the latter. And the food isn't bad either – the tasty burritos for sale on the mall-like concourse are only part of a long list of good and greasy choices. Finally, there's the fireworks – if the Sox hit a home run at night, plumes of color shoot into the air.

Basketball

Chicago is in a similar slump on the basketball court. The Bulls, once the stuff of legend, haven't posed much of a threat since the 1997–98 season, when Michael Jordan was still with the team. The controversial owner Jerry Reinsdorf allowed Jordan, coach Phil Jackson, Scottie Pippen and other key parts of the Bulls juggernaut to leave after that championship year, and since then the team has had a run of largely miserable seasons. In 2004, though, the Bulls showed some spirit, and the fans rallied behind scrappy point guard Kirk Hinrich and rookie Ben Gorden. The team made the play-offs for the first time since 1998, but injuries ended up hampering its scoring potential, and it didn't make it to the championships. The Bulls play on the West Side in the huge United Center.

Football

Once upon a time the Chicago Bears were one of the most revered franchises in the National Football League. Owner and coach George Halas epitomized the team's no-nonsense, take-no-prisoners approach. The tradition continued with players such as Walter Payton, Dick Butkus and Mike Singletary and coach Mike Ditka. In 1986 the Bears won the Super Bowl with a splendid collection of misfits and characters, such as Jim McMahon and William 'the Refrigerator' Perry, who enthralled and charmed the entire city. Over 15 years of mediocrity have taxed all but the most loyal fan's allegiance. And as if they needed more infamy attached to their reputation, the Bears unveiled the $580 million renovation of their home, Soldier Field, in 2003 to almost unanimous derision.

When the Bears' great hope – starting quarterback Rex Grossman – sustained a serious ankle injury in a preseason game in 2005, hopes for a turnaround were dashed. But Chicago's defense is one of the best in the league, and hope springs eternal that the untested new quarterback Kyle Orton may end up bringing a miracle to Soldier Field.

Hockey

The Stanley Cup last came to Chicago in 1961, but Chicago's hockey team, the Blackhawks, wins enough games every year to keep its rabid fans frothing at the mouth.

The fans' fervor is a show in itself, though it never quite reaches the bloodletting antics of the players on the ice. Games against the Detroit Red Wings and the New York Rangers call for extra amounts of screaming, and the crowd always seems to come with bottomless reserves of lung power. The action starts with the traditional singing of the national anthem, which here becomes a crowd performance of raw emotion.

Soccer

Thanks to support from Chicago's Latino and European communities, Chicago's soccer team, the Fire, has been attracting a growing fan base. The team has made the Major League Soccer playoffs several times in recent years and won the championship in 1998.

The Fire played its final season at Soldier Field in 2005; in 2006 it moved to a stadium in the town of Bridgeview, southwest of the Midway Airport.

MEDIA

Newspapers

Chicago is a newspaper town, one of the few cities in the country to support two competing dailies, the *Chicago Tribune* and the *Sun-Times*. The **Tribune** (www.chicagotribune.com), the more highbrow of the two, excels at arts and culture coverage; its writers tend to be articulate experts. For entertainment and dining information, check out the *Tribune*'s www.metromix.com. The **Sun-Times** (www.sun-times.com) is a tabloid and, true to its format, favors sensationalized stories that play up sex, violence and scandal. Recently it has drawn criticism for its palpable lean to the far right under conservative owner Conrad Black. Among other well-known writers, the *Sun-Times* is home to America's most famous movie reviewer, Roger Ebert.

Both newspapers produce digest versions for 20-something readers. The *Tribune* hatched its *Red Eye* first. Sensing a good thing in the making, the *Sun-Times* raced to release its own youth-oriented paper, the *Red Streak*. Both papers look almost identical, and though they're popular (partially because both are given away for free in parts of the city), no one in Chicago can tell you which company puts out which paper.

The best weekly publication in the city is the free **Chicago Reader** (www.chireader.com). The mammoth, four-section *Reader* combines a long cover story with a catalog of virtually everything going on in town, from theater to live music to offbeat films to performance art. Navigating your way through the behemoth, which brims with cool comics and popular advice columns, can take up the better part of a very pleasurable morning.

Other arts papers include **New City** (www.newcitychicago.com), a slim weekly that is a little edgier than the *Reader*; the *Onion* satirical news weekly, which also features

TOP FIVE MULTIMEDIA MUSTS

- **Chicago Historic Plaques** Chicago brings its neighborhood histories to life with these informative historical guides, spread throughout the city.
- **The Devil in the White City** Eric Larson's book is a stunning look into a moment when Chicago was the absolute center of the universe.
- **GapersBlock.com** Chicago's best website, written by and for locals.
- **Chicago Reader** Everything you need to dive into the city's cultural offerings.
- **This American Life** Radio stories of Chicago and the world beyond.

Chicago-specific entertainment listings in its 'AV Club' section); and the monthly *UR*, which offers extensive coverage of DJ and club culture. The **Chicago Free Press** (www.chicagofreepress.com) is the main gay weekly, with local, national and entertainment news.

Magazines

The weekly *Time Out Chicago* launched in 2005, much to the displeasure of the *Reader*. The magazine eschews the deeper journalism of the *Reader* for short, colorful articles and a week's worth of the best entertainment events, shopping sales, museum and gallery exhibits, restaurants, and gay and lesbian goings-on. If you're planning on staying more than a couple days in the Windy City, *Time Out Chicago* is a worthwhile investment.

Monthly **Chicago** (www.chicagomag.com) features excellent articles and culture coverage. But for visitors, the magazine's greatest value lies in its massive restaurant listings. The hundreds of expert reviews are up to date and indexed by food type, location, cost and more. It's worth picking up to find the latest and greatest places in Chicago's vibrant dining scene.

Moguls and would-be moguls consult **Crain's Chicago Business** (www.chicagobusiness.com), a business tabloid that regularly scoops the dailies despite being a weekly.

Chicago also has a wealth of locally produced indie magazines. **Venus Magazine** (www.venuszine.com), a hip and entertaining read, covers up-and-coming women in music. **Roctober** (www.roctober.com) features an array of articles on old and new music, along with a healthy dose of weird comics. Beautifully designed *Stop Smiling* keeps an eye on Chicago's indie rock world. The **Baffler** (www.thebaffler.com) has been dishing out informed cultural criticism for nearly a decade. You can pick up all of Chicago's offbeat publications at Quimby's (p231).

Radio

Thanks to the time they spend driving to and from work, most Chicagoans listen to at least an hour of radio a day. National radio personalities in Chicago include Paul Harvey, the amazingly stalwart conservative on WGN, and Ira Glass, host of WBEZ's *This American Life.*

During some parts of the day, WGN (720AM) broadcasts from its street-level studio in the Tribune Tower on N Michigan Ave. You can press your nose up against the glass and make faces at hosts such as the duo of Kathy O'Malley and Judy Markey, two irreverent delights.

WBEZ (91.5FM), the National Public Radio affiliate, is well funded and popular. It's the home station for the hit NPR shows *This American Life* and *Wait, Wait Don't Tell Me*. Located on Navy Pier, **WBEZ** (☎ 312-832-9150) produces radio dramas and dramatic readings. Some of these recordings are taped before a live audience: call for details.

WBBM (780AM) blares news headlines all day long, with traffic reports every 10 minutes. The left-wing Air America network can be found on WCPT (850AM). Its right-wing counterpoint is located nearby at WLS (890AM). And if you're just hungry for the latest sports scores, tune into the ESPN-run WMVP (1000AM).

You'll find the most interesting music on WXRT (93.1FM), a rock station that aggressively avoids falling into any canned format trap. Other notables in Chicago are WHPK (88.5FM), the eclectic University of Chicago station, and Q101 (101.1FM), a modern rock station that features hyperpopular morning DJ Mancow

TV

Chicagoans love their TVs, though DVD subscription companies like Netflix have definitely reduced the amount of aimless channel surfing that goes on in the Windy City. Chicago's local network affiliates are little different from their counterparts in other large cities. WLS (channel 7, the ABC affiliate) is generally the ratings leader for newscasts, covering the latest murders and mayhem from the streets. WMAQ (channel 5, the NBC affiliate) is a ratings loser after years of being adrift. WFLD (channel 32, the Fox affiliate) features the usual Fox neon effects, but also has the well-respected Walter Jacobsen, who has been around for decades.

Other stations in town each have their own niches. WGN (channel 9) is owned by the Tribune Company. Its meteorologist, Tom Skilling, will tell you more than you could ever

CHICAGOESE 101

You'll be hard-pressed to find the kind of thick accents that *Saturday Night Live* once parodied in skits where heavy-set Chicago sports fans sat around eating 'sassages' and 'sammiches' and referring to their football team as 'Dah Bears' and their city leader as 'Dah Mare.' There is, however, a host of Chicagoisms that you may encounter when talking to locals. Here are some of the most common:

Downstate Used dismissively by Windy City residents to refer to all the backwards areas in Illinois (ie everywhere outside of Chicago city limits).

The Drive Lake Shore Drive (also referred to as 'LSD').

FIB Said about Chicagoans by Wisconsin residents. Short for 'Fucking Illinois Bastards.' Do not use this one unless provoked.

The Friendly Confines Affectionate name for Wrigley Field (named after the 'Welcome to the Friendly Confines of Wrigley Field' sign inside the stadium).

Lincoln Park Trixies Twenty- and 30-something sorority girls who carry Coach purses and drive Volkswagen Jettas around the famously yuppie neighborhood.

The Picasso The unnamed sculpture by Picasso located in front of the Daley Center, often used as a meeting point.

Stoopin' Socializing on the front porch of a home or apartment, usually with friends and beers.

want to know about the weather, but that's good if you're traveling. The station also shows all the games played by fellow Tribune-empire denizens, the Cubs, and carries Bulls games as well. WTTW (channel 11) is a good public broadcasting station, home of the beloved restaurant-review show *Check Please!*, as well as *Chicago Tonight* at 7pm weekdays, which takes an in-depth look at one of the day's news stories.

LANGUAGE

As elsewhere in the US, English is the major language spoken here. In the heart of some ethnic enclaves you'll hear Spanish, Polish, Korean or Russian, but almost all business is conducted in English. Midwestern accents tend to be a bit flat with just a touch of nasal twang, but compared to other parts of the US, most of the English you'll hear is pretty standard – the middle of the country has always produced a large share of plainspoken TV announcers.

In your wanderings you may also encounter 'Black English,' a variation of English that's spoken by many African-Americans. Generally reserved for casual encounters with friends, its lexicon and cadences can be cryptic to non-native English speakers.

ECONOMY & COSTS

First the good news: it's possible to eat and drink very well in Chicago and not spend an arm and a leg. And thanks to the occasional (though increasingly rare) free days at local museums, coupled with the discounts offered in the invaluable *Chicago Guidebook of Special Values* coupon book available in the Visitor Information Center in the Cultural Center (p68), the chances are good you can get in without paying full price at some attractions.

Now the bad news: your hotel room is going to cost you. The rack rates on rooms here are outrageous. This is partially because of the 15.4% hotel tax levied by the city, which Chicago depends on to maintain its parks and public buildings. But the city is only partially to blame for the price tags on hotel and motel rooms. Business travelers are the other culprits. Because of the huge number of conventioneers in Chicago at any given moment, hotel rooms are almost always at a premium. And unlike leisure travelers, the business travelers 1) have to come here whether they want to or not, and 2) get reimbursed for their lodging costs.

The high demand and looser purse strings of conventioneers have put hotels and motels in a position where they charge whatever the market will bear. And with the city getting such a substantial cut of the revenues, there's little incentive for anyone to bring the prices down.

HOW MUCH?

El ticket from O'Hare to Loop $1.50
Near North hotel, one night $150
Art Institute admission $10
Small bag of Garrett's caramel popcorn $2
One hour of meter parking $1
Taxi ride from Loop to Navy Pier $7
Blues club cover charge $15
Martini at the Green Mill $6
Cup of coffee $1.50
Taco in Pilsen $1.25

With visitors being such a heady income stream for the city – around $15 billion in expenditures each year – you'd think they'd try to give them a break. The brutal nature of supply and demand, however, makes that unlikely. Given the facts, there are two things you can do to save money on lodgings in Chicago. First, shop around as much as possible on the Internet before committing to anything – sometimes the room price listed on a discount travel website can be almost $100 lower than the price quoted by the reservation agent at the hotel (see the boxed text, p237, for tips on bidding for travel). Second, start wooing those long-lost family members you have in Chicago. Aunt Bertha's foldout couch is probably sounding better all the time.

GOVERNMENT & POLITICS

Chicago's official motto is 'City in a Garden,' but the late *Tribune* columnist Mike Royko had more than one supporter when he suggested changing it officially to 'Where's mine?' The entire system of Chicago city politics is based on one hand washing the other, with Mayor Daley overseeing a city council of 50 aldermen, each elected every four years.

Maintaining so many politicians and their related offices and staffs is expensive, but proposals to shrink the city council always run aground for the simple reason that the voters like things as they are. Certainly, this amount of bureaucracy is ripe for abuse and corruption (more on that later), but for the average Chicagoan it works well. You got a pothole in front of your house? Somebody stole your trashcan? The neighbor's leaving banana peels all over your stoop? Mundane as they are, these are the kinds of matters that directly affect people's lives, and they can be taken care of with a call to the alderman.

With the districts so small in size, the politicians and their staffs can't afford to anger any voters, because angry voters start voting for somebody else. Because of this, the aldermen (the term refers to both men and women) are constantly trying to put themselves in a position to do someone a favor. During your visit to Chicago, you'll likely see traces of this mercenary friendliness on billboards and bus shelter ads – aldermen rent them out to help spread their phone numbers and offers of help to their constituents.

Politics is a popular spectator sport in Chicago, in part because of the ongoing scandals associated with the aldermen and other elected officials. In 2005 local followers of political

BARACK OBAMA

CNN called him 'the Democrat's calm rock star.' He calls himself 'a skinny guy from the South Side with a funny name.' His supporters are eager to call him 'Mr President.' Whatever the moniker, Chicago resident and freshman Illinois Senator Barack Obama is clearly the man everyone's watching on the political landscape. Obama was raised in Hawaii and Indonesia, the child of a White mother from Kansas and an African father from Kenya. After graduating magna cum laude with a law degree from Harvard, he moved to Hyde Park and began working as a community organizer, helping residents of Chicago's South Side cope with a recent round of steel-plant closings. 'Chicago,' he says, 'is where I found my manhood, my home, my roots.' After teaching at the University of Chicago law school, Obama entered politics as an Illinois State Senator in 1996. Eight years later, he declared his intention to run for a vacant US Senate seat. Though he first seemed destined to be crushed by better funded, more experienced opponents, he ended up winning the seat in the largest landslide victory in Illinois history. And then there was the small matter of 'the speech,' a stirring oration Obama gave at the Democratic National Convention in Boston in 2004. The Democrats scheduled him for the prime-time slot reserved for up-and-comers, and afterwards more than one pundit commented on Obama's presidential bearing. At 44 years old, Obama is likely too young for a 2008 White House bid. But 2012? Who knows. The future is definitely looking bright for this skinny guy from the South Side with a funny name.

sleaze had a field day as details of the 'Hired Truck scandal' began coming to the surface. The city's Hired Truck program was designed to mete out city trucking work to private companies. But it turned out that certain of the companies were paid from the city coffers to simply let their trucks sit idle and contractors were reported to have given monetary incentives for their contracts. By September, 2005, the investigation had resulted in 32 charges and 23 guilty pleas, and a growing number of questions about the Mayor's knowledge of the tit-for-tat patronage systems at work in his administration.

Above Mayor Daley and the pack of aldermen is Illinois governor Rod Blagojevich (blah-*goy*-oh-vich), a Democrat who replaced incumbent George Ryan in 2003. (Ryan was about to begin a trial on federal racketeering charges as the Hired Truck scandal widened.) Blagojevich (referred to in Chicago as 'Blago') immediately made some enemies in the Windy City by rejecting a proposal to allow city-sponsored gambling. And he has continued to remain in the Chicago news for his acrimonious public disagreements with his father-in-law, Richard Mell, a Chicago alderman. Mell has accused Blagojevich's chief fundraiser of offering campaign donors positions on state boards in exchange for contributions to Blagojevich's war chest.

Ah, politics.

ENVIRONMENT

Pity the Chicago River. The ugly stepsibling of majestic Lake Michigan, the river has been rerouted, polluted and abused for most of the city's history. Despite the fact that it essentially saved Chicago's population from gruesome death by waterborne disease (p52), up until the last decade the poor thing has gotten all the respect of a garbage disposal. This was brought up all over again in 2004 in a legendary incident where the driver of the Dave Matthews Band tour bus dumped the vehicle's septic tanks into the river while driving across the Kinzie St Bridge. He missed the river, but managed to score a direct hit on a Chicago Architecture Foundation tour boat that happened to be passing underneath the bridge.

Happily, the dumping was an isolated incident in the river's otherwise-upward trajectory since the 1980s. After monitoring and remediation efforts, the levels of toxic chemicals in the river have declined. Bass fishing has actually become a popular pastime on the upper reaches of the river. The city has also started putting in a series of public river walkways, and mandating developers working along the riverfront to do the same. You won't see Chicagoans inner-tubing down it any time soon, but the river is clearly making a comeback.

Also thriving are the city's populations of wild animals. Coyote and deer both live in the large parks on the outskirts of the city, and sometimes have been known to wander into the Loop. Raccoons are also plentiful, and if you drive through suburban neighborhoods like Oak Park at night, your car headlights are likely to catch them as they bound across the road.

No animal species does better in Chicago than rats. Walk through any alley and you'll see the 'Target: Rats' sign that explains when the most recent dose of poison was laid out for the wee beasties. A pet peeve of Mayor Daley's, the rats have met a formidable foe in the city's Streets & Sanitation department. One brigade of agents actually patrols the alleys of infested neighborhoods, attacking the rodents with golf clubs. 'We work as a team,' one employee reported to the *Sun-Times*. 'One will whack, while the other one will get the final kill.'

Curiously, for a city with so many young people, recycling is not on the radar here. The inconvenient 'blue bag' system the city has in place is just too much bother for most locals, and the absence of a deposit on bottles or cans further lowers the incentive to recycle. News reports about disreputable recycling companies simply throwing the recyclables away after collection has further eroded the program's allure. In 2005 the city sought to lead by example by asking students around the world to submit designs for recycling containers which would be placed next to garbage cans. You can see the winning design in operation on the streets of the Loop from 2006.

Along with rats and recyclables, visitors to Chicago in the summer should be sure to keep an eye out for an infestation of a more beautiful sort. Lightning bugs – a flying beetle with a phosphorescent abdomen – are prevalent in Chicago in July and August. A park full of their twinkling lights is one of the most beautiful things you'll see in the Windy City.

Arts

Arts

It was a supremely fitting moment. The ImprovOlympic comedy theater was celebrating its 25th anniversary in 2005 with a huge improv bash at the Chicago Theatre. Founder Charna Halpern had wooed back famous alumni such as Rachel Dratch, Mike Meyers, Amy Poehler and Andy Richter for the sold-out event. The lights dimmed, the show started and the microphones promptly stopped working. After an hour's delay, the assembled comedians were outfitted with hand-held microphones – not exactly the optimum setup for spontaneous group comedy. But in the end, the impediments simply fueled the show, and the group pushed against the boundaries the way a sprinter would a starting block.

This, in essence, is the story of Chicago arts. As the eyes of the arts world continue to monitor preening locales such as Paris and London, Chicago walks a path of offhand brilliance. In Chicago, plays, art openings and dance performances take place not just in historic theaters and beautifully austere hardwood spaces, but also in storefronts, in alleyways, and anywhere else that will have them. It's a scene that thrives on making its own magic and creating its own momentum. Despite the nonchalance and humility of Chicago artists, the work they do reverberates throughout the world, and visitors to the Windy City get a front-row seat on trendsetting stars and cultural movements that will turn up as tomorrow's headlines in newspapers around the world.

This is an especially good moment for the Chicago visual arts. The gallery scene that was once contained in the River North area has jumped its banks, surged into the West Loop and continued on down to Pilsen. Those who can't get wall space in galleries happily take it to the streets. Art students and graffiti artists undertake midnight 'improvements' with political posters, colorful stickers and that much-maligned Chicago invention, spray paint.

Of all the hot entertainment options in Chicago, though, it is theater that has brought the city its most recent notoriety. Theater is its own universe, with household names like John Malkovich serving time as actors and founding members of local companies. Big theater companies such as the Goodman and Steppenwolf routinely stage premieres by world-famous playwrights, and Chicago's cadre of underground, itinerant companies put on productions wherever they can rent space. (Like theater, the music scene in Chicago is bursting at the seams with talented players and larger-than-life figures. For more on music, see p34.)

Whatever your artistic pleasure, being here is a great opportunity to immerse yourself in the unpretentious scene that has been the launching pad for some of the biggest names in American arts and entertainment. So grab a *Reader* and buy some tickets already.

VISUAL ARTS

Some cities struggle for decades to create one viable arts area. Chicago has given birth to three, and each has its own identity and unique offerings. The cooperation and communication between the three camps can be spotty at best, and it mirrors a certain Chicago split between ragged, warts-and-all avant-garde art, and more traditional object-based or representational pieces that patrons will want to hang in their living rooms.

That high art–low art divide that critics and gallery owners are so conscious of is often gleefully crossed by the artists themselves. Comic artists like Chris Ware (p31) take the art form to an almost architectural level of perfection, painter Kerry James Marshall's recent work plays with comics

Field Museum of Natural History (p108)

TOP FIVE ART MUSEUMS

- **Art Institute of Chicago** (p67) Impressionist masters are just the beginning.
- **Mexican Fine Arts Center Museum** (p97) Ambitious, innovative museum celebrates Mexican and Mexican-American artists.
- **Museum of Contemporary Art** (p79) Controversial, thought-provoking pieces aplenty.
- **Museum of Contemporary Photography** (p108) This small South Loop museum is a divine art snack.
- **Smith Museum of Stained Glass Windows** (p76) Leave the kids playing on the rides and be awed by the glass masters.

and superheroes, and photographer Rashid Johnson gives nods to both 19th-century photographic techniques and hip-hop.

All of this juxtaposition of old and new is a far cry from the Chicago art scene of 100 years ago, which was largely designed to show the world that Chicago was a city 'that got taste.' The industrialists funded works that evoked imperial Europe in their grand scale. Meanwhile, the same industrialists bought up the latest European art. During this period, society matron Bertha Palmer and others gathered much of the Art Institute's collection of impressionist paintings.

During the 1920s Chicago art veered towards modernism and realism, led by the likes of Rudolph Weisenborn and Wassily Kandinsky. The gritty realm of the city was perfect inspiration for these new forms of art, with their hard-edged portrayals of urban life. The essence of life on the South Side was captured by Archibald Motley Jr, one of many who spent most of their creative lives documenting the cultures and subcultures of Chicago.

Styles fragmented with the emergence of surrealism and abstract expressionism in the mid-20th century. Chicago artists who experimented with the new, unconventional techniques included Karl Wirsum and James Falconer.

Today's big names on the contemporary art scene in Chicago include Juan Chavez, who makes sculptural collages and beautiful large-scale mosaics, textile artist Ai Kijima, abstract painters (and brothers) Shan and DaHang Zhou, photographer/interactive machine-maker Sabrina Raaf, and abstract landscape painter William Conger.

The wealth of artists from different parts of the globe working in a host of different media has made it difficult to pinpoint a 'Chicago style' or even define what makes someone a 'Chicago artist.' The issue was brought to the fore in 2005, when former Chicago gallery owner and local arts booster Paul Klein launched a movement to open a modern art museum devoted exclusively to Chicago art. The gallery is still millions of fundraising dollars away from ever being built, but Klein's website (www.artletter.com) is a worthwhile read for his list of current must-see gallery shows, as well as the message board where Chicago artists hold juicy discussions about the local scene.

For a more institutional take on the local scene, check out the **Chicago Art Dealers Association** (CADA; www.chicagoartdealers.org) website or the *Chicago Gallery News* guide. You can get the publication at almost any gallery in River North and West Loop, as well as some of the more established Pilsen galleries. The CADA sponsors the annual two-week VISION art festival, which brings gallery owners and artists from all over the world to Chicago each July.

The other big annual art event is **Art Chicago** (www.artchicago.com), an international contemporary art fair that takes place under a tent in Grant Park's Butler Field. Art Chicago and the VISION festival have also inspired some rival festivals for underground artists, most notably the **Nova Young Art Fair** (www.novayoungartfair.com), which debuted in the West Loop in 2005. The Nova fair – which takes place over four days in late April – is run by artistic gadfly Michael Workman, who writes an articulate column on the local art scene for the *New City* alternative weekly paper.

GALLERIES & EXHIBITIONS

The River North neighborhood (p75) is home to the city's oldest gallery hub. The rents here are some of the most expensive in the city, and the galleries are established places where art patrons might drop $20,000 for a large abstract painting or piece of sculpture from an internationally known late-career artist.

The other 'serious' gallery district is in the still-transitioning West Loop neighborhood (p95). Amid the meatpackers and cold storage warehouses here, you'll find edgier, more

FIVE TO KNOW IN CHICAGO ARTS

- **Liz Armstrong** The take-no-prisoners columnist for the *Reader* drinks like a fish, hits more shows and parties than a dozen of her peers and lives to write about it in her 'Chicago Antisocial' column.
- **Ira Glass** The creator and host of the WBEZ program *This American Life* oversees a show that manages to document all facets of our perplexing, disturbing and ultimately lovable nation.
- **Studs Terkel** At 93 years old, the oral historian and master conversationalist has put a small library's worth of amazing stories into print.
- **Chris Ware** The first comic artist ever to have work in the Whitney Museum's biennial exhibit, Ware has forever raised the bar for the funny pages. Miserable weather? Grab a copy of Ware's *Jimmy Corrigan* at Quimby's and spend a wonderful afternoon under its spell.
- **Mary Zimmerman** As the director and ensemble member of Chicago's Lookingglass Theatre, Zimmerman is one of those bright suns around which entire scenes revolve.

risk-taking art from younger artists, including many painters and photographers, and multimedia collages from Chicago minds. Pieces tend to run anywhere from $500 to $2500 a pop, and the gallery owners are often artist-entrepreneurs in their 30s and 40s who graduated from the School of the Art Institute. To get a closer look at the West Loop art scene, be sure to check out the walking tour on p123.

The third gallery district is in Pilsen (p98). Long the scrappy, shoeless cousin of the West Loop, Pilsen has come into its own in the last two years. In Pilsen, you're most likely to find work by an all-Chicago roster of creative types. The works are also the most affordable in the city; at some shows you can fall in love with a painting and cart it off for under $200.

PUBLIC ART

Much to local sculptors' delight, in 1978 Chicago began to require that developers include financial provisions for public art in their projects, specifically 1% of the total cost. True to the city's art ubiquity, you can see the results throughout the Loop, in parks and along the city's traffic medians.

Chicago is a city that is not afraid to put large-scale public art in very prominent positions. These days, all-weather works by Picasso, Miró and Alexander Calder are as much a familiar part of urban Chicago as the Sears Tower, and the opening of Millennium Park (p69) brought a series of new iconic pieces from international artists to the city.

For a walking tour of public art in the Loop, see p121. And for the scoop on a fun, interactive underground public art project involving music, see the boxed text, p38.

THEATER, COMEDY & IMPROV

If anyone was surprised that the London *Guardian* named Chicago the theater capital of the US in 2004, they sure as hell weren't from Chicago. Acting has long been high art in this town, and Chicagoans are well aware of the treasures they have in local theater companies.

Moviegoers familiar with the scenery-chewing performances of John Malkovich and Gary Sinise already know the tenets of the Chicago style of acting, for which the two Steppenwolf Theater principals receive much credit: a fiery intensity marked by loud, physical acting. Beginning in the 1970s, the tough, machine-gunfire bursts of dialogue in David Mamet's taut dramas only added to Chicago theater's reputation for hard-edged, raw emotion.

The Chicago theater scene today is much more than a bunch of guys having dramatic conversations about life and death. As in the past the focus is on works by local playwrights, but these days those works are as likely to be realized by the nimble puppetry of the Redmoon Theater Company or the funny productions of the House Theatre Company.

And then there's improv, the whole other Chicago universe. Improvisational acting, which forces troupes to create sketches on the fly and change plots and characters according to audience members' whims, came into its own in the 1950s at the University of Chicago.

It's since become a part of life here, and the improv scenes at ImprovOlympic (now called IO after a lawsuit threat from the International Olympic Committee) and Second City have launched the careers of such comedians as Bill Murray, Tina Fey, Rachel Dratch and Stephanie Weir. The genre's openness to newcomers – IO will put on stage anyone who signs up for classes – has made the Chicago improv scene a beacon to office cutups everywhere, stoking the dream that they may someday follow dozens of other Chicagoans to Hollywood or, at the very least, *Saturday Night Live*.

Things only got brighter in the Chicago theater scene in 2000, with renovations and openings in the Loop's 'theater district.' The list of new and renovated theaters includes the gorgeous Cadillac Palace Theater, the Chicago Theater and the Ford Center/Oriental Theater. The former Shubert Theatre was brought back to gilded life as the LaSalle Bank Theatre in 2005, adding yet another option to the vibrant nightlife scene in the downtown area.

DANCE

In the evening, the sidewalks of the Loop theater district are filled with well-dressed patrons making their way into the latest Broadway shows. Even if many of these productions started in New York, the dancing on display inside is pure Chicago. The Windy City is best known for its pioneering work in jazz dance – the razzle-dazzle, high-kicking flamboyant style that forms the heart of musical theater. (Those who saw the 2002 movie musical *Chicago* witnessed some great displays of Chicago-style jazz dance in action.) The man most commonly associated with the style is Chicago's Gus Giordano, who founded Dance Incorporated Chicago in 1962. Four years later, the company evolved into Giordano Dance Company. Many of the best-known names in the genre learned their steps in Giordano's studio, now run by Giordano's daughter.

Chicago is also home to several other well-known groups, including the Joffrey Ballet and the River North Dance Company. Fledgling companies can be seen in and around Chicago, many with recent graduates from the well-respected Columbia College dance program.

LIVE FROM...CHICAGO

Did'ja hear the one about the little comedy troupe that walked into the bar? Yeah, it's a wonder they were ever found, because the bar was in *Hyde* Park! Hyde, you get it? As in hide? *Hide park*? But they were *found*... Yes. Ahem... Take my wife, please. Thank you! You've been a great audience.

Were it not for Chicago's Second City comedy troupe – who first performed loosely structured skits as the Compass Players in a Hyde Park bar in 1955 – you would have thought my joke was hilarious. Thank God they came on the scene to raise the bar, eh? And what a bar-raising. Since 1959, those audience-suggestion-incorporating Compass Players performances have evolved into a form of theater that is so central to what we think of as comedy, that it's hard to imagine funny without it. It's equally hard to imagine what the American comedy landscape would have been like without the actors who learned the give-and-take style of comedy by performing with Second City and its various training programs. Fred Willard, John Belushi, Eugene Levy, Mike Myers, Amy Sederis, Chris Farley, Tina Fey, Bob Odenkirk... the list of alumni reads like a roll call of some of the funniest people from *Saturday Night Live* and *HBO*, as well as classic Christopher Guest movies such as *Waiting for Guffman* and *Best in Show*.

So they redefined comedy, and all got famous and stuff. But what's in store for *you* when you go see a Second City show while you're in Chicago? Well, you never know, exactly. Much like any theater company, Second City has new shows all the time. Depending on which one you see, you may get a program that's heavily pre-scripted, bordering on straightforward topical theater. Or you could see the kind of show where shouting out 'carrot peeler!' at the right moment forever changes the course of the evening. Check any of the Chicago papers for a description of the various shows on offer, and be sure to look through the listings for Second City ETC as well. This is where up-and-coming comedians have a chance to be a little more out-there than the main stage actors.

You may be so enraptured with the whole thing after the show that you decide you want to get in on the act yourself. And you can. Many of Chicago's improv venues around town offer comedy classes where grown-up class clowns can find their improv muses. Check the websites of **Second City** (www.secondcity.com), **IO** (www.iochicago.net) and **Comedy Sportz** (www.comedysportz.com) for more information.

LITERATURE

While it approaches writing with love and dedication, the Chicago writing community has trouble taking itself too seriously. A lit event here is just as likely to take place in a bar as a bookstore, and while there isn't a ton of world-famous authors in the city, there is a vibrant, supportive scene for the writers who do make Chicago their home.

One of the best times for writers and book-lovers is the annual **Chicago Humanities Festival** (www.chfestival.org), which is a two-week bonanza of readings, lectures, and discussions featuring some of the world's most interesting fiction writers and poets. Year-round, you can read the work of Chicago writers in literary magazines such as *Other Voices* and *ACM* (full, self-deprecating title: *Another Chicago Magazine*).

Many contemporary writers take a page from the book of local literary heroes Nelson Algren and Saul Bellow, setting their tales in Chicago and using the distinct personalities of the city's neighborhoods as telling set dressing for each story.

The biggest names on the Chicago scene include the Pulitzer Prize–winning author of *Middlesex,* Jeffrey Eugenides, detective fiction writer Sara Paretsky, bestselling scribe of legal thrillers Scott Turow, literary novelist (and University of Chicago professor) JM Coetzee, and *The Time Traveler's Wife* author Audrey Niffenegger.

Beyond the bestseller lists, you'll find a host of worthwhile works from Chicago authors. A quick reading tour of great Chicago fiction, from the classic to just-published, would start with Theodore Dreiser's *Sister Carrie* (1900). Dreiser was a larger-than-life figure in the Chicago literary set, and his book was somewhat scandalous at the time for its portrayal of female protagonist Carrie Meeber, a small-town girl who moves to Chicago and becomes a 'kept woman,' then, later, a rich New York celebrity. Next up would have to be *The Jungle* (1906) by Upton Sinclair. This novel about the exploited workers in Chicago's South Side meatpacking plants brought the horrible conditions of the plants to the attention of Chicago and the outside world, and ended up being a catalyst for reform. *The Adventures of Augie March* (1953) by Saul Bellow is a must. The engaging portrayal of a dirt-poor Chicago boy growing up during the Depression won Bellow the National Book Award the year it was released.

Bellow died in 2005 but he's still a literary icon in Chicago, matched only by Nelson Algren, whose *The Man With the Golden Arm* (1950) also won the National Book Award. Algren's story of drug addicts struggling for survival along Chicago's Division St shows a side of the neighborhood that has been lost in the ensuing years of gentrification. For more on Algren, see the boxed text, below. A poor Chicago neighborhood also plays a starring role in Sandra Cisneros' *The House on Mango Street* (1983), a series of interconnected vignettes about growing up Mexican-American in a Chicago barrio.

Some great Chicago tales of the last 10 years include *Windy City Blues* (1996) by Sara Paretsky, who pens beloved novels starring detective VI Warshawski, and legal thriller *Personal Injuries* (1999) by Scott Turow. Stuart Dybek won critical acclaim for *The Coast of Chicago* (1990), which is a collection of short stories that add an impressive twist on the

NELSON ALGREN & THE MEAN STREETS OF WICKER PARK

A product of the mean streets of the city, Nelson Algren (1909–81) was the quintessential Chicago fiction writer, crafting realist writing as no-nonsense as the city itself. He lived for many years at 1958 W Evergreen Ave in the then-sordid Wicker Park neighborhood, and he found his characters and places on the surrounding streets.

In 1950 Algren won the first National Book Award, bestowed by American publishers, for *The Man with the Golden Arm,* a novel set on Division St near Milwaukee Ave. Chronicling the lives of people struggling to survive within the confines of their neighborhood, this tale is shaped by varying degrees of desire, hope and loyalty, themes that have defined the lives of generations of Chicagoans. In the following excerpt, Algren explores the relationship between the deeply troubled central character, Frankie, and his sometime friend Sparrow:

> Sparrow himself had only the faintest sort of inkling that Frankie had brought home a duffel bag of trouble. The little petit-larceny punk from Damen and Division and the dealer still got along like a couple of playful pups. 'He's like me,' Frankie explained, 'never drinks. Unless he's alone or with somebody.'

Algren's other works include *The Neon Wilderness* (1974), *A Walk on the Wild Side* (1956) and *The Last Carousel* (1973).

down-and-out narratives of Nelson Algren. One of the current lit scene's stars is Bosnian-born Aleksander Hemon, whose *Nowhere Man* (2002) follows a Bosnian exile in Chicago in the 1990s. Finally, do check out the justly adored *The Time Traveler's Wife* (2004). This tale of a time-traveling Chicago librarian is a funny, thoughtful meditation on love and fate.

COMICS & GRAPHIC NOVELS

When Dave Eggers' cult literary publication *McSweeneys* did an all-comics issue in 2004, it became something of a who's who of contemporary comic illustrators. And of those contributors, nearly half were either from Chicago or had spent their formative years here.

Chicago's central role in the comics world is nothing new. A young man named Walt Disney grew up in Chicago, and studied art at the school on Michigan Ave that would come to be known as the Art Institute. Dalia (aka 'Dale') Messick, the creator of *Brenda Starr, Reporter,* was a Chicagoan. Dick Locher, the illustrator of the Dick Tracy comic strip, lives and works in suburban Chicago. Locher is also a Pulitzer Prize–winning editorial cartoonist, an honor he shares with the late Chicago cartoonist Jeff MacNelly, who created the daily strip *Shoe* as well as contributing single-panel editorial cartoons to the *Tribune.*

Little wonder grown-up readers of comics see Chicago as a dream-town, and its status as an illustrator's mecca is helped by the presence of Quimby's (p231) and Chicago Comics (p226), two great emporiums for comics and graphic novels (essentially novel-length comic books).

If you pick up the *Reader* while you're here, you'll see the work of the genre's master. Chris Ware, who also does illustrations for the *New Yorker* and the *New York Times,* has created an astonishing body of work, much of which follows a series of pathetic, lonely characters as they search for connection in the world. The heartbreaking tales are rendered in exquisitely inventive, multipanel strips that evoke the bygone comics of the early 1900s. Mining the same sad vein in a more autobiographical fashion is the work of Jeffrey Brown, whose coming-of-age graphic novels *Clumsy* and *Unlikely* were published to local acclaim. Brown is part of a collective of talented young graphic novelists called the **Holy Consumption** (www.theholyconsumption.com), which also includes Anders Nilsen, John Hankiewicz and Paul Hornschemeier.

Comic artists working in single-panel and more traditional comic-book forms in Chicago include the bleakly humorous Ivan Brunetti, and Sea and Cake musician Archer Prewitt.

POETRY & SPOKEN WORD

Poetry is a world unto itself in Chicago. In 2002, pharmaceutical heiress (and longtime amateur poet) Ruth Lilly changed the entire landscape of poetry in the country when she bequeathed $100 million to Chicago's Modern Poetry Association, publisher of the humble *Poetry* magazine. The gift stunned everyone in the writing world, including MPA staff. Since then, former Wall St investment banker John Barr has taken over as president of the organization, creating a number of lucrative poetry prizes as well as rolling out the 'American Life in Poetry' project, which aims to steer poetry back from the margins of American literary life.

If you're in the mood for some Chicago-penned poetry, check out Mark Strand, who served as poet laureate for the US from 1990–91.

For a list of regular readings in the city, see p195.

POETRY FROM ON HIGH

The words of a *New York Times* reviewer about Chicago poet Mark Strand were prophetic: 'There are a handful of contemporary poets whom we can consider only by gazing upward.' How far upward? In Chicago, about 50ft. That's the height of the billboard at the busy Near North intersection on which the Poetry Center of Chicago placed a 14ft-tall stanza from Strand's 'Five Dogs' poem. The Poetry Center has made a regular practice of bringing poetry to the streets of the Windy City by placing oversized stanzas where commuters can ponder them. Strand's poetic message to his hometown? 'You there/Come with me into the light and be whole/For the love you thought had been dead a thousand years/Is back in town and asking for you.' The Poetry Center has since rotated in another poem; check the intersection of Chicago Ave and Wells St for their latest poetic mischief.

CINEMA & TV

From shopping-channel infomercials filmed in suburban studios to exploding tanks on downtown streets, Chicago serves as a frequent backdrop for TV shows and movies. Film, especially, has a special place in Chicago's heart from the days when the city was the Hollywood of the Midwest during the second decade of the 20th century (see the Essanay Studios p88).

Part of the city's love of movies is simply the narcissistic joy of getting to see its streets, homes and restaurants projected onto the silver screen. Over the past century, almost every city landmark has had some screen time. In recent years, *Spider-Man 2, Batman Begins* and *The Road to Perdition* all had scenes filmed in Chicago. But the bond between Chicago and the movies goes beyond ego-fulfillment. From the lovingly restored movie houses like the Music Box Theatre (p197) to the beer-soaked, yelling-at-the-screen-is-OK Brew & View (p197) at the Vic, Chicago embraces movies as a part of life. It's no coincidence that Roger Ebert (see the boxed text, p196) lives and writes here. Nor is it an accident that **Cinecast** (www.cinecastshow.com), the Internet's best-known weekly movie review podcast, is produced here.

This hardy love for the moving image also translates into money for the city's coffers. In 2005, Illinois governor Rod Blagojevich signed a bill extending tax breaks to companies filming in the state. (The fact that he chose to do it on the set of the Jennifer Aniston/Vince Vaughn film *The Break-Up,* then being filmed in Chicago, was a corny gesture meant to underscore just how serious Illinois was about wooing filmmakers). Blagojevich's aggressive recruitment of Hollywood productions has been a success, and now local gossip blogs regularly buzz with sightings of celebrities in town to film the latest blockbusters.

TV shows haven't exactly followed Hollywood's Chicago-loving lead, though there are a couple of notable exceptions. Oprah Winfrey films her talk show from her own production facility in the West Loop – Harpo Studios. (Wondering about the name? Spell it backward.) The wildly popular program features celebrities, the occasional serious news investigation and discussions as diverse as racial prejudice and whom to invite to your third wedding.

If Oprah is the class act of daytime TV, Jerry Springer is at the opposite end of the spectrum. Springer's show is taped in Chicago, and being a part of the raucous studio audience is an exercise in high camp and theatrics, with plenty of scripted booing and yelling. For information on how to appear in the studio audiences for either show, see p196.

Apart from the daytime TV juggernaut, only a handful of prime-time shows – NBC's *ER* the most popular among them – ever set foot in Chicago. This doesn't mean that Chicago actors and actresses don't have their mugs appearing on screens big and small across America. *Friends* star David Schwimmer lives here (and directs the Lookingglass Theatre), as do Joan and John Cusack. John Mahoney, who plays Frasier's father on *Frasier,* is an Oak Park resident and comedian Bernie Mac (of Fox's *The Bernie Mac Show*) is a longtime Chicago fixture, as is Cedric 'the Entertainer' (who has been in a host of Hollywood films, most recently as the star of the cringeworthy adaptation of the *Honeymooners*).

TOP FIVE FILMS SET IN CHICAGO

- **Blues Brothers** (1980, director John Landis) In the best-known Chicago movie, Second City alums John Belushi and Dan Aykroyd tear up the city, including City Hall.
- **Ferris Bueller's Day Off** (1986, director John Hughes) A cinematic ode to Chicago, from the director who set almost all of his movies, from *Breakfast Club* to *Home Alone,* in and around the Windy City. This one revolves around a rich North Shore teen discovering the joys of Chicago.
- **High Fidelity** (2000, director Stephen Frears) This Chicago version of Nick Hornby's classic paean to music nerds stars Chicagoan John Cusack as a man uncommitted about commitment. The record-store set for the film was located at Milwaukee Ave and Honore St in Wicker Park.
- **Hoop Dreams** (1994, director Steve James) This stirring documentary follows the high school basketball careers of two African-American teenagers from the South Side. The filmmakers interview the young men and their families, coaches, teachers and friends over several years, showing how the dream of playing college and pro ball – and escaping the ghetto – influences their life choices.
- **The Untouchables** (1987, director Brian De Palma) Chicago playwright David Mamet wrote the screenplay for this edge-of-the-seat drama about Eliot Ness' takedown of Al Capone.

Music

Music

The letter from Billy Corgan was something of a head-scratcher. In 2005, the Chicago resident and former Smashing Pumpkins frontman ran a missive in the *Tribune,* announcing that he had healed from old wounds, he had a new solo album, he was blogging and he had decided to reform his old band. 'This city gave me the gift of my music,' he wrote at the end of the long letter. 'It is my honor to share this love that I have with you from the bottom of my heart.'

Chicago's collective response to the letter ('what a pompous ass') says a lot about the thriving music scene here. Music in Chicago is tireless, spunky and innovative, but it doesn't tolerate prima donnas. Whether it's the free jazz of the Association for the Advancement of Creative Musicians (AACM) or the classical-rock hybrid of the Butchershop Quartet, Chicago is a city that celebrates musicians who hone their own unique, uncompromised vision without regard to major-label record deals, open letters to entire cities, and other trappings of fame.

This independent streak owes a debt to Chicago's rich legacy of pioneering jazz and blues musicians. Ever since the early '20s, when Joe 'King' Oliver brought a young Louis Armstrong to Chicago to play second cornet in his red-hot jazz band, the city has been a beacon for new, untested styles of music. Two decades later, it was the same wide-open musical promise that helped convince a young Muddy Waters to leave Mississippi and come to the place where he could really get his mojo working.

The proletarian ethos remaining from those days – along with the legions of supportive fans – makes Chicago a haven for struggling musicians. Here, you'll find myriad local musicians playing great shows to packed clubs and concert halls. New boutique record labels start up every week in Chicago to release CDs by local bands and rappers, and CD and record shops abound in the city. (See the Shopping chapter p216 for the best places to plunk down the plastic for some hot wax.) Chicago weeklies do their part as well, sparing no ink in their coverage of up-and-coming acts and DJ nights.

Things change, though, when Chicago artists become a national or international phenomenon. An artist who wants to play on the larger stage of Top 40 radio usually ends up relocating to New York or LA at the first sign of a hit. The most widely known Chicago-born musicians right now – rapper-producer Kanye West, rapper Common and R&B singer R Kelly – only see their former hometown from the windows of a tour bus.

That trend has been changing in the last two years. High-speed rapper Twista hit platinum and stayed put in Chicago. Alt-rock band Fall Out Boy did the same. When you combine the growing list of resident megastars with the stratospheric number of scrappy, day job–working independent acts, you'll understand why Chicago is the Midwestern mecca for music.

Accordion player taps into Chicago's rich musical heritage

THE BLUES

Compared to the bustling rock and hip-hop scenes in Chicago, the blues occupies a much smaller, if no less revered, part of the musical pantheon here. This means that very few blues players in the city ever get the kind of arena-sized reputations (or salaries) their rock colleagues enjoy. It also means that visitors to the city can see some of the remaining giants of the scene, from Buddy Guy to Koko Taylor, at small clubs.

The small scale of the blues scene in Chicago breaks wide open in early June, however, when the Chicago Blues Festival (p11) rolls into Grant Park. For three nights, you can see plenty of the legends of the Chicago blues world, many of whom have played with Muddy Waters and other classic players.

Old-time-blues fanatics hungry for the raw, epiphanic feel of the music tend to avoid the North Side clubs (many of which feature gift shops as prominently as they do musicians) and head to the few remaining low-key Black establishments on the South and West sides, such as Rosa's Lounge (p183) or Lee's Unleaded Blues (p182).

Wherever you go, it's good to know a little history of the blues in Chicago. Early on, blues in the city closely resembled the variety played in the bayous of Mississippi and Louisiana. But the demands of noisy clubs and the pressures of urban life soon resulted in a more aggressive, amplified sound that is the basis of Chicago blues. Muddy Waters arrived on the scene in 1943 and is widely regarded as the most important blues musician to work in Chicago. His influence runs deep, extending to early rock groups such as the Rolling Stones and the Paul Butterfield Blues Band. His sideman in later years was Buddy Guy, whose electric-guitar work shaped musicians such as Eric Clapton, Stevie Ray Vaughan and Jimi Hendrix. Guy continues to operate the club bearing his name in the South Loop, Buddy Guy's Legends (p182). Other important blues greats have included Willie Dixon, Sunnyland Slim and Koko Taylor.

TOP FIVE CHICAGO MUSIC EXPERIENCES

- Flipping through the '60s soul records at **Dusty Groove** (p230)
- Dancing at **Lee's Unleaded Blues** (p182)
- Catching a rare Patricia Barber jazz set at the **Green Mill** (p182)
- Hearing the soaring sounds of the **Chicago Gospel Festival** (p11) ringing through Grant Park
- Taking in a fingerstyle guitar maestro at the **Old Town School of Folk Music** (p184)

JAZZ

Many of the great names in jazz – Louis Armstrong, Jelly Roll Morton, Benny Goodman, Bix Beiderbecke and Nat King Cole – lived and worked in Chicago. You can still see smooth crooners and bebop players that evoke the Chicago jazz scene of the '30s and '40s at places like the Green Mill (p182), the ground zero of jazz in the city. Especially worthwhile are singer Kurt Elling's Wednesday night gigs there.

Like Elling, pianist-songwriter Patricia Barber gets the national music press worked into a lather with her voice and incisive lyrics. *Time* has called her a cross between Diana Krall and Susan Sontag and the *LA Times* has said she's 'the coolest singer-songwriter around.' You can find Barber at the Green Mill from time to time.

When you talk about cutting-edge Chicago jazz, the name to know is AACM, a Chicago-based organization that formed in the 1960s, determined to push the envelope of jazz. Many of today's most innovative Chicago jazz players took their inspiration from the AACM, including German Peter Brotzmann, whose group the Chicago Tentet features a rotating lineup of the city's finest improvisers. Another person to keep an eye out for is saxophonist Ken Vandermark, a MacArthur 'genius' grant recipient who packs the Empty Bottle (p183) on his regular gigs there. Other local free-jazz names to watch out for are tenor saxophonist legend Von Freeman, who plays the New Apartment Lounge (p182) on Tuesday nights, and Fred Anderson, who holds court at the club he owns, the Velvet Lounge (p183).

ROCK, POP & INDIE

Chicago is a great town for rock and pop music. For most 20-somethings, going to a club and getting drunk on PBR (Pabst Blue Ribbon, a cheap beer beloved in Chicago) to the caterwauling strains of a local garage band is a rite of passage. This is especially true in Chicago's underground rock world, where music is just one part of a lifestyle that includes thrift store duds, band pins artfully scattered over bike messenger bags and the latest in home-fashioned haircuts. For indie rockers, the venues of choice in the city tend to be the Hideout (p184) and the Empty Bottle (p183), with occasional forays to the Metro (p184) for larger acts.

The reigning fathers of the city's rock scene are Wilco. Headed by former Uncle Tupelo singer-songwriter Jeff Tweedy, the band has been on a 10-year trek that has seen it move

FIVE CHICAGO RECORD LABELS THAT CHANGED THE WORLD

From Chess Records in the '40s and '50s to Thrill Jockey today, Chicago labels have long been the trailblazing leaders in new music. Five labels deserve special credit in making Chicago such a musical hotbed over the past five decades.

Bloodshot (www.bloodshotrecords.com) What do you get when you combine punk rock with old-school country? Ask Bloodshot, which has been Chicago's bastion of brawling twang and barbed-wire heartache for over 10 years. It has put out some of the best records in the left-of-center American genre called No Depression, alt-country or (the label's preferred moniker) insurgent country. Known for releasing CDs by sensitive types like Neko Case and Ryan Adams, Bloodshot also showcases the old-timey side of country with records by Pine Valley Cosmonauts and Wayne Hancock.

Chess Records When the blues left the Delta and took the train for the city, its home in Chicago was Chess Records. Run by two brothers, Leonard and Phil Chess, the label helped launch the careers of Muddy Waters, Howlin' Wolf and legendary harmonica player Little Walter. Chess engineered its records to match the tone of its artists, creating an aggressive, redlining blues sound that remains synonymous with Chicago. The label also served as a catalyst for what would eventually become rock and roll, recording early sessions by Chuck Berry and Bo Diddley.

Delmark Records (www.delmark.com) The oldest independent jazz and blues label in the country, Delmark Records has inspired countless other small startups around the world determined to promote the pioneers and mavericks of the two genres. Delmark was founded in 1953 by a 21-year-old music fan named Bob Koester, who, before his leap into the music recording business, had been selling out-of-print blues and jazz records from his dorm room. Over its 50-year life, the label has released blues works by artists like Junior Wells, Otis Rush, Little Walter and Sunnyland Slim, and jazz records by Art Ensemble of Chicago, Sun Ra and Dinah Washington. Additionally, Koester runs the Jazz Record Mart (p220), a jazz and blues shopping heaven in Near North.

Thrill Jockey (www.thrilljockey.com) When indie rock discovered the nuanced sounds and textures of jazz in the mid-1990s, Thrill Jockey was there to document the 'eureka!' moment. Started by New York transplant Bettina Richards, the independent label has been the celebrated home of local bands like Tortoise, and the Sea and Cake. The label isn't limited to the 'post-rock' bands that made it famous, however, with signings from local countryish acts like Freakwater and Califone to abstract European electronica artists like Mouse on Mars. Thanks to its consistently solid output and stratospherically high cachet, Thrill Jockey has opened the minds of indie music fans worldwide to new genres and styles.

Wax Trax! It's hard to say what would have happened to industrial music in the '80s without the tireless work of local label (and record store) Wax Trax! Along with bringing the raw, electronic mayhem of European artists like KMFDM and Front 242 to the US, Wax Trax! puts out seminal works by fledgling domestic acts such as Ministry, Meat Beat Manifesto and My Life with the Thrill Kill Kult. Though the label is now defunct, you can hear highlights in the extensive, 3-CD box set *Black Box: Wax Trax! Records, The First 13 Years*.

from simple alt-country ditties to experimental epics. It has been the subject of a film documentary (Sam Jones' *I Am Trying to Break Your Heart*), as well as a biography by local writer Greg Kot. For younger listeners, the biggest band out of Chicago is the pop-punk Wilmette outfit, Fall Out Boy, which released its major label debut on Atlantic in 2005. Some lesser-known bands of choice for the hipsters include the Ponys, which straddled the line between rock and dance; the Redwalls, a mop-toppy quintet that sounds like the love children of David Bowie and John Lennon; and the M's has also been making waves.

Also, much of the 'post-rock' scene – bands such as Tortoise, and the Sea and Cake, which married tricky time signatures and cinematic, largely instrumental rock – are still around and making music. Heavy metal and hard rock also have a warm place in the hearts of Chicagoans, thanks to bands like million-selling Disturbed and the fast, intricate guitar bursts of Chevelle. If you'd like to bang your head but there aren't any shows happening, you can get your fix at Neo (p187), where DJ Eleven plays hard rock and thrash for Metal Mondays.

COUNTRY, FOLK & BLUEGRASS

For the most part live country music in Chicago tends to be of the *old* country variety, with a lot of bands drawn to the sounds of '50s and '60s country stars like Johnny Cash and George Jones. The feisty patriarch of Chicago's old-school country scene is Jon Langford, who plays with the Waco Brothers and the Pine Valley Cosmonauts when not spending time touring with his seminal punk rock band, the Mekons. One of the best female country singers in Chicago is Kelly Hogan, one of Langford's compatriots, who you can also find tending bar at the Hideout (p184). Robbie Fulks is a country-tinged folkie who tells great stories in song, and fans of the late Elliott Smith have been singing the praises of lilting singer Kevin Tihista. You can see a lot of these bands at Schubas (p184) or the Hideout, and national folk acts often stop by and play in the converted library of the Old Town School of Folk Music (p184).

Chicago has a popular 'new country' radio station (99.5FM) that plays the likes of Brooks & Dunn and Faith Hill. If you'd like to hear a live band running through its versions of those country hitmakers, you should head to Carol's Pub (p184), where country line dancing is alive, well, and a hell of a lot of fun.

For bluegrass, check out the Bluegrass Wings, which the *Washington Post* named 'one of the finest songwriters of contemporary bluegrass.'

HIP-HOP, SOUL & GOSPEL

In 2004, Kanye West, the son of the head of Chicago State University's English department, put Chicago on the hip-hop map. It was his breakthrough CD *College Drop Out* that did it, and then he did it all over again a year later with his number-one follow-up *Late Registration*.

West's rapping style – light on materialism and free of misogyny – and his ornate, orchestral beats have already had an impact on modern hip-hop. West has also used his newfound power to bring up a host of younger rappers from Chicago, helping artists such as Bump J and Lupe Fiasco get record deals and widespread exposure. He also managed to stir up a new round of political controversy in 2005 when he went off-script during a live NBC TV benefit concert for Hurricane Katrina victims to discuss media portrayals of African-Americans and conclude with the comment that 'George Bush doesn't care about Black people.' The network was aghast, and used the tape delay to censor the comment when it ran in other markets. But the East Coast heard it loud and clear, and it brought outrage, applause and even more attention for the chart-topping rapper.

Along with raising some uncomfortable questions on live TV, West has also made a point of raising the profile of older Chicago rap artists. Before West, the only real success story out of Chicago was Common, a rapper who came up through the ranks in Chicago but moved to New York in 1999. For Common's latest CD, West provided beats for nine of the 11 tracks, bringing the Chicago connection full circle and giving Common a fresh buzz.

Twista is another popular rapper who has been working in Chicago for the past eight years, but who is only beginning to gain a wider following. His 2004 hit 'Slow Jamz' – atypically languid for him – won the American Society of Composers, Authors & Publishers (ASCAP) award for 'Most played R&B song of 2004.'

Chicago was once a hopping place for soul, a genre that primarily emerged from Detroit's Motown sound. Curtis Mayfield, first of soul group the Impressions and later a solo performer and composer, was from Chicago. One of the geniuses of the genre, he wrote hits ('People Get Ready,' 'Beautiful Brother of Mine') for himself and other Chicago singers such as Jerry Butler, Gene Chandler and Major Lance. To hear a fresh take on the socially conscious soul music, look for Andreus (aka Deandrias Abdullah) who cites Mayfield as a major influence.

Apart from Andreus, these days soul is seen mostly as oldies music. It still reverberates through Chicago's mod scene however. This group of tight pants–wearing, Vespa scooter–riding, anorak-toting hipsters is obsessed with '60s sounds and culture, and you can hear a ton of soul at the dance parties thrown once a month by **Mod Chicago** (www.modchicago.com). Check its website for details.

A well-manicured cousin to soul is contemporary R&B, and the current king of the genre is Chicago singer R Kelly, known as much for his early hit 'I Believe I Can Fly' as his later 'Trapped in the Closet' epic.

Chicago's South Side was where gospel really got started, and visitors who head down to the neighborhood for Sunday services can still get an earful of the uplifting spiritual music. The **Pilgrim Baptist Church** (p115; ☎ 312-842-4417; 3301 S Indiana Ave) is located in a former synagogue designed by Adler & Sullivan. This church was headed by gospel's founding father, Thomas Dorsey, and it was here that the careers of gospel greats such as Sallie Martin and Mahalia Jackson began. Dorsey died in 1993, but some members of today's Pilgrim Baptist

Church sang under him. Further south is the **Greater Salem Missionary Baptist Church** (p115; ☎ 773-874-2325; 215 W 71st St), where Mahalia became a member after leaving Pilgrim Baptist, and where old-school gospel still rings out over the pews. For a larger, more modern take on gospel music, head to **Salem Baptist Church** (p115; ☎ 773-371-2300; 11800 S Indiana Ave). It's quite a drive, but choir director Walter Owens is superlative, matched only by the preaching of Rev James Meeks, an Illinois State senator.

Another name to know on the Chicago gospel scene is Mavis Staples. The daughter of bandleader Pops Staples, Mavis Staples had a string of hits ('I'll Take You There,' 'Respect Yourself') with the Staples Singers in the '70s. But as she's gotten older she's put her legendary contralto to work in the service of her own brand of gospel-soul. In 2004, she released the vastly underrated *Have A Little Faith.* In 2005, the City of Chicago declared June 12 'Mavis Staples Day.'

FIVE TO KNOW IN CHICAGO MUSIC

Check over the entertainment listings and if you happen to see any of these names, hop in the next taxi to the club. You won't be disappointed.

- **Buddy Guy** Veteran musician and South Loop club owner is blues royalty in Chicago, but you can still catch him jamming on the city's stages.
- **Jesse de la Pena** One of Chicago's surest-handed DJs, he fills floors around the city with his bottomless crate of hip-hop, house, rock and reggae.
- **Mavis Staples** As part of the Staples Singers, she effortlessly blended pop, soul and gospel. As a solo performer, she puts on one of gospel's most moving shows.
- **Twista** His rapid-fire raps and cameos with biggies like Kanye West have earned him a place in the hip-hop firmament.
- **Wilco** Critics melt at the mere mention of this rock band, whose live shows draw a cult following from all over the country.

DANCE MUSIC & ELECTRONICA

If Chicago had only thought to trademark the term 'house music' when it was invented here in the early '80s, the city's coffers would be forever recession-proof. The genre takes its name from a long-defunct club on the West Side called the Warehouse, where the legendary DJ Frankie Knuckles spliced and diced disco anthems – extending intros, repeating phrases, and adding beats and bits from other songs.

Since then, house music has mutated into a dozen subgenres, from trance to garage to glitchy broken-beat. (In the late '80s, it even spawned another Chicago institution, industrial music – see the boxed text, below.) Whatever the style, house music is still the staple of dance clubs throughout the city.

The club scene in Chicago has come back down to earth after a brief period of wealth-fueled snootiness in the economic boom of the early 2000s. This has been both good and bad for dance fanatics in Chicago. With their smaller budgets, local clubs can't always attract the megastar DJs from New York and Europe. Instead, parties now have a more underground feel; the VIP rooms and big egos that are the hallmark of scenes in Miami or New York don't play much of a role here. Best of all, Chicago patrons rarely endure long lines or discriminatory bouncers who use the velvet rope to inflate their own sense of self-importance.

Mixed crowds of gay and straight dancers are fairly common in the city, with venues like Berlin (p185) being a prime example of a crossover club that everyone loves. While you're in town, keep an eye on the event listings for a set from Jesse de la Pena, who many hail as Chicago's best DJ. Chicago also boasts a larger number of women DJs – some names to look for include Margaret Noble, Teri Bristol, and Psycho-Bitch.

YOUR CHICAGO MIXTAPE IS READY

While exploring Chicago, you may notice a cartoonish cassette tape spray-painted onto the sides of buildings, train trestles and other odd bits of the urban landscape. Pay attention when you see it; the cassette signals a drop-off point for the Chicago Tapes Project. The experiment in sound-sharing is open to everyone, and consists of a number of unofficial nooks throughout the city where audio tapes of music and other recorded bits of life are secreted away. Passersby who recognize the sign and find the tapes are encouraged to take them home. And, should they be so inspired, to eventually make their own tape to leave for someone else. For more on the project, including a map of drop-off spots, check out www.illcutyou.com/tapes.

Architecture

Architecture

In 2005, a local developer made an announcement that would have sent most cities into paroxysms of civic pride. The country's tallest building was going to be erected in Chicago. Even better, the lakefront beauty had been designed by sought-after architect Santiago Calatrava. At its unveiling, the mock-up was a smash hit with architecture critics.

The response from the powers that be? 'Maybe this is the kind of building that should be built elsewhere,' said Burton Natarus, the Chicago alderman overseeing the ward containing the proposed building site.

Chicago is pretty choosy about its architecture. And it can afford to be. For over a century now, the architecture world has brought its best ideas to be planted in Chicago's marshy soil. Ever since William Le Baron Jenney built the first 'skyscraper' at the corner of LaSalle and Adams Sts in 1885, the city's streets have been shaded by an endless succession of unabashedly ambitious marvels (and occasional monstrosities). More so than any other American city save New York, Chicago has always been a place where architects take chances, pushing the envelope on design, height and materials. And the public, far from being passive recipients of the developers' largesse, sees each new addition to the skyline as a wonderful gift or a personal insult.

It makes architecture something of a contact sport in Chicago. Especially now, as the city undergoes a building boom the likes of which haven't been seen in decades. From the beloved outside-the-box buildings of Millennium Park to the controversial condo towers going up in the South Loop, Chicago's architectural heritage is being re-created every day.

THE CHICAGO SCHOOL (1872–99)

Though the 1871 Chicago fire seemed to be an unmitigated disaster at the time, it actually set the stage for a dramatic architectural renaissance in the city. Attracted by the blank canvas of an empty downtown, architects from around the world flocked to the city for commissions. Most were young – the average age was under 30 – and had something to prove. They found a city happy to give them the scorched Loop as a stage, and in a short time they had invented the modern skyscraper, with its steel frame, high-speed elevators and impossibly high (for the time anyway) rooftops. These young architects also defined a new form of architecture that came to be called the 'Chicago School,' stressing economy, simplicity and function.

The maverick architects who defined the new style – Adler & Sullivan, Burnham & Root, Holabird & Roche – closely adhered to the mandate that 'form follows function.' Though the buildings did draw their facades from the underlying logic of the regular steel bracing beneath, it didn't result in a lack of adornment. The architects used a powerful language of simple geometric shapes, primarily strong vertical lines crossed by horizontal bands. Relief from the sharp lines came in the form of bay windows, curved corners, sweeping entrances and other details, which gave the buildings a pragmatic glory that reflected the city around them.

WHAT TO SEE

Named after the pigeons that used to nest here, the **Rookery** (Map pp304-5; 209 S LaSalle St) was built from 1885 to 1888 and remains one of Chicago's most beloved buildings. The original design by Burnham & Root, with its load-bearing walls of granite and brick,

FIVE BUILDINGS THAT CHANGED THE WORLD

These five buildings stunned Chicago when they were first built. If you have limited time on your architectural touring, start with these.

- **Chicago Cultural Center** (p43)
- **Chicago Federal Center** (p44)
- **Jay Pritzker Pavilion** (p46)
- **Robie House** (p42)
- **Rookery** (left)

Prairie Ave Historic District (p112)

surrounds a spectacular atrium space that was remodeled in 1907 by Frank Lloyd Wright. A lavish restoration in 1992 has returned the building to its peak grandeur. Another Burnham & Root classic from the same era is the **Reliance Building** (Map pp304-5; 32 N State St). With its 16 stories of shimmering glass framed by brilliant white terracotta details, it's like a breath of fresh air. The building's lightweight internal metal frame – much of which was erected in only 15 days – supports a glass facade that gives it a feeling of lightness, a style that didn't become universal until after WWII. Narrowly avoiding demolition – a common fate for Chicago's architectural gems in a town where preservation often takes a back seat to commercial interests – the Reliance underwent an exterior restoration in 1995 and reopened as the chic Hotel Burnham (p238) in 1999.

The 1889 **Auditorium Building** (Map pp304-5; 430 S Michigan Ave) to the southeast was designed by Louis Sullivan with Dankmar Adler, and stands as one of the city's greatest structures. Behind its granite and limestone facade hides a magnificent 4300-seat theater with some of the best acoustics and sight lines in the city. Originally a hotel and office space, the building is now largely occupied by Roosevelt University. The 10th-floor library used to be an ornate restaurant. The arcade on Congress Pkwy was created when the sidewalk was sacrificed for the widening of the road in the 1950s.

Daniel Burnham had a hand in the **Marshall Field & Co Building** (Map pp304-5; 111 N State St). Covering an entire block, Marshall Field's was built in five stages by Burnham and others between 1892 and 1914. The southeastern corner (at Washington St and Wabash Ave) went up during the earliest stage and features massive load-bearing walls. On the State St side, the soaring ground-floor retail spaces are topped by Tiffany skylights. The whole store underwent a costly reconstruction in 1992, when a central escalator atrium was added. The structure was to be renamed the Macy's Building at press time, leaving history buffs horrified.

Dating back to the first days of the Marshall Field Building, the **Marquette Building** (Map pp304-5; 140 S Dearborn St) is the work of Holabird & Roche. The architects made natural light and ventilation vital considerations, due to the skimpy light bulbs and nonexistent mechanical ventilation of the time. The same firm took on the building's 1980 renovation. Tiffany and others created the sculptured panels – which recall the exploits of French explorer and missionary Jacques Marquette – above the entrance and in the lobby.

Considered the Loop Lourdes for architecture buffs on a pilgrimage, the **Monadnock Building** (Map pp304-5; 53 W Jackson Blvd) consists of two structures, both dating from the early 1890s. The two parts represent a crucial juncture in American skyscraper development. The original portion of the building consists of traditional, load-bearing walls that are 6ft wide at the base. Working with brick, architects Burnham & Root fashioned a free-flowing facade that becomes almost sensuous around the bottoms of the window bays. Constructed only two years later, the addition lacks the heavy walls and benefits from the latest advance in construction at the time – a then-revolutionary metal frame.

The main structure of the yellowish terra-cotta-clad **Fisher Building** (Map pp304-5; 343 S Dearborn St) was completed in 1896; the simpler northern addition was added in 1907. Inspired by the name of the developer, Lucius G Fisher, architect Daniel Burnham gave the exterior a playful menagerie of fish, crabs, shells and other sea creatures.

Architect Daniel Burnham kept his offices in the sparkling white terra-cotta **Santa Fe Center** (Map pp304-5; 224 S Michigan Ave), which he designed in 1904. The unusual top-floor porthole windows make the structure stand out even more from its neighbors. Enter the lobby and look upward at the vast light well Burnham placed in the center – he gave this same feature to the Rookery. Dating from the same year, the 15-story 1904 **Chicago Building** (Map pp304-5; 7 W Madison St) is typical of many designed by the firm Holabird & Roche during the late 19th and early 20th centuries. The windows fronting State St show classic Chicago style: two narrow sash windows on either side of a larger fixed pane. After a modest career as home to miscellaneous small businesses, the building reopened in 1997 as a dorm for the School of the Art Institute – another innovative use of older Loop office buildings. The preserved cornice is unusual, since most older buildings have had theirs removed for maintenance reasons.

Constructed two years after the Chicago Building, **Carson Pirie Scott & Co** (Map pp304-5; 1 S State St) was originally criticized as being too ornamental to serve as a retail building. You be the judge, as you admire Louis Sullivan's superb metalwork around the main entrance at State and Madison Sts. Though Sullivan insisted that 'form follows function,' it's hard to see his theory at work in this lavishly flowing cast iron. Amid the flowing botanical and geometric forms, look for Sullivan's initials, LHS. The rest of the building is clad simply in white terra-cotta.

PRAIRIE SCHOOL (1895–1915)

The beginning of the 20th century marked the ascent of the Prairie School (or 'Prairie Style') movement, headed by former Sullivan protégé Frank Lloyd Wright. In contrast to the grand edifices, Wright and his contemporaries built on a more modest scale, stressing low-slung structures where the horizontal was the most important axis. You'll know you're looking at a Prairie School home when you notice these ground-hugging lines, along with flat roofs, overhanging eaves and open floor plans.

Like the work of the First Chicago School, the homes of the Prairie School resemble nothing that came before it. Which was precisely Wright's aim. Inspired by Louis Sullivan, Wright sought to create a new kind of architecture – a residential form that was rooted in the aesthetics of the Arts and Crafts movement, and took its inspiration from the flat, unadorned features of the Midwestern landscape. It may sound boring and plain, but the final result was anything but: the homes have both a reassuring weight and a bricky sleekness to them. It's hard to explain but a delight to take in.

While Wright was the best known of the Prairie School bunch, his colleagues such as Walter Burley Griffin, Marion Mahony Griffin, George W Maher and Robert C Spencer also turned out masterful designs in and around Chicago.

WHAT TO SEE

True Prairie School aficionados should start their tour south of the city in Bronzeville, where they can take in an intriguing piece of Frank Lloyd Wright's juvenilia. Built in 1984, the **Robert W Roloson Houses** (Map pp302-3; 3213–3219 S Calumet Ave) comprise a set of row houses that Wright designed soon after striking out on his own. They owe as much to Sullivan's influence as Wright's still-forming ideas about homes. Wright would never do another series of row homes, preferring instead the stand-alone structures more suited to the Prairie School geometries.

Further south, in Hyde Park, you'll see the Wright creation that everyone goes nuts over. The 1910 **Robie House** (Map pp320-1; 5757 S Woodlawn Ave) has been hailed as one of the most important buildings in the country by architecture nerds, and the jutting eaves and wide, horizontal planes were emulated in buildings from Australia to Japan after it debuted.

To see the handiwork of some of Wright's most gifted colleagues, get thee to the **Hutchinson Street District** (Map pp318-19; 600-900 W Hutchinson St), which contains a wealth of Prairie Style homes, including the 839 Hutchinson St property designed by George Maher. Another great structure is **Café Brauer** (Map pp308-9; 2021 N Stockton Dr) on South Pond in Lincoln Park. Before it served up coke and coffee to families heading to the Lincoln Park Zoo, this 1908 building by Dwight Perkins was known as the Refectory.

BEAUX ARTS (1893–1920)

If you could travel back in time and have a conversation with architect Louis Sullivan, he'd tell you that the beaux arts architectural style single-handedly ruined architecture in Chicago. The style, named for the École des Beaux-Arts in Paris, borrows much of its look from antiquity. Walking past the majestic buildings of this era in Chicago – full of columns, cornices, grand entryways, statue-bedecked facades – it's hard to see what Sullivan was grumbling about.

But for Sullivan, like many of those at the forefront of the Chicago School, the obsession with bygone architectural styles was a ridiculous anachronism, akin to lighting one's home with oil lamps a century after the invention of the light bulb.

Even harder for Sullivan to accept was the fact that the popularity of the beaux arts style in the US had its roots in Chicago, thanks to Daniel Burnham choosing to build his 'White City' for the 1893 World's Expo using gleaming, classical buildings, many of which were designed by New York architects enraptured with the beaux arts style.

Those buildings, and the permanent structures they inspired in Chicago, were loved by the populace as much for their soaring stature as the promise they held of being a panacea for urban ills. The early 1890s were boom times for metropolitan areas across the country, but a lack of urban planning meant most cities were facing alarming problems with pollution, sewage and drinking water, and slums. The harmonious beaux arts look on display at the 1893 Exposition offered an alternative to this disorder and chaos. Whether Sullivan liked it or not, it would come to be the dominant paradigm in Chicago architecture for the next 20 years.

WHAT TO SEE

The **Chicago Cultural Center** (Map pp304-5; 78 E Washington St) was born in 1897 as the Chicago Public Library. After the 1871 fire, the British sent over more than 8000 books to establish a free library for the people of Chicago, many of which were autographed by the donors, such as Thomas Carlyle, Lord Tennyson and Benjamin Disraeli. The building was created by Shepley, Rutan & Coolidge to house the collection, then in 1977 it was renovated for use as a cultural center. Today the books have found a home in the Harold Washington Library Center (p46), but the magnificent public spaces remain.

Built in 1893, at the beginning of the beaux arts style's rise to popularity, the Art Institute of Chicago (Map pp304-5) is very much in keeping with the buildings erected in Chicago for the World's Expo the same year. The structure was designed by Shepley, Rutan & Coolidge, and has been expanded several times. Across the train tracks is the large Columbus Dr wing, designed by Skidmore, Owings & Merrill and added in 1977, while the large Rice Building, designed by Hammond, Beeby & Babka, came along in 1988. The bronze lions fronting the main entrance have been beloved mascots since 1894.

Although Union Station (Map pp314-15) was designed in the beaux arts period, it wasn't completed until the style had died out elsewhere.

ART DECO (1928–40)

As the beaux arts look began to peter out, the architects in Chicago once again looked to France for a fresh new direction. They found it in art deco, which shared a love of ornamentation with the beaux arts style, but forsook the classical whites and grays for a more modern palette of blacks, silvers and greens. Instead of urns and heraldic touches, art deco leveraged a decorative vocabulary of sunbursts, stylized gears and machine parts, and zigzag motifs.

As in the rest of the world, the art deco style died out as WWII brought a new sense of austerity to the architectural world.

WHAT TO SEE

The **Chicago Board of Trade** (Map pp304-5; intersection of W Jackson Blvd & S La Salle St) is one of Chicago's few remaining art deco creations. The original 1930 Holabird & Root tower, fronting LaSalle St, is a classic 45-story skyscraper topped with a statue of Ceres, the Roman goddess of agriculture. To the rear, a 1980 addition by Helmut Jahn nicely complements the original. Inside, the earlier building features a sumptuous lobby; the addition contains a 12th-floor atrium with a mural of Ceres that once adorned the original's main trading floor.

On Michigan Ave, you can see the art deco work of Daniel Burnham's sons in the 1929 **Carbide & Carbon Building** (Map pp304-5; 230 N Michigan Ave). Converted into the Hard Rock Hotel in 2004, the lower reaches of the building are covered in black polished granite, with the tower getting a complementary dark green treatment, with orangey-gold terra-cotta highlights throughout. The completion date made it one of the final grand structures to be built in Chicago before the stock market crash put skyscrapers on hold.

THE INTERNATIONAL STYLE (1952–70)

Chicago again became the center of the architectural world after WWII. Led by Ludwig Mies van der Rohe, the new 'International Style' was the pared-down embodiment of Louis Sullivan's mandate. The very structure of buildings – the steel frame – was no longer the inspiration for a building's look, it *was* the look. The oft-copied steel-and-glass towers, similar to the Chicago Federal Center, were built in every country around the world but often without Mies' careful eye for details. And the interiors of Mies' bare-bones structures are as functional as their exteriors, featuring walls that can be moved.

From 1950 through 1980, the Chicago architectural partnership of Skidmore, Owings & Merrill rose to prominence by taking inspiration from Mies' designs.

WHAT TO SEE

Mies' twin modernist landmarks, the **860–880 N Lake Shore Drive Apartments** (Map pp308-9), changed the architectural world when they went up in 1951. Also by Mies, the **Chicago Federal Center** (Map pp304-5; Dearborn St btwn Jackson Blvd & Adams St) bears the same austere look. In 1964 the 30-story Dirksen Building became the first of the Federal Centre buildings to be completed; it holds the federal courts. The 42-story **Kluczynski Building** (Map pp304-5; 230 S Dearborn St) came along in 1974; it serves as a home to various federal agencies. The post office, finished the same year, completes the troika; Mies designed it to be as tall as the lobbies in its two neighbors. *Flamingo,* a bright red sculpture by Alexander Calder, provides a counterpoint to Mies' ebony palette.

In stark, rectangular juxtaposition to the gracious curves of the Perkins & Will–designed Bank One Building (p46), the **IBM Building** (Map pp306-7; 330 N Wabash Ave) was built in 1971, and many consider it to be his signature office building. It was his last American

FIVE WHO BROKE NEW GROUND

- **Daniel Burnham** Designer of 'The Chicago Plan', which stressed an open lakefront and an easy-to-follow street grid, Burnham played a principal role in the development of the Chicago School of architecture and oversaw the beaux arts buildings of the 1893 World's Expo.
- **Helmut Jahn** This controversial architect reversed the Sullivan tenet and designed buildings in which function follows form. His early work, such as the modernist Xerox Centre (1980), is overshadowed by his later showy works, such as the James R Thompson Center (1985) and the masterful United Airlines Terminal One at O'Hare (1988). His latest Chicago creation is IIT's State Street Village dorm (p46).
- **Mies van der Rohe** The legendary architect brought his Bauhaus School ideas to Chicago when he fled the Nazis and Germany in the 1930s. His early '50s buildings set the style for three decades of international architecture.
- **Louis Sullivan** A master of ornamentation, Sullivan brought his skills to bear on the entrance to Carson Pirie Scott & Co (1903) and on the now-destroyed Chicago Stock Exchange; you can see preserved bits of the latter at the Art Institute. Sullivan usually created his work in partnership with engineer Dankmar Adler.
- **Frank Lloyd Wright** A visionary, Wright pioneered the revolutionary Prairie School style of architecture, which derived its form from its surroundings. Buildings were low, heavily emphasizing the horizontal lines of the Midwestern landscape. In contrast to the simple lines of the architecture, Wright added myriad precise details, which you'll notice on closer inspection of his buildings. For more about Wright, see the Oak Park section (p254) and Robie House (p42).

commission. Here, Mies' basic black palette gives way to an almost radical combination of rich browns.

Chicago's other cache of Mies van der Rohe buildings is down on the Illinois Institute of Technology (IIT) campus. Van der Rohe's influence on the campus was extensive; not only did he head the architecture department here for 20 years, but he designed the master plan for the campus layout and created over a dozen classroom and administration buildings (even a frat house – though it was never built). In 2005, the school completed a suitably reverent renovation of his masterpiece **Crown Hall** (Map pp302-3; 3360 S State St), an open, malleable space designed to be altered according to the needs of students and teachers using it. Mies referred to Crown Hall as 'the clearest structure we have done, the best to express our philosophy.'

To see some of the buildings Mies inspired, you'll have to look up. Way, way up. The **John Hancock Center** (Map pp308-9; 875 N Michigan Ave) is Chicago's most recognizable high-rise. The 100-story, 1127ft building combines, from bottom to top, shopping, parking, offices, condos, tourist attractions and broadcast transmitters. The first major collaboration of the Skidmore, Owings & Merrill architect Bruce Graham and engineer Fazlur Khan, this 1970 building muscles its way into the sky atop a series of cross-braces. If you look at the exterior, you can see where the shorter residential floors begin at the 44th floor.

Three years after the John Hancock Center came the **Aon Center** (Map pp304-5; 200 E Randolph St), originally called the Standard Oil building. Chicago's second-tallest building in overall height was originally clad in marble from the same quarry Michelangelo used – at the insistence of Standard Oil's then-chairman, John Swearingen, and his wife, Bonnie. To save money, the marble was cut more thinly than ever before, despite warnings from experts that, structurally, it would be too weak to withstand the harsh Chicago climate. Within 15 years the marble began falling off the building's 1136ft facade. The 43,000 panels covering the exterior had to be replaced with light-colored granite at a cost equal to the original construction.

The only building in Chicago that can look down on the Aon Center, the 110-story **Sears Tower** (Map pp304-5; 233 S Wacker Dr) is one of the world's tallest. Completed in 1973, it also owes its existence to the talents of Skidmore, Owings& Merrill architect Bruce Graham and structural engineer Fazlur Khan. It consists of nine structural square 'tubes' that rise from the building's base, two stopping at the 50th floor, two more ending at the 66th floor, three more calling it quits at 90 stories and two stretching to the full height.

POSTMODERN & 21ST-CENTURY (1980–PRESENT)

During the go-go era of the 1980s, commercial space in the Loop almost doubled, and high-rise offices spread to the Near North. Many of these buildings were influenced by postmodernism, the movement that emphasized eclectic designs drawn from older styles and other art forms. Postmodernism's playful mix of eras and materials made local architects like Helmut Jahn famous in some circles and infamous in others.

The real estate crash at the end of the '80s stalled new construction and the '90s were a timid decade for the architecture scene, with little in the way of innovation or artistic breakthroughs taking place. Much of the building from the late '90s to the early 2000s focused on bringing homes (in the forms of towering condo projects) to the Near North, South Loop and Near South Side areas. The results haven't been so pretty, and the unattractive buildings from this era inspired Mayor Daley in 2003 to write a front-page article in the *Sun-Times* taking local architects and developers to task for failing to employ more eye-pleasing, innovative designs. The article, entitled 'No More Ugly Buildings,' did little to stop the bottom line–focused builders of condos and townhouses. It did, however, resonate with a new breed of up-and-coming Chicago architects – names like Jeannie Gang, Brad Lynch and Doug Garofalo – who have already begun adding their distinctive, modern visions to the city's architectural legacy.

The mayor's malaise was eased in 2003 by a handful of original buildings going up. In 2004, Millennium Park took the city a big step in the right architectural direction. To encourage more buildings like Millennium Park's Pritzker Pavilion (and fewer like the blank-faced condo towers going up in the South Loop), the city passed a new zoning ordinance in 2004 requiring buildings to avoid large, unadorned expanses of windowless walls and other depressing architectural features. Some other fresh new buildings are on their way as well. In 2007, the Spertus Institute will be moving into its dramatic new home designed by Krueck + Sexton just north of its current location on Michigan Ave. And who knows, Chicago might actually see that record-breaking Santiago Calatrava tower some day as well. In the fast-changing world of Chicago architecture, anything is possible.

WHAT TO SEE

For some postmodern fun, check out the twin 'corncob' towers of the 1962 mixed-use **Marina City** (Map pp306-7; btwn Dearborn & State Sts). Designed by Bertrand Goldberg, it has become an iconic part of the Chicago skyline, showing up on the cover of the Wilco CD *Yankee Hotel Foxtrot*. The condos that top the spiraling parking garages are especially picturesque at Christmas, when owners decorate the balconies with a profusion of lights.

Built four years after the Daley Center, the **Bank One Building** (Map pp304-5; Madison St btwn Clark & Dearborn Sts) boasts a gracefully curving shape. The 60-story tower, designed by Perkins & Will and finished in 1969, gives this large bank a distinctive profile. A 2005 remodeling of the interior pushed the bank's staff out into vast rows of cubicles in the lobby, providing a strangely beautiful glimpse into the beating heart of one of the city's economic engines.

The most popular Loop tower to emerge from the 1980s is **333 W Wacker** (Map pp304-5). Completed in 1983, this curving green structure is the work of architect William E Pedersen, who did a masterful job of utilizing the odd triangular site on the curve in the river. Water and sky play across the mirrored glass in an ever-changing kaleidoscope of shapes and colors.

The bulbous **James R Thompson Center** (Map pp304-5; 100 W Randolph St) – completed as the State of Illinois Center in 1986 – features a shape reminiscent of its namesake governor, who commissioned it. Controversial from the start, the oddly shaped structure aroused ire with its all-glass design. Architect Helmut Jahn thought the structure should be a metaphor for open government and left off doors, ceilings and walls from interior offices. As a result he produced a vast greenhouse filled with overheated bureaucrats, who held up thermometers showing temperatures of 110°F and higher for the gleeful media. When the imperious Jahn took a tour of what he had wrought, he was confronted by a secretary who complained about her heatstroke. Jahn suggested she get a new job. Vastly improved air-conditioning has lowered temperatures, and everybody loves the soaring atrium lobby.

Named after the man dubbed 'the people's mayor,' the **Harold Washington Library Center** (Map pp304–5; 400 S State St) serves as 'the people's library.' Appropriately enough, the democratic process played a big role in its design. The city invited architectural firms to submit designs, which were displayed in the Chicago Cultural Center for several months in 1989. Thousands of citizens inspected the proposals and voted for their choice. Robustly traditional, with details derived from many classic Chicago designs, this 1991 Hammond, Beeby & Babka building was the winner. Note the whimsical copper details on the roof, including studious-looking owls.

The modern designs attracting attention are spread throughout the city. In Millennium Park, the Frank Gehry–designed **Jay Pritzker Pavilion** (Map pp304-5; btwn Columbus Dr & Randolph St) has placed the park on the top of 'must-visit' lists for architectural pilgrims. Constructed of 679 steel panels, the bandshell was actually the second design Gehry proposed for the site; a simpler structure was rejected by the park committee as not adventurous enough.

Another local favorite is the **Hotel Sofitel** (Map pp302-3; 20 E Chestnut St). This one comes courtesy of Parisian Jean-Paul Viguier, who took a Miesian fondness for transparent spaces and mapped it across the unique shape of this soaring hotel. The building's white glass and triangle shape are reminiscent of a ship's sail snapping in the wind.

The IIT campus has also opened two new buildings that have made the Bridgeport neighborhood one of the hot spots for architecture in the city. World-renowned Dutch architect Rem Koolhaas contributed the **McCormick Tribune Campus Center** (Map pp302-3; cnr 33rd St & State St), a nook-filled student hangout tucked beneath the El tracks. In a genius move, Koolhaas completely wrapped the El line in a sound-dampening tube, allowing students to more fully immerse themselves in their foosball games without the rumbling distraction of public transportation. Just south of the Campus Center is the Helmut Jahn–designed **State Street Village** (Map pp302-3; cnr 33rd & State Sts). Blair Kamin, the Pulitzer Prize–winning architectural critic for the *Tribune*, called the three pairs of five-story dorms 'dazzling,' and we couldn't agree more.

History

History

THE RECENT PAST

When Millennium Park opened in 2004, the sighs of relief from City Hall were audible for miles. The former no-man's-land turned eternal construction site had been a toad for so long, it was hard to imagine it ever becoming a prince. Four years late and $325 million over the original cost estimate, the park was opened with a three-day celebration in July.

The entire city was invited to the party, as were the philanthropic families and heads of the corporations who had picked up the bill for $205 million of the total cost. Their names hung on every piece of the park; the McCormick Tribune Plaza welcomed visitors and the BP Bridge channeled them back out of it.

The corporate naming of the public space had rubbed many Chicagoans the wrong way. As had the cost-overruns, the ever-lengthening construction period and the allegations of cronyism in handing out contracts to builders. Still, 50,000 people were expected for opening day. As usual, however, the city's estimates proved woefully off. Three hundred thousand curious Chicagoans showed up to take in the new sculptures, wander the paths, play in the fountain and hear the Grant Park Orchestra play a piece composed for the occasion. Even the weather cooperated; the overhanging gray clouds kept their rain to themselves.

The millennium had finally arrived in Chicago. It was four years late. But it was a sight to behold.

Since 2004, Millennium Park has become one of Chicago's great success stories, and it serves as a perfect metaphor for the city itself: dreaming and dedicated, art loving and business oriented, gleamingly pure and scandal filled. And full of challenges.

The 2003 to 2005 era was a challenging one for the city.

On the business front, the number of Fortune 500 companies based in Chicago continued to shrink. Especially painful was the loss of local powerhouse Bank One, which merged with New York–based JP Morgan & Chase and effectively became a New York company. (Perhaps intending to prove to the city that the new company would still be a pillar of Chicago life, the newly merged company picked up the entire tab for the Millennium Park kick-off party.) When Boeing relocated its corporate headquarters to Chicago in 2001, the city had hoped it would inspire other companies to do the same.

That didn't happen. Meanwhile, Mayor Daley's office spent 2005 getting more and more anxious about the amount of time that US Attorney Patrick Fitzgerald had been spending looking into city dealings. After the *Sun-Times* broke a story about a Hired Truck program, where city staff had been accepting bribes in exchange for giving lucrative trucking contracts to companies that never actually did any work, the program was quickly disbanded. But not before Fitzgerald's investigation and subsequent indictment and convictions of city staff opened an unflattering window into the patronage afoot in local government.

As the federal investigation continued through the summer of 2005, it widened to include more aspects of the city's patronage system. In August the mayor himself was interviewed by the Feds. He was not officially named as a target of their investigation, but insiders wondered if that might soon change. For the city's aldermen, who had long been frustrated by Daley's autocratic style, it was an overdue moment of reckoning.

To make matters worse, the city was shrinking again. The 2000 census had revealed a widely touted fact that Chicago had reversed a 50-year decline in its population, and city boosters hailed the revitalized downtown as a major factor in drawing new residents to the formerly undesirable areas. But, though the turnaround of the South Loop area had indeed brought many new residents to the neighborhood, even more Chicagoans were moving

TIMELINE

1779 Chicago's first settler, Jean Baptiste Pointe du Sable, sets up a trading post on the Chicago River

1803 Fort Dearborn built on the south bank of the Chicago River

TOP FIVE CHICAGO HISTORY READS

- **City of the Century: The Epic of Chicago and the Making of America** (1997, Professor Donald Miller) This book looks at the key players in Chicago's explosive growth, and analyzes the Windy City as a model for the changes wrought by urban development throughout America.
- **Chicago Days: 150 Defining Moments in the Life of a Great City** (1997, editor Stevenson Swanson) Put together by the Chicago *Tribune,* this book transcends the saccharine promise of its title to provide intimate snapshots of life throughout Chicago's history.
- **The Devil in the White City: Murder, Magic, and Madness at the Fair that Changed America** (2003, Erik Larson) A riveting book that focuses on the 1893 World's Expo and a gruesome killer who prayed on its attendees.
- **Encyclopedia of Chicago** (2004) A must for lovers of Chicago, this comprehensive guide to the history of the Windy City was put together by the Newberry Library with the help of the Chicago Historical Society.
- **Working** (1974, Studs Terkel) This classic from 1974 features interviews with Chicago traffic cops, shoe shiners, bureaucrats and housewives, all of them discussing the everyday intricacies of their jobs.

elsewhere. Chicago's population dropped by 1.2% between 2000 and 2004 – a blow to the city's hopes that it might once again be on the rise.

Throughout 2004 and 2005, the city's public transportation infrastructure was also in a troubling state. Despite a fare hike for the city's buses, El and Metra trains in 2004, the transit agency was still way short of the funding it needed. In 2005 the Regional Transportation Authority learned it would be receiving hundreds of millions of dollars less than the year before from the Illinois Congress. Overdue purchases were postponed, expansion plans curtailed and yet another fare hike put on the table, much to the consternation of the city's riders.

Even if they grumble at the price of getting around Chicago, residents have to admit that the city itself has never looked better. Mayor Daley's pet projects – parks and beautification – have the city blooming with a host of new and improved green spaces. The long saga of Meigs Field (see p59) left a bitter taste in the mouth of many in the city council. For the public, however, the mayor's seizure of the airport has given it one more beautiful vista to explore. New maps label the former airport simply as 'Northerly Island,' and crowds were already streaming there for outdoor concerts and summer merrymaking.

The Chicago skyline is also continuing to evolve. Donald Trump is busily completing the first stages of construction on his riverfront Trump International Hotel & Tower, a 92-story building that will eventually dwarf its posh riverfront neighbors in Near North. The Art Institute, the Spertus Institute and the DuSable Museum of African-American History have all begun work on ambitious expansion projects. Then there's the open question of the Santiago Calatrava design for the world's tallest building, proposed for construction across Lake Shore Dr from Navy Pier. The hurdles it will have to clear before groundbreaking are numerous, but the developer has wisely hired the law firm of Michael Daley, the mayor's brother, to help clear the zoning process. Even if the tower never gets built, the proposal alone is a testament to the booming building times in the city.

Things on the ground started looking up as well. The Chicago public schools were doing better – test scores continued to rise between 2003 and 2005, while the number of students required to repeat a grade plummeted. Chicago's institutions of higher learning were also making headlines, as University of Chicago professor Steven Levitt's book *Freakonomics: A Rogue Economist Explores the Hidden Side of Everything* rocked the bestseller lists. Meanwhile three of his colleagues expanded Chicago's mighty reputation in the academic fields by taking home the Nobel Prize in physics, economics and chemistry.

From the vantage point of 2005, it was easy to see that the stormy weather of the previous few years was calming. As the Chicagoans who relaxed on the Great Lawn for Millennium Park's opening day party could tell you, a corner had been turned, and the future, like the overture being played by the Grant Park Orchestra, sounded sweet.

1833
Chicago incorporated as a town

1837
Chicago incorporated as a city (pop: 4170)

FROM THE BEGINNING

OUT OF THE SWAMP

No one is sure when Native Americans first lived in the Chicago region, but evidence can be traced back to about 10,000 years ago. By the late 1600s, many tribes made their home in the region, the dominant one being the Potawatomi.

In 1673 Indians directed French explorer Louis Jolliet and missionary Jacques Marquette to Lake Michigan via the Chicago River. The two, who had been exploring the Mississippi River, learned that the Indians of the region called the area around the mouth of the river Checaugou, after the wild garlic (some say onions) growing there.

Various explorers and traders traveled through the area over the next 100 years. In 1779 Quebec trader Jean Baptiste Pointe du Sable established a fur-trading store on the north bank of the river. Of mixed African and Caribbean descent, Pointe du Sable was the area's first non–Native American settler and was possibly the first settler period, given that the Indians dismissed this part of the riverbank as a feverish swamp.

After the Revolutionary War, the United States increasingly focused its attention on the immense western frontier. Because of Chicago's position on Lake Michigan, the government wanted a permanent presence in the area and in 1803 built Fort Dearborn on the south bank of the river, on marshy ground under what is today's Michigan Ave Bridge.

Nine years later, the Potawatomi Indians, in cahoots with the British (their allies in the War of 1812), slaughtered 52 settlers fleeing the fort. During this war such massacres had been a strategy employed throughout the frontier: the British bought the allegiance of various Indian tribes through trade and other deals, and the Indians paid them back by being hostile to American settlers. The settlers killed in Chicago had simply waited too long to flee the rising tension and thus found themselves caught.

After the war ended, bygones were quickly forgotten, as the Americans, French, British and Indians turned their energies to profiting from the fur trade. In 1816 Fort Dearborn was rebuilt. Two years later Illinois became a state, although much of its small population lived in the south near the Mississippi River.

During the 1820s Chicago developed as a small town with a population of fewer than 200, most of whom made their living from trade. Records show that the total taxable value of Chicago's land was $8000.

Indian relations took a dramatic turn for the worse in 1832, when Chief Black Hawk of the Sauk Indians led a band of Sauk, Fox and Kickapoo from what is now Iowa to reclaim land swiped by settlers in western Illinois. The US reacted strongly, sending in hundreds of troops who traveled through Chicago, fueling its nascent economy. The army routed the Indians, and the US government requisitioned the rest of the Indian lands throughout Illinois, including those of the Potawatomi in Chicago. The Indians were forced to sign treaties by which they relinquished their land at a fraction of its worth, and all were moved west, ending any significant Native American presence in the city or region.

Chicago was incorporated as a town in 1833, with a population of 340. Within three years land speculation had rocked the local real estate market; lots that had sold for $33 in 1829 went for $100,000. The boom was fueled by the start of construction on the Illinois & Michigan Canal, a state project to create an inland waterway linking the Great Lakes to the Illinois River and thus to the Mississippi River and New Orleans.

The swarms of laborers drawn by the canal construction swelled the population to more than 4100 by 1837, when Chicago incorporated as a city. But the bullish city boosters turned bearish the same year, after a national economic depression brought the real-estate market crashing down. On paper, Illinois was bankrupt; canal construction stopped for four years.

By 1847 the economy had recovered and the canal was being pushed forward at full pace. More than 20,000 people lived in what had become the region's dominant city. The rich Illinois soil supported thousands of farmers, and industrialist Cyrus Hall McCormick

1865
Union Stockyards open, bacon plentiful

1871
Chicago Fire destroys city, rebrands cows as dangerous pyromaniacs

THE GHOSTS OF CHICAGO

From the victims of Al Capone's henchmen to the restless spirits of river shipwrecks, the Windy City is full of spooky places. Here's a sampling:

Biograph Theater (Map pp308-9; 2433 N Lincoln Ave) Bank robber John Dillinger was shot to death in front of this onetime movie house in 1934, betrayed by the famous 'lady in red' after seeing a Clark Gable film. In the months after the killing, passersby began claiming to see a mysterious figure running down the alley behind the theater, only to collapse and disappear.

Fort Dearborn Massacre Site (Map pp312-13; 16th St & Indiana Ave) In August of 1812, a group of more than 60 soldiers and settlers leaving the fort on the south bank of the Chicago River were attacked and killed by a group of Indians and the fort destroyed. At the site of the attack, people have reported seeing figures dressed in clothes from the era.

Graceland Cemetery (Map pp318-19; 4001 N Clark) The final resting place of many of Chicago's notables is most famous for the grave of a six-year-old girl named Inez Clarke who died in 1880. The grave features a life-size statue of Clarke encased in a Plexiglass box. According to reports, the statue will disappear on stormy nights, reappearing in the morning. Others have reported seeing a girl wandering near the grave wearing 19th-century clothes.

Second Regiment Armory (Map pp314-15; 1058 W Washington Blvd) In 1915 the aging steamer *Eastland* capsized in the Chicago River between the Clark and LaSalle St bridges while still partially moored to the dock. In all, over 800 people lost their lives, and many of the bodies were taken to a makeshift morgue at the Second Regiment Armory. In 1988 Oprah's Harpo Studios bought and completely renovated the building, though something from the building's past has reportedly lingered. Studio employees have allegedly heard mysterious footsteps and seen apparitions believed to be the spirits of the *Eastland* dead.

St Valentine's Day Massacre Site (Map pp308-9; 2122 North Clark St) It was in a garage located on this site that seven men were machine-gunned by Al Capone's men on Valentine's Day, 1929. Though the garage has long since been demolished, the site is claimed to be haunted, and dogs supposedly act strangely when passing by.

moved his reaper factory to the city to serve them. He would soon control one of the Midwest's major fortunes.

In 1848 the canal opened, and shipping flowed through the Chicago River from the Caribbean to New York via the Great Lakes and the St Lawrence Seaway. It had a marked economic effect on the city. A great financial institution, the Chicago Board of Trade, opened to handle the sale of grain by Illinois farmers, who had greatly improved access to Eastern markets.

Railroad construction absorbed workers freed from canal construction. By 1850 a line had been completed to serve grain farmers between Chicago and Galena, in western Illinois. A year later, the city gave the Illinois Central Railroad land for its tracks south of the city. It was the first land-grant railroad and was joined by many others, whose tracks eventually would radiate out from Chicago. The city quickly became the hub of America's freight and passenger trains, a status it would hold for the next hundred years.

RAPID GROWTH

In the 1850s Chicago grew quickly. State St south of the river became the commercial center, as banks and other institutions flourished with the growing economy. The city's first steel mill opened in 1857, the forerunner of the city's economic and industrial diversification. By the end of the decade, Chicago supported at least seven daily newspapers. Immigrants poured in, drawn by jobs at the railroads that served the expanding agricultural trade. Twenty million bushels of produce were shipped through the city that year. The population topped 100,000.

By then, Chicago was no longer a frontier town. Its central position in the US made it a favorite meeting spot, a legacy that continues to this day. In 1860 the Republican Party

1885

The world's first steel-frame 'skyscraper,' the Home Insurance Building, built in Chicago. It is 10 stories (138ft) tall

1886

Haymarket Riot

held its national political convention in Chicago and selected Abraham Lincoln, a lawyer from Springfield, Illinois, as its presidential candidate.

Like other northern cities, Chicago profited from the Civil War, which boosted business in its burgeoning steel and toolmaking industries and provided plenty of freight for the railroads and canal. In 1865, the year the war ended, an event took place that would profoundly affect the city for the next hundred years: the Union Stockyards opened on the South Side, unifying disparate meat operations scattered about the city. Chicago's rail network and the development of the iced refrigerator car meant that meat could be shipped east to New York, spurring the industry's consolidation.

The stockyards become the major supplier of meat to the entire nation. But besides bringing great wealth to a few and jobs to many, the yards were also a source of many problems, including water pollution (see the boxed text, p115).

The stockyard effluvia polluted not only the Chicago River but also Lake Michigan. Flowing into the lake, the fouled waters spoiled the city's source of fresh water and caused cholera and other epidemics that killed thousands. In 1869 the Water Tower and Pumping Station began bringing water into the city through a two-mile tunnel that had been built into Lake Michigan in an attempt to draw drinking water unpolluted by the Chicago River. But this solution proved resoundingly inadequate, and outbreaks of illness continued.

Two years later, the Illinois & Michigan Canal was deepened so that the Chicago River would reverse its course and start flowing south, away from the city. Sending waste and sewage down the reversed river provided relief for Chicago residents and helped ease lake pollution, but it was not a welcome change for those living near what had become the city's drainpipe. A resident of Morris, about 60 miles downstream from Chicago, wrote: 'What right has Chicago to pour its filth down into what was before a sweet and clean river, pollute its waters, and materially reduce the value of property on both sides of the river and canal, and bring sickness and death to the citizens?'

The river still occasionally flowed into the lake after heavy rains; it wasn't permanently reversed until 1900, when the huge Chicago Sanitary & Ship Canal opened.

THE CHICAGO FIRE

On October 8, 1871, the Chicago fire started just southwest of downtown. For more than 125 years, legend has had it that a cow owned by a certain Mrs O'Leary kicked over a lantern, which ignited some hay, which ignited some lumber, which ignited the whole town. The image of the hapless heifer has endured despite evidence that the fire was actually the fault of Daniel 'Peg Leg' Sullivan, who dropped by the barn on an errand, accidentally started the fire himself and then tried to blame it on the bovine. (The Chicago City Council officially passed a resolution in 1997 absolving the O'Leary family of blame.)

However it started, the results of the Chicago fire were devastating. It burned for three days, killing 300 people, destroying 18,000 buildings and leaving 90,000 people homeless. 'By morning 100,000 people will be without food and shelter. Can you help us?' was the message sent East by Mayor Roswell B Mason as Chicago and City Hall literally burned down around him.

The dry conditions set the stage for a runaway conflagration, as a hot wind carried flaming embers to unburned areas, which quickly caught fire. The primitive, horse-drawn firefighting equipment did little to keep up with the spreading blaze. Almost every structure was destroyed or gutted in the area bounded by the river on the west, what's now Roosevelt Rd to the south and Fullerton Ave to the north.

Mayor Mason earned kudos for his skillful handling of Chicago's recovery. His best move was to prevent the aldermen on the city council from getting their hands on the millions of dollars in relief funds that Easterners had donated after the mayor's fireside plea, thus ensuring that the money actually reached the rabble living in the rubble.

1892	1893
First elevated train begins operation	World's Expo opens. Cracker Jack, zipper invented

1893: THE YEAR CHICAGO CHANGED THE WORLD

Imagine walking into a part of Chicago where the buildings were 5000 stories tall, each one capped by a lush redwood forest, and inhabited by residents who teleported to and from work. That's roughly what the 1893 World's Expo was like for those who visited it at the time. Held in Chicago's Jackson Park, the fair was planned by Chicago's Daniel Burnham and landscaped by Frederick Law Olmsted, and offered wonders heretofore unknown to the world at large: long-distance phone calls, the first moving pictures (courtesy of Thomas Alva Edison's Kinetoscope) and the first zipper. Businessmen were in awe of the first vertical file (invented by Melvil Dewey, of Dewey Decimal System fame) and children taken with a new type of gum called 'Juicy Fruit.' It was at the Exposition that Pabst beer won the blue ribbon that has been part of its name ever since. The first Ferris wheel made its debut on the Midway, a long strip of land to the south of the park where the stately calm of the exposition was replaced by a circuslike showmanship. It was here that visitors could see an entire Algerian village, a host of Laplanders, a recreation of a Cairo street (complete with 175 Egyptians) and a wildly popular 'Wild West' show hosted by Buffalo Bill Cody, featuring 97 Indians, 100 former US Calvary soldiers and a female sharpshooter named Annie Oakley. As documented in Erik Larson's excellent *The Devil in the White City: Murder, Magic, and Madness at the Fair that Changed America,* the exposition was also the bait used by one of the city's worst serial killers. Herman Mudgett, better known by the name he used, HH Holmes, ran a hotel and pharmacy near the fairgrounds. The exposition was a time of creation and chaos, and it stands as one of Chicago's most intriguing eras.

Visitors to Chicago looking for traces of the White City can find them throughout the neighborhoods around Hyde Park.

HH Holmes' Hotel The building where Holmes killed at least 26 people is located at 63rd and Wallace in Englewood. A post office now stands on the lot.

Jackson Park Though its hard to imagine it now, the park was once marshy, sandy wasteland. Olmsted's complete overhaul of Jackson Park involved the planting of bushes, trees, flowers and low-lying groundcover, the descendants of which are still living in some parts of the park. A large portion of the fairgrounds is now covered by the Jackson Park golf course.

Lagoon & Wooded Island The body of water immediately to the south of the Museum of Science & Industry was the centerpiece point of Olmsted's designs, and the White City's main buildings were clustered around its edge. The lagoon (along with its watery counterpoint to the south) was created by dredging, and the soil pulled out was used to create hills and other topographical features throughout the park. When dredging, Olmsted had his crew leave an island in the middle of the lagoon, where a Japanese garden stood.

Museum of Science & Industry The fair closed in October of 1893, and by June of 1894 a museum called the Field Museum had opened in the fair's Palace of Fine Art building. Showcasing state-of-the-art exhibits in anthropology and the biological sciences (including many artifacts left over from the fair), it moved to the Loop in 1921. The building reopened in 1933 as the Museum of Science & Industry. The building is the only of the White City's main structures to survive.

Rookery This building was designed by Burnham and his partner, John Root, and the duo had their offices on its top floor. This was the site of many frenzied planning meetings as the fair's opening date drew nearer.

CHICAGO REBORN

Despite the human tragedy, the fire's effect was much the same as that of a forest fire – within a few years there was rapid new growth, a wealth of new life. The world's best architects poured in to snare the thousands of rebuilding contracts, giving Chicago an architectural legacy of innovation. Rebuilding added to the city's economy, which had been scarcely slowed by the conflagration, and by 10 years after the fire, the population of Chicago had tripled.

The later decades of the 19th century saw Chicago on a boom-and-bust economic cycle. While in general the economy grew, it often fell prey to short-lived recessions. During one of these in 1873, thousands of men thrown out of work marched on City Hall, demanding food. The police, who were always on call for governmental and economic interests, beat the protesters, who had dispersed after they were promised free bread. It was the beginning of a history of clashes between labor and police that would stretch over the next 50 years.

In 1876 strikes began in the railroad yards as workers demanded an eight-hour workday. Traffic was paralyzed, and the unrest spread to the McCormick Reaper Works, which was

1900

Chicago reverses flow of Chicago River, forever ingratiating itself with downstate neighbors

1908

Chicago Cubs win the World Series; 'Let's do this again soon,' says team then Chicago's largest factory. The police and federal troops broke up the strikes, killing 18 civilians and injuring hundreds more.

By then, May 1 had become the official day of protest for Chicago labor groups. On that day in 1886, 60,000 workers went on strike, demanding an eight-hour workday. As was usual, police attacked the strikers at locations throughout the city. Three days later, self-described 'anarchists' staged a protest in Haymarket Square where a bomb exploded, killing seven police officers. The government reacted strongly to what became known as 'the Haymarket Riot.' Eight anarchists were convicted of 'general conspiracy to murder' and four were hanged, although only two had been present at the incident and the bomber was never identified.

While the city's workers agitated for better working conditions, other progressive social movements were also at play in Chicago. Immigrants were pouring into the city at a rate of 10,000 a week, and they lived in squalid conditions, enjoying few if any government services. In 1889 two young women from middle-class families, Jane Addams and Ellen Gates Starr, founded Hull House on the city's West Side. The two women opened soup kitchens, set up schools for immigrant children, established English classes for adults and offered other services, such as medical care, to ease the immigrants' hardships.

Meanwhile, the city went on a big annexation campaign, nabbing the independent townships of Lake View, Hyde Park and others to gain their tax revenues. Civic leaders hoped that Chicago's increased population would give it prominence on the world stage.

In 1892 society legend Bertha Palmer followed the lead of other Chicago elite by touring Paris. A prescient art collector, she nabbed Monets, Renoirs and other impressionist works before they had achieved acclaim. Her collection later formed the core of the Art Institute.

The 1893 World's Expo marked Chicago's showy debut on the international stage. Centered on a grand complex of specially built structures on the lakeshore south of Hyde Park, the exposition became known as the 'White City' for its magnificent white-painted buildings, which were brilliantly lit by electric searchlights. Designed by architectural luminaries such as Daniel Burnham, Louis Sullivan and Frederick Law Olmsted, the fairgrounds were meant to show how parks, streets and buildings could be designed in a harmonious manner that would enrich the chaotic urban environment.

Open only five months, the exposition attracted 27 million visitors, many of whom rode the newly built El to and from the Loop. The spectacular buildings surrounded ponds plied by Venetian gondolas. The entire assemblage made a huge impact not just in Chicago but around the world, as the fair's architects were deluged with huge commissions to redesign cities. The buildings themselves, despite their grandeur, were short lived, having been built out of a rough equivalent of plaster of Paris that barely lasted through the fair. The only survivor was the Fine Arts Building, which was rebuilt to become the Museum of Science & Industry.

Chicago's labor troubles reached another critical point in 1894, when a recession caused the Pullman Palace Car Company to cut wages. Worker unrest spread from the huge South Side factory complex, which built railroad cars, to the railroads themselves, and more than 50,000 workers walked off their jobs, paralyzing interstate commerce. Federal troops were called in and gradually broke the strike through a series of battles that left scores of workers injured.

At the turn of the century, Chicago's population had reached 1.7 million, and the city had become a far bigger place than anyone could have imagined just seven decades before. Despite this growth, Chicago still had its wild and woolly elements, many of which could be found in the notorious Levee District, a one-stop Sodom and Gomorrah south of the Loop that was run not by gangsters but by the city's top cops and politicians.

Meanwhile, Chicago's industries continued to prosper at the expense of the environment and worker health. In 1906 Upton Sinclair's fictional account of the stockyards, *The Jungle,* was published. Although Sinclair hoped it would arouse sympathy for exploited workers, it ignited public fury with its lurid portrayal of the factories where public food was prepared.

Though working conditions were bad, they didn't stop the continual flow of immigrants to Chicago. People from Midwestern farms and impoverished nations in Europe continued to pour in, followed, in the early 20th century, by poor Blacks from the South.

1920	1929
Chicagoans raise glasses of beer, whiskey to celebrate onset of Prohibition	St Valentine's Day massacre

THE GREAT MIGRATION

In 1910 eight out of 10 Blacks still lived in the southern states of the old Confederacy. Over the next decade a variety of factors combined to change that, as more than two million African-Americans moved north in what came to be known as the Great Migration.

Chicago played a pivotal role in this massive shift of population, both as an impetus and as a destination. Articles in the Black-owned and nationally circulated *Chicago Defender* proclaimed the city a worker's paradise and a place free from the horrors of Southern racism. Ads from Chicago employers promised jobs to anyone willing to work.

These lures, coupled with glitzy images of thriving neighborhoods like Bronzeville, inspired thousands to take the bait. Chicago's Black population zoomed from 44,103 in 1910 to 109,458 in 1920 and continued growing. The migrants, often poorly educated sharecroppers with big dreams, found a reality not as rosy as promised. Chicago did not welcome Blacks with open arms. In 1919 White gangs from Bridgeport led days of rioting that killed dozens. Employers were ready with the promised jobs, but many hoped to rid their factories of White unionized workers by replacing them with Blacks, which further exacerbated racial tensions. Blacks also found that they were promoted and advanced only so far before reaching an unofficial ceiling. Blacks were also restricted to living in South Side ghettos by openly prejudicial real-estate practices that kept them from buying or renting homes elsewhere in the city.

CHICAGO GOES DRY (SORT OF)

Efforts to make the United States 'dry' had never found favor in Chicago; the city's vast numbers of German and Irish immigrants were not about to forsake their favored libations. During the first two decades of the 20th century, the political party that could portray itself as the 'wettest' would win the local elections. Thus the nationwide enactment in 1920 of Prohibition, the federal constitutional amendment making alcohol consumption illegal, was destined to meet resistance in Chicago, where voters had gone six to one against the law in an advisory referendum. However, few could have predicted how the efforts to flout Prohibition would forever mark Chicago's image worldwide (see the boxed text, p87).

An important year for the city, 1933 saw Prohibition repealed and a thirsty populace return openly to the bars. Another world's fair, this time called the Century of Progress, opened on the lakefront south of Grant Park and promised a bright future filled with modern conveniences, despite the ongoing grimness of the Great Depression. Then, in the same year, Ed Kelly became mayor. With the help of party boss Pat Nash, he strengthened the Democratic Party in the city, creating the legendary 'machine' that would control local politics for the next 50 years. Politicians doled out thousands of city jobs to people who worked hard to make sure their patrons were reelected. The same was true for city vendors and contractors, whose continued prosperity was tied to their donations and other efforts to preserve the status quo.

ENTER THE DALEY

The zenith of the machine's power began with the election of Richard J Daley in 1955. Initially thought to be a mere party functionary, Daley was reelected mayor five times before dying in office in 1976. With an uncanny understanding of machine politics and how to use it to squelch dissent, he dominated the city in a way no mayor had before or has since. His word was law, and a docile city council routinely approved all his actions, lest a dissenter find his or her ward deprived of vital city services.

But Daley and those in the entrenched political structure were oblivious – both by intent and accident – to many of the changes and challenges that Chicago faced in the 1950s and later. After suffering through the Depression, the city experienced sudden affluence during WWII. Factories ran at full tilt, and once again people flocked to Chicago for jobs during the war years. In 1950 the population peaked at 3.6 million. But the postwar economic

1933

Chicagoans raise glasses of beer, whiskey to celebrate repeal of Prohibition

1942

First nuclear chain reaction occurs on a University of Chicago squash court

WHITE FLIGHT

From the late 1950s through the '70s, Chicago's ethnic neighborhoods in the southern, western and southwestern areas of the city underwent rapid change. Whole neighborhoods that had been filled with Irish, Lithuanian and other immigrant residents became populated entirely by Black residents in a matter of months.

The causes were both simple and complex. White residents, raised with racist assumptions about the dangers of having Blacks as neighbors, engaged in panic selling at the first appearance of an African-American on the block. 'For Sale' signs sprouted like weeds throughout the neighborhoods. People who had worked two or more jobs to afford their dream home sold at below-market prices and fled with their families to the suburbs.

The Blacks who could afford to do so fled the slums and snapped up the homes but soon found they had a new set of problems: insurance companies and mortgage lenders engaged in 'redlining,' the practice of refusing to write policies and grant loans in areas that had 'gone Black.' The new homeowners were often forced to purchase mortgages and insurance from unscrupulous businesses – many of them owned by African-Americans – that charged far more than market rates. Soon some families were forced to default on their loans, and their once-tidy homes became derelict, blighting otherwise healthy blocks.

Discrimination also took the form of 'housing covenants,' unwritten agreements in the real-estate industry whereby houses in certain neighborhoods were not sold to people deemed 'unsuitable.'

Government agencies attempted to alleviate these problems by outlawing 'For Sale' signs, punishing firms that engaged in redlining, and requiring banks to open branches in African-American communities and to grant mortgages under the same conditions that applied to White communities. These new policies slowed the destabilizing turnover of neighborhoods, and in the few places where true integration has occurred, neighboring Black and White homeowners find that they share many of the same concerns: good schools, low crime rates, affordable taxes, timely trash removal, instant eradication of snow and a melancholy wish for the return of Michael Jordan and Mike Ditka.

boom also made it possible for many Chicagoans to realize the dream of buying their own homes. Farms and wetlands surrounding the city were quickly turned into suburbs that attracted scores of middle-class people fleeing the crowded city.

The tax base diminished and racial tensions grew. Blacks moved from the ghettos on the South Side to other areas of the city, while Whites, succumbing to racism fueled by fears of crime, grew terrified at the prospect of ethnically integrated neighborhoods.

A 1957 *Life* magazine report that called Chicago's cops the most corrupt in the nation didn't make Chicagoans feel more secure. Although Daley and the machine howled with indignation over the article, further exposés by the press revealed that some cops and politicians were in cahoots with various crime rings. None of this was news to the average Chicagoan.

Chicago's voting practices were also highly suspect, never more so than in 1960, when John F Kennedy ran for president of the US against Richard Nixon, then vice president. The night of the election, the results were so close nationwide that the outcome hinged on the vote in Illinois.

Mayor Daley called up Kennedy and assured him, 'With a little bit of luck and the help of a few close friends, you're going to carry Illinois.' Kennedy did win Illinois, by 10,000 votes, which gave him the presidency. For many, that was the perfect embodiment of electoral politics in Chicago, a city where the slogan has long been 'Vote early and vote often' and voters have been known to rise from the grave and cast ballots.

In 1964 the Civil Rights movement came to Chicago. Martin Luther King, Jr spoke at rallies, demanding better conditions for Blacks and an end to segregation. He led marches through all-White neighborhoods where some racist residents attacked the marchers with rocks and bottles. In one march, King was hit in the head by a brick, foreshadowing events for which Daley and the machine would be ill prepared.

The year 1968 proved an explosive one for Chicago. When King was assassinated in Memphis, Tennessee, the West Side exploded in riots and went up in smoke. Whole stretches of the city were laid to waste, and Daley and the many Black politicians in the machine were helpless

1960

McCormick Place opens, immediately hailed as 'the mistake by the lake'

1968

Chicago cops go nuts at Democratic National Convention

to stop the violence. Worse yet, the city's hosting of the Democratic National Convention in August degenerated into a fiasco of such proportions that its legacy dogged Chicago for decades. With the war in Vietnam rapidly escalating and general unrest spreading through the US, the convention became a focal point for protest groups of all stripes. Regardless of the tempest brewing, conservative old Mayor Daley – the personification of a 'square' if there ever was one – was planning a grand convention. Word that protesters would converge on Chicago sparked authorities' plans to crack the head of anybody who got in the way of Daley's show. Local officials shot down all of the protesters' requests for parade permits, despite calls by the press and other politicians to uphold the civil right of free assembly.

Enter Abbie Hoffman, Jerry Rubin, Rennie Davis, Tom Hayden, Bobby Seale and David Dellinger. They called for a mobilization of 500,000 protesters to converge on Chicago, and their plans steadily escalated in the face of city intransigence. As the odds of confrontation became high, many moderate protesters decided not to attend. When the convention opened, there were just a few thousand young protesters in the city. But Daley and his cronies spread rumors to the media to bolster the case for their warlike preparations. Some of these whoppers included claims that hippie girls would pose as prostitutes to give the delegates venereal disease and that LSD would be dumped into the city's water supply.

The first few nights of the August 25–30 convention saw police staging midnight raids on hippies and protesters attempting to camp in Lincoln Park. The cops went on massive beating sprees, singling out some individuals for savage attacks. Teenage girls were assaulted by cops who shouted, 'You want free love? Try this!' Journalists, ministers and federal Justice Department officials were appalled.

The action then shifted to Grant Park, across from the Conrad Hilton (now the Chicago Hilton & Towers), where the main presidential candidates were staying. A few thousand protesters held a rally, which was met by an overwhelming force of 16,000 Chicago police officers, 4000 state police officers and 4000 members of the National Guard armed with tear-gas grenades, nightsticks and machine guns. When some protesters attacked a few officers, the assembled law enforcers staged what investigators later termed a police riot. Among the lowlights: cops shoved bystanders through plate-glass windows and then went on to beat them as they lay bleeding amid the shards; police on motorcycles ran over protesters; police chanted 'Kill, kill, kill!,' swarmed journalists and attempted to do just that; and when some wounded conventioneers were taken to the hotel suite of presidential candidate Gene McCarthy, cops burst through the door and beat everybody in sight.

The next night Mayor Daley went on national TV and attempted to defend the mayhem with an outright lie. He said he knew of plans to assassinate all the visiting presidential candidates. In reality, what Daley and the police did was play right into the hands of the most extreme of the protesters, who had hoped to provoke just such a sorry spectacle.

The long-term effects of the riots were far greater that anyone could have guessed. The Democratic candidate for president, Hubert Humphrey, was left without liberal backing after his tacit support of Daley's tactics, and as a result Republican Richard Nixon was elected president. Chicago was left with a huge black eye for decades. Once the most popular host to the hugely lucrative political conventions, it saw none return for almost 30 years, until 1996. The stories of police brutality, coupled with reports of rampant corruption in the department, led to decade-long changes that made the Chicago police force more racially balanced than it had ever been; it emerged as one of the most professional departments in the country.

Lyndon Johnson's attorney general refused to prosecute any of the protesters for conspiring to riot in Chicago. But in 1969 President Nixon ordered just such prosecutions, even though the actions of those charged may well have helped elect him. The 'Chicago Seven' trial became a total farce; the accused used it as a platform for protest, and aging judge Julius Hoffman showed a Daley-like tolerance for their antics by sentencing them to prison for contempt of court. However, on the central charges of inciting riots, all seven were acquitted.

Meanwhile, the city's economic structure was changing. In 1971 financial pressures caused the last of the Chicago stockyards to close, marking the end of one of the city's most infamous

1972

Chicagoan Curtis Mayfield releases *Superfly* soundtrack

1974

Sears Tower completed

enterprises. Elsewhere in the city, factories and steel mills shut down as companies moved to the suburbs or the southern US, where taxes and wages were lower. A decade of economic upheaval saw much of Chicago's industrial base erode. Many companies simply went out of business during the recession of the late 1970s. Chicago and much of the Midwest earned the moniker 'Rust Belt,' which described the area's shrunken economies and their rusting factories. The human costs in the city were high; thousands of blue-collar workers lost their high-paying union jobs with virtually no hope of finding replacement work.

But two events happened in the 1970s that were harbingers of the city's more promising future. The world's tallest building (at the time), the Sears Tower, opened in the Loop in 1974, beginning a development trend that would spur the creation of thousands of high-paying white-collar jobs. And in 1975 the Water Tower Place shopping mall brought new life to N Michigan Ave. It was a surprising lure for suburbanites, despite the very same stores in their own malls. Developers realized the urban environment was an attraction in itself.

Daley's death from a heart attack in 1976 began a process of political upheaval and reform that continued through the 1980s. Chicago's normally docile voters were enraged in 1978, when the city council cheerfully voted itself a 60% pay hike at the height of a recession amid record unemployment. Then, in January 1979, 4ft of snow hit Chicago. Daley's 'city that works' didn't, and voters gave Mayor Michael Bilandic a permanent Florida vacation (see the boxed text, p56), electing outsider Jane Byrne.

The colorful Byrne opened up Chicago to filmmakers, allowing the producers of *The Blues Brothers* to demolish part of Daley Center. She appointed her husband, a gregarious journalist, as her press secretary, and he was soon answering questions at press conferences with amusing lines like 'The mayor told me in bed this morning…' As a symbolic overture to minority constituents, Byrne moved into Cabrini-Green, the troubled Near North housing project, but she also showed insensitivity to Blacks on several issues, stoking deep-seated anger.

THE PEOPLE'S MAYOR

In the fall of 1982, a who's who of Black Chicago gathered in activist Lu Palmer's basement on the South Side. The mood was tense. Newspaper columnist Vernon Jarrett was so angry he was ready to punch Harold Washington. So were a lot of other people who had spent months working their butts off to build the incredible movement that was ready to propel Chicago's first African-American mayor – and a reformist to boot – into office. His election would present an obvious change in terms of race, but it was a far bigger challenge to the entrenched interests that had dominated city politics for decades. And now the candidate was dithering about whether he wanted to make the huge commitment to run.

Then-congressman Washington was making it clear that he didn't want to be the sacrificial lamb to a Byrne reelection juggernaut. But months earlier, in another meeting at Palmer's, he had told Jarrett and the rest that he would consider running if they registered 50,000 new voters. They registered 150,000. The movement was bigger than anybody could have hoped.

Eventually, an irate Washington stormed out of the meeting, but he couldn't stop the phenomenon he'd tacitly allowed to take root. He did run, and won the Democratic primary when Byrne and Richard M Daley split the White vote. He then won the general election.

Washington's first term was best described by the *Wall Street Journal*, which called Chicago 'Beirut on the Lake.' The entrenched political machine reacted with all the hostility you'd expect from people who saw their cozy system under attack. Much of the political and social chaos that marked city politics from 1983 to 1987 had ugly racial overtones, but at the heart of it was the old guard refusing to cede any power or patronage to the reform-minded mayor. In retrospect, the chaos benefited the city, because it opened up the political process.

The irony is that when Washington died seven months after he was reelected in 1987, he and his allies were just beginning to enjoy the same spoils of the machine they had once battled. Washington had amassed a solid majority of allies on the city council and was poised to begin pushing his own ambitious programs.

1986

Ferris Bueller's Day Off spikes teens' interest in French impressionist masters

1989

Richard M Daley elected mayor

WHITE BLIGHT

Any Chicago politician can tell you that snow is a substance sent by God to ruin political careers, and because of that, the powers that be view each and every delicate little flake as an invader to be eradicated, whatever the cost.

At the first sign of flurries, official Chicago mounts a counterattack that rivals the Normandy invasion in its fury and single-minded sense of purpose. After all, everybody in city government remembers what happened to Mayor Michael Bilandic, who was sunning himself in Florida in January 1979, when the city was smothered by one of the worst blizzards of the century. Never mind that experts say the volume of snow precluded any response that would have saved the city from being buried for weeks. Images of the tanned Bilandic tut-tutting about the white stuff while people suffered heart attacks digging out their cars stuck with voters when they went to the polls two months later.

Since then every mayor has gone to battle at the fall of the first flake. If you're in Chicago for a snowfall, you'll be treated to quite a show. First, more than 400 salt trucks with plows and flashing yellow lights hit the streets. Next come hundreds of garbage trucks hurriedly fitted with plows, followed by bulldozers, graders, dump trucks and other heavy equipment. Snow-parking rules go into effect, and any mope who leaves his or her car parked on an arterial street will find it towed.

At 10pm watch local newscasts. Each will have breathless reporters live at the command center of the Department of Streets & Sanitation, a milieu much like NASA's mission control, with reports of snow incursions immediately dispatched.

Tiny snowdrift forming at Clark and Diversey? Send in a platoon of plows! Patches of ice on the Randolph Bridge? Get a battalion of salt trucks over there! Homeless man refusing to leave box on Lower Wacker Dr? Send in a squad of cops to arrest him and toss him into a toasty cell. (Less-stubborn sorts can avail themselves of the scores of 'warming centers' the city opens around the city.)

Outsiders might consider this response overkill, but Chicagoans take pride in this can-do attitude. No matter that the thousands of tons of salt dumped every year dissolve concrete, bridges, cars, trees, boots and everything else – nobody complains. In 1992 a deep cold snap hit the Midwest and several cities ran out of salt. 'What's the situation locally?' reporters asked. While cars skated on other cities' streets, everyone was delighted to learn that Chicago still had enough salt for several years, because each year the city buys at least three times what it needs. You can see some of these huge bluish-white mountains on vacant land around town.

Of course, anybody who has been to places such as Washington, DC, Atlanta or Dallas, where just a few flakes can cause pandemonium, might appreciate Chicago's war on the stuff. And they might enjoy the show as well.

A lasting legacy of the Washington years has been the political success of the African-American politicians who followed him. Democrat Carol Moseley-Braun's election to the US senate in 1992 can be credited in part to Washington's political trailblazing. And John Stroger, the first Black president of the Cook County Board of Commissioners, was elected in 1994.

Overall, the 1980s meant good times for the city. The mid-decade economic boom in the US was especially strong in Chicago. Many young urban professionals – the oft-reviled 'yuppies' – found jobs in the fast-growing service and professional sectors and helped spark extensive real-estate development that left large portions of the aging North Side renovated and beautified. As these yuppies aged and started families, many of them stayed in the city rather than following their parents to the suburbs. As a result, gentrification keeps on going and going and going, for two decades and counting. As values in some neighborhoods soar, adjoining areas begin to benefit; the comparatively low prices attract new residents and investors. Development has now spread to portions of the city west and south of the Loop.

A NEW DALEY DAWNS

In 1989 Chicago elected Richard M Daley, the son of Richard J Daley, to finish the remaining two years of Harold Washington's term as mayor. Like his father, Daley owned an uncanny instinct for city politics. Unlike his father, he showed much political savvy in uniting disparate political forces. He shrewdly kept African-Americans within his political power structure, thus forestalling the kind of movement that propelled Washington to the mayor's office.

2001	2002
MTV's *Real World* comes to Chicago, met with protesters	Plans for new Soldier Field unveiled, immediately hailed as 'the mistake by the lake'

After Daley's election, the city enjoyed two years of cooperation between City Hall and then-governor Jim Thompson, who lived in and loved Chicago. Until then, the squabbles in city government had prevented the city from working effectively with the state. These new relations meant that state legislators freed up hundreds of millions of public dollars for the city's use, instead of letting the funds languish in state coffers (as they did through the '80s). Among the projects that bore fruit were an O'Hare airport expansion, the construction of a new South Building and hotel at McCormick Place, and the reconstruction of Navy Pier.

Daley moved to solidify his control of the city in a way his father would have applauded but in a much more enlightened manner. Old semi-independent bureaucracies such as the Park District and Department of Education were restructured under Daley protégés. And the new mayor entertained the city as well. Daley proved himself prone to amusing verbal blabber, such as this classic, his explanation for why city health inspectors had closed down so many local restaurants: 'Whadda ya want? A rat in yer sandwich or a mouse in yer salad?'

Despite falling to third-largest US city, population-wise, in the 1990 census, the '90s were a good decade for Chicago. In 1991 the Chicago Bulls won the first of six national basketball championships. The 1994 World Cup soccer opening ceremony focused international attention on the city. And in 1996 a 28-year-old demon was exorcised when the Democratic National Convention returned to Chicago. City officials spent millions of dollars spiffing up the town and thousands of cops underwent sensitivity training on how to deal with protests. The convention went off like a dream and left Chicagoans believing they were on a roll.

In 1999 Mayor Daley won his fourth mayoral election when he handily beat popular Black congressman Bobby Rush in the primary election. It was an auspicious win that set Daley firmly in control as Chicago headed into Y2K. It was Y2K01, however, that proved to be the more unsettling year for the city. On September 11, the terrorist attacks on Washington, DC and New York City cast Chicago's skyline in a much different light. Long a symbol of the city's strength, the tall buildings suddenly became Chicago's Achilles' heel.

The Sears Tower – which had shared tallest American building honors with the World Trade Center – hastily closed its observation deck. It soon reopened, but with airport-style X-ray machines and security devices. Other less lofty sites followed suit. The Chicago Board of Trade, fearing the financial havoc that could be wreaked by a well-timed bomb, began restricting visitors to its observation deck. The Chicago Mercantile Exchange did the same. For weeks after September 11, just going to work in the Loop felt a little like a brave and reckless act. By the end of October, a no-fly zone encircled the Loop. The no-fly zone was lifted after a couple of weeks, but then reinstated after a good deal of campaigning by Mayor Daley.

Daley won his fifth mayoral election in another landslide victory that year, and things were looking OK. An ambitious, Daley-helmed restructuring of the Chicago public-school system that began in 1989 was showing results, as children who had been kindergartners when Daley took over were now improving their standardized test scores. And Daley's aesthetic dictates – tulips, planters and parks – had the city looking better than it had in decades. Even African-Americans, who had been alienated by Daley's father, turned out in support.

Daley leveraged the turnout in the polls to consolidate his political power in the city. Nowhere was this more apparent than the infamous Meigs Field incident of March 2003. Meigs was a tiny commuter airport on the edge of the Museum Campus downtown, a tantalizingly valuable piece of real estate the mayor had repeatedly argued should be made into a park.

When he ran into opposition from the airport's users – CEOs and other corporate types, mostly – he dropped the plan. Or appeared to, anyway. Then, at 11:30pm on March 30, he shocked the city by sending bulldozers to Meigs under the cover of darkness. The bulldozers made quick work of the airport's runway, as news helicopters flew overhead, capturing images of the affair. The next day, the mayor defended the closure of the airport as a long-overdue move needed to protect the city's skyscrapers from a Meigs-launched terrorist attack. Editorials in both papers bristled at the autocratic action, and the airport's users talked about taking legal action to force the reopening of the airstrip. But legally, the mayor appeared to be within his rights, and the fallout over the incident has passed. For the time being, anyway.

2004

Kanye West puts Chicago hip-hop on the map

2005

Chicago White Sox win World Series; 10,000 Chicago sports fans now able to die happy

Sights

Sights

By the city's official count, Chicago has 198 different neighborhoods. While this seems a little suspect – the city, after all, also counts the Cubs and the Bears as professional sports teams – it's clear that Chicago boasts a great number of distinct neighborhoods, each one marked by its own look, feel and cache of delights.

Tourists to Chicago tend to spend most of their time in the Loop and Near North neighborhoods. These sight-heavy and shop-laden areas could easily occupy you for an entire week. But don't give in to the temptation to spend your whole trip here. Those who squeeze in some trips to the areas outside of the downtown neighborhoods will be rewarded with a wealth of museums, galleries, historical sights, architectural wonders and, most importantly, encounters with everyday Chicagoans in the neighborhoods where they live and play.

Take the expensive Gold Coast, for instance, where tiny, pampered pooches stroll along sidewalks shaded by trees planted when the city's elite migrated up here in the late 1800s.

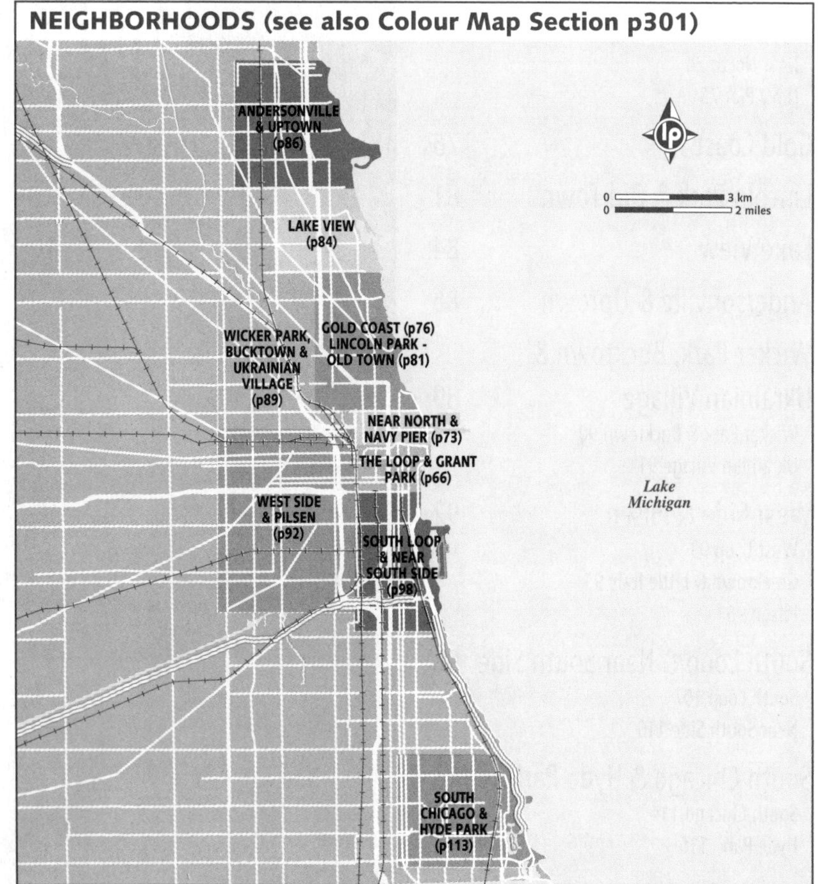

Further north is the historic Old Town area, home of Second City, and the trendy Lincoln Park neighborhood, where college students and yuppies enjoy beautiful parklands and a mouthwatering array of restaurants.

Keep moving north of Lincoln Park and you'll find Lake View – a hub for bars, both gay and straight, as well as the site of the St Peter's Basilica of Chicago baseball, Wrigley Field. Above Lake View is the jazzy destination of up-and-coming Uptown and the European-feeling Andersonville. From there you could swing to the southwest to explore the must-see Wicker Park and Bucktown neighborhoods, as well as the boutique-y bloom afoot in nearby Ukrainian Village.

A quick jog across Congress Ave from the Loop, the West Side has galleries and stunning eateries perched atop layers of turbulent Chicago history. Pilsen, too, is one of the city's most interesting juxtapositions of young and old, with Czech homes housing Hispanic residents who go to hip gallery shows. And then there's the city's condo-central South Loop and Near South Side, where the skyline changes every week and the Chinese food is the best in the city.

ITINERARIES

One Day

Start your day with a plate of eggs and a sweet treat at Lou Mitchell's (p164), followed by a quick cab ride down to the Art Institute of Chicago (p67). Walk off any feelings of art-overload with a short stroll through Millennium Park (p69), and take advantage of the great self-portrait photo opportunity at the Bean. Walk to Rhapsody (p138) for note-perfect lunch, and then take a cab up to Michigan Ave for some top-tier window-shopping. Dinner is deep-dish pizza at nearby Giordano's (p143), followed by sunset after-dinner drinks way, way up on the 96th floor of the John Hancock Center's Signature Lounge (one floor up from the Signature Room, p147). If you're feeling jazzy, take a cab to the Green Mill (p182) afterwards. If not, take in a play at the Lookingglass Theatre (p190) just down the street from the Hancock. Then it's back to the hotel for some well-deserved slumber.

Three Days

Spread out the stops mentioned above over one and a half days, and spend your second afternoon on the water, taking the Chicago Architecture Foundation's riverboat tour (p65). Afterwards, take the Blue Line to Wicker Park (p229), where you can go shopping for souvenirs along Milwaukee and Damen Aves. Dine on the West Side – either communally at Avec (p162) or on vegetarian delights at Green Zebra (p161). No matter how good your dinner, you'll have the blues by the time your cab pulls up at Lee's Unleaded Blues (p182) afterwards. Day Three is a sleep-in day, followed by a late-morning visit to one of the Museum Campus (p107) institutions. Have lunch in the Loop (p136), then spend the rest of the day leisurely exploring the lakefront on a rented bike (p120). Wherever you find yourself for dinner, follow it up with a movie at the classic old Music Box Theatre (p197).

One Week

Tackle the three-day itinerary above, pampering yourself along the way with a visit to one of Chicago's many spas or bathhouses (p214). Make time for a Cubs game (p200) or, if sports aren't your thing, spend a day gallery-hopping in River North (p75) or the West Loop (p93). Relax in Lincoln Park (p83) and visit the superb (and free!) African exhibit at the Lincoln Park Zoo (p83). In your Chicago travels, you are bound to fall in love with one or more of the dozens of colorful neighborhoods here. The city-sponsored walking tours (p65) are a great way to get to know these neighborhoods like a native. Or let a Chicago Greeter (p65) take you on a free, personalized guided tour that you won't soon forget.

ORGANIZED TOURS

Bus Tours

American Sightseeing (☎ 312-251-3100) departs from the Palmer House Hilton and other downtown hotels. The buses are of the big air-conditioned and tinted-glass variety, which means that you're definitely insulated from the sights you see. It runs two- to eight-hour tours of north and south Chicago neighborhoods, starting at $20.

The **Chicago Trolley Co** (☎ 773-648-5000; www.chicagotrolley.com) runs year-round tours in 'San Francisco–style' vehicles and red double-decker buses. Its 13-mile guided tour takes you through downtown and Near North. It covers all the major sights and, best of all, you can hop on and off to your heart's content. Tours start at $10. Call to find out which stop is closest to you.

Boat Tours

Chicago has two main boat-tour companies offering similar 90-minute tours of the river and lake for similar prices. The guides are often perfunctory, offering bad jokes and limited information. Be aware that passing through the locks to and from the lake can take up a fair part of the tour. Boat tours run from May to November.

When the wind blows, which is most of the time, the 148ft **Windy** (Map pp306-7; ☎ 312-595-5555), a four-masted gaff topsail schooner, plies the lake from May to September. The class B tall ship is the only certified four-masted traditional sailing vessel in the US. Passengers can play sailor by helping to raise and lower the sails. A better deal is to play skipper by trying your hand at the wheel. With only the sound of the wind in your ears, the *Windy* is the most relaxing way to see the skyline from offshore. Ninety-minute tours start at $25.

Mercury Chicago Skyline Cruises (Map pp302-3; ☎ 312-332-1353; www.mercuryskylinecruiseline.com) departs from the southeast corner of the Michigan Ave Bridge; tours start at $18. **Wendella Sightseeing Boats** (Map pp306-7; ☎ 312-337-1446; www.wendellaboats.com) departs from the northwest corner of the Michigan Ave Bridge; tours start at $19. Both also offer other tours and night cruises.

Shoreline Sightseeing (Map pp306-7; ☎ 312-222-9328; www.shorelinesightseeing.com) runs tours of Lake Michigan and the Chicago River and also acts as a water taxi, shuttling riders between Navy Pier, the Shedd Aquarium and the Sears Tower. Tours start at $10, and water taxi rides at $6. Printed translations of the tour narration are available in 12 languages including French, Spanish, German, Polish, Arabic, Japanese and Hindi.

If you're looking for a tour of Chicago's skyline with a little more muscle, **Seadog Cruises** (Map pp306-7; ☎ 312-822-7200; www.seadogcruises.com) is happy to assist. Its 2000+HP speedboats will zip you through a 30-minute lake tour, or you can take it slower with a 75-minute architectural tour along the river. Tours start at $17.

Odyssey Cruises (Map pp306-7; ☎ 800-947-9367; www.odysseycruises.com) operates a sleek cruise boat that looks like a huge yacht. Two-hour cruises, which sail throughout the year, include a meal and music. Glamour doesn't come cheap,

IT COSTS WHAT?

Whoever said the best things in life are free definitely spent some time in Chicago. In addition to the free music festivals in Grant Park over the summer and various free museum days, we have plenty of favorite freebies in the Windy City:

- The **Chicago Greeter** (opposite) program involves a friendly local expert showing you exactly the parts of the city you want to see.
- The **Museum of Contemporary Photography** (p108) is a small museum with big-name photographers.
- You think stained glass is for squares? We did too, until we came upon the **Smith Museum of Stained Glass Windows** (p76), stuck in a hallway of Navy Pier.
- **Lincoln Park Zoo** (p83) offers unlimited access to aardvarks and elephants – all day long! What more do you want?
- Your views on Mexican art will never be the same once you have visited the **Mexican Fine Arts Center Museum** (p97) – it's that good.

and the company suggests that you should dress up for the experience. Brunches and lunches start at $39, dinners at $84. A two-hour moonlight cruise during the summer costs $34 and leaves at midnight.

The **Spirit of Chicago** (Map pp306-7; ☎ 866-211-3804; www.spiritcitycruises.com) offers slightly downscale lunch and dinner cruises (wear what you want), departing year-round except when the lake is frozen. The boat offers lots of open space on deck for enjoying the view. Lunch cruises start at $40, dinner cruises at $78 and various party cruises at $25.

Mystic Blue Cruises (Map pp306-7; ☎ 877-299-7783) offers a slightly hipper (read: younger) take on the lakefront tour. Its lunch, noon, dinner, cocktail and moonlight tours start at $23.

Cruising on the Chicago River.

Specialist Tours

Sure, the tourist boat companies run architecture tours. Those in the know, though, make a beeline for cruises run by the **Chicago Architecture Foundation** (CAF; Map pp304-5; ☎ 312-922-3432; www.architecture.org; Santa Fe Center, 224 S Michigan Ave). Staff are ready to answer questions at the foundation's office. The 90-minute boat tours ($25) are lead by volunteers and depart daily from early May through November, from the southeast corner of the Michigan Ave Bridge and the Chicago River. The CAF also runs more than 50 walking tours of the city and suburbs. Two of the most popular are the Historic Skyscrapers walking tour, which departs at 10am daily, and the Modern Skyscrapers tour, which departs at 1:30pm daily. Both start at the Santa Fe Center and cost $12. The Hancock Center office also dispatches a tour of N Michigan Ave at 11am Friday, Saturday and Monday; it costs $12 and lasts about two hours. The CAF also operates bus tours of Chicago, Prairie Ave, Hyde Park, Oak Park and other areas. During the summer it offers architectural bike tours. Call for schedules. One of the best deals is its El tours of the Loop on summer Saturdays. These are free – call for details.

Other highly recommended tours are run by the city's Department of Cultural Affairs. **Chicago Neighborhood Tours** (☎ 312-742-1190; www.chgocitytours.com) covers a different neighborhood every Saturday morning, led by local experts. Tours include many neighborhoods ignored by more mainstream tour companies. To join the $25 tours, be at the Chicago Cultural Center (p68) at 9:30am for the 10am bus departure.

The city is also behind another worthwhile, almost too-good-to-be-true endeavor. The **Chicago Greeter** (☎ 312-744-8000; www.chicagogreeter.com), based out of Chicago Cultural Center, pairs visitors with a local volunteer who will take guests on an informal, free two-hour tour around town. One week's notice is required.

Chicago Supernatural Tours (☎ 708-499-0300; www.ghosttours.com) offers nighttime bus tours that take visitors on a ghoulish itinerary of murder sites, cemeteries, supposedly haunted houses and all sorts of other places with spiritual connections (at least in the minds of the tour leaders). Tours cost $35.

Horse-drawn carriages depart from the Water Tower day and night throughout the year. These attract lots of suburban teens who are in town for a prom and want to smooch. Rates start at $35 for a minimum of 30 minutes; each half hour thereafter costs another $35. Drivers will hope for a tip, whether they give witty commentary or leave you to your romance. You can choose a route or let the driver pick one for you. Carriages can be reserved through **JC Cutters** (☎ 312-664-6014; www.jccutters.com).

Untouchable Gangster Tours (☎ 773-881-1195; www.gangstertour.com) leads comic tours through gangland Chicago daily; tickets cost $24. Confirm pick-up/departure points when booking.

CHICAGO WITH CHILDREN

Chicago is a kid's kind of place. Here are the city's sights that will have them screaming (in a good way).

Adler Planetarium (p107) Where little astronomers are stars.

Chicago Children's Museum (p74) The only problem you'll face on a visit to this educational playland on Navy Pier is making your kids leave come closing time.

Chicago's beaches (p213) The pint-sized waves are perfect for pint-sized swimmers.

Crown Fountain at Millennium Park (p69) It's like swimming in art!

Field Museum of Natural History (p108) Where you'll discover everything from dinosaurs to lost civilizations.

Grant Park (p71) Erupting fountains, proximity to trains and lots of room to run make this a beloved park for youngsters.

John Hancock Center Observatory (p78) Their noses will be stuck to the glass for hours.

Lincoln Park Paddleboat Rides (p83) The water fights are optional.

Lincoln Park Zoo (p83) The new African exhibit includes an entire room full of cockroaches.

Museum of Science & Industry (p117) This huge museum will leave even the most energetic child happily spent after a few educational hours.

Navy Pier fountains and rides (p74) A Ferris wheel, a carousel and a thousand joyful ways to get soaked.

Peggy Notebaert Nature Museum (p84) Where the butterflies frolic freely.

Sears Tower Skydeck (p70) Fantastic views and special kid-friendly history exhibits make this a sky-high treat.

Shedd Aquarium (p109) The top-notch collection of fish and marine mammals makes for a whale of a good time.

'The Picasso' statue (p127) Adults can ponder the meaning of it all while kids whoop it up sliding down the ramp built into the sculpture's base in the Loop.

If you've been forever wanting to try a Segway 'Human Transporter' (you know, those futuristic, two-wheeled scooter contraptions that you saw the Millennium Park security guards whirring around on), there are two companies offering tours on these. The **Segway Experience** (☎ 312-663-0600; www.segwayexperience.com; 224 S Michigan Ave, entrance on Monroe St) runs three two-hour 'park glides' daily, where a guide takes a group to explore Grant Park. Tours are $70 per person, and kids 13 and under can only participate at the discretion of the tour operator. **City Segway Tours** (☎ 877-734-8687; www.citysegwaytours.com/chicago), which also leads Segway tours in New Orleans and Paris, offers similar twice-daily, two-hour tours of Grant Park for $65. Both companies precede the tour with about 40 minutes of Segway training and safety orientation. Tours are run out of the Adler Planetarium.

THE LOOP & GRANT PARK

Eating p136; Shopping p216; Sleeping p237

Caffeine junkies needing a morning fix can skip the latte when they come to the Loop; the surging energy of the city's historic heart is enough to get any pulse racing. The Loop breathes electricity, with the clattering roar of the El trains echoed in the tumultuous tides of office-bound workers. Newspaper hawkers wade into traffic, fishing for sales from executives barking into cell phones. And above the melee, a towering forest of steel and stone soaks in the first rays of the sun.

The vital signs of the Loop weren't always so strong. The 1970s and '80s saw many of the Loop's theaters and restaurants flee to the Near North, the Gold Coast and other neighborhoods. In 1979 a disastrous effort that turned State St into a pedestrian mall proved a 15-year failure that primarily benefited exhaust-belching buses. Most of the remaining entertainment venues in the area closed or moved. At night the streets needed only a few urban tumbleweeds to complete the bleak tableau.

But during this same period the city doggedly kept trying to resuscitate the area. Developers were offered tax breaks, while State St was eventually attractively

TRANSPORTATION

Bus Number 56 runs along Milwaukee Ave from Wicker Park into the Loop; 151 comes down Michigan Ave from the lakefront in the north; 156 travels along La Salle St from River North.

El All lines converge in the Loop; find your destination and take your pick.

Metra Randolph St Station for the north loop; Van Buren St Station for the south.

Parking There is an underground pay lot on Michigan Ave at Washington St and another at Van Buren St. Warning: if you park at a meter along S Columbus Dr, be aware that each meter covers two spaces. If there's no meter at your spot, you likely need to feed the closest one.

remodeled with new street lamps, improved El entrances and other classical details, and reopened to traffic.

Now that the new Loop theater district has further helped to revive the neighborhood, and developers have hit upon innovative schemes for some of the older office buildings. Previously, these architecturally significant buildings would have been torn down because their small floors, low ceilings and other details make them unsuitable for modern offices. Now, however, developers have realized that those small floors are perfect for residences and hotels. As part of this trend, the number of people living in the Loop and its environs has grown by 37% in 10 years.

Grant Park, the green play space that forms a leafy buffer between the Loop and Lake Michigan, shares the Loop's story of grand starts and big slips. Like the Loop, the park has gotten plenty of loving attention from city's budget office in the past decade, turning once-seedy areas into blooming examples of urban planning. Millennium Park is the best example of this, and a stroll through Chicago's latest wonder should be at the top of any visitor's Loop agenda.

Orientation

Wacker Dr (and the Chicago River beyond it) serves as the north and west boundaries of the Loop. The busy Congress Pkwy cuts across the south end of the neighborhood. When looking for an address in the Loop, pay attention to the compass designation that kicks it off; both Madison St (the dividing line for the city's north/south addresses) and State St (the dividing line for Chicago's east/west addresses) are located here. If you arrive at your destination and your hotel has become a Burger King, chances are good that you've swapped an N for an S or an E for a W.

Grant Park acts as a long buffer between the Loop on the west and Lake Michigan to the east. The park is girded by three main north–south thoroughfares, the busy S Lake Shore Dr, Columbus Dr and, on the Loop edge, S Michigan Ave. Millennium Park abuts Grant Park to the northwest. The summer parades for Chicago's ethnic communities often pass through the park, running along S Columbus Dr between E Balbo Dr in the south and E Monroe St in the north.

THE LOOP

ART INSTITUTE OF CHICAGO

Map pp304-5

☎ 312-443-3600; www.artic.edu/aic/; 111 S Michigan Ave; adult/senior/student & child $12/7/7, Tue free; 🕑 10:30am-4:30pm Mon-Wed & Fri, until 8pm Thu, 10am-5pm Sat & Sun

One of the world's premier museums, the Art Institute of Chicago has the kind of celebrity-heavy collection that routinely draws gasps from patrons. Grant Wood's stern *American Gothic*? Check. Edward Hopper's lonely *Nighthawks*? Uh huh. Georges Seurat's *A Sunday Afternoon on La Grand Jatte* (you know, the one that Cameron freaked out over in *Ferris Bueller's Day Off…*)? You bet.

Many of the iconic works that have become part of popular culture – through spoofs in movies, cartoons and advertising –

TOP FIVE LOOP & GRANT PARK

- Staring at reflective self-portraits at the **Bean** (p69).
- Flying along the **Lakefront Bike Path** (p120) on a rented bicycle.
- Enjoying the beer, er, history at the **Berghoff Stand Up Bar** (p170).
- Saying 'hello Dali' to the Surrealist collection at the **Art Institute of Chicago** (above).
- Exploring downtown's groundbreaking **19th-century architecture** (p129).

live in the Art Institute. Its collection of impressionist and postimpressionist paintings is second only to collections in France, and the number of surrealist works – especially boxes by Joseph Cornell – is tremendous.

In the galleries you'll find African and ancient American art; American art from the 17th century onward; ancient Egyptian, Greek and Roman art; Chinese, Japanese and Korean art, beginning 5000 years ago; European decorative arts since the 12th century; European paintings and sculpture from 1400 to 1800; 19th-century European paintings; photography; studies and plans from other buildings; prints and drawings; textiles; furniture; and 20th-century paintings and sculpture.

Don't even think of coming to Chicago without spending at least two hours in the museum. And when you do come, take our 'greatest hits' walking tour (p121), or grab one of the excellent, free museum maps to plan a route that will take you directly to the styles and periods that turn you on. But whatever you do, make a plan: simply wandering through the museum floor by floor will have your feet crying foul before you even make it to the Renaissance.

The main entrance is the original 1893 Allerton Building, where Adams St meets Michigan Ave. The steps themselves become one of the city's prime rendezvous points on fair days. The modern 1977 Rubloff Building, accessed via the Columbus Dr entrance, houses the School of the Art Institute, where the number of pierced body parts far exceeds the student body. The Rice Building was added in 1988, and a brand-new building facing Millennium Park will be opening in 2009.

The museum's good café and restaurant are open for lunch daily and stay open until 7pm on Thursday.

CHICAGO CULTURAL CENTER

Map pp304-5

☎ 312-346-3278; 78 E Washington St; admission free; 10am-7pm Mon-Wed, to 9pm Thu & Fri, to 5pm Sat, 11am-5pm Sun

Think you're just going to swing by the Visitor Information Center and grab some free maps and brochures? Think again. Exhibitions, beautiful interior design and free concerts by up-and-coming Chicago musicians all make the block-long Chicago Cultural Center an easy place to enter and a difficult place to leave. The exhibitions on three floors change frequently; take a moment as you enter on either Randolph or Washington Sts to find out the schedule of events.

The building began its life as the Chicago Public library back in 1897, and the Gilded Age interior is a beautiful mix of white Carrara and green Connemara marble. The building also contains two domes by Louis Comfort Tiffany, including the world's largest stained-glass Tiffany dome on the 3rd floor (where the circulation desk for the library used to be). The splendor of the building was meant to inspire the rabble toward loftier goals.

Excellent, free **building tours** (☎ 312-742-1190; 1:15pm Tue-Sat) leave from the Randolph St lobby. Free lunchtime concerts take place every weekday at 12:15pm.

CHICAGO THEATRE Map pp304-5

☎ 312-462-6363; www.thechicagotheatre.com; 175 N State St; tours noon Thu, 11am & noon on the 3rd Sat of the month year-round, also noon Tue May-Sep); Red Line to Lake

The history is written on the walls of the incomparable Chicago Theatre. Literally: nearly every performer who has appeared here in the last 20 years – from Dean Martin to Prince – has left their John Hancock on one of the backstage walls. You can see all of them on a tour of the theater, though it is the French Baroque architecture of the former movie palace that is the real show-stopper. Opened in 1921, the theater screened silent movies with a full orchestral accompaniment. Working-class Chicagoans were welcomed into the opulent space (which boasted teams of white-gloved ushers), allowing the poor access to the sort of splendor that was previously the reserve of Chicago's upper classes. As well as movies, the theater hosted live concerts, showcasing the talents of artists such as Duke Ellington and Benny Goodman. It closed in 1985, but was reopened as a concert venue in 1987.

MARSHALL FIELD'S Map pp304-5

☎ 312-781-1000; www.fields.com; 111 N State St; 9:45am-7pm Mon-Wed & Fri, to 8pm Thu, 10am-6pm Sat, 11am-6pm Sun; Red Line to Washington

The iconic bronze corner clocks on the outside of Marshall Field's (soon to be renamed Macy's) have been letting busy Loop workers know what time it is for over 100 years now. Along with all the clothes and other department store knickknacks you'd expect to find in this store, fans of Louis Comfort Tiffany will be delighted by the 6000-sq-ft dome capping the atrium in the north end of the building. Tiffany directed the 50 artists who toiled for 18 months to make it.

MILLENNIUM PARK Map pp304-5

☎ 312-742-1168; www.millenniumpark.org; Welcome Center, 201 E Randolph St; 🕑 6am-11pm; Brown, Green, Orange, Purple Line to Randolph or Madison

A 24-acre extravaganza, Millennium Park occupies a prime location on Michigan Ave between Randolph and Monroe Sts. Originally slated to open with the millennium, the park got off to an embarrassingly slow start when the original contractor – a chum of Mayor Daley's – went $100 million over budget, missed various deadlines and was eventually fired. The sailing was much smoother thereafter, and the park's mix of huge, playful art projects, quiet, contemplative nooks, and beautiful gardens have both placated the park's detractors and fast become Chicago icons.

The park has been so popular, in fact, that urban planners from around the country are already taking note of the 'Millennium Park Effect', whereby a huge investment in a free, modern art–filled public space has increased both civic pride *and* the city's fiscal outlook, bringing developers to town who are eager to erect ambitious new buildings that can bask in the park's glow. In fact, many in Chicago have come to see Millennium Park as the modern equivalent of the 'White City' built by Daniel Burnham and his team in Jackson Park for the 1893 World's Expo. Both projects sprang up in very unlikely places (Millennium Park is essentially the roof of the parking garage below it). Both were extremely over-budget and dogged by construction misadventures, and ultimately created complete worlds unto themselves, a universe of new experiences and objects that the world had never before seen.

An hour-long stroll is the best way to take in the park. You can take a walking tour (p131), or drop into the **Millennium Park Welcome Center** (201 E Randolph St), where the Chicago Greeter program runs free **guided park tours** (🕑 10am-4pm Wed-Fri summer only). They depart from the Welcome Center every half hour and are 45 minutes long. If you have an iPod, you can also download the official audio tour for free at www.antenna audio.com/millenniumpark.shtml.

The stately curved colonnades of the **Wrigley Sq and Millennium Monument** replicate the Greek-inspired structure that stood here 50 years ago. Millennium Park was partially financed with gifts from local corporations and deep-pocketed philanthropists; you can see the names of particularly generous cash cows affixed to park features and etched into the base of the monument here. The dramatic colonnade is a godsend for the city's wedding portrait photographers, and those looking to make it into the background of a couple's special moment need only wait a few minutes on sunny days for a blushing bride and groom to come along.

The **McCormick-Tribune Ice Rink** (55 N Michigan Ave; 🕑 Oct-Mar) allows skaters to meditate on the beauty of the Loop's skyline as they practice their figure-eights on the ice. In summer, the rink becomes an extension of the **Park Grill** (☎ 312-521-7275; 11 N Michigan Ave; 🕑 11am-9:30pm Sun-Thu, 11am-10:30pm Fri & Sat) and attached **Park Cafe**, a popular place for parents to have a beer while their kids play in the **Crown Fountain**. The fountain's two 50ft towers are outfitted with LED displays that project a shifting array of faces of everyday Chicagoans who were filmed for the project. Water is pumped up to the top of the towers, where it cascades down onto the black granite below.

To the northeast of the fountain is the huge Anish Kapoor sculpture officially titled **Cloud Gate** but known by everyone in Chicago as the Bean.

Rivaling the Crown Fountain and Cloud Gate for the title of Park's Best Eye-Candy is the **Jay Pritzker Pavilion**. The striking bandshell was designed by Frank Gehry, the trendsetting architect responsible for the Guggenheim Museum in Bilbao, Spain. The freaky curved ribbons of stainless steel, peeling back from above the bandshell, have raised the ire of some conservative Chicagoans, but most people absolutely love it. The acoustics are superb, and the sightlines from the seats and lawn are much better than the area's former setting for outdoor music, the Petrillo Music Shell, across the

WHAT THE EL WAS THAT NOISE?

Novelist Nelson Algren (p30) called them Chicago's 'rusty iron heart.' And Chicago's El trains – short for elevated trains – definitely occupy a prized place in the popular consciousness of the city. From El-related blogs (see www.ctatattler.com and www.thisisgrand.org) to locals wearing T-shirts emblazoned with their favorite transit lines, the El trains have been both a mode of transportation and a mover of souls since they made their debut in the Loop in 1897.

Back then (as now) the Union Loop El trains ran on electricity rather than cables or steam. The whole electric train thing was still a new idea at the time, and the Union Loop was viewed with scepticism and more than a little fear by some residents. The medical profession didn't exactly help matters, either. The New York Academy of Medicine published a paper that year claiming that the elevated trains 'prevented the normal development of children, threw convalescing patients into relapses, and caused insomnia, exhaustion, hysteria, paralysis, meningitis, deafness, and death.'

Though the case for meningitis might have been a *little* overstated, visitors to Chicago who stand under one of the trains as they pass will attest to the risk of deafness. In fact, a group of students from Columbia College conducted a study in 2005 that found the screeching from the train cars exceeded legal levels on several of the tracks. Most Chicagoans, though, just shrug off any attempts to make changes to the system that has been rattling Loop windows and sending cars screeching overhead for over 100 years. It may be rusty, but it's their heart all the same.

The Chicago Office of Tourism runs a free, 40-minute El tour four times daily on Saturdays from May to September. Tours (p65) are led by Chicago Architecture Foundation docents and cover the history of the El and the downtown area it serves. You can pick up same-day tickets at the Visitor Information Center in the **Chicago Cultural Center** (Map pp304-5; ☎ 312-744-2400; 77 E Randolph St).

street in Grant Park. The long-windedly named **Joan W & Irving B Harris Theater for Music & Dance** (☎ 312-629-8696; www.madtchi.com; 205 E Randolph St) is right behind the pavilion. The 1500-seat theater has become a high-profile home for a dozen nonprofit arts groups. While you're in the vicinity of the pavilion, be sure to stop by the **Lurie Gardens**, which uses a blend of native and non-native plants to form a botanical tribute to the tall-grass prairie and Chicago's rebirth after the fire of 1871. Along with being a potent metaphor for Chicago's ability to rise above adversity, the place is just darned pretty. Snaking across Columbus Dr is the **BP Pedestrian Bridge**, which was also designed by Gehry. It functions as a safe way for folks to get from Millennium Park to Grant Park and the lakeshore further east. It also acts as a sound baffle to help keep inadvertent low notes of rumbling semis from making their way into the Grant Park Orchestra programs.

RIVERWALK GATEWAY Map pp304-5

The melding of city finances and local artistry is also on view at the Riverwalk Gateway, Chicago's largest work of public art. Artist Ellen Lanyon created 28 glazed, fired panels that relate key moments in Chicago's river-centric history. The 6ft by 9ft panels depict everything from the 1673 trampings of explorers Jacques Marquette and Louis Jolliet to flag-toting waterskiers celebrating the reduction of river pollution in 2000.

SEARS TOWER Map pp304-5

☎ 312-875-9696; www.the-skydeck.com; 233 S Wacker Dr; adult/child/senior $11.95/8.50/9.95; ⏲ 10am-10pm May-Sep, 10am-8pm Oct-Apr, last ticket sold 30min before closing

It lost the title of world's tallest building years ago (the title goes to Taiwan's Taipei 101 Building), but there's no doubt that the Sears Tower has become a symbol of Chicago. It boasts the kind of stats that make good grade-school presentations: 43,000 miles of phone cable, 2232 steps to the roof, enough concrete to build an eight-lane highway 5 miles long.

Much of what's inside the 110-story, 1454ft building is mundane office space. But the lure of the world's highest observation deck draws more than 1.5 million people a year. The **Skydeck** entrance is on the Jackson Blvd side of the block-size building. Your journey to the top starts with a walk through an airport-style metal detector, followed by a slow elevator ride down to the waiting area where visitors queue for tickets. A sign will tell you how long you'll have to wait to get to the top. On busy days it can be an hour or longer, so this is a good time to confirm the visibility – before you invest your time and money. Even days that seem sunny can have upper-level haze that limits the view. On good days, however, you can see for 40 to 50 miles, as far as Indiana, Michigan and Wisconsin.

After buying your ticket, you'll have to sit through *Over Chicago*. The syrupy narration and dated aerial footage of Chicago in the film may seem endless, but after the 15-minute presentation, you're cleared for takeoff. The 70-second elevator ride will definitely have your ears popping.

Once on the Skydeck, you're bound to think the view was worth the price paid in money and patience. The entire city stretches below, and you can take the time to see exactly how Chicago is laid out. Sunsets can be quite stunning, and the emergence of lights at twilight is charming. Interesting, kid-friendly exhibits on Chicago history wrap around the interior walls, serving as an ideal distraction for those suffering from an unexpected onset of vertigo.

GRANT PARK

Though its charms are very different from the high-tech entertainment provided by neighboring Millennium Park, Grant Park is still an essential piece in the downtown Chicago puzzle. In summer, the park is mobbed with tens of thousands of people gnawing their way through the Taste of Chicago food fiesta, or moving and grooving to the myriad music festivals that blast everything from blues to progressive house out over the waters of Lake Michigan.

When not in the manic moods of summer, Grant Park is a quiet place popular with Loop workers getting a breath of fresh air on their lunch break. Like everything else in the area, it has benefited from the opening of Millennium Park – especially the northern tip of the park, which is now connected via the serpentine Frank Gehry–designed BP Pedestrian Bridge (opposite).

Buckingham Fountain (right)

Known as 'Lake Front Park' when it was officially founded in 1847, the space was originally just a narrow strip of land along the lake. Back in the 1860s, a railroad trestle for the Illinois Central Railroad ran parallel to the area's shoreline out in Lake Michigan. During the clean-up from the fire of 1861, much of the remains of the 18,000 buildings destroyed in the blaze were simply dumped into the lake, much of it between Lake Front Park and the trestle. This trash extended the city into the lake by about three city blocks, increasing the size of Lake Front park and, ironically, creating much of what would eventually become very valuable Loop real estate north of the park.

By the 1890s, though, things had gone downhill for Lake Front Park, which was clogged with several lanes of railroad traffic, and shantytowns had sprouted up throughout the area. The *Chicago Daily News* wrote about the 'great smelly spaces east of Michigan Ave' full of 'dumphills' where 'dog fights alternated with wrestling bouts' and 'the winter's residue of deceased animals lent an added something to the vernal breezes.'

Along with the shantytowns, a host of other smaller buildings – from railroad storage sheds to public-works structures – began to appear in the park. Montgomery Ward came to the rescue (see the boxed text, p72), using a series of lawsuits to clear the land of its occupying armies. Today, the park is the recipient of TLC from the city in the form of new trees and sidewalks, and some interesting sculpture to boot. The park's Rose Gardens contain 150 varieties best viewed from mid-June to September. To watch Chicagoans at a favorite pastime, stop by Hutchinson Field, where scores of amateur league softball games are played each summer.

BUCKINGHAM FOUNTAIN Map pp304-5

🕑 **flows 10am-11pm May-Sep**

The best known of Grant Park's features, this fountain was made nationally famous in the '80s by the opening sequence of the TV show *Married with Children*. Kate Sturges Buckingham, a very wealthy

THE MAN WHO SAVED THE LAKEFRONT

When Chicagoans frolic at the lakefront's vast expanse of beaches and parks, they should thank Montgomery Ward, founder of the department stores bearing his name, who led an impassioned crusade to save the shore from development.

For two decades beginning in 1890, Ward invested a good chunk of his fortune in legal battles to block various projects that would have used a little bit of the shoreline here and a little bit there until all that would have separated the city from the lake was a wall of buildings. Although he was up against the three forces that have shaped the city – greed, power and corruption – Ward steadfastly defended Chicago's original charter, which stipulated that the lakefront should remain 'forever open, clear and free.' Although his many critics thought of him as a populist dilettante, Ward saw the parks as a 'breathing spot' for the city's teeming masses.

After Ward's death in 1913, many others continued fighting for his cause. They had their work cut out for them, as a steady stream of politicians viewed developing the empty real estate of the lakefront and beaches as 'progress.' For example, during the 1960s, Mayor Richard J Daley and his cronies hatched schemes that would have put huge overpasses and cloverleaves at both Oak St Beach and 57th St Beach. Fortunately, both schemes died after massive protest.

widow (who would have likely been none too pleased with her fountain's appearance on the show) gave the magnificent structure to the city in 1927 in memory of her brother, Clarence. She also wisely left an endowment to maintain and operate the fountain. It's twice the size of its model, the Bassin de Latone at Versailles. The central fountain is meant to symbolize Lake Michigan, with the four water-spouting sea creatures representing the surrounding states. The fountain presents a subtle show rather than randomly spraying its 1.5 million gallons. Like so much in life, the spray begins small. Each successive basin fills, stimulating more jets, then climaxes as the central fountain spurts up to its full 150ft. The crowd sighs in awe and is thankful that smoking is allowed. The fountain climaxes once an hour, and mood lighting (colored lights timed to match the fountain's 'moods') comes on at 8pm; the best time to experience the full melodic effect is 9pm. At the four corners of the gravel expanse that surrounds the fountain, pavilions have toilets and sell refreshments.

GRANT PARK SCULPTURE Map pp304-5

Grant Park explorers will be rewarded with a number of beloved statues. Edward Kemeys' bronze **lions** have become Chicago icons since they began flanking the entrance to the Art Institute in 1894. Tucked away in a garden on the northwest side of the Institute sits British sculptor Henry Moore's **Large Interior Form**, a bronze statue that bears Moore's trademark smooth, rounded contours and half-human, half-blob appearance. Augustus Saint-Gaudens' **Sitting Lincoln**, Chicago's second sculpture of Abraham Lincoln, contrasts with the artist's more animated study in Lincoln Park. In this statue President Lincoln shows the isolation of his office as he sits alone in a chair. Architect Daniel Burnham's observation that no one had ever personified the Great Lakes inspired Lorado Taft to create **Fountain of the Great Lakes**, a large bronze work, in 1913. Partially hidden by surrounding shrubs, it's worth seeking out. Here's the artist's description of what the five conch-shell-holding women are up to: 'Superior on high and Michigan on the side both empty into the basin of Huron, who sends the stream to Erie, whence Ontario receives it and looks wistfully after.' This progression duplicates that of the Great Lakes.

The **Bowman & the Spearman** by Ivan Mestrovic consists of two 17ft-high bronze figures of Native Americans. Installed in 1928, they symbolize the struggle between Indians and Whites as the latter moved west. Mestrovic depicted the figures in the act of using their weapons, which are left to the imagination of the viewer. Originally closer together, they were separated by the 1956 intrusion of Congress Pkwy, which destroyed the grand steps that once led to a plaza beyond.

The **Theodore Thomas Memorial** shows a 15ft bronze woman straddling a globe and listening to a chord on her lyre. This 1923 work by Albin Polasek honors the founder of the Chicago Symphony Orchestra. The **Stock Exchange Arch** is not so much a statue as it is a relic amputated from the great Stock Exchange building when it was demolished in 1972. The *AIA Guide to Chicago* calls it the 'Wailing Wall of Chicago's preservation movement.'

TRANSPORTATION

Bus Number 151 runs along N Michigan Ave; 156 is a good north–south bet through River North; 65 travels along Grand Ave to Navy Pier.

El Red Line to Grand for the Magnificent Mile's south end and River North; Red Line to Chicago for the Mag Mile's north end.

Parking The further you get away from the Mag Mile, the more common the metered parking. Parking at Navy Pier is costly – $14 an hour. Instead, look for signed lots west of Lake Shore Dr near the pier and take a free shuttle to the pier.

NEAR NORTH & NAVY PIER

Eating p139; Shopping p219; Sleeping p240

The Loop may be where Chicago fortunes are made, but the Near North is where those fortunes are spent. The song of Near North is a heady choir of salespeople's greetings, excited shoppers cooing and the crackle of luxury goods being swaddled in paper. All of it backed by the steady beat of cash registers opening and closing.

The epicenter of it all is the upscale shopping haven of N Michigan Ave, also known as the Magnificent Mile (Mag Mile). This is a prime place to see Chicago's old money leading their armies of personal assistants in commando raids on the racks at Chanel. You don't have to be a millionaire to enjoy the Magnificent Mile, though, as the whole area – from the Tribune Tower on its south end to the historic Water Tower on its north – glows with a kind of majestic, fairytale warmth. This is especially true from mid-November through January, when as part of the Magnificent Mile Lights Festival (see City Calendar, p9) zillions of little lights are strung through the trees lining N Michigan Ave.

In the River North area, west of State St, art is the big business. What was once a grimy, noisy assortment of warehouses, factories and association headquarters has become Chicago's most prestigious gallery district – a bastion of high ceilings, hardwood floors, and expensive paintings and sculpture.

The area east of Michigan Ave is called Streeterville in honor of George Wellington Streeter, one of the city's great characters. Streeter and his wife were sailing past Chicago in the 1880s, purportedly on their way from Milwaukee to the Caribbean, when they ran aground on a sandbar near what is today Chicago Ave and Lake Shore Dr. Streeter built a little causeway to the mainland and convinced developers to dump excavated dirt on the site. Soon the area had grown to several acres, and Streeter seceded from the city and Illinois.

Various efforts to evict Streeter and a band of loyal squatters ended in the courts in 1918. Streeter lost. Today Streeterville contains some of Chicago's most valuable property, much of it home to hotels, expensive high-rise condos and offices. The River East Center has gone up along several blocks east of Columbus Dr along Grand Ave. The huge project includes hotels, movie theaters, and – you guessed it – more shops.

And speaking of shops! Chicago's most famous tourist attraction, Navy Pier, juts off the eastern end of Near North and is packed with kid- and teen-oriented shops, rides and attractions. Adults, though, will find plenty to do on the pier. It's home to the criminally overlooked Smith Museum of Stained Glass Windows, the Chicago Shakespeare Theater, and plenty of opportunities for romantic, windswept strolling.

Orientation

Near North is surrounded on three sides by water – the lake to the east, and branches of the Chicago River to the south and west. Chicago Ave crops the neighborhood neatly across the top. River North, conveniently,

TOP FIVE NEAR NORTH & NAVY PIER

- Facing death – and fantastic views – on the **Navy Pier Ferris wheel** (p76).
- Checking out the new paintings at the **Zolla-Lieberman Gallery** (p75) in River North.
- Scarfing up handfuls of sticky, sweet Caramel-Crisp from **Garrett Popcorn** (p220).
- Learning how cool stained glass can be at the **Smith Museum of Stained Glass Windows** (p76).
- Spending a week's wages on a jaw-droppingly beautiful room with a view from a bathtub at the **Peninsula** (p242).

has easy access to the Kennedy Expressway. Grand Ave serves as a good east–west thoroughfare for navigating the bottom end of Near North. State St bisects the area on the north-south axis.

Navy Pier juts into Lake Michigan on the eastern edge of the Near North neighborhood. You can hoof it here from Michigan Ave in about 15 minutes. To get to Navy Pier by car, take the Grand Ave exit from Lake Shore Dr. A free shuttle trolley runs daily between the pier and the Grand Ave El stop on the Red Line.

NEAR NORTH

CHICAGO CHILDREN'S MUSEUM

Map pp306-7

☎ 312-527-1000; www.chichildrensmuseum.org; Navy Pier; admission $7, free Thu after 5pm; 🕑 10am-5pm Sun-Wed & Fri, to 8pm Thu & Sat

The target audience of this attraction will love the place. Designed to challenge the imaginations of kids aged toddler through 10, the colorful and lively museum near the main entrance to Navy Pier gives its wee visitors enough hands-on exhibits to keep them climbing and creating for hours.

Among the favorite exhibits, Dinosaur Expedition explores the world of paleontology. The game show 'Face to Face' teaches the young ones how not to grow up to be jerks by cautioning against prejudice and discrimination. Designing your own flight of fancy is the goal at the build-your-own-airplane Inventing Lab. And Waterways lets kids get wet just when they've finally dried out from the Navy Pier fountains. Hint: come in the afternoon to avoid the crowds.

HOLY NAME CATHEDRAL Map pp306-7

☎ 312-787-8040; 735 N State St; admission free; 🕑 7am-7pm

It's ironic that in a town with so many grandiose churches, the Chicago archdiocese would call this modest Gothic church home. It's even more ironic when you consider that the archdiocese has had to close some of its most beautiful churches because of declining membership in some parishes.

Built in 1875 to a design by the unheralded Patrick Keeley, the cathedral has twice been remodeled in attempts to spruce it up. The latter effort in fact covered up bullet holes left over from a Capone-era hit across the street (see the boxed text, p87). The cathedral does provide a quiet place for contemplation, unless the excellent choirs are practicing, in which case it's an entertaining respite. Open most of the day, it holds frequent services.

MEDINAH TEMPLE Map pp306-7

600 N Wabash Ave

The Medinah Temple was built in 1912 by the Shriners, who chose a flamboyant Moorish design for their festival hall. The temple was threatened with destruction in the late 1990s by rapacious developers coveting its location. After an outcry from preservationists in 2000, a typically Chicago deal was cut – the Temple's terra-cotta-bedecked exterior survived, but developers converted the interior to – of all things – a Bloomingdale's home furnishings store.

MERCHANDISE MART Map pp306-7

☎ 800-677-6278; www.merchandisemart.com; 222 Merchandise Mart; 🕑 9am-6pm Mon-Fri, 10am-3pm Sat; Brown, Purple Line to Merchandise Mart

So what if the Sears Tower isn't the tallest building in the world? Chicago still has a record-setter in the Merchandise Mart, the world's largest commercial building (it would be the largest building, period, but for the Pentagon). Spanning two city blocks, the 1931 Merchandise Mart has its own zip code and gives over 50% of its copious space to wholesale showrooms for home furnishing and design professionals. Technically off-limits to nonindustry types, the showrooms are reachable by any civilian brave enough to hop on one of the many elevators. Unless you can fake a wholesaler license, you won't be allowed to actually buy anything from the showrooms. Everyone, though, is welcome to explore the mall on the first two floors of the place; the Merchandise Mart also hosts occasional sales that are open to the public. Check the 'consumer events' section of the website for details.

RIVER ESPLANADE Map pp306-7

Chicago River waterfront, btwn N Michigan Ave & N McClurg Ct

The developers looking to cash in on River East Center were given a mandate by the city – for the proposed shopping area to go through, the company would have to leave the River Esplanade to the Chicago Park District. It was a good deal for both parties, and the River Esplanade makes an excellent place to take a break from your hectic days of unwinding. Beginning with the oddly proportioned curving staircase at the northeast tower of the Michigan Ave Bridge, the landscaped walkway extends east along the river past the Sheraton Hotel.

Every hour on the hour, from 10am to 2pm and again from 5pm to midnight, the esplanade's **Centennial Fountain** shoots a massive arc of water across the river for 10 minutes. The entire exercise is meant to commemorate the labor-intensive reversal of the Chicago River in 1900, which tidily began sending all of the city's wastes downriver rather than into the lake. (Chicago's neighbors downstate, as you can guess, do not go out of their way to celebrate this feat of civil engineering.)

RIVER NORTH GALLERIES

Unlike the ragtag galleries of Pilsen, or the up-and-comers in the West Loop, River North galleries tend to show money artists for a money clientele. The atmosphere here is still welcoming, though, and the gallery owners are happy to let normal folk like you and me wander through their showrooms. You can get a gallery map at any of the galleries to help you find artwork to your liking.

The contemporary art at the **Jean Albano Gallery** (Map pp306-7; ☎ 312-440-0770; 215 W Superior St; 🕑 10am-5pm Tue-Fri, 11am-5pm Sat) includes paintings, drawings, and interesting textile works. **Robert Henry Adams Fine Art** (Map pp306-7; ☎ 312-642-8700; 715 N Franklin St; 🕑 10am-5pm Tue-Fri, from noon Sat) is a friendly, two-floor gallery specializing in works by pre-WWII American impressionist, regionalist and modernist painters. The first gallery to arrive in River North back in the mid-'70s (when it looked more like the West Loop does today), **Zolla-Lieberman Gallery** (Map pp306-7; ☎ 312-944-1990; 325 W Huron St; 🕑 10am-5:30pm Tue-Fri, 11am-5:30pm Sat) continues to show very cool contemporary art by established and emerging artists. If you love photography, drop by **Catherine Edelman Gallery** (Map pp306-7; ☎ 312-266-2350; 300 W Superior St; 🕑 10am-5:30pm Tue-Sat), where the works range from traditional landscapes to mixed-media photo-based collages.

RORA MOSAIC Map pp306-7

Erie St & Chicago River north branch

Artist Ginny Sykes' *Rora* symbolizes the Chicago River. The mosaic of glass tiles is worth a look if you're in the area already.

TRIBUNE TOWER Map pp306-7

435 N Michigan Ave

Colonel Robert McCormick, eccentric owner of the *Chicago Tribune*, collected – and asked his reporters to send – rocks from famous buildings and monuments around the world. All 138 of these are now embedded around the base of the Tribune Tower. In 1999 the *Tribune* added a moon rock brought back by the Apollo 15 mission; look for it on the right side of the building.

NAVY PIER

NAVY PIER Map pp306-7

☎ 312-595-7437; www.navypier.com; 600 E Grand Ave; admission free; 🕑 10am-10pm Sun-Thu, to midnight Fri & Sat, shorter hours Sep-May

Chicago's most-visited tourist attraction, Navy Pier will absolutely blow the minds of children under 12. The pier's collection of high-tech rides, hands-on fountains, kid-focused educational exhibits, fast-food restaurants and trinket vendors will transport your child into the kind of overstimulated, joyful state you haven't witnessed since you finally gave in and got them a puppy for their birthday last year.

For the childless, Navy Pier's charms are more modest. The views out over the city from the pier are spectacular, and the stomach-curdling ride on the gigantic Ferris

Merry-go-round, Navy Pier (above)

wheel is a must. Also, a myriad of themed boat tours depart from the Pier's southern side. The pier isn't all about rides and cotton candy, however. Many of the over seven million visitors to the pier each year actually come here on business – much of the eastern end of the structure consists of exposition space managed in conjunction with McCormick Place. It's a hoot to watch the crowds of laminated-badge-toting conventioneers fighting surly suburban preteens for a table in the pier's McDonalds.

The 150ft **Ferris wheel** (per ride $5) is much more exciting than any Ferris wheel has a right to be. This is due partly to the dizzying heights of the thing, but also because of the almost nonexistent security precautions (make sure the small gate separating you from the Tarmac far below is properly shut!). As long as you don't suffer from acrophobia, though, the ride will be one of your best memories of Chicago. The **carousel** (per ride $4) is another classic, with bobbing, carved horses and organ music. Kids will be clamoring to ride the **Time Escape 3-D** (☎ 415-495-7000; www.timeescape.com; adult/child/senior $10/8/8), a futuristic, virtual roller-coaster ride that takes visitors back in time to Chicago's dinosaur-filled past, and forward 300 years into its zippy future. The flashing, shaking ride lasts 15 minutes, and will likely leave more of an impression on kids than their parents.

A variety of acts appears through the summer at the **Skyline Stage** (☎ 312-595-7437), a 1500-seat rooftop venue with a glistening white canopy. See the Entertainment chapter for details on the **IMAX Theater** (p197) and the **Chicago Shakespeare Theater** (p189).

Some of Navy Pier's free amusements include the fountains at the entrance to the pier. It's as much fun to watch the cavorting kids as the fountains; water jets squirt at unpredictable intervals, and everyone's encouraged to get wet. The upper-level **Crystal Gardens fountains** feature delightful water jets that appear out of nowhere and lazily arc over the heads of the unsuspecting.

If you're looking for further diversions, a flotilla of competing tour boats lines the dock. For the skinny on what's available, see Organized Tours, p64. In summer **Shoreline Sightseeing** (☎ 312-222-9328) runs a water taxi between Navy Pier, the river near the Sears Tower and the Shedd Aquarium.

SMITH MUSEUM OF STAINED GLASS WINDOWS Map pp306-7

☎ 312-595-5024; Navy Pier; admission free; 🕑 10am-10pm Sun-Thu, to midnight Fri & Sat, shorter hours Sep-May

The owners of Navy Pier don't promote this free, impressive attraction very well, but visitors who wander along the lower-level terraces of Festival Hall will discover the country's first museum dedicated entirely to stained glass. Many of the 150 pieces on display were made in Chicago (a stained-glass hub in the late 1800s, thanks to the influx of European immigrants), and most hung at one point in Chicago churches, homes and office buildings. Even if you think stained glass is something for blue-haired grandmas, you should make a point of coming by; the articulately explained collection ranges from typical Victorian religious themes to far-out political designs (the Martin Luther King Jr one is especially noteworthy). And fans of Louis Comfort Tiffany will rejoice to find 13 of his works hanging here.

GOLD COAST

Eating p144; Shopping p221; Sleeping p243

In its most pristine reaches, the Gold Coast outshines even its gilded name, the well-heeled historic mansions glinting with an unself-conscious wealth. When you stroll through the neighborhood, especially in the Astor St area, you'll take in some of the most beautiful old homes in Chicago, if not the country. With a little imagination, you can almost see the late-19th-century moguls who settled the area, brandishing diamond-tipped canes at each other and cradling their tiny dogs on the carriage rides into their Loop offices.

TRANSPORTATION

Bus Number 151 runs along N Michigan Ave; 70 runs along Division St before swooping south to the Newberry Library; 66 swings by the Museum of Contemporary Art.

El Red Line to Clark/Division for the northern reaches; Red Line to Chicago for the southern areas.

Parking Resident-only streets stymie street parking. Try LaSalle St for unmetered parking, or let a restaurant valet find you a spot for around $10.

TOP FIVE GOLD COAST

- Fighting back bitter home envy on **Astor Street** (right).
- Getting high on a 'Gold Coast Martini' at the **Signature Lounge** (above the Signature Room, p147) on the 96th floor of the John Hancock Center.
- Checking out the cool sculptures by Bruce Nauman at the **Museum of Contemporary Art** (p79).
- Seeing some of Chicago's best up-and-coming actors in a **Lookingglass Theatre** (p190) play.
- People-watching from one of the comfy benches beside the 'castellated monstrosity' of the **Water Tower** (p80).

Today, those magnates would have to fight their way to the curb through the throngs of *House and Garden* devotees clinging to the iron gates and drooling. This being Chicago, though, the Gold Coast's historic enclaves like Astor St weren't always so revered. Time has moved on here, and a great number of the beautiful old mansions disappeared 50 years ago to make room for high-rise, high-cost apartments along the lake. So it goes in the Gold Coast. Despite the area's upper-class leanings, the atmosphere is anything but sedate. Teens on gas-powered scooters zoom up the paths alongside Lake Shore Dr, past crowds of beach volleyball players gathering for a lunchtime match. At night, young professionals mix and mingle at Museum of Contemporary Art (MCA) socials, shifting the party to the singles bars around State and Division Sts as the hour grows later.

The further you move away from the lake, the less rarefied the Gold Coast's air. The extreme example being the Cabrini-Green housing projects on the outer western edge of the Gold Coast at Chicago Ave and Sedgwick St. A shorthand for public housing gone awry, the Cabrini-Green apartments look as if a war has been fought (and lost) among their bombed-out towers. Fire-scarred and heartrendingly bleak, the projects are being slowly demolished, the remaining residents relocated far away to the Chicago suburbs. True to Gold Coast form, developers have already drawn up plans for the luxury town houses that will eventually sweep across the valuable 70-acre plot of land. Driving by the smoldering wreck today, it's hard to imagine anyone living here. But in a sign of things to come, the first Cabrini-Green Starbucks has already opened for business.

Orientation

The Gold Coast is just north of Near North and south of Lincoln Park (the park in this case, not the neighborhood). Streetwise, the area stretches languidly along Lake Shore Dr, running up to North Ave in the north and down to Chicago Ave in the south. Astor St is tucked into the northeast corner of the Gold Coast, one block in from the lake. The most hectic parts of the neighborhood are in the south along the posh Michigan Ave and Oak St shopping areas. The Cabrini-Green neighborhood reaches along Division St, between Orleans and Larrabee Sts.

ASTOR STREET Map pp308-9

In 1882 Potter and Bertha Palmer were the power couple of Chicago. His web of businesses included the city's best hotel and a huge general merchandise store later sold to a clerk named Marshall Field. When they relocated north from Prairie Ave to a crenellated castle of a mansion at what's now 1350 N Lake Shore Dr, the Palmers set off a lemming-like rush of Chicago's wealthy to the neighborhood around them. The mansions along Astor St reflect the grandeur of that heady age. We've put their backgrounds together in greater detail as part of the **Lakefront Bike Cruise** (p120).

Originally four, now three, the **1887 homes** at 1308–1312 N Astor St feature a lovely sculptured quality that extends to the turrets, gables and dormers. The architect, John Wellborn Root, was so pleased with his efforts that he moved into 1310. Once one home, now several apartments, the 1887 mansion at 1355 represents the full flower of Georgian revival. Note the alternating skulls and animal heads above the windows.

While he was still working for Louis Sullivan, a 19-year-old Frank Lloyd Wright designed the large but only 11-room **Charnley-Persky House** (☎ 312-573-1365; 1365 N Astor St) and proclaimed with his soon-to-be-trademarked bombast that it was the 'first modern building.' Now home to the National Society of Architectural Historians, the house is sometimes open for tours. Call for times and prices. A late arrival on the street, the 1929 **Russell House** (1444 N Astor St) was designed by Holabird & Root (with the Root in question being the son of John Wellborn Root – this street literally runs in the family). It's art deco French at its most refined.

The neoclassical home at **1500 N Astor** was designed by New York architect Stanford White. Known as the Cyrus McCormick Mansion for its famous owner, the house has since been divided up into condos.

Robert Todd Lincoln, the only surviving son of President Abraham and Mary, was one of the neighborhood's celebrity residents back in its early years. He lived at **1525 N Astor.**

The 1885 mansion that serves as the **Archbishop's Residence** (1555 N State St) spans the entire block to Astor. Built in the Queen Anne style that later became known generically as 'Victorian,' the place is owned by the Catholic Archdiocese of Chicago, and has been home to seven leaders of the Chicago church.

860–880 N LAKE SHORE DR

Map pp308-9

The International Style of high-rises got its start with this Mies van der Rohe work. Built from 1949 to 1951, the twin towers were the manifestation of designs Mies first put forward in 1921. The idea of high-rises draped only in a curtain of glass and steel was so radical at the time that psychologists speculated about the impact of living in a transparent home. Check out the buildings from the lakefront path early in the morning for maximum effect.

GOLD COAST ARCHITECTURE

Map pp308-9

The building styles in the Gold Coast are all over the map, from turn-of-the-century Gothic to '50s sci-fi modern. Going from oldest to newest, some of the highlights include **St Benedict Flats** (42-50 E Chicago Ave), an 1882 series of luxury apartments that's one of the few remaining examples of Victorian Gothic architecture in the city. These apartments almost disappeared like the rest of them in 1992, when Loyola University announced plans to acquire the property and replace it with dorms. Happily, preservationists ruled. It's named for the St Benedictine church that stood on the site until the Great Fire.

The apartments at **1550 N State Parkway** announced the arrival of French elegance in Chicago when they were erected in 1912. The stunning **Archbishop Quigley Preparatory Seminary** (☎ 312-787-8625; 831 N Rush St; admission free) holds the magnificent Chapel of St James, which was ambitiously modeled after the grand 13th-century Sainte-Chapelle in Paris, Louis IX's palace chapel. With 45,000 panes of glass in its impressive array of stained-glass windows, the Chicago version certainly comes close to the original. Local choral groups sometimes perform in the chapel – definitely a recommended and ennobling treat. The **Fourth Presbyterian Church** (☎ 312-787-4570; 126 E Chestnut St; admission free) was built in 1914. It belongs to one of the city's wealthiest congregations and has a long history of reaching out to the poor of the city. Back when it was built, this glitzy stretch of the Magnificent Mile was a sleepy thoroughfare of beautiful mansions known as Pine St. Occasional organ recitals take place in the splendid sanctuary.

INTERNATIONAL MUSEUM OF SURGICAL SCIENCE

Map pp308-9

☎ 312-642-6502; www.imss.org; 1524 N Lake Shore Dr; adult/senior & student $6/3, free Tue; 10am-4pm Tue-Sat

Home to an eclectic collection of surgery-related items, the Museum of Surgical Science features such a poorly marked assortment of medical items that at first it seems like nothing more than a place to escape a vicious lake squall. But start exploring and you'll soon be rewarded with fascinating thematic displays, such as the one on bloodletting – the act of bleeding patients to death to 'cure' them. The undeniable gems of the collection are the 'stones,' as in 'kidney stone' and 'gallstone.' All of the spectacularly large specimens were passed by patients who may have wished instead for a good bloodletting.

JOHN HANCOCK CENTER

Map pp308-9

☎ 312-751-3681; www.hancock-observatory.com; 875 N Michigan Ave; observatory adult/child/senior $9.75/6/7.50; 9am-11pm

The world's tallest 'mixed-use' building (meaning that it contains both residential and commercial space), the Hancock is the third-tallest building in Chicago, at 1127ft. Much less popular than the Sears Tower's

THE END OF LITTLE HELL

The Cabrini-Green housing projects look like hell. Built near the intersection of Sedgwick St and Chicago Ave, the derelict buildings have been a source of embarrassment for the city, a constant battleground for the city's advocates for the poor, and a miserable home for the residents there who have nowhere else to go.

This pocket has been a rough neighborhood since the early 20th century, when it was known as 'Little Hell' for its shoddy homes and the abject poverty of its residents. The city stepped in during WWII, demolishing the structure of Little Hell and replacing it with Frances Cabrini Homes, a low-rise barracks-like apartment complex for war workers. The high rise towers you see today were built in 1958 and 1962, and the new residents were originally a mix of poor Puerto Ricans, Irish, Italians and African-Americans. By the 1970s, though, only the Black residents remained, and the city's maintenance of the properties became abysmal. To prevent children from falling over the open walkways that ran the length of each floor, the spaces were simply enclosed in a floor-to-ceiling steel grill. Rather than keep up the on-site park, the grass was simply paved over, and children played on concrete. Gangs and drug dealers quickly took over control of the buildings. Two police officers were fatally shot at the homes in 1970, and the horrors perpetrated by residents on each other made local news throughout the '80s and '90s.

The irony of the situation was that the miseries of Cabrini-Green were unfolding just six blocks from some of Chicago's smartest Gold Coast homes and shopping strips. And in 2000, those residents breathed a sigh of relief as the city announced a total overhaul of the Cabrini-Green site, one that would demolish or renovate all buildings, replacing them with low-rise mixed-income housing, some of which would be set aside for Cabrini-Green residents. The temporary relocation of some 4000 residents remaining in the building, though, proved to be more difficult than anticipated. In 2005, several of the decrepit, bombed-out buildings were still occupied, even as sparkling new town houses began to rise on the grounds of Little Hell.

Skydeck, the Hancock's viewing platform benefits from having shorter lines and no sappy film. The friendly employees guide you to the fast – 23mph – elevators for the 40-second ride to the 94th floor. In many ways the view here surpasses the one at Sears Tower, and the screened, outdoor area lets you listen in on the sounds of the city. When you're that far above the street, there's something almost lyrical about the dull roar of traffic punctuated by jackhammers and sirens.

However pleasant the view from the top, locals shake their heads sadly at the suckers who pay to make the ascent. The elevator ride to the Hancock's 96th-floor Signature Lounge, one floor up from the Signature Room restaurant (p147), they're quick to point out, is free. Why shell out $10 to go stand around on some windblown viewing deck when the same money could get you a glass of wine, a comfy seat, and almost identical views a few floors higher? They've got a point. The lounge's elevators are to the right of the cashier's desk for the observatory.

Strange factoids: a stuntman in a Spider-Man costume set out to climb to the top of the Hancock Center using suction cups in 1981. The man in question, 'Spider Dan' Goodwin, succeeded despite a questionable intervention attempt by the Chicago Fire Department, who tried to discourage the climb by spraying him with water from the fire hoses. Also, Chicago comedian Chris Farley lived here, and was found dead from a drug overdose in his 60th floor apartment in 1997.

MUSEUM OF CONTEMPORARY ART

Map pp308-9

☎ 312-280-2660; www.mcachicago.org; 220 E Chicago Ave; adult/senior & student $10/6, free after 5pm Tue; ⏲ 10am-8pm Tue, 10am-5pm Wed-Sun

Covering art from 1945 forward, the MCA uses extensive piece descriptions to alleviate a lot of the head-scratching, 'what the hell is it?' befuddlement that tends to accompany encounters with modern art. The museum boasts an especially strong minimalist, surrealist, and book-arts collection, but the works here span the modern art gamut, from Jenny Holzer's LED *Truisms* to Joseph Beuys' austere *Felt Suit*. The permanent collection includes art by Franz Kline, René Magritte, Cindy Sherman and Andy Warhol, with displays arranged to highlight the blurring of the boundaries between painting, photography, sculpture, video and other media. The MCA also regularly hosts dance, film, and speaking events from an international array of contemporary artists. Puck's at the MCA (p146), a café overlooking Lake Michigan, attracts crowds with its fine views of the sculpture garden and the lake beyond, as well as its creative food.

NEWBERRY LIBRARY Map pp308-9

☎ 312-943-9090; www.newberry.org; 60 W Walton St; admission free, must be 16 or older; 10am-6pm Tue-Thu, 9am-5pm Fri & Sat

Humanities nerds and those trying to document far-flung branches of their family tree will have a field day at this research library. Entry requires a library card, but one-day passes are available for curious browsers. Once inside, you can pester the patient librarians with requests for help in tracking down all manner of historical ephemera. (The collection is noncirculating, though, so don't expect to take that first edition of the King James Bible home with you.) The Newberry also often features interesting special exhibits, and has a bookstore where you can pick up such treatises as *Buffy the Vampire Slayer and Philosophy*, and cool vintage Chicago travel posters. Free tours of the impressive building take place at 3pm Thursday and 10:30am Saturday.

OAK ST BEACH Map pp308-9

There aren't many cities outside of Florida that offer this much sand and (miniaturized) surf this close to their major business districts. The Oak St Beach makes for a wonderful respite from the hectic pace of the city. It also offers a good respite from the hectic pace of the beaches further north, where you're likely to get a volleyball spiked on your head if you're not paying attention.

THE (FIRST) PLAYBOY MANSION

Map pp308-9

1340 N State St

The sexual revolution perhaps started in the basement 'grotto' of this 1899 mansion, purchased by Chicago magazine impresario Hugh Hefner as the first Playboy mansion in 1959. Later a dorm for the School of the Art Institute (imagine the pick-up lines!), it was gutted in 1993 and turned into four very staid but very expensive condos. Playboy, now run by Hugh's daughter Christine, maintains its corporate headquarters in Chicago, and Walton St (at Michigan Ave) has been named 'Honorary Hugh M Hefner Way' in an official tip of the hat to Hef.

WASHINGTON SQUARE Map pp308-9

Btwn N Clark St, N Dearborn St, W Delaware Pl, W Walton St

This rather plain park across from the Newberry Library has had a colorful and tragic history. In the 1920s it was known as 'Bughouse Sq' because of the communists, socialists, anarchists and other -ists who gave soapbox orations here.

In the 1970s, when it was a gathering place for young male prostitutes, it gained tragic infamy as the preferred pick-up spot of mass-murderer John Wayne Gacy. Gacy took his victims back to his suburban home, where he killed them and buried their bodies in the basement. Convicted on 33 counts of murder (although the actual tally may be higher), he was executed in 1994.

Delaware Pl and Walton, Clark and Dearborn Sts border the park.

WATER TOWER Map pp308-9

806 N Michigan Ave

Believe it or not, the 154ft Water Tower, a city icon and focal point of the Mag Mile, once dwarfed all the buildings that surround it. Built in 1869, the Water Tower and its associated building, the **Pumping Station** (aka the Water Works) across the street, were constructed with local yellow limestone in a Gothic style popular at the time. This stone construction and lack of flammable interiors saved them in 1871, when the great Chicago fire roared through town.

The Water Tower was the great hope of Chicago when it first opened, one part of a great technological breakthrough that was going to provide fresh, clean water for the city from intake cribs set far out in Lake Michigan. Before then, the city's drinking water had come from shore-side collection basins that sucked in sewage-laden water and industrial runoff from the Chicago River, garnishing it with the occasional school of small fish, all of which ended up in the sinks and bathtubs of unhappy Chicago residents.

Though the fish problem was solved by the new system, the plan was ultimately a failure. Sewage from the river, propelled by spring rains, made its way out to the new intake bins. The whole smelly situation didn't abate until the Chicago River was reversed in the 1890s (p52). By 1906, the Water Tower was obsolete, and only public outcry saved it from demolition three times. Whether Oscar Wilde would have joined the preservationists is debatable: when he visited Chicago in 1881, he called the Water Tower 'a castellated monstrosity with salt and pepper boxes stuck all over it.' Restoration in 1962 ensured the tower's survival, and today it houses the **City Gallery** (☎ 312-742-0808; 10am-6:30pm Mon-Sat, 10am-5pm Sun), showcasing Chicago-themed works by local photographers. The Pumping Station across the street houses a **visitor information center** (p282).

LINCOLN PARK & OLD TOWN

Eating p147; Shopping p223; Sleeping p246

If you've lost track of a Midwestern fraternity brother or sorority sister, chances are good you will find them living happily in Lincoln Park. Ground zero for Chicago's yuppie population, the neighborhood bustles with Banana Republic–wearing residents walking dogs, Rollerblading and pushing babies around in $300 strollers. Local curmudgeons will grouse about Lincoln Park being a soulless victim of gentrification, but the area has some undeniable charms, including many great restaurants, some cute boutiques and the Clark St record-store corridor, where the city's music illuminati pick up tomorrow's hits.

Lincoln Park also has the park itself, a well-loved playland. Almost 50% larger than Central Park in New York, the park offers Chicagoans a chance to celebrate summer with paddleboat rides (aka raucous water fights) on North Pond and with commiserating visits with the polar bears at the zoo.

Fishing at Lincoln Park (p83)

TRANSPORTATION

Bus Number 76 runs along Diversey Pkwy; 74 spans Fullerton; 72 cuts through Old Town along North Ave.

El Brown, Purple or Red line to Fullerton or the Brown or Purple Line to Armitage for Lincoln Park; Brown or Purple Line to Sedgwick, or the Red Line to Clark/Division for Old Town.

Parking Lincoln Park is a headache. If you're stuck for a spot, consider heading out to the meters along Diversey Harbor. Old Town has plenty of cars competing for its plentiful meters. Try the pay garage at Piper's Alley, at North Ave and Wells St.

South of Lincoln Park, Old Town was free-spirited in the 1960s as the epicenter of Chicago's hippie culture. Artists, long-hairs and other freaks flocked to Old Town to tune in, turn on and drop their money on cool black-light posters and bongs from head shops on Wells St. Falling into disrepair in the 1970s, Old Town made a comeback in the 1980s and now is one of the North Side's most expensive places to buy property. Visitors won't find too much in the way of sights, but Old Town outranks its more lively neighbors when it comes to comedy – improv bastion Second City is here, as is Zanies (p192), Chicago's best stand-up club.

Orientation

The streets of Lincoln Park are clogged with all manner of high-end SUVs – if you drive here, you'll likely know the area inside-out by the time you find parking. Lincoln Park is a huge neighborhood, stretching from the park on the east side all the way over to Racine Ave on the west. Armitage Ave runs along the southern end of the neighborhood; Diversey Pkwy serves as Lincoln Park's northern boundary. Oz Park, whose corner abuts Lincoln Ave at its intersection with Geneva Tce, is one of the area's landmarks, as is DePaul University. You'll find DePaul spreading out from the intersection of Sheffield Ave and Fullerton Pkwy.

Old Town is much smaller than Lincoln Park, running from approximately Armitage Ave in the north, Halsted St in the west, and North Ave to the south (though Old Town's Wells St corridor extends a few blocks south of this). The bottom edge of the park forms Old Town's eastern flank.

TOP FIVE LINCOLN PARK & OLD TOWN

- Laughing yourself silly at **Second City** (p191).
- Fighting SAD (seasonal adjustment disorder) with a trip to the lush winter gardens at the **Lincoln Park Conservatory** (opposite).
- Playing with the polar bears (through thick, thick glass) at the **Lincoln Park Zoo** (opposite).
- Bobbing along to a banjo melody at the **Old Town School of Folk Music** (p184).
- Watching crazy foreign movies at **Facets Multimedia** (p197).

CHICAGO HISTORICAL SOCIETY

Map pp308-9

☎ 312-642-4600; www.chicagohistory.org; 1601 N Clark St; adult/child/senior $5/1/3, free Mon; noon-8pm Mon-Wed, 9:30am-4:30pm Thu-Sat, noon-5pm Sun

The histories of the Lincolns, Capones, Daleys and other notables get some attention here, but this well-funded museum focuses on the average person. The role of the commoner in the American Revolution sets the tone for the humanistic exhibits. One, titled 'Fort Dearborn and Frontier Chicago,' shows how settlers and Indians changed each other's lives. The Pioneer Ct offers hands-on demonstrations in the intricacies of making candles, weaving blankets and knitting clothes. None of the work was easy.

Much of the 2nd floor is devoted to Chicago's development and history, with displays that explore the roles of immigration and industry, as well as the problems of slums and the lives of the rich. Special exhibitions – the museum's strong point – cover such diverse topics as how bungalows allowed almost every family to afford a home, and Chicago's role in the birth of gospel music. The Big Shoulders Cafe serves tasty soups and sandwiches, and the bookstore is excellent.

CRILLY COURT Map pp308-9

off Eugenie St

The developer of this pleasant block, Daniel Francis Crilly, was responsible for creating much of the surrounding Old Town area. The facades of the 1890-vintage apartments of Crilly Ct are charming stone variations of Queen Anne architecture. The backs of the properties have surprising wrought-iron porches right out of the French Quarter in New Orleans. The house at 1710 Crilly Ct is the earliest known site associated with the gay and lesbian Civil Rights movement in the US. In 1924 and 1925 Henry Gerber lived in the house, from which he founded the country's first-ever gay civil rights organization – the Society for Human Rights. He also published the groundbreaking homosexual rights publication *Friendship and Freedom* out of the home, managing to get two issues out before police raided the house. Gerber and other organization members were arrested, bringing the organization to an end.

DEPAUL UNIVERSITY Map pp308-9

☎ 773-325-7000; 2320 N Kenmore Ave

DePaul University is charming or ugly, depending where you are. The campus stretches east and west of the El south of Fullerton Ave. Chalmers Pl is a scholarly square east of the El. Here you'll find some beautiful Queen Anne row houses built for a seminary that has since been absorbed by DePaul.

West of the Fullerton El stop, the Academic Center and the University Center were built in 1968 and 1978, respectively, in an architectural style that's aptly named 'brutalism;' both monstrosities look like they're meant to be last redoubts in case of urban assault. The 1992 library marks a new and vastly improved era of DePaul design. Notice how the architects have tried to camouflage some of the Academic Center.

ELKS VETERANS MEMORIAL

Map pp308-9

☎ 773-528-4500; 2750 N Lakeview Ave; admission free; 9am-4pm

The Elks Club, once a hugely popular men's social club, has fallen on hard times all over the US, but during its heyday it built this impressive memorial to honor members killed at war.

FREDERICK WACKER HOUSE

Map pp308-9

1838 N Lincoln Park West

The Frederick Wacker House offers a rare glimpse at how Chicago's houses looked before the 1871 fire. This one was built right afterward – the flames roared through here – but just before the arrival of laws that banned wood structures in the area devastated by the fire.

HENRY MEYER HOUSE Map pp308-9

1802 N Lincoln Park West

The Henry Meyer House is another wooden example built during the same brief window of opportunity as the Wacker House. Imagine whole blocks of these homes and you'll start to get an idea of the horror of the fire.

LINCOLN PARK Map pp308-9

The neighborhood gets its name from this park, Chicago's largest. Its 1200 acres stretch for 6 miles, from North Ave north to Diversey Pkwy, where it narrows along the lake and continues until the end of Lake Shore Dr. The park's many lakes, trails and paths make it an excellent place for recreation. Cross-country skiing in the winter and sunbathing in warmer months are just two of the activities Chicagoans enjoy in Lincoln Park. Many buy picnic vittles from the markets on Clark St and Diversey Pkwy.

Most of Lincoln Park's pleasures are natural, though one of its joys is sculptor Augustus Saint-Gaudens' **Standing Lincoln**, which shows the 16th president deep in contemplation right before he delivers a great speech. Saint-Gaudens based the work on casts made of Lincoln's face and hands while Lincoln was alive. The statue stands in its own garden east of the Chicago Historical Society.

Near the southeast corner of La Salle Dr and Clark St, the **Couch Mausoleum** is the sole reminder of the land's pre-1864 use: the entire area was a municipal cemetery. Many of the graves contained hundreds of dead prisoners from Camp Douglas, a horrific prisoner-of-war stockade on the city's South Side during the Civil War. Removing the bodies from the designated park area proved a greater undertaking than the city could stomach, and today if you start digging at the south end of the park you're liable to make some ghoulish discoveries.

From a little dock in front of pretty **Cafe Brauer**, a 1908 Prairie School architectural creation, you can rent two-person paddleboats and cruise the South Pond, south of the zoo. A more bucolic cruise can be had on the North Pond, which doesn't have the zoo crowds. Rent boats from the little boathouse east of where Deming Pl meets the park. The rental season at both ponds is roughly May through September.

LINCOLN PARK CONSERVATORY

Map pp308-9

☎ 312-742-7736; 2391 N Stockton Dr; admission free; 9am-5pm

The glass bedecked conservatory features 3 acres of lush gardens from a variety of ecosystems, and hosts a rotating array of annual flower shows. Just south of the conservatory, the 1887 statue **Storks at Play** has enchanted generations of Chicagoans. And speaking of plants and birds, the **Alfred Caldwell Lily Pool**, immediately to the northeast of the conservatory, is an important stopover for migrating birds. The stonework here resembles the stratified canyons of the Wisconsin Dells. When not overrun with people, the pool is a magical setting, especially in winter.

LINCOLN PARK ZOO Map pp308-9

☎ 312-742-2000; www.lpzoo.com; 2200 N Cannon Dr; admission free; 9am-5pm, to 7pm May-Sep

The free zoo is one of Chicago's most popular attractions, and its appeal only increased with the 2003 opening of the Regenstein African Journey. The naturalistic African walk-through is a cutting-edge example of zoo exhibits done right – the human visitors are allowed to get surprisingly close to animals who swim, hop and crawl in remarkably lifelike environments. Adults will love the cuddly, perpetually puzzled-looking meerkat, and kids will scream with disgusted glee at the entire room filled with hissing cockroaches.

The rest of the zoo – which opened in 1868 – is fairly typical. **Farm-in-the-Zoo**, the place where many urbanites first learn that milk comes from cows instead of cardboard containers, features a full range of barnyard animals in a faux farm setting just south of the zoo. Frequent demonstrations of cow milking, horse grooming, butter churning and other chores take place. The exhibits don't make any bones about the ultimate fate of most livestock. For instance, those cute piglets head to the slaughterhouse only four to six months after birth.

The exhibits for the lions and other big cats, elephants, monkeys and sea lions are fine but unremarkable. And the cramped penguin habitat borders on the depressing. Still, free is a good price, and if you come during colder months, you'll have many of the exhibits to yourself. You can easily reach the zoo from most parts of the park; there are entrances on all sides. Drivers be warned: parking is among the worst in the city.

MOODY CHURCH Map pp308-9

☎ 312-943-0466; www.moodychurch.org; 1630 N Clark St

Directly across from the Chicago Historical Society stands the hulking Moody Church, a nondenominational church started by Dwight Moody, a 19th-century missionary. Moody, who also founded the Moody Bible Institute in the Gold Coast, was the Billy Graham of his age – a charismatic preacher who took his literal interpretations of the Bible to audiences around the world. During the 1893 World's Expo, Moody organized huge Christian revivalist events under enormous tents in Jackson Park, hoping to warn fair-goers away from the moral ruin awaiting them on the Midway and in Chicago's infamous Levee District. The church, which can hold almost 4000 worshippers, was built in 1925. Tours are available by request.

OZ PARK Map pp308-9

btwn N Larrabee St, W Webster Ave, N Halsted St & W Dickens Ave

This small park is named in honor of Chicago writer Lyman Frank Baum. Though he wrote more than 60 books, Baum was most famous for a story involving a tornado-transported farm-girl named Dorothy and three oddball traveling companions afflicted with various emotional and physical disorders. The story was eventually made into the movie *The Wonderful Wizard of Oz*. Baum lived and wrote in the Humboldt Park neighborhood, located a couple miles west. As you stroll through Oz Park, you'll find the *Tin Man* sculpture in the northeast corner. The 9ft-tall piece by John Kearney is built from car bumpers, and has a bronze companion, the *Cowardly Lion*. A yellow brick sidewalk stretches from that corner into the park.

PEGGY NOTEBAERT NATURE MUSEUM Map pp308-9

☎ 773-755-5100; www.naturemuseum.org; 2430 N Cannon Dr; adult/child/senior $7/4/5, free Thu; 🕑 9am-4:30pm Mon-Fri, 10am-5pm Sat & Sun

This wonderful hands-on museum allows you to do everything from walking among fluttering butterflies to engineering your own river system. Other exhibits show how many different wild animals live in urban Chicago, both inside and outside. A computer lab allows visitors to solve environmental problems, and kids are given free rein to explore, scamper and climb while they learn.

ST CLEMENT'S CHURCH Map pp308-9

☎ 773-281-0371; 646 W Deming Pl

Istanbul's Hagia Sophia inspired the restored Byzantine mosaics that grace the dome of St Clement's Church, a Catholic church built in 1918. When the University of Notre Dame football team loses, Sunday Mass is a sea of red eyes in this parish, which caters to young, single college grads. The church sits on a street lined with gracious mansions that have extra-wide front lawns.

ST MICHAEL'S CHURCH Map pp308-9

☎ 312-642-2498; 1633 N Cleveland Ave

Believe it or not, St Michael's Church was once the Sears Tower of its day. From 1869 until 1885, the Catholic church reigned as the tallest building in Chicago. Built in 1869 by German Catholics, the church was largely destroyed in the 1871 Chicago fire, and completely rebuilt two years later. The Romanesque interior – with its fantastic stained glass – is open to the public.

LAKE VIEW

Eating p151; Shopping p225; Sleeping p247

OK, so the name of this inland neighborhood is a little off. But you know what? No one who lives here is complaining. The 20- and 30-somethings inhabiting the three overlapping Lake View 'hoods of Wrigleyville, Boystown and the Belmont area are too busy checking each other out to notice some dumb lake anyway.

Wrigleyville – named for star attraction Wrigley Field – has become a magnet for singles, who frolic and cruise in the ridiculous number of bars and restaurants that line Clark St and Southport Ave. The tenor of the neighborhood is much like that of the stadium it surrounds: well-mannered by day with an impish dose of carousing by night. Yuppies looking for more bang for their apartment buck have been abandoning their Lincoln Park condos for Wrigleyville

TRANSPORTATION

Bus Number 152 traces Addison St; 22 follows Clark St; 8 runs along Halsted St.

El Red Line Addison stop for Wrigleyville; Brown and Red Line Belmont stop for Belmont and Boystown.

Parking In a word: nightmare. Especially in Wrigleyville, where side streets are resident-only. Take the train or bring a really good book-on-tape to listen to as you try to find parking.

over the past five years. But unlike the hyper-gentrified neighborhoods to the south, Wrigleyville has managed to handle the influx of cell phones and SUVs and still retain its color and atmosphere (read: high-alcohol tolerance).

You don't need a map to know you've arrived in the predominantly gay section of Lake View known as Boystown. If the rainbow flags don't tip you off, the abundance of hot, well-dressed men will. Just south of Wrigleyville, the well-heeled hub of Chicago's gay community bustles on Broadway St during the day and gets hedonistic on Halsted St at night. Boystown is also the place to come if you accidentally left those fur-lined handcuffs at home; the shops here are known for their quirky, fun and sex-friendly vibe.

Though the crowds may be straighter, the shopping scene is equally wild in Belmont, just west of Boystown. This is the youngest-feeling of Lake View's neighborhoods, and the stores here cater to every lifestyle whim of local goths, punks, and hipsters. Whether you need hair dye, a Fender Telecaster, or a vintage Siouxsie Sioux and the Banshees T-shirt, you can count on the endearingly attitude-heavy emporiums here to come through for you.

For all its copious energy, Lake View has little in the way of historic sights or cultural attractions. When you come here, be sure to bring your credit cards.

Orientation

Lake View begins at Diversey Pkwy and stretches from the lake to Ashland Ave, with Irving Park Rd cropping the neighborhood in the north. Wrigleyville occupies the top half of the area, and its bars and restaurants are clustered on Southport Ave, south of Irving Park Rd, and on Clark St, south of Addison St. Boystown is further south and closer to the lake than Wrigleyville; its two main drags are Halsted and Broadway Sts. The charms of the Belmont area are located on Belmont Ave, around where it meets Clark St.

ALTA VISTA TERRACE Map pp318-19

btwn Byron & Grace Sts

Chicago's first designated historic district is worthy of the honor. Developer Samuel Eberly Gross re-created a block of London row houses on Alta Vista Tce in 1904. The 20 exquisitely detailed homes on either side of the street mirror each other diagonally, and the owners have worked hard at maintaining the spirit of the block. Individuality isn't dead, however – head to the back of the west row and you'll notice that every house has grown to the rear in dramatically different fashions.

BOYSTOWN Map pp318-19

btwn Halsted & Broadway Sts, Belmont Ave & Addison St

What the Castro is to San Francisco, Boystown is to Chicago. The mecca of queer Chicago (especially for men), the streets of Boystown are full of rainbow flags and packed with bars, shops, and restaurants catering to the residents of the gay neighborhood. For more info on gay Chicago, see the boxed text, p189.

WRIGLEY FIELD Map pp318-19

☎ 773-404-2827; 1060 W Addison St

This legendary baseball park draws plenty of tourists, who pose year-round under the classic neon sign over the main entrance. Baseball fanatics can take a 90-minute stadium **tour** (☎ 773-404-2827; tours $20)

TOP FIVE LAKE VIEW

- Watching the clouds dawdle across the ceiling of the **Music Box Theatre** (p197) before a movie.
- Catching the *Big Yellow Bus* on Sunday nights at the **Playground Improv Theater** (p191).
- Shopping for retro Cubs shirts at **Strange Cargo** (p227).
- Joining the sports fans cutting work and taking in a day game at **Wrigley Field** (p200).
- Egging on the frantic geniuses at **IO** (p190).

on selected weekends during the baseball season. Reservations are required for the tour, which takes visitors through the clubhouse, dugouts and press box. If you don't have time for a tour, or can't get tickets for a game, stroll over to Sheffield Ave on game day and chat with the guys who hang around, waiting for a ball to be hit out of the park. Notice, too, how the owners of the surrounding three-flats have turned their rooftops into bleachers (an enterprising maneuver that has never sat well with Cubs owners). For details on attending a Cubs game, see p200.

ANDERSONVILLE & UPTOWN

Eating p155; Shopping p228

Andersonville comes out of nowhere. On your way up to this northern neighborhood, you'll pass generic street after generic street, middling blah neighborhoods filled with dollar stores and ugly apartments. And just when you think you've run out of cool Chicago – boom! – that's when Andersonville's oasis of charming shops, fun bars, and top-notch eateries envelops you in a welcoming embrace.

The vibe here is Continental with a friendly, European pace that you won't find in surrounding neighborhoods. Locals linger at cafés and bars long after they should be on their way, and dinners at Andersonville's collection of middle- and highbrow restaurants are hours-long events meant to be savored and recounted later.

You can blame some of that Euro-feel on the Swedes, who started building homes here when Andersonville was little more than a cherry orchard. Their legacy continues today in many of the stores, like the butter-lovin' Swedish Bakery (p157). But the Swedes are only partly responsible for the distinct flavor of Andersonville. The blocks surrounding Clark St from about Argyle St through Bryn Mawr Ave have become popular with young professionals. The once-low rents attracted graphic artists and other creative types in the 1980s and '90s. Many lesbians have found a home among the widely varied residents, and rainbow flags commonly flutter alongside the blue and yellow flags of Sweden. The shopkeepers and condo owners may still routinely sweep their sidewalks each day, as per Swedish tradition, but these broom-wielding businesspeople are as likely to be Lebanese or gay as they are the stolid older Nordic residents.

Uptown, the scrappy neighborhood to the south of Andersonville, has a fascinating history with Al Capone and the mob (see the boxed text, opposite). And before there was Hollywood, there was Uptown. Charlie Chaplin lived here in 1915, when the area was the epicenter of moviemaking in the United States. This ragtag area also hides a surprising nook of gorgeous Prairie School homes around Hutchinson St. If you can't make it down to see Frank Lloyd Wright's masterful Robie House (p117) on the South Side, cruise through here to see some amazing work by those he influenced.

Uptown's most recent contributions to the city have been the kind you eat with chopsticks. Myriad hole-in-the-wall Asian

TOP FIVE ANDERSONVILLE & UPTOWN

- Looking for dead Chicago celebrities at the **Graceland Cemetery** (p88).
- Diving into a bag of velvety rich cookies from the **Swedish Bakery** (p157) and washing them down with tiny cups of free coffee.
- Seeing 30 plays in 60 minutes at Neo-Futurists' **Too Much Light Makes the Baby Go Blind** (p191).
- Ogling the Prairie-style homes on **Hutchinson St** (p89).
- Witnessing the spectacle of the Uptown Poetry Slam at the historic **Green Mill** (p196).

TRANSPORTATION

Bus Number 151 runs along Sheridan Rd; 22 travels along Clark St; 80 covers Irving Park Rd; 78 stretches along Montrose Ave.

El Take the Red Line to Berwyn, six blocks east of Clark St, for Andersonville; take the Red Line to Argyle for Argyle St; the Red Line's Lawrence Ave is good for trips to lower Uptown; Red Line to Sheridan for Graceland Cemetery.

Parking Meter and on-street parking available in Andersonville and Uptown, though big concerts at the Aragon in Uptown can make things hairy.

eateries along Argyle St have earned this area the name 'Little Saigon' and made it a mecca for fans of Vietnamese food. Unlike settled Andersonville, Uptown has some rough spots – keep an eye out at night.

Orientation

Most of the bars, restaurants, and shops in Andersonville are along N Clark St, above W Foster Ave. The Lakewood-Balmoral

CAPONE'S CHICAGO

Chicagoans traveling the world often experience an unusual phenomenon when others ask where they're from. When they answer 'Chicago,' the local drops into a crouch and yells something along the lines of 'Rat-a-tat-a-tat, Al Capone!' Although civic boosters bemoan Chicago's long association with a scar-faced hoodlum, it's an image that has been burned into the public consciousness by TV shows such as *The Untouchables*, movies and other aspects of pop culture.

Capone was the mob boss in Chicago from 1924 to 1931, when he was brought down on tax evasion charges by Eliot Ness, the federal agent whose task force earned the name 'The Untouchables' because its members were supposedly impervious to bribes. (This wasn't a small claim, given that thousands of Chicago police and other officials were on the take, some of them raking in more than $1000 a week.)

Capone came to Chicago from New York in 1919. He quickly moved up the ranks to take control of the city's South Side in 1924, expanding his empire by making 'hits' on his rivals. These acts, which usually involved bullets shot out of submachine guns, were carried out by Capone's lieutenants. Incidentally, Capone earned the nickname 'Scarface' not because he ended up on the wrong side of a bullet but because a dance-hall fight left him with a large scar on his left cheek.

The success of the Chicago mob was fueled by Prohibition. Not surprisingly, the citizens' thirst for booze wasn't eliminated by government mandate, and gangs made fortunes dealing in illegal beer, gin and other intoxicants. Clubs called 'speakeasies' were highly popular and were only marginally hidden from the law, an unnecessary precaution given that crooked cops usually were the ones working the doors. Commenting on the hypocrisy of a society that would ban booze and then pay him a fortune to sell it, Capone said: 'When I sell liquor, they call it bootlegging. When my patrons serve it on silver trays on Lake Shore Dr, they call it hospitality.'

It's a challenge to find traces of the Capone era in Chicago. The city and the Chicago Historical Society take dim views of Chicago's gangland past, with nary a brochure or exhibit on Capone or his cronies (though the CHS bookstore does have a good selection of books). Many of the actual sites have been torn down – some of the more notable survivors:

Capone's Chicago Home (Map pp312-13; 7244 S Prairie Ave) This South Side home was built by Capone and mostly used by his wife Mae, son Sonny and other relatives. Al preferred to stay where his vices were. The house looks almost the same today.

City Hall (Map pp304-5; 121 N La Salle St) This building was the workplace of some of Capone's best pals. During William 'Big Bill' Thompson's successful campaign for mayor in 1927, Al donated well over $100,000.

Green Mill (Map p311; 4802 N Broadway St) This tavern was one of Capone's favorite nightspots. During the mid-1920s the cover for the speakeasy in the basement was $10. You can still listen to jazz in its swank setting today (see p182).

Holy Name Cathedral (Map pp306-7; 735 N State St) Two gangland murders took place near this church. In 1924 North Side boss Dion O'Banion was gunned down in his floral shop (738 N State St) after he crossed Capone. In 1926 his successor, Hymie Weiss, died en route to church in a hail of Capone-ordered bullets emanating from a window at 740 N State.

Maxwell St Police Station (Map pp314-15; 943 W Maxwell St) This station, two blocks west of Halsted St, exemplified the corruption rife in the Chicago Police Department in the 1920s. At one time, five captains and about 400 uniformed police were on the take here.

Mt Carmel Cemetery (Map pp302-3; cnr Roosevelt Rd & S Wolf Rd, Hillside) Capone is now buried in this cemetery in Hillside, west of Chicago. He and his relatives were moved here in 1950. Al's simple gray gravestone, which has been stolen and replaced twice, is concealed by a hedge. It reads 'Alphonse Capone, 1899–1947, My Jesus Mercy.' Capone's neighbors include old rivals Dion O'Banion and Hymie Weiss. Both tried to rub out Capone, who returned the favor in a far more effective manner.

St Valentine's Day Massacre Site (Map pp308-9; 2122 N Clark St) In perhaps the most infamous event of the Capone era, seven members of the Bugs Moran gang were lined up against a garage wall and gunned down by mobsters dressed as cops. After that, Moran cut his losses and Capone gained control of Chicago's North Side vice. The garage was torn down in 1967 to make way for a retirement home, and residents there claim they sometimes hear ghostly noises at night. A **house** (2119 N Clark St) used as a lookout by the killers stands across the street.

neighborhood sits just east of here, between N Broadway St and N Glenwood Ave. Rosehill Cemetery is tucked into the northwest corner of Andersonville.

The exact boundaries of Uptown change depending on who you're talking to, and tend to evaporate entirely if you're talking to image-conscious realtors. In general, Uptown begins below W Foster Ave, reaching as far south as W Irving Park Rd, as far west as N Ashland Ave, and east to Lake Michigan. The 'restaurant row' section of Argyle St is between N Broadway St and N Sheridan Rd.

ARGYLE ST Map p311

btwn N Broadway St & N Sheridan Rd

Like Andersonville, the neighborhood around Argyle St seems to appear out of nowhere. As you come around the corner from Broadway St onto Argyle St, suddenly everything – from the stores to the restaurants to the car-detailing shops – is decked out in Laotian, Vietnamese, and Cambodian script. Even the El train station is topped with a pagoda and painted in the auspicious colors of bright green and red. Many of the residents of the area came here as refugees from the Vietnam war, and their presence has solved Chicago city planners' worries about how to reverse the declining fortunes of this Uptown enclave. The storefronts are all filled now (though the area still looks a little scruffy). The several blocks of Argyle St make a good stopover for lunch, or for a half hour's wandering and window-shopping.

ESSANAY STUDIOS Map p311

1333-1345 W Argyle St

Back before the talkies made silent film obsolete, Chicago reigned supreme as the number one producer of movie magic in the US. In those days Essanay churned out silent films with soon-to-be household names like WC Fields, Charlie Chaplin and Gilbert M Anderson (aka 'Bronco Billy,' the trailblazing star of the brand-new Western genre and co-founder of Essanay). Filming took place at the studio, but it also ventured out into surrounding North Side neighborhoods. At that point, getting the product out the door and into theaters was more important than producing artful, well-made films, so editing was viewed somewhat circumspectly. As a result, it was common in the early Essanay films to see local Chicago children performing unintentional cameos, or bits of familiar neighborhoods poking into the edge of 'California' mesas. Essanay folded in 1917, about the time that many of its actors were being lured to the bright lights of a still-nascent Hollywood. These days, the building belongs to St Augustine College, but the company's terra-cotta Indian head logo remains above the door at 1345.

GRACELAND CEMETERY Map p311

☎ 773-525-1105; 4001 N Clark St; 🕑 8am-4:30pm

Why go to Memphis to see ostentatious memorials to the dead when you can go to Graceland right in Chicago? The local version is in much better taste and is the final resting place for some of the biggest names in Chicago history. Most of the notable tombs lie around the lake, in the northern half of the 121 acres. Buy a 25¢ map at the entrance to navigate the swirl of paths and streets.

Many of the memorials relate to the lives of the dead in symbolic and touching ways: National League founder William Hulbert lies under a baseball; hotelier Dexter Graves lies under a work titled *Eternal Silence*; and George Pullman, the railroad car magnate who sparked so much labor unrest, lies under a hidden fortress designed to prevent angry union members from digging him up.

Daniel Burnham, who did so much to design Chicago, gets his own island. Photographer Richard Nickel, who helped form Chicago's budding preservation movement and was killed during the demolition of his beloved Chicago Stock Exchange Building (the 1972 accident was unrelated to the demolition), has a stone designed by

Carved detail, Rosehill Cemetery (opposite)

admiring architects. Other notables interred here include architects John Wellborn Root, Louis Sullivan and Ludwig Mies van der Rohe (whose sleek, modern tombstone perfectly mirrors his architecture), plus retail magnate Marshall Field and power couple Potter and Bertha Palmer.

HUTCHINSON ST DISTRICT Map pp318-19

Standing in marked contrast to some of Uptown's seedier neighborhoods, the Hutchinson St District is a proud, well-maintained area perfect for a genteel promenade. The homes here were built in the early 1900s, and represent some of the best examples of Prairie-style residences in Chicago. Several of the homes along Hutchinson St – including the one at **839 Hutchinson St** – are the work of George W Maher, famous student of Frank Lloyd Wright. Of special note are the homes at **817 Hutchinson St** and **4243 Hazel St**.

ROSEHILL CEMETERY Map p311

☎ 773-561-5940; W Bryn Mawr & Western Aves

The entrance gate to Chicago's largest cemetery is worth the trip alone. Designed by WW Boyington, the same architect who created the old Water Tower on Michigan Ave, the entry looks like a fantastical cross between high Gothic and low Disney. Through the gates, you'll find the graves of many Chicago bigwigs, from Chicago mayors to a US vice president to meat man Oscar Mayer. You'll also discover some of the weirdest grave monuments in the city, including a postal train and an enormous carved boulder from a Georgia Civil War battlefield. More than one ghost story started here; keep an eye out for vapors as night falls.

SWEDISH-AMERICAN MUSEUM CENTER Map p311

☎ 773-728-8111; 5211 N Clark St; adult/child $4/2; 🕑 10am-4pm Tue-Fri, 10am-3pm Sat & Sun

The permanent collection at this small storefront museum focuses on the lives of the Swedes who originally settled Chicago. In that sense it reflects the dreams and aspirations of many of the groups who have poured into the city since it was founded. At the museum, you can check out some of the items people felt were important to bring with them on their journey to America. Butter churns, traditional bedroom furniture, religious relics and more are all included in the collection.

UPTOWN THEATRE Map p311

www.uptowntheatrechicago.com; 4816 N Broadway St

When it opened in 1925, this grand movie theater cheerily billed itself as 'an acre of seats in a magic city.' Among its other magical amenities, Chicago's largest theater also boasted a space-age 'freezing and air-washing' plant and a 10,000-pipe organ that the theater owners giddily described as being able to produce 'effects of the sublimest beauty or most humorous imitation of the animal kingdom.' A matinee at the 4381-seat Spanish Baroque Revival behemoth was a rite of passage for many Chicago children. It closed in 1981, but the landmark building is currently slated for a $30 million renovation and reopening as the Uptown Theatre and Center for the Arts. Birders will want to swing by with their binoculars to check out Zoom and GG, the two Peregrine falcons who have made a home on the roof here. Four young falcons were born to the proud parents in 2004, and more are likely on the way.

WICKER PARK, BUCKTOWN & UKRAINIAN VILLAGE

Every Chicago hipster worth their jean jacket has a personal story about how they were almost killed in Wicker Park a decade ago. Those stories – from an era when prostitution, gangs and drive-by shootings defined the area – are recounted with the same sort of nostalgic pride that a grandparent uses to explain that they had to ride cows to school in the olden days. For the days of stray bullets are over, and Wicker Park and Bucktown have shot to the top of the list of happening neighborhoods in Chicago.

Just try to make your way along Milwaukee Ave near Damen Ave on a Friday night, and you'll get a sense of the riotous popularity of the neighborhood. Even in these tough economic times, the clubs and bars here are packed, and during the weekend techno dance parties, indie rock concerts and cool author readings all happen within 30ft of

TRANSPORTATION

Bus Number 50 runs up Damen Ave; 72 runs along North Ave; 70 travels along Division St.

El Blue Line to Damen Ave for Wicker Park and Bucktown; Blue Line to Division for Ukrainian Village.

Parking Meter and free on-street parking at a premium in Wicker Park and Bucktown; widely available in Ukrainian Village.

each other. And on any given day, dozens of hip shoe stores, resale shops, boutiques, bookstores, restaurants and salons hold court, providing Chicagoans with the necessary fuel for the modern urban lifestyle.

The neighborhood's transition from slumland to Starbucks didn't happen overnight, though, and there were some memorable snags along the way. In 2001 MTV brought the cast of its reality show *The Real World* to Chicago, renting a Wicker Park loft for the photogenic group. The cameras began rolling, and all seemed to be going according to plan when neighborhood residents, fearing that exposure from the show would speed gentrification, began showing up outside the apartment to protest. What started as a halfhearted, tongue-in-cheek resistance movement soon escalated, and by the time the cast left town there had been 11 arrests and multiple reports of vandalism.

All the hubbub would have been slightly bewildering to the generations of working-class Central European immigrants who originally lived in simple wood-frame residences here. Some of the descendants of those original Wicker Park occupants have found a home in Ukrainian Village, just to the south of Wicker Park. This mostly residential, largely working-class area is closer in feel to the Wicker Park and Bucktown of yore (though without the drug dealers or gang members). It's also home to many of the artists and post-college hipsters who were priced out of Wicker Park, though the slacker class has already started moving on to Logan Sq and Humboldt Park as chic boutiques and spas have begun popping up on Division St, raising interest in the area with Lincoln Park yuppies (and raising rents as well). Ukrainian Village is worth a visit, especially Division St where you'll find an irresistible array of breakfast joints, one-of-a-kind shops and underground bars.

Orientation

All roads lead to Wicker Park and Bucktown. Or at least three of them do, anyway: Wicker Park is centered at the perpetually packed intersection of N Milwaukee, N Damen and W North Aves. Bucktown stretches north along N Damen Ave from the Bloomingdale Ave train bridge. The triangular park itself is a block and a half south of North Ave on N Damen Ave. The area's beautiful old homes are immediately northwest of the park, straddling either side of North Ave.

Ukrainian Village is south of Wicker Park. Its northern boundary is the colorful Division St, though most of its sights are located on W Chicago Ave.

WICKER PARK & BUCKTOWN

Eating p158; Shopping p229; Sleeping p248

FLAT IRON BUILDING Map pp316-17

1579 N Milwaukee Ave

The warren of galleries, studios and workshops in this landmark building has been responsible for a sizable percentage of the artistic zaniness that has long made Wicker Park such a magnet for creative types. Keep an eye on telephone poles around the area for flyers detailing the latest shows and gallery open-houses. (For information on the annual Around the Coyote Arts Festival, see the City Calendar, p9.)

NELSON ALGREN HOUSE Map pp316-17

1958 W Evergreen Ave

In a three-flat one block south of the park, writer Nelson Algren (p30) created some of his greatest works about gritty life in the neighborhood. Algren won the 1950 National Book Award for his novel *The Man with the Golden Arm*, set on Division St near Milwaukee Ave. You can't go into the house, but you can admire it from the street.

POLISH MUSEUM OF AMERICA

Map pp316-17

☎ 773-384-3352; 984 N Milwaukee Ave; adult/senior & student $3/2; 🕑 11am-4pm Fri-Wed

If you don't know Pulaski from a *pierogi*, this is the place to get the scoop on Polish culture. The museum is the oldest ethnic museum in the US, and while you won't find high-tech 3D virtual rollercoaster rides or IMAX screens, you will get a chance to learn about some of the Poles who helped shape Chicago's history. (Pulaski, by the way, was a Polish hero in the American Revolution.) The collection of traditional Polish costumes, WWII artifacts and oddball, amateur food displays feel like they were all lovingly created by Polish retirees living in the area. The group of Polish posters from the '30s – hanging in the hallway by the gift shop – will delight fans of art deco art.

ST MARY OF THE ANGELS CHURCH

Map pp316-17

☎ 773-278-2644; 1850 N Hermitage Ave

With a dome modeled on St Peter's in Rome, the huge St Mary of the Angels church dominates both Bucktown and the view from the Kennedy Expressway. Built with money from Polish parishioners prodded by a zealous pastor, the church features angels on the parapet, in the nave and possibly in the heavens above as well.

Certainly the church is blessed, as proven by its ability to cheat death. Only 60 years after its completion in 1920, its maintenance costs – which had gone through the holey roof – and its declining membership made it a prime candidate for an early demise. But a grassroots campaign arose to save the church, drawing support from the community and people across the city. In 1992 the repairs, which cost more than the original construction bill, were completed, and the invigorated parish has many new members.

WICKER PARK Map pp316-17

btwn N Damen Ave, W Schiller St & N Wicker Park Ave

Sure, Chicago invented the zipper and a handful of other useless bric-a-brac. The city's true legacy, though, will be in a strange softball game invented here. Aptly named, 16-Inch Softball uses the same rules as normal softball, but with shorter games, a bigger, squishier ball and a complete lack of gloves or mitts on the fielders. They've been playing it here for over 75 years, and Wicker Park is a prime place to see the uniquely Chicago sport played by die-hard fanatics. And for travelers suffering withdrawal from the pooch left at home, Wicker Park's dog park is a great way to get in some quality canine time.

TOP FIVE WICKER PARK, BUCKTOWN & UKRAINIAN VILLAGE

- Chowing down on a drunken late night *al pastor* taco at **Flash Taco** (p159).
- Pretending to be a bike messenger at **Handlebar** (p158).
- Watching a reading from the stars of the underground press at **Quimby's** (p231).
- Finding the perfect pair of sunglasses on **Damen Ave** (p229).
- Heading for a late breakfast at one of the cool places on **Division St** (p161).

UKRAINIAN VILLAGE

Eating p161; Shopping p229

CHURCHES OF UKRAINIAN VILLAGE

The domes of the neighborhood's majestic churches pop out over the treetops in Ukrainian Village. Take a minute to wander by **St Nicholas Ukrainian Catholic Cathedral** (Map pp316-17; ☎ 773-276-4537; 2238 W Rice St), which is the less traditional of the neighborhood's main churches. Its 13 domes represent Christ and the Apostles. The intricate mosaics – added to the 1915 building in 1988 – owe their inspiration to the Cathedral of St Sophia in Kiev. Saints **Volodymyr & Olha Church** (Map pp316-17; ☎ 312-829-5209; 739 N Oakley Blvd) was founded by traditionalists from St Nicholas, who broke away over liturgical differences and built this showy church in 1975. It makes up for its paucity of domes (only five) with a massive mosaic of the conversion of Grand Duke Vladimir of Kiev to Christianity in AD 988.

UKRAINIAN INSTITUTE OF MODERN ART Map pp316-17

☎ 773-227-5522; www.uima-art.org; 2320 W Chicago Ave; admission free; 🕑 noon-4pm Wed-Sun

The 'Ukrainian' in the name is somewhat of a misnomer, as this bright white storefront showcases local artists regardless of ethnicity (along with a host of works by people of Ukrainian descent). The space has earned a reputation for putting together some of the best exhibits in Chicago. Shows here range from playfully pretty to perplexingly cerebral works, done in a host of media.

WEST SIDE & PILSEN

The scene near the Linda Warren gallery in the West Loop is about what you'd expect from one of Chicago's hottest art districts. Mod ladies pick at salads on the patio of the upscale eatery Follia. A couple of black-clad guys in punishing German eyewear discuss post-minimalism over a microbrew at the Fulton Lounge. And a man in rubber boots stands across the street, meditatively hosing blood out of the back of his truck.

Wait just a second there…

But yes, that's right. In the West Loop, one of the West Side's up-and-coming neighborhoods, the city's meatpackers and gallery owners exist side-by-side. As weird as it all seems at times, it works. The incongruous pairing of blue collar and black turtleneck is typical for many of the neighborhoods on Chicago's West Side, a patchwork of hard-to-define neighborhoods that includes Little Italy, Greektown and the West Loop, as well as the notoriously rough neighborhoods like Lawndale and Garfield Park further out.

The constant in the West Side is change. In Little Italy (which deserves the diminutive name, consisting as it does these days mostly of Taylor St) the main agent of change is the University of Illinois at Chicago (UIC). The school has teamed up with the city and developers to put in new housing throughout the sometimes-iffy neighborhood. As the UIC has been remaking the neighborhood, so has it been remaking itself. The infamous recipient of one of the ugliest campuses known to humankind (see p94), the university has been healing some old architectural wounds with an extensive remodeling plan.

North of Little Italy, Greektown offers little in the way of sights. Gustatory tourists, though, will revel in the flavors here; the area has enough Greek tavernas and cafés to make Zeus feel at home. No matter how triumphant your *tzatziki* (Greek dip made from yogurt, chopped cucumber, garlic and mint), though, it can't compare with the amazing dish of greens they've cooked up at the Garfield Park Conservatory. When, in 1994, the Conservatory announced plans to do a top-to-bottom renovation of the disintegrating facilities there, it seemed laughable. Twelve years later, the long-shot plan of revitalizing one of the country's biggest plant houses in one of the city's worst neighborhoods has been an unmitigated success.

Safety is definitely a consideration when visiting many sites on the West Side. The areas discussed here are OK during the day, and some are OK at night as well. Individual cautions, as well as transportation options, are covered in each neighborhood section. If you have a car, you can cover the entire area in an afternoon.

TOP FIVE WEST SIDE & PILSEN

- Gulping down a strawberry *agua fresca* (fruit-flavored water) from one of the innumerable food carts along **18th St** (p162).
- Nodding sagely at the canvases of the **West Loop galleries** (p95).
- Learning about the Mexican avant-garde at the awesome **Mexican Fine Arts Center Museum** (p97).
- Grabbing two Polish dogs from **Express Grill** (p160) and eating them in your car.
- Taking in a Bulls game at **United Center** (p201).

TRANSPORTATION

Bus Number 20 runs Loop-bound along Washington St, returns along Monroe St; 8 travels along Halsted St; 9 travels north–south between Pilsen and Irving Park Rd.

El Green Line to Clinton for the West Loop; Blue Line to Clinton for Greektown; Blue Line to Polk for Little Italy; Green Line to Conservatory-Central Park Dr for Garfield Park Conservatory; Blue Line to 18th St for Pilsen.

Parking West Loop free parking is plentiful, especially in the afternoon; Greektown parking can be tough to find but valets abound; Little Italy is fine for free on-street parking. Pilsen has plentiful parking on its side streets.

Orientation

No two ways about it, the West Side is huge. And we're only covering a small portion of it here. If you don't have a car, the distances between neighborhoods are painfully vast. Walking is also impeded by annoying obstructions like Highway 290, which makes an easy stroll between

Greektown and Little Italy all but impossible. Unless you're a long-distance runner, use cabs.

The West Loop area is the northernmost of the West Side neighborhoods we cover. Its main arteries are W Randolph and W Washington Sts, with Halsted St cutting north–south along its eastern edge. Greektown lives just three blocks south on Halsted St from where Halsted St meets W Washington St. If you just keep heading south on Halsted St, you'll pass the smoggy, traffic clogged roundabouts of Highway 290, and find the northeastern edge of the UIC campus. Hull-House (p94) is just a block south, and Taylor St, the main thoroughfare for Little Italy, is one long block south of here. Again, taking a cab through these areas will save you a lot of time, and prevent you from walking through some sketchy neighborhoods on Taylor St near Halsted St.

WEST LOOP

Eating p162

BATCOLUMN Map pp314-15

600 W Madison St

Artist Claes Oldenburg – known for his gigantic shuttlecocks in Kansas City and oversized cherry-spoon in Minneapolis – delivered this simple, controversial sculpture to Chicago in 1977. The artist mused that the 96ft bat 'seemed to connect earth and sky the way a tornado does.' Hmm... See it for yourself in front of the Harold Washington Social Security Center.

CHICAGO FIRE DEPARTMENT ACADEMY Map pp314-15

☎ 312-747-7239; 558 W DeKoven St

Rarely has a public building been placed in a more appropriate place: the fire department's school stands on the very spot where the 1871 fire began – between

THE HAYMARKET RIOT

On May 4, 1886, striking factory workers held a meeting at Haymarket Sq on Randolph St, between Halsted and Des Plaines Sts west of the Loop. A mob of police appeared toward the end of the meeting, which quickly degenerated into chaos – a bomb exploded, killing one policeman and wounding several others. Police began to fire shots into the dispersing crowd, and by the end of the day, six more policemen had been shot and killed (most shot down accidentally by other policemen) and 60 others were injured. Eight anarchist leaders, including some of the most prominent speakers and writers of the movement, were eventually arrested and accused of the crime. Despite the facts that the identity of the bomb-thrower was never known, that only two of the eight accused actually attended the rally (both were on the speaker's platform in view of police when the bomb went off), and that no evidence linking the accused to the crime was ever produced, all eight were convicted of inciting murder and sentenced to hang.

The public outcry against the trial was sizable. Sentiment worldwide had already favored the striking workers, who were demanding an eight-hour workday and were the victims of efforts by the factory owners and their police lackeys to discredit them. After the news came out that both the judge and jury had gone into the case convinced of the anarchist's culpability, the show-trial seemed even more gruesome.

Following an appeal for leniency from the families of the accused, three of the eight were granted life imprisonment. On the morning of the scheduled executions for the others, one of the men to be hanged committed suicide in jail by lighting a dynamite cap smuggled into him by a friend. The other four were draped with hoods, and led, shackled, to the gallows. One of the men, August Spies, uttered the famous words that would later appear on posters and flyers around the world: 'The day will come,' he said from beneath his hood, 'when our silence will be more powerful than the voices you are throttling today.'

The men have become martyrs for the contemporary anarchist and labor activist movements; the monument near their graves at the **Forest Home Cemetery** (Map pp302-3; ☎ 708-366-1900; 863 S Des Plaines Ave, Forest Park) is a popular pilgrimage site, and the graves are still decorated with drawings, flowers, poems and other offerings.

In memory of the dead policemen, a **statue** (Map pp314–15) was erected on the spot some years later: an officer standing with arm upraised, commanding peace 'in the name of the people of Illinois.' The statue has since had a history almost as violent as the event it commemorates. Thieves made away with the plaques at its base several times, and shortly after the turn of the 20th century a bus driver rammed it, claiming to be sick of seeing it every day. In 1928 it was moved several blocks west, to Union Park, where it stood peacefully until the uproarious 1960s, when it was blown up twice. Repaired yet again, the statue has found a home in the inner courtyard of the Chicago Police training center, where no one except for police officers is given access to it.

Clinton and Jefferson Sts. Although there's no word on whether junk mail still shows up for Mrs O'Leary, the academy trains firefighters so they'll be ready the next time somebody or some critter kicks over a lantern (see p52).

JANE ADDAMS HULL-HOUSE MUSEUM Map pp314-15

☎ 312-413-5353; 800 S Halsted St; admission free; 10am-4pm Mon-Sat, noon-5pm Sun

In 1889, at age 29, Jane Addams founded Hull-House. Addams, a middle-class wallflower, graduated from college only to find that there was no meaningful work for bright women. After a tour through Europe, she returned home inspired to turn her energy toward improving the lives of Chicago's poor. When Hull-House first opened (in the decrepit mansion of a family friend), successful models were nonexistent in Chicago. So Addams simply filled the home with like-minded young, middle-class women, who used their energy, smarts and society connections to stage concerts, give classes, and present lectures from such famous figures as suffragist Susan B Anthony and architect Frank Lloyd Wright. In the coming years, the house also provided day-care facilities, a kindergarten, an employment bureau and many other social services to masses of exploited and without-hope Italian, Greek, and Eastern European immigrants. (Bandleader Benny Goodman got his musical start playing in the Hull-House boys band.) Addams also provided space where the burgeoning labor unions could meet. She won the Nobel Peace Prize for her efforts in 1931. She died in 1935, but Hull-House continues her work at locations around the city.

UIC has preserved Addams' house, along with the 1905 dining hall where residents could come for hot meals. A 15-minute slide show on the 2nd floor of the hall details Addams' work. Displays document the struggle for social justice waged by Hull-House and others in the early 20th century.

OLD ST PATRICK'S CHURCH Map pp314-15

☎ 312-648-1021; www.oldstpats.org; 700 W Adams St

A Chicago fire survivor, this 1852 church is not only the city's oldest but one of its fastest-growing, thanks to the strategies of its politically connected pastor, Father Jack Wall. Old St Pat's is best known for its year-round calendar of social events for singles, including the enormously popular World's Largest Block Party, a weekend-long party with big-name rock bands where Catholic singles can flirt. (No less an authority than Oprah has proclaimed the block party the best place to meet one's match.) The social programs have boosted Old St Pat's membership from four (yes, four) in 1983 to thousands two decades later. The domed steeple signifies the Eastern Church; the spire signifies the Western Church. Call to find out when the church is open so you can see the beautifully restored Celtic-patterned interior.

UNION STATION Map pp314-15

☎ 312-655-2385; 2110 S Canal St

This wonderfully restored 1925 building, designed by Graham, Burnham & Company, looks like it stepped right out of a gangster movie. Come during the day when commuters stride through the space, which is dappled with bright shafts of sunlight from the banks of windows near the ceiling.

UNITED CENTER Map pp314-15

☎ 312-455-4650; www.unitedcenter.com; 1901 W Madison St

Built for $175 million and opened in 1992, the United Center arena is home to the Bulls and the Blackhawks (see p201) and is the venue for special events such as the circus. The statue of an airborne Michael Jordan in front of the east entrance pays a lively tribute to the man whose talents financed the edifice. The center, surrounded by parking lots, is OK by day but should be avoided at night – unless there's a game, in which case squads of cops are everywhere in order to ensure public safety. **Tours** (☎ 312-455-4500, ext 2644; $20, 15-person minimum) wind their way through the concourse, press box and scoreboard control room and include lunch.

UNIVERSITY OF ILLINOIS AT CHICAGO Map pp314-15

☎ 312-996-7000; btwn W Harrison St & W 14th Pl, S Halsted & S Morgan Sts

UIC used to be a much more interesting place to visit for all the wrong reasons. Noted Chicago architect Walter Netsch created a design that provoked extreme protests when it opened in 1965. Netsch proclaimed that it was his goal to re-create the sense of wonder one feels when exploring an Italian hill village, but the realities of his design were unremittingly grim. Imagine a maximum security prison without the barbed wire and you have the right idea. By the mid-1980s the whole ugly place was falling apart and despised by its 30,000 students and faculty. In 1990 a rebuilding program began to eradicate much of Netsch's hill town. His voice of protest was lone.

The **University Center Housing & Commons** (700 S Halsted St), an attractive undergraduate dorm that welcomes people onto the campus, became the first major building to break with the past. In the last decade the campus has become a pleasant place to go to school, but there's no reason to make a special trip there. However, if you don't go to the campus, it might just come to you. It has jumped south of Roosevelt Rd in a big way, in the process gobbling up the historic Maxwell St Market and many other surrounding blocks.

WEST LOOP GALLERIES

The residents and realtors are still battling for naming rights to this area of meat processors, cool galleries and chic restaurants. Some say West Loop; others West Loop Gate. And a small number of loft-dwellers just call it home. Either way, the neighborhood galleries – which radiate out from Peoria and Washington Sts – show the kind of maverick, risk-taking art that the established River North galleries won't touch. For a thorough overview of the West Loop scene, with plenty of time for chocolate, check out our West Loop Gallery tour (p123).

You can wander from gallery to gallery all day, but our picks for the best stops include: **FLATFILEgalleries** (Map pp314-15; ☎ 312-491-1190; 217 N Carpenter St; 🕑 11am-6pm Tue-Sat), a gallery that runs multiple shows – including at least one photo exhibition – simultaneously in its large space; **Donald Young Gallery** (Map pp314-15; ☎ 312-455-0100; 933 W Washington St; 🕑 10am-5:30pm Tue-Fri, 11am-5:30pm Sat), which serves as the West Loop's venerable anchor, showcasing work by well-known artists like Sophie Calle and Dan Flavin; and the **Carrie Secrist Gallery** (Map pp314-15; ☎ 312-491-0917; 835 W Washington Blvd; 🕑 11am-6pm Tue-Sat) and **Kavi Gupta Gallery** (Map pp314-15; ☎ 312-432-0708; 835 W Washington Blvd; 🕑 10am-6pm Tue-Fri, 11am-5pm Sat), in the same building and both representing a stable of interesting emerging artists.

Up the street, **Bodybuilder & Sportsman** (Map pp314-15; ☎ 312-492-7261; 119 N Peoria; 🕑 11am-6pm Tue-Sat) was awarded 'best gallery for emerging artists' status by *Chicago* magazine. The shows in the small space often blend elements of humor and commentary. Across the street, about half the exhibits at **moniquemeloche** (Map pp314-15; ☎ 312-455-0299; 118 N Peoria; 🕑 11am-6pm Tue-Sun) are by young Chicago artists, while the other half is by an international group of up-and-comers. A host of worthwhile galleries share the building with moniquemeloche; our favorite of them is **Gescheidle** (Map pp314-15; ☎ 312-226-3500; 116 N Peoria St; 🕑 11am-6pm Tue-Sat), on the 4th floor.

GREEKTOWN & LITTLE ITALY

Eating p163

The Greektown area, located along Halsted St between Van Buren and Monroe Sts, is more of an eat street than anything else, loaded with tasty places to get a plate of spanakopita or flaming cheese. The Greek immigrants who used to give the neighborhood a distinct character, though, have moved on.

That's just slightly less the case in Little Italy. The area south of the Eisenhower Expressway to Roosevelt Rd was a thriving Italian community until the 1950s, when several blows almost killed it. The expressway itself was rammed through the most vibrant part of the neighborhood, the surviving commercial area was demolished for the campus of the University of Illinois at Chicago, and several public housing projects were scattered through what was left. Many people still suspect that the old Mayor Daley intended the entire plan as retribution for the schemes of rival politicians.

Perhaps out of sheer stubbornness, the Italian residents hung on, supporting a commercial district on Taylor St. Meanwhile, professionals drawn to the university and the fast-growing Chicago Medical Center to the west discovered the tree-lined streets of the neighborhood. Beginning in the 1970s, gentrification transformed old homes and added new town houses. And now that the city has spent vast sums beautifying Taylor St, the neighborhood is set to take off.

Although clearly slated for demolition, the remaining blighted housing projects remain a safety concern; visitors to the area should take care to avoid stretches that go from safe to grim in one block. Be extra careful around the blocks between Racine Ave and Loomis St on Taylor St, and in the areas west of Damen Ave and south of Roosevelt Rd.

GARFIELD PARK CONSERVATORY

Map pp314-15

☎ 312-746-5100; www.garfield-conservatory.org; 300 N Central Park Blvd; admission free; 🕑 9am-5pm Fri-Wed, 8pm Thu

With 4½ acres under glass, the Park District's pride and joy, built in 1907, seemed like a lost cause in 1994. Located far away from the heart of the city, in a neighborhood that tended to scare away visitors, the Conservatory nevertheless began a multimillion-dollar restoration campaign. By 2000 it was completed, and the crowds have been pouring in ever since. One of the original designers, Jens Jensen, intended for the 5000 palms, ferns and other plants to re-create what Chicago looked like during prehistoric times. Today the effect continues – all that's missing is a rampaging stegosaurus. The Economic House features a fascinating range of plants that are used for food, medicine and shelter. New halls contain displays of seasonal plants, which are especially spectacular in the weeks before Easter. A children's garden lets kids play with plants that aren't rare or irreplaceable, and a Demonstration Garden was added in 2002 to help answer the questions of the wide-eyed urban gardeners who come here. If you drive, note that the neighborhood is still not the safest.

HELLENIC MUSEUM & CULTURAL CENTER Map pp314-15

☎ 312-655-1234; www.hellenicmuseum.org; 4th fl, 801 W Adams St; admission $5; 🕑 10am-4pm Mon-Fri, 11am-4pm Sat; Blue Line to UIC-Halsted

It's all Greek to you at this museum dedicated to the Greek immigrant experience in Chicago. Artifacts donated by local Greek families – including writings, photographs, and musical instruments – are displayed here in a variety of exhibits.

NATIONAL ITALIAN AMERICAN SPORTS HALL OF FAME Map pp314-15

☎ 312-226-5566; www.niashf.org; 1431 W Taylor St; adult/child & senior $5/3; 🕑 10am-5pm Mon-Fri, 11am-5pm Sat

At the time of writing, the National Italian American Sports Hall of Fame was a medium-sized room filled with an artfully displayed collection of memorabilia. You can see Joe DiMaggio's glove, the football from the famous 1958 NFL Championship game, and a race car once driven by Mario Andretti, along with 100 other bits of sporting history. The Hall of Fame has plans to expand soon; until it does, though, only devoted sports fans will likely feel the $5 admission fee is worth it.

PIAZZA DIMAGGIO Map pp314-15

S Bishop St at Taylor St

As part of the city's beautification campaign, a portion of S Bishop St that meets Taylor St has been converted into Piazza DiMaggio, in honor of Joe DiMaggio, the Italian-American baseball star. A large statue of Joltin' Joe swinging for the bleachers resides here; you can see some of the famous player's artifacts across the street in the National Italian American Sports Hall of Fame.

PILSEN

Eating p165

You won't be in the Windy City for two minutes before a proud resident sidles up to you and explains that, 'You can travel all around the world without ever leaving Chicago.' The best way to respond to these delusional rantings is to nod, smile and back away very, very slowly. For while Chicago boasts a number of thriving ethnic communities, none of them offers the immersive feel of being in another land entirely.

None of them, that is, except for Pilsen. Pilsen is the center of the Latino world in Chicago, and a trip to this convenient neighborhood really is like stepping into the streets of a foreign country. Pilsen thumps with *tejano* (music that's a mix of

Mexican and American styles) and brassy mariachi music, and the streets flow with the sounds of Spanish. The salsas here scald, the moles soothe, and the sidewalks are filled with umbrella'd food carts that tempt passers-by with a rainbow array of cold, pulpy *agua frescas* (fruit-flavored waters) and spicy-sweet *verduras* (thin slices of melon or cucumber dusted with a chili-powder kick).

Chicago's hipster underground has also been quietly relocating here for the last decade. The area around 18th and Halstead Sts has become a hub for storefront art galleries and painter's spaces. Even the taste-making record label Thrill Jockey has its offices here. The mix of sculptors and recent Spanish-speaking immigrants has been a mostly amiable one, and places like the Jumping Bean (p165) give both camps a place to eat, relax and whup each other in games of chess.

The architecture of the neighborhood is another draw. The original Czechoslovakian and Central European settlers here modeled their three-flats and storefronts from the world they'd left behind. In Pilsen, you can also see the city's old vaulted sidewalks, especially along 18th Pl, where one old cottage after another features a front yard several feet below the level of the sidewalks. (The streets were later raised to allow for the construction of sewers.)

Pilsen does have its rough spots, but if you stick to the main drags, you'll be fine. So fine, in fact, that artists and the Latino residents are becoming nervous about the future of their neighborhood. *¡Defienda Pilsen!* (Defend Pilsen!) graffiti appears on walls from time to time, a call to arms against the gentrification transforming neighborhoods to the north. For now, though, Pilsen exists under developers' radars, and life continues apace in one of Chicago's coolest neighborhoods.

The parts of Pilsen you'll be exploring are limited to the corridor of W 18th St, between Halsted St on the far east end and Wolcott Ave on the west. Most of the restaurants and stores cluster around 18th St's intersection with Ashland Ave. The Mexican Fine Arts Museum is located in Harrison Park, a five-minute walk west from the bulk of the other attractions. Many of the storefront galleries are on the eastern end of 18th St, where Hwy 90/94 cuts through the neighborhood.

COOPER DUAL LANGUAGE ACADEMY Map pp314-15

1645 W 18th Pl

The exterior wall of the academy is the canvas for a 1990s tile mosaic that shows a diverse range of Mexican images, from a portrait of farmworker advocate Dolores Huerta to the Virgin of Guadalupe. Each summer, art students add more panels.

MEXICAN FINE ARTS CENTER MUSEUM Map pp314-15

☎ 312-738-1503; www.mfacmchicago.org; 1852 W 19th St; admission free; 🕑 10am-5pm Tue-Sun

Founded in 1982, this vibrant museum has become one of the best in the city. Housed in a renovated field house in Harrison Park, the gleaming exhibit space tackles a bewilderingly complex task (summing up 1000 years of Mexican art and culture), and pulls it off beautifully. The art here ranges from classical-themed portraits to piles of carved minibus tires. The turbulent politics and revolutionary leaders of Mexican history are well represented, including works about Cesar Chavez and Emiliano Zapata.

THE PODMAJERSKY FACTOR

As you walk from gallery to gallery in Pilsen, you'll likely notice the distinctive orange and blue signs for realtor Podmajersky in windows and on business cards laid out on tables. This family-run real-estate company owns much of this neck of Pilsen, and has been promoting it as an artist haven for 30 years now. It has converted old buildings into live-work-show spaces for artists, and sponsors events such as the annual **Pilsen East Open House** (☎ 312-377-4444), which takes place in late September annually. Its latest effort has been renaming the entire area the **Chicago Arts District** (www.chicagoartsdistrict.org). While its clear that Pilsen's arty flavor owes a lot to the efforts of the Podmajersky family, there's also a fear among some artists that subsidising the growth of galleries is just Podmajersky's clever tactic to bring affluent residents to the neighborhood. Whatever the case may be, those looking for affordable, interesting art from some of Chicago's young artists definitely should set aside an hour to explore this gallery-rich eastern edge of a fast-emerging neighborhood.

The museum also sponsors readings by top authors and performances by musicians and artists. And if you are in town during the fall, be sure to check out the exhibits and celebrations relating to November 1, the Day of the Dead, a traditional Mexican holiday that combines the festive with the religious. The events take place for a month on either side of the day.

PILSEN CHURCHES

Some wonderful European-influenced churches remain throughout Pilsen. The 1914 **St Adalbert Church** (Map pp314-15; 1650 W 17th St) features 185ft steeples, and is a good example of the soaring religious structures built by Chicago's ethnic populations through thousands of small donations from parishioners, who would cut family budgets to the bone to make their weekly contribution. The rich ornamentation in the interior of this Catholic church glorifies Polish saints and religious figures. The Poles had St Adalbert's; the Irish had **St Pius** (Map pp314-15; 1901 S Ashland Ave), a Romanesque Revival edifice built between 1885 and 1892. Its smooth masonry contrasts with the rough stones of its contemporaries. Catholics of one ethnic group never attended the churches of the others, which explains why this part of town, with its concentration of Catholic immigrants, is thick with steeples.

PILSEN GALLERIES

Five years ago, the Pilsen galleries were the punk rockers of the Chicago art world. Few of them had phone numbers, most were only open on Saturday, and many were located in the 'curator's' living room. The galleries were run by 20-somethings, showcasing art by 20-somethings, and the rules that governed the commercially oriented 'white cubes' of River North and West Loop galleries didn't apply here.

Since then, though, the scene has matured, and seeing art in Pilsen no longer requires stepping over upended furniture (or upended artists) sprawled out from a party the night before. A great time to come here is on **Second Fridays**, when the dozen or so Pilsen galleries all stay open late on the second Friday of each month to welcome throngs of wandering art patrons with wine, snacks, and freshly hung paintings, ceramics, and photos. The galleries, with a few notable exceptions, are located on S Halsted St, just south of 18th St.

Some of the best bets in Pilsen include the eclectic **Parts Unknown Gallery** (Map pp314-15; ☎ 312-492-9058; 645 W 18th St; 🕑 11am-5pm Tue-Sat), the ceramics-oriented **Dubhe Carreno Gallery** (Map pp314-15; ☎ 312-666-3150; 1841 S Halsted St; 🕑 11am-5pm Tue-Sat), the colorful **Sally Ko Studio** (Map pp314-15; ☎ 312-560-1445; 1743 S Halsted St; 🕑 by appointment), and **4Art Inc** (Map pp314-15; ☎ 312-850-1816; 1932 S Halsted St; 🕑 10am-6pm Tue-Sat), which specializes in large-scale group shows.

THALIA HALL Map pp314-15

1807 S Allport St

Named for the Greek muse of comedy, who casts a bemused gaze from a spot in the arch over the entrance, Thalia Hall brought out the bohemian side of the Czech immigrants, who used it for theater and music productions. Socialists also used it as a rallying place back in the late 1800s; some of the Haymarket Riot testimony centered on meetings held here, and rabble-rousing anarchist Emma Goldman preached to the assembled masses from the stage. Its interior theater was modeled on the Old Opera House in Prague. The building had been abandoned until 2004, when a plan was launched to restore it as a multipurpose venue. We're keeping our fingers crossed.

SOUTH LOOP & NEAR SOUTH SIDE

The Chicago crane, a species that once thrived throughout the city, now resides primarily south of the Loop. No, we're not talking about the shorebirds here. These are the 100ft-tall building cranes, the kind whose presence means only one thing for a neighborhood: that dramatic change is coming.

And it is. The South Loop – which includes the lower ends of downtown and Grant Park along with the historic Printer's Row and Dearborn Park neighborhoods – started the trend in the 1980s. During that time, the South Loop's beautiful, derelict old buildings became homes and super-convenient launching pads for Chicago's downtown workers. Suddenly, the area was alive again. Booming. And the ongoing

(Continued on page 107)

1 *Wrigley Field (p85)* **2** *Chicago skyline* **3** *Swimming, Lake Michigan (p213)* **4** *Leaves, Lincoln Park (p83)*

1 *O'Hare International Airport (p271)* **2** *City skyscrapers* **3** *Platform of the Brown Line El (p274)* **4** *Lion statue, Art Institute of Chicago (p67)*

1 *Historic Water Tower (p80)*
2 *The Chicago Theatre (p68)*
3 *Sears Tower (p70)* 4 *Magnificent Mile Lights Festival (p13), N Michigan Ave*

1 *Adler Planetarium & Astronomy Museum (p107)* **2** *Community art display, Field Museum of Natural History (p108)* **3** *Chinese dragon, Chinatown (p110)* **4** *Clock, Marshall Field's building (p68)*

1 *Prairie Ave Historic District (p112)* **2** *Sculpture, Chinatown (p110)* **3** *In-line skating (p202), Oak St Beach* **4** *Pedestrian, the Loop (p67)*

1 *Lake Michigan from Grant Park (p71)* **2** *Cycling (p202), Oak St Beach* **3** *People, the Loop (p67)* **4** *University of Chicago (p118)*

1 Ferris wheel, Navy Pier (p75) **2** *James R Thompson Center (p46)* **3** *Chicago at night* **4** *Shedd Aquarium (p109)*

1 *Flowers, Lincoln Park (p83)* **2** *Boat tour (p64), Chicago River* **3** *View from John Hancock Center (p78)* **4** *Fountain, Grant Park (p71)*

(Continued from page 98)

TRANSPORTATION

Bus Number 29 to Printer's Row; 12 to Museum Campus/Soldier Field; 4 to Prairie Ave Historic District; 21 to Chinatown.

El Green, Orange and Red Lines to Roosevelt for Printer's Row or Museum Campus/Soldier Field; Red Line to Cermak-Chinatown for Chinatown.

Metra Roosevelt Rd stop for Museum Campus/Soldier Field; 18th St for Prairie Ave Historic District; McCormick Place North Building for McCormick Place.

Parking The Museum Campus boasts plenty of lot parking; meter parking is available but scarce in South Loop and readily available in Near South Side.

renovations of the Museum Campus area added further polish onto a newly gleaming neighborhood.

Developers' eyes then turned southward, toward the Black, poor neighborhoods just inland from the Field Museum, Soldier Field and McCormick Place convention center. Chicago's early millionaires like Marshall Field and George Pullman built their stately mansions along Prairie Ave here in the late 1800s. But when they packed up for the Gold Coast a decade later, the rest of Chicago's money moved with them. By the 1950s, the Near South Side had turned into a bleak zone of boarded up storefronts and dangerous streets.

That era for the Near South Side officially ended in 1993, when Mayor Daley surprised everyone by moving from Bridgeport to the Near South Side town-house development called Central Station. And now the city's wealthy are following his example and flocking to a neighborhood that's been ignored for the last five decades.

The sudden influx of wealthy Whites into a formerly impoverished area makes for a surreal scene. The steel skeletons of high-rise lofts and luxury condos have sprouted everywhere, but essentials like grocery stores, cafés and restaurants haven't yet followed. It gives the Near South Side the feel of a play caught between acts – one set already disappearing as another hastily takes its place.

A few sections of the Near South Side, though, have remained constant through the decades of change. The Prairie Ave historic district still offers an intimate look at the glorious homes that set the tony tone here 100 years ago. And Chinatown continues to bustle day and night – as it has for many years – with the Chicagoans who flock to the ethnic enclave for bubble teas, dim sum and heaping bowls of spicy noodles.

Orientation

The blocks here are long, and, for the time being anyway, uncongested. The South Loop extends between Congress Pkwy in the north and Roosevelt Rd in the south. Printer's Row and Dearborn Park are both part of the South Loop, while the plethora of developments south of Roosevelt Rd fall under the Near South Side jurisdiction. The Museum Campus is located along Lake Shore Dr, on the strip's eastern edge. S Michigan Ave – a far more sedate version of its charmingly opulent cousin to the north – connects the Loop to the Prairie Ave Historic District. Highway 55 runs across the southernmost edge of the Near South Side.

SOUTH LOOP

Eating p166; Shopping p233; Sleeping p249

ADLER PLANETARIUM & ASTRONOMY MUSEUM Map pp312-13

☎ 312-922-7827; www.adlerplanetarium.org; at the end of Solidarity Dr; adult/child/senior $16/14/15, discount for Chicago residents, free Mon & Tue Jan-Feb & mid-Sep–late Dec; 9am-6pm Mon-Sun, shorter hours Sep-Apr

The first planetarium built in the western hemisphere, the Adler Planetarium & Astronomy Museum has seen visitor numbers

TOP FIVE SOUTH LOOP & NEAR SOUTH SIDE

- Soaking in the atmosphere and music at the **Velvet Lounge** (p183).
- Satisfying your inner shutterbug at the **Museum of Contemporary Photography** (p108).
- Feasting on plates and plates of shrimp dumplings at **Shui Wah** (p167).
- Surveying the city from the newly opened **Northerly Island** (p109).
- Making scary faces at Sue, the *Tyrannosaurus rex*, in the **Field Museum of Natural History** (p108).

soar in recent years. From the entrance to the Adler, visitors descend below the 1930 building, which has 12 sides, one for each sign of the zodiac. In the newest wing, a digital sky show re-creates such cataclysmic phenomena as supernovas. Interactive exhibits allow you to simulate cosmic events such as a meteor hitting the earth (this one is especially cool). The original planetarium does a good job planning special events around celestial occurrences, be they eclipses or NASA missions. In the Sky Theater a mechanical Zeiss projector can create a huge variety of nighttime sky effects.

The Adler does a commendable job of involving visitors in astronomy, with live video links to various telescopes around the world and research facilities that are totally accessible to visitors. The sky-show programs last about 50 minutes. The whole place can be easily covered in less than two hours. A cafeteria serves all the usual stomach-filling burgers and sandwiches.

Near the entrance to the Adler, a **12ft sundial** by Henry Moore is dedicated to the golden years of astronomy, from 1930 to 1980, when so many fundamental discoveries were made using the first generation of huge telescopes. About 100yd west in the median, the bronze **Copernicus statue** shows the 16th-century Polish astronomer Nicolaus Copernicus holding a compass and a model of the solar system.

FIELD MUSEUM OF NATURAL HISTORY Map pp312-13

☎ 312-922-9410; www.fieldmuseum.org; 1400 S Lake Shore Dr; adult/child/senior & student $12/7/7, some exhibits extra, discount for Chicago residents, discount days Mon & Tue Jan-Feb & mid-Sep–late Dec; 9am-5pm, last admission 4pm

With over 70 PhD-wielding scientists and 20 million artifacts, you know things are going to be hopping at the Field Museum. The big attraction is the *Tyrannosaurus rex* named Sue, a 13ft-tall, 41ft-long beast who menaces the grand space with ferocious aplomb. Sue, the most complete *T rex* ever discovered, takes its name from Sue Hendrickson, the fossil-hunter who found the 90%-complete skeleton in South Dakota in 1990.

The head honchos at the Field know how large dinosaurs loom in the grade-school imagination, which is why Sue is just one of many dinosaur-related exhibits here. In fact,

Contemporary Chicago sculpture

a new state-of-the-art (and very dinosaur-heavy) exhibit about the history of life on Earth will be opening in May 2006. In the meantime, you can also watch staff paleontologists clean up fossils, learn about the evolution of the massive reptiles, and even learn about *Homo sapiens*' evolutionary ties to the extinct beasts.

A clever blend of the fanciful with a large amount of Field artifacts, the 'Inside Ancient Egypt' exhibit re-creates an Egyptian burial chamber on three levels. The mastaba (tomb) contains 23 actual mummies and is a reconstruction of the one built for Unis-ankh, the son of the last pharaoh of the Fifth dynasty, who died at age 21 in 2407 BC. The bottom level, with its twisting caverns, is especially worthwhile. Those reeds growing in the stream are real.

Other displays worth your time include 'Underground Adventure,' a vast exhibit exploring the habitats of animals and insects that live underground, and the 'Pawnee Earth Lodge,' which allows visitors to explore a complete dwelling of the Great Plains tribe.

MUSEUM OF CONTEMPORARY PHOTOGRAPHY Map pp312-13

☎ 312-663-5554; www.mocp.org; 600 S Michigan Ave; admission free; 10am-5pm Mon-Wed & Fri, to 8pm Thu, noon-5pm Sat

Located in one of the many buildings of Columbia College, this museum focuses on American photography since 1937. Once primarily a venue for student work, it has won widespread support as the only institution of its kind between the coasts. The permanent collection includes the works of Debbie Fleming Caffery, Mark Klett, Catherine Wagner, Patrick Nagatani and 500 more of the best photographers working today.

Special exhibitions augment the rotating permanent collection.

NORTHERLY ISLAND Map pp312-13

Just south of the Adler Planetarium, the once-busy commuter airport of Meigs Field is now well on its way to being transformed into a park. It will feature walking trails, new landscaping, and the (allegedly temporary) Charter One Pavilion outdoor concert venue. The shift from runway to prairie grasses has its root in a controversial 2003 incident that reads a little like a municipal spy thriller, complete with midnight operatives and surprise bulldozings. You can get the whole story on p60. But by 2005, the controversy had already died down, and Chicagoans had begun happily exploring this surprisingly beautiful piece of lakefront that had been largely off-limits to pedestrians for a half century.

OLMEC HEAD NO 8 Map pp312-13

Near the Field Museum, the city has installed Olmec Head No 8. Over 7ft tall, it's a copy of one of the many amazing stone carvings done by the Olmec people more than 3500 years ago in what is now the Veracruz state of Mexico. No one has been able to figure out how the Olmec carved the hard volcanic rock.

PRINTER'S ROW

Chicago was a center for printing at the turn of the 20th century, and the rows of buildings on S Dearborn St from W Congress Pkwy south to W Polk St housed the heart of the city's publishing industry. By the 1970s the printers had left for more-economical quarters elsewhere and the buildings had been largely emptied out, some of them barely making it on the feeble rents of obscure nonprofit groups.

In the late 1970s savvy developers saw the potential in these derelicts, and one of the most successful gentrification projects in Chicago began. The following describes some of the notable buildings in the area as you travel from north to south.

A snazzy renovation of the **Mergenthaler Lofts** (Map pp312-13; 531 S Plymouth Ct), the 1886 headquarters for the legendary linotype company, included the artful preservation of a diner storefront. The **Pontiac Building** (Map pp312-13; 542 S Dearborn St), a classic 1891 design by Holabird & Roche, features the same flowing masonry surfaces as the firm's Monadnock Building, to the north.

A massive and once-windowless wreck, the 1911 **Transportation Building** (Map pp312-13; 600 S Dearborn St) enjoyed a 1980 restoration that assured the neighborhood had arrived. The **Second Franklin Building** (Map pp312-13; 720 S Dearborn St), a 1912 factory, shows the history of printing in its tiled facade. The roof slopes to allow for a huge skylight over the top floor, where books were hand-bound, for this building existed long before fluorescent lights or high-intensity lamps. The large windows on many of the other buildings in the area serve the same purpose.

Once the Chicago terminal of the Santa Fe Railroad, the 1885 **Dearborn St Station** (Map pp312-13; 47 W Polk St) used to be the premier station for trains to and from California. Today it merely sees the trains of parent-propelled strollers from the Dearborn Park neighborhood, built on the site of the tracks to the south.

SHEDD AQUARIUM Map pp312-13

☎ 312-939-2438; www.sheddaquarium.org; 1200 Lake Shore Dr; pass to all exhibits adult/child & senior $23/16, aquarium-only ticket adult/child & senior $8/6, discount for Chicago residents; 🕑 9am-6pm Fri-Wed, to 10pm Thu, shorter hours Sep-May

The world's largest assortment of finned, gilled, amphibious and other aquatic creatures swims within the marble-clad confines of the John G Shedd Aquarium. Though it could simply rest on its superlative exhibits – beluga whales in a 4-million-gallon aquarium anyone? – the Shedd makes a point of trying to tie concepts of ecosystems, food webs and marine biology into its presentation of supercool animals. Permanent exhibits include the multilevel Oceanarium, which mimics ocean conditions off the northwest coast of North America. The beluga whales inside are remarkably cute creatures that come from the pint-size end of the whale scale. Their humped heads and natural 'smiles' make them look eerily human. You'll also see Pacific white-sided dolphins, harbor seals and sea otters. Don't linger only on the main floor – you can go underneath the cement seats and watch the mammals from below through viewing windows. The 'Wild Reef' exhibit will have sharkophiles and sharkophobes equally entranced; over a dozen sharks cut through the waters in a simulation of a Philippines reef ecosystem. And the 'Amazon Rising' exhibits offer a captivating look at a year in the Amazon River and rain forest. Some of the newer and special exhibits sell out early in the morning; consider buying tickets through the website beforehand to ensure entry.

The stretch of grass on the lake between the Shedd and the Adler may be the setting for more amateur and postcard photos than any other place. One look toward the skyline will show you why: the view is good year-round; on clear winter days, when the lake partially freezes and steam rises off the Loop buildings, it verges on the sensational.

SOLDIER FIELD Map pp312-13

www.soldierfield.net; 1410 S Museum Campus Dr

South of the Field Museum is Soldier Field. Built from 1922 to 1926, the oft-renovated edifice has been home to everything from civil rights speeches by Martin Luther King Jr to Chicago Fire soccer games. It got its latest bursting-at-the-seams look in a controversial 2003 makeover. Tours of the stadium are available for groups of 10 or more; call ☎ 312-235-7244 for details. Advance booking is required.

SPERTUS MUSEUM Map pp312-13

☎ 312-922-9012; www.spertus.edu; 618 S Michigan Ave; adult/child $5/3, free Fri; 10am-5pm Sun-Wed, 10am-7pm Thu, 10am-3pm Fri

An excellent small museum devoted to 5000 years of Jewish faith and culture, the Spertus boasts an equally excellent corps of volunteers. The museum's exhibits juxtapose aspects of Jewish life and religion to convey the diversity of both. The Zell Holocaust Memorial – the country's first permanent museum exhibition of its kind – features oral histories from survivors who emigrated to Chicago, as well as the names of Chicagoans' relatives who died.

The museum mounts well-curated special exhibitions that cover topics as diverse as Biblical images in classical art and Jewish humor in the US. The basement is devoted to a children's area called the ARTiFACT Center, where kids can conduct their own archeological dig for artifacts of Jewish life. In 2005 the museum broke ground on its new building just to the north of the current one on Michigan Ave. The strikingly modern space boasts an asymmetrical facade of folded glass that will likely cause much joy and consternation in Chicago architectural circles.

THADDEUS KOSCIUSKO MEMORIAL

Map pp312-13

western end of median btwn Adler Planetarium & Shedd Aquarium

This honors the Polish general who fought on the winning side of the American Revolution and then returned to help his nation fight for freedom. This and the Copernicus statue inspired the city to rename the street Solidarity Dr in 1980 to honor the Lech Walesa–led movement in Poland.

NEAR SOUTH SIDE

Eating p166; Shopping p233; Sleeping p249

CHINATOWN

To experience the full charm of Chinatown, wander its streets and browse in its many varied small shops, especially in the retail heart of the neighborhood, on Wentworth Ave south of Cermak Rd. Other interesting parts include Cermak Rd itself and Archer Ave to the north. The neighborhood is one of the city's most vibrant, and its affluent residents are developing land in all directions even as more immigrants arrive.

The Cermak-Chinatown El stop on the CTA Red Line is just to the east of the action. East of the stop itself is a dicey area dominated by a housing project. But the busy streets of Chinatown itself tend to be safe.

The **On Leong Building** (Map pp312-13; 2216 S Wentworth Ave) once housed various neighborhood service organizations and some illegal gambling operations that have led to spectacular police raids. It now houses the Chinese Merchants Association. Built in 1928 and also known as the Pui Tak Center, the grand structure is a fantasy of Chinese architecture that makes good use of glazed terra-cotta details. Note how the lions guarding the door have twisted their heads so they don't have to risk bad luck by turning their backs to each other.

On much of the rest of Wentworth you'll find a blend of typical Chicago and Chinese architecture. The characteristic arch near Cermak Rd was added in the 1970s, and amateur political scientists can study the 'Four basic values of a nation' inscribed on the back of it. The continually growing **Chinatown Sq** (Map pp312-13; Archer Ave at

Cermak Rd) dates from 1992 and features some of the area's best restaurants.

CHINESE-AMERICAN MUSEUM OF CHICAGO Map pp312-13

☎ 312-949-1000; www.ccamuseum.org; 238 West 23rd St; adult/child & senior $2/1; ⏲ 9:30am-1:30pm Fri, 10am-5pm Sat & Sun

This small museum dedicated to the Chinese experience in Chicago and throughout the Midwest opened in 2005. Along with displays of historical artifacts donated by the community, the museum hosts interesting cultural lectures such as 'Chop Suey: The American Passion for non-Chinese Chinese Food.' Its website contains a great digital guide to the historical buildings and landmarks of Chinatown.

HILLARY RODHAM CLINTON WOMEN'S PARK Map pp312-13

Fronting on Prairie Ave, with the Glessner House to the north and the Clarke House to the west (see Prairie Ave Historic District, p112), the 4-acre park is named for former first lady, now US Senator Hillary Rodham Clinton, who grew up in suburban Park Ridge and calls herself a lifelong Cubs fan (though that slipped her mind when she also pledged her loyalty to both the Mets and the Yankees in her successful bid to become a New York senator). Since Clinton dedicated the park in 1997, landscapers have added a French garden, fountain and winding paths. As bright as its future looks, the park has a notorious past. The Fort Dearborn massacre, in which some Native Americans rebelled against the incursion of white settlers, is thought to have occurred on this very spot on August 15, 1812.

MCCORMICK PLACE Map pp312-13

☎ 312-791-7000; www.mccormickplace.com; 2301 S Lake Shore Dr, main entrance on S Martin Luther King Jr Dr

Called the 'mistake by the lake' before the Soldier Field renovation stole the title, the McCormick Place convention center is an economic engine that drives up profits for the city's hotels, restaurants, shops and airlines. 'Vast' isn't big enough to describe it, nor 'huge,' and 'enormous' doesn't work, so settle for whatever word describes the biggest thing you've ever seen. The 2.2 million sq ft of meeting space spreads out over three halls, making this the largest convention center in the country.

The East Building (now called Lakeside Center) interrupts the sweep of the lakefront. The oldest part of today's complex, it was completed to replace the original fireproof McCormick Place, which burned down in 1967. The *Chicago Tribune* played a disgraceful role in the original building's construction, with its owner Col Robert R McCormick using all of his hefty political weight to get it built on the lake. (Politicians who opposed the project were threatened with investigative stories.)

The North Building, a barn of a place, accrued huge cost overruns during its construction in 1986. The South Building was finished in 1997. The best of the lot, it features the Grand Concourse, a bright and airy hall linking all the buildings. As if 112 meeting rooms weren't enough, the convention behemoth will be opening a new West Building in 2008, located immediately to the west of the current complex.

It's easy to get a cab to and from McCormick Place. A great insider's tip is the 23rd St Metra train station, hidden in the lowest level of the North Building. Trains to and from the Randolph St and Van Buren St Stations, in the Loop, stop often during rush hour. From noon Monday through Saturday, they depart from Randolph St at 20 minutes past the hour and take seven minutes to reach McCormick Place. Parking can be a hike from the buildings and is expensive. The main entrance to McCormick Place now lies on Martin Luther King Jr Dr, just north of the Stevenson Expressway.

NATIONAL VIETNAM VETERANS ART MUSEUM Map pp312-13

☎ 312-326-0270; 1801 S Indiana Ave; adult/child $5/4; ⏲ 11am-6pm Tue-Fri, 10am-5pm Sat, noon-5pm Sun

Opened in 1996, the National Vietnam Veterans Art Museum displays the art of Americans who served in the military during the war in Vietnam. Spread over three floors in an old commercial building, it features a large and growing collection of haunting, angry, mournful and powerful works by veterans.

Cleveland Wright's *We Regret to Inform You* is a heartbreaking look at a mother in her kitchen at the moment she learns of her son's death. Joseph Fornelli's sculpture

Dressed to Kill comments on the role of the average grunt in Vietnam. Some 58,000 dog tags hang from the ceiling, a haunting reminder of the Americans who died in the war. A small café here serves snacks.

PRAIRIE AVE HISTORIC DISTRICT

By 1900 Chicago's crème de la crème had had enough of the scum de la scum in the nearby neighborhoods. Potter Palmer led a procession of millionaires north to new mansions on the Gold Coast. The once-pristine neighborhood, which lined Prairie Ave for several blocks south of 16th St, fell into quick decline as one mansion after another gave way to warehouses and industry. Thanks to the efforts of the Chicago Architecture Foundation, a few of the prime homes from the area have been carefully restored. Streets have been closed off, making the neighborhood a good place for a stroll. A footbridge over the train tracks links the area to Burnham Park and the Museum Campus.

The **John J Glessner House** (Map pp312-13; ☎ 312-326-1480; 1800 S Prairie Ave; tours adult/child $11/7, free Wed; ⏲ tours 1pm & 3pm Wed-Sun) is the premier survivor of the neighborhood. Famed American architect Henry Hobson Richardson took full advantage of the corner site for this beautiful composition of rusticated granite. Built from 1885 to 1887, the L-shaped house, which surrounds a sunny southern courtyard, got a 100-year jump on the modern craze for interior courtyards. Much of the home's interior looks like an English manor house, with heavy wooden beams and

PULLMAN

Railroad magnate George Pullman was nervous. With strikes and labor unrest spreading through the country in the late 1870s, he had become worried that the construction of his luxurious Pullman Palace railroad cars might be affected by the rabble. So he decided to secure the loyalty of his laborers by building a 'workingman's utopia' for them, a company-owned town conveniently located next to the factory. Everybody could walk to work, and the workers' families would have access to a free kindergarten, an excellent library and an unparalleled fitness center.

And he built it. The city of Pullman opened in 1881 – and quickly became the talk of the world, offered up as a beaming example of capital and labor living in harmony with one other. The conditions in Pullman *were* much better than anything else available. While the packinghouse workers of the Bridgeport slums lived in squalor, the Pullman residents were racing in regattas, attending newly built churches, even competing in their own version of the Olympics, called Spring Games and held every Memorial Day.

Pullman automatically deducted rents from workers' paychecks – living here wasn't free, merely affordable – and he got more than rents out of the deal. He also got to keep an eye on his workforce. Political and labor organizations were forbidden in Pullman, the city's newspaper was edited by the company publicist, and workers who wanted to drink alcohol had to leave Pullman to do so. The company even paid some residents to be 'spotters,' spies who reported lapses in morality and loyalty to Pullman heads.

Things worked well enough for the first 11 years. But the 1893 depression hit Pullman's luxury rail-car business hard. The firm laid off some workers and cut the pay of others by as much as 30%. Rents and prices in Pullman's town stayed high, however, leaving workers with little in their paychecks.

Worker resentment grew and finally resulted in a strike in 1894. Three thousand workers walked off the job and poured into the streets of Pullman. Violent clashes between the strikers and thugs hired by Pullman ended with 34 people dead. The strike was finally settled when federal troops were sent in to force the strikers back to work.

It was a pyrrhic victory for Pullman, whose reputation never recovered from the violent crackdown. Censured by a commission authorized by President Cleveland, Pullman was forced by the government to sell off its share in the town. He died a bitter man in 1897. The sale of the town's properties was completed by 1907, and the neighborhood has experienced ups and downs since then. The last part of the complex finally closed for good in 1981.

The southern part of Pullman, where the higher-paid craftsmen and managers lived, has been largely bought up by people determined to preserve it. North Pullman, with simpler housing for laborers, is only now being appreciated for its underlying architectural qualities.

Visit Pullman in the daytime so you can appreciate the buildings. Start at **Historic Pullman Foundation Visitor's Center** (☎ 773-785-8901; www.pullmanil.org; 11141 S Cottage Grove Ave; ⏲ 11am-3pm Tue-Fri & Sun, 11am-2pm Sat), where you can pick up a map, or join a walking tour of the neighborhood. Call for info.

If you're driving, take I-94 south to Exit 66A – 111th St – and make a right as you exit the freeway. Pullman is a half-mile west on your left. By Metra, go to 111th St station.

details. More than 80% of the current furnishings are authentic, thanks to the Glessner family's penchant for family photos.

Tours of the Glessner House include the nearby **Henry B Clarke House** (Map pp312-13; 1827 S Indiana Ave), the oldest structure in the city. When Caroline and Henry Clarke built this imposing Greek Revival home in 1836, log cabins were still the rage in Chicago residential architecture. The sturdy frame paid off – during the past 160 years the house has been moved twice to escape demolition. The present address is about as close as researchers can get to its somewhat undefined original location. The interior has been restored to the period of the Clarkes' occupation, which ended in 1872.

Generally, you can't visit the following houses, but you still can admire them from the outside. Modeled after 15th-century French châteaus, the **William K Kimball House** (Map pp312-13; 1801 S Prairie Ave) dates from 1890 to 1892. Both it and the Romanesque **Joseph G Coleman House** (Map pp312-13; 1811 S Prairie Ave) now serve as the incongruous headquarters for the US Soccer Federation. Limestone puts a glitzy facade on the brick **Elbridge G Keith House** (Map pp312-13; 1900 S Prairie Ave), an early 1870 home.

SECOND PRESBYTERIAN CHURCH

Map pp312-13

☎ 312-225-4951; 1936 S Michigan Ave

Designed by James Renwick, the architect of New York's St Patrick's Cathedral and Washington DC's original Smithsonian Institution, this 1874 church is a neo-Gothic limestone celebration with Tiffany stained glass.

WILLIE DIXON'S BLUES HEAVEN

Map pp312-13

☎ 312-808-1286; 2120 S Michigan Ave; admission $10 incl tour; noon-3pm Mon-Fri, noon-2pm Sat, reservations required

From 1957 to 1967, this humble building was the home of the legendary Chess Records, a temple of blues and a spawning ground of rock and roll. The Chess brothers, two Polish Jews, ran the recording studio that saw – and heard – the likes of Muddy Waters, Bo Diddley, Koko Taylor and others. Chuck Berry recorded four Top 10 singles here, and the Rolling Stones named a song '2120 S Michigan Ave' after a recording session at this spot in 1964. (Rock trivia buffs will know that the Stones named themselves after the Muddy Waters song 'Rolling Stone.')

Today the building belongs to Willie Dixon's Blues Heaven, a nonprofit group set up by the late blues great who often recorded at the studios to promote blues and preserve its legacy. A gift store is open in front, while the old studios are upstairs. There are many artifacts on hand as well.

More often than not visitors will meet AJ Tribble, Blues Heaven docent and Willie Dixon's nephew. During summer, concerts happen at 6pm every other Thursday in the open space next door to the building.

SOUTH CHICAGO & HYDE PARK

A complete history on the rise and fall of the various empires of Chicago's far South Side (including Bronzeville, Bridgeport, Hyde Park, Kenwood and Pullman) reads a little like a Wagner opera. Powerful leaders, decadent wealth, palaces, paupers, epic battles, grand ideas, supernatural destruction and ignominious defeats. From the dark history of Chicago's massive slaughterhouses to the blinding dawn of the nuclear age on a Hyde Park squash court, the personalities of the South Side have long served as a guiding force in the city's fortunes, and, to some extent, the country's destiny.

TRANSPORTATION

Bus Number 1 runs down Michigan Ave to Bronzeville; 8 travels along Halsted St in Bridgeport; 6 runs from State St in the Loop to 57th St in Hyde Park.

El Green Line to 35th St/Bronzeville/IIT for Bronzeville or IIT; Red Line to Sox/35th for Bridgeport.

Metra From 53rd St station for Kenwood; 57th St station for Hyde Park.

Parking Bronzeville has plenty of on-street parking, as does Bridgeport (except for when the White Sox are playing); finding a space in Kenwood isn't a problem, but Hyde Park can be tight. Free parking is available on the street and in University parking lots after 4pm weekdays and all day on weekends. If you're really stumped in Hyde Park, look south of the Midway Plaisance.

That era, for the most part, is over. This area of town, south of the Stevenson Expressway and east of the Dan Ryan Expressway, has had a tough time since WWII. Whole neighborhoods have vanished, with crime and blight driving residents away. The construction of the vast wall of housing projects along the east side of the Dan Ryan Expressway created huge impoverished neighborhoods where community ties broke down and gangs held sway.

But the news isn't all bad. Armchair historians will find some intriguing traces of the South Side gone by. Bronzeville – home to a Black artistic renaissance in the 1940s and '50s that rivaled Harlem – boasts a few worthwhile sights. Irish Bridgeport, former site of the infamous stockyards and the 1968 Democratic Convention debacle, is a must for fans of Mayor Daley. Pullman (see the boxed text, p112) offers a rare look at a capitalists' utopian dream. Kenwood's historic homes look better than ever, and the gargoyle-filled Gothic campus of the University of Chicago in Hyde Park offers visitors more Nobel-lauded brainiacs per square inch than any other place on Earth.

The slow pace and lack of things to do mean South Chicago shouldn't be at the top of anyone's tourist agenda. But if you find yourself curious about Chicago's powerful past, there's plenty to discover.

Orientation

A car is needed to visit Bronzeville and Bridgeport. Conveniently, Highway 90/94, the Dan Ryan Expressway, offers a quick route to both. Bronzeville's main drag is S Martin Luther King Dr (some of the historic sites are three blocks west along S Indiana Ave). Bridgeport is west of Bronzeville, on the other side of Highway 90/94. When you see Comiskey Park you're almost there. The Bridgeport neighborhood runs between 31st St in the north and 43rd St in the south.

For Hyde Park and Kenwood, skip the highway and take Lake Shore Dr, exiting at 57th Dr (also the Museum of Science and Industry exit). Kenwood is immediately north of Hyde Park, between S Drexel Blvd to the west, E Hyde Park Blvd to the south and the lake to the east. Hyde Park is flanked by two huge parks, Washington Park in the west and Jackson Park, where the Museum of Science and Industry is located, to the east. The two parks are connected by the Midway Plaisance, a long green strip of land and accompanying boulevards that run along the south edge of the University of Chicago campus. The intersection of 57th St and S University Ave is a great place to start your explorations of the University of Chicago campus.

TOP FIVE SOUTH CHICAGO & HYDE PARK

- Pretending to be in *Das Boot* while walking through the German U-boat at the **Museum of Science & Industry** (p117).
- Getting the blues at **Lee's Unleaded Blues** (p182).
- Scoping those clean Prairie School lines at **Robie House** (p117).
- Crashing out with a good book in the old-fashioned, Harry Potter–esque **William Rainey Harper Memorial Library** (p118).
- Wandering through the fallen industrial utopia of **Pullman** (p112).

SOUTH CHICAGO

BRONZEVILLE HISTORIC BUILDINGS

Once home to Louis Armstrong and other notables, Bronzeville thrived as the vibrant center of Black life in the city from 1920 to 1950, boasting an economic and cultural strength that matched that of New York's Harlem. Shifting populations, urban decay and the construction of the wall of public housing along State St led to Bronzeville's decline. The same forces that led to the neighborhood's decline can make visiting the area a cautious endeavor. Plan to come with a car during the daytime; it's best to totally avoid the area at night.

Examples of stylish architecture from the past can be found throughout Bronzeville, but note that some of the buildings are in miserable shape and aren't worthy of more than an inspection of the exterior. You can see some fine old homes along two blocks of Calumet Ave between 31st and 33rd Sts, an area known as 'The Gap.' The buildings here include Frank Lloyd Wright's only row houses, the **Robert W Roloson Houses** (Map pp302-3; 3213-3219 S Calumet Ave).

One of scores of Romanesque houses that date from the 1880s, the **Ida B Wells House** (Map pp302-3; 3624 S Martin Luther King

PIG PROBLEMS

In *The Jungle,* Upton Sinclair described the Chicago stockyards this way: 'One could not stand and watch very long without becoming philosophical, without beginning to deal in symbols and similes, and to hear the hog-squeal of the universe.'

These were slaughterhouses beyond compare. By the early 1870s they processed more than one million hogs a year and almost as many cattle, plus scores of unlucky sheep, horses and other critters. All of them trundled through the still-standing **Union Stockyards Gate** (Map pp302-3; 850 W Exchange Ave), one of the first commissions of Burnham & Root's young architecture company. It was a coldly efficient operation. The pigs themselves became little more than a way to turn corn into a denser, more easily transportable substance that was thus more valuable.

The old saying – that once the animals were in the packinghouses, everything was used but the squeal – was almost true. Some bits of pig debris for which no other use could be found were fed to scavenger pigs, who turned the waste into valuable meat. But vast amounts of waste were simply flushed into the south branch of the Chicago River, and it then flowed into the lake. Beyond the aesthetic and health problems that ensued, the packers had to contend with other consequences of their pollution.

Meat processed in Chicago was shipped in ice-packed railroad cars to the huge markets in the East. The ice was harvested from lakes and rivers each winter and then stored for use all year long. But ice that was taken from the Chicago River returned to its stinky liquid state as it thawed over the meat on the journey east, thus rendering the carcasses unpalatable. The packers finally had to resort to harvesting their ice in huge operations in unpolluted Wisconsin.

Jr Dr) is named for its 1920s resident. Wells was a crusading journalist who investigated lynchings and other racially motivated crimes. She coined the famous line: 'Eternal vigilance is the price of liberty.'

Gospel music got its start at **Pilgrim Baptist Church** (Map pp302-3; ☎ 312-842-5830; 3301 S Indiana Ave), originally built as a synagogue from 1890 to 1891. It has a classic exterior that only hints at the vast and opulent interior. Gospel fans will also want to make a pilgrimage to two more places further south where the music soars on Sundays. The **Greater Salem Missionary Baptist Church** (Map pp302-3; ☎ 773-874-2325; 215 W 71st St) is where gospel great Mahalia Jackson was a life-long member. Still further to the south, modern **Salem Baptist Church** (Map pp302-3; ☎ 773-371-2300; 11800 S Indiana Ave) boasts one the city's top choral ensembles, and is helmed by the charismatic state senator Reverend James Meeks.

The **Supreme Life Building** (Map pp302-3; 3501 S Martin Luther King Jr Dr), a 1930s office building, was the spot where John H Johnson Jr, the publishing mogul who founded *Ebony* magazine, got the idea for his empire, which also includes *Jet* and other important titles serving African-Americans. In 2005 the building was renovated after falling into disrepair, a good sign for the rising Bronzeville neighborhood.

In the median at 35th St and Martin Luther King Jr Dr, the **Victory Monument** (Map pp302–3) was erected in 1928 in honor of the Black soldiers who fought in WWI. The figures include a soldier, a mother and Columbia, the mythical figure meant to symbolize the New World.

BRIDGEPORT & UNION STOCKYARDS GATE Map pp302-3

The community of Bridgeport is more important for its historical role than for its ability to draw tourists. The stockyards were once a major attraction, but they are long closed and their land is being rapidly covered by new warehouses. The traditional home of Chicago's Irish mayors (this is where the Daley dynasty grew up), Bridgeport remains an enclave of descendants of Irish settlers. A few Chinese and Hispanic people have moved in, but many African-Americans, who live to the south and east, feel that they're not welcome. While some residents say Bridgeport is more tolerant now, it will probably never live down its role in the 1919 race riots, when thugs went on a killing spree after a Black youth on a raft floated too close to a 'White' beach.

Halsted St from 31st St south to 43rd St is Bridgeport's rather uninteresting main drag. Most of the neighborhood lies west of the huge train embankment that itself is west of Comiskey Park. However, Bridgeport extends north of the park all the way to Chinatown and makes for a good walk after a game if you're in a group and don't stray east of the Dan Ryan Expressway.

A tiny vestige of the stockyards is one block west of the 4100 block of S Halsted

St. The **Union Stockyards Gate** (Map pp302-3; 850 W Exchange Ave) was once the main entrance to the vast stockyards where millions of cows and almost as many hogs met their ends each year. During the 1893 World's Expo, the stockyards were a hugely popular tourist draw, with nearly 10,000 people a day making the trek here to stare, awestruck as the butchering machine took in animals and spat out blood and meat.

The value of those slaughtered in 1910 was an enormous $225 million. Sanitary conditions eventually improved from the hideous levels documented by Upton Sinclair (see the boxed text, p115), although during the Spanish-American war, American soldiers suffered more casualties because of bad cans of meat from the Chicago packing houses than because of enemy fire.

ILLINOIS INSTITUTE OF TECHNOLOGY Map pp302-3

☎ 312-567-3000; 3300 S Federal St

A world-class leader in technology, industrial design and architecture, Illinois Institute of Technology (IIT) owes much of its look to legendary architect Ludwig Mies van der Rohe, who fled the Nazis in Germany for Chicago in 1938. From 1940 until his retirement in 1958, Mies designed 22 IIT buildings that all reflect his tenets of architecture, combining simple metal frames painted black with glass and brick infills. The star of the campus and Mies' undisputed masterpiece is **SR Crown Hall** (3360 S State St), appropriately home to the College of Architecture. The building, close to the center of campus, appears to be a transparent glass box floating between its translucent base and suspended roof. At night it glows from within like an illuminated jewel.

Mies isn't the only architectural hero whose works are on the display at IIT. In 2003 the campus opened two other buzz-worthy buildings by world-renowned architects. Dutch architect Rem Koolhaas designed the **McCormick Tribune Campus Center** (cnr 33rd & State Sts) with its simple lines and striking en-tubing of the El tracks that run overhead. This is Koolhaas' only building in the US. Just south of the Campus Center is the Helmut Jahn–designed **State Street Village** (cnr 33rd & State Sts). Jahn studied at IIT in his younger days, and his strip of rounded glass-and-steel residence halls is a natural progression of the works of the modernist bigwigs he learned from while here. You can get a free **tour** (☎ 312-567-3077; 🕑 1pm Mon, noon Wed & Fri, 5pm Thu) of both buildings from IIT architecture students; tours leave from the welcome center inside the McCormick Tribune Campus Center.

KENWOOD HISTORIC ARCHITECTURE Map pp320-1

Among the treasures of Kenwood is the **Kehilath Anshe Ma'ariv-Isaiah Israel Temple** (☎ 773-924-1234; 1100 E Hyde Park Blvd). Also called KAM Synagogue, this is a domed masterpiece in the Byzantine style. Its acoustics are said to be perfect. Call for opening times. Many classic homes line the shaded Woodlawn Ave, including the **Isidore Heller House** (5132 S Woodlawn Ave), an 1897 Frank Lloyd Wright house with the characteristic side entrance. The house at **4944 S Woodlawn Ave** was once home to Muhammad Ali. Bodyguards around the 1971 **Elijah Muhammad House** (4855 S Woodlawn Ave) indicate that Nation of Islam leader Louis Farrakhan currently lives here.

HYDE PARK

Drinking p177

DAVID & ALFRED SMART MUSEUM OF ART Map pp320-1

☎ 773-702-0200; http://smartmuseum.uchicago.edu; 5550 S Greenwood Ave; admission free; 🕑 10am-4pm Tue-Fri, 11am-5pm Sat & Sun

Named after the founders of *Esquire* magazine, who contributed the money to get it started, the official fine arts museum of the university opened in 1974 and expanded in 1999. The 8000 items in the collection include some excellent works from ancient China and Japan and a colorful and detailed Syrian mosaic from about AD 600. The strength of the collection lies in paintings and sculpture contemporary to the university's existence. Auguste Rodin's *Thinker* occupies a thoughtful place (hey, it's the Smart museum), as do works by Arthur Davies, Jean Arp, Henry Moore and many others.

DUSABLE MUSEUM OF AFRICAN AMERICAN HISTORY Map pp320-1

☎ 773-947-0600; www.dusablemuseum.org; 740 E 56th Pl; adult/child/senior & student $3/1/2, free Sun; 🕑 10am-5pm Tue-Sat, noon-5pm Sun

In a peaceful part of Washington Park, this museum features more than 100 works of

Museum of Science & Industry (below)

African-American art and permanent exhibits that cover African-Americans' experiences from slavery through the Civil Rights movement. The museum, housed in a 1910 building, takes its name from Chicago's first permanent settler, Jean Baptiste Pointe du Sable, a French-Canadian of Haitian descent (see p50).

MUSEUM OF SCIENCE & INDUSTRY

Map pp320-1

☎ 773-684-1414; www.msichicago.org; 5700 S Lake Shore Dr; adult/child/senior $9/5/7.50; 9:30am-5:30pm Mon-Sat, 11am-5:30pm Sun, shorter hours Sep-May

This overstimulating museum will defeat even the most rambunctious six-year-old. (If you're older than six, give in now, as you don't stand a chance.) Nine permanent exhibits thoroughly examine everything on earth, from cerebral concepts like the passage of time to basic questions about the origins of breakfast cereal. Visitors can climb through a German U-boat captured during WWII and press their noses against the window of the Apollo 8 command module. Some of the museum's most famous exhibits are also its simplest. The 'Human Body Slices' exhibit consists of a man and a woman who died in the 1940s – their bodies cut in half-inch sections then pressed between pieces of glass. Eeew, we know. But amazing all the same.

The main building of the museum served as the Palace of Fine Arts at the landmark 1893 World's Expo, which was set in the surrounding Jackson Park. When you've had your fill of space capsules, coalmines and Zephyrs at the museum, the park makes an excellent setting to recuperate.

ROBIE HOUSE Map pp320-1

☎ 773-834-1847; 5757 S Woodlawn Ave; adult/child & senior $12/10; tours 11am, 1pm & 3pm Mon-Fri, continuous tours 11am-3:30pm Sat & Sun

This masterpiece is the ultimate expression of Frank Lloyd Wright's Prairie School style; it makes the otherwise charming surrounding houses look like so many dowdy old aunts. The long, thin Roman bricks and limestone trim mirror the same basic shape of the entire house. The long and low lines, which reflect Midwest topography, are ornamented solely by the exquisite stained- and leaded-glass doors and windows.

The materials used to construct the house were as revolutionary as the design. Poured concrete forms the basis of many of the floors and balconies, while steel beams support the massively overhanging roof – a radical concept for residential construction. Tours of the interior take in the entire house,

A BOMB IS BORN

At 3:53pm on December 2, 1942, Enrico Fermi looked at a small crowd of men around him and said, 'The reaction is self-sustaining.' The scene was a dank squash court under the abandoned football stadium in the heart of the University of Chicago. With great secrecy, the gathered scientists had just achieved the world's first controlled release of nuclear energy. More than one sigh of relief was heard amid the ensuing rounds of congratulations. The nuclear reactor was supposed to have been built in a remote corner of a forest preserve 20 miles away, but a labor strike had stopped work. The impatient scientists went ahead on campus, despite the objections of many who thought the thing may blow up and take a good part of the city with it. Places such as Los Alamos in New Mexico and Hiroshima and Nagasaki in Japan are more closely linked to the nuclear era, but Chicago is where it began.

save the upper floor and servants' quarters. Note that Wright, a control freak if there ever was one, used built-in furniture, windows and other details to prevent the owners from messing with his interior design vision. A gift shop with books and other mementos operates in the garage.

UNIVERSITY OF CHICAGO Map pp320-1

☎ 773-702-1234; 5801 S Ellis Ave

Some universities collect football championships. The University of Chicago collects Nobel Prizes – 78 to the year 2005. In particular, the economics department has been a regular winner, with faculty and former students pulling in 23 prizes since the first Nobel for economics was awarded in 1969. Merton Miller, a University of Chicago economics faculty member and a Nobel winner, explained the string of wins to the *Sun-Times:* 'It must be the water; it certainly can't be the coffee.'

The university's classes first met on October 1, 1892. John D Rockefeller was a major contributor to the institution, donating more than $35 million, which he called 'the best investment I ever made in my life.' The original campus was constructed in an English Gothic style. Highlights of a campus tour include the **Rockefeller Memorial Chapel** (5850 S Woodlawn), the exterior of which will send sculpture-lovers into paroxysms of joy – the facade bears 24 life-sized and 53 smaller religious figures, with even more inside. The **William Rainey Harper Memorial Library** (1116 E 59th St) is another must-see. The long row of arched, two-story windows bathes the 3rd-floor reading room with light and an almost medieval sense of calm. The **Bond Chapel** (1050 E 59th St) is equally serene. Built in 1926, the exquisite 300-seat chapel is the harmonious creation of the architects, sculptors, woodcarvers and glassmakers who worked together on the project.

On Ellis Ave, between 56th and 57th, sits the 1968 Henry Moore bronze sculpture, **Nuclear Energy**, marking the spot where Enrico Fermi and company started the nuclear age (see the boxed text, p117).

Walking & Cycling Tours

Walking & Cycling Tours

Sure, the El is great, and taxis are plentiful. But nothing beats a walking tour for getting to know Chicago's endless array of sights. Every year, Chicago is lauded in national surveys as one of the country's top five most walkable cities, and whether you're into impressionist masterworks or beer-soaked sports bars, you'll find some tailor-made treks in this chapter to put you right in the heart of the action. So fill up those water bottles and strap on the sweatband – Chicago awaits.

LAKEFRONT & HISTORIC HOMES BIKE CRUISE

Biking along the shore of Lake Michigan on the Lakefront Trail is one of the most exhilarating experiences you'll have as a visitor to Chicago. On this tour, you're going to follow the trail from Millennium Park up to the very cusp of Lincoln Park, then swing by historic homes of Astor St on the way back. Along the route, you'll pass two of Chicago's most popular beaches, get fantastic, up-close-and-personal views of the city's skyline, and roll by Chicago's most beautiful historic homes.

TOUR FACTS

Start Brown, Green, Orange or Purple Line to Randolph, walk east two blocks to the Millennium Park Bike Station
End Randolph stop on the Brown, Green, Orange or Purple Line
Distance 6 miles
Duration 2.5 hours
Fuel Stop Oak Street Beachstro

Start at the new **Millennium Park Bike Station 1** (p272), where you can rent a bike if you don't have one. Lock, helmet and maps are included in the rental price, and you should think about bringing a backpack so you don't have to leave the lock dangling from your handlebars – not all bikes are fitted with lock holders. Also, keep in mind that it's illegal to ride your bike on city sidewalks. For most of this adventure, you'll be on a car-free bike trail, but there will be brief forays onto city streets. If riding in the street makes you uncomfortable, you can skip the Astor St detour, or just push your bike on the sidewalk for that portion of the journey.

From the Millennium Park Bike Station, hop in the bike lane and head toward the lake on Randolph. Turn right at Field and follow the signs to the Lakefront Trail. At Monroe, make a left and cross Lake Shore Dr. Pick up the trail marked with a silhouette of a bicycle and pedal north. This is one of the most congested parts of the trail, and if you find your bike lane blocked by some straying pedestrians (or a slow-moving group of cyclists), the etiquette is to call out 'Passing on your left!' and then go around them.

The first thing you'll pass is the moored boat of the Columbia Yacht Club. If you look past the yacht club (to the right of the breakwater), you'll see what appears to be a factory floating on the horizon. This is one of the four **intake cribs 2** that grab freshwater from the lake, feed it through tunnels running underneath the lake and run it through a purification process, and then straight into your hotel's bathroom faucets. Bottoms up!

See the city from ground level

HIGH-VELOCITY ART INSTITUTE TOUR

You could easily spend several days walking through the **Art Institute of Chicago** (p67), with its millennia-spanning collection of American, European and Asian art. But since the human body can only take so much oohing and aahing at amazing works before aesthetic overload kicks in, we've narrowed the museum's treasures down into a sprinter's hour of high-velocity artistic entertainment. Along the way, you'll hit some of the highlights, along with a few curiosities.

Start at the beautiful **Grand Staircase** in the lobby. Go ahead and climb up, enjoying the sunlight-bathed feel, and walk straight ahead into Room 201. Most of the French impressionist art here is courtesy of Bertha Palmer, Chicago's society doyenne of the late 1800s, who had the foresight to collect impressionist works back when many critics decried the 'unhealthy art' with its focus on everyday life as crude and heretical.

The room's main attraction is **Paris Street; Rainy Day** by Gustave Caillebotte. Caillebotte was an engineer by training who inherited a fortune from his father at a young age and used that money to support fellow impressionist artists such as Degas, Monet and Renoir. He straddled the line between the realism that dominated the established art world of his day and the looser, more experimental approach of his impressionist contemporaries.

Exit left to Room 205, where you'll find Van Gogh's **The Bedroom**, a painting picturing the sleeping quarters of the artist's house in Arles. Van Gogh had hoped to create an artist colony in the town, populated by many of the artists you see hanging on the walls around you (the colonization never materialized). This is the second of three versions of the painting, executed during Van Gogh's 1889 stay at an asylum. In the same room is Seurat's pointillist masterpiece of 1884, **A Sunday Afternoon on the Island of La Grande Jatte**. Get close enough for the painting to break down into its component dots, and you'll see why it took Seurat two long years to complete it. Next door, in Room 206, the cavalcade of famous impressionists continues with Monet's **wheatstack** paintings. The 15ft-tall stacks, located on the artist's farmhouse grounds in Giverny, were part of a series that effectively launched Monet's career when they sold like hotcakes at a show he organized in 1891.

Continue through the Gauguin-filled Room 234B and turn right at Room 234A, passing into Room 236. If it seems like the tour just took a turn for the surreal, you're right. The Art Institute has a fantastic surrealism collection, and you can see some honeys of the genre here, from Magritte's whimsical **Time Transfixed**, to Salvador Dalí's nightmarish **Inventions of the Monsters**. In the latter, Dalí's profile is visible in the lower left corner, along with that of his wife, Gala. Painted in Austria immediately before the Nazi annexation, the title refers to a Nostradamus prediction that the apparition of monsters presages the outbreak of war. By way of further explanation, Dalí provided this clear-as-day key: 'Flaming giraffe equals masculine apocalyptical monster. Cat angel equals divine heterosexual monster. Hourglass equals metaphysical monster. Gala equals sentimental monster.' Hmmm…

Continue walking through 237A, where some of the museum's collection of hilarious, weird dadaist publications are on display. The anti-art movement of dadaism went on to inspire surrealist artists. Nonsense is used to great effect, reflecting the dadaists' collective disgust at the senselessness of WWI and the idiocy of those governing art and politics.

Beyond the dadaist works are the remarkable boxes of Joseph Cornell. A solitary man who spent most of his adult life working from the small house he shared with his mother and younger brother in Queens, New York, Cornell built poetic dioramas from juxtaposed objects, photos and bits of newspaper. Associated loosely with the surrealists, Cornell also made short films and even made ends meet by selling illustrations to *Vogue* and *Good Housekeeping*. Note the balance present in **Untitled (Soap Bubble Set)** in Room 237D; this sense of exquisite symmetry is common to all his works.

Head down the stairs at the back of Room 239 to the first level, and then walk straight through to Room 140, the long, armor-filled Gunsaulus Hall. Make a right here, and walk to the end of the hall, turning right at Room 150, and stepping just inside the sculpture court of Room 161, where you take the stairs up to the second level. Room 265, in the back right, features Georgia O'Keeffe's **Black Crosses, New Mexico** along with some other works from the artist's beloved forays into the desert of the American Southwest.

Double back toward the stairwell and stop in Room 263, where Grant Wood's **American Gothic** resides – the Art Institute has been its home since it was painted in 1930 by the then-unknown Wood. The artist, a lifelong resident of Iowa, used his sister and his dentist as models for the two stern-faced farmers.

The final tour stop will be in Room 262, where your eyes instantly fall upon Peter Blume's stunning **The Rock**. The 1944–48 work by the Russian-born American artist depicts the building of the famous Frank Lloyd Wright house, Falling Water, but it is also widely viewed as a reflection of a shattered world attempting to rebuild itself after WWII. In the same room is Edward Hopper's **Nighthawks**. This poignant snapshot of four solitary souls at the center of a sleepless city was inspired by a restaurant on Greenwich Ave in Manhattan. The woman is Hopper's wife, Josephine, who sat in as a model for many of his paintings. The fluorescent lighting depicted was a brand-new invention at the time, and the painter took great pains to capture its particular cast and shadows.

To wrap up the tour (and ponder your own place in a sleepless city over a cup of coffee), ride the Rice Elevator down to level M, and follow the signs to the café.

Past the yacht club, the bike path splits; take the left fork slightly uphill. If you're thirsty, there's a drinking fountain at this juncture (mmm…lake water). Stay on the path as it crosses the Chicago River on the lower deck of Lake Shore Dr, and take a right on Illinois, following the signs for the Lakefront Path as it skirts the western edge of Navy Pier on N Streeter Dr.

At Grand Ave, cross into Jane Addams Memorial Park. The trail signage here briefly changes to 'Chicago Central Trail'; follow the signs for it north through the park and out past **Ohio Street Beach** 3 (p212). This small beach does have a lifeguard on duty if you feel like cooling off, but the Oak St Beach further along will be nicer for a dip.

As you continue north, the **John Hancock Center** 4 (p78) rises to your left, as well as Mies van der Rohe's groundbreaking **860–880 N Lake Shore Drive apartments** 5 (p78). When these were first completed in 1951, the world had never seen anything like them, and psychologists worried aloud about the ramifications of the tenants living in such transparent dwellings. (Apparently the psychological field at the time hadn't investigated those psyche-protecting devices known as 'curtains.')

In a couple minutes, you'll arrive at **Oak Street Beach** 6 (p212). The umbrella-shaded outdoor tables at the seasonal **Oak Street Beachstro** 7 (☎ 312-915-4100) make a great place for a snack or a drink. If you need a bathroom, there are men's and women's toilets in the Oak St pedestrian underpass beneath Lake Shore Dr.

Continue 0.75 miles north to the **Chess Pavilion** 8, built in 1957 for the city's chess fiends. Throw down your bike and get in a game, or turn left at the pavilion, and head west, through the North Ave underpass. You'll emerge on North Ave on the west side of Lake Shore Dr. The greenery to your right is the southern edge of Lincoln Park, another excellent place to explore by bike.

This is the halfway point for your journey; if you're just starting to hit your stride and would like to extend the ride, you can continue one mile north to the free **Lincoln Park Zoo** (p83), and catch up with the tour when you're done exploring.

Otherwise, go a half-block west to Astor St, where you'll make a left and begin the southward trek. This area was an undeveloped marsh when the brilliant real-estate baron Potter Palmer and his wife Bertha bought much of the surrounding land, then built a mansion in the area. Most of Chicago's elite followed their lead, snapping up the suddenly valuable plots from Potter (see what we mean about brilliant?), and leaving a legacy of beautiful, historic urban mansions that rival anything on Park Ave.

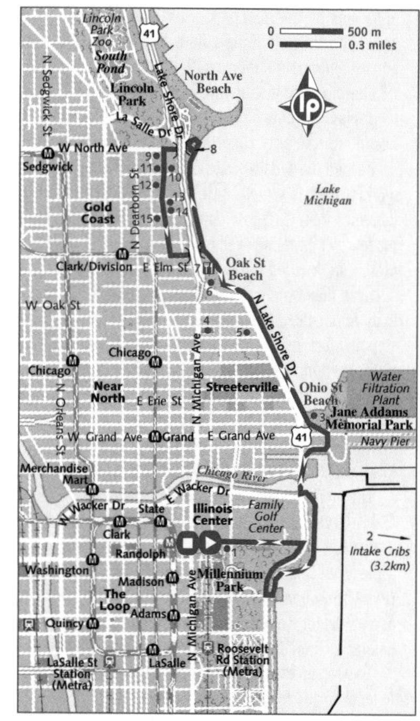

The huge house occupying the corner lot there to your right at Astor and North is just one of the many perks of becoming the Catholic Archbishop in Chicago. Seven of the leaders of the Chicago Archdiocese have lived at the 1885 home, whose block-spanning address is **1555 N State Street** 9 (p78). World leaders, from President Roosevelt to Pope John Paul II, have crashed at the residence while in town.

Further south, you pass **1525 N Astor Street** 10 (p78). Robert Todd Lincoln, son of Abraham and Mary Todd Lincoln, lived here. The Chicago lawyer was a local mover and shaker, eventually taking positions in two US presidents' administrations, and running the Pullman Palace Car Company when George Pullman died in 1897.

Keep pedaling down Astor until you get to E Burton Pl. Here at **1500 N Astor Street** 11 (p78) is one of the neighborhood's standouts, the neoclassical 1893 home designed by New York architect Stanford White. Known as the Cyrus McCormick Mansion for its famous owner, the house has since been divided up into condos.

Russell House 12 (p78) at 1444 N Astor is a 1929 art deco creation built by Holabird & Root. Keep rolling to Astor's intersection with W Shiller St. **Charnley-Persky House** 13 (p77), the rectangular house at 1365 N Astor, was declared by Frank Lloyd Wright as the 'first modern building' in the United States. However, he was in a somewhat less-than-objective position to comment on it – he designed it as a junior draftsman in the firm of Adler & Sullivan. It was completed in 1892 and now houses the Society of Architectural Historians.

Continue cruising southward, passing **1355 Astor Street** 14 (p77) slow enough to notice the alternating skulls and animal heads above the windows. The row of houses at Nos 1308–1312 were designed by storied Chicago architect John Wellborn Root, who enjoyed the results of his handiwork so much he moved into **1310 Astor Street** 15 (p77).

So, you wonder, how much would one of these places cost to buy? Recent sales on the street have ranged from $2 million to $21 million. Renting is a little cheaper, but only in the short run. The two-bedroom penthouse of that art deco stunner at 1444 Astor was available in 2005. The rent? A mere $8500 per month.

Dry your tears with the wind, my friend. Ride the three blocks down to Division, and make a left. At Division you'll find an underpass to the lake. Using it requires you to carry your bike down some stairs. If that's too awkward, follow N Lake Shore Dr (a slower-paced, confusingly named frontage road for the roaring N Lake Shore Dr one block over) south four blocks to Oak, and cross the street. A ramp from there leads under N Lake Shore Dr (the busy one) and back onto Oak St Beach. A leisurely 20-minute retracing of your original route from here will have you back at Millennium Park.

WEST LOOP GALLERY WALK

Tucked between meatpacking plants and warehouses, the galleries of the West Loop are the beachhead for contemporary art in Chicago. The scene in the neighborhood is like nowhere else in the city. Loop-bound bike messengers zip through the rutted streets, dodging chicken-laden semis and beef-toting forklifts, as art patrons carefully make their way over loading docks on their way from one gallery to the next.

Though the galleries here may be less established than their River North peers, the lower rents mean that young galleries can afford to have larger showrooms and take bigger chances on up-and-coming and controversial artists. And the 2005 defection of the heavy-hitting Douglas Dawson Gallery from River North to the West Loop signaled a growing prominence of the neighborhood in the art world. So lace up your walking shoes and set that black beret at a rakish tilt – it's time to explore art, Chicago-style.

The West Loop, located between the Clinton and Ashland stops on the Green line, is awkward to reach via public transportation.

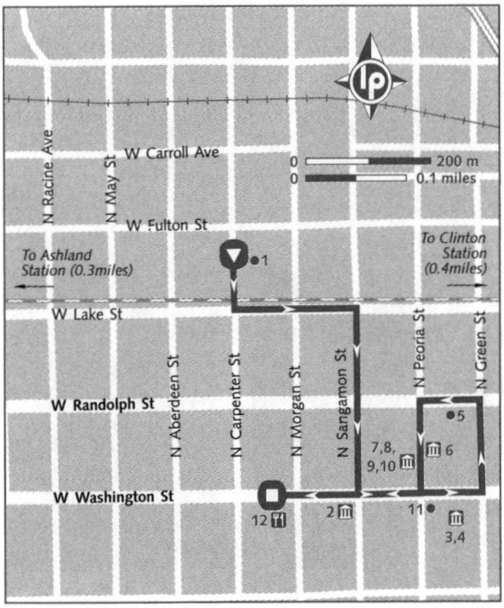

WALK FACTS

Start Taxi direct to FLATFILEgalleries; or Green Line to Clinton, walk west nine blocks on Lake St, making a left on Carpenter St
End Cab from Checker Taxi offices; or walk east up Washington St to S Clinton St, turn left on S Clinton, walk to Clinton stop on El
Distance 0.9 miles
Duration 2 hours
Fuel Stop Chicago Chocolate Company Café

If you don't mind the nine-block walk west along Lake St from the Clinton stop, go for it. If you'd rather save your energy for rigorous art contemplation (our recommendation), take a cab. Regardless, the tour starts on Carpenter St between Fulton Market and Lake, at **FLATFILEgalleries 1** (p95). FLATFILE is like visiting a couple of different art galleries under one roof, with larger-scale shows taking place in the cavernous room upstairs, and a range of photography from international and Chicago-based artists downstairs. Staff members here are young and friendly, and the mix of photographs and occasional contemporary art ranges from slickly futuristic fashion shoots to strange Central European nudes.

When you're done at FLATFILE, head south on Carpenter and make a left on Lake. Follow the El tracks eastward to Sangamon, where you make a right. You'll get a (pleasant) noseful of the light-industrial nature of the neighborhood when you pass the factory for Pastorelli Food Products (162 Sangamon), redolent with the oregano used in its pasta sauces. Be careful crossing the four lanes of traffic on Randolph, and head south to Washington, where **Donald Young Gallery 2** (p95) awaits. Donald Young handles some of the biggest names in contemporary art, including Bruce Nauman, Sol LeWitt and Richard Serra. Unless you look like a deep-pocketed art collector, you'll be amiably ignored by the staff here. The gallery itself is small, and can be explored easily in five minutes.

From Donald Young, make a right and walk east on Washington for two blocks. At 835 W Washington, you'll find one of the several West Loop buildings that contain a veritable warren of galleries. This one includes the **Carrie Secrist Gallery 3** (p95), which consistently shows the most interesting work in the building. With simultaneous minishows from a host of accomplished and thought-provoking artists, this is *the* gallery to hit in the building if you only have time for one. Also top-notch is the **Kavi Gupta Gallery 4** (p95), which represents a hot stable of 30-something contemporary artists, many of them from Chicago. Look for work from conceptual sculptor Danielle Gustafson-Sundell, German nature photographer Yannick Demmerle, and sci-fi painter Scott Anderson.

OK, lest you have an art attack, it's time for a break. Go east a half-block to Green, and walk north for a block, making a left at Randolph and ducking into the **Chicago Chocolate Company Café 5** (☎ 312-243-2888; 847 W Randolph). You could get a tiny snack or something equally bourgeois. Or you could employ some of the radical, outside-the-box thinking we've witnessed at the galleries on the tour and make a meal of a 3lb bag of white-chocolate Turtles, with a side order of Lincoln Park mints. Ask yourself: what would Warhol do?

From the café, waddle west on Randolph, and make a left onto Peoria. Peoria is the West Loop's art hive – the phrase 'Peoria Street galleries' has become almost synonymous with West

Exterior art

Loop art. Start on the east side of the street at 119 Peoria, the home of **Bodybuilder & Sportsman** 6 (p95). You'll have to ring the doorbell for admittance. Hike up one floor, and follow the signs to the gallery. Run by School of the Art Institute of Chicago grad Tony Wight, the space stole the name from the onetime sporting goods shop it used to occupy. Wight, though dead serious about art, uses his small gallery with scuffed floors to show paintings, drawings and video works that tend to poke holes in the overinflated art world.

Walk back downstairs and across the street to the 118 N Peoria St complex. On the ground floor, you'll find **moniquemeloche** 7 (p95). Monique's multilevel gallery has been here since 2001, showcasing Chicago and international artists in a variety of media. Meloche, who also curates traveling shows, is a great resource for local art and artists – ask her about any special one-offs that might be going down while you're in town.

From moniquemeloche, take the elevator up to the top floor to **Gescheidle** 8 (p95), a warm gallery with a sense of humor that draws many of its artists from the Chicago area. On your way back down, visit the worthwhile **Aron Packer Gallery** 9 (☎ 312-226-8984), whose multimedia group shows are always a treat, and the expansive, concrete-floored **Rhona Hoffman gallery** 10 (☎ 312-455-1990), which has been showing art in Chicago since 1983.

At this point, your head is likely an artistic blur. Which is good, as you're almost done. Walk south down Peoria to Washington St. The **Checker Taxi** 11 (☎ 312-243-2537) dispatching office is immediately to your left at 845 Washington. You can hop into one of the cabs waiting out front and head off to your next adventure. Or, if you managed to walk away from the Chicago Chocolate Company with your appetite still intact, you can settle into a delicious Southern meal at **Wishbone** 12 (p164), an Oprah-approved hot spot two blocks west. The choice is yours. (Hint: Wishbone has seats just as comfortable as the taxis, and its biscuits are far more filling than any food for thought your cabdriver might offer.)

WRIGLEYVILLE BAR HOP

On this tour, we'll help you find a watering hole that fits your temperament in the bar-rich Wrigleyville neighborhood of Lake View.

Start at Wrigley Field, a backdrop befitting our first stop. The **Cubby Bear** 1 (☎ 773-327-1622; 1059 Addison St) is one of the two places where 20-something Cubs fans flock after each game to get riotously drunk and console themselves about having wasted so much of their lives rooting for a team that will never win. *Maxim* called the place the best neighborhood bar in Chicago, which it isn't. It is, however, a great place to get a taste of Cubs mania on game day (along with a taste of cheap beer). On away days and during off-season, it is also a surprisingly good place to see rock shows.

WALK FACTS

Start Red Line to Addison
End Wellington stop on the Brown or Red Line, or Southport stop on the Brown Line, depending on bar
Distance 1.8 miles
Duration 3 hours (at least…)
Fuel Stop Pick Me Up Café

If you liked the general atmosphere of the Cubby Bear, but wanted something a little more intimate with outdoor seating, finish off that Pabst and walk east on Addison, making a left onto Sheffield Ave, where you'll duck into **Murphy's Bleachers** 2 (☎ 773-281-5356, 3655 N Sheffield Ave). This is the other beloved Wrigleyville hangout for Cubs fans and their long-suffering significant others. The beers are more expensive here than the Cubby Bear, but the outdoor patio is just as packed and you'll see the same array of young, drunk, excited patrons drinking beer from cans, checking each other out, and discussing why it was a good idea for Dusty Baker to trade Sammy Sosa.

If you don't know who Sammy Sosa is, you probably thought the Cubby Bear was a little obnoxious, and the last thing you'll want to do is go through it all again at Murphy's Bleachers. Instead, head up Clark St one long block to **Ginger Man** 3 (p174). If librarians hung out at dive bars, the scene would resemble Ginger Man. Named for Irish author JP Donleavy's novel about a bohemian hitchhiker in Europe, the bar plays classical music before and

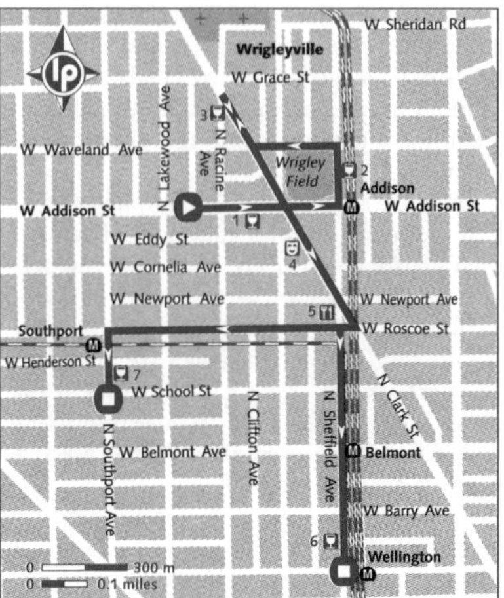

after Cubs games to ward off sporty types. Inside, you'll find over 100 kinds of beers, several pool tables and a mix of interesting neighborhood characters.

You're now either two or three drinks into the tour, depending on your taste for sports bars. And you know what time it is? It's reggae time! Don't tell me you don't like reggae. After a few beers, *everybody* likes reggae. Head out of Ginger Man, and walk three blocks south down Clark to our next stop, the **Wild Hare** 4 (p184). There's no cover here on Tuesday nights or after Cubs games. Otherwise you pay anywhere from $5 to $12 to see local and touring reggae and dancehall bands, and soak in the multicultural vibe of Chicago's diverse world music scene. Also, nightly drink specials mean that you won't be too grumbly about having paid a cover.

You'll likely work up an appetite dancing at the Wild Hare, so you and whatever new friends you made there should walk down the street to the comfy, open-way-late **Pick Me Up** 5 (p155), where you can get an espresso milkshake to help ward off the drowsies.

After eating, the night can end one of two ways: champagne and jazz, or beer and bowling balls. And unless it is a summer night and you have your walking shoes on, you'll need some mechanical assistance. If you choose the classy jazz route, flag a cab and tell your driver you want to go to **Pops for Champagne** 6 (p174), which is eight blocks away. You can also easily get there on the El, by hopping on the Red Line at Addison and getting off at Wellington. At the romantic, dimly lit Pops you'll sip bubbly and be serenaded by a jazz combo for the rest of the evening.

If you want to skip the cover charge (which can be as much as $15) and fancified atmosphere of Pops, tell your cab driver that you want to go to **Southport Lanes** 7 (p211). There, you can take part in an equally refined pleasure: boutique bowling, with human pin-setters. Yep. This convivial, dark-wood bar has a separate room with two bowling lanes where nothing is automatic, and a staff member lurks back behind the pins to retrieve your ball and clear the pins. Tipping – done by stuffing a dollar bill into one of the ball's finger holes and rolling it down the gutter – warms the hearts of the pin-setters and results in friendly 'assistance' when your pins aren't falling on their own.

LOOP SCULPTURE WALK

You'd think the horrible Chicago weather would discourage anyone from leaving *anything* outside all winter. But no – in true can-do, world-be-damned spirit, Chicago has dozens of top-notch sculptures decorating the plazas, courtyards and entryways of the Loop year-round. Where does all the money come from to buy and maintain the art? Good question. In 1967 the arrival of the Picasso sculpture at what's now the Richard J Daley Civic Center began a veritable sculpture frenzy that culminated in the city council 'Percent for Art' decree in 1978, when the powers that be decided new or renovated public buildings had to set aside a certain percentage of building funds to acquire and display art for the public.

It was a rare case of bureaucratic genius, and this walking tour will take you by some of the fruits of that decree, including world-class works by Alexander Calder, Pablo Picasso and Joan Miró.

WALK FACTS

Start Blue Line to Jackson
End Blue, Brown, Green or Orange Line to Clark
Distance 2.1 miles
Duration 1½ hours
Fuel Stop James R Thompson Center

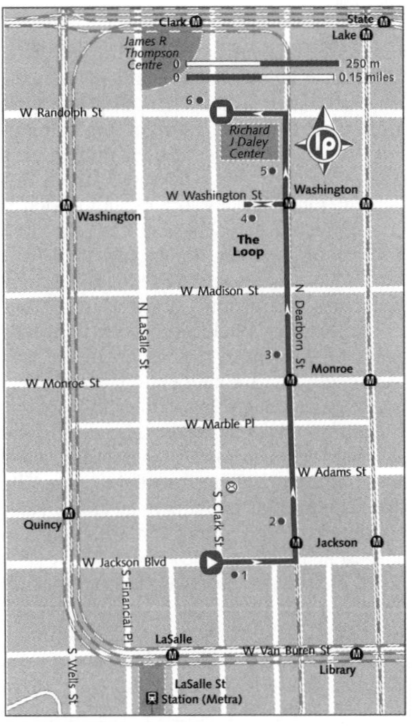

The tour starts down in the southern reaches of the Loop. Exit the Jackson Blue Line station and walk west to 77 W Jackson. The sculpture in the lobby, **The Town-Ho's Story** 1, is by artist Frank Stella and is named for a chapter in *Moby Dick*. The 20ft-tall artwork looks like it was wrenched from the bottom of the Cook County landfill, and it attracted, ahem, *attention* as soon as it was unveiled. One employee in the building – which houses the Environmental Protection Agency (EPA) among other federal bodies – waited all of six days after the sculpture was dedicated before circulating a petition asking for the work to be removed, claiming that 80% of EPA employees objected to the work, and that the 'pile of junk' made the government look bad. The petition garnered over 600 signatures in a matter of days, but the *Story* remains the same.

Double back east on Jackson, turning left onto Dearborn. Alexander Calder's soaring steel sculpture **Flamingo** 2, on S Dearborn St between Adams St and Jackson Blvd, provides some much-needed relief from the stark facades of the federal buildings around it. Calder dedicated the sculpture in October 1974 by riding into the Loop on a bandwagon pulled by 40 horses, accompanied by a circus parade. Note the cement blocks placed on the outskirts of the plaza. These are to prevent car-bombers from driving vehicles into the busy square – utilitarian sculptures of a far more recent vintage than Calder's work.

From here, walk three blocks up Dearborn. Russian-born artist Marc Chagall loved Chicago and in 1974 donated this grand mosaic, called **The Four Seasons** 3, that sits on the Dearborn St side of Bank One Plaza. Using thousands of bits of glass and stone, the artist portrayed six scenes of the city in hues reminiscent of the Mediterranean coast of France, where he kept his studio. Chagall continued to make adjustments, such as updating the skyline, after the work arrived in Chicago.

Keep moving northward on Dearborn and left into Washington St, where you can check out Joan Miró's **Chicago** 4. Miró hoped to evoke the 'mystical force of a great earth mother' with this 40ft sculpture, made with various metals, cement and tile in 1981.

Across Washington St near Daley Plaza, you will find another of Chicago's classic sculptures, **'the Picasso'** 5. Officially the sculpture is untitled, but Chicagoans soon adopted their own no-nonsense name for the huge work in front of the Daley Center. Picasso was 82 when the work was commissioned. It was made to the artist's design specifications at the US Steel Works in Gary, Indiana, and erected in 1967. When Chicago tried to pay Picasso for the work, he refused the money, saying the sculpture was meant as a gift to the city. Bird, ape, dog, woman – you decide. The base of 'the Picasso' makes a great slide for kids.

Continue north along Dearborn St to the end of the block, turning left into Randolph St. Your final stop is at **Monument with Standing Beast** 6, created in 1984 by French sculptor Jean Dubuffet. The fun white fiberglass work looks a little like inflated puzzle pieces and has a definite Keith Haring–esque feel to it. As you can see by the large number of kids crawling around inside the sculpture, this is definitely a hands-on piece of art. Explore to your heart's content, and afterwards, you can get a snack inside the James R Thompson Center right in front of you.

DAMEN AVE SHOPPING SPREE

Chicago's neighborhoods seem to be in a perpetual state of upward mobility. In 2000 MTV tried to film *The Real World* in Wicker Park, and the ensuing protests by residents over the media corporation's presence led to a number of arrests. Gentrification has taken its course in Wicker Park and the adjoining community of Bucktown since then though, and the protests of those days feel like a distant memory. Today, the neighborhood is a commercial zone where some of the city's hottest fashion boutiques and cool little stores have set up shop. The following walk will take you up and down Damen Ave, in the heart of Bucktown. Note: men may want to skip ahead to the part of the tour that begins 'If you happen to have a suffering spouse or significant other in tow…'

WALK FACTS

Start Blue Line to Damen
End Blue Line to Damen
Distance 1.3 miles
Duration 1 hour (at least…)
Fuel Stop The Charleston

The start of the tour is the Damen Ave El stop, where you'll disembark and hit the ground running. Speaking of… If you've been feeling like your feet need some new fashions, make your first stop **City Sole/Niche** 1 (p229). If your budget is under $100, head straight to the City Sole section of the store, where the more affordable fashions live. Looking to go crazy? Have a go at Niche's selection of shoes by European designers. Staff members in both wings of the sizable store pout like fashion models, but they're helpful.

With your shoebox(es) bagged and ready to go, it's time to cross the street. In other parts of town, this is a relatively simple operation, but this intersection is legendary for getting tourists turned around. To make it to the east-side sidewalk on Damen is simple enough, but that's where the fun begins. You'll now have to cross over Milwaukee Ave, then cross North Ave, just to make it back to Damen. Made it? Good.

Heading up Damen on the east side of the street, the first stop is **Clothes Minded** 2 (p230), which offers less over-the-top women's fashions than some of the more avant-garde boutiques on Damen, and the prices are much more down to earth as well. This is the perfect shop for basic cute tops and casual wear.

Keep going on Damen across Wabansia Ave, and you'll hit the **T-Shirt Deli** 3 (p231), a former deli that is now a funky maker of custom T-shirts. Unlike the versions of these stores you used to see in the mall, the T-Shirt Deli sells figure-hugging T-shirts in an array of hipster-approved styles. Pick your shirt, pick your lettering, and, a few minutes later, you walk away with your very own 'Damen is for lovers' baby T.

That's three stores down, and five more to go. Head north for four blocks. Women who wear sizes 12 to 28, looking for hip, stylish clothes beyond the dreadful collections of the corporate 'plus-size' retail chains, should head up Damen to **Vive La Femme** 4 (p231), a one-of-a-kind boutique that also sells bags and accessories. Otherwise, cross Damen a little south of Vive La Femme, and begin the walk southward, down the west side of the street.

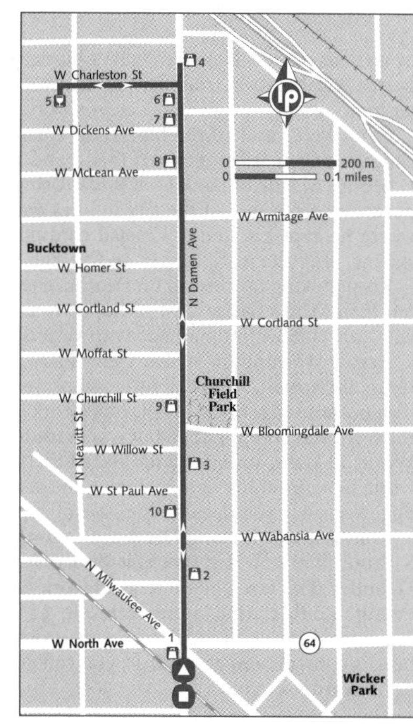

If you happen to have a suffering spouse or significant other in tow, this is the point to set them free. A block west of Damen on Charleston Ave is one of the city's best neighborhood bars, the **Charleston 5** (p176). The beers are excellent and the fashion talk is kept to an absolute minimum, making it a great place to jettison whiny tag-alongs who don't share your love of shopping. You can plan a rendezvous at the Damen El Stop in an hour or so, and continue on your way.

The first store on our southerly route is the wee **Saffron 6** (p231). See it there on the right? Duck in for classic-cut evening wear and accessories, along with jewelry, shawls, and bath and beauty products. Owner Padmaja designs the clothes herself, and she's happy to talk about them.

Further south, you'll find the answer to the eternal question 'What the hell am I supposed to bring to a baby shower?' The coolest kids' store in Chicago, **Red Balloon Co 7** (p231) offers classic children's toys and clothes. And if you're anything like us, you'll end up walking out with some cool goodies for yourself as well. At this point your shopping load is likely becoming burdensome. Take a right on Dickens and run your bags over to the Charleston, dropping the packages off with your SO. Retrace your steps to Damen and continue south along the avenue.

The first of our three remaining stops is **Ms Catwalk 8** (p230), a new boutique that carries lines such as Hazel, Robin Jordan Dresses and Troo, as well as a good selection of jewelry. Next up is **Apartment No 9 9** (☎ 773-395-2999;1804 N Damen), a chic men's store that caters to sophisticated 20- and 30-something Chicago metrosexuals. The pants and shirts are the last word in men's designers, and the shaving kits, complete with brush and lather mug, make good gifts.

And just when you thought your credit card couldn't take anymore, you hit **Climate 10** (p229): a store with absurdly cute cards, stationery, funny books and other essentials. Browse to your heart's content, and don't forget to pick up a 'wish you were here' postcard for all the poor suckers back at home.

HISTORIC LOOP ARCHITECTURE WALK

The Loop abounds with important, beautiful and interesting architecture. Just by walking its streets for about half a day, you can trace the development of modern architecture in Chicago, the US and worldwide. This tour will focus on the landmark buildings in the Loop from 1885 to 1914. For more information on the architects and buildings, check out the Architecture chapter (p40).

Start at the **Reliance Building 1** (p41). This building, a Burnham & Root creation, was finished in 1895. Home of the Burnham Hotel since 1999, the building's owners have gone to considerable lengths to reproduce parts of the interior as they were at the turn of the 20th century, including the decorative metal elevator grills, marble-clad ceiling and walls, and mosaic floor. Head on in for a look.

WALK FACTS

Start Red Line to Washington
End Brown or Orange Line to LaSalle
Distance 1.6 miles
Duration 1¾ hours
Fuel Stop The Chicago Cultural Center Café

Kitty-corner from the Reliance Building is **Marshall Field & Co 2** (p41), at the intersection of State and Washington. Marshall Field's mercantile strategy was to 'dazzle the customer with opulence.' And one kind of customer appealed to him above all: women. In the late 1800s, unescorted women shoppers were frowned upon, but Field welcomed them warmly, and Field was actually the first Chicago retailer to add women's bathrooms to his store. This building was built in stages, starting in 1892 and ending in 1914.

Continuing on, walk east on Washington St to the **Chicago Cultural Center 3** (p43). Built in 1897, the building started its life as the Chicago Library. The impressive hodgepodge of Greek, Roman and European architectural details became all the rage in the city after 1893, when Daniel Burnham designed scores of similar structures for the Chicago-hosted World's

Expo. Duck inside and check out the famous stained-glass domes, and rooms modeled on the Doge's Palace in Venice and Athens' Acropolis. You can also get a quick bite to eat at the café in the lobby.

Turn right (south) and walk along Michigan Ave to the intersection of Madison and then west on Madison two blocks, stopping to admire the Louis Sullivan–designed metalwork facade on **Carson Pirie Scott & Co** 4 (p42). In many ways, this building, completed in 1906, is the finest example of the Chicago School of architecture in the city. Across State St, at 7 W Madison, is another Chicago School masterpiece, the **Chicago Building** 5 (p42). Constructed in 1905 as the Chicago Savings & Trust, the building now houses young artists in its role as School of the Art Institute of Chicago dorms.

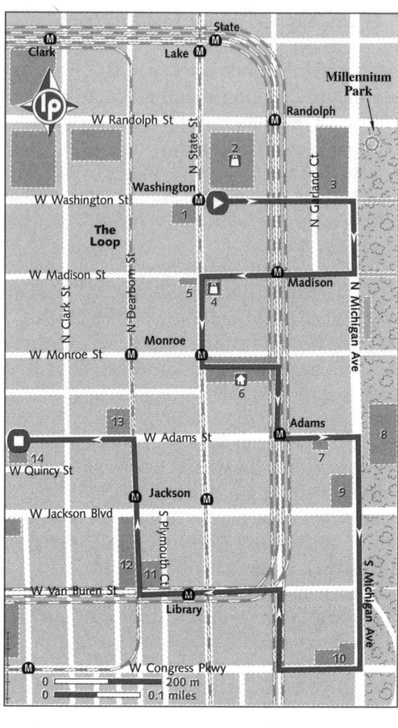

Continue south down State St to Monroe, where you cut through the **Palmer House Hilton** 6. Head up the escalator into the lobby and prepare to begin drooling immediately. This sumptuous space was created by Holabird & Roche, the same folks behind our previous stop. When it was built in 1905, the hotel was the largest in the world. Find the Wabash Ave exit, and walk south one block to Adams. Make a left here, and walk toward the Art Institute. Along the way, you'll pass the remodeled liquor warehouse, which comprises the Adams-facing portion of the **Symphony Center** 7, home of the Chicago Symphony Orchestra.

When you hit the **Art Institute** 8 (p67), stop for a second and take in the classical design details from 1893. This portion of the building was very much of the time, built the same year that the World's Expo was bringing a mania for reinterpreted antiquity to the city's architectural scene. Continue down Michigan to the **Santa Fe Center** 9 (p41). This Daniel Burnham–designed building is the home of the Chicago Architecture Foundation. Head into the lobby to check out the vast well of light Burnham built into the structure – you'll see it repeated in the Rookery, later in the tour.

Taking time out from a stroll in the Loop

Stroll two blocks further on S Michigan Ave, to the **Auditorium Building** 10 (p41). Louis Sullivan and Dankmar Adler collaborated on this fantastic 1889 building, which included the acoustically perfect theater and 400 futuristic hotel rooms. The building's completion was celebrated around the country as a testimony to the can-do spirit of American architects, and President Harrison showed up for its inauguration. Sullivan and Adler proudly moved their offices into the auditorium's tower when it was completed. Roosevelt University has taken over what was originally a hotel portion of the building.

Turn right onto Congress Pkwy, walking the length of the Auditorium Building, before turning right up Wabash Ave and making your first left onto W Van Buren St. Two blocks on, you'll find the **Fisher Building** 11 (p41). This timeless Chicago classic was born in 1896 and absolutely glows in the afternoon sun. Look for all the aquatic details added to the facade, a play on the name of the building's owner, Lucius Fisher.

Make a right-hand turn onto Dearborn St and walk north. That thick-based building you see beside you is the **Monadnock Building** 12 (p41). You'll know if there are any architects nearby, as they'll be staring at the structure in a near-religious reverie. This important building was groundbreakingly tall when it was built in 1891. Ah, how times have changed.

Continue up to Dearborn and Adams Sts, stopping at 140 S Dearborn, home to the 1893 **Marquette Building** 13 (p41). There are more of the beautiful stained-glass panels you see above the entrance located inside the lobby. The final stop on this tour is also one of the most gorgeous. Two blocks east of the Marquette building off of Adams is the **Rookery** 14 (p40). The original design by Burnham & Root, with its load-bearing walls of granite and brick, surrounds a spectacular atrium space that was remodeled in 1907 by Frank Lloyd Wright. The light in here is heavenly, and when you bask in the architectural details inside, try to imagine the building without the pools of light. That's the way it was from the 1940s onward, when the building managers covered over the skylights with tar paper and paint. It wasn't until the building's new owner took over in 1988 that the sun was allowed to shine through again.

MILLENNIUM PARK STROLL

A grand addition to the Loop, Millennium Park is the latest triumph in Chicago's ongoing revitalization of its public spaces. On this tour, you'll walk through the whimsical sculptures, galleries and gardens of the park.

WALK FACTS

Start Red Line to Monroe, walk east two blocks
End Monroe stop on the Red Line
Distance 0.5 miles
Duration 1 hour
Fuel Stop Park Grill

Start at the **Crown Fountain** 1. Built as a place of quiet reflection by Spanish sculptor Jaume Plensa, the two 50ft towers feature the faces of 1000 Chicagoans projected onto light-emitting diode (LED) screens. Water cascades down from the top of the towers onto the black granite floor below. In a whimsical detail, every five minutes the lips on the faces part, and a stream of water shoots from their mouths. The sculptures remained quiet and reflective for all of two minutes after their unveiling before becoming, in the words of the *Tribune*, 'Chicago's Best Water Park' for children. Now the place is mobbed with young art-lovers in swimsuits in the warmer months. In winter, the water is turned off, and the blinking faces are interspersed with nature scenes.

Continue north to the **McCormick Tribune Plaza Ice Rink** 2, which in the winter months features free ice-skating (skate rentals available), accompanied by light shows. Park planners hid the unattractive cooling station needed to maintain the rink across the street in the basement of the Blue Cross, Blue Shield building. In spring and summer, the rink transforms into the outdoor patio of the **Park Grill** 3 (☎ 312-521-7275). Stop here if you need a pick-me-up.

Walk north to the plant-covered stairwell. Straight ahead is the Greek colonnade of **Wrigley Square** 4, a dull nod to a Burnham-inspired peristyle that stood here in 1917. If you get close enough, you'll likely end up in a wedding photo shoot or two. Turn right and walk up the stairs to the park's second level, making a right into the **Chase Promenade** 5, which features public art shows. To your right is the gleaming, iconic **Cloud Gate** 6. Called the 'bean' by locals, the 110-ton sculpture by Brit Anish Kapoor draws its title from the reflections of the sky (and skyline) it provides.

As one of the most photographed pieces of the new park, the 'bean' was the center of a storm of controversy in January, 2005, when security guards told a photographer that he wasn't allowed to take pictures of the sculpture without a city permit. An uproar about copyrighted work in publicly financed spaces followed, and the city fumbled to define its policy. Amateur shutterbugs can snap for free, it turns out, but professional photographers

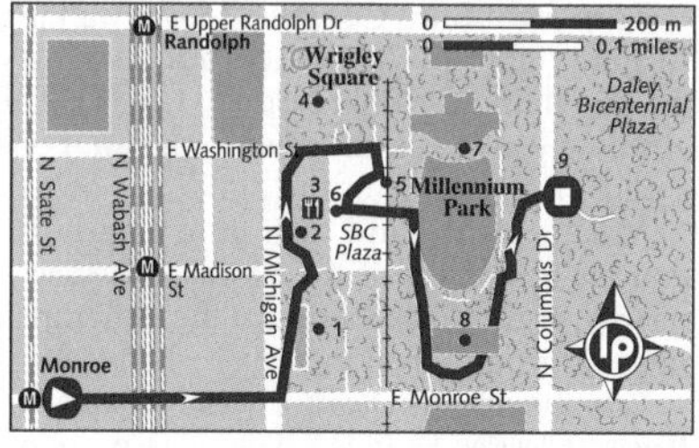

need to get a $325 permit (though even that hasn't been enforced since the flap).

From Cloud Gate, cut due north, through the gap in the hedges, to the **Pritzker Pavilion 7**. Designed by Frank Gehry, the 11,000-capacity performance venue is technically a sculpture rather than a building in order to get around a 1909 law restricting new buildings in Grant Park. A model of the bandshell was tested in a wind tunnel to ensure it could stand up to Chicago's famously blustery winds, and large glass doors keep the stage warm and dry in winter. The original design for the bandshell was modest (and Gehry-free) until local philanthropist Cindy Pritzker got involved, roping Gehry into the project and contributing $15 million of her family's money to make sure it got built. Note the overhead trellises with speakers dangling from them – an innovative way to avoid blocking concertgoers' views with the traditional pole-mounted speakers.

Walk south along the edge of the pavilion to the **Lurie Garden 8**. Divided into two sections, the darker portions of the garden are meant to evoke the prairie that once rolled through Illinois. The brighter, flowering portion of the garden is a botanical nod to Chicago's phoenixlike rebirth after the fire of 1871. Running water separates the two, lined by a boardwalk. Cross the boardwalk now, heading northeast to your final stop, the **BP Pedestrian Bridge 9**. This silver, serpentine structure is the only Gehry-designed bridge in the world. It connects Millennium Park to Grant Park, but was also helps reduce traffic noise from Columbus Dr. As you cross it, you'll get a great view back over the park.

Eating

Eating

Ask any Chicagoan about their favorite local TV shows, and you're going to hear about *Check Please!* A food show totally lacking the usual array of temperamental chefs, professional reviewers, and fussy palates, *Check Please!* sends groups of everyday Windy City natives out to restaurants ranging from haute cuisine to haute dog stands, and then gets them to talk about what they liked and didn't.

The premise could have flopped elsewhere, but not in Chicago. By 2005 the show had received nearly 20,000 applications from would-be food critics eager to come give their two cents on the show. The exuberant reaction to *Check Please!* will come as no surprise to those who have spent any time in Chicago – this is a city where one of the highest civic responsibilities is setting out-of-town visitors straight on exactly which pizzerias they should frequent (and which they should avoid).

The residents of Chicago love to eat well and eat broadly; your average Chicagoan would have no problem explaining the difference between sashimi and Szechwan, tandoori and Thai. But there's also an inherent reluctance to embrace the next big dish or food style out of New York simply because it's new. Or from New York.

This is why Chicago restaurants are some of the best in the world. Because whether they're a hole-in-the-wall or a penthouse bistro, new restaurants here have to prove themselves both capable *and* neighborly. It's a tough balancing act, and, as you might suspect, turnover rates in the Chicago restaurant world are high.

The veterans that do stick around are guaranteed to be worth your time, and fledgling places striving to be the next Blackbird, Charlie Trotter's or Alinea make Chicago a reliably hopping restaurant town. So get out there and enjoy. And if, in your explorations, you're ever looking to strike up a conversation with an attractive local, one three-word phrase will arouse their emotions and unlock their hearts more than any other: 'Thoughts on pizza?'

Opening Hours

Despite the late hours some restaurants keep, Chicagoans tend to have dinner between 6:30pm and 8:30pm. Lunch falls from 11:30am to 2pm, and breakfast tends to be served from 8am to 10am. That beloved creature, brunch, is an amorphous meal that essentially lasts from whenever you wake up on Saturday and Sunday until about 3pm.

Like tipping for counter-service, there are no hard and fast rules for opening hours. The midlevel and budget places usually open around 10am and stay open until around 11pm. Chains, fast-food restaurants and coffee shops get an even earlier start, opening their doors to the harried public around 7am or 8am. Quite a few of the high-end restaurants in Chicago don't serve lunch, and close on Sunday or Monday. In the listings we've noted where venues' hours stray from the standard, as well as any closed days, but if you're going out of your way, it's best to call ahead. Good news for night owls is that Chicago is a late-night diners' paradise. Along with family-style diners like the Golden Apple, an impressive number of smaller restaurants will keep the kitchen open past midnight, especially on weekends.

TOP FIVE EAT STREETS

Good restaurants in Chicago have a magnetic ability to attract other quality eateries. Here are five streets with an embarrassment of dining riches.

- **Clark Street, Lake View** (p151) Between the buffalo-sized burgers, top-notch Thai and supreme sashimi, if you can't find it here, you're not looking hard enough.
- **Damen Avenue, Bucktown** (p157) The boutique street does dining right.
- **Devon Avenue, Far North** (p155) It's a trip, but the Indian and Pakistani food is worth it.
- **Division Street, Ukrainian Village** (p157) This hipster's dining paradise features copious sidewalk seating.
- **Randolph Street, West Loop** (p136) Chicago's best new restaurants are popping up here.

How Much?

In the following restaurant write-ups, we've indicated the range in prices on single mains rather than entire meals. The phrase 'mains $8-23' means that, between the lunch and the dinner menu, the cheapest main course you'll find costs $8, and the most expensive $23. Lunch mains in Chicago restaurants are usually 40% cheaper than the same main course served after the sun goes down.

For an average sit-down lunch in Chicago, including a tip and a drink, expect to pay about $15 per person. Dinner, including drink and tip, will likely be about $25 per person. Eating ethnic foods like Indian, Thai, Chinese or Ethiopian will save you money, as will checking out our 'cheap eats' category. At these good-food-on-a-budget restaurants, you can have lunch for under $8 and dinner for under $15.

Booking Tables

If you would feel uncomfortable wearing a T-shirt to the restaurant in question, that's a good sign that you should probably call ahead and ask about reservations. This is much more true on weekends than midweek. Some places won't take a reservation for parties of less than four or five. But it will save you much aggravation and time spent nursing appetizers at the restaurant's bar if you call ahead to check.

Tipping

If, at the end of your meal, you thought the service was fine, tip a minimum of 15% of the pretax bill. If the service was great, take that number up to 20%. Indifferent or hostile waitstaff deserve whatever pittance you feel like leaving. (If the service was truly abysmal, discuss it with the manager – not only will the waiter get a stern dressing-down later, but you might get your bill reduced for your pain and suffering.) Many restaurants add the tip into the bill for parties of six or more.

At cafés or *taquerías* (places that specialize in selling tacos) where you order food and drinks at the counter, the tipping etiquette is a little less clear (though a tip jar will always be prominently displayed). If you order food that someone has to bring to your table, it's common practice to drop about 10% of your total in the tip jar. If you're getting food or drinks to go, no tip is expected.

Valet parkers should get anywhere from $2 to $5 when they return your car to you (assuming the car is in the same shape as when you surrendered it to them).

Takeout & To Go

With so many parks in Chicago, picnics are going to be a high priority during your visit (if you're here in winter, you can picnic in the car with the heater on). You can pick up groceries and drinks at the ubiquitous **Jewel** (☎ 800-539-3561) stores. **Whole Foods** (Map pp306-7; ☎ 312-932-9600; 30 W Huron St) has top-notch produce and a health-conscious selection of organic foods and baked goods. If you want to do less assembly work, try the deli counter at the incomparable Bari Foods (p162) or pick from the high-class, precooked delicacies at **Charlie Trotter's To Go** (Map pp308-9; 1337 W Fullerton Ave).

If you're looking for snacks fresh off the vine, the city sponsors farmers markets all

City restaurant worker

over Chicago from May to October. Loop locations include Federal Plaza on Tuesday and Daley Plaza on Thursday. Up in Lincoln Park, the **Green City Market** (1750 N Clark) is a favorite for organic and sustainably farmed fruits and veggies, and also includes baked goods and soaps. The markets attract growers from around the region and offer opportunities to try everything from asparagus in May to rhubarb in October. Visit the Chicago farmers markets website (www.cityofchicago.org/specialevents) for a complete schedule.

TOP FIVE THE LOOP

- Savoring the symphony of flavors at **Rhapsody** (p138).
- Passing up the diamonds at the Jewelers Mall to get to the real gem: **Oasis Cafe** (p138).
- Celebrating the end of a busy day with creamed spinach and beer at the **Berghoff** (below).
- Checking out the B&W photos at **Miller's Pub** (opposite) while tucking into a midnight ribs.
- Saving dollars at **Jacobs Brothers Bagels** (p138), set in a priceless Chicago landmark.

THE LOOP & GRANT PARK

The Loop restaurant scene changes with the hour. In the morning, office workers sprint through the Dunkin' Donuts or Starbucks to grab something to scarf at their desks. At noon, the speedy tableau unfurls again, with paper-pushers mobbing sandwich chains like Potbelly or hopping on the escalator down to the food court of the **James R Thompson Center** (Map pp304-5; 100 W Randolph St), where 15 quickie joints serve a range of speed-through vittles (often accompanied by free lunchtime concerts). The Loop's power dining begins at night, as the executive bigwigs who spent the day negotiating mergers and takeovers slide into steak-house booths to seal the deal. Pretheater dining has also become a force in the Loop; if you're planning on getting a bite to eat before a downtown musical or play, be sure to call ahead to make sure a table's available.

Bright lights of the Berghoff (right)

BERGHOFF
Map pp304-5 — German & American

☎ **312-427-3170; 17 W Adams St; mains $8-20; 🕒 closed Sun; Blue, Red Line to Jackson**

The building and this historic restaurant both date from 1898. The first place in Chicago to serve a legal drink at the end of Prohibition, the Berghoff is the only restaurant in town with its own carpentry shop where workers maintain the antique woodwork and furniture. The menu carries old-world classics such as sauerbraten and schnitzel, but the draw here isn't so much the food (which tends to be only so-so), as it is the experience of losing yourself in the bustling atmosphere of a bygone era. The quick and efficient waiters serve a huge crowd of regulars, plus day-trippers from the 'burbs. The adjoining Stand Up Bar has changed little in a century, although women have been admitted for the past 40 years. Sandwiches ($7) are served from a buffet line at lunch, and frosty mugs of Berghoff beer, direct from the Wisconsin brewery, still line the bar.

EVEREST
Map pp304-5 — French

☎ **312-663-8920; 40th fl, One Financial Plaza, 440 S LaSalle St; mains from $30; 🕒 dinner, closed Sun & Mon; Blue Line to LaSalle**

If you're celebrating an anniversary or other romantic milestone while you're in

Chicago, this is your chance to score some *major* points. The 40th-floor views and unfailingly attentive, tuxedo-clad waiters set the scene for a meal your significant other will be talking about for years. The food is French, with a slant toward the Alsace region (the French region near Germany), home of Everest chef Jean Joho, who also runs **Brasserie Jo** (p139). The sommelier here, Alpana Singh, is legendary throughout Chicago's oenophilic circles. The three-course pretheater prix-fixe menu is just $54 per person (seatings at 5:30pm only). Reservations essential.

ITALIAN VILLAGE

Map pp304-5 Italian

☎ 312-332-7005; 71 W Monroe St; mains $12-24; La Cantina Enoteca & Vivere closed Sun; Blue Line to Monroe

There are three restaurants under one roof here, two of which are worth your while. The namesake Village, a good pick for pretheater dining, looks a bit like a Disney set, with twinkling lights and storefronts that evoke the feeling of a southern Italian hill town. The very traditional red-sauce menu includes old-style cuisine such as *mostaccioli* (short, tubular pasta) with sausage. If you're part of a couple you can cozy up in the private booths (but you can't reserve these in advance so you'll have to hope your timing is right). Vivere, a step up from Village in both price and cuisine, boasts more than 1500 bottles in its wine cellar. The menu features high-minded interpretations of standards such as veal scallopini, joined by unusual numbers such as bass-filled squid-ink pasta.

MILLER'S PUB

Map pp304-5 American

☎ 312-645-5377; 134 S Wabash Ave; mains $8-24; to 4am; Brown, Green, Orange, Purple Line to Adams

A photo of your favorite dead celebrity can probably be found somewhere on the walls at this Loop institution, next to Palmer House. Miller's has been serving remarkably tender and candy-sweet ribs for decades. The rest of the menu includes the usual upscale bar staples – salads, burgers and the like. The exceptionally late closing time makes this a popular choice with the post-theater crowd and with office workers burning the midnight oil.

YOUR OWN LOCAL EXPERTS

Want to hear what locals *really* think of the restaurants you're planning on hitting while in town? Check out these food discussion websites, where hungry Chicagoans and Windy City visitors gather to share stories, get advice and offer recommendations.

www.chowhound.com/midwest/index.html The navigation is a touch confusing, but there's a ton of informed opinion here, including heaps of helpful lists for vegans and other niche eaters.

http://forums.egullet.org You'll have to click through to the 'Heartland' section of their extensive forums, but once you're there, you'll find lively conversations about Chicago chefs and restaurants.

www.lthforum.com Wide-ranging, friendly talk about dining throughout Chicagoland that includes lists of farmers markets and maps to some great spots.

NICK'S FISHMARKET

Map pp304-5 Seafood

☎ 312-621-0200; One Bank One Plaza, W Monroe St; mains $16-43; closed lunch Sat, closed Sun; Blue Line to Monroe

Nick's doesn't escape its office surroundings so much as serve as an extension of them, offering a convenient spot for business lunches and dinners. Grab a quick meal upstairs in Nick's Grill, or head down to the main attraction – the dim, cozy confines of Nick's dining room. Long known for its traditional dishes – lobster thermidor, king crab, pepper steak etc – Nick's has been branching out, goosing familiar seafood mains with Asian flavors. Drinkers will enjoy the 11 kinds of martinis on offer, as well as the sizable wine list. Jacket recommended.

PALM

Map pp304-5 Steak & Seafood

☎ 312-616-1000; Swissôtel Chicago, 323 E Wacker Dr; mains $18-125; bus 157

Not picking up the check tonight? Then head to Palm's for the best lobster you've ever had (about $25 a pound). Given that these crustaceans average about 5lb, you can see why you'll want to be sitting on your wallet and brimming with thanks at check time. Equally costly New York strip steaks are also wonderful.

RHAPSODY

Map pp304-5 American

☎ **312-786-9911; 65 E Adams St; mains $9-21; Brown, Green, Orange, Purple Line to Adams**

Tucked inside Symphony Center, the luxurious atmosphere and reasonable prices at this smart-looking restaurant will be music to your ears. Feast on the onion-crusted sturgeon or the succulent beef tenderloin, but leave room for the top-notch desserts, many of which feature chocolate bits cleverly etched with gilded musical notes. This is a great place to regain your strength after a visit to the Art Institute.

RUSSIAN TEA TIME

Map pp304-5 Russian

☎ **312-360-0000; 77 E Adams St; mains $15-28; Brown, Green, Orange, Purple Line to Adams**

The old-world atmosphere and free-flowing vodka at this popular spot near the Art Institute will delight the 70-year-old alcoholic Muscovite in all of us. The czar-worthy menu includes borscht, *pelmeni* (dumplings), beef stroganoff and more. Russian folk songs complete the mood.

TRATTORIA NO 10

Map pp304-5 Italian

☎ **312-984-1718; 10 N Dearborn; mains $14-27; 🕓 closed lunch Sat, closed Sun; Blue Line to Washington**

This lively Italian restaurant's location just a couple blocks from the Loop theater district makes it an ideal candidate for filling your belly pre-play. The simple menu provides exceptionally flavorful takes on familiar items like ravioli (try the asparagus tip, aged buffalo) mozzarella and sun-dried tomato filling) and risotto. If you're in a hurry, the servers will help you get out the door fast; if not, lingering is warmly condoned.

Cheap Eats

BURRITO BUGGY

Map pp304-5 Mexican

☎ **312-362-0199; 206 W Van Buren St; mains $4-7; 🕓 lunch; Brown, Green, Orange, Purple Line to LaSalle**

This quickie lunch option – a favorite with traders from Chicago Stock Exchange – serves the biggest, weirdest burritos you've ever encountered. The barbecue chicken burrito includes tangy chicken alongside corn, cilantro, cheese and mashed potatoes(!). Amazingly, it works. The jerk chicken burrito is equally delicious.

GOLD COAST DOGS

Map pp304-5 American

☎ **312-578-1133; 17 S Wabash Ave; mains $3-6; 🕓 to 6pm; Brown, Green, Orange, Purple Line to Madison**

Get your dog char-grilled and to go at this run-down temple to the legendary Chicago hot dog. 'Chicago dogs' come with the proper sides here: onions, relish, mustard, hot peppers, celery salt and a warm pickle spear. Come at lunchtime when the swarms of hungry diners ensure freshly grilled meat. The atmosphere in the restaurant, which shares space with a fast-food chain, is enough to make you lose your appetite, though – get the dog and take a hike.

JACOBS BROTHERS BAGELS

Map pp304-5 Bagels

☎ **312-922-2245; 53 W Jackson Blvd; mains $1-4; 🕓 lunch; Blue Line to Jackson**

Chicago is not much of a bagel town, making this convenient outpost of Jacobs Brothers all the more noteworthy. The bagels here are almost as substantial as the surrounding 6ft-thick walls of the Monadnock Building (one of Chicago's first skyscrapers).

OASIS CAFE

Map pp304-5 Middle Eastern

☎ **312-558-1058; 21 N Wabash Ave; mains $5-8; 🕓 lunch, closed Sun; Brown, Purple, Green, Orange Line to Madison**

Blink and you'll miss this tiny gem tucked into the back of the Wabash Jewelers Mall. The *Tribune* declared the hummus the best in town, and the chicken pita sandwiches and lamb plates are equally praiseworthy.

SOPRAFFINA MARKET CAFFE

Map pp304-5 Italian

☎ **312-726-4800; 222 W Adams St; mains $6-10; 🕓 lunch, closed Sat & Sun; Brown, Purple, Orange Line to Quincy**

Fast-food Italian with panache, the fresh cuisine here includes a bevy of salads such as chickpea, wheat berry and portobello mushroom and *giardiniera* (hot peppers). You can also order sandwiches, pasta and superthin-crust pizza. This branch of the local chain also serves filling breakfasts.

NEAR NORTH & NAVY PIER

The area north of the Chicago River has some of the best dining options in the city. Whether you're eating tapas or Thai, Near North leans toward creative presentations and lively atmosphere. This is also Chicago's pizza mecca; those up for the challenge could hit Chicago's top five pizza restaurants without leaving the area. Now *that's* amore!

Navy Pier…well…it's about what you'd expect. Plenty of chains whose culinary achievements mostly center on their dexterity with a deep-fat fryer. There is one seafood standout on the pier worth exploring.

TOP FIVE NEAR NORTH & NAVY PIER

- Getting a taste of the future of food at the **Kendall College Dining Room** (p141).
- Falling in love with Mexican food all over again at **Frontera Grill** (p140).
- Popping olives and slurping merlot at **Osteria Via Stato** (p142).
- Building muscles trying to lift an entire pizza at **Giordano's** (p143).
- Making the sushi scene at **Japonais** (p145).

BANDERA Map pp306-7 American

☎ 312-644-3524; 535 N Michigan Ave; mains $10-27; Red Line to Grand

Looking up at the entry to this 2nd-story restaurant on Michigan Ave, you'd have no idea what a gem awaits. The red-bedecked Bandera has the comfortable, retro feel of an expensive supper club, but without the snooty waiters (and at half the price). American classics – such as meat loaf, grilled fish and rotisserie chicken – predominate here. Portions are large, and the food is complemented by live jazz starting nightly around 6:30pm. When you've shopped till you've dropped, this is the place to come pick yourself back up again.

BEN PAO Map pp306-7 Chinese

☎ 312-222-1888; 52 W Illinois St; mains $9-16; closed lunch Sat & Sun; Red Line to Grand

Chinese food reaches new heights under the inspiration of Rich Melman; the high-ceilinged dark interior, with its circular bar, is one of the most chic Asian restaurants in town. The menu – which lands Ben Pao on 'Best Of' lists every year – features many twists, including five-spice shrimp satay and Hong Kong spicy eggplant.

BICE Map pp306-7 Italian

☎ 312-664-1474; 158 E Ontario St; mains $14-28; Red Line to Grand

Milanese export Bice provides an excellent opportunity to savor the delicately spiced foods of northern Italy without the jet lag. Risottos are superb, as are the creamy pastas. At the outdoor tables you can keep your eyes on the sidewalk crowd and ignite the jealousy of the passing rabble by letting your tongue linger on the homemade gelato. Inside, the stylish art deco decor makes a good backdrop.

BLUE WATER GRILL Map pp306-7 Seafood

☎ 312-777-1400; 520 N Dearborn St; mains $14-34; Red Line to Grand

The Midwestern outpost of the New York original serves up fresh fish, lobster, crab, and a number of sashimi and raw-bar selections, along with a Chicago-friendly array of steaks and lamb chops. The large restaurant has a sleek, dark, underwater feel, with a live jazz band from 6:30pm nightly.

BRASSERIE JO Map pp306-7 French

☎ 312-595-0800; 59 W Hubbard St; mains $9-30; dinner; Blue Line to Merchandise Mart

This huge, open place serves wonderful food from Alsace, where owner Jean Joho was born. From the signature beer specially brewed by a local microbrewery to the hot and fresh baguettes, all the details are right. Try the great *choucroute* (smoked meats and sausages on sauerkraut) or the shrimp in a bag. The service is as bright and cheery as the decor. Wear a fancy hat on Thursday and get a free *chapeau au chocolat* (chocolate hat) dessert.

CAFE IBERICO Map pp306-7 Spanish

☎ 312-573-1510; 739 N LaSalle St; meals $15-30; Brown Line to Chicago

Happy diners look like kids in a candy store as they ponder their little plates of tapas.

Among the choices: *salpicon de marisco* (seafood salad with shrimp, octopus and squid), *croquetas de pollo* (chicken and ham puffs with garlic sauce) and *vieiras a la plancha* (grilled scallops with saffron). Finish it off with flan. Most of the small dishes average $5. Iberico's sangria is a force to be reckoned with, and in summer the entire front room will be packed with Loop workers knocking back pitchers of the stuff.

CYRANO'S BISTROT

Map pp306-7 French

☎ **312-467-0546; 546 N Wells St; mains $9-19;** 🕑 **closed Sun; Blue Line to Merchandise Mart**

This popular casual French restaurant is named for the famous Cyrano of Bergerac, the hometown shared by chef and owner Didier Durand. A very cheerful place, Cyrano's serves a menu of southern French favorites, including numerous roasted meats. A few tables line the street and make a good place to sip one of the many wines while watching the after-work hordes march home. The $15 lunch special is a four-course marvel that's served all at once.

FOGO DE CHAO

Map pp306-7 Brazilian Steak House

☎ **312-932-9330; 661 N LaSalle St; lunch $25, dinner $40;** 🕑 **closed lunch Sat & Sun; Brown Line to Chicago**

For those of you who've always dreamed of having Brazilian *gauchos* (cowboys) serve you a never-ending array of meat from a trolley cart, well, we have some good news. And the rest of you will probably like Fogo de Chao as well. This all-you-can-eat meaty import from Brazil revolves around heaps and heaps of well-seasoned lamb, chicken, pork loin and steak. The wonderful dishes are served in a novel way: diners are issued laminated discs on entry – turn it green side up, and servers dressed as *gauchos* will hurry to your table to fill your plate with whatever meats you desire. Other perks include mashed potatoes, fried bananas and unlimited trips to the well-stocked salad bar.

FRONTERA GRILL

Map pp306-7 Mexican

☎ **312-661-1434; 445 N Clark St; mains $14-25;** 🕑 **closed Sun; Red Line to Grand**

Once you've eaten here, you'll never be able to look at the so-so stuff most places pass off as Mexican food again. Chef-owner Rick Bayless has achieved celebrity status with his fresh variations inspired by south-of-the-border fare. His unusual pepper sauces are worth rolling around your palate like a fine wine. Hot tortillas made on-site hold tacos *al carbón*, which are filled with charred beef and grilled green onions. *Chiles rellenos* (stuffed poblano peppers that are batter-fried) await converts to their succulent richness. The place is always mobbed, so expect to wait; reservations are only taken for five or more. See also the listing for **Topolobampo** (p142).

GENE & GEORGETTI

Map pp306-7 American

☎ **312-527-3718; 500 N Franklin St; mains $15-35;** 🕑 **closed Sun; Brown Line to Merchandise Mart**

For once, a place touting itself as one of Frank Sinatra's favorite restaurants can back up the claim, which should tell you everything you need to know about this classic steak house. Out of place in the city, the wooden building looks like it would be more comfortable on a two-lane road in some farm town. Old-timers, politicos and crusty regulars are seated downstairs. New-timers, conventioneers and tourists are seated upstairs. The steaks are the same on both levels: thick, well aged and well priced.

GREEN DOOR TAVERN

Map pp306-7 American

☎ **312-664-5496; 678 N Orleans St; mains $6-14;** 🕑 **closed Sun; Brown Line to Chicago**

The 1872 building housing this veteran bar and grill is one of the oldest structures north of the river. The Green Door Tavern has been around almost as long, serving up great burgers, sandwiches, salads and a few pasta dishes. The walls here are completely covered with ancient photos, signs and memorabilia. If you're in the mood for simple but well-cooked food in a lively, entertaining, old-Chicago setting, this is the place for you.

JOE'S SEAFOOD, PRIME STEAK & STONE CRAB

Map pp306-7 American

☎ **312-379-5637; 60 E Grand Ave; mains $12-37;** 🕑 **closed lunch Sun; Red Line to Grand**

A Chicago restaurateur imported Joe's Stone Crab from Miami Beach and gave it a distinctly local spin, not the least of which is the 'Prime Steak &' in the name. The signature item in this well-appointed, masculine-feeling restaurant is the stone crab – the succulent arthropods are flown in daily from the Gulf of Mexico. The crabs, which may be unavailable in summer months, can run up to $100. The key lime pie here has been known to elicit tears of joy in more-sensitive diners.

KENDALL COLLEGE DINING ROOM

Map pp308-9 New American & French

☎ 312-752-2328; 900 N North Branch St; mains $8-22; 🕑 closed lunch Sat, closed dinner Mon, closed Sun; bus 66

The School of Culinary Arts at Kendall College has turned out a host of local cooking luminaries, and its student-run classroom restaurant is where they honed their chops. The classy space on the river with views out over the Chicago skyline serves inventive French and New American cuisine crafted by eager-to-please hands. A fantastic value, the Dining Room is only open during the school term; call ahead for reservations.

THAT'S AMORE

When pizza first arrived in Chicago it was a scrawny, sickly specimen, and it took about a half century before an enterprising restaurateur named Ike Sewell finally made it well.

Ike, the owner of Pizzeria Uno, rolled out the first 'deep-dish' pizza in 1943. His creation had a flakier crust than the Neapolitan-style pizza, and the thing was *deep* – a full inch of red sauce, chopped plum tomatoes, shredded American-style mozzarella cheese, and a number of optional toppings that ran from Italian-style herb sausage, onions and mushrooms to green bell peppers, pepperoni and black olives.

You may have tried Chicago-style pizza at restaurants in your hometown. But until you've hefted a slice of cheesy Chicago pie in the 312 (or 773) area code, you can't say you've fully lived. You can get a heaping helping at any of the following establishments:

Edwardo's (p166)

Gino's East (p143)

Giordano's (p143)

Pizzeria Uno (p144)

LE LAN Map pp306-7 French-Vietnamese

☎ 312-280-9100; 749 N Clark St; mains $23-36; 🕑 closed Sun; Red Line to Chicago

Tell any self-respecting food-lover in Chicago that you're heading to Le Lan for dinner, and you'll encounter a mix of warm admiration and bitter envy. Helmed by two of Chicago's most respected chefs – Roland Liccioni (of Les Nomades) and Arun Sampanthavivat (of Arun's) – Le Lan offers an exquisite marriage of French and Vietnamese cuisine in a brick-walled setting. Must-tries: the devilishly rich foie gras and the tangy spring rolls.

MIKE DITKA'S RESTAURANT

Map pp308-9 American

☎ 312-587-8989; 100 E Chestnut St; mains $9-22; Red Line to Chicago

When it's too cold for a tailgate party, come to this Near North spot owned by the famously cantankerous former coach of the Chicago Bears. The menu is as meaty as you'd expect (the 'Fridge' burger could feed a family of three for weeks), and football fans can take a trip back to the Bears' glory days with the help of the memorabilia-filled display cases.

NACIONAL 27 Map pp306-7 Latin

☎ 312-664-2727; 325 W Huron St; mains $12-23; Brown, Purple Line to Chicago

The spice at this Latin-American hot spot isn't limited to the menu – salsa dancing breaks out here after 11pm on weekends. Chef Randy Zweiban mixes things up with a zing-filled menu drawing on dishes from 27 different countries in South and Central America; the seviche (raw fish marinated in citrus juice) is some of the best you'll find in Chicago.

NAHA Map pp306-7 New American

☎ 312-239-4030; 500 N Clark St; mains $14-27; 🕑 closed Sun; Red Line to Grand

The gray concrete floors and subdued color palette here help put the focus where it should be – on the food. Chef Carrie Nahabedian draws from her Armenian roots in crafting such popular mains as roast mint-and-lemon-marinated leg of lamb, and halibut with fennel pollen and herbs. Creative salads are another speciality of the house. Don't miss the heirloom tomato and homemade ricotta cheese salad if it's in season. Ask for a table on the south wall for better people-watching opportunities – the power broking going on at Naha is a savory meal all its own.

NOMI Map pp306-7 French

☎ 312-239-4030; 800 N Michigan Ave; mains $10-55; Red Line to Chicago

Named for its stately position on North Michigan Avenue, NoMi has been setting Chicago foodies' hearts afire since opening in 2001. Located on the 7th floor of the Park Hyatt hotel, the sleek, minimalist restaurant is worth a visit for its spectacular views over the Magnificent Mile alone. Acclaimed chef Sandro Gamba's knack for combining French fare with Asian flair is evident in the dishes, which range from roasted Chilean sea bass to frog leg risotto. Reserve a window table around sunset – it's one of the most romantic experiences that Chicago has to offer. Reservations are required.

OSTERIA VIA STATO

Map pp306-7 Italian

☎ 773-642-8450; 620 N State St; mains $18-36; closed lunch Sun; Red Line to Grand

Don't let Osteria Via Stato's location in the Embassy Suites fool you; this prix-fixe Italian delight is miles from your standard hotel-lobby restaurant grub. The three-course dinners ($36) begin with a nibbling array of olives and fresh Parmesan before moving on to family-style antipasti and pasta, and a choice of a half-dozen or so ever-changing meat dishes. The ambience is warm and lively, and the pared-down, two-course lunch ($18) is also worth exploring. The attached wine bar makes a great stopover for a glass of vino and a snack.

RIVA Map pp306-7 Seafood

☎ 312-644-7482; 700 E Grand Ave, on Navy Pier; mains $11-37; bus 66

The high-class option for Navy Pier victuals, Riva offers traditional pasta dishes and fresh seafood. The latter is fitting, given Lake Michigan laps a few feet away. Needless to say, the menu features plenty of calamari and various fresh grilled fish dishes (the tuna is especially good). The inflated prices buy great views of the lake and city skyline.

ROSEBUD ON RUSH

Map pp306-7 Italian

☎ 312-266-6444; 720 N Rush St; mains $14-38; Red Line to Chicago

Huge portions of familiar Italian standards dominate the tables at this outpost of the Rosebud empire (see p165). The prices, quality and weight of the doggie bags are all high. Specialities include veal in its many forms. You'll be unlikely to find enough energy to sing 'Chicago' as you and a companion attempt to plow your way through the Festivale di Sinatra con Amore, a massive meal for two that seems to include half the menu.

SHAW'S CRAB HOUSE

Map pp306-7 Seafood

☎ 312-527-2722; 21 E Hubbard St; mains $10-50; closed lunch Sat & Sun; Red Line to Grand

If you're just going to hit one fish place in Near North, come to Shaw's. Its beautiful old dining room feels like a step back in time to the Jazz Age. Oysters and crab are the way to go here; to find out what's best and freshest, ask one of the friendly and efficient servers. The crab-cake appetizer and the key lime pie make good bookends to the meal. The adjoining Blue Crab Lounge, which has live music several nights a week, is the casual adjunct to the main restaurant.

SUSHISAMBA RIO

Map pp306-7 Fusion

☎ 312-595-2300; 504 N Wells; mains $15-30; Brown Line to Merchandise Mart

The Japanese-Brazilian-Peruvian restaurant has an eye-popping interior, complete with year-round rooftop dining. A DJ spins records on the mezzanine, and patrons can avail themselves of caipirinhas (a Brazilian cocktail made from sugarcane, lime and rum) from the stylish bar. Oh, the food? Sushi rolls, miso-marinated sea bass and small flash-fried crabs, which you eat like oversized popcorn. Dress like you're heading to a chic nightclub and you'll fit right in.

TOPOLOBAMPO

Map pp306-7 Mexican

☎ 312-661-1434; 445 N Clark St; mains $16-33; closed Sun, Mon; Red Line to Grand

Part of the same operation as **Frontera Grill** (p140), this is where chef Rick Bayless lets his creativity flow, unfettered by cost restrictions. Compared with its rollicking neighbor, Topolobampo's mood seems downright serious, as diners sample combinations of flavors most people never knew existed. The menu changes nightly; be prepared for a memorable experience. Reservations required.

TRU Map pp306-7 French
☎ 312-202-0001; 676 N St Clair St; dinner $80-135; ⏲ dinner, closed Sun; Red Line to Grand
Gale Gand (of the Food Network's *Sweet Dreams*) and Rick Tramonto opened one of the city's best restaurants in 1999. The food is French, but with a sense of humor. Starters include a trademark staircase of caviar, with a variety of the little fish eggs waltzing down the steps. The ever-changing and eclectic menu also features a cheese course that's one of the best in the country, and renowned desserts, such as the heavenly roasted pineapple 'carpaccio', which subs in slices of coconut for the meat and infuses the whole thing with pineapple. Expect flawless service in the all-white dining room. Menus include an all-vegetable version ($90) and a chef's special collection ($135).

WILDFIRE Map pp306-7 American
☎ 312-787-9000; 159 W Erie St; mains $11-23; ⏲ dinner; Brown Line to Chicago
A huge grill, rotisserie and wood-burning oven roast shrimp, prime rib, steak and ribs at this haven for barbecuers, with snow-covered grills. Prices for the generous portions average about $19 – not bad for this comfortable and welcoming place. In the best tradition of Chicago smoke-filled rooms (where dubious political deals are cut), you'll emerge smelling of smoke, but at least it's barbecue rather than cigar.

Cheap Eats

BIG BOWL Map pp306-7 Asian
☎ 312-951-1888; 60 E Ohio St; mains $8-12; Red Line to Grand
Big bowls of Asian noodles – more than 30 varieties – are the speciality here, all made with fresh ingredients and a kicking array of sauces. The choices include wheat noodles with shrimp, black beans and snow peas, and barbecued chicken and noodles in broth. The interior is modern and stylish, with huge booths in the shape of – you guessed it – big bowls.

BOSTON BLACKIES
Map pp306-7 American
☎ 312-938-8700; 164 E Grand Ave; mains $5-12; Red Line to Grand
This comfortably divey restaurant is awash in red neon and filled with the kind of old Chicago characters that gentrification usually sends packing. Platters of burgers and sandwiches are made with top-notch ingredients. The cheddar oozes out like volcanic magma under the chives and bacon bits on the potato skins ($6).

DAO Map pp306-7 Thai
☎ 312-337-0000; 230 E Ohio St; mains $6-9; Red Line to Grand
A classic Thai restaurant in a neighborhood lacking in good dining options, Dao is popular with lunching workers. Although the prices are low, the ambience here is a cut above your usual bare-bones Thai eatery, with traditional Thai decorations lending the room a touch of exotic class. Service at all times is quick and cheerful, and all dishes can be made vegetarian, on demand.

GINO'S EAST Map pp306-7 Pizza
☎ 312-943-1124; 633 N Wells St; mains $7-25; Brown Line to Chicago
In the great deep-dish pizza wars going on in Chicago, Gino's is easily one of the top three heavies. And it encourages its customers to do something neither Pizzeria Uno nor Giordano's would allow: customers at Gino's have been covering every available surface (except for the actual food) with graffiti. The pizza is something you'll write home about: the classic stuffed cheese-and-sausage pie oozes countless pounds of cheese over its crispy cornmeal crust.

GIORDANO'S Map pp306-7 Pizza
☎ 312-951-0747; 730 N Rush St; mains $8-26; Red Line to Chicago
The founders of Giordano's, Efren and Joseph Boglio, claim that they got their winning recipe for stuffed pizza from – aww – their mother back in Italy. If you want a slice of heaven, order the 'special,' a stuffed pizza containing sausage, mushroom, green pepper and onions. We think it's the best deep-dish pizza in Chicago.

MR BEEF Map pp306-7 American

☎ 312-337-8500; 660 N Orleans St; mains $4-7; lunch, closed Sun; Brown Line to Chicago

A local classic, the $5 Italian beef sandwiches come with long, spongy white buns that rapidly go soggy after a load of the spicy beef and cooking juices has been ladled on. Past a sign marked 'Classy Dining Room,' you'll find a decidedly unclassy porch with picnic tables and an odd selection of movie posters on the wall. The pictures of Jay Leno aren't fake – he comes here every time he's in town.

PIEROT GOURMET Map pp306-7 French

☎ 312-573-6749; 108 E Superior St; mains $6-12; to 7pm; Red Line to Chicago

This small, casual café next to the Peninsula Hotel is known far and wide for its fantastic breads and pastries, but it also serves excellent open-faced sandwiches and other light, satisfying fare for lunch and (early) dinner in a sunny, friendly environment.

PITA PAVILION Map pp306-7 Mediterranean

☎ 312-335-9018; 8th fl, Chicago Pl, 700 N Michigan Ave; mains $5-10; lunch; Red Line to Grand

On crummy days, the atrium winter garden atop Chicago Pl can be one of the brightest places to eat lunch, amid palm trees and burbling fountains, with a great view along the Magnificent Mile. The pick of the food court has to be Pita Pavilion, which serves a great falafel pita sandwich for $5. Other choices are mall food-court standards.

Local legend Mr Beef (above)

PIZZERIA UNO Map pp306-7 Pizza

☎ 312-321-1000; 29 E Ohio St; mains $8-26; Red Line to Grand

Ike Sewell supposedly invented Chicago-style pizza here on December 3, 1943, although his claim to fame is hotly disputed by rivals. A light, flaky crust holds piles of cheese and an herb-laced tomato sauce. The pizzas take a while, but stick to the pitchers of beer and cheap red wine to kill time and avoid the salad and other distractions, so you can save room for the main event. The $18 classic lands on the table with a resounding thud and can feed a family of four.

PORTILLO'S Map pp306-7 American

☎ 312-587-8910; 100 W Ontario St; mains $2-6; Red Line to Grand

Die-hard hot-dog purists are often heard bemoaning the lack of true dawgs anywhere near the main tourist drags of Chicago, afraid that it gives visitors to the city a watered-down idea of what a real Chicago hot dog is like. Those culinary curmudgeons point to this outpost of the local Portillo's chain – done up in a should-be-cheesy-but-actually-feels-cool '20s, '30s and '40s gangster theme – as the place to get one. You won't find a cheaper lunch outside of McDonald's.

GOLD COAST

The Gold Coast's restaurants consist mostly of mid- to high-end eateries intent on providing pleasant meals without the DJ booths and special effects that mark the scene in hipper neighborhoods. Steak, heavy and rare, is on the menu, and many of the city's power players come here to seal nefarious deals over a table-sized porterhouse. The main eat street is Rush St, though some of the area's more interesting picks are located a little off the beaten path.

BISTRO 110 Map pp308-9 French

☎ 312-266-3110; 110 E Pearson St; mains $10-28; Red Line to Chicago

One of the first bistros to set up shop in Chicago, Bistro 110 has aged well over its nearly two decades. The lively space still feels fresh and modern, and the service is as friendly and attentive as ever. Don't leave here without trying the Robuchon lamb, which is roasted and braised for 20 hours before reaching your table. The spicy pepper steak in cognac-cream sauce is equally memorable. In town over the weekend? The New Orleans–style jazz brunch is a great way to spend your Sunday.

CRU CAFE & WINE BAR

Map pp308-9 French

☎ 312-337-4001; 888 N Wabash Ave; mains $12-24; 🕑 to 1am; Red Line to Chicago

Choose from no less than 500 bottles at this sleek wine bar. The well-dressed patrons speak in lots of European accents, some of them authentic. In summer you can idle away hours people-watching from the outdoor tables. In winter you can gather with a full-bodied red around the roaring fireplace inside. The food ranges from sandwiches to salads to quiche, none of it cheap: a club sandwich is $17. The late-night cheese platters seem a world removed from the late-night weenies you can get elsewhere.

GIBSON'S Map pp308-9 Steak House

☎ 312-266-8999; 1028 N Rush St; mains $20-80; 🕑 closed lunch Mon-Thu; Red Line to Clark/Division

It's a scene nightly at this local original. Politicians, movers, shakers and the shaken-down compete for prime table space in the buzzing dining area. The bar is a prime stalking place for available millionaires. As for the meat on the plates, the steaks are as good as they come, and the seafood is fresh and expensive.

JAPONAIS Map pp308-9 Japanese

☎ 312-822-9600; 600 W Chicago Ave; mains $19-35; 🕑 closed lunch Sat & Sun; bus 66

It's a 'see and be' scene at Japonais, where the dazzling food somehow surpasses the eye candy provided by the preening guests. Expect some of the best sushi and sashimi in Chicago, and Japanese-inspired fusion dishes. The decor, courtesy designer Jeffrey Beers, transports diners to a modern fantasy of sumptuous curves and pooling light.

LE COLONIAL

Map pp308-9 French-Vietnamese

☎ 312-255-0088; 937 N Rush St; mains $13-24; Red Line to Chicago

A colonial outpost of the New York original, Le Colonial re-creates the feel of a swank Vietnamese restaurant during the French era of the 1950s. Fortunately, there's no malaria, and the food shows more imagination than the French exhibited during their rule. The delicately seasoned offerings include warm salads and several seafood and duck dishes. The upstairs bar, with the greenery and languidly turning fans, achieves an atmospheric charm that calls for a tonic.

TOP FIVE GOLD COAST

- Recuperating from art overload on the patio of **Puck's at the MCA** (p146).
- Enjoying omelettes with 50 of your new late-night friends at **Tempo Cafe** (p147).
- Dining next to the moon at the **Signature Room at the 95th** (p147).
- Starting off the morning right with a tall stack at the **Original Pancake House** (p147).
- Elegantly dancing off that second dessert at the **Pump Room** (p146).

MK Map pp308-9 New American

☎ 312-482-9719; 868 N Franklin St; mains $12-36; Brown Line to Chicago

The exposed brick walls hint at mk's industrial past, but this dining hot spot is nothing if not civilized. Chef Michael Kornick (who was nominated for a James Beard award in 2005) wows the mostly business crowds with artfully presented dishes such as seared ahi tuna, roast rack of lamb, and sautéed veal sweetbreads. The desserts are equally scrumptious. Noise levels here on weekends hinder confidential tête-à-têtes, but those looking for imaginative culinary creations paired with excellent people-watching opportunities won't go home disappointed.

MORTON'S Map pp308-9 Steak House

☎ 312-266-4820; 1050 N State St; mains $19-75; 🕑 dinner; Red Line to Clark/Division

With a clubby ambience and prime service, Morton's has remained Chicago's premier steak house long enough for scores of competitors to arrive on the scene. The meat here is aged to perfection and displayed tableside before cooking. See that half a cow? It's the 48oz double porterhouse. Smaller – but still quite dangerous if dropped on your toe – are the fillets, strip

NOUVELLE CHICAGO CUISINE

It took less than a week for the photos to hit the Internet. Shortly after the 2005 opening of Greg Achatz's $200-a-head restaurant Alinea, a Chicago food-lover set the egullet.org message boards abuzz with photographic documentation of her trip there. Amateur gastronomes throughout the city devoured each digital photo, responding with desperate cries for elaboration on everything from food textures to the size of the napkins. 'I can't even imagine how you must've felt throughout your dining experience,' one person wrote in response. 'I can't wait to read more about people's reactions and feelings, and it will all lead up to my May 24th reservation when I will find out just how amazing this restaurant is going to be. I just got goosebumps.'

The instant, vicarious gratification available in online message boards is a new thrill for Chicago foodies. But it's just another twist on Chicago's long-running reverence for restaurants that push the dining boundaries. While you're here, think about getting some goosebumps of your own by breaking the bank and tasting the fruits of some of Chicago's genius chefs. The good news is many of Chicago's four-star restaurants have been around long enough that you can snag same-week reservations, especially if you're willing to eat early or late. Our shortlist of dreamy dining in the city:

Alinea (opposite; prix-fixe menu from $75) They don't have a word yet to describe the sci-fi juxtaposition of flavors and ingredients at Alinea. Some of the courses here are just a single bite. But oh, what a bite.

Arun's (Map pp302-3; ☎ 773-539-1909; 4156 N Kedzie Ave; prix-fixe menu $85) As a diner, your only job at Arun Sampanthavivat's temple to high-end Thai is to pick the spice level. They do the rest, and will do a great job of opening your mind to the marvels of Thai cooking over 12 delectable courses.

Charlie Trotter's (Map pp308-9; ☎ 773-248-6228; 86 W Armitage Ave; average meal for 1 person $200) The king of Chicago cooking. Trotter's eponymous restaurant in Lincoln Park takes seasonal ingredients in note-perfect directions. Pastry chef Della Gossett makes the final act here as memorable as the first.

Spiaggia (Map pp306-7; ☎ 312-280-2750; 980 N Michigan Ave; average meal for 1 person $150) Chef Tony Mantuano won the 2005 James Beard award for Best Midwestern Chef. Visitors to his dramatic dining room savor spectacular Italian cuisine along with dramatic views of the Magnificent Mile.

Tru (p143; prix-fixe menu from $90) Run by head chef Rick Tramato and pastry chef Gale Gand, this New American landmark has been topping best-of lists since it opened in 1999.

steaks and other cuts. The immense baked potatoes could prop up church foundations. Try the hash browns, superb versions of a side dish all too often ignored. Expensive reds anchor the wine list.

PJ CLARKE'S

Map pp308-9 American

☎ 312-664-1650; 1204 N State St; mains $8-23; Red Line to Clark/Division

Hungry for some companionship? PJ Clarke's is an upscale restaurant-pub where Chicago's straight, 30-something singles come to eyeball one another. Both classy and cozy, PJ Clarke's specializes in comfort foods with high-end twists, like the 'béarnaise burger' or the 'teriyaki skirt steak' sandwich.

PUCK'S AT THE MCA

Map pp308-9 New American

☎ 312-397-4034; 220 E Chicago Ave; mains $6-14; 🕓 lunch, closed Mon; Red Line to Chicago

In the Museum of Contemporary Art, this outlet of the irrepressible Wolfgang Puck features strictly contemporary cooking, with dishes that fuse Asian and Mediterranean cuisine. The changing menu features lots of marinated seafood and salads, as well as a few hot items. A deli counter offers sandwiches and more to go. In summer, dine out back on the MCA's patio, one of the city's great hidden gems.

PUMP ROOM

Map pp308-9 American

☎ 312-266-0360; Omni Ambassador East hotel, 1301 N State St; mains $11-38; Red Line to Clark/Division

Book yourself into Booth One at this legendary spot and you'll have something in common with the pantheon of celebrity customers whose photos line the walls. Famous since the 1940s, this Pump Room continues its tradition of understated elegance. Real VIPs, or just lucky poseurs, sit in Booth One, a see-and-be-seen throwback to a previous, glamorous era. There's a dress code, which means you'll be well attired for the cheek-to-cheek dancing that takes places most nights after dinner. Veal porterhouse and grilled sea bass head up the American menu.

SIGNATURE ROOM AT THE 95TH

Map pp308-9 American

☎ 312-787-9596; John Hancock Center, 875 N Michigan Ave; mains $12-39; Red Line to Chicago

Near the top of the Hancock Center – no points for guessing the correct floor – this large room offers stunning views on clear days. Given that diners spend more time looking out the windows than looking at their plates, you'd think the kitchen wouldn't trouble itself over the food, but the fish, steak and pasta dishes are quite good. The lunch buffet ($14), served Monday to Saturday, can be a fine deal, especially if you satisfy your view cravings here as opposed to buying a ticket to the Hancock observation deck. Families come for the Sunday brunch; cheapskates get the same soul-stirring views for the price of a (costly) beer, one flight up in the Signature Lounge.

Cheap Eats

ORIGINAL PANCAKE HOUSE

Map pp308-9 Breakfast

☎ 312-642-7917; 22 E Bellevue Pl; mains $5-10; lunch; Red Line to Clark/Division

Follow your nose to this quaint little cash-only breakfast chain, tucked into a quiet alcove of its busy Near North neighborhood. *Chicago* magazine gave the Original Pancake House (OPH) its Best Breakfast award, and it's easy to see why. With 20 different kinds of pancakes (including the formidable, basketball-sized 'Dutch baby') and myriad egg dishes, the OPH stands head and shoulders above most Gold Coast breakfast options.

TEMPO CAFE

Map pp308-9 American

☎ 312-943-3929; 6 E Chestnut St; mains $6-13; 24hr; Red Line to Chicago

Bright and cheery, this upscale diner brings most of its meals to the table the way they're meant to be served – in a skillet. Its omelette-centric menu includes all manner of fresh veggies and meat, as well as sandwiches, soups and salads. The scene here after the bars close is chaotic and fun.

> **TOP FIVE LINCOLN PARK & OLD TOWN**
>
> - Giggling over the PB&J (and, later, the check) at **Alinea** (right).
> - Watching the theater before the theater at **Boka** (p148).
> - Devouring the freaky sushi rolls of **Tsuki** (p149).
> - Sopping up the sauce at **Robinson's No 1 Ribs** (p151).
> - Getting dogs straight from the source at the **Vienna Beef Factory Deli** (p149).

LINCOLN PARK & OLD TOWN

It's a great time to be opening a restaurant in Lincoln Park, where the trendy locals make dining out an integral part of their busy social calendars. Halsted and Lincoln are the two streets for culinary window-shopping in the neighborhood; on both streets the restaurants tend to be loud, energetic affairs. Having DePaul University in the neighborhood helps keep the roster of cheap eats booming, even as the commercial rents here shoot skyward.

The restaurant scene in Old Town is a quieter version of Lincoln Park. Dining is casual and untrendy, appealing mostly to 30- and 40-somethings in the neighborhood. If you're undecided where to eat come dinnertime, just walk up Wells St and let your nose be your guide.

LINCOLN PARK

ALINEA

Map pp308-9 Tapas

☎ 312-867-0110; 1723 N Halsted St; mains $75-175; dinner, closed Mon & Tue; Red Line to North/Clybourn

This famous restaurant, helmed by superstar chef Greg Achatz, is the kind of place where nervous, awestruck foodies take digital photos of each course before digging in. The options are limited to an eight-course ($75), 12-course ($110) and 30-course ($175) menu. The gasp-inspiring, avant-garde food is an artistic carnival of strange pairings served in steel and glass contraptions created especially for each dish. Expect single-bite dishes such as the famous PB&J (a single grape covered in homemade peanut butter and brioche), and *Harry Potter*–evoking ingredients such as 'dissolving eucalyptus' and 'hyacinth vapor.' Meals tend to take upwards of four hours, and you can add a note-perfect wine pairing for an additional $75.

BACINO'S

Map pp308-9 Pizza

☎ 773-472-7400; 2204 N Lincoln Ave; mains $7-20; Brown, Red Line to Fullerton

This local chain specializes in the stuffed variation of Chicago-style pizza. A very thin crust on the top allows still another layer of cheese to be piled on even higher. The stuffed spinach model – the most popular choice – contains plenty of useful iron to fuel your grueling tourism schedule.

BOKA Map pp308-9 New American

☎ 312-337-6070; 1729 N Halsted St; mains $9-34; 🕑 dinner; Red Line to North/Clybourn

A hip restaurant-lounge hybrid with a seafood-leaning menu, Boka has become the pre- and post-theater stomping ground *du jour* for younger Steppenwolf patrons. Order a cocktail at the bar, or slip into one of the booths for small-plate dishes like grilled Santa Barbara prawns and a radicchio and portobello mushroom salad with a hazelnut bacon vinaigrette. Mains include a glazed Atlantic salmon in a tamari–black truffle sauce and, for the famished, a grilled bison rib-eye steak.

CAFE BA-BA-REEBA!

Map pp308-9 Tapas

☎ 773-935-5000; 2024 N Halsted St; mains $16-30; Brown, Red Line to Armitage

If you plan on kissing anyone after dinner, make certain they've dined with you at this delightfully ersatz tapas joint where the garlic-laced sauces may have you surreptitiously licking the plates. The menu changes daily but always includes some spicy meats, marinated fish and a wonderful potato salad. If you want a main event, order one of the nine paellas ($12 a person) as soon as you get seated – they take a while to prepare.

O'FAMÉ

Map pp308-9 American

☎ 773-929-5111; 750 W Webster Ave; mains $6-18; Brown, Red Line to Armitage

This popular sit-down restaurant started as a takeout business (now tucked into the eatery's eastern edge). Thin-crust pizza and ribs are popular with the neighborhood diners and Steppenwolf theatergoers. Want to stage your own play? You can get picnic versions of everything from the gleaming white-tile takeout area and enjoy them in Oz Park, across the street.

RJ GRUNTS

Map pp308-9 American

☎ 773-929-5363; 2056 N Lincoln Park West; mains $7-14; bus 22

The very first of the now-ubiquitous Lettuce Entertain You stable of restaurants, RJ Grunts came on the scene in the 1970s, when Lincoln Park emerged as the young singles' neighborhood of choice. Now, as then, the huge fruit and vegetable bar and the burgers are the mainstays. This is a fun post-zoo lunch spot; even the pickiest kids (and parents) will find something to love.

ROSE ANGELIS

Map pp308-9 Italian

☎ 773-296-0081; 1314 W Wrightwood Ave; mains $7-15; 🕑 dinner, closed Mon; Brown, Red Line to Fullerton

It must be something they put in the tortellini: you'll see nothing but smiles on diners' faces in this vegetarian-friendly Italian restaurant. The three rooms here all feel like a friend's living room (though the bruschetta and thin-crust pizzas will likely outshine anything your pals have ever concocted).

TILLI'S

Map pp308-9 Fusion

☎ 773-325-0044; 1952 N Halsted St; mains $9-18; Brown, Red Line to Armitage

This comfy restaurant has an eclectic menu (the Thai barbecue salmon is great) that mixes ingredients from all over the globe. Diners are in their late 20s and early 30s, and the young professional crowd gets loud and boisterous on weekends – especially on winter evenings, when everyone basks and drinks by the floor-to-ceiling fireplace. During the week, things are much calmer, and

Tilli's becomes a favorite for the Lincoln Park new-mom scene.

TSUKI

Map pp308-9 Japanese

☎ 773-883-8722; 1441 W Fullerton Ave; sushi $3-12; 🕑 dinner; Brown, Red Line to Fullerton

This large and urbane sushi restaurant opened in 2004 and quickly became beloved in the Windy City for its fresh sashimi and playful touches with sushi rolls. Top picks include the smoked duck nigiri and the intriguing pistachio-salmon teriyaki. Noodles (both soba and udon) and tempura round out the menu, which also includes some vegetarian selections.

VIA CARDUCCI

Map pp308-9 Italian

☎ 773-665-1981; 1419 W Fullerton Ave; mains $7-20; 🕑 dinner; Brown, Red Line to Fullerton

The simple, southern Italian dishes regularly draw moans of delight from diners at this small Lincoln Park gem. Red-checkered tablecloths complement the baroque murals on the walls, and the food leans toward thick tomato-based sauces and amazing sausages (not to mention generous portions, which you'll likely be enjoying for lunch the following day).

VINCI

Map pp308-9 Italian

☎ 312-266-1199; 1732 N Halsted St; mains $9-19; 🕑 closed Mon; Red Line to North/Clybourn

The Steppenwolf brass nameplate on one of the tables shows you this rustic Italian restaurant knows which side its crusty bread is buttered on. Vinci offers much more than proximity to the city's famous stage. The dishes are well-crafted spins on Italian favorites, like the fungus-friendly grilled polenta with portobello and *cremini* mushrooms in porcini mushroom broth, and duck breast with balsamic vinegar sauce.

Cheap Eats

BOURGEOIS PIG

Map pp308-9 Coffee Shop

☎ 773-883-5282; 738 W Fullerton Ave; mains $5-9; Brown, Purple, Red Line to Fullerton

A coffee shop that's powerful brew is only matched by the heartiness of its sandwiches and salads, the Bourgeois Pig is a convivial place to have a bite to eat while working through the voluminous *Reader* or chatting with friends. Tea drinkers will find many options on offer.

FRESH CHOICE

Map pp308-9 American

☎ 312-664-7065; 1534 N Wells St; mains $6-9; Brown Line to Sedgwick

If you're feeling a little burned out on the hot dogs, steaks and mozzarella-laden pizzas, this healthy spot is a great place for a light meal or a vitamin-packed fruit smoothie. Grab an oven-baked sub and sit at the sidewalk tables, or treat your weary body to a salad and a fresh-squeezed carrot juice or a wheatgrass cocktail.

NOOKIES, TOO

Map pp308-9 American

☎ 773-327-1400; 2114 N Halsted St; mains $6-12; Brown, Red Line to Armitage

You can cleanse your previous night's sins with the oat-bran pancakes at this popular brunch spot, or choose from a full complement of eggs, waffles and sandwiches. The fresh-squeezed orange juice is pricey, but worth it if your taste buds are already awake.

PASTA BOWL

Map pp308-9 Italian

☎ 773-525-2695; 2434 N Clark St; mains $6-13; bus 22

You get more than you pay for at this affordable neighborhood pasta joint. The sauces are top-notch; the pesto reeks of garlic and the bolognese is redolent with basil. The meatball sub is also excellent, and the prices are just a fraction higher than what you pay at the Subway store across the street.

VIENNA BEEF FACTORY STORE & DELI

Map pp316-17 American

☎ 773-235-6652; 2501 N Damen; mains $3-6; 🕑 lunch, closed Sun; bus 50

You've eaten them all around town, now come to the source. The out-of-the-way Vienna Beef Factory is the source of the majority of hot dogs sold in Chicago, and the factory's workers' deli is one of the freshest places to try the famous creations. Hot-dog haters can nosh on corned-beef sandwiches or potato pancakes. And Vienna fans can pick up a case of the dogs at the on-site store to share with loved ones at home.

WIENER CIRCLE

Map pp308-9 American

☎ **773-477-7444; 2622 N Clark St; mains $3-6;**
24hr; Brown, Red Line to Diversey

'Order now or get the f*** out!' screams the apron-clad man behind the counter while an addled patron tries to comply. It's 4:30am at this Lincoln Park equivalent of a roadhouse, and the scene has reached its frenetic peak. Wiener Circle is both infamous and revered in Chicago; the place where verbal abuse is a cheerful sport and where the kitchen kicks out some of the best char-grilled hot dogs that money can buy.

OLD TOWN

ADOBO GRILL

Map pp308-9 Mexican

☎ **312-266-7999; 1610 N Wells; mains $10-19;**
closed lunch Mon-Fri; Brown Line to Sedgwick

Like Rick Bayless at Topolobampo, Adobo chef Paul LoDuca takes Mexican foods and flavors to another dimension at his lively eatery near Second City. The yummy guacamole appetizer is made tableside, and the dishes that follow it are no less extraordinary. Try the trout steamed in cornhusk or the tender chicken breast in an Oaxacan black mole sauce. Thirsty? The margaritas are predictably good, but Adobo also has over 80 sipping tequilas on hand.

BISTROT MARGOT Map pp308-9 French

☎ **312-587-3660; 1437 N Wells St; mains $7-20;**
Brown Line to Sedgwick

A visit to Bistrot Margot is like a visit to a little Parisian corner bistro in one of the remoter districts. Roast chicken, steak and *frites*, mussels and other coastal shellfish highlight the classic menu. The interior decor mixes dark wood with bright tiles and red booths, and the busy crowd adds to the atmosphere. It's a good idea to make reservations for the popular Sunday brunch.

FIREPLACE INN Map pp308-9 American

☎ **312-664-5264; 1448 N Wells St; mains $12-27;**
kitchen to 1:30am Fri & Sat; Brown Line to Sedgwick

This local legend has been serving up Chicago-style baby-back ribs for over 35 years. Steaks, burgers and seafood round out the menu. The steak fries are perfectly crisp on the outside and tender on the inside. Blue cheese–lovers will want to pay extra for that dressing on the side salad. The two-level dining room is heavy with wood – almost as much as the namesake fireplace burns up in a night. When the snow is blowing off the lake and the sidewalks are piling up with drifts, you can warm your cockles here. (But you can also air them out in summer at the garden tables.)

¡SALPICÓN! Map pp308-9 Mexican

☎ **312-988-7811; 1252 N Wells St; mains $16-25;**
dinner Mon-Sat; Red Line to Clark/Division

Another favorite among Chicago's high-end Mexican restaurants, Priscilla Satkoff's place has elevated seviche and *chiles rellenos* to an art. Many other items come slathered in heavenly mole. The festive interior features high ceilings and bold colors. Create bright colors in your head by trying some of the 60 tequilas, including some rare, oak barrel–aged numbers.

TOPO GIGO Map pp308-9 Italian

☎ **312-266-9355; 1516 N Wells St; mains $9-23;**
Brown Line to Sedgwick

Roasted peppers and grilled zucchini on the antipasto table are just some of the treats that await at this faithful adaptation of a Roman trattoria, an excellent choice for a relaxing evening of delicious Italian food. The linguini Cinque Terre also scores big points.

TWIN ANCHORS Map pp308-9 American

☎ **312-266-1616; 1655 N Sedgwick St; mains $8-18; Brown Line to Sedgwick**

Twin Anchors is synonymous with ribs, and Chicagoans can get violent if you leave their city without sampling some of Twin Anchors' baby-backs. The meat drops from the ribs as soon as you lift them. Choose among fries, onion rings and baked potatoes for sides. This spot doesn't take reservations, so you'll have to wait outside or around the neonlit 1950s bar, which sets the tone for the place. An almost all-Sinatra jukebox completes the '50s supper-club ambience.

Cheap Eats

CHICAGO BAGEL AUTHORITY

Map pp308-9 Bagels

☎ **773-248-9606; 953 W Armitage Ave; mains $2-6; Brown, Red Line to Armitage**

This lively little spot is packed with DePaul students grabbing a fast breakfast and lunch. The bagels are fine plain or decked out in sandwich fixings.

OLD JERUSALEM

Map pp308-9 Middle Eastern

☎ **312-944-0459; 1411 N Wells; mains $5-9; Brown line to Sedgwick**

The *shwarma* (meat sliced off a spit and stuffed in a pita pocket, with chopped tomatoes and garnish) and falafel are both fantastic at this friendly, 29-year-old Old Town joint. Looking for something leafy? Try the Greek salad, served with Lebanese flatbread. The atmosphere is bare bones; get it to go and have a feast in Lincoln Park.

ROBINSON'S NO 1 RIBS

Map pp308-9 Ribs

☎ **312-337-1399; 655 Armitage Ave; mains $3-8; closed lunch Sat & Sun, closed Mon; Brown Line to Armitage**

In the war of the ribs, this tiny shop has struck some mighty blows against all Chicago comers. Smoky, meaty ribs in a tangy sauce make napkins unnecessary at Robinson's (why waste all that perfectly good flavor on a dumb napkin?). The chicken is also good, and lunch specials run under five bucks for your pick of a meat, french fries and a soda.

LAKE VIEW

Like Lake View itself, the restaurant scenes vary as you move from block to block. Boystown, on Halsted St north of Belmont Ave, has stylish eateries catering to all tastes and preferences. The Belmont Ave area contains a huge variety of restaurants whose quality – but not prices – matches that found closer to the center of town. Scores of moderate- and budget-priced eateries serve food from around the world on Clark St, roughly from Belmont Ave to a little north of Wrigley Field. Some aim their menus squarely at the undiscriminating tastes of suburban day-trippers. Others offer imaginative food at excellent prices. The CTA Belmont and Addison stops are close to either end of the strip.

The name on everybody's lips these days, though, is Southport. The once-quiet Lake View road has turned into a mecca for restaurants and clubs. The stretch of Southport from Belmont Ave north to Irving Park Rd is particularly hopping. Take the CTA Brown Line to the Southport stop to put yourself in the heart of the action.

ANDALOUS Map pp318-19 Moroccan

☎ **773-281-6885; 3307 N Clark St; mains $9-16; Brown, Red Line to Belmont**

There's much more than couscous on the menu at this cheerful Moroccan bistro, which offers numerous veggie options. The *meknes tagine* is a charming concoction of lemony chicken sautéed in onions.

ANN SATHER Map pp318-19 American

☎ **773-348-2378; 929 W Belmont Ave; mains $5-15; Brown, Red Line to Belmont**

In the early 1980s local marketing genius Tom Tunney took a longtime neighborhood coffee shop and gave it a trendy and quirky ad campaign that emphasized its good, basic food. Tunney is now a Chicago alderman (the first openly gay alderman ever elected), and young professionals still flock here for platefuls of reasonably priced chow served in stylish, friendly surroundings. At night Swedish standards such as meatballs and potato sausage join American classics like salmon and meat loaf. Famous for breakfast are Ann Sather's warm and gooey cinnamon rolls, worth a trip in themselves.

TOP FIVE LAKE VIEW

- Savoring salsa by firelight at **Platiyo** (p153).
- Relishing Sunday brunch at **HB** (p152).
- Sharing a superb pizza at **Mia Francesca** (p153).
- Exploring the wonders of a 3am grilled cheese at **Pick Me Up** (p155).
- Soaking up pan-Asian flavors at panned diner prices at **Pingpong** (p153).

ARCOS DE CUCHILLEROS

Map pp318-19 Spanish

☎ 773-296-6046; 3445 N Halsted St; mains $7-17; ⏰ closed Mon; Red Line to Addison

This comfy place avoids the upscale hype of some of the other tapas joints. The owners come from Madrid, and they have faithfully replicated one of that city's family cafés, with a long bar, narrow room and dark wood furniture. Small plates of classics such as sautéed lima beans, chickpea croquettes and tortilla *española* (a cold egg and potato omelette) average $7 each. Don't keep track of how many pitchers of tangy sangria you drink; just keep ordering.

COOBAH Map pp318-19 Latin

☎ 773-528-2220; 3423 N Southport Ave; mains $7-16; ⏰ closed lunch Mon-Fri; Brown Line to Southport

This hopping Latin restaurant and bar in the hot Southport corridor serves up spicy tamales and sweet plantains along with some of the best mojitos in Chicago. Despite the fever pitch of the place on weekend nights (DJs start spinning at 10pm), servers remain attentive and friendly. Try the Coobah pancakes (buttermilk pancakes with cinnamon butter and rum maple syrup) at the weekend brunch.

CULLEN'S Map pp318-19 American

☎ 773-975-0600; 3741 N Southport Ave; mains $7-19; bus 152

Bar chow predominates at this welcoming tavern connected to the Mercury Theatre. Lots of wood and tile evoke a classic Chicago watering hole, though this place dates from more recent times. Baked artichoke appetizers, marinated tuna sandwiches and juicy burgers are typical of the fare. The beer list is long and interesting.

DELEECE Map pp318-19 New American

☎ 773-325-1710; 4004 N Southport Ave; mains $5-25; ⏰ closed lunch Mon-Thu; bus 80

At this upscale café that was once a grocery store, the aromas wafting from the kitchen have an international appeal. Poblano peppers and cilantro add a Mexican touch, ginger chimes in for Asia and olive oil speaks for the Mediterranean. Prices reflect the grocery-store roots, but the soup is definitely not canned. Staff members get praise for being able and affable. Deleece has become a popular Sunday-brunch spot.

DUKE OF PERTH Map pp318-19 Scottish

☎ 773-477-1741; 2913 N Clark St; mains $5-14; bus 22

This genuine Scottish pub offers various Scottish delights like haggis, which may well drive you to drink any or all of the vast number of single malts on offer. However, punters from all around drop in for the excellent fish and chips (all-you-can-eat for $9 Wednesday and Friday). The beer garden is a good refuge.

ERWIN Map pp318-19 New American

☎ 773-528-7200; 2925 N Halsted St; mains $16-19; ⏰ closed Mon; Brown, Red Line to Diversey

'Comfort food' is the trendy term for the kind of rib-sticking fare that Midwestern moms have served for decades. When Mom's not around to heat up the stove, your average Joe might resort to the supermarket's frozen-food section for his comfort. High-class Joes – or at least those with sophisticated palates – resort to Erwin. Dishes on the ever-changing menu feature American ingredients but combine food styles from around the world in imaginative ways. Bring Mom (especially to the delightful Sunday brunch).

HB Map pp318-19 American

☎ 773-661-0299; 3404 N Halsted St; mains $8-14; ⏰ closed lunch Tue-Fri, closed Mon; Brown, Purple, Red Line to Belmont

The owners of this friendly café-turned-restaurant won *The Next Food Network Star* reality TV show in 2005, but the real star is the food – plus the hot waitstaff. Come by on weekends for the justly famous brunch, or drop in at night for an array of comfort foods – from pork chops to pan-fried crabs. HB is BYOB.

JACK'S ON HALSTED

Map pp318-19 New American

☎ 773-244-9191; 3201 N Halsted St; mains $13-25; ⏰ closed lunch Mon-Sat; Brown, Red Line to Belmont

Special of the day? It's always fun food served in an eclectic dining room by highly personable staff. The menu hops around the world, stopping off for American classics like steak or Cajun and then moving on for Italian, French and Asian, with a number of good vegetarian choices along the way. You can wash down every course with the many fine American wines. Be sure to save room for dessert. Sunday brunch is worthy of special occasions.

MATSUYA Map pp318-19 Japanese

☎ **773-248-2677; 3469 N Clark St; mains $6-16; Red Line to Addison**

The wooden boat in the window hints at the sushi-dominated menu here, one of the best-value places on the Japanese dining scene. The sushi offerings include standards such as California rolls down to the square-shaped Osaka-style sushi. The rest of the menu plumbs unusual depths (sample item: octopus marinated in bean paste). Less adventurous types will be happy with the teriyaki-marinated grilled fish.

MIA FRANCESCA

Map pp318-19 Italian

☎ **773-281-3310; 3311 N Clark St; mains $10-25; Brown, Red Line to Belmont**

Diners jam the large room at one of the most popular small, family-run Italian bistros in the city. A buzz of energy swirls among the closely spaced tables, topped with white tablecloths, and the arrangements of fresh flowers. The kitchen is open on one side, allowing full view of your food's preparation. The frequently changing handwritten menu features earthy standards with aggressive seasoning from southern Italy. Other treats include wafer-thin pizzas and the often-overlooked staple of Italian kitchens: polenta. Service can be harried because of the clamoring crowds.

MONSOON Map pp318-19 Indian

☎ **773-665-9463; 2813 N Broadway; mains $12-30; 🕑 dinner, closed Mon; Brown, Red Line to Diversey**

The French-trained Indian chef here spent time at the Peninsula Hotel before helming the kitchen at this beautiful, upscale Indian restaurant. The space is gorgeous, with an open kitchen offering diners up-close views of the work that goes into making the Darjeeling tea–smoked chicken, tandoori rib-eye steak and shrimp *pakoras* (deep-fried, with a spicy batter).

PAT'S PIZZA Map pp318-19 Pizza

☎ **773-248-0168; 3114 N Sheffield Ave; mains $7-22; Brown, Red Line to Belmont**

Thyme is a key ingredient of the sausage here, and combined with a few other toppings, it makes for a great thin-crust combo pizza. A frequent winner of *Chicago Tribune* competitions (which means that the *Sun-Times* regularly dumps on it), Pat's is a family place that still seems a bit overwhelmed by the huge changes in the neighborhood. If you're not here for a thin-crust, skip it.

PINGPONG Map pp318-19 Asian

☎ **773-281-7575; 3322 N Broadway; mains $7-13; 🕑 dinner; Brown, Red Line to Belmont**

This sexy, modern restaurant spices its mix of Japanese, Thai, and Chinese food with a healthy dose of house music. The food is ungreasy, carefully spiced and surprisingly affordable; the hip clientele who wait patiently for one of the few tables in this small space know good value when they see it.

PLATIYO Map pp318-19 Mexican

☎ **773-477-6700; 3313 N Clark St; mains $9-18; Brown, Red Line to Belmont**

The warm dining room of this creative Mexican restaurant is packed with locals who come for the upbeat atmosphere and dishes like mahimahi tacos and the excellent shrimp fajitas. The chef of Platiyo learned his chops working at the superlative **Frontera Grill** (p140), and you can taste the mastery (until you've imbibed too many items from its inventive margarita menu).

PS BANGKOK Map pp318-19 Thai

☎ **773-871-7777; 3345 N Clark St; mains $7-18; 🕑 closed Mon; Brown, Red Line to Belmont**

The shrimp curries burst with hot, plump shrimp at this spot, one of Chicago's best Thai restaurants. The various fish tanks hint at the long list of seafood dishes, many of them the elaborate kind found at banquets in Thailand. Order the Siamese curry noodles for a real treat.

STREGA NONA Map pp318-19 Italian

☎ **773-244-0990; 3747 N Southport Ave; mains $8-15; bus 80**

That hallmark of late-20th-century restaurant design – exposed brick – is the dominant element of the dining room here, which opens on to the street. Locals twirl the typical Italian fare around their forks with glee. The name comes from a witch in Italian children's stories.

TANGO SUR

Map pp318-19 Argentine Steak House

☎ 773-477-5466; 3763 N Southport Ave; mains $11-27; closed lunch Mon-Sat; bus 80

This BYOB Argentine steak house smells great and serves classic skirt steaks and other beefy options. Not in the mood for steak? Then kidneys await. Not in the mood for meat? Go elsewhere. Tables outside expand the seating from the very small and spare interior. This may be the only smoke-free steak place in town.

TUSCANY Map pp318-19 Italian

☎ 773-404-7700; 3700 N Clark St; mains $10-29; Red Line to Addison

A branch of the well-known original on Taylor St in Little Italy, this Tuscany has a real grill to prepare the various steaks on the menu, and a wood-burning pizza oven. The menu draws its inspiration from northern Italy; look for creamy risottos and rosemary-flavored grilled meats. Although rather hoity-toity by Clark St standards, this place is still very casual.

X/O Map pp318-19 Fusion

☎ 773-348-9696; 3441 N Halsted St; plates $6-12; closed lunch Sat, closed Sun; bus 8

This LA-feeling Boystown restaurant refers to its food as 'global tapas,' and its assortment of small plates does indeed run the gamut of the world's cuisines. Though the scene of beautiful young fashionistas sometimes hogs the spotlight, it's chef Bob Zrenner's seasonal, warm plate options that truly shine. Try the Tasmanian line-caught salmon or Vietnamese spicy duck leg with Thai chilis, complemented by a flight of champagne or cognac.

YOSHI'S CAFE Map pp318-19 Japanese

☎ 773-248-6160; 3257 N Halsted St; mains $16-26; closed Mon; Brown, Red Line to Diversey

Yoshi and Nobuko Katsumura preside over one of the most innovative casual places in town. The changing menu focuses on low-fat dishes with a Japanese flair. The kitchen treats all ingredients with the utmost respect, from the salmon and other seafood options to the tofu in the vegetarian dishes. Try to save room for the group dessert, which includes a little bit of everything on the menu. The service is every bit as good as the food.

Cheap Eats

CHICAGO DINER Map pp318-19 Vegetarian

☎ 773-935-6696; 3411 N Halsted St; mains $5-11; Red Line to Belmont

This vegetarian diner has been serving items such as barbecue *seitan* (a meat substitute), wheatmeat and tofu stroganoff for over 20 years now. The hipster staff members are friendly, and the powerful coffee comes from local roaster Intelligentsia. In the morning, the breakfast tofu omelettes are a big hit. In the evening, the mains feature varying amounts of grains and veggies. Vegans take note: even the pesto for the pasta can be had without a lick of cheese.

ORANGE Map pp318-19 American

☎ 773-549-4400; 3231 N Clark St; mains $5-11; brunch, closed Mon; Brown, Red Line to Belmont

When you drive down Clark St on a Saturday and see a place with lines of people winding out the door, you will know you have come across Orange. Serving kooky dishes like French toast kabobs and jelly-doughnut pancakes, alongside the more traditional breakfast staples, Orange is the first thing many Chicagoans want to see in the morning. Check out the restaurant's South Loop location, which is at 75 W Harrison St.

PENNY'S NOODLE SHOP

Map pp318-19 Asian

☎ 773-281-8222; 3400 N Sheffield Ave; mains $5-9; Brown, Red Line to Belmont

Despite the presence of several other excellent Asian choices within a few blocks, this place attracts crowds most hours of the day and night. You'll see people waiting outside in all weather, good and bad. Maybe these hapless hordes are drawn by the place's minimalist decor, low prices or – no doubt – the cheap, tasty noodle soups ($6 average). Penny's is BYOB, so stock up on drinks before you get here.

GETTING CURRIED AWAY

Between the spice shops, sari stores and Indian restaurants, Devon Ave west of Western Ave is one of the most exotic stretches of Chicago. It's also a damn fine place to get a heaping plate of *saag paneer* (soft cheese in a spicy gravy of pureed leafy greens), tandoori chicken, garlic naan and other wonders of Indian cooking. The El doesn't come close to this area, so you'll have to drive, take a cab or ride the El to the Red Line's Morse Ave stop and transfer to the No 155 Morse Ave bus.

Indian Garden (Map pp302-3; ☎ 773-338-2929; 2548 W Devon Ave; mains $6-15; bus 155) Items not found on most South Asian menus dominate here. The cooks use woklike pans and simple iron griddles to prepare a lot of the items. Vegetables go beyond the soggy cauliflower in goopy sauces found at other, less inspired places. Wash it all down with a mango shake.

Sabri Nehari (Map pp302-3; ☎ 773-743-6200; 2511 W Devon Ave; mains $7-16; bus 155) Fresh, fresh meat and vegetable dishes, distinctly seasoned, set this Pakistani place apart from its competitors on Devon. Try the 'frontier' chicken, which comes with a plate of fresh-cut onions, tomatoes, cucumber and lemon, and enough perfectly cooked chicken for two. (The frontier being referred to is Pakistan's mountainous northern frontier.) For dessert, check out the *kheer*, a creamy rice pudding.

Udupi Palace (Map pp302-3; ☎ 773-338-2152; 2543 W Devon Ave; mains $5-10; bus 155) This bustling all-vegetarian Indian restaurant serves toasty, kite-sized rice crepes stuffed with all manner of vegetables and spices, along with an array of curries. The room gets loud with a 20-something Anglo hipster and young Indian crowd.

PICK ME UP Map pp318-19 American

☎ 773-248-6613; 3408 N Clark St; mains $6-9; 3pm-3am Mon-Fri, 24hr Sat & Sun; bus 22

This colorful after-hours hub for the city serves a tasty, oddball array of things like 'sammitches' and 'pizzadillas' to a post-bar (and later) crowd. Designed to look like the inside of a crooked house out of a children's book, the Pick Me Up features brightly painted walls and a cacophonous collection of old signs and advertisements. The coffee's strong and the filling mains are way more interesting than your standard diner fare.

SHIROI HANA Map pp318-19 Japanese

☎ 773-477-1652; 3242 N Clark St; mains $5-12; closed lunch Sun, Brown, Red Line to Belmont

Every large city, if it's lucky, has its Shiroi Hana – the dirt-cheap sushi place where the food is consistently good, if not overwhelming. Lunch is a particularly sweet deal, with most sushi costing just $1.20 per piece.

VILLAGE TAP Map pp318-19 American

☎ 773-883-0817; 2055 W Roscoe St; mains $6-12; bus 50

This neighborhood tavern does everything well: food, drink and atmosphere. And that's the problem – it can get crowded on Friday and Saturday night. Otherwise, it's a real winner. The friendly bartenders give out free samples of the ever-changing and carefully chosen lineup of Midwestern microbrews. The kitchen turns out some great burgers, veggie burgers and chicken sandwiches, and the spiced pita chips are a nice touch. Out back the beer garden contains a fountain; inside the tables enjoy good views of the TVs for ball games. There are also board games available so you and your friends can make your own fun.

ANDERSONVILLE & UPTOWN

Though Andersonville started with the Swedes, the food here has expanded in more cosmopolitan directions. Modern takes on French, Korean, Middle Eastern and Belgian abound on Clark St. Thankfully, one artifact of the neighborhood's Nordic past survives: the must-see Swedish Bakery, where butter and sugar flow like water. Getting up to Andersonville's main drag is best accomplished by car or cab. If you're taking the El, head to the Red Line Berwyn stop.

The star of Uptown's dining scene is Asian Argyle St. Even the Argyle El Station sports an Asian motif in this neighborhood full of restaurants and shops run by people from Southeast Asia. Families in search of the American dream are always opening

TOP FIVE ANDERSONVILLE & UPTOWN

- Munching on a burger and shake from **Huey's Hotdogs** (opposite).
- Romancing the night away at **La Tache** (right).
- Playing cookie monster at the **Swedish Bakery** (opposite).
- Tasting tasty Taiwanese at **Mei Shung** (opposite).
- Washing down the kim chee with a sojutini at **Jin Ju** (below).

someplace new on Argyle St. The same holds true on the adjoining blocks of Broadway and Sheridan Rd (which is three blocks east of Broadway). The restaurants in this area serve up piping hot soup and huge portions of noodles, all at *very* affordable prices. Make sure you bring a big appetite.

ANDERSONVILLE

ANDIE'S Map p311 Mediterranean

☎ 773-784-8616; 5253 N Clark St; mains $6-14; Red Line to Berwyn

The larger Reza's next door may draw the yuppie hordes, but discerning Andersonville locals flock to Andie's for smooth hummus and much more. A recent remodeling has transformed the dining room into a Mediterranean showplace. The cooking occurs in an open kitchen, and smells of grilling meat, eggplant and the world's best lentil soup waft through the air.

JIN JU Map p311 Korean

☎ 773-334-6377; 5203 N Clark St; mains $7-17; dinner; Red Line to Berwyn

One of only a handful of 'nouveau Korean' restaurants in town, Jin Ju throws a culinary curveball by tempering Korean food to Western tastes. The minimalist, candlelit interior of Jin Ju echoes softly with downbeat techno, and the stylish 30-somethings who come here enjoy entrees like *haemul pajon* (a fried pancake stuffed with seafood) and *kalbi* (beef short ribs). In keeping with the current rage for drinks ending in 'tini,' the restaurant offers a scrumptious 'sojutini', made with *soju*, a Korean spirit that is distilled from sweet potatoes.

LA TACHE Map p311 French

☎ 773-334-7168; 1475 W Balmoral Ave; mains $12-27; dinner; Red Line to Berwyn

This art deco–ish space offers a sweet elegance and reasonably priced, high-end bistro fare to a rapidly growing fan base. The kitchen maestro here is Dale Levitski, known for making breakfast place **Orange** (p154) such a success. The veal cheeks here are wonderful, as is Napoleon's favorite postbattle meal, chicken Marengo – this version has chicken served with garlicky crawfish, mushrooms and a poached egg. Looking for a romantic restaurant on the North Side? You've just found it.

RIOJA Map p311 Tapas

☎ 773-275-9191; 5101 N Clark St; mains $3-16; bus 22

A late-20-something crowd fights for the tapas and table space at this hip, bustling Spanish-inspired restaurant. Many of the tapas plates come in mains sizes – a nice touch for those who don't like making a meal of snacks. Weekdays are much calmer than weekends (which border on manic and require long waits).

TOMBOY Map p311 New American

☎ 773-907-0636; 5402 N Clark St; mains $15-23; Red Line to Berwyn

You might wonder about the name, until you realize that Andersonville is a favorite neighborhood of Chicago's lesbian community. Tomboy, with its white tablecloths and exposed brick walls, prepares artful and filling dishes, including a number of meat-free pasta dishes, plus carnivorous items like filet mignon with Gorgonzola cream sauce. An eclectic wine list rounds out the menu.

Sweet treats at Swedish Bakery (opposite)

Cheap Eats

HUEY'S HOTDOGS

Map p311 American

☎ 773-293-4800; 1507 W Balmoral Ave; mains $4-7; bus 22

Those who know hot dogs come to Huey's. Regularly ranked among Chicago's top dine-and-dash greasy spoons, this gregarious hole-in-the-wall makes a perfect pit stop if you're still feeling hungry after a dainty meal at one of Andersonville's upscale eateries. The shakes here are also legendary.

KOPI, A TRAVELER'S CAFE

Map p311 Coffeehouse

☎ 773-989-5674; 5317 N Clark St; mains $5-8; Red Line to Berwyn

An extremely casual coffeehouse with a pile of pillows on the floor in the window, Kopi stocks a large range of travel books, and serves sandwiches and desserts to its lefty clientele. On the bulletin board you'll find ads from people looking for trekking partners for Kazakhstan or looking to unload last year's rock-climbing gear.

SWEDISH BAKERY

Map p311 Bakery

☎ 773-561-8919; 5348 N Clark St; cookies $1; closed Sun; Red Line to Berwyn

You get free coffee in amazingly small cups here, but that's the only thing minimalist about the place, with its butter-laden breads, cookies and pastries. Everything is astoundingly good. Are you in Andersonville? Come here now.

UPTOWN

HAI YEN Map p311 Vietnamese-Chinese

☎ 773-989-0712; 1007 W Argyle St; mains $5-25; closed Wed; Red Line to Argyle

Many of the dishes at this warm Argyle St eatery require some assembly, pairing shrimp, beef or squid with rice crepes, mint, Thai basil, and lettuce. For an appetizer, try the *goi cuon,* fresh rolls of vermicelli rice noodles along with shrimp, pork and carrots. The *bo bay mon* consists of seven (yes, seven) different kinds of beef. Order sparingly, or ask for some help from your server – like the *bo bay mon,* many of the dishes are large enough to feed an army.

MEI SHUNG Map p311 Taiwanese

☎ 773-728-5778; 5511 N Broadway; mains $5-16; closed Mon; Red Line to Argyle

If you've never had Taiwanese food before, Mei Shung will make an excellent first impression. Spicy seafood and peppery crab dishes are served in thick, flavorful sauces. Chicken meals in a special Taiwanese satay sauce are also tops. Filling lunch specials here clock in at just over $4.

TANK NOODLE Map p311 Vietnamese

☎ 773-878-2253; 4953 N Broadway; mains $5-15; closed Thu; Red Line to Argyle

The servers all wear camouflage aprons at this spacious corner eatery, a quirky touch in an otherwise utilitarian restaurant. The crowds, though, aren't here for the ambience: the *bahn mi* (Vietnamese sandwiches), served on crunchy fresh baguette rolls, and the *pho* (beef noodle soup) are both excellent.

THAI PASTRY Map p311 Thai

☎ 773-784-5399; 4925 N Broadway; mains $5-10; Red Line to Argyle

A favorite at lunchtime with workers from both Uptown and Andersonville, this Thai restaurant has a window filled with accolades and awards, and the food to back it up. The pad thai is excellent, and the spot-on curries arrive still simmering in a clay pot.

WICKER PARK, BUCKTOWN & UKRAINIAN VILLAGE

Wicker Park and Bucktown hang somewhere between artist haunt and high-priced loft land, and their restaurants reflect that schism. Along Milwaukee Ave in Wicker Park you'll find a $2 taco joint next to a chi-chi place where $2 won't even cover the tip for the restaurant's valet parking. Bucktown's main eat street, Damen Ave, rolls the two disparate worlds into one – boasting a number of eateries that sell high-end takes on low-end comfort food. It will probably be a few years yet before the Wicker Park–Bucktown area fully comes into its own, food-wise. In the meantime, the mishmash of new and old, and of cheap and pricey is delightful (and delicious). Grab the Blue Line to Damen to start your eating adventures.

Over the past two years, Ukrainian Village has become one of the hot new places for restaurant openings. Especially along Division St near Damen, young restaurateurs have been setting up shop with some encouraging results. The same is true on the eastern edge of the neighborhood, along Chicago Ave near Halsted St. This chunk of town is called West Town, and with the success of places like Green Zebra and the West Town Tavern, it's become an oasis of good eats in a somewhat dingy neighborhood. Cars or cabs are the best way to navigate Ukrainian Village, though the Chicago Blue Line stop will take you close to some of the best options in West Town.

WICKER PARK & BUCKTOWN

HANDLEBAR Map pp316-17 Fusion

☎ 773-384-9546; 2311 W North Ave; closed lunch Mon-Fri; Blue Line to Damen

The cult of the bike messenger runs strong in Chicago, and this bicycle-themed restaurant and bar is a way station for the tattooed couriers and locals who come for the interesting beer list, vegetarian-friendly menu, and back beer garden. Dishes have an international bent – try the samosas, the West African peanut stew or the Handlebar salad, served with arugula, walnuts, slices of pear, and fancy Italian cheese. Bike messengers with ID get special deals on some nights.

HOT CHOCOLATE Map pp316-17 Dessert

☎ 773-489-1747; 1747 N Damen Ave; mains $7-19; closed Mon; Blue Line to Damen

'Come for dessert, stay for dinner' might be the motto at this buzz-heavy Bucktown upstart. Run by renowned pastry chef Mindy Segal, the cute place feels exactly like the irresistible, upscale chocolate desserts it peddles. With five different kinds of hot chocolate available, along with mini brioche doughnuts – served warm with hot fudge for dipping and homemade caramel corn – and a half-dozen other glucose-spiking concoctions, you may forget to order any of the real food on offer, such as Kobe beef skirt steak and mussels.

LE BOUCHON Map pp316-17 French

☎ 773-862-6600; 1958 N Damen Ave; mains $12-23; dinner, closed Sun; Blue Line to Damen

Classic French food at nonclassic prices makes for a winning combination at this quaint spot. Neighborhood types who know a good deal often pack Le Bouchon to feast on all the French standards. The lyonnaise salad is a winner. Other faves on the short menu range from escargot to chocolate *marquisse* (chocolate mousse without the egg whites). Want to see the tiny kitchen? Head to the bathroom – it's on the way.

LULA CAFÉ New American

☎ 773-489-9554; 2573 N Kedzie Blvd; mains $8-22; closed Tue; Blue Line to Logan Sq

Located in the up-and-coming neighborhood of Logan Sq (to the northwest of Wicker Park), this friendly, upmarket café is where hipsters come when they have something to celebrate. Even the muffins here are something to drool over, and that goes double for lunch items like pasta *yiayia* (bucatini pasta with Moroccan cinnamon, feta and garlic) and dinners such as olive oil–marinated rib-eye with braised kale.

MERITAGE CAFE & WINE BAR Map pp316-17 New American

☎ 773-235-6434; 2118 N Damen Ave; mains $24-30; dinner; Blue Line to Damen

The wine list is almost as long as the gaze down the nose you get from the sometimes haughty help at this ode to the Pacific Northwest. But if you're ready for this kind of scene, you'll be rewarded with some really good regional American food featuring lots of fish like salmon, plus mushrooms

TOP FIVE WICKER PARK, BUCKTOWN & UKRAINIAN VILLAGE

- Experiencing a whole new level of doughnut at **Hot Chocolate** (left).
- Having it cheap and chunky with a Costa Rican burrito and oatmeal shake at **Irazu** (opposite).
- Going green at **Green Zebra** (p161).
- Savoring the divine Mac N Cheese at **Milk & Honey** (p161).
- Grabbing a quick *fettia* (dough with egg and cheese baked over it) for the road from **Sultan's Market** (p160).

TOP FIVE VEGGIE DELIGHTS

Some suggestions for when Chicago's bacon fixation gets a little old:

- **Chicago Diner** (p154) The all-vegetarian diner.
- **Earwax** (p176) A hip and arty veggie party.
- **Green Zebra** (p161) Where Chicago's beloved chef Shawn McClain veges out.
- **Lula Cafe** (opposite) Smart, delicious food in cozy surroundings.
- **Sultan's Market** (p160) A place where chickpeas trump chickens.

and game from the forest and various Asian influences. The former corner bar has been renovated just enough to let in the light while still preserving the Victorian character. The covered and heated patio allows you to eat outside in all but the worst weather.

MIRAI SUSHI Map pp316-17 Japanese

☎ 773-862-8500; 2020 W Division St; mains $9-19; ⏰ dinner; Blue Line to Damen

This high-energy restaurant has an even higher-energy lounge upstairs, both packed with happy, shiny Wicker Park residents enjoying some of the freshest sushi in the area. From the trance-hop electronic music to the young, black-clad staff, Mirai is a place where connoisseurs of sashimi and *maki* (rolled sushi) gather to throw back a few cocktails between savory bites of yellowtail and shiitake tempura. Nonsmokers rejoice: chef Jun Ichikawa doesn't allow cigarettes anywhere near his kitchen on the main floor. Smokers should head upstairs or grab a sidewalk table out front.

NORTHSIDE Map pp316-17 American

☎ 773-384-3555; 1635 N Damen Ave; mains $7-13; Blue Line to Damen

The clientele at this sweet spot are mostly Lincoln Park transplants, and it's no wonder why they're here – the covered, plant-filled atrium gives diners a touch of summer no matter how cold it is outside. The cheeseburgers and other pub grub are well cooked. The apple pie is amazing.

SCYLLA Map pp316-17 Seafood

☎ 773-227-2995; 1952 N Damen Ave; mains $9-23; ⏰ closed Mon; bus 50

If something seems fishy about this bilevel restaurant, you know you're in the right place. The seasonal, refined menu of fresh fish and shellfish served with French and Italian touches has garnered rave reviews from diners, and the cozy ambience makes it a great choice for a romantic night out.

SPRING Map pp316-17 New American

☎ 773-395-7100; 2039 W North Ave; mains $15-28; ⏰ dinner, closed Mon; Blue Line to Damen

The seafoody mains at this award-winning place come to your plate by way of Asia, with chef Shawn McClain lovingly dressing up dishes of lobster, grouper, halibut and scallops in mouthwatering soy glazes, hot and sour broth, and fresh wasabi. The restaurant – which was a bathhouse in a former life – looks a little like an Ikea showroom: simple, modern lines and muted greens set the tone.

Cheap Eats

FLASH TACO Map pp316-17 Mexican

☎ 773-772-1997; 1570 N Damen Ave; mains $1-7; Blue Line to Damen

If they ever gave out an award for 'Most Dirt-Cheap Tacos Served to Drunk People,' this well-situated hole-in-the-wall would give Taco Bell a run for its money. And unlike the chains, this place actually has some good items on its dollar menu. Grab a couple of *al pastor* (grilled pork with pineapple) tacos and ask for the salsa – staff keep it behind the counter for some reason – and watch the Wicker Park carnival unfold around you.

HOT DOUG'S Map pp302-3 American

☎ 773-279-9550; 3324 N California; mains $2-5; ⏰ lunch, closed Sun; bus 77

The gourmet sausages served here by owner Doug may be at the forefront of a Chicago hot-dog revolution. With specialities ranging from blueberry-merlot-venison to sesame-ginger-duck, the food at this friendly place has reviewers dragging out their superlatives. On Friday and Saturday, Doug offers fries cooked in thick duck fat (you have to ask for them).

IRAZU Map pp316-17 Costa Rican

☎ 773-252-5687; 1865 N Milwaukee; mains $4-10; ⏰ closed Sun; Blue Line to Western

This unbelievably cheap hole-in-the-wall would be one of Chicago's best value places at three times the price. The Costa

GONE TO THE DOGS

Nobody knows how the classic Chicago hot dog evolved, but it's definitely become a unique creation you won't find anywhere else in the US. More than just a wiener and a bun, a Chicago dog contains a vast array of condiments and flavorings. When done right, it should defy easy consumption, with various ingredients flopping out all over the place and juices and sauces oozing in all directions.

For the record, a Chicago hot dog begins with an all-beef hot dog, preferably a local Vienna brand. Some places steam them, others boil and a few grill. Which method is best is a matter of great debate. However cooked, the 'tube steak' is then laid into a fresh poppy-seed bun. Now the fun begins. A traditional dog will have all of the following toppings, although local variations exist:

- diced onions, white or yellow
- diced tomatoes
- sliced cucumbers, possibly slightly pickled
- shredded iceberg lettuce
- diced green bell pepper
- pepperoncini (Italian hot and pickled peppers)
- sweet relish, usually a virulent shade of green
- bright yellow mustard
- catsup (although some would say 'never!')
- celery salt

The result? Part salad, part hot dog. It's not hard to find a good Chicago hot dog. A great Near North option is **Portillo's** (p144), which started in a Chicago suburb in the '50s. If you like a little theater with your dog, try **Wiener Circle** (p150) in Lincoln Park. For everything from a straight-up Chicago dog to one made with alligator, try **Hot Doug's** (p159), north of Bucktown in Roscoe Village. And if you have a car, head down to Little Italy to enjoy a dog at the brand-new storefront location of the Chicago **Express Grill** (Map pp314–15; ☎ 312-738-2112; 1260 S Union Ave). This place operated out of a box in the Maxwell St Market for generations, and just moved indoors for the first time in 2005.

Rican burritos are plump with chicken, black beans and fresh avocado, and the sandwiches contain a Costa Rican 'mystery sauce' that should be patented. Try the oatmeal shake; it's like drinking a cold oatmeal cookie (that's a good thing). Cash only.

LI'L GUYS DELI Map pp316-17 Deli

☎ 773-394-6900; 2010 N Damen Ave; mains $4-8; Blue Line to Damen

If you need a quick sandwich or salad, this is your place. The eatery roasts its own meats, and everything is made fresh daily.

MARGIE'S Map pp316-17 Ice Cream

☎ 773-384-1035; 1960 N Western Ave; mains $6-11; 🕑 to 1am; Blue Line to Western

This ice-cream parlor on the outer northwest edge of Wicker Park has been making and selling its own luscious sundaes, splits and cones since 1921. It's been almost as long since the crowded place remodeled; the tables are few here, and waits of a half hour or more are common. Once you get a seat, you can forestall the inevitable with a burger or sandwich, or just throw yourself into the cold, creamy main course.

MIKO'S Map pp316-17 Italian Ice

☎ 773-645-9664; 1846 N Damen Ave; drinks $2-4; 🕑 May-Oct; Blue Line to Damen

Pause on a hot day for some cool homemade Italian ice at this seasonal fave. You can sit under the large oak tree and enjoy fruit flavors such as lemon and peach.

NICK'S PIT STOP Map pp316-17 Barbecue

☎ 773-342-9736; 2011 N Damen Ave; mains $4-6; Blue Line to Damen

The scene at this tiny joint is reminiscent of a chicken's version of Dante's *Inferno* – vast rows of wings and breasts roasting over a flaming grill. The bright yellow interior may make it one of the ugliest restaurants, but mmm, are those birds tasty (and cheap!). Get a half-bird or a sandwich, and consider getting it to go: the few seats may be filled.

SULTAN'S MARKET
Map pp316-17 Middle Eastern

☎ 773-235-3072; 2057 W North Ave; mains $5-9; 🕑 closed Sun; Blue Line to Damen

Vegetarians annoyed by Chicago's obsession with all things beef can have their day at this Middle Eastern spot, filled with meat-free delights such as falafel sandwiches, spinach pies, and a sizable salad bar. Especially recommended: the $3 egg *fettia*, a sort of Middle Eastern Egg McMuffin that has dough with egg and two kinds of cheese baked over it.

UKRAINIAN VILLAGE

FLO Map pp316-17 Southwestern

☎ 312-243-0477; 1434 W Chicago Ave; mains $5-14; 🕑 closed Mon; Blue Line to Chicago

The southwestern-flavored dishes at this 20-something brunch favorite have textures and flavors just like fantastic short stories – delicious enough to devour in one sitting, but so well-crafted you want to make them last as long as possible. Think you've had a breakfast burrito before? Not until you've eaten here. The art on the walls is by local artists, and the cheerful staff members keep the coffee flowing.

GREEN ZEBRA Map pp316-17 New American

☎ 312-243-7100; 1460 W Chicago Ave; mains $8-15; 🕑 dinner, closed Mon; bus 66

You don't typically see chicken breast on the menu at vegetarian restaurants, but chef Shawn McClain's veggie haven is anything but typical. With a few nods to the meatily inclined, this celebrated new restaurant focuses most of its energy on delivering amazing odes to meatless meals. The seasonal menu at Green Zebra is heavy on decadent infusions (black-truffle essence, anyone?) and rich broths, and the desserts and cheese plates are also sumptuous.

LEO'S LUNCHROOM

Map pp316-17 American

☎ 773-276-6509; 1809 W Division St; mains $6-13; 🕑 closed Mon; Blue Line to Division

When Wicker Park and Ukrainian Village artists roll out of bed on weekends, they roll directly to Leo's and then stay here all day. The place is run-down, but the mid-end comfort cuisine (biscuits and gravy or pumpkin pancakes for breakfast, spinach salad with goat cheese and salmon over pasta for lunch and dinner) is priced to move. Grab a seat on the deck out back when the sun is out. Cash only.

MILK & HONEY

Map pp316-17 American

☎ 773-395-9434; 1920 W Division; mains $6-10; 🕑 lunch; Blue Line to Division

A bright, stylish space for an excellent breakfast or lunch, Milk & Honey has become the hangout *du jour* for discerning Ukrainian Village hipsters. Most of the dishes are prepared from scratch by co-owner Carol Watson (you can't miss with the Mac N Cheese) and the menu also includes a long list of salads.

SMOKE DADDY RHYTHM & BAR-B-QUE Map pp316-17 Barbecue

☎ 773-772-6656; 1804 W Division St; mains $6-16; Blue Line to Division

Top-notch ribs emerge from the huge wood-fired pit here, and the sweet-potato fries on the side win raves. Live blues and jazz acts play on a small stage every night, and the sidewalk seating out front is bustling.

WEST TOWN TAVERN

Map pp316-17 New American

☎ 312-666-6175; 1329 W Chicago Ave; mains $14-20; 🕑 dinner, closed Sun; bus 66

The owners of the West Town Tavern hoped to create a neighborhood restaurant that evoked Chicago in the '40s, and the exposed brick walls and tin ceiling in the handsome dining area do just that. The atmosphere – casual, ebullient and unpretentious – mirrors the cuisine, and the beef, chicken, and pork mains are all crafted with care by the kitchen.

Cheap Eats

ALLIANCE BAKERY Map pp316-17 Bakery

☎ 773-278-0366; 1736 W Division; mains $5-7; Blue Line to Division

Staff members are friendly and the sandwiches awesome at this independent bakery. Best of all, if you get lunch here, a dessert bar item comes with your meal. Just looking for a pick-me-up after a tough day of shopping? The huge double-fudge-chunk walnut brownie should do the trick. In 2005 the bakery doubled its space, opening a large, comfy room next door where café patrons can sit and enjoy their goodies (with free wireless to boot!).

BARI FOODS Map pp316-17 Deli

☎ 312-666-0730; 1120 W Grand Ave; mains $4-7; lunch; Blue Line to Grand

You'll find the best meats Chicago has to offer in this Italian grocery. If you have a car and plan to picnic, drop by Bari and pick up a sub or two (or three – there's always breakfast tomorrow, right?) along with a nice bottle of Italian red.

LETIZIA'S NATURAL BAKERY

Map pp316-17 Bakery

☎ 773-342-1011; 2144 W Division St; mains $4-7; Red Line to Clark/Division

Early risers can get their fix of fantastic baked goods here starting at 6:30am, and everyone else can swing by at a more reasonable hour for their crunchy, toasty *panini* (bread rolls), slices of gourmet pizza and some mind-expanding coffee. Salads are good too.

TECALITLAN Map pp316-17 Mexican

☎ 312-384-4285; 1814 W Chicago Ave; mains $4-12; Blue Line to Chicago

One of the best burritos in the world is here; weighing more than a pound and costing less than $5, the *carne asada* (roast meat) beef burrito with cheese is not just one of the city's best food values, it's one of the city's best foods. Add the optional avocado and you'll have a full day's worth of food groups wrapped in a huge flour tortilla. For a tasty, greasy change, ask to mix the *carne asada* with pork. The *horchata* (a rice-based beverage made with water, sugar, cinnamon, vanilla and lime) is creamy and refreshing.

WEST SIDE & PILSEN

The West Side is vast, and we've narrowed things down by focusing on the three close-in neighborhoods of the West Loop, Greektown, and Little Italy. Of the three, the burgeoning West Loop area's restaurant scene is the most exciting. The West Loop has long been associated with food, thanks to the large number of meatpackers operating here. But it's only been in the last 10 years that the Randolph St corridor running though the center of the area has become a dining destination. Because the cost per square foot has been so low until recently, owners have been able to let their imaginations roam, teaming with interior decorators and architects to produce fantastical spaces. To get to the West Loop, a cab or car is a must, as the closest El stops on the Green and Blue lines are relatively far away from the action.

The areas of Little Italy and Greektown, though less hip than the West Loop, make for a fun night of dining, offering well-honed recipes from Greek and Italian kitchens. Greektown is easily reached on the El, but you'll need a cab or car to get to Little Italy.

Located south of Little Italy, Pilsen could be a side street in Mexico City. Vendors sell ice cream and especially good rice-pudding pops from carts. Others sell corn on the cob that, once bought, is dipped in melted butter and then rolled in spices. The 18th St stop on the CTA Blue Line puts you at the west end of the strip.

TOP FIVE WEST SIDE & PILSEN

- Getting to know the neighbors at **Avec** (below).
- Finding fish tacos with panache at **De Cero** (opposite).
- Celebrity-spotting Oprah at **Wishbone** (p164).
- Watching the families stream in for a postchurch feast at **Nuevo Leon** (p165).
- Savoring a hot tamale and cool *horchata* (a rice-based beverage) at **Taqueria El Milagro** (p166).

WEST LOOP

AVEC Map pp314-15 New American

☎ 312-377-2002; 615 W Randolph; mains $8-18; closed lunch; Green Line to Clinton

Feeling social? This casual cousin to local fave (and neighbor) Blackbird gives diners a chance to rub elbows at eight-person communal tables. Dishes are meant for sharing (though you only have to share with people you know), and the food from chef Koren Grieveson is exceptional.

BLACKBIRD Map pp314-15 New American

☎ 312-715-0708; 619 W Randolph; mains $26-32; closed lunch Sat, closed Sun; Green Line to Clinton

It's all minimalist vibe and maximalist flavor at this noisy, West Loop hot spot, dining central for Chicago's young and wealthy. The menu changes often, but a diner can expect to encounter intriguing juxtapositions of locally raised foods such as quail with apple-fennel puree, or lamb with goat's-milk feta. The wine list is very short, but well chosen.

DE CERO Map pp314-15 Mexican

☎ 312-455-8114; 814 W Randolph; mains $3-17; closed lunch Sat, closed Sun; Green Line to Clinton

This *taquería* offers a high-end, culinary riff on traditional Mexican cuisine, turning out familiar items such as fajitas with homemade tortillas and spicy chorizo tacos, along with novelties like duck nachos. De Cero's drink list includes several dozen tequilas, along with some one-of-a-kind concoctions such as the locally famous raspberry-basil daiquiri.

FAN CI PAN Map pp316-17 Vietnamese

☎ 312-738-1405; 1618 W Chicago Ave; mains $3-6; bus 66

This cute, bright green box with the eye-catching sign has got some cooking muscle behind it: the chef worked in upscale kitchens such as the Four Seasons Restaurant before opening this tiny 'fast-food' joint that specializes in minty, Vietnamese spring rolls, served alone or over noodles. If you're not in the rolling kind of mood, you can also get Vietnamese sandwiches with chicken or ham.

MARCHÉ Map pp314-15 French

☎ 312-226-8399; 833 W Randolph St; mains $12-30; closed lunch Sat & Sun; Green Line to Clinton

This is forward-looking French food in an eye-catching, futuristic setting. Favored by those en route to the United Center, Marché has a wide-ranging menu, the ingredients are top-notch and the service is highly proficient. The chocolate trio for dessert defies a description that won't leave you drooling.

ONESIXTYBLUE Map pp314-15 French

☎ 312-850-0303; 160 N Loomis St; mains $19-30; dinner, closed Sun; Green Line to Ashland

Though Michael Jordan is a co-owner at this sleek fave, you won't find anything remotely sporty about it. High-end French cuisine carried off with a smile has been the trademark of this place since its opening five years ago. The pepper-crusted ahi tuna is a slam dunk, as is the lengthy wine list.

RED LIGHT Map pp314-15 Asian

☎ 312-733-8880; 820 W Randolph St; mains $17-22; closed lunch Sat & Sun; Green Line to Clinton

Red Light serves up fare that isn't anything like the fortune-cookie standard. In fact, mention 'sweet and sour pork' to the waiters and their attitudes might just freeze you right out the door. Roasted duck and rock shrimp are a few of the stars amid the fresh ingredients. Whole Taiwanese crispy catfish has emerged as a signature item. The entire restaurant glows like a lit-up jewel box at night; this is one beautiful space.

THYME Map pp316-17 Fusion

☎ 312-226-4300; 464 N Halsted St; mains $16-31; dinner; Blue Line to Grand

Thyme's chef-owner John Bubala moved just a few blocks north from his former kitchen at the noted Marché and opened up this spot in a neighborhood where you once went to sell your blood. The food is just as inventive as at Marché, with the menu nabbing ideas and influences from around the globe. On weekends you may have to dine early or late to find a table in the heaving dining room. Better yet, hope for a warm summer night and dine in the verdant garden.

GREEKTOWN

PARTHENON Map pp314-15 Greek

☎ 312-726-2407; 314 S Halsted St; mains $8-17; Blue Line to UIC-Halsted

This veteran has anchored Greektown for three decades. The amount of *saghanaki* (sharp, hard cheese cut into wedges or squares and fried) set ablaze here may

Greektown restaurant

be a principal factor in global warming. The yelps of 'Opaa!' as the cheese ignites reverberate off the walls of the small dining area. Greeks returning to the city from their suburban retreats have made this place a favorite. All the usual suspects are present, and the lamb comes in many forms.

SANTORINI Map pp314-15 Greek
☎ **312-829-8820; 800 W Adams St; mains $10-20; Blue Line to UIC-Halsted**
Fish, both shelled and finned, honor the legacies of Greek fishermen at this popular spot, where fresh whole fish is prepared and served in a tableside display. The boisterous room manages to seem cozy, thanks in part to the large Aegean fireplace. Everything, from the bread to the baklava, goes down swimmingly. Portions are huge, which encourages convivial sharing.

Cheap Eats

ARTOPOLIS BAKERY & CAFE

Map pp314-15 Greek
☎ **312-559-9000; 306 S Halsted St; mains $6-14; Blue Line to UIC-Halsted**
Like a good Greek salad, this one has many ingredients: one of the city's top bakeries – many of the nearby Randolph St joints get their bread here – which sells oozing baklava for $1.50; a café-bar that opens on to the street, with tables along the front; and a food bar with classics like spinach pie, which you can eat in or get to go.

LOU MITCHELL'S

Map pp312-13 Breakfast
☎ **312-939-3111; 565 W Jackson Blvd; mains $5-9;** 🕑 **lunch; Blue Line to Clinton**
Immediately west of the Loop and close to Union Station, this great coffee shop draws hordes who line up to eat elbow to elbow. What draws them? Breakfast dishes that are some of the best in town. Whether it's omelettes hanging off the plates, fluffy flapjacks, crisp waffles or anything else on the long menu, you can expect perfect preparation with premium ingredients. Cups of coffee are bottomless, just like the charm of the staff members, who hand out free treats to young and old alike.

TOP FIVE LATE-NITE EATS

Chicago is a town that understands the importance of a midnight snack. You can get a burger at any hour in the wealth of old-school, 24-hour family restaurants like the Golden Spike or Golden Apple. Or try one of the following:

- **Cru Cafe & Wine Bar** (p145) Toasting sandwiches and clinking wine glasses 'til 1am.
- **Handlebar** (p158) Where you can eat and drink 'til midnight weekdays and 2am on weekends.
- **Miller's Pub** (p137) The Loop legend, open 'til 4am.
- **Pick Me Up** (p155) A bohemian Denny's, open to 3am Monday to Friday, and 24 hours Saturday and Sunday.
- **Tempo Cafe** (p147) Serving eggs and such around the clock.

MR GREEK GYROS

Map pp314-15 Greek
☎ **312-906-8731; 234 S Halsted St; mains $4-7;** 🕑 **24hr; Blue Line to UIC-Halsted**
Although there's no sign of Mrs, Ms or Mr Greek, 'the Mr' is a classic gyros joint with good prices. While the fluorescent lighting and plastic decor may be lacking a little in charm, the gyros have a beauty of their own.

WISHBONE Map pp314-15 Southern
☎ **312-850-2663; 1001 W Washington St; mains $5-10;** 🕑 **closed dinner Mon; Green Line to Clinton**
The perfect corn muffins set the tone for a menu featuring spicy classics such as blackened catfish, fried chicken and baked ham. A big choice of sides includes sweet potatoes that should be a lesson to all the cooks who kill these veggies every Thanksgiving. Breakfasts come with hot, fresh buttermilk rolls. Oprah's Harpo studios are just down the street.

LITTLE ITALY

CONTE DI SAVOIA

Map pp314-15 Italian
☎ **312-666-3471; 1438 W Taylor St; mains $4-8; Blue Line to Polk**
This large grocery sells everything an Italian cook could hope for, including scores of imported rarities and fine wines. The deli counter will make visiting Italians feel right

at home and sells various lunch items you can eat at simple tables inside and out.

MARIO'S Map pp314-15 Italian Ice
1068 W Taylor St; drinks $2-4; ⌚ May-Oct; Blue Line to UIC-Halsted
At this cheerfully ticky-tack box-front store, super Italian ice keeps the crowds coming in the months when there's no ice on the streets.

ROSEBUD Map pp314-15 Italian
☎ 312-942-1117; 1500 W Taylor St; mains $14-22; Blue Line to Polk
Rosebud is not only the beginning of a movie but also the beginning of an empire of Italian restaurants in the city. Massive piles of prime pasta, such as lip-shaped *cavatelli* (round, small pasta), come with one of the finest red sauces in town. Have some good red wine and settle in for some people-watching – you're bound to see several folks who regularly turn up in bold type in the local gossip pages.

TUFANO'S VERNON PARK TAP
Map pp314-15 Italian
☎ 312-733-3393; 1073 W Vernon Park Pl; mains $8-14; ⌚ closed lunch Sat & Sun, closed Mon; Blue Line to Polk
Still family-run after three generations (it opened in 1930), Tufano's serves up the kind of old- fashioned Italian food that has become trendy again. Spaghetti and meatballs and other rib-sticking classics are good, filling and cheap. The blackboards carry a long list of daily specials, which can include such wonderful items as pasta with garlic-crusted broccoli. Amid the usual celebrity photos on the wall you'll see some really nice shots of Joey Di Buono and his family and their patrons through the decades.

PILSEN

CAFE JUMPING BEAN
Map pp314-15 Coffeehouse
☎ 312-455-0019; 1439 W 18th St; mains $4-9; Blue Line to 18th St
This ramshackle café will make you feel like a regular as soon as you step through the door. The Jumping Bean serves excellent, hot focaccia sandwiches, baked goods and

Mexican food at Taqueria El Milagro (p166)

strong coffee to the 20- and 30-something crowd of MFA-wielding artists and local bohemians. Chess and domino games are always breaking out here, and the comfy confines of the place make it an excellent spot for whiling away a couple of hours with a mocha, watching life in Pilsen unfold.

NUEVO LEON Map pp314-15 Mexican
☎ 312-421-1517; 1515 W 18th St; mains $7-14; Blue Line to 18th St
This is where the buses come, disgorging dozens of gringo tourists to sample the famed cuisine of Pilsen's most celebrated restaurant. Sounds horrible, right? Wrong. This huge place deserves to be on the bus tours, and the visiting tourists are just a drop in the bucket of local Latino families who crowd in here to dine daily. Superlative versions of tacos, tamales and enchiladas are available, though the dish most likely to blow any meat-eater's taste buds is the *assado de puerco* – tender roast pork served with homemade flour tortillas.

NUEVO LEON PANDERÍA
Map pp314-15 Bakery
☎ 312-243-5977; 1634 W 18th St; cookies $1; Blue Line to 18th St
This Mexican bakery isn't associated with the other famous Nuevo Leon on the block, but the treats here are equally delicious.

TOP FIVE SOUTH LOOP & NEAR SOUTH SIDE

- Sucking down a banana tapioca smoothie at **Joy Yee's Noodle Shop** (opposite).
- Rolling the lazy Susan to get at more shrimp dumplings at **Shui Wah** (opposite).
- Singing the praises of the Chinese food at **Opera** (right).
- Savoring blistered-crust pizza in the sunken dining room at **Gioco** (right).
- Keeping an eye out for da mayor at da **Chicago Firehouse** (right).

When you walk in, pick up a silver tray, and tong up cinnamon-encrusted buns, fruit-filled empanadas or Mexican sweet-bread, and then take the tray to the counter, where they'll tally your total.

TAQUERIA EL MILAGRO

Map pp314-15 Mexican

☎ 312-433-7620; 1923 S Blue Island Ave; mains $4-7; Blue Line to 18th St

Known for cooking up Pilsen's best steak tacos, Taqueria El Milagro also excels in the tamale corn tortilla arts. BYOB.

SOUTH LOOP & NEAR SOUTH SIDE

As with the neighborhood itself, the restaurant scene in the South Loop and Near South Side is a work in progress. With the dozens of luxury town houses and condo projects that have been built here in the last two years, it seems only a matter of time before this area is filled with hot new eateries. How long it will take for them to come, however, is anybody's guess. For now, a few popular pioneers have set up shop along Wabash and Michigan Aves.

The plodding pace of the restaurant scene in the South Loop and Near South Side would do well to take a page from Chinatown's book, where there seem to be more restaurants than storefronts. From the Red Line Cermak-Chinatown stop, it's an easy walk to dim sum, noodles or a refreshing tapioca bubble tea, all of it so affordable that Chinatown has become the cheap-eats destination for the South Loop and Near South Side.

CHICAGO FIREHOUSE

Map pp312-13 American

☎ 312-786-1401; 1401 S Michigan Ave; mains $10-25; closed lunch Sat & Sun; Red Line to Roosevelt

An old firehouse that's been beautifully restored, this place offers the kind of traditional tasty fare that would light up the face of any firefighter, albeit at prices that might force the firefighter to take a second job. Ribs and steaks headline the show here, although they're pushed out of the spotlight when local resident Mayor Richard M Daley stops by.

GIOCO Map pp312-13 Italian

☎ 312-939-3870; 1312 S Wabash Ave; mains $13-34; closed lunch Sat & Sun; Red Line to Roosevelt

Restaurateurs Jerry Kleiner and Howard Davis made Randolph St on the West Side one of Chicago's hottest dining areas in the 1990s. Now they've opened a whimsical Italian restaurant in a desolate stretch of the Near South Side that hasn't seen this much action since the 1930s, when almost every building was a speakeasy (including, they'd contend, the home of Gioco).
A menu laden with classic Chicago-Italian dishes includes delicate pizzas from a wood-burning oven. Surprises abound, such as the tasty lobster gnocchi.

OPERA Map pp312-13 Chinese

☎ 312-461-0161; 1301 S Wabash Ave; mains $14-25; closed lunch; Red Line to Roosevelt

Owned by the same folks behind Gioco, this upmarket Chinese restaurant is easy on the eyes, exuding a quirky, cinematic pan-Asian ambience (heightened by the intimate 'vault' seating constructed from old film-reel vaults). You'll find familiar dishes on the menu – Peking duck, kung pao beef, general's chicken, etc – remade with boutique meats, sharp spices, and a light touch.

Cheap Eats

EDWARDO'S Map pp312-13 Pizza

☎ 312-939-3366; 521 S Dearborn St; mains $6-18; Red Line to Harrison

Edwardo's, a Chicago-based chain, serves justifiably famous stuffed spinach pizza, as well as some thin-crust models, sandwiches and salads. Everything here is fresh and cheap.

JOY YEE'S NOODLE SHOP

Map pp312-13 Asian

☎ **312-328-0001; 2159 S China Pl (in Chinatown Sq Mall); mains $6-12; Red Line to Cermak-Chinatown**

You'd think Joy Yee was giving its ice-cold homemade fruit drinks and tapioca bubble teas away for free, from the way customers throng this bright restaurant far into the night. Along with the mobbed takeaway drink window, the regular seating area is also packed with diners waiting for their chance to enjoy the big, slurpable bowls of noodles such as *udon* (a thick, wheat-based noodle), *chow fun* (rice noodles) and chow mein. The techno music playing on the stereo is a clear sign that this is not your grandmother's favorite Chinese restaurant.

PHOENIX

Map pp312-13 Chinese

☎ **312-328-0848; 2131 S Archer Ave; mains $7-16; Red Line to Cermak-Chinatown**

This popular spot rises above the old veterans of Chinatown with excellent, fresh food prepared by chefs who are direct from Hong Kong. Midday sees an endless parade of dim sum issuing forth on trolleys from the kitchen. On Sunday the parade is lengthier yet. If you are not coming for the dim sum, you should head elsewhere; the rest of the menu tends toward the bland.

SHUI WAH

Map pp312-13 Chinese

☎ **312-225-8811; 2162 S Archer Ave; mains $3-5; Red Line to Cermak-Chinatown**

It's hard to order a bad dish at Shui Wah, Chicago's best quickie dim-sum joint. Diners tally their choices with a pencil, hand off their picks to the harried waitstaff, and then sit back and wait for the bounty of delicious shrimp dumplings, pan-fried turnip cakes, and sticky rice in lotus leaf to arrive. If, by some miracle of restraint, you're not full after your trip to Shi Wah, you can wander across the minimall's courtyard for a refreshing fruit smoothie at **Joy Yee's Noodle Shop** (above).

SOUTH CHICAGO

Though the South Chicago neighborhoods of Bronzeville, Hyde Park and Kenwood aren't dining destinations in their own right, they do provide their residents with some excellent food. Home of the University of Chicago, Hyde Park, especially, has some great eats in a college-town atmosphere. The people at the table next to yours may well be debating whether a butterfly flapping its wings in Indonesia really is responsible for global warming. To get to Hyde Park, it's best to have a car, but you can also hop on the Metra train from the Loop Randolph station.

The other attraction on Chicago's South Side is soul food, with fried chicken, catfish and juicy collard greens. The soul food places listed below, while not requiring a sizable withdrawal from the bank to pay the bill, will require a car.

ARMY & LOU'S

Map pp302-3 Soul Food

☎ **773-483-3100; 422 E 75th St, near Martin Luther King Dr; mains $6-15; 🕓 closed Tue; bus 75**

If you've never had soul food, start at this warm and welcoming Chicago classic. It rises above the crowd of similar local establishments, many of which are little more than storefronts serving takeout buckets of wings, rib tips and macaroni and cheese. Here you can order fried chicken, catfish, collard greens, sweet-potato pie and all the other classics at prices that are good for your soul. Don't be surprised if you see a few famous Black politicians, led by Jesse Jackson. And don't be surprised if some White politician shows up for a photo op.

CAFFÈ FLORIAN

Map pp320-1 American

☎ **773-752-4100; 1450 E 57th St; mains $6-11; Metra to 59th St**

The menu here traces its heritage back to the original Caffè Florian, which opened in Venice in 1720 and became a meeting place for 'the intelligentsia, with patrons including the most celebrated artists, poets, dramatists, actors, musicians and philosophers of the time,' according to the menu here. The humbler modern version serves lesser mortals, and much of the fare (black-bean nachos, fish and chips) has never graced a tabletop in Venice. But a few Italian items do make the menu, which covers much of the world.

MEDICI

Map pp320-1 American

☎ **773-667-7394; 1327 E 57th St; mains $6-14; Metra to 59th St**

The world's woes have been solved several times over at Medici, chiefly in the form of thin-crust pizza, sandwiches and salads. Burgers come in myriad choices, with optional toppings, and vegetarians can seek refuge in the veggie sandwich. For breakfast, try the 'eggs espresso,' made by steaming eggs in an espresso machine. After your meal, check the vast bulletin board out front. It's the perfect place to size up the character of the community and possibly find the complete works of John Maynard Keynes for sale, cheap. A Medici-run bakery next door serves fresh-baked bread products.

Drinking

Drinking

In the Chicago bar scene, variety is the spice of life. From dive bars where the jukeboxes still drop needles on old Dean Martin 45s, to satellite-TV filled sportaholic havens that resemble a NASA control center, the choice of watering holes facing Windy City natives is staggering. It's no wonder Chicagoans spend so much time drinking; they have to try a lot of places before finding the perfect one.

Though it's hard to imagine, the numbers of bars are actually on the decline in Chicago as a result of a recent citywide tightening in the issuance of new liquor licenses. Still, the sheer variety of bars in the city can make choosing the night's destination a little daunting for visitors. The good news is that once you find your favorite spot, you'll have plenty of time to settle in; Chicago bars are open late on weekends, some until 4am.

Chicagoans tend to drink close to home, but there are a few 'destination strips,' bar-rich streets where taxis are constantly headed to deliver more partying patrons. The Damen Ave corridor of Wicker Park and Bucktown is a bar-hopper's Eden, and Lincoln Ave and Halsted St in Lincoln Park are similarly mobbed with hordes of drinkers. The Boystown area in Lake View is the epicenter of gay nightlife in the city.

In this section, we've only included bars where hanging out is the main attraction. A few listed below may have live music or DJs on the weekends, but the music tends to take a back seat to the sounds of toasts and conversation. If you're looking for the city's best dancefloors or stages, head to the Entertainment chapter (p180).

THE LOOP & NEAR NORTH

The bars in the Loop tend to be attached to hotels (and equally attached to charging $5 for a bottle of Budweiser). Near North is much more interesting, with a selection split between old-school pubs and trendy new places selling New York–style glamour.

BERGHOFF STAND UP BAR Map pp304-5

☎ 312-427-3170; 17 W Adams St; ⏲ 11am-9pm Mon-Thu, to 9:30pm Fri, 11:30-10pm Sat; Blue Line to Jackson

Adjoining the restaurant, this bar has changed little in a century, although women have been admitted for the past 40 years.

BREHON PUB Map pp306-7

☎ 312-642-1071; 731 N Wells St; ⏲ 11am-2am Mon-Fri, noon-3am Sat, noon-2am Sun; Brown Line to Chicago

Forget the gimmicks found in neighboring blocks and experience the real Chicago at this fine example of the corner saloons that once dotted the city. The Brehon purveys 12 kinds of draft beer in frosted glasses to neighborhood crowds perched on the high stools.

CAL'S BAR Map pp304-5

☎ 312-922-6392; 400 S Wells St; ⏲ 7am-8pm Sun-Wed, to 2am Thu-Sat; Blue Line to LaSalle

This legendary dive is a drunken home away from home for the city's bike messengers during the day. On weekend nights, punk-rock bands with names like Lil' Isaac & the Dirty Stank and Johnny Vomit take the stage.

CELTIC CROSSING Map pp306-7

☎ 312-337-1005; 751 N Clark St; ⏲ 2pm-2am Sun-Fri, to 3am Sat; Red Line to Chicago

The fireplace is imported from Ireland – as are the owners and staff – at this comfy Irish pub. Best of all, the pints of Guinness come in *imperial* pints. That's a little over 3oz more!

CLARK STREET ALE HOUSE Map pp306-7

☎ 312-642-9253; 742 N Clark St; ⏲ 4pm-4am Mon-Thu, to 5am Fri & Sat, to 2am Sun; Red Line to Chicago

Come here for the Loop's best beer selection, which includes a rotating selection of tap beer from some of the best Midwestern microbreweries. Work up a thirst on the free pretzels and cool off in the beer garden out back.

TOP FIVE CHICAGO BAR MOMENTS

- Watching weird videos by Chicago artists at the sleek **Rodin** (p177).
- Luxuriating with a glass of bubbly at **Pops for Champagne** (p174).
- Slurping mussels and downing Belgian beer at the **Hop Leaf** (p175).
- Kicking back to the jazz on the jukebox at the eternal **Olde Town Ale House** (p172).
- Winning big-time romantic points for bringing a date to the **Signature Lounge at the 95th** (p79).

ESPNZONE Map pp306-7
☎ 312-644-3776; 43 E Ohio St; 🕐 11am-midnight Sun-Thu, to 1am Fri & Sat; Red Line to Grand
A fantasyland for men whose fantasies consist of watching 20 sports games at once on huge TVs, this bombastic bar features a 'screening room' with a 16ft screen and 'skybox'-style seating.

GREEN DOOR TAVERN Map pp306-7
☎ 312-664-5496; 678 N Orleans St; 🕐 11am-11pm Mon & Tue, to midnight Wed & Thu, to 1am Fri & Sat, closed Sun; Brown Line to Chicago
See the review (p140) in the Eating chapter for details on this old-timey bar.

NARCISSE Map pp306-7
☎ 312-787-2675; www.narcisse.us; 710 N Clark St; 🕐 5pm-2am Mon-Fri, to 3am Sat, 7pm-2am Sun; Red Line to Chicago
It's no jeans, no hats and no athletic apparel at this sumptuous, extravagant spot, one of Chicago's most beautifully lush lounges. Order caviar and sip champagne in gilded splendor while watching the beautiful people orbit around you.

GOLD COAST

The 40-and-over set has a great time in these Gold Coast bars.

GIBSON'S Map pp308-9
☎ 312-266-8999; 1028 N Rush St; 🕐 11am-1am; Red Line to Clark/Division
Gibson martinis (served with a cocktail onion) are the namesake speciality at this lively bar attached to Gibson's steak house. See the review (p145) in the Eating chapter for details. A piano player begins tickling the ivories at 5pm.

LODGE Map pp308-9
☎ 312-642-4406; 21 W Division St; 🕐 5pm-4am Sun-Fri, to 5am Sat; Red Line to Clark/Division
One of those bars that you tend to end up in by accident, only to have the time of

Berghoff Stand Up Bar (opposite)

your life. A Wurlitzer jukebox plays oldies, and the peanuts are free. The crowd of mostly 40-somethings will drink until dawn.

LINCOLN PARK & OLD TOWN

The blood-alcohol levels run pretty high in Lincoln Park's bars, where hard-drinking yuppies who used to socialize over fraternity kegs are now sucking down microbrews and Cosmopolitans and flirting with each other over a Coldplay soundtrack. The bars around DePaul University further heighten the party-hearty feel of the place, serving as beer-soaked launching pads for plenty of awkward conversations the following morning. In Old Town, you'll find the pace is slower and quirkier.

DEJA VU Map pp308-9

☎ 773-871-0205; 2624 N Lincoln Ave; 9pm-4am Sun-Fri, to 5am Sat; Brown, Red Line to Fullerton

Open until 5am (!) on Saturdays, Deja offers more than just an incredibly late last call. This friendly place has a decor that is a mix of opulent Middle Eastern and garage sale art deco. Music is served up live and on record, and the pool is free. Thursday to Saturday, the cover ranges from $4 to $5.

DELILAH'S Map pp308-9

☎ 773-472-2771; 2771 N Lincoln Ave; 4pm-2am Sun-Fri, to 3am Sat; Brown Line to Diversey

From the free artsy movies screened on Saturdays to the non-DJ DJs spinning anything-goes selections from their personal record collections, Delilah's is a happy meeting place for the area's underground rocker scene. Bohemian sophisticates can choose from a bunch of high-end single-malts or opt for a $2 beer.

GIN MILL Map pp308-9

☎ 773-549-3232; 2462 N Lincoln Ave; 4pm-2am Mon-Fri, 11am-3am Sat, to midnight Sun; Brown, Red Line to Fullerton

The slogan here is 'We drink our share and sell the rest.' They're very friendly about it, too, with remarkable $2/pint specials on microbrews some nights. The owners and staff are all fanatical about the Michigan State athletic teams, so watch what you say about the Spartans.

GOOSE ISLAND BREWERY Map pp308-9

☎ 773-915-0071; 1800 N Clybourn Ave; 11am-1am Mon-Fri, to 2am Sat, to midnight Sun; Red Line to North/Clybourn

Chicago's brewpub features the locally made Goose Island beers, including the hoppy Honker's Ale and potent XXX Porter. More sporty than beer-snob tweedy, the brewery has several TVs and gets packed with fans for Bulls and Cubs games. The outdoor area is a must in summer.

KELLY'S Map pp308-9

☎ 773-281-0656; 949 W Webster Ave; 11am-2am Sun-Fri, 11am-3am Sat; Brown, Red Line to Fullerton

DePaul students and fans gather at this classic Chicago bar right under the El – hold onto your glass when a train goes by. Since 1933 – they opened the day after Prohibition ended – the same family has been welcoming all comers with tasty burgers and booze.

LUCILLE'S Map pp308-9

☎ 773-929-0660; 2470 N Lincoln Ave; 5pm-2am; Brown, Red Line to Fullerton

Instead of stale pretzels and day-old popcorn, how do munchies like bruschetta and prosciutto sound? Lucille's is a rarity – a bar where both the food and the atmosphere are top-notch. The alcoholic offerings include an excellent selection of wines by the glass and a bewildering number of martinis.

MOTEL BAR Map pp308-9

☎ 312-822-2900; 600 W Chicago Ave; 2:30pm-2am Mon-Fri, noon-3am Sat, to 2am Sun; bus 66

This chic ode to '60s motel bars (think orange, lime green and chrome) has enough modern industrial touches to keep it from feeling kitschy, and the $8 drinks are strong enough to make you not feel much of anything after awhile.

OLDE TOWN ALE HOUSE Map pp308-9

☎ 312-944-7020; 219 W North Ave; noon-4am Sun-Fri, noon-5am Sat; Brown Line to Sedgwick

A wonderful Old Town neighborhood staple from the days before this was a neighborhood, this bar has been the scene

GAME ON

The weather is miserable, and you're looking for something active to do. Preferably something active you can do with a beer in your hand, while seated in a comfy chair. And you're in luck. Chicago bars provide a range of leisure pursuits in the sporting *and* intellectual realms. Pool tables? Of course. Darts? Check. Cult golfing video game Golden Tee? All over the place. But that's just the tip of the gaming iceberg.

The city's great board-game mecca is the **Blue Frog Bar & Grill** (Map pp312-13; ☎ 312-943-8900; 676 S LaSalle St; 🕑 11:30am-2am Mon-Thu, from noon Fri, 6pm-3am Sat, closed Sun; Blue Line to LaSalle). This haven for retro games resounds with the shouts of players winning and losing at Operation, Sorry and a host of other oldies-but-goodies. Pub quiz contestants will want to make their way to **Ginger's Ale House** (Map pp318-19; ☎ 773-348-2767; 3801 N Ashland Ave; 🕑 11am-2am Mon-Fri, from 10am Sat & Sun; Brown Line to Southport) on Sunday nights. Part of your $5 entry fee goes to cancer charities. European soccer and rugby fanatics will want to hang around to get caught up on their matches; sometimes the bar opens at 6am to show games live via satellite. If you like trivia but want to limit your field of competition, Guthrie's (p174) has a box of Trivial Pursuit cards on most tables for more casual quizzing.

For darts, try Ginger's Ale House, above, or **Mullen's on Clark** (Map pp318-19; ☎ 773-325-2319; 3527 N Clark St; 🕑 5pm-2am Sun-Thu, from 4pm Fri, from 11am Sat; Red Line to Addison). Mullen's is also a great place for foosball warriors to give the little men a spin. Pool sharks can test their mettle against local competitors on the two gorgeous, lovingly restored tables at the Ten Cat Tavern (p175), or ride the felt at one of the six tables at Southport Lanes (p174).

of late-night musings since the 1960s – the last time paint was applied. Come by and grab a book from the lending library, drop some quarters in the old-school jazz jukebox and settle in for a few hours of atmospheric merriment.

RED LION PUB Map pp308-9

☎ 773-348-2695; 2446 N Lincoln Ave; 🕑 noon-11pm Mon-Thu, to midnight Fri & Sat, to 10pm Sun; Brown, Red Line to Fullerton

A British-style pub run by real Brits, this cozy spot features plenty of UK brews and the best onion rings in the city ($4). The Red Lion also hosts regular author talks and readings.

RED ROOSTER CAFE & WINE BAR Map pp308-9

☎ 773-871-2100; 2100 N Halsted St; 🕑 5-10:30pm Mon-Thu, to 11:30pm Fri & Sat, to 10pm Sun; Brown, Red Line to Armitage

Connected to Cafe Bernard, this funky little wine bar makes a great stop before or after meals or the theater. Choose from oodles of wines by the glass.

STERCH'S Map pp308-9

☎ 773-281-2653; 2238 N Lincoln Ave; 🕑 3:30pm-2am Sun-Fri, to 3am Sat; Brown, Red Line to Fullerton

A genial older crowd of writers and would-be poets hangs out at this convivial bar. There's never a shortage of conversation.

WEED'S Map pp308-9

☎ 312-943-7815; 1555 N Dayton St; 🕑 4pm-2am Mon-Sat; Red Line to North/Clybourn

The bras hanging from the ceiling like animal pelts set the tone at this bar where beatnik meets bohemia. Weed's is a bar with a thousand strange stories, most of them courtesy of dada-esque owner Sergio Mayora – whose name has motivated him to run most unsuccessfully for mayor. Spirits stay loose through frequent shots of tequila on the house.

LAKE VIEW

Lake View's bars mirror the distinct neighborhoods it comprises. Wrigleyville, near Wrigley Field, swarms with sports bars, which are mobbed before and after Cubs games. To the west, the Southport corridor between Addison St and Irving Park Rd is booming with new places targeted at the over-25 set. And in Boystown, north of Broadway along Halsted, you'll find Chicago's bustling gay nightlife scene.

CLOSET Map pp318-19

☎ 773-477-8533; 3325 N Broadway St; 🕑 2pm-4am Mon-Fri, noon-5am Sat, to 4am Sun; Brown, Red Line to Belmont

One of the very few lesbian-centric bars in Chicago, the Closet changes mood and tempo at 2am, when the crowd becomes more mixed, the music gets louder and things get a little rowdier.

CULLEN'S Map pp318-19
☎ 773-975-0600; 3741 N Southport Ave; 🕑 11am-1:30am Mon-Fri, 9pm-2:30am Sat & Sun; bus 152
Cullen's fine tavern is connected to the Mercury Theatre, and is an easy walk to the Music Box movie theater. See the review (p152) in the Eating chapter for the details.

DUKE OF PERTH Map pp318-19
☎ 773-477-1741; 2913 N Clark St; 🕑 5:30pm-2am Mon, 11:30am-2am Tue-Fri, to 3am Sat, noon-2am Sun; bus 22
This excellent pub and beer garden boasts almost 80 kinds of single-malt scotch. See the review (p152) in the Eating chapter for all the details.

GENTRY Map pp318-19
☎ 773-348-1053; 3320 N Halsted St; 🕑 4pm-2am Sun-Fri, to 3am Sat; Brown, Red Line to Belmont
This stately piano bar serves as a welcome respite for 30- and 40-year-old gay men tired of the pounding house beats of Boystown's clubs. Live cabaret music nightly.

GINGER MAN Map pp318-19
☎ 773-549-2050; 3740 N Clark St; 🕑 3pm-2am Mon-Fri, noon-3am Sat, to 2am Sun; Brown, Red Line to Diversey
A splendid place to pass an evening, this spot features a huge and eclectic beer selection that's enjoyed by theater types and other creative folks. The G-Man, as it is often called, avoids the overamped Cubs mania of the rest of the strip by playing classical music when the Cubs play at home. There are numerous pool tables in back, and pool is free on Sunday.

TOP FIVE BOOZING BLOCKS

- Rowdy nightowls: **Clark Street** in Lake View (p173).
- Thirty-something hipsters: **Division Street** in Ukrainian Village (p176).
- Collegiate beer-chuggers: **Lincoln Avenue** in Lincoln Park (p172).
- Patio-loving boozehounds: **Damen Avenue** in Bucktown (p176).
- Pangenre bar-hoppers: **Milwaukee Avenue** in Wicker Park (p176).

GUTHRIE'S Map pp318-19
☎ 773-477-2900; 1300 W Addison St; 🕑 4pm-2am; Red Line to Addison
A local institution and the perfect neighborhood hangout, Guthrie's remains true to its mellow roots even as the neighborhood goes manic around it. The glassed-in back porch is fittingly furnished with patio chairs and filled with 30- and 40-somethings. Most tables sport a box of Trivial Pursuit cards.

HUNGRY BRAIN Map pp318-19
☎ 773-935-2118; 2319 W Belmont Ave; 🕑 7pm-4am Sun-Fri, to 5am Sat; bus 77
Sunday nights here are given over to live free jazz, but on other nights the eclectic jukebox reigns supreme. Bartenders are kind and the place has a shambling, well-worn charm.

POPS FOR CHAMPAGNE Map pp318-19
☎ 773-472-1000; 2934 N Sheffield Ave; 🕑 5pm-2am; Brown, Red Line to Wellington
This refined and classy place makes a perfect spot for a post-theater drink, a celebratory toast or a romantic tête-à-tête. You can choose among 12 champagnes by the glass, 140 more by the bottle and scores of excellent wines as well. The snacks are suitably chichi – pâté and the like – and Pops features live jazz nightly (cover averages $10).

ROSCOE'S Map pp318-19
☎ 773-281-3355; 3354 N Halsted St; 🕑 3pm-2am Mon-Thu, from 2pm Fri, 1pm-3am Sat, to 2am Sun; Brown, Red Line to Belmont
Affectionately called 'the gay Bennigan's' (the comfortable but generic restaurant) by some of its 20- and 30-something patrons, Roscoe's has a friendly atmosphere, great menu and inviting beer garden.

SOUTHPORT LANES Map pp318-19
☎ 773-472-6600; 3325 N Southport Ave; 🕑 4pm-1am Mon-Fri, noon-2am Sat, to 1am Sun; Brown Line to Southport
This old-fashioned local bar with a good beer selection has undergone a renaissance under the thoughtful management of some upscale types who oversee the bar itself and an annex with four hand-set bowling lanes. The main bar features an inspirational old

mural of cavorting nymphs. Lots of tables populate the sidewalk in summer.

TEN CAT TAVERN Map pp318-19

☎ 773-935-5377; 3931 N Ashland Ave; 3pm-2am Sun-Fri, to 3am Sat; bus 9

Pool is serious business at the funky Ten Cat – play takes place on two vintage tables that co-owner Richard Vonachen refelts regularly with material from Belgium. The ever-changing, eye-catching art comes courtesy of neighborhood artists, and the furniture is a garage-saler's dream. Regulars (most in their 30s) down leisurely drinks at the bar or, in warm weather, swap pool tales out in the beer garden.

TINY LOUNGE Map pp318-19

☎ 773-296-9620; 1814 W Addison St; 5pm-2am Mon-Fri, to 3am Sat, 7pm-2am Sun; Brown Line to Addison

They aren't kidding about the name. With room to accommodate about 35 in cozy, dark-wooded splendor, this favorite can get a little crowded. The mood is very laid-back and the cocktails (try the Cocotini, a drink made with vodka and Hershey's and Godiva chocolate) are great and well priced.

UNDERGROUND LOUNGE Map pp318-19

☎ 773-327-2739; 952 W Newport Ave; 8pm-2am Sun-Fri, to 3am Sat; Red Line to Addison

This dark, small space was once a speak-easy, and the noir feel of that era remains. Jazz bands sometimes play here, but most nights are cover-free.

ANDERSONVILLE & UPTOWN

Andersonville and Uptown have a handful of character-rich, laid-back drinking options. The area is also a sort of 'Boystown North,' offering a couple of solid gay-bar choices.

BIG CHICKS Map p311

☎ 773-728-5511; 5024 N Sheridan Rd; 4pm-2am Mon-Fri, to 3am Sat, 3pm-2am Sun; Red Line to Argyle

Uptown's Big Chicks has one of the city's most enjoyable bipolar disorders. During the week, the bar is cozily sedate, a place where gay and straight gather to socialize beneath the sizable collection of woman-themed art. On weekends, though, gay men pack the stamp-sized dance floor to boogie until 3am. Then, every Sunday at 4pm, Big Chicks hosts its legendary free brunch.

HOP LEAF Map p311

☎ 773-334-9851; 5148 N Clark St; 2pm-2am Mon-Fri, 11am-3am Sat, to 2am Sun; Red Line to Berwyn

Owner Michael Roper, using the name of the national beer from his ancestral Malta, has created one of Andersonville's best bars. Highlights at the Hop Leaf include an intricate original tin ceiling and a jukebox playing classic country and jazz cuts. The beers are artfully selected by Roper, with an emphasis on Belgian and American brews. In 2003 the Hop Leaf opened a kitchen and now serves Belgian *frites* and mussels.

SIMON'S Map p311

☎ 773-878-0894; 5210 N Clark St; 11am-2am; Red Line to Berwyn

One of Andersonville's few 20-something hangouts, this nautical-themed bar has Clap Your Hands Say Yeah playing on the stereo, and a long bar right out of the '50s. The mural on the wall is of the original owner Simon Lundberg and his friends. Lundberg's son now lovingly runs the place.

WICKER PARK, BUCKTOWN & UKRAINIAN VILLAGE

Take the Blue Line to Damen prepared to party. Wicker Park and Bucktown are both open late, and are perfectly set up for a night's worth of bar-hopping. Ukrainian Village, however, is a little rougher and more spread out – cabbing is a good idea in this neighborhood.

CHARLESTON Map pp316-17

☎ 773-489-4757; 2076 N Hoyne Ave; 3pm-2am Mon-Sat, from noon Sun; bus 50

The resident cats will curl up on your lap at this laid-back Bucktown hangout. Occasional live folk music jibes with the older crowd.

CLUB FOOT Map pp316-17

☎ 773-489-0379; 1824 W Augusta Blvd; 8pm-2am Sun-Fri, to 3am Sat; Blue Line to Damen

This fun bar's cheap drink specials aren't the only sight for sore eyes: the walls at the Club Foot are absolutely packed with three decades of musical and pop cultural ephemera. The crowd varies with the eclectic DJ nights – rockabilly one night, '80s the next.

DANNY'S Map pp316-17

☎ 773-489-6457; 1951 W Dickens Ave; 7pm-2am Sun-Fri, to 3am Sat; bus 50

Little Danny's has become one of the coolest bars in Chicago for the hipster set. DJs lug in everything from old soul 45s to members of Tortoise to add to the mood, and the crowd is friendly and way into it. Blessedly TV-free, Danny's is a great place to come for conversation in the early hours of the evening.

GOLD STAR BAR Map pp316-17

☎ 773-227-8700; 1755 W Division St; 4pm-2am Sun-Fri, to 3am Sat; Blue Line to Division

This friendly dive is where Irvine Welsh hangs out when he's in Chicago teaching. Join Irvine and the bike-messenger set for some cheap drinks and a great jukebox selection.

LEMMINGS Map pp316-17

☎ 773-862-1688; 1850 N Damen Ave; 9pm-4am Mon-Fri, 2pm-3am Sat, noon-2am Sun; bus 50

This mellow bar features a pool table, good beers on tap and a sign in the window telling neighborhood artists how they can get their work displayed in the bar. Lemmings also has one of Chicago's best collections of vintage Schlitz signs – a visual tribute to the glory days of crappy beer.

TOP FIVE COFFEE SHOPS

With Starbucks and Caribou catering to the grab-and-go crowds, Chicago's independent coffeehouses have staked out a more leisurely niche. Most offer a limited menu of tasty food and the type of convivial atmosphere that makes it easy to strike up conversations with the barista or fellow patrons. Many also function as neighborhood community centers, giving locals a place to post flyers about upcoming garage sales or concerts and lost pets. If you want to pick up a gift for a coffee fiend back home, consider picking up a pound of locally roasted beans from any of the Intelligentsia cafés (see below).

- **Bourgeois Pig** (Map pp308-9; ☎ 773-883-5282; 738 W Fullerton Pkwy; 6:30am-11pm Mon-Fri, 8am-11pm Sat & Sun) Plentiful teas, strong coffee, and a nice front patio for Lincoln Park people-watching.
- **Earwax** (Map pp316-17; ☎ 773-772-4019; 1561 N Milwaukee Ave; 9am-11pm Mon-Thu, 8am-midnight Fri-Sun) A freakshow-themed coffee shop and restaurant where neighborhood artists congregate for coffee and vegetarian food.
- **Filter** (Map pp316-17; ☎ 773-227-4850; 1585 N Milwaukee Ave; 7am-midnight Mon-Fri, 8am-midnight Sat, to 10pm Sun) Open late, with plenty of food options, this huge café has zero atmosphere but is a great place to bring your laptop and work all day.
- **Intelligentsia Coffee** (Map pp318-19; ☎ 773-348-8058; 3123 N Broadway St; 6am-10pm Mon-Thu, to 11pm Fri, 7am-11pm Sat, to 10pm Sun) Study, gab or work all day in this cozy Lake View outpost of Chicago's hometown coffee roaster.
- **Uncommon Ground** (Map pp318-19; ☎ 773-929-3680; 1214 W Grace St; 9am-2am) The nonsmoking casual fave in Wrigleyville is great for socializing and also has live acoustic music at night.

WORTH A TRIP

Chicago has a bunch of worthwhile watering holes located well off the well-trod drinking path. This is especially true on Chicago's West and South Sides. Here are some of the standouts:

Hawkeye's (Map pp314-15; ☎ 312-226-3951; 1458 W Taylor St; ⏲ 11am-2am Sun-Fri, to 3am Sat; Blue Line to Polk) This Little Italy institution runs a free shuttle from the United Center to its doorstep when the Bulls or Blackhawks are playing, making it a good place to come to celebrate a victory or agonize over a defeat. Its virtues include a good burger-based menu and fine seasonal tables outside.

Jimmy's Woodlawn Tap (Map pp320-1; ☎ 773-643-5516; 1172 E 55th St; ⏲ 10:30am-2am Mon-Fri, to 3am Sat, 11am-2am Sun; Metra to 55th St) Some of the geniuses of our age have killed some brain cells right here in one of Hyde Park's few worthwhile bars. The place is dark and beery, and a little seedy. But for thousands of University of Chicago students deprived of a thriving bar scene, it's home. Hungry? The Swissburgers are legendary.

Puffer's (Map pp302-3; ☎ 773-927-6073; 3356 S Halsted St; ⏲ 9pm-4am Sun-Fri, to 5am Sat; Red Line to Sox-35th) A cool pub in staid old Bridgeport, Puffer's boasts a bright orange facade and the neighborhood's most amiable clientele, with folks hanging out, talking and sampling from the excellent beer selection. A good choice after a Sox game, it's a 15-minute walk west from Comiskey Park, er, US Cellular Field.

MAP ROOM Map pp316-17

☎ 773-252-7636; 1949 N Hoyne Ave; ⏲ 6:30am-2am Mon-Fri, 7am-3am Sat, 11am-2am Sun; Blue Line to Damen

Drink locally and think globally at this friendly corner café-bar where globes line the walls and a huge map of the world covers the back wall and ceiling. The Map Room features lots of local brews and games for whiling away cold winter days. The volume on the free live music on weekends is kept to a minimum, so your conversations can be kept to a maximum. A great find.

NICK'S Map pp316-17

☎ 312-252-1155; 1516 N Milwaukee Ave; ⏲ 4pm-4am Sun-Fri, to 5am Sat; Blue Line to Damen

This big joint has a friendly, fraternity vibe and a good collection of beers from around the world. Weather warm? Hit the beer garden in back.

QUENCHERS Map pp316-17

☎ 773-276-9730; W Fullerton Ave; ⏲ 11am-2am Mon-Sat, noon-1am Sun; bus 74

At the north end of Bucktown, Quenchers is one of Chicago's most interesting bars. With over 200 beers from more than 40 nations, it offers ample opportunities to find that certain something missing from the swill peddled by the US brewery giants: flavor. Locals, artisans, laborers and visiting brew masters enjoy Earle Miller's hospitality. The prices are the cheapest in town. Live music can get a little loud, though.

RAINBO CLUB Map pp316-17

☎ 773-489-5999; 1150 N Damen Ave; ⏲ 4pm-2am Sun-Fri, to 3am Sat; Blue Line to Damen

Ground zero for the city's indie elite during the week, the boxy, dark-wood Rainbo Club has an impressive semicircular bar and one of the city's best photo booths. The service is slow and the place goes a little suburban on weekends, but it's otherwise an excellent place to meet local artists and musicians.

RODIN Map pp316-17

☎ 773-276-7036; 1530 N Milwaukee Ave; ⏲ 6pm-2am Mon-Thu, 5pm-3am Fri & Sat, to 2am Sun; Blue Line to Damen

This sleek, cinematic hipster spot for 30-somethings slides from restaurant mode to bar mode around 10pm. Arty videos courtesy of Chicago artists are projected on the back wall, and the space often hosts interesting live collaborations between electronic composers and video artists.

SONOTHEQUE Map pp316-17

☎ 312-226-7600; 1444 W Chicago Ave; ⏲ 8pm-2am Wed-Fri, to 3am Sat; Blue Line to Chicago

The DJs here spin genres of electronica so hip they don't even have names yet, a perfect complement to the sleek, next-century space. This kind of bar would be a snooty disaster in New York, but absolutely down-to-earth patrons and reasonable drink prices make it feel like your corner pub.

SOUTH LOOP & WEST SIDE

The South Loop bar scene mirrors the restaurant scene – meager, despite the recent influx of new residents. There is the occasional neighborhood joint worth checking out, however. Bars west of the Loop tend to be scattered far away from any major boozing blocks. Low rents, though, usually mean that their characters remain quirky and unique.

KASEY'S TAVERN Map pp312-13

☎ 312-427-7992; 701 S Dearborn St; 11am-2am Mon-Sat, to 11pm Sun; Red Line to Harrison

This comfortable, casual neighborhood bar has been selling drinks for over 100 years. Golden Tee junkies can get their fix here, and beer fans can choose from one of 20 beers on tap. If it's warm out, Kasey's sidewalk patio is the best place to drink in the South Loop.

RICHARD'S BAR Map pp316-17

☎ 312-421-4597; 725 W Grand Ave; 8am-2am Mon-Fri, from 9am Sat, from noon Sun; Blue Line to Grand

The *younger* of the two main bartenders in this timeless dive is in his 70s. The bar – with its tall, humming refrigerated coolers for to-go orders and strange mix of Rat Pack and *Saturday Night Fever* on the jukebox – feels like something out of a Jim Jarmusch movie. Hang around long enough and the owner may bring out a huge platter of food for everyone.

Entertainment

Entertainment

When Chicago's weekly arts and entertainment paper, the *Reader*, hits the streets every Thursday, there's more than a small risk of someone getting hurt. Not because of poison-pen exposés or yellow journalistic slanderings, mind you. No, the risk caused to the city's populace by the paper is a much more physical one – the four-sectioned thing weighs so much that trying to heft one of them across town could give a grown man a hernia and permanently cripple a small child.

Why does it weigh so much, you ask? Because this is Chicago, and there's at least a pound of goings-on happening every week. Start your weight-lifting regimen now. From theater to dance to experimental musicians playing miked hamster wheels, Chicago has so much going on that you'll need all the stamina you can muster just to read about it.

Tickets & Reservations

From Coldplay concerts to a Steppenwolf drama, Chicago is a city that turns out in droves for big-time shows. For live music, you can expect to pay anything from a $5 cover to $60 (plus handling fees) to see a huge rock band or for great seats at the Chicago Symphony. Popular concert venues tend to sell tickets through the charge-by-phone ticket giant **Ticketmaster** (☎ 312-559-1212). You can also go get Ticketmaster tickets in person at any Tower Records store. Other venues, especially classy ones like the Symphony, will have their own box offices.

For smaller rock and blues clubs, tickets aren't sold ahead of time; you simply show up and pay a cover. The best approach to getting into your concert is to contact the venue directly to find out if advance tickets are on sale. If not, it should be able to advise you on how early you have to show up to make sure you get in.

Scoring theater tickets is a little easier thanks to the League of Chicago Theatres (see the league's website www.chicagoplays.com for Chicago theater news), which operates **Hot Tix** (www.hottix.org) booths, where same-day tickets to participating shows are sold at half-price. The lineup varies every day, with the best selection available on weekends. Hot Tix

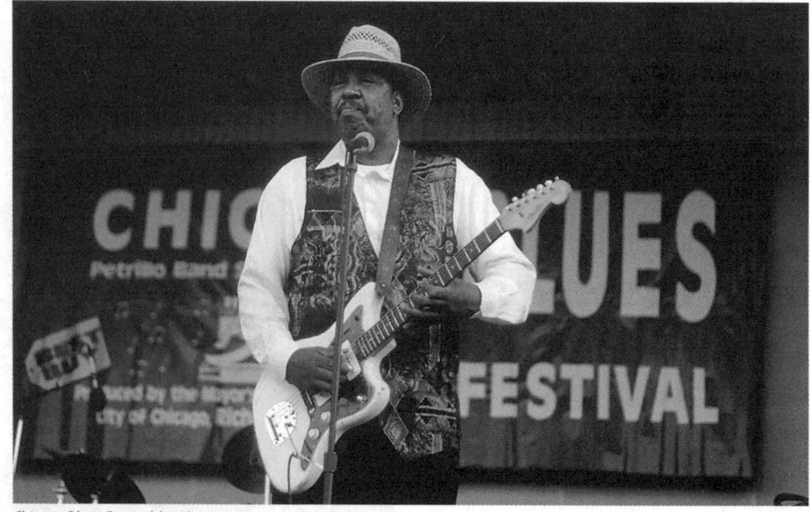

Chicago Blues Festival (p11)

sells weekend tickets beginning on Friday, and the booths also offer regular full-price tickets. To find out what's available, go to the website, which is updated daily, or simply stop by any of Hot Tix's three locations: **Loop** (Map pp304–5; 72 E Randolph St), **Visitor Information Center** (Map pp308–9; 163 E Pearson St) or **Tower Records** (Map pp304–5; 214 S Wabash St).

Also, students, children, senior citizens, the disabled, groups and even actors may qualify for special prices from the theaters themselves. Plus, some places offer low-cost preview shows before the official premiere and last-minute deals right before curtain time. The moral of this story? Always check with the box office for any and all deals before plunking down your bucks – even at Hot Tix.

We've listed opening hours for clubs such as piano bars and the lower-key jazz venues, where performances are likely to continue through the evening. For the start times for concert events, call the venue or check newspaper listings.

TOP FIVE LIVE-MUSIC VENUES

- **Empty Bottle** (p183) From punk to saxy skronking, it's all divey and delicious.
- **Green Mill** (p182) A trip to a jazzier era.
- **Hideout** (p184) Anything goes in this tiny treasure.
- **Lee's Unleaded Blues** (p182) Real-deal blues.
- **Schubas** (p184) Shit-kickin' alt-country and indie music played to well-behaved fans.

LIVE MUSIC

There's more music being played any night of the week in Chicago than you could ever listen to, even if you had a year to spare. Obviously, given the city's blues and jazz roots, you can hear world-class performances in those genres. You can also catch plenty of live rock, by everyone from garage bands to 1960s-revival groups. And with the wealth of ethnic enclaves in the city, you're sure to hear just about anything else you desire.

Festivals

Chicago is one of the best places in the country for free music festivals, and Grant Park is the epicenter of the musical mayhem. The park is packed throughout the summer with fans enjoying free day-long concerts featuring some of the biggest names in blues, jazz, gospel, country and world music. For a complete listing, see p9.

The free festivals, though, are just the tip of the musical iceberg. For those who don't mind paying admission, the city also hosts some smaller music extravaganzas. Bespectacled indie-rock fans swarm the two-day **Intonation Music Festival** (www.intonationmusicfest.com), organized by the staff of *Pitchfork* magazine. In 2005 Lollapalooza, the granddaddy of alternative rock festivals, made a July appearance in Chicago as well. If you love the feel of Lollapalooza but feel it lacks a certain polish, you can take in the all-Polish and Czech music and art festival, **Polapalooza** (www.polapalooza.com), in June.

THEY'RE PLAYING WHERE?

The more you know Chicago's entertainment venues, the more confused you'll be by who plays where. The booking style here involves a lot of club-sharing by wildly different entertainment factions, meaning that the best reggae club in Chicago on Friday is a scooter-filled mod hangout on Saturday. And a gay musical theater group on Sunday. Its a game of musical chairs that keeps different scenes rotating on to and off of the same barstools each night. It's part of the fun mixing of cultures that helps make Chicago so exciting, but it also means that you'd do well to check the club listings carefully before you head back to your favorite reggae bar two nights running.

BLUES & JAZZ

Blues and jazz fans can find a show every night of the week in Chicago. Lovers of gospel, however, will have to cool their jets until Sunday, when they can hear the spiritual music come alive in one of the great, historic South Side churches (p114).

ANDY'S Map pp306-7

☎ 312-642-6805; 11 E Hubbard St; Red Line to Grand

This veteran jazz and blues bar-restaurant doesn't charge a cover for its lunchtime shows. Some workers come at lunch and never quite make it back to the office.

BACK ROOM Map pp308-9
☎ 312-751-2433; 1007 N Rush St; Red Line to Clark/Division
In this tiny place you view the jazz musicians via a mirror. If you're on the small main floor, you might find the intimacy reminiscent of a concert held in your own bedroom.

BLUE CHICAGO Map pp306-7
☎ 312-642-6261; www.bluechicago.com; 736 N Clark St; Red Line to Chicago
The talent lives up to the club's name at this mainstream blues club. If you're staying in the neighborhood and don't feel like hitting the road, you won't go wrong here. Admission to Blue Chicago gets you into the branch two blocks down as well, **Blue Chicago on Clark** (Map pp306–7; ☎ 312-661-0100; 536 N Clark). The latter also offers a Saturday early evening alcohol- and smoke-free 'introduce yourself and your kids to the blues' concert. Call for details.

B.L.U.E.S. Map pp308-9
☎ 773-528-1012; 2519 N Halsted St; Brown Line to Diversey
Long, narrow and crowded, this veteran club crackles with electric moments where the crowd shares in the music. Look for names like Big James & the Chicago Playboys.

BUDDY GUY'S LEGENDS Map pp312-13
☎ 312-427-0333; www.buddyguys.com; 754 S Wabash Ave; Red Line to Harrison
You're likely to find the namesake here, although instead of playing, Buddy will probably be giving the crowd a circumspect gaze as he adds up a stack of receipts. Look for top national and local blues groups in this no-nonsense, cavernous space.

GREEN DOLPHIN STREET Map pp316-17
☎ 773-395-0066; www.jazzitup.com; 2200 N Ashland Ave; bus 6
This classy venue combines excellent and inventive cuisine with good jazz. It's hard to imagine that this riverside club, which looks like it's been around since the 1940s, used to be a junk-auto dealer before the renovation.

GREEN MILL Map p311
☎ 773-878-5552; 4802 N Broadway; Brown Line to Lawrence
You can sit in Al Capone's favorite spot at the timeless Green Mill, a true cocktail lounge that comes complete with curved leather booths. Little has changed in 70 years – the club still books top local and national jazz acts. On Sunday night it hosts a nationally known poetry slam where would-be poets try out their best work on the openly skeptical crowd. Would Al have approved?

HOTHOUSE Map pp312-13
☎ 312-362-9707; www.hothouse.net; 31 E Balbo Dr; Red Line to Harrison
Near Grant Park and the Loop, the jazz, world-music and hip-hop club HotHouse has been called 'indispensable' by *Tribune* critic Howard Reich. It regularly draws top artists from as far away as South Africa and Japan. Look for the great local saxophonist Ernest Dawkins.

JAZZ SHOWCASE Map pp306-7
☎ 312-670-2473; www.jazzshowcase.com; 59 W Grand Ave; Red Line to Grand
Owner Joe Segal presides over an elegant club that caters to jazz purists. Segal's been promoting be-bop jazz in Chicago since he worked as a student booker at Roosevelt University many, many moons ago.

KINGSTON MINES Map pp302-3
☎ 773-477-4646; www.kingstonmines.com; 2548 N Halsted St; Brown Line to Diversey
It's so hot and sweaty here that the blues neophytes in the audience will feel like they're having a genuine experience – sort of like a gritty theme park. Two stages mean that somebody's always on. The club's popularity ensures that it attracts big names.

LEE'S UNLEADED BLUES Map pp302-3
☎ 773-493-3477; 7401 S South Chicago Ave; bus 30
Lee's and **Rosa's Lounge** (opposite) are cut from the same cloth; this is a no-nonsense, nontouristy blues club where the live music runs Thursday to Monday. Dress up.

NEW APARTMENT LOUNGE Map pp302-3
☎ 773-483-7728; 504 E 75th St; bus 3
The only night to come to this simple storefront venue on the far South Side is Tuesday, when saxophonist Von Freeman leads his long-running, roof-raising jam session at 10:30pm. Come early.

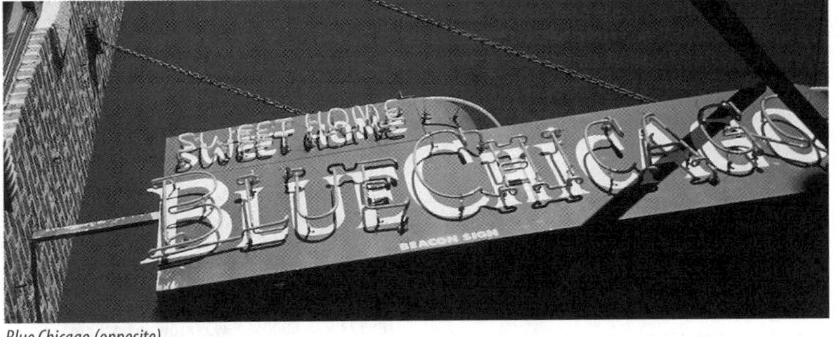

Blue Chicago (opposite)

ROSA'S LOUNGE Map pp302-3
☎ 773-342-0452; www.rosaslounge.com; 3420 W Armitage Ave; bus 73
This is hard-core blues. Top local talents perform at this unadorned West Side club in a neighborhood that's still a few decades away from attracting developers. Take a cab.

UNDERGROUND WONDER BAR
Map pp308-9
☎ 312-266-7761; www.undergroundwonderbar.com; 10 E Walton St; 🕑 4pm-4am Mon-Fri, to 5am Sat, 8pm-4am Sun; Red Line to Chicago
This live-music venue run by musician Lonie Walker features little-known jazz and blues players, along with the occasional rock or reggae player. The club is tiny, and Lonie herself takes the stage for her sultry-voiced show several nights a week.

VELVET LOUNGE Map pp312-13
☎ 312-791-9050; www.velvetlounge.net; 67 E Cermak Rd; Red Line to Cermak/Chinatown
Tenor saxophonist Fred Anderson (one of the founding members of the Association for the Advancement of Creative Musicians; see p35) owns the Velvet, which left its former historic location around the corner and moved here in 2006. Visiting jazz musicians often hang out here late at night. The place rocks during impromptu jam sessions.

ROCK, POP & INDIE

ABBEY PUB Map pp302-3
☎ 773-478-4408; www.abbeypub.com; 3420 W Grace St; Blue Line to Addison
Along with being a good bet for Irish music some nights, Abbey Pub in far-out Irving Park has become one of the city's best small rock venues. An adjoining pub is smoky and crowded. This club is located far from the city center, on the northwest side.

DOUBLE DOOR Map pp316-17
☎ 773-489-3160; www.doubledoor.com; 1572 N Milwaukee Ave; Blue Line to Damen
Hard-edged, alternative rock echoes off the walls in this former liquor store, which still has its original sign out front. If you get confused, the Double Door bouncer will steer you less than carefully to the proper door.

ELBO ROOM Map pp318-19
☎ 773-549-5549; www.elboroomchicago.com; 2871 N Lincoln Ave; Brown, Red, Purple Line to Fullerton
The Elbo Room exemplifies the scene-overlap that goes on in Chicago's music venues. Everything from Spanish-language rock to ska to reggae happens here nightly, and the small size of the place means that even the latest latecomers can get close to the action on stage.

EMPTY BOTTLE Map pp316-17
☎ 773-276-3600; www.emptybottle.com; 1035 N Western Ave; Blue Line to Damen
As the best-known indie-rock venue in Chicago, the Empty Bottle gets its pick of the smaller hot bands to come through town. The impressive programming here doesn't stick to electric guitars and power chords, however – on Tuesday night free-jazz improvisational master Ken Vandermark often plays a set as part of its Chicago Improvisers Series.

HIDEOUT Map pp316-17

☎ 773-227-4433; www.hideoutchiago.com; 1354 W Wabansia; bus 72

Despite its diminutive size and the middle-of-nowhere location, the Hideout has managed to become a darling of Chicago's discerning bar-goers. In its lodgelike back room, folk, country and rock bands perform, and in the dim, cozy front bar, Chicago's local music scene drinks Pabst (or sells it – singers Kelly Hogan and Laurie Stirratt both tend bar here).

HOUSE OF BLUES Map pp306-7

☎ 312-923-2000; www.hob.com; Marina City, 329 N Dearborn St; Red Line to Grand

Blues Brother Dan Aykroyd invested in this spot, virtually guaranteeing that the House of Blues would make a big splash in Chicago. Hip-hop, rock, pop, country, even the occasional DJ Z-Trip dance party – this is where large-draw performers play in Near North. The Sunday gospel brunch features soul-stirring Chicago groups and Cajun chow. Reserve early – it's usually mobbed.

METRO Map pp318-19

☎ 773-549-0203; www.metrochicago.com; 3730 N Clark St; Red Line to Addison

Indie acts teetering on the verge of stardom play this former classic theater, one of the best venues in Chicago, with sweet sight lines and good sound.

NOTE Map pp316-17

☎ 312-489-0011; 1565 N Milwaukee Ave; Blue Line to Damen

Funk and rock bands play until 2am, and are followed by DJs spinning everything from hip-hop to salsa. It's small, it's full. It's a nice kind of dive.

FOLK, COUNTRY & REGGAE

CAROL'S PUB Map p311

☎ 773-334-2402; 4659 N Clark St; bus 22

The closest thing Chicago has to a honky-tonk, Carol's Pub offers boot-stompin' Bud-drinkin' good times to its patrons, who come out on weekends to dance like crazy to the house band, Diamondback. The live music (and the jukebox that fills in during the week) leans more toward old-school 1950s, '60s and '70s country names like Hank Williams and George Jones rather than more recent acts like Garth Brooks.

EXEDUS II Map pp318-19

☎ 773-348-3998; www.exeduslounge.com; 3477 N Clark St; ⌚ closed Tue; Red Line to Addison

This narrow bar fills with smoke and the sounds of good reggae, performed by acts often on their way to or from the Wild Hare.

OLD TOWN SCHOOL OF FOLK MUSIC

Map pp302-3

☎ 773-728-6000; www.oldtownschool.org; 4544 N Lincoln Ave; Brown Line to Western

You can hear the call of the banjos from the street outside this venue, where major national and local acts like John Gorka, Richard Thompson and Joan Baez sometimes play. If you want to join in, you can take classes. The **Old Town School's** (Map pp308–9; ☎ 773-525-7793; 909 W Armitage Ave) original location in Old Town offers classes for kids.

SCHUBAS Map pp318-19

☎ 773-525-2508; www.schubas.com; 3159 N Southport Ave; Brown, Red Line to Belmont

Something of an alt-country legend, Schubas presents a host of twangy, acoustic artists. (Noncountry indie-rock acts too big for the Empty Bottle also might find themselves playing here.) While the bar area itself is lively and boisterous, the back music room is civilized and music-focused (talkers should expect to be shushed).

WILD HARE Map pp318-19

☎ 773-327-4273; 3530 N Clark St; Red Line to Addison

Dreadlocks meet capitalism at this modern reggae club run by guys from Jamaica but financed by local venture capitalists. It books top touring acts. Beware after Cubs games, when the baseball caps outnumber the dreadlocks by a factor of 10.

PIANO BAR & CABARET

COQ D'OR Map pp308-9

☎ 312-787-2200; The Drake, 140 E Walton St; ⌚ 11am-2am Mon-Sat, to 1am Sun; Red Line to Chicago

Cole Porter, Frank Sinatra and others are part of the repertoire of highly talented piano players and singers who rotate

TOP FIVE DANCE CLUBS IN CHICAGO

- **Berlin** (right) Where hot mixed crowds rock hot house mixes.
- **Darkroom** (p186) When DJ Mother Hubbard hits the decks on Thursday.
- **Lava Lounge** (p186) A no-cover favorite with alternative crowds.
- **Smart Bar** (p187) The basement club where two generations of ravers have come of age.
- **Sound-Bar** (p187) The megaclub that's megafriendly.

through this stately lounge. The live music gets going every night at 7pm.

DAVENPORT'S PIANO BAR & CABARET Map pp316-17

☎ 773-278-1830; 1383 N Milwaukee Ave; 🕑 7pm-midnight Mon, Wed & Thu, to 2am Fri & Sat, to 11pm Sun; Blue Line to Damen

Old standards get new interpretations and new songs get heard for the first time at this swank place on an up-and-coming stretch of Milwaukee Ave. The front room is a fun, inclusive (read: sing-along) place, with the back reserved for more fancy-pants cabaret events (where singing along will get you thrown out).

ZEBRA LOUNGE Map pp308-9

☎ 312-642-5140; 1220 N State St; 🕑 2pm-2am Sun-Thu, to 3am Fri & Sat; Red Line to Clark/Division

For a funky night dating back to the days before colorization, try this small, smoky joint decorated entirely in black and white. The piano can get as scratchy as the voices of the crowd, which consists mainly of older people who like to sing along. Regular ivory-stroker Tom Oman is a veteran who knows his stuff.

CLUBBING

The dance clubs in Chicago essentially come in two flavors. The first, and most prevalent, are clubs like Zentra (p188), where your $20 cover will buy you entry into an over-the-top space where the people are good-looking and well dressed, and a gin and tonic will cost you $8. The house or hip-hop at these places will be handled with aplomb by some competent disc-spinner, but ultimately, dancing is secondary to the experience of being in a fantasy land that transcends the bounds of ordinary life for a night.

The second flavor of club is one where fashion is functional, the cover charge is lower and people come to dance. Despite a police crackdown on illegal drugs in dance clubs in the late 1990s, Chicago still has a fairly strong, very friendly dance-music community. And if when you hear 'dance-music community' you think of a bunch of E-d out 19-year-olds with glow sticks, think again: Chicago was one of the hotbeds of house in the early 1980s, and the audiences have aged with the music. When you go out to the more music-focused events like Spundae at Vision or weekends at the SmartBar, you'll see plenty of 30-somethings shaking it out there with the college students.

To find out about dance events, the free monthly paper *UR* is far and away the most helpful guide, including detailed listings of all the best one-offs and regular DJ gigs going down around town. *Time Out Chicago* magazine is also great, with the *New City* and *Reader* providing fairly unhelpful club listings. For the more-underground events, look for flyers at hip record stores like Gramaphone (p227) or any of the rave-themed clothing stores along Milwaukee in Wicker Park.

BERLIN Map pp318-19

☎ 773-348-4975; www.berlinchicago.com; 954 W Belmont Ave; 🕑 8pm-4am Mon, 5pm-4am Tue-Fri, 5pm-5am Sat, 8pm-4am Sun; Brown, Red Line to Belmont

The excitable crowd at Berlin is very mixed, with straights, gays and in-betweens sharing space on the sweaty dance floor. Video monitors play the latest clips from Bjork and Peaches while DJs take the dance floor in a trancey direction.

COTTON CLUB Map pp312-13

☎ 312-341-9787; 1710 S Michigan Ave; 🕑 6pm-3am Sun, Mon, Wed & Thu, 5pm-4am Fri, 7pm-5am Sat; bus 1

A dose of R&B is mixed with hip-hop at this swank place near the South Side. The patrons tend to dress sharply to match the elegant surroundings. Some nights you can catch good live jazz at the piano bar out front.

Berlin dance club (p185)

DARKROOM Map pp316-17
☎ 773-276-1411; 2210 W Chicago Ave; ⏰ 9pm-2am Sun-Fri, to 3am Sat; bus 66
Ground zero for everyone from goths to mods to reggae-heads, this welcoming club changes wildly depending on the day of the week. The famous Life During Wartime indie dance party on Thursday, led by local DJ Mother Hubbard, is a guaranteed good time.

EXCALIBUR Map pp306-7
☎ 312-266-1944; www.excaliburchicago.com; 632 N Dearborn St; ⏰ 7pm-4am Sun-Thu, from 5pm Fri & Sat; Red Line to Grand
Inside its elegant exterior (the building once housed the Chicago Historical Society), Excalibur has three levels of dancing, with mainstream house, hip-hop and '80s booming from various rooms. Other areas in the funhouse include jukeboxes, electronic games, pool and more. Mostly touristy and suburban crowds.

EXIT Map pp308-9
☎ 773-395-2700; www.exitchicago.com; 1315 W North Ave; ⏰ 9pm-4am Sun-Fri, to 5am Sat; Blue Line to Damen
A long-running punk-industrial dance club, where the dance floor comes complete with a cage. You'll want to be wearing leather for self-protection if nothing else.

FUNKY BUDDHA LOUNGE Map pp316-17
☎ 312-666-1695; www.funkybuddha.com; 728 W Grand; ⏰ 9pm-2am Mon-Fri, to 3am Sat, 6pm-2am Sun; Blue Line to Belmont
Though encroachment from suburban types has tarnished the Buddha's cutting-edge rep, this small club is still one of the better dance spots for hip-hop and house in Chicago. Funky Buddha on Titillating Tuesday has women DJs, and no unaccompanied men are allowed.

HYDRATE Map pp318-19
☎ 773-975-9244; www.hydratechicago.com; 3458 N Halsted St; ⏰ 8pm-4am Mon-Fri, 4pm-5am Sat, 6pm-4am Sun; Red Line to Addison
Moving into the former Manhole space, this dance club had some big Boystown shoes to fill. With a more open-air feel (thanks to retractable windows) and crazy-cheap drink specials (how does $1 sound?) it's doing just fine. On Tuesday, $15 gets you a martini and a manicure, and other special events at the gay club include lube wrestling.

KATACOMB Map pp308-9
☎ 312-337-4040; 1916 N Lincoln Park W; ⏰ 8pm-4am Wed-Fri, to 5am Sat, 10pm-4am Sun; Brown Line to Sedgwick
DJs spin soul, house, hip-hop and funk at this weekend favorite with the Lincoln Park crowds.

LAVA LOUNGE Map pp316-17
☎ 773-772-3355; 859 N Damen Ave; ⏰ 7pm-2am Sun-Fri, to 3am Sat; bus 50
Chicago clubgoers love this unpretentious, dim and cover-free club. Well-attended nights include reggae (Tuesday) and hip-hop (Thursday). A different female DJ rocks the club every Wednesday for the long-running Flirt. Better still: the beer supply is wide ranging and the cocktails cheap.

LE PASSAGE Map pp308-9
☎ 312-255-0022; www.lepassage.tv; 937 N Rush St; ⏰ 7pm-4am Wed-Fri, to 5am Sat; Red Line to Chicago
Are you a model? Or just look like one? You've found your niche. If you make it past the doorperson and her clipboard, you'll find a beautiful, vaguely tropical-themed club with French-colonial decor and Polynesian drink specials. Music varies with the night; Wednesday's old-school hip-hop night, 'Back in the Day,' is always fun.

LIAR'S CLUB Map pp308-9
☎ 773-665-1110; 1665 W Fullerton Ave; ⏰ 8pm-2am Sun-Fri, to 3am Sat; bus 9
A hard-drinking rock-and-roll club during the week, the Liar's Club gets slightly softer,

dancier and more carefree on weekends. Still, if you're looking for a scene that's more tattoos-tough than Prada-chic, the Liar's Club has some KISS memorabilia it'd like to show you.

MINX Map pp306-7
☎ 312-828-9000; 111 W Hubbard St; 🕑 9pm-4am Sun, Tue-Fri, to 5am Sat; Red Line to Grand
This slinky lounge serves tapas in its restaurant upstairs, while the music flows over the downstairs booths. Check out Wednesday, with an all-female bill of house DJs called Fierce Bitches.

MODA Map pp306-7
☎ 312-670-2200; www.clubmodachicago.com; 25 W Hubbard St; 🕑 10pm-4am Wed-Fri, to 5am Sat; Red Line to Grand
The frosty fashionistas and wannabe models at this beautiful nightspot – check the art deco–ish leaf series arcing up over the bar – can't risk damaging their outfits by dancing. So despite the great sound system and DJ sets, this is the kind of place where you pay a $20 cover to just come in and feel sexy. Ages 23 and over only.

NEO Map pp308-9
☎ 773-528-2622; 2350 N Clark St; 🕑 10pm-4am Tue-Fri, to 5am Sat; bus 22
This veteran industrial and goth venue dates from the time that Lincoln Park was the city's hottest neighborhood. Though the streets have gone quiet and upscale, this gritty dance club holds its own.

PUMP ROOM Map pp308-9
☎ 312-266-0360; Omni Ambassador East hotel, 1301 N State St; 🕑 6pm-midnight; Red Line to Clark/Division
A certain timelessness prevails at this Gold Coast classic, where jazz and dance trios and vocalists provide slow-dance swing Wednesday through Saturday. The black they insist you wear here should be formal, not grunge. For details on the exquisite food, see p146.

REDNOFIVE Map pp316-17
☎ 312-733-6699; www.rednofive.com; 440 N Halsted St; 🕑 10pm-4am Fri & Sun, to 5am Sat, Blue Line to Chicago
Even after its recent face-lift, this somewhat-cramped two-level place is a little rough around the edges, but the 20-something clientele doesn't seem to mind. Come down for house music.

RESERVE Map pp314-15
☎ 312-455-1111; 858 W Lake St; 🕑 6pm-2am Tue-Fri, 7pm-3am Sat; Green Line to Clinton
If you're looking for one of the most exclusive clubs in Chicago, you've found it. From the selective doorman to the big spending required to even reach the dance floor, this club plays to a limited, well-dressed clientele of big spenders and those who like to live like them for a weekend.

SLICK'S LOUNGE Map pp316-17
☎ 312-932-0006; 1115 N North Branch St; 🕑 5pm-2am Mon-Wed, to 4am Thu, Fri & Sun, to 5am Sat; Blue Line to Chicago
This superhip dance club and restaurant caters to upscale African-Americans. The DJs spin Latin-flavored grooves and soul; all the music reverberates off the nearby waters of the Chicago River's north branch.

SMART BAR Map pp318-19
☎ 773-549-4140; www.smartbarchicago.com; 3730 N Clark St; 🕑 10pm-4am Sun-Fri, 9pm-5am Sat; Red Line to Addison
This downstairs adjunct to the Metro is a dance music–lover's dream, and the DJs who spin here are often far bigger than the space would have you think. Forward-looking breaks, house and trance.

SOUND-BAR Map pp306-7
☎ 312-787-4480; www.sound-bar.com; 226 W Ontario St; 🕑 9pm-4am Sun-Fri, to 5am Sat; Red Line to Grand
This is a megaclub without the megaclub attitude. Superstar trance and house DJs (John Digweed, Dimitri from Paris etc) play on an amazing sound system in a dramatic setting, but the staff members have none of the haughtiness that tends to come with high-profile nightclub ventures.

SPIN Map pp318-19
☎ 773-327-7711; www.spin-nightclub.com; 800 W Belmont Ave; 🕑 10pm-2am Sun-Fri, to 3am Sat; Red Line to Belmont
Though its clientele consists mostly of gay men in their 20s, Spin has also become a

popular destination for hetero men and women looking for a fun place to shake it on the weekends. The serious dancers head to the main floor, while those looking to chat and cruise orbit the large bar by the club's entrance. Don't miss Spin's shower contest every Friday night, when dancing hopefuls of both genders bare (almost) all.

SPY BAR Map pp306-7
☎ 312-587-8779; www.spybarchicago.com; 646 N Franklin St; 10:30pm-4am Tue, Thu & Fri, to 5am Sat; Brown Line to Chicago
The atmosphere at this subterranean spot is cruise-a-rama, as scantily dressed, good-looking 20-something singles cavort to house music. Enter the Spy Bar through the alley and make sure you dress nicely (no jeans) if you want to get through the line more quickly.

SUBTERRANEAN Map pp316-17
☎ 773-278-6600; www.subt.net; 2011 W North Ave; 7pm-2am Mon, 6pm-2am Tue-Fri, 7pm-3am Sat, 8pm-2am Sun; Blue Line to Damen
DJs spin hip-hop and other styles to a stylish crowd at this place, which looks slick inside and out. The cabaret room upstairs draws local bands and popular open-mike events.

VISION Map pp306-7
☎ 312-266-1944; www.visionnightclub.com; 640 N Dearborn St; 10pm-4am Thu, Fri & Sun, to 5am Sat; Red Line to Grand
Located next to Excalibur, Vision throws some of the best techno parties in Chicago. Big-name DJs like Sasha, Doc Martin and Derrick Carter have all spun here, and the crowds come to Vision to dance rather than pose. The recently expanded club also plays hip-hop in the smaller of its two spaces.

ZENTRA Map pp308-9
☎ 312-787-0400; www.zentranightclub.com; 923 W Weed St; 10pm-4am Wed-Fri, to 5am Sat; Red Line to North/Clybourn
Given a Hindi-inspired makeover in 2005, this sumptuous megaclub on a street of steroided sports bars draws in some of the top touring house DJs to play one of four different rooms.

THEATER & IMPROV

They waited on your table at lunch; now see them doing what they *really* love to do. Chicago's actors and playwrights shine every night of the week here, and the lure of potential fame and (somewhat limited) fortune draws young talent to the city's world of companies and acting schools.

Some theater groups have their own venues, others don't. Throughout this chapter we have noted the addresses of those that have regular homes and just the phone numbers (and web addresses) of those that don't. We've also listed a few offbeat venues where the productions are consistently top-notch regardless of who is performing there.

These listings give a small idea of what's being staged. Check the local press to find out what's hot.

Festivals

If you happen to be in town around mid-May, keep your eyes peeled for the **Chicago Improv Festival** (☎ 773-935-9810; www.cif.com), which brings back Chicago's famous comedic names and ensembles for reunion performances on stages throughout the city.

Other festivals include the **Single File Festival** (☎ 312-498-3369; www.singlefilechicago.com), a two-week itinerant celebration of solo shows that starts in mid-August.

Those who enjoy musicals should keep their eyes peeled around the same time for the **Stages Festival** (☎ 773-327-5252; www.theatrebuildingchicago.org), which brings a dozen new musicals, some from Chicago writers, to the Theatre Building (p192).

ABOUT FACE THEATRE
☎ 773-784-8565; www.aboutfacetheatre.com
An itinerant ensemble primarily staging serious plays dealing with gay and lesbian themes and issues.

BAILIWICK ARTS CENTER
Map pp318-19
☎ 773-883-1090; www.bailiwick.org; 1229 W Belmont Ave; Brown, Red Line to Belmont
This facility boasts two stages that see a constant stream of productions, many of them gay-oriented and many by the resident Bailiwick Repertory.

OUT IN CHICAGO

From the time Henry Gerber published his gay rights newsletter *Friendship and Freedom* out of his Crilly Ct residence in 1924, Chicago has been one of the major centers of gay life in the US. And oh, how things have changed since 1924. An openly gay alderman sits on the city council, and Mayor Daley sent a personal letter congratulating the year's inductees into the **Chicago Gay & Lesbian Hall of Fame** (www.glhalloffame.org). Be it in the bars of Lake View or the bucolic streets of Andersonville, same-sex couples walk hand-in-hand and smooch on the street without garnering a second look.

For the low-down on gay and lesbian happenings while you're in Chicago, you can pick up the weekly **Windy City Times** (www.windycitytimes.com) or the **Chicago Free Press** (www.chicagofreepress.com), both of which feature articles about goings-on in the gay and lesbian community, as well as a passable nightlife overview. Better on the nightlife front is the petit *Nightspots* or *Time Out Chicago* magazine, which has a weekly section for gays and lesbians.

Apart from such community-uniting events as the Pride Parade – which rolls up and down Halsted and Broadway on the last Sunday of June – and the **Gay & Lesbian Film Festival** (www.reelingfilmfestival.org) in early November, socializing tends to break down along gender lines. Gay men largely socialize in the area of Lake View known as Boystown, located between Belmont and Addison, and Halsted and Broadway. Lesbians and older gays tend to settle in Andersonville, the former Swedish community in northern Chicago.

Bars and clubs catering to gay men are much more common than lesbian haunts in the Windy City. Roscoe's (p174) and **Sidetrack** (Map pp318–19; ☎ 773-477-9189; 3349 N Halsted St) are the sort of McDonald's and Burger King of the gay bar scene: they attract a clean-cut crowd and offer a friendly, innocuous setting for socializing with friends. Dancing and other forms of higher-paced revelry go down at Spin (p187), Big Chicks (p175), Hydrate (p186) or **Circuit** (Map pp318–19; ☎ 773-325-2233; 3641 N Halsted).

Lesbians looking to meet other women should head to Closet (p173), a friendly bar in Boystown. Another good bet is Women Obsession, a 'weekly lesbian social party' that runs every Wednesday until 4am at Berlin (p185). **Star Gaze** (Map p311; ☎ 773-561-7363; 5419 N Clark St) has become a popular lesbian bar in Andersonville, cooking tasty food late into the night, offering salsa dancing on Friday nights, and packing one of the best back patios in a five-mile radius. Lesbians visiting Chicago should also keep an eye out for anything put on by Chix Mix Productions, which throws sexy, women-oriented bashes. Currently, they're running the show on the first and third Fridays of the month at Circuit.

BLACK ENSEMBLE THEATRE Map p311

☎ 773-769-4451; www.blackensembletheatre.org; Uptown Center Hull House, 4520 N Beacon St; Red Line to Wilson

Original works about the lives of African-Americans are performed by this established group. Its staging of *The Jackie Wilson Story* spawned the national touring production.

CHICAGO DRAMATISTS Map pp316-17

☎ 312-633-0630; www.chicagodramatists.org; 1105 W Chicago Ave; Blue Line to Chicago

Using a small, functional theater space, this organization is one of Chicago's best-known incubators for new playwrights and plays.

CHICAGO SHAKESPEARE THEATER Map pp306-7

☎ 312-595-5600; www.chicagoshakes.com; Navy Pier, 800 E Grand Ave; bus 66

A long-established theater enjoying a beautiful new home out on Navy Pier. As the name implies, the productions are usually adaptations of the Bard's work.

COMEDYSPORTZ Map pp318-19

☎ 773-549-8080; www.comedysportzchicago.com; 2851 N Halsted St; Red, Brown Line to Diversey

The gimmick here is that two improv teams compete with deadly seriousness to make you laugh hysterically. The audience benefits from this comic capitalism, and all the fun is G-rated. Alcohol is allowed but it's BYOB.

CORN PRODUCTIONS Map pp318-19

☎ 312-409-6435; www.cornservatory.org; 4210 N Lincoln Ave

Kitschy and fun, the Corn folks have been expanding of late into more serious shows as well.

COURT THEATRE Map pp320-1

☎ 773-753-4472; www.courttheatre.org; 5535 S Ellis Ave; Metra to 55th St

A classical company hosted by the University of Chicago, the Court focuses on great works from the Greeks to Shakespeare, as well as various international plays not often performed in the US.

FACTORY THEATER

☎ **312-409-3247; www.thefactorytheater.com; 3504 N Elston Ave**

This company has been staging its alternatingly ridiculous (*Poppin' and Lockdown 2: Dance the Right Thing*) and marginally serious plays for 15 years, but still maintains a nervous, irreverent edge that makes its work a must-see.

FREE ASSOCIATES

☎ **312-458-9083; www.thefreeassociates.com**

This comedy improv group is responsible for works such as *BS*, a much-needed skewering of the TV show *ER*. When not laying waste to pop culture, the group also does a send-up of Shakespeare. It's about time.

GOODMAN THEATRE Map pp304-5

☎ **312-443-3800; www.goodman-theatre.org; 170 N Dearborn St; Blue, Brown, Green, Orange Line to Clark/Lake**

The Goodman, named by *Time* magazine as the best regional theater in the US, specializes in new and classic American theater. Its annual production of *A Christmas Carol* has become a local family tradition.

HELL IN A HANDBAG PRODUCTIONS

☎ **312-409-4357; www.handbagproductions.org**

This young group produces hilarious parodies of movies and TV shows, often in musical form.

HOUSE THEATRE

☎ **773-251-2195; www.thehousetheatre.com**

'Chicago's most exciting young theater company' *(Tribune)* presents a mix of quirky, funny shows written by untrained playwrights. Tickets are cheap, though that will likely change as the buzz about it continues to grow.

IO (IMPROVOLYMPIC) Map pp318-19

☎ **773-880-0199; www.improvolympic.com; 3541 N Clark St; Red Line to Addison**

The Olympic Committee forced this comic veteran to change name to its initials in 2005, a suitably laughable development in a long career of chuckles. ImprovOlympic launched the careers of Mike Myers and MTV's Andy Dick, along with a host of other well-known comics. Shows hinge entirely on audience suggestions, and each turn can run 40 minutes or longer. If you're thoroughly motivated by what you see, IO offers a range of courses to suit every temp's budget. The same stage also hosts various improv groups composed of the talented alums, including the legendary Baby Wants Candy, which has been known to improvise entire musicals. Shows here tend to be a little bawdier than at ComedySportz.

LIVE BAIT THEATER Map pp318-19

☎ **773-871-1212; www.livebaittheater.org; 3914 N Clark St; Red Line to Sheridan**

Actors who hoped to lure audiences with the 'bait' of their talent founded this renowned theater in 1987. They've been reeling them in ever since. Mostly the group mounts productions by founders Sharon Evans, Catherine Evans and John Ragir.

LOOKINGGLASS THEATRE COMPANY

Map pp308-9

☎ **312-337-0665; www.lookingglasstheatre.org; 821 N Michigan Ave; Red Line to Chicago**

This company took a step into the big time with the opening of its new spacious digs on Michigan Ave. The ensemble

THE PALACES OF THE LOOP

Chicago boasts some dreamboat old theaters, all of which have been renovated and reopened in recent years as part of the impressive Loop theater district restoration. The city has posted signs in front of each palatial property detailing the zaniness that went on in each during its heyday. Whether they're showing a Cuban ballet company or a Disney musical, these beauties are worth the price of admission alone.

- **Auditorium Theater** (Map pp304–5; ☎ 312-902-1500; 50 E Congress Pkwy)
- **Cadillac Palace Theater** (Map pp304–5; ☎ 312-902-1400; 151 W Randolph St)
- **Chicago Theatre** (Map pp304–5; ☎ 312-443-1130; 175 N State St)
- **Ford Center/Oriental Theater** (Map pp304–5; ☎ 312-902-1400; 24 W Randolph St)
- **LaSalle Bank Theatre** (Map pp304–5; ☎ 312-977-1700; 22 W Monroe St)

cast – which includes co-founder David Schwimmer of TV's *Friends* – loves to use physical stunts and acrobatics to enhance its thought-provoking plays.

MERCURY THEATRE Map pp318-19

☎ 773-325-1700; 3745 N Southport Ave; Brown, Red Line to Belmont

Michael Cullen, owner of the adjoining bar, Cullen's, has created a fast-rising star among North Side theaters with this classy space.

NEO-FUTURISTS Map p311

☎ 773-275-5255; www.neofuturists.org; 5153 N Ashland Ave; Red Line to Berwyn

Best known for its long-running *Too Much Light Makes the Baby Go Blind*, in which the hyper troupe makes a manic attempt to perform 30 plays in 60 minutes. Admission cost is based on a dice throw, and they order pizza when the house sells out.

PLAYGROUND IMPROV THEATER Map pp318-19

☎ 773-871-3793; www.the-playground.com; 3209 N Halsted St; Brown, Red Line to Belmont

This temple of improv hosts irreverent pieces by some of Chicago's best underground improv ensembles. The lineup changes every night, but Sunday's *Big Yellow Bus* show is always a hoot.

PROP THTR

☎ 773-539-7838; www.propthtr.lilyput.com; 3502 N Elston Ave; bus 152

Come see this long-running troupe for fresh stage adaptations of literary works by serious writers, from Nabokov to William Burroughs. The productions are typically dark in theme and well executed.

REDMOON THEATER

☎ 312-850-8440; www.redmoon.org; 1463 W Hubbard St; Green Line to Ashland

Haunting adaptations of classic works such as *Moby Dick* are the speciality of this innovative troupe. Masks, complex costumes and puppets convey universal themes.

ROYAL GEORGE THEATRE Map pp308-9

☎ 312-988-9000; 1641 N Halsted St; Red Line to North/Clybourn

The Royal George is three theaters in one building. The cabaret venue presents long-running mainstream productions such as *Late Nite Catechism*, a nun-centered comedy. The main stage presents works with big-name stars, and the gallery hosts various improv and minor works performed by small troupes.

SECOND CITY Map pp308-9

☎ 312-337-3992; www.secondcity.com; 1616 N Wells St; Brown Line to Sedgwick

A Chicago must-see, this club is best symbolized by John Belushi, who emerged from the suburbs in 1970 and earned a place in the Second City improv troupe with his creative, manic, no-holds-barred style. Belushi soon moved to the main stage, and then to *Saturday Night Live* and fame and fortune. Second City's shows are sharp and biting commentaries on life, politics, love and anything else that falls in the crosshairs of its comedians' rapid-fire, hard-hitting wit. Other famous alums are Bill Murray, Dan Aykroyd, Tina Fey and Elaine May. Try to guess which cast members will be the next to ride the celebrity and success train.

SECOND CITY ETC Map pp308-9

☎ 312-337-3992; www.secondcity.com; 1608 N Wells St; Brown Line to Sedgwick

Second City's second company often presents more-daring work, as actors try to get noticed and make the main stage. Both theaters offer the city's best comedy value after the last show most nights, when the comics present free improv performances to keep everybody's wit sharp.

STEPPENWOLF THEATER Map pp308-9

☎ 312-335-1650; www.steppenwolf.org; 1650 N Halsted St; Red Line to North/Clybourn

This legendary ensemble helped put Chicago theater on the map when it won a Tony in 1985 for regional theater excellence. Among the actors who have starred here and gone on to fame (and regularly come back to perform) are John Malkovich, Terry Kinney, Gary Sinise and John Mahoney, the crotchety old coot on *Frasier*.

STRAWDOG THEATRE Map pp318-19

☎ 773-528-9696; www.strawdog.org; 3829 N Broadway; Red Line to Sheridan

Its great sense of humor helps this company perform quirky works in a highly inventive and fun style.

THEATRE BUILDING Map pp318-19
☎ 773-327-5252; www.theatrebuildingchicago.org; 1225 W Belmont Ave; Brown, Red Line to Belmont
Lots of small troupes present shows in this flexible space.

TIMELINE THEATRE COMPANY
Map pp318-19
☎ 773-281-8463; www.timelinetheatre.com; 615 W Wellington Ave; Brown, Red Line to Belmont
TimeLine has a unique mission of exploring history's place in culture through often-moving theatrical works.

TRAP DOOR THEATRE Map pp316-17
☎ 773-384-0494; www.trapdoortheatre.com; 1655 W Cortland Ave; bus 9
One recent fundraising goal for this ragtag operation was to purchase a bathroom for its tiny theater. Despite the limits of the space, the spirited group stages consistently great productions of European avant-garde plays.

VICTORY GARDENS THEATER
Map pp308-9
☎ 773-871-3000; www.victorygardens.org; 2257 N Lincoln Ave; Brown, Red Line to Fullerton
Long established and playwright-friendly, Victory Gardens specializes in world premieres of plays by Chicago authors. The *Wall St Journal* called it 'one of the most important playwright theaters in the US.'

ZANIES Map pp308-9
☎ 312-337-4027; www.chicago.zanies.com; 1548 N Wells St; Brown Line to Sedgwick
The city's main stand-up comedy venue regularly books big-name national acts familiar to anyone with a TV, and also frequently invites comics you're *going to* hear about on TV. The shows last less than two hours and usually include the efforts of a couple of up-and-comers before the main act. The ceiling is low and the seating is cramped, which only adds to the good cheer.

CLASSICAL MUSIC & OPERA

Chicago may have steaks and pizza aplenty, but audiences hungry for classical music will likely go wanting. Not because Chicago doesn't have an orchestra – the Chicago Symphony Orchestra (CSO) is one of the best in the country – but because tickets are notoriously difficult to get hold of, scooped up by season-ticket holders.

Opera is similarly loved to exclusivity in Chicago. The Lyric Opera is wonderful, but season-ticket holders hog most of the seats in the ornate opera house. Some good vocal and baroque ensembles make use of the city's theaters and churches, though. And in summer, the classical music moves out-of-doors (see p181), where everyone can enjoy it.

If you're truly dying to see the Chicago Symphony or the Lyric Opera, head on down to the show about 30 minutes before curtain. More often than not, some besuited swell will offer you a pair of tickets at a reasonable (or free) price. Check the *Reader* to see what's being performed when you're in town.

Festivals

During the summer-long **Grant Park Music Festival** (☎ 312-742-7638; www.grantparkmusicfestival.com), classical music for the masses is performed at the Petrillo Music Shell (Map pp304–5), in Grant Park at Jackson and Columbus Sts between the Art Institute and the lake. Under the auspices of the Chicago Park District, the Grant Park Symphony Orchestra gives free concerts, usually on Wednesday, Friday, Saturday and Sunday evenings, although events such as the jazz festival can alter the schedule. At present Chicago is the only city in the US to boast a free symphony orchestra. The classical orchestra's solid performances span several genres, from opera to Broadway and 'pop.'

In the summer the CSO and other classical groups (plus a dash of jazz, folk, ethnic and pop) perform at **Ravinia** (☎ 847-266-5100; www.ravinia.org; Green Bay & Lake Cook Rds), a vast open-air festival in Highland Park on the North Shore. The main pavilion contains seating for several hundred in a bowl-like setting with a good view of the stage and the performers. But these tickets sell quickly, and most people end up sitting on the acres of lawn. If you do go, avoid the traffic and take the 45-minute Metra/Union Pacific North Line train from the Ogilvie Transportation Center to Ravinia Station ($5 round-trip). Trains stop both before and after the concerts right in front of the park gates.

APOLLO CHORUS OF CHICAGO

☎ 312-427-5620; www.apollochorus.org

A 150-member vocal group founded in 1872, the Apollo usually performs at the Symphony Center (see **Chicago Symphony Orchestra**, below). Tickets for the chorus' Christmas performance of Handel's *Messiah* sell out every year.

CHICAGO CHAMBER MUSICIANS

☎ 312-819-5800; www.chicagochambermusic.org

This 14-member group has dedicated itself to spreading the sound of chamber music by performing the classics, as well as initiating numerous outreach programs to the community. See local listings for venue information.

CHICAGO OPERA THEATER Map pp304-5

☎ 312-704-8414; www.chicagooperatheater.org; Harris Theater for Music & Dance, 205 E Randolph St; Brown, Green, Orange Line to Randolph

This innovative group stages contemporary and popular works during the summer. Under general director Brian Dickie, Chicago Opera Theater (COT) has scored some artistic success. It concentrates on little-performed 17th- and 18th-century classics as well as contemporary American works.

CHICAGO SINFONIETTA

☎ 312-236-3681; www.chicagosinfonietta.org

This group of notable young musicians, led by the locally well-known Paul Freeman, performs classics as well as adventurous modern works by the likes of Thelonious Monk.

CHICAGO SYMPHONY ORCHESTRA

Map pp304-5

☎ 312-294-3000; www.cso.org; Symphony Center, 220 S Michigan Ave; Brown, Green, Orange Line to Adams

The CSO enjoys lavish support locally. The late Sir George Solti was music director from 1969 to 92 and is credited with propelling the CSO to the very front ranks of world symphony orchestras. The current director, Daniel Barenboim, had the classic big pair of shoes to fill and has done so masterfully. He has molded the group with his personality, and the acclaim continues. The CSO season runs from September to May. In the summer, when the orchestra isn't wowing some European capital, it often performs at Ravinia (see Festivals, opposite). The CSO also oversees the Civic Orchestra of Chicago, the training branch of the symphony. Visiting conductors and musicians often work with the group, which also performs in the Symphony Center. And tickets are free!

LYRIC OPERA OF CHICAGO Map pp304-5

☎ 312-332-2244; www.lyricopera.org; Civic Opera House, 20 N Wacker Dr; Brown, Orange Line to Washington

One of the top opera companies in the US performs in the grand old Civic Opera House, on the south branch of the river. The Lyric's repertoire is a shrewd mix of old classics and much more modern and daring work. You can catch the *Mikado* one week and some totally new but emotionally stunning piece the next.

The company has had excellent luck luring top international names, such as Placido Domingo. It also has joined the international trend of projecting translations of the lyrics onto a screen above the proscenium. Purists shudder with horror; others, whose Italian or German isn't what it could be, sit back and happily read away. Gregarious Sir Andrew Davis, former music director of the BBC Symphony, took the helm of the Lyric in 2000. The season runs from September to March.

MUSIC OF THE BAROQUE

☎ 312-551-1415; www.baroque.org

One of the largest choral and orchestral groups of its kind in the US, Music of the Baroque (MoB) brings the music of the Middle Ages and Renaissance to vibrant life. Its Christmas brass and choral concerts are huge successes.

DANCE

Chicago has long been known as a city for jazz dance, thanks to local pioneers of the form like Gus Giordano. Recent years have also seen an upsurge of smaller modern dance companies, and contemporary and classical ballet continue to flourish. The big news in Chicago's small dance community is the long-awaited opening of the **Joan W & Irving B Harris Theater for Music & Dance** (Map pp304–5; ☎ 312-334-7777; www.madtchi.com; 205 E Randolph Dr), the Millennium

YOUR GIG IN CHICAGO

If the phrase 'open mic' conjures up images of depressed souls plucking acoustic guitars in coffee shops, well, you haven't experienced the high-octane Chicago version yet. Here are four fun opportunities to let your inner extrovert run wild.

- Front a band at **Pontiac Cafe** (Map pp316–17; ☎ 773-252-7767; 1531 N Damen Ave). The bands who play the 'live band karaoke' gigs here know a billion songs, so all you have to do is name the tune, then get up there and rock like there's no tomorrow. It happens every Friday night.
- Join the rhythm section at **Rhythm** (Map pp314–15; ☎ 312-492-6100; 1108 W Randolph St). Patrons are encouraged to make some noise at this drumming bar. Guests bring their own drum or rent one here, then leap into the rhythmic fray of a bar-wide drum circle. It happens most Fridays and Saturdays at 10pm.
- Speak your poetic truths on Sunday night at the **Uptown Poetry Slam at the Green Mill** (p182). This is where slam poetry got started, and you can carve your name into the movement's history during the open session that precedes the slam competition. The open-mike portion of the evening runs from 7pm to 8pm.
- Be the DJ at **Tonic Room** (Map pp308–9; ☎ 773-248-8400; 2447 N Halsted). This Lincoln Park bar hosts iTuesdays, where all are encouraged to bring their iPod or other MP3 player and get up on stage to rock the house for three songs or 15 minutes, whichever comes first. Every Tuesday.

Park performance space that finally gives Chicago's scattered dance scene a centrally located, high-profile home.

You can find complete listings for the biggies and the handful of smaller companies in the *Reader, Tribune* and *Time Out* magazine arts sections. The **Chicago Dance & Music Alliance** (☎ 312-987-9296; www.chicagomusic.org) has a list of upcoming dance performances on its site, and the recently launched site for **See Chicago Dance** (www.seechicagodance.com) also features a calendar and offers online ticket sales.

Festivals

Running for a rhythmic month beginning in November, **Dance Chicago** (☎ 773-989-0698; www.dancechicago.com) brings more than 250 companies to the **Athenaeum Theatre** (Map pp304–5; 2936 N Southport Ave). Styles range from ballet to tap to break dancing. The **Jazz Dance World Congress** (☎ 847-866-9442; www.jazzdanceworldcongress.org) takes place for five days in early August at the Harris Theater for Music & Dance and features performances by some of the top jazz dance companies. For people who want to get in on the action themselves, the city sponsors **Chicago SummerDance** (☎ 312-744-6630; 🕒 evenings Thu-Sat & afternoons Sun Jun-Aug), where ordinary Chicagoans get a chance to practice their ballroom and Latin dance moves in the Spirit of Music Garden (Map pp304–5) to live orchestral accompaniment. Free lessons are included for folks with two left feet.

BALLET CHICAGO

☎ 312-251-8838; www.balletchicago.org

This preprofessional troupe of younger dancers has received acclaim for its precision and skill in performing classical ballet works.

CHICAGO MOVING CO

☎ 773-880-5402; www.chicagomovingcompany.org

This exciting group was founded by Nana Shineflug, one of the pioneers of modern dance in Chicago. The works and performers are all local.

DANCE CENTER AT COLUMBIA COLLEGE Map pp312-13

☎ 312-344-8300; www.dancecenter.org; 1306 S Michigan Ave

More than an academic institution, the Dance Center has carved out a fine reputation by presenting top local and international talent. The center's new state-of-the-art facility within Columbia College should help it to continue attracting quality dance.

GIORDANO JAZZ DANCE CHICAGO

☎ 874-866-6779; www.giordanojazzdance.com

This Chicago company was founded by one of the most important people in jazz dance, Gus Giordano. Now headed by his daughter Nan, the company is out on the road for much of the year, but still comes back for occasional performances in its home town.

HUBBARD ST DANCE CHICAGO

Map pp304-5

☎ 312-850-9744; www.hubbardstreetdance.com; Joan W & Irving B Harris Theater for Music & Dance, 205 E Randolph Dr; Brown, Green, Orange Line to Randolph

Hubbard St is the preeminent dance group in the city, with an international reputation to match. The group has become known for energetic and technically virtuoso performances under the direction of the best choreographers in the world, including founder Lou Conte.

JOFFREY BALLET OF CHICAGO

Map pp304-5

☎ 312-739-0120; www.joffreyballet.org; Auditorium Theatre, 50 E Congress Pkwy; Brown, Orange Line to Library

This famous group has flourished since it relocated from New York in 1995. Noted for its energetic work, the company frequently travels the world and boasts an impressive storehouse of pieces it regularly performs.

MUNTU DANCE THEATER OF CHICAGO

☎ 773-602-1135; www.muntu.com

The word *muntu* means 'the essence of humanity' in Bantu, and this company performs African and American dances that draw on ancient and contemporary movement.

RIVER NORTH DANCE COMPANY

☎ 312-944-2888; www.rivernorthchicago.com

This vibrant young company brings elements of punk, house, hip-hop, mime and more to modern dance.

READINGS, SPOKEN WORD & SHOW TAPINGS

The literary scene in Chicago is small but active, with book fiends arranging a host of events with local and out-of-town authors, often in informal (read: boozy) settings. **Quimby's** (p231; www.quimbys.com) hosts at least a couple of book events and readings each week for underground zinesters, comic-book artists and Chicago celebrity bloggers.

For readings by more-widely known authors, check the website of local bookstore chain **Barbara's Bookstore** (p232; www.barbarasbookstore.com); it hosts more author events than anyone in town, and gets big names for its almost-daily readings and signings.

For those who crave something slightly more performance oriented, you can find several great spoken-word nights around Chicago. And National Public Radio and Oprah fans can have an opportunity to get a behind-the-scenes look at two national shows, both taped in Chicago in front of a studio audience.

DOLLAR STORE

☎ 773-227-4433; www.dollarstoreshow.com; Hideout (p184)

This high-concept, low-pretension lit event hands a small group of young novelists, poets, spoken-word artists and other artistic souls a dime-store object – perhaps a tacky souvenir or a box of Monoxodil – and gives them 30 days to write a piece incorporating the object. The resulting story is then performed by the author at the Dollar Store event, held on the first Friday of every month. It's zany and fun, and a great introduction to some of Chicago's freshest literary talent. There's a $1 cover charge.

HAROLD WASHINGTON LIBRARY CENTER READINGS Map pp304-5

☎ 312-747-4050; www.chipublib.org

Several writers each month come to the country's largest library and give a talk about their recent projects. Recent guests have included John Irving and *Wicked* author Gregory Maguire. The library's author calendar can be seen on its website, or drop by the library for a flyer.

MENTAL GRAFFITI

☎ 312-666-1695; Funky Buddha Lounge (p186)

Mentioned in slam circles in the same reverent tones used for the Uptown Poetry slam, this event at the Funky Buddha Lounge is where hundreds of up-and-coming poets, MCs and freestylers have learned how to work a crowd. There's a $5 cover.

OPRAH WINFREY TELEVISION SHOW TAPING Map pp314-15

☎ 312-591-9222; www.oprah.com; 110 N Carpenter

Yes, Virginia, there is an Oprah. She lives in Chicago, and tapes her hit show on Carpenter St in the West Loop. The good news: the tickets to be in Oprah's studio audience are free. The bad news: it's really, really hard to get them. Reservations can only be secured a month in advance, and you have to call between 9am and 5pm Monday to Friday. Expect to hear *a lot* of busy signal (the Oprah website recommends calling between 1:30pm and 3pm, Chicago time). Alternately, you can check the show's site, where they sometimes announce last-minute openings, allowing would-be guests to request tickets by email.

UPTOWN POETRY SLAM AT THE GREEN MILL

☎ 773-878-5552; www.slampapi.com; Green Mill (p182)

Before slams spread like wordy wildfire across the US, they were happening at the Uptown Poetry Slam. This long-running event is both Adam and the Eve to the many children of slam, and you can come see it every Sunday night. Watch shaky first-timers give it a try from 7pm to 8pm. For an hour after that, a featured guest has a go, and then the slam competition begins in earnest. There's a $6 cover.

WAIT WAIT DON'T TELL ME RADIO SHOW TAPING Map pp304-5

☎ 312-893-2956; www.chicagopublicradio.org; Bank One Auditorium, 10 S Dearborn St

On this chuckly news quiz show, contestants compete to win NPR radio announcer Carl Kassell's deep voice on their home answering machine. Created in conjunction with local NPR station WBEZ, the show is taped before a live studio audience nearly every Thursday. Tickets are $20.

WRITERS ON RECORD RADIO SHOW TAPING

☎ 312-832-6789; Lookingglass Theatre (p190)

The Writers on Record program airs on local station WFMT. For it, host Victoria Lautman sits down for an hour-long chat with a famous writer – recent guests have included Bret Easton Ellis, Michael Cunningham and Louise Erdrich. The tickets are free (but must be reserved in advance), and the event takes place in the beautiful Lookingglass Theatre space on Michigan Ave.

CINEMAS

In summer, nothing feels better than beating the Chicago heat with a frostbite-inducing visit to one of the city's many air-conditioned movie houses. And in winter, toasty buckets of buttery popcorn will allow you to feel your hands again and give you the crucial calories

TWO THUMBS UP

They were the most powerful movie reviewers in history. And they were no taller than a stick of gum. Yes, Roger Ebert's and Gene Siskel's thumbs ruled the film criticism world mercilessly during their 24-year run of televised movie reviewing. The two Chicago newspaper reporters created their first show on Chicago TV station WTTW in 1975. Eleven years and two networks later, the duo went national, inventing the thumb system – which they eventually trademarked. Rather than simply reviewing the Hollywood movies that Americans were most likely to see, the duo saw themselves as advocates for overlooked cinema as well. For an up-and-coming director, getting a 'two thumbs up' rating could transform their film from an art-house also-ran to a commercial success overnight. Siskel's and Ebert's enthusiastic endorsements of offbeat movies like *My Dinner With Andre* and *Hoop Dreams* made them part of the American vernacular, and any time a movie achieved a 'two thumbs up' rating it was sure to be plastered in blockbuster type across posters and advertisements for the film.

However benevolent they could be for a struggling auteur, Siskel and Ebert had an occasionally venomous on-camera relationship with each other. Viewers tuned in for the pair's astute insights on new movies, but the swipes and jabs thrown by the reviewers at each other were also part of the show's draw. 'We would have a fight every taping day over something,' the Pulitzer Prize–winning Ebert recalls in an interview with the *Sun-Times*, the paper for which he's been penning movie reviews since 1967. After Siskel's surprise death from surgery complications in 1999, the Film Center of the School of the Art Institute of Chicago was renamed Gene Siskel Film Center (opposite) in his honor. Roger Ebert can still be read in the *Sun-Times*, and be seen on TV waving his famous thumb with his new cohost and fellow *Sun-Times* writer Richard Roeper. In 2005 the city of Chicago named July 12th 'Roger Ebert Day' throughout the city, placing a plaque dedicated to the legendary man and his discerning thumb in front of the Chicago Theatre (p190).

you need to insulate yourself from the snow piling up outside. It's no wonder that the movies are huge in Chicago.

You'll find out everything you need to know about show times in the *Reader* or *New City*, or in movie sections of either daily paper.

Festivals

Each October, the popular **Chicago Film Festival** (☎ 312-683-0121; www.chicagofilmfestival.org) brings a score of films from around the world to town for two weeks. Check with the festival for each year's schedule. For less mainstream offerings, check out the **Chicago Underground Film Festival** (www.cuff.org), which runs in late August.

Quirkier still, the **Fast Forward Film Festival** (www.fastforwardfilmfest.com) gives local filmmakers 24 hours to make and edit a three-minute video. The results are then shown to excited, sleep-deprived audiences at a BYOB event in one of the area's converted warehouses. The film fest takes place three times a year; check the website for details. The **Midwest Independent Film Festival** (www.midwestfilm.com) is a monthly fest showcasing the best indie films from the Midwest, on the first Tuesday of the month at Landmark's Century Centre Cinema (right).

Chicago is full of movie theaters; following are some of the noteworthy for the traveler.

600 N MICHIGAN THEATERS

Map pp306-7

☎ 312-255-9340; 600 N Michigan; Red Line to Chicago

Despite the name, the entrance to these centrally located theaters is off Rush St. This comfortable complex features six screens of various sizes, plus a café and concessions stand on each of its three floors.

AMC RIVER EAST Map pp306-7

☎ 312-596-0333; 322 E Illinois St; Red Line to Chicago; bus 65

The screens are huge and the sound is rumbling at this high-tech theater – a great option if you're taking in an explosion-filled, special effects–laden blockbuster. Parking is expensive, however; take public transportation.

BREW & VIEW Map pp318-19

☎ 773-929-6713; www.brewview.com; Vic Theater, 3145 N Sheffield Ave; Brown, Red Line to Belmont

Even the worst film gets better when you've got a pizza in front of you and a pitcher of beer at your side. As you watch second-run Hollywood releases here, you can behave as badly as you would at home – in fact, staff members encourage it. You must be 18.

FACETS MULTIMEDIA Map pp308-9

☎ 773-281-9075; www.facets.org; 1517 W Fullerton Ave; bus 74

Facets shows interesting, obscure movies that would never get booked elsewhere. Here you will find the denizens of Chicago's film group between Hollywood contracts.

GENE SISKEL FILM CENTER Map pp304-5

☎ 312-846-2600; www.siskelfilmcenter.org; 164 N State St; Brown, Green, Orange Line to State

The former Film Center of the School of the Art Institute was renamed for the late *Chicago Tribune* film critic Gene Siskel. It shows everything from amateurish stuff by students who should hang on to their day jobs to wonderful but unsung gems by Estonian directors. The monthly schedule includes theme nights of forgotten American classics.

IMAX THEATER Map pp306-7

☎ 312-595-5629; 700 E Grand Ave at Navy Pier; bus 66

The megascreen theater is out on the pier.

LANDMARK'S CENTURY CENTRE

Map pp318-19

☎ 773-509-4949; 2828 N Clark St; Brown, Red Line to Diversey

You'll find a refreshing number of documentaries and independent movies at this seven-screen theater with stadium seating.

MUSIC BOX THEATRE Map ppp318-19

☎ 773-871-6604; www.musicboxtheatre.com; 3733 N Southport Ave; Brown Line to Southport

No matter what's showing, it's worth going to the Music Box just to see the place. This perfectly restored theater dates from 1929 and looks like a Moorish fantasy. Clouds float across the ceiling, which has twinkling stars. The film programs are always first-rate. A second, small and serviceable theater shows held-over films that have proved more popular than expected.

PIPERS ALLEY Map pp308-9

☎ 312-642-7500; 1608 N Wells St; Brown Line to Sedgwick

Located in the complex of the same name, this is a pretty decent multiplex with good sight lines.

THREE PENNY CINEMA Map pp308-9

☎ 773-525-3449; 2424 N Lincoln Ave; Red, Brown Line to Fullerton

The floor boards creak at this ramshackle, family-run complex of tiny theaters in Lincoln Park. But what the family saves in maintenance expenses, you will save in admission prices. The tickets at the Three Penny Cinema are cheap. The offerings include major releases that have passed their prime and a good selection of the better minor films.

VILLAGE THEATER Map pp308-9

☎ 312-642-2403; 1548 N Clark St; Brown Line to Sedgwick

This is a cool old theater that has been broken up into several smaller ones. It shows quirky new releases and second-runs at good prices.

Activities

Activities

It's good to be number five. Just ask Chicago, which jogged away from the dubious distinction of being the second-fattest city in the country in 2005. Now resting in a less-embarrassing fifth place, Chicago is still at a loss to explain how a city where sports are such an integral part of the lifestyle has become one of the five most obese cities in the world.

The answer is pretty clear to anyone who has spent time here. While Chicagoans have a deep-seated love of baseball, football, basketball and soccer, they tend to demonstrate that love by sitting in a comfortable chair or stadium seat, eating hot dogs, drinking beer and cheering their favorite team. This, along with the sedentary nature of most office-bound jobs and a meat- and beer-filled diet, caused a crisis of fat in the Midwestern metropolis.

Enter Mayor Daley and the Chicago Park District. Under the auspices of the **Chicago Works Out** (www.chicagoworksout.com) program, the city has been sponsoring all manner of walking events, biking tours and fitness classes aimed at getting its citizens out of their La-Z-Boy recliners. From free group-yoga classes in Millennium Park to workshops for parents about tricking their children into eating more greens, the city has been putting a chunk of cash behind initiatives to help make Chicago healthier.

Visitors to Chicago will reap the benefits of these programs through improved walking trails, better bike paths, top-notch public tennis courts, skating rinks and easy access to the city's newly beautified parks.

Private health clubs have also been springing up throughout the city to do their part. Most all of them are happy to have you spend a day running around their racquetball courts and scaling their climbing walls. Just ask about a day pass at the most convenient location to where you're staying.

Of course, you *do* owe it to yourself to plant your butt in a stadium seat and take in a game or two while you're here as well. You're on vacation, after all – a couple hours of sedentary living won't hurt.

WATCHING SPORTS

For more detailed information on all of Chicago's sports teams, see the Sports section (p18) of the City Life chapter. Nearly all sports teams save the Cubs use **Ticketmaster** (☎ 312-559-1212; www.ticketmaster.com) as their ticketing outlet.

BASEBALL

Chicago's two Major League baseball stadiums, Wrigley Field and US Cellular Field, are easily reached by public transportation. The baseball season runs from early April to September.

CHICAGO CUBS Map pp318-19

☎ 773-404-2827; www.cubs.com; Wrigley Field, 1060 W Addison St; Red Line to Addison

Chicago is one of only two US cities that boast two Major League baseball teams. By far the local favorite, the Cubs play at Wrigley Field. Tickets are available at the box office, through the team's website, or by calling ☎ 800-843-2827 (within Illinois) or ☎ 866-652-2827 (from out of state).

CHICAGO WHITE SOX Map pp302-3

☎ 312-674-1000; www.chisox.com; US Cellular Field, 333 W 35th St; Red Line to Sox-35th

Less loved – but slightly more successful – than the Cubs, the White Sox play at US Cellular Field (aka Comiskey Park) to the south in Bridgeport. Because the stadium is so enormous, White Sox tickets are much easier to come by. You can get them through the team's website, at the US Cellular Field box office or at any Ticketmaster outlet.

Watching a baseball game at Wrigley Field (left)

FOOTBALL

CHICAGO BEARS Map pp312-13

☎ 847-295-6600; www.chicagobears.com; Soldier Field, 425 E McFetridge Dr

The Bears can be found, sleet, snow or dark of night, at Soldier Field. Since the inauguration of the new stadium, tickets have been hard to come by, and are available only through Ticketmaster.

Soldier Field is tricky to get to on public transportation. Metra trains from Randolph St Station stop at nearby 12th St Station, and Roosevelt Rd El stops are a half-mile stroll away. The greatest joy for Bears fans of late has been their elaborate tailgate feasts in the parking lots before the games.

The football season runs from August to December, when you can get snowed on.

BASKETBALL

CHICAGO BULLS Map pp314-15

☎ 312-455-4000; www.nba.com/bulls; United Center, 1901 W Madison St

No longer the great champions they were in the days of Jordan and Pippen, the Bulls are still heartily loved by Chicagoans. The Bulls hold court at the United Center. Tickets are available through the United Center box office – located at Gate 4 on the building's east side – and at Ticketmaster outlets.

If you're going to take public transportation to the Bulls game, hop on the Brown, Green or Orange Line to Madison, and then take bus 19 or 20 west to the stadium. The season runs from November to April.

HOCKEY

CHICAGO BLACKHAWKS Map pp314-15

☎ 312-455-7000; www.chicagoblackhawks.com; United Center, 1901 W Madison St

After the cancellation of the 2004–05 season over a contentious labor dispute, the National Hockey League (NHL) resumed hockey in time for the 2005–06 season. The Chicago Blackhawks were one of the six founding teams of the NHL and they've been a little off their game for years now. They make their home at the United Center.

Tickets are often sold out, but brokers and concierges can usually obtain them for a minimal markup. Transportation and parking information is the same as for the Bulls (left). The season runs October to April.

SOCCER

CHICAGO FIRE Map pp312-13

☎ 312-705-7200; www.chicago-fire.com; Bridgeview Stadium, 71st & Harlem

Soccer is slowly catching on in Chicago, particularly among the European and

TOP 10 CHICAGO SPORTS HEROES

Should you find yourself in a sports bar anywhere in the Windy City, a misty-eyed mention of any of the names below will help bond you to your fellow drinkers.

- **Ernie Banks** Voted the National League's most valuable player (MVP) twice (1958 and 1959), he was the first baseball player to have his number retired by the Cubs.
- **Dick Butkus** Elected to the Pro Football Hall of Fame in 1979, the Bears player recovered 25 fumbles in his career, a record at the time of his retirement.
- **Mike Ditka** The Chicago Bears star (and current Chicago restaurateur), Ditka is the only person to have won a Super Bowl as a player, assistant coach and head coach.
- **Bobby Hull** Nicknamed 'the Golden Jet,' the Blackhawks left winger is considered one of hockey's all-time greats.
- **Shoeless Joe Jackson** The legendary White Sox player holds the third-highest batting average in baseball's history.
- **Michael Jordan** The Chicago Bulls great ended his career of 15 seasons with the highest per-game scoring average in National Basketball Association (NBA) history.
- **Stan Mikita** The Czech-born hockey star played his entire career with the Chicago Blackhawks, from 1959 to 1980, retiring with the second-most points of any player.
- **Walter Payton** The Chicago Bears great is ranked second on the National Football League (NFL) all-time rushing list, and seventh in all-time scoring.
- **Scottie Pippen** Leading the Bulls through champion seasons throughout the 1990s, Pippen is known for pioneering the point forward position on the basketball court.
- **Ryne Sandberg** The Cubs second baseman played a record 123 consecutive games without an error, and in 2005 became the fourth Cubs player ever to have his number retired.

WINDY CITY ROLLERS

The bang-'em-up sport of roller derby was born in Chicago in 1935, and it's made a comeback in recent years thanks to the battlin' beauties of the **Windy City Rollers** (www.windycityrollers.com) league. Players boast names such as Mob Hit Molley and Annie Maim, and there is a fair amount of campy theater surrounding the bouts. But the action is real (check the injury gallery on the league's website for proof), and the players are dedicated to the derby cause. Matches take place once a month at the Congress Theater, and often feature live rock bands and plenty of booze.

Latino sports fans in the city. The Chicago Fire was the league champ in 2003. Construction began in 2005 for the team's own new stadium, which will open southwest of Midway Airport in 2006.

Tickets are available through Ticketmaster, and are fairly easy to come by. The regular season runs from April to September, with the finals taking place in October.

OUTDOOR ACTIVITIES

RUNNING & WALKING

The lakefront path mentioned on right also has a runner's side for those looking to get a little bipedal workout. Runners hit the trail around 5am. If you're looking for a good starting point, try Oak St Beach on the Gold Coast and head north. The path from the beach northward is largely cinder rather than asphalt, which your feet will appreciate.

If you find yourself getting distracted by the great city and park views, you can regain focus on the free cinder oval track at **Lake Shore Park** (808 N Lake Shore Dr), at the intersection of Chicago Ave and Lake Shore Dr.

Any questions about running should be directed to the **Chicago Area Runners Association** (☎ 312-666-9836; www.cararuns.org), which sponsors training programs and offers free downloadable running maps on its website.

For those looking to move at a more leisurely pace, walking through the city's parks is a great way to get exercise. Again, the **Chicago Park District** (www.chicagoparkdistrict.com) has come through in a big way, offering extensive path lists, maps and ratings of its hundreds of city-maintained walking trails on its website. The site even offers a flower and plant finder to help you identify any flora you discovered en route.

CYCLING & IN-LINE SKATING

Curbs are the highest mountains you'll find in Chicago, making it ideal for biking and in-line skating. The popular, 18½-mile Lakefront Path from Hollywood Ave in the north to 71st St in the south is an excellent way to see the city, and in hot weather the lake offers cool breezes. (For a guided biking tour of the lakefront, see p120.) Lincoln Park is another good spot for biking and rolling, with paths snaking around the small lakes and the zoo. Another surprisingly good option for biking is the Loop on Sundays. The traffic clears out of the business district, giving wheeled tourists an exhilarating, stress-free opportunity to roll through the historic architecture of downtown. There's a map of bike-friendly streets on the **City of Chicago's** (www.cityofchicago.org) website. The advocacy group **Chicagoland Bicycle Federation** (www.biketraffic.org) also publishes a printed guide to biking. You can order a copy on its website.

The city has offered a great gift to bikers in the form of the **Millennium Park Bicycle Station** (www.chicagobikestation.com). The brand-new facility offers bike storage, repairs and gymlike features to make bike commuting an appealing option for workers. It's also a very convenient place to pick up a rental bikes (see p211) to cruise the Lakefront Path.

If you're looking for a very big, very slow group ride while you're in town, **Chicago Critical Mass** (www.chicagocriticalmass.org) organizes rides through the streets on the last Friday of the month. The rides, which are intended to celebrate bike use and disrupt the car-dependent status quo, begin at Daley Plaza (on the corner of Dearborn and Washington Sts) at 5:30pm. The mood is light-hearted and routes unfold spontaneously.

A few places offer bike and skate rental.

BIKE CHICAGO Map pp306-7

☎ 312-595-9600; www.bikechicago.com; Navy Pier, 600 E Grand Ave; 🕑 7am-9pm Apr-Oct

Trek mountain bikes, big cruisers with fat tires, bicycles built for two and kids' bikes are available here. The company's main office is at Navy Pier, and when the weather's nice it also operates out of trailers at

(Continued on page 211)

1 Dining out, Pilsen (p165) **2** *Students, Art Institute of Chicago (p67)* **3** *Pedestrians, North Ave* **4** *Runner, Lasalle Bank Chicago Marathon (p13)*

POLO SPORT

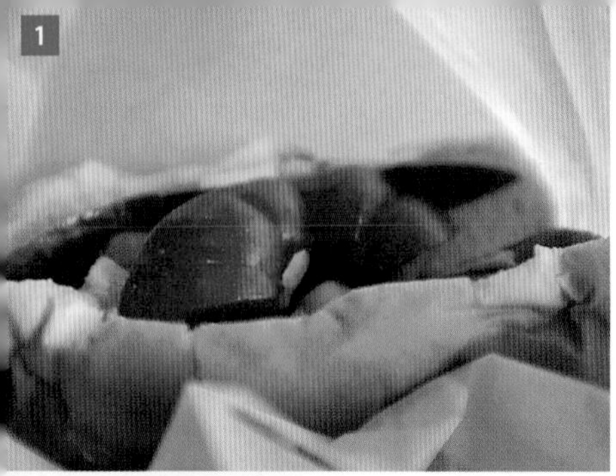

1 *Hot dog (p160)* **2** *Meal at Pizzeria Uno (p144)* **3** *Green Mill (p182)* **4** *Drinks at Nuevo Leon (p165)*

1 *Irazu (p159)* **2** *Making coffee in Greektown (p163)* **3** *Lou Mitchell's (p164)* **4** *Chicago diner*

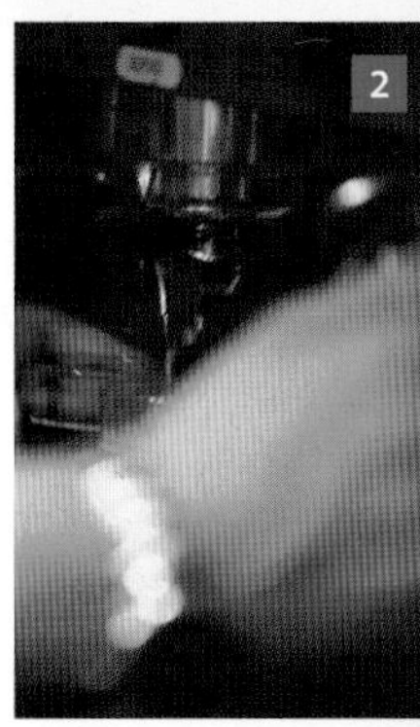

1 *Heroes and artists of Mexico painted on the wall, Mexican Fine Arts Center Museum (p97)* **2** *Monument with Standing Beast (p127)* **3** *One of the River North art galleries (p75)* **4** *Old St Patrick's Church (p94)*

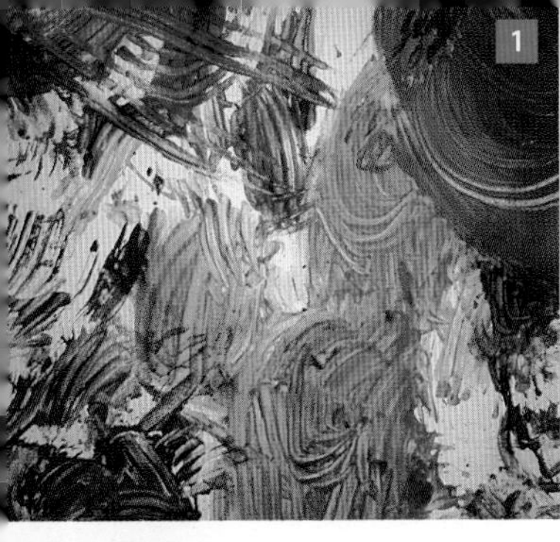

1 *Monkey room, Peggy Notebaert Nature Museum (p84)* **2** *Old Town School of Folk Music (p184)* **3** *The Berghoff (p136)* **4** *Posters, the Metro (p184)*

1 *Electric guitars on sale (p216)*
2 *Art supplies for sale (p216)*
3 *Shopping on Oak St (p221)*
4 *Secondhand music shop (p216)*

1 *The Drake (p244)* **2** *Blue Chicago (p182)* **3** *Hotel Allegro (p238)* **4** *Sofitel Hotel (p244)*

1 *Canyon walls, Starved Rock State Park (p258)* **2** *Fishing (p211) from Montrose Harbour* **3** *Bandstand, Marquette Park, Milwaukee (p260)* **4** *Fresh Water Turtle, Indiana Dunes National Lakeshore (p263)*

(Continued from page 202)

North Ave Beach (☎ 773-327-2706). Bikes run about $34 per day, and can also be had hourly (about $8). Free guided bike tours are available three times a day for renters, and the company also rents in-line skates; rates run about $20 per day.

MILLENNIUM PARK BIKE STATION

Map pp304-5

☎ 888-245-3929; www.chicagobikestation.com; 239 E Randolph St; 🕑 6:30am-7pm Mon-Fri, from 1am Sat & Sun Mar-Oct, 6:30am-6:30pm Mon-Fri Nov-Feb

The brand-new bike station has it all: bike rentals (road, hybrid, tandem and children's), repairs, storage lockers, shower facilities and a coffee bar. Rentals are by the hour, day, week or month. Daily rates start at $34. All rentals include locks and helmets.

ON THE ROUTE Map pp318-19

☎ 773-477-5066; www.ontheroute.com; 3146 N Lincoln; 🕑 11am-8pm Mon-Thu, to 7pm Fri, 10am-6pm Sat, 11am-5pm Sun

For people who want more high-end bikes, On the Route rents hybrids for around-town riding, or mountain bikes for more serious cycling action. You have to rent by the day, weekend or week. Rates start at $35. Helmets and locks are $5 extra.

FISHING

Between the fishing derbies organised by the mayor's office and the state-sponsored Urban Fishing Program, fishing in the city is making a comeback. The waters of Lake Michigan just off Northerly Island (p109) boast good fishing, as do the numerous park lagoons and the Chicago River. If the fish are biting, expect to catch rock bass, smallmouth bass, largemouth bass and the ubiquitous catfish. Anglers over 16 years of age will need a license (available online at www.link2gov.com/il/dnr and at any bait shop for $6 per day). Online resources for maps and tips include **Windy City Fishing** (www.windycityfishing.com) and the **Illinois Department of Natural Resources** (www.ifishillinois.org).

GOLF

Chicago golfers stretch the season as far as possible in both directions. The Chicago Park District has six public golf courses and three driving ranges, all overseen by **Kemper Sports Management** (☎ 312-245-0909; www.cpdgolf.com). You can find out more about the courses and find the next available tee times online or by phone.

Public courses include the following.

CHICAGO'S LUCKY STRIKES

Bowling is a distinctly Midwestern activity. People of all shapes, sizes and ages gather in boisterous groups to send balls crashing into pins. Talent is not a prerequisite, but a willingness to consume copious pitchers of cheap beer is. The lanes draw the most crowds during the cold months.

To try your luck on the lanes, visit one of the following.

Diversey-River Bowl (Map pp302–3; ☎ 773-227-5800; 2211 W Diversey Pkwy)

Southport Lanes (Map pp318–19; ☎ 773-472-6600; www.southportlanes.com; 3325 N Southport)

The Lucky Strike (Map pp308–9; ☎ 773-549-2695; 2747 N Lincoln Ave)

Waveland Bowl (Map pp302–3; ☎ 773-472-5900; 3700 N Western Ave)

DIVERSEY DRIVING RANGE Map pp318-19

☎ 312-742-7929; Diversey Pkwy, Lincoln Park; 🕑 7am-10pm

If you just want to knock a bucket of balls around, this driving range in Lincoln Park will let you whack away to your heart's content. Rental clubs are available, and a bucket is about $7. A reconstruction of the building has won kudos for its creative design.

FAMILY GOLF CENTER Map pp304-5

☎ 312-616-1234; 221 N Columbus Dr

In an inspired move, acres of vacant land have been turned into a golf course just east of the Loop. The center features a driving range, nine short holes with a complex green, chipping greens, and a bar and restaurant. You can make reservations to get a round in ($15) before or after a big meeting.

JACKSON PARK GOLF COURSE

Map pp302-3

☎ 773-667-0524; E 63rd St & Lake Shore Dr

The district's only 18-hole course is moderately challenging. Fees range from $12 to $22. Reservations are recommended.

SYDNEY R MAROVITZ GOLF COURSE

Map pp318-19

☎ 312-742-7930; 3600 N Recreation Dr (Lake Shore Dr) in Lincoln Park

The nine-hole course enjoys sweeping views of the lake and skyline. The course is very popular, and in order to secure a tee time, golfers cheerfully arrive at 5:30am. You can avoid that sort of lunacy by spending a few dollars extra to get a reservation. Fees vary widely through the year, from $8 to $22, with extra charges for nonresidents and reservations. You can also rent clubs here.

PICK-UP GAMES

Those looking to put in a little time on the basketball court will be especially excited by Chicago's offerings; casual hoops happen at almost every park in the city. If you're near Wicker Park (the park, not the neighborhood), you can get a game there. Ultimate Frisbee is also big in Chicago. An informative website dedicated to the sport (www.ultimatechicago.com) will keep you informed about start times. A regular Tuesday evening game is held in Montrose Park in the summer and in Clarendon Park in the winter.

TENNIS

Some of Chicago's public tennis courts require reservations and charge fees, while others are free and players queue for their turns on the court. Place your racket by the net and you're next in line. The season runs from mid-April to mid-October.

At Grant Park's **Daley Bicentennial Plaza** (Map pp304–5; ☎ 312-742-7648; 337 E Randolph St), you can pay a fee to use 12 lit courts. **Waveland Tennis Courts** (Map pp318–19; ☎ 312-742-8515; east side of N Lake Shore Dr where Waveland Ave meets Lincoln Park) charges fees for its 20 lit courts. **Lake Shore Park** (Map pp308–9; ☎ 312-742-7891; 808 N Lake Shore Dr), near the lake, features two very popular (and free) lit courts. In **Grant Park** (Map pp304–5; 900 S Columbus Dr near E Balbo Dr) you'll find 12 lit courts. No reservations are taken, but fees are charged at peak times.

GET YOUR BEACH ON

The Gold Coast's Oak St Beach is just one of the sandy expanses that stretch along the lake, making Chicago the Miami of the Midwest (if only for a few months each year). The city's best beaches, from north to south, are as follows:

Loyola Beach (Map pp302-3) Runs for more than eight blocks from North Shore Ave to Touhy Ave; features an upscale wooden playgrounds for kids. It's fairly close to the Chicago International Hostel and the Loyola El stop.

Montrose Beach (Map pp302-3) A great wide beach with a curving breakwater. The Montrose Harbor bait shop sells ice for coolers. There's ample parking, but the walks to the beach can be long. To get there by bus, take 146 or 151.

Fullerton Beach (Map pp308-9) Fills with zoo day-trippers and Lincoln Parkers. The narrow beach can get jammed on weekends, but a five-minute walk south from Fullerton yields uncrowded vistas.

North Avenue Beach (Map pp308-9) The closest thing Chicago has to a Southern California beach. Countless volleyball nets draw scores of beautiful people wearing the latest skimpy, neon-hued thongs. The steamship-inspired beach house contains a seasonal café. A short walk out on the curving breakwater anytime of the year yields postcard views of the city from a spot that seems almost a world apart.

Oak Street Beach (Map pp308-9) Lies at the north end of Michigan Ave, less than five minutes from the Water Tower. The hulking Lake Shore Dr condos cast shadows in the afternoon, but this popular beach remains packed. The new Oak Street Beachstro provides refreshments.

Ohio Street Beach (Map pp306-7) Nestled between Lake Shore Dr and Navy Pier, is convenient for those who want a quick dip or a chance to feel some sand between sweaty toes.

12th Street Beach (Map pp304-5) Hidden east of Meigs Field and south of the Adler Planetarium, makes a great break from the myriad sights of the Museum Campus. Its out-of-the-way location gives the narrow enclave an exclusive feel.

57th Street Beach (Map pp320-1) Just across Lake Shore Dr from the Museum of Science & Industry; features an expanse of clean, golden sand.

Jackson Park Beach (Map pp302-3) A bit further south of 57th St Beach; contains a stately restored beach house with dramatic breezeways. This beach, next to the yacht harbor, has a charm lacking at the beaches with more modern – and mundane – facilities.

ICE-SKATING

The ice-skating season is depressingly long for sunbathers. Chicago Park District operates a first-class winter rink at **Daley Bicentennial Plaza** (Map pp304–5; ☎ 312-742-7648; 337 E Randolph St) and at the **McCormick-Tribune Ice Rink** (Map pp304–5; ☎ 312-742-1168; 55 N Michigan Ave) in Millennium Park. Both offer skate rental and free admission.

SWIMMING & WATERSPORTS

Between Lake Michigan and Chicago's public pools, there are limitless ways to make a splash in the city.

Lakefront beaches (see the boxed text, opposite) have lifeguards from late May through to early September. However, you can swim at your own risk whenever you want, depending on what you think of the temperature. The water in August is usually in the 70°s F (21° to 26°C). If you're looking for some chlorinated water, try the large and refreshing pool at **Holstein Park** (Map pp316–17; ☎ 312-742-7554; 2200 N Oakley Ave; admission free; 🕑 7am-8pm Mon-Fri, from 9am Sat-Sun) in the heart of Bucktown. You can rent a suit and leave your sweaty duds in a locker. Best of all, the pool has frequent adult-only hours, with no squealing kids.

CHICAGOLAND CANOE BASE

Map pp302-3

☎ 773-777-1489; www.chicagolandcanoebase.com; 4019 N Narragansett Ave

Canoeists and kayakers can retrace the route of French trapper Louis Jolliet by paddling up the Chicago River in a boat from Chicagoland Canoe Base. The outfitter will rent you a canoe for about $45 plus deposit (kayaks are $10 more), and owner Vic Hurtowy will give you tips on where to paddle. Note: the company isn't located on a body of water, so having a car is key to picking up and returning the boats.

CHICAGO KAYAK Map pp302-3

☎ 847-425-9925; www.chicagokayak.com; 2738 Noyes St, Evanston

Based in Evanston and leading trips in the Chicago area and beyond, this company teaches courses in sea kayaking for the novice to the advanced kayaker. Numerous trips on Lake Michigan and the Chicago River depart from points in the city. Rates start at $65 for a four-hour course.

HEALTH & FITNESS

HEALTH CLUBS, YOGA & PILATES

Hotels almost always have either their own facilities or agreements with nearby clubs. If you're looking for something else, here are some good options.

BIKRAM YOGA Map pp316-17

☎ 773-315-9150; www.bycic.com; 1344 N Milwaukee Ave; Blue Line to Damen

For a great yoga-only experience, try this place in Wicker Park, where classes run daily and cost $15 per session.

CRUNCH FITNESS Map pp306-7

☎ 312-828-9777; 38 E Grand Ave; Red Line to Grand

Located in Near North, Gorilla offers more extreme workout opportunities, with martial-arts classes, yoga, boxing and Pilates.

HALSTED STREET MULTIPLEX

Map pp318-19

☎ 773-755-3232; www.fitnessformulaclubs.com; 3228 N Halsted St; Brown, Purple, Red Line to Belmont

A more recent addition to the Chicago gym scene, Multiplex welcomes guests to its half-dozen Chicago locations. Along with the usual workout machines, swimming pools and basketball courts, the clubs offer yoga and Pilates classes. Other branches include the **Gold Coast Fitness Multiplex** (Map pp308–9; ☎ 312-944-1030; 1030 N Clark St) on the, you guessed it, Gold Coast.

HARMONY MIND BODY FITNESS

Map pp308-9

☎ 773-296-0263; www.harmonybody.com; 1962 N Bissell; Brown Line to Armitage

A staff of fully certified Pilates purists offers classes in Pilates, Gyrotonic, yoga and Feldenkrais techniques. Group-yoga classes and Pilates-mat classes cost $15; private sessions run up to $70.

LAKESHORE ATHLETIC CLUB

Map pp308-9

☎ 312-644-4880; 441 N Wabash Ave

Offers pools, full equipment, jogging tracks and more. There are other locations in **Lincoln Park** (Map pp308–9; ☎ 773-477-9888;

GOING TO EXTREMES

Sporty adventurers with a need for speed, altitude and whoop-ass will find some easy adrenaline fixes in Chicago. About five years ago, windsurfers began vanishing from Montrose Beach, replaced by the speedy practitioners of kiteboarding. For the lowdown, check out the website of **Chicago Kiteboarder** (☎ 312-804-5482; www.chicagokiteboarder.com). Along with tips on wind conditions in various parts of the year, it offers suggestions on where to ride in Chicago. Beginners can also sign up for three- to four-hour lessons, starting at $200. For rock climbing, the best action happens at popular climbing destination Devil's Lake, near Baraboo, Wisconsin (about three hours northwest of Chicago). But there are plenty of stellar indoor walls to hit while you're in the city, the most impressive of which is the seven-story wall at the Illinois Center branch of the Lakeshore Athletic Club (p213). Day-use and orientation fees are $40. The **Old Town Multiplex** (Map pp308–9; ☎ 312-640-1235; 1235 N La Salle Dr), an outpost of the Multiplex gym group, also offers a rock-climbing wall. Day-use fees, including a lesson, are about $30. For those looking to climb with the sun on their shoulders, the **Lincoln Park Athletic Club** (Map pp308–9; ☎ 773-529-2022; 1019 West Diversey Pkwy) has a 70ft outdoor climbing wall that features a 30ft overhang and portions of simulated ice climbing (closed in winter and when raining). Use fees total $25. For boxing, try **JABB Boxing Gym** (Map pp316–17; ☎ 312-733-5222; 2nd fl, 410 N Oakley Blvd) where you can take a drop-in boxing class for $12. Call for its schedule. Kickboxers looking for some schooling in the city can find it at **POW!** (Map pp314–15; ☎ 312-829-7699; www.powkickboxing.com; 950 W. Washington), which offers a free first class to visitors.

1320 W Fullerton Ave), Streeterville and the **Illinois Center** (☎ 312-616-9000, 211 North Stetson). Day-use rates average $20. The Illinois Center location has an impressive seven-story indoor climbing wall. Day use and orientation fees cost about $40.

MOVEMENT STUDIO Map pp316-17

☎ 773-489-0484; www.themovementstudio.com; 1811 W North Ave, Suite 202; Blue Line to Damen

If you're serious about Gyrotonic, this spacious Bucktown studio is the place to go. Certified instructors offer the gamut of popular-with-the-stars bodywork techniques (Pilates, Gyrokinesis, yoga) as well as therapeutic massage. Prices start at $15 for a one-hour group class.

MASSAGE & DAY SPAS

Tennis, golf, canoeing…being on vacation can become dreadfully exhausting. After all your activity, head to one of Chicago's day spas to unwind.

FOUR SEASONS SPA Map pp308-9

☎ 312-280-8800; Four Seasons Hotel, 120 East Delaware Pl; Red Line to Chicago

If you really want to do it in style, head to the Four Seasons Spa, where pleasures such as the elixir paraffin wrap and the green tea and ginger mud body mask will 'revitalize your energy meridians.' They also feel pretty great. You can do quick 30-minute sessions or have a luxurious all-day affair. Prices start sky high and go up from there.

SPA SPACE Map pp312-13

☎ 312-466-9585; www.spaspace.com; 161 N Canal St; Green Line to Clinton

Men and women face a dizzying array of massages and body treatments in this sleek, relaxing space. Along with the usual seaweed body wraps, Swedish massages, sports massages and other familiar rubbings, you can get an aromatherapy workout or a 'Heaven and Earth Stone Therapy' massage, where heated river stones are used to melt away tension. Treatments run about $100.

SPACIO Map pp308-9

☎ 773-244-6500; www.spaciospa.com; 2706 N Halsted; Red Line to Diversey

You can get just about everything you need here, from a deep-tissue aromatherapy massage, to a haircut and color, right on down to a pedicure and facial. The 30-minute 'Spacio Tune-Up' ($45) is a relaxing combination of Swedish and Thai massage.

URBAN OASIS Map pp308-9

☎ 312-587-3500; www.urban-oasis.com; 3rd fl, 12 W Maple St; Red Line to Clark/Division

Exactly what the name implies. This calm, friendly place focuses exclusively on massage therapy, offering Shiatsu, Reiki and deep-tissue massages along with a host of other options. Guests are treated to fresh-fruit juices and an array of specialized showers before their massages. Try the invigorating salt-glow massage. Hour sessions cost around $85.

Shopping

Shopping

From the glossy department stores of the Loop and Magnificent Mile to the freak boutiques of Lake View and Wicker Park, Chicagoans have elevated shopping to a pastime almost as revered as baseball. The city's shops can readily satisfy the entire family, and an afternoon spent browsing might result in a half-price Ann Taylor suit for mom, a fine cigar for dad, a nipple ring and Darth Vader guitar for the teenage son in a band, an American Girl doll for little sis and a lucky bingo candle for gramma. Oh, and a sari for the family's foreign exchange student from Bombay.

Though you'll find Gaps and Banana Republics throughout the city, Chicago has also managed to maintain a thriving culture of independent and family-run stores. The friendly atmosphere of a small town pervades the scene, even among the stores along the Magnificent Mile, where low-key kindness prevails despite high-end prices.

Music, new and retro fashions, antiques and ethnic goods are the city's shopping strengths. Easy-to-obtain local souvenirs include sports-logoed gear (a Cubs ball cap being the most popular), jazz or blues CDs or a deep-dish pizza (see the boxed text, below). If all else fails, buy a bag of Tootsie Rolls. They're cheap, they're made in Chicago and you can get them everywhere.

Shopping Areas

The shoppers' siren song emanates from Michigan Ave in the Near North, along what's called the Magnificent Mile. It's stuffed with vertical malls and high-end chains and is the busiest shopping area in town.

The Loop hosts several department stores, especially along State St, which is where you'll find the flagship Marshall Field's and Carson Pirie Scott & Co, Chicago's premier stores from the early 1900s. Ritzy designers from Paris, Milan and Manhattan mix it up in the Gold Coast along Oak St.

Moving north and west of downtown, you'll find boutiques filling Wicker Park and Bucktown (mod), Lincoln Park (tony), Lake View (countercultural) and Andersonville (all three).

Opening Hours

Typical retail shopping hours are 10am to 7pm Monday to Saturday and noon to 6pm Sunday, though it varies depending on the season, the neighborhood and the amount of foot traffic. Prime shopping areas and malls may stay open until 9pm.

THE LOOP

Shopping in the Loop was a legendary experience through the 1970s. Then the rise of suburban shopping malls and the proliferation of stores on N Michigan Ave brought devastation – four of six Loop department stores closed, and scores of smaller stores left. Recently the area has undergone a rebirth, and although it hasn't yet come close to its former glory, numerous national retailers have moved in to serve the huge population of office workers who need to squeeze shopping into their lunch hours.

THE ULTIMATE SOUVENIR

Nothing says 'Greetings from Chicago' like a hulking deep-dish pizza delivered right to one's door. Several local chains will pack their pies on dry ice and ship 'em anywhere in the USA. Two who do it well:

Giordano's (p143; ☎ 800-982-1756; www.giordanos.com) You can ship a single pizza (12in size only), but nothing containing meat. No matter, as the veggie options (especially stuffed spinach) are enough to make you weep with glee. Pizzas cost $16 to $25 depending on the number of toppings; shipping costs an additional $25. Order by phone or online.

Gino's East (p143; ☎ 800-344-5455; www.ginoseast.com) You can add pepperoni or sausage here, but you'll have to order two or more 11in pizzas, costing about $25 each, plus $17.25 for shipping. Pies are sent Monday through Wednesday only. Order by phone or online, then sit back and wait for your friends to swear their undying gratitude.

TOP FIVE SHOPPING STREETS

- **Clark Street** (p225) Everything from human-sized dog collars to humanities tomes on this eclectic street.
- **Damen Avenue** (p229) The mid- to high-end boutiques here will have shopaholics salivating.
- **Michigan Avenue, aka The Magnificent Mile** (p219) Big-city shopping at its best.
- **Milwaukee Avenue** (p229) The funkier cousin to Damen Ave features blocks and blocks of hip stores.
- **Oak Street** (p221) The bastion of New York–style chic in one convenient location.

5 S WABASH AVE

Map pp304-5 — Jewelry

5 S Wabash Ave; Brown, Green, Orange Line to Madison

This old building, located on a block commonly referred to as 'Jewelers Row,' is the center of Chicago's family jeweler trade. Hundreds of shops in here sell every kind of watch, ring, gemstone and bauble imaginable. Most are quick to promise, 'I can get it for you wholesale!'

CARSON PIRIE SCOTT & CO

Map pp304-5 — Department Store

☎ 312-641-7000; 1 S State St; 🕒 9:45am-8pm Mon-Sat, 11am-6pm Sun; Brown, Green, Orange Line to Madison

Carson's has lived in the shadow of Marshall Field's since the former was opened in 1899. Architecturally, the building is a gem, designed by Louis Sullivan with cast-iron filigree dripping over the entrance. And shopping-wise it's pretty good, too, with moderately priced goods and a varied selection spread over six floors. Carson's has attracted a very loyal following of lunchtime shoppers.

CENTRAL CAMERA

Map pp304-5 — Electronics

☎ 312-427-5580; 230 S Wabash Ave; 🕒 8:30am-5:30pm Mon-Fri, 8:30am-5pm Sat; Red Line to Jackson

If you're traveling with a shutterbug, be sure to avoid this place until the very end of your trip, lest you risk seeing the sights all by yourself. Once photo-holics step inside this long, narrow store, it will be days before they surface again.

CHICAGO ARCHITECTURE FOUNDATION SHOP

Map pp304-5 — Chicago Souvenirs

☎ 312-922-3432; Santa Fe Bldg, 224 S Michigan Ave; 🕒 9am-6:30pm; Brown, Green, Orange Line to Adams

Books, posters, postcards and more celebrate local architecture at this heaven for anyone with an edifice complex. The Frank Lloyd Wright section alone contains enough material to research a doctoral thesis.

GALLERY 37 STORE

Map pp304-5 — Arts & Crafts

☎ 312-744-8925; www.gallery37.org; 66 E Randolph St; 🕒 10am-6pm Mon-Fri, 11am-4pm Sat; Brown, Green, Orange Line to Randolph

It's a win-win proposition at this nonprofit entity: painters, sculptors and other artists get paid for creating their wares while teaching inner-city teens, who serve as apprentices, to do the same. Their artworks, including paintings, mosaic tables, puppets and carved-wood walking sticks, are sold in the gallery here. Profits return to the organization.

ILLINOIS ARTISANS SHOP

Map pp304-5 — Arts & Crafts

☎ 312-814-5321; 2nd level, James R Thompson Center, 100 W Randolph St; 🕒 9am-5pm Mon-Fri; Brown, Orange Line to Washington

The best works of artisans from throughout the state are sold here, including ceramics, glass and wood coaxed into jewelry, wine jugs, glassware, mobiles and toys, at prices that verge on the cheap. The enthusiastic staff will tell you all about the people who created the various pieces. The Illinois Art Gallery, next door, sells paintings and sculptures under the same arrangement.

IWAN RIES

Map pp304-5 — Tobacconist

☎ 312-372-1306; 19 S Wabash Ave; 🕒 9am-5:30pm Mon-Fri, 9am-5pm Sat; Brown, Green, Orange Line to Madison

You're witnessing five generations of tobacco know-how at work in this store, which celebrates its 150th birthday in 2007. The setting is jovial and the selection of pipes, pipe tobacco and cigars (100 kinds at last count) can't be beat.

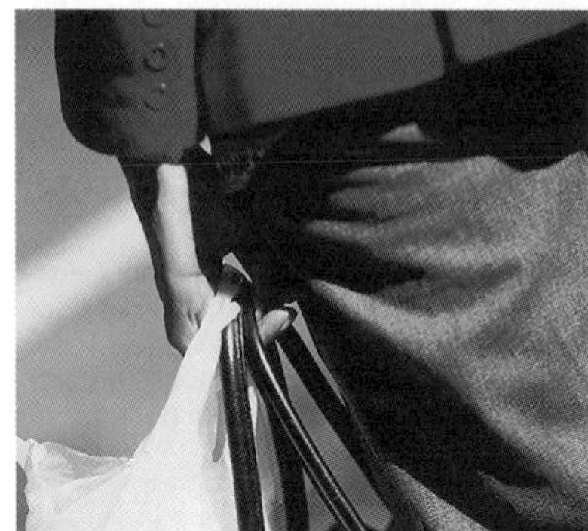
Hitting the sidewalks of the Loop

MARSHALL FIELD'S

Map pp304-5 Department Store

☎ **312-781-1000; 111 N State St; ⌚ 9am-8pm Mon-Thu, 9am-9pm Fri & Sat, 11am-6pm Sun; Brown, Green, Orange Line to Randolph**

The grandest old department store in the country, Field's offers 10 floors of designer clothes, furnishings, gifts, housewares, fine china, crystal and more. Dining under the soaring Christmas tree in the 7th-floor Walnut Room is a local family tradition. The basement gourmet food court is a good place for quick snacks. The bottom level also features a wealth of smaller-merchandise areas selling household items, gourmet food, stationery and more. You can buy the popular chocolate-covered Frango mints throughout the store. But get your Field's fix while you can because, much to locals' chagrin, Macy's has bought the chain and will be changing the name soon, perhaps by the time you read this.

POSTER PLUS Map pp304-5 Fine Arts

☎ **312-461-9277; 200 S Michigan Ave; ⌚ 10am-7pm Mon-Wed, 10am-8pm Thu & Fri, 9:30am-8pm Sat, 11am-6pm Sun; Brown, Green, Orange Line to Adams**

Located across from the Art Institute, this superlative poster store carries reproductions of many of the museum's best-known works, along with a number of fun, Chicago-specific historical prints dating from the late 19th century. Upstairs in the vintage room, European and American poster originals can go for as much as $30,000.

PRAIRIE AVENUE BOOKSHOP

Map pp304-5 Books & Magazines

☎ **312-922-8311; 418 S Wabash Ave; ⌚ 10am-6pm Mon-Fri, 10am-4pm Sat; Brown, Orange Line to Library**

This is easily the classiest and most lavishly decorated bookstore in the city. The beautiful architectural tomes – including many hard-to-find titles – rest on hardwood shelves, and the thick carpet muffles the noise of customers. Soon you'll want to find a smoking jacket, stoke a pipe and curl up in a corner leather chair.

ROCK RECORDS

Map pp304-5 CDs & Records

☎ **312-346-3489; 175 W Washington St; ⌚ 9am-6:30pm Mon-Fri, 10am-4pm Sat; Brown, Orange Line to Washington**

Don't let the sometimes surly staff scare you away from this well-stocked independent record store, which has a good number of listening stations and a wide selection of pop, indie rock, hip-hop and country.

SAVVY TRAVELLER

Map pp304-5 Travel Books

☎ **312-913-9800; 310 S Michigan Ave; ⌚ 10am-7:30pm Mon-Sat, noon-5pm Sun; Brown, Orange Line to Library**

The goal here is to carry every travel-related title in print, which means that you'll find plenty of obscure books tucked in among the comprehensive selection of

TOP FIVE MUSEUM STORES

Remember that many museum shops sell high-quality souvenirs, which may be more meaningful than another T-shirt.

- **Art Institute of Chicago** (p67) Carries an awesome poster selection of the museum's Warhols, Picassos and other famous paintings.
- **Chicago Historical Society** (p82) Stocks hard-to-find local history books.
- **Field Museum of Natural History** (p108) Dinosaur items make this museum store stand out, along with global textiles and pottery aplenty.
- **Mexican Fine Arts Museum** (p97) Brightly painted handicrafts from Mexico fill the shelves.
- **Museum of Contemporary Art** (p79) One-of-a-kind jewelry pieces and colorful children's toys are the strong suit.

Lonely Planet guides. If you can't locate something within the big selection, ask the staffers – who are all travel enthusiasts between vacations – and they'll order it for you. You can also buy gadgets such as electricity converters, luggage and atlases.

SYMPHONY STORE

Map pp304-5 CDs & Records

☎ 312-294-3345; 220 S Michigan Ave; 🕑 10am-6pm Mon-Sat, noon-5pm Sun; Brown, Green, Orange Line to Adams

In this store, in the Symphony Center, the Chicago Symphony Orchestra sells all manner of fun, whimsical, classical music souvenirs (keep an eye out for the Beethoven finger puppets). The shop even carries T-shirts – highly tasteful ones, of course.

NEAR NORTH & NAVY PIER

The city likes to claim that the Magnificent Mile, or 'Mag Mile' as it's widely known, is one of the top five shopping streets in the world. It's hard to argue. The term covers the stretch of Michigan Ave from the Chicago River to Oak St, vacuum-packed with high-end department stores and national chains.

ABRAHAM LINCOLN BOOK SHOP

Map pp306-7 History Books

☎ 312-944-3085; 357 W Chicago Ave; 🕑 9am-5pm Mon-Fri, to 7pm Thu, 10am-4pm Sat; Brown Line to Chicago

In the 'Land of Lincoln' this delightful store is a natural. It carries new, used and antiquarian books about the 16th president, the Civil War and the presidency in general. The knowledgeable staff regularly holds open round-table discussions with Civil War scholars.

AMERICAN GIRL PLACE

Map pp306-7 Dolls

☎ 877-247-5223; www.americangirl.com; 111 E Chicago Ave; 🕑 9am-7pm Sun-Wed, 9am-9pm Thu-Sat; Red Line to Chicago

You know the red shopping bags you see every female under age 12 carrying on Michigan Ave? They come from American Girl Place, a three-story doll store so bizarre you must see it to believe it. Dolls are treated as real people here: the 'hospital' admits them and takes them away in a wheelchair if they need repair; the café seats and treats them as part of the family, including offering them their own tea service. You can even order a doll made to look just like you.

ANTIQUARIANS BUILDING

Map pp306-7 Antiques

☎ 312-527-0533; 159 W Kinzie St; 🕑 10am-6pm Mon-Sat; Brown Line to Merchandise Mart

Look for rare items from five continents in 22 shops. The selection of Asian-focused works is especially strong.

APPLE STORE Map pp306-7 Electronics

☎ 312-981-4104; 679 N Michigan Ave; 🕑 10am-9pm Mon-Sat, 11am-6pm Sun; Red Line to Chicago

Powerbooks, iPods and everything else for Mac enthusiasts are splayed across butcher-block tables in this bright, airy store. The

A MAGNIFICENT PLAN

The Magnificent Mile (Mag Mile) was born from Daniel Burnham's celebrated 'Chicago Plan' (p44) in 1909. The goal: transform Michigan Ave from an Indian trading post into a major commercial boulevard, something along the lines of the Champs-Elysées in Paris.

The action started in 1920, when the Michigan Ave Bridge opened, linking the Loop to the Near North. It sparked a building boom that included many of today's landmarks, the Wrigley Bldg and Tribune Tower among them.

By 1947 the picture looked rosy enough that local developer Arthur Rubloff dubbed the thoroughfare 'The Magnificent Mile.' But the name didn't earn its stripes until the 1970s, with the opening of the Hancock Center, the tallest, most prestigious building in the world at the time, followed by the multistoried Water Tower Pl rising from the ground. The latter brought the concept of vertical shopping malls to Chicago, driving a stake through the heart of State St retail and forever changing the character of N Michigan Ave. Chicago Pl, 900 N Michigan and the Shops at North Bridge were its progeny.

Is it all as magnificent as the name implies? Well, it is if you like gracious, large-scale retailers. And there's no doubt it has become a destination in its own right – one that would make Daniel Burnham smile.

user-friendly setup provides plenty of clued-up staff to answer product questions, a 'genius bar' on the 2nd floor to sort out equipment issues and free Internet access on machines throughout the store.

CHICAGO PLACE MALL

Map pp306-7 Shopping Mall

☎ 312-642-4811; 700 N Michigan Ave; ⌚ 10am-7pm Mon-Sat, noon-6:30pm Sun; Red Line to Chicago

This eight-story mall is occupied mostly by chains like Saks Fifth Ave and Talbots. Smaller stores filling the gaps between the larger retailers feel a little thrown-together, though **Love From Chicago** (☎ 312-787-0838; 8th floor) is one of the best places to get souvenirs, including the elusive Al Capone shot glass. Chicago Pl also boasts one of the most dramatic food courts in the city – the plant- and fountain-filled area has wonderful views.

CHICAGO TRIBUNE STORE

Map pp306-7 Chicago Souvenirs

☎ 312-222-3080; Tribune Tower, 435 N Michigan Ave; ⌚ 9am-5:30pm Mon-Fri, 10am-5:30pm Sat; Red Line to Grand

While this small store doesn't have the selection of other Chicago souvenir places, it does outdo its competitors in *Tribune*-related merchandise. Cubs jerseys and books by noted Chicago authors are also available.

COMPUSA Map pp306-7 Electronics

☎ 312-787-6776; 101 E Chicago Ave; ⌚ 9am-8pm Mon-Fri, to 7pm Sat, 11am-6pm Sun; Red Line to Chicago

A convenient superstore for those looking to pick up laptop supplies, CompUSA offers unbeatable prices on things like wireless cards and hand-held computing devices. Come with a clear idea of what you want – the teenage 'help' rarely knows more than the customers.

GARRETT POPCORN

Map pp306-7 Food & Drink

☎ 312-944-2630; 670 N Michigan Ave; ⌚ 9:30am-9:30pm Mon-Thu, to 11pm Fri & Sat, to 10pm Sun; Red Line to Grand

Like lemmings drawn to a cliff, people form long lines outside this kernel-sized store on the Mag Mile. Granted, the caramel corn is heavenly and the cheese popcorn decadent, but is it worth waiting in the rain for a chance to buy some? Actually, yes. But rather than suffering the lines here, try the store in the **Loop** (Map pp304–5; ☎ 312-630-0127; 26 E Randolph St) across from Field's. It's usually line-free.

JAY ROBERT'S ANTIQUE WAREHOUSE Map pp306-7 Antiques

☎ 312-222-0167; 149 W Kinzie St; ⌚ 10am-5pm Mon-Sat; Brown Line to Merchandise Mart

This vast place boasts more than 60,000 sq ft of antique furniture, clocks and fireplace mantels.

JAZZ RECORD MART

Map pp306-7 CDs & Records

☎ 312-222-1467; 25 E Illinois St; ⌚ 10am-8pm Mon-Sat, noon-5pm Sun; Red Line to Grand

Musicians, serious jazz and blues aficionados, and vintage album collectors flock to this store, which is thoroughly stocked on the jazz and blues genres. Bob Koester and his dedicated staff can find just about anything, no matter how obscure. If you're looking to complete your Bix Beiderbecke collection, the Mart will help you get it done.

MERCHANDISE MART

Map pp306-7 Shopping Mall

☎ 312-527-4141; 222 Merchandise Mart Plaza, W Kinzie & N Well Sts; ⌚ 9am-6pm Mon-Fri, 10am-5pm Sat; Brown Line to Merchandise Mart

Beautifully restored in the early 1990s, the Mart contains a modest collection of chain stores on its lower floors. But the real allure lies on the many floors devoted to distributor showrooms for home furnishings and other interior fittings. As you prowl the halls, you can find next year's hot trends on display today. Technically, only retailers and buyers can shop on most of these floors, though LuxeHome, with its 100,000 sq ft of kitchen and bathroom fixtures, is open to the public. Building **tours** (☎ 312-527-7762; adult/student $10/8) are available when scheduled in advance.

NIKETOWN Map pp306-7 Sporting Goods

☎ 312-642-6363; 669 N Michigan Ave; ⌚ 10am-9pm Mon-Sat, to 6pm Sun; Red Line to Grand

While it's no longer the unique, museum-ish store it once was (outlets have cropped up in many other cities), this Nike temple has all the flash and sparkle you'd expect from the shoe giant. It remains hugely popular, with every swooshed T-shirt, sweatshirt, jersey and hi-top imaginable.

PAPER SOURCE Map pp306-7 Art Supplies

☎ 312-337-0798; 232 W Chicago Ave; 10am-7pm Mon-Fri, to 5pm Sat, noon-5pm Sun; Brown Line to Chicago

Every kind of paper produced is here, with the lightweight merchandise ranging from delicate Japanese creations to iridescent, neon-hued numbers. It's great souvenir shopping for friends with eclectic tastes.

PEARL Map pp306-7 Art Supplies

☎ 312-915-0200; 225 W Chicago Ave; 9am-7pm Mon-Sat, noon-5pm Sun; Brown Line to Chicago

This huge art-supply store sells discounted stock that you can use on the paper you bought from Paper Source.

SHOPS AT NORTH BRIDGE

Map pp306-7 Shopping Mall

☎ 312-327-2300; 520 N Michigan Ave; 10am-8pm Mon-Sat, 11am-6pm Sun; Red Line to Grand

The newest of the classy Michigan Ave malls, Shops at North Bridge appeals to a less aggressively froufrou demographic with stores like Swatch, the Body Shop, Ann Taylor Loft and the LEGO Store. The multilevel mall connects anchor department store Nordstrom to Michigan Ave via a gracefully curving, shop-lined atrium.

SPORTMART Map pp306-7 Sporting Goods

☎ 312-337-6151; 620 N LaSalle St; 9am-9:30pm Mon-Sat, 10am-7pm Sun; Red Line to Grand

In a classic rags-to-riches story, Morrie Mages got his start in his family's store in the old Maxwell St Jewish ghetto, where some of the city's leading retailers launched their careers by selling clothes between WWI and WWII. Mages built the place into the world's largest sporting goods store, eventually moving it from Maxwell St into its own renovated eight-story warehouse here. A few years ago the Chicago-based national chain Sportmart bought out Morrie for a fortune. Now renamed, the store continues his discounting philosophy, albeit without his inveterate promoter's spirit. Check out Mages' *Chicago Sports Hall of Fame*, on the Ontario St exterior wall.

GOLD COAST

Designer boutiques pop up like mushrooms on the tiny blocks just west of Michigan Ave, particularly in the single block of Oak St between Michigan Ave and Rush St; the names read like the advertisers' index in *Vogue*.

900 N MICHIGAN

Map pp308-9 Shopping Mall

☎ 312-915-3916; 900 N Michigan Ave; hours vary by shop; Red Line to Chicago

This huge mall is home to an upscale collection of stores including Diesel, Gucci and J Crew, among many others. Water Tower Pl is under the same management, and they simply placed all the expensive stores over here.

ALTERNATIVES Map pp308-9 Shoes

☎ 312-266-1545; 942 N Rush St; 11am-7pm Mon-Fri, 10am-7pm Sat, noon-5pm Sun; Red Line to Clark/Division

The kinds of shoes that delight the eye and appall the feet are the specialty at this small

CLOTHING SIZES

Measurements approximate only, try before you buy

Women's Clothing						
Aus/UK	8	10	12	14	16	18
Europe	36	38	40	42	44	46
Japan	5	7	9	11	13	15
USA	6	8	10	12	14	16
Women's Shoes						
Aus/USA	5	6	7	8	9	10
Europe	35	36	37	38	39	40
France only	35	36	38	39	40	42
Japan	22	23	24	25	26	27
UK	3½	4½	5½	6½	7½	8½
Men's Clothing						
Aus	92	96	100	104	108	112
Europe	46	48	50	52	54	56
Japan	S		M	M		L
UK/USA	35	36	37	38	39	40
Men's Shirts (Collar Sizes)						
Aus/Japan	38	39	40	41	42	43
Europe	38	39	40	41	42	43
UK/USA	15	15½	16	16½	17	17½
Men's Shoes						
Aus/UK	7	8	9	10	11	12
Europe	41	42	43	44½	46	47
Japan	26	27	27½	28	29	30
USA	7½	8½	9½	10½	11½	12½

store. Alternatives features one of the most cutting-edge collections in town, at prices that gladden the hearts of budding Imelda Marcoses everywhere.

ANTHROPOLOGIE

Map pp308-9 Women's Clothing

☎ 312-255-1848; 1120 N State St; 🕑 10am-8pm Mon-Sat, 11am-6pm Sun; Red Line to Clark/Division

Thirty-something women flock to this classy, unstuffy store that specializes in simple designs in dresses, suits and shoes, as well as housewares and accessories.

BORDERS BOOKS & MUSIC

Map pp308-9 Books & Magazines

☎ 312-573-0564; 830 N Michigan Ave; 🕑 8am-11pm Mon-Sat, 9am-9pm Sun; Red Line to Chicago

This humungous Borders, right across from the Water Tower, is always crowded. Thousands of books, spread over four floors, include lots of special-interest titles. You'll find a good selection of magazines and newspapers near the main entrance. Borders also has opened a much-needed branch in the **Loop** (Map pp304–5; ☎ 312-606-0750; 150 N State St) and a less attractive store in **Lake View** (Map pp318–19; ☎ 773-935-3909; 2817 N Clark St).

CAMPER Map pp308-9 Shoes

☎ 312-787-0158; 61 E Oak St; 🕑 10am-6pm Mon-Sat, noon-5pm Sun; Red Line to Clark/Division

Thanks to an inexplicable dearth of customers, the young employees at the only Midwestern outpost of the hip European shoemaker have plenty of time to talk to you about the fun designs they sell.

Cutting-edge Chicago fashion

CITY OF CHICAGO STORE

Map pp308-9 Chicago Souvenirs

☎ 312-742-8811; Chicago Visitor Information Center, 163 E Pearson St; 🕑 9am-5pm; Red Line to Chicago

This city-run store is a mecca for those wise enough not to try to steal their own 'official' souvenirs. Cheerful city workers will sell you anything from a decommissioned city parking meter ($200) to street signs for famous local streets ($50). The usual array of Chicago books, shot glasses and pint-sized metal replicas of the city's tallest buildings are also available.

EUROPA BOOKS

Map pp308-9 Books & Magazines

☎ 312-335-9677; 832 N State St; 🕑 9am-7pm Sun-Wed, to 8pm Thu-Sat; Red Line to Chicago

As the name promises, this store carries newspapers, magazines and books, primarily in European languages.

H&M Map pp308-9 Department Store

☎ 312-640-0060; 840 N Michigan Ave; 🕑 10am-9pm Mon-Sat, 11am-7pm Sun; Red Line to Chicago

This Swedish-based purveyor of trendy toggery is usually packed with customers clawing the racks for high fashion at low prices. Men and women will find a variety of European-cut styles ranging from business suits to bathing suits. There's another outlet at 22 N State St, but this one is bigger.

JIL SANDER Map pp308-9 Women's Clothing

☎ 312-335-0006; 48 E Oak St; 🕑 10am-6pm Mon-Sat; Red Line to Clark/Division

Jil Sander's minimalist colors and simple designs somehow manage to remain fashionable long after other trendsetters have disappeared from the scene.

KATE SPADE

Map pp308-9 Women's Clothing & Accessories

☎ 312-654-8853; 101 E Oak St; 🕑 10am-6pm Mon-Sat, noon-5pm Sun; Red Line to Clark/Division

Beloved by the women of Lincoln Park, Kate Spade specializes in bags constructed with clean lines. This store also offers jewelry, shoes and sunglasses by a host of designers.

FAMOUS UPSCALE BRANDS

Several big-name, upscale brands have outposts in the 'hood:

Barney's (Map pp308–9; ☎ 312-587-1700; 25 E Oak St; 🕑 10am-7pm Mon-Sat, noon-6pm Sun; Red Line to Clark/Division) A branch of the legendary New York men's clothing store.

Chanel (Map pp308–9; ☎ 312-787-5500; 935 N Michigan Ave; 🕑 10am-6pm Mon-Sat; Red Line to Chicago) Bastion of $2500 sweaters and more for women.

Hermès (Map pp308–9; ☎ 312-787-8175; 110 E Oak St; 🕑 10am-6pm Mon-Sat; Red Line to Clark/Division) Silk scarves, cashmere sweaters and other luxury accessories straight from Paris.

Prada (Map pp308–9; ☎ 312-951-1113; 30 E Oak St; 🕑 10am-6pm Mon-Sat, noon-6pm Sun; Red Line to Clark/Division) A large store that carries the designer's full line of men's and women's clothing.

NORTH FACE Map pp308-9 Outdoor Gear

☎ 312-337-7200; John Hancock Center, 875 N Michigan Ave; 🕑 10am-7pm Mon-Sat, 11am-5pm Sun; Red Line to Chicago

This well-known brand operates a large store that peddles the company's first-rate line of backpacks, sleeping bags and other outdoor gear at full retail prices. You also can buy maps, books and camping doodads.

SUGAR MAGNOLIA

Map pp308-9 Women's Clothing

☎ 312-944-0885; 34 E Oak St; 🕑 10am-6pm Mon-Sat, noon-5pm Sun; Red Line to Clark/Division

One of the youngest-feeling of the Oak St boutiques, Sugar Magnolia specializes in women's clothes by European designers.

WATER TOWER PLACE

Map pp308-9 Shopping Mall

☎ 312-440-3166; 835 N Michigan Ave; 🕑 10am-7pm Mon-Sat, noon-6pm Sun; Red Line to Chicago

Featuring the coolest fountain in all of Chicago mall–land (you'll see it on your ride up the main escalator), Water Tower Pl launched the city's love affair with vertical shopping centers. Many locals swear this first one remains the best one. The mall houses 100 stores on seven levels, including Abercrombie & Fitch, Sharper Image, the Limited, Express and Marshall Field's.

LINCOLN PARK & OLD TOWN

Lincoln Park contains plenty of tony shops, many of which bunch near the intersection of Halsted St and Armitage Ave, and North and Clybourn Aves. Clark St is the main commercial road running through the neighborhood; it offers all sorts of shops but serves record-store hounds particularly well.

ACTIVE ENDEAVORS

Map pp308-9 Outdoor Gear

☎ 773-281-8100; 853 W Armitage Ave; 🕑 10am-7pm Mon-Fri, to 6pm Sat, noon-6pm Sun; Brown Line to Armitage

Prices are high here but so is the quality. If you need lots of personal help choosing top-end outdoor gear, Active Endeavors will serve you well.

BARNES & NOBLE

Map pp308-9 Books & Magazines

☎ 773-871-9004; 659 W Diversey Pkwy; 🕑 9am-11pm; Brown Line to Diversey

This bustling Barnes & Noble location draws crowds every day of the week and has become a prime meeting place for the Lincoln Park yuppies. There's also a **Gold Coast** (Map pp308–9; ☎ 312-280-8155; 1130 N State St) branch.

CHICAGO HISTORICAL SOCIETY STORE Map pp308-9 Chicago Souvenirs

☎ 312-642-4600; 1601 N Clark St; 🕑 noon-8pm Mon-Wed, 9:30am-4:30pm Thu-Sat, noon-5pm Sun; Brown Line to Sedgwick

The shop in the **Chicago Historical Society museum** (p82) boasts an excellent selection of books devoted to local history, many of which are hard to find elsewhere.

TOP FIVE SHOPS FOR LOCAL DESIGNS

- **Chicago Antique Market's Indie Designer Fashion Market** (p232)
- **Mint** (p224)
- **p45** (p230)
- **Saffron** (p231)
- **Studio 90** (p228)

COTÉLAC

Map pp308-9 Women's Clothing

☎ 773-281-2330; www.cotelacusa.com; 1159 W Webster Ave; 12:30-5:30pm Mon, 11am-7pm Tue-Thu, 11am-6pm Fri, 10am-6pm Sat, noon-5pm Sun; Brown Line to Armitage

Cotélac sells basics – earthy blouses, skirts, tank tops and trousers – with a French bohemian flair. Fabrics are soft and floaty, creased and crinkled; they're easy to wash and wear, making them great for stylish travellers.

DAVE'S RECORDS

Map pp308-9 CDs & Records

☎ 773-929-6325; 2604 N Clark St; 11am-8pm Mon-Sat, noon-7pm Sun; Brown Line to Diversey

Dave's is an all-vinyl shop that feels a little like the setting of Nick Hornby's music-nerd classic, *High Fidelity*. Whether or not that's a good thing probably depends on your level of music nerddom. You'll find everything from vocal jazz to techno.

GUITAR CENTER

Map pp308-9 Musical Instruments

☎ 773-248-2808; 2633 N Halsted St; 10am-9pm Mon-Fri, to 7pm Sat, 11am-6pm Sun; Brown Line to Diversey

This large link of the national chain caters to the instrument needs of bands from all over Chicagoland, and has also branched out into DJ equipment like mixers and turntables.

HIFI RECORDS Map pp308-9 CDs & Records

☎ 773-880-1002; 2568 N Clark St; 11am-8pm Mon-Sat, noon-7pm Sun; Brown Line to Diversey

Check out the selection of dirt-cheap old soul and jazz LPs and new indie CDs at this friendly store. The Technics record bags ($45) will make you look cool, no matter what you have in them. HiFi is also a good bet for local music magazines like *Stop Smiling*.

LORI'S, THE SOLE OF CHICAGO

Map pp308-9 Shoes

☎ 773-281-5655; 824 W Armitage; 11am-7pm Mon-Thu, to 6pm Fri, 10am-6pm Sat, noon-5pm Sun; Brown Line to Armitage

Chicago women swear by this place, where designer shoes can be bought for a song. Even if you're not in the market for shoes, drop by on a weekend just to take in the orgy of boxes, tissue paper and frenzied shoppers.

MINT Map pp308-9 Arts & Crafts

☎ 773-322-2944; www.mintboutique.com; 1450 W Webster Ave; 4-9pm Thu, 4-8pm Fri, noon-7pm Sat, noon-4pm Sun; bus 74

Mint's teensy showroom displays handmade handbags, scented candles, jewelry, soaps, greeting cards and other crafty creations by Midwestern artists. Designers rotate in and out, so there's always something new on the shelves.

SAM'S WINE & SPIRITS

Map pp308-9 Food & Drink

☎ 312-664-4394; www.samswine.com; 1720 N Marcey St; 8am-9pm Mon-Sat, 11am-6pm Sun; Red Line to North/Clybourn

From Chilean table wines to first-growth Bordeaux, cavernous Sam's stocks Chicago's largest selection of imported vinos. It's easy to spend half a day here, wandering up and down the aisles and chatting with the casual, informative staff. Beer, spirits, champagne and cheese are sold en masse, too.

TOWER RECORDS

Map pp308-9 CDs & Records

☎ 773-477-5994; 2301 N Clark St; 9am-midnight; Brown, Red Line to Fullerton

Besides all types of mainstream music, this large store sells books and concert tickets, plus an excellent selection of zines and products from the alternative press. There's another Tower location in the **Loop** (Map pp304–5; ☎ 312-663-0660; 214 S Wabash Ave).

UNCLE DAN'S Map pp308-9 Outdoor Gear

☎ 773-477-1918; 2440 N Lincoln Ave; 10am-8pm Mon-Thu, to 7pm Fri & Sat, 11am-6pm Sun; Brown, Red Line to Fullerton

The smell of leather hits you in the face as you walk into this outdoor gear store, which offers a big selection of hiking boots and equipment, plus camping supplies and many brands of backpacks. It's a relaxed place to buy outdoor gear, without the derisive looks of lurking sales dudes who consider anything less than a frontal assault on K2 to be for wimps.

TOP FIVE MUSIC STORES

Independent record stores flood Chicago's neighborhoods, supported by the rockin' live-music scene in town (see p34). Vinyl geeks will discover heaps of stacks to flip through, while jazz, blues and hip-hop lovers are well positioned for obscure finds.

- **Dusty Groove** (p230)
- **Evil Clown** (p226)
- **Gramaphone Records** (p227)
- **Jazz Record Mart** (p220)
- **Reckless Records** (p231)

VOSGES HAUT-CHOCOLAT

Map pp308-9 — Sweets

☎ 773-296-9866; www.vosgeschocolate.com; 951 W Armitage Ave; 11am-8pm; Brown Line to Armitage

This tiny purple shop produces enormous flavors in its succulent chocolates by folding in exotic ingredients like curry powder, chili peppers and wasabi. There's another branch in the **Peninsula hotel** (Map pp306–7; ☎ 312-644-9450; 520 N Michigan Ave).

LAKE VIEW

Stuff that's never worn – let alone sold – on Michigan Ave is de rigueur on Halsted and Clark Sts in Lake View. Even if you're not buying, the browsing is entertainment in itself. Near Belmont Ave several stores serve the rebellious needs of full-on punks and teenagers. On weekend days the sidewalks attract a throng of characters – rich teens from the North Shore, black-clad punks with blond roots, the rest of Lake View's diverse tribes and people selling socialist newspapers. If you'd prefer a nice, solid designer dress to a nipple ring and PVC bikini, head to Southport Ave, where a string of clothing boutiques have laid down roots.

AIR WAIR

Map pp318-19 — Shoes

☎ 773-244-0099; 3240 N Clark St; noon-8:30pm Mon-Sat, to 6:30pm Sun; Brown, Red Line to Belmont

The Air Wair features perennial sales on huge, heavy boots of minimal practical value outside of a steel mill (read: Doc Martens). Celebrate your third piercing with a pair.

ALLEY

Map pp318-19 — Men's & Women's Clothing

☎ 773-525-3180; 3228 N Clark St; noon-10pm Sun-Thu, to midnight Fri, 10am-midnight Sat; Brown, Red Line to Belmont

A vast emporium based on counterculture and pop trends, the Alley offers everything from pot pipes to band posters to human-sized dog collars. Loud, obnoxious punk-rock tees ('I've got the biggest dick in the band' etc) are a specialty of the house. The labyrinth of rooms includes one devoted to the Alley's 'Architectural Revolution' store, which sells plaster reproductions of gargoyles, Ionic pillars and other items that have found a mainstream market with non-dog-collar-wearing interior designers.

ARCHITECTURAL ARTIFACTS

Map pp318-19 — Antiques

☎ 773-348-0622; www.architecturalartifacts.com; 4325 N Ravenswood Ave; 10am-5pm; Brown Line to Montrose

This mammoth, 80,000-sq-ft salvage warehouse, located a bit northwest of Lake View proper, is a treasure trove that prompts continual mutterings of 'Where on earth did they find *that*?' Italian marionettes, 1920s French mannequins and Argentinian cast-iron mailboxes rest alongside decorative doors, tiles, stained-glass windows, fireplace mantels and garden furnishings. Be sure to step into the free, attached Museum of Historic Chicago Architecture.

ARMY NAVY SURPLUS USA

Map pp318-19 — Outdoor Gear

☎ 773-348-8930; 3100 N Lincoln Ave; 8am-5pm Mon-Fri, 10am-5pm Sat; Brown Line to Southport

The merchandise area here would send a drill sergeant into a conniption. The place is a huge mess. But among the torn boxes and shambles of merchandise are actual military surplus items of the highest quality the taxpayer can afford.

BOOKWORKS

Map pp318-19 — Used Books

☎ 773-871-5318; 3444 N Clark St; noon-10pm Mon-Thu, to 11pm Fri & Sat, to 6pm Sun; Brown, Red Line to Belmont

This small, used-title bookstore has an excellent Chicago-specific section, and also sells used jazz and blues records. Contemporary fiction is a specialty.

BROWN ELEPHANT

Map pp318-19 Secondhand

☎ 773-549-5943; 3651 N Halsted St; 11am-6pm; Red Line to Addison

Everything from furs to studs lines the simple pipe coat racks at this resale shop, which helps to raise funds for the Howard Brown Health Center, an acclaimed clinic serving the gay, lesbian and bisexual community. Among last year's satin dresses you can find some gems, price- and style-wise. The used CD selection is especially good.

CHICAGO COMICS

Map pp318-19 Comics & Collectibles

☎ 773-528-1983; 3244 N Clark St; noon-8pm Mon-Thu, to 10pm Fri, 11am-10pm Sat, noon-6pm Sun; Brown, Red Line to Belmont

This comic emporium has won 'best comic book store in the US' honor from all sorts of people who should know. Old Marvel *Superman* back issues share shelf space with hand-drawn works by cutting-edge local artists (Chris Ware, Ivan Brunetti and Dan Clowes – who lived here during his early *Eightball* days – among them). *Simpsons* fanatics will 'd'oh!' with joy at the huge toy selection.

CHICAGO MUSIC EXCHANGE

Map pp318-19 Musical Instruments

☎ 773-477-0830; 3270 N Clark St; 11am-7pm Mon-Fri, to 6pm Sat, noon-5pm Sun; Brown, Red Line to Belmont

This is the place for vintage and classic guitars and other instruments. Watch out for the drool left by garage-band hopefuls.

CUPID'S TREASURE

Map pp318-19 Sex & Fetish

☎ 773-348-3884; 3519 N Halsted St; 10am-midnight Sun-Thu, to 1am Fri & Sat; Red Line to Addison

Here's where you can buy all those things you wondered if your neighbors owned. Spread through three large rooms, the adult toys on display leave adult browsers giggling like children. The goods – frilly, aromatic, battery-powered, leathery and more – should satisfy even the most imaginative of consenting adults. If you're having trouble deciding, ask the friendly staff, who are always eager to help and are earnest in their advice. Consider the following guidance given to one couple: 'The whip requires more skill. With the paddle, it's easy – you just spank.'

DISGRACELAND

Map pp318-19 Men's & Women's Clothing

☎ 773-281-5875; 3338 N Clark St; 11am-7pm Mon-Sat, noon-6pm Sun; Brown, Red Line to Belmont

You won't find loud '70s polyester shirts at this used clothing store, which specializes in secondhand (but up-to-date) fashions, mostly from companies like Gap, Banana Republic and Abercrombie & Finch. The men's stuff is downstairs.

EVIL CLOWN

Map pp318-19 CDs & Records

☎ 773-472-4761; 4314 N Lincoln Ave; noon-9pm Mon-Sat, to 7pm Sun; Brown Line to Montrose

This small store is covered with posters from Radiohead, Weezer, the Flaming Lips and other alternative favorites. Evil Clown sells used CDs acquired from people liquidating their collections ahead of the creditors. The staff knows where to find the good stuff. If you want to check out some local bands live, take a look at all the fliers advertising performances.

FOURTH WORLD ARTISANS

Map pp318-19 Arts & Crafts

☎ 773-404-5200; 3727 N Southport Ave; 11am-7pm Mon-Fri, to 6pm Sat, noon-5pm Sun; Brown Line to Southport

This exotic bazaar provides local artisans, recent immigrants and small importers with a market for their handicrafts, and with assistance in learning entrepreneurial skills. Reasonably priced folk art, textiles, masks, musical instruments and jewelry from Vietnam, Ghana, Pakistan and other far-flung countries fill the shelves.

GAY MART

Map pp318-19 Toys & Novelties

☎ 773-929-4272; 3457 N Halsted St; 11am-7pm Sun-Wed, to 8pm Thu, to 9pm Fri & Sat; Red Line to Addison

The Woolworths of the strip sells toys, novelties, calendars, souvenirs, you name it. One of the top sellers is Billy, the heroically endowed 'world's first out and proud gay doll.' Ken would just wilt in Billy's presence – that is, if Ken had anything to wilt.

GRAMAPHONE RECORDS

Map pp318-19 CDs & Records

☎ 773-472-3683; 2843 N Clark St; 🕑 11am-9pm Mon-Fri, 10:30am-8:30pm Sat, noon-7pm Sun; Brown Line to Diversey

Gramaphone is the hippest record store in Chicago – you'd have to either be a DJ or be dating a DJ to have heard of most of the hip-hop and electronic music sold here. Along with its collection of trendsetting sounds, Gramaphone offers record needles and DJ supplies, and a host of info on upcoming parties.

MEDUSA'S CIRCLE

Map pp318-19 Men's & Women's Clothing

☎ 773-935-5950; 3268 N Clark St; 🕑 noon-8pm Mon-Sat, 1-6pm Sun; Brown, Red Line to Belmont

Not sweating enough? Medusa's carries everything for raven-haired folks who like to wear dark velvet clothes on hot days. It's mostly girly tough stuff, like T-shirts of kittens armed with guns, and purses decorated with skulls wearing pink bows.

MIDWEST STEREO

Map pp318-19 Electronics

☎ 773-929-5523; 2806 N Clark St; 🕑 11am-8pm Mon-Fri, 10:30am-7pm Sat, noon-6pm Sun; Brown, Red Line to Belmont

A hub for DJ gear, both used and new. If you're looking for a basic mixer or a Technics turntable (or a PA system that will quickly make you the talk of your neighborhood), this is your store.

SOLILOQUY

Map pp318-19 Books

☎ 773-348-6757; 1724 W Belmont Ave; 🕑 11am-6pm Mon-Sat; Brown Line to Paulina

What would a great theater town be without a great theater bookstore? Soliloquy takes its bow in this category with more than 5000 volumes, including plays, anthologies, dialect CDs and titles on technique, writing and directing.

SPORTS WORLD

Map pp318-19 Chicago Souvenirs

☎ 312-472-7701; 3555 N Clark St; 🕑 9am-8pm; Red Line to Addison

This store across from Wrigley Field is crammed with authentic Chicago sports duds. All-wool Cubs and White Sox caps

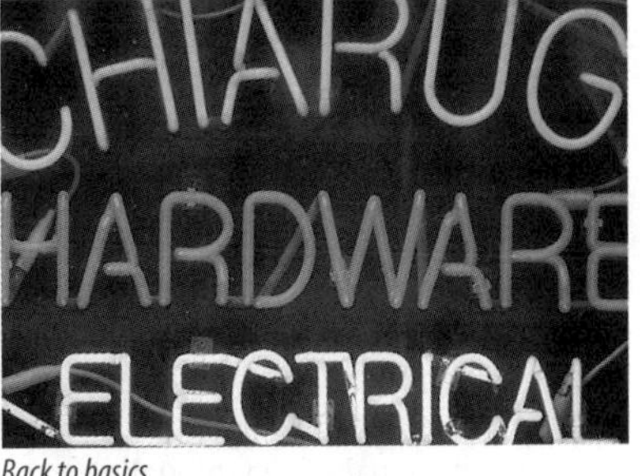

Back to basics

just like those worn by the players are $25. All-synthetic baseball caps just like those worn by nerds are $10.

STRANGE CARGO

Map pp318-19 Men's & Women's Clothing

☎ 773-327-8090; 3448 N Clark St; 🕑 11:30am-6:45pm Mon-Fri, 11am-6:45pm Sat, 11:30am-5:30pm Sun; Red Line to Addison

One of the coolest stores in Chicago for retro T-shirts and thrift-store-esque hipster wear, Strange Cargo also sells wigs, clunky shoes and leather jackets. Have something you want to get off your chest? You can use its iron-on machine to enliven vintage-style tees (or, ahem, panties) with the message of your choice. It also carries nice, cheesy decals of Mike Ditka, Harry Caray and other local sports heroes, which make excellent souvenirs.

UNCLE FUN

Map pp318-19 Toys & Novelties

☎ 773-477-8223; 1338 W Belmont Ave; 🕑 noon-7pm Tue-Fri, 11am-7pm Sat, 11am-5pm Sun; Brown, Red Line to Belmont

This weird toy and novelty shop is one of the best spots in Chicago for goofy gifts, kitschy postcards and vintage games. The shelves are overflowing with strange finds such as fake moustache kits, 3-D Jesus postcards and Chinese-made tapestries of the US lunar landing (just $5, baby).

WINDWARD SPORTS

Map pp318-19 Sporting Goods

☎ 773-472-6868; 3317 N Clark St; 🕑 11am-6pm Mon & Thu, to 5pm Wed, Sat & Sun, to 8pm Fri; Brown, Red Line to Belmont

One-stop shopping for sporty gear, whether you're into windsurfing, in-line skating, snowboarding or the see-it-to-believe-it 'flowboarding' (kind of like a cross between skateboarding and snowboarding). Ask at the store about various beach rentals of windsurfing equipment during the summer.

YESTERDAY

Map pp318-19 Toys & Novelties

☎ 773-248-8087; 1143 W Addison St; 1-7pm Mon-Sat, 2-6pm Sun; Red Line to Addison

If you've ever actually lived through the classic tale about discovering that your mom has thrown out all of your baseball cards, you can come here to find out what a fortune you've lost. Old sports memorabilia is the specialty of this shop, which is older than some of the goods on sale.

ANDERSONVILLE & UPTOWN

Clark St, north of Foster Ave, is the main commercial drag, hosting fashion and furnishing stores with reasonable prices. The Swedish-goods shops that are sprinkled between attest to the neighborhood's former inhabitants.

ALAMO SHOES

Map p311 Shoes

☎ 773-784-8936; 5321 N Clark St; 9am-8pm Mon-Fri, to 6pm Sat, 10am-6pm Sun; Red Line to Berwyn

This throwback to the 1960s focuses on comfortable Swedish shoes and Birkenstocks for both men and women, all at really good prices. The enthusiastic staffers hop off to the back room and emerge with stacks of boxes until you find what you want or you're entirely walled in by the possibilities.

EARLY TO BED

Sex & Fetish

773-271-1219; www.early2bed.com; 5232 N Sheridan Rd; noon-9pm Tue-Sat, to 6pm Sun; Red Line to Berwyn

This low-key, women-owned sex shop is good for novices – it provides easy to understand explanatory pages and customer reviews throughout the store, so you'll be able to know your anal beads from cock rings from bullet vibes. Also on hand are feather boas, bondage tapes, and videos and books (including serious resources like sex manuals for rape victims).

TOP FIVE BOOKSTORES

- **Barbara's Bookstore** (p232) Tops for serious fiction.
- **Quimby's** (p231) Ground Zero for comics, zines and graphic novels.
- **Savvy Traveller** (p218) If it's a travel book, they've got it.
- **Seminary Cooperative Bookstore** (p233) One of the world's best scholarly bookstores.
- **Women & Children First** (opposite) Women-penned fiction and other feminist tomes.

LAUNDRÉ

Map p311 Men's & Women's Clothing

☎ 773-769-2890; 5205 N Clark St; noon-7pm Tue-Sat, to 5pm Sun; Red Line to Berwyn

Scurry into Laundré for hi-top shoes, Puma T-shirts, track jackets and high-end jeans (Blue Cult, Paper Denim and True Religion etc), all of which sell for about 30% less than they do downtown.

PAPER TRAIL

Map p311 Greeting Cards & Gifts

☎ 773-275-2191; 5309 N Clark St; 10am-6:30pm Tue-Fri, to 6pm Sat, 11am-4pm Sun; Red Line to Berwyn

Here's where you find the cards the designers at Hallmark probably want to create, if only such creativity wouldn't cost them their jobs. The store's Chihuahua card collection is matched in scope only by the 'boxing rabbi' puppets.

STUDIO 90

Map p311 Women's Clothing

☎ 773-878-0097; 5239 N Clark St; 11am-7pm Mon-Fri, 10am-6pm Sat, 11am-5pm Sun; Red Line to Berwyn

Everything here is designed by the owners, who have built a growing reputation on their loose-fitting, sophisticated women's clothes. Studio 90 also houses the best $10 earring rack in town.

WIKSTROM'S GOURMET FOODS

Map p311 Food & Drink

☎ 773-275-6100; 5243 N Clark St; 9am-6pm Mon-Sat, 11am-4pm Sun; Red Line to Berwyn

Scandinavians from all over Illinois flock here for homemade limpa, herring and lutefisk. It sells over 4000lb of Swedish meatballs around Christmas time.

WOMEN & CHILDREN FIRST

Map p311 Books & Magazines

☎ 773-769-9299; 5233 N Clark St; 🕑 11am-7pm Mon & Tue, to 9pm Wed-Fri, 10am-7pm Sat, 11am-6pm Sun; Red Line to Berwyn

Hillary Clinton caused a mob scene when she came to this Andersonville feminist mainstay for her 2003 reading. High-profile book-signings and author events happen every week at the welcoming shop, which features fiction and nonfiction by and about women, along with children's books.

WICKER PARK, BUCKTOWN & UKRAINIAN VILLAGE

Damen and Milwaukee Aves in Wicker Park are two of the city's best shopping drags. You'll find the more oddball and youth-oriented resale shops residing on Milwaukee, while Damen holds a wealth of women's clothing boutiques. Division St is honing in on this territory with its young designer and home-furnishing stores, though it's rougher around the edges.

AKIRA'S

Map pp316-17 Men's & Women's Clothing

☎ 773-489-0818; 1837 W North Ave; 🕑 noon-9pm Mon-Sat, to 7pm Sun; Blue Line to Damen

Several fashion design students work here, manning (and woman-ing) the denim bar that's stocked with 20-plus different brands of jeans. There's a focus on up-and-coming and newly popular lines.

BOTANICA

Map pp316-17 Religious Paraphernalia

☎ 773-486-5894; 1524 N Milwaukee Ave; 🕑 9am-5pm Mon-Fri, 10am-5pm Sat; Blue Line to Damen

This slightly spooky, old-world storefront sells sacred candles, tarot cards, herbal remedies and devotional paraphernalia amid the dust and clutter.

CASA DE SOUL

Map pp316-17 Clothing & Accessories

☎ 773-252-2520; 1919 W Division St; 🕑 noon-8pm Mon-Fri, 11am-7pm Sat & Sun; Blue Line to Division

While the turntable in front blasts groovy tunes, check out the shell-inlaid coin purses, beaded handbags, unique clothing and earrings, and African wood-carved items (from the owner's homeland).

CITY SOLE/NICHE

Map pp316-17 Shoes

☎ 773-489-2001; 2001 W North Ave; 🕑 11am-8pm, to 9pm Thu, to 6pm Sun; Blue Line to Damen

One of the hippest men's and women's shoe stores in Chicago is divided into two sections. Niche is where high-priced designs dwell, and City Sole is its more down-to-earth cousin. Together they service the neighborhood: punks, young housewives and old Polish women alike.

CLIMATE

Map pp316-17 Greeting Cards & Gifts

☎ 773-862-7075; 1702 N Damen Ave; 🕑 11am-8pm Mon-Fri, 10am-9pm Sat, 11am-6pm Sun; Blue Line to Damen

'Eclectic' doesn't do justice to the array of items packed into this small store, including cocktail party kits, sassy dating guides and other tongue-in-cheek essentials for urban living.

RETRO CHIC CHICAGO

Much to the chagrin of fashion-forward metropolises New York City and Los Angeles, Chicago is fashion-backward, and proud of it. Place the blame – or praise, as the case may be – on its denizens' thrifty, Midwestern sensibilities. Folks here don't throw out their old bowling shirts, pillbox hats, faux-fur coats and costume jewelry. Instead, they deposit used duds at vintage or secondhand stores, of which there are hundreds. These places provide a shopping bonanza for bargain seekers patient enough to comb through the racks. The payoff is when you find that perfect 'My Name is Bob' gas station attendant work shirt or chestnut-colored fake mouton coat – both for $5.

For those less patient, several stores have popped up that offer retro-style clothes, but you'll be the first one to wear them.

Lake View and Wicker Park/Bucktown present the most fertile hunting grounds for retro chic styles:

Lilly Vallente (p230)

Strange Cargo (p227)

T-Shirt Deli (p231)

Una Mae's Freak Boutique (p231)

US #1 (p231)

CLOTHES MINDED
Map pp316-17 Women's Clothing
☎ 773-227-3402; 1735 N Damen Ave; 11am-7pm Mon-Fri, to 6:30pm Sat, noon-5pm Sun; Blue Line to Damen
A regular winner in Chicago 'best of' lists, Clothes Minded offers everyday women's fashions in a fun, inviting shop.

DUSTY GROOVE
Map pp316-17 CDs & Records
☎ 773-342-5800; 1120 N Ashland; 10am-8pm; Blue Line to Division
Be sure to check out the battery-powered record players ($100) at this mecca for soul, jazz and electronica.

JOHN FLUEVOG SHOES
Map pp316-17 Shoes
☎ 773-772-1983; 1539-1541 N Milwaukee Ave; 11am-7pm Mon-Sat, noon-5pm Sun; Blue Line to Damen
Bold and colorful shoes by the eccentric designer are the order of the day at this close-out haven. They come as tough-girl chunky or sex-kitten pointy as you like, with equally hip selections for men.

LILLY VALLENTE Map pp316-17 Secondhand
☎ 773-645-1537; 1746 W Division St; noon-7pm Tue-Sat, to 5pm Sun; Blue Line to Damen
Tackling the racks of clothes and junk at this resale shop is a pleasure, and it won't take long to stumble across a find or four. You'll rarely leave empty-handed.

MEBLE Map pp316-17 Home Furnishings
☎ 773-772-8200; 1462 N Milwaukee Ave; 11am-6pm Tue-Sun; Blue Line to Damen
Chandeliers, chimes, couches, chairs – it's worth browsing here to see the weird and wonderful mix of pricey props, antiques and conceptual art pieces. If you're thinking of buying beware – much of it is made of metal and won't work as carry-on baggage.

MS CATWALK
Map pp316-17 Women's Clothing
☎ 773-235-2750; www.mscatwalk.com; 2042 N Damen Ave; 11am-6pm Mon-Sat, noon-5pm Sun; Blue Line to Damen
Ms Catwalk stocks fun, flirty clothing and garnishes for women. T-shirts feature images from Buddha to Supergirl to Junior Mints candies; hoodies, lo-rise corduroy pants and big silvery bags accessorize your selection.

MYOPIC BOOKS Map pp316-17 Used Books
☎ 773-862-4882; 1564 N Milwaukee; 11am-1am Mon-Sat, to 10pm Sun; Blue Line to Damen
An eclectic used-book store with an enormous fiction collection, Myopic contains large sections for special interests such as lesbian, gay, geek and more.

NOIR Map pp316-17 Men's & Women's Clothing
☎ 773-572-6084; 1726 W Division; 11am-8pm; Blue Line to Damen
A cool store with affable staff and simple, affordable fashions, Noir is a must for those put off by the showy clothes and snooty attitudes of most boutiques. The pants, shirts and shoes are unpretentious, and classic cuts from the '50s predominate.

P45 Map pp316-17 Women's Clothing
☎ 773-862-4523; 1643 N Damen; 11am-7pm Mon-Wed, Fri & Sat, to 8pm Thu, noon-5pm Sun; Blue Line to Damen
The international buyers at this ultrahip boutique ensure that the latest styles arrive in Chicago roughly the same time they hit the coasts. Whether it's a black mesh vest by Tree or a bright orange leather blazer from Ulla Johnson, the clothes here deliberately push the fashion envelope. The shop also features jewelry created by local designers.

PENELOPE'S
Map pp316-17 Clothing & Accessories
☎ 773-395-2351; 1913 W Division St; 11am-7pm Mon-Sat, noon-6pm Sun; Blue Line to Damen
Named after the owners' ridiculously cute pug, Penelope's is a warm boutique for 20- and 30-somethings. Offering both women's and men's fashions along with nifty gifty things, Penelope's further ups the ante by providing an arcade-style stand-up Ms Pac-Man game to keep significant others occupied while loved ones try on clothes.

PORTE ROUGE Map pp316-17 Kitchen
☎ 773-269-2800; www.porterouge.biz; 1911 W Division St; 11am-7pm Mon-Sat, to 5pm Sun; Blue Line to Division
This sunny, French-kissed shop offers hand-painted crockery and chic kitchen

accessories that make even the most marginal, grilled cheese–burning cooks among us look gourmet.

QUIMBY'S Map pp316-17 Comics & Zines

☎ 773-342-0910; 1854 W North Ave; ⏲ noon-10pm Mon-Fri, 11am-10pm Sat, noon-6pm Sun; Blue Line to Damen

The epicenter of Chicago's comic and zine worlds, Quimby's is one of the linchpins of underground culture in the city. You can find everything here from crayon-powered punk-rock manifestos to slickly produced graphic novels.

RECKLESS RECORDS

Map pp316-17 CDs & Records

☎ 773-235-3727; 1532 N Milwaukee Ave; ⏲ 10am-10pm Mon-Sat, to 8pm Sun; Blue Line to Damen

Chicago's best indie-rock record and CD emporium allows you to listen to everything before you buy. If you're looking for CDs by local bands like Tortoise or Gastro del Sol, come here first.

RED BALLOON CO Map pp316-17 Kids

☎ 773-489-9800; 2060 N Damen Ave; ⏲ 11am-6:30pm Mon-Thu, to 6pm Fri & Sat, noon-5pm Sun; Blue Line to Damen

When hipsters get good jobs and start having kids, this is where they outfit the li'l pups. Adorable clothes, classic children's books and '50s-ish toys prevail in the cozy space.

SAFFRON

Map pp316-17 Women's Clothing

☎ 773-486-7753; 2064 N Damen Ave; ⏲ 11am-6pm Tue-Sat, noon-5pm Sun; Blue Line to Damen

Elegant Saffron specializes in women's classic-cut evening-wear, along with indulgent jewelry, shawls and bath and beauty products. The owner designs many of the items.

TOMMY'S ROCK & ROLL CAFÉ

Map pp316-17 Musical Instruments

☎ 773-486-6768; www.tommysguitars.com; 2500 W Chicago Ave; ⏲ 7am-3pm Mon, to 6pm Tue-Fri, to 3:30pm Sat; bus 66

Located at the edge of Ukrainian Village, Tommy's is hands-down the most rawkin' guitar store in town. So grab a doughnut or Polish sausage at the tiny front café, then strum (after you wash your hands!) the vintage axes in all their polka-dotted, snake-skinned, heart-shaped and Darth Vader–painted glory. Elvis impersonator photos, letters from Tom Petty, big-ass amps and a whole lot of handcuffs ratchet up the entertainment.

T-SHIRT DELI

Map pp316-17 Men's & Women's Clothing

☎ 773-276-6266; www.tshirtdeli.com; 1739 N Damen Ave; ⏲ noon-7pm Tue-Fri, to 6pm Sat, to 5pm Sun; Blue Line to Damen

They take the 'deli' part seriously: after they cook (aka iron a retro design on) your T-shirt, they wrap it in butcher paper and serve it with potato chips. Choose from heaps of shirt styles and decals, of which Mao, Sean Connery, Patty Hearst and a red-white-and-blue bong are but the beginning.

UNA MAE'S FREAK BOUTIQUE

Map pp316-17 Men's & Women's Clothing

☎ 773-276-7002; 1422 N Milwaukee Ave; ⏲ noon-7pm Mon-Thu, to 8pm Fri, 11am-8pm Sat, noon-6pm Sun; Blue Line to Damen

It's unlikely that the solid suburban women who once wore the pillbox hats and fine Republican cloth coats on sale here would ever have thought of themselves as freaks. Along with the vintage wear, Una Mae's has a growing collection of new accessories like scarves, hats and cosmetics.

US #1 Map pp316-17 Men's Clothing

☎ 773-489-9428; 1509 N Milwaukee Ave; ⏲ 11am-7pm; Blue Line to Damen

From the outside this place looks like a dump. Inside, however, you'll find rack after rack of affordable, vintage '70s bowling, Hawaiian and western-wear shirts, as well as towers of old Levi's jeans.

VIVE LA FEMME

Map pp316-17 Women's Clothing

☎ 773-772-7429; 2115 N Damen Ave; ⏲ noon-8pm Mon-Fri, to 5pm Sat & Sun; Blue Line to Damen

Plus-size shops for women are often woefully lacking in style. Not so at Vive La Femme, where larger women can find cutting-edge designs in a variety of sizes from 12 and up.

WEST SIDE & PILSEN

Ethnic shops (primarily Greek and Mexican) and used-goods and antique markets are percolating in the West Side neighborhoods. Keep an eye on the West Loop's up-and-coming **Fulton Market** (www.explorefultonmarket.com; Fulton & Lake Sts btwn Desplaines & Racine Sts), which comprises a slew of galleries and studios in what used to be a fish and meat shipping zone.

ATHENIAN CANDLE CO

Map pp314-15 Religious Paraphernalia

☎ 312-332-6988; 300 S Halsted St; 9:30am-6pm Mon, Tue, Thu & Fri, to 5pm Sat; Blue Line to UIC/Halsted

Whether you're hoping to get lucky at bingo, remove a jinx or fall in love, this store promises to help with its array of candles, incense, love potions and miracle oils. Though candles have been made in the back room for the city's Orthodox churches since 1919, the owners aren't devoted to one religion: you'll find Buddha statues, Pope holograms, Turkish evil eye stones, tarot cards and door mezuzahs. Unlike other stores of the ilk, which can be creepy, Athenian is tidy and the staff amiable.

BARBARA'S BOOKSTORE

Map pp314-15 Books & Magazines

☎ 312-413-2665; 1218 S Halsted St; 9am-10pm Mon-Sat, 10am-8pm Sun; bus 8

For serious fiction, you can't touch this locally owned store. Staff members have read what they sell, and touring authors regularly give readings. There's another location near the entrance to **Navy Pier** (Map pp306-07; ☎ 312-222-0890).

BLOMMER CHOCOLATE STORE

Map pp314-15 Sweets

☎ 312-492-1336; 600 W Kinzie St; 9am-5pm Mon-Fri, to 1pm Sat; Blue Line to Grand

Often in the Loop, a smell wafts through that's so enticing you'd shoot your own mother in the kneecaps to get to it. It comes from Blommer Chocolate Factory, which provides the sweet stuff to big-time manufacturers like Fannie May and Nabisco. Luckily, the wee outlet store sells a line of Blommer's own goodies straight to consumers at cut-rate prices. The dark chocolate, especially with covered almonds, reigns supreme.

CHICAGO ANTIQUE MARKET

Map pp314-15 Antiques

☎ 312-951-9939; www.chicagoantiquemarket.com; 1300 block of W Randolph St; admission $8; 8am-4pm last Sun of the month May-Oct; free trolley hourly from Tribune Tower, 435 N Michigan Ave

This market has become quite a ta-do in town. More than 200 dealers hock collectibles, costume jewelry, furniture, books, Turkish rugs and pinball machines. One of the coolest facets is the Indie Designer Fashion Market, where the city's fledgling designers sell their one-of-a-kind skirts, shawls, handbags and other pieces; it takes place inside the Plumbers Hall.

NEW MAXWELL ST MARKET

Map pp314-15 Flea Market

S Canal St btwn Taylor St & roughly 16th St; 7am-3pm Sun; Blue Line to Clinton

Every Sunday morning hundreds of vendors set up stalls that sell everything from Cubs jerseys in the wrong colors to tube-sock 10-packs to tacos for $1. This isn't your father's Maxwell St Market, which city officials forcibly relocated in 1994 after it became the sort of place where drug dealers and vendors of stolen hubcaps openly competed for customers. It's not even on Maxwell St any more, but a half-mile east. Still, you can nosh well and buy hubcaps, but the odds that the latter are fresh from your own car are somewhat diminished.

ANTIQUE ALLEYS

Chicago is a magnet for the best antiques and collectibles between the two coasts. Serious shoppers can easily make a week of it. The city hosts several antique malls that bring scores of dealers together under one roof. Dealers also cluster in the blocks around the Merchandise Mart and Kinzie St in River North, along the stretch of Lincoln Ave north from Diversey Pkwy to Irving Park Rd and along Belmont Ave west from Ashland Ave to Western Ave. Cruising that last strip is like driving along a country road laced with wheezy old stores, yet you're in the thick of the city. Notable stores:

Antiquarians Building (p219)

Architectural Artifacts (p225)

Chicago Antique Market (above)

Jay Robert's Antique Warehouse (p220)

Kane County Flea Market (p234)

SOUTH LOOP & NEAR SOUTH SIDE

Chicago's Chinatown sells the same things as every other Chinatown the world over: inexpensive groceries and housewares, Hello Kitty trinkets and all the Buddhist altar goods the ancestors require. It makes an entertaining shopping spree post dim sum or other noodle-y meal.

AJI ICHIBAN Map pp312-13 Sweets

☎ 312-328-9998; 2117-A S China Pl (in Chinatown Sq Mall); 🕒 11am-8pm Mon-Thu, to 9pm Fri, 10am-9pm Sat, 10am-8pm Sun; Red Line to Cermak-Chinatown

The front sign at this Asian snack and candy store says 'Munchies Paradise,' and so it is. Sweet and salty treats fill the bulk bins, from dried salted plum to chocolate wafer cookies, roasted fish crisps to fruity hard candies. It's all packaged in cool, cartoon-y wrappers, with plenty of samples out for grabs.

GIFTLAND Map pp312-13 Toys & Novelties

☎ 312-225-0088; 2212 S Wentworth Ave; 🕒 10am-9pm Sun-Thu, to 10pm Fri & Sat; Red Line to Cermak-Chinatown

After you see it, you'll wonder how you've lived without it: a toast-scented Hello Kitty eraser. Giftland stocks a swell supply of pens, stationery, coin purses and backpacks donning the images of Kitty as well as Mashi Maro, Pucca, Doraemon and other Asian cartoon characters.

HOYPOLOI Map pp312-13 Home Furnishings

☎ 312-225-6477; 2235 S Wentworth Ave; 🕒 11am-7:30pm Sun-Thu, to 8:30pm Fri & Sat; Red Line to Cermak-Chinatown

Hoypoloi is more upscale than most Chinatown stores, filled with Asian artwork, glassware and other funky interior items.

TEN REN TEA AND GINSENG CO

Map pp312-13 Food & Drink

☎ 312-842-1171; 2247 S Wentworth Ave; 🕒 9:30am-7pm; Red Line to Cermak-Chinatown

Ten Ren is *the* place to buy green, red, white and black teas, plus the teacups and teapots to serve them in. Thirsty shoppers can quench with a bubble tea sold at the counter.

WOKS N THINGS Map pp312-13 Kitchen

☎ 312-842-0701; 2234 S Wentworth Ave; 🕒 9am-7pm; Red Line to Cermak-Chinatown

This busy store carries every kind of utensil and cookware you could want. Don't miss the baseball-bat-shaped chopstick holders.

SOUTH CHICAGO & HYDE PARK

Bibliophiles should hop on the next Metra train to Hyde Park to check out the great selection of bookstores around the University of Chicago campus.

57TH STREET BOOKS

Map pp320-1 Books & Magazines

☎ 773-684-1300; 1301 E 57th St; 🕒 10am-9pm Mon-Fri, to 8pm Sat & Sun; Metra to 57th

A vast selection of general-interest titles here fills the basements of two buildings. The travel section features a commendable choice of Lonely Planet guides, a table and chairs for careful choosing and a chilled-water dispenser to cool the sweaty tourist.

AFROCENTRIC BOOKSTORE

Books & Magazines

☎ 773-924-3966; 4655 S Martin Luther King Dr; 🕒 10:30am-6:30pm Mon-Fri; bus 3

'Seeing the world through an Afrikan point of view' is the slogan at this store, where big-name Black authors give readings.

POWELL'S Map pp320-1 Used Books

☎ 773-955-7780; 1501 E 57th St; 🕒 9am-11pm; Metra to 57th

This leading used-book store can get you just about any book ever published – for a price. Shelf after heaving shelf prop them all up. Another outlet is located in **Lake View** (Map pp318–19; ☎ 773-248-1444; 2850 N Lincoln Ave). Both stores are well arranged.

SEMINARY COOPERATIVE BOOKSTORE Map pp320-1 Books & Magazines

☎ 773-752-4381; 5757 S University Ave; 🕒 8:30am-9pm Mon-Fri, 10am-6pm Sat, noon-6pm Sun; Metra to 57th

This is the bookstore of choice for several University of Chicago Nobel Prize winners, including Robert Fogel, who says, 'For a scholar, it's one of the great bookstores of the world.'

OTHER NEIGHBORHOODS

Lincoln Sq and Devon Ave are two shop-stuffed neighborhoods in the city's northern quarter. They are a bit off the beaten path, but worth the schlep.

Antique-o-philes will want to make the pilgrimage to suburban St Charles, about 45 miles west of Chicago, to the **Kane County Flea Market** (☎ 630-377-2252; www.kanecountyfleamarket.com; 525 S Randall Rd, btwn Rtes 64 & 38 in St Charles; admission $5; noon-5pm Sat, 7am-4pm Sun 1st weekend every month), where hundreds of dealers sell everything from junk to books to rare curios.

LINCOLN SQUARE

Lincoln Sq is an old German neighborhood that has gentrified, yet retains European roots. The area is located between Andersonville and Lake View, to the west; the shopping district is next to the intersection of Lincoln, Lawrence and Western Aves.

CHOPPING BLOCK Map pp302-3 Kitchen

☎ 773-472-6700; www.thechoppingblock.net; 4747 N Lincoln Ave; 10am-7pm Mon-Fri, to 6pm Sat, to 4pm Sun; Brown Line to Western

Let's say your recipe calls for Hungarian cinnamon, gray sea salt and Balinese long pepper. Instead of throwing up your hands in despair after searching the local grocery, and then calling for a pizza delivery, stop in at Chopping Block. Specialty foods, high-end cookware and hard-to-find utensils (corn butter brush or ravioli stamper, anyone?) are the name of the game. The store also offers cooking classes ($20 to $125 for a two- or three-hour session), like Summer Fruit Pies.

MERZ APOTHECARY

Map pp302-3 Bath & Beauty

☎ 773-989-0900; 4716 N Lincoln Ave; 9am-6pm Mon-Sat; Brown Line to Western

Merz is a true, turn-of-the-century European apothecary. Antique pharmacy jars contain herbs, homeopathic remedies, vitamins and supplements, and the shelves are stacked high with skin care, personal care, bath and aromatherapy products from around the world. It's perhaps the only place in town with an extensive hot-water bottle selection. The staff speaks seven languages altogether.

TIMELESS TOYS

Map pp302-3 Kids

☎ 773-334-4445; 4749 N Lincoln Ave; 10am-6pm Mon-Wed & Sat, to 7pm Thu & Fri, 11am-5pm Sun; Brown Line to Western

This charming independent shop is better described for what it does *not* carry – no Barbies, Harry Potter books or trendy kiddie togs. Instead you'll find high-quality, old-fashioned toys, many of which are made in Germany and other European countries. Have fun playing with the bug magnifier, microscopes, glitter balls, silk wings, wooden spinning tops and Bozo the Clown bop bag.

DEVON AVENUE

Known as Chicago's 'International Marketplace,' Devon Ave is where worlds collide – Indian women in jewel-toned saris glide by Muslim men in white skullcaps, and Nigerian women in bright-print robes shop beside Orthodox Jewish men in black yarmulkes. It is one of the most diverse communities you'll see, and makes a festive shopping destination.

Devon Ave at Western Ave is the main intersection. Indian sari and jewelry shops start near 2600 W Devon; to the west they give way to Jewish and Islamic goods stores, while to the east they trickle out into a gaggle of electronics and dollar stores. Stock up here on low-priced film, over-the-counter medicines, luggage and your other travel necessities.

INDIA SARI PALACE

Map pp302-3 Women's Clothing

☎ 773-338-2127; 2534 W Devon Ave; Red Line to Morse, transfer to bus 155)

One of the avenue's top shops for beautifully decorated, silky saris.

ROSENBLUM'S WORLD OF JUDAICA

Map pp302-3; Religious Paraphernalia

☎ 773-262-1700, 2906 W Devon Ave; 9am-6pm Mon-Wed, to 7pm Thu, to 3pm Fri, 10am-4pm Sun; Red Line to Morse, transfer to bus 155)

Rows of *dreidels*, menorahs, *shofars* and other *tchotchkes*.

Sleeping

Sleeping

As the most popular convention city in the US, Chicago abounds with hotels. In the Loop and North Side, more than 100 hotels of all types offer more than 25,000 rooms. That's the good news. The bad news is that the conventions can attract tens of thousands of visitors, who fill up even the most remote locations and pay top dollar for the chance to do so.

To find out if your intended visit coincides with a major show, you can try calling the **Chicago Convention & Tourism Bureau** (☎ 312-567-8500; www.choosechicago.com), but these folks – the ones who market McCormick Place – may not give you complete information on upcoming shows because of contractual agreements. The best sources are probably the major convention hotels, such as the Hyatt, the Sheraton and the Hiltons. If they have room for the dates of your visit, then most other places will as well.

Happily, the Internet has dramatically lowered the price of a stay in Chicago for savvy self-bookers (see the boxed text, opposite). Without an Internet deal, the average downtown room rate runs about $150. During nonholiday weekends in the dead of winter, the best hotels sometimes offer rooms for $125 a night. Ask about package deals, which may include in-room treats such as champagne, as well as free theater tickets and parking.

And speaking of parking: hotels in the Loop and Near North charge around $30 per night to leave your car in their lot. If you're staying in the Loop, or along the Magnificent Mile, there are no free on-street alternatives. This makes the West Side (p248) and other neighborhoods away from downtown cheaper bets for travelers who will be driving during their stay.

Finally, if you do arrive in town and everything seems to be full, try the hotels by the O'Hare and Midway Airports. Because these are a trek from the city center, they often have a few beds available when no one else does.

Check-in at most hotels begins at 3pm; checkout time is typically noon. Many hotels will allow you to store your luggage with them on the day of checkout.

Price Ranges

When we list room rates in this chapter, we are listing average prices for a standard double-occupancy room with bathroom (unless otherwise indicated). The range noted takes into account seasonal fluctuations and the vagaries of weekend versus weekday lodging. We use the term 'Cheap Sleeps' to indicate places where a room for two people averages less than $100 per night. Use the prices quoted for comparison purposes only, since a large convention in town can make them laughably off-base. And beware of a nasty surprise you will find on your bill – the hotel tax is a gnarly 15.4%.

B&Bs

Chicago is slowly catching on to the bed-and-breakfast concept. **Bed & Breakfast Chicago** (www.chicago-bed-breakfast.com), a booking service, handles rooms at more than 60 places in the city, most of them in the Gold Coast, Old Town and Lincoln Park areas. The units run the gamut from bedrooms in upscale old graystones to whole apartments where you're left to your own devices. This is an excellent way to experience life in the more interesting neighborhoods. The service provides you with a list of places based on your desires for price, location and proximity of the owners. Rates for singles and doubles range anywhere from about $95 to over $300. The minimum stay at most of the places is two or three nights.

Longer-Term Rentals

Lucky enough to have to extend your time in Chicago? Hotels often offer very attractive rates for stays of a week or longer, so you can start your hunt for a long-term stay with them. You can also look in the *Yellow Pages* under 'Apartments': several of the large management companies run advertisements of their furnished apartments, geared toward corporate clients.

THREE-STAR SLEEPS AT ONE-STAR PRICES

At first glance, Chicago's array of budget sleep options may seem pitiful. But in reality, the Loop and Near North neighborhoods abound with centrally located, posh hotel rooms that cost slightly more than a private room at a hostel. Where are the rooms hiding? On your computer. By using the right booking websites (and being open to a little randomness) you can save a jaw-dropping amount on your accommodations.

The savings are particularly great in Chicago because the hotels here are so danged large. With 500 or more guest rooms, the Hyatts, the Sheratons and other oversized Goliaths for business travelers have blocks of unsold rooms most nights of the week. Getting *somebody* into those beds, even at half-price, is better than letting them go empty. But because they don't want to undercut their own (full-price) Internet bookings, the hotels dump the extra rooms through third-party sites like Hotwire.com and Priceline.com.

Some drawbacks come with the great rates. Oftentimes, you don't get to see the name of the hotel until after you've made your reservation and paid for the room. The truly astounding deals ($50 per night for a three-star room is common) tend to only occur at the larger (read: blander) hotels. And making changes to existing reservations can be harder than crossing Lake Shore Dr at rush hour.

Still, in most situations, it's worth it. No, you don't get to see what hotel you're booking until you've already committed yourself to it. But you do get to see the hotel's neighborhood, star rating, and list of amenities. And who wouldn't like a little more spontaneity and unpredictability in their lives? In exchange for living with a little mystery, you'll pay about half what you would if you called the hotel directly. Some of the sites to know:

Hotels.com (www.hotels.com) Like Orbitz, this site can find deals on Chicago hotels that other sites miss.

Hotwire.com (www.hotwire.com) The king of hotel-hunting sites is typically $50 cheaper than all its competitors. You can find four-star downtown rooms on it for around $80, even in the high season. It's also great for rental cars.

Orbitz (www.orbitz.com) If you don't care for the notion of mystery hotels, this straightforward booking site turns up slightly better rates for the Windy City than its competitors.

Priceline.com (www.priceline.com) Unlike Hotwire, Priceline asks you to actually to 'bid' on a room, picking the neighborhood and amenities you'd like, then offering a price you'd be willing to pay. If Priceline finds a room that matches your requirements, it's automatically booked and your credit card is charged. Hot tip: visit the Chicago forums of www.biddingfortravel.com before putting in your offer. Priceline users post their recent winning bids here – along with the hotels they got for those bids – giving you an inside track on how much you should offer.

Another good resource is the **Habitat Corporate Suites Network** (☎ 312-902-2092, 800-833-0331; www.habitatcsn.com), which manages many of the city's upscale high-rises in the Near North. The fully equipped rental units come with cable TV and voice mail, and they enjoy good locations, in buildings with door attendants. Rates tend to run $70 to $120 per day.

If you don't want to work through a middleman, try the **Residence Inn by Marriott** (Map pp308–9; ☎ 312-943-9800, 800-331-3131; www.residenceinn.com; 201 E Walton St). It offers apartment-sized units, each with a full kitchen. The Gold Coast hotel also provides breakfast every day, as well as a free buffet (with beer and wine) in the lobby on evenings from Monday to Thursday. Rooms are bigger than typical hotel rooms and make good homes for the person stuck on the road. There's even a laundry room where you can wash your dirty duds.

THE LOOP & GRANT PARK

Loop hotels are convenient to Grant Park, Millennium Park, the museums and the central business and financial districts. They are usually no more than a 15-minute walk away from River North and N Michigan Ave (and for those near the river, much less).

FAIRMONT Map pp304-5 Hotel

☎ 312-565-8000, 800-527-7544; www.fairmont.com; 200 N Columbus Dr; r $169-389; Brown, Green, Orange Line to Randolph

Tall people will be thrilled with the extralong beds here, and less lofty-heighted souls will enjoy the spacious rooms, well-equipped work areas, opulent bathrooms and other luxuries provided by this Toronto-based company. Rooms near the top of the hotel's

45 stories can enjoy excellent views if they face the park or lake. The public spaces are equally grand, and the hotel is spitting distance from the celebrated spitting fountains of Millennium Park.

HOTEL ALLEGRO Map pp304-5 Hotel

☎ 312-236-0123, 800-643-1500; www.allegrochicago.com; 171 W Randolph St; r $179-249; Brown, Orange Line to Randolph

Located next door to the Cadillac Palace Theater, the Allegro was once known as the Bismarck Hotel, home to various Chicago political organizations and dubious dealings. Thanks to a hip makeover and nice features for the price, the 483-room hotel now attracts a broad demographic to its velvety, primary-toned interior. Boutique touches, such as a complimentary wine hour, flat-screen TVs and free wireless Internet, add to the attraction.

HOTEL BURNHAM Map pp304-5 Hotel

☎ 312-782-1111, 877-294-9712; www.burnhamhotel.com; 1 W Washington St; r $169-399; Red Line to Washington

One of the finest boutique hotels in Chicago, this historic gem began its life as the Reliance Building in the early 1890s. The offices in the Burnham-designed building have since been transformed into cute, cheery hotel rooms, adorned with granite counter tops, Aveda bath products and a simple French feel throughout. Some rooms still bear the original wood-and-glass doors from the building's previous life (complete with a beautiful old brass key to open them). The Burnham offers a complimentary wine reception every night, and the hotel's Atwood Café is a worthwhile destination in its own right. The proprietors brag that the hotel has the highest guest-return rates in Chicago; it's easy to see why. Free wired Internet available.

HOTEL MONACO

Map pp304-5 Hotel

☎ 312-960-8500; www.monaco-chicago.com; 225 N Wabash Ave; r $199-329; Brown, Orange Line to State

Posh and quirky, Hotel Monaco offers free nightly wine happy hours, 'Tall Rooms' for NBA-sized travelers and your own in-room goldfish. Service is classy without being snooty, and the rooms are bright and stylish, with extras including yoga props and

Hotel Allegro (left)

CD players. Free wireless Internet service is available throughout the building, and a business center and 24-hour fitness room are also on-site.

HYATT REGENCY CHICAGO

Map pp304-5 Hotel

☎ 312-565-1234, 800-233-1234; www.chicago.hyatt.com; 151 E Wacker Dr; r $179-289; Brown, Green, Orange Line to State

A vast convention hotel with 2019 rooms, the Hyatt Regency was best known for being big. And kind of blah. A $60 million renovation completed in 2002, however, has given the rooms a more modern look, and added free DSL Internet access for all guests. Drinkers will rejoice at the fact that the Hyatt boasts the longest freestanding bar in North America. The big downside: no swimming pool. Lots of specials keep all those rooms filled in off-peak times.

PALMER HOUSE HILTON

Map pp304-5 Hotel

☎ 312-726-7500, 800-445-8667; www.hilton.com; 17 E Monroe St; r $94-219; Brown, Green, Orange Line to Adams

Built in 1892, the Palmer House hotel features the kind of 'Oh my God' opulence in its lobby that makes a trip here imperative, even if you don't stay here. The home of many worldwide hotelier firsts (first to use electric lighting, first to have in-room telephones, inventor of the brownie), the Palmer House has been a pampering home to four generations of visitors. It boasts a surprisingly friendly and welcoming vibe for a place so resplendent in Tiffany statues and

BEST FOR BUSINESS

Working in Chicago? We salute you. Fighting off the delectable distractions of the Windy City is going to take some doing, and these hotels will help you stay focused and productive.

Courtyard by Marriott Chicago Downtown (p240) The hotel chain 'designed by business travelers' delivers the goods.

Hyatt Regency McCormick Place (p250) This sleek Hyatt is part of McCormick Place, allowing you to sleep late and still make it to the convention floor before your colleagues.

Peninsula (p242) Speakerphones in the bathrooms have built-in noise-canceling technology so your clients will never know you're holding the meeting from the tub.

Sheraton Chicago Hotel & Towers (p242) Large desks give toiling workers plenty of room for paper pushing.

W Chicago City Center (below) Kids running rampant in the hallways? Not at this subdued place, where business travelers make up the bulk of the guests.

acres of glittering gold. The Hilton's 1639 rooms vary greatly in size, so ask for a big one when you check in. The pool and fitness club are both above average, and the management works to make the hotel especially appealing to gay and lesbian travelers. Wired Internet is available for a fee.

RENAISSANCE CHICAGO HOTEL

Map pp304-5 Hotel

☎ 312-372-7200, 888-236-2427; www.renaissancehotels.com; 1 W Wacker Dr; r $159-389; Brown, Green, Orange Line to State

This luxury hotel, next to the offices of advertising giant Leo Burnett, is lavish in its decor and amenities, but feels a touch dated. The public spaces are actually much nicer than the somewhat bland exterior would suggest, with ornate tapestries and other elegant touches. The rooms are large and include sitting areas, which will be appreciated by those who don't want to spend all their time in their room in bed. Bay windows offer good views of the skyline and the river. All rooms contain modem ports, and the business-traveler rooms come with fax machines and printers. In addition, a 24-hour Kinko's business-service facility is on the premises. The hotel offers packages that include tickets to shows in Loop theaters.

SILVERSMITH Map pp304-5 Hotel

☎ 312-372-7696, 800-227-6963; www.crowneplaza.com/silversmith; 10 S Wabash Ave; r $189-234; Brown, Green, Orange Line to Madison

Another Loop architectural gem that has been converted into a hotel, the Silversmith was built in 1894. Although the exterior was designed by Daniel Burnham's firm, the hotel's interior recalls Frank Lloyd Wright. The rooms are big, and the furniture has a distinct Prairie-style charm. The views leave something to be desired: some overlook the El track, and others look right into another building. However, the atmosphere is pleasantly relaxed, and the location is ideal for exploring the city's great attractions on foot.

SWISSÔTEL CHICAGO

Map pp304-5 Hotel

☎ 312-565-0565, 800-654-7263; www.chicago.swissotel.com; 323 E Wacker Dr; r $179-599; Brown, Green, Orange Line to Randolph

On the eastern frontier of Illinois Center, the Swissôtel – in a striking triangular mirrored-glass high-rise – is easy to spot. The 632 large rooms offer the expected good views from their individual sitting areas. Separate showers and bathtubs mean that one can douse while the other dunks. The casual Cafe Suisse bakes its own bread and pastries, and the Palm is a notable steak house. Anyone wandering through can lay waste to the huge bowl of mini Swiss chocolates on the concierge counter. This place fills up for weekday stays *months* in advance, so reserve early.

W CHICAGO CITY CENTER

Map pp304-5 Hotel

☎ 312-332-1200, 877-946-8357; www.whotels.com; 172 W Adams St; r$199-499; Brown, Orange Line to Quincy

The employees all wear black at this hip hotel, where the soaring, beautiful lobby feels a little like a European cloister remade into a sleek dance club. The smallish rooms are simple to the point of starkness, using lots of grays and dark-wood trim to maintain the Euro feel. Rooms have wireless web TV and high-speed Internet access. Look for deals on weekends, when the moneyed folks working in the surrounding financial district have gone home and you can expect to find a tumbleweed rolling up the street.

NEAR NORTH & NAVY PIER

North of the river you can't go a block in any direction without finding a hotel. If you want to be near the center of Chicago's tourist action, stay here and enjoy all the eating, drinking, shopping and entertainment you could possibly desire.

BEST WESTERN CHICAGO RIVER NORTH Map pp306-7 Hotel

☎ **312-467-0800, 800-727-8088; www.bestwestern.com/rivernorthhotel; 125 W Ohio St; r $89-225; Red Line to Grand**

Surprisingly cheery, well-maintained rooms make this one of the better-value options in River North. The large rooms have a vaguely Asian flair, and the pool and sundeck overlook the Loop. In-room coffeemakers and free parking (!) sweeten the deal. Free wired Internet access.

CHICAGO MARRIOTT HOTEL

Map pp306-7 Hotel

☎ **312-836-0100, 800-228-9290; www.marriott.com; 540 N Michigan Ave; r $199-369; Red Line to Grand**

Recent renovations and upgrades have improved the somewhat gloomy 46-story Marriott, now sporting features like high-speed Internet access in every room, sleeker furniture, downy bedding, and flat-screen TVs in some of the generally smallish rooms. Three restaurant-bars are on-site, and you have nice city views from upper floors.

COMFORT INN & SUITES DOWNTOWN Map pp306-7 Hotel

☎ **312-894-0900, 888-775-4111; www.chicagocomfortinn.com; 15 E Ohio St; r $129-249; Red Line to Grand**

Classier than the typical Comfort Inn, the hotel is housed in an art deco–style 1920s building. Nice amenities include continental breakfast, fitness room with whirlpool and sauna, and high-speed Internet access. Rooms tend to be dark and some are on the small side, but if you stick to lower end of the price range you'll find a good value in a great location.

COURTYARD BY MARRIOTT CHICAGO DOWNTOWN

Map pp306-7 Hotel

☎ **312-329-2500, 800-321-2211; www.courtyard.com; 30 E Hubbard St; r $179-309; Red Line to Grand**

Billing itself as 'the hotel designed by business travelers,' this outpost charges rates that fall at the high end of the moderate range. Rooms on the high floors in the fairly new building enjoy excellent views, and all contain good work areas for travelers needing to pound away at the laptop. There's also a sundeck, a whirlpool and an indoor lap pool. The management has cut deals with several nearby restaurants, so you can charge your meals at those places to your room account.

EMBASSY SUITES CHICAGO-DOWNTOWN

Map pp306-7 Hotel

☎ **312-943-3800, 800-362-2779; www.embassysuites.com; 600 N State St; r $179-279; Red Line to Grand**

A good deal for families, this chain hotel offers all the expected suite features, including the two-room layout with beds in one room and a sofa bed in the other. The kitchenette has a microwave, which means you can nuke up some sort of popcorn and pizza delight for the kids and then head out into River North for some real food. Speaking of food, you can feast on a free full – not continental – breakfast served in the atrium each morning, and the indoor pool is a great way to wake up.

EMBASSY SUITES CHICAGO-RIVER EAST Map pp306-7 Hotel

☎ **312-836-5900, 866-866-8095; www.chicagoembassy.com; 511 N Columbus Dr; r $209-245; Red Line to Grand**

It's the usual Embassy Suites deal – an all-suite layout with complimentary happy hour and breakfast. True to Embassy Suites form, the rooms all overlook a central atrium. This version, though, is way more stunning than most, with a chic airplane-hangar feel and a small forest of trees growing in the lobby. The River East location is a 10-minute walk from Navy Pier. Wired Internet is available for a fee.

HAMPTON INN & SUITES-CHICAGO DOWNTOWN Map pp306-7 Hotel

☎ 312-832-0330, 800-426-7866; www.hamptoninn.com; 33 W Illinois St; r $109-239; Red Line to Grand

The relatively new Hampton features 230 rooms (including 100 suites, some with full kitchen), an indoor pool, a hot tub, a sauna, an exercise room, a free continental breakfast buffet, a guest coin laundry and a business center. The Prairie School–style lobby tends to be a little overrun with kids, but the staff members maintain a general sense of friendly calm, and the rooms are nice places to settle into. As you head to your room, check out the wonderful collection of oversized B&W photos of historic Chicago. Free wired and wireless Internet.

HILTON GARDEN INN Map pp306-7 Hotel

☎ 312-595-0000, 800-774-1500; www.hilton.com; 10 E Grand Ave; r $149-224; Red Line to Grand

This 23-story hotel features bright, good-sized rooms with microwaves and plenty of Neutrogena products to help get guests into a lather. A complete renovation will wrap up in 2006, bringing the single-orchid-in-classy-vase simplicity of the lobby to all the guest rooms. There's a tiny pool, Jacuzzi and the usual – for this price range – business center. Grill-o-philes will be happy to note that the adjoining restaurant is run by the Weber Grill company. There's free wireless Internet.

HOLIDAY INN-CHICAGO CITY CENTRE Map pp306-7 Hotel

☎ 312-787-6100, 800-465-4329; www.chicc.com; 300 E Ohio St; r $136-230; bus 66

Though nearly generic, this hotel is better than many of its namesake brethren, but it's still unremarkable in most respects. Views aren't bad, and you're in close proximity to Navy Pier. Guests have access to a fitness center with an indoor pool and tennis courts, and all rooms have free high-speed Internet access.

HOTEL INTER-CONTINENTAL CHICAGO Map pp306-7 Hotel

☎ 312-944-4100, 800-327-0200; www.chicago.intercontinental.com; 505 N Michigan Ave; r $179-429; Red Line to Grand

The Inter-Continental has a split personality. The older portion, on the south side, was once a health club for rich men and holds such classic details as a beautifully mosaicked indoor swimming pool in a setting worthy of William Randolph Hearst. The rooms have a similar elegant, heavily draped atmosphere, overlaid with all the facilities business travelers expect. Just north is an addition that used to house the Inter-Con's budget chain. The rooms in the newer addition feel fresh and fun; whimsical touches such as funky lamps and polka dots abound. At $50 less than the south wing, it's a great value in a top-tier hotel. Swimmers should note that the pool is the largest inside any hotel in the city. Wired Internet is available for a fee.

HOUSE OF BLUES HOTEL Map pp306-7 Hotel

☎ 312-245-0333, 800-235-6397; www.loewshotels.com; 333 N Dearborn St; r $170-229; Red Line to Grand

As the hotel component of the adjacent **House of Blues** (p184) club, the House of Blues Hotel specializes in festive, entertaining lodgings. The huge gold Buddha near the door is your first indication of the quirky, vibrant decor. The rooms are spacious, with bathrooms bordering on huge. The music scene next door is never far from view: musicians playing at the House of Blues often stay here, and each day hotel staff members print a list of live-music offerings around the city. Wired Internet is available for a fee.

LE MERIDIEN Map pp306-7 Hotel

☎ 312-645-1500; www.lemeridien.com; 520 N Michigan Ave (main entrance at 521 N Rush St); r $219-469; Red Line to Grand

If you're looking for a little urban pampering, this chic hotel connected to the upscale North Bridge Shops is for you. The Euro-sleek, blond-wood rooms – each with a CD player, voice mail, a thick bathrobe and free high-speed Internet – are discreetly luxurious. During the day you can visit the spa to massage and whirlpool the urban din away.

LENOX SUITES

Map pp306-7 Hotel

☎ 312-337-1000, 800-445-3669; www.lenoxsuites.com; 616 N Rush St; r $139-239; Red Line to Grand

While none of the rooms is striking, the location and prices of the Lenox are hard to beat. Some of the suites are barely bigger than one room, others are fairly sizable, and all house a full kitchen. Be sure to request one of the much-preferable remodeled rooms, though with further room renovations on the way, the improved suites should all be similarly attractive. A free continental breakfast (aka muffin basket) is delivered to your room daily.

OMNI CHICAGO HOTEL

Map pp306-7 Hotel

☎ 312-944-6664, 800-444-6664; www.omnihotels.com; 676 N Michigan Ave; r $199-379; Red Line to Chicago

One of the nicest properties on Michigan Ave (the entrance is just west on Huron St), the modern all-suite Omni rises high above a retail and office building. The rooms are decked out in rich colors and cherrywood. The living room of each of the 347 units features an excellent work area with a two-line phone, and all suites now boast plasma TVs. Other amenities include free high-speed wireless Internet access, an indoor pool, whirlpools and an exercise room.

PENINSULA Map pp306-7 Hotel

☎ 312-337-2888, 866-288-8889; www.peninsula.com; 108 E Superior St; r $445-515; Red Line to Chicago

Hailed as the best place to stay in Chicago by everyone from Zagat Survey to *Condé Nast Traveler*, the Peninsula is truly an experience. Each of the large, luxurious rooms comes equipped with no fewer than five phones, three of which are located in the bathroom. Lighting and electronics are all tied into impressively complicated high-tech systems, and DVD players come standard in the rooms. Some of the rooms have views from bathtubs, and the rooftop, glass-enclosed pool is enough to weep over. How's the service? Staff members here are all required to take personal grooming classes to ensure there's never a hair out of place.

RADISSON HOTEL & SUITES

Map pp306-7 Hotel

☎ 312-787-2900, 800-333-3333; www.radisson.com/chicagoil; 160 E Huron St; r $159-309; Red Line to Chicago

This Radisson is excellent value. Many of the rooms come with microwaves and refrigerators, and the hotel contains a small heated rooftop pool and sundeck. The minuscule exercise room feels a little like a garage sale waiting to happen, but at these rates, you won't sweat it. The furniture has a funky, fun feel. Great weekend Internet deals at the Radisson can drop the room rates down to as little as $89 for two people. Wired Internet is available at the hotel for a fee.

SHERATON CHICAGO HOTEL & TOWERS Map pp306-7 Hotel

☎ 312-464-1000, 877-242-2558, 800-325-3535; www.sheratonchicago.com; 301 E North Water St; r $199-219; bus 56

The best of the monster convention hotels, the Sheraton contains 1204 rooms, all with excellent views, especially those on the river. The vast public spaces feature huge plate-glass walls and fountains made with black granite, while the room decorations are typical of corporate hotels – nice but nothing particularly special. The lower level lies on the River Esplanade, which runs east from Michigan Ave. The hotel's bizarre address means it is just behind the NBC Tower, one block east of Michigan Ave along Columbus Dr.

W CHICAGO-LAKESHORE

Map pp306-7 Hotel

☎ 312-943-9200, 877-946-8357; www.whotels.com; 644 N Lake Shore Dr; r $209-329; bus 66

This Near North outpost of the clubby, cushy hotel is located within walking distance of Navy Pier and the Oak St beach, making it a good choice for those with children. The hotel's location on the inner access road away from other high-rises means that the rooms are sunny and the views of either the lake or the city are good. Rooms are less gray-feeling than those of its Loop counterpart. Low rooms on the Lake Shore Dr side suffer from traffic noise. Wired Internet access is available for a fee.

WESTIN RIVER NORTH

Map pp306-7 Hotel

☎ 312-744-1900, 877-866-9216; www.westinriver north.com; 320 N Dearborn St; r $199-359; Brown, Green, Orange Line to State

On the north bank of the river, the former Hotel Nikko continues to reflect its Asian roots; the rock garden, for example, is still carefully tended. But fans of the Westin chain can now rest easily in a hotel that's much better than its older sibling further north. Rooms are large, views are good and the service is splendid. The lobby bar, with its minimalist decor and open feel, makes an excellent place for a casual meeting.

Cheap Sleeps

BEST WESTERN INN OF CHICAGO

Map pp306-7 Hotel

☎ 312-787-3100, 800-557-2378; www.bestwestern .com; 162 E Ohio St; r $89-169; Red Line to Grand

One of the neighborhood's best values, the Best Western Inn of Chicago offers less-than-fancy rooms in an older building, but you can't beat the location. Staff members are friendly, and the hotel completed a renovation in 2004, creating a bare-bones rooftop deck for picnicking patrons. If you're looking for rooms that are basic without being depressing, this is a good choice. It's a favorite with tour groups, so book early. Free wireless access is available on some floors.

CASS HOTEL Map pp306-7 Motel

☎ 312-787-4030, 800-227-7850; 640 N Wabash Ave; r $69-119; Red Line to Grand

'It was a big deal for us to start offering washcloths,' laughs the manager here, when asked about the amenities at his budget hotel. You do get a washcloth here, along with a towel and TV, but not a whole lot more. Rooms are very simple and rather small – 'hostelesque' is probably a good word – but the location is fantastic and the price is unbeatable.

HOWARD JOHNSON INN

Map pp306-7 Motel

☎ 312-664-8100, 800-446-4656; www.hojo.com; 720 N LaSalle St; r $85-125; Brown Line to Chicago

The parking lot here is filled with the cars and trucks of contractors and other budget-minded passers-through. The Howard Johnson Inn (HoJo) offers free parking and free cable, and has coffeemakers in every room. The furniture, however, is about five years past due for a renovation, and those expecting more than something cheap and functional should definitely look elsewhere. There's free wired Internet access.

OHIO HOUSE MOTEL

Map pp306-7 Motel

☎ 312-943-6000; 600 N LaSalle Dr; r $85-115; Red Line to Grand

Make your reservations quick at Ohio House, before developers turn it into a trendy restaurant. This throwback auto-court motel, with its cement-block detailing, has remained resolutely unchanged since JFK was president. Though you may not think it to look at it, the bare-bones rooms are clean and well maintained; most have even been remodeled in the past couple of years. Another huge selling point: the parking is free. Wireless Internet is available for a fee.

RED ROOF INN Map pp306-7 Motel

☎ 312-787-3580, 800-466-8356; www.redroof .com; 162 E Ontario St; r $80-109; Red Line to Grand

The couches in the lobby are stained, but this motel is just steps from the Michigan Ave shopping bonanza, and the remarkably cheap room prices will leave enough change in your pocket to pick up a souvenir or two in the stores. Rooms are the definition of utilitarian, bordering on cell-like. Wireless Internet is available for a fee.

GOLD COAST

Home to many of the city's best hotels, the Gold Coast also has a few moderately priced gems.

DOUBLETREE GUEST SUITES HOTEL

Map pp308-9 Hotel

☎ 312-664-1100, 800-222-8733; www.doubletree .com; 198 E Delaware Pl; r $179-359; Red Line to Chicago

Dysfunctional couples love it here: each room includes two TVs, two phones and other amenities in pairs, including the freshly baked cookies. There's only one indoor pool, however. The striking modern lobby rises a few notches above the usual hotel entry.

DRAKE Map pp308-9 Hotel

☎ 312-787-2200, 800-553-7253; www.thedrakehotel.com; 140 E Walton St; r $229-329; Red Line to Chicago

The ageless Drake is Chicago's grandest hotel. Listed on the National Register of Historic Places, the hotel has hosted the likes of Queen Elizabeth and other glitterati since opening in 1920. It enjoys a commanding location at the head of Michigan Ave and offers convenient access to Oak St Beach, a short stroll through the pedestrian tunnel under Lake Shore Dr. The quiet rooms are built like bank vaults, with heavy old doors and marble baths. The suitably grand public places include restaurants and bars many notches above the norm. The Cape Cod Room serves excellent seafood. The attached Coq d'Or is one of the classiest bars in town.

FOUR SEASONS HOTEL

Map pp308-9 Hotel

☎ 312-280-8800, 800-332-3442; www.fourseasons.com/chicagofs; 120 E Delaware Pl; r $355-675; Red Line to Chicago

Rising high above the 900 N Michigan Ave mall, the Four Seasons is often considered the best hotel in Chicago. It pampers guests and firmly believes in the old maxim 'your wish is our command.' For instance, room service will endeavor to rustle up whatever you desire, whether or not it's on the menu, 24 hours a day. Each of the 343 rooms is unique, thanks to the handmade rugs and other decor, though all include marble baths, DVD players and wired Internet access (the latter for a fee). Needless to say, the amenities include an indoor pool, a health club, a whirlpool, a sauna and just about anything else spa-related short of a mud bath. (Though if you'd like one…) Seasons restaurant serves superb American cuisine in a plush setting. The casual café is good as well, and the commodious bar overlooking Michigan Ave makes an excellent meeting place.

Hotel Sofitel (right)

GOLD COAST GUEST HOUSE

Map pp308-9 B&B

☎ 312-337-0361; www.bbchicago.com; 113 W Elm St; r $129-199; Red Line to Clark/Division

Visitors from abroad will be especially welcomed by innkeeper Sally Baker at the Gold Coast Guest House. Baker has been steadily refining her 1873 classic three-flat for 15 years. Her experience as a travel guide based in London helps her understand the needs of travelers new to the US or to Chicago. Each of the four guest rooms includes a private bath, individual air-conditioning controls, DVD and CD players and wireless Internet access. Guests receive a bounteous continental breakfast and can help themselves to sodas and snacks in the refrigerator at other times. The enclosed, ivy-laden garden out back makes a pleasant escape from the city.

HOTEL INDIGO Map pp308-9 Hotel

☎ 312-787-4980, 866-246-3446; www.hotelindigo.com; 1244 N Dearborn; r $169-259; Red Line to Clark/Division

Formerly the Claridge Hotel, the nicely renovated Indigo is tasteful and comfortable, with a flair for cozy Scandinavian-minimalist style. Rooms are on the small side, but hardwood floors, colorful interiors and comfy, oversized furniture duly compensate. The excellent Gold Coast location means shopping, dining, the lake and nightlife are all short strolls away. Amenities include a fitness room and free wireless Internet in the 24-hour lounge.

HOTEL SOFITEL Map pp308-9 Hotel

☎ 312-324-4000, 800-763-4835; www.sofitel.com; 20 E Chestnut St; r $169-369; Red Line to Chicago

The Sofitel looks a little like some state-of-the-art Mac computing device from the outside, its triangular glass tower leaning gracefully forward into space. Inside, stylish staff members tend to stylish 30- and 40-something guests, who come here for the luxuriously minimalist vibe. Rooms feel a little like they were decorated from a high-end IKEA, all blond-wood and rectangular lines. All rooms come with high-speed Internet access and a cute bottle of European water.

OMNI AMBASSADOR EAST

Map pp308-9 Hotel

☎ **312-787-7200, 800-843-6664; www.omnihotels.com; 1301 N State St; r $169-259; Red Line to Clark/Division**

In Hitchcock's *North by Northwest*, Cary Grant gets to hang out at the Ambassador East with Eva Marie Saint before he meets that crop-duster in the Indiana cornfield. Your stay may lack the same glamour or danger, but you will still be in swank surroundings that include the famous **Pump Room** (p146) off the lobby. Grand touches abound, from the marble floors to the heavy woodwork. Rooms vary widely in size and style, with some seemingly untouched since Grant and Saint made eye contact. Aim for one of the large, bright ones. To reflect its chain affiliation, the hotel has added 'Omni' in front of its name.

PARK HYATT Map pp308-9 Hotel

☎ **312-335-1234, 800-633-7313; www.parkchicago.hyatt.com; 800 N Michigan Ave; r $285-480; Red Line to Chicago**

This flagship of the locally based Hyatt chain spares no expense, from the flat-screen TVs to the DVD players to the oodles of phones in every one of the 203 rooms. For once, the word 'stunning' adequately describes the **NoMi** (p142) restaurant and bar , with its views over Michigan Ave and the Water Tower, plus a nice outdoor area looking west. The hotel's amenities include a pool and concierges ready and willing to jump at your request. Suites come with balconies and cost the moon.

RITZ-CARLTON Map pp308-9 Hotel

☎ **312-266-1000, 800-621-6906; www.fourseasons.com/chicagorc; 160 E Pearson St; r $350-930; Red Line to Chicago**

One of the city's finest hotels, it occupies 32 stories above Water Tower Pl. The lobby, mostly understated, bursts with stunning floral arrangements. The large rooms embody refinement, with antique armoires and floral prints. The concierges have earned a reputation for being able to conjure up the answer to any guest's demand. The well-equipped health club includes an indoor pool. The Dining Room is an excellent French restaurant serving prix-fixe and degustation menus, including vegetarian options.

SENECA Map pp308-9 Hotel

☎ **312-787-8900, 800-800-6261; www.senecahotel.com; 200 E Chestnut St; r $149-229; Red Line to Chicago**

Another boutique hotel, the Seneca is popular with people who want a nice room but don't need all the accoutrements of a major hotel. The place has the feel of a well-maintained older apartment complex from the 1920s. Most rooms are on the large side, and many include full kitchens. Amenities at the dignified Seneca include laundry facilities, fitness room and rooftop sundeck. Free wireless Internet is available.

SUTTON PLACE HOTEL

Map pp308-9 Hotel

☎ **312-266-2100, 800-606-8188; www.suttonplace.com; 21 E Bellevue Pl; r $189-329; Red Line to Clark/Division**

This hotel works hard at staying true to its European roots. Built as a German-owned Kempinski Hotel in the mid-1980s, it was bought by the French chain Le Meridien in the early 1990s before adopting its rather anonymous name now. Electronics freaks will enjoy the rooms, which all come with CD players, VCRs and stereo TVs. When not exercising your finger on the remotes, you can work out at the nearby health club or check in to the 'Aerobics Suite' and feel the burn. The contemporary decor is accented by Robert Mapplethorpe's lush floral photos (the controversial stuff is over at the Museum of Contemporary Art.) Gaunt models haunt the Whiskey Bar, off the lobby.

TREMONT Map pp308-9 Hotel

☎ **312-751-1900, 800-621-8133; www.tremontchicago.com; 100 E Chestnut St; r $129-229; Red Line to Chicago**

The Tremont is one of several of boutique hotels in this well-placed location, adjacent

TOP FIVE BOUTIQUE HOTELS

Because so many of Chicago's hotels are built for business, a certain bland luxury tends to reign over the city's sleeping options. Happily, Chicago's boutique hotels buck this trend, placing an emphasis on unique decorating touches, and staff members who go the extra mile to make stays memorable. Five great Chicago boutique properties:

- **City Suites Hotel** (opposite) One of Chicago's best-kept secrets, in a neighborhood bustling with nightlife.
- **Hotel Burnham** (p238) You couldn't ask for a more central Loop location, and the Landmark building is one of Chicago's coolest structures.
- **Hotel Monaco** (p238) Free wine happy hours and a great riverside location make this stylish boutique property a find.
- **Tremont** (p245) Personal service and marble baths just steps away from Michigan Ave.
- **Willows Hotel** (opposite) Peace and quiet in a beautiful building not far from Lincoln Park.

to the fine shopping of the Magnificent Mile and Water Tower Pl. The rooms of the Tremont are spacious and equipped with marble baths, though short on the technological gizmos of otherwise comparable hotels. The decor – sort of whimsical European – is fairly bright for an older, somewhat staid building like this one. The clientele leans toward the tasseled loafer–lawyer set, who enjoy the speakerphones in the rooms and the small fitness room and sauna on-site. In colder seasons, you may find yourself lingering by the fireplace or on one of the leather couches in the sophisticated, cozy lobby.

WESTIN HOTEL, CHICAGO

Map pp308-9 Hotel

☎ 312-943-7200, 888-625-5144; www.westinmichiganave.com; 909 N Michigan Ave; r $199-399; Red Line to Chicago

This 751-room hotel is a shopper's dream, located within pouncing distance of all the Michigan Ave malls. The hotel got a facelift recently, and the work has transformed what was a dark, homely hotel into a cheerier place to stay. Rooms come with high-speed Internet plus all the basics like coffeemakers, CD players and in-room safes. Note that the hotel entrance is well east of Michigan Ave, on Delaware Pl.

LINCOLN PARK & OLD TOWN

These hotels and inns, often cheaper than the big ones downtown, place you near a lot of the city's best nightlife. Daytime pleasures at the museums and in the Loop and Near North are a short El or bus ride away.

DAYS INN LINCOLN PARK NORTH

Map pp308-9 Motel

☎ 773-525-7010, 888-576-3297; www.lpndaysinn.com; 644 W Diversey Pkwy; r $105-151; Brown, Red Line to Diversey

With 122 rooms near the busy intersection of Clark St, Diversey and Broadway, the Days Inn is situated in an old retail building above one of the North Side's gazillion coffee bars. The rooms are average sized, well kept, and a bit dull, though nice amenities (free wireless Internet, free pass to next door Bally's Health Club, free continental breakfast) and a good location (a short walk to Lincoln Park, the lakefront, and neighborhood dining and bars) make this a desirable spot. A 15-minute train ride will take you to downtown.

Cheap Sleeps

DAYS INN GOLD COAST

Map pp308-9 Motel

☎ 312-664-3040, 800-329-7466; www.daysinn.com; 1816 N Clark St; r $89-119; Brown Line to Sedgwick

Once a flophouse called the Hotel Lincoln, this place has been upgraded to the low standards of Days Inn. However, it's clean, and the furniture is much younger than you are. The best feature, besides the rate, is the excellent location across from the zoo and in the midst of Old Town. You can easily walk to many of the top destinations on the North Side from here.

INN AT LINCOLN PARK

Map pp308-9 Motel

☎ 773-348-2810, 866-774-7275; www.innlp.com; 601 W Diversey Pkwy; r $99-169; Brown, Red Line to Diversey

The Comfort Inn sits right on enjoyable Diversey Pkwy, east of Clark St, and about five minutes' walk from Lincoln Park and the lake. Built in 1918, the building was modernized in the 1980s. The rooms are clean

CHICAGO'S HOSTELS

Arlington House (Map pp308-9; ☎ 773-929-5380; www.arlingtonhouse.com; 616 W Arlington Pl; per person dm $24, r $54-68; Blue Line to Washington) This occupies an excellent location in the heart of Lincoln Park, one block west of Clark St. The rooms in the classic brick building look pretty beat up, but recent management changes have brought a new energy to the place. Choose a renovated room if you have a choice. Open year-round, 24 hours a day.

Chicago International Hostel (Map pp308-9; ☎ 773-262-1011; www.chicagointernationalhostel.com; 6318 N Winthrop Ave; dm $21; Red Line to Loyola) Near Loyola University, this major year-round hostel housed in a 1960s building lies three blocks south of the Loyola El stop on Sheridan, then two blocks east. A recent renovation vastly improved the hostel's attractiveness. Though the location is safe enough, you're far from the action. The El takes at least 35 minutes to get you to Chicago Ave.

Hostelling International-Chicago (Map pp302-3; ☎ 312-360-0300; www.hichicago.org; 24 E Congress Pkwy; dm $35-45; Blue, Red Line to Jackson) OK, so the prices are a little outrageous for a hostel. But oh, what a hostel. Opened in 2000, this bright and cheery place is the best hostelling option in Chicago by far, with a superconvenient location and clean, cared-for sleeping areas. It does double duty as Columbia College dorms during the academic year, so the number of available beds is lower September to May. If you can get a room here, you'll enjoy 24-hour access (hello, nightclubs!) and a kitchen. Check-in starts after 2pm.

and reasonably priced, though slightly unattractive and worn. The finest feature is the location. Some rooms come with king beds, and a couple feature whirlpool tubs. Amenities include free continental breakfast and free parking. Internet access is available for a fee.

LAKE VIEW

These places all lie near great nightlife spots and away from the tourist bustle of N Michigan Ave.

BEST WESTERN HAWTHORNE TERRACE Map pp318-19 Hotel

☎ 773-244-3434, 888-675-2378; www.hawthorneterrace.com; 3434 N Broadway St; r $139-189; bus 36

A very good northern option, this hotel in a 1920s residential building is in a fine location in which to explore the city from any direction. Amenities include in-room fridges and microwave, wired and wireless Internet access, a fitness room with sauna and whirlpool, and a pleasant outdoor terrace for when the weather agrees. An array of good dining options is a couple of blocks west on Halsted St.

CITY SUITES HOTEL Map pp318-19 Hotel

☎ 773-404-3400, 800-248-9108; www.cityinns.com; 933 W Belmont Ave; r $109-209; Brown, Red Line to Belmont

Location, location, location. The City Suites Hotel, between Clark St and the El, definitely has it. You won't go hungry or thirsty or get bored in this stylish, art deco–tinged place, full of brightly redone rooms (not all of which are suites), right in the middle of a neighborhood bustling with nightlife. This is one of the best-kept lodging secrets in Chicago, and it will remind European visitors pleasantly of home. The hotel is run by Neighborhood Inns of Chicago, which also operates the Majestic and Willows Hotels. All three serve complimentary continental breakfasts. Wireless Internet access is available for a fee.

MAJESTIC HOTEL Map pp318-19 Hotel

☎ 773-404-3499, 800-727-5108; www.cityinns.com; 528 W Brompton Ave; r $109-209; bus 151

The Majestic, located close to both Wrigley Field and the Halsted St neighborhood, is nestled into a row of residential housing. From the lobby fireplace and dark-wood furnishings to the Laura Ashley floral decor and jewel-toned accents, the interior has the stately, cozy feel of an English manor. Rooms are slightly larger than those of the other two Neighborhood Inns properties, while the continental breakfasts and fee-based Internet access remain the same.

WILLOWS HOTEL Map pp318-19 Hotel

☎ 773-528-8400, 800-787-3108; www.cityinns.com; 555 W Surf St; r $119-219; bus 22

The architectural pick of the Neighborhood Inns of Chicago trio, the Willows puts up an ornate terra-cotta facade on a very narrow strip of property. The rooms are soft-hued and sizable, and even in the busiest times the hotel remains blessedly quiet. It's located a stone's throw from the many attractions of Clark and Halsted Sts, as well as Lincoln Park and the lakefront. Continental breakfast is served daily, and wireless Internet is available for a fee.

Cheap Sleeps

VILLA TOSCANA Map pp318-19 B&B

☎ 773-404-2643, 800-404-2643; www.villatoscana.com; 3447 N Halsted St; r $99-139; bus 8

Comprising eight rooms in an 1890s Victorian, Villa Toscana provides comfortable lodging in the heart of Boystown, home of the city's gay nightlife. Rooms are on the small side, but each has a private phone line, TV and free wireless Internet. Five have private bathrooms. Front and back yards provide outdoor space to barbecue or hang out, and continental breakfast including waffles is served daily.

WICKER PARK

Unless you have a friend with a foldout couch in Wicker Park, chances are pretty slim that you'll end up sleeping here. The neighborhood, despite its copious charms, has yet to attract any major hotels. There is, however, a handful of B&Bs in the area that are worth exploring.

HOUSE OF TWO URNS BED & BREAKFAST Map pp316-17 B&B

☎ 773-235-1408, 877-896-8767; www.twourns.com; 1239 N Greenview Ave; r $99-185; Blue Line to Division

At the edge of still-gentrifying Wicker Park, the House of Two Urns has an artsy, funky feel – more hip than the typical quaint B&B. Situated on a classic Chicago residential street, the four rooms are split between two buildings: the main house, a former two-flat brownstone (where you'll be served homecooked breakfast), and the more apartment-like digs across the street (with a full kitchen and a patio with grills). Amenities include a roof deck, free laundry, Internet access, fireplaces and Jacuzzis. Owner Kapra Fleming can chat you up in German, Spanish and French (and Anglaise, *oui*).

WICKER PARK INN BED & BREAKFAST

Map pp316-17 B&B

☎ 773-486-2743; www.wickerparkinn.com; 1329 N Wicker Park Ave; r $115-135; Blue Line to Damen

Located in a classic Chicago brick row house, the three rooms of the Wicker Park Inn make up in character and value for what they lack in space and privacy. The worldly young owners are on hand for advice if you need them, and an ample library of travel guides and city information will answer many questions too. The hipster scene of Wicker Park is right outside your door, with good coffee, chic boutiques and fine food aplenty. Daily do-it-yourself breakfast at the inn includes baked goods from the owners' adjacent bakery. One room has a private deck. Free wireless Internet is available.

WEST SIDE

Unless you have a compelling reason to stay on the West Side, your Chicago trip will be much more enjoyable at one of the places that's more central.

CHICAGO MARRIOTT AT MEDICAL DISTRICT/UIC Map pp314-15 Hotel

☎ 312-491-1234, 800-356-3641; www.marriott.com; 625 S Ashland Ave; r $149-269; Blue Line to Racine

If you happen to be visiting someone who goes to University of Illinois at Chicago (UIC) or want to *really* get to know Little Italy, this hotel is a good option. Boasting a vaguely European vibe, this upscale Marriott has a new fitness center and recently outfitted its rooms with fluffy new bedding. Free wireless Internet is available.

HOLIDAY INN-CHICAGO DOWNTOWN Map pp304-5 Hotel

☎ 312-957-9100, 800-465-4329; www.basshotels.com/holiday-inn; 506 W Harrison St; r $129-209; Blue Line to Clinton

On the west side of the river, this Holiday Inn offers convenient access to exciting attractions like Union Station, the bus station and the post office. OK, so there's not a lot going on in the neighborhood, but the amenities include a guest laundry and a business center, and a small rooftop pool with a view of Sears Tower. All rooms come with high-speed wireless Internet access.

CATCHING SOME SLEEP (& A PLANE IN THE MORNING)

Chicago's array of airport hotels may come in handy if you have a very early flight (or if all other accommodations in the city have been sucked up by visiting conventioneers). Most of the hotels in Rosemont are linked to an enclosed pedestrian walkway that leads to the Rosemont Convention Center. If you're stuck at one of these places, you're probably within walking distance of the Rosemont CTA station for the 30-minute ride to downtown.

All the following places offer free shuttle service to and from O'Hare. But remember, the same traffic that plagues the expressways around O'Hare will swallow up your hotel shuttle bus; many people instead use the CTA for its five-minute ride to O'Hare from Rosemont.

Chicago O'Hare Rosemont Travelodge (Map pp302-3; ☎ 847-296-5541, 800-578-7878; www.travelodge.com; 3003 Mannheim Rd, Des Plaines; r $69-109; Blue Line to O'Hare) The sleepy bear comes alive at this Travelodge – the enthusiastic management provides free incoming fax service, cable TV, newspapers, coffee and more. The place looks like a throwback, but staff members really do aim to please. It's also the closest cheap hotel to the airport.

Excel Inn of O'Hare (Map pp302-3; ☎ 847-803-9400, 800-367-3935; 2881 Touhy Ave, Elk Grove Village; r $60-85; Blue Line to O'Hare) A favorite dumping ground for airline passengers whom the airlines don't like (eg nonfrequent fliers with dirt-cheap tickets) but who still have to be put up for the night, the Excel is a simple motel in a town that claims to be America's largest industrial park. All rooms include coffeemakers, ironing boards and other useful touches.

Holiday Inn Chicago-O'Hare Kennedy (Map pp302-3; ☎ 773-693-2323, 800-465-4329; www.holiday-inn.com; 8201 West Higgins Rd, Chicago; r $99-199; Blue Line to Cumberland) Amenities here include one noteworthy bonus for the kids: in-room video games, in addition to the standard cable. Other features include an outdoor pool, fitness center and free wireless Internet.

Hotel Sofitel (Map pp302-3; ☎ 847-678-4488, 800-763-4835; www.sofitel.com; 5550 N River Rd, Rosemont; r $99-199; Blue Line to O'Hare) The pick of the O'Hare litter is the Sofitel, a member of the friendly French chain of the same name; the hotel even makes especially flaky croissants in its own bakery. The large rooms include a number of amenities.

Hyatt Regency O'Hare (Map pp302-3; ☎ 847-696-1234, 800-233-1234; www.hyatt.com; 9300 W Bryn Mawr Ave, Rosemont; r $129-229; Blue Line to O'Hare) This ever-expanding property contains 1099 rooms, many with views of the expressway or the enclosed parking garage. It's across from the convention center and a short walk from the El.

Marriott Suites Chicago O'Hare (Map pp302-3; ☎ 847-696-4400, 800-228-9290; www.marriott.com; 6155 N River Rd, Rosemont; r $169-229; Blue Line to O'Hare) Compared with the O'Hare Marriott, this one offers much bigger rooms in a much newer building.

O'Hare Hilton (Map pp302-3; ☎ 773-686-8000, 800-445-8667; www.hilton.com; r $139-279; Blue Line to O'Hare) If you want a real airport hotel, you can't get closer than the Hilton – it's right in the middle of the airport, across from Terminals 1, 2 and 3. Underground tunnels link the hotel with the terminals, the shuttle tram and the CTA. The rooms are large and soundproof. Amenities include an indoor pool, sauna, whirlpool and exercise center. The restaurants aren't bad, either – definitely better than what you'll find in the terminals.

O'Hare Marriott (Map pp302-3; ☎ 773-693-4444, 800-228-9290; www.marriott.com; 8535 W Higgins Rd, Chicago; r $109-209; Blue Line to O'Hare) This Marriott often becomes a temporary home for bumped passengers. It's big and has a big parking lot, but it's otherwise unremarkable.

Ramada Plaza Chicago O'Hare (Map pp302-3; ☎ 773-693-5800, 800-272-6232; www.ramada.com; 5616 N Cumberland Ave; r $119-209; Blue Line to Cumberland) Recent renovations (including a name change) have spruced up this hotel. You can work out in the fitness room or swim (weather permitting) while killing time before that flight.

SOUTH LOOP & NEAR SOUTH SIDE

Sleeping options in this neighborhood offer convenient access to both the Museum Campus and McCormick Place, but are a long way from all the action on the North Side.

BEST WESTERN GRANT PARK INN

Map pp312-13 Hotel

☎ 312-922-2900, 800-472-6875; www.bestwestern.com; 1100 S Michigan Ave; r $119-139; Green, Orange Line to Roosevelt

This hotel is not much to look at, though it does have a pool and great views over Grant Park. The neighborhood is still in transition – it's not bad, just dead – but the hotel lies close to the Museum Campus, only about a mile from McCormick Place and three blocks from the Roosevelt El stop. Rooms are better than you'd think from the clunky exterior. Free wireless and wired Internet is available (for your first 30 minutes of use per day).

CHICAGO HILTON & TOWERS

Map pp312-13 Hotel

☎ 312-922-4400, 800-445-8667; www.hilton.com; 720 S Michigan Ave; r $109-359; Red Line to Harrison

When it was built in 1927, this was the largest hotel in the world, with close to 2000 rooms. A renovation in the mid-1980s brought that total down to a still huge 1544. Some of the resulting rooms now have two bathrooms, perfect if one member of a party locks themselves away for hours of ablutions. If the bathroom isn't relaxing enough, you can head up to work on your backstroke in the Olympic-sized swimming pool. The hotel boasts three bar-restaurants, a welcome feature in the slightly lifeless South Loop neighborhood. The lobby bar that overlooks Michigan Ave at the north end of the block-sized building has also played a minor role in history: Chicago police tossed protesters through the plate-glass windows here at the height of the riots during the 1968 Democratic National Convention. Wireless Internet is available for a fee.

HYATT REGENCY MCCORMICK PLACE

Map pp312-13 Hotel

☎ 312-567-1234, 800-633-7313; www.mccormickplace.hyatt.com; 2233 S Martin Luther King Jr Dr; r $279-319; Metra to McCormick Place

If you're manning a booth at McCormick Place during a show, this is the most convenient arrangement imaginable: after a short walk you can pass out in bed with memories of a day spent glad-handing dolts – er, potential clients – dancing in your head. The 800 rooms come with all the usual conveniences and boast good views of the Loop, more than 2 miles north. If you're not doing anything at McCormick Place, then there's no reason to stay down here, so far from most of the city's action.

Cheap Sleeps

CHINATOWN HOTEL SRO LTD

Map pp312-13 Hotel

☎ 312-225-8888; 214 W 22nd Pl; r $55-85; Red Line to Cermak-Chinatown

This hotel is a dirt-cheap option for adventurous travelers who are willing to put up with basic, slightly shabby rooms and a staff whose command of English isn't the strongest. The location, though, is just a couple of blocks from the El stop, in the heart of Chinatown (think of the dim sum!). Free Internet is available in the lobby (though it doesn't always work). If you're broke, and can't find a good room on any of the bidding sites (see the boxed text, p237), this is a fine place to spend a night or two.

TRAVELODGE CHICAGO DOWNTOWN

Map pp312-13 Motel

☎ 312-427-8000, 800-211-6706; www.travelodgehoteldowntown.com; 65 E Harrison St; r $99-149; Red Line to Harrison

The rooms at this budget-chain option feel cheap, and they are. They're clean, though, and recent improvements in staff friendliness makes the Travelodge a fine choice for those traveling on a very tight budget. The motel offers in-room coffeemakers and free HBO and Showtime, but the real treat is outside the room: the location puts you within an easy walk to Grant Park, the museum campus and other downtown attractions.

Excursions

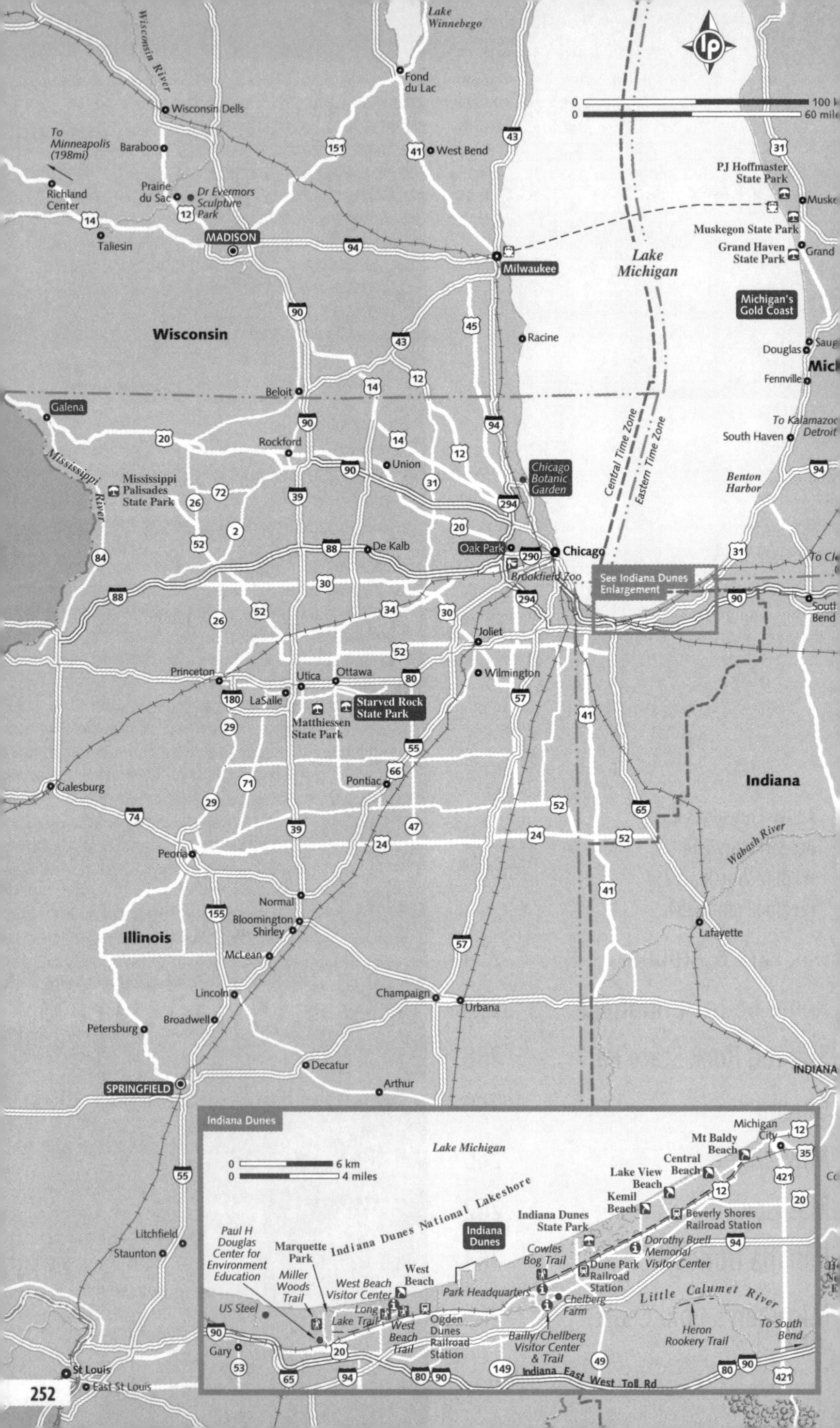

Lake Winnebego
Fond du Lac
Wisconsin River
Wisconsin Dells
To Minneapolis (198mi)
Baraboo
West Bend
Richland Center
Prairie du Sac
Dr Evermors Sculpture Park
Taliesin
MADISON
Milwaukee
Lake Michigan
PJ Hoffmaster State Park
Muskegon State Park
Grand Haven State Park
Michigan's Gold Coast
Wisconsin
Racine
Douglas
Fennville
Beloit
Galena
Rockford
Union
Mississippi River
Mississippi Palisades State Park
Chicago Botanic Garden
Central Time Zone
Eastern Time Zone
To Kalamazoo
Detroit
South Haven
Benton Harbor
De Kalb
Oak Park
Chicago
Brookfield Zoo
See Indiana Dunes Enlargement
South Bend
Joliet
Wilmington
Princeton
Utica
Ottawa
LaSalle
Starved Rock State Park
Matthiessen State Park
Pontiac
Galesburg
Indiana
Wabash River
Peoria
Normal
Bloomington
Shirley
Illinois
McLean
Lafayette
Lincoln
Champaign
Urbana
Broadwell
Petersburg
Decatur
Arthur
SPRINGFIELD
INDIANA
Litchfield
Staunton
St Louis
East St Louis
Indiana Dunes
Lake Michigan
0 6 km
0 4 miles
Indiana Dunes National Lakeshore
Michigan City
Mt Baldy Beach
Central Beach
Lake View Beach
Kemil Beach
Beverly Shores Railroad Station
Indiana Dunes State Park
Dorothy Buell Memorial Visitor Center
Paul H Douglas Center for Environment Education
Marquette Park
Miller Woods Trail
West Beach
West Beach Visitor Center
Cowles Bog Trail
Dune Park Railroad Station
Park Headquarters
Chelberg Farm
Little Calumet River
US Steel
Long Lake Trail
West Beach Trail
Ogden Dunes Railroad Station
Bailly/Chellberg Visitor Center & Trail
Heron Rookery Trail
To South Bend
Gary
Indiana East West Toll Rd

Excursions

With all its tall, steely buildings, rockin' live-music clubs, lakefront parks and endless neighborhoods of Indian, Mexican, Vietnamese and global eats, why on earth would you want to leave Chicago? Let us break it to you gently: the city does lack a few things – towering sand dunes, surging waterfalls and top-quality corn dogs, among others – and to experience them, you'll have to hit the road. The eight destinations in this chapter range from 20-minute jaunts to 3½-hour journeys, and fan out beyond Illinois into Wisconsin, Indiana and Michigan.

Oak Park is a short El ride from downtown, though it seems a world away with its huge old houses, wraparound porches and sprawling green yards. Frank Lloyd Wright designed many of the town's buildings and had his studio here. Ernest Hemingway was born a few blocks away, and his home is now a museum, too.

Route 66, the nostalgic Mother Road, starts in downtown Chicago in front of the Art Institute, then carries travelers south through a trail of kitschy roadside attractions, drive-in movie theaters and scattered shrines to local hero Abe Lincoln.

Two other Illinois destinations make inspiring stops: Starved Rock State Park, with its waterfall-filled canyons and ridgetop hiking trails; and genteel Galena, a B&B-stuffed, Civil War–era town near the Mississippi River.

Next it's time to turn north toward Wisconsin, aka 'The Dairy State.' Folks here refer to themselves as 'cheeseheads' and emphasize it by wearing foam rubber cheese-wedge hats for special occasions (most notably during Green Bay Packers football games). Lest there be any doubt about dairy pride, check out the state's quarter – yep, there's a cow and big hunk of cheese right on the back. Two cities are particularly excursion-worthy: Milwaukee, a down-to-earth city if ever there was one, which admirably balances Harleys and beer with world-class art and cultural festivals; and liberal, leafy Madison, the small state capital loaded with walkable coffee shops, bookstores, brewpubs and cheap, international places to grab a bite.

Beach bums will want to proceed east to Indiana Dunes and Michigan's Gold Coast for sand, surf and mango-colored sunsets.

The prices listed here are for peak season, which runs from late May to early September. During the off-season, many places reduce their hours and some even close entirely.

ACTIVE ENDEAVORS

Don't give us the 'it's too cold' or 'it's too hot' whine. The region offers activities to match a variety of weather moods and personal tastes. Visitors can hike and raft in **Starved Rock** (p258); kayak and bicycle in **Madison** (p262); hike, swim and cross-country ski in **Indiana Dunes** (p263); and tramp over rugged, wooded sandbanks in the parks along **Michigan's Gold Coast** (p265). For a great bike ride that's close to home, pedal to the **Chicago Botanic Garden** (p257).

Modern totem pole, Starved Rock State Park (p258)

ART & HISTORY

Architecture buffs can be unleashed in Oak Park to view **Frank Lloyd Wright's studio** (below) and a couple of streets' worth of homes he designed; **Taliesin** (p263), outside Madison, is his übersite. The **Milwaukee Art Museum** (p260) sports unusually cool folk and outsider art galleries. To see folk art beyond a museum's confines, visit **Dr Evermor's Sculpture Park** (p262) and gape at the futuristic Forevertron. Novelist Ernest Hemingway hails from Oak Park, where the **Hemingway Museum** (below) tells his story (using words sparely, of course). Springfield houses a trio of historical **Abraham Lincoln sights** (p256), including his tomb. Galena offers historical insight on another Civil War–era president at the **Ulysses S Grant home** (p259).

WILDLIFE WATCHING

Eagles (p258) descend on Starved Rock in January and February. Indiana Dunes harbors a breeding ground for the **great blue heron** (p264), which prefers to live much closer to a stinky steel mill than you'd imagine. For those who like to experience their nature in a more corralled environment, try the **Brookfield Zoo** (opposite).

FEEDING FRENZY

Make sure you wear expandable trousers when you embark. Route 66's **Cozy Dog Drive In** (p256) birthed the corn dog, and it's still frying up a mean one. **Crane's Pie Pantry** (p267) near Saugatuck is famed for its fruit pies; the blueberries, raspberries and other fillings come straight from the surrounding orchard. Beer, cheese and bratwursts are Wisconsin specialties. Milwaukee is home to several breweries, including **Miller** (p260) and **Sprecher** (p260), and the world's best brats, grilled at **Miller Park** (p260). Don't dare leave town without knocking back a frozen custard at **Kopp's** (p261). Madison's **Dane County Farmers' Market** (p262) offers beer-cooked brats and artisanal cheese.

OAK PARK & AROUND

The suburb of Oak Park spawned two famous sons: Ernest Hemingway was born here, and architect Frank Lloyd Wright lived and worked here from 1898 to 1908. The town's main sights revolve around both men.

During Wright's 10 years in Oak Park, he designed a helluva lot of houses. Stop at the **visitors center** and ask for the architectural walking-tour map (usually a free, photocopied page), which gives their locations. Ten of them cluster within a mile along Forest and Chicago Aves; the homes are privately owned, so all gawking must occur from the sidewalk. **Moore House**, on Forest Ave, is particularly noteworthy. It's Wright's bizarre interpretation of an English manor house that was first built in 1895. In his later years, Wright called the house 'repugnant' and said he had only taken the commission because he needed the money. He claimed that he walked out of his way to avoid passing it.

To actually get inside a Wright-designed dwelling, you'll need to visit the **Frank Lloyd Wright Home & Studio**, nearby on Chicago Ave. Staff offer hour-long tours of the complex. It's a fascinating place, filled with the details that made Wright's style distinctive. Note how he molded plaster to look like bronze and how he stained cheap pine to look like rare hardwood. Always in financial trouble, spendthrift Wright was adept at making the ordinary seem extraordinary. Staff members also offer tours that combine the Home & Studio with a neighborhood walkabout. Self-guided audio tours are available, too. Both the Home & Studio and the visitors center sell tickets for whatever combination you desire.

The **Unity Temple** is the only other Wright building that devotees can go inside; it requires a separate admission fee. If you're short on time or money, skip this one and head to the Home & Studio instead.

Oak Park honors another famous local at the **Ernest Hemingway Museum**. The exhibits begin with his middle-class Oak Park background and his innocent years before he went off to find adventure. The ensuing displays focus on his writings in Spain and during WWII. Admission includes entry to **Hemingway's birthplace**, where you can see his first room. 'Papa'

MORALITY FOR A THINKING MAN

The public reveres Frank Lloyd Wright today, but that wasn't always the case for the acerbic and philandering architect.

Born in Wisconsin in 1867 and always a prodigy, Wright came to Chicago in 1887 to work for Louis Sullivan as a drafter. But in 1893 that relationship soured when Sullivan found out that Wright was moonlighting and not cutting in the firm on his profits.

Wright then based his studio in Oak Park, and worked there until he ran off to Europe in 1908 with Mamah Borthwick Cheney, a client, leaving behind his wife and six kids. Upon return, he worked from studios at his rural Wisconsin home (see p263), where he lived with Cheney although he was still married to his first wife. Public condemnation was harsh. On Christmas Day in 1911, Wright held a press conference to explain his infidelity, proclaiming that he, as a 'thinking man,' did not have to follow the rules of 'the ordinary man.'

In 1914 a deranged servant murdered Cheney. Wright found consolation with Miriam Noel, who had sent him a letter of sympathy. They married in 1923 and divorced in 1927. In 1928 Wright married his third and final wife, Olga Hinzenberg, with whom he had had a child in 1925.

Wright spent most of his later years working at his Arizona desert home, where he died in 1959 at the age of 91.

was born here in 1899 in the large, turreted home of his maternal grandparents. It's pretty forgiving of the town to pay homage to Hemingway, since he once called Oak Park a 'village of wide lawns and narrow minds.'

To see the array of animals Hemingway likely shot and killed on his famed hunting expeditions, head from Oak Park southwest to the **Brookfield Zoo**. With 2700 animals and 215 acres, the zoo can easily sustain a day's wanderings. More extensive than the free Lincoln Park Zoo in Chicago, Brookfield features dolphin shows, African- and Australian-themed exhibits, several primate areas, a kids' zoo and a ton more.

Because most visitors use the north gate and tend to stop at the nearby attractions first, you can avoid some of the crowds by starting in the southern part of the zoo and working back north.

Information

Oak Park Visitors Center (☎ 708-848-1500; 158 N Forest Ave; 🕑 10am-4pm winter, 9am-5pm summer)

Sights

Brookfield Zoo (☎ 708-485-0263; www.brookfieldzoo.org; 8400 W 31st St, Brookfield; adult/3-11yr $8/4; 🕑 9:30am-6pm, shorter hours Sep-May)

Ernest Hemingway Museum (☎ 708-848-2222; 200 N Oak Park Ave; admission included with Hemingway's Birthplace; 🕑 1-5pm Sun-Fri, from 10am Sat)

Frank Lloyd Wright Home & Studio (☎ 708-848-1976; www.wrightplus.org; 951 Chicago Ave; adult/7-18yr $12/10; 🕑 tours 11am, 1pm & 3pm Mon-Fri, continuous 11am-3:30pm Sat & Sun)

Hemingway's Birthplace (☎ 708-848-2222; www.ehfop.org; 339 N Oak Park Ave; adult/child $7/5.50; 🕑 1-5pm Sun-Fri, from 10am Sat)

Moore House (333 N Forest Ave)

Unity Temple (☎ 708-383-8873; www.unitytemple-utrf.org; 875 Lake St; adult/child 5yr & under/student $7/free/5; 🕑 10:30am-4:30pm Mon-Fri, 1-4pm Sat & Sun)

TRANSPORTATION

Distance from Chicago To Oak Park 8 miles; Brookfield Zoo 14 miles.

Direction West.

Travel time To Oak Park 20 minutes; to Brookfield Zoo 25 minutes.

Car To Oak Park, take I-290 west, exiting north on Harlem Ave; take Harlem north to Lake St and turn right. For the zoo, go west on the Eisenhower Expressway (I-290) to the 1st Ave exit, then south to 31st and follow the signs.

El Take the Green Line to the Oak Park stop, which lands you about 1 mile from the visitors center. The trip (one way $1.75) takes 20 minutes; be aware that the train traverses some bleak neighborhoods before emerging into Oak Park's wide-lawn splendor.

Metra The Union Pacific West Line has an Oak Park stop; trains depart from Ogilvie Transportation Center. Brookfield Zoo is reachable via the Burlington Northern Santa Fe (BNSF) Line from Union Station; exit at the Hollywood stop (one way to Oak Park/zoo $2.05/2.90).

ROUTE 66 TO SPRINGFIELD

The classic highway from Chicago to Los Angeles once cut diagonally across Illinois to St Louis and beyond. Though now almost totally superseded by I-55, the old route – which is affectionately called Main St, USA – still exists in scattered sections, and its associated Americana survives in towns bypassed by the interstate. You'll encounter a serious trail of corn dogs, pies and other eats along the way, so get ready to loosen those belts.

The 'Mother Road' kicks off at the corner of Adams St and Michigan Ave in downtown Chicago. Our first stop: the Gemini Giant, a 28ft fiberglass spaceman proffering burgers and fries south of Joliet. Leave I-55 at Joliet Rd, following Hwy 53 southbound to Wilmington. This is where the Giant stands guard outside the **Launching Pad Drive-In.**

On the outskirts of Pontiac, look for the **Log Cabin Inn**. When Route 66 was realigned, the restaurant was jacked up and rotated 180 degrees to face the new road. The **Route 66 Hall of Fame** is also in town.

Cruise by Bloomington and Normal and stop off in Shirley at **Funk's Grove**, a 19th-century maple-syrup farm. Further south in Broadwell, the mythical 1930s **Pig-Hip Restaurant** has been renovated as a **museum**.

The small state capital of Springfield harbors a trio of Route 66 sights. All must stop to hail the corn-dog's birthplace at the **Cozy Dog Drive In**. It's a Route 66 legend, with all sorts of memorabilia and souvenirs, plus homemade doughnuts to chase down the main course. **Shea's Gas Station Museum** lets visitors fill up with Route 66 pumps and signs. And there's nothing better on a warm summer evening than catching a flick under the stars at the **Route 66 Drive In.**

Springfield also has a certifiable obsession with local hero Abraham Lincoln, who practiced law here from 1837 to 1861. The city's Abe-related sights offer an in-depth look at the man and his turbulent times, which only some cynics find overdone. Many of the attractions are walkable downtown and cost little to nothing. Get your bearings with maps from the central **visitors center**. At the time of writing a new center was scheduled to open next to the Lincoln Presidential Library & Museum in 2006.

To visit the top-draw **Lincoln Home**, you must first pick up a ticket at the **Lincoln Home Visitors Center**. The site is where Abe and Mary Lincoln lived from 1844 until they moved to the White House in 1861. You'll see considerably more than just the home: the whole block has been preserved, and several structures are open to visitors.

The **Lincoln Presidential Library & Museum** contains the most complete Lincoln collection in the world, everything from his Gettysburg Address and Emancipation Proclamation to his shaving mirror and briefcase. You'll have to wade through some Disney-esque exhibits to get to the good stuff, but it's worth it.

After his assassination, Lincoln's body was returned to Springfield, where it lies today. The impressive **Lincoln's Tomb** sits in **Oak Ridge Cemetery**. The gleam on the nose of his bust, created by visitors' touches, indicates the numbers of those who pay their respects.

For more information on the Mother Road, contact the **Route 66 Association of Illinois** or get Lonely Planet's *Road Trip: Route 66* book, which will guide you all the way to LA, baby.

TRANSPORTATION

Distance from Chicago To Wilmington 60 miles; Springfield 200 miles.

Direction Southwest.

Travel time To Wilmington one hour; Springfield 3½ hours.

Bus Greyhound (☎ 800-231-2222; www.greyhound.com) runs frequent buses from Chicago to Springfield ($37 to $45, 4½ hours); the station (☎ 217-544-8466; 2351 S Dirkson Pkwy) is southeast of downtown.

Car Take I-55 south out of Chicago and follow it all the way to Springfield. Old Route 66 often parallels the interstate.

Train Amtrak (☎ 800-872-7245; www.amtrak.com) runs three trains per day between Chicago and Springfield ($16 to $45, 3½ hours); the station (☎ 217-753-2013; cnr 3rd & Washington Sts) is downtown.

Information

Lincoln Home Visitors Center (☎ 217-492-4150; 426 S 7th St, Springfield; admission free; 8:30am-5pm)

DETOUR: CHICAGO BOTANIC GARDEN

The **Chicago Botanic Garden** (☎ 847-835-5440; www.chicagobotanic.org; 1000 Lake Cook Rd, Glencoe; admission free; 🕑 8am-dusk) blooms year-round in tony Glencoe, 25 miles north of the city. The Chicago Horticultural Society runs the facility, which features thousands of plants in 26 settings on 385 acres. It's a magnet for urban gardeners who don't have room to plant their own pine forest and put in a waterfall.

A tram runs through the site, but come on, it's not that big and what better way to smell the roses than via a slow meander on foot? Among the highlights are a prairie garden, a herb garden, a Japanese garden and a rose garden. Although admission is free, keep your wallet handy if arriving by car: the Society charges $12 per vehicle for parking.

By car, take I-90/94 west out of the city, and stay on I-94 when it splits off. I-94 eventually merges with US 41; follow signs for the latter from here onward. Exit at Lake Cook Rd and travel a half-mile east to the garden. The trip takes 30 minutes and parking costs $12. Public transportation is not an easy option, but if you must: take the Union Pacific North Line from Ogilvie Transportation Center to the Glencoe stop (one way $3.30). Outside catch PACE bus 213 'Northbrook Court' (one way $1.50), which drops you off garden-side.

Lots of people prefer to make the journey on two wheels, as the garden connects to one of Chicagoland's best bicycle routes. The North Branch Trail starts at Clayton Woods on the corner of Devon and Caldwell Aves. From there you pedal north on a paved trail along the Chicago River, mostly through forest preserves. Eventually North Branch connects to the Skokie Trail, which takes you through the Skokie Lagoons to the botanic garden – a wonderful trek of about 30 miles.

Route 66 Association of Illinois (www.il66assoc.org)

Springfield Visitors Center (☎ 800-545-7300; www.visitspringfieldillinois.com; 109 N 7th St, Springfield; 🕑 8am-5pm Mon-Fri)

Sights

Funk's Grove (☎ 309-874-3360; Shirley; 🕑 seasonal)

Lincoln Home (☎ 217-492-4150; 426 S 7th St, Springfield; admission free; 🕑 8:30am-5pm)

Lincoln Presidential Library & Museum (☎ 217-558-8844; www.alplm.org; 212 N 6th St, Springfield; adult/5-15yr $7.50/3.50; 🕑 9am-5pm, to 8:30pm Wed)

Lincoln's Tomb/Oak Ridge Cemetery (☎ 217-782-2717; north of downtown Springfield; admission free; 🕑 9am-4pm, to 5pm summer)

Log Cabin Inn (☎ 815-842-2908; 18700 Old Route 66, Pontiac; 🕑 5am-4pm Mon & Tue, to 8pm Wed-Fri, to 2pm Sat)

Pig-Hip Restaurant Museum (☎ 217-732-2337; Broadwell; admission free; 🕑 10am-5pm Mon-Sat usually)

Route 66 Drive In (☎ 217-698-0066; Recreation Rd, Springfield; adult/under 13yr $5/3; 🕑 nightly Jun-Aug, weekends mid-Apr–May, Sep & Oct)

Route 66 Hall of Fame (☎ 815-844-4566; 110 W Howard St, Pontiac; admission free; 🕑 11am-3pm Mon-Fri, 10am-4pm Sat)

Shea's Gas Station Museum (☎ 217-522-0475; 2075 Peoria Rd, Springfield; admission free; 🕑 7am-4pm Tue-Fri, to noon Sat)

Eating

Cozy Dog Drive In (☎ 217-525-1992; 2935 S 6th St, Springfield; items $1.50-3.50; 🕑 8am-8pm Mon-Sat)

Launching Pad Drive-In (☎ 815-476-6535; 810 E Baltimore St, Wilmington; items $2-5; 🕑 9am-10pm)

Chicago Botanic Garden (above)

Sleeping

All options listed here are in Springfield.

Carpenter Street Hotel (☎ 217-789-9100, 888-779-9100; www.carpenterstreethotel.com; 525 N 6th St; r $70) Bland but decent nonsmoking downtown option with pool and air-con.

Inn at 835 (☎ 217-523-4466; www.innat835.com; 835 S 2nd St; s/d from $100/115) A fine historic B&B with pool and parking.

Motel 6 (☎ 217-529-1633; 6010 S 6th St; r $35-50) One of many chain hotels lining I-55 east of town with pool, parking and air-con.

STARVED ROCK STATE PARK

One of the most popular parks in Illinois, **Starved Rock State Park** features more than 2800 acres of woodlands along the Illinois River, 1 mile south of the small town of Utica. The park's distinctiveness comes from the 18 canyons that slice dramatically through tree-covered, sandstone bluffs. After a heavy rain, waterfalls cascade down the head of each canyon.

According to legend, a band of Illinois Native Americans got trapped atop the park's 125ft butte during a battle with the Ottawa and starved to death – hence the park name. Today you can climb the namesake rock via a congested, rat-maze system of wooden stairs and decks, but you're better off wandering the park's other 13 miles of hiking trails; several ascend to the top of ridges, offering spectacular views.

For those who prefer to take to the water, the Illinois River and canyon waterways provide opportunities for paddled canoe jaunts. White-water-rafting enthusiasts can get their thrills zipping through the Class II and III rapids of the nearby Vermillion River with **Vermillion River Rafting**.

The park **visitors center** offers full information on the many outdoor opportunities and rentals in the area – including canoes, horses, bikes and skis – as well as the hiking trails and other park features. Although the park gets very crowded on summer weekends, you can always leave the throngs behind by hiking beyond Wildcat Canyon, which is less than a mile east of the main parking area. Less than a mile from this point is La Salle Canyon, where a waterfall turns into a glistening icefall in the winter. Indeed, January and February are good times to visit if you don't mind the cold weather, as this is when **bald eagles** flock to the Rock to chow down on the Illinois River's fish-abundant waters. (A nearby dam creates a kind of holding pen for slippery swimmers – and thus an easy meal for the eagles.) The park conducts sporadic trolley tours to view the creatures during these months; call the visitors center for details.

The park's 133 electric **campsites** can be crowded, and they're not particularly leafy. The **Starved Rock Lodge** is a cool stone-and-log affair built by the Civilian Conservation Corps in the 1930s. It's perched on a high bluff facing the Illinois River, and offers guest rooms as well as cabins with fireplaces. If you'd prefer to stay in Utica, try the **Starved Rock Inn**.

And if the crowds at Starved Rock are too much, try **Matthiessen State Park**, just across Hwy 178. It features dramatic limestone cliffs and chasms formed by water runoff to the river. Hiking, cross-country skiing and equestrian trails meander through the park.

Information

Starved Rock Visitors Center (☎ 815-667-4906; www.dnr.state.il.us; admission free; 🕑 9am-9pm Jun-Aug, shorter hours Sep-May)

Sights

Matthiessen State Park (☎ 815-667-4868; www.dnr.state.il.us; admission free; 🕑 5am-9pm)

Starved Rock State Park (☎ 815-667-4906; www.dnr.state.il.us; admission free; 🕑 5am-9pm)

TRANSPORTATION

Distance from Chicago 90 miles.

Direction Southwest.

Travel time 1½ to two hours.

Car Take I-90/94 south to I-55. Take I-55 south to I-80. Go west on I-80, 45 miles to Exit 81 (Rte 178, Utica). Go south (left) 3 miles on Rte 178 and follow the signs into the park. Matthiessen State Park is across Rte 178.

Sleeping

Starved Rock Inn (☎ 815-667-4238; www.shopcattails.com; cnr Rtes 6 & 178; r from $69) An old-fashioned inn, the eight rooms are decorated with handmade wood furnishings.

Starved Rock Lodge (☎ 815-667-4211, 800-868-7625; www.starvedrocklodge.com; cnr Rtes 178 & 71; r & cabins $95-115) Features 72 rooms and 22 cabins; restaurant, lounge and café on site.

Starved Rock State Park Campgrounds (☎ 815-667-4726; www.dnr.state.il.us; campsites $20 plus reservation fee $5) There are 133 electric sites total; 100 can be reserved.

GALENA

Though just a speck on the map, Galena, Illinois, draws hordes of Chicagoans to its perfectly preserved, Civil War–era streets. The town spreads across wooded hillsides near the Mississippi River and manages to maintain its charm, despite a slew of tourist-oriented antique shops and restaurants.

Lead was mined in the upper Mississippi area as early as 1700, but industrial demands in the mid-19th century resulted in a boom. Galena (named for the lead sulfide ore) became a center for the industry and major river-port town, and a collection of businesses, hotels and mansions, in both Federal and Italianate styles, shot up here. The boom ended abruptly after the Civil War, and Galena was all but deserted until restoration began in the 1960s.

The main **visitors center** is on the eastern side of the Galena River, in the 1857 train depot. Get a walking guide, leave your car and explore on foot.

Elegant old Main St curves around the hillside and the historic heart of town. Among the sights is the **Ulysses S Grant Home**, a gift from local Republicans to the victorious general at the end of the Civil War. Grant lived here until he became the 18th president of the United States. Tours are provided, sometimes conducted by a uniformed guy who pretends he 'is' Grant.

The elaborate Italianate **Belvedere Mansion** is another fine old dwelling, stuffed with antiques and holding a special claim to fame: it sports the green drapes from *Gone With the Wind* (remember the ones Scarlett O'Hara rips down and sews into a dress?).

Six miles north you can tour the underground **Vinegar Hill Lead Mine & Museum**. On weekend evenings, set out on the hokey but fun **Annie Wiggins Ghost Tour**. Yes, she wears a costume, but so does everyone it town, it seems.

Galena brims with B&Bs – you can't throw a quilt without it landing on a four-poster bed at one of the zillion properties in town. They add to the old-fashioned ambience, and it's easy to see why so many city dwellers pack up their cars on Friday, anxious to escape to the country and drift back into another, slower age (at least until Sunday).

En route to Galena, east of Rockford off I-90, is Union's **Illinois Railway Museum**, one of the best of its kind in the US. The grounds boast more than 200 acres full of historic trains dating from the mid-1800s to the present. Models on display include steam, diesel and electric locomotives, plus passenger and freight cars, many of which are protected by large sheds. This is ground zero for the state's train nerds, and part of the fun is just watching the older patrons and museum volunteers giddily discussing the intricacies of each engine, coupler and car.

TRANSPORTATION

Distance from Chicago To Galena 165 miles; Union 60 miles.

Direction Northwest.

Travel time To Galena three hours; Union one hour 15 minutes.

Car Take I-90 west out of Chicago (tolls apply). Just before Rockford, follow US 51 and I-39 heading south for 3 miles, and then merge onto US 20 west, which runs all the way into Galena. To reach the rail museum, depart I-90 for US 20 at the Marengo exit; go northwest about 5 miles to Union Rd north and follow the signs.

Information

Galena Visitors Center (☎ 815-777-4390, 877-464-2536; www.galena.org; 101 Bouthillier St; 🕑 9am-5pm Mon-Sat, from 10am Sun, extended hours in summer)

Sights

Annie Wiggins Ghost Tour (☎ 815-777-0336; www.anniewiggins.com; 1004 Park Ave; 1hr tour $10; 🕑 evenings Fri & Sat May-Oct)

Belvedere Mansion (☎ 815-777-0747; 1008 Park Ave; adult/child $10/3; ⌚ 11am-4pm Mon-Fri, to 5pm Sat & Sun, late May-Oct)

Illinois Railway Museum (☎ 815-923-4000; www.irm.org; 7000 Olson Rd; adult $6-9, child over 4yr $4-7; ⌚ varying hours Apr-Oct) Take US 20 to Union Rd.

Ulysses S Grant Home (☎ 815- 777-3310; www.granthome.com; 500 Bouthillier St; adult/child $3/1; ⌚ 9am-4:45pm Wed-Sun Apr-Oct)

Vinegar Hill Lead Mine & Museum (☎ 815-777-0855; 8885 N Three Pines Rd; adult/child over 6yr $7/2.50; ⌚ 10am-4pm daily summer, Sat & Sun only Sep & Oct)

Eating

Clarks Again (☎ 815-777-4407; 200 N Main St; dishes $3-6; ⌚ breakfast & lunch year-round, dinner in summer) Biscuit-and-gravy breakfasts or lunchtime sandwiches.

Log Cabin (☎ 815-777-0393; 201 N Main St; mains $10-17; ⌚ from 4pm) Huge dinner portions served amid Americana ambience.

Sleeping

Most B&Bs cost at least $85 nightly. The visitors center can help get you a room; call or check the website. Except during winter, many places are full, especially on weekends.

DeSoto House Hotel (☎ 815-777-0090; www.desotohouse.com; 230 S Main St; r $108-200) Grant and Lincoln stayed in the well-furnished rooms, and you can, too. The hotel dates from 1855 and has air-con.

Grant Hills Motel (☎ 815-777-2116; www.granthills.com; US 20; s/d $63/73) A cozy motel 1.5 miles east of town, with fine views, air-con, pool and a horseshoe pitch.

MILWAUKEE

No one gives much consideration to Milwaukee, Wisconsin, standing as it does in Chicago's shadow, and that's a shame, because with its lineup of beer, motorcycles, world-class art and a ballpark with racing sausages and mystery condiments, it makes a rollicking getaway.

Germans first settled the city in the 1840s. Many immigrants started small breweries soon thereafter, but the introduction of bulk-brewing technology in the 1890s turned beer into a major Milwaukee industry. Schlitz ('the beer that made Milwaukee famous'), Pabst and Miller were all based here at one time, but among the majors, only Miller remains today.

So why not make **Miller Brewing Company** your first stop, and join the legions of drinkers lined up for the free tours? Though the watery beer may not be your favorite, the factory impresses by its sheer scale: you'll visit the packaging plant where 2000 cans are filled each minute, and the warehouse where a half-million cases ship out. And then there's the generous tasting session at the tour's end, where you can down three full-size samples. Don't forget your ID.

For more swills, head to **Sprecher Brewing Company**, a small microbrewery with a museum of memorabilia from long-gone Milwaukee suds-makers and a beer garden replete with oompah music. It's 5 miles north of downtown.

In 1903 William Harley and Arthur Davidson, local Milwaukee schoolmates, built and sold their first Harley-Davidson motorcycle. A century later, the big bikes are a symbol of American manufacturing pride, and the **Harley-Davidson plant**, in the suburb of Wauwatosa (20 minutes from downtown), is where the engines are built. The one-hour tours are kind of technical, but the ultimate payoff comes when you get to sit in the saddle of a vintage bike.

Even those who aren't usual museumgoers will be struck by the lakeside **Milwaukee Art Museum**, which features a stunning winglike addition by Santiago Calatrava. There's a permanent display on Frank Lloyd Wright, and fabulous folk- and outsider-art galleries. Pick up the free, self-guided audio tour.

The Milwaukee Brewers play baseball at top-notch **Miller Park**, which has a retractable roof and real grass. It's famous for its 'Racing Sausages,' a group of people in giant sausage costumes who sprint down the field at the end of the 6th inning. Hot dogs and bratwursts come imbued with the Secret Stadium Sauce; no one knows for sure what it is, other than damn delicious.

Good places to scope for eats include **N Old World 3rd Street** downtown; the fashionable **East Side** by the University of Wisconsin Milwaukee; hip, Italian-based **Brady Street** by its intersection with N Farwell Ave; and the gentrified **Third Ward**, anchored along N Milwaukee St south of I-94. The **Friday night fish fry** is a highly social tradition observed at restaurants throughout Wisconsin and all over Milwaukee. Frozen custard is another local specialty; it's like ice cream only

TRANSPORTATION

Distance from Chicago 92 miles.

Direction North.

Travel time 1½ hours.

Boat For those planning more extensive excursions, Milwaukee is the jump-off point for the Lake Express ferry (☎ 866-914-1010; www.lake-express.com), which sails to Muskegon, MI (one way adult/child $50/24, car/bicycle $59/7.50, 2½ hours, daily mid-May to December), and provides easy access to Michigan's beach-lined Gold Coast (p265). The terminal is a few miles south of downtown; take I-794 East and follow the Port of Milwaukee signs.

Bus Greyhound (☎ 800-231-2222; www.greyhound.com) runs frequent buses from Chicago to Milwaukee ($13 to $28, two hours). The station (☎ 414-272-2156; 606 N James Lovell St) is centrally located downtown. Across the street, Badger Bus (☎ 414-276-7490; www.badgerbus.com; 635 N James Lovell St) goes to Madison ($15, 1½ hours).

Car Take I-90/94 west from downtown, and follow I-94 when it splits off. The interstate goes all the way into Milwaukee. It's a busy road, and travel times can be horrendous in peak hours. It's also a toll road part of the way, costing about $2.50.

Public transportation The Milwaukee County Transit System (☎ 414-344-6711; www.ridemcts.com) provides efficient local bus service (fare $1.75). The main Amtrak station has route maps. Bus 31 goes to Miller Brewery from the corner of 6th and Washington Sts.

Train Perhaps the quickest way to Milwaukee given the snail-crawl pace of highway traffic is via Amtrak (☎ 800-872-7245; www.amtrak.com), which runs the Hiawatha train seven times per day to/from Chicago ($20, 1½ hours). The main station (☎ 414-271-0840; 433 W St Paul Ave) is downtown; there's also one at Milwaukee's airport (☎ 414-747-5300; www.mitchellairport.com).

smoother and richer. **Kopp's** is a popular purveyor, advertising flavors of the day (Midnight Chocolate Cake! Grand Marnier Blueberry Crisp!) from a flashing highway billboard.

The city's festival schedule is endless. **Summerfest** is the granddaddy, with 11 days of music and merriment in late June–early July. There's also **PrideFest, Polish Fest, Irish Fest, German Fest** and a host of others. Call the **visitors center** for details. The center also supplies attraction information, maps and 'A Taster's Guide to Wisconsin Cheese, Beer and Wine.'

Information

Milwaukee Visitors Center (☎ 414-908-6205, 800-554-1448; www.visitmilwaukee.org; 400 W Wisconsin Ave; 8am-5pm Mon-Fri) In the Midwest Airlines Center.

Sights

German Fest (www.germanfest.com) Late July.

Harley-Davidson plant (☎ 414-343-7850; www.harley-davidson.com; 11700 W Capitol Dr, Wauwatosa; admission free; usually 9:30am-1pm Mon-Fri) No open-toed shoes permitted.

Irish Fest (www.irishfest.com) Mid-August.

Miller Brewing Company (☎ 414-931-2337; www.millerbrewing.com; 4251 W State St; admission free; 10:30am-3:30pm Mon-Sat)

Miller Park (☎ 414-902-4000, 800-933-7890; www.milwaukeebrewers.com; 1 Brewers Way, near S 46th St; tickets $5-44)

Milwaukee Art Museum (☎ 414-224-3200; www.mam.org; 750 N Lincoln Memorial Dr; adult/13-18yr $8/4; 10am-5pm, to 8pm Thu)

Polish Fest (www.polishfest.org) Late June.

PrideFest (www.pridefest.com) Mid-June.

Sprecher Brewing Company (☎ 414-964-2739; www.sprecherbrewery.com; 701 W Glendale Ave; admission $3; tours at 4pm Fri then hourly at noon, 1pm & 2pm Sat) Reservations required.

Summerfest (☎ 800-273-3378; www.summerfest.com; day pass $12)

Eating & Drinking

Check the free, weekly **Shepherd Express** (www.shepherd-express.com), or for additional restaurant and entertainment listings try www.onmilwaukee.com.

African Hut (☎ 414-765-1110; 1107 N Old World 3rd St; mains $9-13; 11:30am-9:30pm Mon-Sat) Exotic meat and vegetarian dishes with ingredients like pounded yam, cassava and cooked peanuts with herbs.

American Serb Memorial Hall (☎ 414-545-6030; www.serbhall.com; 5101 W Oklahoma Ave; meals $7-10; ⌚ noon-9pm Fri) Sizzles up a mighty fish fry.

Kopp's (☎ 414-961-2006; 5373 N Port Washington Rd, Glendale; ⌚ 10:30am-11:30pm) Divine frozen custard.

Palm Tavern (☎ 414-744-0393; 2989 S Kinnickinnic Ave) Located in the south side neighborhood of Bay View, this warm, jazzy little bar has a mammoth selection of unusual beers and single-malt scotches.

Von Trier (☎ 414-272-1775; 2235 N Farwell Ave) Long-standing German favorite with plenty of brews on tap and a *biergarten*.

Sleeping

You should book ahead in summer to ensure you get a room.

Astor Hotel (☎ 800-558-0200; www.theastorhotel.com; 924 E Juneau Ave; r $79-129) This 1918 hotel with air-con and Internet access has bright, spacious rooms, some of them with cool old furnishings. The Astor Hotel is located near the lake, east of downtown's core. Parking is $4.

Best Western Inn Towne Hotel (☎ 414-224-8400; www.inntownehotel.com; 710 N Old World 3rd St; s/d from $89/99) This old hotel has good-quality air-con rooms with a vintage ambience in the heart of downtown. Parking is $10.

MADISON

Wonderfully ensconced on a narrow isthmus between Mendota and Monona lakes, Madison, Wisconsin, is an irresistible combination of small, grassy state capital and liberal, bookish college town. To get an indication of the hipness factor at work here, consider that the city birthed the cheeky, farcical newspaper the *Onion*.

The heart of town is marked by the X-shaped **State Capitol**, the largest outside Washington, DC. Tours are available on the hour most days. On warm-weather Saturdays, Capitol Sq is overtaken by the **Dane County Farmers' Market** – a good place to sample the Wisconsin specialties of cheese curds and beer-cooked bratwursts.

Take advantage of the city's lakes and 200 miles of trails. For rentals, try **Yellow Jersey** for bicycles, and **Carl & John's Paddlin'** for canoes and kayaks – both within a mile of Capitol Sq.

State Street runs from the capitol west to the University of Wisconsin. The lengthy street is lined with free-trade coffee shops, parked bicycles, and incense-wafting stores selling hackey-sacks, skirts from India, used CDs and books. A smorgasbord of restaurants – Nepali, Turkish and Afghani among them – peppers the strip amid the pizza and cheap-beer joints.

The campus has its own attractions, including the 1240-acre **Arboretum**, dense with lilac, and the **Memorial Union**, with its festive lakeside terrace. The Union also offers free live music, films, Internet access and budget travel information in its 2nd-floor travel center.

Monona Terrace Community Center, two blocks from the square, has a fabulous rooftop garden overlooking Lake Monona. It finally opened in 1997, 59 years after Frank Lloyd Wright designed it. Tours are offered daily.

Dr Evermor's Sculpture Park sprawls 11 miles northwest of Madison on US 12. The doctor welds pipes, carburetors and other salvaged metal into a hallucinatory world of futuristic creatures and structures. The crowning glory is the giant, egg-domed Forevertron, cited by Guinness as the world's largest scrap-metal sculpture. The good doctor himself – aka Tom Every – is often around and happy to chat about his birds, dragons and other pieces of folk art. Look for sculptures along the highway marking the entrance.

Madison's **visitors center** is six blocks east of Capitol Sq, though you'll likely find all you need at the Memorial Union.

TRANSPORTATION

Distance from Chicago 150 miles.

Direction Northwest.

Travel time Three hours.

Bus Climb aboard Van Galder Bus (☎ 800-747-0994; www.vangalderbus.com), which runs between Chicago (either O'Hare or downtown) and Madison's Memorial Union (one way $24, 3½ hours) several times daily. Badger Bus (p261) goes to Milwaukee ($15, 1½ hours); it also originates at Memorial Union.

Car Take I-90/94 west out of Chicago; stay on I-90 when it splits off. Stay on the interstate going west to Rockford, then north. On the outskirts of Madison get onto US 18/12 west for about 6 miles, and then look for the Park St exit into downtown. Parts of I-90 require tolls.

Information

Madison Visitors Center (☎ 608-255-2537, 800-373-6376; www.visitmadison.com; 615 E Washington Ave; 8am-5pm Mon-Fri)

Sights

Carl & John's Paddlin' (☎ 608-284-0300; www.paddlin.com; 110 N Thornton Ave, btwn E Jansen & E Washington Sts; kayak or canoe per day $30; 10am-6pm Mon-Thu, to 8pm Fri, to 5pm Sat & Sun)

Dane County Farmers' Market (www.dcfm.org; Sat May-Nov)

Dr Evermor's Sculpture Park (www.drevermor.com; US 12; admission free; 9am-5pm Mon & Thu-Sat, from noon Sun)

Memorial Union (☎ 608-265-3000; 800 Langdon St)

Monona Terrace Community Center (☎ 608-261-4000; www.mononaterrace.com; 1 John Nolen Dr; admission free, tours adult/student $3/2; 8am-5pm, tours 1pm) Parking costs $3.

Onion (www.theonion.com)

State Capitol (☎ 608-266-0382; admission free; 8am-6pm Mon-Fri, 8am-4pm Sat & Sun)

University of Wisconsin Arboretum (☎ 608-263-7888; 1207 Seminole Hwy; admission free; 7am-10pm)

Yellow Jersey (☎ 608-257-4737; www.yellowjersey.org; 419 State St; bikes per day $10; 10am-6pm Tue, Wed & Fri, to 8pm Mon & Thu, 9am-5pm Sat, from noon Sun)

Eating

Himal Chuli (☎ 608-251-9225; 318 State St; mains $8-13; 11am-9pm Mon-Sat, from noon Sun) Cheerful, cozy place serving homemade Nepali fare, including vegetarian dishes.

Kabul (☎ 608-256-6322; 541 State St; mains $8-12; 11am-10:30pm Sun-Thu, to 11pm Fri & Sat) Nicely done Afghani food.

Michelangelo's (☎ 608-251-5299; 114 State St; mains $2-5; 7am-11pm) Coffees, sweets and sandwiches.

Sleeping

HI Madison Hostel (☎ 608-441-0144; www.madisonhostel.org; 141 S Butler St; dm $18-21, r $41-44; year-round) By the capitol; has Internet access.

University Inn (☎ 608-285-8040, 800-279-4881; www.universityinn.org; 441 N Frances St; r $79-139) A handy hotel with parking and air-con, by the State St action.

INDIANA DUNES

Lake Michigan's prevailing winds created the 21 miles of sandy beaches and dunes that comprise **Indiana Dunes National Lakeshore**. Behind the sands, large areas of woods and wetlands have become major wildlife habitats and the breeding ground for an incredible variety of plant life. Everything from cactus to hardwood forests and pine trees sprouts here.

Preserving this rare ecosystem, which stretches from Gary east to Michigan City, has always been a struggle. The vast and stinky steel mills that pop up amid the bucolic beauty show which way the fight often has gone, and gives visitors a whiff (literally – just breathe in that rotten Gary air) of the horrors that might have spread had activists like Dorothy Buell and Illinois Senator Paul Douglas not stepped in to protect the region.

Today the area attracts huge crowds in summer months, when people from Chicago to South Bend flock to the shores for good swimming and general frivolity. Swimming is allowed anywhere along the national lakeshore. On busy days a short hike away from the folks clogging up a developed beach will yield an almost deserted strand. In winter the lake winds and pervasive desolation make the dunes a moody and memorable experience. You may well hear the low hum of the 'singing sands,' an unusual sound caused by the zillions of grains of sand hitting each other in the wind.

DETOUR: TALIESIN

Forty miles west of Madison and 3 miles south of Spring Green, Taliesin was the home of native son Frank Lloyd Wright for most of his life and is the site of his architectural school. It's now a major pilgrimage destination for fans and followers. The house was built in 1903, the Hillside Home School in 1932, and the **visitors center** (☎ 608-588-7900; www.taliesinpreservation.org; Hwy 23; tours $15-80; 9am-6pm May-Oct) in 1953. A wide range of guided tours covers various parts of the complex; reservations are required for the more lengthy ones. The two-hour walking tour ($15, no reservation needed) is a good introduction. For additional Wright sights, visit Oak Park (p254).

Relaxing beside Lake Michigan, Indiana Dunes (p263)

A good place to start your trip is the **Dorothy Buell Memorial Visitor Center**. The helpful center features a section on the local flora and fauna, as well as free park and hiking trail maps. From the visitors center, it's time to hit the beaches. Of the developed ones, Central Beach is a good place to escape the masses, and it leads to a set of steep dune cliffs. Mt Baldy Beach boasts the highest dunes, with namesake Mt Baldy offering the best views all the way to Chicago from its 120ft peak. Don't look east or you'll see the environmental travesty of downtown Michigan City's coal-powered electric plant and huge cooling tower. This beach is by far the busiest of the lot. West Beach, which is nearest to Gary, draws fewer crowds than the others and features a number of nature hikes and trails. It's also the only beach with an on-duty lifeguard.

If you'd rather be on your feet than flat on your back on the sand, the park service has done a fine job of developing hiking trails through a range of terrain and environments. The Bailly/Chellberg Trail begins at the **Bailly/Chellberg Visitor Center**, a major site that's some distance from the beaches. The 2½-mile trail winds through the forest, passing restored log cabins from the 1820s and a farm built by Swedes in the 1870s. Among the diverse plants growing here are dogwood, arctic berries and cactus.

The nicely varied 5-mile walk at Cowles Bog Trail combines marshes and dunes. The 1½-mile Miller Woods Trail passes dunes, woods and ponds, plus the **Paul H Douglas Center for Environmental Education**, which offers day programs. At West Beach the Long Lake Trail is a classic wetlands walk around an inland lake. The easy, 2-mile Heron Rookery Trail rewards with an amble past a breeding ground for the **great blue heron**; it's located inland, southeast of Buell Visitor Center. The best times for viewing are dawn and dusk, when you can catch the tall, regal birds wading into the water and spearing food with their pointy-sharp bills. Since the birds can be elusive, it's wise to stop into the center first and have staff give you sighting tips.

Much of the national park area is good for cycling, although the traffic and the narrow shoulders on Hwy 12 can make that road dangerous. However, the Calumet Bike Trail runs west from near Michigan City almost to the Chellberg Farm, in the middle of the national lakeshore. There is cross-country skiing inland, especially along the trails described above.

Indiana Dunes State Park is a 2100-acre shoreside pocket within the national lakeshore. It has more amenities, but is also more regulated (and crowded). Away from its mobbed beaches, the park features secluded natural areas. In winter cross-country skiing is popular, while summertime brings out the hikers. Seven numbered trails zigzag over the sandscape: Trail 4 climbs up Mt Tom, the highest dune at 192ft; Trail 2 is good for spring flowers and ferns and is well-used by skiers; and Trail 8 surmounts three of the highest dunes, paying off with killer views of the region.

Other than a couple of snack bars sprinkled along the major beaches, you won't find much to eat in the parks, so pack a picnic or stop at homey, Italian **Lucrezia** in Chesterton or the sophisticated, foodie-favorite **Miller Bakery Café** in Miller Beach.

TRANSPORTATION

Distance from Chicago 50 miles.

Direction Southeast.

Travel time 75 minutes.

Car Take I-90 through Gary to US 12; most sites are located off US 12. Note that I-90 is a toll road, so be prepared to pay $3 to $4 en route.

Metra South Shore Line trains (☎ 800-356-2079; www.nictd.com) depart frequently from Randolph St Station in the Loop and stop at Miller, Ogden Dunes, Dune Park and Beverly Shores (one way $5 to $8).

Parking at the national lakeshore's beach lots is a nightmare on weekends unless you arrive before 10am; West Beach is your best bet, though it charges $6 per car. The state park has bigger lots. Or take the South Shore train from Chicago, which allows you to avoid the parking mess if you don't mind walking a mile or more from the various stations to the beaches.

It's certainly satisfying to visit the dunes as a day trip, but many folks prefer to linger and pitch a tent at the state park's renovated **campground.** Be sure to book ahead in summer.

The **Porter County Convention & Visitors Bureau** produces handy ecotourism, birding, hiking and biking guides for the area; call them to order the freebies, or pick them up at the park's Buell Visitor Center. Unfortunately, the parks do not rent bicycles or skis, so you'll have to bring your own.

Information

Bailly/Chellberg Visitor Center (☎ 219-926-7561; Mineral Springs Rd; 11am-4:30pm Sat & Sun) South of Hwy 12.

Dorothy Buell Memorial Visitor Center (☎ 219-926-7561 ext 225; Kemil Rd; 8am-5pm, to 6pm summer) Just off Hwy 12, about 1 mile from the Beverly Shores rail station.

Porter County Convention & Visitors Bureau (☎ 800-283-8687; www.indianadunes.com)

Sights

Indiana Dunes National Lakeshore (☎ 800-959-9174; www.nps.gov/indu; admission free except West Beach, which charges per car $6)

Indiana Dunes State Park (☎ 219-926-1952; www.dnr.in.gov/parklake; per car $8; beaches 9am-sunset, park 7am-11pm, shorter hours Sep-May) Located at the end of Hwy 49, near Chesterton.

Indiana Dunes State Park Camping (☎ 866-622-6746; www.camp.in.gov; campsites $8-24; year-round)

Paul H Douglas Center for Environmental Education (☎ 219-926-7561) Call for program schedule.

Eating

Lucrezia (☎ 219-926-5829; 428 S Calumet Rd, Chesterton; mains $11-25; 11am-10pm Sun-Thu, to 11pm Fri & Sat)

Miller Bakery Café (☎ 219-938-2229; 555 Lake St, Miller Beach; lunch mains $8-16, dinner mains $16-28; lunch 11:30am-2pm Tue-Fri, dinner 5-9pm Tue-Fri, to 10pm Sat, 4-8pm Sun)

MICHIGAN'S GOLD COAST

Michigan's west coast – aka its Gold Coast – is the place to come to watch incredible sunsets while waves tickle your toes. The 300-mile shoreline features endless stretches of beach and is dotted with coastal parks and small towns that boom during the summer tourist season.

Saugatuck – known for its strong arts community, numerous B&Bs and gay-friendly vibe – is one of the most popular resort areas. The best thing to do in town is also the most affordable. Jump aboard the **Saugatuck Chain Ferry**, and the operator will pull you across the Kalamazoo River. On the other side you can huff up the stairs to the grand views atop **Mt Baldhead**, a 200ft-high sand dune. Then race down the north side to beautiful **Oval Beach**. The **Saugatuck Dune Rides** provide a half hour of good, cheesy fun spent zipping through the sand.

Several galleries line the Blue Star Hwy between Saugatuck and South Haven (yes, it's south, as the name implies, by about 20 miles), offering pottery, paintings, sculptures and glasswork. **Blue Star Pottery** – known for its sturdy bowls and platters with leaf-print designs – stands out. The area also sports a slew of antique shops where you can buy old traffic lights, Victorian sleds

TRANSPORTATION

Distance from Chicago To Saugatuck 140 miles; Grand Haven 170 miles; Muskegon 185 miles.

Direction Northeast.

Travel time To Saugatuck 2½ hours; Muskegon 3½ hours.

Boat The Lake Express ferry (☎ 866-914-1010; www.lake-express.com; Great Lakes Marina, 1920 Lakeshore Dr) sails from Muskegon to Milwaukee, Wisconsin (one way adult/child $50/24, car/bicycle $59/7.50, 2½ hours, mid-May to December).

Car Take I-90 east toward Indiana for about 30 miles (be prepared to pay about $4 worth of tolls). After Gary, merge onto I-94 east, and stay on it for about 65 miles. After Benton Harbor merge onto I-196/US 31, and take it for about 40 miles, until you see exits for Saugatuck. The state parks are all off US 31 to the north.

or $100 china teacups. Start at the whopping, 50,000-sq-ft **Blue Star Antique Pavilion**, which can absorb buyers and browsers alike for the better part of a day. If you're too lazy to drive far, mosey around downtown Saugatuck, near Water and Butler Sts, where more galleries and shops proliferate.

To commune with nature, head north to Grand Haven and Muskegon. Three state parks cluster between these two towns, all offering the opportunity to hike and camp on or near Lake Michigan beaches. Resorty Grand Haven is all about silken sand, boardwalks and lighthouses. Oh, and there's a giant musical fountain that squirts 90,000 gallons of water sky-high each evening in summer. **Grand Haven State Park** sprawls along the beach and is connected to downtown restaurants by a scenic walkway along the Grand River. Between Grand Haven and Muskegon is **PJ Hoffmaster State Park**, providing a 10-mile trail system with several sections that hug Lake Michigan. North of Muskegon is **Muskegon State Park**, with 12 miles of trails through rugged, wooded dunes. The town of Muskegon itself is no great shakes, but it is the jump-off point for the Lake Express ferry to Milwaukee (see p261).

For a more in-depth exploration of Michigan's Gold Coast, get Lonely Planet's *Road Trip: Lake Michigan* book.

DETOUR: MIDWESTERN METRO GETAWAYS

Minneapolis, Detroit and Cleveland aren't far from Chicago. They range from five to nine hours away by car, and little more than an hour by air if you cop a cheap flight (check Southwest or Northwest Airlines; the latter has hubs in Minneapolis and Detroit). Amtrak also runs to all three cities. Pick up a copy of Lonely Planet's *USA* for more in-depth explorations.

Detroit

Ah, the Motor City. Once the pride of the nation for its car savvy (GM, Ford and Chrysler all launched here), the city fell to pieces when the auto industry tanked. Today, once-grand buildings lie boarded up with trash blowing about their bases, and wide swaths of downtown are downright vacant. It's a grim but fascinating destination.

A trio of top-tier attractions is part of the reason why. Spend a day wandering and wondering through the **Henry Ford Museum/Greenfield Village complex** (☎ 313-982-6001; www.thehenryford.org; 20900 Oakwood Blvd; adult/5-12yr $26/20; 🕒 9:30am-5pm, Ford open year-round, Greenfield Village closed in winter) in suburban Dearborn. The two museums contain a fascinating wealth of American culture such as the chair Lincoln was sitting in when he was assassinated, Edgar Allan Poe's writing desk, the bus on which Rosa Parks refused to give up her seat and, of course, vintage cars. The **Motown Museum** (☎ 313-875-2264; www.motownmuseum.com; 2648 W Grand Blvd; adult/child $8/5; 🕒 10am-6pm Tue-Sat) is a string of unassuming houses that became known as 'Hitsville USA' after Berry Gordy began Motown Records – and the careers of Stevie Wonder, Marvin Gaye et al – with an $800 loan in 1959. Diego Rivera's mural *Detroit Industry* fills a room at the renowned **Detroit Institute of Arts** (☎ 313-833-7900; www.dia.org; 5200 Woodward Ave; adult/child $4/1; 🕒 10am-4pm Wed & Thu, to 9pm Fri, to 5pm Sat & Sun).

The 'coney' – a hot dog smothered with chili and onions – is a Detroit specialty. When the craving strikes (and it will), take care of business at **Lafayette Coney Island** (☎ 313-964-8198; 118 Lafayette Blvd; items $2-3; 🕒 24hr). The minimalist menu consists of burgers, fries, pies, doughnuts and beer, in addition to the signature item. Cast-iron stomach required.

Detroit may be Motown, but in recent years it's been rap, techno and hard-edged rock that have pushed the city to the forefront of the music scene; homegrown stars include the White Stripes and Eminem. **St Andrew's Hall** (☎ 313-961-6358; www.standrewshall.com; 431 E Congress St) and **Magic Stick** (☎ 313-833-9700; www.majesticdetroit.com; 4120 Woodward Ave) are where the coolest bands plug in their amps.

Shorecrest Motor Inn (☎ 313-568-3000, 800-992-9616; www.shorecrestmi.com; 1316 E Jefferson Ave; s/d $69/89) provides inexpensive downtown lodging with air-con and parking.

Cleveland

Does it or does it not rock? You'll have to visit to decide.

Certainly Cleveland's top attraction is the **Rock & Roll Hall of Fame & Museum** (☎ 216-781-7625, 888-764-7625; www.rockhall.com; 1 Key Plaza; adult/9-12yr $20/11; 🕒 10am-5:30pm, to 9pm Wed year-round, to 9pm Sat Jun-Aug). It's more than a collection of rock-star memorabilia, though it does have Janis Joplin's psychedelic Porsche and Ray Charles' sunglasses. Interactive multimedia exhibits trace the history and social context of rock music and the many performers who created it. Why is the museum in Cleveland? Because this is the hometown of Alan Freed, the

Sights

Note all **state parks** (www.michigandnr.com/parksandtrails) listed require a vehicle permit (per day/year $8/29) to enter.

Blue Star Antique Pavilion (☎ 269-637-5787; 337 Blue Star Hwy; 🕑 11am-5pm Fri-Sun May-Nov, by appointment rest of time)

Blue Star Pottery (☎ 269-857-6041; 2948 Blue Star Hwy; 🕑 10am-6pm)

Grand Haven State Park (☎ 616-847-1309; 1001 Harbor Ave; 🕑 8am-11pm, closed Nov-Mar) Take US 31 to the Franklin St exit.

Muskegon State Park (☎ 231-744-3480; 3560 Memorial Dr; 🕑 9am-10pm) Take US 31 to the Hwy 120 exit.

Oval Beach (Oval Beach Rd; vehicle $5)

PJ Hoffmaster State Park (☎ 231-798-3711; 6585 Lake Harbor Rd; 🕑 8am-10pm) Take US 31 to the Pontaluna Rd exit.

Saugatuck Chain Ferry (Water St; fare $1; 🕑 9am-9pm)

Saugatuck Dune Rides (☎ 269-857-2253; www.saugatuckduneride.com; 6495 Blue Star Hwy; adult/child $14.50/9.50; 🕑 10am-5:30pm Mon-Sat, from noon Sun May-Sep)

Eating

Crane's Pie Pantry (☎ 269-561-2297; 6054 124th Ave, Fennville; 🕑 9am-8pm Mon-Sat, from 11am Sun May-Oct, reduced hours rest of year) Off Hwy 89, a few miles

disc jockey who popularized the term 'rock 'n' roll' in the early 1950s, and because the city lobbied hard and paid big. Be prepared for crowds.

Cultural attractions cluster around Case Western Reserve University (aka 'University Circle'), 5 miles east of downtown, including the excellent **Cleveland Museum of Art** (☎ 216-421-7340; www.clemusart.com; 11150 East Blvd; admission free; 🕑 10am-5pm Tue-Sun, to 9pm Wed & Fri). Busy **Little Italy** is along Mayfield Rd, near University Circle (look for the Rte 322 sign).

For stylish eating and drinking, head to **Ohio City** and **Tremont**, which straddle I-90 south of downtown. **West Side Market Café** (☎ 216-579-6800; 1979 W 25th St; mains $4-7; 🕑 breakfast Mon, Wed, Fri & Sat, lunch Mon-Sat) is a smart stop if you're craving well-made breakfast and lunch fare, and cheap fish and chicken mains. The **West Side Market** (www.westsidemarket.com; cnr W 25th St & Lorain Ave; 🕑 Mon, Wed, Fri & Sat) is adjacent, overflowing with fresh produce and prepared foods. **Great Lakes Brewing Company** (☎ 216-771-4404; 2516 Market Ave) wins prizes for its brewed-on-the-premises beers. Added historical bonus: Eliot Ness got into a shootout with criminals here; ask the bartender to show you the bullet holes.

For sleeping try **Brownstone Inn** (☎ 216-426-1753; www.brownstoneinndowntown.com; 3649 Prospect Ave; r $75-135), a five-room B&B between downtown and University Circle. It has air-con and parking.

Minneapolis

Minneapolis is young, forward thinking and environmentally aware, with all the fixings of progressive prosperity – a cache of coffee shops, organic and ethnic eateries, rock and roll clubs and enough theaters to be nicknamed Mini-Apple (second only to the Big Apple, New York City, in per capita venues).

Top attractions include the **Walker Art Center** (☎ 612-375-7622; www.walkerart.org; 725 Vineland Pl; adult/12-18yr $8/5, Thu eve free; 🕑 11am-5pm Tue-Sun, to 9pm Thu & Fri), with big-name US painters and great US pop art, and the whimsical **Sculpture Garden** (admission free; 🕑 6am-midnight) next door. Walk the 2-mile trail by **St Anthony Falls** (on the north edge of downtown at the foot of Portland Ave), the power source of the timber and flour mills that gave rise to this Mississippi River city. Within a mile or two of downtown, a ring of lakes circles the inner-city area. **Cedar Lake**, **Lake of the Isles**, **Lake Calhoun** and **Lake Harriet** are all surrounded by parks and paths.

Browse for food and drink in the punk-yuppie **Uptown** neighborhood. **French Meadow Bakery & Café** (☎ 612-870-7855; www.frenchmeadow.com; 2610 Lyndale Ave S; sandwiches $7-8, mains $14-18; 🕑 6:30am-10pm Sun-Thu, to 11pm Fri & Sat) focuses on local and organic ingredients. In warm weather (true, there isn't that much, so seize this opportunity when it comes) you can't beat a plate of Belgian waffles with fresh berries while sitting curbside in the sun.

Acts such as Prince and protogrunge bands like Hüsker Dü and the Replacements cut their chops in Minneapolis. **First Avenue & 7th St Entry** (☎ 612-338-8388; www.first-ave.com; 701 1st Ave N) is the bedrock of the city's music scene, and it still pulls in top bands and big crowds. **Triple Rock Social Club** (☎ 612-333-7499; www.triplerocksocialclub.com; 629 Cedar Ave) is a popular punk-alternative club.

Cheery, 10-bedroom **Wales House** (☎ 612-331-3931; www.waleshouse.com; 1115 Fifth Street SE; r with/without bathroom $65/55) caters to scholars at the nearby University of Minnesota, and is a fine place to lay your head. It has air-con and parking.

south of Saugatuck; located smack-dab in the middle of a fruit orchard, which is where the blueberry, apple, red raspberry and other luscious fillings come from.

Everyday People Café (☎ 269-857-4240; 11 Center St, Douglas; mains $12-22; ⏲ lunch & dinner, closed Wed) A few miles south of Saugatuck; a hip, upscale café with dishes like chipotle barbecue pork and stuffed portobello mushrooms.

Loaf & Mug (☎ 269-857-3793; 236 Culver St; mains $6.50-13; ⏲ 8am-9pm, closed Tue) Just-baked bread, sandwiches, breakfast dishes and tapas.

Sleeping

B&Bs abound in Saugatuck. Most are tucked into century-old Victorian homes and range from $100 to $200 a night per couple in the summer high season.

Bayside Inn (☎ 269-857-4321; www.baysideinn.net; 618 Water St; r $75-180) A former boathouse with 10 rooms, air-con and an outdoor hot tub.

Michigan State Park campsite reservations (☎ 800-447-2757; www.midnrreservations.com; campsites $18-25, reservation fee $2)

Pines Motorlodge (☎ 269-857-5211; www.thepinesmotorlodge.com; 56 Blue Star Hwy; r $125-165) Mom-and-pop motel with comfy, air-con rooms at Saugatuck's edge.

Twin Gables Inn (☎ 269-857-4346, 800-231-2185; www.twingablesinn.com; 900 Lake St; r $90-210) Fifteen-room inn with air-con, overlooking Lake Michigan.

Directory

Directory

TRANSPORTATION

AIRLINES

Between O'Hare and Midway airports, you'll likely find a way to get anywhere in the US and abroad. Airlines flying into and out of Chicago include the following:

Air Canada (☎ 888-247-2262; www.aircanada.ca)

Air France (☎ 800-237-2747; www.airfrance.com)

America West Airlines (☎ 800-247-5692; www.americawest.com)

American Airlines (☎ 800-433-7300; www.aa.com)

ATA (American Trans Air; ☎ 800-883-5228; www.ata.com)

British Airways (☎ 800-247-9297; www.britishairways.com)

Continental Airlines (☎ 800-523-3273; www.continental.com)

Delta Airlines (☎ 800-221-1212; www.delta.com)

Japan Airlines (☎ 800-525-3663; www.jal.com)

KLM Royal Dutch Airlines (☎ 800-447-4747; www.klm.com)

Lufthansa (☎ 800-645-3880; www.lufthansa.com)

Northwest Airlines (☎ 800-225-2525; www.nwa.com)

Southwest Airlines (☎ 800-435-9792; www.southwest.com)

United Airlines (☎ 800-864-833; www.united.com)

US Airways (☎ 800-428-4322; www.usairways.com)

Virgin Atlantic (☎ 800-821-5438; www.virgin-atlantic.com)

Flights

In addition to the airline companies' own websites, which often offer Internet-only deals, a number of third-party sites can be helpful in finding you discounts on flights:

www.cheaptickets.com

www.expedia.com

www.go-today.com

www.hotwire.com

www.orbitz.com

www.priceline.com

www.site59.com

www.smarterliving.com

www.travelocity.com

www.travelzoo.com

If you're trying to work out a complex itinerary or would like someone to handle the bookings for you, try **STA Travel** (Map pp308-9; ☎ 312-786-9050; www.statravel.com; 429 S Dearborn St), which has another branch in **Lincoln Park** (Map pp308-9; ☎ 773-880-8051; 2570 N Clark St).

AIRPORTS

Chicago is served by two main airports. O'Hare International (ORD) is the world's busiest hub and located 17 miles northwest of the city. Midway (MID) is smaller and located 10 miles to the south of the city center.

As for shuttle vans, **Airport Express** (☎ 312-454-7800, 800-654-7871; www.airportexpress.com) has a monopoly on services between the airports and hotels in the Loop and Near North. Once downtown, you may have to ride around while others are dropped off before you. You also may have to wait until the van is full before you leave the airport. If there are two or more of you, take a cab – it's immediate, direct and cheaper per person. A ride with Continental Airport Express from Midway to the Loop costs $19 per person. From O'Hare the fare is $24 per person, plus the usual 10% to 15% tip. For shuttle rides between Midway and O'Hare airports use the **Omega Shuttle** (☎ 773-483-6634; per person $16).

Midway

Midway is a modern, attractive airport with three concourses. You'll enter and exit through the magnificent New Terminal, home to almost all of the airport's services and amenities. Midway is mostly known as a home to cut-rate carriers such as Southwest and ATA.

Airport Information/Customer Service (☎ 773-838-3003), airport police, ATMs and Travelers Aid are in the New Terminal building.

AIRPORT SECURITY

Since the September 11, 2001 terrorist attacks, airport security in the US has adopted a zero-tolerance policy for even the slightest infractions of airport rules. These rules mean that confiscations of tiny pocketknives and other entirely innocuous-seeming (but potentially malicious) instruments are routine at the X-ray detectors: plan on checking any belongings that might be construed as threatening. Also, know that if the **Transportation Safety Administration** (www.tsa.gov) decides to screen your checked luggage and you have a lock on it, agents will simply break off the lock. Visit the website for more information.

Expect to have to take off your shoes and belt as you go through the metal detectors, and know that the people waving those wands over you are now federal employees; however inept they may seem at times, they do carry the weight of the government and can cause you no end of delays if angered.

Additionally, there are two City Information Centers; the first is in the baggage-claim area of the New Terminal building, and the other is on the top floor, near the ATA counter. Both primarily offer brochures and maps, as well as the city's official visitor's guide.

Follow the signs to ground transportations to catch a taxi. The taxis are available on a first-come, first-served basis, and you can split the costs by sharing a ride. Tell the driver you'd like to ride-share before heading off. Costs are based on the meter (there are no flat-rate rides), and will likely run about $25 plus tip into the Loop.

You can take the CTA Orange Line from Midway to the Loop. A one-way ride will cost you $1.75, and transfers within the El system are free. To reach the CTA station, follow the signs from the New Terminal.

If you're renting a car at the airport, take S Cicero Ave north to I-55N. You can tune in to the airport radio station – 800AM – for traffic and airport-parking updates.

O'Hare

O'Hare's four operational terminals bustle day and night. Terminal 1, designed by architect Helmut Jahn, is the most striking. Terminal 4 is no longer used.

For general airport info call ☎ 773-686-2200. You'll find ATMs and phones (including TTY phones) available in every terminal. Airport information and customer-service counters are in Terminals 1, 3 and 5. The Children's Museum (p74) runs an exhibit space for children 12 and under in Terminal 2. The 24-hour **currency exchanges** (☎ 773-462-9973) are in Terminals 3 and 5. Police kiosks/lost-and-found counters can be found on the upper levels of all terminals. The **Travelers & Immigrants Aid Office** (☎ 773-894-2427; 🕑 8:30am-9pm Mon-Fri, from 10am Sat & Sun) is on the upper level of Terminal 2. It provides information, directions and special assistance to travelers.

For medical help, the University of Illinois at Chicago's Medical Center runs a **clinic** (☎ 773-894-5100) on the upper level of Terminal 2. There's also a **post office** (🕑 9am-5pm Mon-Fri) on the upper level of Terminal 2. If you're looking to hook into email or other business services, **Laptop Lane** (☎ 773-894-3100), in Terminal 1, offers faxing, printing and Internet access.

Each terminal has one taxi stand outside the baggage-claim area; you may have to line up. The fare to the Near North and Loop runs $35 to $40, depending on tip (usually about 10% to 15%) and traffic (taxi meters keep running even when the car is at a standstill). If there are other travelers heading downtown, it may make sense to share a cab. Inform the driver you want to share the cab before you start off.

The Chicago Transit Authority (CTA) offers 24-hour train service on the Blue Line to and from the Loop. Unfortunately, the O'Hare station is buried under the world's largest parking garage. Finding it can be akin to navigating a maze – directional signs are variously marked as 'CTA,' 'Rapid Transit' and 'Trains to City.' Unless you are staying right in the Loop, you will have to transfer to another El or bus to complete your journey. For recommendations on which one to take, ask your hotel when you reserve your room. A good alternative is to ride the El as close as you can get to your hotel and then take a taxi for the final few blocks. Again, ask your hotel or consult the neighborhood map in this book to see which El stop is closest to your hotel.

For trips further afield, regional bus companies serve southern Wisconsin, suburban

Illinois and northwest Indiana from the bus-shuttle center, installed in the ground level of the central parking garage. Use the tunnels under the Hilton Hotel to get there from Terminals 1, 2 and 3. Terminal 5, the international terminal, has its own pickup area.

If you're renting a car, take I-190 east from the airport to I-90 east into the Loop.

BICYCLE

Bikes can be rented for about $35 per day. Try the following:

Bike Chicago (Map pp306-7; ☎ 312-595-9600; www.bikechicago.com; Navy Pier; bus 66)

Millennium Park Bike Station (Map pp304-5; ☎ 888-245-3929; www.chicagobikestation.com; 239 E Randolph St; Brown, Green, Orange, or Purple Line to Randolph)

On the Route (Map pp318-19; ☎ 773-477-5066; www.ontheroute.com; 3146 N Lincoln Ave; Red, Brown Line to Belmont)

Bicycles on Trains & Buses

Bikes are allowed on all CTA trains, save for during high-use commuter hours (7am to 9am and 4pm to 6pm Monday to Friday). When entering the station, tell the customer-service assistant you have your bike and look for the handicapped-accessible swing gate. Go through the gate, depositing your bike on the other side, and then return through the same gate, running your transit card through the scanner-turnstile. If there is no swing gate, the customer-service person will open a gate for you. To get to the platform, use elevators when possible. Only two bikes are allowed per train car.

Bikes are allowed on Metra trains all day and evenings on weekends, and from 9:30pm to 3pm and again from 7pm onward weekdays. The number of bikes is limited to two per train car, and cyclists under 12 are not allowed on the trains with bicycles, regardless of parental accompaniment.

Many CTA buses and all Pace buses are equipped with bike racks on the front. These racks accommodate two bikes at a time, and there is no extra cost associated with using them. Tell the driver you have your bike with you, and that you will need to access the rack attached to the front of the bus. Before boarding the bus, swing the rack's support arm down over your bike to secure it. When getting off, alert the driver at your stop that you will be removing your bike.

BUS

Long-distance bus carrier **Greyhound** (Map pp314-15; ☎ 312-408-5800, 800-231-2222; www.greyhound.com; 630 W Harrison St) sends dozens of buses in every direction every day. Trips are slower than they would be by car, with the bus making many stops along the way to pick up people traveling from small towns. Sample one-way fares and times include Minneapolis ($67, 10 hours), Memphis ($70, 10 hours) and New York City ($88, 18 hours). The station's ticketing windows are open 24 hours. The Clinton El stop on the Blue Line is two blocks away.

CAR & MOTORCYCLE

Driving in Chicago is a challenge. The pace is speedy and reckless, and Chicago drivers have little patience for slow-driving tourists. And during rush hour, the highways and surface roads become a crawling mess. With public transportation being what it is, there is little reason to use a car, unless you're heading out of town.

Parking

Parking in Chicago can range from effortless to excruciating. Meter spots and on-street parking are plentiful in outlying areas, but the Loop, Near North, Lincoln Park and Lake View neighborhoods can require up to an hour of circling before you find a spot. Valet parking, even at $11, can be worth it in these congested neighborhoods.

Parking-meter rates vary from neighborhood to neighborhood, but in many, 25¢ will buy you 30 minutes or more of time, up to the posted limit. Watch out for streets where parking meters are only posted at every other parking spot. These are 'double' meters, and you'll need to examine them closely to figure out which meter applies to your spot.

Some common curb colors and their meanings include the following:

Blue Disabled parking only; identification required.

Green Ten-minute parking zone from 9am to 6pm.

Red No parking or even stopping.

White For picking up or dropping off passengers.

Yellow Loading zone from 7am to 6pm.

The biggest rule of parking in Chicago is to never park in a spot or parking area marked 'Tow-Away.' Your car will be towed. Period. Tow-truck drivers in Chicago are like vultures, circling the streets on the lookout for illegally parked cars. Towing fees run to $125, plus the cost of the cab ride to retrieve your car from the lot. Almost every Chicago driver has had their car towed at some point. It's not pretty.

Parking in a garage can be expensive, but will save you time and traffic tickets. Try the downtown garages off Michigan Ave at Washington St and at Van Buren St.

Rental

Both O'Hare and Midway have a plethora of car-rental options, supplementing the in-town branches. Online bookings have become common for all major rental agencies; reserving your car through the Web is also a good way to take advantage of Internet-only rates. You'll need a credit card to rent a car, and many agencies rent only to those 25 and older. Of the agencies listed here, Enterprise sets itself apart by picking up customers.

Expect to pay $30 to $45 per day for a compact car, with rates going down somewhat if you rent for an entire week. Rates are also lower on weekends, sometimes dramatically so. Most agencies offer unlimited mileage on their cars; if they don't, ask about it – the per-mile costs can add up quickly. Also, be aware of redundant insurance coverage – liability and medical insurance provided by the car-rental companies are optional and can often add 50% to the cost of your rental. Many credit cards have built-in liability coverage on car rentals – check with yours before renting so you know exactly how much supplemental insurance you need to get from your rental-car company.

Some of the larger car-rental agencies in Chicago include the following:

Alamo (☎ 800-327-9633; www.alamo.com)

Avis (☎ 800-331-1212; www.avis.com)

Budget (☎ 800-527-7000; www.budget.com)

Dollar (☎ 800-800-4000; www.dollar.com)

Enterprise (☎ 800-867-4595; www.enterprise.com)

Hertz (☎ 800-654-3131; www.hertz.com)

National (☎ 800-227-7368; www.nationalcar.com)

Thrifty (☎ 800-527-7075; www.thrifty.com)

For motorcycle rental, contact **Illinois Harley-Davidson** (Map pp302-3; ☎ 708-749-1500, 888-966-1500; www.eaglerider.com; 1301 S Harlem Ave, Berwyn). The range of motorcycles includes several Harley-Davidson touring models and Buell sports bikes. Rentals start at $75 per day.

LOCAL TRANSPORTATION

The **Chicago Transit Authority** (CTA; ☎ 312-836-7000; www.transitchicago.com) consists of the El trains and local buses. Between the two systems, you will be able to get most everywhere you want to go in the city. **Pace** (www.pacebus.com) buses and **Metra** (www.metrarail.com) trains handle outlying suburbs. For help on all routes, call the **travel information line** (☎ 312-836-7000) or visit the helpful **trip-planning website** (http://tripsweb.rtachicago.com).

Fares for single adult riders on both CTA buses and the El are $1.75, with transfers costing an additional 25¢. The plastic tickets have a magnetized strip that allows you to add as much fare as you'd like (up to $100). Fares (and transfers) are deducted automatically when you enter the El system or board the bus.

Single- and multiday passes are available for one day ($5), two days ($9), three days ($12), five days ($18), seven days ($20) and 30 days ($75). Inexplicably, these passes are not available at all CTA stations. You can buy them at the O'Hare and Midway airport El stops, in local retail outlets such as Jewel, and at tourist attractions such as the Sears Tower, Shedd Aquarium and Field Museum. You can also buy them through the CTA website.

You can get free, useful system maps at all CTA stations.

Bus

Local CTA buses go almost everywhere, but they do so on erratic schedules. The bus stops are clearly marked, with signs showing which buses stop there, but little else. The buses make frequent stops and don't go very fast. At rush hour you will probably have to stand and many buses lack air-conditioning, making for a hot ride in summer.

Pace buses handle Chicago's outlying suburban areas. Each ride costs $1.50, with a transfer costing 25¢.

Taxi

Taxis are easy to find in many of the northern parts of the city, from the Loop through Wrigleyville. Stand on the curb and raise your arm to hail one. In other parts of the city, you can either call a cab or face what may be a long wait for one to happen along. Fares start at $1.90 when you enter the cab and $1.60 for each additional mile; extra passengers cost 50¢ apiece. Drivers expect a 10% to 15% tip. All major companies accept credit cards. Of the four reliable companies listed below, Flash is very popular with locals because it has a reputation for hiring older, more experienced drivers. To report a taxi, call the **taxi complaint hotline** (☎ 312-744-9400).

Checker Taxi (☎ 312-243-2537)

Flash Cab (☎ 773-561-1444)

Yellow Cab (☎ 312-829-4222)

American-United Taxi (☎ 773-248-7600)

Train

THE EL

The El train system is an efficient, air-conditioned way to get around Chicago, though only the Blue Line from O'Hare to the Loop and the Red Line from Howard to 95/Dan Ryan run trains 24 hours.

METRA

A web of commuter trains running under the Metra banner serves the 245 stations in the suburbs surrounding Chicago. The primary riders are people who work in the city and live elsewhere.

The clean, timely trains have two levels, with the second offering tight seating but better views. Some of the Metra lines run frequent schedules seven days a week; others operate only during weekday rush hours. The four end-of-the-line Metra stations in Chicago are Ogilvie Transportation Center, Union Station, La Salle St Station and Millennium Station. Each station has schedules available for all the lines, as well as other information.

Short trips start at $1.85; buy tickets from agents and machines at major stations. At small stations where nobody is on duty, you can buy the ticket without penalty from the conductor on the train; normally there is a $2 surcharge for doing this.

TRAIN

Amtrak

Chicago's **Union Station** (Map pp304-5; 225 S Canal St btwn Adams St and Jackson Blvd) is the hub for **Amtrak** (☎ 800-872-7245; www.amtrak.com), and it has more connections than any other US city. Trains leave regularly for Midwestern cities like Milwaukee ($20, two hours) and Indianapolis ($33, five hours), as well as long-haul destinations like Boston ($106, 23 hours). During much of the year it's crucial to reserve your Amtrak tickets well in advance. Amtrak is usually faster than traveling by Greyhound, and much, much more comfortable.

PRACTICALITIES

ACCOMMODATIONS

Because of the near-constant stream of business travelers coming to Chicago, the city has no off-season rates when it comes to lodging. That said, more rooms tend to be available on the weekend, and you can sometimes find special weekend deals that will knock up to 50% off the normal rates. See the Sleeping chapter (p236) for more information.

Along with the hotels' own websites, some helpful Internet resources for finding discounted rooms include those listed under Flights (p270) and the sites that allow you to 'bid' for rooms (see the boxed text, p237).

BUSINESS

The pace of business in Chicago is bounding, though it's much less manic than New York. You'll find that the larger stores keep late hours, but few – save Walgreens and a handful of other chain retailers – are open all night. If you're burning the midnight oil and are looking for some place to make some quick photocopies, send a fax, check your email, or overnight a slice of Chicago-style pizza to a colleague back home, head to the Near North **FedEx Kinko's** (Map pp306-7; ☎ 312-670-4460; 444 N Wells) or the branch in **Wrigleyville** (Map pp318-19; ☎ 312-975-5031; 3524 N Southport); both stay open 24 hours.

Business Hours

Normal business hours:

Banks From 8am to 5pm Monday to Friday.

Bars and pubs Until 2am Sunday to Friday, until 3am Saturday.

Shops From 10am to 7pm Monday to Saturday, noon to 6pm Sunday.

Restaurants From 11am to 10pm.

CHILDREN

Chicago is a welcoming place for children. From the dinosaurs at the Field Museum to the carousel on Navy Pier to a bike ride along the Lakefront Path, the city will come across as endlessly thrilling for kids. For more on specific child-friendly attractions, see the boxed text, p66. And for a comprehensive overview on traveling with kids, check out Lonely Planet's book *Travel With Children*.

A helpful Internet resource is **GoCityKids** (www.gocitykids.com), which provides a list of recommendations for children visiting Chicago based on the weather that day, the level of intellectual rigor or athletic activity desired, and the child's age. The results can be sorted by neighborhood, making it a breeze to find something great for your kids to do even after you've already exhausted the delights of Navy Pier and all the museums.

Baby-Sitting

Check with the concierge at your hotel for a list of recommended sitters. **American ChildCare Services Inc** (☎ 312-644-7300; www.americanchildcare.com) is the official babysitter for the Chicago Cubs; it'll send sitters to hotel rooms throughout Chicago. Rates start at $16.50 per hour, with a four-hour minimum, and there is a supplementary $20 'agency fee' to pay for the sitter's transportation. **North Shore Nannies** (☎ 847-864-2424; www.northshorenannies.com; 520-B Lee St, Evanston) offers rigorously screened sitters who will do in-hotel sitting. Rates start at $10, plus parking and a placement fee. Booking a couple of days ahead is recommended.

CLIMATE

The nickname 'Windy City' actually has nonmeteorological origins. It was coined by newspaper reporters in the late 1800s in reaction to the oft-blustery boastfulness of Chicago's politicians. Nevertheless, Chicago is windy, with everything from cool, God-sent lake breezes at the height of summer to skirt-raising gusts in the spring to spine-chilling, nose-chiseling blasts of icy air in the winter. The city experiences all four seasons, with late spring and early fall being generally warm, clear and dry times. Winter and summer behave as expected (see climate chart), but early spring and late fall can freely mix nice days with wretched ones. Chicago has no true rainy season; its 34in of average annual precipitation are spread throughout the year. For a blow-by-blow on Chicago's annual weather, see the City Calendar (p9).

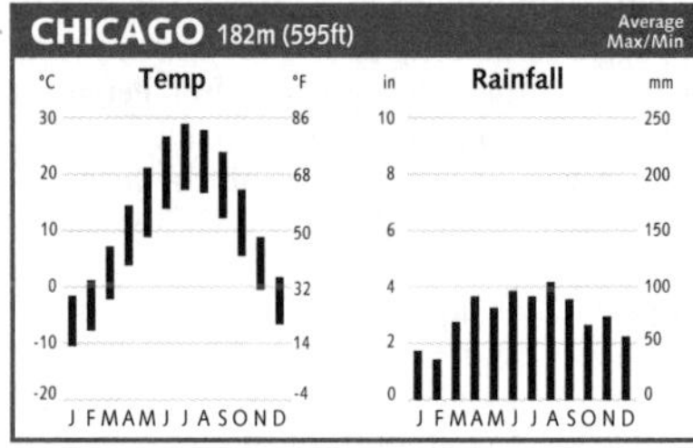

CONSULATES

Australia (Map pp304-5; ☎ 312-419-1480; Suite 1330, 123 N Wacker Dr)

Austria (Map pp306-7; ☎ 312-222-1515; Suite 707, 400 N Michigan Ave)

Brazil (Map pp306-7; ☎ 312-464-0246; Suite 3050, 401 N Michigan Ave)

Canada (Map pp304-5; ☎ 312-616-1860; Suite 2400, 180 N Stetson Ave)

France (Map pp304-5; ☎ 312-327-5200; Suite 3700, 205 N Michigan Ave)

Germany (Map pp306-7; ☎ 312-580-1199; Suite 3200, 676 N Michigan Ave)

Ireland (Map pp306-7; ☎ 312-337-1868; Suite 911, 400 N Michigan Ave)

Italy (Map pp306-7; ☎ 312-467-1550; Suite 1850, 500 N Michigan Ave)

Japan (Map pp306-7; ☎ 312-280-0400; Suite 1100, 737 N Michigan Ave)

Mexico (Map pp314-15; ☎ 312-738-2833; 204 S Ashland Ave)

New Zealand (Map pp302-3; ☎ 773-714-9461; Suite 500, 8600 W Bryn Mawr)

South Africa (Map pp304-5; ☎ 312-939-7929; Suite 600, 200 S Michigan Ave)

Sweden (Map pp304-5; ☎ 312-781-6262; Suite 1250, 150 N Michigan Ave)

Switzerland (Map pp306-7; ☎ 312-915-0061; Suite 2301, 737 N Michigan Ave)

UK (Map pp306-7; ☎ 312-970-3800; Suite 1300, 400 N Michigan Ave)

CUSTOMS

International travelers will be familiar with the red-and-green line system at O'Hare. Those with nothing to declare can opt for the green line, which is still subject to spot checks. Those with something to declare should definitely do so, because if you try to smuggle something in and are caught, your day will immediately go downhill. Penalties for drug smuggling are especially severe. Remember, until you clear all the formalities, you have no rights. Non–United States citizens over the age of 21 are allowed to import 1L of liquor and 200 cigarettes (or 100 non-Cuban cigars) duty free. Gifts may amount to no more than $100 in value. You may bring any amount of money less than $10,000 into or out of the US without declaration. Amounts greater than $10,000 must be declared.

Certain goods such as ivory and tortoiseshell anything are a no-no, as are drug paraphernalia. For more information, visit the website www.customs.gov.

DISABLED TRAVELERS

Chicago can be a challenge for people with reduced mobility. The preponderance of older buildings means that doorways are narrow and stairs prevalent. Much of the El is inaccessible. If you do find a station with an elevator, make sure that there's also one at your destination. The CTA has, however, made progress on making its buses wheelchair-friendly, installing lifts in over 80% of the routes. To see a list of wheelchair-accessible routes and El stations, head to www.transitchicago.com/maps/accessible.html or call ☎ 312-836-7000.

For hotels, you are best off with the newer properties. But call the hotel itself – not the 800 number – and confirm that the room you want to reserve has the features you need. The phrase 'roll-in showers' is interpreted very loosely by some properties.

The **Mayor's Office for People with Disabilities** (☎ 312-744-6673, TTY 312-744-7833) is a good place to call to start asking questions about the availability of services.

DISCOUNT CARDS

Chicago **CityPass** (www.citypass.net) costs $49.50 for adults and $39 for children (ages three to 11) and gets the bearer into the Hancock Observatory, the Art Institute of Chicago, the Field Museum, the Shedd Aquarium, the Adler Planetarium and the Museum of Science and Industry. You can buy the passes at the attractions themselves, or at any of Chicago's visitor information bureaus (see Tourist Information, p282).

ELECTRICITY

Electric current in the US is 110–120V, 60Hz AC. Outlets accept North American standard plugs, which have two flat prongs and an occasional third round one. If your appliance is made for another system, you will need a converter or adapter. These are best bought in your home country. Otherwise, try a travel bookstore.

EMERGENCIES

For all emergencies (police, ambulance, fire), call ☎ 911. For nonemergency police matters call ☎ 311.

GAY & LESBIAN TRAVELERS

The heart of Chicago's large and vibrant gay and lesbian community lies on N Halsted St between Belmont Ave and Addison St, but Andersonville, Lincoln Park, Bucktown and other neighborhoods are also gay- and lesbian-friendly. Outside the Halsted neighborhood, however, open affection between same-sex partners often draws confused or disapproving stares. Some good local gay weeklies include the **Chicago Free Press** (www.chicagofreepress.com) and the **Windy City Times** (www.windycitytimes.com). For a list of gay-owned and gay-friendly businesses found in Chicago, contact the **Chicago Area Gay & Lesbian Chamber of Commerce** (Map pp302-3; ☎ 773-303-0167; www.glchamber.org; 1210 W Rosedale Ave).

HOLIDAYS

Chicago's governmental offices and services shut down on public holidays, as do many of the city's shops. To find out how you can join in on Chicago holiday celebrations, see the City Calendar (p9). Major public holidays include the following:

New Year's Day January 1

Martin Luther King, Jr Day Third Monday in January

President's Day Third Monday in January

St Patrick's Day March 17 (government offices remain open)

Memorial Day Last Monday in May

Independence Day July 4

Labor Day First Monday in September

Columbus Day Second Monday in October

Veteran's Day November 11

Thanksgiving Day Fourth Thursday in November

Christmas Day December 25

INSURANCE

A travel insurance policy to cover theft, loss and medical problems is a good idea, especially when traveling in the US, where dismal medical coverage means routine trips to the doctor can cost the uninsured hundreds of dollars. Some policies specifically exclude 'dangerous' activities, which can include motorcycling.

You may prefer a policy that pays doctors or hospitals directly rather than requiring you to pay on the spot and claim later. If you have to claim later, ensure you keep all documentation.

Check that the policy covers ambulances or an emergency flight home.

INTERNET ACCESS

Free Internet access has become a thing of the past at many of Chicago's higher-end hotels. Wi-fi, however, has taken off in Chicago, and even though you'll have to pay about $5 per hour to use it, you'll have no trouble getting connected either in your hotel room, lobby or nearby café. For those hotels that haven't gone wireless yet, it's also a good idea to bring 5ft or so of Ethernet cable with you. If you need to buy any computer equipment while you're in town, try CompUSA (p220).

For those traveling without a laptop, you can access the Internet for free at any public library (try the Harold Washington Library in the Loop – you'll have to get a 'day pass' at the counter), or visit FedEx Kinko's (p279) or an Internet café, where you can get on a machine right away. Costs range from $6 to $9 per hour. A reliable Internet café for Net-surfers is **Screenz** (Map pp308-9; ☎ 773-348-9300; www.screenz.com; 2717 N Clark St; 🕒 8:30am-1am Mon-Fri, from 9am Sat & Sun; Brown, Red Line to Diversey).

LEGAL MATTERS

The basics of Chicago's legal system are identical to other US cities. If stopped and questioned by the police, you should cooperate, though you are not required to give them permission to search either your person or your car (though they can do both if they determine they have 'probable cause'). If arrested, you have the right to remain silent – which you should do – and the right to make one phone call from jail. If you don't have a lawyer or friend or family member to help you, call your consulate. The police will give you the number upon request.

It's generally against the law to have an open container of alcoholic beverage in public, whether in a car, on the street, in a park or at the beach. But during festivals and other mass events, this rule is waived. The drinking age of 21 is pretty strictly enforced. If you're younger than 35 (or just look like it), carry an ID to fend off overzealous barkeeps and the like. The legal driving age is 16, the age of consent is 17 and the voting age is 18. There is zero tolerance at all times for any kind of drug use.

MAPS

Maps are widely sold at hotels, drug stores and newsstands. Try Lonely Planet's *Chicago* city map, a laminated map that folds into a compact size. Any bookstore, from Barbara's (p232) to Borders (p222) will carry it. You can pick up free maps of the Chicago transit system at any CTA station, or download one from www.transitchicago.com.

MEASUREMENT

Chicago uses the imperial measurement system.

MEDICAL SERVICES

If you are ill or injured and suspect that the situation is in any way life threatening, call ☎911 immediately. This is a free call from any phone.

If you have a less serious malady, such as the flu or a sprained ankle, and want to see a doctor, ask your hotel for a recommendation. Though Chicago is filled with clinics and doctors, none of their services come cheap, so make sure you have insurance, or try the free John H Stroger Jr Hospital of Cook County.

Clinics & Emergency Rooms

The following hospitals offer medical services through their emergency rooms. If your condition is not acute, call first, because many also operate clinics that can see you in a more timely and convenient manner. If you are broke and have no insurance, head to John H Stroger Jr Hospital of Cook County. If your problem is not life threatening, you will be seated in a waiting room where you will do just that for perhaps 12 hours while you're surrounded by people sicker than yourself.

Children's Memorial Hospital (Map pp308-9; ☎773-880-4000; 2300 N Lincoln Ave; Brown, Red Line to Fullerton)

Illinois Masonic Hospital (Map pp318-19; ☎773-975-1600; 836 W Wellington Ave; Brown, Purple Line to Wellington)

John H Stroger Jr Hospital of Cook County (Map pp314-15; ☎312-633-6000; 1901 W Harrison; Blue Line to Medical Center) Two blocks south of the El stop.

Northwestern Memorial Hospital (Map pp306-7; ☎312-926-2000; 251 E Huron St; Red Line to Chicago)

University of Chicago Hospital (Map pp320-1; ☎773-702-1000; 5841 S Maryland Ave; Metra to 57th)

MONEY

The US currency is the dollar ($), divided into 100 cents (¢). Coins come in denominations of 1¢ (penny), 5¢ (nickel), 10¢ (dime), 25¢ (quarter), 50¢ (half dollar – rare) and $1 (silver dollar – rare). A gold-colored $1 coin, introduced in 2000, features the face of Native American Sacagawea. Notes (bills) come in denominations of $1, $2 (rare), $5, $10, $20, $50 and $100.

See p22 for where the money goes in Chicago.

ATMs

You can find ATMs everywhere in Chicago, with many convenience stores such as White Hen getting in on the action as well. All machines are connected to Cirrus and Plus, the world's two largest banking networks.

Unless you find an ATM belonging to your bank, you will be charged a fee of around $2 to withdraw money from one of the machines. The exchange rate you get by taking money out of the ATM is usually the very best available (though the fees may nullify that advantage).

Changing Cash & Traveler's Checks

You'll find that exchanging foreign cash and non–US dollar traveler's checks in Chicago is a hassle, although it can be done. One cautionary note: shortly after arriving in Chicago, you will begin noticing 'currency exchanges' on many street corners. These primarily serve people without bank accounts who want to cash checks, and will not exchange foreign currencies. Head instead to the banks and exchange places listed here.

Traveler's checks are usually just as good as cash in the US, provided they are in US dollars. Most places will accept them as long as you sign them in front of the cashier, waiter etc.

To exchange international monies or traveler's checks for dollars, you can visit the arrivals areas of O'Hare's Terminals 3 or 5, which have foreign-exchange services. Otherwise, you could try one of the following:

American Express (Map pp304-5; ☎312-541-5440; 55 W Monroe St; 🕑 8:30am-5:30pm Mon-Fri; Blue Line to Monroe)

Bank One (Map pp304-5; ☎312-732-6009; 21 S Clark St; 🕑 7:30am-6pm Mon-Fri; Blue Line to Washington)

Northern Trust Bank (Map pp304-5; ☎312-630-6000; 50 S LaSalle St; 🕑 8am-5pm Mon-Fri; Brown, Orange Line to Washington)

Travelex (Map pp304-5; ☎312-807-4941; 19 S LaSalle St; 🕑 9am-5pm Mon-Fri; Brown, Orange Line to Washington)

World's Money Exchange (Map pp304-5; ☎312-641-2151; Suite M-11, upper fl, 203 N LaSalle St; 🕑 9am-5pm Mon-Fri; Blue, Brown, Green, Orange Line to Clark)

Credit Cards

Major credit cards are widely accepted by car-rental firms, hotels, restaurants, gas stations, shops, large grocery stores, movie theaters, ticket vendors, taxicabs and other places. In fact, you'll find certain transactions impossible to perform without a credit card: you can't reserve theater or other event tickets by phone without one, nor can you guarantee room reservations by phone or rent a car. The most commonly accepted cards are Visa and MasterCard. American Express is widely accepted but not as universally as the first two. Discover and Diners Club cards are usually good for travel tickets, hotels and rental cars, but they're less commonly accepted in other situations.

If your credit card is lost or stolen, call the card issuer.

American Express (☎ 800-528-4800)

Diners Club (☎ 800-234-6377)

Discover (☎ 800-347-2683)

MasterCard (☎ 800-307-7309)

Visa (☎ 800-336-8472)

NEWSPAPERS & MAGAZINES

For specifics on Chicago's newspapers and magazines, see p20. Daily papers include the following:

Chicago Sun-Times (www.suntimes.com)

Chicago Tribune (www.chicagotribune.com)

Weekly arts and entertainment papers include the following:

Chicago Reader (www.chireader.com)

New City (www.newcitychicago.com)

UR (www.urchicago.com)

Worthwhile local magazines include the following:

Baffler (www.thebaffler.com)

Chicago Magazine (www.chicagomag.com)

Crain's Chicago Business (www.chicagobusiness.com)

Roctober (www.roctober.com)

Time Out Chicago (www.timeout.com)

PHARMACIES

Both Walgreens and Osco pharmacies are convenient places to get your prescriptions filled. The following branches are open 24 hours:

Osco (Map pp318-19; ☎ 773-871-8242; 2940 N Ashland Ave; Brown, Red Line to Diversey)

Walgreens (Map pp306-7; ☎ 312-664-8686; 757 N Michigan Ave; Red Line to Chicago)

Walgreens (Map pp306-7; ☎ 312-587-1416; 641 N Clark St; Red Line to Grand)

POST

At press time, it cost 37¢ to mail a 1oz 1st-class letter within the US. Each additional ounce cost 23¢. Domestic postcards cost 23¢ to mail. It costs 60¢ to mail a 1oz letter to Canada or Mexico, 80¢ for other international destinations. Attach 50¢ of postage for postcards to Canada and Mexico, 70¢ for those going overseas. All aerograms cost 70¢.

Parcels mailed to foreign destinations from the US are subject to a variety of rates. First class can be very expensive. If you're not in a hurry, consider mailing your items 4th class, which goes by boat. Those rates can be very low, but delivery to Europe, for instance, takes six to eight weeks. If all you are sending is printed matter such as books, you qualify for an extra-cheap rate.

If you'd like to get mail while traveling but don't have an address, have it sent to you in Chicago via 'general delivery.' This is the same as poste restante. Letters should be addressed as follows: Your Name, c/o General Delivery (Station Name), Chicago IL (Zip Code), USA.

General-delivery mail is held for at least 10 days (sometimes as long as 30) before being returned to the sender. Bring some photo ID when you come to pick up your mail. Full-service post offices that also accept general delivery include the following:

Cardiss Collins Postal Store (Map pp304-5; ☎ 312-983-8182; 433 W Harrison St, Chicago, IL 60699; 24hr)

Fort Dearborn Station (Map pp306-7; ☎ 312-644-3919; 540 N Dearborn St, Chicago, IL 60610; 7:30am-5pm Mon-Fri, to 1pm Sat, 9am-2pm Sun)

Loop Station (Map pp304-5; ☎ 312-427-4225; 211 S Clark St, Chicago, IL 60604; 7am-6pm Mon-Fri)

Shipping Services

Shipping companies such as **UPS** (domestic ☎ 800-742-5877, international 800-782-7892; www.ups.com) and **FedEx Kinko's** (domestic ☎ 800-463-3339, international 800-247-4747; www.fedex.com) specialize in getting packages across the country and around the world in the blink of an eye. Call them to find the closest Chicago location to you.

RADIO

Of the options listed, WBEZ can be heard on the Internet, at www.wbez.com.

Q101 101.1FM (modern rock)

WBEZ 91.5FM (national public radio)

WHPK 88.5FM (eclectic)

WMVP 1000AM (ESPN sports talk)

WXRT 93.1FM (rock)

SAFETY

Serious crime in Chicago has been dropping over the last few years, and the areas written about in this book are all reasonably safe during the day. At night, the lakefront, major parks and certain neighborhoods (especially south and west of the Loop) can become bleak and forbidding places. The Loop, Near North, Gold Coast, Old Town, Lincoln Park and Lake View, on the other hand, are tolerably safe (and bustling) night and day. For those who like to know (in great detail) before they go, you can visit www.chicagocrime.org, the pet project of a Chicago computer programmer. The site breaks down crime by type and neighborhood, and probably shouldn't be viewed by those who are on the fence about coming to the Windy City. (It's safe! We swear!)

TAXES

The basic sales tax is 9%. Some grocery items are taxed at only 2%. Newspapers and magazines, but not books, are tax-free. The hotel tax is 15.4%; the car-rental tax is 18%. And for meals in most parts of town you are likely to visit, there's an extra 10.25% added to the bill.

TELEPHONE

Area Codes

The city has two area codes, with more soon to come as the proliferation of pagers, faxes and Internet connections sops up the available supply of numbers. The area code ☎ 312 serves the Loop and an area bounded roughly by 1600 North (ie 1600 block, north of Madison St in the Loop), 1600 West and 1600 South. The rest of the city falls in area code ☎ 773. The northern suburbs use area code ☎ 847, those close to the west and the south ☎ 708, and the far west suburbs ☎ 630.

Cell Phones

The US uses a mess of incompatible formats for cell (or 'mobile') phones. Many still use an old analog format, while the newer digital models primarily use the competing TDMA or CDMA formats. Few use the GSM format that is popular in the rest of the world. If you really can't be separated from your cell phone, it is a good idea to check with your service provider to see if there's any hope it will work in the US.

Places that rent cell phones for short terms in Chicago are surprisingly scarce. If you really need your own phone (and phone number) during your stay in Chicago, you can order a phone through a New York company such as **Roberts Rent-A-Phone** (☎ 800-964-2468; www.roberts-rent-a-phone.com), which will mail you overnight a phone that will work in Chicago. Between the $5 daily charges and the additional $1.75 per minute charges, though, the bill will add up quickly.

Collect Calls

You can call collect (reverse the charges) from any phone; just dial ☎ 0 to begin the call. Rates, however, end up being *much* more expensive than walking to Walgreens or Jewel and purchasing a prepaid calling card. So if you have the cash to spring for a card, try to avoid making collect calls. Collect calls from the US to foreign countries are especially expensive, sometimes running $2 per minute. The operator should be able to tell you how much the rates will be before you place the call.

Dialing

All phone numbers within the US and Canada consist of the three-digit area code followed by a seven-digit local number. If you are calling locally, just dial the seven-digit number. If you are calling from within the US to another area code, dial ☎ 1 + the three-digit area code + the seven-digit local number. In the city, if you don't use the area code when you should or you do use it when you shouldn't – both of which are common mistakes – you'll get an ear-shattering screech, followed by advice on what to dial.

The country code for the US is ☎ 1. The international access code is ☎ 011 for calls you dial directly; dial it first, before you dial the country code. To find out the country code of the place you're trying to call, look in the front of the local phone directory.

Toll-free phone numbers start with the area codes ☎ 800, ☎ 877 or ☎ 888. Numbers that begin with ☎ 900 will cost you a small fortune (up to several dollars per minute). You'll most often see such numbers advertised late at night on TV in ads asking, 'Lonely? Want to have some hot talk?'

Local directory assistance can be reached by calling ☎ 411. If you are looking for a number outside of your local area code but know what area code it falls under, dial ☎ 1 + the area code + 555-1212. These calls are no longer free, even from pay phones. To obtain a toll-free phone number, dial ☎ 800-555-1212.

Pay Phones & Hotel Phones

Unfortunately, pay phones do not use the same high-tech card systems in the US that they do in Europe. This is fine for local calls, which cost 35¢ for about 10 minutes of talk time. But trying to make a long-distance call at a pay phone if you don't have a credit-card calling card or a prepaid calling card requires an outrageous amount of change. When using hotel phones, know that some places will charge up to $2 per local call. Ask in advance to avoid a shock later.

Prepaid Calling Cards

Convenience stores and other places sell telephone cards good for a prepaid amount of long-distance phone time; these are typically available in amounts of $5, $10, $20 and $50. To use one, you dial an ☎ 800 number and then enter the code number on your card. At a prompt from an automated operator, you simply enter the number you are calling. The company's computer keeps track of how much value you have left on the card. These cards are often a good deal and a good way to circumnavigate the swamp of phone-call-making minutiae.

TIME

Chicago falls in the US Central Standard Time (CST) zone. 'Standard time' runs from the last Sunday in October to the first Sunday in April. 'Daylight saving time,' when clocks move ahead one hour, runs from the first Sunday in April to the last Sunday in October, when clocks go to standard time.

Chicago is one hour behind Eastern Standard Time, which encompasses nearby Michigan and Indiana, apart from the northwestern corner of Indiana, which follows Chicago time. The border between the two zones is just east of the city. Note that Indiana doesn't take a cotton to notions like daylight saving time. In the summer Indiana keeps the same time as Chicago; in winter, with the exception of its northwestern corner, it is one hour ahead.

The city is one hour ahead of Mountain Standard Time, a zone which includes much of the Rocky Mountains, and two hours ahead of Pacific Standard Time, the zone which includes California. Chicago is six hours behind Greenwich Mean Time (but remember daylight saving time).

TIPPING

Restaurant wait staff, hotel maids, valet car parkers, bartenders, bellhops and others are paid a mere pittance in wages and expect to make up the shortfall through tips. But whom to tip? And how much?

Bartenders Per drink $1.

Bellhops From $2 total to $1 per bag or more, depending on the distance covered.

Cocktail servers Per drink $1, when they bring the drinks.

Concierges Nothing for answering a simple question, $5 or more for securing tickets to a sold-out show.

Doormen For summoning you a cab $1 to $2, depending on the weather.

Hotel cleaning staff Per day $1 to $2, left on the pillow each morning.

Restaurant wait staff Standard is 15%, but leave 20% if you're really pleased with the service; an easy rule is to pay the same amount as the tax (which is 18.5% in Chicago restaurants).

Skycaps At least $1 per bag.

Taxi drivers From 10% to 15% of the bill.

Valet car parkers $2 to $5, when the keys to the car are handed to you.

For more on tipping in restaurant situations, see p135.

TOURIST INFORMATION

For sheer tonnage of leaflets, maps and coupon books, you can't beat the Visitor Information Center in the Chicago Cultural Center. (Friendly staff members don't hurt either.) The second location, in the Water Tower Pumping Station, is close to both Near North and Gold Coast sights and shops. The Chicago Office of Tourism has also set up a 24-hour hotline to answer questions about sights, events and lodging – call ☎ 877-244-2246.

Chicago Cultural Center Visitor Information Center (Map pp304-5; ☎ 312-744-2400; 77 E Randolph St; 10am-6pm Mon-Fri, to 5pm Sat, 11am-5pm Sun; Brown, Green, Orange Line to Randolph)

Illinois Marketplace Visitor Information Center (Map pp306-7; ☎ 312-744-2400; 700 E Grand Ave; 10am-8pm Mon-Thu, to 10pm Fri & Sat, to 8pm Sun; bus 66)

Water Tower Pumping Station Visitor Information Center (Map pp308-9; ☎ 312-744-2400; 163 E Pearson St; 7:30am-7pm; Red Line to Chicago)

Internet Resources

The best Internet resource on the city's restaurant and nightlife scene is the review-heavy www.metromix.com website, which is run by the *Chicago Tribune*. The website of the **Chicago Reader** (www.chireader.com) also has top-notch dining reviews. **Citysearch Chicago** (http://chicago.citysearch.com) offers up broad coverage of venues, and its 'best of' lists in dozens of genres are a good way to get a handle on the city's latest places.

The most interesting takes on Chicago, though, tend to be on blogs and homespun efforts. The best of these is www.gapersblock.com, which reports on the latest news, cultural happenings and political shenanigans afoot in the Windy City. The **Chicagoist** (www.chicagoist.com) site offers a snarky, 20-something viewpoint on life in the city.

Various wings of the city's tourism powers that be have also set up several websites to help spread the word about Chicago.

www.877chicago.com Offers travelers entertainment packages and on-site room reservations.

www.chicago.il.org This business traveler–oriented site allows you to book rooms and offers some nightlife and dining tips.

www.cityofchicago.org For tourists and residents, this site is packed with information about the city's events and programs, but you have to do some digging to find the good stuff.

VISAS

A reciprocal visa-waiver program applies to citizens of certain countries, who may enter the US for stays of 90 days or fewer without having to obtain a visa. Currently these countries are Andorra, Australia, Austria, Belgium, Brunei, Denmark, Finland, France, Germany, Iceland, Ireland, Italy, Japan, Liechtenstein, Luxembourg, Monaco, the Netherlands, New Zealand, Norway, Portugal, San Marino, Singapore, Slovenia, Spain, Sweden, Switzerland, the Netherlands and the UK.

In order to travel to the US visa-free, visitors from the above countries must have a machine-readable passport. If your passport cannot be scanned by a computer, you'll need to get a visa regardless. Consult with your airline or the closest US consulate or embassy for more information.

With heightened security concerns showing no sign of abating, travelers should be aware that US visa rules are subject to change with little warning. Check the **government website** (http://travel.state.gov) for the latest developments.

Visa Extensions

Tourists using visas are usually granted a six-month stay on first arrival. If you try to extend that time, the first assumption will be that you are working illegally, so come prepared with concrete evidence that you've been behaving like a model tourist: receipts to demonstrate you've been spending lots of your money from home in the US or ticket stubs that show you've been traveling extensively. Requests for visa extensions in Chicago are entertained at the office of **US Citizenship & Immigration Services** (Map pp304-5; ☎ 800-375-5283; www.uscis.gov; Suite 600, Kluczynski Building, Chicago Federal Center, 10 W Jackson Blvd). Meetings are all by appointment only, though, and to make an appointment, you have to visit the fine, robotic folks at http://infopass.uscis.gov. Be sure to get the paperwork moving well before your visa expires.

WOMEN TRAVELERS

Women will be safe alone in most parts of Chicago, though they should exercise a degree of caution and awareness of their surroundings.

The El is safe, even at night, though you might want to seek out more populated cars or the first car, to be closest to the driver. Or you can take one of the buses that parallel many train lines.

In the commonly visited areas of Chicago, you should not encounter troubling attitudes from men. In bars some men will see a woman alone as a bid for companionship. A polite 'no thank you' should suffice to send them away. Chicagoans are very friendly, so don't be afraid to protest loudly if someone is hassling you. It will probably send the offending party away and bring helpful Samaritans to your side.

WORK

It is very difficult for foreigners to get legal work in the US. Securing your own work visa without a sponsor – meaning an employer – is nearly impossible. If you do have a sponsor, the sponsor should normally assist or do all the work to secure your visa. Contact your embassy or consulate for more information.

If you're interested in doing some volunteer work while you're in town, check out the listings on the Chicago **Community Resource Network** (www.chicagovolunteer.net) or look through the opportunities listed in the community section of the **Craigslist message board** (http://chicago.craigslist.org).

Behind the Scenes

THE LONELY PLANET STORY

The story begins with a classic travel adventure: Tony and Maureen Wheeler's 1972 journey across Europe and Asia to Australia. There was no useful information about the overland trail then, so Tony and Maureen published the first Lonely Planet guidebook to meet a growing need.

From a kitchen table, Lonely Planet has grown to become the largest independent travel publisher in the world, with offices in Melbourne (Australia), Oakland (USA) and London (UK). Today Lonely Planet guidebooks cover the globe. There is an ever-growing list of books and information in a variety of media. Some things haven't changed. The main aim is still to make it possible for adventurous travelers to get out there – to explore and better understand the world.

At Lonely Planet we believe travelers can make a positive contribution to the countries they visit – if they respect their host communities and spend their money wisely. Every year 5% of company profit is donated to charities around the world.

THIS BOOK

This fourth edition of *Chicago* was researched and written by Chris Baty with assistance from Karla Zimmerman, who wrote the Shopping and Excursions chapters. Chris wrote the third edition as well. The first and second editions of the book were written by Ryan Ver Berkmoes. This guidebook was commissioned in Lonely Planet's Oakland office, and produced by the following:

Commissioning Editor Jay Cooke

Coordinating Editor Jennifer Garrett

Coordinating Cartographer Jack Gavran

Coordinating Layout Designer Cara Smith

Managing Cartographer Alison Lyall

Assisting Editors Katie Lynch, Andrea Dobbin, Jackey Coyle, Joanne Newell, Susannah Farfor, Tom Smallman, Kate Evans

Assisting Cartographers Wayne Murphy, Emma McNicol, Owen Eszeki, Barbara Benson, Kusnandar, Herman So

Cover Designer Daniel New

Project Managers Sarah Sloane, Nancy Ianni

Thanks to Greg Benchwick, Heather Dickson, Stephanie Pearson, Charles Rawlings-Way, Indra Kilfoyle, Lara Jane, Sally Darmody, Adriana Mammarella, Justin Flynn, Laura Gibb, Helen Koehne, Kate McLeod, Celia Wood

Cover photographs by Lonely Planet Images: Detail of Citibank building, Richard Cummins (top), Cubs baseball fans, Ray Laskowitz (bottom); Oak St Beach jogger, Ray Laskowitz (back).

Internal photographs by Ray Laskowitz/Lonely Planet Images except for the following: p253, p101 (#4), p210 (#1, 2) Charles Cook/Lonely Planet Images; p2 (#4, 5), p264, p99 (#2), p100 (#4), p101 (#2), p102 (#1, 2), p105 (#3), p210 (#3, 4) Richard Cummins/Lonely Planet Images; p103 (#1) Lee Foster/Lonely Planet Images; p206 (#1) Rick Gerharter/Lonely Planet Images; p101 (#1) Mark & Audrey Gibson/Lonely Planet Images; p205 (#3), p209 (#3) Tom Given/Lonely Planet Images; p100 (#1) Peter Hendrie/Lonely Planet Images; p180 Raymond Hillstrom/Lonely Planet Images; p101 (#3), p106 (#3) Richard I'Anson/Lonely Planet Images; p99 (#3) Lou Jacobs Jnr/Lonely Planet Images; p2 (#3) Peter J Schulz/City of Chicago.

All images are copyright of the photographer unless otherwise indicated. Many of the images in this guide are available for licensing from Lonely Planet Images: www.lonelyplanetimages.com.

THANKS

CHRIS BATY

Thanks to the magnificent, lifesaving Elly Karl, as well as Regan Kappe, Shawn Regan, Jay Cooke, Marie Marasovich, Julia Cardis, Amy Lombardi, Bob Mehr, Sam Hallgren, Jeff Ruby, John Hindman, Chai Lee, Tim and Katie Tuten, Anna Woehrle, Marie Chiart, Karla Zimmerman, Diana Slickman, and anyone who told me about their favorite restaurant or took me to their favorite bar. Thanks also to Jennifer Garrett, Jack Gavran and the rest of the wonderful Lonely Planet folk in Melbourne.

KARLA ZIMMERMAN

Thanks the following people for sharing their considerable knowledge of all things Chicago and beyond: Brian Austin, Sam Benson, Carmine Cervi, Frances Ginther, JoAnn Hornak, Dave Jacobson, Valerie Liberty, Tim McKeon, Diana Slickman, Mary Visconti and Ray Zielinksi. My gratitude to fellow Chicagoan Chris Baty, especially for his beyond-the-call-of-duty map help. Thanks to Jay Cooke for the frequent idea-slinging. Thanks most of all to Eric Markowitz, who is, quite simply, the world's best partner-for-life.

OUR READERS

Many thanks to the travelers who used the last edition and wrote to us with helpful hints, useful advice and interesting anecdotes:

Roberto Altavilla, Jens Bonefeld, James Borkman, Jane Boxall, Elizabeth Cook, Andrew Cosgrave, Zac Drumsticks, Ronalie Green, Matt Hodson, Danika Kopanke, Bryan Krefft, Russell Levine, Daniel Mann, Greg Marshall, Elena Mosca, Henk-Jan Nusman, Barry Popik, Kelly Ross, Richard Royston, Jason Smith, Michelle Sofge, Morten Stryhn, Brian Tiernan, Jared Wouters

ACKNOWLEDGEMENTS

Many thanks to the following for the use of their content:

Chicago Transit Authority Rail Map © 2005 Chicago Transit Authority

SEND US YOUR FEEDBACK

We love to hear from travelers – your comments keep us on our toes and help make our books better. Our well-traveled team reads every word on what you loved or loathed about this book. Although we cannot reply individually to postal submissions, we always guarantee that your feedback goes straight to the appropriate authors, in time for the next edition. Each person who sends us information is thanked in the next edition – and the most useful submissions are rewarded with a free book.

To send us your updates – and find out about Lonely Planet events, newsletters and travel news – visit our award-winning website: www.lonelyplanet.com/feedback.

Note: We may edit, reproduce and incorporate your comments in Lonely Planet products such as guidebooks, websites and digital products, so let us know if you don't want your comments reproduced or your name acknowledged. For a copy of our privacy policy visit www.lonelyplanet.com/privacy.

Index

See also separate subindexes for Eating (p297), Drinking (p298), Entertainment (p298), Shopping (p299) and Sleeping (p300).

Abbreviations
Michigan (MI)
Minnesota (MN)
Wisconsin (WI)

INDEX

000 map pages
000 photographs

INDEX

000 map pages
000 photographs

DRINKING

ENTERTAINMENT

INDEX

SHOPPING

SLEEPING

MAP LEGEND

ROUTES

Tollway
Freeway
Primary Road
Secondary Road
Tertiary Road
Lane
Under Construction
Track
Unsealed Road
One-Way Street
Mall/Steps
Tunnel
Walking Tour
Walking Tour Detour
Walking Trail
Walking Path
Pedestrian Overpass

TRANSPORT

Ferry
Metro
Monorail
Bus Route
Rail
Rail (Underground)
Tram
Cable Car, Funicular

HYDROGRAPHY

River, Creek
Intermittent River
Swamp
Water

BOUNDARIES

International
State, Provincial
Disputed
Regional, Suburb
Ancient Wall

AREA FEATURES

Airport
Area of Interest, Campus
Beach, Desert
Building, Featured
Building, Information
Building, Other
Building, Transport
Cemetery, Christian
Cemetery, Other
Forest
Land
Park
Sports
Urban

POPULATION

CAPITAL (NATIONAL)
Large City
Small City
CAPITAL (STATE)
Medium City
Town, Village

SYMBOLS

Sights/Activities
Beach
Christian
Monument
Museum, Gallery
Other Site
Trail Head
Zoo, Bird Sanctuary

Eating
Eating

Drinking
Drinking

Entertainment
Entertainment

Shopping
Shopping

Sleeping
Sleeping

Transport
Airport, Airfield
Bus Station
General Transport
Parking Area

Information
Bank, ATM
Embassy/Consulate
Hospital, Medical
Information
Internet Facilities
Police Station
POI, Information
Post Office, GPO
Telephone

Geographic
National Park

Maps

See Andersonville & Uptown Map (p311)
See Lake View Map (pp318–19)
See Gold Coast & Lincoln Park Map (pp308–9)
See Near North & Navy Pier Map (pp306–7)
See The Loop & Grant Park Map (pp304–5)
See Wicker Park, Bucktown & Ukrainian Village Map (pp316–17)

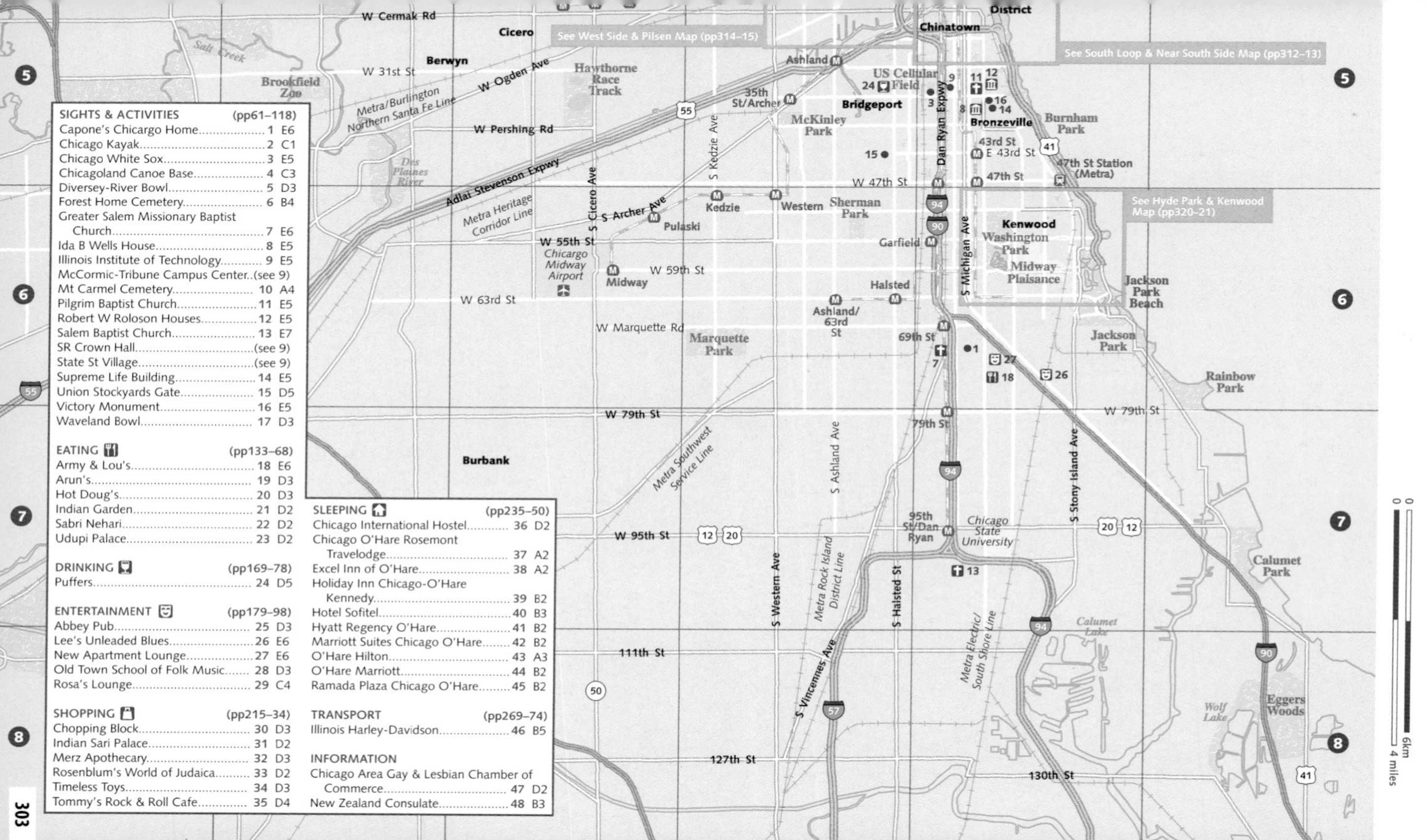
SIGHTS & ACTIVITIES (pp61–118)
Capone's Chicargo Home.................. 1 E6
Chicago Kayak.................. 2 C1
Chicago White Sox.................. 3 E5
Chicagoland Canoe Base.................. 4 C3
Diversey-River Bowl.................. 5 D3
Forest Home Cemetery.................. 6 B4
Greater Salem Missionary Baptist Church.................. 7 E6
Ida B Wells House.................. 8 E5
Illinois Institute of Technology.................. 9 E5
McCormic-Tribune Campus Center..(see 9)
Mt Carmel Cemetery.................. 10 A4
Pilgrim Baptist Church.................. 11 E5
Robert W Roloson Houses.................. 12 E5
Salem Baptist Church.................. 13 E7
SR Crown Hall..................(see 9)
State St Village..................(see 9)
Supreme Life Building.................. 14 E5
Union Stockyards Gate.................. 15 D5
Victory Monument.................. 16 E5
Waveland Bowl.................. 17 D3
EATING (pp133–68)
Army & Lou's.................. 18 E6
Arun's.................. 19 D3
Hot Doug's.................. 20 D3
Indian Garden.................. 21 D2
Sabri Nehari.................. 22 D2
Udupi Palace.................. 23 D2
DRINKING (pp169–78)
Puffers.................. 24 D5
ENTERTAINMENT (pp179–98)
Abbey Pub.................. 25 D3
Lee's Unleaded Blues.................. 26 E6
New Apartment Lounge.................. 27 E6
Old Town School of Folk Music.................. 28 D3
Rosa's Lounge.................. 29 C4
SHOPPING (pp215–34)
Chopping Block.................. 30 D3
Indian Sari Palace.................. 31 D2
Merz Apothecary.................. 32 D3
Rosenblum's World of Judaica.................. 33 D2
Timeless Toys.................. 34 D3
Tommy's Rock & Roll Cafe.................. 35 D4
SLEEPING (pp235–50)
Chicago International Hostel.................. 36 D2
Chicago O'Hare Rosemont Travelodge.................. 37 A2
Excel Inn of O'Hare.................. 38 A2
Holiday Inn Chicago-O'Hare Kennedy.................. 39 B2
Hotel Sofitel.................. 40 B3
Hyatt Regency O'Hare.................. 41 B2
Marriott Suites Chicago O'Hare.................. 42 B2
O'Hare Hilton.................. 43 A3
O'Hare Marriott.................. 44 B2
Ramada Plaza Chicago O'Hare.................. 45 B2
TRANSPORT (pp269–74)
Illinois Harley-Davidson.................. 46 B5
INFORMATION
Chicago Area Gay & Lesbian Chamber of Commerce.................. 47 D2
New Zealand Consulate.................. 48 B3
See West Side & Pilsen Map (pp314–15)
See South Loop & Near South Side Map (pp312–13)
See Hyde Park & Kenwood Map (pp320–21)
W Cermak Rd
Cicero
Berwyn
Chinatown
District
W 31st St
W Ogden Ave
Brookfield Zoo
Hawthorne Race Track
Metra/Burlington Northern Santa Fe Line
W Pershing Rd
Adlai Stevenson Expwy
Metra Heritage Corridor Line
S Cicero Ave
S Archer Ave
S Kedzie Ave
Ashland
35th St/Archer
US Cellular Field
Bridgeport
McKinley Park
Dan Ryan Expwy
Bronzeville
Burnham Park
43rd St
E 43rd St
47th St
47th St Station (Metra)
W 47th St
Kedzie
Western
Sherman Park
Pulaski
Kenwood
Washington Park
Midway Plaisance
Garfield
S Michigan Ave
W 55th St
Chicago Midway Airport
Midway
W 59th St
W 63rd St
Halsted
Ashland/63rd St
Jackson Park Beach
Jackson Park
W Marquette Rd
Marquette Park
69th St
Rainbow Park
W 79th St
79th St
Burbank
Metra Southwest Service Line
S Ashland Ave
S Stony Island Ave
W 95th St
95th St/Dan Ryan
Chicago State University
S Western Ave
Metra Rock Island District Line
S Halsted St
Metra Electric/South Shore Line
Calumet Park
Calumet Lake
111th St
S Vincennes Ave
Wolf Lake
Eggers Woods
127th St
130th St
6km
4 miles

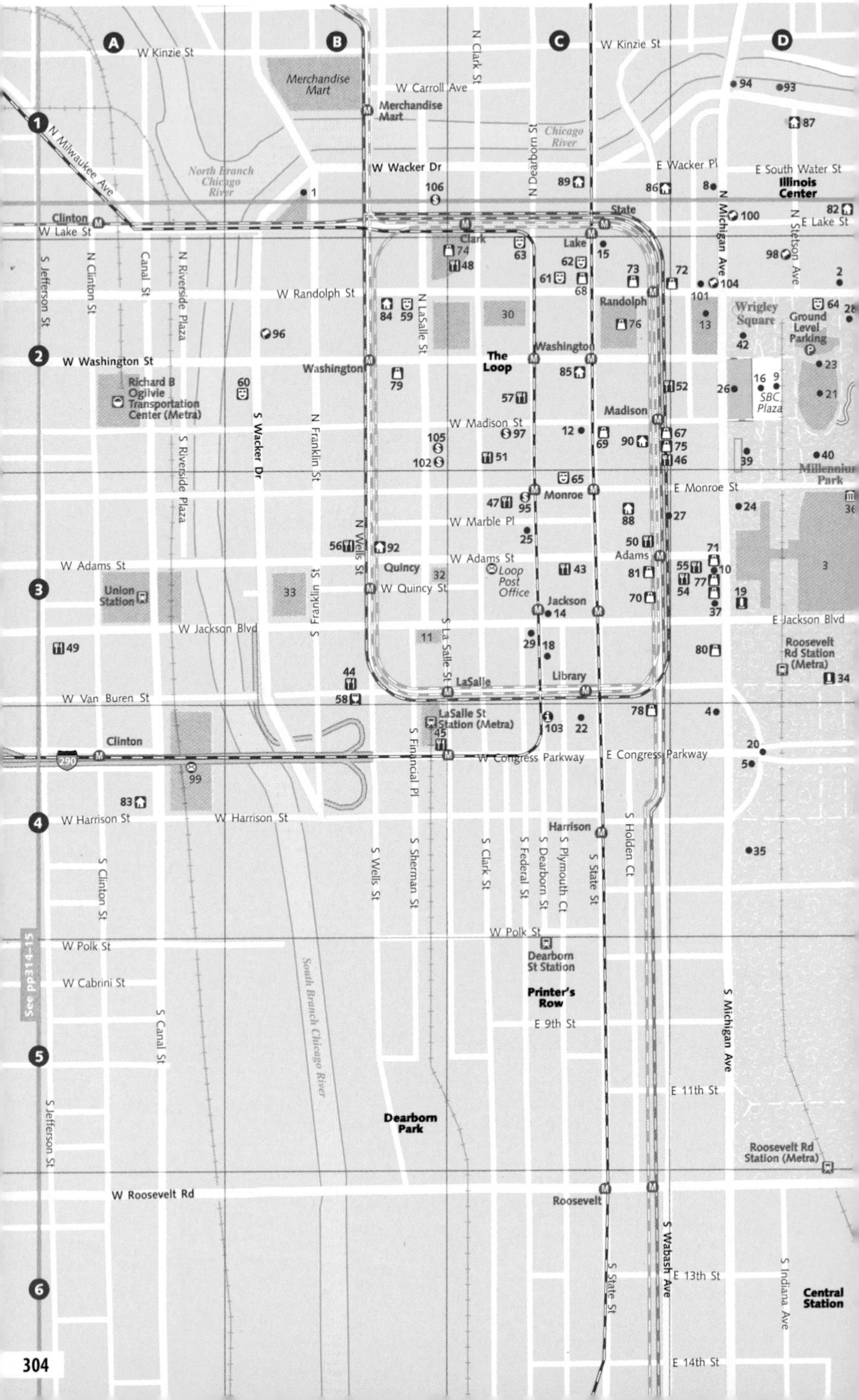

THE LOOP & GRANT PARK

A
B
C
D
1
2
3
4
5
6

W Kinzie St
Merchandise Mart
W Carroll Ave
N Clark St
Merchandise Mart
N Milwaukee Ave
North Branch Chicago River
Chicago River
N Dearborn St
W Wacker Dr
106
89
E Wacker Pl
86
8
E South Water St
Illinois Center
94
93
87
1
Clinton
W Lake St
State
Clark
Lake
100
82
E Lake St
74
48
63
15
62
61
68
73
72
101
104
98
N Michigan Ave
N Stetson Ave
2
S Jefferson St
N Clinton St
Canal St
N Riverside Plaza
W Randolph St
84
59
N LaSalle St
30
Randolph
76
13
Wrigley Square
64
28
Ground Level Parking
42
96
W Washington St
Washington
The Loop
Washington
85
23
Richard B Ogilvie Transportation Center (Metra)
60
79
57
52
26
16
9
SBC Plaza
21
S Wacker Dr
N Franklin St
W Madison St
97
Madison
12
69
90
67
75
46
105
102
51
39
40
Millennium Park
S Riverside Plaza
65
Monroe
95
47
E Monroe St
24
36
W Marble Pl
88
27
25
56
N Wells St
92
50
Adams
W Adams St
71
W Adams St
Quincy
32
Loop Post Office
43
81
55
10
3
Union Station
33
S Franklin St
W Quincy St
77
54
19
70
Jackson
14
37
W Jackson Blvd
E Jackson Blvd
11
29
18
80
Roosevelt Rd Station (Metra)
49
S La Salle St
LaSalle
Library
34
44
W Van Buren St
58
78
4
LaSalle St Station (Metra)
103
22
45
Clinton
290
W Congress Parkway
E Congress Parkway
20
5
S Financial Pl
99
83
W Harrison St
W Harrison St
Harrison
S Holden Ct
35
S Clinton St
S Wells St
S Sherman St
S Clark St
S Federal St
S Dearborn St
S Plymouth Ct
S State St
W Polk St
W Polk St
Dearborn St Station
W Cabrini St
See pp314–15
South Branch Chicago River
Printer's Row
S Canal St
S Michigan Ave
E 9th St
E 11th St
S Jefferson St
Dearborn Park
Roosevelt Rd Station (Metra)
W Roosevelt Rd
Roosevelt
S Wabash Ave
E 13th St
S State St
S Indiana Ave
Central Station
E 14th St

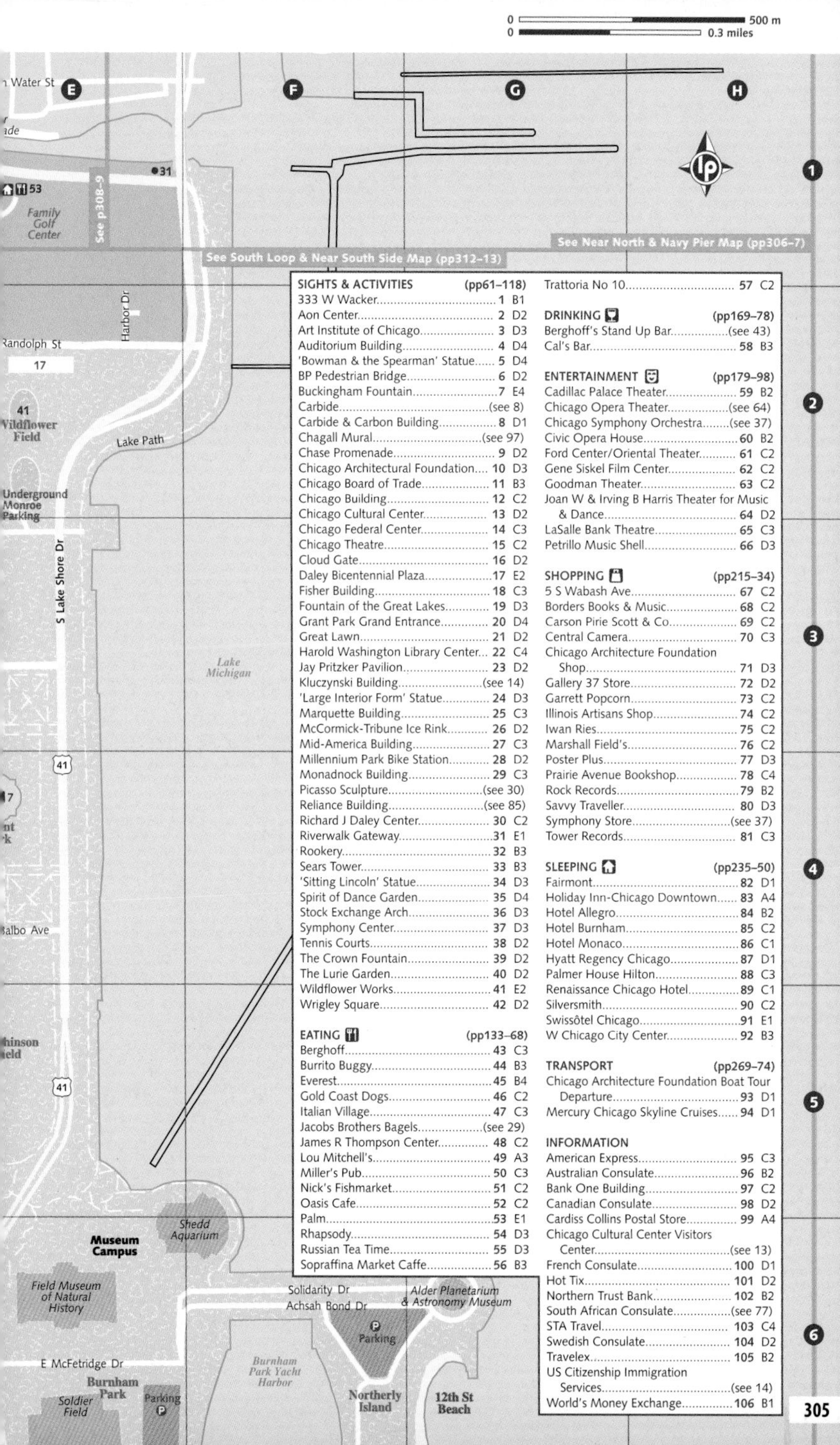

SIGHTS & ACTIVITIES (pp61–118)

333 W Wacker.......1 B1
Aon Center.......2 D2
Art Institute of Chicago.......3 D3
Auditorium Building.......4 D4
'Bowman & the Spearman' Statue.......5 D4
BP Pedestrian Bridge.......6 D2
Buckingham Fountain.......7 E4
Carbide.......(see 8)
Carbide & Carbon Building.......8 D1
Chagall Mural.......(see 97)
Chase Promenade.......9 D2
Chicago Architectural Foundation.......10 D3
Chicago Board of Trade.......11 B3
Chicago Building.......12 C2
Chicago Cultural Center.......13 D2
Chicago Federal Center.......14 C3
Chicago Theatre.......15 C2
Cloud Gate.......16 D2
Daley Bicentennial Plaza.......17 E2
Fisher Building.......18 C3
Fountain of the Great Lakes.......19 D3
Grant Park Grand Entrance.......20 D4
Great Lawn.......21 D2
Harold Washington Library Center.......22 C4
Jay Pritzker Pavilion.......23 D2
Kluczynski Building.......(see 14)
'Large Interior Form' Statue.......24 D3
Marquette Building.......25 C3
McCormick-Tribune Ice Rink.......26 D2
Mid-America Building.......27 C3
Millennium Park Bike Station.......28 D2
Monadnock Building.......29 C3
Picasso Sculpture.......(see 30)
Reliance Building.......(see 85)
Richard J Daley Center.......30 C2
Riverwalk Gateway.......31 E1
Rookery.......32 B3
Sears Tower.......33 B3
'Sitting Lincoln' Statue.......34 D3
Spirit of Dance Garden.......35 D4
Stock Exchange Arch.......36 D3
Symphony Center.......37 D3
Tennis Courts.......38 D2
The Crown Fountain.......39 D2
The Lurie Garden.......40 D2
Wildflower Works.......41 E2
Wrigley Square.......42 D2

EATING (pp133–68)

Berghoff.......43 C3
Burrito Buggy.......44 B3
Everest.......45 B4
Gold Coast Dogs.......46 C2
Italian Village.......47 C3
Jacobs Brothers Bagels.......(see 29)
James R Thompson Center.......48 C2
Lou Mitchell's.......49 A3
Miller's Pub.......50 C3
Nick's Fishmarket.......51 C2
Oasis Cafe.......52 C2
Palm.......53 E1
Rhapsody.......54 D3
Russian Tea Time.......55 D3
Sopraffina Market Caffe.......56 B3
Trattoria No 10.......57 C2

DRINKING (pp169–78)

Berghoff's Stand Up Bar.......(see 43)
Cal's Bar.......58 B3

ENTERTAINMENT (pp179–98)

Cadillac Palace Theater.......59 B2
Chicago Opera Theater.......(see 64)
Chicago Symphony Orchestra.......(see 37)
Civic Opera House.......60 B2
Ford Center/Oriental Theater.......61 C2
Gene Siskel Film Center.......62 C2
Goodman Theater.......63 C2
Joan W & Irving B Harris Theater for Music & Dance.......64 D2
LaSalle Bank Theatre.......65 C3
Petrillo Music Shell.......66 D3

SHOPPING (pp215–34)

5 S Wabash Ave.......67 C2
Borders Books & Music.......68 C2
Carson Pirie Scott & Co.......69 C2
Central Camera.......70 C3
Chicago Architecture Foundation Shop.......71 D3
Gallery 37 Store.......72 D2
Garrett Popcorn.......73 C2
Illinois Artisans Shop.......74 C2
Iwan Ries.......75 C2
Marshall Field's.......76 C2
Poster Plus.......77 D3
Prairie Avenue Bookshop.......78 C4
Rock Records.......79 B2
Savvy Traveller.......80 D3
Symphony Store.......(see 37)
Tower Records.......81 C3

SLEEPING (pp235–50)

Fairmont.......82 D1
Holiday Inn-Chicago Downtown.......83 A4
Hotel Allegro.......84 B2
Hotel Burnham.......85 C2
Hotel Monaco.......86 C1
Hyatt Regency Chicago.......87 D1
Palmer House Hilton.......88 C3
Renaissance Chicago Hotel.......89 C1
Silversmith.......90 C2
Swissôtel Chicago.......91 E1
W Chicago City Center.......92 B3

TRANSPORT (pp269–74)

Chicago Architecture Foundation Boat Tour Departure.......93 D1
Mercury Chicago Skyline Cruises.......94 D1

INFORMATION

American Express.......95 C3
Australian Consulate.......96 B2
Bank One Building.......97 C2
Canadian Consulate.......98 D2
Cardiss Collins Postal Store.......99 A4
Chicago Cultural Center Visitors Center.......(see 13)
French Consulate.......100 D1
Hot Tix.......101 D2
Northern Trust Bank.......102 B2
South African Consulate.......(see 77)
STA Travel.......103 C4
Swedish Consulate.......104 D2
Travelex.......105 B2
US Citizenship Immigration Services.......(see 14)
World's Money Exchange.......106 B1

NEAR NORTH & NAVY PIER

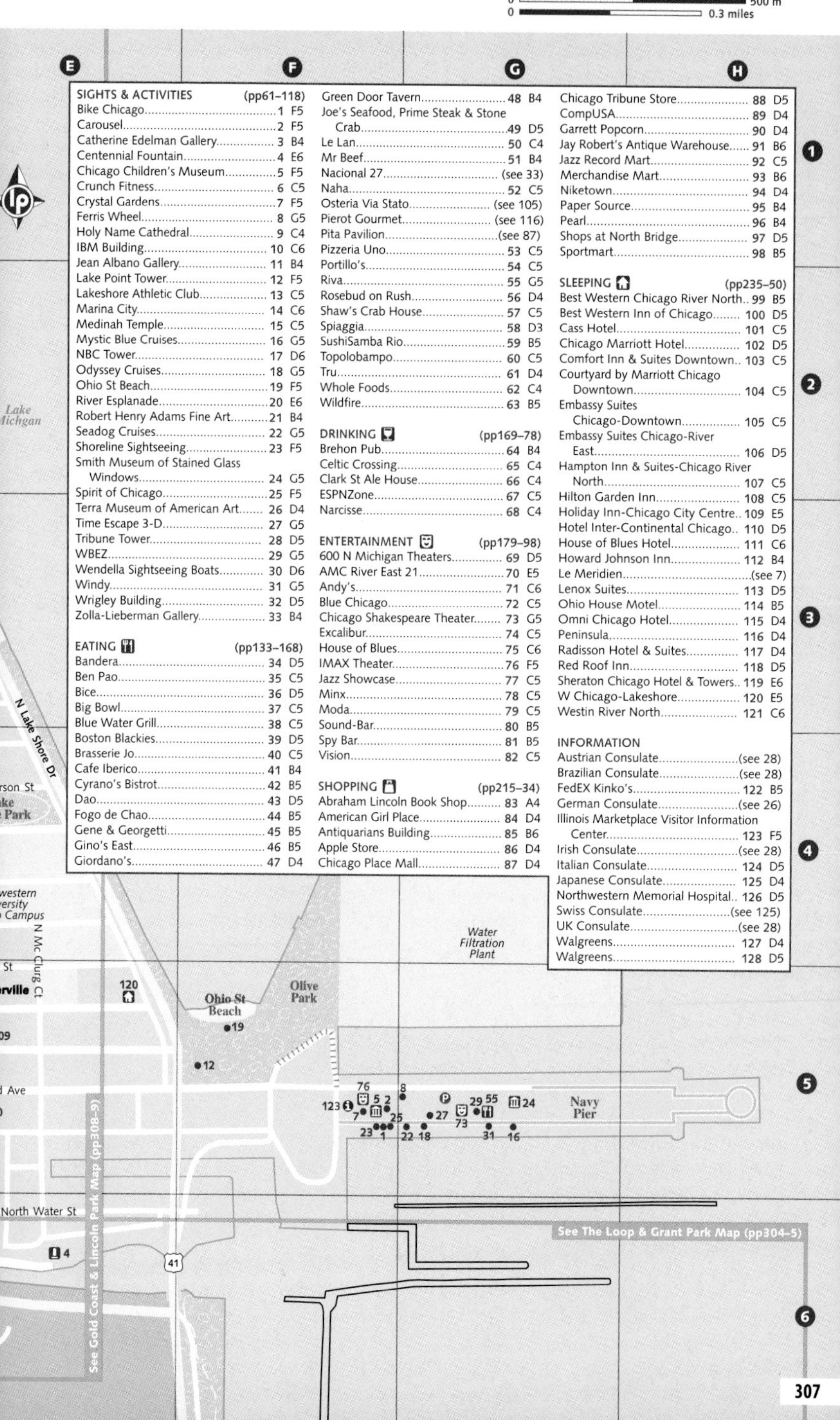

0 500 m
0 0.3 miles
E
F
G
H
1
2
3
4
5
6
SIGHTS & ACTIVITIES (pp61–118)
Bike Chicago....1 F5
Carousel....2 F5
Catherine Edelman Gallery....3 B4
Centennial Fountain....4 E6
Chicago Children's Museum....5 F5
Crunch Fitness....6 C5
Crystal Gardens....7 F5
Ferris Wheel....8 G5
Holy Name Cathedral....9 C4
IBM Building....10 C6
Jean Albano Gallery....11 B4
Lake Point Tower....12 F5
Lakeshore Athletic Club....13 C5
Marina City....14 C6
Medinah Temple....15 C5
Mystic Blue Cruises....16 G5
NBC Tower....17 D6
Odyssey Cruises....18 G5
Ohio St Beach....19 F5
River Esplanade....20 E6
Robert Henry Adams Fine Art....21 B4
Seadog Cruises....22 G5
Shoreline Sightseeing....23 F5
Smith Museum of Stained Glass Windows....24 G5
Spirit of Chicago....25 F5
Terra Museum of American Art....26 D4
Time Escape 3-D....27 G5
Tribune Tower....28 D5
WBEZ....29 G5
Wendella Sightseeing Boats....30 D6
Windy....31 G5
Wrigley Building....32 D5
Zolla-Lieberman Gallery....33 B4
EATING (pp133–168)
Bandera....34 D5
Ben Pao....35 C5
Bice....36 D5
Big Bowl....37 C5
Blue Water Grill....38 C5
Boston Blackies....39 D5
Brasserie Jo....40 C5
Cafe Iberico....41 B4
Cyrano's Bistrot....42 B5
Dao....43 D5
Fogo de Chao....44 B5
Gene & Georgetti....45 B5
Gino's East....46 B5
Giordano's....47 D4
Green Door Tavern....48 B4
Joe's Seafood, Prime Steak & Stone Crab....49 D5
Le Lan....50 C4
Mr Beef....51 B4
Nacional 27....(see 33)
Naha....52 C5
Osteria Via Stato....(see 105)
Pierot Gourmet....(see 116)
Pita Pavilion....(see 87)
Pizzeria Uno....53 C5
Portillo's....54 C5
Riva....55 G5
Rosebud on Rush....56 D4
Shaw's Crab House....57 C5
Spiaggia....58 D3
SushiSamba Rio....59 B5
Topolobampo....60 C5
Tru....61 D4
Whole Foods....62 C4
Wildfire....63 B5
DRINKING (pp169–78)
Brehon Pub....64 B4
Celtic Crossing....65 C4
Clark St Ale House....66 C4
ESPNZone....67 C5
Narcisse....68 C4
ENTERTAINMENT (pp179–98)
600 N Michigan Theaters....69 D5
AMC River East 21....70 E5
Andy's....71 C6
Blue Chicago....72 C5
Chicago Shakespeare Theater....73 G5
Excalibur....74 C5
House of Blues....75 C6
IMAX Theater....76 F5
Jazz Showcase....77 C5
Minx....78 C5
Moda....79 C5
Sound-Bar....80 B5
Spy Bar....81 B5
Vision....82 C5
SHOPPING (pp215–34)
Abraham Lincoln Book Shop....83 A4
American Girl Place....84 D4
Antiquarians Building....85 B6
Apple Store....86 D4
Chicago Place Mall....87 D4
Chicago Tribune Store....88 D5
CompUSA....89 D4
Garrett Popcorn....90 D4
Jay Robert's Antique Warehouse....91 B6
Jazz Record Mart....92 C5
Merchandise Mart....93 B6
Niketown....94 D4
Paper Source....95 B4
Pearl....96 B4
Shops at North Bridge....97 D5
Sportmart....98 B5
SLEEPING (pp235–50)
Best Western Chicago River North....99 B5
Best Western Inn of Chicago....100 D5
Cass Hotel....101 C5
Chicago Marriott Hotel....102 D5
Comfort Inn & Suites Downtown....103 C5
Courtyard by Marriott Chicago Downtown....104 C5
Embassy Suites Chicago-Downtown....105 C5
Embassy Suites Chicago-River East....106 D5
Hampton Inn & Suites-Chicago River North....107 C5
Hilton Garden Inn....108 C5
Holiday Inn-Chicago City Centre....109 E5
Hotel Inter-Continental Chicago....110 D5
House of Blues Hotel....111 C6
Howard Johnson Inn....112 B4
Le Meridien....(see 7)
Lenox Suites....113 D5
Ohio House Motel....114 B5
Omni Chicago Hotel....115 D4
Peninsula....116 D4
Radisson Hotel & Suites....117 D4
Red Roof Inn....118 D5
Sheraton Chicago Hotel & Towers....119 E6
W Chicago-Lakeshore....120 E5
Westin River North....121 C6
INFORMATION
Austrian Consulate....(see 28)
Brazilian Consulate....(see 28)
FedEX Kinko's....122 B5
German Consulate....(see 26)
Illinois Marketplace Visitor Information Center....123 F5
Irish Consulate....(see 28)
Italian Consulate....124 D5
Japanese Consulate....125 D4
Northwestern Memorial Hospital....126 D5
Swiss Consulate....(see 125)
UK Consulate....(see 28)
Walgreens....127 D4
Walgreens....128 D5
Lake Michigan
N Lake Shore Dr
N Mc Clurg Ct
Water Filtration Plant
Ohio St Beach
Olive Park
Navy Pier
North Water St
See Gold Coast & Lincoln Park Map (pp308–9)
See The Loop & Grant Park Map (pp304–5)
41

Lake Michigan
Belmont Rocks
Fullerton Beach
Lake Shore Dr
See Lake Viw Map (pp318–19)
See Wicker Park, Bucktown & Ukrainian Village Map (pp316–17)
Diversey Harbor
Lincoln Park
Lincoln Park Zoo
North Pond
South Pond
Oz Park
De Paul University
Lake View
Belmont
Wellington
Diversey
Fullerton
Armitage
Randolph St Station (Metra)
N Cannon Dr
N Stockton Dr
N Lincoln Park West
N Commonwealth Ave
N Lakeview Ave
N Clark St
N Lincoln Ave
N Sedgwick St
N Broadway
N Orchard St
N Halsted St
N Mildred Ave
N Geneva Tce
N Sheffield Ave
N Kenmore Ave
N Seminary Ave
N Clifton Ave
N Racine Ave
N Magnolia Ave
N Surrey Ct
N Lakewood Ave
N Wayne Ave
N Southport Ave
N Janssen Ave
N Greenview Ave
N Ashland Ave
N Marshfield Ave
N Paulina St
N Clybourn Ave
N Elston Ave
N Maud Ave
N Larrabee St
N Howe St
N Burling St
N Dayton St
N Fremont St
N Bissell St
W Belmont Ave
W Briar Pl
W Barry Ave
W Wellington Ave
W Oakdale Ave
W Diversey Pkwy
W Hampden Ct
W Wrightwood Ave
W Deming Pl
W St James Pl
W Arlington Pl
W Altgeld St
W Lil Ave
W Lill Ave
W Montana St
W Fullerton Parkway
W Belden Ave
W Webster Ave
W Dickens Ave
W Armitage Ave
W Menomonee St
W Wisconsin St
W Cortland St
W Melrose St
W Fletcher St
W Nelson St
W George St
W Wolfram St
Ridge Dr
North Ave

See pp306-7
See p304-5
See West Side & Pilsen Map (pp314–15)
Gold Coast
Oak St Beach
Goose Island
Stanton Schiller Park
Washington Square
Cabrini-Green
River North Gallery District
Near North
Streeterville
Northwestern University Chicago Campus
Fort Dearborn Post Office
North Branch Chicago River
Kennedy Expressway
Elkhart Park
West Side
Seneca Park
Lake Shore Park
Merchandise Mart
Illinois Center
River Esplanade
Family Golf Center
W North Ave
N North Ave
N Lake Shore Dr
E Lake Shore Dr
N Michigan Ave
N Rush St
N Wabash Ave
N State St
N Astor St
N Dearborn St
N Clark St
N La Salle St
N Wells St
N Franklin St
N Orleans St
N Sedgwick St
N Larrabee St
N Kingsbury St
N Clybourn Ave
N Ogden Ave
N Milwaukee Ave
N Halsted St
N Elston Ave
N Racine Ave
N Noble St
N Ashland Ave
N Marshfield Ave
N Paulina St
W Division St
E Division St
W Chicago Ave
E Chicago Ave
W Grand Ave
E Grand Ave
E Wacker Dr
W Wacker Dr
Sedgwick
North/Clybourn
Clark/Division
Chicago
Grand
Division
0 500 m
0 0.3 miles

GOLD COAST & LINCOLN PARK (pp308–9)

SIGHTS & ACTIVITIES (pp61–118)

- 860–880 **1** F7
- 1308-1312 N Astor St **2** E6
- 1340 N State St **3** E5
- 1355 N Astor St **4** E5
- 1500 N Astor **5** E5
- 1525 N Astor **6** E5
- 1550 N State St **7** E5
- Alfred Caldwell Lily Pool **8** D3
- Archbishop Quigley Preparatory Seminary **9** E7
- Archbishop's Residence **10** E5
- Biograph Theater **11** C3
- Cafe Brauer Paddleboat Rental **12** E4
- Charnley-Persky House **13** E5
- Chess Pavilion **14** E5
- Chicago Historical Society **15** E5
- City Gallery (see 51)
- Couch Mausoleum **16** E5
- Crilly Court **17** D5
- DePaul University **18** B3
- Elks Veterans Memorial **19** D2
- Farm-in-the-Zoo **20** E4
- Four Seasons Spa (see 159)
- Fourth Presbyterian Church **21** E7
- Frederick Wacker House **22** D4
- Fullerton Beach **23** E3
- Gold Coast Fitness Multiplex **24** E6
- Harmony Mind Body Fitness **25** C4
- Henry Meyer House **26** D4
- International Museum of Surgical Science **27** E5
- John Hancock Center **28** F7
- Lakeshore Athletic Club **29** E8
- Lincoln Park Athletic Club **30** B2
- Lincoln Park Conservatory **31** D3
- Lincoln Park Zoo **32** D4
- Lucky Strike **33** B2
- Moody Church **34** E5
- Museum of Contemporary Art **35** F7
- Newberry Library **36** E6
- North Ave Beach **37** F4
- Oak St Beach **38** F6
- Old Town Multiplex **39** E6
- Paddleboat Rental **40** D2
- Peggy Notebaert Nature Museum **41** D3
- Pumping Station (see 51)
- Russell House **42** E5
- Spacio **43** C2
- St Benedict Flats **44** E7
- St Clement's Church **45** C2
- St Michael's Church **46** D5
- St Valentine's Day Massacre Site **47** D3
- 'Standing Lincoln' Statue **48** E5
- 'Storks at Play' Statue **49** D3
- Urban Oasis **50** E6
- Water Tower **51** E7

EATING (pp133–68)

- Adobo Grill **52** D5
- Alinea **53** C5
- Bacino's **54** C3
- Bistro 110 **55** E7
- Bistrot Margot **56** D5
- Boka **57** C4
- Bourgeois Pig **58** C3
- Cafe Ba-Ba-Reeba! **59** C4
- Charlie Trotter's **60** C4
- Charlie Trotter's To Go **61** B3
- Chicago Bagel Authority **62** C4
- Cru Cafe & Wine Bar **63** E7
- Fireplace Inn **64** D5
- Foodlife (see 51)
- Fresh Choice **65** D5
- Gibson's **66** E6
- Japonais **67** C7
- John Barleycorn Memorial Pub **68** C3
- Kendall College Dining Room **69** C6
- Le Colonial **70** E6
- Mike Ditka's Restaurant **71** E7
- mk **72** D7
- Morton's **73** E6
- NoMi (see 164)
- Nookies, Too **74** C3
- O'Famé **75** C3
- Old Jerusalem **76** D5
- Original Pancake House **77** E6
- Pasta Bowl **78** D3
- PJ Clarke's **79** E6
- Puck's at the MCA (see 35)
- Pump Room (see 153)
- RJ Grunts **80** D4
- Robinson's No. 1 Ribs **81** C4
- Rose Angelis **82** B2
- ¡Salpicón! **83** D6
- Signature Room at the 95th (see 28)
- Tempo Cafe **84** E7
- Tilli's **85** C4
- Topo Gigo **86** D5
- Tsuki **87** A3
- Twin Anchors **88** D5
- Via Carducci **89** A3
- Vinci **90** C4
- Wiener Circle **91** C2

DRINKING (pp169–78)

- Deja Vu **92** B2
- Delilah's **93** B2
- Gin Mill **94** C3
- Goose Island Brewery **95** B4
- Kelly's **96** C3
- Lodge **97** E6
- Lucille's **98** C3
- Motel Bar (see 67)
- Olde Town Ale House **99** D5
- Red Lion Pub **100** C3
- Red Rooster Cafe & Wine Bar **101** C4
- Sterch's **102** C3
- Weed's **103** C5

ENTERTAINMENT (pp179–98)

- B.L.U.E.S. **104** C2
- Back Room **105** E6
- Coq d'Or (see 158)
- Exit **106** B5
- Facets Multimedia **107** A3
- Hot Tix (see 51)
- Katacomb **108** D4
- Kingston Mines **109** C2
- Le Passage (see 70)
- Liar's Club **110** A3
- Lookingglass Theatre Co (see 51)
- Neo **111** D3
- Old Town School of Folk Music **112** C4
- Pipers Alley **113** D5
- Royal George Theatre **114** C5
- Second City **115** D5
- Second City ETC **116** D5
- Steppenwolf Theatre **117** C5
- Three Penny Theater **118** C3
- Tonic Room **119** C3
- Underground Wonder Bar **120** E6
- Victory Gardens Theater **121** C3
- Village Theater **122** E5
- Zanies **123** D5
- Zebra Lounge **124** E6
- Zentra **125** C5

SHOPPING (pp215–34)

- 900 N Michigan **126** E6
- Active Endeavors **127** C4
- Alternatives **128** E6
- Anthropologie **129** E6
- Barnes & Noble **130** E6
- Barney's **131** E6
- Borders Books & Music **132** E7
- Camper **133** E6
- Chanel **134** F6
- Chicago Historical Society Store (see 15)
- City of Chicago Store (see 51)
- Cotélac **135** B3
- Dave's Records **136** C2
- Europa Books **137** E7
- Guitar Center **138** C2
- H&M **139** E7
- Hermes **140** E6
- HiFi Records **141** D2
- Jil Sander **142** E6
- Kate Spade **143** E6
- Lori's, the Sole of Chicago **144** C4
- Mint **145** A3
- North Face (see 28)
- Prada **146** E6
- Sam's Wine & Spirits **147** B5
- Sugar Magnolia **148** E6
- Tower Records **149** D3
- Uncle Dan's **150** C3
- Vosges Haut-Chocolat **151** C4
- Water Tower Place **152** F7

SLEEPING (pp235–50)

- Ambassador East **153** E6
- Arlington House **154** C3
- Days Inn Gold Coast **155** D4
- Days Inn Lincoln Park North **156** C2
- DoubleTree Guest Suites Hotel **157** F6
- Drake **158** F6
- Four Seasons Hotel **159** E7
- Gold Coast Guest House **160** E6
- Hotel Indigo **161** E6
- Hotel Sofitel **162** E7
- Inn at Lincoln Park **163** D2
- Park Hyatt **164** E7
- Residence Inn by Marriott **165** F6
- Ritz-Carlton **166** F7
- Seneca **167** F7
- Sutton Place Hotel **168** E6
- Tremont **169** E7
- Westin Hotel, Chicago **170** F6

INFORMATION

- Children's Memorial Hospital **171** C3
- Screenz **172** C2
- STA Travel **173** D2
- Visitor Information Center (see 51)

ANDERSONVILLE & UPTOWN
0 500 m
0 0.3 miles
A
B
C
D
1
2
3
4
5
6
W Victoria St
W Rosehill Dr
W Edgewater Ave
N Ridge Ave
W Hollywood Ave
W Olive Ave
Rosehill Cemetery
3
N Hermitage Ave
N Winthrop Ave
Bryn Mawr
W Bryn Mawr Ave
W Gregory St
W Catalpa Ave
W Rascher Ave
W Balmoral Ave
W Summerdale Ave
W Berwyn Ave
W Farragut Ave
W Foster Ave
W Winona St
W Carmen Ave
W Winnemac Ave
W Argyle St
W Ainslie St
W Lawrence Ave
W Leland Ave
W Wilson Ave
W Sunnyside Ave
W Montrose Ave
N Wolcott Ave
N Ravenswood Ave
N Paulina St
N Ashland Ave
N Clark St
N Glenwood Ave
N Wayne Ave
N Lakewood Ave
N Magnolia Ave
N Broadway
N Kenmore Ave
N Winchester Ave
N Dover St
N Beacon St
N Malden St
N Racine Ave
14
41
Lakewood-Balmoral
Andersonville
Berwyn
To Early to Bed (100m)
Argyle
St Boniface Cemetery
Lawrence
Chase Park
Uptown
To Hutchinson St District (0.3mi)
See Lake View Map (pp318–19)
Wilson
Montrose
Graceland Cemetery
SIGHTS & ACTIVITIES (pp61–118)
Argyle St 1 D4
Essanay Studios 2 C4
Rosehill Cemetry 3 A1
St Ita's Church 4 D2
Swedish-American Museum Center 5 B3
Uptown Theatre 6 D5
EATING (pp133–68)
Andie's 7 B3
Hai Yen 8 D4
Huey's Hotdogs 9 B2
Jin Ju 10 B3
Kopi, A Traveler's Cafe 11 B3
La Tache 12 C2
Mei Shung 13 D2
Rioja 14 B4
Swedish Bakery 15 B2
Tank Noodle 16 D4
Thai Pastry 17 D4
Tomboy 18 B2
DRINKING (pp169–78)
Hop Leaf 19 B3
Simon's 20 B3
ENTERTAINMENT (pp179–98)
Black Ensemble Theater 21 C6
Carol's Pub 22 C5
Green Mill 23 D5
Neo-Futurists 24 B3
SHOPPING (pp215–34)
Alamo Shoes 25 B3
Laundré 26 B3
Paper Trail 27 B3
Studio 90 (see 29)
Wikstrom's Gourmet Foods 28 B3
Women & Children First 29 B3
311

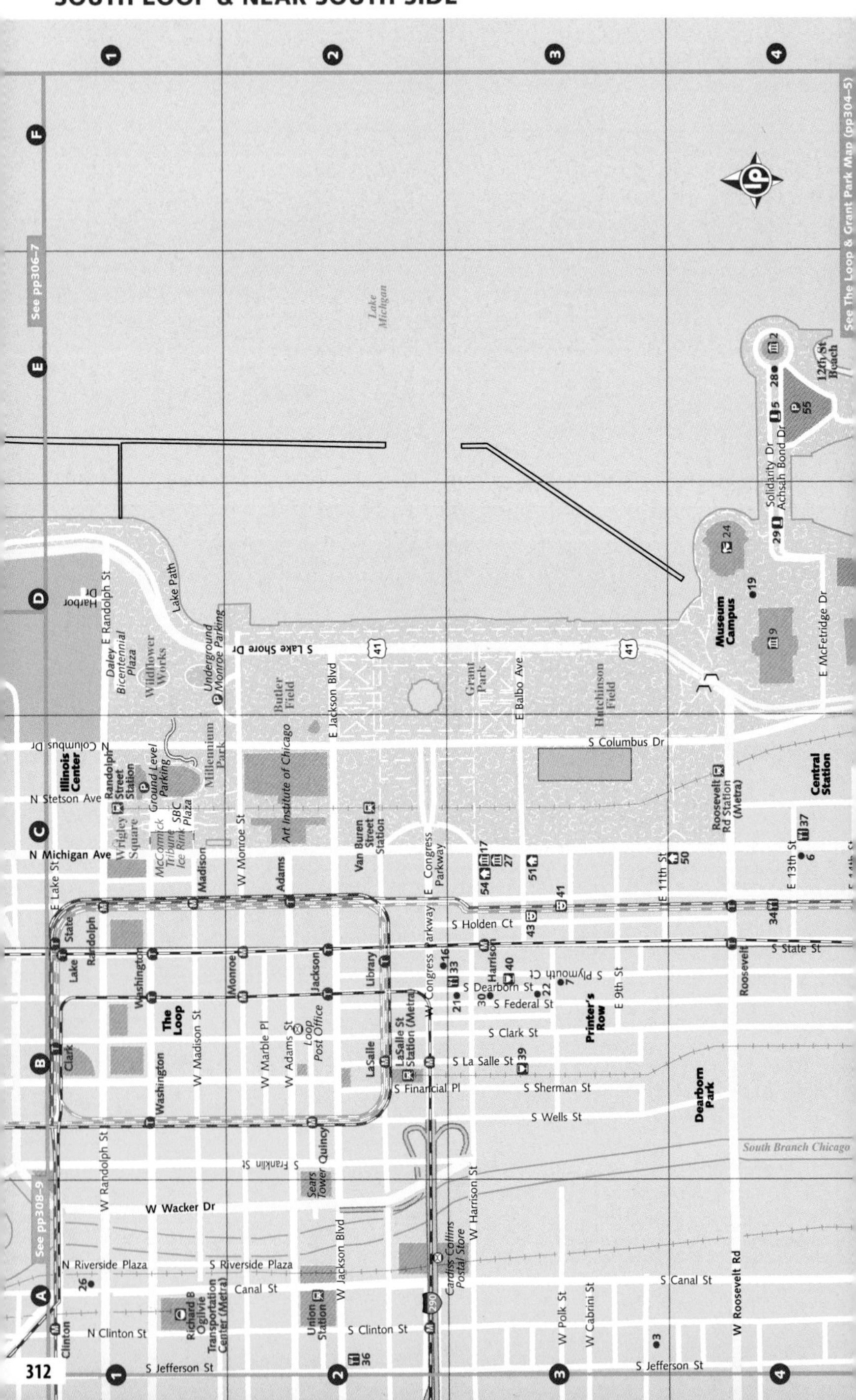

See pp306-7
See The Loop & Grant Park Map (pp304-5)
See pp308-9
Lake Michigan
Lake Path
Harbor Dr
E Randolph St
Daley Bicentennial Plaza
Wildflower Works
Underground Monroe Parking
Millennium Park
Butler Field
E Jackson Blvd
S Lake Shore Dr
Grant Park
E Balbo Ave
Hutchinson Field
S Columbus Dr
N Columbus Dr
Illinois Center
N Stetson Ave
Randolph Street Station
Ground Level Parking
Wrigley Square
McCormick Tribune Ice Rink
SBC Plaza
Art Institute of Chicago
Van Buren Street Station
E Congress Parkway
N Michigan Ave
Museum Campus
E McFetridge Dr
Solidarity Dr
Achsah Bond Dr
12th St Beach
Roosevelt Rd Station (Metra)
Central Station
E 11th St
E 13th St
S Holden Ct
S State St
S Plymouth Ct
S Dearborn St
S Federal St
E 9th St
Printer's Row
S Clark St
S La Salle St
S Sherman St
S Wells St
S Financial Pl
LaSalle St Station (Metra)
Dearborn Park
South Branch Chicago
The Loop
W Madison St
W Marble Pl
W Adams St
Loop Post Office
W Congress Parkway
W Jackson Blvd
W Harrison St
S Franklin St
Sears Tower
Quincy
W Randolph St
W Wacker Dr
N Riverside Plaza
S Riverside Plaza
Canal St
S Canal St
Richard B Ogilvie Transportation Center (Metra)
Union Station
Cardiss Collins Postal Store
N Clinton St
S Clinton St
S Jefferson St
W Polk St
W Cabrini St
W Roosevelt Rd
E Lake St
State
Randolph
Lake
Washington
Monroe
Madison
W Monroe St
Adams
Jackson
Library
LaSalle
Clark
Harrison
Roosevelt
Clinton

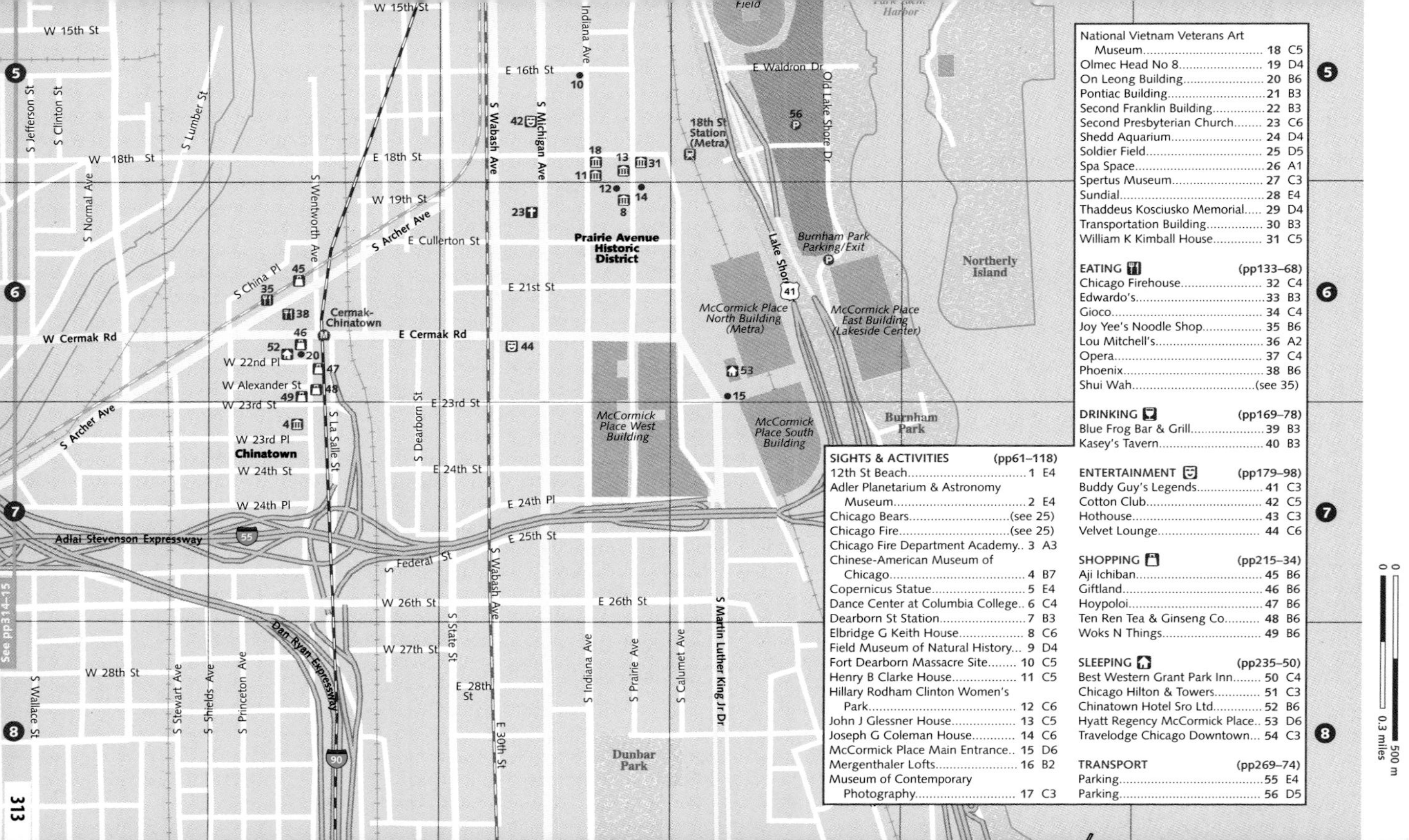
SIGHTS & ACTIVITIES (pp61–118)
12th St Beach 1 E4
Adler Planetarium & Astronomy Museum 2 E4
Chicago Bears (see 25)
Chicago Fire (see 25)
Chicago Fire Department Academy 3 A3
Chinese-American Museum of Chicago 4 B7
Copernicus Statue 5 E4
Dance Center at Columbia College 6 C4
Dearborn St Station 7 B3
Elbridge G Keith House 8 C6
Field Museum of Natural History 9 D4
Fort Dearborn Massacre Site 10 C5
Henry B Clarke House 11 C5
Hillary Rodham Clinton Women's Park 12 C6
John J Glessner House 13 C5
Joseph G Coleman House 14 C6
McCormick Place Main Entrance 15 D6
Mergenthaler Lofts 16 B2
Museum of Contemporary Photography 17 C3
National Vietnam Veterans Art Museum 18 C5
Olmec Head No 8 19 D4
On Leong Building 20 B6
Pontiac Building 21 B3
Second Franklin Building 22 B3
Second Presbyterian Church 23 C6
Shedd Aquarium 24 D4
Soldier Field 25 D5
Spa Space 26 A1
Spertus Museum 27 C3
Sundial 28 E4
Thaddeus Kosciusko Memorial 29 D4
Transportation Building 30 B3
William K Kimball House 31 C5
EATING (pp133–68)
Chicago Firehouse 32 C4
Edwardo's 33 B3
Gioco 34 C4
Joy Yee's Noodle Shop 35 B6
Lou Mitchell's 36 A2
Opera 37 C4
Phoenix 38 B6
Shui Wah (see 35)
DRINKING (pp169–78)
Blue Frog Bar & Grill 39 B3
Kasey's Tavern 40 B3
ENTERTAINMENT (pp179–98)
Buddy Guy's Legends 41 C3
Cotton Club 42 C5
Hothouse 43 C3
Velvet Lounge 44 C6
SHOPPING (pp215–34)
Aji Ichiban 45 B6
Giftland 46 B6
Hoypoloi 47 B6
Ten Ren Tea & Ginseng Co 48 B6
Woks N Things 49 B6
SLEEPING (pp235–50)
Best Western Grant Park Inn 50 C4
Chicago Hilton & Towers 51 C3
Chinatown Hotel Sro Ltd 52 B6
Hyatt Regency McCormick Place 53 D6
Travelodge Chicago Downtown 54 C3
TRANSPORT (pp269–74)
Parking 55 E4
Parking 56 D5
0 500 m
0 0.3 miles
Prairie Avenue Historic District
Chinatown
Northerly Island
Burnham Park
Dunbar Park
McCormick Place North Building (Metra)
McCormick Place East Building (Lakeside Center)
McCormick Place South Building
McCormick Place West Building
Burnham Park Parking/Exit
18th St Station (Metra)
Cermak-Chinatown
Adlai Stevenson Expressway
Dan Ryan Expressway
Lake Shore Dr
Old Lake Shore Dr
S Martin Luther King Jr Dr
S Michigan Ave
S Wabash Ave
E Cermak Rd
W Cermak Rd
S Archer Ave
See pp314–15

WEST SIDE & PILSEN

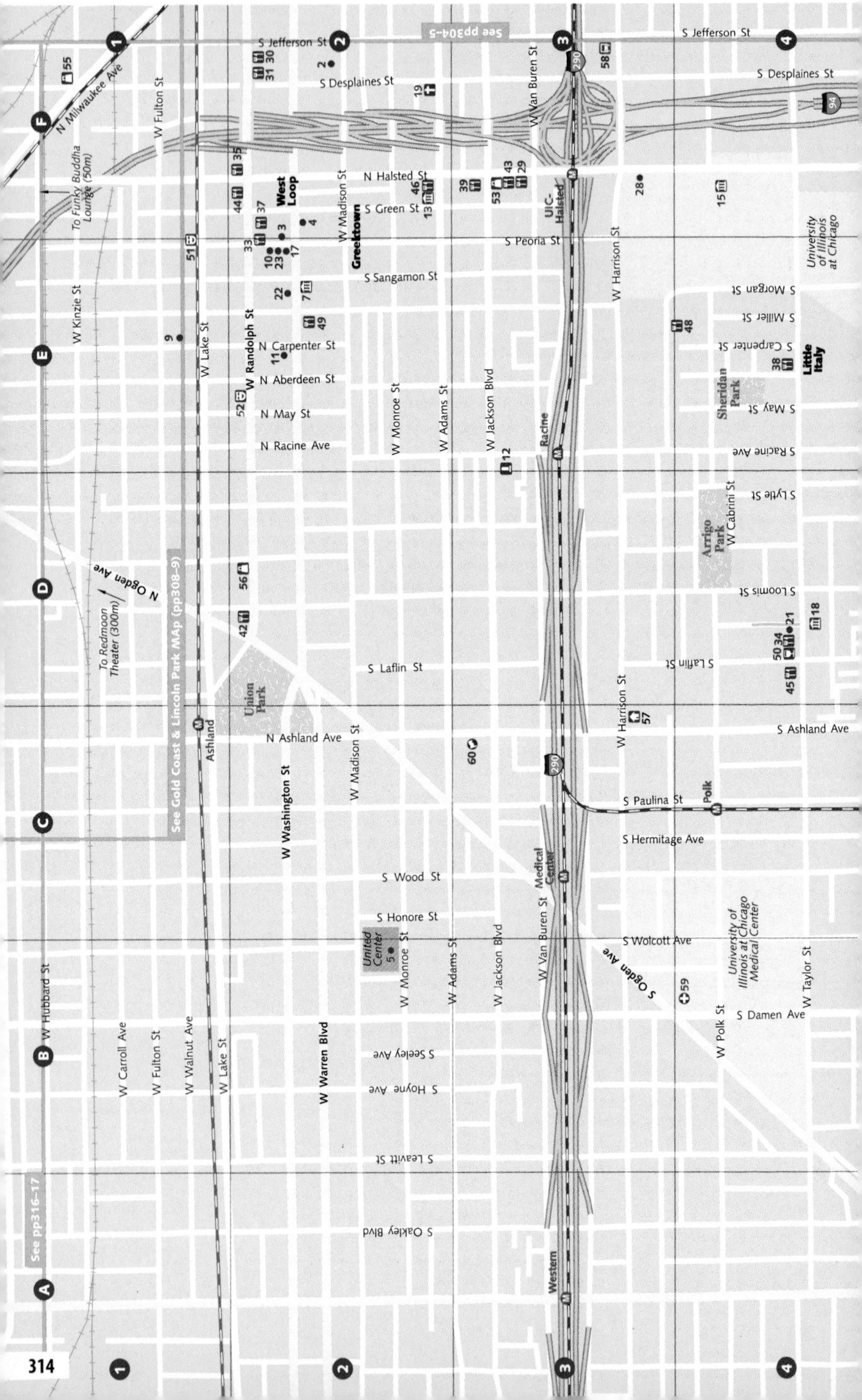

See pp304–5

See Gold Coast & Lincoln Park MAP (pp308–9)

See pp316–17

To Funky Buddha Lounge (50m)
To Redmoon Theater (300m)
N Milwaukee Ave
N Ogden Ave
S Ogden Ave
W Hubbard St
W Kinzie St
W Carroll Ave
W Fulton St
W Walnut Ave
W Lake St
W Randolph St
W Washington St
W Warren Blvd
W Madison St
W Monroe St
W Adams St
W Jackson Blvd
W Van Buren St
W Harrison St
W Polk St
W Taylor St
W Cabrini St
S Jefferson St
S Desplaines St
N Halsted St
S Green St
S Peoria St
S Sangamon St
N Carpenter St
N Aberdeen St
N May St
N Racine Ave
S Morgan St
S Miller St
S Carpenter St
S May St
S Racine Ave
S Lytle St
S Loomis St
S Laflin St
N Ashland Ave
S Ashland Ave
S Paulina St
S Hermitage Ave
S Wood St
S Honore St
S Wolcott Ave
S Damen Ave
S Seeley Ave
S Hoyne Ave
S Leavitt St
S Oakley Blvd
West Loop
Greektown
Little Italy
Union Park
Sheridan Park
Arrigo Park
United Center
University of Illinois at Chicago
University of Illinois at Chicago Medical Center
UIC-Halsted
Racine
Medical Center
Western
Ashland
Polk

SIGHTS & ACTIVITIES (pp61–118)
4art Inc. 1 F6
Batcolumn 2 F2
Bodybuilder & Sportsman 3 F2
Carrie Secrist Gallery 4 F2
Chicago Blackhawks 5 B2
Chicago Bulls (see 5)
Cooper Dual Language Academy 6 C6
Donald Young Gallery 7 E2
Dubhe Carreno Gallery 8 F6
FLATFILEgalleries 9 E1
Gallery 1R (see 3)
Gescheidle Gallery 10 E2
Harpo Studios 11 E2
Haymarket Riot Monument 12 E3
Hellenic Museum & Cultural Center 13 F2
Holy Family Church 14 E4
Jane Addams Hull House 15 F4
Kavi Gupta Gallery (see 4)
Mexican Fine Arts Center Museum 16 C6
moniquemeloche 17 E2
National Italian-American Sports Hall of Fame 18 D4
Old St Patrick's Church 19 F2
Parts Unknown Gallery 20 F6
Piazza DiMaggio 21 D4
POW! 22 E2
Rhona Hoffman 23 E2
Sally Ko Studio 24 F6
Second Regiment Armory (see 11)
St Adalbert Church 25 C6
St Pius Church 26 C6
Thalia Hall 27 E6
University Center Housing & Commons 28 F3

EATING (pp133–68)
Artopolis Bakery & Cafe 29 F3
Avec 30 F2
Blackbird 31 F2
Cafe Jumping Bean 32 D6
Chicago Chocolate Co 33 E2
Conte di Savoia 34 D4
De Cero 35 F2
Express Grill 36 F5
Marché 37 F2
Mario's 38 E4
Mr Greek Gyros 39 F3
Nuevo Leon 40 D6
Nuevo Leon Panderia 41 C6
onesixtyblue 42 D2
Parthenon 43 F3
Red Light 44 F2
Rosebud 45 D4
Santorini 46 F2
Taqueria El Milagro 47 D6
Tufano's Vernon Park Tap 48 E4
Wishbone 49 E2

DRINKING (pp169–78)
Hawkeye's 50 D4

ENTERTAINMENT (pp179–98)
Oprah Winfrey Show (see 11)
Reserve 51 E1
Rhythm 52 E2

SHOPPING (pp215–34)
Athenian Candle Co 53 F3
Barbara's Bookstore 54 F4
Blommer Chocolate Store 55 F1
Chicago Antique Market 56 D2

SLEEPING (pp235–50)
Chicago Marriot at Medical District/UIC 57 C3

TRANSPORT (ppXXX–XXX)
Greyhound (see 58)
Main Bus Station 58 F3

INFORMATION
John H Stroger Jr Hospital of Cook County 59 B4
Mexican Consulate 60 C3

WICKER PARK, BUCKTOWN & UKRAINIAN VILLAGE

SIGHTS & ACTIVITIES	(pp61–118)	
Bikram Yoga	1	C6
Diversey River Bowl	2	A1
Flat Iron Building	3	B5
Holstein Park	4	A3
JABB Boxing Gym	5	A8
Nelson Algren House	6	B6
Polish Museum of America	7	D7
Saints Volodymyr & Olha Church	8	A7
St Mary of the Angels Church	9	C4
St Nicholas Ukrainian Catholic Cathedral	10	A7
Ukrainian Institute of Modern Art	11	A7
Wicker Park	12	B5

EATING	(pp133–68)	
Alliance Bakery	13	C6
Bari Foods	14	E8
Fan Si Pan	15	C7
Flash Taco	16	B5
Flo	(see 53)	
Green Zebra	17	D7
Handlebar	18	A5
Hot Chocolate	19	B4
Irazu	20	A4
Le Bouchon	21	B4
Leo's Lunchroom	22	C6
Letizia's Natural Bakery	23	B6
Li'l Guys Deli	24	B4
Margie's	25	A4
Meritage Cafe & Wine Bar	26	B3
Miko's	27	B4
Milk & Honey	28	B6
Mirai Sushi	29	B6
Nick's Pit Stop	30	B4
Northside	31	B5
Pontiac Cafe	32	B5
Scylla	33	B4
Smoke Daddy Rhythm & Bar-B-Que	34	C6
Spring	35	B5
Sultan's Market	36	B5
Tecalitlan	37	C7
Thyme	38	F8
Vienna Beef Factory Store & Deli	39	B2
West Town Tavern	40	D7

DRINKING	(pp169–78)	
Charleston	41	B3
Club Foot	42	B7
Danny's	43	B3
Earwax	44	B5
Filter	(see 3)	
Gold Star Bar	45	C6
Lemmings	46	B4
Map Room	47	B4
Nick's	48	B5
Quenchers	49	A2
Rainbo Club	50	B6
Richard's Bar	51	F8
Rodin	52	B5
Sonotheque	53	D7

ENTERTAINMENT	(pp179–98)	
Chicago Dramatists	54	E7
Darkroom	55	A7
Davenport's Piano Bar & Cabaret	56	C6
Double Door	57	B5
Empty Bottle	58	A7
Funky Buddha Lounge	59	F8
Green Dolphin Street	60	C3
Hideout	61	D4
Lava Lounge	62	B7
Note	63	B5
rednofive	64	F8
Slick's Lounge	65	E6
Subterranean	66	B5
Trap Door Theatre	67	C4

SHOPPING	(pp215–34)	
Akira's	68	C5
Botanica	69	B5
Casa de Soul	70	B6
Climate	71	B5
Clothes Minded	72	B5
Dusty Groove	73	C6
John Fluevog Shoes	74	B5
Lilly Vallente	75	C6
Meble	76	B5
MS Catwalk	77	B3
Myopic Books	78	B5
Noir for Men	79	C6
p45	80	B5
Penelope's	81	B6
Porte Rouge	82	B6
Quimby's	83	B5
Reckless Records	84	B5
Red Balloon Co	85	B3
Saffron	86	B3
Tshirt Deli	87	B4
Una Mae's Freak Boutique	88	C5
US #1	89	B5
Vive la Femme	90	B3

SLEEPING	(pp235–50)	
House of Two Urns Bed & Breakfast	91	D6
Wicker Park Inn	92	C6

See Lake View Map (pp318–19)

To Hot Doug's (0.3mi); Factory Theater (0.5mi); Prop Thtr (0.5mi)

To Lula Cafe (0.6mi)

W Diversey Ave · W Fullerton Ave · W Webster Ave · W Shakespeare Ave · W Charleston St · W Dickens Ave · W McLean Ave · W Armitage Ave · W Homer St · W Cortland St · W Moffat St · W Churchill St · W Willow St · W Bloomingdale Ave · W Montana St · W Medill Ave · W Belden Ave · W Lyndale St · W Altgeld St · N Ashland Ave · N Wolcott Ave · N Paulina St · N Leavitt St · N Damen Ave · N Elston Ave · N Winchester Ave · N Hermitage Ave · N Marshfield Ave · N Clybourn Ave · N Dominick St · N Magnolia Ave · N Racine Ave · N Clifton Ave · N Seminary Ave · N Kenmore Ave · N Maud Ave · N Marcey St · N Kingsbury St · N Sheffield Ave · N Bissell St · N Fremont St · N Dayton St · N Halsted St · N Burling St · N Orchard St · N Howe St · N Larrabee St · N Wilmot Ave · N Milwaukee Ave · N Winnebago Ave · John F Kennedy Expwy · North Branch Chicago River · Churchill Field Park · Bucktown · Wellington · Armitage · Western

0 500 m
0 0.3 miles
pp 306-7
See Gold Coast & Lincoln Park Map (pp308-9)
W North Ave
North/Clybourn
N Clybourn Ave
N Dayton St
W Blackhawk St
N Halsted St
W Evergreen Ave
Stanton Schiller Park
W Scott St
N Ogden Ave
W Division St
N Crosby St
N Howe St
N Larrabee St
Hobbie St
N Kingsbury St
N Hooker St
N Hickory Ave
N Cherry Ave
N North Branch St
Goose Island
N Sangamon St
W Chicago Ave
N May St
N Elston Ave
N Racine Ave
N Milwaukee Ave
Chicago
W Erie St
Grand
W Grand Ave
N Magnolia Ave
Throop St
Elston Ave
Besly Ct
N Cleaver St
N Greenview Ave
N Bosworth Ave
N Ashland Ave
N Noble St
Elkhart Park
W Cortez St
W Thomas St
Division
West Side
N Marshfield Ave
N Paulina St
N Hermitage Ave
N Paul
N Wood
N Honore
W Le Moyne St
W Julian St
W Blackhawk St
N Wicker Park Ave
N Elk Gve Ave
W Schiller St
W Rice St
N Wolcott Ave
N Winchester Ave
W Superior St
N Damen Ave
W Concord Pl
Caton St
W Pierce Ave
Damen
Wicker Park
W Evergreen Ave
W Potomac Ave
W Crystal St
W Haddon Ave
W Augusta Blvd
W Iowa St
W Chicago Ave
Ukranian Village
W Huron St
W Erie St
W Ohio St
W Race Ave
W Grand Ave
W Ferdinand St
N Leavitt St
N Bell Ave
N Oakley Ave
N Oakley Blvd
N Claremont Ave
N Western Ave
W Cortez St
W Hirsch St
W Division St
W Le Moyne St

LAKE VIEW

Western
A
B
C
D
W Wilson Ave
W Sunnyside Ave
Montrose
See Andersonville & Uptown Map (p311)
W Montrose Ave
76
W Cullom Ave
N Ravenswood Ave
58
W Berteau Ave
Graceland Cemetery
2
Western Ave
W Belle Plaine Ave
N Clark St
17
W Irving Park Rd
W Irving Park Rd
Irving Park
Hebrew Cemetery
N Hermitage Ave
N Paulina St
N Marshfield Ave
N Ashland Ave
49
63
W Byron St
41
W Grace St
33
32
64
16
66
83
W Waveland Ave
8
35
42
50
Addison
N Lincoln Ave
N Southport Ave
N Lakewood Ave
100
W Cornelia Ave
6
15
W Roscoe St
Southport
Paulina
W Henderson St
48
W School St
W Melrose St
N Damen Ave
N Ravenswood Ave
92
89
W Belmont Ave
W Belmont Ave
68
54
43
N Ashland Ave
5
W Fletcher St
77
W Barry Ave
N Lincoln Ave
W Nelson St
W Wellington Ave
See Wicher Park, Bucktown & Ukrainian Village Map (pp316–17)
53
W Oakdale Ave
North Branch Chicago River
N Western Ave
N Paulina St
W George St
N Southport Ave
N Lakewood Ave
W Wolfram St
102
88
W Diversey Ave
1
2
3
4
5
6

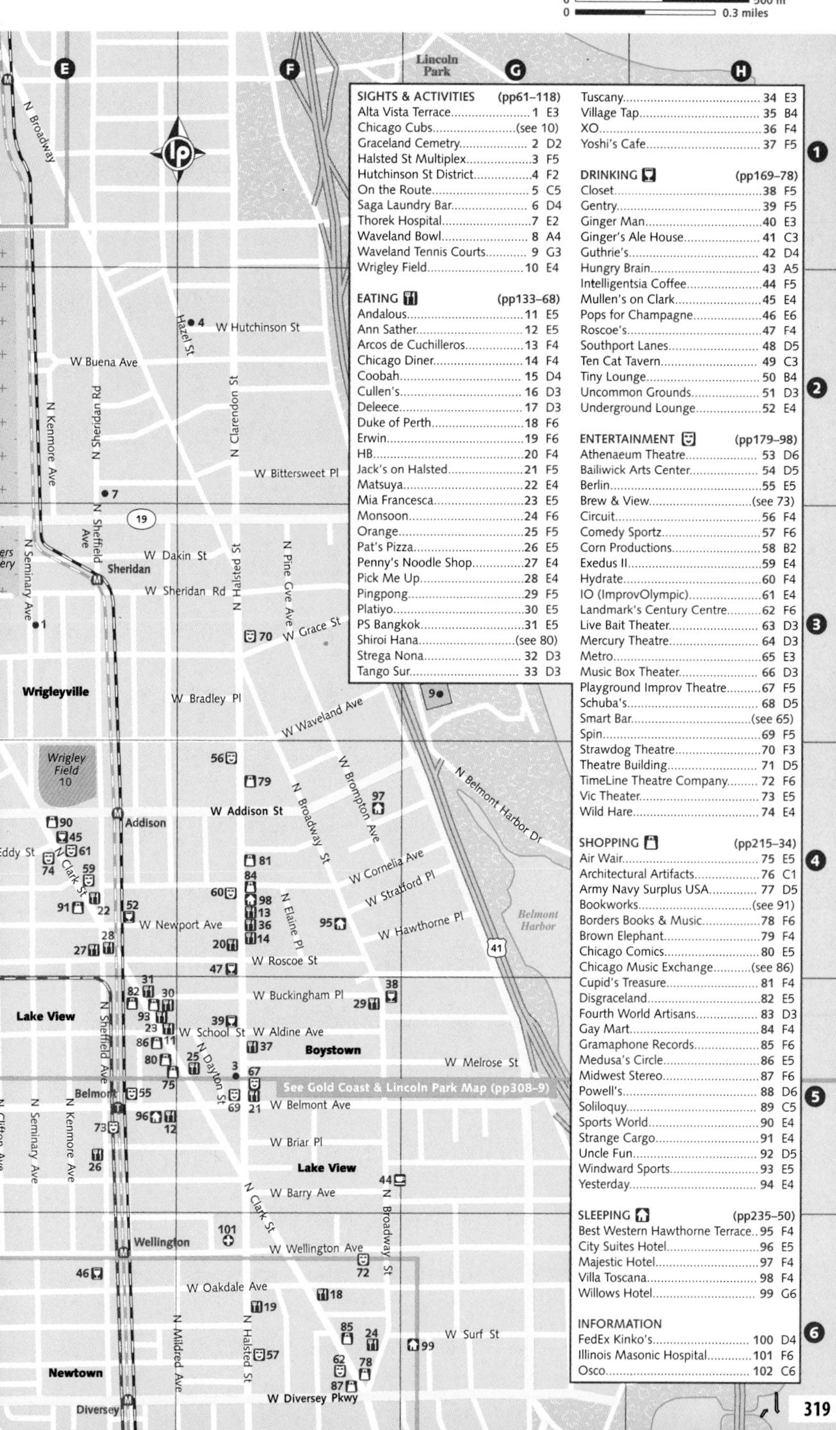
0 500 m
0 0.3 miles
Lincoln Park
E
F
G
H
1
2
3
4
5
6
SIGHTS & ACTIVITIES (pp61–118)
Alta Vista Terrace 1 E3
Chicago Cubs (see 10)
Graceland Cemetry 2 D2
Halsted St Multiplex 3 F5
Hutchinson St District 4 F2
On the Route 5 C5
Saga Laundry Bar 6 D4
Thorek Hospital 7 E2
Waveland Bowl 8 A4
Waveland Tennis Courts 9 G3
Wrigley Field 10 E4
EATING (pp133–68)
Andalous 11 E5
Ann Sather 12 E5
Arcos de Cuchilleros 13 F4
Chicago Diner 14 F4
Coobah 15 D4
Cullen's 16 D3
Deleece 17 D3
Duke of Perth 18 F6
Erwin 19 F6
HB 20 F4
Jack's on Halsted 21 F5
Matsuya 22 E4
Mia Francesca 23 E5
Monsoon 24 F6
Orange 25 F5
Pat's Pizza 26 E5
Penny's Noodle Shop 27 E4
Pick Me Up 28 E4
Pingpong 29 F5
Platiyo 30 E5
PS Bangkok 31 E5
Shiroi Hana (see 80)
Strega Nona 32 D3
Tango Sur 33 D3
Tuscany 34 E3
Village Tap 35 B4
XO 36 F4
Yoshi's Cafe 37 F5
DRINKING (pp169–78)
Closet 38 F5
Gentry 39 F5
Ginger Man 40 E3
Ginger's Ale House 41 C3
Guthrie's 42 D4
Hungry Brain 43 A5
Intelligentsia Coffee 44 F5
Mullen's on Clark 45 E4
Pops for Champagne 46 E6
Roscoe's 47 F4
Southport Lanes 48 D5
Ten Cat Tavern 49 C3
Tiny Lounge 50 B4
Uncommon Grounds 51 D3
Underground Lounge 52 E4
ENTERTAINMENT (pp179–98)
Athenaeum Theatre 53 D6
Bailiwick Arts Center 54 D5
Berlin 55 E5
Brew & View (see 73)
Circuit 56 F4
Comedy Sportz 57 F6
Corn Productions 58 B2
Exedus II 59 E4
Hydrate 60 F4
IO (ImprovOlympic) 61 E4
Landmark's Century Centre 62 F6
Live Bait Theater 63 D3
Mercury Theatre 64 D3
Metro 65 E3
Music Box Theater 66 D3
Playground Improv Theatre 67 F5
Schuba's 68 D5
Smart Bar (see 65)
Spin 69 F5
Strawdog Theatre 70 F3
Theatre Building 71 D5
TimeLine Theatre Company 72 F6
Vic Theater 73 E5
Wild Hare 74 E4
SHOPPING (pp215–34)
Air Wair 75 E5
Architectural Artifacts 76 C1
Army Navy Surplus USA 77 D5
Bookworks (see 91)
Borders Books & Music 78 F6
Brown Elephant 79 F4
Chicago Comics 80 E5
Chicago Music Exchange (see 86)
Cupid's Treasure 81 F4
Disgraceland 82 E5
Fourth World Artisans 83 D3
Gay Mart 84 F4
Gramaphone Records 85 F6
Medusa's Circle 86 E5
Midwest Stereo 87 F6
Powell's 88 D6
Soliloquy 89 C5
Sports World 90 E4
Strange Cargo 91 E4
Uncle Fun 92 D5
Windward Sports 93 E5
Yesterday 94 E4
SLEEPING (pp235–50)
Best Western Hawthorne Terrace 95 F4
City Suites Hotel 96 E5
Majestic Hotel 97 F4
Villa Toscana 98 F4
Willows Hotel 99 G6
INFORMATION
FedEx Kinko's 100 D4
Illinois Masonic Hospital 101 F6
Osco 102 C6
N Broadway
W Hutchinson St
Hazel St
W Buena Ave
N Sheridan Rd
N Kenmore Ave
N Clarendon St
W Bittersweet Pl
N Sheffield Ave
W Dakin St
Sheridan
W Sheridan Rd
N Halsted St
N Pine Gve Ave
N Seminary Ave
W Grace St
Wrigleyville
W Bradley Pl
W Waveland Ave
Wrigley Field
N Broadway St
N Brompton Ave
N Belmont Harbor Dr
W Addison St
Addison
Eddy St
N Clark St
W Cornelia Ave
W Stratford Pl
N Elaine Pl
W Newport Ave
W Hawthorne Pl
Belmont Harbor
W Roscoe St
W Buckingham Pl
Lake View
W School St
W Aldine Ave
Boystown
N Dayton St
W Melrose St
See Gold Coast & Lincoln Park Map (pp308–9)
Belmont
W Belmont Ave
N Clifton Ave
W Briar Pl
W Barry Ave
Wellington
W Wellington Ave
W Oakdale Ave
W Surf St
N Mildred Ave
Newtown
W Diversey Pkwy
Diversey

HYDE PARK & KENWOOD

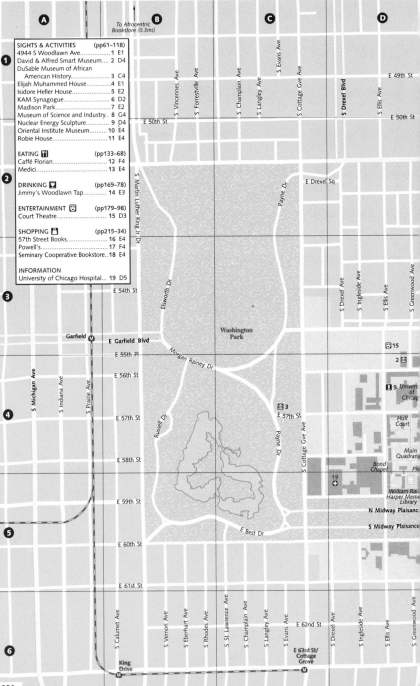

SIGHTS & ACTIVITIES	(pp61–118)
4944 S Woodlawn Ave	1 E1
David & Alfred Smart Museum	2 D4
DuSable Museum of African American History	3 C4
Elijah Muhammed House	4 E1
Isidore Heller House	5 E2
KAM Synagogue	6 D2
Madison Park	7 E2
Museum of Science and Industry	8 G4
Nuclear Energy Sculpture	9 D4
Oriental Institute Museum	10 E4
Robie House	11 E4
EATING	(pp133–68)
Caffé Florian	12 F4
Medici	13 E4
DRINKING	(pp169–78)
Jimmy's Woodlawn Tap	14 E3
ENTERTAINMENT	(pp179–98)
Court Theatre	15 D3
SHOPPING	(pp215–34)
57th Street Books	16 E4
Powell's	17 F4
Seminary Cooperative Bookstore	18 E4
INFORMATION	
University of Chicago Hospital	19 D5

0 500 m
0 0.3 miles
E
F
G
H
1
2
3
4
5
6
Lake Michgan
S Woodlawn Ave
S Dorchester Ave
Kenwood Park
S Blackstone Ave
S Lake Park Ave
S Chicago Beach Dr
S East End Ave
E 50th St
Kenwood
E Hyde Park Blvd
Lake Shore Dr
41
E 52nd St
53rd St Station (Metra)
E 53rd St
E 54th St
S Kimbark Ave
S Kenwood Ave
S Ridgewood Ct
S Cornell Ave
E Hyde Park Blvd
S Everett Ave
E 55th Pl
55th-56th-57th St Station (Metra)
E 55th St
E 56th St
Hyde Park
S Harper Ave
E 57th Dr
E 57th St
57th St Beach
E 58th St
Rockefeller Memorial Chapel
59th St Station (Metra)
Columbia Dr
E 59th St
Midway Plaisance
E 60th St
S Stony Island Ave
East Lagoon
E 61st St
West Lagoon
Jackson Park
Jackson Park Beach
63rd St Station (Metra)

CHICAGO TRANSIT MAP

PURPLE LINE continues downtown weekday rush periods

Linden, Central, Noyes, Foster, Davis, Dempster, Main, South Blvd, Howard

YELLOW LINE

Skokie

RED LINE

Howard, Jarvis, Morse, Loyola, Granville, Thorndale, Bryn Mawr, Berwyn, Argyle, Lawrence, Wilson, Sheridan, Addison, Belmont, Fullerton, North/Clybourn, Clark/Division, Chicago, Grand, Harrison, Roosevelt, Cermak-Chinatown, Sox-35th, 47th, Garfield, 63rd, 69th, 79th, 87th, 95th/Dan Ryan

BROWN LINE

Kimball, Kedzie, Francisco, Rockwell, Western, Damen, Montrose, Irving Park, Addison, Paulina, Southport, Belmont, Wellington, Diversey, Fullerton, Armitage, Sedgwick, Chicago, Merch Mart

BLUE LINE

O'Hare, Rosemont, Cumberland, Harlem, Jefferson Park, Montrose, Irving Park, Addison, Belmont, Logan Square, California, Western, Damen, Division, Chicago, Grand, Clinton

BLUE LINE (Forest Park branch)

Forest Park, Harlem, Oak Park, Austin, Cicero, Pulaski, Kedzie-Homan, Western, Medical Center, Illinois Medical District, Racine, UIC-Halsted, Clinton

BLUE LINE (54th/Cermak branch)

54th/Cermak, Cicero, Kostner, Pulaski, Central Park, Kedzie, California, Western, Damen, 18th, Polk

GREEN LINE

Harlem, Oak Park, Ridgeland, Austin, Central, Laramie, Cicero, Pulaski, Conservatory-Central Pk. Dr., Kedzie, California, Ashland, Clinton

Roosevelt, 35th-Bronzeville-IIT, Indiana, 43rd, 47th, 51st, Garfield

GREEN LINE (Ashland branch): Ashland/63rd, Halsted

GREEN LINE (East 63rd branch): boarding inbound only King Dr, East 63rd Cottage Grove

ORANGE LINE

Midway, Pulaski, Kedzie, Western, 35th/Archer, Ashland, Halsted, Roosevelt

See Downtown Inset

LAKE MICHIGAN

Downtown Inset

Brown Line, Purple Line, Green Line, Red Line, Blue Line

use card or pass; walk between elevated & subway

Lake St., Clark, State, Lake, Randolph, Washington, Washington, Madison, Monroe, Adams, Quincy, Jackson, LaSalle, Library, Van Buren St., LaSalle, Congress Pkwy

Wells St., Dearborn St. subway, State St. subway, Wabash Ave., Orange Line, Green Line, Red Line, Blue Line

NORTH

Free connection between routes

Accessible station

Park & Ride Lot

cta

July 2005

Map © 2005 Chicago Transit Authority. All rights reserved. Used with permission.

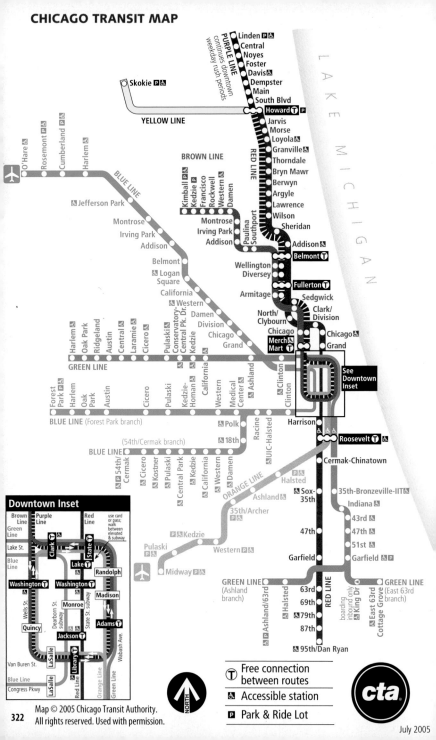

PENGUIN BOOKS

THE COMPETITIVE RUNNER'S HANDBOOK

BOB GLOVER is founder and president of Robert H. Glover and Associates, Inc., a sports and fitness consulting firm. Since he founded the program in 1978, Glover has directed the running classes for the 32,000-member New York Road Runners Club. More than 3,000 students participate each year in these classes at the beginner, advanced beginner, intermediate, advanced intermediate, basic competitive, competitive, and advanced competitive levels. He is a regular training columnist for the NYRRC's *New York Running News*, and the American Running and Fitness Association's *Running & FitNews*. Glover's Official New York City Marathon Training Program is followed annually by thousands of runners. Each year since its founding in 1990, Glover has directed over 1,000 boys and girls aged five to thirteen in the City-Sports-For-Kids track-and-field program sponsored by the New York Road Runners Club. A high school (Dansville, New York) county champion at 2 miles and a three-time gold medalist at the Hue Sports Festival during the Vietnam War, he has competed for nearly forty years at distances ranging from the quarter-mile to the 50-mile ultra-marathon, and has completed over thirty marathons. He now places frequently in local races as a masters age fifty-plus competitor, and coaches the Great New York Racing Team. Glover has coached over forty women athletes under the three hour barrier for the marathon, with three of them ranking in the top ten in the United States. He has coached his various running teams to several national and international titles at a variety of distances in both the open and masters categories. With over thirty years' experience coaching all levels of runners, more than 50,000 men and women have participated in his classes and nearly a million runners have followed his training program in his books since *The Runner's Handbook* was first published and became an immediate national best-seller in 1978. He and his wife, Shelly-lynn, live in Sleepy Hollow, New York, where they love to run together along wooded trails made famous by the Headless Horseman. They often win awards together in couples races.

ALSO BY BOB GLOVER AND SHELLY-LYNN FLORENCE GLOVER

The Runner's Handbook

The Runner's Training Diary

The Injured Runner's Training Handbook

The Family Fitness Handbook

The Competitive Runner's Handbook

The Bestselling Guide to Running 5Ks Through Marathons

Revised Edition

Bob Glover and
Shelly-lynn Florence Glover

Penguin Books

PENGUIN BOOKS
Published by the Penguin Group
Penguin Group (USA) Inc., 375 Hudson Street, New York, New York 10014, U.S.A.
Penguin Books Ltd, 80 Strand, London WC2R 0RL, England
Penguin Books Australia Ltd, 250 Camberwell Road, Camberwell, Victoria 3124, Australia
Penguin Books Canada Ltd, 10 Alcorn Avenue, Toronto, Ontario, Canada M4V 3B2
Penguin Books India (P) Ltd, 11 Community Centre, Panchsheel Park, New Delhi – 110 017, India
Penguin Books (N.Z.) Ltd, Cnr Rosedale and Airborne Roads, Albany, Auckland, New Zealand
Penguin Books (South Africa) (Pty) Ltd, 24 Sturdee Avenue,
Rosebank, Johannesburg 2196, South Africa

Penguin Books Ltd, Registered Offices: 80 Strand, London WC2R 0RL, England

The Competitive Runner's Handbook by Bob Glover and
Pete Schuder first published in the United States of America in
Penguin Books 1983
Revised edition published 1988
This second revised edition by Bob Glover and
Shelly-lynn Florence Glover published 1999

20 19

Copyright © Robert H. Glover and Associates, Inc., 1983,
1988, 1999
All rights reserved

A Note to the Reader
The ideas, procedures, and suggestions contained in this book are not intended to substitute for medical or other professional advice applicable to specific individuals. As with any activity program, yours should be prepared in consultation with a physician or other competent professional.

LIBRARY OF CONGRESS CATALOGING-IN-PUBLICATION DATA
Glover, Bob.
The competitive runner's handbook: the bestselling guide to
running 5Ks through marathons / by Bob Glover and
Shelley-lynn Florence Glover. —Rev. ed.
p. cm.
Rev. ed. of: The new competitive runner's handbook. 1988.
Includes index.
ISBN 0 14 046.990 7
1. Running—Training. 2. Running—Psychological aspects.
3. Running races. I. Glover, Shelly-lynn Florence. II. Glover,
Bob. New competitive runner's handbook. III. Title.
GV1061.5.G54 1999
796.42'4—dc21 98-33345

Printed in the United States of America
Set in Sabon
Designed by Betty Lew

Except in the United States of America, this book is sold subject to the condition that it shall not, by way of trade or otherwise, be lent, re-sold, hired out, or otherwise circulated without the publisher's prior consent in any form of binding or cover other than that in which it is published and without a similar condition including this condition being imposed on the subsequent purchaser.

Dedication

So many men and women have contributed to the development of running for fitness and competition that it is difficult to choose the single man or single woman who has had the most profound influence. For me, however, it was an easy choice. Both the third edition of *The Competitive Runner's Handbook* and the third edition of *The Runner's Handbook* are proudly dedicated to two good friends who contributed the most to my career as a running coach and writer. For many reasons they can be called "The Marathon Man" and "The Marathon Woman."

Fred Lebow died in 1994, just four weeks prior to the twenty-fifth anniversary of his pride and joy, the New York City Marathon. When Fred took the reins as president of the New York Road Runners Club, the organization had fewer than 200 members. When he died, the NYRRC was over 30,000 strong. A charismatic, innovative leader, Fred's most publicized accomplishment was his direction of the New York City Marathon. In a bold move in 1976, he took the event from the confines of Central Park out onto the streets of all five boroughs. He brought the marathon to the people. His concept excited the media, which further promoted the sport and helped fuel the big running boom of the late 1970s. Just as important, thousands of spectators caught up in the excitement took up running themselves—first running for fitness and then training to run the marathon itself. Cities around the world started marathons through their streets and sought out Fred and his staff for advice. Fred's fame spread and spread as three U.S. presidents met with him at the White House and even the pope had an audience with him. Despite all this, Fred remained a dedicated middle-of-the-pack—and later, as he battled cancer—back-of-the-pack runner. He immediately endorsed and promoted the many ideas that I presented to him concerning expansion of the NYRRC's educational services to runners. Together, we presented running clinics years before anyone else was doing them. More programs followed: Saturday morning group fun runs, long runs for marathon training, brochures on training for all levels of runners, the official New York City Marathon training schedule. Two programs that we developed remain very special. While he was in the hospital the first time in his battle with cancer, Fred gave the go-ahead to start our very successful City-Sports-For-Kids track-and-field program. From a humble beginning with 23 kids in our first session, we expanded to include over 1,000 boys and girls aged five to thirteen in our fun-and-fitness program each year. Fred loved to stop by and cheer the kids on. Ironically, I was at this program, started from his hospital room, when I learned that Fred had died. Through misty eyes I looked around the field and saw over 300 kids having fun at Fred's sport—running. Back in 1978, I approached Fred with the idea of starting classes for running. To our knowledge at that time, such a thing did not exist. Coached workouts were for high school and college teams and a few Elite adult runners, not for the average man and woman. "Even if one person shows up, we should try," was Fred's command. We started with 25 runners—including Fred—and now get as many as 850 runners per ten-week session; more than 3,000 students per year. Fred made it to the classes as often as he could, fighting it out with the intermediates during speed workouts. He was always ready to offer encouragement to even the slowest runner in the class. His advice to runners entering his races was the same whether it was a back-of-the-packer or a world record-holder: "Whatever you do, just try your best." All of these programs, and this book, remain as a legacy to Fred's commitment to the average runner.

Nina Kuscsik is a pioneer athlete and a leader in the women's running movement. More important, she has been a good friend for more than two decades and is my heroine. Nina has completed more than eighty marathons, which, to my knowledge, is more than any other female in the world. She was a world-class marathoner who was ahead of her time as an athlete. Until 1971, women were still trying to break the 3-hour barrier for the marathon, and Nina was one of the few athletes competing back then capable of such a feat. That year in the New York City Marathon she came within a minute of becoming the first woman in the world to race a marathon under 3 hours—Beth Bonner held off her challenge to win in 2:55:22 to Nina's 2:56:04. This was a remarkable achievement considering that the event consisted of four loops of hilly Central Park. The following spring, Nina became the first official women's finisher of the Boston Marathon, and in the fall won New York to become the first woman to win both of these prestigious races in the same year. She won New York again in 1973 to become the first athlete—male or female—to win consecutive titles in this event. Nina went on to win several marathons and lower her time to 2 hours, 50 minutes. I was there to cheer her on—again over those Central Park hills—when she set an American record for 50 miles. Nina's many contributions to running were far from restricted to her racing accomplishments. She was politically active in the sport back when the men had the say and they said that women were inferior and could harm themselves by running too far. Thus, women were banned from competing in distances longer than a mile on the track and were outlawed by Boston Marathon officials. But Nina attacked this thinking with her body and her mind, proving that women can run long and fast, and boldly challenged the rules at boring meeting after meeting with crusty AAU officials. By 1972, Boston officials finally gave in and stood by shaking their heads as Nina not only led the women to the finish line, but finished well ahead of the majority of the "superior" men. The battleground shifted that fall to the New York City Marathon, which that year was the National AAU championship. The unenlightened AAU agreed to sanction women to run that race, but ruled that they couldn't start with the men—they were to begin 10 minutes earlier. Ladies first. Nina fixed that! She spearheaded a well-publicized protest: The women sat down at the starting line and refused to budge until the men started. Nina organized a civil rights lawsuit against the AAU

Contents

PART IV: SPECIFIC TRAINING FOR RACING

PART V: MARATHON TRAINING AND RACING

PART VI: MENTAL ASPECTS OF COMPETITIVE RUNNING

PART VII: RUNNING FORM AND SHOES

PART VIII: FOOD AND DRINK FOR HEALTH AND PERFORMANCE

PART IX: THE RUNNING ENVIRONMENT

PART X: SPECIFIC COMPETITORS

PART XI: ILLNESS AND INJURY

PART XII: SPECIAL TRAINING

PART XIII: BALANCE

Introduction: The Challenge of Competitive Running

There is a competitive side to everyone's personality, whether they know it or not, or admit to it. Competition surrounds us. You compete for grades in school, for business, to get the guy or gal you favor. You have to compete for attention with your friends, family, and—in my case—with your dogs. Some people bad-mouth competition. But it's what makes the world function. Without it, life would be monopoly and monotony. With it, it's challenging and exciting. The stress of competition may improve or hinder performance at work, school, or sports. Competition can be enjoyable and rewarding, but it can also be frustrating and defeating.

Many runners don't start running with competition in mind, but the urge to compete against yourself and others eventually presents a challenge that many embrace. It becomes a goal in itself, a reason to keep running, a means to test your physical and mental limits.

Like many runners, I have a love-hate relationship with racing. I love to train for races. But as race day approaches I wonder, "Why am I doing this?" After all, I'm asking my mind to push my aging body to its very limits. As the race begins a new surge of confidence pumps my blood and drives me onward! How do I feel during a race? I hate it. I want to quit over and over. But I love it, too, so I keep going. The challenge of defeating fatigue, battling peers, and reaching my potential keeps me going forward. When finished, I look back at the discomfort I experienced as mere fleeting moments. Instead of dwelling on how much work it was, I glow with the feeling of accomplishment. I'm motivated, inspired to race once again to improve myself.

We suffer individual hardships together in races. All of us, you and me, the winner and the final finisher. We test ourselves against ourselves and against the elements and, if we wish, against each other. Competitive running is exciting. You play the edges, challenge boundaries. You see how far or how fast you can run. Taking a chance at success or failure is a heart-thumping, mind-numbing experience.

Competitive running gives your running life a focus. Circle the race date on your calendar and train for that day. Thinking of the upcoming race motivates you to get out the door and get going with your training. Competition measures progress. You set a goal and accomplish it. As racing distances and times improve, you feel proud, ready to take on new challenges in running—and in the rest of your life.

Competitive running isn't all hard work and pain. It's fun too. Races are a large social gathering, a party in running shorts. For every runner that grunts and groans, huffs and puffs in an all-out effort to win a trophy, there are hundreds behind him or her that are chatting away with friends or perfect strangers, smiling all the way from start to finish. Of course, if you want to run your best times, save the chatter until after you've crossed the finish line. For many runners the best part isn't the race itself, but the chance to relax and socialize with similar people afterward. Most events provide refreshments and a gathering area where runners can bask in their glory, brag and complain, exchange excuses (too hot, too hilly, started too fast, started too slow . . .), compare blisters, look for old friends, make new ones, or even check out the runner with the nice legs that passed you with a mile to go. It's this atmosphere of shared accomplishment that often hooks runners on racing.

In the average race, there are hundreds, perhaps thousands of runners, but only a handful of elite athletes. Most runners are just like you, battling not against the leaders but against themselves. You will have plenty of company at your pace. And remember this: The first and foremost goal of all runners in a race, from the front to the back of the pack, is the finish line. We all have that common bond.

PART 1

BASIC TRAINING

CHAPTER 1

Categories of Competitive Runners

In this book, runners are divided into categories by their race times. By indentifying your level, you can structure your own training program. The categories are used to establish guidelines for weekly mileage, long runs, and speed workouts. Sample training schedules for specific race distances, from the 5K to the marathon, are included for each category. Use the categories as a goal: Train to move up to the next category for the various race distances.

The open class (age 20–34) is based on the race time charts presented in Chapter 25. All other age groups are based on age-adjusted formulas detailed in Chapter 38. Categories are organized by percentages of the approximate world record (which represents 100 percent) for age and gender:

FIGURE 1.1	
Novice Competitor	below 50 percent (slower than Figure 1.2/1.3)
Intermediate Competitor	below 50 percent (slower than Figure 1.2/1.3)
Basic Competitor	50 percent (Figure 1.2/1.3)
Competitor	60 percent (Figure 1.4/1.5)
Advanced Competitor	65 percent (Figure 1.6/1.7)
Local Champion	75 percent (Figure 1.8/1.9)
Semi-Elite	85 percent (Figure 1.10/1.11)
Elite	90 percent

NOVICE AND INTERMEDIATE COMPETITORS (BELOW 50 PERCENT)

Runners new to competition, "casual" competitors, and anyone whose race performance level is less than 50 percent are categorized as Novice and Intermediate Competitors. Their race times would be slower than those listed in Figure 1.2 for the Basic Competitor. A good goal for these competitors is to reach the 50 percent performance level.

BASIC COMPETITOR (50 PERCENT)

This is the majority of the runners in the middle of the pack. This performance standard is achievable by most runners willing to train diligently and wisely. Over time, with proper training, this runner may be able to move up to the next category.

COMPETITOR (60 PERCENT)

Runners at this level usually finish in the top one-third of the field and may place in some local races. This is the highest level of competition most runners can achieve because of limited natural ability, or lack of time or discipline. Moving up to the next category requires discipline and hard work.

ADVANCED COMPETITOR (65 PERCENT)

The 65 percent level is the qualifying standard to be a member of our Greater New York Racing Team. The Advanced Competitor is blessed with a fair amount of talent and/or a strong work ethic. The Advanced Competitor usually places in the top 10 to 25 percent of the field in races and may win awards in local events. Moving up to the next category is a big jump. It requires a serious commitment to training combined with a strong talent base.

LOCAL CHAMPION (75 PERCENT)

This level is achieved by those with the talent, dedication, and energy to reach at least the top local class. This is a serious level of competitive training. The Local Champion usually finishes in the top five or ten of his or her age group in local races, and sometimes wins. It's a big step from here to the Semi-Elite level.

SEMI-ELITE (85 PERCENT) AND ELITE (90 PERCENT)

Since some Local Champions may aspire to the Semi-Elite level, I have included racing times for this category, but not for the Elites. I have coached several athletes who have reached the Semi-Elite performance level. These runners often win smaller races and place high in big ones. Elite Competitors are the cream of the crop, the fleet ones that run off with all the big prize money in top races around the world. I do not set specific training guidelines for Semi-Elites and Elites since most of them have individual coaches. There is little anyone can teach these runners except, perhaps, to remind them that they wouldn't be at the top if the rest of us weren't behind them!

GUIDELINES FOR THE CHARTS

Obviously, these categories are only approximate guides to help you determine what program is best for you.

A runner may qualify as one level for one race distance, and another level for a different race distance. For example, you may be categorized as a Basic Competitor for 5K and 10K distances, but because of a lack of mileage or experience be classified as a Novice or Intermediate Competitor due to slower relative race times in longer distances. Determine the appropriate category for you based upon your present fitness level, not what you used to be able to run or what you dream about running.

Interpolate if your age falls between those listed. Or, use the charts in Chapter 38 to determine your exact performance rating for each of your races.

FIGURE 1.2: MEN: BASIC COMPETITOR (50%)						
Age	5K	5M	10K	10M	Half-Marathon	Marathon
12	28:35	46:51	59:16	Not recommended for this age		
15	27:00	44:25	56:11	1:33:03	2:03:01	Not recommended
18	26:05	43:04	54:29	1:30:14	1:59:18	4:16:14
20–34	25:56	42:38	53:56	1:29:20	1:58:06	4:13:40
40	26:57	44:25	56:11	1:33:03	2:03:01	4:24:14
45	27:57	45:51	58:00	1:36:03	2:06:59	4:32:46
50	29:03	47:54	1:00:36	1:40:22	2:12:42	4:45:01
55	30:16	49:34	1:02:43	1:43:53	2:17:20	4:54:58
60	31:40	52:00	1:05:46	1:48:57	2:24:01	5:09:21
65	33:17	54:39	1:09:09	1:54:32	2:31:25	5:25:13
70	35:13	57:40	1:12:55	2:00:20	2:39:28	5:43:03

FIGURE 1.3: WOMEN: BASIC COMPETITOR (50%)						
Age	5K	5M	10K	10M	Half-Marathon	Marathon
12	31:22	51:25	1:05:02	Not recommended for this age		
15	29:40	48:46	1:01:41	1:41:49	2:15:40	Not recommended
18	28:53	47:47	1:00:26	1:39:46	2:12:56	4:40:30
20–34	28:47	47:18	59:50	1:38:46	2:11:36	4:37:42
40	30:13	49:47	1:02:59	1:43:58	2:18:32	4:52:19
45	31:31	51:59	1:05:45	1:48:32	2:24:37	5:05:10
50	32:57	54:22	1:08:46	1:53:31	2:31:16	5:19:12
55	34:35	56:59	1:12:05	1:59:00	2:38:33	5:34:35
60	36:27	59:52	1:15:44	2:05:01	2:46:35	5:51:31
65	38:38	1:03:34	1:20:20	2:12:20	2:56:30	6:11:00
70	41:17	1:07:40	1:25:20	2:19:40	3:06:40	6:31:30

FIGURE 1.4: MEN: COMPETITOR (60%)						
Age	5K	5M	10K	10M	Half-Marathon	Marathon
12	23:48	39:07	49:29	Not recommended for this age		
15	22:49	37:24	47:19	1:18:22	1:43:36	Not recommended
18	21:44	35:50	45:19	1:15:04	1:39:15	3:33:10
20–34	21:37	35:32	44:57	1:14:27	1:38:25	3:31:23
40	22:27	36:53	46:42	1:11:42	1:42:15	3:39:35
45	23:17	38:25	48:35	1:20:29	1:46:24	3:48:32
50	24:13	39:51	50:24	1:23:29	1:50:22	3:57:04
55	25:14	41:23	52:22	1:26:44	1:54:40	4:06:17
60	26:23	43:30	55:02	1:31:09	2:00:31	4:18:51
65	27:44	45:36	57:41	1:35:32	2:06:18	4:31:20
70	29:21	48:27	1:01:17	1:41:31	2:14:12	4:48:15

FIGURE 1.5: WOMEN: COMPETITOR (60%)						
Age	5K	5M	10K	10M	Half-Marathon	Marathon
12	26:08	43:00	54:24	Not recommended for this age		
15	24:43	40:47	51:35	1:25:09	1:53:27	Not recommended
18	24:05	39:45	50:17	1:23:00	1:50:35	3:53:22
20–34	24:00	39:25	49:52	1:22:18	1:49:40	3:51:25
40	25:11	41:29	52:29	1:26:38	1:55:26	4:03:36
45	26:16	43:24	54:54	1:30:37	2:00:44	4:14:46
50	27:28	45:03	56:59	1:34:04	2:05:20	4:24:29
55	28:48	47:18	59:50	1:38:46	2:11:36	4:37:42
60	30:23	49:47	1:02:52	1:43:58	2:18:32	4:52:19
65	32:12	53:09	1:07:14	1:50:58	2:27:52	5:12:01
70	34:24	56:19	1:11:14	1:57:35	2:36:40	5:30:36

FIGURE 1.6: MEN: ADVANCED COMPETITOR (65%)						
Age	5K	5M	10K	10M	Half-Marathon	Marathon
12	21:59	36:08	45:42	Not recommended for this age		
15	20:45	34:06	43:09	1:11:28	1:34:29	Not recommended
18	20:04	33:03	41:49	1:09:15	1:31:33	3:16:38
20–34	19:57	32:48	41:29	1:08:43	1:30:51	3:15:06
40	20:44	34:06	43:09	1:11:28	1:34:29	3:22:56
45	21:30	35:14	44:34	1:13:50	1:37:36	3:29:39
50	22:21	36:45	46:30	1:17:01	1:41:49	3:38:41
55	23:17	38:25	48:35	1:20:29	1:46:24	3:48:32
60	24:21	40:02	50:44	1:23:55	1:50:32	3:58:11
65	25:36	42:13	53:24	1:28:27	1:56:56	4:11:09
70	27:05	44:25	56:11	1:33:03	2:03:01	4:24:14

FIGURE 1.7: WOMEN: ADVANCED COMPETITOR (65%)						
Age	5K	5M	10K	10M	Half-Marathon	Marathon
12	24:08	39:45	50:17	Not recommended for this age		
15	22:48	37:32	47:29	1:18:23	1:44:27	Not recommended
18	22:13	36:40	46:23	1:11:05	1:42:01	3:35:16
20–34	22:08	36:23	46:02	1:15:58	1:41:14	3:33:37
40	23:12	38:09	48:15	1:19:39	1:46:08	3:43:57
45	24:15	39:45	50:17	1:23:00	1:50:35	3:53:22
50	25:21	41:52	52:57	1:27:24	1:56:28	4:05:45
55	26:36	43:48	55:24	1:31:27	2:01:51	4:17:08
60	28:02	45:55	58:05	1:35:53	2:07:46	4:29:37
65	29:42	48:46	1:01:41	1:41:49	2:15:40	4:46:17
70	31:45	51:59	1:05:45	1:48:32	2:24:37	5:05:10

FIGURE 1.8: MEN: LOCAL CHAMPION (75%)

Age	5K	5M	10K	10M	Half-Marathon	Marathon
12	19:03	31:21	39:39	Not recommended for this age		
15	17:59	29:36	37:27	1:02:02	1:22:01	Not recommended
18	17:24	28:37	36:12	59:57	1:19:16	1:50:15
20–34	17:17	28:25	35:57	59:33	1:18:44	2:49:07
40	17:58	29:36	37:27	1:02:02	1:22:01	2:56:09
45	18:38	30:40	38:48	1:04:16	1:24:58	3:02:30
50	19:21	31:49	40:15	1:06:40	1:28:08	3:09:18
55	20:11	33:10	42:00	1:09:30	1:31:57	3:17:24
60	21:07	34:40	43:51	1:12:38	1:36:01	3:26:14
65	22:11	36:26	46:06	1:16:21	1:40:56	3:36:49
70	23:29	38:35	48:45	1:20:50	1:46:54	3:49:30

FIGURE 1.9: WOMEN: LOCAL CHAMPION (75%)

Age	5K	5M	10K	10M	Half-Marathon	Marathon
12	20:54	34:17	43:21	Not recommended for this age		
15	19:47	32:37	41:16	1:08:00	1:25:30	Not recommended
18	19:16	31:45	40:09	1:06:17	1:28:15	3:06:10
20–34	19:11	31:32	39:53	1:05:51	1:27:44	3:05:08
40	20:09	33:05	41:50	1:09:04	1:32:02	3:14:12
45	21:01	34:32	43:40	1:12:06	1:36:04	3:22:42
50	21:58	36:06	45:40	1:15:24	1:40:27	3:31:59
55	23:03	37:50	47:52	1:19:01	1:45:17	3:42:10
60	24:18	40:00	50:35	1:23:30	1:51:00	3:54:40
65	25:46	42:14	53:25	1:28:11	1:57:30	4:07:57
70	27:30	45:29	57:32	1:34:58	2:06:32	4:27:01

FIGURE 1.10: MEN: SEMI-ELITE (85%)						
Age	**5K**	**5M**	**10K**	**10M**	**Half-Marathon**	**Marathon**
12	16:48	27:41	35:01	Not recommended for this age		
15	15:52	26:00	32:53	54:28	1:12:01	Not recommended
18	15:21	25:14	31:55	52:51	1:09:53	2:30:06
20–34	15:15	25:05	31:44	52:33	1:09:28	2:29:13
40	15:51	26:00	32:53	54:28	1:12:01	2:34:40
45	16:27	26:59	34:08	56:32	1:14:45	2:40:33
50	17:05	28:03	35:29	58:46	1:17:42	2:46:53
55	17:48	29:12	36:56	1:01:11	1:20:53	2:53:45
60	18:36	30:40	38:48	1:04:16	1:24:58	3:02:30
65	19:35	32:18	40:52	1:07:41	1:29:28	3:12:10
70	20:43	34:06	43:09	1:11:28	1:34:29	3:22:56

FIGURE 1.11: WOMEN: SEMI-ELITE (85%)						
Age	**5K**	**5M**	**10K**	**10M**	**Half-Marathon**	**Marathon**
12	18:27	30:19	38:21	Not recommended for this age		
15	17:27	28:50	36:29	1:00:13	1:20:15	Not recommended
18	17:00	27:59	35:24	58:26	1:17:53	2:44:21
20–34	16:56	27:49	35:12	58:06	1:17:25	2:43:21
40	17:47	29:12	36:56	1:00:58	1:21:14	2:51:25
45	18:32	30:31	38:36	1:03:43	1:24:54	2:59:10
50	19:23	31:58	40:26	1:06:44	1:28:55	3:07:38
55	20:21	33:33	42:26	1:10:03	1:33:20	3:16:57
60	21:44	35:50	45:20	1:14:49	1:39:42	3:30:23
65	22:44	37:32	47:29	1:18:23	1:44:27	3:40:24
70	24:17	40:05	50:42	1:23:42	1:51:32	3:55:20

CHAPTER 2

Key Ingredients to Successful Racing

Do you have "the right stuff?" There are several key ingredients to successful racing. You should be aware of the factors that can limit, or enhance performance. None of them stands alone as the essential factor in successful racing; many of them are dependent upon each other. Most researchers, however, agree that the trainable physiological components that are the most important determinants of distance running performance are aerobic endurance, aerobic capacity, lactate threshold, running economy, and speed. Your training then should concentrate on these areas, but not overlook other factors. Competitive running, just like good health, demands a holistic approach. Follow the guidelines in this book to improve on your areas of weakness and take advantage of your areas of strength.

Aerobic and anaerobic energy systems. When you run, energy is supplied two ways: aerobically ("with oxygen") and anaerobically ("without oxygen"). Here's how the aerobic energy system works: You breathe in oxygen which is then absorbed by the blood as it passes through the lungs. The heart then pumps oxygen-enriched blood to the muscles where energy to run is produced. The energy nutrients, stored carbohydrates (glycogen), fat, and, to a small degree, protein provide the fuel for this process. The anaerobic energy system works differently. Chemical processes (glucose metabolism) within the muscles produce a limited amount of anaerobic energy, forming lactic acid as a by-product.

How fast and how far you run determine how much each energy system contributes to fueling your muscles. At rest, all energy needs are met aerobically. But when you start running aerobically (within your training heart rate range), some energy needs are met anaerobically. The faster you run, the more you need anaerobic energy. You can't last long at fast speeds because the sudden energy demands quickly exhaust aerobic energy supplies, forcing you into "oxygen debt."

As the distance of the race gets shorter and the pace faster, the more you run anaerobically. It is estimated from various research that a 100 yard sprint is 92 percent anaerobic, 8 percent aerobic; an all-out mile is 75 percent anaerobic, 25 percent aerobic; a 5K race is 7 percent anaerobic, 93 percent aerobic; a 10K race is 3 percent anaerobic, 97 percent aerobic; and a marathon is 1 percent anaerobic, 99 percent aerobic. Think anaerobic energy doesn't amount to much for long-distance racing? First of all, if you surge during a race, charge a big hill, or kick to the finish, you'll suddenly be running more anaerobically. Further, anaerobic conditioning is important to raise your lactate threshold. At any race distance if you push the pace above this threshold you'll be forced to slow down.

So runners need to train both the aerobic and anaerobic energy systems to perform well at all distances. The shorter the race distance, the more important it is to increase the amount of anaerobic training.

Aerobic endurance. This is your body's ability to sustain prolonged running. It is primarily developed over time with plenty of mileage and long runs, as well as with lactate threshold training runs. Jogging along at very slow paces will produce some benefits, but some research suggests that running at an intensity of 70 to 80 percent of maximum heart rate results in maximum gains in aerobic endurance. Packing in the miles and "going long" produces many specific benefits. It enhances the oxygen transport system. Cardiac output, the maximum amount of blood the heart can pump per minute, becomes stronger. Lots of changes happen within the hard-working leg muscles that improve performance. In fact, it's within the muscle cells that most of the adaptations and processes of aerobic endurance occur. This includes increases in the:

- number and size of the mitochondria (where aerobic metabolism takes place) in your muscle fibers, which produces more energy for running;
- number of capillaries, the smallest blood vessels that carry oxygen and nutrients to the muscles, so you can run farther and faster;
- amount of myoglobin in your muscles, which means oxygen is transported to the mitochondria faster—and, again, you can run farther and faster;
- number of aerobic enzymes in the mitochondria, which speeds up energy production.

With aerobic endurance training the leg muscles improve their ability to conserve glycogen and metabolize fat for energy, thus improving your ability to run for longer periods of time. Muscular endurance is also improved, and slow-twitch muscle fibers are trained to enhance their aerobic power.

Aerobic capacity (VO_2max). This is the body's maximum capacity to consume, transport, and use oxygen for energy in a given time period. The higher your aerobic capacity, the faster you can run long distances with less effort. It is also known as maximal oxygen uptake (VO_2max). Runners often confuse this "max" and maximum heart rate (MHR is detailed in Chapter 47), which is the fastest your heart can beat when exercising very hard. What gets confusing is that although 100 percent of VO_2max and 100 percent of MHR are of equal effort, they're not equal at lower intensities (75 percent of MHR, for example, would be reached at about 50 percent of VO_2max), and you can (at least for a few seconds) go above 100 percent of VO_2max, but 100 percent of MHR is as far as you can go. So to minimize the maximal confusion, I'll refer to VO_2max in this text as aerobic capacity.

Aerobic capacity can be measured in a laboratory while running on a treadmill and is expressed as milliliters of oxygen per kilogram of body weight per minute (ml/kg/min). Women have a lower average aerobic capacity than men due to a combination of physiological differences between genders. Studies of Elite runners found an average value of 76.9 for men and 67.0 for women. The highest score ever recorded, to my knowledge, for distance runners was 84.4 by the late Steve Prefontaine, former American record-holder for the 5K on the track; and for the women Norway's Grete Waitz, former world record-holder for the marathon, at 73.5. Aerobic capacity declines with aging, but not too quickly if you train properly.

Aerobic capacity is largely inherited. Once you reach around 20 miles per week of training, no matter how much more you train, it can only be increased by 5 to 15 percent. Since the average healthy person's aerobic capacity is only around 30.0 to 50.0, they'll never catch up to the scores of the genetically endowed Elites. But anyone can improve, and even a little improvement makes a big difference in performance. A 1 percent increase in aerobic capacity results in approximately a 1 percent improvement for race times. How much is that? If you run 49:43 for a 10K (8:00 pace), a 1 percent improvement would drop that time to 49:13—a half-minute improvement!

Aerobic capacity can be enhanced by aerobic endurance exercise: packing in the miles and aerobic cross-training. Losing weight improves aerobic capacity, so more mileage will help here, too, by burning off more calories. Research indicates that aerobic capacity increases significantly if runners up mileage from 20 or 30 miles a week to 40 or 50. But improvements slow down after that and level off at about 80 miles a week. According to exercise physiologists, the best way to improve aerobic capacity once you've hit about 40 or 50 miles a week is with speed workouts at intensities that approach your maximum aerobic capacity. That's 5K race pace or slightly faster, pushing heart rates to 90 to 98 percent of maximum and reaching 95 to 100 percent of aerobic capacity. For this reason, the majority of workouts with our classes are run at this intensity. A continuous training run at these fast paces can't be tolerated for much more than 10 minutes. Therefore intervals at these paces are used to boost total training time for a single workout to 15 to 30 minutes. The most effective workouts are intervals of approximately 660 yards to 1 mile, or about 2 to 6 minutes.

Highly conditioned runners have higher aerobic capacities and can race at a faster pace more comfortably than less-conditioned runners. However, among runners with similar aerobic capacity scores, a runner with a higher aerobic score may lose to another runner since performance is affected by such factors as running economy, lactate threshold, muscular fitness, mental toughness, pacing, and so forth. For example, most fit marathoners perform at 75 to 80 percent of their aerobic capacity. However, some runners are able to handle a higher percentage than this. Frank Shorter, the 1972 Olympic Marathon champion, had a relatively low aerobic capacity for an Elite runner. But he had great running economy and his lactate threshold was so high he could run marathons at 85 percent of his aerobic capacity, allowing him to outrun many runners with a higher value. Some Elites may reach 90 percent of aerobic capacity in marathons. Most of us mere mortals couldn't last 10 miles at that relative intensity.

Anaerobic capacity and anaerobic endurance. Anaerobic capacity is the opposite of aerobic capacity: Now we're dealing with your limit to exercising without oxygen. You've approached your anaerobic capacity when you have to suddenly slow down due to muscle fatigue. Never experienced it? Go to a track and take off running as fast as you can. By the time you finish a lap you'll know what track runners mean when they say "The Bear jumped on my back," or "I rigged up." That's rigged as in rigor mortis, or "dead meat." Anaerobic endurance is the ability to maintain a very fast running speed even when exhausted. This reminds me, painfully, of my days as a high school half-miler.

Since fast running requires anaerobic energy, it's important to be as anaerobically fit as possible. The body's capacity to perform without sufficient oxygen is limited; but, with training, anaerobic capacity and anaerobic endurance can be improved somewhat. Short, fast interval sprints of 30 to 90 seconds will train the anaerobic system in measured doses, improving your ability to ward off "The Bear." This enables your body to limit the degree to which muscles become acidic and produces chemical agents that "buffer" the lactic acid that does build up, slightly increasing your tolerance to running in oxygen debt.

These runs push heart rates to 95 to 100 percent of max, reaching 100 to 130 percent of aerobic capacity. (You can go over 100 percent for short periods of time due to the contribution of anaerobic energy.) But this type of training is more important for sprinters and short-distance runners, like half-milers and milers, than it is to long-distance runners covering 5K to the marathon.

Plus, running that fast places a tremendous strain on the muscles, which increases risk of injury. I don't emphasize specific workouts to enhance anaerobic capacity in this text. For the average runner, it's more important to train anaerobically just enough to improve lactate threshold.

Lactate threshold. Lactate threshold (LT), sometimes referred to as anaerobic or fatigue threshold, is the pace beyond which large amounts of lactic acid begin to accumulate in the blood at a rapid rate and muscle efficiency falls off significantly with fatigue. Your muscles produce more lactate than can be cleared. This process is accompanied by a noticeable difficulty with breathing. You can't talk comfortably in complete sentences. This is called the "ventilatory threshold." Most people lump all these similar effects together and just call it LT, so I shall, too, in an effort to simplify things. Whatever you call it, training to improve it is critical because once these thresholds are exceeded, fatigue will quickly follow. LT is the key to how fast you can race for long distances.

An untrained person may reach their threshold as low as 30 to 40 percent of their aerobic capacity, an average fitness runner may reach 50 to 60 percent, and a fairly well-trained competitive runner may reach 70 percent. For all these runners there is plenty of room for improvement in their threshold and race times. A well-trained competitive runner's threshold intensity is about 80 to 85 percent of aerobic capacity (as much as 90 percent for some Elites).

There exists no definite aerobic-anaerobic borderline at which you suddenly switch from one type of energy system to the other. Rather, a continuum exists. When racing hard you need more anaerobic energy because you are running so fast you can't supply enough oxygen by normal aerobic means to fuel the working muscles. As you go into oxygen debt, lactic acid is produced faster than it can be removed. The faster you run and the higher you drive your heart rate above training range limits, the more oxygen debt you will incur, and more lactic acid is produced. At easy- and medium-paced running the lactic acid that is produced is easily whisked away by the blood before it can accumulate and interfere with muscle function. However, as the pace approaches or exceeds a certain level (your threshold), the muscles produce more lactic acid than the body can remove. It accumulates in the muscles, forcing you to slow down. For most runners LT would be about 85 to 92 percent of maximum heart rate.

All racing includes some aerobic and some anaerobic running. When racing 5Ks and 10Ks, you run at or slightly above your LT—but fortunately you don't have to run for long. Half-marathon pace is close to your LT, and marathon intensity is mostly slightly below it. For these long-distance races, having a high LT is critical to being able to handle a strong pace for the duration of the event.

Intense speed training at faster than race pace will challenge the anaerobic system and improve your threshold. It can be raised, however, more safely at less intense speeds; this allows for a greater volume of work. Physiologists recommend that you train at or slightly faster than LT pace in order to improve it, enabling you to run faster and farther before fatigue sets in—whether it be for a 5K or a marathon. LT is approximately 15K to half-marathon pace, or about 20 seconds slower than 10K pace for most trained runners. Speed training at this threshold pace, especially tempo runs, will help train you to handle this intense pace. Weight training may help, too. A study at the University of Maryland demonstrated a 12 percent increase in LT with a strength training program.

Running economy and form. Running economy is how efficiently you use oxygen when running at a given pace. If you have the same aerobic capacity as another runner but are also the hard-earned owner of a superior running economy, you will most likely defeat that opponent in races. That's because you run along at a lower percentage of your aerobic capacity. Here are the advantages: You will feel more comfortable maintaining the same pace as the less efficient runner; and for the same effort you can run a faster pace. Miles and miles of running make you a more efficient runner. The best way to sharpen running economy according to researchers is with short, fast running (faster than 5K pace) with track intervals and steep-hill repeats. These workouts help you learn to minimize wasted motion with poor running form, recruit fast-twitch fibers, and feel comfortable at fast speeds. As a result, you'll save energy in races. Research shows that a runner's economy may be good on the flats, but not on uphills or downhills. Practicing ups and downs will make you more efficient here, too. Weight training improves the strength of key muscle groups, thus less effort is required to run.

Muscular fitness. Improved muscular strength, power, and endurance enhance running economy, lactate threshold, resistance to muscle fatigue, and speed, and minimize injury. Muscular fitness is improved in general with weight training and more specifically with strength training runs such as hill training and fast intervals. See Chapter 43 for a detailed description of muscular fitness.

Fast-twitch and slow-twitch muscle fibers. All muscle fibers tend towards one of two types, which actually are a continuum rather than two separate fibers. You inherit a certain ratio of fast- to slow-twitch fibers. Fast-twitch fibers (there's a type A—the most important—and a type B) contract rapidly and exhaust glycogen quickly during fast sprinting. The more of these fibers you have, the faster you can run. World-class sprinters have a predominance of fast-twitch fibers. If you lack leg speed, it is largely because you weren't born with enough of them. Slow-twitch fibers, the stuff Elite marathoners are made of, are the key to aerobic endurance since with training these fibers can work for long periods of time without tiring. If you lack endurance, it is largely because you weren't born with enough of these fibers. A few fast-twitch runners, however, have excelled in the marathon, and a few slow-twitch runners have been successful sprinters. But, for most people, your muscle fibers largely determine how fast you can be.

For the general population, and the average runner, slow-twitch fibers make up about 45 to 55 percent of the total. Top runners with approximately 70 percent slow-twitch and 30 percent fast-twitch fibers are usually better at the 5K to 10K. Most top marathoners have a higher percentage of slow-twitch fibers: 80 to 90 percent. Unfortunately, you can't change the ratio you were born with, but you can improve the capabilities of what you've got to a certain degree with training. As a result, you'll be able to improve performance.

The endurance capabilities of slow-twitch fibers are enhanced with easy- to moderate-paced training runs, especially long runs, since these are the fibers that are recruited most often during low-intensity training. But fast-twitch fibers are recruited some, too, and are increasingly called into action as slow-twitch fibers become fatigued. This is both good and bad news. On the good side, distance running can improve the endurance capabilities of fast-twitch fibers somewhat. You'll be able to run slow, longer. This is important even to a slow-twitcher. And it offers hope to those fast-twitchers who have the muscles of a sprinter but the heart of a marathoner. If that's you, don't give up. With proper training you can still enjoy finishing a marathon. But you'll finish behind a whole bunch of those slow-twitch folks. Your best bet at maximizing performances as a distance runner probably lies in the 5K and under distances. Now, the bad news about the effects of distance running on fast-twitch fibers: Too much long, slow distance running results in loss of the effectiveness of what fast-twitch fibers you were born with. Running slow too often will make you slower.

On one hand, you won't excel at long distances if you have too many fast-twitch fibers because your muscles will fatigue easily. On the other, you need enough fast-twitch fibers to be able to run those distances fast, and to kick at the end of races. Ideally, distance runners are born with mostly slow-twitch fibers along with enough of the fast-twitch stuff so they can race fast over long distances.

Here's more good news. Whether you have a higher than average fast-twitch fiber count, or if you were born to be a long, slow, keep-plugging-away runner, you can retain and improve the efficiency of your fast-twitch fibers, and your speed, somewhat. With speed training you'll be able to switch into faster gears, but you're still not going to outsprint the sprinters. But then they can't outsprint you if you've left them a mile behind down the road.

Some final bad news here: At any age, but more for masters runners, fast-twitch fibers become less effective with lack of use. Use it or lose it. That's why I recommend at least some type of speed training year-round.

Sprint speed. Sudden, explosive bursts of speed, whether for a midrace surge or a finishing kick, is dependent upon anaerobic energy, your percentage of fast-twitch muscle fibers, muscular strength and power, and coordinated running form. Although heredity determines whether you can be really fast or not, everyone can improve their speed with specific speed training.

Flexibility. Improvements here minimize injury and contribute to smoother, longer strides.

Injury and illness prevention. Perhaps the single greatest cause of improvement among runners is remaining injury-free long enough to attain consistent training. Running improves immunity to illness, but overtraining lowers it.

Fuel and hydration. After 60 to 90 minutes of running, you begin to deplete glycogen supplies—carbohydrates stored in muscles that are the critical fuel for long-distance racing. Fueling up with carbs before and during running along with long training runs helps you avoid "hitting the Wall" where you run low on glycogen. Lack of fuel prior to running can cause mental fatigue. Dehydration not only limits performance, it can be life-threatening.

Body weight. Runners need a light chassis and strong engine for optimal performance. But you do need sufficient weight and body fat to be healthy.

Age. You slow down with aging and must accept that fact. However, you can greatly minimize this slowing process with proper training.

Adjusting for weather. Heat, humidity, cold, wind, and more. Mother Nature presents obstacles to performance.

Mental fitness. Train the mind as well as the body if you want to reach your potential.

Strategy. Whether racing against yourself, the course, or competitors, a successful race requires a well-prepared plan of action.

Goals and motivation. To succeed, you need realistic, challenging goals and the motivation to train to meet those goals.

Heredity. To be a great runner, pick the right parents. That doesn't necessarily mean that if your parents were either great or poor athletes you will follow suit. But if one or both of your parents were athletically gifted, your chances of being athletic are increased. A nonathletic parent(s) may have the genetic ability to be a good athlete but never took advantage of it. You also have to inherit the right genes for your sport. The height, weight, and skills necessary for basketball or football aren't of much value in competitive running.

Body type affects weight, and thus performance. If you were given genes to be tall, big-boned, or for a "well-cushioned" body type, you weigh too much to excel at running. You can run well for your weight, and use running to control your weight—but your ability is hindered by genetics. I remind myself of this when dragging my 6′1″, 165- to 170-pound body up hills next to my shorter, featherweight competitors. But then I wasn't given enough height or weight to excel at basketball either.

Some of us are naturally strong, some much weaker; some are born to be speedier, some much slower. Your heart-lung machine is also inherited. The ability to exercise aerobically and anaerobically is greatly affected by genetics. Fortunately, all of us can improve in these areas with proper training. Certain biomechanical features and weaknesses that may limit performance are also inherited. Examples: a leg that is longer than the other, weak arches, and the tendency to overpronate.

Few of us are born to be natural Elite runners. You can achieve performances—despite genetic imperfections—that will satisfy you and amaze your competitors. While genetics is important, what you do with what talent you were given may be even more important. I outrace lots of more naturally talented runners and you can, too. How? Superior training—both physical and mental.

PUTTING IT ALL TOGETHER: THE TRAINING PROGRAM

How fast you can race isn't primarily dependent on how fast you can run over short distances. Innate speed is handy to have certainly, but the key to faster race times is the ability to hold a speed slower than all-out for long distances. Possessing the ability to do this is the key ingredient to successful racing. But how do you put together all the ingredients discussed above in order to achieve racing success? You're holding that key ingredient in your hands. Train wisely for successful performance.

Don't just go for a run each day—with the distance dependent upon your time constraints, and the pace on your mood. How far, fast, and often you run should be determined in advance with a well-thought-out training schedule. The schedule should include at least a general progression of training phases—base, strengthening, sharpening, and tapering—as discussed in Chapter 14.

A mix of these four running intensity zones is essential to optimal performance:

- *Aerobic endurance training* includes a balanced amount of short, medium, and long runs at 60 to

80 percent of maximum heart rate. This primarily improves overall aerobic and muscular endurance. These runs are essential for all race distances.

- *Lactate threshold training* is primarily at a pace slightly slower than 10K race pace (15K to half-marathon pace). Tempo runs are the most effective way to improve lactate threshold. These workouts are particularly important for half-marathon and marathon training, but still valuable for 5Ks and 10Ks.
- *Aerobic capacity training* is primarily at 3K to 5K race pace. Interval, fartlek, and long-hills training at this pace is the most effective way to improve aerobic capacity. These workouts are particularly important for 5K and 10K training, but still valuable for half-marathons and marathons.
- *Anaerobic training* is primarily at much faster than 5K pace. Short, fast intervals, hard fartlek bursts, and short hill repeats are the most effective ways to improve anaerobic fitness, speed, muscular strength and power, efficiency of fast-twitch fibers, and running economy. These workouts are mostly used when training for distances of 5K and less.

In summary, the right combination of the key types of training will help you, as much as possible, get "the right stuff."

CHAPTER 3

Basic Training Principles

Training methods are based on established principles. Some are determined by physiological research. Others come from personal experiences of runners and coaches. Each runner "borrows" hints from this or that person and processes them through trial and error. The result is different applications of the same basic knowledge. We are greatly indebted to those pioneer coaches, runners, and scientists who contributed to the resource bank we draw on. Other books or other coaches may tell you to train differently—they are neither right nor wrong. They simply have interpreted the basic training principles in a different way.

The following ten principles form the backbone of this book:

PRINCIPLE #1: BASE TRAINING AND SHARPENING

When you construct a house, you start with the base and build on that. The same is true of competitive running. First build a base of aerobic endurance. Do this by progressively increasing weekly mileage, and then, sharpening with speed training to peak for key races. Then recover and rebuild with base training. The better the base, the harder you can work as you sharpen for races, and the more likely you are to meet performance goals.

PRINCIPLE #2: DON'T OVERTRAIN: ADAPTATION TO PROGRESSIVE TRAINING

If the training load remains the same over a period of time, performance will stagnate. Fortunately, the body is a remarkable organism and will surprise you in its ability to get stronger in order to adapt to progressive increases in training. But, it can also surprise you by breaking down if you overstress it. The work load shouldn't be too little or too much. It must be intense enough and regular enough to promote adaptation to a higher level of racing fitness—the "training effect." If the stress is nearly equal to your body's capacity to handle the work, your body will adapt by increasing its capacity. As fitness improves, your body will be able to handle a greater training load (and race intensity) with the same effort. On the other hand, if the stress is too much (overtraining), you overtax the adaptation system, causing fatigue, injury, burnout, or poor performance.

This principle is sometimes incorrectly translated by runners and coaches as "no pain, no gain." Instead, "train, don't strain" is the rule to follow. Train hard enough to improve, but don't strain so much that you defeat the improvement. More—faster and longer—isn't always better. You will need to work your heart, lungs, and muscles harder by increasing pace or distance—but not necessarily both. Progressively increase the stress load on the body, but not by excessive amounts. Overload gently. Follow the 5 & 10 rule: never increase mileage or speed by more than 10 percent, preferably 5 percent, from one week to the next, or one month to the next.

It's amazing how much you can progress if you allow for gradual training increases. I remember when my goal was to finish a 2-mile race in high school; by my senior year I was the county champion. Once my greatest dream was to run under a 6-minute-per-mile pace for 5K; a few years later, I could run that pace and faster for the marathon. My goal after finishing my first marathon was to break 3:30 to qualify for the Boston Marathon; a few years later I ran almost an hour faster than that. Those results didn't happen overnight. I trained following the principle of progressive training.

By pushing themselves progressively farther and faster, runners of all levels can reach performances they never dreamed possible. If I can improve that much with limited natural talent, why can't you improve dramatically, too? You can, but you need to take it one step at a time.

PRINCIPLE #3: RECOVERY—THE HARD-EASY METHOD

In daily training, sandwich hard days with easy ones. Hard days are runs that are faster or longer than usual—brisk runs, speed training, long runs, and races. Easy days are short or medium runs over not too difficult courses at a comfortable, conversational pace. What is easy for one runner may be difficult for another. It may take longer to recover after certain runs. Perhaps you ran a workout too hard, the course was unusually hilly, it was a very hot day, or you were short on sleep and long on stress. Further, the older we get, the longer it takes to recover. Many runners may be wise to follow the "hard-easy-easy" system!

It usually takes forty-eight hours to recover from hard runs, and seventy-two hours or more from races. Rest (taper) before a race, and slowly rebuild afterward. A common mistake is to rush back into training, especially if you raced extremely well or poorly. Either extreme naturally drives runners to immediately work harder—to get even better or to reclaim fitness. Whoa! Listen to reason, not emotion. First recover, then gradually increase training intensity. Take it easy for a few days after short races; a few weeks after a marathon.

The hard-easy concept is perhaps the most difficult principle to teach in our classes. Runners will race on Sunday, do a brisk run Monday while they're still on a high, and then on Tuesday wonder why they are outsprinted by the grandmas in our group. Also, don't be a "weekend warrior." The average working person must be careful not to squeeze in hard days on both Saturday and Sunday—the result can be total fatigue by Monday or Tuesday, or worse, an injury. A common error: racing Saturday and then doing a long run on Sunday to take advantage of the full weekend. Folks, you can't have it all.

Sometimes your body tricks you. You may feel very strong the day after a hard workout or race and, pumped up from the excitement of doing well. You may be tempted to run hard again. Don't! You will pay for it the next day. Beware of the "two-day lag": The first day after an intense run leaves you feeling high and invincible, the second day your body finally crashes as the principles of physiology catch up. My toughest training day is always two days after a hard effort. If you ignore the principle of recovery, you could dig yourself into a very deep hole.

Some runners take a full week of recovery training each month. After three weeks of vigorous running, they cut mileage by 25 to 50 percent and refrain from speed training and long runs for the week. This system is especially good for the runner who has a tendency to overtrain, since it has its own built-in physical and mental relief.

The human body responds best to the stress of exercise if allowed to recover and adapt. Stress applied on top of stress equals breakdown; stress followed by recovery equals progress. If sufficient recovery does not occur, then the body's resources are depleted. Runners at all levels may wisely choose to recover from strenuous workouts with a day off or with "active rest" the following day (or days) rather than an easy run. Active rest could be an exercise such as walking or swimming that is gentle to the musculoskeletal system.

The basic rule here is *listen to your body* and recognize its warning signs—sore muscles, aches and pain, and fatigue. Take a few days off when your body complains. Do not run the same pace or number of miles every day. Hard-easy training involves mixing the distance and speed of your runs in such a way as to induce the right amount of stress and recovery that will benefit your running. Follow this simple formula: Vigorous exercise plus rest equals improved fitness.

PRINCIPLE #4: SPECIFICITY OF TRAINING

The best way to train your body for running is by running. No matter how many hours you spend swimming, biking, or lifting weights, you still won't use the same muscles the same way as you do in running. And you need to train specifically for upcoming races to adapt to the specific stresses you will encounter on race day. These include the race distance, terrain, and weather.

The longer the race, the more important it is to train with higher weekly mileage and longer single runs. Twenty or 30 miles a week with long runs of 10 miles may be sufficient for a 10K runner, for example, but the specific demands of the marathon would require perhaps 40 miles a week or more with long runs of 20 miles or more.

To perform your best, do specific speed training at race pace or faster so that you can better handle your goal race pace. The

5K runner would do specific training faster than the 10K runner, since, obviously, the required pace is quicker. On the other extreme, marathoners don't need to run workouts as fast as 5K runners and should do some training at their specific marathon pace (although they'll benefit from speed training at 5K to 10K pace). Typically, speed training for short races involves workouts run at a faster pace, over a shorter distance than for longer races. For example, eight or more quarter-miles at an intense pace are the staple of a 5K runner's training; whereas a marathoner's key workout may be four to five times a mile at 5K to 10K pace, or a 10- to 13-mile run at marathon pace.

Train at specific speed training paces to produce specific physiological improvements. For example: slightly slower than 10K pace to raise your lactate threshold, about 5K pace to boost aerobic capacity, and faster than 5K pace to improve running economy and leg speed.

Prepare for the lay of the land, too. Get ready for a hilly race by running over hilly terrain a few times a week at your normal training pace. Add some speed workouts on hills (repeats, fartlek). Include hills similar to those you'll face on race day. If possible, train over the hills you'll be racing. Train specifically also for a flat, fast course on a track or road. The race pace may be quicker than you're used to, so sharpen with short, fast runs on flat surfaces. Include long intervals of 1 to 2 miles, and tempo runs of 3 to 4 miles over flat terrain to get used to holding a steady, quick pace. Also, train specifically to prepare for racing in the heat, cold, and at altitude.

PRINCIPLE #5: CONSISTENCY OF TRAINING

Base training is based on steady, *consistent* work. Constant training—fifty-two weeks a year—is necessary to be a successful competitive runner, although you don't need to train at high levels year-round. You run when it's hot or cold, when you're high or low, alone or with friends, when aiming for a big race or when you've reached your goal.

Train consistently all week, too—not just on Saturday and Sunday. Even small amounts of training on a regular basis are better than sporadic running followed by days of inactivity. Develop a minimal fitness base—anywhere from 50 to 75 percent of your peak mileage—and don't fall below it except in case of injury or illness. For example, if you normally build to 50 miles a week for the marathon, don't fall below a base of 25 to 35 miles a week during lulls in training. If you do, it will be harder to build back up. Train consistently all year in order to grow stronger year after year.

Consistency requires discipline. Force yourself out the door. A top-level runner usually puts in some mileage every day; less serious competitors run four to six days a week. It is easy to take a day off when things get hectic. A day or two off here and there won't hurt, but skipping workouts too often will. Instead of not running at all, shorten runs when faced with obstacles; force yourself to do a minimal amount to keep the habit of consistency alive. Schedule, in advance, hard training days and don't skip them—and it sure is more tempting to pass on them than easy days.

To succeed as a competitive runner, you need to be a little compulsive about getting in your daily run. If possible, schedule runs for the same time every day; make it an important appointment with yourself. Set weekly goals, and stick with them. In 1978, I ran exactly 100 miles each week for twelve consecutive weeks of base work. If I needed a few miles before midnight at the end of the week to hit this goal, out I went into the dark; if I hit my 100-mile mark while still on the run, I'd walk home from there. This consistency may seem a bit fanatical, but it worked for me. After lowering the mileage and sharpening with quality speed training, I enjoyed two months of racing times I never dreamed I could accomplish—including a 30K race at 5:30 pace. As I turned fifty and made a comeback, I ran exactly 3,000 miles for the year. That's about 60 miles a week. All but a handful of those training weeks were within 5 to 10 miles of that average. I took off only one day per month (although less experienced runners should take more), never two days in a row. Consistency paid off once again as my age-adjusted times were nearly equal to my peak times twenty years earlier.

Set weekly mileage ranges to help with being consistent. For example, run not less than 30 miles in a single week, but not more than 40; that would mean 35 miles on the average. Be consistent with speed training, too. Students that show up regularly for our speed classes outperform those that don't in local races. Be compulsive, but be practical. If your body asks for a day or more off—take it. But only sound reasons like severe physical fatigue, injury, or illness should excuse you. A diary helps here. Logging your training each day will force you to be consistent.

PRINCIPLE #6: DIMINISHING RETURNS AND REVERSIBILITY OF TRAINING

As you build mileage or increase speed training, you often see significant results: Workouts are better and race times may improve significantly. But adding more and more mileage or more and harder speed training will not result in continued benefits at the same rate. You'll still improve with progressive increases in training, but the returns will be at a diminished rate.

What happens when you do less work? Fortunately, it takes less work to maintain a level of fitness than it took to achieve it. Unfortunately, your body builds fitness slowly and loses it quickly. It takes only a few weeks to lose most of the adaptation to training that you have worked so hard to achieve if you stop, or sharply curtail training. It takes less time to get out of shape than to get in shape. If you stop exercising completely, most or all of your conditioning will be lost in five to ten weeks. You will have detrained. Use it or lose it!

PRINCIPLE #7: INDIVIDUALITY AND FLEXIBILITY OF TRAINING

Not everyone has the same capacity to adapt to a specific training program. Genetically determined physical capacities make each runner unique in terms of how he or she will adapt to training. All exercise must be flexible and adapted to the specific needs of the individual. Find out what training routines work best for you. Not every method works equally well on all people. A coach or a book shouldn't establish a single training schedule for all runners. Each of us has personal likes and dislikes, strengths and weaknesses. Your ability level and goals are unique to you. We are all different. Yet the basic training principles discussed here apply to all of us. You determine how to best adapt them for your individual needs, which will change as you develop as a competitive runner. That's why the training programs detailed in this book are samples.

Find out through experience what training and racing strategies work best. Some runners thrive on a steady diet of high mileage and weekly 20-milers, while others would break down following this program. They may do best with low mileage and more speed training. Some may benefit most from 1-mile speed workouts, while others perform better by doing shorter, faster quarters. How often you can race, and how much recovery time you need varies from one individual to another.

Learn to "go with your strengths." Try to improve in the areas you have less talent in, such as speed or endurance, but don't waste a lot of time on them if you will get better results and enjoy running more by maximizing your natural ability in other areas. So don't force yourself to run high-mileage, for example, if you're a fast-twitch speedy type that'll improve most with a low-mileage, high-intensity program.

Be flexible with your training. Adapt to weather conditions, available facilities, your health, and family and work responsibilities. Alter training to fit your needs—be stubborn about getting in your runs, but practical.

PRINCIPLE #8: PATIENCE AND EXPERIENCE

Fast race times will not come overnight. For the competitive runner, success is measured in months and years, not days and weeks. Each day you put more miles in the bank and build for the future. With experience, you become a wise and efficient competitor. You *experience* your first marathon, for example, then *race* the next. Important lessons have to be learned: dressing for races, drinking and fueling on the run, handling heat and cold, pacing and race strategy. No matter how many times you have read what to do in this book, until you have experienced it and learned by doing—possibly learned through error—you won't be a skilled competitor. You learn from every race you run—even after you've raced for over thirty years like myself. The more races you log in your diary, the more knowledgeable you will be. Be patient as you progress slowly, but steadily.

PRINCIPLE #9: MODERATION AND BALANCE

Too much of anything—food, drink, work, book writing, sex, running—isn't good. Be moderate in your approach to life. Balancing the major stresses—work, school, family, friends—with running is as important as balancing the individual parts of your training program.

PRINCIPLE #10: EXTENDED GOALS

Competitive running offers never-ending challenges. There always seem to be new goals—longer distances to conquer or more minutes and seconds to knock off the clock. Even as we slow with age, we are presented with new opportunities as we move into new age classifications, with new standards of excellence. Our sport gives us a tremendous incentive to keep improving—the extended goal. No matter how far or fast you run a race, once it is over you can plan to improve on that effort.

CHAPTER 4

The Warm-up and Cool-Down

Many runners lace up their running shoes and head out the door full-speed. "Don't have time for a warm-up," they say. When returning, they often don't stretch tired muscles, or even let their heart rates gradually lower. Follow the "1-2-3 approach" to exercise: warm-up, peak work, cool-down. Peak work includes not only running but also other aerobic exercise and weight training. Treat the warm-up and cool-down as part of a three-step process that improves the quality of runs, helps avoid injury, and reduces muscle soreness after hard training runs.

THE WARM-UP

Warm-ups let your body gradually adjust to exercise, preparing it for harder work to come and actually making that work easier. Warming up allows heart and breathing rates to gradually make the transition from resting state to vigorous exercise, increases blood flow to the heart, brings more oxygen and blood to the muscles, and raises body temperature. The warm-up improves muscle efficiency, increases the speed of nerve impulses which improves coordination, and increases muscular elasticity as well as the flexibility of connective tissue. Not only does a good warm-up help prevent muscle strains, but research from the University of Massachusetts has shown that warm-up runs also help prevent the microscopic damage to muscles that causes muscle soreness. This means you will recover more quickly from a hard workout so you can resume hard training sooner.

Ideally, the warm-up consists of three steps:

Relaxation. Try beginning with a few minutes of relaxation exercises (Chapter 44) to loosen up muscles that are tense.

Stretching. Five to ten minutes of gentle limbering and stretching prepare muscles and connective tissue for exercise. Many experts suggest only stretching after running, since muscles should be "heated up" to allow a more thorough, safe stretching program. Others recommend running slowly for at least 5 to 15 minutes to warm muscles, then stretching prior to continuing the workout. Here's a compromise: Bike or walk before stretching to warm muscles, then complete a cardiorespiratory warm-up before running.

Cardiorespiratory warm-up. It may be okay to skip the prerun relaxation and stretch, but this part is essential. This phase, lasting at least 5 to 15 minutes, is critical since it actually warms the body. Gradually it increases your resting heart rate to training range and increases body temperature by 1 or 2 degrees Celsius to produce sweating. A 1-degree increase in muscle temperature during warm-ups makes muscles 13 percent more efficient. A warm muscle contracts more forcefully and relaxes more quickly, minimizing injury while enhancing speed and strength.

After walking briskly (or riding a stationary bike) for 5 to 15 minutes, start running slowly, gradually increasing pace for 5 to 10 minutes until leveling off at a steady rate. Please note: If I can't get you to do a walking warm-up before you run, then at least start runs at a slow pace. You may require a longer warm-up to feel loose on a cold day than on a hot day. Also, early-morning athletes may require a longer warm-up than those who have been up and moving for part of the day.

You can compare your warm-up to warming up a car on a cold day. You don't just jump into your car, start it, and take off at 60 miles an hour down the highway. Well, you could, but it would strain the engine and you wouldn't have a very efficient ride. Let it warm up for a few minutes, then start off gradually before reaching cruising speed. Most of us treat our car engine better than ourselves. Respect your body; warm it up gently prior to vigorous exercise.

THE COOL-DOWN

Many runners can't resist the urge to sprint to the finish of the run and then head for the easy chair or couch to recover. Sorry, your body needs to cool down first and then you can hang out. The cool-down is the warm-up in reverse and is equally important. Stopping an activity abruptly may cause the pooling of blood in your extremities and the slowing of waste product removal in your system. It may also cause cramps, soreness, dizziness, or an abnormal strain on your heart. Never sit immediately or enter a warm shower or sauna without first properly cooling down.

The purpose of the cool-down is to help your body return to its pre-exercise level. Cooling down helps your heart rate and breathing return to normal and minimize muscle soreness and tightness. Why do you think they walk prize racehorses after workouts and races? Take care of your prize body, too.

After your run or other aerobic workout, keep moving at a slow pace for at least 5 to 10 minutes. Walking slowly is usually the best cardiorespiratory cool-down. The important thing is to keep moving around so that blood is pumped from the extremities, especially the legs, back into the central circulatory system. Before moving on to stretching, you should be breathing normally and feel relaxed; your heart rate should be within twenty beats of your prerun level. If not, walk around some more until you have properly recovered from the workout.

Your postrun stretching routine should last 10 to 15 minutes (or more). You may repeat the same exercises that you do during the warm-up, or add others. See Chapter 44 for recommended stretches. Ideally, end with relaxation exercises. Properly done, the cool-down routine should leave you feeling very relaxed and energized instead of fatigued. At the completion of it you should no longer be sweating; heart rate should be close to normal and muscles fully relaxed.

WARMING UP AND COOLING DOWN FOR HARD RUNS

Refer to Chapters 8 and 28 for specific guidelines for speed training and races.

CHAPTER 5

Training Pace

How fast should you run in daily training? Fast enough to gain fitness, but slow enough for your run to be safe, comfortable, and enjoyable. It's the easy- and moderate-paced runs that build the base upon which you can sharpen for races with faster speedwork. The aerobic endurance benefits detailed in Chapter 2 are primarily a function of how much time you spend running, not how fast you run. Too many runners train at a pace faster than necessary, leaving them prone to injury, fatigue, and burnout, and unable to properly recover from previous speed sessions, long runs, or races.

The simplest way to make sure you're training at the appropriate pace is to *listen to your body.* That is, run according to how you feel. You should be able to carry on a conversation as you run, or hum a tune if you run alone. If you can say a few words, but not full, coherent sentences you are running harder than necessary. You haven't passed the "talk test." Monitor your "perceived exertion." If you're getting breathless, tired, or are feeling overheated or uncomfortable, slow to a more moderate pace.

Many runners err on the too fast side: They strain to run and strain to talk. Train, don't strain. If you are running with friends make sure the pace is slow enough that you can chat back and forth. After all, why bother to run with others if you can't socialize? The formula here is simple: Run fast enough for perspiration, but slow enough for conversation. Many runners monitor training intensity by heart rate (see Chapter 47).

Most runners monitor training by pace per mile. You should

have a flexible range for your training pace: from easy to brisk. I use three types of training paces:

Brisk Pace:	10K race pace + 1 minute (or 5K race pace + 1 min, 15 sec).
Base Pace:	10K race pace + 1½ minutes (or 5K race pace + 1 min, 45 sec).
Easy Pace:	10K race pace + 2 minutes (or 5K race pace + 2 min, 15 sec).

These pace formulas are only estimates. They should be determined by your *present* fitness level for a 5K or 10K race. Be honest! These formulas are most accurate for experienced, fit competitors with an adequate mileage base. If your paces seem too easy based on these formulas, perhaps you can race faster: Taper for your next race and give it a good effort. On the other hand, if training paces based on these formulas seem too hard, perhaps you've overestimated your fitness level (or mismeasured your training routes).

Base pace is the comfortable training pace you naturally settle into for a typical unstructured run. This pace should be the target for most runs since some research indicates it is the best intensity for improving aerobic fitness. It equals about 70 to 75 percent of maximum heart rate and is a conversational pace. My 10K race pace is about 6:15 per mile, thus my base pace is approximately 7:45 per mile (closer to 8:00 on my hilly courses).

Brisk pace is the estimated fastest pace you can run at and still stay within your training heart rate range. You'll be at approximately 80 percent of maximum heart rate and may not be able to talk comfortably in full sentences. This is too fast for a daily pace. It's only a notch below tempo pace. Do not run this fast on consecutive days, the day before or after hard runs, or too frequently. One or two brisk-paced runs of 30 minutes to an hour each week will help keep you fit if you're not doing regular speed training or if your mileage is low. With a 10K race pace of 6:15 per mile, my brisk pace is about 7:15 per mile.

Easy pace is recovery running. It equals approximately 60 to 70 percent of maximum heart rate. Use these runs the day after hard workouts and races, the day before races, and whenever you're tired and want to take it real easy. Usually these are short runs of 3 to 5 miles, although some runners may do long runs at this pace. On easy pace days I dawdle along at 8:15 per mile (sometimes as slow as 9:00), two minutes slower than 10K race pace.

Remember, these are *approximate* pace goals based on your present fitness level. As you become more fit, the pace of your training runs will naturally become a little faster. On the other hand, cut back training paces if you lose fitness. Also adjust for age-related slowdown. Some twenty years ago my base pace was about 6:45 per mile. But now, regrettably, with the same effort I train (and race) a minute per mile slower.

If running high mileage, you may benefit from doing most runs at your easy pace. However, running too slowly too often—for whatever reason—can lead to bad running form habits and a feeling of sluggishness. Experienced, fast runners sometimes train a little faster than these guidelines for brisk runs—especially if training for short races or doing low mileage. They feel lighter on their feet and peppier. Even speedsters need to exercise caution; don't leave your race on the training paths. Faster isn't always better.

Ideally, start runs at your easy pace and then settle into your even, comfortable base pace. Most veteran runners have a good idea of what their pace-per-mile should be and how their body feels at that effort—in terms of heart rate, talk test, and perceived exertion. When in doubt, go by how you feel rather than stubbornly trying to stick to a certain pace. Of course hills, wind, heat, fatigue, slippery footing, and other factors may require you to slow the pace in order to maintain the same effort.

If you know some of the mile markers along the course you can check your pace—just like you would in a race. Or, check it for a mile or two at the local track. If you run the same course or courses regularly and know the approximate distance, you can establish landmarks along the way that let you know if you are running faster or slower than usual, or if you are pacing evenly.

I suggest you do as I do, learn to pace by all of the methods described. Effective monitoring of intensity requires a simultaneous monitoring of heart rate, subjective feeling, and pace. When in doubt, slow down the pace, take it easy. Keep training days for training and racing days for racing.

FIGURE 5.1: TRAINING PACE GUIDE

10K Race Time (Minutes: Seconds)	10K Race Pace	Brisk Pace (10K + 1 Min)	Base Pace (10K + 1½ Min)	Easy Pace (10K + 2 Min)
32:00	5:09	6:09	6:39	7:09
32:30	5:14	6:14	6:44	7:14
33:00	5:19	6:19	6:49	7:19
33:30	5:24	6:24	6:54	7:24
34:00	5:29	6:29	6:59	7:29
34:30	5:33	6:33	7:03	7:33
35:00	5:38	6:38	7:08	7:38
35:30	5:43	6:43	7:13	7:43
36:00	5:48	6:48	7:18	7:48
36:30	5:53	6:53	7:23	7:53
37:00	5:58	6:58	7:28	7:58
37:30	6:02	7:02	7:32	8:02
38:00	6:07	7:07	7:37	8:07
38:30	6:12	7:12	7:42	8:12
39:00	6:17	7:17	7:47	8:17
39:30	6:22	7:22	7:52	8:22
40:00	6:27	7:27	7:57	8:27
40:30	6:31	7:31	8:01	8:31
41:00	6:36	7:36	8:06	8:36
41:30	6:41	7:41	8:11	8:41
42:00	6:46	7:46	8:16	8:46
42:30	6:51	7:51	8:21	8:51
43:00	6:56	7:56	8:26	8:56
43:30	7:00	8:00	8:30	9:00
44:00	7:05	8:05	8:35	9:05
44:30	7:10	8:10	8:40	9:10
45:00	7:15	8:15	8:45	9:15
45:30	7:20	8:20	8:50	9:20
46:00	7:25	8:25	8:55	9:25
46:30	7:29	8:29	8:59	9:29
47:00	7:34	8:34	9:04	9:34
47:30	7:39	8:39	9:09	9:39
48:00	7:44	8:44	9:14	9:44
48:30	7:49	8:49	9:19	9:49
49:00	7:54	8:54	9:24	9:54
49:30	7:58	8:58	9:28	9:58
50:00	8:03	9:03	9:33	10:03
50:30	8:08	9:08	9:38	10:08
51:00	8:13	9:13	9:43	10:13

FIGURE 5.1: TRAINING PACE GUIDE (continued)

10K Race Time (Minutes: Seconds)	10K Race Pace	Brisk Pace (10K + 1 Min)	Base Pace (10K + 1½ Min)	Easy Pace (10K + 2 Min)
51:30	8:18	9:18	9:48	10:18
52:00	8:23	9:23	9:53	10:23
52:30	8:27	9:27	9:57	10:27
53:00	8:32	9:32	10:02	10:32
53:30	8:37	9:37	10:07	10:37
54:00	8:42	9:42	10:12	10:42
54:30	8:46	9:46	10:16	10:46
55:00	8:51	9:51	10:21	10:51
55:30	8:56	9:56	10:26	10:56
56:00	9:01	10:01	10:31	11:01
56:30	9:06	10:06	10:36	11:06
57:00	9:10	10:10	10:40	11:10
57:30	9:15	10:15	10:45	11:15
58:00	9:20	10:20	10:50	11:20
58:30	9:25	10:25	10:55	11:25
59:00	9:30	10:30	11:00	11:30
59:30	9:35	10:35	11:05	11:35
60:00	9:40	10:40	11:10	11:40

Note: Runners slower than 60 minutes for the 10K often train close to race pace.

CHAPTER 6

Training Mileage

"Beyond each racing mile lies hundreds of miles of groundwork which establish how the race will go" wrote Joe Henderson in the *Guide to Distance Running* back in 1971. That basic theme guided my training then as I made the transition from track racer to road racer, and it guides me, and you, now.

You need to put mileage in the bank—lots of it in progressive, moderate doses, accumulated day after day, week after week, month after month, year after year. Training mileage is the backbone of every runner's program. Too little and you fade before the finish line; too much and you don't make it to the starting line healthy. A balance is needed. You need enough mileage to meet realistic race goals, but need to be aware of your limitations and not force yourself to go beyond these realistic boundaries.

So how far and how often should you run? The answers to these questions are determined by other questions: What is the purpose of your training? What race distance are you training for? How much can you tolerate physically and mentally? How much time and energy can you realistically invest in training? How strong is your desire to reach challenging goals?

Training mileage includes daily easy- and base-paced runs, as well as the miles you accumulate with speed training and races. Faster-paced mileage tears you down; slower runs build you up for hard efforts and help you recover from them. The slower runs build a base and maintain fitness. Runs within a training heart rate range of 60 to 80 percent of maximum heart rate improve aerobic endurance, thus they are referred to as aerobic endurance runs. They improve the efficiency of the oxygen transport system—the heart and lungs are strengthened and the muscles' ability to use oxygen is enhanced. Aerobic training miles improve the strength and endurance of leg muscles, as well as neuromuscular efficiency. Long runs improve the endurance capabilities of slow-twitch muscle fibers, and train the muscles to store more glycogen.

Since performance is greatly dependent upon your muscles' ability to use oxygen to produce energy, aerobic capacity sets the upper limit for your distance-running performances. It can be raised by increasing training volume. According to studies by Michael Pollock, Ph.D., at the University of Florida, untrained individuals who built to 25 miles per week increased their aerobic capacity by about 30 percent after several months. When they doubled their mileage to 50 miles per week for several more months, their aerobic capacity increased by another 13 percent. But according to studies at Ball State University by David Costill, Ph.D., improvements slow down after that, increasing by only 3 percent at 75 miles a week and even declining slightly at 100 miles a week.

Although packing in the miles and long runs is important to performance, it isn't enough by itself. Running slow teaches you to run slow. Fast-twitch fibers aren't activated, the anaerobic system isn't challenged, and race pace running form isn't rehearsed at aerobic speeds. Also, research demonstrates that speed training at approximately 5K race pace is even more effective in raising aerobic capacity than mileage, especially if you're already at 40 to 50 miles a week. That's good news for those that can't tolerate higher mileage or are already putting in as much mileage as their schedule permits. Think of mileage as the base of fitness which is then brought to peak performance with speed training. Both aspects of training, quantity with mileage and quality with speed, are essential to success as a competitive runner.

TYPES OF AEROBIC ENDURANCE RUNS

Mileage is divided into three distances: short, medium, and long.

The short-distance run (2 to 5 miles). This is used primarily as a recovery or tapering run at your easy or base pace. It usually precedes or follows long runs, speed workouts, and races. Short runs are about 20 to 45 minutes, ideally over reasonably flat terrain. Runs less than 2 or 3 miles won't help you enough to be worth the effort; runs longer than 5 miles won't be easy days for most runners. The emphasis is on staying relaxed.

The definition of a short run varies according to your training level. It generally is about half the distance of your daily average. For Novice Competitors, a short run may be 2 or 3 miles. Local Champions, on the other hand, might average 8 to 10 miles per day and consider a 5-mile run to be short and easy. My short runs are either a 3- or 5-mile loop or 30 to 45 minutes on the treadmill. I'll go short when my body tells me it needs rest, when babying an injury, and when packing in mileage with two-a-days.

The medium-distance run (3 to 10 miles). This is your average daily run, which makes up the bulk of your training. Balance it with long and short runs. Medium runs take about 30 to 90 minutes, depending upon your fitness level and pace. The distance ranges from about 3 miles for Novice Competitors to 10 miles for Local Champions. If you average 5 miles a day, your medium-distance run will be in the 4- to 6-mile range. The primary goal for these runs is to "pack in the miles" without placing great stress on your body and mind. Most of these runs will be at base pace to better promote fitness, although some may be at easy or brisk pace.

The long-distance run (5 to 24 miles). These are about two to three times the length of medium-distance runs. If your normal daily run is 6 miles, for example, long runs would usually be in the 12- to 18-mile range. These workouts give you the strength and confidence to go the distance on race day. Long runs are considered *hard* workouts, even if you're running an easy pace. They fatigue the legs and deplete energy reserves, especially on runs of 90 minutes and longer. Don't "go long" more than once a week; twice a month may be often enough for most runners, although some thrive on three or four long runs a month.

On the average, the long run shouldn't be more than one-half (preferably no more than one-third) of weekly mileage. For example, average at least 20 miles per week to support long runs of 10 miles, and at least 40 miles per week to support long runs of 20 miles. Runners should do at least three, preferably five or more, long runs over the three months prior to a key race.

How long should you run? A rough rule of thumb for Novice

and Intermediate Competitors is to build gradually to runs of at least two-thirds the race distance, and preferably run the race distance or slightly longer. Basic Competitors should at least run the distance of the race regularly. Competitors, Advanced Competitors, and Local Champions should go at least slightly longer than race distance. These guidelines change for marathon training since Novice Competitors may not be able to handle long runs of more than 18 to 20 miles and experienced marathoners should limit their stress to runs of no longer than 22 to 24 miles. See Chapter 21 for guidelines for long runs in marathon training.

FIGURE 6.1: LONG-RUN MILEAGE GUIDE

Race Distance	Novice/ Intermediate Competitor	Basic Competitor	Competitor/ Advanced Competitor	Local Champion
5K	3–6	5–8	8–10	8–12
10K	5–8	6–10	8–12	10–15
Half-marathon	10–13	11–15	12–20	13–20
Marathon	18–20	18–20	20–22	20–24

HOW MUCH MILEAGE?

Many runners are obsessed with mileage. They record it in a diary, track it on charts and graphs, count and discuss, brag about and exaggerate mileage. Some even categorize themselves by mileage and may be driven to log more mileage than their friends and competitors, as if mileage were the only goal in running.

More mileage is many runners' solution to almost any problem: the "more is better" syndrome. High mileage, however, is not the goal of training; performance is. Others don't put in enough mileage to support their goals. Whether due to fear of injury, lack of time or commitment, or the attitude of getting by with less work, they undertrain and thus underperform.

But what about those studies showing that aerobic capacity doesn't improve much after you reach about 50 miles a week? Obviously there are still some additional advantages to running higher mileage—why else would most Elites run 100 to 150 miles a week? High mileage produces other benefits that affect performance. These include training the body to burn more fat along with glycogen, enhancing the endurance capacity of both slow-

and fast-twitch fibers, maintaining body weight at an ideal performance level, and developing the mental discipline to run despite fatigue. You feel strong when you come down off high mileage for an important race, the legs feel much fresher as you taper, and mentally you just *know* you're ready. I feel most confident and fit on high mileage. But one man's meat is another man's poison. Others run much better on lower mileage with plenty of rest days.

Should you run as much per week as you can get away with, or run as little as you can get away with? For most runners, the commonsense answer is somewhere in between. Unfortunately, what you need and what you can do are not always the same. You must determine how much mileage you need to meet realistic goals and how much you can tolerate. Let the Elites have their triple-digit mileage weeks. The average runner needs much less to both improve and be healthy.

WEEKLY MILEAGE GUIDELINES

Most competitive runners fit into our recommended weekly mileage goals below. These figures should be averaged for six to twelve weeks prior to tapering for your key race. You do not need to maintain this mileage year-round. Take a break after the big race, and lower mileage before rebuilding again.

FIGURE 6.2: WEEKLY MILEAGE GUIDE

Race Distance	Novice/ Intermediate Competitor	Basic Competitor	Competitor/ Advanced Competitor	Local Champion
5K	10–20	15–25	30–40	30–60
10K	15–25	20–30	30–50	40–70
Half-marathon	20–30	25–35	30–50	50–70
Marathon	30–40	40–50	40–60	50–80

FACTORS THAT AFFECT MILEAGE

Your mileage depends on more than just desire. Consider these factors:

Age. The more we get beyond age forty, more off days and short-run days are needed to recover from hard training. This results in less weekly mileage. Further, pace slows with age, causing us to run more minutes to get in the same mileage as younger runners of the same age-adjusted ability. Again, the answer is to lower mileage. Ten-mile training runs that took me 70 minutes to complete twenty years ago may now take 85 minutes. To keep up with the mileage standard of my youth I'd have to pound the roads and trails for more time. This would mean I'd actually be training harder. The answer: I swallow my pride and compromise. I'll run 50 to 60 miles a week at age fifty instead of the 70-mile-plus weeks my thirty-year-old body enjoyed. I suggest you compromise, too. When considering the weekly mileage recommendations in Figure 6.2 for your race category, factor in age. For example, a thirty-year-old Basic Competitor's 50-mile training week in preparation for a marathon might be ideal, but a 40-mile week (or even less) might be best for a sixty-year-old Basic Competitor. This allows for more recovery days and additional time on your feet due to a slower pace.

Experience. Runners who have accumulated many miles for several years may find they can race well at a lower mileage level than in previous years.

Pace. Elite male runners average about 6 minutes per mile for their normal 10-mile training runs. That's 10 miles in an hour. The average male or female may run between 9 and 12 minutes per mile for a 10-miler. That's 10 miles in one and one-half to two hours. For a 40-mile training week, this average runner would run six to eight hours longer than an Elite runner. So who's working harder anyway? The point here is that you shouldn't compare mileage with other runners, especially if they run those miles much faster than you. The slower you train, the less mileage you should attempt. Otherwise, you spend too much time pounding the roads. Most runners who train and race at approximately the same pace can handle similar weekly mileage work loads.

It is harder to keep mileage up if you: are carrying extra pounds; run often over very hilly terrain or in bad weather; must train in the reduced light of early morning or late evening; don't have training partners to help you along, especially on long runs; have an inflexible work schedule, or many career and family responsibilities; don't fuel and hydrate properly on a daily basis; don't get adequate sleep; are frequently battling injury or illness; race often, or train too hard too often. The solution may be to reduce mileage, correct the problems above, or both.

GUIDELINES FOR INCREASING MILEAGE

Follow the principle of adaptation to progressive training to improve fitness and avoid overtraining. How you increase mileage depends first on how often you run. If you are running less than five days a week, gradually add more days until you are running five to six days consistently. Don't add too much mileage on the new days at first. Once you get up to your maximum number of training days per week (5 to 7), stay at that level for a few weeks. Then increase the distance of your long run, and then your medium runs. Maintain a balance of short, medium, and long runs. Be sure to include easy recovery days as you build mileage. When building for a race, start with a solid base. For example, if building to 40 miles a week, average at least 20 miles a week for a month before starting the buildup.

Avoid any sudden increases in mileage from day to day, week to week, month to month, even year to year. Don't increase weekly mileage or long runs by more than 5 to 10 percent per week, or better yet every other week. Be patient, not *a* patient. A common mistake is to increase mileage quickly when feeling good or in a hurry to build up for a race. The usual result of increasing the work load too rapidly is either fatigue or injury. It may not seem like much if you jump your mileage from 20 to 30 miles per week over a week or two—that's only 10 miles a week. But that's a 50 percent increase in your work load and your body most likely isn't ready for it. A 5 to 10 percent increase can range from 1 to 2 miles a week (for the 20-mile-per-week runner) to 3½ to 7 miles a week (for the 70-mile-per-week runner). This is a safe way to progress. Don't continuously move your mileage upward. Here's a math riddle. Add 10 percent each week, week after week, until you're running twenty-four hours a day. How long will this take you? Get the message?

Every few weeks you may benefit by either leveling off for a few weeks, or dropping back for a week before adding more mileage. Plateaus and cutbacks help reduce the pressure of constantly building up mileage. You do not have to increase every week. Here's a sample ten-week gradual progression using plateaus: 20-20-22-22-24-26-26-26-28-30. A schedule using cutbacks may be like this: 20-22-24-20-24-26-26-28-24-30. Injury rates increase most after about 40 miles a week. So, before you reach this figure, plateau for a few weeks to build resistance to injury. Shelly-lynn and I prefer building to a weekly mileage level and staying there to build fitness. We'll lower it slightly to peak for races. After running a series of races, or completing a marathon, we'll recover at a lower mileage level until ready to build to peak mileage again.

You don't have to keep climbing the mileage ladder. You can get off any time. More isn't always best. Success is measured by race times, not training mileage. If you are happy with the level where you are now and have achieved a comfortable balance between running and the rest of your life, don't let peer pressure or inner guilt feelings drive you to do more. You can always move up later—if you want.

Determine the upper limits of mileage you have time for and can handle physically and mentally. Decide how badly you want to reach your goals. Establish how much of a time and energy commitment you can invest. Don't compare yourself to others, especially if those runners are more experienced and talented. It's natural to think that if Ken Smith runs 50 miles a week and beats you, that if you run 60 miles a week you can beat him. It may not work that way. But then again, maybe it will. I often beat runners with more talent by out-training them. Few runners, however, have my thirty-plus years of running experience.

TIPS FOR MANAGING YOUR MILES

Set weekly mileage ranges when training for key races. This may be more practical than aiming to run the same mileage week after week. For example, run no less than 30 miles in a single week, but no more than 40; that would mean 35 miles on the average. Adjust ranges as you are able to handle more (or less) training. As I was writing this chapter, my weekly goal range was at least 50 miles per week, but no more than 60. When marathon-training, I change that range to a minimum of 60 and a maximum 70. Using ranges helps to maintain motivation and consistency.

If you miss a few days, don't try to make it up all at once. Add a mile or two a day, or forget missed mileage. Running twice as far one day to make up for a lost day is not the answer. It's better to continue the next day at the rate of training you would normally have followed for the week. By setting monthly mileage goals rather than weekly ones, you can be more flexible with your training week.

Don't count "junk" miles. Running a mile to the gym, for example, may save time and be enjoyable, but it isn't part of training. Don't log mileage unless you run at least 2 or 3 miles at a time and are running in your training heart rate range. Don't look for every excuse to put miles in your diary. It's important that the miles you claim are of reasonable quality. In the end, it is the blend of quantity and quality mileage that will help you improve times, not how many miles you log each week. Don't feel you absolutely have to run once more late on Sunday night in order to reach your goal (But I do!). But do plot mileage goals regularly in advance—this gives you the motivation to keep it up.

If you don't know exactly how long your course is, estimate it—on the conservative side. My wooded trails certainly aren't certified, but my estimate of their distance is good enough for me. If you feel you are running 7:30 a mile, that equals 8 miles in an hour. If traveling over unknown territory at that pace, run for a half hour and return. Log it as 8 miles. That's close enough.

Don't run the same distance every day over the same course at the same time of day with the same people at the same pace. Variety makes it easier and more enjoyable to pack in mileage. On the other hand, putting in high mileage is often a robotlike task, so being familiar with a few basic courses is quite helpful when you just want to push automatic and cruise without thinking. Having a trusty course is a kind of security blanket—you feel comfortable with it. I run my basic 7- or 10-mile courses almost every day, but look for a different route once a week for a change of scenery.

Lower mileage a few times a year, especially after a marathon or a series of peak races. But don't drop too much below your peak level for too long or it'll be tougher to get back to your peak mileage. The cutback should be about 25 percent, certainly no more than 50 percent. So, for a 40-mile-a-week runner this maintenance range would be 20 to 30 miles a week.

GETTING BY ON LESS

If you don't have the time, health, desire, or ability to handle a more ideal weekly mileage program, you at least should concentrate on being as efficient as possible. Perhaps, for example, you should run 40 to 50 miles a week to meet your racing goals, but choose, for whatever reason, to get by on 30 miles a week (This program can be adapted to as low as 20 miles a week). Although you would be stronger and perhaps faster at the higher mileage, you still may be able to accomplish some reasonably good performances. The key is to include the basics each week: one long run, one or two fast days, two or three recovery days, two or three off days. Here's a sample breakdown of a realistic, efficient 30-mile training week for 5K to half-marathon racing:

- A long run of 10 miles (one-third the weekly mileage total). This will only work for races up to the half-marathon. Adapt this "get-by-on-less" system for the marathon by alternating 40-mile weeks that include a long run of at least 18 to 20 miles with 30-mile weeks that don't.
- One or two fast days: A track interval or hill repeat workout; and a fartlek, tempo run, or at least a brisk-paced run of 4 to 6 miles. Note: For most Novice and Intermediate Competors, and many Basic Competitors, only one speed workout per week is recommended.
- Two easy days. Run short (3 to 5 miles) at your easy or base pace.
- Two days off. Either don't run or cross-train for 30 to 45 minutes.

After 6 to 10 weeks, you'll be reasonably fit. A key to performance is to race often when you want to do well—twice a month for two months, and then take a break. But don't let mileage slip too much—you're already at a low level.

RUNNING FOR MINUTES, NOT MILES

Some runners prefer to log their training by minutes run rather than mileage. It keeps things simple: An hour is an hour no matter where you run or what the weather. Since the key to aerobic fitness is time spent in your training heart rate range, how many miles you run or exactly what pace you run per mile isn't critical. Many runners find that tracking minutes keeps them from overtraining since they don't get obsessed with weekly mileage figures or try to run training courses in a certain time. Maintaining mileage goals and training pace when running over hilly courses or in hot, muggy weather can be frustrating. Instead, just start your watch and run by effort. Since races are held over mileage distances and most runners talk in terms of mileage, we'll stick to mileage guidelines in this book. But feel free to adjust our weekly mileage guidelines to weekly minutes run.

HOW OFTEN SHOULD YOU RUN?

You need some form of aerobic exercise at least three times a week to gain and then maintain a minimal level of fitness, but that's not enough for optimal performance. A study of British marathoners reported in the *Journal of Sports Science* indicated that the frequency of runs better predicted superior racing times than any other variable, including weekly mileage and years of running experience.

But should you run every day? Some runners argue that you must in order to build a habit you won't break: It's too easy to take more days off if you give in and take one, they say. This is nonsense! Most runners need at least one, and perhaps two, days off a week to recover. Studies show that consecutive days run and weekly mileage are major predictors of injury. Taking at least one day off per week is linked with reduction of injury frequency.

The average Novice and Intermediate Competitor should run four or five days a week. Experienced competitors will have trouble reaching mileage goals and keeping fit enough for racing on less than five or six days of running per week. Many Local Champions and most Semi-Elites and Elites run every day. I seldom take a day off. Why? It's difficult to reach my 60-plus miles a week with an off day. It would require averaging 10 miles per day or more on the other days. And I feel better if I run every day. For experienced, fit runners, an easy run of 3 to 5 miles is like a day off.

Still, one or two days off each week is recommended for most runners. Give the body a day of rest and it will respond better for the rest of the week. Which days to take off will be determined by your schedule—when you do your long runs, speed work, and races. Take your day off on a regularly scheduled day, or save it for a busy workday or a day when you feel tired or overstressed. Monday is often a preferred rest day (although others like myself prefer to get a good jump on mileage for the week) following a weekend of high mileage or racing: It allows for an easier transition into the work week. A good choice is to take a day off following long runs while marathon training, or after a hard race or workout. No sense pounding the roads with tired legs.

But beware. Taking days off can get too easy. If you don't keep a consistent running schedule going, you will not achieve the desired level of fitness. Keeping a weekly training diary helps here; too many big zeros entered will make you feel guilty. If you really need to train every day, for whatever reason, try substituting non-impact cross-training once or twice a week.

Spread the exercise out over the entire week. Most runners can find the time to run on weekends but have trouble getting out during the week. Don't be a "weekend warrior," cramming in all your mileage on Saturday and Sunday. This sets up injury. Schedule at least two short or medium runs during the week.

A good minimal goal for Novice Competitors is to run every other day. Some coaches and runners advocate running every other day even for experienced competitors. The theory behind this strategy is that it takes approximately 48 hours for the body to recover properly from a run. Running fewer days per week, while accumulating the same or nearly the same mileage as running five or six days a week, certainly saves time warming up, cooling down, dressing, undressing, and showering. More recovery between runs minimizes injury and allows you to feel fresher and run with better form. Because of time constraints or susceptibility to injury, you might find this system helpful. Many older runners in their sixties and beyond discover that every-other-day running keeps them healthy, and most important—they enjoy their runs more.

Many runners enjoy running more often. They may run as

much for pleasure or stress management as for performance. Runners often feel very antsy if they don't get in their daily run. My legs get twitchy and I can't sleep if I take off two days in a row. As long as you take a few days easy each week and are injury-free, run as often as you want. But you don't have to run every day.

SHOULD YOU RUN TWO-A-DAYS?

Researchers haven't decided which is more beneficial to fitness—a single run of 10 miles, for example, or two 5-milers. Two-a-days take time. Running once a day gives you the most miles per hour of time invested. You waste time duplicating changing clothes, showering, stretching, warming up, and cooling down. And then there is the extra energy spent worrying about getting in your next run. Running two-a-days may encourage some runners to try for more mileage than they can safely handle. Few runners at the Novice, Intermediate, and Basic Competitor levels should consider running twice a day. Many runners above those levels may benefit.

Here are some of the advantages of breaking up daily mileage:

- If you're running through or recovering from an injury, two 4-mile runs (for example) rather than an 8-miler may allow you to stay within the limits of what your body can safely tolerate.
- Running in bad weather—whether extreme heat or cold, or hard rain or wind—can be safer and more comfortable with two-a-days. No matter how bad the weather, you won't get too uncomfortable for the first 30 to 45 minutes. During heat waves, some runners survive by running as the sun is coming up and again after it goes down. If footing is bad due to snow or ice, the longer you run the more muscles fatigue and injury risk increases. To minimize this, limit runs in poor footing to 30 to 45 minutes at a time. I often compromise in bad weather by running once outside in the elements and either earlier or later in the day inside on my treadmill.

- Two-a-days may be more practical if you have a busy schedule. It's that or sacrifice mileage. If you don't have time to get in your 8-miler in the morning because of a work or family obligation, try running 4 miles and add a second 4-miler later in the day. Running to and from work a few times a week saves time and money.
- In the day or days following a hard run or race, it may be beneficial to run two short workouts for recovery. For example, an easy 2- or 3-miler the next morning and another in the evening.
- If your race or speed workout is in the evening, a short run in the morning or at noon will loosen you up. I run better workouts with this system. Not only that, speed training days may interfere with mileage goals. With our evening classes, total mileage for the workout ranges from 4 to 6 miles. For me to get my average of 8 or more miles a day, I'll run 3 to 5 miles easy earlier in the day.
- Two-a-days help keep your mileage up. It's especially difficult to run high mileage without at least a few two-a-days. I prefer that most runners only run once a day unless they average at least 8 miles a day. Otherwise, it isn't efficient. But if you average 10 miles a day or more, it's very stressful running only once a day. I once experimented with running 15-milers every day for a week, then breaking it up the next week into a 5-miler and a 10-miler each day. The single-run days were a lot more difficult. Runs of over an hour result in more dehydration and glycogen depletion. Further, you'll run more slowly and be more prone to sloppy running form and injury late in runs when doing high-mileage weeks in single workouts.

Experiment with breaking up your days to see if it agrees with your body and mind. It won't work for everyone. If you decide to try two-a-days, start with a few easy 3-milers in the morning once or twice a week in addition to your evening run. Later, you may move up to 4- or 5-milers. When doing two-a-days, any run much shorter than 30 minutes will provide limited fitness benefit. You can break runs up evenly, or make one a short run and the other a medium run. For example: do a 3-miler and a 7-miler, or a pair of 5-milers. I find the combination of a short run and a medium run works best. Don't eliminate the long run. At least two or three single runs each month should be 15 miles or longer for high-mileage runners, or those marathon training. Limit two-a-days to three days a week or less. That provides variety to your training schedule without becoming too stressful.

WHAT TIME OF DAY SHOULD YOU RUN?

For many runners running schedules are determined by their work and family schedules. You fit in runs when you can, usually before or after work during the week and on weekend mornings. But often we have some flexibility in determining when to run. Our bodies have their own individual cycles, and most of us run when it feels best for us and when we enjoy it most.

Morning runs. Early-morning runs start your day on a pleasant note. Getting in your run early certainly has its advantages. Those who develop the first-thing-in-the-morning routine tend to be more consistent in their training. Makes sense. You don't run the risk of last-minute business or personal demands causing you to miss a run, cut it short, or force you to rush through it. Morning runs also avoid the heat and peak air pollution. You can enjoy your run without carrying along all the stress that builds up during the day. Early-morning runs are more guilt-free. You're not stealing prime time from your family or skipping out of work early to squeeze in a run. They save time too by combining your morning and postrun shower.

There are disadvantages, too. Winter brings cold, dark mornings that are easy to skip unless you are very dedicated. It's not easy to find early-morning running partners that will show up on time. An early-morning run following an evening run may not leave sufficient recovery time. Unless you go to bed early enough to compensate, getting up early to run will rob you of much-needed sleep. Some of the most restful sleep is during the last two hours, and to wake up before your body is ready may leave you fatigued rather than refreshed. Don't cut an hour of sleep out of your schedule to run early. Go to bed an hour earlier. Most runners need at least seven or eight hours of sleep every night. If you cut into that, you may pay for it with lousy running and sluggishness at work.

According to a survey by podiatrist Dr. John Pagliano, early-morning runners get injured more frequently than noontime or evening runners. Why? Cooler air temperature may be a factor. But a more important ingredient may be body temperature. According to our daily rhythms, body temperature is lowest between 4:00 and 6:00 A.M. So, before about 6:00 A.M. and for the next few hours your muscles are going to be stiff and cold, and much more prone to injury. Counteract the risks of early-morning running by warming up properly. Too many early-morning runners are in a hurry and skip warm-ups. Better to skip a few minutes of running than to risk injury. Don't attempt aggressive stretching exercises—your muscles are too "cold" to stretch properly. Do some easy limbering exercises. Walk for 5 to 10 minutes before running. On cold mornings, I warm up on my elliptical trainer or with a walk on the treadmill. Once out the door, start running slowly, gradually moving into a steady, but controlled, pace after a mile or two. An early-morning running pace may be slower than a pace you run later in the day. That's okay as long as you are within your training heart rate range. Avoid hard running or races until you have been up and about for at least two hours. Then there's the value of compromise: A mid-morning run, if you can fit it into your schedule, allows for many of the advantages of early-morning runs and minimizes many of the disadvantages.

Since most races are scheduled in the morning, at least do a few race-time morning runs to get accustomed to awakening and running early. That's why I drag myself out of bed for hard 10-milers with the local 8:30 A.M. running crew. Upon returning, I reward myself for my dedication: I go back to bed.

Midday runs. This is my time to run. If you have flexible hours, a midday run is a great option. You don't have to worry about darkness and it's the warmest part of the day in winter. You also aren't as stiff as in the morning. A run will lessen your appetite; a light lunch afterward will help you maintain weight control. A midday run helps clear the mind and provides a break from daily stresses. Like early-morning runs, it may eliminate hassles at home when your spouse or kids want and need your attention after work. However, running in the heat of the day is tough. A steady diet of it could result in chronic dehydration or fatigue. If you must stick to a midday routine, consider indoor alternatives a few times, including biking, swimming, and treadmilling.

Evening runs. This is when most runners are on the road. The pressures of the day are left behind. It is usually the easiest time of day to find running partners. According to a study at the Cooper Clinic Research Institute in Dallas, exercising in the evening was the most effective in controlling weight in runners.

These runs, however, are most likely to interfere with the rest of your social life, and dinners often have to be rescheduled to accommodate the evening runner. It's too easy to come home from work feeling tired and just skip the workout, although if you force yourself to run you'll most likely feel better. Getting stuck with a late workday or in traffic coming home from work can also result in a big zero-mileage day. During the winter, you have to cope with the dark and cold. Running too hard late in the day may make it hard for you to get to sleep.

DO YOU NEED TO TRAIN AT THE SAME TIME OF DAY AS RACES?

Are you at a disadvantage if you don't train at the time of day you race? Penny Burgoon, Ph.D., directed a study at California State University which tested folks who identified themselves as morning, midday, or evening runners. They performed a maximal exercise test in the early morning (7:30 to 8:30 A.M.), noon, and evening (7:30 to 8:30 P.M.). The results? Runners don't gain an advantage by racing at the same hours they train; nor do they lose anything by racing at hours other than when they train. In short, the morning runners didn't outperform the evening runners on early-morning exercise tests, and the evening runners didn't outperform the morning runners on the evening tests. Nevertheless, it is recommended that you do some training at the time of day you plan to race. At least you'll be better prepared mentally.

A noteworthy outcome was that all runners, regardless of

when they trained or preferred to run, performed best in the evening. Several studies have indicated that aerobic capacity peaks in the late afternoon and early evening. If you can find a few evening races, you might find it easier to turn in a good race time. In fact, several world track records for distance events have been set at night.

ALTITUDE

How much mileage you can tolerate and race performance are affected by high altitude. Above 3,000 feet you will notice the decrease in oxygen and may tire more quickly. The higher the altitude, the greater the effect. Above 5,000 feet, each 1,000-foot increase in altitude decreases your aerobic capacity 3 to 4 percent. Maximal heart rate decreases, lactic acid levels increase, and the amount of oxygen passing through your lungs into the bloodstream also decreases. As I found out the hard way, air at higher altitudes is cool and dry, which is tough on the respiratory system. You also dehydrate quicker, overheat more readily, and may be exposed to greater amounts of sunshine and therefore sunburn.

If visiting at altitude, start with short runs at a reduced pace. Within a week, you may gradually increase the intensity and duration of runs. The higher the altitude, the longer the period of acclimatization. At 3,000 feet you may adjust in about a week. At 6,500 feet—Denver's altitude—it will take two weeks; at 8,000 feet, four weeks.

Many Elites train at altitude because they believe it improves performance. Many studies, however, show otherwise. Because you can't train (or race) as fast as you can at sea level, high-altitude training may not benefit you much (Of course it will help some if you *think* it does). On the other hand, if you live at a high altitude and speed-train and race at a low altitude, you may have an advantage. This may be a key reason for the success of the many great African distance runners that live at high altitudes. Also, runners who live and train at altitude can perform relatively better at altitude than those who do not have this advantage. This was proven at the 1968 Mexico City Olympics.

RUNNING SURFACES

God gave our ancestors the soft earth to cushion the barefoot runner. Then along came shoes and pavement to mess up the system. Here are the various running surfaces you may encounter in running and racing:

Dirt and cinder. This surface provides excellent shock absorption. I estimate I can handle at least 25 percent more mileage when training on dirt versus pavement. Running on dirt requires extra energy. But this builds strength and you feel faster when you hit paved race courses. But beware of rocks, ruts, slippery mud, and other perils.

Grass. A favorite workout I do with our classes is fartlek on the grassy sections of Central Park. The constant changing of surface eliminates the repetitive stress of road-running. Grass reduces impact, but the uneven surfaces and tricky footing can throw you off stride or trip you. Running on grass strengthens muscles in the feet, ankles, and legs that don't get as much work as you push along on smooth pavement.

Sand, beaches. Running along the beach may look like fun, but it can be dangerous. I don't recommend it. The beach is soft and, closer to the water where it is firmer, it's slanted. Footing is uncertain and there are hidden objects buried in the sand, from shells to such refuse as glass. Your heels will sink into the sand, causing Achilles tendon strain. If you insist on running on the beach, run out and back to compensate for the slant and wear shoes for protection. Limit beach-running at first to 10 minutes and build to no more than 30 minutes. Better yet, try the boardwalk.

Pavement. Concrete, used on most sidewalks and some roads, is the worst surface in terms of shock absorption. If the choice is between concrete and asphalt, take asphalt since it is much more forgiving. Hopping on and off sidewalks at intersections can contribute to injury. Many runners prefer asphalt to grass or dirt since the surface is more dependable. Most park trails are paved with asphalt since they can also be used as bike trails. However, they are often slanted for drainage, as are roads. This can contribute to injury. Find paved areas that are not slanted too much, or when it is safe to run on the crown of the road. Otherwise, alternate the direction you run every few miles to minimize the strain.

Tracks. If you don't mind going around and around, running on your local school track may be an option for putting in a few miles. Most are made of a synthetic material that provides some cushioning. The faster tracks are harder than the softer ones. Running two long turns per lap of a quarter-mile track will place extra stress on the ankles, knees, and hips. Indoor tracks, which are smaller, have even tighter turns and are usually banked—which causes even more strain on the body. Usually you cannot reverse direction on a track; everyone must run the same way.

So where to run? Only run on grass and dirt trails if you are in good shape and have strong, flexible ankles and feet. Asphalt is the best paved choice. If you intend to race on paved surfaces, you should do some training there to prepare your body for its stresses. Variety is best for conditioning and injury prevention. But beware of sudden changes in running surfaces. Start cautiously. Try new surfaces just for short runs at first. Don't run on it two days in a row until you have adjusted. A final option for running surfaces—a treadmill. These handy devices offer a well-cushioned ride indoors where you can control your environment.

HILLS

Training involves three types of grades: flat, up, and down. Too much or too little of any of them isn't good for you. Running on the flats all the time is boring, and works the same muscles over and over, neglecting those that get strengthened on hills. Even if you mostly race on the flats, running hills will benefit you. But too many hills will make it harder to reach mileage goals and cause long runs to be too difficult. Don't run hilly courses two days in a row. Also, if you haven't been running much mileage on hilly courses, don't suddenly shift to lots of it. Lots of uphills or downhills may cause injury, especially late in long runs when you're tired. Downhill running at aerobic training paces doesn't do anything for you except make it easier. But the price you pay may be soreness the next day as a result of the increased shock and eccentric motion caused by the mechanics of downhill running.

All runners complain about hills. Then they brag about conquering them on their training courses. Sure, running up hills tires your legs and makes you huff and puff. But making it up them brings you strength and confidence, and adds variety to your training routine.

Running hills can be a lot of fun. One of my favorite training routines, especially when traveling, is to run to the top of the nearest big hill. At the peak I'm rewarded with a lovely view and the confidence of knowing I was strong enough to conquer all the land below!

CHAPTER 7

The Runner's Training Diary

Since 1973 I have faithfully maintained a training diary, and Shelly-lynn's been keeping one since 1978. My diary has been with me during all my ups and downs. I brag to it about significant mileage weeks, and good workouts and races. I complain to it about fatigue, and poor runs and races, as well as injuries and illnesses. I pull my good friend off the shelf every day and talk to it. It's my very valued training partner.

I strongly recommend that you keep a diary, too. It will become a record of training and competition over a period of days, weeks, months, and years. A diary is essential to understanding what does and doesn't work in your running. You can study the past to succeed in the future. It documents your progress as a runner. You'll refer to it regularly for guidance. How did I train for my best races? How many long runs did I do going into my previous marathons? What was my weight when I was racing well? What training errors contributed to shin splints? What shoes did I wear in my last marathon? Your diary will have the answers to these questions as well as a summary of your running highlights (and low points).

The diary gives you perspective. It is sometimes difficult to see the successes and failures of your training while they are going on. But if you look back, you notice a pattern. You see improvement with peaks followed by valleys, and then followed by peaks again. A diary kept over the years offers the opportunity to reflect upon a memorable running career. I find an old training diary enjoyable reading. Reviewing my past successes in the "good ol' days" pumps me up.

Planning and recording runs is one of the secrets of success. A diary helps you set goals, train consistently and progressively. It contains the facts and feelings of your running program. Your diary doesn't forget. Its accurate recording of workouts will be there when you analyze your training. Look back at the weeks preceding a poor performance and find the telltale entries. More positively, review what training preceded good races and build on this knowledge. You learn what works best for you by trial and error. By experimenting with your running and keeping a detailed diary, you can write your own personalized training book, which is more valuable than any book you could buy.

Be consistent. Fill in information after each run, before you forget details. It is easier to reach weekly mileage goals if you record runs daily. A diary keeps you honest. Nobody likes to see too many unplanned zeros—*in writing*. But don't become a slave to recording mileage. Remember, fitness and performance are the goals, not accumulating mileage in your diary. By keeping a diary, you can make sure you do enough, but not too much, running to meet your goals. Your diary—like any good coach or running partner—should be a motivator, not an overbearing stress. It should act like your conscience, urging you to get out the door to keep on schedule; but it should also be a voice of caution, reminding you of past training errors.

Daily and weekly records should at least include the basics: date, course, distance, running time, and pace. I write in fast milage (speed workouts and races) in red, and training pace mile mileage in black so I can more easily monitor hard-easy training. Log details of key speed workouts and long runs in order to measure progress. Record the important details of races so you can compare them to past and future results. It may be useful to record even more information such as weight, heart rate, shoes, weather, time of day, injuries, sleep, cross-training, and on and on. General comments such as how you felt during your run may prove helpful, too. Some runners make personal entries unrelated to running. Wouldn't it be fun to browse through the diaries of some running friends!

The diary can be a simple wall calendar or a more formal log such as our *Runner's Training Diary*.

PART II

SPEED TRAINING

CHAPTER 8

Introduction to Speed Training

SPEED! All runners want it. Speed thrills. It's fun to change gears, pick up the pace. The sense of your body moving fast, the exhilaration of it, is just as rewarding to you and me as it is to Elites. It's especially exciting to kick by other runners at the end of a race. Speed is critical to success. After all, the goal in racing is to run as fast as you can for the distance, and faster than as many other runners as possible. Speed is relative. Getting faster is just as important to a 10-minute per mile 5K runner as a 5-minute per mile runner. All of us can get faster—within our genetic limits—by training for speed.

Most Novice and Intermediate Competitors run their first few races at a nice easy pace. Speed isn't the goal, enduring is. They're happy just to reach the finish line. But once that's accomplished, they begin to think beyond "just finishing"—they want to run faster. At this point, speed can be improved somewhat by getting stronger through steady runs, but you'll make more progress if you train your body to run a fast pace with speedwork. But that very word scares people away. Many runners are intimidated by the prospect of speed*work*. You shouldn't be. The brutal "no pain, no gain" workouts some competitors brag about aren't for you (Besides, they're probably exaggerating). To safely improve race times, you need only run at race pace and a little faster over a distance shorter than your race, and learn to handle a modest amount of discomfort. Think of it as speed*play*. If new to speed training, keep it light and playful and you'll benefit and have fun.

Many competitors do all or most of their training at a slow, conversational pace. After all, it takes much less planning and work to "just go for a run" than for a structured speed session. To perform at your best you need specific speed training. Although some runners avoid it and still race well, most will benefit. You can improve with even moderately hard speed training.

If you don't mind some extra discomfort in workouts, you may be able to race even faster. Sure, training fast hurts, but so does racing hard. Some training on the edge of pain will prepare your mind and body for the distress of all-out racing. Here's some consolation: Even the Elites up ahead of us suffer some in workouts and races. They just get the pain over with faster and look better while doing it.

Speeding is a double-edged sword. You can't run your best times without speed training. On the other hand, if you overdo it you may get injured, burn out, or peak too soon. Certainly the downsides of speed training are a concern. Take your choice. Take limited risks by speeding wisely and improve race times, or play it cautiously to minimize both injury and performance.

So if your choice is to fulfill your potential, don't think about getting into speed work; do it. Designed properly, it supercharges your running many ways:

Physiological benefits. Training at race pace—or slightly slower or faster—mimics the physiological stresses of racing. Chapter 2 explains several key physiological ingredients improved with speed training including aerobic capacity, lactate threshold, running economy, efficiency of fast-twitch muscle fibers, and muscular strength and power. Basically speed training makes you a stronger, speedier, more efficient runner. You'll run faster paces more easily, and run farther at race pace before fatigue sets in. As you enter the masters ranks, speed training becomes even more important to minimize the loss of muscular strength and fast-twitch muscle fibers with aging.

Everyone benefits from speed training, especially if:

- It is difficult for you to hold a fast pace during a race, but you finish feeling as though you could have run farther at the same pace.

- You feel uncomfortable with the pace at the start (assuming you didn't start too fast for your fitness), or cannot generate a kick at the end.
- You lack the strength to generate power during a race, especially up hills.

The physiological benefits of speed training will not show up immediately in your race results. It takes about two weeks or more for a complete training effect to take place after a good workout. And one quality session isn't enough—you need a few weeks of consistent speedwork to see progress. Be patient.

Psychological benefits. You may get some results immediately. I've had many students rejoice about significantly improved race times after only one or two of our speed sessions. I wish I could brag it was because of my coaching, but you won't get significant physiological benefits that soon. Rather, these runners improved because they learned there was an athlete hidden within themselves. They *thought* they could race faster, therefore they did.

Many runners underestimate their ability. Working through small doses of discomfort in training helps them realize they can push a strong, controlled pace in races without falling in a heap. Experienced competitors, too, benefit psychologically from speed training. They build confidence going into key races after running more easily and faster in speed workouts. They feel more comfortable starting races at a little faster pace and know from feelings they had in speed sessions that they can hang in there to the end, even pick it up for a finishing kick.

Biomechanical benefits. Footstrike, stride, body posture, and arm motion are different when running fast than at easy training paces. Breathing pattern changes, too. During speed workouts, you exaggerate proper biomechanics: You drive the arms faster, lift the knees higher, quicken the stride, increase foot pushoff, and really concentrate on relaxed breathing. You prepare the body to adjust to differences between training and race pace. Speed sessions help improve running form and economy as stride length and stride rate are increased. You'll be more efficient, coordinated, relaxed, and faster on race day.

Strategic benefits. How do you know what pace to start at and hold for races? Many runners find out the hard way by trial and error. They may start too slow and wish they had tried harder, or start too fast and wish they had been more conservative. Either way, they most likely would have run a faster time with better pacing. Speed training mimics the pacing of races and helps you learn to be aggressive, but sensible, about your starting pace. You can practice race pace over and over again to learn what it feels like. On race day you can slip into that gear more easily.

Speed sessions may also familiarize you with pack running. By working out in a group, you learn to hang on when you want to drop out, or hold back and be patient. You feel what it's like to run elbow-to-elbow with others, to "draft" off them, or to lead a group. All these methods help you, and the runners working out with you, run faster workouts and faster races. In our classes, we group runners by 5K race pace and encourage them to hang together in a tight pack. But you should also run some race pace workouts by yourself to learn how to judge your own pace.

Speed training measures fitness, helping you establish race time goals. Comparing recent speed session results with previous times will show you where you stand. For example, if my mile interval times dip under 5:50, or my run to the Ridge under 40:00, I know I'm ready to challenge my age fifty-plus race records. I'll start my next race at a challenging, but realistic, goal pace. On the other hand, if these test runs aren't up to previous standards, I have sad but true feedback that I've got more work to do. I'll pick a more conservative race goal.

WHAT'S MORE IMPORTANT, HIGHER MILEAGE OR MORE SPEED TRAINING?

In the early days of road racing, runners favored long, slow distance training and did very little fast stuff except for racing. Then, spurred by the success of Emil Zatopek, the great Czech who ran large quantities of speed workouts on a track, runners shifted to speed training, the new formula for success. Said Zatopek, "Why should I practice running slow? I already know how to run slow. I want to learn to run fast." Run fast he did, and with mind-boggling quantity. Want to try out his training? Leading up to the 1952 Olympics, this training animal ran 400-meter intervals sixty times for ten consecutive days. The result: He won Olympic gold in the 5K, 10K, and marathon.

By the 1960s, most top runners hit the track often and trained there intensely. In the 1970s as the popular running boom began, many runners shifted back to an emphasis on long, slow distance training (now called LSD). By the 1980s, however, track-trained stars like Grete Waitz and Alberto Salazar took over road-running events. Many runners agreed that "long, slow running only teaches you to run slow," and they took off for the track. Speed training once again became the secret formula for success.

In the 1990s, moderation took control. High mileage was replaced with moderate, even low mileage for many runners. High-volume, high-intensity speed training was replaced with more moderate speed training. But no one told the Africans about the advantages of doing less. Training with high mileage and frequent speed training, they dominated road races around the world as more moderate-trained U.S. stars no longer could keep up, let alone match American times from the 1980s.

Okay, but you're not out to beat the Kenyans, just your own best time or perhaps other runners in your age group. What should you concentrate on? More mileage or more speed? Evidence is mounting for reasonable quality over excessive quantity. Research at the University of Medical Hospitals in Germany found that runners who kept mileage at a steady 45 miles a week while increasing training intensity improved their fitness dramatically. On the other hand, runners that more than doubled mileage while skipping speed training showed little improvement. The high-mileage runners also suffered more complications of overtraining: fatigue and muscle soreness.

Other studies show that after reaching and maintaining a solid mileage base, you can lower it while working on intensity; the result is improved fitness and less risk of injury. The studies seem to indicate that the answer is first to build a reasonable base of mileage your body can tolerate, then sacrifice mileage (if necessary due to time or energy constraints) while concentrating more on speed for a limited period of time.

David Costill, Ph.D., studied the advantages of mileage versus speed training at Ball State University. He states in *Inside Running: The Basics of Sports Physiology*: "The major disadvantage on 'volume' in training is that long, slow distance training is considerably slower than racing pace. Such training fails to develop the neurological patterns of muscle fiber recruitment that will be needed during races that require a faster pace. Since the selective use of muscle fibers differs according to running speed, runners who train only at speeds slower than race pace will not train all of the muscles needed for competition."

What does all this mean to you? The higher your goals, the more important it is to put in the hard work, both mileage and speed. Neither high mileage nor frequent speed training alone is a successful training program. You need both LSD and speed. The key is blending them together into a balanced schedule. Experience teaches you what combination works best for you. Ideally, a base of endurance running should be topped by speed workouts on the track, hills, trails, and roads to sharpen for key races.

Generally, 90 percent of your training should be endurance work, and only 10 percent speed. On a 30-mile training week aim for no more than 3 miles of speed mileage. For example: three times a mile, or six times a half-mile. Experienced competitors may (or may not) be able to handle twice-a-week speed training and up to 20 percent or so of their weekly mileage may be speed training. On a 50-mile training week, they may run up to 10 miles of speed mileage. But be careful here. Also, the shorter the race distance, the less mileage and more speed training you need—it will be a higher percentage of weekly mileage.

For the average runner, a moderate amount of both mileage and speed is best for both performance and good health: for example, 20 to 30 miles and one speed session per week. For more advanced runners with higher goals, the numbers get a bit bigger. I'll run 50 to 60 miles combined with one or two speed sessions on most weeks. If you have a limited amount of time and want "more bang for the buck," limit mileage while concentrating on one or two quality runs per week. That's exactly what I did while on deadline for this book. I cut mileage to 40 to 50 miles a week while retaining one track interval session and one tempo run.

TYPES OF SPEED WORKOUTS

Four basic types of speed training are used in this book and detailed in the following chapters: intervals, hills, fartlek, and tempo runs. They complement each other. Each contributes in special ways. All of them improve your ability to withstand the physical and mental stress of racing. Include a combination of these types of workouts—on the track, roads, trails, and hills—in your training program to promote all the benefits of speed training discussed in this chapter and add variety. As a result, your training will be more interesting and productive.

Don't worry about exactly what type of workout you should do, or that you can't fit them all in your schedule. Almost any speed training will help. In our classes we do a variety of workouts since our students have a variety of needs and are training for a variety of distances. They are at all stages of their training. Yet they all benefit from whatever workouts we give them, especially since it's most often more productive to do any kind of speedwork with a group than a specific one on your own. The more you can fine-tune your specific speed training, however, the better your chances of reaching your potential.

THE 1-2-3 APPROACH TO SPEEDWORK: WARM UP, RUN FAST, COOL DOWN

Don't just jump on a track or head for the hills without first warming up, and then head for the shower after your last interval. It's not wise to either start or stop these body-straining workouts too quickly. Improve the quality of speed sessions and minimize risk of injury by warming up and cooling down properly. It's preferable to warm up and cool down for longer than the typical 10 to 15 minutes you might do for your normal training run. If possible, set aside up to 30 minutes of easy running plus 10 to 20 minutes for stretching both before and after speed workouts. For intervals and hill training, it's ideal to stretch thoroughly after running easily for at least 10 to 15 minutes. Then run another 5 to 10 minutes and do a few strides (short, brisk pickups) prior to starting the speed workout. Afterward, cool down by running at an easy pace prior to a quality stretch session. I'll change to training shoes and put on dry, warm clothes to make this cool-down run safer and more comfortable.

THE BASIC VARIABLES: DISTANCE, QUANTITY, INTENSITY, RECOVERY

Speed training is based on the variables above. They can be maneuvered in various ways to make the workout more difficult as you get in better shape. Increasing the distance, quantity, or pace of the runs, or shortening recovery between them, makes the workouts harder. For the most part, it's best to gradually increase the stress of one variable at a time.

Distance and quantity. The length of speed runs used in this text ranges from 220 yards for intervals to 13 miles for a marathon-paced tempo run. Most workouts range from a quarter-mile to one mile. Complete enough speed runs ("reps") to give yourself a good workout, but not so many that you can't finish the last one at nearly the same pace as your average. If new to speed training, minimize the number of reps in a workout. With experience and fitness, you may increase the quantity of reps per session. Generally, the longer or faster the interval, the fewer the reps. Total speed mileage for a workout (excluding warm-up, cool-down, and recovery runs) generally ranges from 2 to 6 miles, depending upon your fitness level and goals, and the intensity, type, and distance of the workout. Three to 4 miles of speed mileage is appropriate for most runners and most workouts.

Intensity (pace). This is how fast you run workouts. The speed is usually race pace or faster, which would generally reach 85 to 98 percent of your maximum heart rate. It should be based on the pace you are capable of now, not what you used to be able to run or the pace you fantasize about. Generally, the longer the distance, the more reps, and the less recovery—the slower the pace.

Adjust workout paces as your race paces improve. The best way to judge the proper intensity is by monitoring consistency. If you aren't able to maintain the desired pace, or at least be near it, for the entire workout, that usually means you're running too fast. If you had too little, or too much, left at the end, adjust your pace for the next speed session. It's better to run slower and more consistently than to start fast and tighten up, finishing the workout exhausted and frustrated. Complete speed training knowing you could have run just a little faster. The key is to run fast enough to challenge your limits yet stay relaxed and under control.

The range I use in this book is from a low-intensity marathon pace to near-sprint. As an introduction to speed training, I recommend a pace range between your 5K and 10K race pace. If you haven't raced enough to know your race pace then just run at an effort that will leave you slightly breathless. Don't sprint—ever. Hard, all-out sprinting will make you more prone to injury.

I use seven basic speed training intensities in this book (see Chapter 10, Figure 10.6 for more guidelines):

* **Near-sprint pace:** Approximately half-mile to one-mile all-out race pace, or a bit faster than hard pace. It's not an all-out sprint, but it's just a notch below. This intensity is used for Power Intervals to build raw speed and muscular strength and power; improve running economy, anaerobic capacity, neurological recruitment, and development of fast-twitch fibers. At this pace you'll reach 98 to 100 percent of maximum heart rate and 100 to 130 percent of aerobic capacity. This speed is generally only used in bursts of 30 to 90 seconds for two to four reps with a complete recovery period. It should be used only by very fit, experienced runners.
* **Hard pace:** Ranges from slightly slower than near-sprint pace when running 220s to 5 percent faster than 5K pace for mile runs. This is the fastest pace most runners need to use in speed training. Improves leg speed and muscular fitness, aerobic capacity, anaerobic energy production, and running economy. At this pace you'll reach 95 to 98 percent of maximum heart rate and 95 to 100 percent of aerobic capacity.
* **Fast pace:** Ranges from slightly slower than hard pace when running 220s to 2.5 percent faster than 5K pace for mile runs. This is the fastest pace I recommend for Novice and Intermediate Competitors. It improves aerobic capacity, running economy, and sharpens leg speed.
* **5K pace:** Present or goal race pace. Develops a feel for pacing at this intensity and improves aerobic capacity. Develops speed for longer races. At this pace you'll reach 90 to 95 percent of maximum heart rate and up to 98 percent of aerobic capacity.
* **10K pace:** Present or goal race pace. Develops a sense of pacing for mid-range distances, and improves aerobic fitness and lactate threshold. Used for Pace Intervals when training from 10K to the marathon. This is a good pace to start at when new to speed training. At this pace you'll reach about 90 to 92 percent of maximum heart rate and aerobic capacity.

* **Tempo:** Approximately 10 to 30 seconds per mile slower than 10K pace, or 25 to 45 seconds per mile slower than 5K pace. Primarily used to improve lactate threshold. At this pace you'll reach about 85 to 92 percent of maximum heart rate and aerobic capacity.
* **Marathon tempo:** Present or goal race pace. This speed develops a feel for pacing at a relaxed marathon pace. At this pace you'll reach about 80 to 85 percent of maximum heart rate and about 75 percent of aerobic capacity.

Recovery. Here's the easy part—how much rest you take between reps. The theory behind speed training is that you can manage hard work in small quantities if the body is rested in between. If you ran very hard with no rest breaks, you would be racing. The body can't handle too many races, but it can handle weekly or twice-weekly speed sessions. Basically, you recover by allowing the heart rate, breathing, and body temperature to get back down to about the level you would be at for a slow run or brisk walk. Your pulse should be below 120 after the rest period.

For hill repeats, recovery is a slow jog back down to the start. Fartlek recovery is usually at training pace for about the same distance as the burst. The jogging or walking recovery for intervals ranges from 30 seconds to 6 minutes, or approximately the same time period as the interval run or slightly less. Make sure you are breathing comfortably before running fast again. If you're still uncomfortable after your intended recovery period, then take more time before you run hard again, slow the pace, or abort the rest of the training session.

FACTORS INFLUENCING SPEED WORKOUTS

The quality of speed workouts depend on these factors:

Goals. Each workout should relate specifically to your racing goal and present training phase. To build strength and staying power, emphasize long hill training, fartlek, and tempo runs. To develop a sense of race pace, run intervals at your goal race pace. To sharpen speed as a key race nears, go with faster intervals.

Fitness and experience. The more you have, the more speed you can safely manage—and the more you will benefit. But you still need to be cautious and patient. All runners must ease back into speedwork after a layoff. Don't fool yourself into thinking you are still in good shape. Remembering how well you ran in the past and thinking you can do it now leads to shattered egos and injury.

Bad weather. The best temperature for running is 40 to 60 degrees Fahrenheit. If it gets much warmer or colder, adjust the workout. In hot and humid conditions, be prepared to reduce the pace and/or the distance or number of reps. Recovery is a battle to bring both your heart rate and temperature down. Take longer recovery breaks. Walk instead of jog, and drink more fluids while recovering. Don't compare hot-day workout times with those run in more ideal weather. In fact, we seldom time very hot weather workouts with our classes; they are meaningless compared with the effort. Be aware of how your body is responding to warning signs of heat stress.

Never speed-train on a hot day without fluids and shade handy. Bring fluids to workouts, or plan your runs for tracks, trails, or roads that have access to water. If possible, warm up and run your workout in the shade. This may mean switching your planned workout from a sunny track to a shaded trail. If you do hard speedwork in the sun, at least try to stay in the shade during recovery periods. Perhaps the better option is to switch your workout to the cooler evening.

Cool, crisp weather allows you to run and recover fast. Below 32 degrees Fahrenheit, however, speedwork can cause injury. Take extra time to warm up before running hard on a cold day, and then do your first few reps conservatively to further ease into faster running. Don't run extremely fast when it is extremely cold: You may not be able to loosen up adequately, resulting in a lack of efficiency in your motion and possible injury. Do intervals in extremely cold weather at race pace or slower. Besides, you won't be able to run fast times anyway due to the combination of cold and extra clothing. Keep moving to keep warm and prevent muscles from tightening. Run slowly during the recoveries on intervals; fartlek and tempo runs are good choices for these reasons. Never attempt to run hard on snow or ice; you may fall or strain a muscle. Look for bare spots during a continuous run and then pick up the pace. Or look for dry hills and work out there. A good option is to speed on a treadmill.

A strong wind can ruin your workout. First it blows you faster, then slower; you can't keep a steady pace and your times will be slowed. Just run at your intended effort level and forget time goals. In a cold, steady rain, starting and stopping for intervals could cause muscle strain or tightness. Further, footing may be slippery. Under these conditions, it may be better to change your workout to another day.

Of course there are also benefits to suffering through foul-weather workouts. The feisty champion, Zatopek, recommends it: "There is a great advantage in training under unfavorable conditions, for the difference is then a tremendous relief in a race." If I've scheduled a team workout or class training session, I expect committed runners to show up "come Hell or high water." I might alter the workout a little to compensate for the conditions, but I believe a tremendous amount of mental toughness is accomplished by not wimping out. Besides, they don't ever cancel races due to weather (except for very icy roads).

Physical. A minor illness, such as a cold, or a minor injury requires that you run fewer and less intense reps and take more time for recovery. Stay away from speedwork if the illness or injury becomes more serious. Fatigue, whether due to lack of sufficient sleep or overtraining, obviously requires a more conservative approach.

Psychological. Performance is affected by the runner's mental state. Anxiety and mental stress may cause occasional poor workouts. Back off. Don't take out your stresses on the track, hills, or roads. Run a more controlled workout.

GROUP WORKOUTS

Why do over 2,000 people pay to take our speed training classes each year? Because they would never work as much on their own. Hard running is more bearable, even enjoyable, when accomplished in a group setting. You're more likely to get in consistent workouts, too. It sure is easier to cook up excuses to skip a scheduled hard run, or bail out halfway through one, if you have no one to account for but yourself. Miss a few group training sessions, and you risk falling behind your peers. Just as important, you'd be missed by your training partners and you would miss them. The social atmosphere of shared hard work brings people closer together. Team up with others of similar ability to push and pull each other to new levels of fitness. This is the biggest secret to success of the teams I have coached. As the infamous Villanova University track coach Jumbo Elliott was fond of saying: "Runners make runners." All of this translates into faster race times.

To make workouts more beneficial, everyone works together at a similar pace and effort. If you sprint way ahead, you mess up the group pacing. If you lag behind, either you work too hard trying to keep up or the group has to slow to keep you in contact. For our classes, runners of similar pace are teamed up so they will help each other as a team. Ideally, you'll be close enough in ability so you can flow together at a steady pace. You can push and pull each other to times much faster and easier than if you ran alone. The key here is to run together as a team, not to try to run each other into the ground.

What happens if you can't find anyone to run speed workouts at your pace, or your small training group has a wide range of abilities? The answer is the staggered start. Whether a tempo run, interval, or hill repeats, give the slower runners a head start so that everyone in the training group will finish at about the same time. This makes the workout more fair and fun for everyone. It offers a challenge for the slower runners to hold off the faster ones, and for the faster runners to catch and pass the slower ones. Here's another option: Slower runners can do part of speed workouts at the same pace as the faster runners. For example, I sometimes do hard workouts with younger, faster runners. I can't keep up with them for the full length of each interval, but I can keep up for part of it. So, I may run less distance, but at their speed. On 4-lappers on the track, for example, I'll hang on for 3-laps and then drop out before I start to deteriorate too badly. This way I get high-quality training with high-quality company. Of course I'm sure to remind them that twenty years ago the roles would have been reversed!

EASING INTO SPEED TRAINING

If you are new to speed training, one speed workout per week—or even one—every other week—is plenty unless you are supervised by an experienced coach for a second session. You still need to build and maintain enough mileage to get to the finish line in reasonable comfort, and you can't do that safely if you are doing too much speed training. Allow your body and mind to make a safe transition into faster running rather than thrash yourself until running is no longer fun. The key words here are caution and patience. Start carefully and allow your body to adapt to the new stress. Chapter 10 details how to use transition intervals before attempting faster speed training. With any type of speed workout, start with fewer reps, take plenty of recovery time between them, and run them at a controlled pace before intensifying the work as your body adjusts. See Chapter 9 for a sample 12-week program ideal for easing into speed training.

SAFE SPEEDING

I've never met a runner that didn't want to run faster. But I've also never met one that didn't get injured at least a few times trying. The healthiest form of running is aerobic running. Just run nice and easy for a few miles a few times a week and you'll minimize injury and maximize health. Once you start trying to run fast, the more likely you are to get hurt. Speed training can be high-risk activity unless you learn to speed safely. Avoid sudden changes in surface, type, quantity, or intensity of speed workouts.

Here are some tips to make your workouts safer and more productive:

You need an aerobic base. It's safer to hold off on speed training until you have reached a mileage base of 15 to 20 miles per week. Besides, until you reach that level you'll improve race times significantly by just increasing aerobic endurance. More experienced competitors should be within the mileage ranges recommended in Chapter 6 to be able to handle the speed training recommended for their level in the following chapters. Once you've reached your desired mileage base and start to intensify speed training, you may need to lower mileage at least some weeks to guard against overtraining or injury, and to allow for quality workouts. When peaking, choose intensity over mileage.

Ease into each speed session. Start each session slightly slower than you'll finish it. Finish all of your workouts feeling exhilarated and tired, but not exhausted.

Ease into faster shoes. Test them out first in shorter or slower-paced workouts before using them for longer or faster ones. Practice in your race day shoes before you race in them. It'll make your workouts faster and provide a safer transition for racing. But they'll have less cushioning, less support, and less heel-lift to go along with less weight. I compromise. I wear medium-weight training shoes for fartlek, tempo runs, hill training, and long races; lightweight training shoes for track intervals and short races. Those super lightweight racing shoes may allow you to train and race fast, but for the average runner they'll bring injury, too.

Listen to your body. If it protests about overstress; pay attention, and ease back. Drop out immediately if you feel anything unusual happening—a muscle tighten, a sharp pain. You can keep going, but you may regret it.

Don't get greedy. If you've improved with a consistent schedule of once per week speed training don't assume you'll get even better with two hard runs per week. Some runners find out the hard way due to injury or fatigue, especially as they age, that one quality run per week, or every other week, is best.

Follow the hard-easy method. Once again: Always take it easy the day before and one or two days after speed workouts. This is probably the most important rule of speed training. It is during recovery that your body gets stronger. Consider active recovery the day after a speed session: Instead of running, walk briskly or train with a non-weight-bearing activity such as biking or swimming.

Schedule wisely. Most runners speed-train during the middle of the week so that it doesn't interfere with races or long runs on weekends. Don't try to pack in more than one type of stressful training—speedwork, races, long runs—on any weekend.

Don't speed too close to racing. Your last speed workout prior to a race should be at least three days in advance; your last peak workout at least ten days in advance. After racing, a good rule to follow is not to run a hard speed workout for at least a day for every mile of the race: three to four days for a 5K, six to seven days for a 10K, two weeks for a half-marathon, and four weeks for a marathon.

Don't race during training. If you do, you may leave your race on the training runs, or get injured. No sprinting allowed! Do your speed runs evenly. Don't show off on one and sandbag another.

Log your complete workout. Include quantity, intensity, rest, weather, and more if helpful. Then you can more accurately compare workouts and measure progress.

Speed consistently. If you're sporadic with your speed training, you not only will minimize the benefit, you'll be more vulnerable to injury. Try to speed-train at least every other week. If you skip it more than two weeks, you'll lose fitness.

Don't speed-train hard week after week, year-round. It's too hard on your body and mind. Sharpen for a few races, then back off.

SPEED-TRAIN WHEN YOU'RE INJURED

What? If you stop speed training completely when injured, you may lose more fitness than if you cut your mileage and kept speed-training. But most injuries will get worse, and may have been caused by speed training. What to do? Speed-train with cross-training options as detailed in Chapter 45. But first, check with your sports doctor to make sure it won't affect your injury recovery. You can continue to do some cross-training speedwork as you're easing back into speed training with running.

MAINTAINING A SPEED BASE

Many programs recommend eliminating speed training during training lulls, including rebuilding phases and during the base buildup. But research shows that you'll actually lose more fitness by maintaining aerobic training and cutting speed training than if you cut back on mileage and continue to speed-train consistently. Accumulating mileage keeps you fit, but only for running slow.

You do need to back off from hard speed training periodically, but that doesn't mean you should completely stop for several weeks or months. Skipping a couple of weeks or even a month won't damage fitness too much, but if you take any longer it'll take a long time for the speed to come back. Your fast-twitch fibers will think you don't want them anymore. Your brain and nervous system have to be trained regularly to control fast running with proper coordination. Take off too much time from speed training and your body will have to relearn the skills of fast running. Many of our students take our speed classes year-round, but they ease up occasionally, especially during the winter months where we don't emphasize timed intervals as much. For our classes I suggest that runners move back a group and run at more controlled speeds when they're in between more intense training periods. That way they have a speed base to draw on when they're ready to intensify training again.

During speed training lulls, aim to get in a light speed session weekly or at least every other week. Good choices include strides and fartlek. Another is a modified cutdown interval workout. Run two laps of the track at faster than 5K speed, then one and a half laps, one lap, and one half-lap. Concentrate on running quick to keep your fast-twitch fibers from going on vacation, and on plenty of recovery (jog a lap or more) to keep the workout from getting too hard. Save the hard-core speed training for when it counts: as you are peaking for key races.

GOOD DAYS, BAD DAYS

Some days you have it, some you don't. You may feel awesome, or you may feel awful. Most workouts, like most races, will be somewhere in between. Don't let either extreme fool you. A great workout doesn't mean you're ready for much tougher ones. It takes more than one great workout to justify that.

When you're having a bad workout you've got three choices:

1. Abort it and go out for a beer, back to bed, or both. Just forget about it and go into the next workout with a clear conscience. Don't let a bad day ruin your confidence. All runners have bad workouts, even the Elites.
2. Tough it out. As long as you don't slow too badly, it may pay off to hang in there. It'll teach you to overcome bad patches in races. Of course if you're feeling ill or injured, trash the workout before it trashes you.
3. Save the workout by adjusting. Cut back your goal pace, decrease the distance or number of reps, or lengthen recovery. Make all these concessions if needed. For example, if you planned to run 4 times a mile at 5K pace but couldn't hit that time on the first one because you just weren't up to it—whether due to the weather, fatigue from a long run a few days earlier, stress at

work, or whatever—shorten the workout to a few quarters. It's a lot easier mentally to only have to run one lap at a time and you'll be running faster, so you'll salvage some benefit from the workout. At least you'll have something positive to write in your diary rather than "dropped out." The switch may even perk you up so you end up having a good day after all!

CHAPTER 9

A Simplified 12-Week Speed Training Program

Okay, you've heard enough talk and want some action. You're ready to run fast! Many runners, especially at the Novice, Intermediate, and Basic Competitor levels, don't care to know about speed training theories. You just want to run fast enough to meet modest goals: "Tell me what workouts to do and I'll do them."

What follows is a sample 12-week speed training program modeled on the typical schedule we use for our New York Road Runners Club classes. Thousands of runners have benefited from these workouts and you will, too. Use this easy-to-follow model as an introduction to speed training, or as a balanced program for experienced competitors. It's conservative, but effective. Too little training when it comes to speedwork is always better than too much. The key is to run a few quality workouts within a limited time period to help you get faster without overtraining. It includes each of the four basic types of speed workouts—intervals, hills, fartlek, and tempo—discussed in more detail in the following chapters. Review that information if you want to design your own speed program.

The program assumes you've developed a good fitness base (at least 15 to 20 miles a week for at least a month) and are ready to "sharpen" for races with some speedwork. To further prepare for a key race, you'll benefit from running one or two races during the 12-week buildup program—say a 5K and a 5-miler before a 10K race, or a 10K and a half-marathon before your marathon. Time the program so the last hard speed session is ten to twelve days before your big race. Don't run too hard too close to the race. After key races, take a break from hard training, and then come back to the trusty schedule again when you are ready to prepare for another good race effort. Or, if you're adventurous, move on to the advanced workouts in the following chapters.

This sample program is just that—a sample. Use it exactly as explained, or adapt it to fit individual needs. You may choose to expand it to 14 to 16 weeks, or to cut it to 8 to 10 weeks. It is designed to allow average runners to progress week-by-week, resulting in improved performances. Just as important, it includes a variety of workouts to keep your training interesting. More experienced, advanced runners may choose to increase the work load slightly from the following recommendations.

Be sure to warm up and cool down for speed sessions with easy running for at least 10 to 15 minutes. The program assumes you are only ready or willing to handle one speed workout per week. Keep these workouts separated from long runs by at least two days, and at least four days from races.

This program starts with transition intervals, as recommended in Chapter 10, before moving on to faster speed training. Experienced competitors will benefit from a few sessions of strides, short brisk pickups of 100 yards followed by complete recovery, prior to starting this program. Less-experienced runners haven't yet developed a good enough sense of pace to do these workouts under control, so they should start with week #1.

TWELVE SAMPLE WORKOUTS

If you're new to speed workouts I'll give you a suggested range for pace: between a little faster than 5K and a little slower than 10K pace. If you're experienced and fit, you may run a little faster. See guidelines for intensity in Chapters 8 and 10. You may choose to count down to a key race with the following sample program:

12 Weeks to Go: Fartlek

What the heck is a fartlek, you ask? It's a few bursts of speed included within your normal endurance run. This is a great way to make the transition between easy running and speed training. You run intervals just like you would on the track, but not over an exact, timed distance. If possible, find an interesting park or trail to explore while fartleking—ideally over grass or dirt to add even more variety. As an introduction to speed training, start first with the Modified Fartlek Run over level or gently rolling terrain.

After a proper warm-up, start fartleking. Do surges at a variety of speeds (not faster than race pace at first) for a variety of distances (50 yards to a half-mile) in a variety of combinations. The recovery period is at training pace or slower and should cover approximately the same distance or time as the interval. Pick landmarks, such as lightposts, and run to them. Many people prefer a little structure if they fartlek on their own. Thus, running for a certain time period works best. To get you started, I recommend a simple workout: Run four to eight bursts of 2 minutes each with 2 minutes of slow running recovery in between.

You might like fartlek so much you'll choose to do it again, replacing one of the following runs. If you do, experiment with a combination of shorter and longer bursts, and slower and faster paces. As you get used to this workout, progressively increase the number of fartlek pickups. Total mileage for this run, including warm-up and cool-down, will range from 4 to 8 miles, depending upon your experience and fitness.

11 Weeks to Go: Long-Hill Repeats

"Ugh, are you really going to make me run up a *big* hill," you complain. Long hills improve muscular fitness and mental toughness. Find one that is about a quarter-mile to a half-mile in length and not too steep. It should take about 2 to 5 minutes to run up it. Run the hill at 5K to 10K race pace a total of three to six times, depending on your fitness level. Recover by running back down nice and easy. This workout increases leg strength and bolsters your confidence in racing up hills.

10 Weeks to Go: Tempo Run

Tempo runs mimic the race itself, but not the whole race. These runs improve concentration while teaching you to stay relaxed and hold a strong pace for several minutes. These are great workouts to raise your lactate threshold.

After a proper warm-up, move into an effort that is comfortably hard, about 85 to 90 percent of your maximum heart rate. This should be a brisk, steady pace you can hold for the distance.

Aim for running 20 to 30 seconds per mile slower than 10K race pace, or about 35 to 45 seconds slower than 5K race pace. Hold this pace for 2 to 4 miles (or 15 to 30 minutes) and then ease into a cool-down run. An option is to do intervals at tempo pace, such as three times a mile with a 1-minute recovery period.

9 Weeks to Go: Mile Intervals

This one isn't really an interval workout yet. It's a training session to start developing a sense of race pace as you get used to running on a track. Run each of the four laps at approximately the same pace—about your race pace for the distance you are training to run. This way you are learning to keep a steady race pace. Hold back on the first lap, just as you must at the start of a race. If you feel you can run a little faster on the third or fourth lap, go ahead. If you hardly broke a sweat, start a bit faster for your second one. If you struggled to finish and were slowing down at the end, start slower on the next one. Ideally you ran the whole way at the same pace, finishing tired but not exhausted. Aim to do the same for your second mile interval. Novice and Intermediate Competitors should start with just two reps; Basic Competitors with three; and faster categories with three or four. Take a 3- to 5-minute walking or jogging recovery between intervals.

8 Weeks to Go: Short-Hill Repeats

Now the work gets more intense, but at least the suffering doesn't last long. Muscular power and running economy are really boosted with this workout. Pick a hill that's 50 to 200 yards in length and steep enough to challenge you, but not so steep it interferes with good form. You don't have to run these real hard since fighting gravity will take care of the intensity. Drive up the hill as if you are finishing a 5K race. Do not sprint all-out. Emphasize good running form. It should take about 30 to 90 seconds to get to the top. Do four to eight hill repeats. Recovery is a very slow run downhill.

7 Weeks to Go: Half-mile Intervals

Back to the track for halves—two-lappers. Now it's time to really work on speed and enhancing aerobic capacity by holding 5K race pace or slightly faster. Try to run each lap of the track in the same time—this is called running even "splits." You also should try to run each half-mile interval in about the same time. This is even pacing just like you should run in your races. While doing these intervals, visualize yourself running at the start or midway point of your race. Stay relaxed. Maintain good form. Keep on pace. Do four to six intervals, depending on your fitness level, with a 3- to 4-minute walking or jogging recovery.

6 Weeks to Go: Tempo Run

Do the same workout as in week #3. But this time you may run a little longer or a little faster.

5 Weeks to Go: Quarter-mile Intervals

Back to the track for quarters—one lappers. These are short and fast, but don't sprint all-out. Run faster than 5K race pace to improve leg speed, muscular fitness, running economy, and ability to handle lactic acid buildup. Concentrate on pumping your arms, pushing off your feet, and lifting your knees to go faster. This workout will make your starting race pace seem less intimidating and help you get ready for your finishing kick. Run four to eight quarters, depending on your fitness level, with a 2- to 3-minute recovery walk or jog between each one.

4 Weeks to Go: Mile Intervals

Back to miles, but this time you run them faster as a peak workout. This one is for the mind. It toughens you for maintaining a strong pace in a race. Hang in there and you'll be stronger on race day. Do three to four intervals at 5K race pace or slightly faster with a 3- to 5-minute recovery walk or jog in between. Try to keep a steady pace for each quarter-mile split. Just like in a race, you'll need to hold yourself back for the first mile or two in order to save energy for the last 1 or 2 miles. For the middle interval(s), stay calm and concentrate on your pace—again, mimicking your race strategy. The last mile will feel similar to the last mile of your race. Concentrate on good form while remaining mentally strong. Don't give up here or you'll mess up your average time just as letting go toward the end of a race will cost you precious seconds.

You can use this workout to test your fitness level and help predict your race day potential. Ideally, you'll run these miles at a faster pace and more comfortably than you did during the fourth week of this program.

3 Weeks to Go: Half-mile Intervals

It's back to two-lappers. But this time either add one or two more intervals or run at a slightly faster pace. See how much you've improved!

2 Weeks to Go: Cutdowns

Cut what? This is just a psychological trick to help runners practice their finishing kick and peak for races. It adds variety to your training since you are now getting away from running the same distance for each interval. With cutdowns, each successive interval is a shorter distance and is run at a slightly faster pace. Here, I recommend a mile, half-mile, and then a quarter-mile (An option is to insert a three-quarter-mile interval after the mile). Visualize that each run is your finishing kick. As you get closer and closer to the finish line, pick up the pace. Run your mile and three-quarter mile at race pace, your half-mile at faster than race pace, and your finishing quarter-mile quick, but not full steam. Take a 3- to 4-minute recovery walk or jog between intervals. As an option, do a pyramid workout: Build up in distance and then back down. For example, run a quarter-mile (not too fast!), half-mile, mile, and then another half-mile and quarter-mile.

1 Week to Go: Strides

This should be a light, controlled workout similar to week #1. Run it about two to four days before your big race. This peppy run, perhaps over the race finish line, should leave you mentally ready but not physically fatigued. Strides—a few brisk but not too hard pickups of about 100 yards—is detailed in Chapter 10.

SUMMARY

Remember, this is a flexible, *sample* program. Make whatever changes you feel will benefit you and keep your running enjoyable. This simplified 12-week program will help you get ready, with a modest amount of work, for a quality race effort. You will learn to run faster. Good luck!

CHAPTER 10

Interval Training

Interval training is based on a simple formula: Run at race pace or faster for segments that are much shorter than your race distance, with recovery breaks to minimize the stress on the body. The first really scientific approach to such training was developed during the 1930s by German cardiologist Dr. Hans Reindell, who used intermittent running to strengthen the hearts of some of his patients. He had them run repetitive short distances with short rest periods in between. The subjects pushed their heart rate to 170 to 180 beats per minute during the run, allowing it to drop to below 120 beats during the rest period. It worked; his patients became more fit. He then teamed with Woldemar Gerschler, a coach and exercise physiologist, to research this training method on more than 3,000 individuals. They found that a key to improved fitness with this method was controlling the rest intervals. Thus, they named their radical program "interval training." Technically, the rest breaks you take between each speed run is the "interval." Over the years, however, coaches have come to call the actual speed runs "intervals"—thus I shall in this text.

Intervals are the heart and soul of most competitive training programs. They are the best way to improve race performances according to decades of practical experience by runners and coaches as well as several studies. One such study at Texas Southwestern University by Dr. Peter Snell found that 30 minutes of weekly interval training at 5K pace produced twice the improvement in aerobic capacity and 10K race times compared to training with tempo runs. By the way, Snell knows his way around the track! The New Zealander is considered one of the greatest half-milers and milers of all-time, having set world records and won Olympic gold at both distances.

Intervals can make or break runners. That is, you can either get faster or, if you're not careful, get injured. The intermittent work allows you to train much faster than you would at a steady, hard pace. This is where you really learn race pacing and increase speed. When intervals follow a logical sequence of progression, you can carefully monitor improvement which is a strong motivating factor. Intervals can also be used to help predict your racing fitness. Check your diary to compare your interval times with those going into previous races. It'll give you an idea of how much faster (or slower) you're capable of racing.

Intervals at race pace and faster improve several key factors to racing success, including aerobic capacity, anaerobic tolerance, lactate threshold, running economy, muscular strength and power, and the efficiency of fast-twitch fibers. Intervals also train you to concentrate and constantly monitor your body.

Many runners, especially beginner racers, may race at only a slight discomfort level. By learning to push harder and keep going in shorter intervals of concentrated discomfort you realize that you can give your all on race day. Intervals benefit runners training for all distances in all phases of a training program.

TRACK INTERVALS

Ah, the track, the almighty mecca of speed! Many runners, including myself, started running with school track teams. The sacred track may be intimidating. But don't worry, you don't have to be a track racer to train on a track. Anyone can benefit from track-training, whether fast or slow, as individuals or in groups. Remember this: You're working just as hard running laps at your 5K race pace as those fleet-footed folks are at their 5K pace. Not only that, you'll spend more time per lap suffering at that intensity. So the faster runners should be respectful of you, not the other way around. Many local clubs have regular track workouts and welcome all levels of runners.

I love track intervals. I also hate them. That's because they're a lot like races and I have a love-hate relationship with them, too. If you work hard at intervals, they sure aren't easy. But neither is a hard race effort. And just like a race, the pressure of anticipated time goals looms. Both interval times and race times get better and better if you put in the necessary effort. After a few quality interval sessions on the track each spring, I feel like a new runner—almost young again. I have new spring in my step, and am more coordinated. It never ceases to amaze me: Consistent track intervals bring your speed back every time after a training lull, and really sharpen you for peak racing performances. The track allows for the precision of knocking off exactly measured laps. Progress can be more easily measured. Track workouts can get the most out of you—especially if your coach is watching. You can cheat a little out on a road when no one is looking, but there's no place to hide on a track.

Most tracks nowadays are 400 meters rather than the quarter-mile (440 yards) ovals used when I was a trackman. The metric lap is less than 3 yards short of a quarter-mile, so this little difference is of no significance to your workouts—about 1 second short per lap for most runners. In this text we'll refer to quarters, halves, three-quarters, and miles for intervals rather than 400, 800, 1200, and 1600 meters since most American runners think in terms of mileage. Other than the difference between quarter-mile and 400-meter tracks, all tracks should be the same precise distance. But be sure to run as close as possible to the curb or you'll run a longer distance; tracks are measured 1 foot from them. Not all tracks are the same speed either. Some artificial surface tracks are soft; some are hard. The hard ones are faster, but the soft ones offer more cushioning. Cinder and dirt tracks, especially if not in good repair, are slower than artificial surfaces—perhaps by as much as 2 seconds per lap.

What about indoor tracks? It's great to be able to escape the elements and really let your legs fly on an indoor circuit. But running on indoor tracks can cause injury. Most are eight laps to a mile or worse. I used to work out on one (until I got injured) that was twenty-three laps to a mile. The tight turns and banked surfaces indoors create unusual leg stress. Also, indoor air is often dry and dirty, which may trigger respiratory problems. Most runners are better off running intervals on a treadmill than on indoor tracks. Save those speedy little ovals for tracksters who are experienced at running around and around while leaning inward. Besides, you shouldn't try to do hard speed training year-round, so use the cold-weather months to take a natural break.

You don't have to run intervals on a track. Perhaps you can't get to one easily, the surface bothers your legs, or you just don't like the intensity it involves. No problem. Measure off your own distances on trails or roads. Keep them flat if possible since the goal here is to build speed. We don't have a track in Central Park yet we have several loops on paved paths we use for intervals for our classes. I've coached several runners that developed into national class competitors without ever stepping foot on a real track. If you have the luxury, the best place to make up your own track is on dirt trails shaded by trees. Don't have exact courses? Simply run hard at your desired intensity for intervals by time, rather than distance. If, for example, you run half-mile intervals at about 3 minutes each on a track, just run hard for 3 minutes for your intervals off the track. It's not as precise, but you still get a solid workout. These speedwork variations allow you to interval-train wherever you go.

INTERVAL WORKOUT VARIABLES: DISTANCE, QUANTITY, INTENSITY, RECOVERY

Effective interval training depends on the proper combination of the basic variables above. Don't just juggle the variables and hope to come up with the right combination. Plan carefully. Guidelines for these variables and the various factors that influence speed workouts are detailed in Chapter 8. When designing interval sessions, examine the key variables individually and consider all these factors.

The Interval Training Guide (Figures 10.1–10.5) that follows minimizes guesswork choosing the key variables. Charts for each competitive category recommend a range of quantity, intensity, and recovery for the key interval distances. Adding to the number or distance of intervals run, quickening the pace, or shortening the recovery period—but not all at once—make the workout harder. Don't make significant changes in more than one variable at a time. Start workouts conservatively by using the easier ends of the ranges. For example, the Basic Competitor chart for faster than race pace intervals (Figure 10.2) shows the following ranges for half-mile intervals: four to six reps, at 5K race pace or faster, with a recovery period of 3 to 5 minutes. So if you're new to speed training or are just coming back to faster training, it may be wise to start with four reps at 5K pace with a 5-minute recovery.

INTERVAL DISTANCE AND QUANTITY

In general, run longer interval distances to prepare for longer races, and shorter ones for shorter races. Miles are the backbone of speed training for many marathoners, and quarters are the key for many 5K runners. Yet all runners benefit some from a mixture of long intervals for strength, endurance, and stamina for holding race pace, and short ones for speed and power. You'll need both types to improve your race times.

The longer the distance and faster the intensity, the fewer reps you run. For example, my suggested range of reps for Basic Competitors for race pace intervals is five to ten quarters, but only three to four one-milers; and the suggested number of quarters drops to four to eight when the intensity switches to faster than race pace. So how many reps should you run? Start at the low end of the suggested ranges. A good rule of thumb is to stop the workout before, not after, your pace falls off too much and your form deteriorates. One rep too many can leave you frustrated (or injured) rather than proud of your training session. With experience and fitness, you may increase the number of intervals for each workout, but be conservative. It's better to run with controlled quality than to boost the quantity of intervals too much.

To add variety, increase the number of quality reps by running *sets*. These are groups of intervals separated by a longer recovery period. To run eight times a quarter-mile instead of six, for example, run four reps separated by a 2-minute recovery period to complete one set, then take a 5-minute recovery break before completing a second set of four reps, each with a 2-minute recovery.

The total speed mileage of each interval workout (not including warm-up, cool-down, and recovery running) ranges from 1 to 2 miles for Novice Competitors (for example, four to eight times a quarter-mile) to 5 miles or more for Local Champions. For the average competitor, most workouts (except intervals less than half-miles) should total about 3 miles of speed training. A general rule of thumb is that total speed mileage in an interval session shouldn't exceed about 8 to 10 percent of your average weekly mileage. So that's about 2 miles or less if you average 20 miles a week, 3 to 4 miles if you average 40 miles, and 5 to 6 miles if you average 60 miles.

Six different distances—from 220 yards to 2 miles—are used for the basic workouts in this text. I keep the distances fixed for the entire workout. This keeps things simple and it's easier to measure progress and make adjustments in the variables. But as you improve you may wish to add other distances, or combine a variety of distances in a single workout. Hill repeats are similar to interval workouts and other interval options include tempo intervals and intervals injected into steady-paced runs (fartlek). The interval distances:

220s. These are half-lappers (220 yards or 200 meters) and are primarily used to train for distances of 5K or less, or to sharpen speed for a finishing kick. I only include this option for experienced, fit Advanced Competitors and up since the shortness of this workout entices runners to blast away faster than their muscles can tolerate.

Quarters. One-lappers (440 yards or 400 meters) are the long-time favorite of track coaches. In quantity and at race paces, they are used to improve general aerobic conditioning and develop a "feel" for race pace. But generally they are used to improve running economy and to sharpen speed in the final few weeks before shorter races of 5K to 10K. Experienced, fit runners may run these at a controlled near-sprint. Here's where you really work on honing leg turnover, knee lift, foot pushoff (and increased stride length), arm drive, and staying relaxed while running anaerobically.

My college coach loved this workout. We didn't. But by doing them we ran faster, and you will, too. If you run them hard, you'll cuss me just like I cussed my cranky ol' coach. You may even find out why our coach placed a bucket at the finish line for these workouts. But you don't have to run that intensely to benefit from quarters, and perhaps you shouldn't. For this reason, the ranges I recommend here are less in quantity and intensity than what some coaches would recommend and certainly less than what those young Elites run. Short, fast intervals cause far more injuries than slower, longer ones. Stay under control, ease into fast training.

Halves. On two-lappers (880 yards or 800 meters) you work on both pacing and speed. Aim to run the same split times for each of the two laps, or run negative splits—picking up the pace slightly on the second lap to simulate a finishing kick. Warning: Run too fast on the first lap and that Bear will find you the second time around. Like quarters, in quantity and at race pace they improve general aerobic conditioning whereas at faster paces they hone your ability to run fast in races. Halves are valuable in training for races from the 5K to the marathon. An option used by many runners is 1000 meter intervals. That's a half-lap longer than halves, just enough extra distance to really hurt.

Three-quarter (1200 meters). Three-lappers are a bridge between the short, fast intervals and long ones. They'll build the strength and speed to handle mile intervals and add variety to your program if you're tired of a steady diet of halves and miles. Run the first two laps slightly slower than your normal pace for half-mile intervals and then concentrate on maintaining form and speed over the last lap.

Miles (1600 meters). Now we're in distance-running territory. Those fast sprinters don't cross this line! Four-lappers develop the ability to hold a strong pace over a significant distance, and improve concentration. Miles are tough, even at 10K race speeds. That's because they mimic the race itself. You need to start aggressively for each mile interval to meet your goal, yet not start too fast. The middle laps demand a combination of patience and pushing, and the final lap forces you to concentrate on good form while digging down deep for the guts to keep on pace. Try to run each lap the same pace or gradually pick it up over the last two. The complete set of intervals also teaches proper distribution of energy: Run the first one or two intervals too fast and you'll be struggling on the last one or two.

Miles are the key workouts in my class and team workouts for training for 10K to the half-marathon, but especially for the marathon. Miles can be introduced during the base phase, increased during the strength phase, and really emphasized as you sharpen for longer races. By comparing progress over the course of a few sessions of mile intervals you'll know you're getting in good shape.

1¼ to 2 miles. Not many runners dare venture beyond mile intervals. But if you do, you'll be rewarded with increased fitness and mental toughness. Hanging on to a strong pace beyond a mile isn't easy, but neither is it on race day. You've got to be really disciplined to do five- to eight-lappers on a track. But this way you get constant feedback on pacing. I run my long intervals on dirt trails to decrease the pounding to my body, but running them on roads will best simulate racing conditions. To make this workout more valuable when off the track, mark each half-mile. We do two types of these long intervals with our classes, primarily when marathon training. One course is a 1¼-mile loop through the north hills of Central Park, the other is an out-and-back course—2 miles each way. The longer your long-interval choice and the faster your pace, the more recovery you should take and less reps you should do.

Optional Combination Intervals. The possibilities for variety are endless. I'll give you a few examples:

* ***Ladders.*** Run up the ladder, for example, with a 440, 660, half-mile, three-quarter mile, and mile interval. I use these to build strength and confidence.
* ***Cutdowns.*** Run down the ladder, for example, with a mile, three-quarter mile, half-mile, 660, 440. I use these to practice the finishing kick. Quicken the pace as the distance shortens. Another good choice is to start workouts with a warm-up interval. For example: Run a mile interval at 10K pace, then six times a half-mile at a faster pace.
* ***Pyramids.*** Run up and back down the ladder. For example, run a quarter-mile, half-mile, three-quarter mile, mile, mile, three-quarter mile, half-mile, quarter-mile.
* ***Groups.*** Run a few reps of one distance and then move to another. For example: two times a mile followed by four times a half-mile.
* ***Sets.*** For example, a mile followed by a half-mile to complete a set. Do two to three sets with a 3-minute recovery between the intervals, but a full 5 minutes between sets.
* ***Cut times.*** For example, start running a set of six halves at 10K pace. Cut the pace by 5 seconds per interval until the final one is 30 seconds faster than 10K pace.

* ***Shifting gears.*** For example, run four times three-quarter mile. Run the first two laps at 10K pace and then drop the final lap to faster than 5K pace. Work on your finishing kick.
* ***Out-and-backs.*** This is run off the track, ideally over trails. Run in one direction for 1 minute, then return to the start at the same pace. Take a 2- to 3-minute recovery. Repeat this sequence going out (and back) for 2-, 3-, 4- or more minute intervals. It's a great workout to do with runners of varying speeds since when you turn around the last-place runner is now the leader that can try to hold off the charge of the faster runners. We make this a fun workout with our classes by calling it "Chase the Coach." Our coaches lead to the turnaround time, then try to catch all the students going back.
* ***Over and unders:*** For example, run a steady 2 miles while alternating quarter-miles at 5 to 10 seconds faster than 10K pace with recovery quarters at 5 to 10 seconds slower than 10K pace.
* ***5K or 10K race distance intervals.*** You can do this on a track, but it will be less boring off-track. The best location is over a measured race course for the distance you are training to run. For example, alternate running hard and slow for a 5K distance. Run 10 seconds faster per mile than 5K pace for a half-mile (or about 3 minutes), then run easy for 220 yards (or about 1 minute). Keep this up until you finish the goal distance. Your final time should be 1 to 3 minutes slower than your present race time for this distance. Ease into this workout since it is tough. Start at one-half to two-thirds the race distance and with longer recoveries.

INTERVAL RECOVERY

Recovery isn't glamorous. After all, runners want to brag about how fast they go, not how much time they spend resting. But how much you rest between intervals is just as important as the intensity or distance of the run. Incomplete recovery is important to interval training for two key reasons: (1) it keeps you from running too fast, and (2) it is essential to the development of your aerobic and anaerobic systems.

The simplest way to determine how much recovery to take between intervals is to use Coach Gerschler's old-fashioned, but still accurate way: When your heart rate drops to 120 beats, start the next interval. The time between each interval may vary with this system, depending on how hard you run and the weather. But here's the built-in beauty of this system: Run one too fast and you're forced to recover longer.

Most runners prefer a set recovery time between intervals. But how do you know how long to take? In general, the harder you run, the more reps, and the longer the distance—the more recovery time required. A rule of thumb is to take as much recovery time as the time spent running the interval, or slightly less. Many coaches simply have runners jog a lap between intervals for quarters and halves, and two laps for miles. Okay, you're waiting for me to make it easy for you by telling you how much recovery you should take at various intensities and distances. My recommended recovery periods on the following *Interval Training Guide* range from 30 seconds to 6 minutes, depending upon the speed and distance of the intervals and your category.

Remember, the amount of rest you take controls how fast you can run. If you require more than these recommended recoveries to keep on pace with your workout, you may be running too fast. If necessary, rest longer than planned, cut the intensity, or cut the workout short. On the other hand, don't take too long a recovery period. The goal is *incomplete recovery.* Start again after you've had enough rest to complete the next interval at the same pace and effort as the previous one. Don't wait so long that you're so fresh you can run too easily or much faster. Keeping recovery periods challenging is essential to mimicking the stress of competition. After all, you don't get any recovery breaks in races!

These are just guidelines. Adjust them to fit your individual needs. More rest may be required for Novice Competitors, for runners coming back to speed training after a layoff, on a hot day, et cetera. The average runner should start conservatively with recovery times. With experience, find a set recovery time for each interval distance that works best and stick with it. Keep the recovery period constant and slightly increase the pace and number of intervals. That's the kind of improvement your stopwatch can capture, and it builds confidence as you approach your races. When peaking for a race, however, some coaches like to sharpen their athletes by emphasizing cutbacks in recovery.

What do you do during recovery? The temptation is strong to

lie down and take a nap! Whatever you do, don't lie down, sit down, or stand still. Besides not promoting blood flow to remove lactic acid, your muscles are likely to get stiff if you stop moving. Further, blood may pool in your legs and cause dizziness or fainting. So keep moving, at a slow jog or fairly brisk walk. Most track coaches prefer a running recovery to keep their athletes loose and ready to go. If you don't have the energy to run slowly after each interval, you ran too fast. Research demonstrates that you'll actually recover quicker between each rep if you jog easily at a pace that is approximately 3 to 4 minutes per mile slower than 10K pace. That's a shuffle, but it keeps blood flowing through your legs. Nevertheless, I use a walking recovery for our classes of average runners since it minimizes the pounding on the legs (especially if running hard on hard pavement), and helps bring down body temperature (particularly on hot days).

INTERVAL INTENSITY (PACE)

Before each interval workout I tell our classes: "Run anywhere from faster than 5K pace to a little slower than 10K pace. If you're just coming off a race, or going into one, take it a little easy. But if you're healthy, well-rested, and feeling good, push the pace if you want to improve your fitness. How much push is up to you. But whatever pace you run, you should be able to maintain it for the complete set of intervals."

Interval pace is largely dictated by your training goals. Run faster to train for short, fast races; longer and not as fast to train for longer races. Run 10K pace or slightly slower than 10K pace to best improve lactate threshold, at or near 5K pace to best improve aerobic capacity, and faster than 5K pace to best improve running economy, speed, and power. Run at race pace to learn how to parcel out energy, faster than race pace to make race pace seem easier. Ease into interval training with race pace training before moving on to faster paces.

Intervals are run in three general categories: at or near race pace, faster than race pace, and near-sprint. It's often confusing when comparing interval training advice from one coach to the next since many of them use different terms, or the same terms with a different meaning. Some define intervals as race pace and others as much faster than race pace. Some use the term repeats or repetitions instead of intervals for faster than race pace speedwork. To simplify things, I refer to all intermittent training in this book as intervals. I break them down into four basic types: Pace, Fast, Hard, and Power Intervals.

By running intervals at race pace you become familiar with the pace you'll run for races. This effort should drive the heart rate up to about 85 to 90 percent of maximum. The stress of Pace Intervals comes from shorter recoveries and more reps, not hard intensity. You have two choices here: present race pace or goal race pace. I recommend starting with your present fitness level and increasing the intervals to your realistic, challenging race goal pace as your fitness improves. Also, use Pace Intervals as a transition to Fast Intervals. Every interval and every split within each interval should be run at the same pace, preferably within a few seconds of each other. This improves your sense of pace and trains you to hold back when fresh, save energy for later, and keep pushing when tired—just like in a race.

Obviously, you should run 5K pace intervals to pace-train for the 5K distance, and 10K pace intervals to pace-train for the 10K distance. But what about longer races? Some half-marathon and marathon-paced intervals are helpful to learn the feel for these speeds, but at those paces you're really running tempo intervals (Chapter 13). On the following *Interval Training Guide*, use 10K pace for race pace intervals when training for half-marathons and marathons. This speed is quick enough to challenge, and slow enough to practice pacing.

Intervals at faster than 5K pace mimic or exaggerate the intensity of racing and are uncomfortable, thus making it easier to handle a fast pace on race day. Fast and Hard Intervals drive heart rates up to 90 to 98 percent of maximum, about the level reached in short, fast races. A continuous run at this pace couldn't be held for more than 10 minutes or so.

Start your interval build-up program at conservative paces and increase the speed of your workouts as you sharpen for races. Interval speed depends on the amount of rest between intervals, distance run, and quantity of reps. The shorter the recovery period, and the greater the distance and number of reps—the slower the pace.

A key to successful interval training is not to run more speed mileage than your weekly mileage supports, or at faster paces than dictated by your present racing fitness. General guidelines for intensity for speed training are detailed in Chapter 8.

POWER INTERVALS OR REPEATS

Many coaches have runners train at even faster paces than recommended above for intervals, especially when training for the 5K distance and shorter. They promote short, fast runs of 30 to 90 seconds (110 to 660 yards) at 90 percent all-out effort. I call this near-sprint pace and it may be as fast as half-mile or mile intensity. Some pain-loving veterans may run almost all-out for halves, even miles. These workouts are best kept for the young, talented, experienced runners who are more prepared to safely handle these intensities. There is a limit on how fast we can safely speed so I don't promote these workouts for the average runner. They are not included on my *Interval Training Guide*.

But if you can handle them, they'll sure help you get stronger, more powerful, and faster. They'll give you plenty of experience at running with high levels of lactic acid as that Bear jumps on your back. Running economy is enhanced. In fact, researchers at Arizona State University found that Steve Scott improved his running economy by 5 percent over a nine-month period after adding hard repeats to his training. The result: He set American records for 1500 meters and the mile.

Generally, only two to four reps are recommended since the intensity is so high. Recovery time is up to five times that of the hard run. Take more if you need it, less if you don't. Don't think you're a goof-off by taking so much time. Unlike regular intervals that require incomplete recovery to be most beneficial, here you take *complete* recovery. You want to be rested enough to run the next rep as fast as the previous one. Walk, jog, or even lie down if you want during these lengthy recoveries. As I recall, I spent most of mine puking. So if you have a high threshold for pain and want to speed to the max, give repeats a try. Be warned: Your hamstrings might rebel.

IMPROVING INTERVAL TIMES

If the main goal of racing is to improve your pace per mile, then the goal of interval training should be to do the same. What's the best way to improve interval times? For whatever interval distance(s) you choose to key on, first determine the number of reps and the length of recovery you want to use as your measuring sticks. For example, you may choose to build to running four times a mile with a 4-minute recovery period since that is what you did as key workouts going into your last marathon. You might ease back into this type of workout doing three reps with a 5-minute recovery. For the next workout, cut the recovery to 4 minutes. Ideally, you'll be able to run the same pace for the intervals even as you cut recovery. Once you've adjusted to your target recovery time and moved up to four reps, it's time to target your pace.

A good goal is to aim to cut it by 1 or 2 seconds per 440 yards. In this example, by 4 to 8 seconds for the mile. When aiming to increase the pace of your intervals, you may want to lower the reps slightly to adjust. So for this example, cut back to three reps but aim to run each lap slightly faster. Once you can accomplish that goal, move to four reps until you can run goal pace for the complete set of four times a mile. As you get comfortable with this pace, repeat this method to bring your times down by a few more seconds per lap.

Remember, add only one or two intervals at a time while keeping the pace and recovery the same, and then bring down the pace. Don't be obsessed with time, however. Concentrate on maintaining a steady pace and speed will come. Use the *Interval Training Guide* to choose the number of reps and recovery times. You don't have to reach the maximum number of reps on the charts before starting to work on running faster.

Increase speed in steps to allow your body to adapt to the increased work loads. Trying to run too fast too soon for intervals may lead to frustration. Interval training brings quick gains at first, then smaller ones later. For experienced runners, each time you sharpen for races you should gradually see smaller, but steady gains. Be flexible. Be patient. The speed will come (or come back). I promise.

ADJUSTING INTERVAL WORKOUTS

In a perfect workout, you'll finish feeling you have a little left and are not exhausted. The first, middle, and last interval would be the same pace. But perfect workouts don't always happen. If you run the entire workout faster than planned, don't think it was just luck. You need more of a challenge. Cut back on the recovery period if it may be excessive, add more intervals, or lengthen the distance. On the other hand, perhaps you can't run the workout as fast as planned. Make adjustments. Maybe you need more rest. Giving yourself 15 to 30 seconds of extra recovery can be a big help. Or, cut back on the number of intervals planned. This way you may be able to do the remaining ones at your goal pace. Stop the workout at any point where your pace falls off dramatically. Minimize loss in confidence and the beating you're giving your body. Analyze what went wrong. You may have misjudged your fitness and set too fast a goal pace. Perhaps the weather was a factor, or you just weren't feeling good. A common cause: starting too fast on the first interval. Don't fret. Adjust.

GENERAL GUIDELINES FOR INTERVAL TRAINING

Keep the following points in mind:

- Warm up and cool down for intervals following guidelines in Chapter 8.
- Jog into the start of intervals. Don't start flat-out as if you were in a race. This places stress on your legs.
- Be careful not to leave your best performances on the track. Intervals should be challenging but controlled. Save your all-out efforts for race day. Although it helps to have another runner or a pack of runners to flow with, racing each other will ruin the workout. Work together, or work alone at your own pace.
- Develop a relaxed rhythm and try to stay with it through the workout. If you begin to lose form, back off slightly while staying relaxed rather than tensing up and trying to muscle your way around the track.
- Focus on the workout and your running form. Some runners in our classes carry on a conversation while running intervals. I ask them to save their energy for the work. Besides, it interferes with the concentration of other runners in the group. Save the socializing for the warm-up and cool-down periods.

- Don't do the same workout each week—look for variety. But go back to some of the workouts periodically to measure progress.
- The average runner should limit themselves to one interval workout per week. Experienced runners may balance a track workout with a fartlek, tempo, or hill training session at least two days before or after interval sessions. Only very fit, experienced runners should attempt two hard interval sessions per week.
- You may need an extra recovery day as you ease into, or back into intervals.

TRANSITION INTERVALS

To minimize injury and maximize the quality of interval training, avoid suddenly going from just running at your aerobic training pace to interval pace. Whether new to interval training or coming back to it after injury, a winter break or other training lull, ease your body into faster running with transition intervals.

Novice and Intermediate Competitors in our classes start with modified fartlek to introduce them to switching gears, and 1-mile intervals to give them a feel for running evenly at race pace for long distances before we teach faster running. For more experienced competitors, fartlek, tempo intervals, and both uphill repeats and downhill intervals and strides are good choices as a transition to interval training. When you're ready to hit the track for regular intervals, start first with 10K pace and with longer intervals as a further transition before moving on to shorter distances and faster speeds.

Strides. These simple "semi-sprints," also called "accelerations" and "pickups," can be helpful during all phases of training. Besides being an excellent way to ease into regular interval training, strides serve many other purposes. They are used as a drill to improve form; to maintain some leg speed during training lulls and while base-building rather than skipping speedwork entirely; to help recover from stiffness at the end of a medium- or long-distance run; as a second, but light speed session during the week when building toward fast racing; as a final peppy workout two to four days before a race; as the final warm-up factor prior to speedwork and racing; or just to liven up your running a bit if you're feeling sluggish or bored with a steady diet of slow running.

They can be run on any reasonably flat surface with good footing. A grassy field is a good choice, but even a flat stretch of pavement will do. First, warm up thoroughly. An option is to do strides in the middle or the end of a short- or medium-distance run. Whether used as a separate workout or as part of a training run, when you're ready to pick up speed run briskly for about 20 seconds, or about 100 yards (such as the straightaway on a track). These are short enough that they won't leave you tired like a hard workout, but yet will add a little quality to your training. To minimize straining muscles, gradually increase your speed for the first 20 yards, hold it for 60 yards, and then ease back down over the final 20 yards. Then recover with 100 yards or so of easy jogging (such as the curve on a track, or the rest of the lap). Use a complete recovery since the goal is to work only on speed.

These aren't all-out sprints and this isn't meant to be a full-blown speed session. Run with smooth, controlled speed: 80 to 90 percent effort. This may range from half-mile to slightly faster than 5K race pace. Start with just a few strides and gradually build to ten or more when used as a transition to speed training. Don't panic if you huff and puff alot when you first start doing strides. That's why you're doing them, to ease your body back into faster running. The breathing, relaxed form, and speed will return.

Peaking with Intervals. Time your progression so you don't peak too soon. Increase the intensity of interval workouts over the last two to four weeks prior to a key race. Your last hard interval session should be ten to fourteen days before your goal race; if it's much earlier, you may peak too soon; if it's later, you may not get sufficient adaptation in time and may not recover adequately prior to race day. Make sure peak workout goals are challenging, but reachable. Pick some workouts you've done a few times as you built up your training and have proven in the past to be a good measure of your fitness, such as six times a half-mile. Your goal is to run the workout faster than you have this training cycle, maybe even ever. Popping a good interval session here proves you're ready.

Unfortunately, high levels of fitness achieved after sharpening with a progressive interval program can't be maintained for more than a few weeks. So after improving interval times over a period of two to three months or so with intervals, take advantage of it. Race. If you've got it, flaunt it! Then back off a bit before sharpening again.

Going Beyond. Many experienced, fit runners have a favorite, tough workout they like to do only as they get close to an important race. They use it as an important measure of their race readiness. It isn't a workout that should be used too frequently, may be once or twice a year—maybe even once in your life. These workouts aren't easy, in fact I call them "going beyond" workouts since their perceived difficulty is beyond the imagination of most runners. But to enter a new dimension as a competitive runner, you have to train your body and mind to go beyond. These callousing workouts should be a significant physical and mental test.

My most grueling workout was 20 times a quarter-mile at faster than 5-minute mile pace on a hot day. After that mind-boggling workout, I knew I could run a great race even in the heat. And I did, blasting a 4 miler in 20:09—a PR by over a minute. Another of my key workouts from the past was 6 times the 1¼ mile hilly northern loop in Central Park. By comparing how much faster I ran this workout than in previous training sessions going into past marathons, I knew I was peaking for a great race. My workout time dropped from 5:30 per mile to 5:15. For the marathon, I set a personal record by 10 minutes, averaging under 6:00 per mile. These are all times I wouldn't have dared to attempt if I hadn't "gone beyond" in training. If you dare, find a few challenging workouts to push you into a new dimension. But make sure you are very fit first, and give yourself at least 2 or 3 weeks to recover before the big race. Don't let me scare you. The workouts don't have to be killers for you to benefit, but they should challenge you enough that you can brag about them, too.

SIX STEPS TO WRITING YOUR PERSONAL INTERVAL WORKOUT

Not everyone has a coach to take the mystery out of writing interval workouts. But you can use this book as your coach! By using my six-step approach and the following *Interval Training Guide* anyone can play coach.

Step 1: Determine your fitness category. Choose the category in Chapter 1 that best describes your present racing shape. Follow the guidelines for the interval variables on the following charts for this category. These are just guidelines. Some runners blessed with natural speed may move up a group for speed training. Others not blessed with speed, inexperienced with interval training, or coming back from injury or a layoff may need to move down a group. Masters runners may need to move back a group. For this example, I'll choose a Basic Competitor.

Step 2: Determine the goal of the workout. Are you training for a 5K or a marathon? Are you sharpening for a peak race or just reintroducing speedwork during your base training? Do you want to work on race pace or hone speed? These are just some of the questions you must answer before planning intervals. For this example, our Basic Competitor is sharpening for a 10K race.

Step 3: Determine the interval distance. For this example, our Basic Competitor chooses a peak workout of half-miles.

Step 4: Determine the interval pace. Is it race pace or faster than race pace? For this example, the runner wants to run faster than race pace. This Basic Competitor has already run several workouts at 5K pace and a few at Fast Pace. The choice here is to go with the more challenging Hard Pace for a final peak workout about twelve days before the race. The *Goal Time Ranges for Intervals Guide* (Figure 10.7) can be used to establish a time goal.

Step 5: Determine the quantity of intervals. In this example, our runner has built to running five times a half-mile and chooses to bring the pace down while keeping at five intervals.

Step 6: Determine the recovery of the intervals. The range from the charts for this example is 3 to 5 minutes. This runner has been using 4-minute walking recoveries for this workout and will stick to it as a measuring stick.

Note: *Consult the more detailed guidelines for writing interval workouts for specific distances in the racing chapters: 5K, 10K, half-marathon, marathon.*

INTERVAL TRAINING GUIDE

Okay, you want me to make it simple for you. So just follow this general guide to determine the quantity, intensity, and recovery of your intervals. The distance on the charts is in yards or miles, and recovery (jogging or walking) is in minutes. The intensity on these charts relates to the paces described in the *Interval Pace Guide* (Figure 10.6).

FIGURE 10.1: INTERVAL TRAINING GUIDE—NOVICE AND INTERMEDIATE COMPETITOR

Distance	Pace Intervals			Faster Than Race Pace Intervals		
	Quantity	Intensity	Recovery	Quantity	Intensity	Recovery
Quarters	4–8	5K–10K	2–3	4–5	F–5K	3–4
Halves	4–6	5K–10K	3–4	3–4	F–5K	3–5
¾ miles	3–4	5K–10K	3–4	2–3	F–5K	4–5
Miles	2–4	5K-10K	4–5	2–3	F–5K	4–6
1¼–2 miles	1–2	5K–10K	4–6	1	F–5K	

FIGURE 10.2: INTERVAL TRAINING GUIDE—BASIC COMPETITOR

Distance	Pace Intervals			Faster Than Race Pace Intervals		
	Quantity	Intensity	Recovery	Quantity	Intensity	Recovery
Quarters	5–10	5K–10K	2–3	4–8	H–5K	3–4
Halves	5–8	5K–10K	3–4	4–6	H–5K	3–5
¾ miles	3–5	5K–10K	3–4	2–3	H–5K	3–5
Miles	3–4	5K-10K	3–5	2–3	F–5K	3–5
1¼–2 miles	2–3	5K–10K	4–5	1–2	F–5K	4–6

FIGURE 10.3: INTERVAL TRAINING GUIDE—COMPETITOR

Distance	Pace Intervals			Faster Than Race Pace Intervals		
	Quantity	Intensity	Recovery	Quantity	Intensity	Recovery
Quarters	6–10	5K–10K	2–3	5–8	H–5K	3–4
Halves	6–8	5K–10K	3–4	4–6	H–5K	3–5
¾miles	3–5	5K–10K	3–4	3–4	H–5K	3–5
Miles	3–4	5K-10K	3–4	3–4	F–5K	3–5
1¼–2 miles	2–3	5K–10K	4–5	1–3	F–5K	4–6

FIGURE 10.4: INTERVAL TRAINING GUIDE—ADVANCED COMPETITOR

Distance	Pace Intervals			Faster Than Race Pace Intervals		
	Quantity	Intensity	Recovery	Quantity	Intensity	Recovery
220s	8–12	5K–10K	1–1½	6–10	H–F	1–2
Quarters	8–12	5K–10K	1–2	6–10	H–5K	2–3
Halves	6–8	5K–10K	2–3	5–8	H–5K	3–4
¾ miles	4–6	5K–10K	3–4	3–5	H–5K	3–5
Miles	4–5	5K-10K	3–4	3–4	H–5K	3–5
1¼–2 miles	3–4	5K–10K	4–5	2–3	F–5K	4–6

FIGURE 10.5: INTERVAL TRAINING GUIDE—LOCAL CHAMPION

Distance	Pace Intervals			Faster Than Race Pace Intervals		
	Quantity	Intensity	Recovery	Quantity	Intensity	Recovery
220s	10–16	5K–10K	½–1½	8–12	H–F	1–2
Quarters	8–16	5K–10K	1–2	8–12	H–F	2–3
Halves	8–12	5K–10K	2–3	6–10	H–F	3–4
¾ miles	5–8	5K–10K	2–4	4-6	H–5K	3–4
Miles	4–6	5K-10K	3–4	4–5	H–5K	3–5
1¼–2 miles	3–4	5K–10K	4–5	2–4	F–5K	3–6

FIGURE 10.6: INTERVAL PACE GUIDE

The following paces are used on the *Interval Training Guide*. Actual time ranges for these paces is charted on the *Goal Time Ranges for Intervals Guide*.

PACE INTERVALS

5K Pace (5K): Present or goal race pace.

10K Pace (10K): Present or goal race pace. Use this pace to ease into faster interval training.

FASTER THAN RACE PACE INTERVALS

Hard Pace (H): This is the fastest pace most runners need to use for interval training. Most Novice and Intermediate Competitors and many Basic Competitors shouldn't use this pace, or at least should run it with caution. Hard Pace is approximately:

*5 percent faster than 5K to 10K race pace for mile intervals.
*7.5 percent faster than 5K to 10K pace for three-quarter mile intervals.
*10 percent faster than 5K to 10K pace for half-mile intervals.
*12.5 percent faster than 5K to slightly slower than one-mile pace for quarter-mile intervals.
*15 percent faster than 5K to slightly slower than one-half-mile pace for 200 yard intervals.

Fast Pace (F): This speed is the fastest interval pace I recommend for Novice and Intermediate Competitors. It is approximately:

*1 to 2 percent faster than 5K to 10K pace for 1¼ to 2-mile intervals.
*2.5 percent faster than 5K to 10K pace for mile intervals.
*5 percent faster than 5K to 10K pace for three-quarter-mile intervals.
*7.5 percent faster than 5K to 10K pace for half-mile intervals.
*10 to 12.5 percent faster than 5K to 10K pace for quarter-mile intervals.
*12.5 to 15 percent faster than 5K to 10K pace for 220-yard intervals.

5K Pace (5K): For training for races longer than 5K.

GOAL TIME RANGES FOR INTERVALS GUIDE

Figure 10.7 establishes suggested time ranges for intervals. Use it as a general guide to pick the best pace to start, and stay at, for intervals at the various distances. When running Faster Than Race Pace Intervals, most runners push the pace more the shorter the distance. That is, they'll run a faster pace for quarters than for miles. For example, I run 5Ks at 6:00 per mile. I generally do my fastest mile intervals at 5:45 pace, three-quarter miles at 5:40 pace (4:15), halves at 5:30 pace (2:45), and quarters at 5:20 pace (80 seconds).

I use Hard Pace as the fastest end of the recommended interval pace range. For the slower end, I use 5K pace (although you can use 10K pace if you choose). So my range for halves on the chart, for example, would be 2:42 to 3:00. Figure out the math yourself, or use the chart below. This is just an estimated, suggested range. Adjust if the paces are too fast for you to complete your selected number of reps.

The following guide uses 5K race pace as the reference point since that is the pace you should reach to maximize aerobic capacity gains, and faster paces than this provide the most improvement in running economy and muscular strength. Although most runners will benefit from running at these speeds even when marathon training, many runners, especially Novice and Intermediate Competitors, may be safer to run interval times based on a percentage of 10K pace rather than 5K pace.

The goal should be to run each interval in the same time, or even slightly increase the pace for the last few. Some coaches recommend that the last interval should be the fastest, and that the last lap of each interval should be the fastest. This may work for you. But don't be one of those hot dogs that hold way back for the last one so they can sprint to glory. I tend to run a bit slower on the last few intervals since, frankly, I really put out and I'm running out of steam. But that's what racing involves, at least for me. As long as I just slow a little and don't die then I know I'm okay.

Here's a general guide for interval pacing:

- Each mile interval shouldn't vary by more than 5 to 10 seconds. For example: 6:01, 5:59, 6:03, 6:08.

Although this runner slowed some on the last interval, it was still within an acceptable range.

- Each half-mile interval shouldn't vary by more than 3 to 5 seconds.
- Each quarter-mile interval shouldn't vary by more than 2 to 3 seconds.
- Runners (particularly Novice, Intermediate, and Basic Competitors) may have the speed to run faster than these interval ranges based on their present 5K fitness. There are four common reasons: 1) They should be able to race faster; 2) Their mileage is low so they have fresh legs for speed training but lack endurance for race distances. They don't yet have the endurance, strength, and experience to hold a strong pace for long distances; 3) The pushing and pulling of a fast group and the motivation of their coaches inspire them to run faster than they would on their own; 4) They are running the workout too fast and may pay for it the next day.

At any level, if you can safely hold faster paces than the following *approximate* recommendations for the complete workout, go right ahead. However, don't overdo it. It would be safer, and still beneficial, to stick to the recommended ranges.

Note: Goal ranges are purposely not included for 220s and quarters since standards for short intervals are difficult to establish for long-distance runners.

FIGURE 10.7: GOAL TIME RANGES FOR INTERVALS GUIDE

5K Pace	Halves Hard Fast 5K	¾ Miles Hard Fast 5K	Miles Hard Fast 5K
5:00	2:15-2:19-2:30	3:28-3:34-3:45	4:45-4:53-5:00
5:10	2:20-2:23-2:35	3:35-3:41-3:53	4:55-5:02-5:10
5:20	2:24-2:28-2:40	3:42-3:48-4:00	5:04-5:12-5:20
5:30	2:29-2:33-2:45	3:49-3:56-4:08	5:14-5:22-5:30
5:40	2:33-2:37-2:50	3:56-4:02-4:15	5:23-5:32-5:40
5:50	2:38-2:44-2:55	4:03-4:10-4:23	5:33-5:41-5:50
6:00	2:42-2:46-3:00	4:10-4:17-4:30	5:42-5:51-6:00
6:10	2:47-2:51-3:05	4:17-4:24-4:38	5:52-6:00-6:10
6:20	2:51-2:56-3:10	4:24-4:31-4:45	6:01-6:11-6:20
6:30	2:56-3:00-3:15	4:31-4:38-4:53	6:11-6:20-6:30
6:40	3:00-3:05-3:20	4:37-4:45-5:00	6:20-6:30-6:40
6:50	3:05-3:10-3:25	4:45-4:53-5:08	6:30-6:40-6:50
7:00	3:09-3:14-3:30	4:51-4:59-5:15	6:39-6:50-7:00
7:10	3:14-3:19-3:35	4:59-5:07-5:23	6:49-6:59-7:10
7:20	3:18-3:23-3:40	5:05-5:13-5:30	6:58-7:09-7:20
7:30	3:23-3:28-3:45	5:13-5:21-5:38	7:08-7:19-7:30
7:40	3:27-3:33-3:50	5:19-5:28-5:45	7:17-7:29-7:40
7:50	3:32-3:37-3:55	5:27-5:35-5:53	7:27-7:38-7:50
8:00	3:36-3:42-4:00	5:33-5:42-6:00	7:36-7:48-8:00
8:10	3:41-3:47-4:05	5:40-5:50-6:08	7:46-7:58-8:10
8:20	3:45-3:51-4:10	5:47-5:56-6:15	7:55-8:08-8:20
8:30	3:50-3:56-4:15	5:54-6:04-6:23	8:05-8:17-8:30
8:40	3:54-4:00-4:20	6:01-6:10-6:30	8:14-8:27-8:40
8:50	3:59-4:05-4:25	6:08-6:18-6:38	8:24-8:37-8:50
9:00	4:03-4:10-4:30	6:15-6:25-6:45	8:33-8:47-9:00
9:10	4:08-4:14-4:35	6:22-6:32-6:53	8:43-8:56-9:10
9:20	4:12-4:19-4:40	6:29-6:39-7:00	8:52-9:06-9:20
9:30	4:17-4:24-4:45	6:36-6:47-7:08	9:02-9:16-9:30
9:40	4:21-4:28-4:50	6:42-6:53-7:15	9:11-9:26-9:40
9:50	4:26-4:33-4:55	6:50-7:01-7:23	9:21-9:35-9:50
10:00	4:30-4:37-5:00	6:56-7:07-7:30	9:30-9:45-10:00

Times are in minutes: seconds

CHAPTER 11

Hill Training

Hill training is called "speedwork in disguise." That's because you don't have to run as fast to work hard. I don't know about you, but my effort to get up hills in races sure isn't disguised! Let's face it, hills hurt. They tire you out. They slow you down. Big guys like me are at a disadvantage compared to those skinny, featherweight Elites. Many runners avoid hill training because it is too much work. So why bother?

Because there's pleasure in them thar hills. Well, at least there is once you've finished your workout. Overcoming their challenge is fun! Right? Okay, at least it is satisfying. As I tell our students when they groan after finding out I've scheduled hills, "I hate hills, too, but they're good for you." This fact is sure: If you're going to race on hills, you've got to train on them. Exercise physiologist Bob Fitts, who ran away from me on the hills when I competed against him in college cross-country, advises: "Hill training is the foundation upon which all the other principles of successful hill racing must stand. There is a simple reason for this. When running up a hill, extra muscle fibers are used to perform the extra work. These fibers recruited for hill running are not generally used while running on level terrain. Therefore, if you race on hills without training on hills, you are asking untrained muscle fibers to work. Such muscle fibers will fatigue rapidly, and your performance will fall off."

Fortunately, running hills is an acquired skill. Anyone can improve, even you and me. Look at it this way, the better you get on them the more runners you can pass (or avoid getting passed by) on hills in races, and the less time you'll lose on the finishing clock. See Chapters 29 and 30 for the strategy and tactics of racing up and down hills. If you avoid hilly races, like some wise runners I know, that's no excuse to avoid training on them. Even if you race on the flats, hills will help improve performance.

When a student misses a speed class and calls to ask what they can do to make it up, I send them to the hills. Why? It's a great workout to do by yourself since the hill will make sure you get enough of a challenge.

Running fast for long-distance races depends on a combination of endurance and speed. But muscular fitness—strength, power, and muscular endurance—is important, too. A big advantage of hill training is that it allows you to simultaneously work on aerobic, anaerobic, and muscular fitness. Running hills, like lifting weights, is resistance training. Although weight training is also recommended for both the upper and lower body, it doesn't use the same neuromuscular patterns as running. Hills strengthen the leg muscles to meet the specific demands of running even when you're not on hills. By working hard on hills, you force the muscles to overcome the incline and resistance of gravity. This strengthens the driving muscles—the hamstrings, calves, buttocks, and particularly the quadriceps which don't get much work on the flats. Fatigued quads are particularly a problem late in races, especially marathons. It's hard to pick your feet up and move them forward if the quads are growing tired of this important repetitive task. Ankles strengthen as the feet push off to bound up hills. Since you have to really pump the arms to get up hills, your upper body is strengthened, too.

A study at the Karolinska Institute in Stockholm, Sweden found after 12 weeks of running hill repeats on a moderately-steep 400-meter slope, a group of runners improved running economy by 3 percent. With hill training, you'll also increase resistance to fatigue during races. That will help you maintain good running form and a steady pace. Since you have to concentrate on driving the arms, lifting the knees, and pushing off the feet to get up hills in training, running form will be exaggerated and improved. As with Fast Intervals, you'll also be able to tolerate greater levels of lactic acid, and extend your lactate threshold.

Hill training bolsters your confidence. Hey, you don't have to do repeats up the same hill in a race, so a few scattered hills on race day don't seem so bad. As you develop courage by hill training you won't be intimidated by one of those killer hills during a race. You'll better tolerate the discomfort of overcoming hills and be psychologically prepared to "hang on" to the top. In fact, you may even look forward to tough hills since you'll gain on your competition. You'll be able to attack the hill before it attacks you.

Running hills can cause or prevent injury. Ease into hill training or you'll risk lower leg injuries. Be sure to warm up and stretch carefully before and after these workouts. Run easy coming off hill workouts for a day or more. If you're bothered by lower leg injuries, skip hills and ease into speed training on the flats. But running hills can also help prevent knee problems by strengthening the quads, and hills allow you to go anaerobic without the pounding trauma of track intervals. In fact, a study by Tom Clark at the Nike Research Laboratory found that running a 7-minute-mile pace up a steep hill produced only 85 percent of the shock felt by the same runner at the same pace on the flats.

Hill training is valuable when preparing for all distances, particularly marathons. Add it at the beginning of the strengthening phase of your training cycle, as a transition to fast track intervals. By strengthening muscles before you start training fast you'll minimize injury and increase the quality of track workouts. But hills can also be used to sharpen for races, especially hilly events. You can fine-tune workouts for the speed and power for 5Ks with short, steep hills, or enhance aerobic and muscular endurance for marathons with long hills. Ideally, mix the various types of hill training to get maximum benefit.

There are two basic types of hill training: repeats (long and short) and continuous runs (rolling hills fartlek and long climbs).

HILL REPEAT GUIDELINES

Hill training is different from hill running. In daily runs you try to get up hills as economically as possible. The goal is to minimize effort. Although running hills often at training pace improves overall strength, it won't make you faster. To get that benefit, you have to repetitively work the hills hard. During hill training you run harder than when hill running. You exaggerate form and effort to be able to run up hills in races more efficiently—and to run faster on the flats, too. Before starting any type of hill training, ease into it by running over hilly courses two or three times a week, increasing the intensity slightly on the uphills. When you're ready for hill repeats, start conservatively with moderate hills. Ease into hill repeats if you're new to it or coming back to it by running 10K race pace or tempo pace. To increase distance-running strength, progressively increase the grade, speed, and number of hill repeats—but not all at once—a little at a time as you get more fit.

Hill repeats are basically like track intervals, but you go up instead of around. Run easy for 15 to 30 minutes on the flats, then run slightly faster than training pace up the hill to further prepare the body for the intensity of these workouts. Then, start the workout using the Hill Repeat Guide (Figure 11.1). Run the first repeat slightly slower than your goal intensity. Try to run the rest of the workout at goal intensity. Don't sprint like mad up them. That wears you out more than it builds you up, and invites injury. Rather, run fast, but under control. Think of it as about 85 percent effort, or about as hard or slightly faster than you would work the hills in a typical race. Emphasize good running form—push off your feet, drive your arms, lift your knees. Run all the way through an imagined finish line at the top. If your pace slows dramatically or form and breathing become ragged, reassess the intensity or abort the workout.

Begin your effort 20 yards from the base of the hill so you can gather speed before starting up the grade. This eliminates the strain of a standing start on a steep slope. Continue running hard for another 20 yards on the flats, if possible, at the top of the hill. This tactic helps you pull away from competitors on race day.

At the top, don't stop. This is a continuous run at intermittent paces. Recover by running back down nice and easy. The recovery run should take about three times as long as it took you to run up a short, steep hill. Return somewhat faster on a longer, gentler hill: about twice the time it took you to go up. If you have to walk down all or part of the way, you've run up too fast. Don't run too fast or "brake" coming downhill or you'll risk injury. The steeper the hill, the less shock you'll get going up, but the more shock you'll get going down. Relax and run down gently. Better yet, when climbing very long or steep hills, have your chauffeur drive you back to the start to save your legs (like some Elite runners).

How can you run hill repeats if you can't find appropriate inclines? Be creative. Highway, bridge, and parking garage ramps are possibilities, although they may pose obvious safety problems. Stadium steps are a favorite of mean coaches. Stairs in apartment or office buildings are used by some runners. After coming down with shin splints from racing too zealously at the first Empire State Building Run (eighty-six flights), I've retired from stair running. For many runners the answer is the treadmill. With a flick of a button you can make a hill appear. Better yet, you can make it disappear. A big advantage of treadmill hill training is that you can recover on level ground rather than risking injury by jogging down steep hills. One more challenging option: stairclimbers. At my gym I attack a big monster called "The Gauntlet." The computer throws out a variety of challenging hills forcing me to pick up the effort or get tossed off the machine. Another advantage here is that you have minimal shock at impact.

LONG HILL REPEATS

These are tough. They're analogous to running long intervals on the track. Find a moderate-grade (5 to 8 percent, or 3 to 4 degrees) hill just steep enough to try the legs and just long enough to try the mind. After running a few of these workouts, you'll really gain confidence for conquering hills in races. Long hills are particularly good for building strength and endurance for races of half-marathon to the marathon. Find one that is about a quarter-mile to a half-mile in length. It should take about 2 to 5 minutes to run up at your race pace effort or slightly faster. If the hill is too long, the recovery coming back down will be too long. If available hills are too long, run your first repeat until you get to 4 minutes, for example. Mark the spot, then use this as your finish for the remainder of the workout. If you can't find a long-enough hill, run hard on the flats going into the hill so your total hard effort is at least 3 minutes.

Experienced, fit competitors may run up to a mile for hill repeats. One star athlete I coach, Toshi d'Elia, used measured miles up a hill for key workouts as she trained for marathons. She did as many as five, mile long hill repeats. The result: At fifty, she became the first woman in the world over that age to break the 3-hour barrier for the marathon with a 2:57 in the Masters World Championship in Glasgow, Scotland. A tough workout we do in class to prepare for the New York City Marathon is 1¼ mile loops of the northern hills in Central Park. The course divides into approximate thirds: up, down, up. Recovery is a ½ mile jog on the flats from the finish to the start. The goal is to do them at 5K to 10K race pace. After conquering 3 to 5 repeats of this loop the runners are ready for any hills they may face on race day.

SHORT HILL REPEATS

These are short, but not sweet. Rather, they are steep. This workout is sure to elicit groans from our students. It hurts. Hey, a short-hills workout is over quickly and really prepares your body and mind for racing. They're particularly good for sharpening speed for races of 5K to 10K since they are run at faster than race pace effort. They are of similar benefit to short, hard- and fast-paced intervals on the track.

Pick a hill that's 50 to 200 yards in length and steep enough (10 to 15 percent, or 7 to 9 degree grade) to really challenge you, but not so steep that it makes good form impossible. It should take about 30 to 90 seconds to get to the top. If the hill is too steep or too long, you won't be able to maintain a strong effort to the top. Shorten hills that are too long by running for a minute, for example, on your first repeat, marking the spot, then using this as your finish for the remainder of the workout. You don't have to run these too hard since gravity will take care of the intensity. Do not sprint all-out. Envision that you're running to a finish line at the crest of the hill. These are excellent for improving form, strength, and speed.

FIGURE 11:1: HILL REPEATS GUIDE

Category	Long Hills Quantity	Long Hills Intensity*	Short Hills Quantity	Short Hills Intensity*
Novice and Int. Competitor	3–4	5K–10K	4–5	5K–10K
Basic Competitor	4–5	5K–10K	5–6	F–10K
Competitor	5–6	5K–10K	6–8	F–10K
Advanced Competitor	6–8	F–10K	8–10	H–10K
Local Champion	8–10	F–10K	8–12	H–10K

Recovery: Jog slowly downhill to start.

Intensity: Note: Paces listed are the effort for that pace. Actual pace per mile will be slower since you're running uphill. A good guide is to aim for a heart rate of about 85 to 90 percent for long hills, and 90 to 95 percent for short hills. The following intensities are used on this *Hill Repeats Guide*:

Hard Pace (H): Approximately 20 seconds per mile faster than 5K pace, or 30 seconds per mile faster than 10K pace.

Fast Pace (F): Approximately 10 seconds per mile faster than 5K pace, or 20 seconds per mile faster than 10K pace.

5K Pace (5K): Present or goal race pace.

10K Pace (10K): Present or goal race pace.

ROLLING HILLS FARTLEK

This continuous strength training run is detailed in Chapter 12.

LONG CLIMBS

Now we're talking hills, even mountains. These workouts aren't for Novice, Intermediate, or most Basic Competitors. I run to "the Ridge" most Sunday mornings with my training group. I'll often run it as fast as tempo pace. I warm up with a 2-mile jog before I meet the group since we start off at a brisk pace. The run to the ridge takes about 40 minutes, most of which is uphill on dirt trails. We often push each other, which simulates racing conditions. I record my times for these runs, and at landmarks along the way, to monitor my fitness. As my Ridge run times come down, so do my race times. But these runs are child's play compared to some Elite workouts. Kenyan and Mexican runners have been dominant in road racing in large part due to their fabled runs up mountains and volcanos. They'll climb for 20K or longer at high altitude. They believe it builds a strong body and an even stronger mind.

DOWNHILL TRAINING

We minimize downhill training in our classes. Why? I'm not totally against downhill training. But in a group setting it often leads to sprinting to an injury. Downhill training is best done by yourself. It's easier to concentrate on what is safe for you. Clark's Nike study demonstrated the danger: A runner going downhill at a 7-minute pace experiences 40 percent more leg shock than on the flats. The amount of shock generated is directly related to the pace and steepness of the downhill. The quads absorb much of this shock in addition to generating much of the force needed to run uphill. Also, eccentric motion, where the muscles lengthen while they are trying to shorten as they contract, is greatly increased when running downhill. This increases the amount of minute tearing in connective tissue that occurs with running, especially for the quads. In other words, running downhills too often or too fast is likely to cause injury. Here's the Catch-22: Avoiding training on downhills sets you up for injury when racing downhills.

For most races you spend as much time going down hills as you do going up. So it makes sense to practice it at least a little. Used with caution, downhill training can be very beneficial. Running down hills efficiently saves as much time as running up the hills efficiently. The trick is to develop a feel for good downhill racing form (Chapter 31) by practicing it until it becomes subconscious to relax, and almost throw yourself downhill at quick paces. The key, however, is to not recklessly throw yourself downhill which wastes energy and invites injury, nor to be too conservative by braking which also wastes energy besides giving up speed.

Downhills, if run correctly, can be used to teach relaxation and improve leg turnover since you can get going quite fast with less effort. Hip flexibility is enhanced resulting in increased stride length. Downhill training prepares the quads for the extra work they must perform running up and down hills late in races when they're already fatigued. Research shows periodic training on downhills minimizes the amount of muscle damage that occurs in races. The muscles develop more of a tolerance to the stress of the downhills, and as a result postrace muscle soreness is reduced. Legs beaten up early on tough downhills have less strength later in the race to negotiate uphills such as is the case with the Heartbreak Hills of the Boston Marathon. And with sore quads it's impossible to take advantage of the final downhill stretches at Boston and other races. Spectators can shout "It's all downhill from here, you've got it made" all they want; it won't help unless they lend you their quads. Conservative downhill training will help you conquer these late race weaknesses.

Then there's the psychological advantages. Running downhill fast means giving up some control, letting go. Runners are often afraid to let go on downhills, just like many skiers. But letting go while staying relaxed is safer and faster—both skiing and running downhills. Both demand practice until the action becomes less intimidating, more natural. With practice, you'll gain confidence with your downhill racing ability. When you believe you're a good downhill racer, you probably are.

Don't expect too much from your first downhill workouts. They may feel awkward and uncomfortable. With practice, you'll develop a feel for it. It'll gradually become a fluid, effortless, flowing motion. Listen to your body during and after these workouts. If your hamstrings are tight or the shins are sore, you may be overstriding. If your quads are sore, you may be braking too much. Wear well-cushioned shoes when training downhill to help absorb shock.

How often should you train on downhills? Once a week for a few weeks until you've got the hang of it is adequate for technique improvement. Once you've mastered it, just like riding a bike your body won't forget how to do it. But you need to go back to it occasionally to keep your technique from getting rusty. Train on downhills consistently for a few weeks to prepare for the strain of upcoming races that include substantial downhills. Research demonstrates that the muscle-soreness prevention benefits of eccentric training, such as downhill running, last for about four to six weeks. Train enough to provide protection but not so much as to cause damage. A good choice is to practice downhills once a week for three or four weeks before a downhill-loaded race. Stop this training two weeks prior to the event to allow the muscles to fully rest. Then race the hills confidently knowing that your leg muscles are primed for the action, although not fully protected.

Warning. Downhill training can be dangerous. Not every runner will be able to master the techniques well enough to benefit. Be cautious. So if you want to give it a try, here's how to do it.

Downhill Intervals. First a reminder. This is not a speed workout; rather, it's training to improve your ability to race downhills, minimize postrace muscle soreness, improve running form, and as a transition to faster track interval training. Hold back on the intensity. Pick a gentle hill, ideally on grass or dirt, about 100 yards long with a flat area of at least 50 yards at the bottom. Make sure you're well warmed-up before starting these workouts. Begin with 50-yard downhill runs and gradually extend them to 100 to 200 yards after a few sessions. Experienced, fit runners may build up to quarter-milers. The first two intervals of each session should be run at a moderate pace to further prepare the muscles for faster downhill training. Then, run quick, but not all-out down the hills. The object is to train yourself to run with controlled speed, not to do a hard speed workout. Concentrate on staying relaxed and maintaining good form. Do two or three quick intervals and gradually build up to six to ten, or a total of 15 to 20 minutes of brisk downhill training. Continue your momentum and stride rate for several strides (about 20 to 30 seconds) when you hit the bottom (as you should in a race to take advantage of gravity's assistance) and then gradually slow down. Recovery is simply an easy jog back to the top. Take your time.

Shelly-lynn and I discovered "Gescheidt downhills." The demanding, perfectionist photographer had us run interval after interval down a dirt trail while he shot several roles of film. Our job was to make downhill running look fun, fast, and exciting. It was. How do we look on the cover? We just hope the next cover idea isn't for us to look like we're enjoying running hard up a steep hill!

CHAPTER 12

Fartlek Training

Fartlek is not something you do when running after eating Mexican food. The Swedish term *fartlek* means "speed play"—and that's exactly what you do with this continuous strength-training run. It was invented by former Swedish Olympic coach Gusta Holmer after reviewing his country's military training exercises, which used varied pace brisk walks and jogs to increase fitness. Fartlek involves changes of pace over varying terrain and distances. It's a steady-paced, short- or medium-distance endurance run injected with dashes of some or all of the other basic types of speed training: intervals, hill repeats, and even tempo runs. Therefore it captures many of the benefits of each of these workouts. Physiologists characterize this kind of training as the exercise continuum; every system of the body is affected by fartlek. It can be used to improve aerobic capacity, running economy, lactate threshold, and muscular fitness.

Fartlek offers many advantages. It's a good way to introduce speed training prior to hitting the track for more intense work. Your legs get accustomed to switching gears. Since you don't have the pressure of running a precise distance in a certain time as with track intervals, you can concentrate on a relaxed, economical form while running fast. Fartlek is a great change of pace from the confined atmosphere and structure of track intervals. You'll accumulate more mileage than you would with most other speed options. It offers plenty of flexibility to adjust on the run for how you feel and the weather. Fartlek is much easier to do on your own than track intervals, yet it is fun and challenging in a group. It's a great workout for mental training over all or parts of race courses. Most important, fartlek offers plenty of variety, bringing more zest to your training routine. Fartlek can be a blissful, carefree light workout, or very demanding.

You can fartlek on a track or your regular road courses, but it's most fun and beneficial when you get off the beaten path and go sight-seeing over trails, or across grassy fields. The more varied and unexpected the experience, the better. It's just like being a kid again. Going exploring can be ageless fun. The favorite workout for our classes is a 5- to 8-mile fartlek loop of Central Park. We stay off the pavement whenever possible as I lead the adventurous group into the park's nooks and crannies. We run on grass, dirt, cinder, and up huge rock formations. I've even led groups up and down a playground slide and through a water fountain. The workout includes bursting to the top of Belvedere Castle for a spectacular view, a timed quarter-mile around the track after charging the Great Hill, a flower-scented loop of the Conservatory Garden, a visit to the zoo, a winding tour of the Ramble, the long drive up Cat Hill, and, of course, a practice kick into the New York City Marathon finish.

On all types of fartlek, start with a warm-up run of at least 10 to 15 minutes. Then, burst at a variety of speeds (from 1-mile to marathon pace, but mostly 5K pace or slightly faster) for a variety of distances (50 yards to 1-mile, but mostly 100 yards to a quarter-mile) in a variety of combinations. Recovery is generally at about base-training pace (not an easy walk or jog as you would do for track intervals). The faster the bursts, the slower the recovery. The recovery period usually consists of two-thirds to approximately the same distance or time as the fartlek burst. It's okay, and advisable, to take brief time-outs to hydrate.

How long you fartlek depends on your fitness and intensity of effort. Total fartlek time ranges from 20 to 60 minutes (or about 2 to 8 miles). Start and finish the workout with an easy run of at least 10 to 15 minutes. As with any type of speedwork, ease into it. Don't run too fast or too long too soon. At first do 20 to 30 minutes of light fartleking; only experienced, highly fit runners should fartlek for more than 40 minutes.

You can fartlek three ways—by landmarks, by time, or in combination. Pick targets, of varying distances away, to run briskly to—such as the top of a hill or the next streetlight. Be sure to pick a nonmoving target. A former slightly crazed training partner once called out for a burst to the dog ahead and then yelled for it to run. We chased it for nearly a mile! Many runners prefer running hard for a set time period, ranging from 30 seconds to 5 minutes. Timed pickups can all be the same, such as 2-minute bursts followed by 2-minute recoveries, or they can gradually increase or decrease in time or distance. Although many runners prefer structure, fartlek is most enjoyable when run spontaneously: Pick it up when the mood strikes or you see something challenging to run to or over.

A fartlek workout can be as easy or hard as you choose. For example, it can be used as an intense peak workout over key sections of a race course ten to fourteen days prior to a race, or as a light, peppy run a few days before a race. It can be used during all phases of the training cycle.

I break fartlek into four types: modified, rolling hills, advanced, and group.

MODIFIED FARTLEK

This is a recommended run for Novice, Intermediate, and Basic Competitors just beginning speed training, or for all levels of runners easing back into strenuous training after a layoff. Modified fartlek is run over easier terrain (flat, not hilly; smooth not rough), for shorter distances and slower speeds than regular fartlek. The object is to minimize the stresses on the body as it eases into harder work. Stick to one overload factor, speed. Adding another, such as the resistance of steep hills, would make the workout too difficult at this stage of your training. At first, limit fartlek bursts to 10K pace, and periods of about a quarter-mile or approximately 2 minutes. Start with four to eight bursts during 20 to 30 minutes of fartleking. Total mileage, including warm-up and cool-down, will range from 3 to 6 miles depending on your fitness level. Be conservative with pace and recovery. Keep the speed under control and don't go again until you feel ready. Remember the object of modified fartlek: easing into speed training while having fun doing it.

ROLLING HILLS FARTLEK

Now you'll incorporate the resistance of hill training into the continuous run. This workout is best used during the strengthening phase and prior to hilly races. If possible, include a variety of hills ranging in grade from moderate to fairly steep, and distance from 100 yards to three-quarter mile. Ideally, choose a course with a series of hills that aren't spaced too far apart. Accelerate up and over the top of each hill you encounter at race pace, then run between them at base- to brisk-training pace. Throw in a few short bursts between hills if you go too long (more than 5 minutes) between hills. As you become stronger, search out steeper hills, and increase the number of hills and total mileage.

ADVANCED FARTLEK

Here's where pleasure and pain coincide. These runs train both the mind and body. They can be very stressful, since they combine a continuous distance run, intensity (speed), and resistance (hills) in one workout. Include some hard running on the flats along with both up- and downhills. Run between a bit harder than modified fartlek to almost as grueling as race intensity. If you want to be challenged, push yourself to the edge of what you can tolerate, then go again before fully recovering.

Advanced fartlek can be used for specific purposes: strength training on hills, race pace training, sharpening with faster than race pace intervals, or a combination. It can replace hard intervals on the track or hill repeats for those that don't enjoy or can't physically handle those workouts. As you get more fit, you may increase the number of fartlek bursts and the total mileage for the workout. The number of pickups per workout may range from six to twenty; go as you feel. Some fit runners shorten the recovery time or quicken the recovery pace. But be careful here. Total mileage, including a 1- to 2-mile warm-up and cool-down, can range from 5 to 12 miles, depending on your fitness level and the intensity of the bursts. Vary the workout according to your goals: Include more short, fast intervals when training to build speed; longer intervals at race pace when building stamina for longer races; plenty of hills when gearing up for a hilly race.

Here are some advanced fartlek options:

Fartlek ladders, cutdowns, and pyramids. Burst "up the ladder" 1, 2,

3, 4, and 5 minutes, for example, at race pace or slightly faster. Or, reverse the order, running cutdowns a little faster as the distance decreases to simulate your finishing kick. Try pyramids by running up the ladder, then back down.

Fartlek surges. This is surging off a strong recovery pace. Instead of running hard and then jogging for recovery, run harder than 5K or 10K race pace for 1 to 3 minutes off a brisk pace (about a minute slower than 10K race pace) or tempo pace (10 to 30 seconds slower than 10K pace). After surging, hold the quick recovery pace for another 2 to 6 minutes before surging again. Limit this type of fartleking to 10 to 20 minutes. These runs simulate race conditions, where you may have to pick up the pace to pass or move away from a runner. This gives you the skill to pick up the pace in a race even when you are already running hard. Caution: Fartlek surging is only for those with a strong body and mind.

Marathon fartlek. This is the same as above, except that you surge off marathon pace. By bursting at faster paces and then settling back to marathon pace, marathon intensity seems easier. This workout also develops a feel for marathon pacing, and the confidence that you can pick up the speed in a marathon if you need to get back on pace or as a tactical move against your competition.

Long-run fartlek. Add a little spice to long runs by throwing in a few fartlek pickups. It'll teach you to change gears during long races and build confidence. But don't burst too hard, too soon, or too often.

Heart rate fartlek. Here's still another chance for variety. Run fast until your heart rate reaches 90 to 94 percent of maximum, then run at training pace until it returns to 75 percent of maximum. Pay no attention to how long it takes to reach those levels.

Advanced fartlek can be intense and different. But it can be so much fun you can easily overdo it. Be cautious on the intensity of pickups and allow adequate recovery between bursts. Too much stress can lead to injury or several days of fatigue-slowed runs. A hard fartlek run may require two or more easy days of running for full recovery since it mimics the stress of a race.

GROUP FARTLEK

Both pleasure and misery enjoy company! You can fartlek with a single training partner or a group of up to thirty or so of similar ability. The simplest way to run this workout is to agree in advance how long you'll run each burst, and everyone runs hard for that time at their desired pace. To regroup, the leaders jog back toward the slowest runner. Be sure the recovery time and pace suits everyone in the group. Usually a leader calls out landmarks. With our classes I'll suddenly announce "pick it up to the top of the hill," or "run fast to the next traffic light." The students never know where we will run next, when we'll start a burst, or what pace I'll throw at them. You learn to run hard when required, not when you're ready. This prepares you for responding to tactical moves in a race. Here's a fun option: Take turns being the leader and see who offers the biggest surprise!

Fartlek can lead to overtraining or injury if runners get in over their heads trying to keep up with more fit training partners. It's okay to back off when needed rather than hanging on stubbornly after you've lost good form. I plan suggested stopping points during a session for those not ready to complete the full workout with the main group. If a coach or leader can run or bike with the group, they can control the duration and intensity and look for runners that should cut the run short. Some coaches have their team run on a track or on short loops through fields so they can control the workout by blasts from their whistle: Pick it up on the first blast, slow it down on the next, sprint on two sharp blasts. In fact, this was a favorite of my college cross-country coach until one of the guys stuffed gum in his whistle! "But coach, we didn't hear the whistle so we just went for a fun run." I won't describe the next workout he made us do!

CHAPTER 13

Tempo Training

Tempo runs are the simplest of all speed workouts: Just warm up, run at a challenging, steady pace (over reasonably level terrain) you can hold for the distance, and cool down. They are also called lactate, anaerobic, or fatigue threshold runs. When you go above your threshold, lactic acid builds up, breathing becomes labored, form gets ragged, and muscles tense and tighten as fatigue sets in. You're forced to slow down. With tempo runs, you train close to your threshold without exceeding it. As a result, you'll raise it, enabling you to run faster and farther before fatigue sets in. Holding a tough pace is crucial to performance. Chapter 2 details the physiology of lactate threshold (LT).

Most competitive runners manage to get in a reasonable amount of aerobic endurance runs, and perhaps weekly track intervals or hill repeats, yet neglect specific LT training. Tempo runs offer many advantages. Although LT can be improved with shorter, faster intervals, tempo runs allow for a higher quantity of threshold training per workout, and at safer speeds. Since the pace of tempo runs isn't as hard as other types of speed training, recovery is quicker and injury less likely. It's less stressful than intervals, both physically and mentally. Tempo running is controlled so it guards against the tendency to train as hard as you can.

Tempo training helps runners develop a feel for even pace (thus the term "tempo"), so you'll run more evenly in races. The Russians first introduced these runs, wanting to simulate race conditions without exposing their runners to the full physical and mental stress of actual races. Tempos get you used to running briskly, but not too intensely, for a sustained period. Concentration is improved: The pace is just hard enough to force you to focus on your running and endure discomfort for an extended period. You can get into a groove while staying relaxed and visualizing yourself cruising along during the middle miles of a race. You gain confidence that you can hold a strong pace. Running form and economy are improved.

Research indicates that aerobic capacity won't change significantly over a training season for fit runners, but LT can. In a study at the Karolinska Institute in Stockholm, Sweden, a group of runners added one 20-minute tempo run each week to their training program. Fourteen weeks later, their LT had improved by 4 percent and 10K race times by over a minute. Here's another advantage: With aging, aerobic capacity slowly fades away but your LT may still be improved. You can beat some younger runners (or, for that matter, runners of your age) with a higher aerobic capacity if you develop a higher LT, allowing you to work at a higher percentage of your aerobic capacity than the competition.

Tempo runs will help your performance at any race distance, but they are especially valuable when half-marathon and marathon training. You get used to running for several minutes at a slightly uncomfortable pace that is near half-marathon and slightly faster than marathon pace. This makes these paces seem more comfortable on race day. For most experienced marathoners, the speed of tempo runs is about half-marathon pace. Tempo workouts can be used during all phases of training.

I break tempo training into three types: continuous, intervals, and marathon.

THE CONTINUOUS TEMPO RUN

Start and end all continuous tempo runs with an easy run of at least 10 to 15 minutes. The key to tempo training is to balance pace and mileage. Run 2 to 5 miles (or 15 to 40 minutes) at a challenging pace you can hold for the distance. You can determine the right tempo pace by perceived exertion. This should be "comfortably hard." Breathing becomes faster, but you're not gasping for air. You can think clearly and talk, but not in full sentences. You should run in some discomfort, but not the kind of pain that causes you to abruptly end the workout. The goal is to run at an even pace that can be held constant for the distance, but doesn't feel easy.

Most runners need some help in determining the appropriate tempo intensity. So here are some imperfect guidelines to follow. For Novice, Intermediate, and Basic Competitors, tempo pace is approximately 15 to 30 seconds per mile slower than 10K race pace, or 30 to 45 seconds slower than 5K pace; and training heart rate should be approximately 85 percent of maximum. For more advanced runners, recommended tempo pace is 10 to 20 seconds per mile slower than 10K pace, or 25 to 35 seconds slower than 5K pace; and training heart rate should be 85 to 92 percent of maximum. Another common guide is to run at 15K to half-marathon pace. According to research by Jack Daniels, Ph.D., at this intensity most runners' breathing rate pattern switches to a 2-2 rhythm (two footsteps, right and left, while breathing in, and two while breathing out) from a 3-3 rhythm used for easy training. Most runners will get adequate results with a simple "20-20" formula: a 20-minute tempo run at 20 seconds per mile slower than 10K pace.

Control is the key to tempo runs. Resist not turning them into a race against the clock. This isn't supposed to be a killer workout. Stick to the goal: running slightly slower than your *present* 10K race pace. You don't get extra benefits (in fact, you may lose some) by running faster. If you slow considerably during a run, your lactate level is increasing too quickly and you need to start slower next time. On the other hand, the effort should be enough that you are challenged at the end. If you hold a steady pace and still have lots of pep at the end, you didn't raise your lactate level enough. Next time run faster or longer. If you haven't yet developed a good sense of pace, do your first few tempo runs at a conservative pace and distance. With experience, you'll develop a feel for the desirable training zone between too fast and too slow that allows for steady gains.

As you become more fit, concentrate first on running the same pace and distance with less effort rather than trying to run faster. Your heart rate may drop by a few beats per minute while at the same pace. Don't try to run faster every time you do a tempo run. But if you know you're getting fitter but don't have a race scheduled soon, go ahead, gradually improve your tempo time (for the same effort) over the same distance. As you build toward a key race and fitness improves, increase tempo pace by 3 to 5 seconds per mile every three to six weeks. If you run the same course at least periodically, you can monitor fitness improvement. If, for example, you run 4 miles (or an unknown distance) in 32 minutes at 85 percent of your maximum heart rate, a month later you may be able to run the same course (under similar weather conditions) at the same heart rate level in 31:40.

You can do tempo runs anywhere. They can be run more precisely on a treadmill (just set the pace and keep up for 20 minutes), or track (getting time splits every lap). Or, wear a heart rate monitor and set it so that it beeps if you stray more than a few seconds from tempo heart rate pace wherever you run. Wooded trails offer shade, scenery, and softer footing; roads a better race simulation. Knowing the exact distance isn't as important as running at the proper effort level. If possible, know where a few mile marks are so you have pacing feedback. A simple solution: Run out to a landmark, then return. Try to run each segment in the same time. Since the goal is a steady effort, avoid hills, strong winds, and excessive heat as much as possible. Tempo pace per mile may vary from run to run according to how you feel, the course, and the weather. That's okay, but strive to keep an even, controlled pace within each run. Don't be obsessed with keeping to an exact pace per mile, especially when confronted with hills or winds. In these situations, concentrate on even effort, not even pace. These are all reasons why many runners use perceived exertion or heart rate monitors as their guide when tempo running rather than pace per mile.

Here are a few advanced options for continuous tempo runs:

Tempo group runs. Run with training partners to get a feel for hanging with runners in a race. Be careful to group up with runners that will run at or near *your* tempo pace. Don't turn group tempo runs into competition. You're running to stay at and improve your threshold pace, not race other runners. If you get caught up with competing against others and push the pace above your threshold, fatigue will quickly set in and you won't be able to complete the workout as planned. Just like in races, running hard for several minutes at a steady pace is easier to do with others. But you don't always have the benefit of runners to pull you along in races at your desired pace. Solo tempo runs teach discipline. You learn to hold pace on your own and to tough it out through bad patches.

Tempo racing. Here's a convenient way to get in a tempo run: Enter a short race (5K to 4 miles) and hold back the effort to your tempo pace. Or do a 10K race, using the first 2 miles to warm up at training pace and then go into your tempo pace. The key here is to refrain from competing. Your goal is to run a steady tempo pace, not a good race time. Tempo racing also gives you practice at adjusting to mile splits. But don't tempo-race too often: It may become too easy to slip back to tempo pace rather than push your all-out race pace.

Tempo ridge runs. This is my secret workout (well, it used to be). Two or three times a month I run with a group up, up, and up the trails to the top of a ridge. We start at training pace to warm up, then gradually up the pace until we start to climb at a strong pace. The total run to "the Ridge" takes 40 minutes; 20 to 30 minutes of that is at tempo intensity. Then we run steady for another 30 to 40 minutes to complete the run.

Fast tempo runs. These are only for very fit, experienced competitors. It is one notch higher in intensity than regular tempo. After warming up, run between 10 seconds per mile slower than 10K race pace and 10K pace for 20 to 30 minutes. It's a good way to sharpen for a hard 5K to 10K race. But don't try these runs too often.

Long run tempo. Run at training pace for 10 miles (up to 15 miles for Advanced and Local Champion Competitors), then switch to a controlled tempo gear for 20 to 30 minutes. Keep this in the 20 to 30 seconds slower than 10K pace range. Add a cool-down run of 10 to 20 minutes to complete a long run of 15 to 20 miles.

Or do it the other way around with a workout Daniels gives top marathoners: Run for 3 to 4 miles to warm up, then run tempo pace for 4 to 5 miles (up to 8 for Elites), then run training pace for 6 to 10 miles to complete a long run. Notes Daniels, "The idea behind this demanding workout is that the threshold pace running forces the running muscles to use up glycogen stores more rapidly than would be the case in a steady, easy, long run. By the latter stages of the workout the feeling you get mimics the feeling during the final stages of a marathon race—but you haven't had to run so far." But you better be fit before you try this "hitting the Wall" training. Ease into it and don't try it too often.

TEMPO (CRUISE) INTERVALS

Many Novice, Intermediate, and Basic Competitors don't have the discipline, experience, and mental and physical fitness to complete a 20- to 30-minute continuous tempo run. When we've tried these runs with our classes, most of the runners couldn't hold a steady pace to the end, and the runners spread out a lot. So, we break the workout up. We run out for 2 miles at tempo pace, take a 60- to 90-second brief recovery, and then run back for 2 miles. This works well. They get halfway splits for each run, and can compare their going-out to coming-back 2-mile times for consistency. It is mentally easier for them to do the workout.

Advanced runners also benefit from tempo intervals. Not only do they add variety from the stress of continuous tempo running and thus are a bit easier; but you can accomplish more LT training. For example, you may be able to do three 10-minute tempo intervals with a 1-minute recovery in place of a single 20- to 25-minute continuous tempo run. However, you do lose some specificity of training with tempo intervals: The workout doesn't mimic the continuous stress of racing as well as continuous tempo.

Tempo intervals, or "cruise intervals" as popularized by Daniels, are run at regular tempo pace, but for shorter distances. Don't run any faster than 10 seconds per mile slower than 10K pace. If the pace is too easy for these intervals, increase the distance or decrease the recovery periods. Tempo intervals range in length from 3 to 15 minutes (or half-mile to 2 miles). Short recovery periods of 30 seconds to 2 minutes are used to keep blood lactate from lowering too much before starting again. The total tempo running time should be 20 to 40 minutes, about 4 to 6 miles. Here are some examples of tempo intervals: two to three times 2 miles with 1½ minute recoveries, four to five times a mile with 1-minute recoveries, or eight to ten times a half-mile with 30-second recoveries. These workouts are usually done on the track, but can also be run on the roads or on hills. Tempo intervals can be used to sharpen for races of 10K and longer, and as a transition to faster-paced intervals for shorter races.

MARATHON TEMPO RUNS

This fast continuous run is a little slower and longer than traditional tempo runs. After warming up, run 4 to 6 miles at half-marathon pace, or 6 to 13 miles at marathon pace. A good option is to run a 10K race at half-marathon pace, or a 10-mile or half-marathon race at marathon pace. Start at the low end of these distance ranges and gradually increase the length, but not speed, of these runs. The key is to maintain the entire workout at your steady race goal pace and at a heart rate range of 80 to 85 percent of maximum. These workouts specifically train you to handle half-marathon and marathon race pace. They build strength and endurance, enable you to practice running form biomechanics at these race paces, improve your feel for these race paces, and give you confidence in holding goal pace.

PART III

PLANNING YOUR TRAINING

CHAPTER 14

The Training Schedule

Many runners just run and when a race comes along they feel like doing, they enter. They have no plan; they don't train for better racing. Other runners follow very detailed training plans that separate the year into cycles and phases. This method is referred to as "periodization" because the schedule for a training cycle (or season) is divided into periods of time (phases), each with a specific training goal.

With periodization each phase prepares the runner for the next, more advanced one. The most rigid programs consist of a base phase of endurance running, followed by a strengthening period emphasizing hill training, then sharpening concentration on track intervals. This series of phases builds to a peak for a key race or series of races to complete the training cycle. Many running books preach the necessity of following a detailed three- to six-month training schedule using periodization in order to reach peak performance. This one won't. I'll modify it for the average runner.

It would be ideal to follow a very structured program. But, let's face it, the majority of runners don't have a coach to monitor a fancy training plan nor the desire to be *that* serious. Typical runners in our classes want to enjoy doing well in several races, not just one. They prefer to race once or twice a month rather than building gradually for one key race. After all, they're interested in self-improvement and having some fun, not winning prize money.

Periodization in its truest sense is best left for the Elites. It's too demanding and too boring for the rest of us. Besides, skip speed training for several weeks as recommended in those long-term buildups and your fast-twitch fibers feel neglected. They take a long time to retrain. Suddenly switching from endurance runs to hills and then to track intervals may cause injury. It's better to gradually blend from one phase and one type of training to the next.

I'm not telling you a training plan is a waste. The more you plan your overall training schedule and individual workouts the more likely you will perform well. But the more complex and lengthy the schedule, the less likely you'll follow it. So I'll give you a compromise program. This chapter reviews the key phases of a training program. Follow them specifically if you wish with a well-designed periodization program. Or, follow them in a general sense using my recommendations.

THE TRAINING CYCLE

This is your running season, from the start of your buildup to your final peak race. For school and college teams this is well-defined: cross-country in the fall, indoor track in the winter, outdoor track in the spring. Their seasons end with the championship meets. But for adult road-runners seasons are built around individual goals and the weather, not team schedules.

Mother Nature helps determine racing seasons with her four seasons: winter, spring, summer, and fall. In colder climates, most runners back off over the winter. Spring brings us back to faster training with renewed commitment and enthusiasm. PRs (personal records) here we come! Mother Nature also forces runners to back off in the heat of summer, but allows them to peak in the coolness of fall. Runners living in areas such as Southern California where natural seasons blend together are more tempted to overtrain and overrace. So next time you're cussing about a long stretch of bad weather, think of it as Mother Nature asking you to take a break.

There are two extreme approaches to road racing: the one-race season and the year-round season. Some runners may train for four to twelve months following a periodization program aiming for one race. Elites often do this when preparing for a major event. During this time every workout is designed to prepare for the big day. These runners sacrifice less significant race results along the way to reach a very high peak for that key race. This training philosophy isn't recommended for the average runner because it offers no rewards along the way. Further, you risk having one bad day and losing a whole training season.

At the other extreme is the runner who trains to race almost every week. We have lots of them in our classes. They enjoy challenging themselves and the spirit of the racing scene so much that they don't want to miss out. Overracing is hard to avoid since there is at least one event within jogging distance of almost every runner each weekend. When these overracers start a training cycle it is often for one of two reasons: They're coming back from injury, or they just signed up for a marathon. Sound familiar?

If you're a fun racer and the fellowship aspect is more important than performance, then go right ahead, have fun. But, chances are, you really would like to run faster or you wouldn't be reading this book. You will increase your chances of running faster if you race less often, and train to do well in a few races. If you insist on racing almost every weekend, at least take a month or two off twice a year to let yourself recover. Usually this type of runner does just that—because of injury.

THE MULTIPLE-PEAK BLENDING METHOD

A compromise between the extremes of the one-race season and the year-round season is the plan I recommend for most of us. I call it the multiple-peak season. Build to a high-fitness level and enjoy racing with success one to two times a month. Race well for two months or so, then take a break. Then do it all again. Following this modified periodization program you may be able to enjoy two to four peaks each year, each consisting of a few good race performances. You might not reach as high a peak as with a more highly disciplined periodization approach, but you'll have more good race results and more fun.

This is the approach I take. I race year-round, but aim to peak three times: in the spring when the weather warms, the summer when I do fast group track intervals, and the fall when the weather cools. I get good results when I run a series of races two to three weeks apart, with my best results coming after three or four races. In between these training cycles, I'll take a month or two off from racing and hard training. But I maintain a good mileage and speed base (weekly less intense workouts such as fartlek, tempo, and strides) so that when it comes time to up the training again I'll be fresh, but not out-of-shape. Ideally, I choose when to take the breaks. Often, however, other factors play a part in my scheduling: bad weather (cold streaks, extended snowstorms, heat waves), work (this book!), injury, allergies, asthma.

Most runners can build and maintain fitness fairly easily for races in the 5K to 10K range on moderate weekly mileage, long runs of 6 to 10 miles, and consistent speed training. You can race fairly often, and you get more than one chance for a good performance with each training cycle. You may be able to squeeze in three or four peaks a year. But the marathon demands higher mileage, longer long runs, and a longer training cycle. For many marathon specialists, this means up to two training cycles each year—for a spring and fall marathon. But you can reach some mini-peaks along the way—for example, popping a PR for a half-marathon and 10K within a few weeks of your marathon.

Many runners train exclusively for one distance. For variety and improvement, try training primarily for a longer or shorter distance for a training cycle. This is especially valuable for marathon specialists. They'll benefit by the faster training required for 5Ks and 10Ks. By improving their speed for these shorter races, they'll be able to race faster over the marathon distance. On the other extreme, a 5K specialist benefits by concentrating on the 10K for a while to improve strength and endurance.

The following chapter leads you through a ten-step process to write your own training schedule. Chapter 9 details a sample 12-week speed training program to improve race times. Sample 12-week training schedules for 5K, 10K, and the half-marathon and 16-week schedules for the marathon are included in this text. All these samples are based on the general concept of the periodization approach. However, they don't build from one isolated phase to the next. Rather, they blend from one phase to another, and blend together all the key types of speed training—fartlek, hills, tempo, and intervals—along with short, medium, and long endurance runs.

THE TRAINING PHASES

Five phases are used in a training cycle: endurance base, strengthening, speed-sharpening, race-peaking, rebuilding. Other coaches may use different names for phases, but all programs are based on the same training principles. The phases follow in a specific order and each serves the purpose of preparing for the next phase. The first four phases build to peak fitness and are diagrammed in Figure 14.1. *Coach Glover's Training Pyramid.*

The endurance base phase. This is the easiest phase to do, and the one most neglected by the average runner. Build a good foundation of aerobic and muscular endurance. The stronger the base, the higher you can aim for racing and the longer you can hold a high level of fitness. You need a good base to support the faster speed training and racing to come.

In the traditional periodization program, runners spend four to six weeks in this phase when training for 5Ks and 10Ks, eight to twelve weeks or longer for the marathon. With this approach, you gradually build to your peak mileage and long-run distance goals for the training cycle within the endurance base phase while concentrating only on aerobic endurance running. The theory is if you cheat on endurance and jump into early speedwork and racing, you may get some fast early season race times but you'll falter in your key races late in the racing season.

With the multiple-peak blending method, you start the sample training schedules in this book with a mileage base that should be at least 50 percent of your peak mileage goal, preferably 75 percent of it. For example, if you aim to peak at 40 miles a week, your base should be at least 20 miles a week, preferably 30. The base period also should include a weekly long run that is at least one-third to one-half the length of the peak long run for your cycle. For example, at least 6 or 7 miles, preferably 10 miles or more, if the peak goal is 20-milers. From this level, expand the base over approximately the next four to six weeks for 5K to half-marathon training, and for approximately the next six to twelve weeks for the marathon. Follow the guidelines in Chapter 6 for increasing mileage.

During this endurance-base expansion, start to blend in some hill training, fartlek, tempo runs, and race pace intervals. These workouts shouldn't be too intense. The object is to ease into faster training. Also, include a low-key race or two for motivation and to establish a baseline for your racing fitness. Don't be depressed if race times this early in the schedule aren't as good as you'd like. Be patient. Top fitness is only a few weeks away. I promise.

The strengthening phase. This is a transition between easy endurance running and fast sharpening work. With the periodization method, you maintain the mileage base while adding hill training twice a week to strengthen muscles so they'll be better prepared for the track intervals to come. This phase typically lasts from two to four weeks for 5K training, four to six weeks for marathoners.

With the multiple-peak blending method, the endurance base phase starts to blend into the strengthening phase after the first two weeks, continuing until peak mileage is reached and you start to blend into the sharpening phase. This process takes about three to six weeks. During this period the speed-training emphasis should be on gradually intensifying hill training, fartlek, and tempo runs; improving the intensity and quantity of race pace intervals; and easing into faster than race pace intervals. One or two races during this phase to build strength is recommended. Examples: a 10K when aiming for a 5K peak; a half-marathon to build for a 10K; a half-marathon to toughen up for a faster half- or a full marathon. Expect the quality of this race to be a little higher than your race during the base period. Don't race too often here or instead of building strength, you'll lose it. Or you may peak too early.

The speed-sharpening phase. This is where the intensity increases. With the periodization method, you lower mileage and cut out all types of speed training except track intervals. These workouts consist of some race pace intervals, but mostly more intense work ranging from half-mile to 5K race pace. This phase typically lasts from three to four weeks for 5K training, four to six weeks for marathons. With this method you might aim to run one quality race at a distance shorter than your goal race. For example, a 5K to help sharpen for a 10K, or a 10K or half-marathon to sharpen for a marathon.

With the multiple-peak blending method, this phase is a gradual transition from strength-oriented to speed-oriented training. It lasts about three to six weeks. All the major types of speed training are used here with an emphasis on intervals at race pace and faster. A race every three weeks or so can be used to practice various racing strategies without being concerned yet with top performances. Sometimes important races will occur during this phase, several weeks prior to your training peak. If you're feeling fit, go for a good time. Take it when you can get it! Hey, you could be in peak shape later only to have bad weather or come down with the flu. But don't race too hard too often just yet. With more sharpening you've still got a few weeks to go before peak fitness.

Ideally, time your training so you move from speed-sharpening to race-peaking right when you want to run your best races. If you feel close to peaking, however, consider moving up your plans. For example, if you're aiming for a marathon in November but your workout and race times in September indicate you're already near top shape, don't despair. Adjust. Just move right into the race-peaking phase earlier than planned. So, you've peaked a little early—better early than never! Look for a good marathon in October and go for it. It can work the other way, too. If workout and race times aren't up to your expectations—perhaps due to lost time to injury or illness, work or family obligations—consider taking longer to move into your speed-sharpening phase and pushing back your race-peaking phase by a few weeks. Now that November marathon might be moved to December.

Speed-sharpening is less intense for novice racers. They don't need the stress of fast speed training on top of the new mileage levels. They should emphasize mileage and long runs along with some strengthening workouts and race pace intervals. Some experienced competitors may benefit by lowering mileage by some 10 to 15 percent (but keep up the long runs, especially if half-marathon or marathon training) while making the transition to the race-peaking phase.

The race-peaking phase. This is where you put it all together—endurance, strength, and speed—to race your best times. With the periodization program, this phase consists of tapering for one, perhaps two key races. Tapering (detailed later) for a key race ranges from a few days for a 5K to two or three weeks for a marathon.

With the multiple-peak blending method, you try to stay fit for as long as possible in order to get in several good races. Peak fitness can only be held for about three to six weeks because the intensity of the training and the stress of racing drain you physically and mentally. But you may race well for a few weeks longer if you don't overtrain or get injured trying to squeeze too many hard speed workouts and fast races into your schedule. A danger is believing that you can still add to your fitness during this phase. But you need very little training just to maintain it. How many races can you get out of peak fitness if you're not just aiming for one big performance? Approximately four to six hard efforts is a good goal.

During this phase quality is more important than quantity. Keep mileage levels high enough to hold strength, but low enough to allow for fast racing. Keep up the long runs until two to three weeks prior to key races. As you get closer to your key races, modify speed training. Cut back on the number of reps while still running them at fast but controlled paces, and allow for more recovery. The goal now is to maintain your peak. To do so you need to work hard enough to keep sharp, but not so hard as to pass your peak. Concentrate on speedwork aimed at specific race distances or courses. For example, mile intervals for marathon training, or long hills if you're going to be racing on a hilly course.

Go after some PRs in a series of races of varying distances to measure fitness, gain confidence, and have fun. Space these races to allow for recovery. Taper for them more than you did in previous phases; don't train through these, but go hard while your fitness is high. After adequate recovery from each race, resume your speedwork if you have more races on your schedule.

Peaking is more art than science. It involves developing a feel for putting together the key elements—quality speed workouts, rest, mental training—at the right time. With experience you'll become a better peaking artist. Runners often ask, "How do I know if I've reached my peak?" Times and feelings from workouts and build-up races often are key indicators. One of the first books I read about training was written in 1967 by Tom Osler. I still refer to this classic twenty-nine-page *Conditioning of Distance Runners* often. In it he details some of the symptoms of peaking. During speed workouts, the runner "feels as though there is nearly no effort on his will-power as his body thirsts to accelerate." The body "surges forward of its own free will." After hard training "instead of the mild feeling of physical depression which followed workouts, he should feel unusual leg lift and zip."

Osler added in *Runner's World*, "There are definite symptoms which the athlete can detect within himself when the attempt at peaking is progressing successfully. These include 1) an increase in competitive drive; 2) a great eagerness to race; 3) general feeling of alertness and a desire to do things; 4) increased sexual drive. When these symptoms are not observed, it is likely that the attempt at peaking will be unsuccessful."

How do you know if you've passed your peak? In speed workouts and races you'll start out feeling fast and comfortable, but run out of gas before the end. Remember that endurance base you built up? All those strengthening runs? When you cut mileage to concentrate on speed and racing you'll eventually run low on endurance and strength. After the last race of your season—whether by plan or because you've run out of steam—break and move into the rebuilding phase. Dr. George Sheehan advised runners to make the decision on a high note: "When you set a personal record, take a week off and tell people about it." If you try to milk your peak for all it's worth, you could end up regretting it. Overtraining leads to a very anticlimactic end to your training season. You have to learn to quit while you're ahead.

The rebuilding phase. Rebuilding consists of two parts. The rest period required after each race is termed recovery. The rest period after your racing cycle is completed is long-term rebuilding. This is true for both the periodization and multiple-peak blending method.

Recovery. Races require even more easy recovery time than hard training runs. A good rule of thumb: Run easy for the same number of days after a race as the number of miles of the event. That means three or four days of easy running after a 5K, about a week after a 10K, about two weeks following a half-marathon, and about four weeks after a marathon. In other words, take these recovery periods or more before training hard or long again, and prior to your next race. You may get away with returning to hard days sooner, but then again you might not. Generally, the less fit you are and the harder you pushed yourself, the longer the recovery period. It may take longer to recover from racing in extreme heat and humidity, or from exceptionally hilly courses—

particularly if they have lots of steep or long downhills. By racing only when you are fit enough for the distance, pacing yourself wisely, and going into the race with flexible, strong muscles and a proper diet, you minimize the tearing-down process that is part of racing. Fluid and fuel taken during the race will also aid recovery.

Keep moving when you finish. After leaving the chute, drink fluids, put on warm clothes, walk. For races of 10K or less, try a little jogging. Do some gentle stretching. Eat carbohydrates, particularly after long races, to replenish lost energy sources. Do this within 15 minutes of finishing running and over the rest of the day. Apply ice—immediately after the race and over the next few days—to any sore or tender areas.

Later in the day after racing, go for a walk, swim, or bike-ride to aid recovery. Try dancing—believe it or not, it will make an incredible difference the next day. If you're too tired or sore to run the next day, don't. Stick to non-weight-bearing exercise and walking until you feel like running and can run with good form. This may be for several days after a long race. Research indicates rest is more important to recovery than running after hard efforts. So why abuse the body by compelling it to run on blistered feet and tired legs? Do plenty of stretching a few times a day over the next few days, but don't force it on stiff muscles. Put the restorative power of extra sleep (including naps) to work for you for several days after racing. Massage within a day or two of a race (or hard workout) helps me recover.

Beware of a "false high" you may get a few days after a big race. Hold back on your training for a few days. Gradually increase mileage back to your normal (but not necessarily peak) level. This will usually take two or three days after a 5K, three to five days after a 10K, five to seven days after a half-marathon, and a week or two after a marathon.

Rebuilding. This is recovering from the entire cycle. After your last peak race, take a long break. Although this phase may seem anticlimatic, it is essential. Plan for it in advance, and don't cut it short by rushing back into hard training. You need time off to relax and allow your mind and body to recover and regenerate from the intense training and racing.

Here's a good rule: All runners should take at least two or three breaks from hard training and racing each year; each break

FIGURE 14.1: COACH GLOVER'S TRAINING PYRAMID

should last about a month or more. The rebuilding stage consists mostly of easy runs (or cross-training) and should lead into the endurance base phase when you're ready to start another training cycle. First, recover from your last race like you would for any other. Follow the guidelines above. But after you're over the fatigue from the race, continue taking it easy. Cut mileage by 10 to 25 percent or more below your peak, but certainly not by more than 50 percent. If you cut by too much, you will need much longer to build a base for the next cycle. Also cut out long runs. You may wish to do a few light speed workouts to help spruce up your running and keep the fast-twitch fibers active. But no racing! You can't rebuild if you keep tearing yourself down.

RACE-
PEAKING
PHASE
Taper mileage, specific speed training, mental preparation, peak for key races
SPEED-SHARPENING PHASE
Faster speed training concentrating on track intervals, transition races to practice strategies
STRENGTHENING PHASE
Maintain mileage base and long runs, emphasis on strength-training runs (hills, fartlek, tempo), improve quantity and intensity of race pace intervals, introduce faster than race pace intervals, overdistance racing
ENDURANCE BASE
Build mileage and long runs, introduce speed training at controlled paces, low-key racing for fun and motivation

TAPERING

Some programs include tapering as the final phase before a peak race. Although the taper is more concentrated prior to a big race, it should be used before any race you want to do well in—no matter what training phase you're in. When racing during your build-up phases, you will probably not taper as much. You may just back off a little the day or two before less important races. This way you can "train through" the race with minimal interruption to your mileage and speed training schedules. But to race your best, you need to be well rested. You can't have it all: high mileage, speed training, and a good race—all in one week.

Tapering involves allowing time to recover from the physical and psychological demands of heavy training. You want to achieve this goal without losing fitness and confidence, and while sharpening your speed. How do you pull this off? Gradually decrease mileage while maintaining some quality speed training.

With tapering, muscles repair the microdamage that comes with regular training and minor injuries have time to heal. You'll feel refreshed, peppier both physically and mentally. A study by David Costill, Ph.D., found that highly competitive athletes who reduced training by 60 percent for 15 days before a competition improved their performance times by almost 4 percent over when they didn't taper.

In a study at the University of Alberta in Canada a group of well-trained runners trained vigorously for one hour, five days a week for six weeks. Then, one group followed a six-day taper in which volume of training was reduced, but not intensity. In successive days they followed this program: run 40 minutes, day off, run 40 minutes, run 20 minutes, run 20 minutes, day off, race. In other words, they cut their training time over the six-day taper from 300 minutes to 120 minutes. The researchers found that the runners increased glycogen storage by 25 percent and lactate threshold by 12 percent. They also increased aerobic enzyme concentrations which translates into quicker oxygen delivery to the muscles. A group that only tapered for 3 days got similar results for lactate threshold and aerobic enzymes, but increased glycogen storage by only 12 percent. Those runners that trained through the test by continuing running hard for an hour a day only showed increases in aerobic enzymes. The no taper group's lactate threshold levels decreased and glycogen levels dipped by 12 percent.

I have tried the dramatic tapers recommended by some researchers. They may work for some runners, but not for me. I start to feel too stale, less fit. I'm more irritable than when training too much, and my leg muscles twitch, making it hard to sleep at night. So I taper more moderately. With experience, you will learn what is best for you. Here's what I recommend:

- How long you taper depends on the distance of the race, your fitness level, and what feels best for you. Sample tapering schedules are included in each specific racing distance chapter. Generally, the longer the race and the less fit or experienced you are, the more you need to taper. If you taper too much, you may lose a little of your racer's edge. If you taper too little, you may not perform well because you're not fully recovered from previous training. With experience, you will learn what's best for you.
- Taper for approximately the same number of days as for the length of the race in miles: three days for a 5K, 6 days for a 10K, 13 days for a half-marathon, and up to twenty-six days for a marathon. The week prior to a race cut mileage by as much as one-half for 5Ks, 10Ks, and half-marathons. For the marathon reduce mileage by as much as 25 to 50 percent after your last long run (two or three weeks prior to the marathon) and gradually ease down to about one-third peak mileage for the six days before a marathon. If you're already a low-mileage runner, reduce mileage by less for all distances—about 25 to 30 percent. Do endurance runs at a pace you are comfortable with. Be careful not to pick up the intensity since you'll have extra energy, but also don't run too slow—it may make you feel slow.

- The last long run should be no closer than one week prior to races in the 5K to half-marathon distances (two weeks if you're aiming for a top performance); two to three weeks prior to the marathon.
- Don't cut out speed training. Small amounts of controlled fast running as you cut mileage will keep you sharp by fine-tuning fast-twitch fibers and remind you that you are very fit. The shorter the race, the more important this is. The last hard speed workout should be ten to fourteen days prior to a peak performance. Your last moderate speed workout, four to six days prior to a race, should be at 5K to 10K race pace with a reduced number of reps. Fartlek or strides is a good choice here.
- It's okay to take a few extra days off from running while tapering, but not too many. You'll feel sluggish. I prefer a day off two days before a race followed by a short, easy run the day before; others prefer to not run at all for two days before.

When tapering, get plenty of sleep, especially the second and third night before the race. Extra sleep will help your body recover more quickly from training and help make up for any loss of sleep over the last few days due to prerace jitters. Control your weight by reducing caloric intake to match the reduction in calories burned off with higher mileage. Keep off your feet as much as possible and minimize any physically or emotionally taxing activities over the last few days prior to a race. I'll get a massage a day or two before races to help my muscles get ready for a strong effort. Follow the guidelines in this book for fueling and hydrating during the tapering period.

Many runners love the taper. At last, they have more time and energy. But others feel uncomfortable cutting back. They're afraid they are going to lose their hard-earned fitness. They may stubbornly cling to their training like a security blanket. After all, runners are used to working hard to get ahead. They don't want to rest. But tapering isn't being a wimp. It takes at least ten to fourteen days for the training effect to occur, so any work you do in that time period before a race may help you mentally, but could hurt you physically.

As coaches, Shelly-lynn and I find that our toughest task is convincing runners to taper enough. We tell them that sacrificing some mileage and hard runs in order to be rested for a good effort is worth it. After all, the purpose of training is to race well, not to post impressive numbers in your diary. There have been many examples of runners, from back-of-the-pack to Olympic champs, who were injured or ill over the last few weeks going into a big race and were forced to cut back training. In many cases, they probably performed better than if they were able to continue with their normal training routine.

OVERRACING

You can stress yourself physically and mentally with too much racing. Don't race more than twice a month; seldom race two weeks in a row, particularly long races. Wait at least six weeks, preferably six months, before running another marathon. Select races wisely, space them properly, and recover before training hard or racing again.

OVERTRAINING

Overtraining occurs when the body can't adapt to hard training because the work load is too much, the recovery is not enough, or both. It can lower resistance to disease, increase the risk of injury, deplete glycogen, exhaust fast-twitch fibers, and undermine performance.

In *Better Training for Distance Runners*, David Martin, Ph.D., and Peter Coe define overtraining as a "combination of 1) inability to train or race at an acceptable level, 2) an extended period of fatigue, and 3) often an increased occurrence of sickness. This represents a complex combination of psychophysiological signs and symptoms of a more far-reaching nature than simple fatigue. It suggests a trend toward actual cellular injury, profound fuel exhaustion, breakdown of the body's defense mechanisms, neurological and endocrine disturbances, or perhaps all of these together."

The key is to keep things under control. There is a fine line between training to the max and overtraining. It's better to undertrain slightly than to overtrain. The most frequent cause we see of long-term overtraining comes when a runner finishes one marathon and then—in an effort to get even better after a good performance, or to make up for a subpar one—jumps back into another one within a few weeks. They may or may not pull off a good second effort, but they are quite likely to feel the effects of overtraining for six months or more. Greed has its price.

The same training program—even for runners of the same ability—can be too much for one runner, but not for another. What may not be too much for you when you are in top shape may be too much at other times, such as when coming back after a training lull. What's happening with the rest of your life may be a factor, too. Training you should be able to tolerate may be too much when under stress in other areas.

When planning your training schedule, be sure to make gradual increases in mileage, long runs, and speed workouts. Don't overrace. Pay attention to how your body responds to your training schedule and be prepared to back off if necessary. As Dr. George Sheehan warned: "Listen to your body. It will tell you when you are doing too much." Here are some signals your body may send out:

- A loss in competitive desire and enthusiasm for training. A desire to quit or an unexplained poor performance in workouts or races.
- A sluggish feeling that lasts for several days. This usually starts with a few runs in which your pace is the same as usual, but it feels more difficult. Next comes "heavy legs." Now you're tired and slow. You have no zip in your step. You may think you're running 8-minute miles, but your watch says it's a 9-minute pace. Your ability to kick during speed workouts and races disappears.
- A tired feeling after a full night of sleep. It may be difficult to get out of bed in the morning. You may also have difficulty falling asleep, or may wake up often in the night and find it difficult to go back to sleep. An occasional poor night's sleep should not

be a concern, but if it persists for two or three nights, take notice.

- An increase in morning resting heart rate of ten beats or more for the average runner, or five or more for the highly trained competitor. Significant increases are a sign you are not fully recovered from the previous day or days of stress—whether from running or life.
- A pale, sallow, dejected look.
- More frequent or persistent colds, headaches, and respiratory infections. Minor cuts heal slowly. Swollen lymph glands. An early sign for me is a sore throat.
- Upset stomach, loss of appetite, sudden weight loss, constipation, or diarrhea.
- Mild tenderness or stiffness that doesn't go away after a day of rest or after the first few minutes of your daily run. Soreness for a day or two after hard runs is normal, but soreness that accumulates from high mileage or persists for several days after hard running isn't. Be aware of any indications that your musculoskeletal system has been overtaxed.
- Increased irritability, feelings of tension, short-temper, mild depression, loss of confidence, difficulty making decisions, lack of concentration, poor coordination. Spouses are often the first to know when cranky mates are overtraining.
- An uncharacteristic lack of interest in running. This is often called "the blahs" or "burnout." You may also have feelings of apathy about your life in general (possibly including sex). These are sure signs of the overtraining syndrome.

What to do if these symptoms strike? Don't do what most runners do if they have a bad workout or race. They think it means they have to train even harder so they dig themselves into a deeper hole. Instead, pull the plug. Cut back the distance and pace of your runs or take a few days off. It may be necessary to forgo an upcoming competition, even skip the rest of your season. Sometimes athletes can't make this decision by themselves. They need to be counseled by family, friends or their coach. If you wait too long to back off, it may take a long time to return to top shape: weeks, months, or even longer.

When overtraining symptoms appear, eat plenty of carbohydrates to restock muscle glycogen and drink lots of fluids since chronic dehydration may be a factor in your fatigue. Get plenty of sleep. Take a break to do some of the relaxing things you used to enjoy before you started training so much: reading, watching TV, going to movies, listening to music, doing normal things with family and friends. If the symptoms are severe, stop exercising completely for a week. If the various steps I've recommended don't solve the problem within a week, see a sports doctor to make sure the symptoms don't become too severe. Serious illnesses can result.

The best way to fight off overtraining is with a detailed diary. If you write in how you *feel* every day you'll be more likely to take notice. Compare those feelings with your training for the previous few days, and previous training seasons. By analyzing entries in your training diary often, you'll avoid many of the pitfalls of overtraining.

UNDERTRAINING

Prepare properly for races to do well and avoid injury. A sufficient mileage base and speed training are essential for racing. If you train only 20 miles a week and then run a marathon, you're asking for trouble. The same is true if you do all your running at 9-minute miles and then attempt to race at a much faster pace. Overtraining breaks you down before reaching the starting line. Undertraining breaks you down before reaching the finish line.

CHAPTER 15

How to Write Your Own Training Schedule

We can't write a detailed training schedule for each and every runner in this book like Shelly-lynn does for her private clients. This text can only give sample schedules to follow. You can plan and write your own schedule, however, by following the guidelines in this chapter. After all, only you know what goals you want to pursue, what training has and hasn't worked for you in the past, and how much training you can tolerate.

You may not even need to write a schedule. As long as you follow the general scheme of things, you don't necessarily have to formalize your training schedule. I don't. I'll have a general plan and then adjust month-by-month, week-by-week, even day-by-day according to how I feel. I don't write it down until I've recorded it in my diary, after it's been accomplished. But then after nearly forty years of racing I have a lot of experience to reflect on. I don't like to plan details in advance. It's just my personality. I will, however, have a general theme in the back of my mind—such as peak mileage and long run goals. Most runners, however, benefit from a well thought-out written training schedule. Some get quite anxious without a detailed plan. It's their security blanket.

A model training program for each category of competitive runner is included within each specific racing chapter, from 5K to the marathon. Follow them fairly closely, or use them as a general guide to design your own training schedule. Your schedule must remain flexible enough to adjust at the warning signs of overtraining or injury, or for life's stresses. That would be the action a personal coach would take. Don't blindly follow any training schedule.

The previous chapters detail the various types of runs—short, medium, and long aerobic endurance runs; hills, fartlek, tempo, and interval speed training runs—and why, how, and when they should be used in your training program. Chapter 14 shows you how, if you wish, to develop a training program using the key phases—endurance base, strengthening, speed-sharpening, and race-peaking—to build for a race. Now it is your turn to do the writing.

In formulating a training schedule—whether you're training for a 5K, 10K, half-marathon, or a marathon—work backwards. Start with your race date, then figure out how many weeks in advance of it you should start your schedule. Then, follow this ten-step approach.

TEN STEPS TO WRITING YOUR OWN TRAINING SCHEDULE

Step #1: Select Your Race and Time Goal

Choose the particular race or set of races for which you want to train. The selection of your key race should be made carefully. Some may choose a hyped-up big race that attracts thousands of runners, including many Elites. These races are exciting for all levels of runners, from front to back. Others may want to do well in their annual hometown event, a corporate race, or a favorite event they run each year to judge their fitness. A good choice is to find one of the fastest courses around at the time of year that increases the odds for good racing conditions. Of course many runners choose a marathon to train toward. Whatever race you choose, it should be important enough to you that you will dedicate yourself to twelve to sixteen weeks of solid training. Write the date of your key race in your calendar, then write it down on your training schedule.

Step #2: Determine the Starting Point and Phases for Your Training Schedule

Your race choice should be far enough into the future so you have sufficient time to build mileage and long runs, and sharpen with speed training. For the marathon, this should be at least sixteen weeks in advance, for 5K to half-marathons at least twelve weeks in advance. If you already have a reasonable mileage base and have been doing some speedwork, you may be able to get away with a shorter schedule. Pick a date well in advance and use this as the starting point of your training schedule.

You may choose to run for four weeks or more at a base level prior to building up mileage with your twelve- or sixteen-week schedule. If, for example, you choose to build to 40 miles a week for a marathon, it would be ideal to establish a base of at least 20 miles a week for at least a month before you start building mileage. If you choose to follow the more structured approach of training with a precise base, strengthening, sharpening, and tapering phase, use the guidelines in the previous chapter to develop your training cycle.

Step #3: Select Your Fitness Category

To develop the best training program to fit your needs, decide which of the categories of competitive runners detailed in Chapter 1 you will use as your flexible guide for weekly mileage, long runs, and specific speed workouts.

Step #4: Select Your Build-up Races

Twelve to sixteen weeks is a long time to train without racing. Build-up races keep you motivated, measure progress, and help you sharpen for a key race. Choose at least two races that fit your individual needs. For example, you may pick a 10K and a 5K prior to peaking for an important 5K race; or, two half-marathons and a 10K to peak for a marathon. Write them into your schedule early so you can plan your mileage and long run goals around them. Of course be flexible enough that you can make a change in which races you use in your buildup. Spread them out. Run them with more conservative goals early in the schedule and with more challenging goals as you get in better shape. For example, a half-marathon at marathon pace and then, a few weeks later, another half in personal record time. It's good to get in more than one race when you're in peak shape. If you "put all your eggs in one basket," you could get bad weather or just have a bad day for your big race and have nothing to brag about after all that training. Plan for at least one build-up race close to your peak where you can show off your stuff. Being fit is fun. Don't save it for one race. With proper training and planning, you can run a few good performances within your training cycle.

On the other hand, too many build-up races can make it difficult to design and follow a progressive training program. Racing more often than every three weeks may hurt you more than it would help. You need time to taper and recover. For most runners, one build-up race each month is about right.

Step #5: Determine Your Long Runs

Using the guidelines in Chapter 6, determine the number and length of your long runs, and when to fit them into your schedule. Schedule them to gradually increase in distance. Particularly when marathon training, it is important to place these into your schedule and then plan mileage goals around them. Write long runs in your calendar, too, so you can make it a priority when planning other aspects of your life.

Step #6: Determine Your Weekly Mileage Goals

Use the guidelines in Chapter 6 to determine weekly mileage goals for the entire training cycle. Wait to schedule weekly mileage until races and long runs are planned since those will affect how much mileage is appropriate for the week, and perhaps the next. Write it down before you start figuring in how far you're running on individual days. Be sure to progress slowly and take a few cutbacks or plateaus to rest. You may choose to lower mileage some as you intensify speed training. Plan a significant taper in mileage for a week or two prior to your key race, perhaps somewhat less for the build-up races.

Step #7: Determine Your Speed Training Workouts

Use the speed training guidelines in Chapters 8 to 13 to determine which types of speed training to do when, and the distance, quantity, intensity, and recovery of each workout. Or, follow the sample 12-week program in Chapter 9. Determine the exact quantity and intensity of each workout a few days before to make adjustments for training progress. Try to determine a set day (or days) of the week for these workouts to ease planning and maximize commitment. When scheduling far in advance be flexible. It isn't always possible to run the exact planned workout, or fit it in on the exact day as planned. But by writing it down, you will be motivated to stay reasonably close to your predetermined schedule.

If you have a group to speed-train with under the direction of a coach, you don't have to worry about planning your speed workouts unless you want to follow an exact plan. For most runners, the value of training partners outweighs ideal speed workout schedules. Our students just write "speed class" into their schedule on Tuesday or Thursday evening and let us take care of the rest.

Step #8: Determine Your Off Day(s)

Plan your rest. A good choice for most runners is Mondays and/or Fridays to ease out of or into heavier weekend training. The day after a long run or race is a preferred choice for many competitors. Others plan off days to accommodate work and family commitments. Whatever your reasons or choices, write them into your schedule and try to stick with them. Of course, feel free to change them around or to take more if your body, mind, work, or family schedule demand it. Most runners benefit from one or two (maybe even three) off days each week. Too many off days require a lot of compensation to reach weekly mileage goals. You could end up running too far on some days.

Step #9: Determine Your Daily Mileage Goals

Why did I save this for last? Because you need to schedule your short- and medium-distance aerobic endurance run days around the other key factors that total weekly mileage: races, long runs, speed workouts, off days. Include one, or preferably at least two, aerobic endurance run days (or off days) before and after any race, long run, or speed session.

Shelly-lynn usually doesn't write in the exact distances of these filler days for her clients in order to give them more flexibility. Manipulate the blank days according to fatigue and mileage goals. Or, write down ideal daily mileage goals and use this as a general guide, adjusting here and there to fit your changing needs. Others prefer to have a set schedule and keep to it no matter what. Use the training schedules at the end of each specific racing distance chapter, from 5K to the marathon, as models for how to spread mileage out over each week.

Some runners prefer to start their weekly schedule on Sundays. However, that sometimes means starting your training week with a race or long run. The sample schedules in this book start on Mondays. It makes the most sense to start your training week when most people start their work week, and to train toward weekend races or long runs. Also, having both Saturday and Sunday available to make up a few miles lost during the week makes it easier to reach weekly mileage goals.

Step #10: Analyze and Modify Your Schedule

Analyze your schedule periodically and make modifications as necessary for such factors as injury, illness, bad weather, stress, or your wedding. Shelly-lynn does this for clients and you should, too. However, it is important to have faith in your carefully planned schedule and stick to it as closely as possible. Of course, go ahead and make minor upgrades if workouts and races show that you're progressing ahead of schedule and can handle more work.

Don't forget to plan your rebuilding phase after your key race. Follow guidelines in Chapter 14.

PART IV

SPECIFIC TRAINING FOR RACING

CHAPTER 16

The Novice Competitor

I love converting runners to racers. Why? It's fun and inspiring to watch runners set challenges to run farther or faster, reach those goals, and then raise them again. "Hooray! I did it, Coach Glover!" you can exclaim.

Racing isn't for everyone. But I think every runner should try a few races to see what it's like. For one thing, the era of the "fun racer"—the average racer—has emerged. For most of the runners in most races, the race is not to win, but to better personal goals and to have fun doing it.

The goal for your first race is simple: Finish. *Experience* your first race; don't race it. You will be a hero just for finishing, so don't put pressure on yourself by announcing a time goal. Look at it this way: The slower you run the distance, the easier it will be to show off by improving your time the next race!

Participating in races adds a special kind of enjoyment to your running, making it that more likely you'll stick with it for a lifetime. So what are you waiting for?

SELECTING YOUR FIRST RACES

The distance should be long enough to challenge you but short enough to be completed with a reasonable effort. Your first races should be slightly longer or faster than your normal runs. I recommend a distance between 2 miles and 5K (3.1 miles), but not more than 10K (6.2 miles). These are popular racing distances so you will have many events to choose from. Choose a local race—traveling adds to your excitement and stress. Be a "hometown hero" finishing in front of friends and family. Pick a low-key "fun run" or charity event. Or, enjoy a mass-participation event with plenty of novice and casual racers. If possible, stay away from very hilly courses and avoid hot weather for your first race experiences. In other words, minimize your obstacles. Women may prefer women-only races at first.

TRAINING FOR YOUR FIRST RACES

If you run for at least 30 minutes at a time, three to five times a week, you are ready to train for your first race. Concentrate on building endurance so you can run the race distance comfortably. You need a minimum amount of mileage and long runs to reach the finish line with reasonable comfort. My basic guidelines are the following:

- Weekly mileage should be at least two to three times the distance of the race itself (I prefer three). For example, 12 to 18 miles per week for a 6-mile race.
- Hold that mileage for at least four to eight weeks prior to tapering for the race.
- Complete at least three long runs, covering at least two-thirds of the race distance, in the eight-week period prior to the race. For example, a 4-mile long run for a 6-mile race. If you can safely build up to long runs equal to or beyond the race distance, that is even better.
- Don't cram mileage in during the last week or two before a race. Build gradually. Alternate three types of conversational endurance runs—long, short, medium. Do not concern yourself yet with speedwork. Your goal is merely to hold a steady, easy pace to the finish. After you have experienced the thrill of finishing your first race, increase the intensity of a few of your runs so that you can run faster in races.
- Taper. Take it easy the last days before the race. Take some days off. When you do run, go short and

easy. No additional training will help at this point, but it could hurt your race performance. It's too late to get in better shape for the race. Let your body rest up for the big effort.

Figures 16.1 and 16.2 are sample first-race schedules for you to use. One is a specific eight-week training program, including a tapering week, for the 5K race distance; the other is for the 10K. Please note that these schedules are designed to help you make it to the finish line with a minimal amount of training. If your goal is to improve race times beyond this level, then move on to the more advanced schedules for various race distances in the following chapters.

FIGURE 16.1: SAMPLE EIGHT-WEEK TRAINING PROGRAM FOR YOUR FIRST RACE (5K)

Weeks to Go	Mon.	Tues.	Wed.	Thurs.	Fri.	Sat.	Sun.	Total Mileage
8	Off	2	2	2	Off	2	Off	8
7	Off	2	2	2	Off	2	2	10
6	Off	2	2	2	Off	2	2	10
5	Off	2	3	2	Off	2	3	12
4	Off	2	3	2	Off	2	3	12
3	Off	2	3	2	Off	2	3	12
2	Off	2	3	2	Off	2	3	12
1	Off	2	2	2	Off	2	race (5K)	8 + race

FIGURE 16.2: SAMPLE EIGHT-WEEK TRAINING PROGRAM FOR YOUR FIRST RACE (10K)

Weeks to Go	Mon.	Tues.	Wed.	Thurs.	Fri.	Sat.	Sun.	Total Mileage
8	Off	2	3	3	Off	2	4	14
7	Off	2	3	3	Off	2	4	14
6	Off	3	3	3	Off	2	5	16
5	Off	3	4	3	Off	3	5	18
4	Off	3	4	4	Off	3	4	18
3	Off	3	4	3	Off	3	5	18
2	Off	3	4	3	Off	2	4	16
1	Off	2	2	2	Off	2	race (10K)	10 + race

TIPS FOR BEGINNER RACERS

Here are some important tips:

Organize yourself. Take care of all the important prerace details (Chapter 28).

Shoes and clothing. Wear your faithful, well-cushioned, well-broken-in training shoes. You don't need a fancy new pair just for the race, nor are you ready for racing shoes. Beginner racers usually wear too much clothing. Start the race feeling slightly underdressed. Your body will heat up during the race, and even clothing that was comfortable for training runs may now feel too warm. If the weather is cold, dress in layers. In the heat, wear a minimal amount of light, loose, breathable clothing.

Walk if necessary. You can walk during a race if you wish. If someone gives you a hard time just tell them Bob Glover said it was okay. Nowhere on the race application does it say you can't walk. Pace yourself and try to run all the way, but be smart and walk if necessary so you can finish. As a beginner racer, you might need a light breather here and there, especially if the hills or heat may be too much for you. But walk briskly and keep moving toward that finish line. Since you should drink water at the stations, walk with your cup of water as you slowly drink it. Everyone will think you are only walking so you can drink! And if you walk up steep hills, I can guarantee you won't be alone. But be sure to run across the finish line smiling.

Fear not. Afraid of finishing last? That's unlikely if you are well prepared and follow these guidelines. Some runners start too fast and struggle in last, or attempt to run the distance without proper mileage "in the bank" beforehand. Gain confidence by planning your race strategy (Chapter 29) in advance. Turn your fear around and use this energy to help you get to the finish line. Look forward to this opportunity to show off. After all, you only get to run your first race once!

FIRST-RACE TIPS

At the starting line, position yourself in the very back or near the back so you won't get trampled by the speedsters, or get dragged out at too fast an early pace. One strategy for first-time racers is to let as many people start ahead of you as possible. This will help ensure that you start slowly, and instead of having lots of people passing you during the race, they'll be plenty of people for you to pass.

Standing there among a crowd of runners who you may think look younger, sleeker, and faster, you may begin to feel all alone, insecure, intimidated. Be assured, all runners go through this—even the Elite. Before you panic and look for escape routes, think about all the good training you did to prepare for this first-race experience. You can do it! Give yourself a good pep talk. Soon it will be too late to chicken out—you will be saved by the starter's horn.

The blast of the starter's horn will propel you along with the flowing mass of runners down the road. "Why did I let Bob Glover start me on this madness?" your inner voice screams. But you're off. You fight adrenaline and hold back. Maintain a comfortable, slightly slow pace. Find a group of runners going at your pace and join them. Don't race against anyone who passes you or whom you pass early in the race—you'll lose your sense of an even pace. Chat with the runners around you, wave to your fans, laugh, have fun. This is a fun race for you, not a serious race, as it is for those up ahead. Hang in there; set goals to run from one landmark to the next.

After a while, if you feel good, pick up your pace. Start picking off runners; you're the tortoise passing the hares who went out too fast. This gives you confidence and the excitement of passing runner after runner over the last mile or two of the race. Finish in good form. Look good for the photos of you completing your first race.

Now comes the fun: You can brag to everyone in sight (and then go home and call all your friends) about how great you felt in your first race. You can cheer the top runners as they receive their trophies, and know that you, too, are a winner.

WHAT'S NEXT?

After the race, take it easy the next few days with less and slower running. Even though you will not be racing hard, you will still be under a lot of stress from the excitement and exertion of your first race. Recover carefully. Avoid the temptation to immediately train harder right away for your next race.

While recovering, analyze your race. Use the experience as

background to help you prepare for your next race. Reevaluate your training program and select new racing goals. Make them either farther or faster, but not both—not yet.

Here are some goals that you can set for yourself:

1. The safest, least competitive goal is to extend the distance of your longest race. If you have run a 5K, enter a race that's in the 4-mile to 10K range, then one from 10 miles to a half-marathon, then perhaps a marathon. Finishing will continue to be a reward; only now the distance will be tougher. However, you don't have to keep racing longer and longer distances, and if you aren't properly prepared for them, you shouldn't. Don't be in a hurry to make the transition from beginner racer to a more serious competitor, or to move up to the marathon distance (if you even choose to accept this challenge).
2. Another goal is to improve your time over the same distance, then improve your time over a variety of distances. You'll soon hear other runners talk about setting PRs (personal records). Record your PR for different race lengths and then set a goal of improving those times.
3. A more competitive goal is to aim for a certain place (overall or within your age and/or gender category) in a race, like the top 100 or even the top 10,000. I faintly remember the days when I often aimed for the top ten. Or, aim for finishing within a certain percentage of the field, or your age group. Percentages sometimes sound better when you want to brag. Instead of saying that you finished 15,132nd in the New York City Marathon, you can say that you finished in the top 50 percent!

MEMORIES

Most runners remember their first race vividly, and each of their tales is instructive and often inspiring. My first race was as a sixteen-year-old. For the first time, high schoolers in New York State (boys only, girls weren't yet allowed to run long distances) were allowed to run longer than a mile. In preparation for the 2-mile event being added to the high school track program the following season, the folks in Hornell, New York, added to their adult 7-mile road race on Memorial Day a 2-mile road race for boys. One of my best friends, Bob Elliott, challenged me to do it with him. I was very nervous about running my first road race. Not only that, this would be the first time I had ever run 2 miles! I finished with a lot left, passing a lot of experienced distance runners. Afterward, my friends in school called me "marathon man." They thought 2 miles must be a marathon, and they certainly had never heard of anyone back in those days who could run that far. Little did I know that I would one day run a marathon at a faster pace per mile than I ran my first 2-miler. Who would have dreamed that I would run 2 miles faster as a fifty-year-old than as a sixteen-year-old? This very event helped shape the rest of my life. The following track season at Dansville High School I became a pioneer—the first ever Livingston County 2-mile champion. I found something to give me the confidence to excel in whatever I chose to do. Perhaps you, too, will be inspired by finishing your first race.

CHAPTER 17

5K Training and Racing

The 5K may be short, but it isn't easy. What it lacks in distance it makes up for in intensity. It's one of the most popular racing distances, but that wasn't the case when I first started road racing. 5Ks were hard to find in those high mileage days since most long-distance runners didn't want to waste a run by only racing 3.1 miles. Now many major events include a choice between a 5K and a longer race. In many cases, the 5K draws more participants.

The 5K offers benefits to all runners, even marathoners. It's the perfect distance challenge for novices. Most runners are capable of good 5K performances with limited training. 5Ks are a refreshing break from the physical and mental stresses of longer races. It allows for quick recoveries. The legs bounce back to life within two to four days. Its fast pace is exhilarating to speed lovers. Heat and humidity affect performance less than long distances. I've showed up for a half-marathon on a miserable day and wisely decided to switch to the companion 5K.

Many competitors use 5Ks as part of their overall training program. I often use them as a second speed workout of the week. Training and racing at 5K pace is the perfect intensity for improving aerobic capacity. That translates into better performances for longer distances, too. If 10K training, 5Ks hone speed and running form. 5K pace is slightly faster (about 15 seconds per mile) than 10K pace. After racing at this faster intensity, 10K pace seems easier. Our 10K training programs include 5Ks as key sharpening races. Some 10K specialists devote a whole training cycle to the 5K to improve speed. Every 15 seconds of improvement in 5K time translates to about a 30-second drop in 10K time. If training for the half-marathon or marathon, 5Ks are helpful, too. Use them for a speed workout, or for motivation. The 5K requires less time for tapering and recovering than longer races so it won't interfere as much with your mileage goals.

We often see runners who are successful at short distances struggling to be marathoners. Make the most of your ability at 5K first, then move up gradually in racing distance if you choose. Okay, get your first marathon out of the way if you insist, but then go back to the 5K until you have developed enough endurance and strength to transfer your 5K speed to longer races.

Some runners specialize at this distance. If you race better at shorter distances than longer ones, why not concentrate on your talent? You may have the muscle fiber ratio and psychological makeup more suited to 5K racing. Not everyone is blessed with the speed to run fast 5Ks. If you've got it, flaunt it. Don't waste your time and beat up your body trying to be a long-distance runner you're not, especially if you don't really enjoy it. Instead, sharpen your speed and invite the marathoners to take you on at *your* distance. For runners not able to handle the mileage required for longer races due to limited time or vulnerability to injury, the 5K offers a chance to still excel. Here's perhaps the biggest advantage for 5K specialists: You can race more often. It's okay to race this distance two weekends in a row. But don't get too greedy. Limit yourself to two 5Ks a month.

THE 5K TRAINING PROGRAM

Although you don't need a lot of mileage and long runs to be successful at 5Ks, you do need a good foundation of endurance and strength to support faster speed training.

Most 5K racing goals can be achieved with a 12-week training cycle. Chapter 14 details the various training phases; Chapter 15 guides you in writing your own 5K program. Or, use the sample 12-week training schedules in Figures 17.2–17.5 (pages 178–181) to blend the various training phases and types of endurance and speed training runs.

Mileage and Long Runs

Novice and Intermediate Competitors achieve modest goals on as little as 10 to 15 miles a week; even Local Champions can be competitive with as little as 30 or 40 miles a week. Running too much mileage or running long too often takes away from your ability to handle intense speedwork.

The following sample schedules include a recommended base mileage to be held for at least a month prior to starting the program. It should be at least 50 to 75 percent of your peak mileage goal. During the base period long runs should be at least one-third to one-half the peak long-distance runs for the program. Follow the flexible guidelines in Figure 17.1. Gradually increase weekly mileage and the length of long runs until you reach your goal range. Hold at that level for a few weeks, then gradually cut back distances to allow for faster training and racing as you begin to peak.

FIGURE 17.1: MILEAGE AND LONG-RUN GUIDE FOR 5K TRAINING

Category	Weekly Mileage	Long-Run Distance
Novice/Intermediate Competitor	10–20	3–6
Basic Competitor	15–25	5–8
Competitor/Advanced Competitor	30–40	8–10
Local Champion	30–60	8–12

Speed Training

The speed workouts in our schedules make a gradual transition from continuous strength training runs (fartlek and tempo), hill training, and race pace intervals to faster than race pace intervals. Since aerobic capacity is the most important physiological determinant of success in distance races lasting up to 20 minutes or so, an emphasis should be placed on training at 95 to 100 percent of your aerobic capacity. Thus, 5K training includes plenty of shorter intervals (220s, quarters, halves) at intensities ranging from 3K to 5K race pace. Power Intervals at one-mile race pace boost your anaerobic system and muscular power. See the speed training section for specific guidelines for speed workouts, including how to choose the quantity, intensity, and recovery. Feel free to replace our suggested workouts with others detailed in those chapters.

Our schedules include only one of many possible combinations of speed workouts to improve your 5K race times.

In our schedules, speed sessions are included on Wednesdays—the middle of the week—to allow for adequate rest going into and coming off weekend races and long runs. Include them whatever day of the week works best for you. If you need more time to taper or recover for races and long runs, shift or minimize our suggested speed workouts. Since the 5K requires building plenty of speed, a second speed workout most weeks would be helpful to most runners. For example, schedule a speed workout on Tuesday and either Thursday or Friday, rather than on our suggested Wednesday only. If adding a second speed session to our suggested one, keep these taxing workouts at least 48 to 72 hours apart. Balance the two speed sessions within a week. Unless you are very fit and highly experienced, avoid doing two hard track workouts each week, or two hill sessions. Good choices for adding a second workout to our suggested one: strides, tempo runs, fartlek, hill repeats. Most runners can't handle two very hard workouts in the same week, so run one of them well under control.

Build-up Races

The sample schedules include one overdistance race of 10K early in the schedule to build strength, and three races at the 5K distance to build toward a peak performance. You may race slightly more often, but don't overdo it. Overracing invites injury and interferes with speed training. You may compete slightly less often, but regular racing toughens you for competition. The races in the sample schedules are on Sundays—the most common race day. If your race is on another day, adjust your training accordingly using the basic principles of the sample schedules.

The range of the overdistance race can be from 4 miles to 10K. Anything longer tears you down when you need to keep the legs fresh for fast racing. An option is to replace a 5K on the sample schedule with a 5-mile or 10K two or three weeks prior to your final 5K so that you can go for a good time at that distance, too.

Underdistance races of approximately 2 miles, if you can find them, improve speed for 5K racing. Race at least one other 5K close to the final 5K on your schedule. This familiarizes you with the distance and effort required for a peak performance. You may be blessed with great weather, feel good, and run a great race prior to your scheduled peak race. Here's a big advantage of 5K racing: You can race it a few times until you get it right. Although the goal is to run each 5K faster with the fastest being the last peak effort, racing often doesn't work that way. That's why I put a series of three 5Ks in the sample program. It improves the odds that you'll reach your goals. You may choose to taper more or less than the sample schedules for races, and run more or less mileage as you recover from races.

SAMPLE 12-WEEK 5K TRAINING PROGRAMS

Don't follow the training schedules in Figures 17.2–17.5 (pages 178–181) blindly. Understand the concepts behind them. Modify the training programs by varying the daily and weekly mileage, the exact day and type of speed workouts, and the timing and distance of races to suit your needs. Be prepared to adjust for progress, fatigue, health, or injury. For speed training and race days the mileage figure includes warm-up and cool-down running as well as interim recovery runs.

A sample rebuilding phase isn't included. That doesn't mean it isn't important. See Chapter 14 for guidelines.

BREAKING BARRIERS

Breaking barriers can be very rewarding, whether it's the 30-minute or the 15-minute mark. Following are some time goals to motivate you. Running the *approximate times* listed for fast to hard paced intervals, and a range of race distances predicts your ability to break the corresponding 5K time barrier.

5K LOGISTICS

Review the general prerace logistics guidelines in Chapter 28. A thorough warm-up is especially important for short races. Your body blasts off from a standing start to maximum aerobic capacity pace within seconds. Don't overdress; the high intensity of 5K racing heats you quickly. If you want to experiment with lightweight training or racing shoes, here's the place to do it. The lighter the shoe, the faster you'll feel on your feet. In a short, quick race, you may be able to tolerate the reduced cushioning.

The Sub-16:30 5K (5:18 per mile)
Intervals: miles in 5:02–5:10, ¾ in 3:41–3:47, ½ in 2:23–2:27.
Races: 2 miles in 10:15, 4 miles in 21:36, 5 miles in 27:10, 10K in 34:20.
The Sub-17-Minute 5K (5:28 per mile)
Intervals: miles in 5:12–5:20, ¾ in 3:48–3:55, ½ in 2:28–2:32.
Races: 2 miles in 10:32, 4 miles in 22:13, 5 miles in 27:50, 10K in 35:15.
The Sub-6-Minute-Pace Mile 5K (sub-18:39)
Intervals: miles in 5:42–5:51, ¾ in 4:10–4:17, ½ in 2:42–2:46.
Races: 2 miles in 11:35, 4 miles in 24:30, 5 miles in 30:40, 10K in 38:48.
The Sub-20-Minute 5K (sub-6:26 per mile)
Intervals: miles in 6:06–6:16, ¾ in 4:28–4:35, ½ in 2:54–2:59.
Races: 2 miles in 12:22, 4 miles in 26:10, 5 miles in 32:50, 10K in 41:30.
The Sub-7-Minute-Pace 5K (sub-21:45)
Intervals: miles in 6:39–6:50, ¾ in 4:51–4:59, ½ in 3:09–3:14.
Races: 2 miles in 13:29, 4 miles in 28:20, 5 miles in 35:45, 10K in 45:15.
The Sub-7½-Minute-Pace 5K (sub-23:18)
Intervals: miles in 7:08–7:19, ¾ in 5:13–5:21, ½ in 3:23–3:28.
Races: 2 miles in 14:23, 4 miles in 30:34, 5 miles in 38:10, 10K in 48:10.
The Sub-8-Minute-Pace 5K (sub-24:52)
Intervals: miles in 7:36–7:48, ¾ in 5:33–5:42, ½ in 3:36–3:42.
Races: 2 miles in 15:16, 4 miles in 32:30, 5 miles in 40:40, 10K in 51:30.
The Sub-8½-Minute-Pace 5K (sub-26:25)
Intervals: miles in 8:05–8:17, ¾ in 5:54–6:04, ½ in 3:50–3:56.
Races: 2 miles in 16:16, 4 miles in 34:40, 5 miles in 43:20, 10K in 54:50.
The Sub-9-Minute-Pace 5K (sub-27:58)
Intervals: miles in 8:33–8:47, ¾ in 6:15–6:25, ½ in 4:03–4:10.
Races: 2 miles in 17:12, 4 miles in 36:44, 5 miles in 45:55, 10K in 58:00.

Hydrate before the race, but not during it. Whatever fluids you take in won't be fully absorbed for at least 20 minutes. Most runners will be finished or nearly finished before then. But if you're running for a half hour or more on a hot day, take fluids early in the race. You won't dehydrate much during the time period of a 5K race, so fluid replacement isn't a big issue anyway. Save the precious seconds lost trying to drink on the run. I'll grab water quickly during a 5K to rinse my mouth and pour over my head. It's mentally refreshing. "Hitting the Wall" due to glycogen depletion isn't a factor in 5Ks, but brain drain is a potential problem. Fasting overnight lowers your body's blood sugar. The leg muscles have enough glycogen to perform, but the brain lacks fuel. The

FIGURE 17.2: SAMPLE NOVICE AND INTERMEDIATE COMPETITOR'S 12-WEEK 5K TRAINING SCHEDULE

Weeks to Go	Monday	Tuesday	Wednesday	Thursday	Friday	Saturday	Sunday	Total Mileage
Base	Off	3	3 (strides)	3	Off	4	Off	13
12	Off	3	3 (modified fartlek)	2	Off	5	2	15
11	Off	3	3 (3–4 x long-hill repeats)	2	Off	5	2	15
10	Off	3	3 (2-mile tempo run)	3	Off	5	3	17
9	Off	3	3 (3–4 x half-mile, 5K pace)	3	3	Off	6 (race 10K)	18
8	Off	3	3 (4–5 x short-hill repeats)	3	Off	6	3	18
7	Off	4	4 (2–3 x mile, 5K–fast pace)	3	Off	6	3	20
6	Off	4	4 (3–4 x half-mile, fast pace)	3	Off	6	3	20
5	Off	4	3 (4–5 x quarter-mile, fast pace)	4	3	Off	4 (race 5K)	18
4	Off	3	4 (2–3 x mile, 5K–fast pace)	3	Off	5	3	18
3	Off	3	3 (4–5 x quarter-mile, fast pace)	2	3	Off	4 (race 5K)	15
2	Off	3	4 (cut down: mile, $\frac{3}{4}$, $\frac{1}{2}$, $\frac{1}{4}$; fast–hard pace)	2	Off	4	2	15
1	Off	3	3 (strides)	2	2	Off	4 (race 5K)	10 + race

FIGURE 17.3: SAMPLE BASIC COMPETITOR'S 12-WEEK 5K TRAINING SCHEDULE

Weeks to Go	Monday	Tuesday	Wednesday	Thursday	Friday	Saturday	Sunday	Total Mileage
Base	Off	4	3 (strides)	3	Off	5	Off	15
12	Off	3	4 (fartlek)	3	Off	6	2	18
11	Off	3	4 (4–5 x long-hill repeats)	3	Off	7	3	20
10	Off	3	5 (3-mile tempo run)	3	Off	8	3	22
9	Off	3	4 (5–6 x half-mile, 5K pace)	3	4	Off	8 (race 10K)	22
8	Off	4	4 (5–6 x short-hill repeats)	4	Off	8	5	25
7	Off	4	5 (2–3 x mile, 5K–fast pace)	4	Off	8	4	25
6	Off	4	5 (4–6 x half-mile, fast pace)	4	Off	8	4	25
5	Off	5	4 (6–8 x quarter-mile, fast pace)	4	4	Off	6 (race 5K)	23
4	Off	3	5 (2–3 x mile, 5K–fast pace)	3	Off	6	3	20
3	Off	4	4 (6–8 x quarter-mile, fast–hard pace)	3	3	Off	6 (race 5K)	20
2	Off	4	5 (cut down: mile, ¾, ½, ¼; fast–hard pace)	3	Off	5	3	20
1	Off	3	3 (strides)	3	3	Off	6 (race 5K)	12 + race

FIGURE 17.4: SAMPLE COMPETITOR'S AND ADVANCED COMPETITOR'S 12-WEEK 5K TRAINING SCHEDULE

Weeks to Go	Monday	Tuesday	Wednesday	Thursday	Friday	Saturday	Sunday	Total Mileage
Base	Off	5	4 (strides)	4	4	6	3	26
12	Off	4	5 (fartlek)	4	4	8	3	28
11	Off	4	6 (5–8 x long-hill repeats)	4	4	8	4	30
10	Off	5	5 (3-mile tempo run)	5	5	10	3	33
9	Off	6	6 (6–8 x half-mile, 5K pace)	6	6	3	8 (race 10K)	35
8	Off	6	5 (6–10 x short-hill repeats)	5	5	10	4	35
7	Off	6	6 (3–4 x mile, 5K–fast pace)	6	6	8	5	37
6	Off	6	6 (5–8 x half-mile, fast pace)	6	6	8	6	38
5	Off	6	5 (6–8 x quarter-mile, fast–hard pace)	6	4	3	6 (race 5K)	30
4	Off	6	6 (3–4 x mile, 5K–hard pace)	5	5	8	5	35
3	Off	6	5 (6–8 x quarter-mile, fast–hard pace)	6	4	3	6 (race 5K)	30
2	Off	6	6 (cut down: mile, 3/4, 1/2, 1/4; fast–hard pace)	5	4	6	3	30
1	Off	4	4 (strides)	4	3	Off	6 (race 5K)	15 + race

FIGURE 17.5: SAMPLE LOCAL CHAMPION'S 12-WEEK 5K TRAINING SCHEDULE

Weeks to Go	Monday	Tuesday	Wednesday	Thursday	Friday	Saturday	Sunday	Total Mileage
Base	Off	6	6 (strides)	5	6	8	4	35
12	Off	6	6 (fartlek)	5	6	10	5	38
11	Off	6	6 (8–10 x long-hill repeats)	6	6	10	6	40
10	Off	6	6 (4-mile tempo run)	6	6	12	6	42
9	6	8	7 (8–10 x half-mile, 5K pace)	8	6	Off	10 (race 10K)	45
8	Off	6	6 (8–12 x short-hill repeats)	7	8	12	6	45
7	Off	8	7 (3–4 x mile, 5K–fast pace)	6	8	10	6	45
6	Off	6	7 (6–10 x half-mile, fast–hard pace)	6	7	10	6	42
5	6	6	6 (8–10 x quarter-mile, fast pace)	6	4	Off	7 (race 5K)	35
4	Off	6	7 (4–5 x mile, 5K–hard pace)	6	7	8	6	40
3	6	6	6 (8–12 x quarter-mile, fast–hard pace)	6	4	Off	7 (race 5K)	35
2	Off	6	7 (cut down: mile, $3/4$, $1/2$, $1/4$; fast–hard pace)	5	6	6	3	33
1	Off	5	5 (strides)	5	3	Off	7 (race 5K)	18 + race

result could be a sluggish race. Follow the prerace fueling guidelines in Chapter 33 for avoiding brain drain. Fueling up during a 5K won't help performance and wastes time.

5K RACE STRATEGY

The 5K issues this special challenge: too short to relax and too long to sprint. You'll be running at close to your maximum aerobic capacity (about 95 percent) and slightly above your lactate threshold. At this intensity there isn't much room for pacing errors. The goal is getting to the finish line before lactic acid takes control of your body. If you start too fast or surge too quickly, you'll soon be running too slow; your muscles will accumulate lactic acid very quickly. But if you start too slow or lose contact with your peers, it isn't easy to get back on goal pace or to catch competitors.

Lining up in the right spot is crucial. Starting too far up front risks getting stampeded by the faster starters behind you, or getting pulled out too fast by the speedsters ahead. Starting too far back traps you behind slower starters, costing precious seconds. Line up aggressively, but not foolishly. Be alert and ready to go when the starter sets you off. Start no more than 5 to 10 seconds per mile faster than you want to average. A good bet is to start at the pace you think you can average and pick it up a little along the way if you feel good. The start-slow-and-pick-it-up-later strategy works better for races longer than 5K. It's critical to keep pushing a steady pace while monitoring your body signals. Slack off, and you'll fall off pace. But if you push the pace too much at any point in the race, you'll crash and burn. Racing 5K requires constant concentration. Lose it for a few seconds and you'll add a few seconds to your finishing time. Unlike longer races, where you strive to improve by minutes, 5K improvements come in seconds—so every second counts that much more. Here's the value of running a few 5Ks before your peak effort: You perfect race pacing and concentration with practice.

I break the 5K mentally into four segments: first-, second-, and third-mile marks, and the finishing tenth of a mile. During the first mile, find your rhythm; settle into a steady, strong pace. Hit the 1-mile mark at or slightly faster than race goal pace. In the second mile, pick up the effort slightly to keep on pace. Find a runner or a pack of runners going your pace and hang with them. Let them pull you along. Push a little more the third mile to stay on pace and to move up a few places. Focus on good form. With about 400 to 600 yards to the finish, gradually accelerate. Pick out other runners as targets. At the 3-mile mark, envision the last turn at a track workout, switch to all-out gear, and kick in over the last tenth of a mile to beat the clock and your competition. One of the perks of 5K racing is that you can race often, producing plenty of opportunities to test different pacing and race tactics.

Review the general tips for racing strategy and tactics in Chapters 29 and 30.

CHAPTER 18

10K Training and Racing

The 10K (6.2 miles) is the yardstick of performance: the ideal distance to compare 5K specialists from one end of the road racing spectrum and marathoners at the other. You can fairly accurately predict 5K, half-marathon, and marathon performances from 10K results. There are plenty of 10Ks to choose from on most racing calendars. You can run a few each training season since recovery usually takes less than a week.

This is the perfect racing distance for most runners. It's long enough to challenge the endurance of beginner and casual racers, and short enough to challenge the speed of experienced competitors. If you don't want to suffer too intensely or for too long, the 10K offers a middle ground—combining the speed of the 5K with the endurance of the marathon. Many experienced runners specialize at this distance. They may lack the raw speed to excel at 5K, or the endurance or time and ability to tolerate the higher mileage required for quality marathoning.

Many 10K runners make the mistake of racing in excess. You won't be able to improve 10K times week after week. Take a break from the stress of being measured by the same yardstick. Compete at a variety of distances, coming back to the 10K when you feel ready for a good performance. Improving times for experienced competitors depends on speed. A good way to improve speed is to lower 5K times. Look at it this way, improving your 5K time by 15 seconds should whack about 30 seconds off your 10K.

Overdistance racing helps, too. 15K to half-marathon distances improve your strength and endurance for the 10K.

If you're in good 10K shape, you can train for other race distances with only slight modifications in your program. That's exactly what many experienced competitors do. They basically train as 10K runners year-round and make specific adjustments for racing longer or shorter. 10K races can be used to prepare for other race distances. They improve strength for the 5K, and build speed for the half-marathon and marathon. Alberto Salazar simultaneously held American records for the 5K, 10K, and marathon and believed that the strength and speed that come with 10K training contributed to his ability to race well at all three distances. He states, "I believe that to run your fastest marathon you should be as close as possible to your fastest 10K shape a few months before." Try concentrating on the 10K for a training cycle before returning to marathon training. An improvement of 1 minute for 10K increases your potential for the marathon by 5 minutes. If training for 5-mile (or 8K) races, use these 10K training guidelines since there is only a difference of about 5 seconds per mile in race paces.

THE 10K TRAINING PROGRAM

Success at this distance involves blending more mileage but less speed than required for the 5K, but less mileage and more speed than needed for the marathon. Most 10K racing goals can be achieved with a 12-week training cycle. Chapter 14 details the various training phases; Chapter 15 guides you in writing your own 10K program. Or use the sample schedules in Figures 18.2–18.5 (pages 189–192) to blend the various training phases and types of endurance and speed training runs.

Mileage and Long Runs

If moving up from 5K to 10K, you don't need to do double training to race twice the distance. Increase mileage and long runs by about 10 to 25 percent to build enough endurance and strength to carry you through the last 5K of the race.

The sample schedules include a recommended base mileage to be held for at least a month prior to starting the program. It should be at least 50 to 75 percent of your peak mileage goal. Long runs during the base period should be at least one-third to one-half the longest runs for the training program. Generally, run long at least twice a month. Follow the flexible guidelines in Figure 18.1. Gradually increase weekly mileage and the length of long runs until you reach your goal range. Hold at that level for a

FIGURE 18.1: MILEAGE AND LONG-RUN GUIDE FOR 10K TRAINING

Category	Weekly Mileage	Long Run Distance
Novice/Intermediate Competitor	15–25	5–8
Basic Competitor	20–30	6–10
Competitor/Advanced Competitor	30–50	8–12
Local Champion	40–70	10–15

few weeks, then gradually cut back distances to allow for faster training and racing as you begin to peak.

Speed Training

The speed workouts in our sample schedules make a gradual transition from continuous strength training runs (fartlek and tempo), hill training, and 10K pace intervals to faster than race pace intervals. Aerobic capacity and lactate threshold are physiologically equally important to 10K success, so both are emphasized in training. 10K training isn't as intense as 5K training, yet it is generally run at faster paces than marathon training. You run longer intervals (especially halves and miles) more often and with more reps than with 5K training. Include training at 5K pace to boost aerobic capacity, faster than 5K pace to improve anaerobic tolerance and muscle power, at 10K pace to develop a feel for race pace, and at tempo pace to raise lactate threshold. See the speed training section of this book for specific guidelines for speed workouts, including how to choose the distance, quantity, intensity, and recovery. Feel free to replace our suggested workouts with others detailed in those chapters. Our sample schedules include only one of many possible combinations of speed workouts to improve your 10K race times.

In our schedules, speed sessions are included on Wednesdays—the middle of the week—to allow for adequate rest going into and coming off weekend races and long runs. Include them whatever day of the week works best for you. If you need more time to taper or recover for races and long runs, shift or minimize our suggested speed workouts. Since speed is important in 10K racing, a second speed workout most weeks may be helpful to many runners. For example, schedule a speed session on Tuesday and either Thursday or Friday, rather than on our suggested Wednesday only. If adding a speed workout to our suggested one, keep these taxing workouts at least 48 to 72 hours apart. Balance the two speed sessions within a week. Unless you are very fit and highly experienced, avoid doing two hard track workouts each week, or two hill sessions. Good choices for adding a second workout to our suggested one: strides, tempo runs, fartlek, hill repeats. Most runners can't handle two very hard workouts in the same week so run one of them well under control.

Build-up Races

The sample schedules each include one overdistance race of 10 miles early in the program to build strength and raise lactate threshold, two races of 5K to sharpen speed and boost aerobic capacity, and two races at the 10K distance to run for peak performance. You may race slightly more often, but don't overdo it. Overracing invites injury and interferes with speed training. You may compete slightly less often, but regular racing toughens you for competition. The races in the sample schedules are on Sundays—the most common race day. If your race is on another day, adjust your training accordingly using the basic principles of the sample schedules.

The overdistance race can be from 15K to half-marathon. Anything longer tears you down when you need to keep the legs fresh for fast racing. An option for your underdistance races is to replace a 5K on the schedule with a 4- or 5-miler. Race a 10K two to four weeks before the final 10K on your schedule. This familiarizes you with the distance and effort required for a peak performance. You may be blessed with great weather, feel good, and run a great race prior to your scheduled peak race. Getting more than one chance at 10K improves the odds you'll reach your goals. You may choose to taper more or less than the sample schedules for races, and run more or less mileage as you recover from races.

SAMPLE 12-WEEK 10K TRAINING PROGRAMS

Don't follow the training schedules in Figures 18.2–18.5 blindly. Understand the concepts behind them. Modify the training programs by varying the daily and weekly mileage, the exact day and type of speed workouts, and the timing and distance of races to suit your needs. Be prepared to adjust for progress, fatigue, health, or injury. For speed training and race days the mileage figure includes warm-up and cool-down running, as well as interval recovery runs. A sample rebuilding phase isn't included. That doesn't mean it isn't important. See Chapter 14 for guidelines.

BREAKING BARRIERS

Breaking barriers can be very rewarding, whether it's the half-hour or the 1-hour mark. Following are some time goals to motivate you. Running the *approximate times* listed for intervals and race distances predicts your ability to break the corresponding 10K time barrier.

10K LOGISTICS

Review the general prerace logistics guidelines in Chapter 28. Warm up properly to allow for a quick start. Don't overdress; the intensity of 10K racing heats you quickly. Many runners wear racing shoes for the 10K; lightweight trainers may be the best choice for most runners. Hydrate before the race and for the first 5K, but not after that. Taking fluids late in the race wastes seconds. It takes about 20 minutes for the fluids to absorb. After 5K, I'll just rinse my mouth and pour the fluids over my head for a quick mental boost. "Hitting the Wall" due to glycogen depletion isn't a factor in 10Ks since most runners are finished within an hour. But you do need some fuel in the morning to counteract brain drain and low blood sugar. Avoid a sluggish race and poor concentration with prerace fueling (Chapter 31). Fueling up during a 10K won't help performance and wastes time.

10K RACE STRATEGY

You'll be racing along at about 92 percent of maximum aerobic capacity, and at or slightly above lactic threshold. At 10K pace you have a little more room to operate below your limit than for the 5K, but starting too fast or surging too quickly along the way

FIGURE 18.2: SAMPLE NOVICE AND INTERMEDIATE COMPETITOR'S 12-WEEK 10K TRAINING SCHEDULE

Weeks to Go	Monday	Tuesday	Wednesday	Thursday	Friday	Saturday	Sunday	Total Mileage
Base	Off	3	3 (strides)	2	Off	5	2	15
12	Off	3	4 (modified fartlek)	2	Off	6	3	18
11	Off	3	4 (3–4 x long-hill repeats)	2	Off	8	3	20
10	Off	3	4 (2-mile tempo run)	2	2	8	2	21
9	Off	3	4 (4–6 x half-mile, 5K–10K pace)	3	2	Off	10 (race 10K)	22
8	Off	4	4 (4–5 x short-hill repeats)	4	Off	8	4	24
7	Off	4	4 (3-mile tempo run)	4	4	3	5 (race 5K)	24
6	Off	4	4 (2–3 x mile, 5K–fast pace)	4	Off	8	4	24
5	Off	4	4 (4–5 x quarter-mile, fast pace)	4	3	Off	7 (race 10K)	22
4	Off	4	4 (3–4 x half-mile, fast pace)	3	Off	8	2	21
3	Off	3	5 (tempo intervals, 2 x 1½ miles)	4	3	Off	5 (race 5K)	20
2	Off	4	4 (2–3 x mile at 5K–fast pace)	3	Off	6	3	20
1	Off	3	4 (strides)	3	2	Off	7 (race 10K)	12 + race

FIGURE 18.3: SAMPLE BASIC COMPETITOR'S 12-WEEK 10K TRAINING SCHEDULE

Weeks to Go	Monday	Tuesday	Wednesday	Thursday	Friday	Saturday	Sunday	Total Mileage
Base	Off	4	3 (strides)	3	Off	5	3	18
12	Off	4	4 (fartlek)	3	Off	6	3	20
11	Off	4	4 (4–5 x long-hill repeats)	3	Off	8	3	22
10	Off	3	5 (3-mile tempo run)	4	Off	10	3	25
9	Off	4	5 (5–6 x half-mile, 5K–10K pace)	3	3	Off	10 (race 10K)	25
8	Off	5	5 (5–6 x short-hill repeats)	4	Off	10	3	27
7	Off	6	5 (3-mile tempo run)	5	5	Off	6 (race 5K)	27
6	Off	6	5 (2–3 x mile, 5K–fast pace)	5	Off	8	4	28
5	Off	6	4 (5–8 x quarter-mile, fast–hard pace)	4	5	Off	8 (race 10K)	28
4	Off	4	5 (4–6 x half-mile, fast–hard pace)	5	Off	8	4	26
3	Off	4	5 (tempo intervals, 2 x 1½ miles)	4	3	Off	6 (race 5K)	22
2	Off	5	5 (2–3 x mile, 5K–hard pace)	4	Off	8	3	25
1	Off	3	4 (strides)	3	2	Off	8 (race 10K)	12 + race

FIGURE 18.4: SAMPLE COMPETITOR'S AND ADVANCED COMPETITOR'S 12-WEEK 10K TRAINING SCHEDULE

Weeks to Go	Monday	Tuesday	Wednesday	Thursday	Friday	Saturday	Sunday	Total Mileage
Base	Off	6	5 (strides)	6	Off	8	5	30
12	Off	6	5 (fartlek)	6	Off	10	5	32
11	Off	6	6 (5–8 x long-hill repeats)	6	Off	10	6	34
10	Off	6	6 (3-mile tempo run)	6	Off	12	6	36
9	Off	8	6 (6–8 x half-mile, 5K–10K pace)	6	4	Off	12 (race 10K)	36
8	Off	6	5 (6–10 x short-hill repeats)	5	6	12	6	40
7	7	8	6 (4-mile tempo run)	6	6	Off	7 (race 5K)	40
6	Off	6	6 (3–4 x mile, 5K–fast pace)	5	5	12	6	40
5	6	6	6 (5–8 x quarter-mile, fast–hard pace)	5	5	Off	8 (race 10K)	36
4	Off	6	6 (4–8 x half-mile, fast–hard pace)	5	6	12	5	40
3	7	8	6 (tempo intervals, 2 x 2 miles)	6	6	Off	7 (race 5K)	40
2	Off	6	6 (3–4 x mile, 5K–hard pace)	5	5	8	5	35
1	Off	6	6 (strides)	5	3	Off	8 (race 10K)	20 + race

FIGURE 18.5: SAMPLE LOCAL CHAMPION'S 12-WEEK 10K TRAINING SCHEDULE

Weeks to Go	Monday	Tuesday	Wednesday	Thursday	Friday	Saturday	Sunday	Total Mileage
Base	Off	8	8 (strides)	8	Off	10	6	40
12	Off	8	7 (fartlek)	8	Off	12	7	42
11	Off	8	7 (8–10 x long-hill repeats)	8	Off	13	6	42
10	Off	8	8 (4-mile tempo run)	6	5	13	6	46
9	Off	8	8 (8–12 x half-mile, 5K–10K pace)	8	7	3	12 (race 10K)	46
8	Off	8	6 (8–12 x short-hill repeats)	6	8	15	7	50
7	3	8	8 (4-mile tempo run)	8	8	3	8 (race 5K)	46
6	5	8	8 (4–5 x mile, 5K–fast pace)	8	8	15	8	60
5	8	8	7 (8–12 x quarter-mile, fast–hard pace)	8	6	3	10 (race 10K)	50
4	5	8	8 (6–10 x half-mile, fast–hard pace)	6	8	12	8	55
3	8	8	8 (tempo intervals, 3 x 2 miles)	8	6	4	8 (race 5K)	50
2	Off	8	7 (4–5 x mile, fast–hard pace)	6	8	10	6	45
1	Off	6	6 (strides)	6	4	Off	10 (race 10K)	22 + race

The Sub-34-Minute 10K (5:28 per mile)
Intervals: miles in 5:00–5:15, ¾ in 3:38–3:56, ½ in 2:22–2:26, ¼ in 1:09–1:11.
Races: 5K in 16:20, 5 miles in 27:00, 10 miles in 56:30, half-marathon in 1:15:00.

The Sub-35-Minute 10K (5:37 per mile)
Intervals: miles in 5:09–5:25, ¾ in 3:46–4:04, ½ in 2:27–2:31, ¼ in 1:11–1:13.
Races: 5K in 16:50, 5 miles in 27:40, 10 miles in 58:00, half-marathon in 1:17:00.

The Sub-6-Minute-Pace Mile 10K (sub-37:17)
Intervals: miles in 5:28–5:45, ¾ in 4:00–4:19, ½ in 2:36–2:40, ¼ in 1:15–1:18.
Races: 5K in 17:53, 5 miles in 29:25, 10 miles in 1:01:45, half-marathon in 1:21:30.

The Sub-40-Minute 10K (6:26 per mile)
Intervals: miles in 5:52–6:10, ¾ in 4:17–4:38, ½ in 2:47–2:51, ¼ in 1:21–1:23.
Races: 5K in 19:13, 5 miles in 31:35, 10 miles in 1:06:00, half-marathon in 1:27:30.

The Sub-7-Minute-Pace 10K (sub-43:30)
Intervals: miles in 6:25–6:45, ¾ in 4:41–5:04, ½ in 3:03–3:08, ¼ in 1:29–1:31.
Races: 5K in 20:55, 5 miles in 34:20, 10 miles in 1:12:00, half-marathon in 1:35:15.

The Sub-7½-Minute-Pace 10K (sub-46:47)
Intervals: miles in 6:49–7:10, ¾ in 4:59–5:23, ½ in 3:14–3:19, ¼ in 1:34–1:37.
Races: 5K in 22:20, 5 miles in 34:20, 10 miles in 1:12:00, half-marathon in 1:35:15.

The Sub-50-Minute 10K (8:02 per mile)
Intervals: miles in 7:20–7:40, ¾ in 5:20–5:45, ½ in 3:27–3:35, ¼ in 1:41–1:44.
Races: 5K in 24:00, 5 miles in 39:30, 10 miles in 1:22:45, half-marathon in 1:49:30.

The Sub-8½-Minute-Pace 10K (sub-52:50)
Intervals: miles in 7:46–8:10, ¾ in 5:40–6:08, ½ in 3:41–4:05, ¼ in 1:47–2:03.
Races: 5K in 25:20, 5 miles in 41:45, 10 miles in 1:27:30, half-marathon in 1:55:30.

The Sub-9-Minute-Pace 10K (sub-55:56)
Intervals: miles in 8:14–8:40, ¾ in 6:01–6:30, ½ in 3:54–4:00, ¼ in 1:54–1:57.
Races: 5K in 26:53, 5 miles in 44:10, 10 miles in 1:32:30, half-marathon in 2:02:30.

The Sub-60-Minute 10K (9:39 per mile)
Intervals: miles in 8:47–9:15, ¾ in 6:25–6:56, ½ in 4:10–4:17, ¼ in 2:01–2:05.
Races: 5K in 28:50, 5 miles in 47:20, 10 miles in 1:39:30, half-marathon in 2:11:30.

The Sub-10-Minute-Pace 10K (sub-1:02:09)
Intervals: miles in 9:02–9:30, ¾ in 6:36–7:08, ½ in 4:17–4:24, ¼ in 2:05–2:08.
Races: 5K in 29:50, 5 miles in 49:00, 10 miles in 1:43:00, half-marathon in 2:16:00.

will still cause significant fatigue due to lactic acid accumulation. Race pace is about 15 seconds per mile slower than 5K pace. But that's still much quicker (1 to 2 minutes per mile) than your training pace.

10Ks require a combination of the aggression of 5Ks and the patience of marathoning. You don't need to concentrate as keenly for the 10K as for the 5K, but still you can't let your mind wander too much. You have more time to make up for pacing and tactical errors than in shorter races, but the race isn't so long that you can make up a lot. The key to 10K racing is to start off at the proper pace, concentrate on the middle miles, and then push it home the last mile. The first half-mile or mile sets the tone for your race. Going out too fast or too cautiously ruins your chance for a good time. For 10Ks, I prefer to start slightly faster (no more than 5 to 10 seconds per mile) than race goal pace for the first mile or two and then settle into a steady pace. Most runners race best starting at race goal pace and trying to stay there; others start slow and then pick it up after the first mile. Experiment with various pacing strategies in build-up races.

The first mile or two should be relatively easy. It's the same pace or slower than your mile intervals on the track. Think of that first mile rep when doing speed training. You're pushing and holding back at the same time in a tug-of-war that helps you be right on pace. Look for runners you want to beat or stay close to. Unless you start much too fast or much too slowly, you will not pass or be passed by many runners after the 5K mark. Get into the proper position relative to fellow competitors early.

The middle miles are critical. This is where time is lost. You're no longer fresh and you can't yet get pumped for the finishing kick. Don't let your mind wander. Concentrate on good form and relaxed breathing. From mile 1 through 5, think of the middle mile intervals in your speedwork. Here you're pushing to stay on pace more than holding back to keep from going too fast. Use the 5K mark as a mental spur: You're heading home; it's now only a 5K race.

In the first 5K, concentrate on pace, not runners trying to pass you or vice versa. For the second half of the race, try to move up from runner to runner to help you maintain a good pace, or "hitch a ride" when a competitor goes by you. Look to move up a few places. Don't be satisfied with just holding your place. Most likely many of the runners around you are slowing down. This presents a mirage. You think you're on pace but you may not be. Instead of slowing with them, use the runners up ahead as targets to keep you on pace. Look for your peers—runners in your age group or those who run similar times. Go after them. Use them to pull you in or to try to beat and thus move up another notch. To do this, you may have to increase the effort slightly to gain ground on your competition and to keep from slowing from your goal pace. But don't get excited and surge. That could push you over your lactic threshold. The goal here is a steady push at your limit.

Gather your physical and mental resources for the final mile. Reflect on how hard the last reps were in your mile intervals. You made it through the discomfort then and you will make it to the 10K finish by being mentally tough. Fight off oxygen debt and leg fatigue by relaxing and really concentrating on good running form and controlled breathing. Position yourself for changing into your final gear at the 6-mile mark. Pick out a runner ahead to go after. Only two-tenths of a mile to go. That's less than a lap of the track. Switch to your one-lap kick mode and go.

Review the general tips for racing strategy and tactics in Chapters 29 and 30.

CHAPTER 19

Half-Marathon Training and Racing

The half-marathon (13.1 miles) is the middle ground between the trendy 10K and the classic marathon, offering many of the challenges and benefits of both these distances. The half is about midway between 10K and marathon paces, but closer in distance to 10K. In fact, at 21K it is only about one-third the distance between 10K and the 42K marathon.

Unlike the 5K, 10K, and marathon, the half isn't an Olympic event. Nevertheless, it has become a significant road race distance. Many marathons offer a companion half which outdraws its "big brother." Certainly the half deserves a spot on your racing calendar and recognition with its own training chapter in this book. If training for a 15K (9.3 miles), 10-mile, or 20K (12.4-mile) race, use these half-marathon guidelines, too, since there is only a few seconds difference in race paces.

There are many reasons to run half-marathons. Some runners are just getting warmed up when a 10K race is nearly over. The half offers the challenge of long distances, but without the more lengthy time commitment to training and the hard pounding of a full marathon. You can recover in time to get back to regular training in about a week. The half can be raced a few times a year. The pace of this race doesn't demand intense speed training. In fact, many runners use frequent short races as their speed training for the half. Some runners prefer the relative comfort of half-marathon pace. You race at about 20 seconds slower per mile than for 10K. Yet at about 20 seconds per mile faster than marathon pace and about a minute quicker than aerobic training pace, it's a quick workout. Also, the half doesn't require those exhausting weekend-wrecking 20-milers that are essential to the full marathon. A few runs of an hour or two are usually a sufficient investment of time and energy. For all these reasons and more, the half-marathon is a goal in itself for many runners.

Many competitors use this racing distance as part of their overall training program. The 15K to half-marathon distance is run at or near lactate threshold (LT) pace. Racing at this intensity boosts your threshold, translating into better performances at all racing distances. The half builds strength and confidence for 5K and 10K racing. In comparison, these events feel short, making the last mile or two easier both physically and mentally. The half is a good proving ground for aspiring marathoners. I advise marathon hopefuls to first complete a half before taking on a full marathon. It'll give you a chance to experience the training and style of racing you will need to run the full distance. For all levels of runners, the half can be used as a marathon dress rehearsal. It's long enough to require patient pacing and sufficient fueling and hydrating on the run. Use the half to practice and refine your techniques in these areas and test shoes and clothing. If you're in half-marathon shape, you're not that far out of marathon shape. Many marathon specialists concentrate on half-marathons until they're ready to key on their next marathon effort. Only slight adjustments in mileage and long runs are necessary.

Half-marathon races are used several important ways in marathon training. Run them at training pace to facilitate long runs. Early in a marathon training cycle, 13 miles may be as long as you're ready to train. Later, add a few miles before the race to accumulate your desired long run goal. An option is to run the race at marathon pace to get a feel for that race effort. Another option is to run a hard half-marathon as a good tune-up 3 to 5 weeks before a marathon. Use it to predict marathon times.

To succeed at racing half-marathons, you need to hold a strong pace for an extended period of time, ranging from an hour for Elites to over 2 hours for most Novice, Intermediate, and Basic Competitors. Runners above these levels should train for the half more like a 10K specialist than a marathoner. 10K racing will make half-marathon pace feel less stressful. Improving 10K times will improve half-marathon performances. Reduce 10K time by 30 seconds and you should be able to race 75 seconds faster for the half. If you'll be racing for over two hours, train more like a marathoner than a 10K runner. The stresses you'll experience, including glycogen depletion and dehydration, will be similar to the marathon. Emphasize sufficient mileage and long runs. For these runners, the half is more a grueling distance challenge than a race for time.

The half-marathon will be your first really long race? Treat it like you're training for your first marathon. Concentrate on building endurance and increasing long runs up to close to the race distance. Your main goal for your first half is to experience the distance by completing the race in reasonable comfort. How fast you run isn't as important as finishing. In succeeding half-marathons you work on improving your time.

THE HALF-MARATHON TRAINING PROGRAM

Most half-marathon goals can be achieved with a 12-week training cycle. Since endurance is such a key to success at this distance, it's essential the cycle begin with at least a solid month of mileage. In effect, this becomes a 16-week cycle. Chapter 14 details the various training phases; Chapter 15 guides you in writing your own half-marathon program. Or use the samples in Figures 19.2–19.5 to blend the various phases and types of endurance and speed runs.

Mileage and Long Runs

If moving up from 10K to the half, you don't need to double train to race twice the distance. Increase mileage and long runs by about 10 to 25 percent to build enough endurance and strength to carry you through the last 10K of the race.

The sample schedules include a recommended base mileage to be held for at least a month prior to starting the program. It should be at least 50 to 75 percent of your peak mileage goal. Long runs during the base period should be at least one-third to one-half the longest runs for the program. Run long two to three times a month. Follow the flexible guidelines in Figure 19.1. Gradually increase weekly mileage and the length of long runs until you reach your goal range. Hold at that level for a few weeks, then taper the final two weeks or so for your key half-marathon. The last long run is two to three weeks prior to the race. First-timers build to long runs of at least two-thirds the race distance. The recommended long run minimum for experienced competitors is similar to that for the marathon—run for as many minutes in training as you will on race day. For half-marathoners, this is about 11 or 12 miles. Those glycogen-depleting runs of 20 miles and more aren't necessary for half-marathon training. But if they give you added strength and confidence, include some in your program.

FIGURE 19.1: MILEAGE AND LONG-RUN GUIDE FOR HALF-MARATHON TRAINING

Category	Weekly Mileage	Long Run Distance
Novice/Intermediate Competitor	20–30	8–13
Basic Competitor	25–35	11–15
Competitor/Advanced Competitor	30–50	12–20
Local Champion	50–70	13–20

Speed Training

Once you have the endurance to cover 15K to half-marathon in easy training runs, the best way to improve race performance at these distances is by boosting your LT. This is because 15K to 10-mile race pace roughly equals LT intensity, and half-marathon pace is about 2 to 3 percent slower than LT pace. Speed training for half-marathons is basically the same as for the 10K, except for an increased emphasis on LT training. The sample schedules include these threshold lifting workouts: 3- to 5-mile continuous tempo runs, tempo intervals, 4- to 6-mile runs at half-marathon goal pace, and 10K pace intervals. The schedules also include workouts at 5K pace and slightly faster to improve aerobic capacity and running economy. To race longer distances, speed-train longer distances. Emphasize intervals ranging from half-miles to 2 miles. See the speed training section of this book for specific guidelines for speed workouts, including how to choose the distance, quantity, intensity, and recovery. Feel free to replace our suggested workouts with others detailed in these chapters. Our sample schedules include only one of many possible combinations of speed workouts to improve your half-marathon race times.

In our schedules, speed sessions are included on Wednesdays—the middle of the week—to allow for adequate rest going into and coming off weekend races and long runs. Include them whatever day of the week works best for you. If you need more time to taper or recover for races and long runs, shift or minimize our suggested speed workouts. Experienced competitors may benefit from a second speed session on some weeks. For example, schedule a speed session on Tuesday and either Thursday or Friday, rather than our suggested Wednesday. If adding a speed workout to our suggested one, keep these taxing workouts at least 48 to 72 hours apart. Balance the two speed sessions within a week. Unless you are very fit and highly experienced, avoid doing two hard track workouts each week, or two hill sessions. The extra workouts should primarily be tempo runs, half-marathon-paced tempo, or fartlek, which help build endurance and are run at controlled speeds. One speed session a week may be best for many runners when running at increased mileage. Don't speed-train for at least a week after a half-marathon.

Build-up Races

The sample schedules include a variety of race distances to enhance motivation and provide a wide range of benefits. Modify them to meet your preferences and race availability. Some competitors race half-marathons monthly, building to their fastest performance. Others like to save their long race effort for one peak race. You may race slightly more often than these schedules, but don't overdo it. Overracing invites injury and interferes with quality training. You may compete slightly less often, but regular racing toughens you for competition. The races in the sample schedules are on Sunday—the most common race day. If your race is on another day, adjust your training accordingly using the basic principles of the sample schedules.

A 10-miler is slated early in the program to test endurance and enhance lactate threshold. A 5K boosts aerobic capacity and adds a dash of speed. A 10K race two to three weeks before your key half-marathon is great for final sharpening. An option is a half-marathon four to six weeks prior to your key half to familiarize you with the distance and effort required for a peak performance. You may be blessed with great weather, feel good, and run a great

The Sub-1:15 Half-Marathon (5:43 per mile)
Intervals: miles in 5:04–5:20, ¾ in 3:42–4:00, ½ in 2:24–2:28.
Races: 10K in 34:20, 10 miles in 56:50, marathon in 2:41.

The Sub-6-Minute-Pace Half-Marathon (sub-1:18:36)
Intervals: miles in 5:15–5:35, ¾ in 3:49–4:10, ½ in 2:29–2:34.
Races: 10K in 36:00, 10 miles in 59:30, marathon in 2:48:30.

The Sub-1:20 Half-Marathon (6:06 per mile)
Intervals: miles in 5:20–5:40, ¾ in 3:55–4:14, ½ in 2:32–2:37.
Races: 10K in 36:30, 10 miles in 1:00:15, marathon in 2:50.

The Sub-1:25 Half-Marathon (6:29 per mile)
Intervals: miles in 5:42–6:00, ¾ in 4:10–4:30, ½ in 2:42–2:46.
Races: 10K in 38:40, 10 miles in 1:04:00, marathon in 3:00.

The Sub-1:30 Half-Marathon (6:52 per mile)
Intervals: miles in 6:01–6:20, ¾ in 4:24–4:45, ½ in 2:51–2:56.
Races: 10K in 41:00, 10 miles in 1:08:00, marathon in 3:11.

The Sub-7½-Minute-Pace Half-Marathon (sub-1:38:15)
Intervals: miles in 6:35–6:55, ¾ in 4:48–5:11, ½ in 3:07–3:12.
Races: 10K in 44:45, 10 miles in 1:14:00, marathon in 3:30.

The Sub-1:45 Half-Marathon (8:00 per mile)
Intervals: miles in 7:03–7:25, ¾ in 5:09–5:34, ½ in 3:22–3:26.
Races: 10K in 47:50, 10 miles in 1:19:00, marathon in 3:43.

The Sub-1:50 Half-Marathon (8:23 per mile)
Intervals: miles in 7:22–7:45, ¾ in 5:23–5:49, ½ in 3:29–3:35.
Races: 10K in 50:00, 10 miles in 1:22:30, marathon in 3:52.

The Sub-2:00 Half-Marathon (9:09 per mile)
Intervals: miles in 8:05–8:30, ¾ in 5:54–6:23, ½ in 3:50–3:56.
Races: 10K in 55:00, 10 miles in 1:31:00, marathon in 4:15.

The Sub-9½-Minute-Pace Half-Marathon (sub-2:04:27)
Intervals: miles in 8:24–8:50, ¾ in 6:08–6:38, ½ in 3:59–4:08.
Races: 10K in 56:45, 10 miles in 1:34:00, marathon in 4:25.

The Sub-10-Minute-Pace Half-Marathon (sub-2:11)
Intervals: miles in 8:47–9:15, ¾ in 6:25–6:56, ½ in 2:01–2:05.
Races: 10K in 59:50, 10 miles in 1:39:00, marathon in 4:39.

The Sub-2:15 Half-Marathon (10:18 per mile)
Intervals: miles in 9:02–9:30, ¾ in 6:36–7:08, ½ in 4:17–4:45.
Races: 10K in 1:01:30, 10 miles in 1:41:30, marathon in 4:47.

race prior to your scheduled peak. Getting more than one chance at the half-marathon while you're in good shape improves the odds that you'll reach your goals.

You may choose to taper more or less than the sample schedules for races, and run more or less mileage as you recover from races. I don't recommend racing any distance for at least two weeks after a half-marathon, nor another half-marathon or a marathon for at least three to four weeks.

SAMPLE 12-WEEK HALF-MARATHON TRAINING PROGRAM

Don't follow the training schedules in Figures 19.2–19.5 blindly. Understand the concepts behind them. Modify the training programs by varying the daily and weekly mileage, the exact day and type of speed workouts, and the timing and distance of races to suit your needs. Be prepared to adjust for progress, fatigue, health, or injury. For speed training and race days, the mileage figure includes warm-up and cool-down running, as well as interval recovery runs. A sample rebuilding phase isn't included. That doesn't mean it isn't important. See Chapter 14 for guidelines.

BREAKING BARRIERS

Breaking barriers can be very rewarding, whether it's the one-hour or the two-hour mark. In the chart on page 201 are some time goals to motivate you. Running the *approximate times* listed for intervals and race distances predicts your ability to break the corresponding half-marathon time barrier.

HALF-MARATHON LOGISTICS

Review the general prerace logistics guidelines in Chapter 28. Since a quick start isn't needed and the length of the race is quite long, minimize your warm-up run. Running a few miles before the race hastens glycogen depletion. Jog a half-mile to a mile to loosen up. Include a few easy strides if starting faster than training pace. Racing shoes may be okay for those racing at faster than 7-minute miles. Lightweight trainers offer more cushioning for runners pounding the pavement for one and a half hours and longer. If you'll be out there over two hours, consider wearing regular training shoes. Hydrating during the race is essential, especially in warm weather. Follow guidelines in Chapter 34. Glycogen depletion becomes a factor in races over an hour. Carbo-load going into the race and fuel up during it following guidelines in Chapter 33.

FIGURE 19.2: SAMPLE NOVICE AND INTERMEDIATE COMPETITOR'S 12-WEEK HALF-MARATHON TRAINING SCHEDULE

Weeks to Go	Monday	Tuesday	Wednesday	Thursday	Friday	Saturday	Sunday	Total Mileage
Base	Off	3	3 (modified fartlek)	2	Off	6	2	16
12	Off	2	4 (2-mile tempo run)	2	Off	8	2	18
11	Off	2	4 (3–4 x long-hill repeats)	2	Off	10	2	20
10	Off	2	5 (tempo intervals, 2 x 1½ miles)	2	Off	12	3	24
9	Off	4	5 (2–4 x mile, 5K–10K pace)	4	4	Off	10 (race 10K)	27
8	Off	5	5 (3-mile tempo run)	5	Off	13	2	30
7	Off	5	5 (4–6 x half-mile, 5K–10K pace)	5	Off	13	2	30
6	Off	5	5 (1–2 x 1½-miles, 5K–10K pace)	4	4	2	6 (race 5K)	26
5	Off	5	5 (2–3 x mile, 5K–fast pace)	5	Off	13	2	30
4	Off	5	5 (tempo run, 4 miles, half-marathon pace)	4	4	Off	8 (race 10K)	26
3	Off	4	5 (3–4 x half-mile, fast pace)	4	Off	10	2	25
2	Off	4	5 (2–3 x mile, 5K to fast pace)	4	Off	8	2	23
1	Off	3	4 (tempo intervals, 6 x ½ mile)	2	2	Off	13 (race half-marathon)	11 + race

FIGURE 19.3: SAMPLE BASIC COMPETITOR'S 12-WEEK HALF-MARATHON TRAINING SCHEDULE

Weeks to Go	Monday	Tuesday	Wednesday	Thursday	Friday	Saturday	Sunday	Total Mileage
Base	Off	4	4 (fartlek)	3	Off	6	3	20
12	Off	3	5 (3-mile tempo run)	3	Off	8	3	22
11	Off	4	5 (4–5 x long-hill repeats)	3	Off	10	3	25
10	Off	4	5 (tempo intervals, 2 x 1½ miles)	4	Off	12	3	28
9	Off	5	5 (3–4 x mile, 5K–10K pace)	5	5	Off	10 (race 10K)	30
8	Off	6	5 (3-mile tempo run)	5	Off	13	4	33
7	Off	5	5 (4–6 x half mile, 5K–fast pace)	5	Off	15	3	33
6	Off	6	6 (2–3 x 1½ miles, 5K–10K pace)	6	6	Off	6 (race 10K)	30
5	Off	6	6 (2–3 x mile, 5K–hard pace)	6	Off	13	4	35
4	Off	6	5 (tempo run, 4 miles, half-marathon pace)	6	5	Off	8 (race 10K)	30
3	Off	6	6 (4–6 x ½ mile, fast–hard pace)	5	Off	13	3	33
2	Off	5	6 (2–3 x mile, 5K–fast pace)	4	Off	10	3	28
1	Off	3	4 (tempo intervals, 6 x ½ mile)	3	2	Off	13 (race half-marathon)	12 + race

FIGURE 19.4: SAMPLE COMPETITOR'S AND ADVANCED COMPETITOR'S 12-WEEK HALF-MARATHON TRAINING SCHEDULE

Weeks to Go	Monday	Tuesday	Wednesday	Thursday	Friday	Saturday	Sunday	Total Mileage
Base	Off	6	6 (fartlek)	6	Off	8	6	32
12	Off	6	6 (3-mile tempo run)	6	Off	10	5	33
11	Off	6	6 (5–8 x long-hill repeats)	6	Off	12	5	35
10	Off	6	7 (tempo intervals, 2 x 2 miles)	5	Off	15	5	38
9	6	7	6 (3–5 x mile, 5K–10K pace)	5	4	Off	12 (race 10K)	40
8	Off	6	6 (4-mile tempo run)	6	5	15	4	42
7	Off	6	6 (4–8 x half mile, fast–hard pace)	5	5	18	5	45
6	6	7	8 (2–4 x 1½ miles, 5K–10K pace)	8	8	Off	8 (race 5K)	45
5	Off	6	6 (3–4 x mile, 5K–hard pace)	5	5	18	5	45
4	6	7	6 (tempo run, 5 miles, half-marathon pace)	6	5	Off	10 (race 5K)	40
3	Off	7	6 (4–8 x half-mile, fast–hard pace)	6	6	15	5	45
2	Off	6	6 (3–4 x mile, 5K–hard pace)	6	6	10	6	40
1	Off	3	4 (tempo intervals, 6 x ½ mile	3	2	Off	15 (race half-marathon)	12 + race

FIGURE 19.5: SAMPLE LOCAL CHAMPION'S 12-WEEK HALF-MARATHON TRAINING SCHEDULE

Weeks to Go	Monday	Tuesday	Wednesday	Thursday	Friday	Saturday	Sunday	Total Mileage
Base	Off	7	7 (fartlek)	8	5	10	6	43
12	Off	7	7 (4-mile tempo run)	7	6	12	6	45
11	Off	7	7 (8–10 x long-hill repeats)	7	6	15	6	48
10	Off	8	8 (tempo intervals, 3 x 2 miles)	8	6	15	5	50
9	8	8	8 (4–6 x mile, 5K–10K pace)	8	3	3	12 (race 10K)	50
8	Off	8	7 (4-mile tempo run)	7	8	18	5	53
7	6	7	7 (6–10 x half-mile, fast–hard pace)	6	6	18	5	55
6	8	8	8 (3–4 x 1½ miles, 5K–10K pace)	8	8	5	10 (race 5K)	55
5	5	7	7 (4–5 x mile, 5K to hard pace)	6	7	18	5	55
4	8	8	8 (6-mile tempo run, half-marathon pace)	6	5	Off	10 (race 10K)	45
3	Off	8	8 (6–10 x half-mile, fast–hard pace)	8	6	12	8	50
2	Off	8	8 (4–5 x mile, 5K to hard pace)	8	5	10	6	45
1	Off	3	4 (tempo intervals, 6 x ½ mile	3	3	Off	15 (race half-marathon)	13 + race

HALF-MARATHON RACE STRATEGY

Racing half-marathons involves a compromise strategy between that of the 10K and the marathon. Like the marathon, it is important to be patient in the early miles. The pace may seem too easy after racing 10Ks and zipping through speed workouts at 5K pace and faster. But if you start too fast, you'll use up extra fuel. The last few miles can really drag out if your glycogen tank is on empty. Sure, you won't struggle for as long or as painfully as in the marathon, but a too-fast start will still bring enough agony.

You'll race at about 85 to 90 percent of aerobic capacity. The key is to run slightly below your LT so you don't fatigue an hour or so into the race due to lactic acid accumulation. Push the pace above your LT at the start or along the way and you'll regret it. The higher your LT, the faster you can run at half-marathon pace.

The first mile or two sets the tone for your effort. Going out too fast sets you up for failure. If you go out a bit too slow, you have adequate time to make up for it. So it's better to err on the side of caution. But don't line up too far back in the pack. You'll lose time getting to the starting line and weaving through slower runners. Look at the first mile as a warm-up. Run it at goal pace or slightly slower. This settles you safely under LT pace. By the second mile, start looking for your competitors. Try to flow along with a pack of runners if they're running a pace that's good for you. Draft off other runners, saving energy. Resist the urge to race too early. Don't be lured into chasing competitors if they're going too fast. Let them go. Most likely you'll catch them later—at your pace. Holding pace with reasonable effort shouldn't be a problem for the first half if you're properly trained, unless you tense up due to panic. But can you hold back the pace to reserve energy for the second half? Concentrate on staying relaxed. You have some room to let your mind wander, but don't let your pace slip.

If your goal pace is tough during the first few miles, you're in trouble. Either your goals were way higher than your fitness, the course or weather are too difficult, or you're just having a bad day. Try slowing the pace slightly. Perhaps you'll feel better later in sufficient time to get back on pace. If not, adjust your pace and time goal. Stubbornly pushing ahead during the first half will lead to an even slower, more miserable second half. Look around you.

You may be still doing well compared to your peers even if you're not able to hold your desired pace.

To achieve your goal time you need to push the effort over the second half like you do in the middle miles in the 10K. This requires mental toughness since by halfway through the race you're in unfamiliar territory with holding a pace at or near LT. You're well beyond your 20- to 30-minute tempo runs. Move from runner to runner to help maintain a good pace, or "hitch a ride" when a competitor goes by you. Don't be satisfied with just holding your place. Most likely many of the runners around you are slowing down. This presents a mirage. You think you're on pace but you may not be if you're slowing with them.

The first 10 miles are for pacing, the final 5K for racing. Use the 10-mile mark as a motivational landmark: It's now only a 5K race. Reel in runners. Use runners up ahead as targets. Increase the effort slightly to gain ground on them and to keep from slowing from your goal pace. But don't surge too much. That could push you over the threshold. The goal here is a steady push at your limit.

Gather your physical and mental resources for the final mile. You won't be able to push it in as fast as in shorter races, but still you can gain ground on your competition and slice seconds off your finishing time with a strong final mile. Reflect on how hard the last few reps were in your mile intervals and the last mile in your long runs. You made it through the discomfort then and you will make it to the finish line of the half-marathon with mental toughness. Fight off fatigue by relaxing and focusing on good running form and controlled breathing.

Position yourself to change into your final gear over the last quarter-mile. That's just a lap of the track. Even though you've been running for well over an hour, you can muster the energy to push for another 2 minutes or so. Remember this as you're getting close to the finish line: In long races seconds don't count as much as minutes, but a second or two can make the difference in being, for example, a 1:30 half-marathoner or a 1:29 half-marathoner. That is, run 1:29:59 and you can say you're a "1:29 half-marathoner." At 1:30:01 you're just a "1:30 half-marathoner."

Review the general tips for racing strategy and tactics in Chapters 29 and 30.

PART V

MARATHON TRAINING AND RACING

CHAPTER 20

The First-Time Marathoner

Becoming a marathoner isn't easy, but anyone can be one no matter who you are, how much you've run, or how slow afoot you are. A marathon, says the dictionary, is any test of endurance. Runners know it as a 26.2 mile (42.195 kilometer) test of physical and mental toughness.

Marathoners consist of three basic types. **Marathon participants** may walk all or part of the way. They enjoy the event—and finish—any way they can. **Marathon runners** train to run all or most of the way at whatever pace will get them to the finish line, earning full conquering-hero status. **Marathon racers** train to cover the distance as fast as they can. Most first-timers are participants or runners.

THE ADVANCED FIRST-TIMER

If you have some speed training and racing experience, you may choose to use the schedule for Novice and Intermediate Competitors in the next chapter. It is similar to the mileage program here, but adds suggested speed workouts. Be careful, however; you can finish the marathon by sticking to my suggested first-timer's program. Too much mileage and fast training can lead to failure. It may be wise to save more advanced training for your next marathon.

If you've run several races and have accumulated plenty of mileage over the years, your first marathon won't be the same as for most runners. You may even choose to set a time goal based on results from races in the 10K to half-marathon range. Find the category that best describes your achievements—Basic Competitor, Competitor, Advanced Competitor, or Local Champion—and follow the training guidelines for them in Chapter 21. But be conservative. It may be best to train a little less than those recommendations since it's your first marathon. Some runners have popped exceptional times in their first attempt. But they trained properly, raced wisely, made friends with Lady Luck, and are blessed with natural talent.

Read on, advanced first-timers; much of the advice in this chapter still pertains to you. After all, you are prone to typical rookie mistakes.

WHY?

Why would anyone in their right mind want to run a marathon? The training involves a lot of time and effort, and increased risk of injury. The race itself is grueling and unpredictable. It's long enough to fully tax your body, mind, and soul. Your energy supplies, muscular endurance, emotions, and psychological strengths are fully tested. Therein lies its appeal to participants and spectators alike: It isn't easy. The marathon is an epic struggle.

Marathon training tones the body and, by greatly increasing calorie-burning, helps you lose weight. This, more than competitive reasons, is why many runners are attracted to not only their first marathon, but to running one or more each year. It works. For others, it's the challenge. The glamour and tradition of "the classic distance" captures the imagination. It's "there," like the highest mountain to climb. As the longest of mainstream running events, it's the ultimate test of fitness and courage. The marathon is larger than life, having a profound impact on all those who successfully meet its rigorous training and racing demands. Finishing a marathon proves you can set a lofty goal and achieve it. It gives you the confidence to take risks and make important changes in other aspects of your life.

Being a marathoner makes you feel important—to others, but mostly to yourself. Most of all, finishing a marathon makes you a hero! I challenge first-timers: "Once you've crossed the finish line of the marathon, there isn't anything you can't do."

YOU CAN DO IT

"If you want to run, run a mile," said Emil Zatopek, the Czech 1952 Olympic champ at 5K, 10K, and the marathon. "If you want to experience another life, run a marathon." Still want to run a marathon? You won't be alone. Thousands of first-timers take up the challenge each year. For over twenty-five years, I have been the speaker for a series of clinics for the New York City Marathon. We always have a standing-room-only crowd of over 500 people. At the start of each lecture I ask the same question: "How many of you are thinking about running your first marathon?" I'm amazed every year when I ask them to stand, because over 90 percent of the audience consists of first-timers. It's fun to watch their confidence rise as they look around and see the hundreds of others about to take on the same daunting task. So if you are thinking of running your first marathon, be assured that you have a lot of company. Also, take heart in the fact that my Official New York City Marathon Training Program, which is included in this chapter, is sent to every marathon entrant, and we have a better than 95 percent finishing rate for that event each year.

The marathon is the longest and most difficult challenge most runners ever experience. To complete it, you don't need to be a superior athlete. You don't even need to be very athletic. But you do need to train properly, pace yourself wisely, and have the will to endure discomfort on race day. Dick Traum has completed a dozen marathons with an artificial leg and each year enters over 100 physically challenged runners in the New York City Marathon from his Achilles Track Club. Some of them "run" by propelling themselves with canes and crutches. One, who can't walk and has no use of his hands, kicks with his feet to propel his wheelchair backwards toward the finish line. These athletes run this way for hours on end. If they can finish, what's your excuse? According to Traum, who started running in my beginner's class and caught the marathon bug from me, "Anyone who honestly takes the time to train can finish a marathon. You just have to be patient and disciplined. You have to put in the time." And you're never too old to run a marathon—more than half of the runners each year in the New York City Marathon are over the age of forty, and some are twice that age.

SELECTING YOUR FIRST MARATHON

Don't pick a hot or hilly one; nor a race that won't include a large crowd to cheer you on, plenty of novices at your pace to keep you going, and lots of volunteers to provide support. That usually means a highly promoted big-city event which offers exciting perks—music, banners, a pasta party, postrace celebration. It's hard not to finish one of these big events. The spectators and officials along the way almost demand that you keep going. They plead: "Don't stop now, you can do it!" You're running it for them, too. But they would rather let you do the suffering.

If possible, choose a marathon near your home to avoid the excitement of both travel and an unfamiliar environment. Another key factor: If you run near home, you'll have that many more friends and family available to support you during the race and congratulate you after the finish! Some runners prefer traveling to their first marathon. They look at it as an exciting treat after all the hard work. The marathon is a popular challenge. It is run through almost every major city in the United States and the world. Hundreds of marathons are held each year, involving thousands of runners. It has become a vacation attraction offered by travel agents in such exciting spots as San Francisco, Honolulu, New York, London, Rome, and Paris. What a way to see a city! Wherever you decide to run, pick a marathon far enough into the future to allow proper training.

BASIC REQUIREMENTS BEFORE STARTING MARATHON TRAINING

I know many people who started running because they wanted to run a marathon. Some had athletic backgrounds, but many were "couch potatoes." Entering a marathon may be a great motivator for improving fitness, but don't rush into it. I suggest that first-timers meet these basic requirements prior to starting training:

1. Be in reasonably good health. Have a thorough medical exam before greatly increasing your physical activity. Don't start marathon training if you're injured or ill. Get healthy first. If you're carrying extra weight, lower it to minimize the stress on your body.

2. Establish a solid fitness base. Run three times a week or more for at least six to twelve months to allow your body time to adjust to running before increasing the work to marathon proportions. Build to at least 15 to 20 miles a week for a month or two prior to starting a marathon build-up program. That's about halfway to my recommended peak level. If you don't start here, it'll be a strain to reach your mileage goal.
3. Establish a long-run base of at least one-third your peak goal of 18 to 20 miles. Believe it or not, if you can run 10K (6.2 miles), you can add 20 miles to that distance by marathon day if you train properly.
4. Ideally, run at least a 10K race before commiting to marathon training. Complete at least one race of 10 miles to half-marathon somewhere between the start of your buildup and three weeks before the marathon. This longer race provides a good feel for the required marathon effort.
5. Marathoning is a sport for the fully mature. You should be at least sixteen years old, preferably eighteen to twenty-one, before attempting a marathon. Regardless of whether marathoning presents a risk to a youth's growing bones, it certainly involves an emotional struggle that is better reserved for adults. On the other hand, I have coached runners in our classes in their sixties, seventies, and even eighties, who have enjoyed their first marathon. These folks certainly should check first with their doctor and may be wise to train and race with a run-walk participatory theme.
6. Do you have the necessary time and energy to invest in marathon training? Marathon training requires sacrifices. If you're already overburdened with stress at home or at the office, or if you're about to make a major change in your life—such as moving—hold off on adding the energy-sapping physical and mental stress of marathon training until your life is better balanced.

What if you don't meet all or most of these requirements? Take your time. Gradually build up your mileage and racing distances. Enjoy conquering the 10K and then the half-marathon. These challenges may be enough to satisfy you. Or, they may be a beneficial stepping-stone to a marathon in the future.

TRAINING FOR YOUR FIRST MARATHON

If you don't sabotage yourself by trying to do too much too soon, or by not starting your training well in advance, completing a marathon is within reach of any healthy man or woman. Don't wait until it's too late. Give yourself plenty of time to build mileage and long runs. Ideally, put in two months of base training and four months of specific marathon training. Becoming a marathoner isn't easy, and it's time-consuming. Many runners comment that it's like having a part-time job.

Some runners do more training than I suggest, some less. Don't undertrain, but don't do too much, either. The trick is to avoid the obstacles of overtraining, injury, and discouragement. The percentage of first-time marathon starters who cross the finish line is much higher than the percentage of runners who start marathon training and make it to the starting line. My minimum and maximum training guidelines will help you survive both marathon training and your first marathon.

Here are the key components to your marathon training program: weekly mileage, cross-training, rest days, long runs, speed training, practice races.

Mileage. From my recommended fitness base of 15 to 20 miles a week, gradually build to a peak mileage range of 30 to 40 miles. Use my sample 16-week build-up programs outlined in Figures 20.1 and 20.2 as a guide. Hold at your peak mileage range for at least six to eight weeks prior to tapering over the final two to three weeks. The sample schedules include a suggested taper. Review guidelines for increasing and maintaining mileage in Chapter 6, marathon mileage in Chapter 21, the taper in Chapter 22, and motivational tips on how to stay on schedule in Chapter 26.

Cross-training. Minimize the wear and tear on your body by replacing up to 20 percent or so of mileage with nonimpact aerobic exercise following guidelines in Chapter 45. For example, replace a 3-mile run that would take 30 minutes with biking or swimming for that time period. Or, to increase your overall aerobic training, add a 30-minute cross-training workout on a scheduled off day.

Rest days. Take days off to recover and adapt to training. This is especially important for beginner marathoners who are running more mileage and longer distances than ever before. On off days, either don't exercise at all, do a light cross-training workout, or go for a walk. The sample schedules include off days on Mondays and Fridays, bracketing the weekend which normally includes long runs or races. If you can reach your mileage goals with three off days per week at any point, or throughout your schedule, go right ahead if that's what works best for your body and time schedule. Take rest days any day you choose, but I prefer off days during the work week when time is short and stress is high.

Long runs. Here's the key to finishing. But how far and how often do you need to run long? Beginner marathoners gradually build up the distance from a base of at least 6 miles. Complete at least three runs, preferably four or five, of 18 to 20 miles (my minimum range to be considered a long run) prior to the marathon. That's about two-thirds to three-fourths the marathon distance.

My recommended long-run limit for first-time marathoners is 20 miles. The potential gain beyond three and a half to four hours (my recommended time limit) isn't worth the risk. Past this distance, fatigue accumulates more rapidly, and running form deteriorates. Additional pounding greatly increases chance of injury as each stride pounds the pavement with three times the force of your body weight. Runs beyond 20 miles seriously deplete energy reserves, leaving marathon hopefuls not only very tired but susceptible to illness.

Why not go 26 miles to make sure you can do it? A few trainers suggest that even first-timers should do this so you know what it's like to run this far, making it easier on race day. I strongly disagree. Why not save the mystery and excitement of finding out if you can really run the marathon distance when you've got lots of other people to share it with? Complete your first marathon with all the fanfare and with witnesses to your glorious feat, not in practice. Training runs this long would put you on your feet—often alone and in the heat—for four to six hours. This leaves you more vulnerable to injury and to failing to finish, or finishing exhausted, leaving you wiped out for days. This would be a severe confidence-crusher. Save the excitement of those last few miles for when you have plenty of support. Don't worry; on race day your mileage base and the enthusiasm of the crowd will carry you over the last 6.2 miles.

If you increase the distance too soon or run long too often, you'll likely get discouraged or injured. That's why it's best to increase the distance of these runs by no more than 2 or 3 miles at a time. Transition runs of 8, 10, 13, and 15 miles or so should be incorporated along the way prior to the long runs of 18 to 20 miles. As you get up to runs of the half-marathon distance and more, run long every other weekend to minimize buildup of physical and mental fatigue. Schedule long runs well in advance so you can plan the rest of your training, and your life, around them. It can be intimidating for beginners to even think of running these distances, so make sure you clear the calendar ahead of time so there aren't any excuses for getting out the door.

All long runs should be at an easy, conversational pace. Concern yourself with getting in the distance, not with breaking your training course records. After all, you're training for surviving, not racing your first marathon. Think of it this way: "If you can chatter, exact pace doesn't matter." Take a few walk breaks if necessary, especially on hills and in hot weather. I don't agree with the strategy promoted by a few trainers of taking planned walk breaks every mile or so during long runs. Sure, it may make it easier, but it'll also keep you out there longer. This system is okay if you'll be satisfied with frequent walk breaks for your marathon, but why not train to run all the way?

Taper long runs as you taper weekly mileage. The last long run should be two, preferably three weeks prior to marathon day to minimize the risk of injury and maximize recovery time. The weekend before the marathon, run no farther than 6 to 8 miles. See the following chapter for detailed information on benefits and training guidelines for long runs. Most of these tips apply to all levels of runners.

Speed training. Speedwork isn't essential for first-time marathoners since their goal isn't to speed, but to endure. But properly run, speed training offers benefits. First-timers will most likely run the marathon distance at a pace slower than their daily runs, so they don't need to push hard in speed training. Short, intense workouts aren't necessary. Emphasize longer speed workouts such as half-mile and mile intervals. Controlled running at 5K, 10K, and tempo pace improve aerobic capacity, running economy, lactate threshold, sense of pacing, and confidence. Hill training strengthens the mind and body for marathon hills. Include some marathon pace training to get used to that speed. More than 500 first-time marathoners take our New York Road Runners Club speed classes in preparation for the New York City Marathon each year for these reasons.

Don't attempt fast running if you haven't fully recovered from long runs or if feeling tired from high mileage. See the speed training section for specific guidelines.

Practice races. Many first-timers do not race at all in preparation for their marathon. A few races are recommended as dress rehearsals to practice pacing, drinking and fueling on the run, to test shoes and clothing, and so on. They break up the monotony of training by giving you intermediate goals and rewards. Races are also a great place to meet other marathoners and share experiences—even add a training partner. They can be used as part of long runs, to practice marathon pacing, and to measure fitness and better select your marathon starting pace. Long races are a proving ground. Complete a half-marathon before taking on a full marathon. The experience will give you a good idea if you're ready for marathon training. Don't run these long races all-out. Use them to build you up, not tear you down.

THE FIRST-TIME MARATHONER 16-WEEK TRAINING PROGRAM

Thousands of first-time marathoners have successfully reached the finish line by following my program, which is not only printed in this book but is also available in brochure form as the "Official New York City Marathon Training Program." That schedule is slightly different from the one here because it is adjusted to fit in New York Road Runners Club races and long training runs.

Please note that these are *sample* schedules. Follow them exactly, as many runners around the world do, or adapt them to fit your needs. Be dedicated about it, but flexible. Follow the theme of the schedules if you make up your own program: progressive increases in weekly mileage with a few plateaus and cutbacks, gradual increases in well-spaced long runs, off days and short runs for recovery to balance long runs and medium runs, a gradual tapering of mileage and long runs over the final two or three weeks. Long runs are scheduled on Saturdays to allow for more recovery time before going to back to your job on Monday, but you may wish to change them to Sundays or other days. Carefully adjust your program to fit in a few races—this may mean switching around long runs and making sure to run easy the day before and after races. Half-marathons are especially valuable.

Two sample schedules are included: The bare minimum schedule in Figure 20.1 building from a 15-mile-a-week base for at least a month to 35 miles at the peak; and Figure 20.2 starting at a 20-mile-a-week base building to 40 miles a week. The second schedule is my preferred program. If you are not yet at 15 miles per week, you are not ready to build up for a marathon. If you are at more than 20 miles a week when starting the schedule, you may choose to stay at your present level until you are on schedule. Runners who choose to run more than 40 miles a week can just add a few miles to each week on the program.

A sample rebuilding program isn't included. See Chapter 24 for "aftermarathon" guidelines.

TIPS FOR FIRST-TIME MARATHONERS

In many ways running your first marathon is like running your first race all over again. Review the tips for beginner racers in Chapter 16. Guidelines for the marathon countdown, including the physical and mental preparations over the last few weeks, days, and hours, are detailed in Chapter 22.

STRATEGY FOR FINISHING YOUR FIRST MARATHON

Review the general tips for racing strategy in Chapter 29 and the marathon-specific strategy guidelines in Chapter 23. Here are a few key strategic tips for rookies:

Establish your goal: to finish in reasonable comfort. This dictates your training and racing plans. It makes no sense to set a time goal; you are entering the land of the unknown. Take the pressure off and train to finish with a smile. Your friends will be impressed enough that you made it all the way, and nonrunners won't know the difference between a three-hour and a five-hour marathon anyway.

FIGURE 20.1: SAMPLE 16-WEEK FIRST-TIME MARATHONER TRAINING SCHEDULE: BUILDING FROM A 15-MILE-A-WEEK BASE FOR AT LEAST ONE MONTH

Weeks to Go	Mon.	Tues.	Wed.	Thurs.	Fri.	Sat.	Sun.	Total
Base	Off	3	Off	3	Off	6	3	15
16	Off	3	Off	3	Off	8	3	17
15	Off	3	Off	4	Off	10	3	20
14	Off	3	Off	3	Off	13	3	22
13	Off	4	Off	4	Off	8	4	20
12	Off	3	Off	3	Off	15	3	24
11	Off	4	6	4	Off	10	3	27
10	Off	4	4	3	Off	16	3	30
9	Off	4	4	6	Off	12	4	30
8	Off	4	3	4	Off	18	3	32
7	Off	6	6	6	Off	12	5	35
6	Off	4	4	4	Off	20	3	35
5	Off	5	4	5	Off	12	4	30
4	Off	4	4	4	Off	20	3	35
3	Off	5	5	5	Off	15	3	33
2	Off	4	6	4	Off	6	5	25
1	Off	4	4	4	Off	2	26.2 marathon	14 + race

FIGURE 20.2: SAMPLE 16-WEEK FIRST-TIME MARATHONER TRAINING SCHEDULE: BUILDING FROM A 20-MILE-A-WEEK BASE FOR AT LEAST ONE MONTH

Weeks to Go	Mon.	Tues.	Wed.	Thurs.	Fri.	Sat.	Sun.	Total
Base	Off	3	4	4	Off	6	3	20
16	Off	3	4	4	Off	8	3	22
15	Off	4	4	4	Off	10	3	25
14	Off	4	4	3	Off	13	3	27
13	Off	5	4	5	Off	13	3	30
12	Off	4	5	5	Off	15	3	32
11	Off	6	6	6	Off	12	5	35
10	Off	6	4	4	Off	18	3	35
9	Off	6	6	6	Off	12	5	35
8	Off	5	6	6	Off	20	3	40
7	Off	5	4	5	Off	13	3	30
6	Off	5	6	6	Off	20	3	40
5	Off	6	6	6	Off	13	4	35
4	Off	5	6	6	Off	20	3	40
3	Off	6	6	5	Off	15	3	35
2	Off	5	6	5	Off	5	5	26
1	Off	4	4	4	Off	2	26.2 marathon	14 + race

Surviving to the end will give you plenty to brag about. Enjoy the experience.

Scared? If you have the guts to do the training, you have the guts to finish the race. Fear not. You won't finish last, and someone will still be at the finish when you get there. Most reasonably fit people can walk a marathon at 20-minutes-per-mile pace, taking just under nine hours. A combination of fast walking and slow running should get you to about a 15-minute-per-mile pace, which would bring you to the finish in just under seven hours. By running all, or most of the way, most reasonably trained runners can average a 12-minute-per-mile pace, putting them just over five hours. Most first-timers run between four (about 9-minute-per-mile pace) and five hours; many finish more slowly than that. Here's a good goal to keep in mind: Run your first marathon as slowly as possible. That way it'll be easier to impress your friends with how much you improve that time for your next marathon!

Lining up and starting out. Line up at or near the back of the pack. Purposely let most of the runners start ahead of you. This way you prevent yourself from starting too fast, and you'll spend most of the race passing people, which will lift your spirits. If, on the other hand, you line up too far up front, hundreds of runners may pass you, especially at the end when you are physically and mentally fatigued. That is depressing.

In crowded marathons it may take several minutes just to reach the starting line and a few miles to settle into your pace. One way to compensate is to deduct, for your personal records, the time it took you to get to the starting line from your finish time. Don't weave in and out of people in an effort to move up: You'll waste energy and risk injury. If you find yourself stuck with the masses, relax and enjoy yourself. After all, it's your first marathon and without all those other runners surrounding you the 26.2 mile run would be much tougher. I assure you, over the last few miles you will be happy to have a lot of company in your struggle.

Pacing. Start at the same trusty pace you averaged for your last long training run and hold that evenly to 20 miles. Think of the marathon as an extension of your long run. If you can pick it up a bit from there, go ahead. If you start faster than this because of the excitement, or because you set a faster time goal, you may run out of steam over the last miles. If starting with a friend, promise each other to keep the starting pace reasonable. The best bet is to get stuck in the crowd so you have to start with a slow walk progressing to a brisk walk, slow jog, and finally your training pace. I repeat. Beware of starting too fast. This is the most common error for marathoners. If it's hot or if you face a headwind, slow your starting pace by as much as a minute per mile.

Walk if you have to. Nowhere on the application form does it say you must run every step. Even if you've trained adequately, be prepared to take brief walk breaks if you start to feel too hot or tired. Good times to take walk breaks: (1) going up hills; (2) after getting water. Carry the cup with you and take your time sipping. It makes walking seem more necessary. If you're really struggling on hills, break it up with walking. Most likely you won't be alone. If necessary over the last few miles, alternate running and walking the rest of the way. This just might get you in faster than the survival shuffle some call running. Keep moving. Don't sit down no matter how strong the urge. It'll be too tough to get going again.

A few trainers preach the value of planned walk breaks during marathons. A typical schedule calls for one minute walk breaks at each mile mark. They say it's a kinder, gentler form of marathoning. I say phooey. If your goal is to participate in a marathon then fine, take pleasure in your run-walk experience. This is a sensible approach if you're undertrained or you just want to experience the excitement of the marathon event. But if you want to be a marathon runner, a conquering hero, train to run all the way. Besides, many runners who've tried this find it's hard to regain momentum when they resume running. Hey, it's your choice.

Keep fueling and hydrating. First-timers are out there a long time. That means you'll require even more fuel and fluids than the average runner.

Quitting. If you are badly favoring an injury, feeling weak and dizzy because of the heat or illness, or are extremely fatigued—use common sense. Bail out and look for medical help. Don't feel like a failure if you drop out for reasons of personal safety. There are plenty more chances down the road to become a marathon hero. You won't be the first, or last, to drop out in your first marathon attempt. Even Bill Rodgers, four-time winner of both New York and Boston, dropped out in his first marathon.

But if you trained properly and aren't ill or hampered by injury, then you should finish as long as you can handle it mentally. Dig down deep for extra strength and keep going. Everyone feels like quitting many times and everyone has aches and pains and stiffness along the way. You might even need to limp it in. You're not alone. But don't give up unless you need to stop for significant health reasons.

Mental toughness. To finish, call on your fortitude. The marathon is popular because it's challenging. If it was easy, anyone could do it. That's why you're different—you can do it. When periods of physical and mental weakness hit you, and I assure you they will, remember all the training you did for this race (especially those tough long runs) and all the people who supported you and are cheering for you now. Draw from the support of all the runners around you (many of them first-timers, too), the spectators along the course, and your personal commitment to finish.

Think about your friends and family waiting for you at the finish line—preparing for a hero's welcoming. Relax, and believe in yourself. Have faith in your training program. Talk tough to yourself: "Come on, let's get going!" Push through periods of self-doubt by internalizing the cheers from the crowd to pull you along. Most likely, if you keep moving you will feel better again. Accept discomfort. It's real. But use all of your mental resources and your background of solid training to keep it from slowing you down. If you followed my program from this book, don't let me down! Visualize Coach Glover exhorting you toward glory. Review the mental techniques for outrunning fatigue and discomfort in Chapter 27.

"The Wall." Here comes the real test. Most likely you will experience a taste of "the Wall" (See Chapter 21) somewhere around 20 miles. But if you trained well, tapered, carbo-loaded, and took in sports drinks and gels since just before the start, you will pass through the Wall in reasonably good shape.

10K to go. The 20-mile barrier represents the start of a new race. For most beginner marathoners this is the farthest you have ever run. You are entering new and untested territory. From here to the finish do what you have to do to finish. That may include walking;

it definitely will include plenty of soul-searching. Chapter 23 gives tips for how to conquer this final distance.

The finish. As you near the finish line, the spectators will be cheering wildly for you. They recognize your incredible feat. Here you come—head up, legs tired but still churning, arms pumping. After finishing, you hug the runner in front of and behind you. You congratulate each other. You smile, you laugh, you cry. Rejoice; you've conquered! Congratulations, marathon hero.

But you haven't finished yet. You have to stay in line (don't sit down or you might not get back up!) and pass through the chutes in order of finish or you may not get proper credit for your victory. Don't forget to eat and drink right away. See the guidelines for "the aftermarathon" in Chapter 24. Finally, and most important, enjoy your first marathon. It's one of those first experiences you'll never forget.

THE UNDERTRAINED MARATHONER

No matter what I say, some of you are still going to start your first marathon unprepared. I did it myself, so I can't be too harsh. I suggest that if you insist on doing it anyway—whether undertrained due to injury, inadequate planning, or lack of desire to train more—that you review the following guidelines. The whole premise is that you must promise to "participate" in the marathon rather than race it.

- If you can't run more than 5 miles at a time, then alternate running for 5 to 10 minutes with brisk walking breaks of a minute or more. Be sure to begin using this strategy from the very start. Don't make the mistake of trying to run as far as you can before you switch over to walking. By then you will have pushed yourself over the brink, and even walking will prove difficult. So swallow your pride from the very beginning, run slowly and walk briskly, keep moving, and keep smiling.
- If you have built up your long runs to somewhere between 6 and 15 miles, run nonstop for no more than two-thirds that distance. Then switch off running for a mile and walking for a minute or two.

After you've participated in a marathon in this manner—and I'd prefer you trained better for it so you could run all the way the first time—you may be motivated to train to run all the way for your next one.

SOME CONCLUDING WORDS

You don't ever have to run a marathon. Don't let anyone push you into something you don't want to do. The lure of this popular event creates a lot of peer pressure. Desire is the only emotion that will get you through your training and to the finish line. You have to really want it, for yourself. Also, if you've entered the marathon but your training is not up to par, don't go. Instead, make plans for another marathon down the road. There are plenty to choose from. Treat the marathon with respect. Better to postpone than to have a miserable experience.

WHAT'S NEXT?

Almost every first-time marathoner says the same thing at the finish line: "Never again." After you've conquered the marathon and rejoiced, once may indeed be enough. You may go back to being a fitness runner, or take up the challenge of improving times at shorter distances. That's fine. That incredible accomplishment will be forever remembered and continue to inspire you throughout your life.

But many runners catch the marathon bug. You may like the way you look and feel as the result of your training, or want to experience the excitement over a different course in another city. Being cheered as a celebrity by hundreds of adoring spectators can be habit-forming. Many are fascinated with seeing how much faster they can push themselves over that long road to the marathon finish line. But improvement isn't an easy task. It will require more work—more mileage, long runs, speed training. If you want to improve your marathon time, you are ready to graduate to the training programs in the following chapter.

CHAPTER 21

Marathon Build-up Training

The marathon isn't just difficult to race, the training is difficult, too. That's part of the attraction: You set a lofty goal that requires hard work to achieve. Many runners agree the training is harder than the race itself. A major investment of time and energy is required. You have to work for an hour or so five or six days a week—three hours or more when going long—for four months or longer. All these training hours and miles are part of the essential marathon buildup that allows you to race the 26.2 miles to glory in as few hours and minutes and seconds as possible.

Running a marathon and racing a marathon are not the same. If your goal is to run all or most of the way without much concern for time, the first-timer survivor's program in the previous chapter will suffice. But to race a marathon it's not just the distance that's the obstacle, but your willingness to test your physical and mental limits against the clock. Knowing how much it takes to run a marathon and yet pushing yourself to do it again, but even faster, involves taking a big risk. Racing a marathon isn't about playing it safe, it's about doing your best. To do that, you make sacrifices, pay the price in training and in the race. No sugarcoating here—marathon racers discover the peace inside of pain. And here lies the marathon lure: to see what we can take, to climb an even higher mountain, to experience the agony and the ecstasy of human performance.

It's your choice—comfort and participatory fun, or push to

your limits. There is a compromise position: moderate training, modest racing goals, reasonable racing discomfort.

As a veteran of more than thirty marathons and as the coach of thousands of marathoners, I've learned many "secrets" of marathon success. I share them with you here. Proper training, pacing, and so forth are important, but among the elusive elements that make the marathon special are the combination of Mother Nature and Lady Luck, and your mental ability to overcome the enormous physical demands of the 26.2 mile marathon monster.

THE MARATHON TRAINING PROGRAM

The marathon demands respect. If you don't train properly or you race foolishly, it will humble you whether a back-of-the-packer or an Olympian. That I can guarantee—from personal experience. Ideally, it takes six months of work to build up for a good marathon effort: two months of base training and four months of specific marathon training. If you've maintained a good mileage base you've reduced your commitment to four months of work. Training for much longer isn't likely to work any better than a too-short program: You'll likely pass your peak, lose interest, or get injured. The key to marathon training is balancing the right amount of mileage, long runs, speed training, build-up races, and rest. You must be willing to put in the time and not take shortcuts. Don't undertrain; but don't do too much either. The trick is to avoid the obstacles of overtraining, injury, and discouragement.

Chapter 14 details the various training phases; Chapter 15 guides you in writing your own marathon program. Or, use the sample schedules in Figures 21.2–21.5 to blend the training phases and types of endurance and speed runs.

MILEAGE

Marathoning requires more mileage than 5Ks to half-marathons to establish enough endurance and strength to support longer training runs and quality speed training. This is a very demanding schedule, but running as fast as you can for 26.2 miles is a very demanding task.

The sample schedules include a recommended base mileage to be held for one to two months prior to starting the buildup program. This base should be at least 50 to 75 percent of your peak mileage goal. Following guidelines in Chapter 6, gradually increase weekly mileage until you reach your goal. Maintain your peak mileage range for at least six to eight weeks, then taper for two to three weeks before the marathon. Follow the flexible mileage goals in Figure 21.1.

What if you get behind mileage goals due to one reason or another? If you've been consistent up to the point of disruption, you can ease back into your schedule. Whether you couldn't run at all, or had low mileage for a week or two, don't just start again where you would have been. Rather, move back a week or two from the highest level you reached, and then gradually catch back up to the program. Don't panic. By starting four to six months before the marathon, you develop a reservoir of endurance to draw on if you lose a few days along the way. A long-term schedule allows you to miss even a few weeks. If you miss a month or more and don't keep in shape with cross-training, seriously consider postponing your marathon.

LONG RUNS

The most important ingredient to marathon success is the long run; it mirrors the marathon itself. "Going long" is a hallowed weekend tradition that is despised and loved, feared and revered, bragged and complained about.

Some runners concentrate on weekly mileage instead of long runs. For marathoning success, a 40-mile training week of five 8-milers isn't equal to one of four 5-milers and a 20-mile-long run. You are not training to run 40 or so miles in a week, but to run 26.2 miles all at once. To do that, you need long training runs more than impressive weekly mileage figures.

FIGURE 21.1: MILEAGE AND LONG-RUN GUIDE FOR MARATHON TRAINING

Category	Weekly Mileage	Long-Run Distance
Novice/Intermediate Competitor	30 – 40	18 –20
Basic Competitor	40 – 50	18 –20
Competitor/Advanced Competitor	40 – 60	20 –22
Local Champion	50 – 80	20 –24

Long-Run Benefits

- Improve the ability of muscles to store glycogen and use fat efficiently as fuel, sparing glycogen.
- Force the body to search for help from fast-twitch (speed-oriented) muscle fibers, which can be trained to assist slow-twitch fibers for a marathon effort.
- Improve aerobic and muscular endurance.
- Teach you to run relaxed with efficient form for long periods despite fatigue.
- Develop patience.The long run forces you to slow down and pace yourself wisely—just as you must in the marathon.
- Provide a "dress rehearsal" for testing potential race day shoes and clothing, fueling and hydrating, and so on under marathonlike conditions.
- Provide an effective way to maintain or lose weight.
- Develop friendships. There's nothing like sharing conversational-paced long runs for bonding.
- Above all, the long run is for the mind. It builds psychological endurance and confidence. You finish despite the objections of the mind and body. After several long runs, you know you can handle the marathon distance.

How long is long enough? For marathoners, 18 to 20 miles qualifies as a long run. That's about two-thirds to three-fourths the marathon distance. Experienced marathoners benefit from some runs as long as 22 to 24 miles.

A sufficient mileage base is needed to support long runs. Ideally, the long run is no more than one-half your average weekly mileage. For example, average at least 40 miles a week to support 20-milers. Establish a base level of long runs before starting your build-up schedule. This makes it easier and safer to increase to runs of 20 miles and more. The sample schedules include recommended runs for the base period that are at least one-third to one-half the peak long distance run for the training program. For Novice and Intermediate Competitors the goal is at least 6 miles; 10 or more miles for more advanced marathoners. During the base period try to build to once- or twice-per-month runs of 8 to 13 miles. Then, ease into running these distances three or four times a month. During the 16-week specific marathon training program, gradually increase long-run distances by no more than 1 to 3 miles at a time until you reach your goal range. This progression from moderately challenging to longer and longer runs allows the body to adapt to running for longer and longer periods and still recover sufficiently for quality workouts a few days later.

Some runners prefer going long by time rather than mileage. The advantage is you're not under pressure to run the distance in a certain time, racing the workout against your previous times. You're also free to explore on the run since you're not confined to a measured route. A three-hour run over an unknown distance is a three-hour run, no matter how fast or slow you go, or where you go. When running by time, gradually increase long runs by no more than 15 to 30 minutes at once. Estimate how much time it'll take to run your desired distance and set that as your goal. Experienced, fit marathoners should aim to build to at least one run of approximately the same time period (but not the same distance since you'll be running slower) you will be running on marathon day.

I usually combine the two systems of measuring long runs. I'll set a mileage goal and then run for the time period necessary to reach that figure at my estimated 8-minute-mile pace. For example, a 23-mile run at 8-minute pace would take 3:04—a good goal if I'm aiming for a three-hour marathon. Sure, it's not likely to be exactly 23 miles, but who cares. It's close enough for me and goes in my diary that way.

My recommended limit for any level of runner, however, is 22 to 24 miles or three and a half to four hours of running—whichever comes first. The potential gain beyond this time isn't worth the risk of fatigue, injury, and frustration. And the longer the run, the longer the recovery. Follow the flexible long-run guidelines in Figure 21.1.

Although some marathoners put in runs of marathon length or longer, the average runner suffers more than benefits from such practice. Not only is it a long way to run, it's a long time to run. It takes about a half hour longer to run the marathon distance at training pace than at race pace. That's 30 more minutes to battle dehydration, glycogen depletion, and fatigue. Additionally, runners attempting such long runs are more vulnerable to failing to finish. That's a severe psychological blow.

How can a runner who has to work hard to finish a 20-mile training run expect to hold a strong pace for a full marathon? According to Dr. David Costill, "A 20-mile run during training is not equivalent to the first 20 miles of the marathon. With proper tapering and nutrition, the runners should start the marathon better prepared for the distance than when the 20-miler was run in training."

How often do you need to go long? Run long more frequently if your goal is to race a marathon and not just finish. Ideally, complete at least five or six long runs (of 18 to 24 miles) during the 16-week marathon program. You may be able to do a few more, but running long too often increases risk of injury and overtraining. On the average, go long every other weekend once you reach 18-milers; some veteran marathoners may schedule two of every three, or even three of every four weekends. Race or do medium-distance runs of 10 to 15 miles on alternate weekends.

Don't put off long runs until the marathon looms a few weeks away. Cramming one in every weekend to make up for lost time isn't advisable. If you plan well, you can get in an adequate number of long runs by doing two per month. Many veteran marathoners, myself included, developed the tradition in the 1970s of running long every weekend. Unless you have a fun group to run with you may soon burn out with this routine. It may result in chronic fatigue; you never completely recover from previous long runs. Besides, your family will be happy that you won't ruin every weekend.

When's the last long run? Many runners used to go long the weekend before the marathon to help deplete glycogen reserves prior to carbo-loading. Thankfully, research proved that wasn't necessary. The last long run became a tradition two weeks prior to the marathon as a kickoff to the mileage taper. Some research suggests that this process should start three weeks before the marathon to maximize recovery. Dr. Costill emphasizes in *Inside Running*: "Although most runners feel an urge to perform one long run a week or two before the competition, there is little justification for such action. The training gains from a 20-mile run are usually not realized for three to four weeks. The risk of injury far outweighs the conditioning effect or the psychological boost of an overdistance run within the last two weeks before the race." A few conservatives recommend a full month between the last long run and the marathon.

What should you do? For the average marathoner, three weeks before the marathon may work best. If you're fit and have put in several long runs, a two-weeks-to-go long run is okay. But to allow for adequate recovery this shouldn't be your longest run. That should be three to five weeks before. I may go long two weeks prior to my marathons, but won't go longer than 18 to 20 miles at an easy pace. A good compromise is a 15- to 16-mile run with two weeks to go to build confidence and minimize recovery time.

If you're not in top shape, are nursing a minor injury, or prefer a more conservative approach, give yourself a three- or four-week interval after the last long run. Also consider your racing schedule and the rest of your life. If your last sharpening race is two weeks before the marathon, go long the week before that. What if you've scheduled your last key race (or you have a business trip or family obligation) with three weeks to go and don't want to run long any closer than that to the marathon? It's okay to do your last long run a month before the marathon as long as you have plenty of them logged in your diary. Don't space the last long run any farther away or you'll lose benefits. The weekend before the marathon, run no further than an 8- to 10-miler.

How slow should you go long? This is where many runners go wrong. Speed isn't as important as getting in the distance, and time on your feet. Running too fast risks injury and leaves you fatigued and sore, interfering with quality workouts for days. Running long and slow trains the body to use fat efficiently as fuel. Running too fast on long runs on the other hand burns glycogen quickly, causing you to "hit the Wall."

Control the pace. For most runners, long runs should be at conversational pace: "If you can chatter, exact pace doesn't matter." For Novice and Intermediate Competitors, and some Basic Competitors, the best long-run pace is at or near your goal marathon pace—which is a relaxed finisher's effort rather than a push for a fast time.

Many Basic Competitors, and most Competitors, Advanced

Competitors, and Local Champions (but not Novice and Intermediate competitors) race a marathon at a pace faster than their short- and medium-distance runs. For these experienced, fit runners the best long run pace is about 1 to 1½ minutes per mile slower than marathon race pace (or about 1½ to 2 minutes per mile slower than 10K race pace). Some runners may be able to run as fast as 30 to 45 seconds quicker than projected marathon pace, and some benefit by running as slow as 2 minutes above marathon pace. Some runners, myself included, favor starting long run at 1½ to 2 minutes slower than marathon pace and gradually lowering it to 30 to 45 seconds slower than marathon pace by the end. Running too fast can tear you down, but running exceptionally slow can, too. Run slow enough to be in control and finish in reasonable comfort, but fast enough that you're not compromising good running form. Start at a slower speed than for short- and medium-distance runs to prevent early fatigue.

You should be completely recovered from long runs in two or three days. To do this, train and not strain while going long. To prevent going too fast, try running measured courses without wearing a watch. Or, forget measured courses and run by time. Run out one and a half hours, for example, and then return to complete a three-hour run that would be about (at a perceived 9-minute pace) 20 miles.

Another good way to keep pace under control is to wear a heart rate monitor. For most runners the recommended intensity for long runs is 60 to 70 percent of maximum heart rate, although experienced marathoners may run at 70 to 80 percent. During the second and third hour of runs, heart rates tend to go up by five to fifteen beats per minute despite a steady pace, especially under conditions of heat stress. This is due to "cardiac drift" as detailed in Chapter 47. It's okay to let heart rate increase slightly late in long runs as long as you can maintain a comfortable pace.

Experienced, fit marathoners may quicken the pace to marathon intensity over the last few miles of some long runs. This teaches leg muscles to function at this pace when already fatigued, and trains the mind that it is possible to run strong to the end of the marathon. At his peak, Olympic Marathon champ Frank Shorter ran most of his 20-milers by running a 10-mile loop at an easy (for him) 6-minute pace, then pushing a second loop at his marathon tempo (5-minute pace). For most of us, picking it up to marathon pace at the end of a long run should be restricted to the last 3 to 5 miles or so of running. Another option is to do pickups of 5 minutes or so at marathon pace every 20 to 30 minutes during some long runs. This teaches you to be able to move into race gear at various stages of fatigue. The best way, however, for the average runner to practice marathon race pace for extended periods is with fast continuous runs of up to 13 miles, not during long runs.

Some veterans are fond of combining going long with a tempo run. They'll run 10 or 12 miles at their normal long-run pace to develop leg fatigue. Then, they'll pick up the pace to about 10 seconds per mile faster than marathon pace for 3 or 4 miles. This is followed by 2 miles of easy running to complete the long run and cool-down. These workouts train you to run fast when you're already tired and are a great psychological boost. When facing bad patches in the marathon you can reflect on these runs as a reminder that you can run through fatigue. Use this variation with caution.

Long-run tips. Many runners look forward to long runs. You can do plenty of deep thinking on solitary runs or enjoy the company of others. If you look at the long run as something to savor rather than a dreaded task that you must get out of the way, it will be easier, even enjoyable. Here are some tips to make them more productive and fun:

- Treat the long run as a hard day, even though running at an easy pace. Take it easy the day before; follow it with at least one, if not two easy days. Starting tired may result in a poor run, causing more harm than good. If very sore or tired the day after a long run, take a day or more off.
- Set up running partners. Solo long runs may be okay occasionally, but for most runners they soon become depressing. Be sure your partner is willing to run at your conversational pace. If your friend can't run the whole distance, hook up for the last miles. Fresh conversation brings a rush of energy. Try a relay of friends who take turns keeping you

going. If you can't find a running partner, ask someone to ride along on a bike. Join or start a long-run group. Such groups make long runs as much a social outing as a training run.

- A long race at training pace adds spice to long runs. Or, run the opposite direction of a race and enjoy cheering on friends while getting in your mileage.
- Avoid as much as possible extremes of heat and cold, hills, and headwinds. Start early in the morning or late in the day to avoid the heat, and seek shaded courses. Slow the pace if running in the heat, and stop if you feel the warning signs of heat illness or your pace drops dramatically. In the winter, plan to avoid freezing headwinds, or at least run into the wind on the way out rather than facing it (and potential frostbite) when you are tired and sweat-soaked on the way back. If the weather is very bad, postpone long runs until the next day or even the next weekend. If you start and the weather gets worse, cut it short. Be tough, but reasonable. Incorporate some hills into your course to toughen you, but avoid too many killer hills—long runs are taxing enough as it is! Be wary of steep downhills, particularly late in runs when the legs are tired or injury may result.
- Run long on Saturday if possible so you can rest Sunday. That makes it easier to go to work Monday morning with a clear head. It also provides a backup if the weather is lousy on your scheduled day.
- For the most part, stick to a few trusty courses where you know the distance and where to get fluids. As a change of pace, occasionally run over new terrain.
- Beware of running long on slanted surfaces as it leaves you prone to injury. If you must run on them, change direction (and the slant) every few miles. Avoid congested areas—especially late in the run when dodging cars, bikes, and people is not easy be-

cause of physical and mental fatigue. Dirt trails absorb more shock, an important factor over the course of two or three hours.

- Take walk breaks if needed, especially when it is hot or when hills cause your heart rate to soar. But keep moving. It is okay to stop running for a few minutes to drink fluids or use the toilet, but if you stop for too long and stand around or sit down you will stiffen up. Some trainers promote planned walk breaks every mile. This is okay if you're undertrained or if you simply enjoy running more by taking it easier. Unless you plan to take walk breaks in the marathon, I don't recommend them in training.
- Keep drinking, ideally every 30 minutes or so, even in cool weather. If possible, take in the same type of sports drink you'll have access to for your marathon. Plan runs with fluid and fuel supplies in mind. Either bring them with you (such as gels tucked in your pocket and a bottle of fluid strapped to your body), have them available en route at water fountains or faucets, get supplied by a support team, or loop back home or to the car to refuel and rehydrate. Take in fluids, carbs, and protein immediately after running to aid recovery.
- Do not run long if not fully recovered from illness or injury. Bail out if you feel an injury coming on, or if you turn an ankle, fall and bang a knee, and so on. Favoring an injury may cause additional problems. When returning from injury, ease into long runs with a combo run and bike or swim for a workout totaling two or three hours.
- Wear well-cushioned, broken-in (but not broken-down) shoes. The effect of inadequate shoes is greatly exaggerated over the course of a long run.
- Be flexible. If you have built up mileage and long runs well in advance, you can skip a long run here and there and not lose out. But don't make a habit of it. Discipline yourself to go long on schedule.

SPEED TRAINING

Many experienced marathoners race a marathon at a faster pace than their daily runs of 5 to 10 miles or so. For example, my marathon pace is a minute faster than my normal training pace. These runners need to learn to push the pace. But even if your marathon pace is the same or slower than your training pace, speed training can improve your marathon time.

Speed training improves running form, sense of pacing, and mental discipline. Run some long intervals and continuous runs of 6 to 13 miles at your intended marathon pace to get used to the feel of that speed. Workouts at 5K race pace or faster improve aerobic capacity, running economy, and confidence. They make marathon intensity seem easy, allowing you to run relaxed. Marathoners emphasize longer intervals of 1 to 2 miles at 10K pace or faster to simulate the stress of race pacing. My preferred workout is four to six times a mile at slightly faster than 5K intensity. Hill training strengthens the legs for the marathon effort and prepares the mind for conquering marathon hills.

Marathon pace is about 5 percent slower than lactate threshold pace. Raising your threshold allows you to push faster without excessive fatigue caused by lactic acid accumulation. As a result, you can improve marathon performance. Continuous tempo runs of 20 to 40 minutes and long tempo intervals are the answer here. A good tempo choice is 6 or more mile intervals at 15 to 30 seconds per mile faster than marathon goal pace (which is the same as about 20 to 30 seconds slower than 10K race pace).

Hundreds of marathoners take our New York Road Runners Club speed classes each year for the reasons above. But don't attempt fast running if you haven't fully recovered from long runs or races, or you are overly tired from high mileage. The last hard session should be ten to fourteen days before the marathon. The final speed workout should be four to six days before the event. It should be brisk, not hard, and include extra recovery time and a reduced number of intervals. It's a mental tuneup, not a real speed session, so control your body, which is rested and raring to go. See the speed training section of this book for specific guidelines for speed workouts, including how to choose the distance, quantity, intensity, and recovery of your intervals. Feel free to replace our suggested workouts with others detailed in these chapters. Our sample schedules include only one of many possible combinations of speed workouts to improve your marathon race times.

In our schedules, speed sessions are included on Wednesdays—the middle of the week—to allow for adequate rest going into and coming off weekend races and long runs. Include them whatever day of the week works best for you. If you need more time to taper or recover for races and long runs, shift or minimize our suggested speed workouts. Once a week speed training is enough for most marathoners while increasing mileage and long runs. Experienced marathoners may benefit from a second speed session some weeks. If adding a speed workout to our suggested one, keep these taxing workouts at least 48 to 72 hours apart. Balance the two speed sessions within a week. Unless you are very fit and highly experienced, avoid doing two hard track workouts each week, or two hill sessions. The extra workouts should primarily be tempo runs, marathon paced runs of 6 to 13 miles, hill training, or fartlek, which help build endurance and are run at controlled speeds. Don't return to speed training too soon after build-up races, especially long ones.

BUILD-UP RACES

The sample schedules include a variety of build-up races to increase motivation and provide a wide range of benefits. Modify them to meet your preferences and race availability. You may race slightly more often than these schedules, but don't overdo it. Overracing invites injury and interferes with packing in mileage, long runs, and quality speed training. You may compete slightly less often than these schedules, but regular racing toughens you for competition.

Some marathoners do not race at all in their buildup. A few races are recommended to practice pacing, drinking and fueling on the run, test shoes and clothing, and so on. Besides, races are motivators. They give you something to aim for; four to six months is a long time to train without intermediate goals and rewards. Don't "put all your eggs in one basket" by keying only for the marathon. Race day could bring bad weather or you could just have a bad race. Ideally, race at least once a month over the four months going into your marathon. This builds valuable experience.

Your last long race of 15K to half-marathon should be at least three weekends before the marathon; don't race longer than 10K two weekends before. Racing any distance the weekend before the marathon is not advisable unless it is a controlled race of 10K or less at marathon pace. Do not race more than twice a month; seldom race two weekends in a row. Do not race on a Saturday and then do a long run on Sunday in an effort to get everything in. You will invite injury if you don't recover from races properly and space them wisely. The best choice is to plan your races and then schedule long runs around them.

Races in the 15K to half-marathon range test pacing and endurance, and enhance lactate threshold. 5Ks boost aerobic capacity and add a dash of speed for motivation. 10Ks sharpen speed for a fast marathon. Use races early in the schedule for fun and to build strength. "Train through" some of these events without complete tapering to keep mileage up. Select a few races in your last month or two to go for a good time, perhaps even a PR, while you're in good shape. Recording good performances will give you increased incentive to continue training for the marathon.

The sample schedules include a series of races: a 10K, half-marathon, and 5K early to increase fitness, motivation, and race experience; a half-marathon with four weeks to go and a 10K with two weeks to go to sharpen and go for good times to predict marathon fitness. Choose other distances or combinations if you wish. You may choose to taper more or less than the sample schedules for races, and run more or less mileage as you recover. Taper adequately for key races.

Races can be used three ways:

1. **To get in long training runs** with water stations and split times along the way to help you learn pacing. You get to run with lots of people. Create a beneficial long run by running a few miles prior to a race of any distance and then running the race at training pace. For example, run 12 miles prior to the start of a 10K and then run through the race (register so you can use the water stations) for a total run of 18.2 miles. This is sure easier than going long alone. Be careful here. Don't get caught up in the excitement and combine both the

stresses of a long run and a race. Hold back your competitive nature and run at a conversational pace.

2. **Practice marathon race pace.** Running a few races of 10K to half-marathon distance at marathon pace will help you become familiar with that effort. Don't think this is an easy run. It isn't. This is a controlled speed workout. How can you keep this pace for the whole marathon? On race day you'll be rested and pumped-up with excitement and confidence.
3. **To measure progress and better select your time goal.** If, for example, you struggled to run an 8-minute pace for a half-marathon, you know you are not ready to hold that pace for the marathon. On the other hand, if your race went well it may predict a faster marathon than you had planned. For guidelines for predicting marathon times from other race distances and setting goal times see Chapter 25. Don't be dismayed if your times early in your buildup don't match your goal marathon time. You're still building fitness. The best test is within a month of the marathon when you're rounding into top shape.

CROSS-TRAINING

Minimize the wear and tear on your body by replacing up to 20 percent of mileage with nonimpact aerobic exercise. For example, replace a 5-mile run on your training schedule that would take 40 minutes with a swim for that time period. Or, to increase overall aerobic training, add a 30- to 60-minute cross-training workout on a scheduled off day or as a second workout on an easy run day.

REST: EASY AND OFF DAYS

It's hard to get marathoners to appreciate the value of taking it easy. They often consider rest as quality training time lost rather than as an investment in quality workouts to come. Don't let the urgency of preparing to race 26.2 miles force you into neglecting recovery. Rest days aren't glamorous, but they should be considered just as important as fast or long-run days. With its higher mileage and longer runs, marathoning demands quality rest days or overtraining and injury will result. Rest includes easy days of short- and medium-distance runs at conversational pace, and days off with no running. They allow the body to recover from and adapt to hard training during the rest of the week—long runs, speed workouts, and races.

The sample schedules include, on the average, two hard days—one speed workout and either a long run or a race. That's enough hard work when you're also increasing mileage, although some experienced marathoners may be able to handle an additional speed workout some weeks. Generally, five days are devoted to recovery—at least one of them a day off. Resist the temptation to run longer or faster on easy days, and to skip off days in an attempt to increase mileage.

Off days are especially important if running more mileage, harder speed workouts and races, and longer distances than ever before. On off days, either don't exercise at all, do a light cross-training workout, or go for a walk. The sample schedules include off days on each Monday and some Fridays, bracketing the weekend which normally includes long runs or races. If you can reach mileage goals with two or more off days per week at any point, or throughout your schedule, go right ahead if that's what works best for your body and time schedule. If you're an experienced high-mileage marathoner like myself, you may be able to eliminate off days—replacing them with an easy run. But I'll still take occasional unscheduled days off when my body (or wife) demands it. Take rest days any day you choose, but I recommend them during the work week when time is short and stress levels are high.

INJURY AND ILLNESS

Runners often refuse to heed injury or illness signals because they're desperate to run a particular marathon. If your health is threatened as you approach a marathon, postpone it. Continuing hard training, or starting a marathon when injured or ill could result in a very serious health problem.

SAMPLE 16-WEEK MARATHON TRAINING PROGRAM

Thousands of marathoners have successfully reached the finish line and achieved PRs by following my schedules, which are not only printed in this book but are also available in brochure form as the "Official New York City Marathon Training Program." That program is slightly different from the one here because it is adjusted for New York Road Runners Club races and long runs.

The schedule for Novice and Intermediate Competitors is similar to that in the previous chapter for first-time marathoners. But the program here includes suggested speed workouts and thus is a little more advanced. It is for more advanced first-time marathoners, and for those who have run a marathon but don't have the ability or desire to train at a higher level.

For all levels the training programs in Figures 21.2–21.5 (pages 246–253) are *sample* schedules. Follow them exactly, as many runners around the world do, or adapt them to fit your needs. Be dedicated about it, but flexible. Follow the theme of the schedules if you make up your own program: progressive increases in weekly mileage from the base to peak level with a few plateaus and cutbacks, gradual increases in well-spaced long runs, off days and short runs for recovery, a gradual tapering of mileage and long runs over the final two or three weeks. Modify the training programs by varying the daily and weekly mileage, the exact day and type of speed workouts, and the timing and distance of races to suit your needs. Adjust for progress, fatigue, health, or injury. For speed training and race days, the mileage figure includes warm-up and cool-down running, as well as interval recovery runs.

A sample rebuilding phase isn't included. That doesn't mean it isn't important. See the guidelines for the "aftermarathon" in Chapter 24.

BREAKING BARRIERS

Breaking barriers can be very rewarding, whether it's the three-hour or the four-hour mark, and can spur you to even greater achievements. A common standard of excellence for runners is to meet the age-adjusted qualifying times for the Boston Marathon. The average finishing time in most major marathons is about four hours for men and four and a half hours for women. Use getting into the upper half as a motivator. Following are some time goals to motivate you. Running the *approximate times* listed for intervals and race distances predicts your ability to break the corresponding marathon time barrier.

The Sub-2:40 Marathon (6:06 per mile)
Intervals: miles in 4:50–5:15, ¾ in 3:38–3:57, ½ in 2:22–2:26.
Races: 10K in 34:30, 10 miles in 57:00, half-marathon in 1:15.
The Sub-2:50 Marathon (sub-6:29 per mile)
Intervals: miles in 5:23–5:40, ¾ in 3:56–4:15, ½ in 2:33–2:37.
Races: 10K in 36:30, 10 miles in 1:00:15, half-marathon in 1:20.
The Sub-3:00 Marathon (sub-6:52 per mile)
Intervals: miles in 5:42–6:00, ¾ in 4:10–4:30, ½ in 2:42–2:46.
Races: 10K in 38:40, 10 miles in 1:04, half-marathon in 1:25.
The Sub-3:15 Marathon (7:26 per mile)
Intervals: miles in 6:06–6:25, ¾ in 4:27–4:49, ½ in 2:53–3:12.
Races: 10K in 41:30, 10 miles in 1:09, half-marathon in 1:32:30.
The Sub-3:30 Marathon (8:00 pace per mile)
Intervals: miles in 6:35–6:55, ¾ in 4:48–5:11, ½ in 3:07–3:12.
Races: 10K in 44:45, 10 miles in 1:14, half-marathon in 1:38:15.
The Sub-3:45 Marathon (8:34 pace per mile)
Intervals: miles in 7:03–7:25, ¾ in 5:09–5:34, ½ in 3:20–3:26.
Races: 10K in 47:45, 10 miles in 1:19, half-marathon in 1:46.
The Sub-4:00 Marathon (9:09 pace per mile)
Intervals: miles in 7:27–7:50, ¾ in 5:27–5:53, ½ in 3:32–3:37.
Races: 10K in 51:00, 10 miles in 1:25, half-marathon in 1:53.
The Sub-4:15 Marathon (9:43 pace per mile)
Intervals: miles in 8:05–8:30, ¾ in 5:54–6:23, ½ in 3:50–3:56.
Races: 10K in 55:00, 10 miles in 1:31, half-marathon in 2:00.
The Sub-4:30 Marathon (10:17 pace per mile)
Intervals: miles in 8:28–8:55, ¾ in 6:11–6:42, ½ in 4:01–4:08.
Races: 10K in 57:30, 10 miles in 1:35, half-marathon in 2:06:30.
The Sub-4:45 Marathon (10:52 pace per mile)
Intervals: miles in 8:52–9:20, ¾ in 6:29–7:00, ½ in 4:12–4:19.
Races: 10K in 1:01, 10 miles in 1:41, half-marathon in 2:14.
The Sub-5:00 Marathon (11:26 per mile)
Intervals: miles in 9:21–9:50, ¾ in 6:50–7:23, ½ in 4:26–4:33.
Races: 10K in 1:04, 10 miles in 1:45:30, half-marathon in 2:20.

TRAINING TO BEAT "THE WALL"

Hitting the Wall means running very low on glycogen, the carbs stored in your running muscles. After about 90 minutes of running, you begin to deplete. The longer you run, the more you deplete. If you deplete too much, you'll be engulfed by fatigue. For most marathoners, that will be somewhere between 10 miles and the halfway mark. Most trained runners can store about 18 to

20 miles' worth of carbs. That's why this distance is known as the theoretical location of the Wall. But some runners may deplete glycogen reserves a few miles sooner, some a few miles later.

Here's what happens. When the muscles start to run low on glycogen, a chain reaction takes place. Your body attempts to conserve what glycogen remains by burning more fat for energy. As less and less glycogen is available to help keep you going, fat becomes the primary fuel. The result: You have to slow down to provide extra oxygen to metabolize fat. Glycogen stored in the liver also depletes, causing a shortage of blood sugar, which is needed to feed the brain. As a result, mental fatigue sets in. You feel lightheaded, uncoordinated, confused, depressed, unmotivated. Now you not only can't run any faster, you don't care.

Okay, so how can you beat the Wall? Truth is you can't beat it, but you can greatly minimize its effect on your performance. Here's how:

Train your muscles. High mileage and long training runs cause muscle cells to adapt to store more glycogen. According to a study by Dr. Costill, well-trained muscles store 20 to 50 percent more glycogen than untrained muscles. Long runs develop mitochondria in cells to metabolize oxygen so that fat can be used more efficiently as fuel. This "spares" some glycogen for later use. If you only burned glycogen you would run low and "hit the Wall" much earlier and much harder. By conserving glycogen and utilizing some fat, you'll have sufficient energy reserves to keep a good pace in the late stages of a marathon. It's during this transition from glycogen to fat for fuel that much of the discomfort associated with the Wall takes place. The more glycogen-depletion runs you do, the better trained your muscles become to make this transition.

Taper and carbo-load. Cutting back training as the marathon gets close, as described in the next chapter, means you'll be burning off less muscle glycogen. Resting the muscles allows them to store more carbs for the marathon effort. In conjunction with tapering, fueling with a carbo-loading program will saturate your muscles with glycogen to help power you past the Wall. This includes carbs consumed in the days going into the race, on race morning, and on the run. Here's where those high-tech sports drinks, energy bars, and gels can really help you out.

FIGURE 21.2: SAMPLE NOVICE AND INTERMEDIATE COMPETITOR'S 16-WEEK MARATHON TRAINING SCHEDULE

Weeks to Go	Monday	Tuesday	Wednesday	Thursday	Friday	Saturday	Sunday	Total Mileage
Base	Off	3	4 (modified fartlek)	4	Off	6	3	20
16	Off	3	4 (2-mile tempo run)	4	Off	8	3	22
15	Off	4	4 (3–4 x long-hill repeats)	4	Off	10	3	25
14	Off	3	5 (2–4 x mile, 5K–10K pace)	3	Off	13	3	27
13	Off	6	5 (3–4 x long-hill repeats)	4	4	3	8 (race 10K)	30
12	Off	4	5 (fartlek)	5	Off	15	3	32
11	Off	6	5 (4–6 x half-mile, 5K–10K pace)	6	Off	12	6	35
10	Off	5	5 (2–3 x mile, 5K–fast pace)	4	Off	18	3	35
9	Off	6	6 (tempo intervals, 2 x 1½ miles)	6	4	Off	13 (race half-marathon)	35

FIGURE 21.2: SAMPLE NOVICE AND INTERMEDIATE COMPETITOR'S 16-WEEK MARATHON TRAINING SCHEDULE (continued)

Weeks to Go	Monday	Tuesday	Wednesday	Thursday	Friday	Saturday	Sunday	Total Mileage
8	Off	5	6	6	Off	20	3	40
7	Off	6	5 (1–2 x 1½ miles, 5K–10K pace)	5	5	3	6 (race 10K)	30
6	Off	6	6 (4-mile tempo run, half-marathon pace)	5	Off	20	3	40
5	Off	6	6 (tempo intervals 2 x 2 miles)	6	4	Off	13 (race half-marathon)	35
4	Off	5	6	6	Off	20	3	40
3	Off	6	6 (3–4 x half-mile, fast pace)	6	6	Off	8 (race 10K)	32
2	Off	5	5 (2–3 x mile, 5K–fast pace)	4	Off	8	3	25
1	Off	4	4 (3 miles at marathon pace)	3	Off	2	race marathon	13 + race

FIGURE 21.3: SAMPLE BASIC COMPETITOR'S 16-WEEK MARATHON TRAINING SCHEDULE

Weeks to Go	Monday	Tuesday	Wednesday	Thursday	Friday	Saturday	Sunday	Total Mileage
Base	Off	5	5 (fartlek)	4	Off	10	6	30
16	Off	4	6 (3-mile tempo run)	4	Off	12	6	32
15	Off	6	6 (4–5 x long-hill repeats)	4	Off	15	4	35
14	Off	6	6 (3–4 x mile, 5K–10K pace)	4	Off	18	3	37
13	Off	6	6 (4–5 x long-hill repeats)	4	6	5	10 (race 10K)	37
12	Off	6	6 (fartlek)	4	3	18	3	40
11	Off	6	6 (4–6 x half-mile, 5K–fast pace)	5	5	12	6	40
10	Off	6	6 (2–3 x mile, 5K–fast pace)	5	3	20	3	43
9	Off	6	6 (tempo intervals, 2 x 1½ miles)	4	4	Off	15 (race half-marathon)	35

FIGURE 21.3: SAMPLE BASIC COMPETITOR'S 16-WEEK MARATHON TRAINING SCHEDULE (continued)

Weeks to Go	Monday	Tuesday	Wednesday	Thursday	Friday	Saturday	Sunday	Total Mileage
8	Off	5	6	6	4	20	4	45
7	4	8	6 (2–3 x 1½ miles, 5K–10K pace)	5	6	3	8 (race 5K)	40
6	Off	5	9 (6–8 miles, marathon pace)	3	4	20	4	45
5	Off	6	6 (tempo intervals 2 x 2 miles)	6	3	Off	14 (race half-marathon)	35
4	Off	5	6	6	3	22	3	45
3	Off	8	6 (4–6 x half-mile, fast–hard pace)	6	4	3	8 (race 10K)	35
2	Off	6	6 (2–3 x mile, 5K–fast pace)	4	Off	10	4	30
1	Off	4	4 (3 miles at marathon pace)	3	Off	3	race marathon	14 + race

FIGURE 21.4: SAMPLE COMPETITOR'S AND ADVANCED COMPETITOR'S 16-WEEK MARATHON TRAINING SCHEDULE

Weeks to Go	Monday	Tuesday	Wednesday	Thursday	Friday	Saturday	Sunday	Total Mileage
Base	Off	6	6 (fartlek)	5	5	12	6	40
16	Off	6	6 (3-mile tempo run)	5	5	15	6	43
15	Off	8	6 (5–8 x long-hill repeats)	6	6	13	6	45
14	Off	7	6 (3–4 x mile, 5K–10K pace)	6	4	18	4	45
13	Off	8	7 (5–8 x long-hill repeats)	7	6	4	10 (race 10K)	42
12	Off	6	7 (fartlek)	6	6	20	3	48
11	Off	8	8 (4–8 x half-mile, 5K–fast pace)	8	6	15	5	50
10	Off	8	8 (3–4 x mile, 5K–fast pace)	8	6	20	5	55
9	Off	8	8 (tempo intervals, 2 x 2 miles)	6	6	Off	15 (race half-marathon)	43

FIGURE 21.4: SAMPLE COMPETITOR'S AND ADVANCED COMPETITOR'S 16-WEEK MARATHON TRAINING SCHEDULE (continued)

Weeks to Go	Monday	Tuesday	Wednesday	Thursday	Friday	Saturday	Sunday	Total Mileage
8	Off	8	8	8	6	22	3	55
7	Off	8	8 (2–4 x 1½ miles, 5K–10K pace)	8	8	5	8 (race 5K)	45
6	Off	8	11 (8–10 miles, marathon pace)	5	6	20	5	55
5	Off	8	8 (tempo intervals 2–3 x 2 miles)	6	4	Off	14 (race half-marathon)	40
4	Off	8	8	7	6	23	3	55
3	Off	8	8 (4–8 x half-mile, fast–hard pace)	7	6	3	10 (race 10K)	42
2	Off	5	7 (3–4 x mile, 5K–fast pace)	5	Off	10	5	32
1	Off	4	5 (3–4 miles, marathon pace)	3	Off	3	race marathon	15 + race

FIGURE 21.5: SAMPLE LOCAL CHAMPION'S 16-WEEK MARATHON TRAINING SCHEDULE

Weeks to Go	Monday	Tuesday	Wednesday	Thursday	Friday	Saturday	Sunday	Total Mileage
Base	Off	7	7 (fartlek)	7	8	15	6	50
16	Off	7	7 (4-mile tempo run)	7	7	18	6	52
15	Off	8	7 (8–10 x long-hill repeats)	7	7	20	6	55
14	Off	8	7 (4–6 x mile, 5K–10K pace)	7	7	20	6	55
13	4	8	8 (8–10 x long-hill repeats)	8	8	3	11 (race 10K)	50
12	Off	8	7 (fartlek)	7	8	22	6	58
11	4	8	8 (6–10 x half-mile, 5K–fast pace)	8	8	18	6	60
10	Off	8	8 (4–5 x mile, 5K–fast pace)	8	8	22	6	60
9	Off	8	8 (tempo intervals, 2–3 x 2 miles)	8	8	3	15 (race half-marathon)	50

FIGURE 21.5: SAMPLE LOCAL CHAMPION'S 16-WEEK MARATHON TRAINING SCHEDULE (continued)

Weeks to Go	Monday	Tuesday	Wednesday	Thursday	Friday	Saturday	Sunday	Total Mileage
8	Off	10	8	8	9	23	7	65
7	4	8	8 (3–4 x 1½ miles, 5K–10K pace)	8	10	3	9 (race 5K)	50
6	Off	8	12 (10–11 miles, marathon pace)	7	8	23	7	65
5	3	8	7 (tempo intervals, 2–3 x 2 miles)	5	Off	15 (race	45 half-marathon)	
4	Off	10	8	8	9	23	7	65
3	6	10	8 (6–10 x half-mile, fast–hard pace)	8	8	Off	10 (race 10K)	50
2	Off	8	8 (4–5 x mile, 5K–hard pace)	6	Off	10	6	38
1	Off	4	5 (3–4 miles, marathon pace)	4	Off	3	race marathon	16 + race

Don't start too fast. Starting too fast will burn off glycogen prematurely. A conservative starting pace helps save glycogen for later in the marathon, pushing back the Wall and lessening the sensation of stress when you do hit it.

Fight dehydration. As you dehydrate, heart rate increases even if you don't increase the pace. As you work harder to keep pace, you burn off glycogen more rapidly. Drinking plenty of fluids before and during the race (ideally, sports drinks that also include carbs) will minimize dehydration.

Train your mind. You will run short of glycogen at some point in the marathon. The question is when and how badly you "hit the Wall" and how well you cope with it mentally. You will hit bad patches in the race as your body adjusts to burning fat for fuel. How tough will it get? That you'll never know until it happens. If you've prepared for it properly, it most likely will be just a few miles of manageable discomfort.

Racing a marathon is tricky business. Even if you train well, push just a little too much too soon, or not get quite enough fluids and fuel in you, and you could crash. Don't waste time and energy worrying about the Wall. Instead, be positive. Monitor your body's feedback and make adjustments. Use the mental techniques in Chapter 27 to prepare for the fatigue associated with the Wall. Take it as a mental challenge: Your sugar-starved brain is trying to trick you into slowing or quitting. In many cases you can talk yourself through the Wall. But if you're struggling too much, don't try to force the pace. Stay relaxed, take in some fluids and fuel, slow the pace, walk for a while if necessary. By staying calm and channeling your mental and physical resources you can minimize the loss and still finish in a reasonable time.

CHAPTER 22

Marathon Countdown

The marathon countdown begins two weeks or so before marathon day. Concentrate on rest and mental preparation from this point on to gear up for a peak performance. Errors during the marathon countdown may cost four or more months of carefully planned training. Unlike a 5K or 10K race, you can't do it again in a week or two, so count down to your marathon wisely.

THE PHYSICAL COUNTDOWN: THE MARATHON TAPER

Tapering is critical for marathoners. That's because they need plenty of rest to recover from a lofty training peak to prepare for the trauma of racing for three or four hours or so. Refer to Chapter 14 for general information on tapering; following are specific guidelines for the marathon taper.

The last two or three weeks of training pose a dilemma for the nervous marathoner: How to maintain a high level of fitness and yet rest up for a good marathon effort? Runs here should be geared toward maintaining a fitness base and rebuilding mental and physical reserves. When in doubt about how far or fast to run, choose the conservative path. Even if you aren't as fit as you'd like to be, the taper is essential. If you're not in marathon shape with two weeks to go, devote your energy to prayer, not last-minute training. Trying to get just a little more fit will do more harm than good. There is very little physiological value in any mileage, long runs, or speed training you do within two weeks of a marathon. You will be as fit as you will get. Here's where less is better than more. Less training minimizes the chance of injury, gives your mind and muscles an opportunity to rest up for a big effort, and allows the body to stock up on carbohydrates to energize your marathon effort. Moderate training over the last two weeks, however, is important to prevent unwanted weight gain and minimize the anxiety and depression that often accompany dramatic reductions in running.

Be warned: This is the most dangerous period of the entire marathon-training program. Your body and mind are well-rested and peaking for a top performance. It's hard to hold back when you feel so good and are so psyched-up. Rein yourself in. Don't run too far or too fast or you'll blow your entire 16-week buildup.

If nursing an injury, taper extra. This is a great time to heal. But the taper may seem to bring on injuries. You may develop all kinds of minor aches and pains, or feel sluggish and irritable as the race approaches. You train less but worry more. This is normal. These problems disappear as race day adrenaline pumps you up and your well-trained body and relaxed, confident mind take over.

How soon and how much should you taper for a marathon? Many experts recommend at least a 50 percent cutback in mileage over the final two weeks. Dr. David Costill's advice based on his research: Cut back to one-third normal mileage for two weeks before the marathon. For example, reduce from 60 miles to 20 miles a week. This conservative advice may be too radical for many runners. The ideal tapering program may require a little more running because of the psychological stress of cutting back. With experience you'll find what works best for you.

COACH GLOVER'S MARATHON TAPER

Following is a general tapering formula that will work for most runners.

Three weeks to go: Do either your last long run or your last race (10K to half-marathon) three weekends before the marathon. For the following week of training (three weeks to go), consider cutting mileage to 75 to 85 percent of normal. If you've been running 50 miles a week, for example, cut back to about 37 to 42 miles. Some fit runners prefer to hold mileage steady and only taper for the final two weeks; others gradually taper over four weeks.

Generally, the higher your mileage, the more and sooner you need to taper. If at less than 50 miles, you probably don't need to start tapering until two weeks to go.

Two weeks to go: Do either your last long run of 18 to 20 miles (be careful), last race (10K or less), or a moderate long run of 15 miles or so with two weekends to go. For the following week of training (two weeks to go), cut mileage to 50 to 75 percent of normal. If you've averaged 50 miles a week, cut back to about 25 to 37 miles.

One week to go: Now's the time for serious tapering. Cut further to about 14 to 20 miles (about one-third normal mileage) in the six days prior to the marathon. Take at least one or two days off on marathon week. I don't take off the day before the race since tension is high and a short run is relaxing. Some take off Friday before a Sunday marathon, others prefer a day or even two off right before the race. Still others take off two days and then run 2 or 3 miles the day before. Here's a suggested final week: Monday: off, Tuesday—4 miles, Wednesday—4 miles, Thursday—3 miles, Friday—off, Saturday—3 miles, Sunday—marathon.

Although you're tapering mileage, don't also cut back pace. Run at your normal training pace within your training heart rate range. Slowing to an uncomfortable jog causes you to alter form and feel sluggish. Here's a good time to do a few short runs of 3 or 4 miles at marathon pace. Sample tampering programs for each category of runner are included in the training schedules in Chapter 21.

THE MENTAL COUNTDOWN

Your mind must be trained to take advantage of your physical training. Review Chapter 25 for guidelines for setting your marathon time goal and starting pace. Mental training—including coping with prerace anxiety, maintaining concentration while racing, and running through discomfort and fatigue—is explored in detail in Chapter 27. Of particular importance is the section on visualizing your race. Set goals to get to certain mile markers or landmarks and then set out to knock them off one at a time. If possible, run part of the course (especially the hills and the finish) or drive over it so you can better prepare your mind for the race.

LOGISTICS

Take care of prerace details to free yourself to focus on physical tapering and mental preparation. Make a checklist of what must be done before the race, and do it. Chapter 28 offers general tips for logistical concerns both in the days and hours prior to arriving at the race site, and on race day. Most of them apply to marathoners. Be sure to get plenty of sleep, carbo-load effectively, and keep hydrated during the marathon countdown. Here are some marathon specific tips:

Pre Race Day

- The logistics of race day are likely to be more complicated and stressful than for shorter races, especially in big city events. Often the start and finish aren't in the same place. Double-check how you'll get to the starting line and home after finishing. Have a backup plan in place for anything that could go wrong: the car doesn't start, you miss the bus to the start, and so on.
- Runners tend to do stupid things at the last minute out of nervousness. Whether it's trying out a different workout, switching to fast-looking new shoes, or stuffing yourself with a magical food or supplement, if you're not used to it, don't do it. Avoid introducing anything new into your life during these final weeks, such as starting a new job or work project, moving or remodeling. These changes will take away needed mental energy.
- At least a month in advance, pick out the shoes and clothing you'll wear. This gives you plenty of time to break them in. Only the lightweight, quick-footed runners should consider racing shoes for marathoning. Lightweight trainers are the best choice for most marathoners; regular trainers for those pounding the pavement more than four hours and for heavier runners. Feet swell over the marathon distance, so make sure shoes don't feel too

tight. They should be broken in, but still have most of their cushioning ability. Aim for 50 to 100 miles on your shoes, including your last long run, and then set them aside for marathon day. I'm extra careful. I'll get two pair of shoes broken-in and set them aside just in case something happens to one set.

- Use your last long run and race as a full dress rehearsal. Practice carbo-loading with the foods you intend to eat for energy in the days and hours before the marathon. Before and during these runs, drink the same sports drinks that will be available on the course and eat the same sports gels or other fuels you'll consume during the marathon. Wake up and run at the same time of day you will for the marathon. Wear the same clothes; shoes, too, if they're training shoes. If you'll be using lightweight trainers or racing shoes for the marathon, test them for part of the long run, then switch to more-cushioned training shoes to minimize injury.
- Carbo-load and hydrate properly, but taper off caloric intake slightly as you cut back mileage to avoid unnecessary weight gain. About 100 calories equals a mile.
- Avoid catching a last-minute cold or flu. This is a common problem. Although you're in peak marathon shape, your immunity may be down. How to minimize getting sick at this crucial time? Taper early, get enough sleep, wash your hands often, and keep away from as many potentially germ-carrying people as possible.
- Cut out cross-training and weight training over the final two weeks to more completely rest.
- As you taper, you'll have lots of extra time and energy. Too many runners use it to clean out the garage, et cetera. Stick to less-physical ways to spend your time—read a book or go to the movies—and save every ounce of extra physical en-

ergy for the marathon. Don't waste mental and emotional energy either. Avoid tasks requiring prolonged heavy thinking, or producing stress.

- Stay off your feet as much as possible the last three days and on marathon morning. Sight-seeing is a problem for runners who travel to an exciting place, such as New York. Plan your trip so you can stay for a few days after the race. Enjoy sight-seeing once the stress of the marathon is out of the way.
- Avoid the premarathon hoopla. Don't spend hours at prerace clinics, exhibits, and so forth. Attend a few of them for a few minutes to enjoy the atmosphere, but don't spend a lot of time on your feet. Hanging around large crowds at prerace events tends to make you more nervous and drain off energy. In the last two days, minimize your contact with others. Hang out with a few calm, confident, supportive friends and relax.
- Organize your support crew. They can pass you fluids and fuel, and cheer you on at strategic spots—such as the top of a big hill, the 20-mile mark, and 1 mile before the finish line. Encourage lots of people to be on the course to give you a cheer. Review how you will meet running partners at the start, and friends and family at the finish area.
- If you want the crowd along the way to give you an extra boost, wear something distinctive. Print or write on your singlet a name or slogan to give spectators something to cheer about. I've run along with "Go Mo," "Marathon Mom," "Elvis Lives," "Texas," "Fast Grandpa," and "Slow Motion" among others. They all seemed to thrive on the crowd cheering them on. Our Greater New York Racing Team singlets elicit plenty of "Go New York" shouts. Believe me, it helps.
- Throughout the marathon countdown, think calm. Focus on staying relaxed. Expect to feel edgy as the big day approaches. This is normal and happens to all marathoners. Your body has energy to spare,

and it misses the hard training. You will have to deal with withdrawal symptoms at the same time you are coping with prerace anxiety. Don't start worrying about losing your fitness and panic. You are not losing fitness; you are ready. There is nothing you can do now to improve your fitness, but you can make training errors or mental mistakes that could mess up your race.

Race Day

- Wake up at least three hours before starting time to give yourself plenty of time to fuel up, dress, recheck your bag, et cetera. Many runners like to take a warm shower to loosen up and calm down. Arrive at the race at least two hours early. Why so early? There's too much at stake if you arrive late. Large crowds make simple tasks take longer. Arrive in time to take care of prerace concerns without feeling rushed.
- At the staging area, turn in extra clothing to the baggage area or to a friend. If it's warm, stay in the shade as much as possible and wear a hat to the start to help keep the sun off you. If it's cool, wear a throwaway outfit or a plastic bag to keep warm until the race starts. You may start the race with an extra shirt you can toss away after you've warmed. But don't overdress since you'll heat up during the race. Weather conditions often change over the course of a few hours of running. It could get much hotter, or much cooler. It could also rain and then stop, or rain could dampen your spirits late in the run. Be prepared as much as possible for changes in the weather. A good choice is to position your support crew along the course with extra clothing.
- Don't waste energy with a running warm-up on race morning. But don't get stiff by standing or sitting too long either. Every 15 minutes or so move around. Go for a short walk. Stretch only after a

walking warm-up and make sure not to overstretch while excited and nervous.

- Know where the starting line is and as the race gets close, particularly in large events, position yourself so not to get caught in a crowd and not be able to make it to your planned starting spot. This may require standing in a tight crowd for several minutes—both prior to the actual lineup and after the runners have been called to the start. Since you may not be able to get free to get a drink or use the toilet, carry a plastic container of fluids to the start and use innovative techniques (which I won't describe) for relieving yourself of last-minute urges to urinate. Be mentally prepared for all of these inconveniences. Don't panic. It's part of the show in big races and everyone around you is affected by it too.

CHAPTER 23

Marathon Strategy

The marathon is unforgiving. Start too fast or don't take proper fluids, for example, you blow your race. Not only do you suffer physically and mentally in order to make it to the finish line (or before dropping out), you can't redeem yourself in another marathon in a week or two. Nor can you try again in a few days if you finish feeling you could have pushed harder and run faster.

Here are some strategic tips to help you reach your marathon goals:

MARATHON RACE DAY STRATEGY

Chapter 29 discusses racing strategy in more detail. Here are some marathon-specific strategies:

Pacing. This is where many marathoners err. You'll suffer for a long time if you don't pace wisely. You must combat the triple terrors—lactic acid accumulation, dehydration, and glycogen depletion—which may work individually or in combination—to destroy your race. Most marathoners run at a pace that is about 95 to 97 percent of their lactic threshold pace. If starting too fast, or surging too quickly, you'll exceed your threshold and waste glycogen supplies. You'll also increase body heat, contributing to dehyration which in turn increases heart rate and accelerates glycogen burning. Going out too fast sets you up for failure. Don't think you can build a time cushion by starting faster. This strategy usually backfires. The likely result is either a long struggle over the last several miles or dropping out.

What's a good starting pace? Statistical studies show that runners starting a marathon at more than 2 percent (about 10 seconds a mile) faster than their average pace slow significantly over the last 6 miles compared to those who run with even pacing or negative splits. Most experienced marathoners should start at their goal pace. Determine this from predicted times from build-up races and experience in previous marathons. Most fit marathoners race at a pace that is about one minute faster per mile than their long run training pace. A good bet for Novice and Intermediate Competitors is to start at the same pace as you averaged for your last long run and hold that speed to 20 miles. From there, hang on as best you can. You may even be able to pick up the pace if you've trained well.

Some marathoners benefit from starting slow (up to 10 seconds a mile) for the first 2 or 3 miles and then picking it up. Others like myself prefer to start slightly faster (no more than 5 to 10 seconds) than goal pace in order to run more by equal effort. Some prefer running the first half a minute or two slower than they will run the second half (negative splits). Chapter 29 details various pacing options. If you go out a bit too slow, you have adequate time to make up for it. So it's better to err on the side of caution. If you can pick it up a bit from there, go ahead. If it is a warm day, be prepared to start slower than your original goal pace. If starting with a friend or a group of friends, promise each other to keep the starting pace reasonable.

What about pacing by heart rate monitor? A good goal for runners who will be out there for over three and a half hours is to start out at about 70 percent of maximum heart rate (MHR) for the first 3 miles and then gradually increase to about 80 percent by the finish. Faster marathoners should start out at 70 to 75 percent of MHR for the first 3 miles and gradually increase to about 85 percent by the finish. Some Elites may be able to handle heart rates of 85 to 90 percent of MHR without exceeding their lactate threshold. These ranges take into consideration the phenomenon known as "cardiac drift"—a natural increase in heart rate with prolonged running. Chapter 47 includes guidelines for dealing with "drift" and using heart rate monitors for marathon pacing.

Crowded starts. Due to crowded conditions in large marathons, it may take a few minutes just to reach the starting line and a mile or more to settle into your pace. Don't panic. Weaving through runners to get back lost time wastes energy. Stay calm. Ease through as best you can while gradually picking up the pace. Once you hit your intended rate of speed, settle into that rhythm. If, for example, your goal was an 8-minute opening mile and you hit 9:30, look to run the second mile in 8:00, not faster. Stay at this pace until you feel relaxed and in a groove. Now you have a choice to make: Accept the time lost at the start or try to make some or all of it up. If you didn't lose too much time you can make it up by gradually quickening the pace. Aim to make up no more than 5 seconds or so per mile. At that rate, you get back a minute lost at the start over 12 miles. In some congested events like the New York City Marathon, you just need to accept the inevitable. Count on losing time at the start and factor that into your time goal.

Take note of your time when you cross the starting line. For your records, deduct that time. The Boston Marathon and other events use computer chips placed in the runners' shoes to record actual time from starting line to finish. Even if you deduct this time, the first mile still may be slowed by runners that wrongly lined up ahead of you. Try looking at a slow start as a blessing, preventing going out too fast and setting up lots of runners to pass along the way. Make the best of it. A bad start doesn't mean your race is doomed to failure. You've got a long way to go. Stay calm; get to work.

Watch your watch. Many races have each mile marked but only give times every 5 miles. Wear your runner's watch so you can monitor your pace. You can't always depend on the times given along the course being accurate. Markers are sometimes misplaced, but you should be able to quickly detect major errors since you will know approximately what time you should arrive at each mile. Be prepared, keep an eye on your watch, and don't panic if some mile markers or splits seem to be off. By regularly consulting a watch, you help yourself concentrate on the race; you keep in tune with your goal pace. Play a little game: See how close you can come to running mile after mile at the same pace. It's not always the same effort, however, to run at the same pace. Be prepared for slower mile splits when running up hills or into headwinds as well as faster times with downhills and tail winds.

Walking. If your training hasn't been sufficient, the weather is very hot, you're struggling on hills, or you're just having a bad day, take walk breaks if necessary. Most likely you won't be alone. Over the last few miles, walk breaks may be the key to surviving. Try alternating running with walking if your body just can't keep running nonstop. Better to finish than to stubbornly run until you can't take another step, or cause serious injury. But it's better still if you've trained and paced yourself properly so walking isn't needed.

A few trainers promote planned walk breaks at each mile mark during marathons. They claim even experienced runners will run faster times this way—with walk breaks of 15 seconds to a minute per mile. True, this strategy will keep runners who can't hold back the pace from starting too fast and dying too soon. It'll help undertrained runners finish stronger; otherwise they run as long as they can and then walk. By then they can't walk very fast either. This planned walk approach is appealing to runners that don't or won't put in the necessary time to train properly. So if you want to take it easy for whatever reason, go ahead—walk-run the marathon. But don't brag to people that you ran the marathon. You participated, enjoyed yourself, and finished. That's an achievement and has its own rewards. But to be a conquering hero, train to do your best. To do that, you'll need to race the marathon on the run.

The first few miles: Test the water. Ease into the race both in terms of your running pace and emotional involvement. Look at the first 2 miles as a warm-up run, shortening your race to 24 miles. Slow down gradually and remain calm if you find that your first mile or two are too quick. Emotionally, stay as calm as possible. Save your mental energy for the second half of the race when you'll need it to convince your body to keep going. Try to get in with a pack of runners who are flowing comfortably and help each other. You have some room to let your mind wander, but don't let the pace slip. Start looking for your competitors, but resist the urge to race too early. The marathon is more a race of attrition than head-to-head battles. Don't be lured into chasing your competitors if they're going too fast. Let them go. Most likely you'll catch up to them later—at your pace.

By 5 miles you should be into a good flow. From here to 10 miles is a good test. Hopefully, you'll feel comfortable at goal pace. But it's too early to get cocky! If your goal pace is already tough, you're in trouble. Either your goals were way higher than your fitness, the course or weather too difficult, or you're just having a bad day. Try slowing the pace slightly. Perhaps you'll feel better later in sufficient time to get back on pace. Stubbornly pushing ahead during the first half will lead to an even slower, more miserable second half. Look around you. You may still be doing well compared to your peers even if you're not able to hold your desired pace.

Halfway analysis. This is a critical point psychologically for most runners. If you hit the halfway mark at or slightly ahead of goal time and feel pretty good, you get a mental lift. If you are slightly behind schedule, don't panic. You may still be able to run a negative split and reach your goal. If you're on pace but struggling, or way off your mark, readjust your time goal. You can still finish in a respectable time if you keep your wits and keep working.

The second half: concentration, mental toughness. This is where the race begins, where fatigue tries to capture you. Concentrate on pace, good form, and the runners around you. Keep relaxed, and remain confident and goal-directed. Occasionally change form a little to provide relief. When you hit bad patches where you are physically and mentally fatigued—and you will—hang in there. Don't give in to periods of self-doubt and discomfort. Have faith in your training program. Think about all the work invested in the race. Accept discomfort. It's real. Use all of your mental resources to keep it from slowing you down.

Move from runner to runner to help you maintain a good pace, or "hitch a ride" when a competitor goes by you. Don't be satisfied with just holding your place. Most likely many of the runners around you are slowing down. This presents a mirage. You think you're on pace but you may not be if you're slowing with them.

Bail out. If you are favoring an injury or bad blister, feeling weak and dizzy because of the heat or illness, or are extremely fatigued—use common sense. Bail out and look for medical help.

Don't feel you are a failure by making an intelligent decision to drop out for personal safety. You can always try another marathon down the road.

But if you trained properly and do not feel ill or are not hampered by an injury, keep going. Dig down deep for extra strength. Everyone feels like quitting many times; you are not alone. No one said it would be easy. That's why so many people want to take on the marathon.

"The Wall." This is mostly a myth if you are properly prepared. Most likely you will experience a taste of it somewhere around 20 miles—the approximate point where glycogen supplies run low. But if you followed the Wall-beating guidelines in Chapter 21—trained well, tapered, carbo-loaded, didn't start too fast, and took in sports drinks and gels since just before the start of the race—you will pass through "the Wall" in reasonably good shape.

10K to go. You pass two key mile markers in the marathon: halfway and 20 miles. 13.1 miles is halfway in distance, but the final 10K seems like half the race or more in effort. Running 20 miles is something you've done several times in training. You know you can do it. But few runners have run 26.2 miles in training, nor should they. Here is the reason I recommend a few training runs of 22 to 24 miles. They put you on your feet for the approximate time period for your marathon, better preparing you physiologically and psychologically for the rigors of the last 10K of the marathon.

From here on it's a new race, a 10K. Of course, it isn't anywhere near the same effort as starting a 6.2-mile race without already logging 20 long miles. But convince your mind that you are familiar with the 10K distance and use that now as a distance goal. Now, the mind must take over from the body. Outrun fatigue and discomfort by using the mental techniques detailed in Chapter 27. You've come this far and your body certainly will be tired. The willpower that forced you to train through heat, cold, rain, and snow now be unleashed. Keep pumping the arms and picking up the feet. Somehow you will keep going forward if you can keep the arms and legs in motion.

Break up the course now mile marker by mile marker, landmark by landmark, even block by block—but keep knocking them off, counting down the miles to the mile-to-go marker, then the

26-mile sign, and then the finish line. Work on the runners around you; use them to push or pull you along. Think in terms of time left until the finish. First get under the 30-minutes-to-go barrier, then 20, then 15, and finally 10: You know you can suffer for these amounts of time which may seem less threatening than mileage to go.

Establish a time goal for the 25-mile mark, and what time you'll need to run from there to the finish to meet your goal. It'll give you something to key on. For example, if you're trying to average under 8 minutes per mile for the marathon, with even pacing you'll hit 25 miles in 3:20. That'll give you 10 minutes to get to the finish line. Hit that mark in 3:19, you'll have an extra minute to spare; arrive in 3:21, you'll have to push it in under 9 minutes. This mental game gives you a boost to help spur you to the finish.

The finish. As you cross the 26-mile mark you have only 385 yards—less than a quarter mile—to go. Use the noise of the crowd and the spirit of the runners around you to energize one last push. But don't surge too fast. I've seen many poor souls cramp up within reach of the finish as a result of a sudden sprint. Keep the push steady. Work the arms and lift the knees. Keep this in mind as you're getting close to the finish: In marathons seconds don't count as much as minutes, but seconds can make the difference in being, for example, a 2:59 marathoner or a 3:00 marathoner. That is, run 2:59:59 and you can say you're a "2:59 marathoner."

As you catch sight of the digital clock over the finish, use it to pull you in to your personal victory. Don't forget to stop your watch when you cross the line (but try to do it while not looking down or you will ruin photos of you finishing): It may be a long time before you get the official results. Believe it or not, fatigued runners often forget to stop their watch, and then they don't remember the exact time that was on the finish clock. Most importantly don't forget to congratulate the runners around you who helped you in and, of course, congratulate yourself on a job well done. Way to go, conquering heroes and heroines!

CHAPTER 24

The Aftermarathon

This is the unglamorous recovery and rebuilding stage which starts when you cross the finish line. Most runners carefully plan their training going into marathons, but few plan for the aftermarathon. After all, you're tired and the mind is undisciplined. Your goal has been achieved. A postmarathon runner is very vulnerable to injury and illness in the days and weeks that follow. How well you are able to return to good running is determined by the following:

Fitness, experience, age. The better your training and the more experienced you are at marathoning, the better the odds are you'll recover sooner. Generally, a high-mileage runner recovers faster than a low-mileage runner. Age also slows recovery.

Prerace injuries (or those that occur during the race). If you take a chance and run a marathon when injured or ill, the odds are high you'll be a double loser. You'll likely run poorly and make the condition worse, laying you up for several weeks.

Flexibility and muscular strength. The marathon severely taxes runners with poor flexibility and relatively weak muscles. Recovery will take longer.

Race pacing, fueling, hydration. Starting too fast or insufficient fuel and fluid intake affect recovery. So, too, does hot, humid weather and lots of downhills.

Postrace recovery procedures. Your job isn't over at the finish line. Fight the urge to lie down, hoping the pain and fatigue will go away. Force yourself to begin the very important but largely neglected postmarathon recovery process. If you fail to take care of your aching, glycogen-depleted, dehydrated body, recovery will take longer.

THE FIRST FEW HOURS AND DAYS

What's more painful than running a marathon?—the fatigue and soreness you experience as soon as you stop and over the next few hours and days. Expect it; it's part of the deal. You may really want to just lay down and brag and/or moan about your marathon while you lick your wounds, but you can lessen the agony and quicken recovery by taking the following steps. You have four immediate concerns: rehydrating, refueling, treating injuries and blisters, and delayed-onset muscle soreness (DOMS).

Keep moving when you finish. You usually have to anyway to get out of the chutes and to the baggage claim or family reunion area. Put on dry, warm clothes to prevent stiffness and increase comfort, drink fluids, and take in carbs as soon as possible. Unless too injured or dehydrated, keep walking for a total of a mile or so (about 15 to 20 minutes) after the race. Then, do what your body really wants to do—sit or lie down in the shade. Continue eating and drinking. Have any blisters or injuries treated immediately by medical personnel at the finish area. Apply ice to any painful areas, and repeat the process along with taking ibuprofen for the next few hours (and days) to combat inflammation. When sitting or lying down, keep your feet elevated, and don't stay in one position for too long: You might not be able to get out of it! After you have gained some strength, go for another 10- to 20-minute walk and eat and drink some more. Do some very light stretching, but don't overstretch fatigued muscles.

Go ahead, hang around after the race to celebrate with others for a while. Share the stories of agony and glory. As soon as you've gathered the strength, or friends have arrived to assist you, head for your home or hotel. Force yourself into the shower. You'll feel better once you do. Some find that a hot bath or whirlpool relaxes them, aiding recovery. Many experts advise against it since it may increase inflammation and body temperature. They suggest something I refuse to try: cold showers or baths. If you do take a hot bath, treat any injured areas first with ice. Nap if you can sneak one in. You may not fall asleep, but just resting with your eyes shut will help with restoration. Later in the day, go for another walk (15 to 30 minutes) and stretch lightly, or swim to combat stiffness and help you relax. Shelly-lynn's solution to movement and relaxation: going shopping. Every good effort deserves a reward!

The morning after take a bath to relax, but remember to treat injured areas with ice first. Take a walk and do more gentle stretching. A professional massage 24 to 48 hours after the race and then again in a few days helps speed recovery. Get plenty of sleep for several days. Go to bed early, and take naps if possible. It is extremely important to get more than the normal amount of sleep to boost immunity (which will be down) and help your traumatized body heal. For the first few days after a marathon, runners often have trouble sleeping due to the excitement, although some sleep much more deeply and longer than normal. If you have trouble sleeping, at least lay in bed and rest often. Don't worry about oversleeping, your body deserves the extra shut-eye.

REFUELING AND REHYDRATING

As soon as possible after finishing, drink at least 16 ounces of fluids and consume 50 to 100 grams of carbs. Continue drinking and reloading with carbs over the next few hours and days. Make sure to include some protein to enhance glycogen replacement and repair damaged muscle tissue. According to Dr. David Costill, "Probably the first meal after the marathon should be like the last big meal before. It often takes three to five days to recover the glycogen. That's part of the problem of recovering from a marathon. A lot of people don't go after the carbohydrates hard enough, and that is part of the cause for the fatigue and difficulties getting back into running form again." Follow the general guidelines for refueling and rehydrating after races as detailed in Chapters 33 and 34.

REBUILDING—GETTING BACK TO RUNNING AND RACING

Beware of a false high you may experience a few days after a strong marathon effort. Hold back. Even if you feel strong, you're not. A rule of thumb is to take one recovery day for every mile that you race. Thus, you'll need about twenty-six days—a month or so—to rebuild. Some runners may recover sooner; some need longer. You may recover more quickly from one marathon than another. Biopsies done on marathoners have shown muscle cells take up to a month to recover from the microscopic damage inflicted during a race. Besides recovering from muscle soreness and blisters, you need time to restore body chemistry and glycogen stores to normal levels, and regain the desire to train for the next challenge.

Recovery deserves as much planning as your premarathon schedule. Think of it as the premarathon taper in reverse—a few off days, then a few short runs, then a gradual increase in weekly mileage until you reach your normal, premarathon peak level. Many veterans insist on running the next day, perhaps even the evening of the marathon. They believe it helps them recover sooner. But a study by Dr. Costill at Ball State University in Indiana indicates you may be better off not even running a step for the first week. Researchers compared a group that didn't run for a week with a group that ran easily for 20 to 40 minutes a day. The nonrunners scored better in tests for muscle strength and endurance three days and a week after the marathon.

I recommend that you not run for three to seven days after a marathon even if you feel good enough. Why compel the body to run on blistered feet and tired, sore legs? Don't pound away on muscles that need time to repair. If you think some exercise will help you recover by forcing blood to your legs, or to satisfy your habit, stick to 30 to 60 minutes of nonimpact aerobic exercise. Swimming is particularly good because of its natural massaging action. Frequent walks help, too, whether several short ones throughout the day or longer ones of an hour or more.

After three to four days of nonrunning, you may be ready to run easy (on soft surfaces if possible) for 2 to 4 miles per day the rest of the week. It may be a good choice to run every other day, or to alternate running and walking. Increase mileage the second week to no more than 25 to 50 percent of normal and to no more than 50 to 75 percent during the third and fourth postmarathon week (but less than this is okay). By the fourth or fifth week you may be ready to resume normal mileage. For example, this may be 40 miles a week compared to 50 miles when at peak marathon training.

Forget about how fast you run for a while. Run easy according to how you feel. The first goal is to gradually get back to running comfortably at your normal training pace without undue stiffness or soreness. Speed training isn't necessary for a month or more if you have no immediate race goals—and perhaps you shouldn't. But if you want to return to running fast sooner, ease into speedwork. If your body is ready and willing, about ten to fourteen days after the marathon a light speed workout, such as a controlled fartlek or tempo run, will help you ease into quicker running. Repeat this (or put it off) the next week, or try a few long intervals at 10K pace or slower. By the fourth or fifth week, you may be able to run harder speed sessions.

If at any point during this four-week "reverse taper," you feel unduely fatigued or sore, then run less. Take plenty of extra rest days until you're back to normal. Don't run if favoring an injury—you'll do even more damage than usual due to post-marathon muscle damage. Remember, recovery is your priority for at least four weeks after a marathon. There's no need to rush: Research shows you won't lose much, if any, fitness by cutting back for a month.

Even if you ran a good race, you may feel depressed for a few weeks. Just as in postpartum depression, your "baby" has reached the finish line and your long-sought-after goal, around which your life revolved for months, has been achieved, leaving you feeling empty. It's okay to take some time off from serious running and enjoy activities that you had to give up because you were spending so much of your nonworking time running. Cutting out speed training, racing, long runs, and higher mileage for a few weeks or months may be a good investment in your future training. Maintain minimal mileage levels, however, by doing a few easy runs per week.

WHAT'S NEXT?

Almost every marathoner, from Novice to Elite, swears at the finish line (or perhaps sooner): "Never again." It's that draining, physically and mentally. If you choose to enjoy shorter races and retire from rigorous marathoning, that's fine. You're a hero for life for achieving challenging marathon goals. But many runners catch the marathon bug. They want to explore different marathon courses—with all the excitement that comes with the travel. For some, it becomes a vendetta: Getting even with that marathon monster. For others, its a new challenge: further improving PRs.

What's the best way to improve your marathon performance? Don't do what many runners attempt—jump into the next marathon they can find to try to lower their time. It may work, but it's more likely to result in injury and failure. Besides getting lucky with good weather, your best bet to improve is to take a break from marathon training and lower your times for shorter distances. Improve 10K and half-marathon PRs and come back to marathon training a faster, more complete runner. Then, aim to increase mileage and the number of long runs slightly above your previous marathon training cycle to become stronger, while continuing to work on speed training. Improve your mental training and racing strategy, too. So then you'll be both faster and stronger, smarter and more confident. And hungry. Go for it!

Most marathoners shouldn't race any distance for at least four weeks. Ideally, another marathon shouldn't be considered for at least six months, preferably a year for first timers; some experienced marathoners may be able to run another marathon in three or four months. If you marathon too often and too close together, you increase risk of injury and decrease the chances for a good performance.

Okay, I'm asked this question a lot: How to adjust training for a second marathon in a few months? If you insist on it, first recover adequately for a month following the guidelines in this chapter, then gradually build up mileage until you're back on the schedule you followed for the last month or two before your previous marathon. You don't need to be concerned about long runs for at least a month since the marathon itself takes care of that. But then a long run every other week is recommended along with a race or two to determine sharpness.

PART VI

MENTAL ASPECTS OF COMPETITIVE RUNNING

CHAPTER 25

Goal-Setting and Race Time Prediction

Goal-setting is one of the most powerful tools any runner can use to improve performance. Goals challenge you, mark progress, keep you going. They become the framework that guides training and competition.

Competitive runners have three goals: finishing, running a good time (perhaps a personal record), and placing high among their peers. For the first-time racer and marathoner, the goal is finishing. For most veteran competitors, the goal isn't finishing or winning, but improving their times. In effect, they race against themselves.

Choose both short- and long-term objectives. Short-term goals may include your next race or series of races. These stepping stones bring you closer and closer to your final goals for the racing season. Successes and failures in reaching short-term goals provide critical feedback for adjusting long-term goals. Long-term goals provide general direction over the course of a racing season or longer. The most important goal you set is the one for a year from now. This goal should change as you improve, but always be a year away—a carrot dangling out of reach guiding you in the direction of improvement. By reserving a goal or two for the future, you won't be in a rush to try to do too much too soon.

The value of setting goals is cumulative. As you reach your first goals, you gain confidence and become inspired to challenge yourself further and work toward higher ambitions. You move step by step toward seemingly unreachable long-term objectives. For example, the goal for my first marathon was just to finish, then it became qualifying for the Boston Marathon (3½ hours in those days), then breaking three hours, and finally breaking 2½ hours. When I crossed the finish line of my first marathon in 3:36:31, I certainly thought it impossible for me to ever run an hour faster.

Goals should be challenging, but realistic. A goal that is too easy and quickly attained provides no sense of accomplishment. But a goal set too high only leads to frustration and disappointment. Be realistic about your talent, fitness level, and ability to do the quantity and quality of training necessary to achieve goals. Factor your lifestyle into goal setting. Base goals, for example, on how much training you can accomplish with a full-time job and a family rather than if you were single or only worked part-time. If your family or career takes too much time and energy from training to achieve lofty running ambitions, back off and postpone serious training until it can better blend in with the rest of your life. There is a big difference between realistic goals and ideal goals. Few of us train under ideal conditions.

Establish several goals for each race. That will increase the opportunities for success. Set a goal for both time and place, or for time splits along the way. You might, for example, miss your time goal but still place well.

Setting goals is the first step. Then commit to them! You can't just dream about running fast times; you have to work hard to produce a great performance. Choose goals you believe in, that you will pursue with dedicated training. The stronger the commitment, the better your chance of success.

Build flexibility into your goals and continuously evaluate how you're doing. Don't expect to reach goal time after goal time at a rapid rate of improvement. Most often progress comes quickly at first and then more slowly, in amounts that will still be satisfying. Runners often reach plateaus, or even regress slightly, before moving ahead again. Reassess goals frequently and, if necessary, adjust goal times or how long you give yourself to meet them. You will attain many of your goals and miss others. But at least you will have the satisfaction of knowing you tried to reach them all.

COACH GLOVER'S THREE-GOAL SYSTEM

For each race, establish three goals:

The acceptable goal represents a minimum—for example, improving your best time by a small amount, or completing your longest race. It may take into account factors of weather, training, personal health, and so forth. It represents reasonable progress. This may not always be a personal record (PR) for the distance, but it may show improvement for your current racing season.

The challenging goal represents a significant improvement. It's a tough but realistic goal requiring you to put in solid training and a strong effort. It's reachable if everything goes well. For example, improving your 10K time by a solid margin, or running your best quality race of the year. Determine challenging goals by analyzing recent workouts and races and comparing them to past training and race times.

The ultimate goal is your dream time—a performance that represents a major breakthrough. If everything goes perfectly on race day, maybe you can hit this very demanding goal. Usually it takes at least six months to a year to reach this goal. It may be a long-term rather than a short-term project. But "going for it" and "popping" one of these fast times may allow you to enter a new dimension as an athlete.

Use the race time comparison and prediction system detailed in Figures 25.1–25.2 to help establish goals. Don't be satisfied with setting a "soft" PR if your training and other race times indicate you're capable of more. Also, look at what your peers are doing. If your teammates and competitors make significant improvements, maybe you can too. The saying "What you can conceive you can achieve" fits here. Go for it!

GOAL-SETTING FACTORS

Prerace goals and postrace analysis should take into consideration many factors. The goal in some cases may be to just finish feeling strong rather than to make an improvement. Factors that influence goal-setting include fitness level, aging, weather, course difficulty, physical and mental health, and number of runners in the race and spectators along the course.

RECORD AND MAKE PUBLIC YOUR GOALS

To be effective, goals need to be specific and measurable. Write them down in advance and adjust them as you record actual race times. Use a training diary for this purpose or make a simple chart like the one below to establish tangible, written goals.

Date	Race Distance: 10K Acceptable Goal	Personal Record: 51:00 Challenging Goal	Ultimate Goal
Short-term (within 30 days)	50:30	50	49
Intermediate (within 3 months)	50	49:30	48
Long-term (in 1 year)	49	48	45

In the above example, the runner has established a realistic goal system that is quite flexible. The 10K goal times present a solid challenge to motivate the runner to keep training. This runner may progress faster or slower than this goal system so adjustments along the way should be made. By establishing written goals, this runner is more likely to succeed. So are you. Establish a separate chart for each of your key racing distances. Adjust your goals as race times improve. Compare performances at different distances using the charts in Figures 25.1–25.2 to help establish new goals at all distances after a good race.

Post your goals where you will see them often: on your refrigerator or bathroom mirror for example. Carry written goals in your wallet or purse and pull them out to review often. Make your goals public. Make a claim, and then you are forced to back it up! Running partners and teammates with similar goals can be a great help here. At least share your goals with a friend or family member who can provide support and motivate you to achieve them. Going it alone is a tougher route to your goal.

PREDICTING RACE TIMES

Knowing in advance what your finishing time *should* be—approximately—and therefore what your starting pace should be, is a great advantage. When predicting future race times from previous ones, consider all of the above factors related to goal-setting. Be fair to yourself. Disregard super race times which are questionable measures of performance owing to special circumstances: strong tail wind, downhill course, or the possibility of a short course. With experience at measuring the factors that influence race times, and a feel for your ability, race-prediction systems can help you accurately forecast racing times.

There are many systems available to predict race times. Of course they are only estimates and their reliability depends on comparing performances on similar courses and in similar weather conditions. They also depend on specificity of training. You can't predict 5K times from longer distances if you don't put in adequate fast speed training, and you can't predict marathon times from shorter distances if you don't put in enough mileage and long runs.

Many prediction systems are based on statistics which relate how much we slow down over distance. They are formulated after analyzing thousands of race times. One of the best of these is contained in the classic *Computerized Running Training Program* by James B. Gardner and J. Gerry Purdy, first printed in 1970. Their amazingly accurate charts detail race time comparisons from 100 meters to 50K. Some simplified formulas are fairly reliable. Here are some examples:

- **To predict 10K times from 5K times,** multiply 5K time by 2 and add 1½ minutes. To predict 5K times from 10K times, reverse the formula: Subtract 1½ minutes from 10K time and divide by 2. These formulas seem to work best for those racing between 6 and 8 minutes per mile for 5K. Faster runners should subtract about 1 minute; slower runners about 2 minutes.
- **To predict 10-mile times from 5-mile times,** multiply 5-mile times by 2 and add 3 minutes. To predict 5-mile times from 10-mile times, reverse the formula: Subtract 3 minutes from 10-mile time and divide by 2.
- **To predict marathon times from 10K times,** the ratio of approximately 1:5 exists between 10K times and marathon times. Starting with a 10K time of 30 minutes equaling a marathon of 2:20, add 5 minutes for every change of 1 minute in 10K time.
- **To predict marathon times from half-marathon times,** multiply the half-marathon time by 2 and add 10 minutes. Or, to reverse it, subtract 10 minutes from marathon time and divide by 2 to yield half-marathon time.

RACE TIME COMPARISON AND PREDICTOR CHARTS

The performance charts in Figures 25.1–25.2 are highlighted here because they are simple to use and understand. They establish scores for runners of all ability levels at popular race distances from 5K to the marathon. A perfect score is 1,000 points, which is 100 percent of the world record for each race distance when the charts were compiled. All other scores represent a percentage of this standard. For example, 510 points for a male runner who runs 25:25 for 5K is 51 percent of the world record standard time of 12:58:4. Statistical analyses of race times for all levels of runners demonstrate that runners tend to perform at a constant percentage of the world record at all distances. In other words, the runner noted above would race at about 51 percent of world record pace for distances from 5K to the marathon.

These charts can be used for three important purposes:

1. **Predict race times and establish race goals.** If your training is of equal quality for different distances, you can predict your race times from a recent race. For example, a woman runs 21:03 for a 5K a month prior to a 10K race. That's a 720-point-value performance equal to a 41:17 for 10K. She can use this information to establish her race time goal and starting pace for the 10K. The predictor charts are more accurate the closer the racing distances. For example, it is much more accurate to predict a 5-mile or 10K result from a 5K race than from a marathon, or a marathon from a half-marathon result than from a 5K. Time predictions are most accurate when based on your performance in a series of races peaking for a big race.
2. **Analyze race results.** After you have finished the race, analyze your time and compare it with recent races at the same and other distances. When making time comparisons, adjust for weather as well as course difficulty. If your score has improved, then you've moved up a notch. Record in your diary your race time, pace per mile, and performance score. Use this information to set goals for your next races.
3. **Rate best performances for all distances.** Use the chart to compare lifetime PRs as well as best times for each racing season. You can compare scores between different race distances to determine your best racing distance or

range. The charts may reveal more ability or better training at certain distances. Example: A runner scores 600 points for 5K, 570 for 10K, and 520 for the marathon. The frequency of racing a certain distance is likely to result in superior scores at that distance. For example, if you race 5Ks often you are more familiar with the intensity and pacing required and thus are likely to score higher than with a longer distance that you race only occasionally. Further, you are more likely to score your best after at least one recent "practice" race at that distance.

The charts can be used to compare male and female times on an equal basis. For example, a female's 750-point score for a 5K time of 19:11 is equal to a male's time of 17:17. At distances beyond half-marathon, statistical time differences between men and women become more sizeable and favor women over men. According to the numbers, if a man and woman have similar 10K times the woman will outscore the man in the marathon. For example, a 10K time of 40:15 for a male predicts a 3:09:18 marathon; and a 10K time of 40:09 for a female predicts a 3:06:23 marathon. So, if you guys have been hanging on to a group of women in shorter races, be prepared to see them leave you in the dust in longer races! See Chapter 38 for age-adjusted time comparisons.

Race times on a track are usually about 10 points faster than a flat, certified road race at the same distance. A score of 750 points (19:11) for a female on a flat 5K road race is approximately equal to a score of 760 points (18:56) on the track. Cross-country times run on dirt or grass tend to be at least 10 points slower than a road race of the same distance and difficulty. But since most cross-country courses are unforgivably hilly, don't forget to adjust the comparison further. I find my 5K times over the rugged Van Cortlandt Park trails in the Bronx are at least a minute slower than most paved courses.

NOTE: If your race time falls between 2 point scores, either round off to the nearest score or interpolate to establish an intermediate score. These charts are based purely on race time statistics and should be used as a general guide. Other charts and systems may yield slightly different results.

FIGURE 25.1: MEN'S RACE TIME COMPARISON AND PREDICTOR CHART

Rating	5K	8K/5M	10K	15K	10M	20K	½ Marathon	Marathon
1000	0:12:58	0:21:19	0:26:58	0:41:26	0:44:40	0:56:20	0:59:03	2:06:50
820	0:15:49	0:26:00	0:32:53	0:50:32	0:54:28	1:08:42	1:12:01	2:34:40
810	0:16:00	0:26:19	0:33:18	0:51:09	0:55:09	1:09:33	1:12:54	2:36:35
800	0:16:12	0:26:39	0:33:42	0:51:47	0:55:50	1:10:25	1:13:49	2:38:32
795	0:16:19	0:26:49	0:33:55	0:52:07	0:56:11	1:10:52	1:14:17	2:39:32
790	0:16:25	0:26:59	0:34:08	0:52:27	0:56:32	1:11:18	1:14:45	2:40:33
785	0:16:31	0:27:09	0:34:21	0:52:47	0:56:54	1:11:46	1:15:13	2:41:34
780	0:16:37	0:27:20	0:34:34	0:53:07	0:57:16	1:12:13	1:15:42	2:42:36
775	0:16:44	0:27:30	0:34:48	0:53:28	0:57:38	1:12:41	1:16:12	2:43:39
770	0:16:50	0:27:41	0:35:01	0:53:49	0:58:01	1:13:10	1:16:41	2:44:43
765	0:16:57	0:27:52	0:35:15	0:54:10	0:58:23	1:13:38	1:17:11	2:45:48
760	0:17:04	0:28:03	0:35:29	0:54:31	0:58:46	1:14:07	1:17:42	2:46:53
755	0:17:10	0:28:14	0:35:43	0:54:53	0:59:10	1:14:37	1:18:13	2:47:59
750	0:17:17	0:28:25	0:35:57	0:55:15	0:59:33	1:15:07	1:18:44	2:49:07
745	0:17:24	0:28:37	0:36:12	0:55:37	0:59:57	1:15:37	1:19:16	2:50:15
740	0:17:31	0:28:48	0:36:26	0:55:59	1:00:22	1:16:08	1:19:48	2:51:24
735	0:17:39	0:29:00	0:36:41	0:56:22	1:00:46	1:16:39	1:20:20	2:52:34
730	0:17:46	0:29:12	0:36:56	0:56:45	1:01:11	1:17:10	1:20:53	2:53:45
725	0:17:53	0:29:24	0:37:12	0:57:09	1:01:37	1:17:42	1:21:27	2:54:57
720	0:18:01	0:29:36	0:37:27	0:57:33	1:02:02	1:18:14	1:22:01	2:56:09
715	0:18:08	0:29:49	0:37:43	0:57:57	1:02:28	1:18:47	1:22:35	2:57:23
710	0:18:16	0:30:01	0:37:59	0:58:21	1:02:55	1:19:21	1:23:10	2:58:38
705	0:18:24	0:30:14	0:38:15	0:58:46	1:03:21	1:19:54	1:23:46	2:59:54
700	0:18:31	0:30:27	0:38:31	0:59:11	1:03:49	1:20:29	1:24:21	3:01:11
695	0:18:39	0:30:40	0:38:48	0:59:37	1:04:16	1:21:03	1:24:58	3:02:30
690	0:18:48	0:30:54	0:39:05	1:00:03	1:04:44	1:21:39	1:25:35	3:03:49
685	0:18:56	0:31:07	0:39:22	1:00:29	1:05:12	1:22:14	1:26:12	3:05:09
680	0:19:04	0:31:21	0:39:39	1:00:56	1:05:41	1:22:51	1:26:50	3:06:31
675	0:19:13	0:31:35	0:39:57	1:01:23	1:06:10	1:23:27	1:27:29	3:07:54
670	0:19:21	0:31:49	0:40:15	1:01:50	1:06:40	1:24:05	1:28:08	3:09:18
665	0:19:30	0:32:03	0:40:33	1:02:18	1:07:10	1:24:43	1:28:48	3:10:44
660	0:19:39	0:32:18	0:40:52	1:02:47	1:07:41	1:25:21	1:29:28	3:12:10
655	0:19:48	0:32:33	0:41:10	1:03:15	1:08:12	1:26:00	1:30:09	3:13:38
650	0:19:57	0:32:48	0:41:29	1:03:45	1:08:43	1:26:40	1:30:51	3:15:08
645	0:20:06	0:33:03	0:41:49	1:04:14	1:09:15	1:27:20	1:31:33	3:16:38
640	0:20:16	0:33:18	0:42:08	1:04:44	1:09:48	1:28:01	1:32:16	3:18:11
635	0:20:25	0:33:34	0:42:28	1:05:15	1:10:20	1:28:43	1:33:00	3:19:44
630	0:20:35	0:33:50	0:42:48	1:05:46	1:10:54	1:29:25	1:33:44	3:21:19
625	0:20:45	0:34:06	0:43:09	1:06:18	1:11:28	1:30:08	1:34:29	3:22:56

FIGURE 25.1: MEN'S RACE TIME COMPARISON AND PREDICTOR CHART (continued)

Rating	5K	8K/5M	10K	15K	10M	20K	½ Marathon	Marathon
620	0:20:55	0:34:23	0:43:30	1:06:50	1:12:03	1:30:52	1:35:15	3:24:34
615	0:21:05	0:34:40	0:43:51	1:07:22	1:12:38	1:31:36	1:36:01	3:26:14
610	0:21:15	0:34:57	0:44:12	1:07:55	1:13:13	1:32:21	1:36:48	3:27:55
605	0:21:26	0:35:14	0:44:34	1:08:29	1:13:50	1:33:07	1:37:36	3:29:39
600	0:21:37	0:35:32	0:44:57	1:09:03	1:14:27	1:33:53	1:38:25	3:31:23
595	0:21:48	0:35:50	0:45:19	1:09:38	1:15:04	1:34:41	1:39:15	3:33:10
590	0:21:59	0:36:08	0:45:42	1:10:14	1:15:42	1:35:29	1:40:05	3:34:58
585	0:22:10	0:36:26	0:46:06	1:10:50	1:16:21	1:36:18	1:40:56	3:36:49
580	0:22:21	0:36:45	0:46:30	1:11:26	1:17:01	1:37:08	1:41:49	3:38:41
575	0:22:33	0:37:04	0:46:54	1:12:03	1:17:41	1:37:58	1:42:42	3:40:35
570	0:22:45	0:37:24	0:47:19	1:12:41	1:18:22	1:38:50	1:43:36	3:42:31
565	0:22:57	0:37:44	0:47:44	1:13:20	1:19:03	1:39:42	1:44:31	3:44:29
560	0:23:09	0:38:04	0:48:09	1:13:59	1:19:46	1:40:36	1:45:27	3:46:29
555	0:23:22	0:38:25	0:48:35	1:14:39	1:20:29	1:41:30	1:46:24	3:48:32
550	0:23:35	0:38:45	0:49:02	1:15:20	1:21:13	1:42:25	1:47:22	3:50:36
545	0:23:48	0:39:07	0:49:29	1:16:01	1:21:57	1:43:22	1:48:21	3:52:43
540	0:24:01	0:39:29	0:49:56	1:16:44	1:22:43	1:44:19	1:49:21	3:54:53
535	0;24:14	0:39:51	0:50:24	1:17:27	1:23:29	1:45:18	1:50:22	3:57:04
530	0:24:28	0:40:13	0:50:53	1:18:11	1:24:17	1:46:17	1:51:25	3:59:18
525	0:24:42	0:40:36	0:51:22	1:18:55	1:25:05	1:47:18	1:52:29	4:01:35
520	0:24:56	0:41:00	0:51:52	1:19:41	1:25:54	1:48:20	1:53:33	4:03:55
515	0:25:11	0:41:23	0:52:22	1:20:27	1:26:44	1:49:23	1:54:40	4:06:17
510	0:25:25	0:41:48	0:52:53	1:21:15	1:27:35	1:50:27	1:55:47	4:08:42
505	0:25:41	0:42:13	0:53:24	1:22:03	1:28:27	1:51:33	1:56:56	4:11:09
500	0:25:56	0:42:38	0:53:56	1:22:52	1:29:20	1:52:40	1:58:06	4:13:40
495	0:26:12	0:43:04	0:54:29	1:23:42	1:30:14	1:53:48	1:59:18	4:16:14
490	0:26:28	0:43:30	0:55:02	1:24:33	1:31:09	1:54:58	2:00:31	4:18:51
485	0:26:44	0:43:57	0:55:36	1:25:26	1:32:06	1:56:09	2:01:45	4:21:31
480	0:27:01	0:44:25	0:56:11	1:26:19	1:33:03	1:57:22	2:03:01	4:24:14
475	0:27:18	0:44:53	0:56:46	1:27:14	1:34:02	1:58:36	2:04:19	4:27:01
470	0:27:35	0:45:21	0:57:23	1:28:09	1:35:02	1:59:51	2:05:38	4:29:51
465	0:27:53	0:45:51	0:58:00	1:29:06	1:36:03	2:01:09	2:06:59	4:32:46
460	0:28:11	0:46:20	0:58:37	1:30:04	1:37:06	2:02:28	2:08:22	4:35:43
455	0:28:30	0:46:51	0:59:16	1:31:04	1:38:10	2:03:49	2:09:47	4:38:45
450	0:28:49	0:47:22	0:59:56	1:32:04	1:39:16	2:05:11	2:11:13	4:41:51
445	0:29:08	0:47:54	1:00:36	1:33:07	1:40:22	2:06:36	2:12:42	4:45:01
440	0:29:28	0:48:27	1:01:17	1:34:10	1:41:31	2:08:02	2:14:12	4:48:15
435	0:29:49	0:49:00	1:02:00	1:35:15	1:42:41	2:09:30	2:15:45	4:51:34

FIGURE 25.2: WOMEN'S RACE TIME COMPARISON AND PREDICTOR CHART

Rating	5K	8K/5M	10K	15K	10M	20K	½ Marathon	Marathon
1000	0:14:23	0:23:39	0:29:55	0:45:51	0:49:23	1:02:10	1:05:48	2:18:51
820	0:17:32	0:28:50	0:36:29	0:55:55	1:00:13	1:15:49	1:20:15	2:49:20
810	0:17:45	0:29:12	0:36:56	0:56:36	1:00:58	1:16:45	1:21:14	2:51:25
800	0:17:59	0:29:34	0:37:24	0:57:19	1:01:44	1:17:42	1:22:15	2:53:34
795	0:18:06	0:29:45	0:37:38	0:57:40	1:02:07	1:18:12	1:22:46	2:54:39
790	0:18:12	0:29:56	0:37:52	0:58:02	1:02:31	1:18:42	1:23:17	2:55:46
785	0:18:19	0:30:08	0:38:07	0:58:24	1:02:55	1:19:12	1:23:49	2:56:53
780	0:18:26	0:30:19	0:38:21	0:58:47	1:03:19	1:19:42	1:24:22	2:58:01
775	0:18:34	0:30:31	0:38:36	0:59:10	1:03:43	1:20:13	1:24:54	2:59:10
770	0:18:41	0:30:43	0:38:51	0:59:33	1:04:08	1:20:44	1:25:27	3:00:19
765	0:18:48	0:30:55	0:39:06	0:59:56	1:04:33	1:21:16	1:26:01	3:01:30
760	0:18:56	0:31:07	0:39:22	1:00:20	1:04:59	1:21:48	1:26:35	3:02:42
755	0:19:03	0:31:19	0:39:37	1:00:44	1:05:25	1:22:20	1:27:09	3:03:54
750	0:19:11	0:31:32	0:39:53	1:01:08	1:05:51	1:22:53	1:27:44	3:05:08
745	0:19:18	0:31:45	0:40:09	1:01:33	1:06:17	1:23:27	1:28:19	3:06:23
740	0:19:26	0:31:58	0:40:26	1:01:58	1:06:44	1:24:01	1:28:55	3:07:38
735	0:19:34	0:32:11	0:40:42	1:02:23	1:07:11	1:24:35	1:29:31	3:08:55
730	0:19:42	0:32:24	0:40:59	1:02:48	1:07:39	1:25:10	1:30:08	3:10:12
725	0:19:50	0:32:37	0:41:16	1:03:14	1:08:07	1:25:45	1:30:46	3:11:31
720	0:19:59	0:32:51	0:41:33	1:03:41	1:08:35	1:26:21	1:31:23	3:12:51
715	0:20:07	0:33:05	0:41:50	1:04:08	1:09:04	1:26:57	1:32:02	3:14:12
710	0:20:15	0:33:19	0:42:08	1:04:35	1:09:33	1:27:34	1:32:41	3:15:34
705	0:20:24	0:33:33	0:42:26	1:05:02	1:10:03	1:28:11	1:33:20	3:16:57
700	0:20:33	0:33:47	0:42:44	1:05:30	1:10:33	1:28:49	1:34:00	3:18:21
695	0:20:42	0:34:02	0:43:03	1:05:58	1:11:03	1:29:27	1:34:41	3:19:47
690	0:20:51	0:34:17	0:43:21	1:06:27	1:11:34	1:30:06	1:35:22	3:21:14
685	0:21:00	0:34:32	0:43:40	1:06:56	1:12:06	1:30:45	1:36:04	3:22:42
680	0:21:09	0:34:47	0:44:00	1:07:26	1:12:37	1:31:25	1:36:46	3:24:11
675	0:21:19	0:35:02	0:44:19	1:07:56	1:13:10	1:32:06	1:37:29	3:25:42
670	0:21:28	0:35:18	0:44:39	1:08:26	1:13:42	1:32:47	1:38:13	3:27:14
665	0:21:38	0:35:34	0:44:59	1:08:57	1:14:16	1:33:29	1:38:57	3:28:48
660	0:21:48	0:35:50	0:45:20	1:09:28	1:14:49	1:34:12	1:39:42	3:30:23
655	0:21:58	0:36:06	0:45:40	1:10:00	1:15:24	1:34:55	1:40:27	3:31:59
650	0:22:08	0:36:23	0:46:02	1:10:32	1:15:58	1:35:38	1:41:14	3:33:37
645	0:22:18	0:36:40	0:46:23	1:11:05	1:16:34	1:36:23	1:42:01	3:35:16
640	0:22:28	0:36:57	0:46:45	1:11:38	1:17:10	1:37:08	1:42:49	3:36:57
635	0:22:39	0:37:15	0:47:07	1:12:12	1:17:46	1:37:54	1:43:37	3:38:40
630	0:22:50	0:37:32	0:47:29	1:12:47	1:18:23	1:38:41	1:44:27	3:40:24
625	0:23:01	0:37:50	0:47:52	1:13:22	1:19:01	1:39:28	1:45:17	3:42:10

FIGURE 25.2: WOMEN'S RACE TIME COMPARISON AND PREDICTOR CHART (continued)

Rating	5K	8K/5M	10K	15K	10M	20K	½ Marathon	Marathon
620	0:23:12	0:38:09	0:48:15	1:13:57	1:19:39	1:40:16	1:46:08	3:43:57
615	0:23:23	0:38:27	0:48:39	1:14:33	1:20:18	1:41:05	1:47:00	3:45:46
610	0:23:35	0:38:46	0:49:03	1:15:10	1:20:57	1:41:55	147:52	3:47:37
605	0:23:46	0:39:05	0:49:27	1:15:47	1:21:38	1:42:45	1:48:46	3:49:30
600	0:23:58	0:39:25	0:49:52	1:16:25	1:22:18	1:43:37	1:49:40	3:51:25
595	0:24:10	0:39:45	0:50:17	1:17:04	1:23:00	1:44:29	1:50:35	3:53:22
590	0:24:23	0:40:05	0:50:42	1:17:43	1:23:42	1:45:22	1:51:32	3:55:20
585	0:24:35	0:40:26	0:51:08	1:18:23	1:24:25	1:46:16	1:52:29	3:57:21
580	0:24:48	0:40:47	0:51:35	1:19:03	1:25:09	1:47:11	1:53:27	3:59:24
575	0:25:01	0:41:08	0:52:02	1:19:44	1:25:53	1:48:07	1:54:26	4:01:29
570	0:25:14	0:41:29	0:52:29	1:20:26	1:26:38	1:49:04	1:55:26	4:03:36
565	0:25:27	0:41:52	0:52:57	1:21:09	1:27:24	1:50:02	1:56:28	4:05:45
560	0:25:41	0:42:14	0:53:25	1:21:52	1:28:11	1:51:01	1:57:30	4:07:57
555	0:25:55	0:42:37	0:53:54	1:22:37	1:28:59	1:52:01	1:58:34	4:10:11
550	0:26:09	0:43:00	0:54:24	1:23:22	1:29:47	1:53:02	1:59:38	4:12:27
545	0:26:23	0:43:24	0:54:54	1:24:08	1:30:37	1:54:04	2:00:44	4:14:46
540	0:26:38	0:43:48	0:55:24	1:24:54	1:31:27	1:55:07	2:01:51	4:17:08
535	0:26:53	0:44:12	0:55:55	1:25:42	1:32:18	1:56:12	2:02:59	4:19:32
530	0:27:08	0:44:37	0:56:27	1:26:31	1:33:11	1:57:18	2:04:09	4:21:59
525	0:27:24	0:45:03	0:56:59	1:27:20	1:34:04	1:58:25	2:05:20	4:24:29
520	0:27:40	0:45:29	0:57:32	1:28:10	1:34:58	1:59:33	2:06:32	4:27:01
515	0:27:56	0:45:55	0:58:05	1:29:02	1:35:53	2:00:43	2:07:46	4:29:37
510	0:28:12	0:46:22	0:58:40	1:29:54	1:36:50	2:01:54	2:09:01	4:32:15
505	0:28:29	0:46:50	0:59:14	1:30:48	1:37:47	2:03:06	2:10:18	4:34:57
500	0:28:46	0:47:18	0:59:50	1:31:42	1:38:46	2:04:20	2:11:36	4:37:42
495	0:29:03	0:47:47	1:00:26	1:32:38	1:39:46	2:05:35	2:12:56	4:40:30
490	0:29:21	0:48:16	1:01:03	1:33:34	1:40:47	2:06:52	2:14:17	4:43:22
485	0:29:39	0:48:46	1:01:41	1:34:32	1:41:49	2:08:11	2:15:40	4:46:17
480	0:29:58	0:49:16	1:02:20	1:35:31	1:42:53	2:09:31	2:17:05	4:49:16
475	0:30:17	0:49:47	1:02:59	1:36:32	1:43:58	2:10:53	2:18:32	4:52:19
470	0:30:36	0:50:19	1:03:39	1:37:33	1:45:04	2:12:16	2:20:00	4:55:26
465	0:30:56	0:50:52	1:04:20	1:38:36	1:46:12	2:13:42	2:21:30	4:58:36
460	0:31:16	0:51:25	1:05:02	1:39:40	1:47:21	2:15:09	2:23:03	5:01:51
455	0:31:37	0:51:59	1:05:45	1:40:46	1:48:32	2:16:38	2:24:37	5:05:10
450	0:31:58	0:52:33	1:06:29	1:41:53	1:49:44	2:18:09	2:26:13	5:08:33
445	0:32:19	0:53:09	1:07:14	1:43:02	1:50:58	2:19:42	2:27:52	5:12:01
440	0:32:41	0:53:45	1:08:00	1:44:12	1:52:14	2:21:17	2:29:33	5:15:34
435	0:33:04	0:54:22	1:08:46	1:45:24	1:53:31	2:22:55	2:31:16	5:19:12

CHAPTER 26

Motivation

Motivation involves having the incentive to keep on going—staying with a training schedule. You need better reasons to continue than excuses to quit. If you're not highly motivated you won't achieve your potential no matter how much physical talent you're blessed with.

What motivates athletes to keep going, to do the hard work necessary to succeed? Sports psychologists break down motivation into two categories: extrinsic and intrinsic. Extrinsic motivation includes rewards such as trophies and prize money, as well as recognition and praise from others. These factors can certainly influence your desire to succeed, but the drive must come from within to produce long-term success. Intrinsic motivation involves a strong inner desire to accomplish goals: feelings of personal accomplishment and pleasure. If competitive running doesn't provide satisfaction and enjoyment, then it will not provide sufficient rewards to keep you in the sport—or at least as a competitor.

Clear, reachable goals—winning an award, achieving a time, finishing your longest race, beating a competitor—give you the focus to train. They provide challenges that peak your interest. But it's hard to keep it up year-round, year after year. Sometimes running loses its zest. The list of excuses may begin to mount: "I don't have the time"; "The weather is too bad"; "I don't have anyone to run with"; "I couldn't stick with a schedule"; or even "It just isn't fun anymore." Add your top excuses to this list. Go ahead; it will make you feel better.

Motivation doesn't just happen. You have to plan it, just like you plan your training schedule. Following are some strategies to improve your motivation, race times, and, most importantly, your enjoyment of running. Try several of them in various combinations, or make up your own.

Are you ready? Well, okay then. Let's get motivated!

COACH GLOVER'S MOTIVATIONAL TIPS

Here are my top motivational tips to keep you going:

Have fun. If you don't, you won't stay with running. Do the majority of your runs at a relaxed pace and enjoy life around you. Or just tune out and escape from the pressures. Maybe you'll even experience that euphoric state called a "runner's high." Doesn't that sound like fun? Don't make running another stress in your life. If you do, you'll burn out and running won't be fun. Instead of thinking "no pain, no gain," think "no fun, no run."

Below are some more tips for enjoying running. Add to them: The amount of fun you can have is only limited by your creativity and enthusiasm.

Run together. The social aspects are one of the key reasons people start, and stick with, running. Training alone can be very demanding. Running with others greatly reduces the mental strain that comes with training. Even though this requires some planning, it's well worth the effort considering all the benefits. Line up a few runners your pace to train with. Dependable, enjoyable training partners are worth their weight in gold. Friendships grow more readily when running with one or two partners at a time, but sometimes the more the merrier. Support each other when the weather turns bad, or when excuses blow in the wind. If you make an appointment with your training partner you are much more likely to get out the door and enjoy a good run. Many runners set a standing date at least once a week. Include a few new running partners from time to time to add variety to your schedule.

Many running clubs have informal group runs that are open to anyone. I used to lead a group run at New York City's West Side YMCA. We'd get as many as 100 runners and many of us would head to the local bar afterward to eat, drink, and be merry. One of our regulars was Robin Williams—back when he was a pretty good runner and an aspiring actor. His sense of humor sure kept running fun for our group!

Our training classes with the New York Road Runners Club attract hundreds of men and women of all ages and abilities. They enjoy the camaraderie of working out together—even through my sometimes grueling workouts. Many come to our classes as much for fellowship reasons as for fitness. They hang out and socialize before, during, and after class. Some show up even if they're injured or coming off a race just so they won't miss the party. And then there is the dedicated pizza crowd. They work hard in class so they can eat guilt free afterward with "the gang."

You may enjoy joining a team. Many offer regular speed sessions and long runs, and an increased source of training partners and social friends. Teams organize exciting trips to races, regular social gatherings, and newsletters full of race results and gossip. Teammates pick each other up and help motivate one another. "Belonging" makes you feel like a better, more dedicated runner. If you feel that way, then you are. Pride in wearing a team uniform and not wanting to let your teammates down can certainly contribute to your performance. When we formed the Greater New York Racing Team I was overwhelmed with how much most of the runners improved. Each runner's success inspired his and her teammates to raise their goals. Just as important, it's fun belonging to a team full of people with similar interests. The biggest benefit from running with a team: the support that members give each other, both athletically and socially.

Whether running with a group or with an individual training partner, observe a few important rules. Don't get in over your head. If you get carried away with the fun and fellowship—or, if not careful, the competitive nature of some runners—you could run too fast or too far. Time and miles fly by when running and talking. But do talk. After all, if you can't run alongside your running partners and talk, why should they run with you? However, if you run too slow too often your fitness will be affected.

Involve family and nonrunning friends. Let them share in the excitement so they can help keep you going. Encourage them to help you with your training and attend races. Having them cheering along the course and waiting at the finish line, and knowing they'll be there, will inspire you to work harder in training and racing.

You can have friends or family keep you company on training runs by riding along on a bike or on inline skates. Nonexercisers can help by meeting at various points along the course to give you drinks and encouragement. Or they can time track workouts. Their help will give you a boost, and respite from the often lonely training.

Use your spouse or friends as a support group. It's their job to help you reach goals by being available to listen to you brag and complain about running and offer cheerful encouragement. But don't let a spouse or friend who is not experienced and qualified at coaching become your coach. Use them as motivational cheerleaders, not running experts, or they could innocently lead you astray. Motivate your supporters to keep up their job, too. Reward them by taking them along for a vacation when you run a race, or buy them a present when you go shopping for running equipment.

Get a coach. A coach, or at least an advisor, is very helpful. He or she can give you feedback about your training, help establish goals, give you pep talks, and listen to you brag about your achievements. If you don't have a coach, use this book to help pep you up, and brag about your achievements to anyone who will listen.

Read about running. Enjoy an inspiring book about running, or pick up a copy of a running magazine and read about successful runners. I love to read about mentally tough Elites such as Emil Zatopek and Steve Prefontaine. Their stories stoke my competitive fires, and I reread them close to big races.

Watch races. You don't have to run in races to be motivated by them. Just watching gets you pumped up. The enthusiasm at races is infectious. Go to a track meet or road race and view the excitement of the up-front racing. Tape highlights of an exciting race on TV and replay them before a race to "feel" yourself in the middle of the action.

Surround yourself with mental stimuli. Find what gets you psyched and surround yourself with it—posters, quotes, photos, videos.

Seek variety. If you do the same thing over and over it gets boring. You don't have to run all the time to be a runner. Cross-training with other aerobic sports may add a dash of fun to your fitness routine. Many runners travel the same course, at the same time of day, day after day. Although such a routine adds discipline, it would be more enjoyable to vary it. Run short some days and longer others; or faster or slower some workouts. You can even vary the same course by running it in the opposite direction—it's amazing how different things look. I often leave my trusty routes to explore new areas. Where does that road lead to? What is at the top of that hill? Tired of the same workouts on the track? Try out the options in the speed training section such as ladders, pyramids, fartlek, and tempo.

Some runners enjoy listening to music as they run. In fact, studies at Springfield College show people who listen to music exercise longer and with less feeling of fatigue. Just be sure to only wear headsets in a safe environment away from car and bike traffic, and potential muggers.

Heart rate monitors are motivational toys. If I've been running alone too much, bringing along a monitor provides a training partner. I'll check it frequently to see if I'm going too fast or too slow, or how my heart responds to the hills. Sometimes I'll challenge myself with it—trying to keep at, above, or below a certain number.

Take off your watch. You'll be surprised how relaxing it is to run with no time goals or restraints. Just run as you feel. Or, run for time, but not over a measured distance.

Race by seasons. You can't be in peak shape or keep highly motivated about training all year. Build to a series of races or one key race, and then take a break. When you feel motivated to start training again, build toward a different goal.

Race a variety of distances. Some runners do one 10K race after another and expect improvement with each race. Others may only train for the 5K or marathon. It becomes increasingly harder to meet time goals and stressful to face yet another race at the same distance. The greater variety of race distances, the more opportunity you have to set PRs. Get away from some of the most common distances, coming back to them when you're hungry to be measured again. Try something new like racing a mile, a relay, or cross-country. Don't run the same races year after year. It's okay to run a favorite race or two each year, but if you race too many of the same events over and over you'll lose your enthusiasm.

Race often, but not too often. Overracing makes people stale, tired of racing. It is particularly common when people start to improve and don't want to miss the feeling of doing well. They race too often, even every week. Race at least a few times a year for motivation, but not more than twice a month.

Adjust goals. You can't beat the clock forever. Eventually, due to age, injury, or lack of time or commitment, you'll no longer be able to run PRs. But you can still use time goals for motivation by adjusting your thinking. I keep four sets of records as goals: all-time (unfortunately those will never change again), 5-year age group (such as 50–54), single-age (each birthday wipes the slate clean), and calendar year (a new year brings a new set of goals). Look for different goals that still satisfy you, such as staying in the top half of race finishers or completing your local race each year.

Keep a diary. This record helps maintain consistency. Finishing another week on schedule and writing it into your diary gives you a sense of accomplishment. That's why we wrote *The Runner's Training Diary*. Use it as a motivational tool.

Reward yourself. How about a trip to the local running store for new gear as a treat for your hard work. New duds make you feel spiffy, and reinforce your commitment.

Change shoes. If your runs are feeling real slow, try switching to a pair of lightweight shoes for a run. It may let you feel peppy and help you get out of your slow-poke rut.

Remember the health benefits. Many competitors began running to improve the way they look and feel. Periodically remind yourself of the health improvements you've made. Check your weight, measure your waist and hips. Can you wear sleek outfits that you wouldn't dare be seen in before you started running? Think about how much more energy you have now, how much better you can handle stress.

Adjust for weather. Be flexible about running in bad weather. Facing too many days in a row of lousy conditions will sap the enthusiasm of even the most dedicated runner. Take a day or two off, alternate running one day with a day off the next, or switch to cross-training to ride out a heat wave or freeze.

Run away or quit running. Got your attention didn't I? One of the best motivators is to occasionally run away. Go on a trip and run with new people and explore new places. Got the midwinter blues? So take a break and head to exciting locations with plenty of sunshine and no ice or snow underfoot. Many resorts provide fun options so you can keep your exercise program going.

Sometimes you may need to stop running for a few days due to burnout from work or heavy training. All the tricks described above stop working. So quit. After a few days off my body starts twitching. I get more and more irritable until finally the urge to run returns. Your spouse may even force you to run to improve your disposition! When I'm back running I appreciate it even more.

So run away, quit and come back, or just keep running toward reasonable goals. Whatever you do, remember that the key to keeping motivated is to keep running fun. Enjoy!

CHAPTER 27

Mental Training

To achieve your potential, it is important to train mentally as well as physically. Too often runners set reachable racing goals and put in the necessary workouts to meet them, but fall short. They arrive at the starting line in superb shape, but something happens along the way. If you're not mentally prepared your body can't pull off a great race—and perhaps not even an acceptable performance.

Sports psychologist Dr. Jerry Lynch asked Elite runners what is most important: natural ability, diligent training, positive mental attitude, or good coaching. Their key to success by an overwhelming majority: positive mental attitude. If you enter competition in the same physical shape as another racer, most often the one who finishes first will be the one that's stronger mentally. Even if your goal is just defeating the clock, mental training offers benefits.

Your mind can work for you, or against you. Push aside self-doubts and excuses, let your talent and training go to work. Rather than allow your mind to hold you back and cause failure, prepare it to drive you down the road to success. Roger Bannister, who had the physical and mental toughness to be the first to break the "impossible" four minute barrier for the mile in 1954, stated: "Though physiology may indicate respiratory and circulatory limits to muscular effort, psychological and other factors beyond the ken of physiology set the razor's edge of defeat or victory and determine how close an athlete approaches the absolute limits of performance." In the next year and a half after Bannister's barrier-buster, several other runners followed. It was now possible.

Take control of your mind to control your body. But running isn't an easy sport in which to control behavior. John Elliott states in *The Competitive Edge*, "The mental aspects of performance often seem elusive and inaccessible. It is far easier to control pace during a race than it is to control thoughts. It is easy to log mileage, but not so easy to chart emotions. Building sprint speed is a fairly straightforward process—building confidence is not. The way to train for a hilly race is obvious, but how does one train to relax through the near-panic felt during unremitting discomfort?" One of the biggest challenges runners face is uncertainty. You don't always know what to expect from the course, weather, your competitors, and your own body. Unlike other sports, you can't call a time-out to rethink your game plan. You have to make decisions while you, and the clock, are still running. The longer the race, the more uncertainties you encounter—and the more time you have to think, worry, lose concentration, and erode confidence. You establish mental barriers.

Mental training can't improve your physical ability. That's determined by a combination of genetics and competitive training. But by training the mind, you'll be able to make full use of your talents. You may very well discover that you had more in you than you thought possible.

KEY MENTAL ATTRIBUTES

There are many important ingredients to mental training. Setting challenging goals and developing the motivation, desire, and discipline to keep training toward those goals are detailed in the previous chapters. The development and execution of strategy and tactics are explored in the following chapters.

Following are additional characteristics of a mentally strong competitive runner as well as strategies for improving psychological skills:

The Stimulus-Belief-Response System

All behavior comes down to a stimulus producing a response. The race horn sounds, you run. But not everyone responds in the same way to the same stimuli, and each person may respond differently at times. Why? Before you respond to a stimulus you think about it, however briefly. Psychologists call this middle step the "belief system." Performance depends on the strength of your beliefs, which are ever changing. They may change positively, or negatively; you can control the change, or let it control you. In races you are subjected to many stimuli: pace, fatigue, heat, hills, competitors, and more. How you respond depends on how your mind processes these stimuli.

A key factor here is your self-image. Feeling worthwhile as an athlete doesn't come easily. Your self-image needs to be constantly reinforced to strengthen your belief system and the way you respond to stimuli. Think of yourself as an athlete. Yes, you! Whether you run a 5-minute or a 10-minute mile, are twenty years old or sixty. You strive to do your best just like the Elites up front. Feel proud of yourself as a runner. Don't compare yourself to others and feel substandard. Another key to self-image: positive rather than negative feedback from family, friends, teammates, and coaches.

Positive thinking is essential to building a powerful belief system. Set imposing, perhaps seemingly impossible, ultimate goals for down the road. Your in-between goals will then no longer be intimidating. Australian coach Percy Cerutty advised, "Run hard, be strong, think big!" Don't back-pedal before a race thinking: "I'm just running through the race," or "I didn't taper, I'm just doing the race easy." This talk doesn't really diffuse anxiety and it doesn't prep your mind for a good performance. In fact, if you think and act negatively, you will most likely perform that way.

Confidence

To do your best, you've gotta believe in yourself. There is a functional link between physiology and psychology. If you have the confidence to do something, your body will respond. With confidence you can cope with various race day obstacles, but even slight problems are magnified if you lack it. Achieving goals—long training runs, consistent mileage, increasingly faster times in speed workouts and races—builds confidence, which results in further improvements in performance. Reflect on these successes as you approach a race and during it to keep your confidence strong.

Runners often improve race times by a lot after only one or

two of our speed training classes. Can our workouts be that great? No. But our pep talks are. We challenge people to search for the athlete within and work hard. In group speed sessions you can push harder than ever imagined. Transferring this knowledge to racing results in improved performances. These runners didn't get physically better in such a short time, rather they didn't underperform from lack of confidence.

When we started our Greater New York Racing Team we established time standards for membership. One runner was very excited about the team, but said she wasn't good enough. "You won't be good enough if you think you aren't good enough," was my reply. I had seen her progress in speed sessions and believed she was not performing to her ability due to lack of confidence. I gave her a lesson in mental preparation. First, she was given a challenging time goal and an ambitious, but realistic starting pace. Then, she was asked to mentally practice running her goal time over the course. "But do you really think I can run that fast?," she asked nervously. My reply: "I don't think you can, I know you can." "Okay, I'll do it if you say I can" was her resolve. She ran a personal record time and qualified for the team. Why? Because she was trained, talented, and believed she could.

POSITIVE AFFIRMATIONS AND SELF-TALK

Negative thoughts can creep into our minds, undermining confidence and self-image. These fleeting moments of self-doubt are particularly damaging during prerace hours and at critical junctures during competition. Sports psychologists recommend combating potentially damaging self-talk by developing a list of positive self-talk (affirmations). If you get very nervous during a race and tighten up, for example, your positive statement could be "I get calmer as the race gets longer."

Try writing down negative thoughts, then change them to positive affirmations and physically get rid of the negative ones. Affirmations counterattack self-doubt and reinforce self-image and goals. Look at them regularly; think about them while running and racing, and throughout the day. Use them to pump yourself up with self-talk during races. Change them periodically. Try making up inspirational sayings that rhyme and are easy to remember, or, memorize famous quotes.

Affirmations should be phrased in a positive form and present tense ("I run relaxed" rather than "I won't get tense"), be active statements, and focus on what *you* will do, rather than on your competition. Here are some examples of affirmations: "I am loose and fast"; "I am strong and powerful"; "I am focused and relaxed"; "I am strong on hills"; "I run well in the heat"; "I am a sub-three–hour marathoner"; "I will beat ___________ in our next race." (Please don't pick me.)

CREATIVE IMAGING

Sports psychologists recommend forming creative images of what you feel like when running well. The idea is to combine the feeling of confidence with that of moving strongly and smoothly. Do you run fast "like a cheetah," gracefully "like an antelope," flow smoothly "like a mountain stream," or move powerfully "like the wind?" I used to envision myself running "like Frank Shorter" after he won the Olympic Marathon. Call up these images during training runs and prerace visualization so it will be easier to call upon them at critical points in races when you need a boost. Use a variety of images: a powerful one to help you up hills, a smooth one for flowing downhill, and a fast one to gear up for the finishing kick.

PRERACE ANXIETY AND AROUSAL

Let's face it, racing is a huge strain on the nerves. Most runners experience varying degrees of stress prior to competition. They may become anxious about their opponents, their goal time, the weather, or the course. This is perfectly normal.

The body reacts to a threatening stimulus—be it an impeding race or a group presentation—and prepares for action. The brain signals for the release of adrenaline into your bloodstream, which initiates a number of physical reactions: You start to perspire, your heart rate speeds up, muscles tighten, breathing becomes shallow, your stomach churns, you develop "cotton mouth." You may experience difficulty thinking clearly.

And that's not all! Coordination may become impaired, making it difficult to perform such simple tasks as tightening your shoelaces, or getting your warm-up pants off without tripping over them. You may need to use the toilet, only to get back in the long line because you have to go again. A college teammate used to heave before every race as part of his warm-up. Does any of this sound familiar? If not, then you either have nerves of steel or aren't very serious about your racing.

But as annoying as all this stress is, it's essential to a good performance. Think of nervousness as an aid. Psychologists refer to this state of tension as "arousal." According to research by Dr. Brent Rushall, author of *Psyching in Sport*, lack of sufficient arousal prior to competition leads to disinterest; whereas excessive arousal leads to being overwhelmed by emotions. Both extremes result in impaired performance.

The goal is to achieve a balance—a state of "optimum arousal" in which you get psyched up for the big effort and become stimulated to do your best, but don't get overwhelmed by the emotions and have an "anxiety attack." For some runners, the optimum arousal state is a narrow peak from which it is easy to slide in either direction; for others it is broader. Through experience you will become aware of your optimal level of arousal which may vary for different-length races. Getting "psyched up" for a short race may help you get off to a good, confident start, but such a tactic could backfire in longer races. Long-distance racing requires the ability to spread out emotions and energy over long periods of time. Dr. George Sheehan warned, "Strong emotions often contribute nothing but stupidity. It is the fired-up, psyched-up runner who runs the most irrationally paced races." Try to save emotion for late in the race where it is needed to help you overcome fatigue and battle your competition.

It's not unusual for negative thoughts to pass through your mind, or to look for excuses not to run well, or to even think about skipping the race altogether. As long as you recognize these as normal fleeting thoughts, you can keep them from taking over. A debate takes place in your mind: "Can I, or can't I?" The physically and mentally prepared athlete recognizes this as a normal question and knows the answer.

On race day, the competitive runner must be prepared to manage thoughts of the physical and mental stress he or she will face during the actual race. The best way to prepare for this is with regular, demanding workouts and build-up races, and with some mental training. Elliott has a simple recommendation for race day worrywarts: Go ahead and worry in the days prior to the race, and then set it aside. Worry about the weather, the course, the competitors, whatever. "Stay with each situation until you feel your anxiety drop," he suggests. "Worry systematically and intensely . . . and humorously. Make your scenarios crazy and outrageous. Creative worrying is a way of desensitizing yourself to worries."

One of the major sources of anxiety is worrying about factors that are beyond your control, such as the fitness of your competition. Focus on things that are within your control, and on your strengths, not your weaknesses. Besides thinking positively yourself, surround yourself with positive-thinking people. Avoid running friends who are emotional wrecks before the race, full of negative statements. Seek calm, strong-minded runners to socialize with in the final hours before a big race. Or seek out nonrunning friends who are confident people and are very supportive of your race efforts. Before races I prefer to avoid everyone as much as possible. There is only one strong, confident runner I want to talk to as the race approaches: myself.

A familiar prerace routine reduces prerace anxiety. It encompasses all the basic race-day logistics, relaxation and visualization, warm-up running, and stretching. It gives you something positive to focus on, minimizing the time available for worry. The next chapter includes a sample routine.

RELAXATION

Running itself is a form of relaxation. But competitive running causes tension to build. That's why the lines are so long at toilets before races! Tension affects more than your bladder and bowels. An overanxious runner is prone to mental errors—such as starting too fast or losing concentration—and often experiences loss of confidence. Tense muscles are less flexible, more prone to injury, and fatigue more easily. Tightness in running form contributes to inefficiency.

The simplest way to stay relaxed prior to hard workouts and races is to take a time-out for at least 15 minutes (some prefer an hour or more) to do quiet, pleasurable activities. This may include listening to music, knitting, reading, doing a crossword puzzle, talking with friends, or taking a hot shower. More formal relaxation techniques include meditation, yoga, zen, biofeedback, and progressive relaxation.

Deep breathing is a key part of most relaxation programs, and is a simple technique. Set aside a few minutes before key workouts and races to unscrew the nervous head, and screw on the relaxed, confident head. If possible, find a quiet place away from others. Either sit quietly or lay down, and close your eyes. Inhale slowly through the nose while belly-breathing (push the stomach out), and slowly raise the shoulders up and back. Hold a deep breath for a few seconds, then slowly exhale through the mouth (Some prefer to inhale to a count of five, hold for a count of five, and then release to a count of five). Focus on the feeling of relaxation as you exhale tension out of your body. Repeat until you feel relaxed, about 5 to 10 minutes.

During prerace warm-ups, scan your body for muscle tension. If you locate a tight area, do a modified version of progressive relaxation: Tense the area, then release it. Say and think "calm" before races and even during a race when you start to feel tense. Repeat a slogan "*calm, calm, calm*" a few times along with deep breathing. Try "explosive exhaling": Inhale deeply and then exhale forcefully and loudly, blowing away the tension.

VISUALIZATION

Visualization is a mental game used by athletes in every sport to enhance performance. You program the mind to respond in a certain way at certain times. As long as you have a solid goal and a strong desire to reach it, all you need is a good imagination. Visualization is a psychological trick that allows you to take what you would like to do and convince yourself to do it. You see and feel success so that when it's actually happening you are not afraid to succeed, but rather embrace it as an old friend.

Visualization trains athletes to mentally experience events as if they were living it. You can also benefit from reliving your best performances over and over. It's like putting a videotape into your brain. Rerun some of your best races and workouts to give you a feel for visualization. Then imagine an upcoming race. You control the imagery; you should actually imagine your muscles in action as you rehearse your race.

The central nervous system reacts in much the same way

whether you're actually running or imagining yourself as running. In *The Mental Athlete* Dr. Kay Porter and Judy Foster note, "Each time you 'see' yourself performing exactly the same way you want with perfect form, you physically create neural patterns in your brain. These patterns are like small tracks permanently engraved on the brain cells. It is the brain that gives the signal to the muscles to move. It tells each muscle how to move, when to move, and with how much power. Our performance will be tremendously more powerful if we have also trained our minds and created the neural patterns to help our muscles do exactly what we want them to do perfectly." Neurons will fire just as they do in a race, and muscles contract in minute but detectable amounts.

The technique works because it follows the psychological principle that the closer one comes to simulating an actual situation, the greater one's chances of developing the skill to perform it. By imagining yourself successfully running, you actually improve form and performance. By training the subconscious mind to perform in the way you want, it will "tell" your conscious mind to perform in that manner.

Visualization is a three-step process: (1) set a goal and create a positive self-image; (2) achieve a state of deep relaxation; (3) imagine yourself succeeding.

Set your goals, believe in them, and expect them. The next step is to achieve a state of deep relaxation. Relaxation gets rid of mental tensions to free up the mind for positive visualization. Find a quiet place and do deep belly-breathing for 5 to 10 minutes as described earlier. Or, follow the progressive relaxation routine (Chapter 44). This should leave you relaxed enough to clearly visualize your upcoming race.

Then, focus on your goal. Mentally rehearse the entire race, being as specific and positive as possible. Use all of your senses: "See" the landmarks along the way, "hear" the crowd cheering, "smell" the air, "feel" your body moving smoothly. Visualize the warm-up area, starting-line scene, course, spectators, competitors, et cetera. See, hear, smell, and feel the entire race experience. Visualize yourself starting the race full of energy, conquering hills, running with good form, and reaching mileage markers at your goal times. Segment the course in your mind and visualize reaching each segment goal. Imagine yourself crossing under the finish line clock within your goal time. Repeat the whole mental process several times before a key race. You become a movie director and run the dramatic film of your race through your mind. It may take a few sessions to get the hang of the technique. Be patient.

Visualization can be practiced at quiet times during the days leading into races, and before training runs. It can be reinforced by running the course, or key portions of it, in advance if that's possible. Some runners continue visualizing in brief flashes into their runs and races by "seeing" themselves running up an approaching hill, or finishing the race strongly. But don't overdo it here or you'll interfere with your concentration. When visualizing, practice the "perfect" race. But, on occasion also incorporate some unforseen problems and see yourself reacting to them calmly. For example: your shoelace comes untied, or you lose time at the start.

Avoid too much mental rehearsing the night before races. It may leave you emotionally drained. Instead, you may wish to do relaxation exercises to help you get to sleep. On race day, you may benefit from rehearsing your race one more time as a final tune-up. Others find that this leaves them either too hyped or too relaxed.

Whether you follow these visualization techniques conscientiously, or merely occasionally daydream a race, you can see yourself as a confident, successful runner. But you must have a solid training program and race strategy to back up visualization. It's not enough just to dream about running fast.

I carry visualization one step further. After returning home from a race, I'll rerun the race highlights in my mind while I can still "feel" and "see" them. This process reinforces good racing habits and builds confidence.

CONCENTRATION: ASSOCIATION AND DISSOCIATION

Dr. William Morgan, an exercise psychologist at the University of Wisconsin, conducted a study that showed most top runners totally focus on the race, closely monitoring running form, pace, and body signals. This is called "association." In contrast, he found most middle-of-the-packers "dissociate." They think of things other than the race and feedback from their body: planning personal or work matters, the environment, reflections on high and low points in their personal or running lives, listening to music, or chatting with other runners. These distractions serve as a way of handling boredom, negative messages, fatigue, and pain.

If your goal is to merely finish a race despite discomfort, dissociation will certainly help. But it may detract from performance. Although a few top runners have success with this method—entering a trance state by repeating a mantra over and over, reliving part of their lives, or staring at another runner's back or ear—most attempt to "associate" with the pain and discomfort of the race which tells them how hard they can push themselves. It's hard to maintain pace unless you concentrate on what your body is doing. The runner who associates can better preserve fuel and avoid injury or heat illness.

Concentration can be difficult with so many stimuli competing for your attention. These include internal cues (running form, feelings of fatigue, sense of pace and effort, thoughts about strategy) and external cues (competitors, coach's instructions, demands of the course, weather, spectators' cheers). During the race, narrow the focus when necessary, such as when running up a steep hill or passing a competitor, then widen it to fit your needs. Monitor body signals for breathing rate, body temperature, state of dehydration, heat illness, fatigue, muscle tightness, and other factors that allow you to better adjust effort. Keep in tune with your body so you'll know when you can run a little harder and when you need to hold back. Pay attention also to your racing strategy and the actions of your competitors.

Morgan found that Elite runners concentrate on running the race one segment at a time, without worrying about what's up the road. Focus on the next landmark or mile marker you practiced with visualization, and knock 'em off one at a time. Keep alert with self-talk: "Come on, use your arms up that hill." I talk to myself off and on throughout races, issuing reminders, strategies, and encouragement. It helps me concentrate, keeps me going.

Decide if you're running for fun or racing for peak performance. Don't waste energy waving and smiling at the spectators if you want to run your best. Look straight ahead, focus on a narrow strip of road, or the opponent ahead. You're not sight-seeing if you're going for a good race result.

One of the biggest problems with distance races is they last a long time and are extremely repetitive. The mind has too much opportunity to wander, and to worry. You basically repeat the same action stride after stride, minute after minute, mile after mile. "Your concentration is taxed," states Elliott. "You get inattentive, you 'go to sleep,' and then mistakes happen. You suddenly find the runner you wanted to stay with is now twenty yards ahead. Or you feel chilled and dizzy, and realize you haven't attended to your body. Of course, the fatigue of a race and the monotony of it only accentuate this strain on your attention."

No runner can maintain a complete focus during a race. At least be sure to concentrate hardest at the most critical times. This is usually the opening mile until you can settle into a smooth pace, and the last half of the race. If you lose concentration in a short, fast race, you'll quickly lose contact with your opponents. It's harder to make up distance and time lost to mental errors in short races. Although you have more time to reel in opponents and pick up seconds after falling asleep mentally in marathons, a prolonged lack of attention will destroy months of hard training. You don't get many shots at a good marathon, so stay alert.

Concentration must begin before the race. Zero your thinking in on the race as it approaches. Distractions like too many running clinics and parties will interfere with your concentration and drain away mental energy. So, too, will stressful business and family responsibilities. Try to arrange for a time-out from other responsibilities for the last few days going into a really important race. Spend the night before the race relaxing: Read a book or watch television. Don't work late into the night, draining your mental energy. On race day it's okay to spend some time warming up and talking to your friends, but be sure to take a few minutes to be alone—especially as the start nears. Joan Benoit Samuelson, winner of the first women's Olympic Marathon, enters what she calls the "cocoon" of concentration before races.

It's okay to dissociate much of the time in most of your training runs. After all, that's the time when you can enjoy the scenery, converse with friends, think over life's decisions, or just zone out. But use some of your workouts to improve concentration. Running a few long runs alone while associating over the last half improves concentration late in a race. So, too, do long speed sessions such as 1- or 2-mile intervals and tempo runs. If you speed-train with others, don't chat while running hard. Not only does it develop a bad habit for you, it will distract others from maintaining concentration. Brisk treadmill runs force me to concentrate. If I don't, I'll be thrown off the back! Running mindlessly with headphones will do the opposite: teach you to lose concentration. Runners with headphones have been known to run into the sides of moving cars and stationary street signs. I'm not kidding, I've seen it happen!

All runners have momentary lapses in concentration while racing. The average runner may find that by purposely dissociating while running up a troublesome hill, for example, he can conquer it. Some mind-wandering is inevitable, whether purposely or not, but the key is to recover quickly and get back into your concentrated effort, or you will lose precious seconds. Make sure that these are passing thoughts you don't dwell on. Pay attention to your race or you'll daydream away all you worked hard for in training, and up to that point in the race. The average competitor probably associates less than half the time. A good goal is to associate at least two-thirds the time in races; a peak performance requires 90 to 100 percent mental concentration on the body's effort.

SISU: NO GUTS, NO GLORY

Sisu is a word that defines the mental toughness of the Finnish character, especially that of its many great "Flying Finns" such as Paavo Nurmi and Lasse Viren. "*Sisu* is working really hard for something you want to do and not giving up," says Viren. "That's the main point, never giving up." The late Steve Prefontaine, once America's greatest distance runner, summed up his race day mindset: "A lot of people run a race to see who's the fastest. I run to see who has the most guts."

If you run races just for the fun, you experience very little discomfort. But to get the most out of your body you run through discomfort, make a gut check. How much can you take? Some runners are mentally tough, others are softies. The average competitor who wants modest race results can handle a reasonable amount of discomfort. But to excel, you have to go beyond that.

My college cross-country coach challenged us to dig deep into our soul at critical moments in hard workouts and races by shouting out our team motto: "Pay the price." Believe me we did, and on race day we ran over our heads. The opponents paid the price. Our rugged band of overachievers placed second in the state championship despite being picked for last in the preseason.

Work to improve your psychological strength during races. If you give in when the going gets tough, you'll never reach your potential. Think "when the going gets tough, the tough get going." If you run a truly great race, you'll run a tightrope of discomfort and maintain—somehow—physical and psychological balance. But learn the difference between discomfort and serious pain. You can handle the discomfort of tiring muscles and a reasonable amount of pain, but trying to "gut it out" when in severe pain is foolish. The warning sign of injury is pain. You're likely to injure yourself seriously if you neglect serious pain.

The "King of the Roads" revealed his inner thoughts in *Bill Rodgers' Lifetime Running Plan*: "When testing the limits of your potential, racing can be harder mentally than physically. After all, your body is in pretty substantial distress, and your mind's main task seems to be to figure out how to better the situation as soon as possible. If they could be illustrated, the battles that go on in racers' minds would be far more interesting to watch unfold than most road races. That's one of the things I love about running—thanks to what it takes to push yourself, you really get to know yourself, and what kind of mental toughness you have. Once you've realized what you're capable of, and that the negative voice inside your head shouldn't always win, this can have a powerful impact on how you conduct the rest of your life." Indeed, the mental toughness and confidence gained on the race course, especially in marathons, has spurred many runners to take risks that greatly enhanced their careers.

The great runners thrive on adversity, accept discomfort, and overcome difficult challenges from the weather, course, and competitors. You can, too. Speed workouts and practice races help you adjust physiologically and mentally to the discomfort of oxygen debt and hard-worked muscles. Long training runs prepare you for dealing with physical and mental fatigue. You'll learn to run with these feelings. Henry Rono, the great Kenyan runner, said: "If you train only to *take* the pain, you will never be any good; but if you train to *break* the pain, you can move on to a new level."

MENTAL TRICKS FOR FIGHTING OFF FATIGUE AND PAIN

Fatigue and pain limit performance. It's a physical reality, but much of it is psychological and thus can be dealt with. Anxiety and fear magnify fatigue. When confidence goes during a race fatigue rushes in for the kill. Once fatigue has taken charge, it's a long way to the finish line. The key is to accept discomfort as part of the deal, and be confident you will run well despite it. Shellylynn advises her clients who are new to competition to welcome pain as a sign of success. Be proud to be so uncomfortable: It takes a lot of effort to hurt!

Following are some mental tricks to occupy your mind at a time it's searching for reasons to concede to distress. You can't outrun fatigue, but maybe you can bluff your way through it.

Acknowledge discomfort, minor pain, and fatigue when they attack you, says New York City physical therapist Robert Kropf, who uses mental techniques to help runners recover from injury and race more efficiently. Fighting fatigue causes tension, loss of confidence and concentration, and further fatigue. Instead of thinking "Oh no, my hamstring is tightening up," think, "Hello hamstring, are you reminding me to loosen up and relax?" This technique reduces anxiety, although it sure sounds silly. Carry on a conversation with fatigue and pain (but not out loud or they'll lock you up!). By recognizing the problem, you will not let it take control.

Kropf suggests that at the first sign of pain or fatigue—or even before it appears in anticipation—heighten your awareness in the area. If you feel tightness in your quads late in a race, for example, tighten those muscles momentarily and then let go. This reduces anxiety, helping fight off fatigue with relaxation. Repeat a relaxation slogan, such as "*calm, calm, calm,*" if you feel fatigue or pain setting in. Kropf recommends specific visualization. Become familiar with anatomical drawings of the various muscles of the body, particularly ones that often cause you trouble in a race.

"See" those muscles widening and lengthening as they are being relaxed. This wards off the tension that causes fatigued muscles to tighten and shorten.

Attention to breathing and posture is important here. Control discomfort by controlling breathing. If you're struggling, focus on deep, steady breathing. This relaxes you, allowing you to concentrate on effort, not pain. When fatigue sets in, the chest moves forward, the low back arches, the spine shortens, and the head lowers. The arms and shoulders tend to come up, and you hit farther back on the heels. A series of compensations take place that shorten your stride, placing key muscle groups in biomechanical disadvantage. This leads to poor form and the inability to maintain pace. Kropf recommends that at first you give in to the tension and fatigue. Let your body go in the direction it wants. Exaggerate the poor form that fatigue creates only momentarily rather than fight it. Then, after breaking the pattern of fighting fatigue, you can concentrate on relaxed, good form as described in Chapter 31. Feel your jaw loosen, your neck and shoulders relax, the torso widen and lengthen, and imagine the head floating into a hat 1 inch above your head. Feel yourself getting taller, feeling relaxed and more efficient.

A trick I use to fight discomfort is talking to myself. Actually, it's more of a strong lecture. Remind yourself how much you—and your family and friends—have sacrificed to prepare for this race. Reflect on how you pushed through fatigue in hard workouts. Remember how badly you want to beat your opponent or break your time barrier. Concentrate on how you don't want to let down your teammates. Tough pep talks will help you through bad patches of fatigue. This is a good time to call up affirmations, such as this one: "I'm going to beat you because I've got *sisu.*" The bottom line: Are you going to let brief periods of discomfort negate all you have invested?

Sometimes when being attacked by fatigue it's wise to back off the pace a bit to allow yourself a chance to regroup, physically and mentally. Stay composed, relax, and then, once you've regained some control, get back to work. Ease up a little, but don't slow dramatically. Otherwise, look for mental tricks to prevent slacking off. Replace pain with other thoughts. Think about your running form, pace, or the competitor up ahead. Taking a break from thinking about pain (dissociation) may break the pain cycle and at least minimize its grasp on your body. Try picking up the pace to fight off discomfort. That's right. Believe it or not, by slightly picking it up you may be able to shake off fatigue. A quicker pace uses different muscles, allowing some of the tired ones to rest momentarily. After 100 yards or so, return to your goal pace. A course with gently rolling hills offers a natural way to use different muscle groups. Try getting mad. When a runner passes, get angry—but remain reasonably relaxed. Or get mad at a comment made by a spectator or competitior. Get aggressive when the going gets tough. Flash back to previous races or hard workouts where you ran tough. A sudden rush of adrenaline provides a psychological boost, and may break the hold of fatigue.

Segmenting the race helps too. I try to hold off fatigue late in races by concentrating on how close I'm getting to the end of all this torture. I'll count it down, 3 miles to go, 2, 1, half-mile. It may be easier to think in terms of time to go rather than distance; it seems less threatening when battling fatigue. I'll set time goals: 30 minutes to go, 20, 10, 5, 3, 1. Think that discomfort's grip on you is slowly fading away as you get closer and closer to the finish line.

John Elliott has a good feel for pain. He writes, "Races always evoke some dread about the pain that will come. But we can't escape the fact that the more discomfort we can accept in a race, the faster we will run. Successful racing means *courting the pain.*"

Elite runners associate with pain. By paying close attention to it, they can better adjust effort. What do they do if they're running below their pain threshold? Yep, they push harder until they're paying the price again. They understand the bottom line: Without pushing themselves to the edge, experiencing just the right amount of fatigue and pain, they'll never find out what they're made of. The same is true for you. Make peace with pain, court it, in order to enjoy racing success. Recognize pain and fatigue as a challenge, not a barrier to your racing goals. Finally, keep reminding yourself when you're feeling fatigue that the runners around you probably are in just as much, or more, distress than you. So who is going to give in to fatigue first?

THE WARRIOR ATTITUDE

The key ingredient, in my opinion, to successful mental training is what I refer to as a "warrior attitude." A warrior prepares fully and purposely for war. He focuses on the impending battle and trains his body, mind, and soul to act with strength and cunning. He lives a spartan existence, denying luxuries that would sap his resolve. He has the desire, motivation, discipline, belief, self-esteem, confidence, courage, and mental toughness to win in battle. He prepares a wise strategy, dwells on it, and executes it while staying calm in battle and fending off pain and fatigue. The warrior prepares to fight the ultimate fight, and face the ultimate defeat—death.

The runner doesn't need to, and shouldn't, prepare for competition with such seriousness. After all, it's not a matter of life or death (although it may feel that way during some races). However, most runners would benefit from modeling themselves somewhat after these fierce ancient warriors. You need to make sacrifices to be a warrior runner. Every time you think about skipping a workout because you're "too busy" or "too tired," remind yourself that you are a warrior. When you think about wolfing down that big dessert after dinner, be a warrior and pass it up. Call upon that warrior attitude to get you to complete long runs and interval sessions after fatigue has partially taken over your mind and body. Unleash the warrior in you as you fend off negative thoughts, lactic acid buildup, glycogen depletion, heat buildup, surges by opponents, steep hills, muscle fatigue and all those other demons that attack during competition. Being a fierce warrior is all about preparation, sacrifice, and bravery.

Don't think of yourself as just a jogger that races recreationally on occasion. It's okay to admit to yourself and others that you are a serious athlete (warrior) in training. The warrior attitude shouldn't be reserved just for professional athletes. I think of myself several times a day as being a warrior: when preparing to run, while lifting weights, while fueling and hydrating, while preparing to nap. It drives me to make the sacrifices I need to make to become a better athlete.

A warrior is willing to let his mind take his or her body to the ultimate test. I am a warrior. Are you?

MENTAL TRAPS TO SUCCESS AND ENJOYMENT

Competitive runners face disappointments and mental stresses that not only affect performance, but take away the fun of running. Developing strategies to cope with them is also an important aspect of mental training.

Surviving a bad race. If by some chance you have a bad race, don't panic. You can't have a good race each time out; you're entitled to a few disappointments. Figure out the likely causes for a bad outing: too hot, started too fast, unrealistic expectations, coming off the flu, too much stress at work, lack of motivation, poor mental preparation or execution of race strategy. Whatever the reason(s), you're frustrated you didn't get the race time you were capable of achieving.

What to do? Go ahead, bitch about it to as many people who will listen to get it out of your system. Then, congratulate yourself on having the courage to take risks. Accept mistakes as learning experiences. Analyze, get back to training, and go stick your neck out again at the next race. Bad races actually help me. They make me realize I wasn't prepared physically or mentally for a top effort. A bad race motivates me to increase my commitment. Watch out! I'm likely to run really well in my next race.

Surviving a DNF. Almost every runner has a few "DNFs" in his or her diary: a Did Not Finish. When the going gets tough most runners think about dropping out. The pain and pressure get difficult and you may momentarily lose confidence. Mentally tough, well-trained runners hang in there and quickly regain confidence and finish well. If you are overwhelmed with a desire to quit because you feel very unhappy, then quit. Walk off the course without feeling like a failure. Analyze your problem—perhaps overtraining, too much pressure at home or work, et cetera—and deal with it. If you find yourself favoring an injury or are very uncomfortable because of bad weather, or the effects of illness, drop out. Dropping out for intelligent safety reasons will save your body and mind a lot of abuse. You will recover from the effort much faster than if you forced yourself to finish no matter what.

But will you recover from the disappointment and embarrassment of a poor performance, or being a DNF? If you're a confident runner, you know that the runner who was struggling out there isn't the real you and that you'll return next time and do well. I've quit a few times, due to both physical and mental reasons. My all-time classic DNF? I was struggling on a hot day when a runner came alongside and asked: "Aren't you Bob Glover?" I blurted, "What's left of him." He gushed, "I started running with your book, thanks!" He left me in the dust. Crushed, I walked off the course!

If at all possible, avoid DNFs. Finishing despite having a bad day makes you that much tougher when things are going good for you. Learn to differentiate between troubles that are fleeting and not a threat to your health—physical and mental—and those that justify a DNF.

After a bad race or DNF, take a few easy training days, set a new goal, and get back to work. It may be helpful to start racing again with a low-key effort before taking another shot at a highly competitive race. Concentrate on the previous good race and how well you will do in the next one. Stay confident. But if you still feel lousy several days after a race, you are headed for injury or burnout and should take an extended break from competitive racing and training.

Surviving burnout. A runner approached me as I was writing this chapter. She had improved by leaps and bounds since starting our running classes. In fact, she dropped her 10K time from 45 to 40 minutes in a few months. She ran PRs week after week. But then her times didn't improve. Worse, she began to hate competition. Racing too often left her body tired; she could no longer get mentally up for each race. Competition had lost its excitement. Instead, it was a heavy burden.

You can't train and race hard year-round and expect to keep improving indefinitely. Either your body or your mind will fail. Take several time-outs a year. Rest, regenerate. The mind must be prepared to race or the body won't respond the way it did when you were "psyched up." Work in streaks of energy and mental buildup. In between, take a break before racing breaks you.

My advice for the "burned out" runner is to back the mileage down, stop hard speed training for a few weeks, and don't race again until you're hungry for competition. Don't toe the line until you can fully enjoy the challenge of competition. Set a goal for a few months away, and then gradually build toward it. Don't just jump into the next race on the schedule. Build excitement toward a new PR, for moving up to a marathon, down to a 5K, a trip to a new and exciting, perhaps faraway, race.

The Fast-Time Syndrome. One of the great delights in our sport is running fast times, setting PRs. But you can't run one every time, and you shouldn't expect to always be at the top of your game. Some runners search out flat courses, or even downhill ones and those suspected to be a bit short, so they have a better chance for the almighty fast time. If you "cheat," you're not being fair to yourself. Don't get too cocky if your time on a very fast course is superior to your PR, or your peer's times on a tougher course. That's not a true comparison of your ability. On the other hand, if most races you run are on "slow" courses, setting sail on a fair course and running a fast time brings about a well-deserved reward for your hard training.

Don't ruin running by overemphasizing the importance of fast times. Enjoy races even if the result isn't a time you can gloat over. Look for rewards other than *the fast time:* doing well against the competition or previous races on the same course, gaining strength for upcoming key races, having fun taking part in your sport with others. Reaching for fast times motivates and strengthens you mentally; obsessing over fast times tears you down, leaving you prone to burnout and poor performances.

Fear of failure. Fear can drive you to a great performance, but it can also be overwhelming. Many of us run harder when scared a bit, whether fearful of not reaching our goal time or by being passed by a competitor. The cost for giving in to fear is anxiety, the loss of confidence, and a less-than-ideal performance. A poor performance often has more to do with the anxiety caused by the fear of failure than any lack in training or talent.

All runners worry to some degree about failing. Some athletes run superior workouts and race well in low-key races but then perform poorly in big races. They "choke." Others come up with creative cop-out or avoidance tactics before, during, or after races to cover the fact they fell victim to the fear of failure. You've heard them all, and maybe even used some of them. They include: "I'm just doing it as a workout," "I think I'm catching a cold," and "I started too far back."

Runners set up for failure by putting pressure on themselves to meet lofty goals, or allow others to do so. Then they worry about letting down their coach, teammates, family, or friends. They don't want to become embarrassed in front of others. It's okay to fear not meeting expectations. Failing to reach goals is part of the sport. Success is, after all, much sweeter when balanced by occasional defeat. If you aren't willing to risk failure, you'll never fully succeed.

Porter recommends taking on fear head-on: "Instead of fighting or resisting fear, acknowledge it and let it go. In this way you decrease your own resistance to it, and it will not get in your way. You control it instead of it controlling you. After acknowledging the fear, take positive actions to begin thinking differently. Wallowing in the fear accomplishes nothing." The combination of setting realistic, short-term goals, developing positive affirmations, practicing relaxation techniques, and race visualization will help overcome fear of failure. Be practical about your fears: Can you live with yourself if you fail in your race? Look at the potential setback long-term rather than short-term in order to decrease its magnitude.

Despite all these suggestions, if you can't resolve your fears, discuss them with others you can trust. A well-trained sports psychologist may be of help.

Fear of success. What? That's right, many runners don't know how to accept success. Timothy Gallwey summed up much of the problem for athletes in *The Inner Game of Tennis*: "Most of us find something frightening about surpassing our own or others' expectations, and this fear usually keeps us from doing it. We identify with these expectations, and don't like to rock the boat by exceeding them." Sometimes runners fall victim to "the pecking order syndrome." They are afraid to pass other runners because they are comfortable with their position on the ladder of success. To try to move up would be risky. They lack the confidence to challenge status quo. Others fear if they are too successful, they will have to take the sport too seriously, or others will expect too much from them, or even resent them. Still others fear knowing their full potential, since that would require them to do something with it. These prospects can be frightening. You may back off when the action heats up in a race feeling "I'm not a serious competitor." It is safer to not be serious than to accept the pressure that comes with wanting to do your best.

Dr. Martha Friedman, author of *Overcoming the Fear of Success*, theorizes that the main problem is the inability to feel good about what you really want. This may be largely due to a lack in self-esteem, perhaps caused by being ridiculed in the past for a lack of athletic success. The result may be self-sabotage. In various subtle ways you attempt to avoid the discomfort of success by giving less than your best.

How can you be more successful at success? First, acknowledge a fear exists. Then, pump yourself up with positive affirmations and visualize yourself succeeding. Most importantly, see yourself accepting success. This is a real weakness in many runners. Athletes in most sports are full of self-claims after their events. "I am the greatest" was the infamous brag of the highly successful boxer Muhammad Ali. But runners mostly wander around meekly after a race waiting for someone to compliment them, only to immediately reject it.

Why do we do this? And most of us are guilty at least occasionally. If not careful, modesty may turn to self-deprecation. Learn how to accept achievement and compliments. Don't pull yourself down. Build yourself up. When another runner says, "Nice race," reply, "Thanks. I worked hard for it." You did; don't reject a compliment with "I was just lucky" or "I should have done better." Internalize the compliments, allow them to build your self-esteem as an athlete. Politely take in compliments from others even if you didn't do well. It's rude to blow people off, especially your opponents. On the other hand, don't make a fool of yourself by bragging endlessly about your successes. Muhammad Ali's act wouldn't sit well with competitive runners. Be quietly confident before the race, show reserved pride after the race.

The Expectations Trap. Jonathan Beverly, who coaches with our running classes, wrote about this and the following common mental traps in *Runner's World*: "Problems begin when expectations exceed abilities," states Beverly. "This leads to remarks such as, 'Oh, it was a PR but not nearly what I should have run.' " Make a commitment to be the best you can be, but keep your expectations in balance. According to Beverly, a key to happiness is to "celebrate what we achieve rather than reinforce what we have yet to accomplish."

The Comparison Treadmill. "We compare ourselves to better runners and assume that faster times will make us happier," writes Beverly. "They won't and can't. Someone else is always faster. Worse, he probably trains less than you do." Comparing yourself to other runners and setting goals to beat faster runners motivate you to improve. But don't get obsessed with it. "All runners are not created equal," adds Beverly. "We do not start with the same genes or have the same time and resources for training." Jonathan and I compare his race times with my age-adjusted performances. But we keep it in perspective. As long as we enjoy the comparing and use it to motivate each other, it's okay.

The Perfection Myth. "We believe that we will someday run the perfect race on the perfect course on the perfect day following the perfect training season," writes Beverly. "We believe that then (finally!) we will run the way we have always known we could." Accept imperfect success. Don't beat yourself up with the "I should'ves" and the "I could'ves." You did succeed if you took risks and tried your best. Look for at least a small aspect of each race that represents achievement. Keep things in perspective. "Strive for excellence, not perfection" advises Lynch. Sums Beverly, "We must accept that this—this very day, with all its distractions, imperfect conditions and running impediments—may be as good as it gets."

The Pheidippides syndrome. Beverly points out that this Greek messenger, who allegedly dropped dead after running 24 miles from Marathon to Athens to announce victory over the invading Persians, symbolizes ultimate effort. He notes runners often complain "We could have (and should have) given much more" of ourselves in order to knock off a few more seconds or places in a race. "The only way out of our Pheidippides trap," says Beverly, "is to find peace within ourselves. To believe that you could do more if you only pushed harder is yet another way to avoid accepting reality. Yes, we will always wonder what we could accomplish at the outer limits. But we can only appreciate what we actually accomplish today."

CHAPTER 28

Prerace Logistics and Day-of-Race Routine

Planning ahead for all your logistical needs in the prerace hours will make race day less stressful. There's nothing worse than last-minute worries, or disasters such as forgetting your racing shoes or number. A familiar race-day routine controls prerace anxiety and race readiness. It allows you to control the physical and mental buildup to peak when the race starts.

LOGISTICS PRIOR TO ARRIVING AT RACE SITE

Here's a checklist for the days before the race:

Preregister. Otherwise you may miss the entry deadline. Most events allow race-day entry. Higher fees and longer lines are great incentives to preregister. Many events allow you to pick up your number, T-shirt, and registration materials prior to race day, freeing you of time and worry on race day. I feel more comfortable traveling to a race if my number is already pinned to my singlet.

Race-day trips. Double-check the start time, travel directions, how long it will take to get there, and parking facilities. Traveling more than one or two hours on race day is too hectic and exhausting. Instead, arrive the day before (but not too late at night) and stay over, starting race day relaxed and rested.

Overnight trips. Confirm transportation and housing arrangements. Use the most comfortable means of travel you can arrange and afford. Driving for several hours should be avoided if possible. If not, stop every two hours or so for walk and stretch breaks. Take turns driving unless you have a designated driver that won't be racing. If traveling by plane, schedule an early arrival time. If you have delays you won't be arriving late at night, upsetting your sleep pattern. See Chapter 48 for more tips on traveling.

Meals. If eating at home, make sure you have the foods available you'll want the night before and on race morning. If away from home, find out what restaurants will be open and have the foods you want. Don't eat too late the night before, or too close to the start on race day.

Sleep. Keep to a normal sleeping pattern for several days going into races. If you'll be awakening on race day earlier than normal, get to bed early enough in the preceding days to get enough rest. If you've slept well all week, then losing sleep to jitters the night prior to competition won't affect performance according to researchers. Most experts agree that a good night's sleep is most important over a period of a few nights before the race (particularly two nights prior) than the night before. If you do sleep poorly the night before and think you'll run poorly as a result, you probably will. Don't worry about losing sleep since it's too late to matter.

Nevertheless, it's better to get a good night's sleep if possible. Here are some tips:

- Taking a nap the day before is a great idea to help compensate for any sleep you might lose to nerves. But napping for too long or too late in the day will make it harder to get to sleep that night. Going to bed more than an hour earlier than normal is likely to backfire, too. You're more likely to toss and turn rather than get extra sleep.
- Don't eat too close to bedtime. An unsettled stomach may hinder sleep. Avoid caffeine and other products that may contribute to sleeplessness from noon on. Minimize fluid intake in the last two hours before bedtime to minimize middle-of-the-night toilet trips.
- Develop a routine to promote relaxation and sleep. For each race, do the same activities at the same time: eat dinner, watch television or read, shower or take a bath, go to bed, et cetera.

- Answer all your questions before bedtime. Know everything you have to know about the race and be confident all your prerace logistics are taken care of so you don't lie in bed thinking of things.
- Don't race the race in bed. This is not the time to get pepped up mentally rehearsing the race. Try to think of other things that help you feel relaxed.
- If you can't sleep, at least lay still. Try to minimize tossing and turning. Don't get up and work or nervously pace the floor. Think of it this way: Your goal isn't necessarily to sleep, but to at least spend time resting and relaxing in bed, off your feet.
- If your bedmate is also racing and you're tossing and turning keeping him or her awake, one of you should head for the sofa.

On race day, get up at least two hours before the event. Have someone awaken you as a backup to your alarm. If traveling, don't depend on the hotel wake-up call; too many runners have missed the start for this reason. Research indicates being suddenly awakened by a loud alarm or phone ring may interfere with peak performance. Awaken by a gentle ring, door knock, or a hug from your mate.

Sex? I'll bet I've got your attention now. Should you or shouldn't you the night before? Will it drain away strength needed for the race? The fear of sex is deeply rooted in athletic tradition. Ancient Greek athletes were prohibited from engaging in sex and many modern athletes from around the world have been discouraged to enjoy sex the night before games. But "the ol' professor," New York Yankee manager Casey Stengel, summed it up best: "It ain't the sex that wrecks these guys, it's staying up all night looking for it." Want a note from your doctor? The American Medical Association states, "Sexual relations the night before competition do not hinder athletic performance provided that sex is a regular part of the athlete's life." Some researchers even believe sex the night before a race may be advised since it promotes relaxation.

Weather. The weatherman isn't always right, but at least you'll have a head start on planning clothing needs and last-minute strategy if you keep up with the latest forecast. Don't let early reports get you too depressed and take away from your mental preparation. Besides, the weather may very well change! Anyway, the weather is the same for your competitors too.

Set out race-day clothing, shoes, runner's watch, and entry form. Do this the night before the race. Stick some money into your shoe or shorts for emergencies. Pin your number to your racing singlet or shirt the night before, too, so you don't misplace it. Review again the entry form for specific directions.

Pack your running bag carefully. The night before, place in your bag *everything* you might need on race day. Pack running shoes first (I wear racing shoes to the event but pack training shoes to wear afterward). Then toss in necessities by working your way from your feet up the body to your head. Include extra clothing of everything, and pack for the weather. Include a towel for drying off afterward and a plastic bag for sweaty clothing. Pack prerace hydration and fuel needs. Remember the little necessities (I tuck these in a separate small bag): toilet paper, blister and sun-burn protection, bronchial sprays, safety pins, pain relievers, postrace snacks. Include pen and paper for recording race results, or writing down phone numbers of new friends you make. Double-check the bag in the morning before leaving. When traveling overnight, pack running equipment separately from regular clothing. Never check essential racing gear with an airline. Carry it with you—and that includes your race number!

THE RACE-DAY ROUTINE

The time period from arriving at the race site to the blast of the starting horn is critical to success. This nerve-racking part of racing is the part I hate the most, demanding careful attention or the race risks ruin. All activities that affect your psychological and physical readiness should be closely planned and monitored. Develop a regular routine that comforts and prepares you for action. Some runners listen to music during their prerace routine; others take a break and read. Many find that warming up and hanging out with teammates keeps them calm; others prefer to be alone. Let your routine become a "friend" you can trust with your emotions as excitement builds before races. With experience, you'll learn what works best. By following the same pattern of activity on race mornings you'll feel more confident and perform better. It may change somewhat from race to race—longer races and extreme weather, for example, require special preparations.

Here are some guidelines:

Arrive early. Get to the event one to two hours prior to the start. The bigger the race, the earlier you should arrive to cope with the logistics of parking and getting around. Registering and getting your number in advance will save precious minutes on race morning. Sometimes it's not a good idea to be extra-early. If it's very hot or cold, don't arrive too early unless you have a plan for shelter. Many races don't provide a building for prerace comfort. Your heated or air-conditioned car may be the solution if you're able to park near the race site.

Keep prerace fluids and fuel handy. Most races at least have water at the start, but few have sports drinks and gels. I get nervous before a race and can't find things easily so I pack my gels in a blue plastic bag that can easily be picked out of my runner's bag. For fuel on the run, I'll pin gel packs to my shorts, or tuck them in pockets, several minutes prior to the start.

Take care of business. Runners get nervous before races and have to use the toilet repeatedly. To minimize distress, make a toilet stop just prior to arriving at the race site. That'll cut out one waiting line. At the race site, check out the location of the toilets and various options (such as a gas station up the street) if the line is long. I use my warm-up run for scouting. Use the bushes if they're your only reasonable choice. But don't tell anyone I told you where to go and make sure the local police aren't looking. As the race nears, modesty gives way to prerace nerves. As the saying goes, "Just do it." But be equipped: Carry toilet paper to races. The facilities often run out, and of course the bushes don't come equipped. A good tip here: Stick paper towels in your shorts for emergencies before and during the race. It holds up when wet with rain or sweat. Toilet paper doesn't.

Apply skin protectors and take medications. This includes protection you use for blisters or chafing (feet, nipples, crotch) and sunburn, as well as asthma sprays.

Shoes. Warm up in the shoes you will race in. That way you're used to the feel of the shoe, and most importantly—you know where they are! Some prefer waiting to the last minute to put on their lighter racing shoes. It makes them feel faster. Make sure the laces are snug, but not too tight. Double-knot for security.

Final clothing adjustments. Have a plan for last-minute needs and postrace requirements. Many races offer a baggage check. If not, have a friend watch your bag or try to park your car close by. Gradually peel off clothing as the race start approaches. If it's cool, wait until the last possible minute to strip down to racing essentials. Reminder: You'll heat up as you start racing so don't overdress. For mass events, check your bag extra-early to avoid last-minute crowds and, if needed, wear throwaway clothing to keep warm until the start. Be sure to include plenty of dry, warm clothes and an extra pair of shoes in your runner's bag for postrace comfort.

Final mental preparation. As the race gets close, narrow your focus. The mental warm-up heightens. Think positively and minimize personal interactions. Concentrate on how well you are going to start and run the first mile. At this point, don't dwell on what's further down the road.

THE RACE-DAY WARM-UP AND COOL-DOWN

Few runners warm up properly for races. Just tugging at your toes a few times and jogging to the starting line isn't enough. Stretching before a race is only part of a proper warm-up. Without a sufficient aerobic warm-up, you're asking your body to go from a standing start to full race speed within a few seconds. To do this safely and efficiently, you need to make a transition from just hanging around getting nervous to race mode. A proper warm-up gradually increases heart rate, reducing stress on the heart as you increase speed. It dilates blood vessels, allowing for more efficient transportation of oxygen to the leg muscles. A key part of the warm-up is to actually warm up the muscles, elevating their temperature to improve flexibility and function. A cold muscle is more likely to pull. Warming up helps head off such nuisances as side stitches and exercise-induced asthma. It provides a time to focus your mind, warming it up for the race, too. A good warm-up improves confidence, helps you feel more relaxed and loose as you start off, minimizes risk of injury, and slightly improves performance.

Walk around for a few minutes on race morning to get your

muscles moving before starting the warm-up. I use the walk from my car to the start area for this purpose. About 45 to 60 minutes before the start, jog slowly for 15 to 30 minutes, finishing about 15 to 30 minutes prior to the start. On cool days, wear warm-up clothing right up until the start to help keep muscles warm. On hot days, don't jog for too long to keep body temperature from rising too much before the race even begins. For marathons, skip the jog and stick to periodic walks to keep loose and save energy. Half-marathoners may also follow this advice, especially if they won't be starting fast. In longer races think of the first 2 miles of the race as your warm-up run.

After your aerobic warm-up, stretch lightly for 5 to 10 minutes. Be careful not to nervously force a stretch. Finally, alternate easy jogging with five to ten short, brisk strides right up until the start. These are controlled pickups of about 50 to 100 yards at approximately race pace or slightly faster. Don't sprint here, just run fast enough to make your start feel more comfortable. Strides are more beneficial for short races; skip them for the marathon.

Warming up is important whether racing long or short, or in hot or cold weather. But it is even more critical in the cold since muscles are more tight, and in shorter races when you'll start off at a faster pace. Ideally, the warm-up should end no sooner than 30 to 60 seconds prior to the start of a race to keep your heart rate and body temperature up. Except for small races, or for Elites up in the front row, this is next to impossible since you have to get lined up. Try to time it as close as you can. For most races you can warm up until about 5 minutes before the start. It's impossible to warm up the last 15 minutes or longer before big races because you require more time to secure your place in the start area. At least jog as long as you can and then try to move around a little to stay loose while remaining relaxed.

Don't forget the value of a cool-down. It'll help you recover from the race effort. Keep moving through the chutes. Don't stop and stand still or sit after you've passed through them. If you do, you may get faint. After drinking plenty of fluids and taking in some carbs, go for a walk or an easy jog. Running after a race is optional. Some runners consider it part of the postrace celebration. They look forward to unwinding with friends on the run while recapping the race, or jogging in the opposite direction to cheer on runners still finishing. You may choose to use this time to run alone while analyzing your race. Others have had enough running and prefer to let their body begin to heal. But at least walk around to minimize postrace stiffening.

If you choose to do a postrace run, it's a good idea to change into training shoes before jogging to provide maximum cushioning and support for tired legs, and into drier and warmer clothing. Be careful not to let postrace adrenaline pump you up and push you along too fast here. It's surprisingly easy to do, which risks injury, especially if cooling down with other jabbering runners. This is a recovery jog, not a training run! For some runners, a jog of a mile or two is sufficient; some veterans may run 5 or 6 miles. Most runners are up for some running within a few minutes of finishing a 5K or 10K, but few choose to run at all after races of a half-marathon and longer.

After your aerobic cool-down, whether a jog or walk, drink more fluids and, particularly after a long race, continue to take in carbs. Get out of wet clothing, especially in cool weather, to prevent hypothermia. Yes, this may be the second time you switched to dry clothes after the race. Stretch moderately. Don't overdo it when muscles are tight after a race. For the remainder of the day, take periodic walking and stretching breaks to aid recovery.

PRERACE RITUALS

Prerace rituals go beyond routine. They involve sometimes trivial, yet meaningful actions that serve no purpose other than to provide a security blanket at a time of great stress. Some runners, for example, never shave before a race: It makes them feel meaner. Many runners follow superstitious patterns: wearing a "lucky" singlet that represents a good race, setting their alarms to go off at exactly two hours prior to the race start, not crossing the finish line in warm-up runs, always wearing a bracelet or necklace that brings special strength. If you're convinced that a certain ritual makes you a better runner, then it does. Just don't share some of the more bizarre ones with nonrunning friends or they'll think you've been running too much!

CHAPTER 29

Race Strategy

Race *strategy* is a game plan for how to race. Race *tactics,* detailed in the next chapter, is putting prerace strategy into action in head-to-head competition. Strategic planning and its execution are important to racing success. Mistakes here can wipe out weeks of great training. In short races they will affect your time and place, but in long races they may determine if you finish at all.

A good strategy is essential to the motivation and confidence of any competitor. It gives you a mental edge. There are three strategic ways to run a race: against the course for time or survival, against yourself for a PR (personal record), and tactically against your competitors. An effective strategy factors in your running strengths and weaknesses (both physical and mental), weather, difficulty of the course, personality, and fitness.

RACE PACING

Overall race pace is your average per mile for the entire distance, for example, 8:00 for 10K. But how do you know what pace you can average and at what pace to start? Chapter 25 helps you predict race times and establish realistic time goals. Knowing approximately what finishing time you can expect will help determine your pacing strategy. Pacing involves the distribution of energy over the length of the course. Since you have a finite amount of energy available, it's critical to ration it wisely. Do this by monitoring your body and your watch.

Body monitoring. Some runners pay little attention to their times along the way. Perhaps they don't even wear a watch. They monitor energy use by effort, not time. The legendary Arthur Newton wrote in 1935, "So long as you watch your wind carefully and treat it kindly you can average a better pace than any other method will give you. Nothing but the wind can tell you whether your pace is correct for the conditions at the time, for your breathing is entirely dependent on the amount of energy you are bringing to use." Breathing rate (Chapter 31) will indeed guide you. If you're breathing too fast or out of control, slow the pace. If you're comfortable, pick it up until you're in that ideal effort zone—not in too much discomfort or comfort. Of course, runners have different opinions of what's a comfortable effort. "Associate" with your body (Chapter 27). Some runners use heart rate monitors (Chapter 47) to guide their effort. Back in Newton's racing days digital watches and heart rate monitors weren't even dreamed about. But I doubt he would have used these high-tech toys. After all, they don't measure your wind.

Some competitors pace themselves by "red-lining." They push to the edge of their physical and mental limits. This strategy demands superior fitness and precise body monitoring. If you push just enough, you'll run a peak performance. But if you cross the line the result is often disaster. With experience you'll learn to tolerate racing just within that red line.

Time monitoring. Most competitors parcel out energy by monitoring both their body and watch. Time pacing is measured by "splits," segments from one mile marker to the next. Luxury watches flash time for each mile passed while continuing to record total race time, and recall splits for postrace analysis. Some watches have a pacer that beeps precisely when your feet hit the ground at your desired pace. To me, this robot-racing is almost cheating, and the distracting noise is annoying to others.

STARTING TOO FAST

Here's the biggest sin in racing. "But I was feeling so strong the first few miles." I hear this over and over even from experienced competitors who should know better. If you run well ahead of goal pace while you're feeling good, you're ahead of the game. Right? Wrong. A fast early pace is the reason most runners slow over the second half. As pace starts to slip away, so does confidence, particularly if many runners pass. As you slip mentally you slow even more, maybe even dropping out.

The majority of runners in every race start too fast. Joe Henderson, who has paced himself well as a running writer for over three decades, advised in *Racing Techniques*: "A super-fast start isn't 'money in the bank.' It's a severe drain on limited reserves. Physiologists have estimated that every second faster than level pace in the first half of the race costs a second or two at the end; 2 seconds cost you 4 or more; 3 seconds slows you by . . . Well, they say there's a geometric progression." And the longer the race the longer you'll suffer.

David Costill, Ph.D., explains in *Inside Running*, "The primary source of energy during the early stage of a race will be the glycogen stored in the muscles. If the pace is unusually fast in the first few minutes, the quantity of glycogen used will be markedly greater and the muscles' stores will be seriously depleted. At the same time, the by-products of rapid glycogen breakdown may result in a large production of lactic acid, which increases the acidity of the muscle fibers. Proper pacing can minimize the threat of glycogen depletion and lessen the chance of premature exhaustion." Start too fast in a short race and "the Bear jumps on your back" as lactic acid builds up; start too fast in a long race and you'll "hit the Wall" due to glycogen depletion. Which is worse? In either case, you'll slow dramatically. Although the discomfort is more intense, you're likely to be able to finish a short race since glycogen supplies won't run out. In a long race, you'll suffer longer and may run so low on energy that you can't finish.

The problem is the first half of a race seems too easy. Henderson sums it up: "You know you should be saving something for later, but your body is crying 'faster.' It's hard to hold back. Then comes the second half, which is a different problem altogether—almost a different race. This is where you begin to hurt. Where did all that energy go? Your body now cries 'slower,' and you know you should be going faster. It's hard to hold on."

This start-fast strategy isn't much fun (for long); in fact, it's painful. Go ahead, start fast if you want. You surely won't be alone. It may work out. But when it doesn't, let these words haunt you: "I told you so!"

PACING OPTIONS

So what is the best pacing strategy? Since research demonstrates that energy requirements increase dramatically with even the slightest acceleration, most exercise physiologists advocate even pacing. Many coaches and runners, however, promote the advantages of other options. Find what works best for you through experience. And what works best for one race course or distance, or weather condition, may not be ideal for another. Following are some options:

Even pacing. You'll get the best mileage per gallon of gas by driving your car at an even, not-too-fast speed of about 50 miles per hour. You'll be less likely to "run out of gas." This may be the most efficient system for most runners, too. The goal here is to run the same time split mile after mile. I've run some big PRs with even pacing, including a marathon in which I ran every mile within 5 seconds of each other. I felt like I was on automatic cruise control, locked into a steady gear, driving myself with perfect energy efficiency. With even pacing the first few miles seem easy and warm you up. Yet, you won't give away time as you would in a slower-start system.

With even paced racing, however, you will have to really push in the middle of the race on because you don't build up a time cushion. As the miles go by, the effort needed to keep the same pace increases. Lack of concentration can quickly put you behind goal pace. Play a little game: Run from mile marker to mile marker, seeing how close you can come to hitting your goal pace at each split. A good goal is to run each mile within 5 seconds of goal pace.

Henderson promotes two-part racing: Divide the race distance in half; the more equal the half-times are, the more efficient your pacing. Most of the world records in distance races have been set with a deviation of less than 1 second per mile from the first and second half times. Notes Henderson in *Masters Running and Racing*, "The lesson for you from the fastest and best-trained runners is this: If you start faster than you finish, you lost considerably more speed in the last half than you gained in the first. And if you drop too far behind an even pace in the first half, you can't make up that lost time in the second."

If the course is mostly flat, straight, and without strong winds or excessive heat, running an evenly paced race can be accomplished almost flawlessly. Keep an even effort when faced with hills, winds, and turns, and try to make up some or all of lost time on easier sections of the course. Despite superb training and perfect pacing, too much exposure to these obstacles won't allow even pacing. Take comfort that your competitors are slowed, too.

Hold back at the start, then run even pacing. The body, just like a car, runs more efficiently when properly warmed up. It's nearly impossible in most races to keep a running warm-up going right up until the start. Most likely, you'll be squeezed together like sardines and held there for several minutes. By easing out for the first half-mile to mile in short races, and for the first 1 to 3 miles in longer races, you'll warm-up gradually, save energy for the work ahead, minimize lactic acid buildup, and keep body heat from building too rapidly. Many runners feel less tense in the early going if they start slowly, and gain confidence as they pass runners after picking up the pace.

How slow to start? About 10 seconds per mile slower than what you want to average. Then, gradually pick it up to even pacing at goal pace or up to 5 seconds faster than that pace. At the end, you may have enough energy saved to reclaim, and more, what you lost in time at the start.

Negative splits. Many coaches insist this is the most effective way to race. The idea is to run the second half faster than the first. Jogging the first half and then sprinting the second will guarantee a great split differential to brag about, but it won't result in a optimal performance. Run the first half slightly slower (5 to 10 seconds per mile) than goal pace, and the second half slightly faster. For example, a good goal for a 40-minute 10K would be splits of 20:15 and 19:45. Ideally, you'll gradually gain speed as you get closer to the finish line, although you may slow the pace somewhat as you tire. You'll also pass a lot of runners, feeding your resolve to keep pushing and passing.

Negative split strategy won't work if the second half of courses are more difficult than the first, or if the weather worsens. However, saving effort for the second half may still improve performance relative to the competition. In good weather and on fast courses, negative splitting may produce fast times. Yet, except for long races, it's difficult to catch your competition if you're not reasonably close. For this reason, most Elites maintain contact with the leaders. Negative splits are harder to do in marathons due to increasing fatigue and glycogen depletion.

Negative splitting is especially valuable when moving up in distance and for hot weather racing. This, or the previous start-slow method, may be the only pacing strategy available in a crowded start. But it's easy to chicken out with these methods: Take it too easy for too long, and you'll never reach your potential. This style doesn't work well for me. I get anxious being behind schedule, costing confidence, and I'm not good at pushing to pick up the pace. And remember, there's less time to make up for a slower start in shorter races than longer ones.

Train with negative splits to race this way. After all, you need to program your mind and body to do the opposite of how most people race. To practice this strategy, run easy the first half of a steady run, then pick it up for the second half. A good way to run this workout is on out-and-back courses. Go easy to the turnaround (whether a set distance or time period) and then run harder coming back.

Start slow, push in the middle, and hang on. This is favored by many top runners as the best way to combine race pacing with head-to-head tactics. They flow with or behind the lead pack until they're ready to pick it up. Then they start moving away from runners as they "lower the hammer." Bill Rodgers was a master at employing this strategy, often busting open races with his fastest pacing in the middle miles. He then had the physical and mental strength to hang on for the win. The lead pack in most road races run this way. When the pace quickens, the race becomes a matter of attrition. If the pace were run more evenly, the pack would stay together longer. The average runner can't body-monitor as precisely as an Elite, and can't handle pace changes as efficiently. Actually, many top runners find out the hard way they can't either.

Pace by even effort. On a flat course, the first few miles don't take as much effort as the last few. So a 6:50 pace at the start may be equal in effort to a 7:00 pace in the middle miles, and a 7:10 pace in the final miles. Ideally, you'll save a little energy to pick up the effort and pace for a finishing kick. Following this strategy, you may average 7:00 for the race.

Building a slight time cushion, which increases by a few seconds each mile early in the race, develops the confidence that you can run your goal time. Or, you may dare yourself to move to a new level. If you're having a good day, you may pop a good race by maintaining your starting pace to the end. Many of my breakthrough races came with this pacing method. Of course, you're taking the chance you could misjudge the effort and pay the price late in the race.

PACING TIPS

Here are some general guidelines:

- Don't panic if you start too fast. If you catch yourself soon enough, you may be able to salvage the race by using your head. You'll throw your rhythm off by slamming on the brakes. Pull in the reins a little at a time, but do "hold your horses." You may feel great at this point, but risk falling apart down the road. Cut the pace back gradually by about 5 to 10 seconds per mile slower than goal pace. Do this for a half-mile to mile of a short race, up to 2 to 3 miles for a long one. Then, get back on goal pace. Slowing more than that, you'll lose too much momentum and find it difficult to bring the pace back to goal pace after you're under control. Further, the extra cut in pace probably won't help you recover any more. Runners with a goal of just finishing may be wise to take a walk break until getting under control and back on pace.
- Adjust according to splits and your body signs. Remember, uphills and headwinds cause slow splits, and downhills and tail winds contribute to fast ones. Also, heat gradually slows despite your determined effort to keep on schedule. If you're expending too much energy to keep on pace, back off a bit. The sooner you adjust, the less the damage.
- Memorize or write down and carry your split-goal times. Write them on paper and wrap the paper in

plastic for protection, or write them on your hand or arm. Use waterproof ink and write large enough to see while on the run.

- Split times are occasionally inaccurate. Wear your own watch to check splits at each mile marker. In some cases, mile markers are accidentally placed improperly. Develop a sense for accurate pacing and an awareness of the quality of the runners around you to help protect you against these errors. Don't panic if splits seem way off. The more they're off, the more you can be sure they are inaccurate. Have confidence in your pacing and fitness.
- When you begin to tire, the effort necessary just to hold a decent pace will increase. Think of how you stayed strong late in your long runs, and over the last few long intervals in speed training.
- If you're way off pace and feeling real bad, cut back and use the race as a training run, or drop out to minimize risk of injury or fatigue. Persevere if possible, but don't try to be a hero if you're fighting injury or illness, overheating or cold, extreme fatigue or mental burnout.
- If you're past the halfway point and feeling good, don't be afraid to pick it up slightly and go for a really good time. Take advantage of days when everything feels great; we don't have a lot of them.
- It's not easy for most runners to know how fast they're running, and whether they can hold that pace to the finish. Getting a feel for race pacing is largely a matter of trial and error. With experience you'll develop a feel for the right speed, especially if you race the same distances frequently. You'll automatically flow into the proper pace, learning it is right for you by monitoring not just your watch, but your breathing as well. You will know when to pick it up or slow it down, despite what the watch says.
- Don't let the watch cause undue pressure. Many runners run better when "listening to their body."

In fact, I ran my best race as a fifty-year-old over a course that had no mile markers.

PRACTICING PACING

Most competitors run slower than race pace day after day in training. It's not easy to suddenly switch to a faster pace when the starting horn goes off. Develop a feel for the running form, breathing, and rhythm of a particular race pace by practicing it at least a few times before key races.

Intervals. Running intervals at or near race goal pace gives you a feel for that pace. To make race pace seem easier, practice pacing with faster than race pace intervals. Intervals mimic the race: You have to hold back in the first ones, push a little in the middle, and really work to stay on pace in the end. Aim to run each interval at the same pace. Also, run splits—such as each quarter-mile in a one-mile interval—near the same time. If you can't hold pace as these workouts progress, it's because you ran too fast at the start. Better to learn that on the practice track than the race course!

To prepare for races using other pacing strategies, mimic them with your intervals. Start slower than race pace and gradually lower the times for the intervals (or the second half of each interval) to prepare for negative split races. Run intervals and splits by equal effort if that's your race strategy. Throw in some fast intervals in the middle of the workout (or pick it up in the middle of each interval), or run the last one hard (or the last 100 yards of each interval) if you want to practice those pacing techniques.

Steady-paced runs. To get a feel for pacing, time yourself each mile over reasonably flat, measured courses. See how close you can come to running them all at your goal time. You can run these at your normal training pace, or slightly slower than 10K race pace as tempo runs of 2 to 5 miles. With our running classes we offer steady-paced workouts over an out-and-back measured course. Our students use this route to practice going out and coming back in the same time, or playing the negative split game. Runs of 4 to 6 miles at half-marathon pace, or 6 to 13 miles at marathon pace will help develop a feel for pacing for longer races.

Practice races. Run some races slower than full effort to practice pacing for a longer race distance. For example, run a 5K at 10K pace; or a half-marathon at marathon pace. Run some build-up races hard, but try out different pacing strategies. It's better to experiment in low-key races than in your peak events.

KNOW AND SEGMENT THE COURSE

To perform well in a race, make sure you're familiar with the course. Eliminate surprises and look for places to gain an edge. By knowing what it actually looks and feels like, your visualized "rehearsals" will be more effective. If you live near the race course, practice the route (or at least key sections) before race day. If this isn't possible, perhaps you can drive the course. Some runners get "psyched out" by touring a course: It may seem long and very difficult. But the confident runner has the advantage of knowing the location of all the key landmarks.

If you can't see the course in advance, the next choice is to get to the race early and jog parts of the route. Also, ask other runners for advice about the course, and try to get hold of a course map. The first thing I do is find where and how tough the hills are on the course. Then, I'll make sure I'm familiar with at least the first half-mile to mile at the start and the last half-mile to mile at the finish. For most runners these are the most important sections.

Whether you're strong or not on the hills, knowing when to expect them helps prepare mentally for their challenges. It's no fun being suddenly surprised by a steep hill. If you catch one near the start, you'll want to plan for a more cautious starting pace. If you're aware a hill is coming at a critical point late in the race, you'll save a little physical and mental energy for the climb. Knowing about long stretches of early downhills, you'll be careful not to get going too fast or risk paying for it later. You'll know in advance that time splits aren't as good as they seem due to the friendly terrain. Some courses offer long stretches of flats or downhills in the middle of the race which are good places to pick up some time and places.

Get off to a good start by being knowledgeable of key obstacles—turns, hills, narrow sections—in the opening mile. You'll have periodic mental letdowns during the race, and by knowing the challenges coming up throughout the course you can set short-term goals: "Make it to the top of that next hill and then I get to go downhill for a while." Know where to expect faster and slower miles. If the first mile is mostly downhill, for example, a 7:15 effort may end up a 7:00 mile. You'll know it won't be necessary to put on the brakes if the effort is easy. If the last mile includes a big hill, you may need a 7:00 effort to produce a 7:15 mile. You'll know to build up a slight cushion prior to the last mile in order to hit your time goal.

The most important aspect in prerace course preparation is being totally familiar with the last mile and knowing, *for sure,* exactly where the finish line is located. Most races start and finish near the same spot so there usually is no excuse for not knowing where the finish line is at.

Pick landmarks in advance that you'll use on race day to trigger your final attack, whether against the clock or other competitors. Some examples: a traffic light with a half-mile to go, a turn with 660 yards to the finish, a building a quarter-mile to the end. Or, station family and friends at a key location near the finish. Sighting them jumping up and down, and hearing them shouting your name, can be the signal for you to dig down deep for more strength. You'll gain confidence with their support, and the knowledge that the battle is almost won.

SEGMENT THE COURSE

Break the race distance up in your head. It makes the race go by easier. According to research by Dr. Brent Rushall at Lakehead University in Ontario, Canada, performance improves if the athlete attains goals along the way rather than just a single, final goal. You can segment the course by mile markers, landmarks, or both. Some runners concentrate only on hitting each mile marker in a certain goal time. Others prefer keying on major landmarks, such as the top of a hill, a turnaround point, or key spots where they've placed cheering fans. By breaking the course into bite-sized pieces, you can keep yourself pushing to a goal that is possible to reach. When you begin thinking only of a finish line miles away, it's too easy to get mentally fatigued. Set short-term goals along the course to concentrate on, and to provide you with successful experiences to keep you going. Each segment provides an intermediate finish line, and a new starting line.

The more you know the course, the better you can segment and visualize your successful race. I break down a 10K in Central Park into six segments: starting mile, north hills, west hills, flat lower loop, Cat Hill, Museum to finish. If I didn't segment courses in advance, I'm not sure I'd have the staying power to keep on a strong pace, or hang on to a competitor. Know your race courses, segment them in your mind, and then develop a race strategy for each segment.

FIGHTING THE ELEMENTS

Race strategies need to account for heat, cold, wind, hills, and turns.

Heat and cold. Try to run on the shaded side of the road if it's sunny, and the sunny side if it's cold. In all weather, position yourself in advance to get to fluid stations with a minimal loss of extra effort. Know in advance which side of the road has water or sports drinks, and at which miles. Follow guidelines in Chapter 34 for saving time while hydrating. Chapters 36 and 37 detail how heat and cold affect performance, and various strategies you can use to minimize it.

Wind. Even on the calmest of days, we run into a resistance produced by our bodies pushing through the air. At a 9:00 pace, you use 2 percent of your energy each step just plowing through those billions of invisible molecules of still air. The faster you run, the more energy required to overcome that resistance. A pace of 6:00 in calm air is equivalent to running into a headwind of 10 MPH; nearly 5 percent of energy is used to overcome your own air resistance. Drop that pace to 4:00 and you're creating a headwind of 15 MPH. When running outdoors you face the combined air resistance you create and any headwind provided by Mother Nature. How much headway can you make against a headwind? The energy required to run a 6:00 mile against a 15 MPH wind is similar to running a 5:00 mile in calm air. The stronger the wind, the greater the percentage increase in effort, according to studies at Penn State University by Dr. Peter Cavanagh.

Tail winds with speeds up to your running pace act to vacuum the air out of your way. Velocities greater than your running speed actually give you a push. But let that wind speed blow against you and that feeling of effortless running soon becomes a struggle. Studies by Dr. Mervyn Davies of Great Britain found a tail wind produces an energy gain about half as much as you lose with the same headwind. You read that right: Mother Nature doesn't play fair! A headwind slows you more than a tail wind of the same speed helps. The lesson learned: If race day arrives with strong headwinds, set sail for another race (or convince the race directors to run the course in the reverse direction!).

The slower the runner, the more time lost due to a headwind. According to Dr. Jack Daniels, a three-hour marathon runner loses 11 seconds per mile when running into a 5-mile-per-hour headwind and 25 seconds per mile when facing a 10-mile-per-hour headwind. That's an extra 5 to 11 minutes over the marathon distance; but a four-hour marathoner running the entire race into the wind loses approximately 15 to 32 minutes with the same winds.

Now the good news: A tail wind helps the slow runner more than the fast. The three-hour marathoner runs 8 seconds per mile faster with a 5-mile-per-hour tail wind and 18 seconds faster with a 10-mile-per-hour tail wind. The four-hour marathoner, however, gets pushed along even more at between 10 and 24 seconds per mile!

When running into the wind, lean forward slightly to decrease the resistance. Stay relaxed maintaining good running form and conserving energy. Try to tuck in behind others to reduce the wind resistance. Look for a big runner and keep as close as you can to properly "draft." Chester Kyle, a professor of mechanics at California State University, reports you cut wind resistance by 31 percent if you stay 10 feet behind another runner; by 51 percent if you're within 5 feet. If you're with a pack of runners on a windy day, take turns shielding each other from the wind. Hang with a group as long as you can. The effort will be far easier than if battling headwind alone. When you have a tail wind, try to take full advantage of it by moving away from the pack—go behind the others or to the side in order to better sail.

Adjust your pacing for the winds. The best strategy for windy days is the same as with up and downhills: Maintain equal *effort*. You'll lose time if you have an equal amount of head and tail winds in the race. Don't be disappointed if you run much slower than your goal time because of strong winds. On the other hand, don't think you've entered a new dimension if you run a super fast time with a strong tail wind.

If it's a windy day, know in advance where it'll help and hinder your efforts. Look for open stretches (such as fields or bodies of water) that present challenges, as well as that are sheltered from wind. If you know that certain turns in the course will bring about a sudden change in wind, you can mentally prepare better.

Hills. This is for sure: You can't run as fast on a course with significant uphills as on the flat. Researchers at Springfield College and the U.S. Army Research Institute of Environmental Medicine in Natick, Massachusetts, studied runners as they raced for 30 minutes on three types of courses: flat, early uphills and later downhills, and early downhills and later uphills. They ran about 3 percent faster on the level course (equivalent to about a minute for a 10K race) as both types of hilly routes.

Even if you race over a hilly course with an equal amount of ups and downs, you lose. You can't totally make up the loss of energy and time on uphills when you come down the other side. According to research by Dr. Daniels, the theoretical energy cost increases about 12 percent on a 1-degree slope, but you only gain back 7 percent coming down that slope. So you get back only about half the time you lose going up the same hill. Further, many runners make the mistake of trying to run too fast on the uphills and not taking enough advantage of the downhills. The best way to handle a hilly course is to try to maintain an even *effort,* not necessarily pace per mile, going up and down hills.

Push too much going up and you'll greatly increase heart rate, breathing rate, body temperature, and lactic acid accumulation. This will make it difficult to return to your goal pace when you return to the flats. To minimize this, cut the pace back to keep effort about the same. Adjust more the steeper and longer the hill. The effort shouldn't feel substantially tougher than on level ground at race pace. Be especially cautious on hills early in the race. The Springfield research demonstrated that, contrary to what one would think, killer hills affect performance more when confronted early than late in the race. Why? Most runners charge up hills too fast early in the race while feeling fresh. As a result, blood lactate levels rise quickly and remain high throughout the remainder of the race. If a runner is well warmed up and then runs fast up a hill late in a race, the buildup is less. Advises researcher Jeffrey Staab, slow the pace in the early uphill sections enough so that your breathing rate doesn't increase. You'll lose a little time in the early going, but save time in the end.

Okay, so hitting the hills too fast too early will set you up for a bad performance. But have those researchers faced a tough hill near the end of a race? "Hills are great levelers," said Dr. George Sheehan in *Running & Being*. "If there is anything that cuts a runner down to size, it is a reasonably long hill with a fairly steep grade. And particularly if it is placed near the end of a race. Hills make all men brothers." I agree with Sheehan; I'd prefer to get hills out of the way earlier, not later.

You can minimize lost time on hills by shifting to an efficient hill-running gear and using sound strategy. Don't let hills beat you psychologically. Attack them gently with confidence gained from hill training. When running uphill, pick landmarks along the way as short-term goals to make it easier, and use the runners around you to help you up. I focus on a spot between the shoulder blades of a runner in front of me, mentally attach a rope, and allow that runner to pull me uphill. Flash back to some of those tough hill workouts to make your charge up the hill easier.

It's a different story on downhills. You can increase pace by about 10 to 15 percent on moderate downhills without an increase in heart rate or lactic acid accumulation. You gain a significant advantage (although this shrinks some as the downhill grows steeper). This is why race results on "aided" courses that have a significant net elevation drop aren't accepted for record purposes.

But many runners don't take full advantage of downhills. They "brake" due to fear, or haven't perfected downhill racing technique. Combine a little bravery with some caution here. Run too slow on the downhills and you risk falling behind other runners, but freewheel too fast and you risk injury due to the eccentric forces on the leg muscles. When going down let gravity go to work and pick up the pace. Go ahead, push it a bit even if you feel you're going a little too fast. But stay under control, and don't push hard on steep downhills. The trick is to take off the brakes and run with relaxed form. This you learn with race experience and downhill drills (Chapter 11). Chapter 31 details proper racing form for making the most of downhills and minimizing the loss on uphills.

Curves, turns, and slants. Curvy courses and those with sharp turns are longer and slower. Why? Rounding turns forces you to slow down and interrupts even pacing. Race directors don't measure courses as if runners were driving a car, always staying in the right lane and making rounded turns. Rather, they take every possible shortcut a runner could possibly use on curves and turns. They measure perfect tangents at all times. You can't possibly run that precisely. Besides, you have other runners and spectators in the way. So you actually run longer than the measured race distance. Don't assume the shortest possible distance is next to the curb. Minimize distance lost by running tangents, cutting straight lines at curves to cut off excessive distance. This will save precious seconds, and gain some distance on competitors who don't take advantage of this strategy. Turns can be dangerous, so be cautious. You can strain a muscle on a tight turn, slip and fall if the footing isn't good, or get tripped up by other runners. Unfortunately, some races include hairpin turns (even within the first half-mile!). Be especially prepared for them.

Most roads are crowned or banked to facilitate drainage, not runners. Running on a slant causes an imbalance of stress on muscles which may result in performance loss or injury. Run on the flattest part of the road as much as possible. That may be in the middle or off on the shoulder.

LINING UP

If you don't get a fairly good start, nothing you do in the middle or final miles will make up for it. Make sure you position yourself well at the start line. Where you stand at the start of a race is a good measure of your level of confidence and common sense. Don't just line up next to your friend—he or she may be too fast or too slow for you. Don't line up in the front of the pack with the 5-minute milers if you're a 10-minute miler. Not only will you get in the way of others, but you will most likely start too fast and ruin your race. On the other hand, if you seed yourself too slow, you'll end up tripping over other runners for the first mile or two. If slower runners are crowding the way you'll lose valuable time at the start. Line up with confidence with or slightly ahead of other runners of your ability level. Many races post lineup signs according to your expected pace per mile. Since most people cheat at this, line up slightly ahead of the appropriate pace signs. Look for runners you know and position yourself accordingly. If you see a runner who is slightly better than you and runs a good steady pace, line up behind him or her and use that runner as a guide in the early going. Top women and masters runners who want to be competitive with their peers usually line up close to the front even if they aren't as fast as many of the runners around them. But they need to get a good start for their "race within a race."

Be prepared when the starting time gets close. Don't rush off to the toilet or to change a shirt and miss the start. Often, races start late so try to keep moving, but stay near the start area. Sometimes races suddenly start with little or no warning.

STARTING OUT

Your first goal is avoiding getting trampled by the crowd, and getting into a good position and a steady race pace as soon as possible. Keep your hands up to ward off runners in a crowded start, keep your feet low to avoid tripping. Flow with the crowd, whether it is faster or slower than your intended starting pace, until you can establish your own pace.

Don't take off too fast in an effort to get a good start, but be alert and get out quickly or you'll find yourself trapped behind slower runners. Up-front competitors try to establish a position over the first 100 to 200 yards with a controlled acceleration before settling into a fast steady pace. Beware of the vacuum effect: A wave of runners up front starts off fast and sucks everyone behind them out too fast. Once you've managed a good start, the next goal is to reach the one-mile mark relaxed and under control, effectively shortening the race by a mile.

If you're stuck in a slow start, don't panic and swerve in and out of people, passing like a lunatic. Not only will you risk injury to yourself and others, you will waste a lot of physical and mental energy. Instead, calmly make your way through the crowd. As space opens up, gradually get to your race pace. Later, if you feel comfortable, pick up your pace slightly in an effort to make up for time lost at the start. But be careful or you could blow your race. It may be best to just write off the lost time and note in your diary: "Lost 2 minutes at start."

In mass races with thousands of runners, you most likely will have no choice but to start slowly, writing it off as a fun run. If you wish, start your watch when you get to the starting line and time your personal effort. In these events, jog through the first few miles and then gradually pick up steam, and pick off runners, as you go along. Make the goal to have fun and pass lots of runners rather than set a PR.

THE MIDDLE MILES

These are the Rodney Dangerfields of running: They get no respect. Most runners plan strategies for starting at a proper pace and finishing with a strong effort, but not for the unglamorous middle miles. Here's the toughest part of the race. It's easy to run well at the beginning, or to get psyched up for a sprint to the finish. But during the middle miles you're far enough along to be hurting, but too far from the finish to start kicking. If you fade during those miles midway between the starter's gun and the finish line, you won't reach your goals.

Maintaining pace, form, and concentration here is difficult. Few people are watching, the pack has thinned, and the euphoria of the early miles has been replaced by the reality of fatigue. If you've ever thought about quitting midway through a race, you're not alone. Your ability to concentrate on the task at hand may be the first thing to go. Invariably, your mind will start to wander. That's natural; nobody can concentrate with the same intensity for an entire race. But you can blow your race by not maintaining pace. It's easy to lose focus, and pace, in the middle miles. Call upon the various mental tricks in Chapter 27 to battle fatigue. Try staying close with a pack of other runners. Draw on their energy. It gives you something to focus on instead of the fatigue. Most of all, think about protecting your investment—all the training you did to get to the starting line, and all the effort expended to get to the middle miles. Here's the easiest place to let off the gas. Don't. Keep pushing, just like you keep pushing in the middle intervals of your speed sessions. Recognize you'll have midrace mental letdowns and recover from them quickly to focus again on the road straight ahead. The ability to recognize negative thoughts that strike midrace and not panic or dwell on them comes from racing experience.

THE FINISH

Your final strategic move, the finishing kick, is detailed in the next chapter. Run all the way through the finish line. The only thing worse than not reaching the finish is to get beat a few steps from it or to just miss your goal time. Don't slow as you approach the finish; rather, run hard until a few steps beyond it to maximize your performance. Don't immediately shut off your watch as you reach the finish. First, lowering your arms to do so will cost you a second or two. Second, many races snap your picture at this memorable moment. Don't let the photo and your race lose intensity. Turn off your watch after you're a few strides past the finish. Keep your momentum until you are in the chute. Once in the chute, the race isn't over. Pay attention. Don't pass anyone or let anyone pass you until you've been accurately recorded by officials.

POSTRACE ANALYSIS

Most races aren't all good or all bad. While the experience is still fresh in your mind (within a few hours of the finish) revisualize it. Then analyze the race: Write down what went right—and wrong—to reinforce what you did well and learn from mistakes. Ask yourself some questions: How was your mental preparation? Was your fueling and hydration adequate? Did your clothes and shoes serve you well? Were your pacing and head-to-head tactics effective? Did you maintain concentration and good form? How did you handle the heat, hills, or wind? Did you start and finish well? Were you mentally tough?

Record all the key race details in your diary: splits for each mile, average pace, finishing time and place, weather, course difficulty, et cetera. Compare your time with other races using the charts in Chapter 25. Analyze how you did against your peers. Ask yourself still more questions: Did you meet your time and place goals? If not, why? How can you improve next time? What goals do you have for your next race?

CHAPTER 30

Race Tactics

Note: Please do not read this chapter if you compete near me in races. I prefer to have the advantage.

Some runners enjoy racing against competitors as much as the clock. They are head-to-head racers, not pacers. For these runners, it's a combination of pacing and tactical racing that brings success. When racing head-to-head, you may have to adjust the pace in order to stay in contact with competitors. If you ignore the competition and focus only on your goal pace, you may limit yourself. When runners get caught up in the competition they often achieve big performance breakthroughs. Sometimes employing head-to-head tactics can inspire you to run fast times, but it may also yield slower results. You may have to choose to go for either time or place.

The tactics of competition are largely a matter of outsmarting and discouraging competitors, making them believe they can't beat you. Do this by creating a stressful situation you're prepared to handle, but they're not. A well-paced, fast time may not be good enough to beat you if you've slipped away with a tactical move.

Don't use the same tactics every race. Besides getting boring, your opponents may catch on and be prepared to counterattack. I was undefeated in the county league as a high school two-miler until my faithful game plan didn't work. I had been easily winning races by taking the lead and running a strong, steady pace. After a few laps I'd be alone having worn everyone down. But then in the last meet of the regular season, a big, muscular runner hung on my shoulder until one lap to go and shocked me by sprinting by. I couldn't respond in time to catch him.

The following week in the county two-mile event I had to beat my rival or York High would would win the championship. He lined up next to me full of confidence. He was ready to do it again. But I had a new strategy. The gun went off and I just stood there. Off went the field of 20 runners, including my very confused nemesis. Starting in last place, I gradually moved up through the pack. With three laps to go my opponent grew anxious and took the lead. Confidently, I moved to his shoulder. "Let's see how he likes it now," I said to myself. Sure that he was preparing for a final all-out quarter-mile sprint, I put my secret plan to work. This time I had the surprise advantage as I started my kick with two laps to go. He was completely unprepared for such a long finishing drive and I won by 100 yards. I didn't lower my county record, but I got revenge—and the county championship for the good ol' Dansville Mustangs!

Some race tactics can be carried out as determined well in advance. But often you must respond to situations as they unfold, such as a competitor making an unexpected surge. Practice stressful tactical moves in workouts, and mentally rehearse various tactical possibilities so you can more readily respond in the heat of competition. To win "your race," try the following tactics:

Race the clock. Pace to run your best time and be confident this will be good enough to defeat your competitors. This isn't a real exciting duel, but it may be the most effective way to compete for most runners.

Take the lead. Burst out and lead from the start, whether leading the entire race or certain opponents. Push for the first mile or so and then ease into a pace you can handle to protect your lead. This tactic boosts yours and undermines your opponent's confidence. But it's risky. Unless you're able to get out of sight quickly, your opponents know where you are and can track you down from behind if you falter. You may be able to steal a victory, but unless you're sure you can break away and keep going don't burst to the lead. It's a painful way to lose.

The best way to counter this type of tactician is with confidence in your own fitness. Maintain a reasonable distance behind, keep a pace you can handle, stay relaxed. Don't give up. That's what they want you to do. As the runner eventually slows, and they most likely will, try to gradually close the distance. The tables are now reversed: The momentum is now on your side.

Some runners prefer to lead, but with more caution. Instead of bursting to a lead in an attempt to break away, they'll set a strong steady pace designed to gradually wear out opponents. This is a good way to take away the kick of fast finishers. Some would rather be in control of race pace, setting the tempo for the competition. This allows them to be more relaxed than if trying to hang with or follow their competition. The danger is that this strategy will make it easier for your competitors. If they can draft off you and stay relaxed, you're helping them run a great race.

It's a tremendous burden to know you're being followed. Cautioned Dr. George Sheehan in *Running & Being*: "Running in front may be good for your ego but it is a severe drain on your physiology. Leading is a lonely and often stupid business. The leader should know that he requires more effort to do the job than those running behind him. They are shielded from air resistance by his body; and free from the tension and anxiety and mental effort of setting the pace."

Hang and surge. Run with or follow, working off your opponents, and move away from them in midrace. This is usually the most effective head-to-head tactic. You can gradually quicken the pace until your opponent "breaks," or "surge" away. Surges are short, quick accelerations that rapidly open up a gap. Pass or surge decisively. Lower "the hammer." Break away with a strong move while concentrating on good form and controlled breathing. Create the illusion, at least, that you can keep going at that pace. After these surges of 100 yards or so, ease back into a race pace you can maintain to the finish. The lead you gain with a surge is likely to remain to the end. If your opponent catches back up, try a series of surges to soften them up.

According to Bill Rodgers, a noted race tactician, "To be able to surge is the key when you're battling with a specific opponent. This is true for all levels of runners, but to achieve this, you have to train for it. I model my training to this end." To practice surging tactics, he starts interval workouts at a fast, but controlled pace to mimic the start of races. Then, somewhere in the middle of the session, he throws in a very fast one, a surge. He then finishes with a few reps while tired, just like holding on for the win in a race. I have our classes practice surging with fartlek training.

Most runners prefer to follow by a few yards (but no more than 5 to 10) when employing this tactic. It's generally more comfortable than running stride for stride, or off the shoulder of an opponent. It's easier this way to maintain your own comfortable rhythm; your opponent's stride length or rate may differ from yours. You'll also maintain an element of surprise when you suddenly move ahead. Most up-front racing involves competing side-by-side or off one's shoulder: It's easier to make sudden moves, and respond to them quickly. But this isn't considered sportsmanlike back in the pack in road races and it could cause tripping. The best way to madden and distract an opponent is to shadow him or her by staying a step behind.

What if you're being shadowed? If you sense a runner following you closely they have one of two things in mind: They're tired and are using you to pull them along until they feel better, or they're feeling good and are waiting for the right spot to pass. If you can handle it, a strong surge will allow you to break away from these hangers-on. Or, slow the pace allowing them to pass, then reverse the shadowing strategy.

When is the best time to make a move in a race? You can predetermine where you will make tactical moves. Decide this after studying the race course. For example, you may push on a downhill to open a lead. Often it's best to react to how you or your opponent is running rather than follow a set strategy. If you're feeling peppy, or if your competition seems to be struggling a little (sloppy form, heavy breathing, erratic pace), that may be the best time to go. Another good time to surge by an opponent is at fluid stations. You can occasionally skip one and pick the pace up while your opponent is drinking, or take fluids quicker than your competition.

Be prepared to counter surgers. If an opponent gradually increases the pace, try to hang on. If they surge away with a sudden burst, mentally toss a lasso over their shoulders and gradually pull yourself back into contact. Don't respond immediately. Don't panic or give up. Remember the distance gained by a competitor on a surge may be the distance between you at the finish if you don't react.

Most races up-front are won or lost with hang-and-surge tactics. But this plan is risky for non-Elites since it requires superb physical and mental conditioning. Don't try to blast away from an opponent too early in a race or the tables may be turned later.

Hang and kick. If you have superior speed, maintain contact and then outkick foes to the finish line. Ah, yes. The finishing kick is so glorious it deserves more discussion.

THE FINISHING KICK

There's nothing more exhilarating than a strong kick in front of all the finish line spectators. Even a mediocre race is more acceptable if you can muster up a good-looking kick, passing back at least a few of the runners that caught you struggling earlier. On the other hand, there's nothing more frustrating than to run the whole race ahead of a competitor, only to have him or her sprint by at the end. Or, to just miss your goal time because you couldn't pick up the pace as you neared the finish clock. It doesn't have to be this way! Develop a strong finishing kick. This might be a strong move to defeat others, or to shave precious seconds off your time.

Kicking demands more than pure speed at the end of a race. It involves the ability to shift suddenly into a higher gear at a point where the natural urge is to just hang on. It requires the will to go fast in the face of fatigue. Generating a kick depends on several other factors. The form mechanics of switching to a "finishing gear" is detailed in Chapter 31. If you don't pace yourself properly, or your legs aren't strong enough to handle the hills and distance, you won't have enough strength to kick. Most competitors have enough strength to support a kick, even if they're not sure about it due to fatigue; but, they may not be able to sprint because they lack leg speed. You're either born with plenty of fast-twitch fibers, or you have to work to slightly improve what speed you have.

The kick is as much a mental as a physical weapon. The ability to finish fast gives you the psychological edge of having another gear you can use. You know you can "turn it on" when needed. If you're confident in your ability to kick, it will be there for you. But if you believe you don't have a good kick, you won't.

All of the elements of a successful kick are pulled together with practice. Speed training helps you learn to stay relaxed at race pace and faster, improves anaerobic capacity, hones running form, trains fast-twitch muscle fibers so they can be called into play when needed, and, most important, develops a strong kicker's mentality. Speed workouts of 220 to 440 yards are especially helpful. When doing fartlek training incorporate some short, fast accelerations to simulate the finishing kick. We practice the finishing kick with our running classes with cutdown workouts. For example, we'll run intervals of one mile, three-quarter mile, half-mile, and one-quarter mile. Each is run as if it's the final distance to the finish line and you're kicking it in. Since each interval is progressively shorter, the speed gets faster, too. This builds confidence to generate speed at the end of a race. By running speed workouts with, and against, other runners you practice the intensity of racing opponents to the finish line. Where possible, do speed workouts into the finish line of upcoming races to develop a pattern of familiarity and success.

Where do you start your finishing kick? Dr. Sheehan noted: "Even in the end there is strategy. It is not enough to have the speed. Not enough to give your all. That sprint, that giving, must be done at the right time, at the precise moment that allows no adequate response. It must be checkmate."

If you're a fast kicker, the closer to the finish you can wait before starting a kick the better. This may be 50 to 100 yards. But if you're not blessed with lots of speed, you may need to kick from farther out, enabling you to get away from a faster sprinter. This takes careful timing. You can sprint too soon, run out of gas, and be passed back. If you can't break a faster opponent early with surges or a hard pace, start your final kick one-quarter to a half-mile from the finish. This tactic may wear them down, negating their speed, or catch them by surprise, defeating them mentally. On the other hand, don't wait too long to reel in an opponent. Get close with a mile to go to be well-positioned to kick. A wait-and-kick tactic may defeat your opponent, but it can result in a time slower than your ability. Respond to kickers by moving with them, staying close, and then, if possible, outkicking them from behind.

Continue your kick beyond the finish line. By letting up too soon, you may get passed before the line, or lose seconds off the clock. Make it a habit to run hard until you reach a point 5 to 10 yards beyond the actual finish line. Finish strong, but please don't jog through the race and then sprint by hard-working runners with a mad, all-out sprint to the cheers of the crowd (who don't know you held back earlier in order to show off). Be a strategic kicker, but not a hot dog finisher.

TACTICAL TIPS

The following additional tips may help you defeat your competitors, whether you're fighting for the win or to beat a "friendly" rival back in the pack.

Adjust tactics for race distances. In a short race such as the mile or 5K, if you don't hold close contact with your opponents from the start, you can't make up the distance. Go out and run with or near them from the start. In longer races you can follow, relax, set your pace, and have plenty of time to go after opponents.

Don't let others psych you out. Focus on yourself, not comments by other runners. You run the race with your legs, not your mouth.

Run with packs. Don't just focus on runners in your age or gender category. They'll be your main interest, but use the other runners in the field to your advantage, too. Use them to hold or push your pace, break the wind, or pull you up hills. Take turns sharing the lead so everyone gets a fair ride. If the pace slows, make a move toward the next individual or group. If it's too fast, back off and look for runners coming up.

Hitch a ride. Sometimes you may find yourself being continuously passed, perhaps because you started too fast or are having a bad day. Minimize the damage by hitching a ride. Drop in behind someone who passes and stay with the pace as long as possible. If you have to let go, take a break and then try to hook up with another runner. Think of competitors as tow ropes.

Team up. By running with teammates or friends of similar ability, you can help each other stay on pace. Hold each other back from starting too fast; push and pull each other to pick up the pace or to surge past other competitors. In team races, the total place score wins. So the more runners each of you passes, the better the team score. Help each other race against teams and individual runners. Don't race against your teammates. Assist each other as long as it's mutually beneficial and then finish according to who is stronger on that day.

Set a place marker and work on it. Perhaps your goal is to place in the top fifty in a race. In the early miles you can count up ahead and determine approximately where that place is and keep it in sight. It's easiest to do this on turns where you'll get a good view. If the course is out-and-back, you can easily determine your place and eyeball the place you're after. Friends stationed along the course can help keep track of where you stand in this game. Of course, this task is tough in mass races if you're behind a few hundred (or thousand) runners.

Set passing goals. As the race progresses, get aggressive. Set small goals of passing runners one by one. See how many runners you can catch over the second half of the race, and over the final mile. That will keep you going strong when tiring.

Passing tactics. Arthur Newton shared his passing secrets in *Commonsense Athletics*: "If I wanted to pass a man, I used to keep behind him for a minute or so—he would be going just too slow for me and therefore I'd be saving up a trifle of energy during this period to make up for extra expenditure. This would be required when I started to pass him. As soon as I was ready I would go slightly faster, and if he still stuck to me would keep it up and listen to his breathing. I nearly always learnt what I wanted in this way. If a couple of hundred yards made much difference to his respiration I knew I was safe and kept going till he dropped back; if however he still managed to get along quite comfortably I might try even half a mile an hour faster and again 'listen in.' All this time I would be going somewhat faster than I wanted to and if my rival still appeared to be quite perky I should deliberately drop behind him until, a mile or two later, I'd start the business all over again."

Pass decisively. Accelerate to passing gear, go by quickly, build a good lead, and don't look back. Make sure your form looks good and your breathing is under control when passing. Leave the impression you "own them." This tactic discourages opponents from battling to hang on to you. After you've gained at least 30 yards, settle back into your pace.

Pass smoothly. Tactical bursts expend energy. For most of the race, especially back in the pack, pass at your even race pace. Often passing really means going past runners who started too fast.

Practice passing. How? In speed sessions, practice surging by runners. When out for training runs, sight runners up ahead, reel them in, and pass smoothly. You can usually pass at least a few runners without having to run too hard. If everyone on your training course is passing you, find a better place to run. I visualize passing runners when I'm driving down the highway, passing cars. I put on my blinker, switch lanes, accelerate, and zoom—I've left another opponent in the dust. But don't speed. Can you imagine explaining to the cops you weren't really speeding, you were visualizing a surge!

Stay alert. If an opponent tries to break away or pass, be mentally prepared to go with him or her. A move can come at any time, so be ready.

Pass 'em back. If an opponent passes, don't give up. Keep them within striking distance, watch for signs of fatigue, and glide back into contention gradually. Newton advised, "When another tries to pass let him get on with it. If you're in better condition he's bound to make the discovery later on." Don't panic. Stay relaxed.

Take advantage of turns. If you're leading an opponent, throw in a burst right after you go around a turn. When they come around and see you again, you'll have gained distance and given yourself a psychological advantage. Or, if the course has several turns, put in a "hide and seek" move: Gain enough distance so that your competitor can't see you, creating the illusion of a bigger lead. Shorten the distance on your opponents by running tangents along curvy courses. Perhaps the most famous example of the advantage gained with this tactic was when Rod Dixon came from behind to win the 1983 New York City Marathon by cutting tangents in Central Park while Geoff Smith followed the traffic lane. Turns are a good place to sneak a peak at who's tailing you. Even better are out-and-back sections where you see who is ahead and behind. You can be motivated by seeing Elite runners duking it out up front, and cheered by all the runners back in the pack. Just be sure to look strong when you cross paths with your competitors on the out-and-backs.

Respect the hills. If you're a strong uphill runner and are in good shape, you'll naturally pull away from some runners without having to pick up effort on hills. Pain-loving runners may surge on hills to pass or break opponents. If you're super-fit and have practiced hard surges on hills, it may work. This strategy can backfire. If you insist on surging on hills, make sure you're well into the race before you try it and that you can handle the extra fatigue buildup more than your opponent.

The advice for most runners: Don't blast up hills; you'll most likely pay for it later. It'll take a lot more energy to gain a few yards going uphill than on the flats. If competitors surge on a tough hill, let them go but try to maintain a reasonable distance behind. They are likely to come back to you later. The best place to make a move is at the crest of the hill, just before the top. This is where many runners take a break to catch their breath. You'll deliver a psychological blow by passing a runner just as they've conquered a hill. I like to stay close to my competitors going uphill, using them to help me to the top. If that uphill is followed by a downhill, then I've got them right where I want them. I'll zoom by with confidence going down.

Don't give up; go for it. *The Quotable Runner* by Mark Will-Weber contains several gems on racing tactics. Here are some that are especially enlightening:

- Alf Shrubb, a champion British distance champ in the early 1900s, advised: "Never really give in as long as you have any earthly chance, and above all don't allow yourself to fancy that you are in this predicament until the gruesome knowledge is absolutely forced upon you. For however bad you may be feeling, it is by no means impossible that the other fellows may be feeling quite as much, if not even more, distressed."
- Bill Rodgers, the "King of the Roads" in the seventies, stated: "My whole feeling in terms of racing is that you have to be very bold. You sometimes have to be aggressive and gamble." Rodgers adds, "If

you want to win a race you have to go a little berserk."

- Herb Elliott, the Australian who set the world record in the 1500 meters at the 1960 Olympics, had a simple philosophy: "The only tactics I admire are do-or-die."

KNOW YOUR COMPETITION

Whether racing up front for the win, further back for age-group honors, head-to-head for bragging rights with your friends (or enemies), or just enjoying spirited competition with runners of similar ability, knowing your competitors can be just as important as knowing the course.

In most races I have a shot at placing high in my age group, perhaps even winning. I track race times of my age-group competitors (as well as men and women of all ages who are often near me in races). After my races, I analyze the results, looking for who I was near, who was in reach, who I beat, and who I should have beaten. I search local race results on the Internet and figure out approximately where I would have placed in comparison to others (Some of my best races I didn't even run!).

Knowing what my competitors are capable of running is to my advantage. If Harry Smith has been running much faster than I'm capable of going, I'll be prepared to keep him in sight, but I won't be foolish enough to go out with him from the start. This runner is my future target. If I see Eddie Jones has been running the times I want, I pace off him, and try to pass him late in the race. This runner is my immediate target. If I'm aware that Joe James has been improving, and is getting closer and closer to me, I'll be prepared to try to hold him off. This runner has me as his target!

Knowing your competitors' times keeps you motivated on tough courses and in bad weather. If your splits are off, but your strong competitors are near, then you know you're running a good race for the conditions. I've had many races where I was disheartened by my times but then decided to tough it out when I realized my competition wasn't having such a great day either. After the race, if you hang tough, you can play the comparison game: "Eddie always runs under 39 minutes for 10K, and he ran 40:30, so my time of 41 flat isn't so bad."

I also learn if competitors are much stronger at longer or shorter distances, how they pace themselves, and how they fare on hills, in heat, and in the finishing kick. This gives me an edge. One thing I never take into consideration: a competitor's assessment of their racing fitness. We all lie here!

A few warnings:

- It isn't always easy to find the runner(s) you're aiming for in races. Try lining up near them at the start. Keep track of them. If you lose sight, forget them and find other runners to key off, or concentrate on time goals.
- It's hard to tell who is in your age group. If my goal is to beat as many age fifty-plus runners as possible, I have to guess by appearance at some of them. I've had races where I busted my gut catching and passing a balding runner, only to find out he was in an older age group. On the other hand, I've seen guys up ahead that looked thirty or forty take first place in my age group. Could I have challenged them if I'd known? One advantage of wearing a hat for us balding folks is for camouflage against those masters runners looking for a target up ahead! Women can't always tell from a distance if runners ahead are women or men. The best strategy for all runners is to assume that everyone within reach is your competition.
- Don't get bogged down with the "pecking order syndrome." If you analyze your competition and know that you should place behind certain runners, you will. Challenge the pecking order; dare yourself to move up to a new level.
- It's fun and motivating to play the comparison game. But constantly comparing yourself to others can be self-defeating (and annoying to others) if you don't keep it under control. Besides, there's always someone faster. Don't beat yourself up because someone keeps getting better and better than you. Don't announce to others that your goal is to kick

their butt. Motivate and support each other in a positive way. Running is just a sport. Be a good sport.

- Knowing your competitors may inspire some runners, but for others it's self-defeating, even nauseating. They may just not have the type of personality to go with head-to-head strategy. They do better competing against themselves and the course.
- One last warning: If you beat me, I'll be looking to get even. I do have a competitive personality. But, I try to keep it in perspective.

EMBRACE THE COMPETITION

Running isn't boxing—the goal isn't to knock out opponents. It isn't combat—you don't kill your enemies. The humane goal of competitive runners is to make it to the finish line ahead of others. Running, for the most part, emphasizes sportsmanship and cooperation more than many sports.

How can you embrace the competition, be a good sport? Wish your competitors luck (or at least recognize them with a nod) before the race; congratulate them afterward, whether you beat them or not. Share the pace and wind-shielding chores occasionally during the race. Be considerate: Look before cutting, or spitting. Share a drink if you see your competitor missed out. Help each other whenever you can. The theory that "nice guys always finish last" need not apply to runners. On the other hand, don't get so carried away with being a good sport that you negate your mental toughness, lose your focus on beating the clock, and, where possible, the competition. A true competitor appreciates an opponent that did his or her best to defeat them. View opponents as partners who, because of their efforts, inspire you to reach new heights. In the end you all win for helping each other do your best.

PART VII

RUNNING FORM AND SHOES

CHAPTER 31

Running Form and Economy

Running economy is how efficient you use oxygen when running at a certain pace. Good running form, along with speed training and weight training, is essential to good economy. Inefficient form wastes energy, detracting from performance. The secret then is to channel energy into efficient movement in order to run your best. Theoretically, runners may defeat more aerobically blessed, but less economic competitors. So if you're up against a competitor that's moving more smoothly than you, hope you're a lot more fit.

Runners have individual styles—their running "signatures." Some shuffle, some flow, some rock, and some roll. I can spot a running friend's form at a distance. Naturally born runners are blessed with a well-coordinated, economical running form. Most of us are given less efficient biomechanics.

But the more you run, the more efficient you get as the body finds ways to conserve energy. Many experts say that little should be done to change the way you run. In fact, some Elites have form quirks due to their body compensating for a biomechanical abnormality. No one is going to change their form for better results.

Most coaches feel that improvements can and should be made for most runners, especially if you have obvious form faults. Besides enhanced running economy, improving form helps prevent injuries. For example, running high on the toes or leaning too far forward can contribute to shin splints or Achilles tendinitis.

Learn the basic principles of good form and spot-check them periodically. They apply to everyone, fast and slow. The main thing is to have good biomechanical form and still run relaxed. Running, when done properly, should be a complete, flowing action that occurs unconsciously. There are four basic parts to good form: arm drive, footstrike, stride, and body posture.

ARM DRIVE

Your arms are not just along for the ride. In fact, they provide the momentum that pulls you along. Try running up a hill with your arms behind your back. You'll soon discover how important the arms are to performance. Penn State University biomechanics professor Dr. Peter Cavanagh found runners need 4 percent more oxygen to run the same speed without using their arms at all compared to when using them. Proper arm drive helps you gain speed, maintain balance, and conserve energy.

The starting position for the arm drive is important. The arms hang loosely from the shoulders with the forearms approximately parallel to the ground between the waistline and chest. Keep the elbows unlocked and slightly away from the body. Pressing the arms rigidly against the body or letting them flop around interferes with efficiency. High arm carriage causes muscle fatigue and tension in the shoulders and upper back, and a shortened stride. Low arm carriage results in excessive forward lean and an inefficient, bouncy stride. Every runner varies slightly in an arm position that allows them to run relaxed and efficiently.

Arm action begins with the hands. Hold them loosely, so the thumb and forefinger or middle finger just touch, "cupping." Don't clench the fists or point the fingers stiffly. The result will be tension and fatigue that can spread to the rest of the body. Shellylynn uses a "potato chip drill" to teach students to hold their hands loosely: They run intervals holding a chip in each hand. Those that break the fewest are the winners! Rotate the wrists so the thumbs are on top. The wrists should be relaxed, but not too loose. Some prefer a cocking and snapping of the wrists when running fast. As you raise the arm up, cock the wrist slightly upward. On the downswing, flick the wrist in a snapping motion, while turning the palm slightly downward and inward. This motion helps focus on good arm drive mechanics.

From the starting arm position, with the hands leading the

way, the arms move in synch with your legs. The opposite arm and leg go up or down in concert to stabilize the torso. As one leg drives into the ground, the opposite arm drives downward to add to the force. Keep the elbows bent at approximately a right angle, but this angle will close slightly on the upswing and open slightly on the downswing.

When running easy, hold your arms in a comfortable position and keep their action to an easy up-and-back small arc. The arms at this pace primarily help keep balance and establish a smooth rhythm. Arm swing is more vigorous and moves through a larger arc with faster running. Leg power is affected by the power of the thrust of the arms. The faster the arms go, the faster the legs can go. The upswing brings the hand close to your body at about the pectoral muscle. On the downswing, the hand should drive to just past the hips, brushing the area just below the side of your waistband. If you don't drive the arms through this full range of motion, you will not be able to run as powerfully; exceeding it wastes energy. Arm motion isn't perfectly up and down. On the upswing the arms move inward slightly. They shouldn't cross the midline of the chest or they'll cause side-to-side movement. The arms move slightly outward on the downswing as the elbow moves slightly away from the body.

Most of the arm movement should be in the lower arms; the upper arms shouldn't move very much, and the shoulders only roll slightly as the hips turn during the stride. Concentrate on driving from the forearm, swinging the arms from the elbow down, with the elbow acting as a hinge, opening and closing a little with each swing. If you lock the elbow and start the arm action with the powerful shoulder and chest muscles, you'll waste energy and tighten up. Proper arm swing is very similar to pushing yourself along a trail with cross-country ski poles. You lead first with the hands, wrists, and forearms—not the elbows.

A strong upper body enhances arm drive. Weight training is highly recommended along with cross-training activities that involve vigorous arm motion. A good exercise to improve arm drive is dumbbell arm pumps: Stand with one foot up on a bench or step for balance and pump the arms rapidly, with the same motion as running, while holding light dumbbells in each hand.

FOOTSTRIKE

Running involves a pushoff and an airborne "float" before the next landing. Footstrike includes how you land and push off. Suggested footstrike for the average runner is *gently* on the heel, allowing the forefoot to come down quietly as your body moves forward. The ankle, knee, and hip joints are slightly flexed to cushion impact at landing and stretch the muscles of the calves, quadriceps, and buttocks. Like pulling on a rubber band, this stretching builds up energy in these muscles and their tendons. The foot should strike the ground near your center of gravity (under the hips) and while the leg is moving backward to minimize braking. An instant after landing, the hips pass over the foot. Footstrike ends as you push off the ball and toe of your foot with a flick of the ankle and a little spring. This releases the "rubber band" energy. The body is propelled upward (but not too high) and forward as the drive foot and leg push against the ground, exerting backward and downward force.

Point the toes straight forward so the feet land in a straight line—as if running on a balance beam. Your foot first hits the ground slightly on the outside edge of the shoe and then rolls inward lightly to the ball of the foot, allowing the foot and body to absorb shock. Pronating too much inward or supinating outward at footstrike increases injury risk. Caress the ground in a rocking motion, spreading out the shock over the whole foot. Since you hit the ground with the force of three times your body weight, it's essential that you land gently.

Minimize footstrike angle. If you land with the sole angled upward at 30 to 45 degrees, as many runners do, touchdown occurs with your foot in front of your body, causing a braking effect. Excessive heel strike produces added shock, and forces you to run with a short, choppy stride. The angle should be slight, almost flat-footed in a midfoot strike. This eliminates much of the braking action and reduces shock.

Heel-ball versus ball-heel footstrike. There are two basic types of footstrike: heel-ball (rearfoot), and ball-heel (forefoot). Running shoes are designed with thick heels to accommodate heel-ball running. But if you run barefoot, you'll notice that natural running form is ball-heel. Most fast runners don't run heel-ball, they run ball-heel. A study of Elites by Dr. Cavanagh found that 60 percent landed on the forefoot, 10 percent on the heel, and 30 percent on the midfoot. Elites run ball-heel so swiftly and smoothly it appears they are running on their toes. With this method you land lightly on the back of the ball of the foot, on the outside edge. As the foot rolls inward, the knee bends slightly to absorb shock as the heel gently touches the ground, so the entire sole of the shoe makes contact. Then, you roll up to the ball of the foot for lift-off, pushing off the big toe. Just before you begin flight, extend the ankle so only the toes touch the ground. Concentrate on "popping" off the ground with a light flick of the ankle rather than pounding the foot into the ground.

The ball-heel method allows you to gain speed by increasing both stride length and stride rate, whereas stride length is minimized with heel-ball running. Proper ball-heel form allows the Achilles tendon and arch to help absorb shock and produce energy for pushoff rather than relying on the muscles. Excessive toe strikers, however, land too high on their toes. This form error minimizes cushioning, increases the strain on the lower leg, and results in too much bouncing and, therefore, wasted energy.

I run heel-ball in training and ease into ball-heel for short races and speed sessions. For longer races, I'm somewhere in between. Runners may not benefit from the more advanced ball-heel footstrike unless they're lightweight, have strong and flexible leg muscles, and can race at least at 7-minute-per-mile pace. Most middle-of-the-pack and back runners will be safer and more efficient using the heel-ball (or actually midfoot strike) method. The best footstrike method is whatever allows you to run relaxed and efficiently.

If you decide to switch from heel-ball to ball-heel running for fast-paced runs, or if you are a ball-heel striker and want to minimize injury by switching to heel-ball for most of your mileage, do so gradually. Give your body a chance to adjust to this new method. Periodically during training runs and races, concentrate on using the new footstrike. Switching to heel-ball running is particularly recommended for marathon training and racing. Switching to ball-heel form may be best for short, intense speed training and races of 5K and less. To minimize injury when switching to ball-heel, be sure to strengthen and stretch key muscles and tendons that will be asked to do additional work. Not all runners can safely change their footstrike. This may not work for everyone; it's practically like learning to walk all over again. You may be better off and safer running with the footstrike that is most natural for you.

If you develop a powerful ball-heel foot drive, keep it fine-tuned. It's easy to fall into the pattern of lazy heel-ball footstrikes which require less effort. If you don't use those springing and driving muscles, you won't be able to call on them to help you run safe and fast on race day. Practice in speed training or form drills.

Whatever footstrike you use, strive to hit the ground lightly and quietly. The sound of your feet decreases as you become more efficient. If runners around you in races are pounding the ground making a lot of noise, chances are your quiet, more energy-saving footfalls will soon be all you'll hear.

STRIDE

Running speed is the product of stride length and stride rate. *Stride length* is the distance covered between footstrikes. Each time you land on either the right or left foot, you complete one stride, or step. A stride cycle consists of two successive strides, beginning and ending with the same foot striking the ground. *Stride rate* is the total number of steps (one with each foot) or stride cycles (one right, one left) per minute. The exact combination of stride length and rate used by each runner differs due to factors such as leg length, muscular strength, flexibility, coordination, and fatigue. As you run faster, stride rate increases slightly; stride length increases even more. To improve performance, improve stride length, stride rate, or both.

The running stride consists of two phases: support (ground contact from landing to pushoff) and flight (or recovery). You should spend approximately equal time in each phase, although at faster speeds you'll automatically propel through the air somewhat longer. If you spend too much time in flight, or too much time on the ground (causing braking), you'll lose speed. When striding, as the right arm drives down, you drive off the left foot. At the same time you raise the left arm while lifting the right knee upward. You propel through the air, landing on the right foot to complete one stride. To complete the full stride cycle, repeat the action to the opposite side.

Video analysis of races show that top runners have better running economy: less vertical displacement (how high the runner raises himself with each stride, the greatest energy cost in running), less overstride, and less time that the driving foot is in contact with the ground (reducing braking). They also have a quicker stride rate and a greater controlled stride length. Top runners maintain stride rate and stride length better throughout the race. Many runners unknowingly slow their cadence and/or shorten stride as they tire late in races. As a result, they slow as the race progresses.

Stride length. As you stride forward, the lead or reaching foot, after it has stretched forward and already started to swing back, should strike the ground more or less directly under your hips. Studies show at least 20 percent of runners overstride. If the foot hits the ground too far ahead of your center of gravity and before the knee begins flexing back, you're overstriding. This causes additional shock and braking. A long, leaping stride is inefficient; you spend too much time in the air. Conversely, a short, choppy stride is wasteful; you spend too much energy to advance a short distance. This is understriding. At least understriders are more efficient than overstriders. Runners with pronounced or distorted knee lift or back kick are also wasting energy.

Stride length shouldn't be copied from any other runner nor imposed by coaches. At any given pace, everyone has a stride length that's best for them; usually it's the most comfortable. A runner's most efficient stride length typically occurs subconsciously.

How to improve stride length? Not by consciously stretching the lead leg out in front of the body as many runners do (resulting in overstriding), but by increasing rear leg drive and range of motion. With strength and flexibility training, speed and hill workouts, and the drills detailed later, you can develop a more powerful stride: lifting the knees slightly higher, pushing off harder at toe-off, and extending each of the three major leg joints—ankle, knee, and hip.

Stride rate. According to Dr. Cavanagh's research, Elites don't stride out as far as the slower runners (who often overstride), but have a quicker turnover rate: 180 to 190 steps per minute compared to just 160 to 170. For most runners, 180 steps per minute

(90 stride cycles) is considered optimal, regardless of race distance. A slow stride rate may contribute to injury as well as loss of speed: You spend more time in the air and raise your center of gravity too high, causing a harder landing.

How do you know if your stride rate is quick and efficient? Dr. Cavanagh suggests testing yourself while running at your regular training pace on a flat surface while counting the times the right foot (or left if you prefer) hits the ground per minute. If your stride rate per minute is less than 90 cycles, you'll probably benefit from shortening your stride and increasing its frequency.

You can't consciously improve stride length, but you can consciously improve stride rate. To do this most effectively, concentrate on taking quick, soft, relaxed steps. Keep your body upright and feet low to the ground. Don't worry here about changing footstrike or stride length. One thing at a time. However, you may need to shorten stride length somewhat at first to speed up your cadence.

Here are some helpful drills:

- Weekly speed workouts run at faster than race pace, concentrating on a quick stride rate, will teach your legs to turn over faster.
- Run up and down a few flights of stairs to train yourself to take smaller, quicker steps. Do this once a week for a few weeks.
- Practice running at a faster stride rate. First, run for a minute at a time while counting your current stride rate. Then, quicken your stride while counting again for a minute. Do a series of three to six of these runs until you can get the feel for running at a rate of 90 stride cycles (180 steps) per minute or slightly faster. An easier way to do this drill, for runners like myself that can't get the hang of counting and running at the same time, is to use a runner's watch that includes a pace beeper. Set it to beep at your goal stride rate. Start running at your normal stride rate and then turn on the beeper. Keep pace with it for a few minutes at a time during your daily runs. Little by little, run at the quicker

> stride rate for more and more of your run. Eventually, you may be able to run the entire workout at a faster stride rate without the pacer.

Stride rate improvements may come quicker and easier than enhanced stride length. But you can only get so much faster this way. Once you perfect the most efficient rate for you, improved performance depends on increasing stride length.

Stride types. There are two basic types of running stride: the shuffle and power stride. The shuffler moves along very efficiently with few extraneous motions. He or she uses the heel-ball footstrike and runs very low to the ground with little vertical lift, skimming the surface with short, quick strides and little knee lift. Speed is gained by increasing stride rate, and only minimally by increasing stride length. The shuffle stride is efficient for long races and for handling high mileage. Most marathoners shuffle for economy.

The power stride is used by most Elites, even in the marathon. Many average runners use the shuffle stride for easy runs and switch to the power stride for speed workouts and races of 10K and less. The power strider uses the ball-heel footstrike, runs with a slight forward lean, and has more knee lift and a longer stride. The power runner rockets through the air rather than skimming the earth's surface. To gain speed, drive hard off the ball of the foot, lift your knee, and naturally extend your stride. How high you lift the knees is relative to the speed. The faster the pace, the higher the lift. Sprinters lift their knees very high; marathoners very little. If you bring the knees up too high you'll lean back, lessening forward drive. The faster you move the upper legs forward, the longer the stride and the quicker the pace. With the power stride you can more effectively increase pace by increasing both stride rate and stride length.

Powerful quads are important to the power stride, as well as strong lower leg muscles so the ankles can help you lift off the ground, saving the hamstrings and other major muscles from being overworked. These key muscles are strengthened by running hills and drills, and with weight training. Stretching for the arch, Achilles tendon, and calf muscles are also important.

The key to running faster is to quicken controlled strides, whether shuffling or powering along. Find a stride that naturally works best for you at a comfortable pace, then switch gears to adjust power and speed for hills, speed training, and racing. I'm basically a slight shuffler in easy training runs and when marathoning, but I'll switch over to the power stride when running shorter and faster.

BODY POSTURE

Former U.S. Olympic coach Bill Bowerman emphasizes that posture is the most essential element in a smooth and efficient running form. He notes: "The best postural position for a distance runner is an upright one. You should be able to drop a plumb line from ear level and it would fall straight down through the line of the shoulder, the line of the hip and then into the ground." This position will keep the greatest majority of body weight directly over the point of ground support and minimize the strain on postural muscles.

Allow your body to move as freely and with as little rigidity as possible. Keep your back straight and chest high. New Zealand coach Arthur Lydiard suggests that you imagine a rope attached to the center of your chest, pulling you toward a three-story-high rooftop a block away. By "tucking in" the buttocks, you can run in an erect, comfortable position. When the hips are under and forward, the calf muscles can be properly used, taking the load off the hamstrings. Leaning too far forward, one of the most common mistakes, cuts down stride length, and places an extra burden on the leg muscles, contributing to lower leg injuries. If the upper torso leans too far forward, bending at the waist, you will force the hips too far back and drastically cut down on the length of your stride. On the other extreme, leaning too far back has a braking effect, and places a severe burden on the legs and back. Heel-ball runners using the shuffle stride run nearly erect, but relaxed. While running fast with the ball-heel footstrike, use a slight forward lean to generate speed. This is the body's natural reaction to the increased drive of the legs.

I often see runners working hard with their heads down, especially at the end of races. A study at Central Washington University determined that running economy is approximately 1 percent more efficient when looking straight ahead instead of looking down at your feet. Why? Your head helps keep you erect. If looking down, you lean forward, ruining your efficient upright running style. Bring the head too far back, and you'll lean backward. Tilting the head to one side or the other will also throw off the efficiency of your movement. Your head weighs about 10 pounds (perhaps more for some of my thickheaded friends), so keep it centered on your shoulders in a natural, relaxed position. Envision balancing this book on your head as you run.

Good running posture is essential to good body mechanics. Maintaining proper body angle while running for long periods of time requires strong postural muscles. Strength training for the upper torso, hip, and abdominal muscles is recommended.

RACING FORM

It's one thing to have good running form at a relaxed training pace, and another to have good racing form. Efficient racing form improves running economy, shaving seconds, even minutes, off your time and giving you an edge over competitors who have poor form. To maximize your potential, develop the ability to maintain form throughout a race and when switching gears to run hills, surge, pass, or kick.

To go faster: 1) *Drive off* the back foot; 2) *Drive up* with the knees; 3) *Drive down* with the arms. As a result of emphasizing "the three drives," you slightly increase stride length (without overstriding) and increase stride rate. You run faster.

Starting gear. Shifting suddenly from a standing start to race pace isn't ideal. If you're fit and ready for a fast time, start quickly to establish a good position and then ease back to a steady race pace. A quick start begins with vigorous arm swings to help you overcome inertia. Lift the knees high and run with "quick feet." Start quick, not all-out. Stay relaxed and under control. After 50 to 100 yards, throttle back to your goal pace. If stuck in a crowded start, run cautiously with your hands up in front of you to ward off other runners and maintain balance. Take short strides and keep your feet close to the ground to minimize tripping. Start slow and then ease into your race pace.

After settling into your race pace, concentrate on the racing form you've practiced in speed training and form drills. Check yourself periodically: arm motion, footstrike, knee lift, body posture, breathing. Have someone meet you at various points along the course to shout out corrections or reminders to you: "Lift your knees"; "Get off your heels"; "Drive your arms."

Passing gear. Passing requires deftly changing gears to pick up the pace until you're ready to ease back to race pace. The strategy of passing runners and surging is discussed in Chapter 30. Passing form starts with an increased arm swing. Quicken the arm drive to get the legs to move into passing speed. Slightly increase foot and knee drive. Passing gear isn't all-out; it's controlled acceleration—just like passing cars when driving. After you've smoothly passed, slow down the tempo of "the three drives." Stay relaxed and keep your breathing under control during passing.

Uphill gear. When you round the bend and see the Big Hill, don't wince. Attack the hill before it attacks you by shifting to a powerful uphill gear to propel yourself to the top. Run the hills at a strong pace, but not all-out. Conquer them with a minimum loss of energy, whether in training or racing. Attack with finesse, not muscle, by climbing with good form and reasonably controlled breathing. Slight modifications in form can improve your racing time over hilly courses.

The key to success is in maintaining the same effort, breathing rate, and stride rate as on the flats. If breathing becomes too labored, you picked up the effort. Don't try to maintain the same pace as on the flats. That'll cost energy. To maintain even effort, pace will slow somewhat as gravity slows you down. But don't slow stride rate. Cortland (NY) State track coach Jack Daniels, Ph.D., emphasizes, "Once you let your turnover slow down going up a hill, fatigue will make it hard to regain your fast rhythm at the top. By shortening your stride and maintaining your stride rate, it will be easier to keep moving at your desired race velocity once you reach the crest. Since the rate is already there, you'll only have to extend your stride length to regain your preferred race speed."

Increase knee lift slightly to allow the feet to get up and out in front of you. It's like climbing stairs: You want to pick your feet up more, but still keep them low to the ground. The steeper the hill, the shorter the stride and the more you need to lift the knees. Quicken the arm drive and push harder off the back foot to help overcome the pull of gravity. But don't exaggerate the arm and leg drive. Keep your head up and eyes focused on an object 20 to

30 yards ahead. Stay relaxed. Tension diverts energy from the real struggle of running uphill.

When running very fast uphill in speed training, or to break a competitor in a race, increase forward lean (but not from the waist), shorten stride, and further increase arm, foot, and knee drive. The steeper the hill or faster the pace, the more you increase "the three drives." The need to switch from heel-ball to ball-heel footstrike, and from shuffle to power strides, also increases. Blast off with controlled power. But if facing a very steep or long hill, you won't be able to maintain powerful form for long. Adjust: Maintain efficiency by cutting back on the foot drive and concentrating on short, quick steps and arm action.

Practice switching gears when you approach hills during some of your daily training runs.

Downhill gear. Most runners ignore downhill form, but you can actually improve race times more by perfecting downhill rather than uphill technique. It seems simple: Take off the brakes and roll. But many runners are hesitant to let go. They fight the downhill by leaning back, shortening stride, landing way back on the heels, and raising the arms to "brake." This slows you down and overtaxes muscles. Others lean too far forward, dramatically lengthen stride, and flail their arms wildly, resulting in an awkward downhill freefall. They gain speed, but at increased risk of injury and with wasted energy. The trick is to increase the descent speed while conserving energy; to harness the force of gravity while staying under control. Concentrate on proper form to maintain momentum, balance, and efficiency. Develop a feel for downhill running so you flow smoothly with the hill like a mountain stream.

How fast you flow is determined by body lean, stride rate, and stride length. Let gravity provide much of the energy. To do this, increase forward lean slightly, but don't bend at the waist. Tilt from the pelvis. Keep the body approximately perpendicular to the surface while falling forward as if you will land on your face. Forward momentum will allow you to catch yourself, please, with each footstrike. To keep a steady, relaxed pace, maintain a body lean that allows the center of gravity to remain over the lead leg. Leaning too far forward produces too much speed; leaning back causes you to slow.

Although you'll stride out slightly longer than on the flats, the key to downhill speed is a quicker turnover. At the start of a downhill, slightly shorten stride length and gradually let stride rate and pace increase as gravity allows. As you get into a good flow, gradually lengthen stride somewhat. The steeper the hill, the quicker the stride rate and faster the pace. Shorten stride length slightly if necessary to control yourself if you start to go too fast, or are on a steep descent. On a slight decline, however, push off the back foot with more power and lengthen stride to take advantage of the opportunity to really pick up speed. As the pace picks up, lift the knees to allow for an increase in stride length. Find the stride length that takes maximum advantage of gravity but allows you to stay under control.

If the downhill isn't too steep and the pace too quick, you should be able to maintain heel-ball footstrike if that is the most efficient and comfortable technique for you. Land as gently as possible and quickly roll forward to push off the ball of the foot. Don't let your foot slap against the ground. Run with "quick feet." Keep them low to the ground, strike lightly, and quickly lift them off the ground to minimize the pounding. When the slope increases or the pace quickens, podiatrist Dr. Steve Subotnik suggests: "Concentrate on landing on the ball of the foot. If you're landing on your heels, you're overstriding. This is important because the foot and leg absorb shock much better on downhills when you land on the ball of the foot under a bent-knee, than when you land on the heel in an almost straight-knee position." If you run ball-heel, it's easier to generate speed similar to pushing off the angle of a sprinter's starting blocks.

The arms aren't needed to provide power, but rather maintain balance and rhythm. On uphills, the arms lead the legs, but on downhills the arms follow the legs. Keep the shoulders relaxed, elbows away from the body, and just let the arms keep in synch with the legs.

If you're going down a very steep or long hill, adjust form for safety. Daredevils zooming down these are often injured, from falling or from overtaxed muscles. Slip into a cautious gear: Shorten the stride to baby steps, bend the knees slightly at footstrike to maximize shock absorption, maintain a slight forward lean or even lean back slightly, and bring the arms away from the body more for increased stabilization. The most important thing is to stay relaxed. If you tense the muscles, you'll be more vulnerable to injury. The most sensible thing to do when you come across a very steep downhill in training is to use the Coach Glover method: Walk it. For me, steep downhills put too much stress on my back and hips. I just turn off my watch until it's over and then start again at the bottom of the hill.

But I don't walk down hills in races (actually, if they are absurdly steep I won't run the race). I fly down hills, and so should you if you want to run your best. Because of my height, I weigh more than most of my competitors, that places me at a disadvantage on uphills where I have to pull my weight against gravity. But my long legs really cover ground on the downhills, and I use my weight to advantage by allowing gravity to force me downward. Use good downhill technique to pick up speed and pass competitors. To race downhill, increase forward lean, stride rate, and stride length. The more you lean forward, the faster you'll have to move your legs to maintain balance. It's simple: Either the legs keep up, or you fall flat on your face. Remember, stride length isn't increased by reaching out more with the lead foot, but by increasing foot pushoff and knee lift with the support leg. The arms don't drive hard, but they must move faster to balance the quicker stride rate. Keep the arm movement up and down, rather than let them flail from side to side. Keep breathing under control and stay relaxed. Learn to "let go" and allow your body to "fall" downhill. Just as with racing down a slope on skiis, you are less likely to fall and will be able to reach the bottom much faster if you push fear out of your mind and concentrate on proper form.

Downhill running form is best practiced on a gentle slope, preferably a more forgiving surface than pavement. Because of the eccentric motion involved, don't practice this form too often. See Chapter 11 for downhill running workouts.

Finishing gear. The better your finishing form, the more runners you'll outkick and the more time you'll shave off the clock. The kick may be a gradual shifting of gears as you gain steam over the last quarter- or half-mile of a race, or a more sudden acceleration of 50 to 100 yards. You'll usually have enough for a finishing kick, even if you don't think you will. The key is to practice your finishing kick in speed workouts and to make form adjustments to gain speed. I take our running classes to the finish line of races in Central Park and have the students practice their speed and form over the last quarter-mile. When they hit that section in a race they go on "automatic," switching to the form they rehearsed.

The finishing kick is dependent on intensifying "the three drives." The kick starts with a vigorous arm drive. Concentrate on getting up more on your toes with the ball-heel footstrike, pushing powerfully at toe-off. Knee lift increases dramatically in order to increase stride length. Whee, we're sprinting now! Stride rate is also quickened somewhat, but the major change is in stride length. Heel-ballers not able to get up on their toes will have to rely on short, compact, very fast strides to kick to the finish. It's important to keep your finishing form going until you drive beyond the line; if you let up as you approach it you'll lose speed, and time.

Well-paced races leave you with enough strength for a strong finishing kick. In reality, you'll sometimes finish just holding on or tailing off. If you've expended yourself too early, concentrate on maintaining proper form as well as possible. Stay relaxed, and keep pumping the arms. If you do, the legs will keep up as best they can. When I'm shot, I concentrate on a shortened arm swing, a compact, efficient stride, and keeping my breathing under control. Running economically will help make up for loss of power as you approach the finish. Think of it this way: The better your form as you're finishing in fatigue, the more runners you'll hold off and the less time you'll lose. On the other hand, if you see your competitors' form deteriorating near the end of a race, go for the kill.

Here's a motivator: You'll want to look good for the finish line photos! At least try to look better than the other runners you're kicking in with. Chapter 30 discusses how the finishing kick fits into your racing strategy.

RACE-FORM WORKOUTS AND DRILLS

You don't win awards or set PRs by looking good at conversational pace. You need to have good form at race intensity to perform your best. Even if you have mastered good racing form, over a period of time inefficiencies can appear for various reasons. Perhaps an injury, or loss of flexibility or postural muscle strength affects your form. Maybe high mileage has turned you into more plodder than sprinter. Regular speed training and drills helps maintain good racing form, and iron out flaws that may develop.

Race-paced training practices the biomechanics and breathing rate required to hold pace. Speedwork at faster than race pace and form drills exaggerate proper form, forcing you to focus on it. They strengthen runners, increase flexibility, and enhance fast-twitch fibers. As a result, running economy is improved. These workouts optimize stride length and rate, and teach you to efficiently power along while staying relaxed. By pumping the arms, lifting the knees, and driving off the back foot much harder in these workouts than in daily training runs, it will be easier to maintain good form habits in races, as well as in easy-paced training runs. Do speed workouts and/or drills once or twice a week for a while to help you improve racing form. Once you've mastered good form, don't completely eliminate these training sessions. It's easy to lose good racing form if you don't keep practicing it.

Here are a few adaptations of speed workouts that'll improve racing form:

- ***Strides.*** These short, brisk accelerations are detailed in Chapter 10. Concentrate on staying relaxed, and the mechanics of "changing gears," not running hard.
- ***Downhill intervals.*** A slight downhill is favored by many coaches to improve leg speed and form for both flat and downhill racing. Here, you can get moving much faster with less effort, getting a feel for increased stride rate and length, and staying relaxed at a very fast pace. See Chapter 11 for guidelines.
- ***Steep-hill intervals.*** Hills force you to concentrate on the "three drives"—foot pushoff, knee lift, and arm motion—to overcome gravity. You naturally change gears to make forward progress. Therefore, I find it easier to teach running form to our classes on a short, steep hill than on the flats. Pick a short (100 yards or so), fairly steep hill. After warming up thoroughly, run three to six reps at 5K pace, jogging

slowly back down. Don't run all-out. This is a drill, not a speed workout. Bound up the hill gracefully like a deer rather than pound up it like a lumbering elephant. Steep hills (Chapter 11) are great for improving muscular power.

Here are some specific form drills. Do about 30 to 50 yards at a time. Start with four or five sets of each, taking a few minutes of rest between. Warm up first with easy running and stretching to minimize injury. If you're new to drills, it might take a few sessions to get used to the coordination and technique involved. It's better to do them on grass or a track than pavement to minimize pounding.

- ***High knees.*** Perform a marching action, walking forward while using an exaggerated arm drive and lifting the knees as far as you can. Just rise up on your toes; you don't leave the ground during this drill. After you've mastered it, try doing it while running. Take very short strides so that you are almost running in place. This drill strengthens the hip flexors and improves power at pushoff.
- ***Butt kicks.*** Run in place, up on the balls of your feet, but instead of lifting the knees, kick the legs back so the heel lightly touches the buttocks. Take short steps while running with a 10 degree forward lean. The flexibility and strength of the quads are increased with this drill.
- ***Skipping.*** Just like when you were a kid, skip, land on the heel, and roll quickly to the ball of the foot. Push off the ground by driving the foot downward, lifting off with a flick of the ankle. Lift the knee as high as possible while driving the opposite arm down. Coordination and pushoff power are improved with skipping.
- ***Fast feet.*** While staying up on the balls of your feet, move the feet forward as fast as you can with small steps. Move the arms rapidly in coordination with the feet. This improves coordination and stride rate.

More advanced plyometrics drills, such as bounding, are better left for high school and college athletes under the guidance of an experienced coach. If they aren't done properly, injury may result.

BREATHING

Efficient breathing is important to performance: It consumes approximately 10 percent of total energy while running. There are two basic rules to breathing on the run: It should follow "belly breathing" principles and be relaxed. The belly should expand as you inhale, and flatten as you exhale. Lie on your back and place this book on your stomach. Take a deep breath. If you are "belly breathing" properly, the book rises as you inhale, and falls as you exhale. The expansion of the abdomen indicates that the diaphragm is fully lowered, inflating the lungs to their fullest. At rest, you only need to use a small part of your lung capacity. The faster you run, the more you'll need. Consciously lift the chest as you belly-breathe to free the action of the diaphragm. This allows you to utilize more of your lung capacity. Belly breathing will also help prevent the dreaded side stitch.

Breathing should be as relaxed as possible, given the conditions imposed by your effort. Many runners tense up and hyperventilate, especially when running up hills or when excited or fatigued during races. When you get tense, the muscles that assist breathing get tight, causing you to breathe in shallow, quick breaths—"panic breathing." This can cause the whole body to tense up. Take deep breaths that are regular, relaxed, and rhythmic.

Use your breathing like a metronome, measuring the pace of your runs. Most runners breathe in time with their footsteps, whether they realize it or not. We tend to breathe in a "footed" pattern, breathing in and out when landing on a particular foot. Most runners are right-footed breathers, inhaling and exhaling off the right foot. The stride to breathing ratio is mostly unconscious, and varies from person to person. Most runners use a 2-2 rhythm: They inhale while taking two steps (one with each foot), and then exhale while taking two steps. They take one complete breath (an inhalation and exhalation) per four steps. Given the ideal stride rate of 180 steps per minute, a complete breath per four steps results in an ideal breathing rate of 45 breaths per minute. If your breathing rate is slower, you may not be taking in enough oxygen. A too-fast rate may result in shallow breathing, a cause of side stitches.

Most runners don't know or care what their breathing rates are. They just do what comes naturally. In most cases, this is a 2-2 breathing pattern. A 3-3 pattern is good for very easy days. You may start warm-up runs at 3-3, switching to 2-2 after a few minutes. The 3-3 ratio may be beneficial for the first few miles of marathons, but for most racing the 2-2 pattern works best. Switching to a 2-1 pattern (exhale for two steps, inhale for one) may be more productive for your finishing drive (the last mile or so), or speed workouts. To maximize breathing intake, some runners quickly exhale as completely as possible every three or four breaths. In between they breathe normally. The noisy ones moan when they do it. I often do this in races and speed training. It seems to help me keep under control and keep moving. But I've been told by competitors who beat me that they burst ahead so they didn't have to listen to me moan anymore!

Then there's the theory that runners should breathe in through the nose and out through the mouth. This supposedly promotes relaxation and filters the air. That's fine if you think it works for you, and it may at easy paces. But competitive running calls for lots of air to satisfy the body's need for oxygen. You can get a lot more air breathing through the mouth: The opening in the back of your throat is almost ten times larger than those two little holes in your nose. Most runners automatically shift from nose to mouth breathing as their bodies require more and more air. I suck it in through both my mouth and nose—I'd breathe through my ears, too, if it worked.

What about those breathing aids that you tape across your nose? They may make breathing more comfortable, especially if you have a stuffy nose, by opening the nasal passages. I tried one in a race and felt my breathing was easier. After finishing a great race, thinking I had found *the answer*, I realized the darn thing had fallen off! Research says it doesn't improve performance. Besides, if you're running hard you'll need to breathe through your mouth. If you think they help, go ahead and use them. Breathe any way you want as long as you stay relaxed and under control.

When racing, listen to your competitors' breathing. If they're breathing loudly and rapidly, he or she is probably struggling. This can be a sign of weakness, allowing you an opportunity to surge away. On the other hand if you're trying to fight off other runners, try to keep your breathing quiet and controlled or you'll tip them off that you're struggling to stay with them. Use your breathing rate to monitor even race effort, particularly to keep from starting too fast and on hills. If you're breathing too hard and fast, slow the pace; if breathing rate slows on downhills, or in the middle miles due to loss of concentration, pick up the pace.

FORM ANALYSIS

Periodically do a mental check of the key ingredients to proper form, especially your personal problem areas. Try to correct inefficient movements and clean up bad habits. You can improve by concentrating on just one or two things at a time. If you check your form consciously and consistently, it'll become a habit and you'll do it unconsciously. Then, at least in your mind, you'll flow like a mountain stream.

I practice and analyze my form on the treadmill. I'm not going anywhere so I can easily focus on it. One at a time, I pay attention to footstrike, body posture, stride, arm action, and breathing. Sometimes I'll count my stride and breathing rates to see if they're at optimal levels. Occasionally, try running on a treadmill in front of a mirror. You'll get very helpful feedback and can make form improvements as you watch yourself looking better and better. Who is that runner anyway!

You may choose to have a coach analyze your form and offer suggestions for improvement. In our running classes I give our students an overview of good running form without telling them how to run every step. Then, I'll just allow them to run naturally. I'll watch for obvious faults in their form and help them make corrections. But I don't overcoach. It's better that a runner feel comfortable than have perfect form. Most runners naturally develop the footstrike and stride that works for them. I leave them alone and concentrate on their upper body form.

Whether on a treadmill, track, or road, analyzing running form isn't easy when your body parts are rapidly moving. An effective way of analyzing and improving form is by video. Have someone film you during workouts and races like Shelly-lynn does with her clients. You can review it in slow motion, freezing the key phases of your stride. If possible, film yourself from three directions—front, side, and rear. You may be surprised at the things you are obviously doing wrong.

PUTTING IT ALL TOGETHER AND STAYING RELAXED

Confused? It's not really that complicated. Don't worry too much about having to remember all these points about running form. You don't have to carry this book with you on your runs for reference. Learning good running form is largely second nature. For the most part, the more you run the better your form will get without having to even think about it. Your body teaches you what works best. A good way to perfect running economy and form is to run speed workouts at 5K pace or faster with other runners. You'll naturally learn to run more efficiently in order to hold speed, and by osmosis you'll pick up good form from the runners around you.

The most important thing is to run relaxed. A key to doing this, according to *Relax and Win* author Bud Winter, is learning to work at 90 percent effort rather than 100 percent. Running all-out slows you down, whereas holding back a bit stimulates relaxation and allows muscles to stay loose. Of particular importance is the ability to "turn off" the hamstrings when the opposing quadriceps are contracted, and vice versa. Tension here causes the leg muscles to tighten. Make sure your hands, wrists, and elbows remain loose. Release any building tightness by occasionally letting your head roll from side to side, shrugging and lowering the shoulders, and dropping the arms loosely. Let the muscles not directly involved with running—such as in the face, neck, and shoulders—relax. Keep your mouth slightly open and loosen your jaw, don't clench your teeth. By occasionally allowing the chin to lower and flap—as in talking—you can keep the jaw and neck muscles relaxed. All your muscles should feel loose. As Winter put it: "Let the meat hang on the bones."

If you feel good when you run—relaxed and comfortable—you're no doubt doing far more things right than wrong. There's no need to become obsessed with attaining perfect form; nobody's got it, not even the world's best.

CHAPTER 32

Running Shoes

The most important investment any runner makes is a good pair of running shoes. Look at them as an essential training tool, not just a piece of equipment. Each of them strikes the ground about 800 times per mile. Hitting with the force of about three times your body weight, at 40 miles a week each shoe pounds the ground more than 1,600,000 times a year! Running shoes protect the feet from the environment, cushion impact, stabilize the foot, and neutralize biomechanical imbalances.

When I recall the flimsy items my high school coach told me were running shoes back in 1963, my feet ache. They had canvas uppers and gum soles so thin I could feel every stone. My first running injury was a cut from a piece of glass that worked its way through my shoe. Well-cushioned running shoes didn't start appearing until the 1970s. My first pair came from a mail-order outfit. They didn't fit very well and the leather uppers got crusty after getting wet, causing blisters. But they provided some cushioning and I sure was proud to wear them. Now there are so many shoe choices I gave up trying to keep track of them. The list of specialization is almost endless.

ANATOMY OF THE RUNNING SHOE

Shoes have five major parts: last, outer sole, midsole, heel counter, and upper.

Last and lasting. The word "last" has two important meanings: It describes both the shape of the shoe and a method of construction. Companies use a model of the foot called a last. It's a foot-shaped piece of wood, plastic, or metal on which the shoe is built. It's an average shape based on the impressions of many feet. Each company might use a slightly different last, and even within a company the last used may vary from one shoe style to another. The shape of the last affects the shape, fit, flexibility, and stability of shoes. There are two basic shapes used for a last—straight and curved. A straight last has little or no curve from the heel to toe and provides greater support under the medial arch. A curved last turns inward from the heel to the toes. Variations are slightly curved (closer to straight) and semi-curved (closer to curved).

There are three lasting techniques used in shoe construction: board, slip, and combination. In board lasting, the upper materials are glued to a fiberboard before it's attached to the midsole. Straight, board-lasted shoes aren't very flexible, but they give you a firm ride and provide a good platform for orthotics. Unfortunately, fewer straight-lasted shoes are made so your selection may be limited. With a slip lasting, the upper material is stitched together and then glued to the midsole. This makes a lighter, more flexible shoe with a softer feel. Combination lasting uses the board method in the heel for stability and the slip method in the forefoot for flexibility. Many runners prefer combination-lasted shoes that provide some of the benefits of both types. If you're used to one type of last, it may be difficult adjusting to another.

Outer sole. This treaded part resists wear, provides traction, and absorbs some shock. It should not wear out quickly. In fact, unless you wear them down unevenly, it should still be in good shape after you discard your shoes due to loss of midsole cushioning. The outer sole should wear primarily on the extreme outer edge of the heel and in the center of the ball of the foot. There are many sole designs, but most provide adequate traction. Some sole types, however, make better snow tires. In general, soles are hard or soft: Harder soles are heavier, have less cushion, and wear longer; softer soles are lighter, have more cushion, and wear out faster.

Midsole. Located between the outer sole and the foot bed, this is the hidden heart of the running shoe. It absorbs shock, flexes at toe-off, and adds stability. It's constructed from various types of foam. Air bags, gel, and other material may be inserted to increase cushioning. Shock-absorbing properties deteriorate with use. Also, studies at the University of Osaka in Japan indicate that midsoles may lose up to 50 percent of their cushioning when exposed to running in cold temperatures.

Heel counter. This is the firm wrapping around the back of the shoe that stabilizes the shoe and, therefore, the foot. A rigid counter covering the entire heel is desirable, especially for pronators. It's usually made from plastic. Squeeze it to see if it's firm and supportive. Above the counter is the cushioned ankle collar, which provides protection and helps prevent Achilles tendinitis. A heel wedge, located above the midsole, adds height to the heel, increases shock absorption, and reduces strain on the foot and leg. A wedge of ½ to 1 inch is desirable.

Uppers. Most shoe uppers are either nylon, nylon mesh, or a combination. This creates a lightweight, breathable, washable, soft shoe that requires little break-in and dries fast when wet. The mesh uppers make the shoes cooler in the summer.

Lacing system. This is an important part of the upper. It holds it all together by securing the shoe to the foot. Improper lacing can cause discomfort and injuries. Pulling laces too tight cuts off circulation and may cause tendinitis on the top of the foot; too loose, and shoes fit sloppily. There are three types of lacing systems: variable width with staggered eyelets to adjust width, speed lacing with plastic D-rings, and conventional eyelets. Various lacing methods besides the standard crisscross system can be used to meet individual needs. For example: Use the eyelets closest to the centerline of the shoe in a variable-width system, skipping those farthest to the outside to adjust for wide feet (Do the opposite to adjust for narrow feet); drawing the laces across the top in a parallel system rather than crisscrossing if you have high arches; cross-over loop through the upper laces to make the shoe fit more snug in the heel. Have a shoe salesperson show you the variations on lacing.

Some laces aren't agreeable. They don't feel right or are too long or too short. I struggled with a pair of unruly laces for weeks until the bright light went off: I replaced them with another style. For some reason I have problems with my shoes coming untied. I never mastered the art in kindergarten. It can be a serious nuisance if they untie during a race. It happened to me the first time I raced in a new pair of shoes that had round, rather than flat, laces.

I stopped a total of three times—including halfway up a killer hill—to retie them. My shoe guy came to the rescue, showing me a special way to double-knot them he learned from a fisherman. Or, you can buy special clips that keep laces from running away from you.

INSOLES AND ORTHOTICS

Removable insoles, or sockliners, come with shoes and absorb moisture and reduce blistering. They are usually constructed of plastic foam that molds to the shape of your foot. Although they may provide some motion control and absorb shock, their function is minimal. They can be tossed out if you don't like them or need more room. Commercial insoles may offer more cushioning and motion control. Use them to adjust shoe size. Heel pads or cups reduce shock, but don't take up as much space as full insoles. Do padded insoles really increase cushioning? Some studies say yes, others say no. I've found that well-cushioned insoles make a difference when I'm doing high mileage on hard surfaces. But they're too heavy for racing.

Orthotics are inserts to support and correct footstrike. They give you help where you need it, such as support under the arch or behind the metatarsal heads in the ball of the foot. They can raise the heel to eliminate Achilles tendon or calf strain, or correct differences in leg length. They place the foot in a neutral position and allow it to strike the ground "normally."

Orthotics are not a panacea for all pain or injury. Surveys show that 40 to 75 percent of runners wearing orthotics report great improvement or complete recovery from a long list of painful conditions. In the 1960s, when orthotics were not available, I suffered from knee pain that ended my collegiate athletic career. I was told surgery would be necessary and I'd never play sports again. I was forced to accept this condition until 1975 when Dr. Richard Schuster, a pioneer in sports podiatry, crafted customized orthotics to correct the severe pronation that was causing the knee pain. Within three years I was running 100 miles a week pain-free and racing marathons. Now, Dr. Schuster periodically upgrades my orthotics to keep me on the run.

Surveys show 50 percent of high-mileage runners wear orthotics, although they probably aren't necessary for some. Sometimes they are overprescribed by doctors. Schuster advises: "Unless there are several imbalances, or pain related to imbalances, the indiscriminate use of orthotic foot devices could stir up a hornet's nest of other problems." If your outer soles wear out unevenly or too fast, or if the heel counter breaks down, you are a likely candidate for orthotics.

First try commercial over-the-counter orthotics. Available at most running stores, they are contoured to the shape of the average foot, and modified to reduce excessive pronation. They may help with mild biomechanical problems. If they don't, consult a sports podiatrist. Most custom devices are fashioned in a lab from a mold of your feet. The orthotic can be made from a variety of substances. Most are constructed from strong, light, and relatively flexible polypropylene or fiberglass.

When breaking in orthotics, first wear them walking and then gradually add running. If they do not feel right, have them adjusted. Orthotics may need to be readjusted or replaced as they wear and your needs change. Remove the insoles that came with your shoes, or cut out the arch support to avoid interference with the orthotics' function. Ask your podiatrist and running shoe salesperson about the best shoes to accommodate orthotics. They should be straight-lasted or slightly curved.

What about racing in orthotics? Researchers at the Spaulding Rehabilitation Hospital in Spaulding, New Hampshire, tested runners with and without orthotics on a treadmill. There was no difference in performance. They theorized the orthotics made up for their extra weight by allowing the subjects to run more economically.

In summary, orthotics are an expense but are worth every penny if they keep you running injury-free. Just like my running shoes, I always have a backup pair. I wear them in all my shoes—street shoes, training shoes, and racing shoes.

FOOT SHAPE AND BIOMECHANICS

Every runner's foot shape and biomechanics is slightly different. Approximately 50 percent of runners have normal arches, 25 percent have high arches, and 25 percent have low arches. Most runners fit into one of the following three general types (which use one of three categories of shoes used by running companies):

Medium-arched, semi-curved foot, neutral pronation. These folks pronate properly, allowing for good motion control and cushioning, and probably use semi-curved shoes with either slip- or combination-lasting. Shoe category: Stability.

Low-arched, straight foot, overpronator. If your foot rolls inward a great deal you may be overpronating. Runners with this condition, but not all of them, tend to have highly flexible, straight feet and low arches. Overpronators tend to break down shoes on the inner border. They often suffer from runner's knee, shin splints, or iliotibial band syndrome. In general, a straight, board-lasted shoe with a hard heel counter and firm midsole is best for this foot type. Shoe category: Motion control.

High-arched, curved foot, underpronator. If your foot doesn't pronate enough (underpronation), or rolls excessively outward (supination), your shoes may compress to the outside. Runners with this condition, but not all of them, have high, curved, rigid arches. You don't absorb shock well and are prone to ankle strains, stress fractures, shin splints, plantar fasciitis, and knee pain. In general, a curved, slip-lasted shoe with lots of cushioning, and a flexible forefoot will serve you best. Shoe category: Cushion.

How do you know what type you are? Take the wet foot test. Place a piece of white paper on a hard floor, wet your foot, and step on the paper. If the imprint shows the forefoot and heel connected by a curved band about 2 inches or more wide, you are the medium-arched, semi-curved foot, neutral type. A large impression that shows no or little arch indicates you are the low-arched, straight-foot, overpronator type. If the footprint shows the forefoot and heel connected by a very narrow, curved band, you are the high-arched, curved-foot, underpronator type.

HOW TO CHOOSE YOUR SHOES

Walk into any sports store and you are soon overwhelmed by a wall full of running shoes to choose from. Not only are there several manufacturers offering choices, but each company has lots of styles. Further, new models are introduced frequently and old ones are revamped. Read the latest recommendations from running magazines and they often have contrasting opinions. Ask runners for advice, and they'll each recommend a different shoe. I go through agony trying to buy the right pair—and I've had over thirty-five years of experience at it.

What to do? The best bet is to do what I do: Go to a local running specialty store for recommendations that fit your personal needs. Take your time and make your selection as carefully as possible. Most veteran runners, including myself, have a closet littered with discarded running shoes that "just weren't right." Invest in the best shoes you can find and afford. Don't buy too cheap or you'll likely pay for it down the road. Shoes are important and your only major investment on the road to fitness and performance. On the other hand, the most expensive shoes aren't necessarily the best.

Shoes should provide five basic things: flexibility, cushioning, durability, motion control—and comfort. Ultimately, these factors are the most important, not price, looks, or brand name. Don't be influenced by marketing gimmicks proclaiming the latest breakthrough in technology or by what shoes are on the feet of Elite runners (who are paid to wear those brands!).

Here are my recommended steps for buying running shoes:

Step #1: Know your foot style and biomechanics. Follow the guidelines above for determining these factors and for deciding which of the three general categories of shoes—stability, motion control, and cushion—are best for you.

Step #2: Consider special factors. These include: injury pattern (ask your sports doctor for recommendations), body weight, running surfaces, and how much you run and race. For example, I run high mileage and at 6′1″ am a big runner, thus I need a shoe with plenty of cushioning. Further, they need to accept orthotics and have a wide toe box to take pressure off my foot neuroma. They also need to be very stable or they will start tilting inward after a few miles due to my severe pronation. Most runners should train in a regular-weight or heavyweight shoe. Some runners feel most comfortable and can tolerate lightweight trainers.

Step #3: Go to your local running shoe guy (or gal). Narrow potential shoes by following Steps 1 and 2 above. Discuss these choices and your running history with the salesperson. According to my shoe guy, Andy Kimerling of the Westchester Road Runner in White Plains, New York, "Bring in your old running shoes. They will clearly show the type of shoe you need. The tread wear and stress on the shoe upper will give the salesperson information to guide in his or her advice as to your individual needs." Try to stay with a shoe type you've used successfully in the past.

A good local store has experienced salespeople who have test-driven many of the shoes in the store and have been trained to assess your training and biomechanical needs. They learn from customers about what does and doesn't work, and the store manager keeps on top of shoe trends and runners' needs. Over a period of time your shoe guy becomes familiar with the best choices for you. Local stores also know the best places to run in the area, local races you may want to enter, or special group runs or classes that may help your training. Often they get involved in promoting the sport in your community. Return the favor when it comes time to buy running gear. What to do if there isn't a running specialty store in your area? Your best bet is to analyze the reviews of shoes in the running magazines, review this chapter carefully, and become the best shoe guy or gal possible. Then shop at a sports-related store that at least has a wide selection of running shoes.

Step #4: Make sure the shoes fit. Here's the most important step. Worry more about comfort than technology and looks. Have the shoe guy or gal measure your foot for length and width. Be sure to measure both feet, since they may differ (like mine). Your shoe size may change—get bigger—as you run more, age, or as a result of injury. Try on both shoes of the pair; do not assume that since one fits they both will. Always try on the shoes while wearing your normal running socks (if you change sock thickness, it will affect fit) and, if you wear them, orthotics. Allow some room for expansion: Feet swell by as much as half a size on long runs in warm weather. For this reason, shop in the afternoon or evening—or, better yet, after a run—when your feet are slightly larger.

Tight shoes pinch your feet, resulting in discomfort or injury. Shoes that are too long may slide and create blisters. Give the shoes the thumb test: You need about a thumbnail's width between the longest toe (not necessarily your big toe) and the end of the shoe. You should be able to wiggle the toes freely inside the shoes. If you are uncertain about which size to go with, take the larger. You can always fill in with insoles. Running shoe size is often a half to a full size larger than for dress shoes.

The width should be snug but not pinched. Your foot should

not bulge over the midsole material. A shoe too tight in width will not give good support and may cause the feet to numb and cramp due to lack of circulation. On the other hand, if it's too loose your foot may slide, causing blisters and leg problems. Try different models to find the width that feels best. Most shoes come in a D width for men and a B for women. Some models come in a variety of widths. Be sure that the heel counter fits firmly but not too tightly. Your heel should not slide up and down as you walk or run. The upper should fit snugly and hold the foot in place securely. It shouldn't press too tightly or be too loose in any area of your foot.

Take your time. Ask more questions. Try on a few shoes for comparison. Once you find a shoe you like, try on one size larger or smaller for comparison—to be sure. Finally, the shoes should be comfortable right away. Don't rely on a break-in period.

Step #5: Test the shoes. Many stores let you take a test job around the block. Some even let you exchange shoes if they don't quite fit after you've run once or twice with them for a few miles (as long as you don't get them too dirty). Check the workmanship of the pair of shoes you buy—quality control in the factories isn't perfect. Check for flexibility. Bend the shoe. It should flex about 30 to 35 degrees in the forefoot as you bend it with both hands—about the same as when you run. Hopefully, you'll have several choices in your size and type. Of those, the best bet is to pick the shoe that feels best when running.

WHY WOMEN'S RUNNING SHOES?

For years, women were neglected by the shoe companies, primarily because they were only a small percentage of the running market (which was predominantly male, like the shoe company executives). At first, women had to get by with men's shoes, then shoe companies offered scaled-down versions of the men's models in colors that appealed to women. That compromise was insufficient because the anatomy of a woman's foot is different from, and not simply a smaller version of, a man's foot. For example, in general, a woman's forefoot is wider and her heel is narrower relative to length than a man's. A woman's size 10 shoe is roughly equivalent to a man's size 8½, but a woman's size 10 is ¼- to ½-inch narrower in the heel. (Generally, women's shoes are one and a half sizes larger in number than men's for the same approximate foot size). Women who bought small men's running shoes found that their heels slipped. If they fit the shoes for a snug heel, then the shoes were too tight in the forefoot. Today, women make up a significant share of the running shoe market. Not surprisingly, shoe companies now produce several shoes designed only for women, incorporating technology specific to them. Moreover, women with wide feet also have the choice of buying men's running shoes.

WHAT ABOUT THE HEAVY RUNNER OR UNUSUAL FOOT SIZES?

The more you weigh, the greater the impact when you run. Heavier runners frequently have wide, flat feet and overpronate. Look for shoes with a wide toe box and lots of support for pronation. The heavier runner should exchange shoe lightness for cushioning, durability, and support. Ask your shoe guy or gal for recommendations.

Running shoes are sized up to 15 for men and 11 for women. Half sizes are usually not available in shoes larger than 13. Women with large feet may be able to select a men's shoe. Most shoe models have one width. New Balance offers most of its shoes in four or more widths to accommodate those runners with wide or narrow feet. Other companies may make some models in widths but may not publicize it. Again, ask your running salesperson for assistance. You can also make a wide shoe fit better by adding insoles or by using shoes with a variable-width lacing system.

WHO SHOULD WEAR RACING SHOES?

Racing shoes may allow you to run your best. According to the accepted standard, for every ounce you take off your feet, you will save about a second per mile. The average racing shoe is 3.5 ounces lighter than training shoes; a typical size 9 men's training shoe weighs 11 to 12 ounces and a racing shoe weighs 7 to 8 ounces (How's this for progress?: In the early seventies, the average racing shoe was about 13 ounces!). A 40-minute 10K runner wearing racing shoes could theoretically improve by about 24 seconds and a three-hour marathoner by 1:48. That's the theory.

But racing shoes are made for speed, not injury-prevention. In exchange for lightness and flexibility, the racing shoe takes away cushioning (about 15 percent less), support, durability, and stability. The lighter the shoe, the sooner they will break down. There is less heel-lift, which may injure your Achilles tendons, and the curved last may fit much differently from your trainers. If your body is taking more of a beating, you may actually run slower in racing shoes despite the advantage of less weight.

Racing shoes may be okay for those who race at 7-minute-per-mile pace or faster, are light on their feet, and without biomechanical problems. Beginner racers should stick to training shoes for at least their first several races and first few marathons. More experienced runners may benefit from compromise—using lightweight training shoes. These rate about halfway between racers and trainers in terms of weight, flexibility, cushioning, support, stability, and durability. I use very heavy, stable training shoes that weigh nearly 14 ounces per shoe. For speed workouts, brisk continuous runs, and races, I switch to my lightweight trainers that weigh 10 ounces. I sure feel lighter and faster when I make the switch. And feeling ready to zoom in fast shoes is a big step! Other runners compromise this way: They use lightweight trainers for half-marathons and marathons, and switch to racing shoes for races of 10K and less. At these distances the benefits of lighter shoes most likely "outweigh" the disadvantages. Very few runners should wear racing shoes for the pounding the body takes during marathons. What about spikes? If you race over rugged cross-country courses, they will help you gain traction and improve performance. But, they are very flimsy and may increase risk of injury.

Whether you switch from regular trainers to lightweight trainers, or to racing shoes, break them in with a few short runs and speed workouts before racing. Wear them in races of 10K and under before trying them in longer events. Warm up before races in the shoes you will compete in to adjust to the lower heels and different shape. Cool down after races in training shoes to increase comfort and minimize injury.

"TO BE DISCONTINUED"

It sure gets annoying when I find the perfect running shoe—and then the company discontinues it. Why do they do this to us?

Some of the changes reflect improvements as technology advances. Much of the reason, however, is marketing. Regardless, the replacement shoe doesn't feel exactly like the old shoe. If you learn that your favorite running shoe is phasing out, stock up on a few pairs of them. But sooner or later you will literally run out. Ask your shoe guy or gal for help finding a shoe with features similar to your old ones. This may mean switching brands. If you're lucky, you may even find a shoe you like better.

STREET SHOES ARE IMPORTANT, TOO

Your feet spend more hours a week inside street shoes than running shoes. Poorly fitting street shoes with little support can cause problems for your feet and your running. Many runners try solving this problem by wearing running shoes all day. But this may cause problems from the lack of variety of stress for the foot. On the other hand, wearing shoes that have thin, hard soles may hurt your feet. The lack of shock absorption may injure your back or knees. High, loose-fitting heels in boots can irritate the Achilles tendon and loose-fitting casual shoes lack support and may cause heel spurs. Boots and shoes with pointed toes can cause trouble, too.

The worst, however, are high heels. Wearing any shoe, women's or men's, with a heel higher than one inch is detrimental to your feet. High heels can cause injuries, especially to the feet and lower leg. If you must wear heels, at least get low ones with a wide heel platform to distribute weight more evenly and aid balance. Minimize the time you wear them. Many women walk to and from work in running shoes, saving their modest heels for the office.

Fortunately, several brands of health shoes provide good cushioning and support with reasonable fashion. Some running shoe companies make dress shoes for walking. To air out your feet and still get good support (instead of slippers or flimsy sandals), try specially designed sport sandals. They provide a foot bed similar to a running shoe and adjustable straps to secure the feet. I wear a combination of running shoes, health shoes, and hiking boots throughout the day, and go with sport sandals for around the house, especially after running when my feet are swollen and tired. Make sure your street shoes are in good repair. I found this out the hard way. My worn-out dog-walking shoes aggravated a hip problem.

BREAKING IN SHOES

Most running shoes today are easy to break in. The uppers are very soft and the soles are flexible. Still, in general try these steps recommended by Andy Kimerling for breaking in new running shoes: 1) Walk around in them for a mile or two. Stay alert to any conditions that might give you difficulty; 2) Try them out on a short run; 3) If all goes well after a short run, go ahead and run regularly in your new shoes. As you break them in, alternate running in a well-broken-in pair to make your transition more gradual. Run short and medium distances in your new shoes for at least a week before going distances over 10 miles, or for racing.

HOW LONG WILL SHOES LAST?

Sorry, no running shoe can last forever. Some runners, however, stubbornly keep pounding away in their faithful partners long after they've outlived their effectiveness. It used to be that the uppers or outer soles of running shoes were the first to go. With modern technology, the durability of running shoes is now usually determined by the compression of the midsoles. Midsoles break down with use as well as with exposure to heat, sunlight, salt, and such. When running shoes lose their shock absorption that shock has to go somewhere. Your body pays the price. Various studies indicate that most midsoles lose some of their cushioning properties as early as 150 miles, and that by 300 to 500 miles they have lost 50 percent of their capabilities. So most shoes should be replaced after about 300 to 500 miles, although some midsole types may last longer. Heavy runners and over- or underpronators may wear out shoes sooner. Running on soft trails rather than hard pavement will extend shoe life. Racing shoes wear out much sooner and should be replaced after 200 to 300 miles, or when they lose their bounciness.

You can't tell shoes need replacing by looking at them. For most runners by the time wear appears on the outer sole, the midsole is shot. I number and date my shoes and log the mileage on each pair in my diary. When I hit 300 miles, I start checking the cushioning. You can tell this by pressing the midsole with your thumb to check the material's "bounce" or cushion. It should compress and not be rigid. Your shoe guy can also test this for you. My body tells me when to switch to new shoes: My back and legs start to feel tight after a few miles, especially if running on pavement. Another test is to put on a new pair of shoes with the same or similar type cushioning and run around the block in them, followed by a run in your old shoes. If you feel a significant difference in cushioning between the two, you probably should make the switch. When in doubt, throw the old ones out. The money you save by squeezing out a few more miles won't cover the doctor's bills.

Some runners wear down the outersoles unevenly. You could resole them or even use specially made materials to patch them up. But if you've logged several miles in them the midsoles are likely to be worn out. Get another pair of shoes. Sometimes the heel counter breaks down. Give them this test: Put the shoes on a flat table and look at them from behind. If they roll too much in or out, discard them.

CARE AND REPAIR—HOW TO MAKE RUNNING SHOES LAST LONGER

Treat your running shoes like you treat a new car. The better you take care of them, the longer they will last and the more comfortable your ride. Runners can be tough on shoes. Here are a few tips to help your shoes last longer:

Rotate shoes. Studies show that by alternating two pairs of shoes they'll last longer than three pairs used consecutively. Rotated shoes have 80 percent of cushioning after sixty runs of an average of 5 miles compared to only 60 percent for those not rotated. Midsoles compress when you run, taking twenty-four to forty-eight hours to re-expand to their full cushioning capacity. Alternating shoes if you run two days in a row allows the midsole materials to bounce back better. It may be beneficial to alternate similar but not identical shoes to change the stress pattern on your feet. Since midsoles compress some even with walking and standing, don't train in the shoes you wear around all day. Further, if you keep two pairs going you have a broken-in backup if you lose one or if the dog eats a shoe!

Let shoes dry out. Dry for at least twenty-four hours if they get wet from sweat, rain, or snow. Loosen the laces, open the tongue, and pull out the insoles. Stuff the shoes with newspaper to wick out the moisture and help retain shape and fit. Air-dry shoes—the heat of a radiator or clothes dryer may damage them. Drying in front of a fan is okay. Studies at Tulane University indicate that shoes that are wet provide significantly less shock protection. Besides, who enjoys putting on a pair of wet running shoes? Enough of a reason to have at least two pairs of running shoes ready for action.

Store and clean shoes properly. Let them air out adequately after running. Don't stuff them in a locker, sports bag, or a stuffy stairwell. Keep them in a cool, dry place. Don't jam shoes into your bag or you could cause damage to their shape and support. Avoid exposing shoes to heat and cold. Don't leave them out in the direct sunlight or in the hot trunk of a car for a long time. Heat damages the materials in the shoe and may change the way it fits your foot. Avoid storing shoes in the cold as it affects its cushioning properties. Tossing shoes in the washing machine or soaking them may cause damage. Wash them by hand with a soft brush, mild soap, and cold water.

Minimize perspiration buildup. Wear socks and use foot powder to keep shoes dry, kill fungus and bacteria, control odor, and neutralize the corrosive acids in sweat.

Don't wear running shoes to play other sports. The lateral movement of activities such as tennis, basketball, or aerobics classes could disturb the balance of the shoe. So, too, can normal household activities such as mowing the lawn.

PART VIII

FOOD AND DRINK FOR HEALTH AND PERFORMANCE

CHAPTER 33

Fuel and Nutrition for Running

Competitive runners need to fuel themselves properly for good health and peak performance. This means not only eating a healthy daily diet, but also consuming the right fuels before, during, and after running.

GOOD NUTRITION FOR HEALTHY RUNNERS

A balanced diet includes six nutrients essential to good health and performance—carbohydrates, fats, protein, vitamins, minerals, and even water. Runners need a diet high in carbs, with sufficient protein, and low in fats. Sports nutritionists recommend 60 to 70 percent of a distance runner's caloric intake should come from carbs, mostly from the complex variety, which are packed with vitamins, minerals, and fiber. Include plenty of grain products, vegetables, and fruits. Fats contain more than double the calories per gram as carbs and protein. A high-fat diet has the potential to quickly pack on the pounds. No more than 20 to 25 percent of the total diet should come from fats. Concentrate on foods low in saturated fat and cholesterol. Especially avoid fats prior to running as they are slow to digest.

Protein makes up 15 to 20 percent of the recommended diet. Protein needs increase with competitive training according to research by Peter Lemon, Ph.D., at Kent State University. Extra protein is used for energy (5 to 6 percent of total fuel) and to repair tissue damage incurred during hard training or racing. Distance runners should consume 0.5 to .75 grams of protein per pound of body weight. Concentrate on sources low in fat and cholesterol such as lean meats, fish, low-fat dairy products, poultry, beans, whole grains, and cereals. There is no evidence that protein supplements improve performance.

Vitamins and minerals aren't energy nutrients, but they're still important. As antioxidants, vitamins C, E, and A (in the form of beta-carotene) neutralize toxic compounds, called free radicals, that damage cells. Stress and intense exercise may produce lots of these dangerous free radicals. Some minerals, called electrolytes, produce ions that can be involved with chemical reactions. They are lost in small amounts with sweat during exercise. Sodium and chloride are lost in the greatest amounts; calcium, copper, magnesium, potassium, and zinc in lesser amounts. Usually, electrolytes lost with sweating can be easily replaced with a balanced diet. If you find yourself craving salty foods, that may be your body's way of telling you to consume more sodium. Try a few potato chips, crackers, or pretzels and wash them down with a sports drink (which contains sodium and other electrolytes).

Calcium and iron are key minerals for runners. A program of weight-bearing exercise such as running, weight training, and a calcium-rich diet are important to keeping bones strong and preventing stress fractures and osteoporosis. Good sources include low-fat milk and dairy products, calcium-fortified fruit juices, beans, cauliflower, oranges, eggs, and dark leafy vegetables. Milk-intolerant runners should drink lactose-reduced milk, or calcium-fortified rice or soy beverages.

Iron is necessary for the production of hemoglobin in your red blood cells. Hemoglobin carries oxygen from the lungs to the muscles, and if your level is low, running performance suffers. As much as one-quarter of the world's population is iron-deficient. This results in anemia—a condition in which the blood's oxygen-carrying capacity is decreased. Symptoms include fatigue, loss of energy, headaches, behavior change, and impaired intellectual performance. Iron also bolsters resistance to disease and stress, and benefits muscle contraction. Women are prone to anemia because they lose iron in blood during menstruation. They need approximately twice as much iron as men. Iron-deficient anemia occurs more frequently in runners than in the general population. An estimated 30 to 50 percent of menstruating women runners have iron-poor blood. As many as 10 percent of male runners may be iron-deficient.

"Runner's anemia" may result in high-mileage runners, men or women. According to the U.S. Olympic Committee, training affects iron status in many ways, including losses through sweating, decreased iron absorption, and the impact of hard footstrikes that may destroy normal blood cells. This type of anemia usually doesn't occur until runners reach at least the 40- to 50-mile-per-week level. Runners who don't eat meat are particularly prone to iron deficiency.

A sports doctor or nutritionist can determine iron deficiency with blood tests. Standard hemoglobin and hematocrit tests may not detect the problem. They test only for anemia, the final stage of iron deficiency. Have a complete blood count and iron profile which measures other factors including ferritin, a marker of stored iron. If you are feeling tired and sluggish, the cause may be iron deficiency. Studies show aerobic performance improves significantly within a few weeks with iron supplementation but only to the extent that a deficiency exists—that is, iron supplements do not allow you to run farther if you are not iron-deficient. In fact, excess iron is dangerous to your health.

Natural sources of iron include lean beef, lamb and pork, liver, dark meat poultry, leafy green vegetables, nuts, lentils, dried fruits, blackstrap molasses, shrimp, scallops, iron-fortified cereals and breads. Combine iron-rich foods with those high in vitamin C to enhance iron uptake. Cooking in a cast-iron skillet also contributes.

SHOULD YOU TAKE VITAMIN AND MINERAL SUPPLEMENTS?

Many scientists are uncertain whether taking supplements is as healthful as food sources, but most agree taking supplements providing 100 percent of the RDA is safe (even if it sends total intake above the RDA). RDAs may be too low for some vitamins and modern health stressors, including poor air quality, creating a need for additional vitamins. Natural and synthetic vitamins are equally beneficial, and tests have shown that most cheap supplements are as good as expensive ones.

If your diet isn't well balanced, then supplements may help keep you healthy and prevent a loss of performance. I take a "one-a-day" vitamin and mineral supplement to make sure I'm covered and take an additional gram of vitamin C daily. Most Elites take supplements with an emphasis on vitamin C, calcium, and iron. The best bet is to discuss your diet and potential needs of supplements with your sports doctor or nutritionist. They can advise you according to the latest research.

SNACKING

Three well-balanced meals every day combined with healthy snacking prevents a wide change in blood sugar, which in turn affects your appetite, energy level, and ability to handle stress. Healthy snacking is essential to most runners in heavy training. "Grazing" during the day results in more energy for performance and mental alertness. Healthy snacks include cereal, pretzels, low-fat popcorn, raisins, fresh or dried fruits, juice, sports drinks, energy bars, low-fat granola bars, low-salt crackers, low-fat yogurt, baked potatoes, nuts, seeds, bagels, fig bars, and carrots. A few cookies here and there won't hurt—and a treat now and then is good for the spirit.

WHERE DO WE GET OUR ENERGY FOR RUNNING?

Carbs, protein, and fats are the energy nutrients. Although protein and fats are important fuel sources, carbs are most important to runners. During digestion, they are broken down to simple sugars like glucose which is used by the body in three ways:

Blood glucose. A small, but significant amount of glucose circulates in the blood (blood sugar) to keep us exercising and feed the brain, preventing mental fatigue.

Liver glycogen. Some glucose is converted to glycogen and stored in the liver. It can be reconverted to glucose and released into the blood to meet energy needs.

Muscle glycogen. The majority of glucose is converted to glycogen and stored in muscle fibers; it is available only to the specific fiber where it is stored. This muscle glycogen is the key to vigorous exercise.

According to Nancy Clark's *Sports Nutrition Guidebook:* "The average 150-pound active male has about 1,800 calories of carbohydrates stored in his liver, muscles, and blood in approximately the following distribution: muscle glycogen—1,400 calories, liver glycogen—320 calories, blood glucose—80 calories." In contrast, the average runner has over 60,000 calories of fat stored in fat cells throughout the body as well as within muscle fibers.

At any level of effort, a mixture of fuels is used. The body doesn't just run out of one fuel and switch to another. The intensity and duration of exercise determines the proportion of fuels used. At low intensities where lots of oxygen is readily available to burn fat for fuel, the body prefers fat. It releases 9 calories per gram compared to only 4 for carbs and protein. But fat, unlike carbs, isn't an efficient fuel for vigorous exercise. It takes approximately three times more oxygen to burn a gram of fat as it does a gram of carbohydrate. At higher levels of intensity, with increased oxygen demands, a higher percentage of energy comes from carbs.

Little energy is needed to read this page and there's lots of oxygen available; so, fats supply most of your needs. At rest or light activity, you burn approximately two-thirds fat and one-third carbs. At a slow walk, 60 percent of energy comes from fat. Start to run and this mix changes. More fuel is needed, and you need it fast, so your body increases the amount of carbs it burns. During the first few minutes of exercise, you burn about 80 percent carbs and 20 percent fats. Once settled into an easy training pace, you use fat and carbs about equally. Thus, most easy-paced runs will be supplied with approximately 50 percent of energy from carbs and 50 percent from fat. The longer or harder the run, the greater the use of carbs. With high-intensity running, such as in racing or speed training, 70 to 80 percent of energy needs are met from carb sources. Glycogen stores (and fueling on the run) determine how long you can exercise at higher intensities. Marathon racing demands lots of carbs: for the average runner, up to 70 percent (up to 80 percent for Elites) of the total energy used comes from carbs compared to 30 percent from fats. In the late miles of a marathon, as carb stores deplete, fat becomes more valuable as a supplemental energy source as does a small amount of protein. Running improves the muscles' ability to burn fat, thus helping to conserve valuable stored carbs.

As mentioned, the body has plenty of fat stores—enough to run for many hours. Unfortunately, glycogen stores are much more limited. They deplete during intense exercise, such as repeated sprints, racing half-marathons and longer, or after long training runs of 90 minutes or more. Trained runners can store about 18 to 20 miles worth of carbs. You will still have enough fat to offset the lack of glycogen as it depletes, but fat has a higher oxygen requirement and thus performance will suffer. When you run low on glycogen, you will slow down and feel tired. "Hitting the Wall" is associated with the marathon, but you may experience at least a bit of it in races from 10 miles and up. See Chapter 21 for guidelines for beating the Wall.

Glycogen depletion can also result from chronic heavy training. During successive days of high mileage or intense running—such as marathon training—glycogen stores can progressively deplete, resulting in fatigue. To keep muscle glycogen well-stocked, eat a diet high in carbs and follow a sensible training program that provides for rest days. Runners require about 4 grams of carbs per pound of body weight per day. Those who put in 50 miles a week or more probably need to consume about 700 additional calories a day, most of it carbs.

What about the theory that a balanced diet of 40 percent carbs, 30 percent fats, and 30 percent protein is better for endurance athletes? This theory hasn't been scientifically proven and most sports professionals side with the high-carb diet.

The Food Energy Index: Quick and Slow Carbs How quickly carbs digest and enter the bloodstream is measured by the Food Energy Index (Glycemic Index). Foods are ranked according to their glycemic response (their ability to elevate blood sugar). Low- to moderate-glycemic foods release glucose slowly over several hours, providing sustained energy. Emphasize these foods an hour or two before long runs, and for races lasting more than 90 minutes. High-glycemic foods produce a rapid rise in blood glucose, providing quick energy. Emphasize these foods during runs to boost performance, and after to quickly reload depleted energy reserves. The index can change due to many factors, including the amount of food eaten, fiber content, amount of added fat, and how it was prepared. Low-glycemic sources include: fructose, apples, pears, grapefruit, underripe bananas, low-fat frozen yogurt and milk, lentils, green beans, energy bars. Moderate-glycemic sources include: oranges, overripe bananas, rice, spaghetti, sweet potatoes, boiled potatoes, corn. High-glycemic sources include: pure glucose supplements, sports drinks, baked potatoes, corn flakes, Cheerios, oatmeal, jelly beans, hard candy, honey, bagels, white and whole wheat bread, bran muffins, raisins.

SHOULD YOU EAT BEFORE RUNNING OR RACING?

It used to be that eating before exercise was a no-no. In fact, I avoided food before all of my races until the 1990s when more and more research convinced me of the value of fueling up before and during running. Like many runners, I used to roll out of bed and skip eating before morning runs, convinced food would upset my stomach and slow me down. Prerun eating has several important functions:

1. ***To fuel the muscles and prevent "hitting the Wall."*** This is particularly valuable prior to long runs and races to minimize running low on glycogen.
2. ***To prevent "brain drain."*** When blood sugar is low, the body boosts it by converting liver glycogen to glucose. But if liver glycogen depletes, you experience "brain drain," or "bonking." Says Clark: "Despite adequate muscle glycogen, an athlete may feel uncoordinated, lightheaded, unable to concentrate, and weakened because the liver is releasing inadequate sugar into the bloodstream. Although the muscles can store glucose and burn fat, the brain does neither. This means that food must be consumed close enough to strenuous events to supply sugar to the blood, or the brain will not function optimally. Athletes with low blood sugar tend to perform poorly because the poorly fueled brain limits muscular function and mental drive."

   It's several hours between dinner and a race the next morning. Glycogen stores may be full when you go to bed, but overnight you may burn off much of the limited glycogen stored in the liver just from normal bodily functions. The body will be ready to run but it may lack fuel for the brain. The result could be a sluggish workout or race.
3. ***To help you feel comfortable and confident.*** Many runners can't run well on an empty stomach, although others find that food combined with stress causes stomach

problems. If you feel hungry, or if you are worried that you aren't properly fueled, you can't perform with confidence.

PRERUN FUELING

Fueling may include the following stages:

1. *A small high-carb meal* (500 to 1000 calories) two to four hours prior to running.
2. *A high-carb snack* (such as a bagel or energy bar) an hour before running.
3. *A sports drink or sports gel* 5 to 15 minutes prior to running.

Research by Michael Sherman, Ph.D., at Ohio State University found that performance improved by 12.5 percent when carbs were consumed an hour before exercise. Fifteen to 75 grams of carbs are recommended in the hour before running. Sherman suggests that a good guide is to consume 0.5 grams of carbs per pound of body weight about an hour before exercise to boost performance. More than this isn't likely to produce additional benefits. Please note that heavier runners need more prerun energy than lighter ones.

Here are a few suggestions that may help with prerun meals:

- How much to eat varies from person to person, depending upon food tolerance and how hard and long you will be running.
- When running for more than 90 minutes, emphasize slow-releasing carbs with a low to moderate glycemic effect. Avoid foods with a high sugar content or a high-glycemic effect, especially in the hour before running. These include soft drinks and candies. They give you a quick "sugar boost," and then turn around and give you a "sugar low" during the run. Suggests Clark: "If you simply must have a little bit of something sweet, eat it within 5 to 10 minutes of exercise. This short time span is too brief for

the body to secrete insulin, the hormone that causes low blood sugar. Because the body stops secreting insulin when you start to exercise, you should be able to handle this sugar fix safely *if* the food settles comfortably."

- Also avoid high-fat proteins, like cheese and red meat, that take a long time to digest. Milk causes problems for many runners so be careful about having it prior to running (including with your cereal). Fructose (the sugar in fruit and honey) may cause stomach distress. The best bet is to choose high-starch, low-fat foods—trusty carbs such as breads, bagels, pasta. The key here is selecting easily digestible, high-energy foods which you should eat daily for good health and running performance.
- Prior to racing, don't eat anything you haven't tried before a training run. Experiment before your regular runs, not your races. Don't be unpleasantly surprised by trying something new on race day—or the night before for that matter.
- Allow plenty of time for digestion. This may vary from an hour or two for a small snack, energy bar, or a liquid carbohydrate meal to two to four hours (or even more) after a meal. Your last meal before exercising should be a light one, not a heavy feast. Allow extra time for digestion before intense exercise. What works well before training runs doesn't always hold up—or stay down—during races. During an easy run, your stomach gets about two-thirds of normal blood flow, which allows near-normal digestion. Intense exercise diverts more blood to the muscles. Digestion slows dramatically because the stomach may get only 20 percent of its normal blood flow.
- If you can't handle food before running in the morning, make sure to eat well the day before. Try a bedtime snack instead of breakfast. Remember that overnight fasting reduces liver glycogen stores.

If this isn't replaced prior to running, it may result in a poor performance due to a shortage of available blood glucose.

- What works well for you before nonimpact activities such as biking or swimming may differ from what works with running. The up-and-down movement associated with running may contribute to abdominal stress.
- Drink plenty of water and other nonalcoholic and noncaffeinated fluids with meals to aid digestion and to prevent dehydration.

CARBO-LOADING

Carbo-load to improve performance for races lasting more than 90 minutes or so. The goal is to avoid "hitting the Wall." You may load for a 10-mile or half-marathon race, but for most runners this ritual is mainly for marathoning. Loading works for the average runner as well as faster ones. In fact, the middle-of-the-packers may benefit most. David Costill, Ph.D., author of *Physiology of Sports and Exercise,* notes:

> The difference between elite and average marathoners is that even if both started out with the same amount of glycogen, the elite marathoner would spare it by burning a higher ratio of fat. Although more oxygen is required to burn fat, the highly developed oxygen transport system of the elite runner allows this. Furthermore, he moves more economically, which means that he uses less oxygen to accomplish the same task. The average runner, on the other hand, depletes his glycogen supply sooner and doesn't have as efficient an oxygen transport system to burn fat. That's why hitting the wall is so devastating and why carbohydrate loading is more important for the average runner than for the elite runner.

Not only that, the average marathoner has to keep running much longer than those sub-three-hour runners after becoming glycogen-depleted. Loading, however, may not work as well for poorly trained runners. Those long runs help you load better.

The key to loading is to rest muscles going into the race (hoarding glycogen) while increasing the carbs in your diet (adding to glycogen stores). This combination allows the body to "load" glycogen for improved long distance performance. Here are the basic ingredients for carbo-loading:

- Start tapering two to four weeks before a marathon. Especially minimize running the last three to seven days. While tapering, you'll burn less glycogen for fuel and can store more for the marathon race. Also taper caloric intake to prevent weight gain. A general guide is to take in 100 calories less for each mile cut out. But don't overdo it.
- Stick to your normal diet of approximately 60 percent carbs until three days before the event. Then, increase carbs to 70 percent. Increase the percentage of carbs in your diet, not the calories. Aim for about 500 grams of carbs per day while being careful not to take in too many high-calorie fats.

  Some sports nutritionists recommend carbo-loading every day during training, not just before the big event. A daily diet of up to 70 percent carbs helps avoid glycogen depletion during periods of heavy training. Clark recommends consuming 4 grams of carbs per pound of body weight per day.
- Stick to your normal eating routine. Try to schedule meals at the same time. If traveling, it's tougher to stick to a routine and you may have less control over what you eat and how it is prepared. Plan ahead by finding out how restaurants and food stores can meet your nutritional needs. Bring along plenty of high-carb snacks such as energy bars and fig bars to help keep you carbo-loaded.
- Carbo-loading with too many refined wheat products will cause constipation; too many fruits will cause diarrhea. Take in adequate protein to aid muscle recovery. Not only that, research at the University of Texas found that glycogen storage rates were 38 percent higher when protein was added to

sports drinks. Beware of fats hidden in a high-carb diet. This includes ice cream, cookies, extra cheese on pizza. Skip the butter on your toast, pancakes, and baked potatoes; cream cheese on your bagel; and rich sauces on pasta.

- Drink plenty of water during loading. Water is stored in muscle tissue along with glycogen, and muscles will take from other organs if enough isn't supplied from the outside, which could lead to dehydration. You may gain a few pounds (2 to 4) and feel bloated while loading, but don't worry about it. This is to be expected since your body stores 2.6 grams of water for every gram of glycogen you load. Most of that is water weight, and you'll lose that and more on the run as you start to sweat. Pack in about 3 ounces of water for each ounce of carbs consumed.
- The day before the marathon, snack frequently throughout the day with high-carb foods that you are familiar with.
- Eat a high-carb meal (800 to 1000 calories) that agrees with your stomach the night before a marathon or long race. Years ago most coaches promoted a big steak to build muscle as the pre-event meal. Indeed, my college cross-country team used to eat a big steak dinner the night before races. Now the meal of choice is often pasta. Spaghetti, macaroni, noodles, steamed or boiled rice, potatoes, fruits, starchy vegetables, and breads are good carb sources. I like to load up on pancakes or waffles. Drink plenty of water or other nonalcoholic and noncaffeinated fluids to help you pack in the carbs and hydrate for the race. Avoid gas-forming foods such as beans and any type of food that may upset your stomach or interfere with sleep.
- This "last supper" is an important meal. Don't eat too much for dinner or too late at night. Carbo-load, don't overstuff. Eat about 6:00 P.M. when

preparing for a morning race the next day. A light snack, such as an apple or banana or energy bar, around 10:00 P.M. may help you feel more prepared. Select carefully where you eat the night before. Make reservations, or if dining out at the prerace feed, get there early so you don't have to wait to eat. Don't attend that spaghetti feast for the masses if the scene is too exciting for you. Don't eat anything that is unfamiliar. The best option may be the dullest and safest one: a quiet meal at home or hotel room.

- Eat a light, high-carb breakfast two to four hours prior to racing (no matter how early it starts) if you have found that doing so before a long run and practice race works for you. This should be 500 to 1000 calories, including about 200 grams of carbs. Include a combination of low- and high-glycemic foods. Good choices: bagels, toast, bananas, raisins, rice, pasta, liquid carbs. Don't limit yourself to traditional breakfast food—pasta is a great way to start the day. An energy bar or bagel an hour before the race will give you an extra boost. Drink 8 to 16 ounces of a sports drink (with 6 to 8 percent carb levels) 5 to 15 minutes before the start of the race and suck down a gel pack.

SHOULD YOU EAT BEFORE SHORT RACES?

Races of less than 90 minutes, particularly less than 60 minutes, don't diminish glycogen stores nearly as much as marathons. Thus, carbohydrate intake isn't as critical. Nevertheless, muscle glycogen still plays an important role since you burn plenty of carbs to fuel an intense effort. One study demonstrated that the ability to sprint at the end of a 15K race was enhanced for runners that consumed sports drinks an hour prior to the event. Follow a daily high-carb diet of at least 60 percent carbs. Prerace meals or snacks aren't necessary for short races to push back the Wall, but they ward off "brain drain." If you choose not to eat a meal, it may be helpful to take in an energy bar an hour before, or sports drink and a gel 15 minutes before. The amount and types of foods you can eat the morning of a slower-paced marathon may not work for you at the more intense pace of a short race.

FUELING UP ON THE RUN

Research demonstrates that for races lasting more than 60 minutes, long training runs longer than 90 minutes, and for intense speed workouts, fueling during the run will boost performance. Early in these runs, most of your energy comes from stored muscle glycogen. Later, the sugar in your blood (blood glucose) and liver glycogen become more significant as you start to deplete stored muscle glycogen. Carb intake during a run will help meet this energy need.

But how do you fuel on the run? One simple way is to drink fuel in a sports drink that has a 6 to 8 percent carbohydrate solution. Not only do they boost performance by sustaining blood glucose levels and sparing muscle glycogen, they help keep you hydrated. They also provide fuel for the brain to fight mental fatigue.

What about eating solid foods? Studies at the University of Texas found that solid carbs were as effective as liquid carbs. Their conclusion was it may be helpful to eat small pieces of bananas, energy bars, or gels during long, hard workouts since they pack in more carbs than liquids do. Drink plenty of water with them to facilitate absorption. This works for some—others find anything solid eaten on the run causes stomach distress.

What should you do? Again, experiment in long runs and practice races, not during an important race. Shelly-lynn directs long runs for marathoners. She sets up feeding stations en route with a smorgasboard of bagels, pieces of energy bars and bananas, and Mike and Ike's candy. Guess which is the most popular? Yep, Mike and Ike's! Other runners prefer hard candy, or glucose tablets.

I take in sports drinks every 2 miles in long races and consume a gel pack (or Ike and Mikes) about every 30 minutes as well. In between, I drink water. For example, at the New York City Marathon, they give sports drinks every 2 miles and water every mile. I'll drink water at the odd miles, and sports drinks and water at the even miles. The best strategy appears to be to take in

8 to 16 ounces of a sports drink or a sports gel about 5 to 15 minutes before a long run or race. Then, every 15 to 30 minutes for races and every 30 to 60 minutes for long training runs, take in more carbs either in liquid (about six to twelve swallows), solid, or gel form, or in any combination. Whatever the source, consume 30 to 60 grams of carbs per hour for long races to keep blood glucose levels up. This is about 24 ounces of a sports drink (three full 8-ounce cups), one or two gel packets, one energy bar, or any combination. This strategy fights off dehydration, hypoglycemia, and glycogen depletion resulting in a more comfortable, improved performance. It is important to point out that fatigue cannot be prevented by fueling up on the run. It can, however, be delayed.

Runners have all kinds of tricks to keep themselves moving toward the marathon finish line. A friend of mine, Jerry Mahrer, packs twenty-six jelly beans into a plastic bag and pins them to his shorts before each marathon. He pops one into his mouth at each mile mark. This technique keeps his blood sugar up and gives him short-term goals to keep him going. As long as he thinks this helps that may be half the battle! Other runners have a support crew waiting for them at key spots along the course as an oasis with favorite foods and drinks to give them a physical and emotional boost. I was once handed a banana Popsicle by a little girl on a hot day during the Boston Marathon. It hit the spot and perked me up for my 2-mile drive to the finish line. After the race, I wondered whether she meant to give it to me, or did I plunder it! Some hungry marathoners have been known to detour into a corner deli to grab a quick snack. If you are out there just to make it to the finish line, then a midmarathon munch stop won't slow you down nearly as much as it will keep you going. I've taken a snack break at delis on my long training runs. Sometimes not being a purist makes hard training more enjoyable, so bring along some money in case you have a snack attack.

Then there is Zoe Koplowitz, who has multiple sclerosis and "runs" with the aid of crutches. She bills herself as the world's slowest marathoner, taking over twenty-four hours to complete the distance. During the New York City Marathon she has a midnight snack when a McDonald's in the Bronx opens just for her. Her fuel stop strategy works: Zoe has successfully placed last for over ten years!

REFUELING AFTER RUNNING

Carbo-"reloading" is important too. A high-carb daily diet will easily replenish glycogen used within twenty-four hours of runs of less than 60 minutes. But if you run much longer, you need to reload after running. Eating soon after a long race or training run will restore glycogen stores sooner, and allow you to run stronger the next day.

According to research by John Ivy, Ph.D., at the University of Texas, muscles are most receptive to glycogen replacement if you eat within the first 15 minutes. The sooner you ingest carbs after running, the better. According to Ivy, "The longer you wait before consuming carbohydrates, the less hungry your muscles become. If you wait longer than 15 minutes, the rate of absorption is decreased by roughly 50 percent." At least eat within 30 minutes of running.

What should you eat after running hard and long? Carbs, again. Take in about 50 to 100 grams of carbs within the first 15 minutes. Your goal should be to consume 600 grams (or 2,400 calories) of carbs in the next 24 hours. That's about 50 grams every 2 hours. The emphasis should be on high-glycemic foods such as bagels, bread, and raisins that can quickly refuel muscles. It may not be practical to sit down to a big meal after you've finished a long training run or race. A quick way to get large amounts of carbs into your system when you have a reduced appetite is to consume high-carbohydrate drinks.

Don't forget to take in a sufficient amount of protein too. Heavy training or intense racing will cause microscopic muscle tissue damage and protein is needed to repair it. Protein will help prevent injuries and speed recovery so you can return sooner to quality training. It also increases glycogen replacement immediately after hard exercise. The body absorbs the most protein within the first two hours after exercise. The recommended postrun ratio is 1 gram of protein for every 3 grams of carbs consumed (for example, cereal with milk).

LIQUID CARBS

Sports drinks are either low- or high-carb concentrations. Low-carb drinks like Gatorade supply energy for exercise *and* help with hydration. They have carbohydrate concentrations of 6 to 8 percent and improve performance by maintaining blood glucose levels, delaying fatigue in runs of an hour or longer. Use these before, during, and after running. They are available at fluid stations during most major marathons. These low-carb sports drinks are discussed in more detail in Chapter 34.

High-carb sports drinks such as GatorLode help build energy stores before and after running. They contain carbohydrate concentrations of 20 to 25 percent. That's three to four times the concentration of regular sports drinks. They're not really drinks, but rather liquid meals ingested an hour or two before running, or after running. Don't drink these during your runs—they are not intended for that purpose. They provide a mix of complex and simple carbs, and usually contain no fat or protein. They leave the stomach faster than solid foods, allowing you to pack in carbs easily and quickly.

If you are having problems eating 60 to 70 percent of daily calories as carbs, try high-carb drinks as a supplement. It may be difficult to eat enough carbs without feeling full when carbo-loading, or during periods of intense training when you don't feel like eating. Shelly-lynn uses them regularly when packing in heavy mileage, but I find that they don't agree with my stomach. An 8-ounce glass may provide as many carbs as 2 cups of pasta. If you don't have time to cook a high-carb meal, you can load up with these liquid carbs. But don't look to liquid meals as a replacement of your balanced diet—they don't contain all the essential nutrients needed for good health.

ENERGY BARS AND GELS

Energy bars, such as PowerBar and Clif Bar, are ideal for a pre-exercise fuel boost, energy pickup during a long run, postrun recovery food, quick snack, or light meal. We buy them by the case (partially because our dogs love them, too). I'll eat one for energy before my prebreakfast runs when a full meal would cause stomach stress, and munch on one when I return to satisfy my hunger until I've recovered enough to enjoy a meal. They are particularly helpful to reload carbs after a long run when I have a limited appetite. Also, instead of grabbing a candy bar when I'm hungry for a snack, I'll grab an energy bar instead. However, don't chow down a bunch of them during the day because they each contain approximately 100 to 300 calories—less than candy, but they add up. Some runners eat small pieces of bars during races, but I find that they bog me down.

Choose a bar with less than 30 percent fat and more than 60 percent carbs (some bars follow the 40-30-30 theory previously discussed). Most energy bars provide lots of carbs (25 to 50 grams per bar) as well as some amounts of protein, vitamins, minerals, and fiber. Most bars include both high-glycemic carbs for quick energy, and low-glycemic carbs for energy later in the run. The early energy bars tasted like mud. Now they are quite tasty and come in all kinds of flavors and textures.

Snacks such as bagels, bananas, and fig bars pack as many carbs per calorie for less money as these high-tech options. But, like many runners, I feel more like an athlete when I eat an "official" athletic energy food! Energy bars are handier than traditional snacks: They don't spoil or crush, and can be easily stuffed into a sports bag, office desk, or car glove compartment.

But energy bars aren't easy to carry or open on the run, and they cause digestion problems for some if taken too close to running, or on the run. Hence, the invention of concentrated carbohydrate gels, such as PowerGel and GU. They pack about 100 calories from carbs (about 25 grams) into a small packet weighing about an ounce. Just tear them open and squeeze out the carbs for an easy-to-chew (or slurp) energy boost. Gels contain mostly carbs, are more easily digested than bars, and provide quicker energy boosts. They come in a variety of exotic flavors such as Chocolate Outrage, and Orange Burst. Unlike bars, I'll use them immediately prior to running as well as on the run. Use one or two packets within an hour of running, and one every 30 to 60 minutes during a long run or race. We buy them by the case, too. Pin them to your shorts, or stuff them into shorts with built-in carrying pouches. We admit our initial skepticism until we tried them out. They really make a difference in how we feel late in runs and races.

There is nothing special about the carbs in gels. They are just easier to use. Some runners prefer to suck on hard candy or glucose tablets, or chew jelly beans. Sports drinks supply a low concentration of carbs. You'll have to drink a lot to equal the fuel power of a gel. But sports drinks are recommended to add some fuel as well as hydration.

Experiment with various energy sources before, during, and after training runs and practice races until you find what works for you. Don't eat them for the first time before or during an important race since they may upset your stomach. Energy bars and gels purposely have a low water content so that they can be compact and easily carried. Drink plenty of water (at least 6 to 8 ounces) to aid in digestion and absorption. I try to grab two cups of water, figuring I'll get about one and a half cups in me to go with my gel. Time race fueling just before a fluid station—and don't litter!

CAFFEINE

Will caffeine improve performance? Depends upon who you ask. Some runners swear by it, others swear at it. For every runner (like Shelly-lynn and myself) for whom caffeine perks up runs, there is another for whom it causes "the runs." For some a cup of coffee is too much. For others, it won't even give them a mild jolt.

Some scientific evidence indicates that caffeine can improve performance. In fact, Frank Shorter drank defizzed cola while winning the 1972 Olympic Marathon. Why the physical and mental boosts many runners experience? Caffeine stimulates the central nervous system, thus increasing mental alertness and concentration. It may decrease the perception of fatigue, thereby making running seem easier. Caffeine may boost performance by forcing the body to use fatty acids for fuel, conserving glycogen and delaying fatigue. It may also increase the force of muscle contraction, delaying muscle fatigue during extended periods of hard effort. It may aid some people with asthma by widening blood vessels in the lungs.

Doses of just 1.5 to 3 milligrams of caffeine per pound of body weight can improve performance. For most runners, one or two cups of coffee or a can of cola or iced tea prior to a run, or perhaps a caffeinated gel just prior to running and about once an hour on the run, is sufficient. Some runners prefer higher doses of caffeine in tablet form. The International Olympic Committee considers caffeine a performance-enhancing drug. But an average-sized runner would have to consume the equivalent of six to eight cups of coffee within a short period of time to get enough caffeine to be banned.

Regular caffeine users experience less of a boost than infrequent users. For this reason, I limit caffeine use to key workouts and races. I'll often drink cola and/or take a caffeinated gel 15 minutes prior to a training run to help me get off to a good start. A quick dose of caffeine late in a long run or race helps me regain alertness and gives me a perception of feeling stronger. It really seems to aid my running. Caffeine may provide just a psychological boost, but I'll take all the help I can get!

But caffeine-boosting isn't for everyone. The potential performance-impeding and health-risk side effects need to be considered. Sensitivity to caffeine may cause increased nervousness and anxiety before races, impeding performance. Sleeplessness may occur for several hours after caffeine-boosted races and workouts, affecting recovery. It may cause diarrhea, nausea, and headaches before, during, and after races. It's a diuretic, which means it forces the body to urinate frequently. This can lead to dehydration if too much caffeine is consumed throughout the day and after running. Some research suggests that caffeine consumed prior to running doesn't increase urine production while on the run. However, some runners may lose time if too much caffeine intake before and during the event causes a comfort stop.

Experiment in training and practice races before trying caffeine for a big race. Don't rely on caffeine to produce fast times. You still have to train properly.

FASTING

Some believe fasting cleanses and "detoxifies" the body, preparing its metabolism for the stress of long-distance racing when glycogen supplies are low. But there are many health-risk side effects, and fasting appears to have the opposite effect of carbo-loading—it "unloads" the runner. Dr. David Nieman and researchers at Loma Linda University in California showed runners who fasted, compared to those who ate, had a 45 percent decrease in endurance. The fasting runners also had a harder time holding pace. Prior to the run, the fasting runners had leg muscle glycogen levels 17 percent lower than the fed runners. The researchers analogy:

FIGURE 33.1: SUMMARY OF FUEL INTAKE FOR RUNNERS	
Daily	Low-fat, high-carb (60 to 70 percent of calories) diet.
Before running	Eat a small high-carb meal (500 to 1000 calories) two to four hours prior to running, and/or a liquid carb meal or energy bar one to two hours prior. Emphasize low- to moderate-glycemic foods. Try a sports gel 15 minutes before running. Drink 8 to 16 ounces of a sports drink 5 to 15 minutes prior to runs. 15 to 75 grams of carbs is recommended in the hour before running (0.5 grams per pound of body weight).
During running	Fuel every 15 to 30 minutes during long races, every 30 to 60 minutes or so on long runs. Drink 6 to 12 ounces of a sports drink or eat gels, banana and energy bar pieces, hard candy, and glucose supplements. Thirty to 60 grams of carbs per hour is recommended in long races.
After running	After long runs and races, consume 50 to 100 grams of carbs within 15 minutes, another 50 grams every two hours until you eat a regular meal. Aim for about 600 grams of carbs within twenty-four hours.

"Fasting for 24 hours prior to a competition is like running for 90 minutes prior to the competitive event." If fasting for religious or other reasons, cut back training until getting back to a regular healthy diet.

CHAPTER 34

Hydration and Running

Runners must drink, drink, drink and drink—before, during, after runs, and throughout the day. The closer you come to replacing all the fluids lost during running, the better for both performance and good health. Hydration is important no matter what the temperature, but be especially attentive in warm weather. Chapter 36 discusses dehydration and its impact on race times and heat illness.

Water is the most important substance to human life except for oxygen. You need a good supply every day to function normally. This key nutrient makes up 50 to 60 percent of body weight. It provides the medium in which most of the body processes occur. As the main component of sweat, it stabilizes body temperature by acting as a coolant. Water is the major component of blood and thus helps transport energy nutrients to the exercising muscles, and carry away waste products such as carbon dioxide and lactic acid. As the main component of urine, it helps dissolve waste products. Water lubricates joints, cushions organs and tissues, and softens food for digestion.

Balancing water intake and loss is essential. How is it lost? Sixty percent through urine, 5 percent through fecal loss, 15 percent with evaporation from the skin, 15 percent as air is humidified during respiration, and 5 percent through normal sweating (as you run, you lose much more). About 60 percent of daily fluid intake comes from drinking; 30 percent from the water in foods we eat; and 10 percent is produced in cells during the metabolism of carbohydrates, fats, and protein. Good food sources for water include watery fruits and vegetables, juices, milk, and soups. The best drink is water. There is little danger of consuming too much; any excess is flushed away by the kidneys. On the other hand, not drinking enough when running a lot can place a strain on the kidneys, as I found out after developing painful kidney stones.

A general guideline for nonrunners is to drink at least eight 8-ounce glasses (2 quarts) of fluids daily. A rough rule of thumb is to drink at least an additional 16 ounces of fluid per 500 calories expended. That's about two 8-ounce cups per 5 miles of running. Most competitive runners should consume 3 to 4 quarts of fluids or more each day, at least half of this should be calorie-free water. It is not unusual for runners training at high mileage in warm weather to require 5 to 10 quarts of fluid daily.

The more you run, especially in hot weather, the more fluids needed in the daily diet. Set a goal of drinking a glass or two of fluids with each meal as well as at least a glass of fluids midmorning, midafternoon, and in the evening. This is in addition to what you drink before, during, and after running. Make sure during hot weather that you drink more than thirst dictates. If you are carboloading, you need still more fluids.

Don't look to caffeinated and alcoholic drinks to help meet hydration needs. Drinking lots of coffee, cola, and beer will not rehydrate you; in fact, it dehydrates. They are diuretics that may, if consumed in excess, increase the amount of fluids lost through urination. If you are used to it, one beer the night before, or a cup of coffee the morning of a race will have little effect on dehydration.

When pouring in fluids, remember you are also pouring in calories. Each glass of soda or juice is worth about a mile of running (about 100 calories per 8 ounces). At least the sports drinks are a better deal—at about 50 calories per serving. But the beer I like to drink in the evening is worth 150 calories per 12-ounce bottle! Do you know how many calories are in a glass of water? Yep, zero.

To keep my weight down, I literally replace my high-calorie drinks with no-calorie ones by filling an empty soda bottle with tap water and putting it in the refrigerator outside my office. By keeping water handy, I pass on the urge to grab something else. For me, the key is keeping the water very cold. In most parts of the country, ice-cold tap water tastes great. If yours doesn't, try filtering it or buy bottled water. Water bores you? Spice it up with a slice of lime or lemon and a few ice cubes, or drink seltzer water, which is full of sparkles but has no calories.

SPORTS DRINKS

Water was the main choice for fluid replacement on the run until the high-tech sports drinks became popular during the 1970s running boom. Before then, a few wily runners concocted their own drinks or downed juices or sodas on the run. I even competed against old-timers who drank brandy during races—and beat me!

Sports drinks, such as Gatorade and Exceed, are valuable for several reasons:

Improve absorption. Drinks containing a 6 to 8 percent concentration of carbs and small amounts of sodium are absorbed into the body up to 30 percent faster than water, and much faster than drinks such as soda or juices with higher concentrations. Drinks with more than 8 percent concentrations are more likely to cause stomach distress because they are absorbed too slowly. Experiment with drinks in training runs and build-up races. If you are running an important marathon, find out what type of sports drinks will be offered and get used to it prior to the race.

Supply fuel. They improve performance by quickly supplying glucose.

Electrolyte source. They replace sodium, chloride, and potassium lost in sweat. These are crucial contributors to optimal performance. Some claim that potassium loss while sweating might cause cramping and impair the body's normal functioning. Studies by Dr. David Costill and others, however, indicate that electrolyte loss is very small during running and that a balanced diet supplies enough replacement electrolytes.

Stimulate drinking, retains fluids. Water shuts off the thirst mechanism and stimulates the kidneys before a runner is fully hydrated—so you lose water in the form of urine. Studies show that the sodium in the drinks helps retain fluids and stimulate thirst. Also, runners choose to drink more when offered lightly flavored, moderately sweet sports drinks than when offered plain water. Taste is important when you need to take in plenty of fluids.

Daily fluid replacement. Replace soda and other high-calorie sugar drinks with sports drinks for meals and snacks.

We highly recommend sports drinks. We buy them by the case. They'll supply fluids faster than water along with needed carbs for energy. But water lovers take heart. Good old-fashioned H_2O is still of great value to runners. Drink plenty of it during the day to supply needed body fluids without extra calories, during training runs when sports drinks aren't available, and along with sports drinks during races.

DRINKING BEFORE RUNNING OR RACING

Research demonstrates that fluid intake before running helps keep body temperature and heart rate lower than that of runners who don't drink before running. The well-hydrated runner will experience less strain on the body and a reduced perception of exertion at a given pace than the underhydrated runner. Being well-hydrated is the difference between surviving and thriving.

The American College of Sports Medicine (ACSM) recommends drinking about 17 ounces of fluid about two hours before exercise. If you do not have to urinate within an hour, drink another 8 ounces. Don't drink too much after this until just prior to your run: You'll need 60 to 90 minutes to eliminate excess fluids through urination. Drink 1 or 2 cups (8 to 16 ounces) of fluids 5 to 15 minutes prior to running according to the ACSM. If you don't know exactly how much you're drinking, a good estimate is one big swallow equals an ounce. The kidneys shut down (for the most part) when you start running, so last-minute fluid intake will remain in your body. These fluids will help replace fluid loss from sweating as you start running. If running for less than an hour, this drink can be water or a sports drink. Beyond an hour run, choose a sports drink that will provide fluids plus additional carbs for energy.

Look for fluid stations at the starting area of races. Most good races offer a choice between water and sports drinks. Again, heed the warning: Don't drink something before or during key races that you haven't tested in training runs and build-up races.

DRINKING ON THE RUN

If you wait until you are thirsty to drink, it may be too late. You can lose 2 quarts of water before getting thirsty. Don't wait until late in the run or until you feel hot; it takes up to 20 minutes for the fluid to be absorbed.

How much should you drink on the run? The ACSM recommends consuming 6 to 12 ounces (or six to twelve big swallows) every 15 to 20 minutes when racing, especially in the heat. In hot weather races you may need to drink more frequently, especially if you are not able to consume the recommended volume while on the run. Drink at least every 30 to 45 minutes for easy training runs in hot weather; at least every hour in cool weather. Water is adequate to replace lost fluids for runs up to an hour; but, beyond that, replace fluids and improve performance by hydrating with sports drinks.

Most athletes voluntarily consume fluids equal to one-half to two-thirds of sweat losses during exercise. Ideally, you should replace 100 percent of fluid lost. To do this, you would need to match your fluid intake with your sweat rate. This may be impossible under many conditions. The goal should be to replace at least 80 percent of fluids lost while on the run.

The more you sweat, the more you need to replace. You can estimate the amount of fluid you need to replace by determining your sweat rate. The average sweat rate during running is about 1 to 1½ quarts per hour. You lose about 2 pounds of body weight per quart of sweat produced—about 2 to 3 pounds per hour of running. This rate of loss increases at a faster pace. Running at intense paces can cause losses of more than 2 quarts of sweat (4 pounds of body weight) per hour. To find your average sweat rate weigh yourself without clothes immediately before and after several runs. Your rate likely will be more during the hot weather months. If your sweat rate is about 2 pounds per hour, you will need to consume about 32 ounces per hour (8 every 15 minutes).

These amounts are much higher than you are used to and may cause stomach stress. Ingesting a lot of fluid while running may be uncomfortable at first, so ease into it to expand your tolerance. Besides sweat rate, also consider the rate at which your stomach empties fluids. If you drink too much, surplus fluids may slosh around in your stomach, causing discomfort. Should you drink less in races to prevent this? Runners differ significantly in both their rates of sweating and gastric emptying. Most runners' stomachs can empty about 6 or 7 ounces every 15 minutes during a race. Some runners can handle more, some less. You may be able to absorb fluids more efficiently some days than others. Experiment in training runs and practice races—with the types, frequency, and volume of drinks. Few drink too much in races, since it's highly unlikely that you'll consume full cups of fluid while running hard.

Unfortunately, you will most likely lose more fluid per hour on the run than your stomach can absorb. Try as you might, you can't drink enough to keep up. The best you can do is to minimize the loss by drinking early and often.

Some studies show that cold fluids are absorbed more quickly; others indicate warm drinks are better. The ACSM recommends "ingested fluids be cooler than ambient temperature (between 59 and 72 degrees Fahrenheit) and flavored to enhance palatability and promote fluid replacement." But, don't be fussy here; drink up no matter how warm or cold the drinks, or how they taste.

Runners don't gain much in performance by drinking during runs lasting less than 30 minutes. They will be finished before any fluids are absorbed. This includes short races and the last few miles of longer ones. But if you feel the need to drink anyway, it may help you psychologically. Prerace and postrace fluid intake for short distances, however, is still recommended.

Do you need to drink on the run even in cold weather? In cold conditions you don't feel like you're sweating much since there is a significant difference between body and air temperature. Also, humidity is usually low so heat dissipates through evaporation quickly. You may not notice sweating, even though it occurs. Although you usually don't sweat as much in cold weather, you'll still have some sweat loss. Also, cold, dry air draws water out of your respiratory system. Since breathing rate increases with running, significant amounts of fluid can be lost through respiration while running for long periods.

You may drink somewhat less on cooler days, but it is still important. For training runs of less than an hour, a glass of water or sports drink prior to running will probably be enough unless you are overdressed and thus will sweat more. You still should drink on long runs of over an hour—at least every 3 to 5 miles—despite the temperature. What about races? You'll benefit from drinking during races of 30 minutes or longer on cold days—running will raise your body temperature and deplete fluids even when the spectators are wearing winter coats. And in races of over an hour, sports drinks are recommended. Be careful, however, not to overdrink on cold days and cause stomach distress.

Where can you find fluids during training runs? Plan ahead. Know where to find water. Most parks and playgrounds have drinking fountains. Scout out a friendly gas station, school, or home along the way. Look for water faucets or hoses. If I've run for too long without finding water, I'll look for a place where I can buy some bottled water or sports drinks. On long runs, I'll loop back home at least once to get sports drinks. You can also plant sealed bottles of drinks along your route. Some runners prefer to carry their drinks. The simple solution is to carry a water bottle in your hand. But that may interfere with good form and relaxation. Hands-free hydration systems with exciting names like FastDraw and CamelBak are available at running stores. They range from simple handheld flasks to high-tech fanny-pack models that contour to the shape of your body and include a plastic tube to allow hands-free, over-the-shoulder drinking. I can't stand to carry drinks with me, but I know many runners that don't mind it at all. But they *do* mind not having enough to drink. The best solution may be a support crew. Have family or friends meet you along the way with your favorite drink, or accompany you on a bike.

Enhance the quality of runs and protect your health by taking fluids frequently. Fluid deprivation during training runs will not toughen you for hot weather races. The body can't adapt to running without fluids. I'll stop two or three times on hot days at water fountains for each 6-mile loop of New York's Central Park. Don't worry that you are cheating when you take a break from running to get a drink. It takes just a few seconds. You don't need to jog in place while waiting behind someone at the fountain, but try to get running as soon as possible after drinking or your muscles will get stiff.

HOW TO DRINK DURING A RACE

Drinking during a race can be tricky. You have to get to it, get it in you, and get back into your pace. What's more important, getting in plenty of fluid or keeping moving? A little time lost drinking is more than recovered down the road. Pace slows by 2 percent for every 1 percent of body weight lost in sweat.

All races should provide fluid stations at least every 2 or 3 miles. If they don't, don't run them, especially in hot weather. Race directors should tell you where the fluid stations are located. Many long races offer a choice between water and a sports drink. The New York City Marathon, for example, offers water every mile and a sports drink every 2 miles. I try to pour some of each in me during long races. You have three choices on how to take in fluids during a race:

1. Completely stop and drink a full cup.
2. Grab the cup and take swallows while walking. When finished, ease back into running.
3. Grab a cup and do your best to keep running while drinking.

With the first option, beware of gulping the drink down too fast, which could cause stomach distress. Although unusual for Elites, Bill Rodgers came to a dead stop to drink four times while winning the Boston Marathon in 2:09. Taking a few walk breaks while making sure you take in enough fluids will give your muscles a break from the pounding of the running while allowing your body to cool off a bit. Look at it as a good excuse to rest. If you are holding a cup of water while walking, doesn't it seem justified to take a break? Your goal is to finish, and by making sure you get plenty of fluids you increase your chances of reaching your goal. So go ahead, walk, drink, and then run. I give you permission. You may lose 5 to 10 seconds per stop but lose less time in the end than if you tried to clumsily drink on the run. If concerned about time loss if you drink frequently, combine drinking on the run for some stops and drinking while walking for others.

If you are an experienced racer and want to minimize time lost while drinking in order to run a good time, you'll need to master the art of drinking on the run. No doubt about it, drinking from a cup while on the run is an awkward business. I still get more up my nose than down my throat. Here are some tips to help speed you on your way:

- Be on the lookout for fluid stations. As you get close to one, maneuver to that side of the road. If you suddenly cut to a water table you may cut off another runner.
- Plan ahead, look for your best shot at getting fluids quickly. Usually, it is more crowded at the beginning of the stations, so take a quick glance to see if fluid is available a few feet farther along. I try to grab a cup at the beginning and another at the end of each fluid station. Sometimes it's faster to grab a cup off the table yourself, but usually the volunteers can save you time by handing it to you. Thank them if you have the energy. Without their often thankless efforts you'd be in trouble.
- Run defensively. Runners of all sizes, shapes, and speeds converge at fluid stations. Be aware of the traffic heading into and out of the area. Some will be running full-speed and want their drinks in a hurry; others will be staggering and fuzzy-brained. I've been both. It isn't unusual to see runners cut off or knocked down. Also be warned that the footing may be slippery around the water stations—the roadway will be wet and strewn with discarded cups.
- To take a cup on the run, keep your eye on it and watch as your hand reaches for the cup. It is easy to miss if you don't pay attention. If you are grabbing a cup from a volunteer, yell out or point to them, making eye contact so they can assist in the transfer. If you need to grab a cup from a table, slow down slightly and move your arm back as you make contact with the cup. This way you won't hit it at full running speed and it will be easier to pick it up and

minimize spillage. If you fail to grab a cup on the run, stop and make sure to get the fluids. Especially in hot weather or in long races it is important to consume fluids despite losing a few seconds in attaining it.

- Try to take in at least six big swallows (6 ounces) of each cup. You should get that much even if you spill some. Many races hand out 8- to 10-ounce-sized cups, so you have room for error. You must slow down some to drink on the run. Experiment with the best way to hold the cup. Some runners pinch the top of the cup together as soon as they get it to prevent too much of the fluid from splashing out. Then they'll sip it a little at a time. I just hold it in one hand and take a mouthful, swallowing it a little at a time before taking another mouthful. Stay relaxed, breathe normally between swallows, and take time finishing the cup while maintaining a steady pace. Others try to gulp it down quickly in one or two big swallows and off they go again. Budd Coates, fitness director for Rodale Press, passed on this tip in *Runner's World*: "Grab a cup, using your fingers as pincers. Place one or more fingers inside the cup and your thumb on the outside, and squeeze the wall of the cup between them. Then, with your free hand press the side rims of the cup together, and drink from one end of the slit."

If you are concerned about your drinking technique, run a few practice races that have fluid stations. Or, set up a table along your training route and every 5 to 15 minutes loop by it and practice your drinking form. Shelly-lynn has our running classes practice grabbing cups of water on the run.

You don't have to wait until reaching stations to drink. By supplementing the official fluid tables, you don't need to consume as much fluid each time—drinking 6 to 8 ounces at a time without spilling it isn't easy. Some races don't supply fluids often enough to meet your demands. In some big races, it is very hard to get fluids without literally standing in line and fighting for them. And sometimes they run out for those folks in the back of the pack. So it is helpful to have a backup fluid-supply system.

In many races spectators along the course may offer drinks. A good, safer way to make sure you consume enough fluids is to form a support team—friends, relatives, kids—and make them a part of your racing success. Position them along the course with cups of fluids or small plastic squeeze bottles filled with water or your favorite road-tested sports drink or concoction. Just be sure to be precise as to where they will meet you. Be prepared to yell out their names so they can find you—it's hard to pick out runners as they run by.

Sometimes, in an effort to break away from competitors or save precious seconds, a runner will skip a few fluid stations. Some races and personal records have been won this way. But others have been lost by competitors who suddenly fell apart from lack of fluids. Compare the drawbacks (slowing some during the race to drink fluids, and possibly suffering some gastrointestinal discomfort) of drinking plenty of fluids when racing with the benefits (minimizing the loss of running speed late in the race, and increasing safety). I slow slightly as I drink and then fartlek to catch up to the group I was with. I estimate I only lose 3 seconds or so per stop which I can make up in 100 yards or so. But in the last 20 minutes of races I'll just pour water on my head to minimize slowdown. If racing, don't be so obsessed with getting fluids that you lose focus on your pace and competition.

POUR IT ON YOU, TOO

Pouring water on you may not help cool the body, but it may help you feel better. If nothing else, it provides a great psychological boost. You need plenty of help coping with the mental stress of running on a hot day. During training runs I'll cup my hands under water fountains and splash my head and chest with water. During races, I take two cups of water at each station. I drink one and pour the other over my head (Warning: Sports drinks get quite sticky when poured over your head by mistake!). Be careful not to get your shoes and socks too wet which may cause blisters. Try pouring water down your back rather than your front to minimize this.

DRINKING AFTER RUNNING

Start drinking immediately after finishing runs to replace lost fluids and help bring down your body temperature. Aim for at least 16 ounces (2 cups) for every 30 minutes of running. But drink more than that if you sweated a lot. A common guideline is to drink at least 2 cups of fluids (16 ounces) for every pound of body weight lost running to replace fluid lost with sweating. You may need to drink even more than that to properly rehydrate. You also need to replace fluid lost with urine production. Research shows that 125 to 150 percent of total fluid loss is usually enough fluid to fully rehydrate. For example: If you lose 3 pounds running, you lost about 48 ounces of fluid. Ideally, consume 60 to 72 ounces of fluid within two to three hours after running.

Marathoners often lose 6 to 12 pounds, or the equivalent of as much as 1 to 1.5 gallons of fluids. This is not permanent weight loss, but a temporary fluid loss. The sooner you get that fluid level back to normal the better you will recover. Even if the scale doesn't show lost weight after a run, drink plenty of fluids. A good rule: Continue drinking until you have a good flow of clear or pale yellow urine. How much you drink before and during runs minimizes postrun dehydration and fluid replacement needs. To rehydrate adequately following a long, hard run may take one or two days. So continue drinking heavily for a day or two. Weigh yourself before and after every long run and race to see how much fluid weight you are losing.

The key to rehydration is salt intake. Research by Ronald Maughan, Ph.D., at the University of Aberdeen in Scotland, and Dr. Hiroshi Nose at Yale University, indicates that drinking plain water or sugary drinks is ineffective at restoring fluid balances after exercise because it suppresses thirst and increases urine output. Much of the fluid is lost in urine over the next two hours. When fluids contain sodium, the thirst drive is stimulated, resulting in greater amounts of fluid intake, and urine production decreases, resulting in increased fluid retention. Sports drinks (which contain some sodium) help, but studies show that only 69 percent of body weight is restored with them. How do you increase salt intake? Eat some salty foods (a small bag of salty pretzels or potato chips), and take a sports drink to assist in the retention of the fluids you consume. Or, add some salt to water or a sports drink.

Dr. Maughan's research has demonstrated that a well-balanced meal with foods rich in electrolytes, especially sodium and potassium, combined with plenty of water (one and a half times that lost during running) resulted in complete rehydration within six hours of exercising. On the other hand, consuming only a sports drink resulted in a 10- to 11-ounce body-water deficiency. If you want to enjoy a postrun beer, first drink plenty of water and eat some food. If you are dehydrated and don't have food in your stomach, the alcohol will hit you much harder. Drink plenty of water to go along with the beer, since alcohol causes you to urinate more and thus adds to dehydration, not hydration. Remember: Don't run, drink alcohol, and then drive.

FIGURE 34.1: SUMMARY OF RECOMMENDED FLUID INTAKE FOR RUNNERS

Daily	3 to 4 quarts or more, at least half of it calorie-free water.
Before running	17 ounces two hours before running, particularly long runs in hot weather. Drink 8 to 16 ounces 5 to 15 minutes prior to running. A sports drink is recommended for runs and races longer than one hour.
During running	6 to 12 ounces (six to twelve large swallows) every 15 to 20 minutes when racing; at least every 30 to 45 minutes for easy runs in warm weather; at least every hour when cool. Take sports drinks for runs and races longer than one hour.
After running	At least 16 ounces for every 30 minutes of running; at least 16 to 24 ounces for each pound of body weight lost within two to three hours of running. Keep drinking for several hours on hot days. Drink until urine is clear or pale yellow.

CHAPTER 35

Performance Weight

Most Elites are natural featherweights, but most runners need to work at reducing body fat and weight. Strive for a strong engine, light chassis, and good health. According to a Harvard University study, being as lean as possible, while keeping healthy, increases your defense against major diseases. Researchers found that those who weighed the least lived longest. The way I figure it, that means we get that many more years of running!

Extra weight affects running, putting extra stress on the cardiorespiratory and thermoregulatory systems. You pound the road with greater force, thus increasing the risk of injury. And you cannot run as fast.

HEALTHY VERSUS PERFORMANCE WEIGHT

Don't feel lonely if you weigh more than you did when you were younger and more active. I weighed in at 155 to 160 pounds as a high school and college runner. This weight continued through my twenties and into my thirties when I was a serious marathoner. But then, as I retired from competitive training and marched toward the half-century mark, the scales somehow tipped 190! My running shorts and business suits didn't fit anymore unless I sucked it in and held my breath. I didn't feel or look the way I wanted. When I ran my legs and knees ached from the added weight. Worse, I was *much* slower. Despite appearing fit to others, I felt like an elephant on the run. Then one day—this is a true story!—while running I was passed by an elderly lady wearing headphones as she ran and skipped rope! That was the last straw!—time to lose weight and get back into good shape. I hadn't really increased my food intake, but the stress of a business combined with a continuing bout with asthma and a bad back reduced my exercise level dramatically. At the same time, I discovered that the research was true. You really do gain weight as you age and metabolism slows down.

What weight is desirable for optimal health? The experts have many theories and no one agrees on a single formula. Not only that, they keep changing their recommendations. Most weight charts are based on what the average American weighs, rather than should weigh. They allow for a higher weight than may be ideal for health. If you feel and look good, chances are you are near healthy weight.

But you can be within an acceptable healthy weight range and still not be at your ideal performance weight. Competitive runners may be 10 to 20 percent below standard healthy weight ranges. Not everyone can be skinny like the Elites, but most can at least be lighter. Generally, competitors arrive at their ideal performance weight by the process of self-selection. As mileage approaches a high, consistent level, the body establishes a comfortable and efficient weight. Indeed, most Elites answer when asked about their best running weight: "I wait until I'm in shape, then I weigh myself."

Being overweight can dramatically slow race times. Up to a point, the more weight you lose, the better your race times. In general, for every 1 percent reduction in total body weight, there is a 1 percent increase in running speed capacity. Check your diary for what you weighed when you ran your best races. Record weight regularly. This will keep you from gradually gaining or losing weight without realizing it. Don't record weight after running when you have temporarily lost body fluids. Rather, step on the scales (nude and after emptying your bladder) after getting up each morning.

PERFORMANCE WEIGHT CHARTS

Figures 35.1 and 35.2 list recommended performance weight ranges for competitive runners. The target weight for men is based on this formula: twice your height in inches (the average weight for Elites) plus 10 percent. The target for women is based on this formula: Start with 5′6″, 120 pounds. Add 3 pounds for each inch above this height; subtract 3 pounds for every inch below it. The recommended performance weight range is from 10 percent below to 10 percent above the target weight. For most runners, their best performance weight will be at the target weight or slightly under it. At 6′1″, my target is 161 pounds; my performance range 146–175. I was 155 to 161 pounds during my peak running years, and at age fifty-plus strive to keep close to my target while maintaining good health. As I finish this chapter, I'm down to 168 pounds! Shelly-lynn, at 5′6″, has a target weight of 120 pounds; a performance range of 108–132. Her racing weight fluctuates between 108 and 120 depending upon mileage.

NOTE: Weight loss below or weight gain above the ranges indicated on the charts could result in loss of health and performance. These ranges are based on statistics and are estimated guidelines only. They do not account for individual differences. Small-framed and/or shorter runners may weigh a little less than the charts; large-framed and/or taller runners may weigh a little more than the charts.

BODY COMPOSITION: FAT VERSUS MUSCLE

What you weigh is one thing. How lean you are is another. The body consists of water and two types of tissues: fat and lean body tissue—bone, organ, and muscle. The percentage of body weight

FIGURE 35.1: PERFORMANCE WEIGHT CHART FOR MALE RUNNERS

Height	Target Weight	Weight Range
5′6″	145	132–158
5′7″	147	134–161
5′8″	150	136–163
5′9″	152	138–166
5′10″	154	140–168
5′11″	156	142–170
6′	158	144–173
6′1″	161	146–175
6′2″	163	148–178
6′3″	165	150–180

FIGURE 35.2: PERFORMANCE WEIGHT CHART FOR FEMALE RUNNERS

Height	Target Weight	Weight Range
5′1″	105	95–116
5′2″	108	97–119
5′3″	111	100–122
5′4″	114	102–125
5′5″	117	105–129
5′6″	120	108–132
5′7″	123	111–135
5′8″	126	113–138
5′9″	129	116–142
5′10″	132	119–145

that is fat is called body fat percentage. It's determined by dividing total body weight by the weight of your fat. David Costill, Ph.D., director of the Human Performance Laboratory at Ball State University, found that each pound of fat added or lost can result in an increase or decrease of body fat percentage by as much as half a percent, which affects performance.

Body-fat percentage can be measured in many ways. The most accurate assessment is hydrostatic (underwater) weighing done by technicians in a laboratory. Skinfold tests measure fat under the skin using calipers; this may be fairly accurate. You can take this test at most fitness clubs or Ys. They may also offer a bioelectrical impedance analysis, a computerized method that sends minute electrical currents through the body to determine body fat percentage. Or, you can just save the money by taking the nude jump test: Stand in front of a full-length mirror and jump; anything that shook (that shouldn't) when you landed is fat.

Standard error for body fat percentages is plus or minus 3 percent. For this reason, place your emphasis on a range and carefully monitor significant changes over time. Serious competitors may find that these tests aren't as accurate in the lower ranges. Using formulas designed for athletes rather than the general population increases accuracy.

Some people may weigh within the standard ranges for good health but have a high percentage of body fat. They are of standard weight but overfat. This may include some runners that are slim, but flabby. These runners would benefit from weight training to increase muscle tone. On the other side, some athletes, such as professional football players, weigh above the standard range for their height. Their rigorous training produces muscle and decreases body fat far below average. Their bulk is in muscle, not fat. Some big-boned, heavy runners with low body fat just will not be able to lose weight. But they can train wisely and be the best they can be for their given body type. Women have more body fat than men of the same size, weight, and activity level. These genetically designated fat stores are geared for reproduction. Very fit women, however, may have a lower body fat percentage than less active men.

Most people assume the less fat on your body the better. This is true to a point. But, all of us need a certain amount of fat for our bodies to function normally. For men, essential body fat is 3 to 5 percent; for women, it's 11 to 13 percent. Fat isn't all bad. In fact, it performs a variety of important functions. Body fat is an essential structural component of cell walls and nerve fibers, supports and cushions vital body organs, helps make hormones and healthy skin, and insulates the body from the environment. Stored fats in the body are an important source of energy. As much as 70 percent of our energy at rest comes from fat.

A person 5′10″ tall weighing 150 pounds carries about 90 of those pounds as water, 30 as fat, and 30 as lean tissue. To lose weight, you want to lose fat, not critical lean tissue. To gain weight, add lean tissue and fat in proportion, not just fat. What should your body fat percentage be? Figure 35.3 provides an approximate guide.

FIGURE 35.3: BODY FAT PERCENTAGE RANGES

Classification	Percent fat	
	Men	Women
Essential fat	3 to 5	11 to 13
Elite distance runners	5 to 8	13 to 17
Advanced and Champion Competitors	8 to 12	17 to 20
Novice, Intermediate, and Basic Competitors	12 to 15	20 to 23
Average American	15 to 20	23 to 26
Overweight	20 to 25	26 to 35
Overfat (obese)	over 25	over 35

YOU CAN BE TOO THIN, TOO

Many people aspire to a weight and body shape that's probably unrealistic for them. Pressure to be thin, whether for looks or performance, can result in serious psychological and health costs. You can perform poorly and be prone to injury and illness if you are underweight. Without sufficient caloric intake, muscles burn their protein for fuel resulting in strength loss. The quest for thinness may result in eating disorders. The American College of Sports Medicine (ACSM) reports that up to 62 percent of women competing in college endurance sports suffer some sort of eating disorder, either anorexia (self-induced starvation), bulimia (binge-eating, followed by self-induced vomiting), laxative abuse, crash diets, or other unhealthy practices. Some men are similarly affected. If you have a running friend who may have an eating disorder, encourage him or her to seek professional counseling.

BODY IMAGE

Look around at the starting line of any race. Most runners up front look very lean and muscular. Are you unhappy if you don't measure up to this standard? Actually, as many Elite runners as middle-of-the-packers are concerned about body image.

Men and women inherit one of three standard body types from their parents:

- *Ectomorph* (slender and small-boned like most Elites)
- *Mesomorph* (big-boned and heavily muscled)
- *Endomorph* (round and soft)

Make the best of what you were born with. A balanced program of running, weight training, and eating properly will result in the healthiest, fittest body you can achieve. Don't waste time and energy fussing about the "perfect" body. You can improve running times with your natural body by training properly. Next time you are nearing the finish line of a race and you see one of those perfect bodies up ahead, pick up speed and power right by. At least you got faster genes!

CLYDESDALE RUNNERS

Not everyone was born to be a featherlight distance runner. Some are so tall they can't help but weigh more than the runners around them, or built more for football than marathoning. Some are over-fat (but not overweight) but have the talent to help compensate for it. Many runners who weigh at the high end of the chart (or above it) in Figures 35.1 and 35.2 aren't overfat. Their body-fat percentage may even be lower than many skinny runners. Take heart with this comment big guys and gals: You just may outnumber those ectomorphs in most races. Don't believe me? Skip past the first few rows at the starting line of most races and you'll find plenty of heavyweight (but fit) and slightly overweight (but working at slimming down) runners.

Heavy runners should wear well-cushioned shoes in training and racing to absorb the extra impact—you pound the ground at about three times your body weight. Shoes will need to be replaced more often, too, since the midsoles will take more of a beating. Bigger and fitter runners sweat a lot and thus need extra fluids and slower paces on hot days.

Road race awards are dominated by lightweight runners. Many race directors have responded to this inequity by including awards in the "Clydesdale" division (named for those huge, but fit horses). A typical breakdown for men: 185 to 199 pounds, and 200 pounds and over. For women: 140 to 159 pounds, and 160 pounds and over. The competition in these categories is just as fierce as the regular age divisions. Some runners have been known to bulk up a few pounds so they qualify!

CALORIES, EXERCISE, AND WEIGHT MANAGEMENT

Food intake is measured in kilocalories, more widely known simply as calories. A calorie is the measure of energy required to heat 1 gram of water 1 degree centigrade. A pound of body fat stores about 3,500 calories. To lose that pound, you must take in 3,500 calories less than you use; to gain it, you must take in 3,500 calories more than you use. In general, a deficit or excess of 500 calories a day brings about a weight loss or gain, respectively, at the rate of 1 pound per week; a deficit or excess of 1,000 calories a day, 2 pounds a week.

Carbohydrates, fats, and proteins contain calories; water, minerals, and vitamins do not. Calories in the form of fat build up easily: A gram contains 9 calories, whereas a gram of protein or carbs contain 4. Even if you eat mostly carbs, too much food intake results in too many calories and excess pounds. Too few calories also affects performance and health. A recommended standard: Multiply your ideal body weight by 15 and add about 100 calories for every mile you run each day on the average. Another general rule: Take in 20 to 23 calories per pound each day if you're a high-mileage runner, or 17 to 19 calories per pound if you're a low-mileage runner. For the average runner, the break-even point is about 2,500 calories per day.

Three factors contribute to burning off calories. First, and most important, is resting metabolic rate. Most of us burn 60 to 75 percent of our total calories each day by breathing, thinking, maintaining body temperature, and pumping blood through our bodies. Resting metabolic rate depends on body composition. The more muscle you have the faster the metabolic rate; muscles burn more calories at rest than fat. Women have less muscle than men of comparable size and activity level, resulting in metabolic rates about 10 percent lower.

Second, physical activity accounts for 15 to 35 percent of calorie burning. This may be running, weight training, working at your desk, mopping the floor, and such. Running not only boosts calorie burning during exercise, it also continues the consumption afterward.

Third, and least significant, is the energy your body burns processing food. This burns 10 to 15 percent of calories per day. But this thermic effect of food (TEF) can be significant over a period of time. A lower than normal TEF can cause weight gain.

We lose muscle mass after age fifty, lowering resting metabolic rate and burning fewer calories per day. Thus, we need fewer calories as we grow older. A seventy-year-old generally needs 10 to 15 percent fewer calories than a twenty-year-old. As we age, we should eat less and/or run more, thereby leveling off our weight rather than continuing to gain. Most Americans take in more calories as they get older. I don't agree with charts allowing us to gain weight with aging. They're based on what average Americans do, not what they should do. I'll concede 5 pounds to aging, but no more.

RUNNING AND CALORIES

Running burns about 100 calories per mile depending on your weight and the intensity of your workout. The more you weigh and the faster you run, the more calories you will burn per minute. Figure 35.4 lists the number of calories you can burn at various paces per 30 minutes of running.

What about the controversial idea that slower-paced running is better for burning fat and losing weight than faster-paced running? According to the theory, the "fat-burning zone" is between 50 and 60 percent of your maximum heart rate (MHR). Research at the University of Texas indeed found that fat provides 90 percent of calories burned at that pace. At 75 percent of MHR, only 60 percent of calories burned comes from fat since your body switches to burning carbs as you run faster. So should you run slower to burn off more fat? According to the Texas study, running at the higher intensity, but still at a conversational pace, actually resulted in more fat calories burned. Why? The 50 percent intensity workout burned only 7 calories per minute while the 75 percent intensity workout burned twice that.

FIGURE 35.4: APPROXIMATE CALORIES EXPENDED PER 30-MINUTE RUN

Weight (Pounds)	Pace (Minutes Per Mile)						
	12:00	11:00	10:00	9:00	8:00	7:00	6:00
100	200	215	230	262	300	350	400
110	208	225	242	276	315	362	418
120	216	233	250	284	325	370	432
130	234	252	270	305	350	410	468
140	255	273	292	320	380	450	510
150	272	293	315	356	408	476	544
160	294	317	340	378	440	500	588
170	310	338	365	410	465	540	620
180	328	354	380	431	490	574	656
190	344	372	400	452	518	602	688
200	360	392	425	473	540	630	720

Note: 3,500 calories expended equals one pound of weight loss.

TIPS FOR HEALTHFUL WEIGHT LOSS

Gradually increase mileage. Upping mileage by 10 miles a week burns about 1,000 extra calories. If you hold caloric intake constant, this results in a loss of about 1 pound a month. Because of increased mileage, the average runner drops 5 pounds or more during marathon preparation.

Weight-train. Include two to three strength-training sessions a week to increase muscle mass. Muscle is more metabolically active than fat: A pound of fat burns 2 calories a day at rest to maintain itself, but a pound of lean body mass burns 30 to 50 calories a day. Weight training helps minimize muscle-mass loss, and therefore weight gain, with aging. At first you may not lose weight with weight training and running, but you will lose inches because muscle weighs more than fat but takes up less space.

Lose weight gradually. Rapid loss affects metabolism which may be a health risk and increases the likelihood that any weight lost will not only come back, but that you will gain back additional weight. A loss of no more than 1/2 to 2 pounds a week helps ensure that the loss is coming from body fat rather than lean muscle tissue. The signs of muscle loss are much the same as those of overtraining: sleep problems, increased susceptibility to illness, and irritability. To safely lose weight, the ACSM recommends a negative caloric balance of up to 500 to 1,000 calories per day. Reach this goal by consuming 250 to 500 calories less per day while burning off 250 to 500 calories more each day with exercise. A net loss of 500 calories per day over the course of one week is 3,500 calories, which equals 1 pound. On the other hand, that formula can work the other way, which is how we gain weight. Err by a few calories each day on the wrong side of this balance and you pay for it over time. An excess of merely 30 calories a day adds up to 10 pounds over three years or so. This is exactly how weight creeps up on many of us!

Eat enough calories. A sufficient amount of calories are needed to fuel your running. If you are too tired to exercise, you probably are dieting too strictly. It's asking a lot of your body to push its limits and at the same time restrict food. Provide your body with enough fuel to train. After the energy needs are met, a runner can choose to maintain weight or lose it for a lighter chassis.

Don't skip meals. This makes you hungrier, increasing the temptation to binge. Eat several small meals and snacks throughout the day if necessary.

Choose the right parents. Studies show that genetics may play a significant role in determining body weight. Some of us are born to outweigh those Elite runners.

Consider professional help. This support can help you reach goals safely. This may be a sports doctor, nutritionist, or psychologist.

Be consistent, patient, and disciplined. To succeed, you don't have to be perfect. Just be as consistent as possible with exercising and eating right. Set a reasonable goal, like 5 to 10 pounds off in two or three months.

Eat the right foods. Fats have more than twice as many calories per gram as carbs and proteins. Emphasize high-energy carbs. Eat low-fat or nonfat dairy products, lean cuts of meat, skinless poultry, and lean fish. Switch to lower-calorie items—water instead of soda, an apple instead of a candy bar. Minimize desserts and high-calorie snacks. But don't reduce your fluid intake. No one loses weight permanently from sweating. You need to replace lost body fluids.

Keep a nutrition log. Write down what you eat every day and analyze total fat, carbohydrate, protein, and calorie intake. To make it easier, try one of the software packages available for computers. If you periodically track food intake for a few days, you may be shocked. You may wish to have your diet analyzed by a sports nutritionist.

Change eating habits. Eat more slowly and until you feel comfortable, not stuffed. Keep those evening meals light, especially if you get home late from work or if you run late at night before dinner. Nancy Clark, author of *The Sports Nutrition Guidebook*, warns: "Many runners diet at breakfast and lunch, drag themselves through a midday workout, are famished at dinner and eat everything in sight. They end up gaining weight."

PART IX

THE RUNNING ENVIRONMENT

CHAPTER 36

Hot Weather Running

Runners hit the roads and trails more often in the warmer months. The extra daylight hours make it easier to get runs in and wearing light clothing allows you to have more zip. There's a race almost every weekend, giving you plenty of motivation. Most runners look forward to warmer weather after having struggled through winter. Let's face it, it's a lot easier getting out the door to run when it's warm and bright than when it's cold and dark.

The comfort of warm weather is one thing, training and racing in hot, muggy conditions is another. Just running along at an easy pace is taxing, but hard efforts including long runs, speed training, and racing require additional adjustments. Combined with humidity, air pollutants, and sun exposure, heat causes many problems. It threatens all runners, no matter how fast or slow you run.

Heat affects some runners more than others and even the same runners differently from day to day. I sweat profusely and am not a good heat runner, although I can improve my hot weather race times somewhat by heat training. Shelly-lynn, on the other hand, thrives in the heat. Although women tend to sweat less, they cope with heat as well as men. What about us older runners? Research indicates sedentary oldsters may tolerate heat less effectively, but active masters runners cope well.

Following the guidelines in this chapter and common sense, you can cope with hot weather running and racing.

HEAT AND PERFORMANCE

The combination of heat exposure and running causes a serious challenge. A dual role develops for the blood: It must cool the body by transporting heat to the skin's surface, and supply oxygen and fuel to the working muscles. Running in cool weather at a moderate pace, there is enough blood for both functions. In hot weather, when body-cooling blood is pumped to the skin, less blood flows back to the heart. Each heartbeat pumps out less blood than in cooler weather and the heart compensates by beating faster to keep up with the needs of the body. Blood volume is reduced even further if you dehydrate. As a result, the heart beats even faster. This quicker heart rate, however, isn't enough to offset the lost blood volume and the heart is overworked, resulting in reduced aerobic power. Heat further sabotages running times by increasing the rate of glycogen depletion and lactate buildup in the muscles. The result of these excessive demands is discomfort, a greater subjective sensation of effort, and impaired performance.

Temperatures in the 40 to 60 degree Fahrenheit range are ideal for most runners looking for fast times. Warmer than that and most runners begin to slow. But by how much? Here's a rough formula: You will slow by at least one second per mile for every 1-degree Fahrenheit increase in temperature above 60 degrees Fahrenheit. At 80 degrees, for example, you'll most likely run at least 20 seconds slower per mile—that's an extra 2 minutes slower than an ideal weather 10K. High humidity and direct sunlight add to slowdown.

Dehydration is the key factor here. On a hot day, sweat loss can total 2 to 3 pounds of body weight per hour or more. Runners are forced to slow their pace by about 2 percent for each percent of body weight lost by dehydration. Performance can be affected in as little as 30 minutes of running; the longer you run the more you dehydrate and the more your pace will decline.

Mental performance also declines in the heat. Various studies indicate that sustained attention, error rate, response time, and task accuracy are negatively affected by heat exposure. If mental performance deteriorates, physical performance will be affected. Recognize that reduced performance is unavoidable when faced with heat and dehydration. Lower expectations for race times and adjust starting pace. The key to training and racing in these conditions is to not let it get to you mentally. Think of it as just another challenge that you will overcome, an inspiration. Handle it better than your competition.

HOW YOUR BODY DISSIPATES HEAT

Dependent upon the combination of the severity of the environmental conditions and the intensity of the run, your body may not be able to dissipate heat as fast as it is produced. As a result your internal temperature may rise to over 100 degrees Fahrenheit (98.6 degrees is normal) causing deterioration in health and performance. In an attempt to regain optimal efficiency, the body transfers heat to other areas. Four mechanisms are involved in heat loss: conduction, convection, radiation, and evaporation.

Conduction. This method transfers heat to the environment by direct contact. As blood passes through the muscles, it is heated and transports heat to the skin. It is then conducted by direct contact to clothing or the surrounding air. Ice or cold water on the skin conducts heat away from the skin because heat will move from a higher concentration to an area of lower concentration. Try jumping into a swimming pool after a run on a hot day for quick cooling by conduction. Conversely, this thermal energy could be transferred by conduction the other way if the contact is warmer than the skin temperature, as in a warm bath which would transfer heat to the body.

Convection. This mechanism involves the transfer of heat similar to a conveyor belt. Air is always in constant motion, although we may not always feel it. As the air around us warms due to body heat, it rises and is replaced with cooler air. This allows the body to continue to transfer heat to the cooler environment. Conduction and convection work to move heat away from the body as long as the air temperature is lower than the temperature of your skin. When the air surrounding the body is very hot, the combination of convection and conduction can cause the body to heat up rather than cool off. The more the movement of the air around the body, the greater the heat transfer by convection. Thus the wind (as well as fanned air and the breeze you create while running) works effectively to convey heat away from the body. In cold weather a headwind can convey too much heat to the environment and hypothermia may result. Conduction and convection account for 10 to 20 percent of dissipated body heat.

Radiation. Like a radiator in a cold room, body heat moves to the skin and out to the cooler environment. Heat transfers from the body to any nearby object—such as clothing, walls, or furniture—whose surface temperatures are lower than the skin temperature. At rest, radiation is responsible for the majority of heat loss. At normal room temperature (70 degrees), it accounts for about 60 percent of total heat lost by the body. Radiation works the other way, too, such as when moving into the sun on a cool day to get warmer, or when direct and indirect (reflected off streets and buildings) sunlight produces an overabundance of heat. This is why you should seek the sun in the winter, but avoid it in the summer. Feel the difference in the air when you run on the sunny versus the shady side of the street and you'll better understand the effect of radiation. Direct sunlight and hot, paved streets should be avoided when possible.

Evaporation. Here's the one you've been waiting for—it's time to talk about good ol' sweat, the status symbol of hard-working runners. Evaporation of sweat is the most effective mechanism for heat loss. Perspiration absorbs heat from the skin by conduction. This fluid is converted from liquid to vapor by this heat from the skin and then evaporates into the environment, cooling the body further. Heat is not lost through sweating; it is lost only when the sweat actually evaporates. Headwinds enhance evaporation and humidity hinders it. Twenty percent of heat loss at rest is produced from evaporation, but it is responsible for about 80 percent of heat dissipation during exercise. Approximately 90 percent of water lost during exercise is sweat; the rest is through respiration.

SWEATING AND DEHYDRATION

Here is why you sweat. Heat is produced as a by-product of muscle contractions as calories are burned for energy. While running, your core and blood temperatures increase. When the hypothalamus, the part of the brain that controls body temperature, senses the temperature rise it dilates blood vessels near the skin. The warm blood flows into these capillaries. If the blood temperature becomes warm enough, the sweat glands are activated. So when we run, we sweat. Sweating cools the body—4 ounces of sweat prevents a 1-degree rise in body temperature. Sweat consists mostly of water, but it also includes other nutrients such as sodium, chloride, and potassium. This is why sports drinks contains these nutrients.

Sweating is the most important thermoregulatory response. It's good for you since it cools the body, but it's bad for you—in fact, dangerous—if you lose too much water. When body fluid is lost through sweating and not replaced, you dehydrate. When dehydrated, body cells work inefficiently, sweating decreases, heart rate and body temperature increase, blood volume decreases, and less blood is available to circulate oxygen and glucose through the body. For example, every liter (2.2 pounds) of water lost will result in an increase of approximately eight heartbeats per minute.

Dehydration impairs performance and increases risk of heat illness. Prevention of dehydration is even more important than carbohydrate replacement for the long-distance runner. If you are low on carbs, you just slow down. But you can die from dehydration.

It is critical to hold down body temperature by replacing lost fluids. Studies by Dr. David Costill showed rectal temperatures in runners stayed 2 degrees Fahrenheit cooler when the runners drank fluids during a two-hour run than when they didn't. Chapter 34 details specific guidelines for hydration.

Dehydration can result from a single run, or from training several days in a row without adequate rehydration. After an extended period of training in high heat and humidity it's not unusual to feel fatigued later in the day or even several days later. Because of the chronic effects of dehydration, it's tougher to recover from one run to the next. Your legs will be sorer and your overall energy level lower. Warning: Dehydration can occur even in cold weather if you don't drink enough fluids.

How much you sweat depends upon several factors. The hotter it is and the harder you run, the more you'll sweat. Bigger people perspire more. The fitter the runner, the more and larger the sweat glands resulting in increased sweat production, and the sooner you will sweat during a run. High humidity increases sweating, but interferes with evaporation. Headwinds cool the body, reducing sweat production. Finally, how much you sweat is partly determined by genetics. The average person has two to three million sweat glands spread over most of the body. But some of us have sweat glands as much as five times bigger than other individuals, which helps account for why some of us sweat much more than others.

Thirst is not an early warning sign of dehydration. Runners need to drink more fluids than thirst demands. Any one of us can lose as much as 2 quarts of fluids before getting thirsty. The easiest way to know if you have sufficiently replaced lost fluids is to check the color and frequency of your urine. A good flow of clear or pale yellow urine indicates that the body has a normal fluid balance. Dark or reduced urine indicates, among other things, the need to replace lost fluids. If you urinate frequently over the next few hours after a run then most likely you're getting enough fluid.

Another good monitor is to weigh yourself each morning. If your weight is 2 pounds or more below that of the previous morning, your sudden weight loss is no need to celebrate. It is most likely due to too much water loss. Drink up! Besides monitoring urine and weight, also pay attention to how you feel. If tired several days in a row, especially when training a lot in hot weather, suspect chronic dehydration.

HUMIDITY

This is a critical factor in hot weather running too. Under very humid conditions, little sweat can evaporate since the air is saturated, and it becomes difficult for the body to lose heat. Sweat just drips off the skin, providing less cooling.

The National Weather Service uses a Heat Index to measure discomfort and the potential danger of heat-related illnesses. The Heat Index (Figure 36.1) is expressed as an "apparent temperature." It is basically the summertime equivalent of winter's windchill factor. It expresses what a combination of temperature and relative humidity feels like. How bad can it get? It's not unusual in the United States for summer weather to reach 90 degrees Fahrenheit with 70 percent humidity. That combination creates an oppressive 106 degrees Fahrenheit in "apparent temperature." The basic premise of the Heat Index is simple: The higher the temperature and the higher the humidity, the higher the Heat Index. An actual air temperature of 80 degrees Fahrenheit combined with

85 percent humidity is more dangerous than an air temperature of 90 degrees Fahrenheit in a dry climate.

When the Heat Index goes above 90 degrees Fahrenheit, the possibility of heat-related illnesses increases sharply. The National Weather Service issues a heat advisory when the Heat Index exceeds 105 degrees Fahrenheit. At that point you should exercise outdoors only with extreme caution. Better yet, head inside for an air-conditioned workout. Okay, I'll admit that I run at this level of discomfort, but I keep the pace under control and will not race under these conditions. When the Heat Index exceeds 130 degrees, do not exercise outdoors! That includes me.

Here's a simple formula for deciding whether it is safe to run: Add the temperature in degrees Fahrenheit and the percentage of

FIGURE 36.1: HEAT INDEX

	Air Temperature (F°)										
	70°	**75°**	**80°**	**85°**	**90°**	**95°**	**100°**	**105°**	**110°**	**115°**	**120°**
RELATIVE HUMIDITY	APPARENT TEMPERATURE (WHAT IT FEELS LIKE)										
0%	64°	69°	73°	78°	83°	87°	91°	95°	99°	103°	107°
10%	65°	70°	75°	80°	85°	90°	95°	100°	105°	111°	116°
20%	66°	72°	77°	82°	87°	93°	99°	105°	112°	120°	130°
30%	67°	73°	78°	84°	90°	96°	104°	113°	123°	135°	148°
40%	68°	74°	79°	86°	93°	101°	110°	123°	137°	151°	
50%	69°	75°	81°	88°	96°	107°	120°	135°	150°		
60%	70°	76°	82°	90°	100°	114°	132°	149°			
70%	70°	77°	85°	93°	106°	124°	144°				
80%	71°	78°	86°	97°	113°	136°					
90%	71°	79°	88°	102°	122°						
100%	72°	80°	91°	108°							

APPARENT TEMPERATURE	HEAT STRESS RISK WITH PHYSICAL ACTIVITY AND/OR PROLONGED EXPOSURE
90°–105°	Heat cramps or heat exhaustion *possible*
105°–130°	Heat cramps or heat exhaustion *likely* Heatstroke *possible*
130°+	Heatstroke *highly likely*

humidity. If the sum is over 150, don't run or run with caution. For example, if the temperature is 80 degrees Fahrenheit and the humidity is 80 percent, the sum total is 160, meaning that the conditions are not good for running. I call these the dreaded "80-80 days."

Get in the habit of checking the air temperature and the relative humidity prior to runs and races. Check out the local weather report. I have an outdoor thermometer and humidity gauge in my window which I examine prior to picking out what clothes I will wear, how far I will run, and at what pace.

HEAT-RELATED ILLNESSES

High temperatures, humidity, and direct sunlight in combination with heat generated internally by the exercising body can lead to heat stress. Your body may produce more heat than it can give up into the environment. If the cooling system can't keep up, your internal temperature rises. A significant increase in body temperature may cause your body to malfunction. As you sweat, you lose fluids and this in itself may interfere with your body's ability to regulate heat. Too much heat buildup combined with too much fluid loss is a dangerous combination.

The earliest warning signs of heat stress are fatigue, anxiety, irritability, dizziness, or visual impairment. If you recognize and respond to these symptoms you can head off serious problems. Listen to your body's warning signals and stop running or slow to a walk and drink lots of fluids. If you stop early enough, you may be able to resume easy running after you have cooled off and rehydrated.

Heat-related illnesses are listed here in progressive order of seriousness:

Heat cramps. Severe cramping is most likely caused by mineral losses and dehydration from heavy sweating. For most runners, the calf muscles are the most vulnerable. Although not as serious as the following illnesses, heat cramps can be very painful. Drink lots of fluids immediately; include replacement liquids such as sports drinks since loss of electrolytes may have caused the cramping. Try massaging the cramped muscles and cool the body with cold water and wet towels. Move out of the sun to a cooler location.

Heat exhaustion. This is the extreme fatigue that may develop during exercise in hot weather and is caused by dehydration and the body's inability to cool itself. This is a potentially dangerous condition that may lead to heatstroke. Symptoms may include headache, goose bumps, an uncoordinated gait, breathlessness, dizziness, nausea, a weak but rapid pulse, weakness in the legs, cramping, profuse sweating, dilated pupils, and/or vomiting. You may feel a flushed, hot sensation around your head and shoulders. The skin may become pale, moist, and cold. Body temperature will be elevated. If you experience any of these symptoms, stop running immediately. Seek help and medical attention. Find a cool, shaded spot and lie down with your feet elevated. Loosen or remove excess clothing. Drink fluids as soon as possible and continue doing so until you feel better.

Heatstroke. This is an extreme emergency situation and can be fatal. It involves the sudden failure of the thermoregulatory system. Symptoms are similar to heat exhaustion but progress to disturbances of the central nervous system (disorientation, unsteady gait, inability to think clearly, bizarre or combative behavior, loss of consciousness, seizures). Heatstroke may be accompanied by profuse sweating, but usually involves cessation of sweating and skin that is hot and dry. It usually is accompanied by rapid pulse and respiration as body temperature rises above 104 degrees Fahrenheit. The runner may develop convulsions, suddenly collapse, or go into a coma.

Too often determined competitors ignore the warning signs of heat exhaustion and run themselves into heatstroke. By then they may not be able to understand the warning signs; others will have to help. You may have to physically pull this runner off the road since he may not understand the seriousness of his condition. Get the runner to a cool, shaded area and find a way to lower body temperature immediately: Rub the body with ice, immerse the person in cold water, or wrap the body in wet sheets and fan the victim. Seek medical help immediately—even if the runner claims to feel better. The runner will need fluid replacement, probably intravenously.

SUN AND HEALTH

It used to be a well-tanned body was a sign of fitness. Like many runners, I ran shirtless all summer to get a good tan. No more!

Now we know that too much exposure to the sun increases the risk of skin cancer and eye damage. Indeed, I know of several runners that have been affected. Why the problem? The ozone layer in the atmosphere that screens the sun is deteriorating. Damage is a year-round threat—not just in the summer. Sunburn is considered a first-degree burn. All sunburn and suntans are visible evidence of injury to the skin which may lead to premature aging of the skin and accelerate the development of skin cancers. The American Cancer Society recommends examining the skin for new moles or pigment spots. Apply the "ABCD rule" to recognize melanoma, the prevalent type of skin cancer:

A) Asymmetry: The two sides don't match.
B) Border irregularity: The borders aren't smooth, but are indented.
C) Color: It contains areas of different colors—black, brown, tan, red, blue.
D) Diameter: The spot is larger than 6 millimeters wide—the size of a pencil eraser.

To minimize sun exposure, avoid running in open areas between 10 A.M. and 3 P.M., the peak period for ultraviolet B radiation from sunlight. Sand, concrete, water, and snow reflect the sun's rays and increase exposure to harmful UV rays. The skin is more vulnerable at high altitude. Ultraviolet radiation penetrates cloud cover. Avoid tanning salons and sunlamps. Apply sunscreen liberally on all exposed areas. Choose a waterproof or water-repellent sunscreen with a sun protection factor of at least 15. Test the product in training runs before using it in races. I once applied a sun block on my face prior to a race and then I sweat so much it ran into my eyes, temporarily blinding me until I washed it out at a fluid station. Some studies indicate that oil-based sunscreen may contribute to overheating on hot, dry days by blocking the evaporation of your sweat. Use water-based sunscreen.

The sun can damage your eyes, too. Extended UV exposure triples risk of cataracts and increases the chance of developing keratitis, inflammation of the cornea. The sun's heat can also dry out the eyes and cause eye fatigue and other ailments. Exposure to sunlight causes eyestrain from constant squinting. This tension can then spread to other parts of the body.

Most quality sports sunglasses come in a wraparound style to ensure maximum UV protection. You can get them with interchangeable lens tinting that adjusts to variations in sunlight. Each tint provides a different balance of light transmission, color, absorption, and light reflection. Sunglasses make runs more comfortable by reducing eyestrain and shielding eyes from wind, sun, and airborne pollen. Runners sure look faster wearing them! I resisted these sleek-looking gadgets until Shelly-lynn bought a pair for me. They really do help me stay relaxed when running in the sun. Although most valuable in warm weather, they can be of help, too, on sunny winter days. Here's the big bonus: They protect eyes from bugs (now if I can just remember to keep my mouth shut, too!).

Don't run shirtless. If running in direct sunlight, wear a loose-fitting shirt that covers at least your shoulders, along with a hat or visor and sunglasses. Although it may be warmer, dark-colored clothing absorbs UV light, protecting your skin better than light-colored clothing, which lets light through. If you go with this choice out of concern for skin protection, be sure it's made of a wicking fabric. In an effort to publicize the danger of sun exposure, the National Weather Service and Environmental Protection Agency developed a daily UV Index for many major U.S. cities. The listings forecast danger by skin type for the next day. Use the combination of Heat Index and UV Index to help guide your dress and training in hot weather.

TIPS FOR RUNNING IN HOT WEATHER

Make adjustments in your training and racing to maximize safety and performance on hot, humid days.

Drink, drink and drink. Drink before, during, and after runs to replace lost fluids. If you don't, first you will be uncomfortable, then performance falters, and finally you could get ill. The longer the run and the hotter the weather, the more important it is to drink lots of fluids.

Pour fluids on you. This may help conduct heat away from you. Studies at the University of Wisconsin, however, showed that skin wetting doesn't increase the rate of body cooling or help prevent dehydration. Nevertheless, the study concludes, "If wetting your skin increases your personal comfort while running, by all means do it." It sure helps me psychologically and I feel cooler. But if you have to make a choice whether to pour fluids in you or on you, drink up. A pint of water in the stomach is worth a gallon on the outside. Many races provide hose sprays or mists to cool runners. Be careful, however, when training or racing to minimize the amount of water you get on your feet. Socks and shoes can become soaked and blisters are more likely to occur.

Some races offer wet sponges. By rubbing them vigorously over the body you remove oil and accumulated salt from sweat, which results in more efficient sweating.

Dress cool. Choose a lightweight, breathable fabric that wicks away sweat. Don't overdress! Even on mild days you can overheat if you do. On hot days minimize clothing to maximize skin surface from which perspiration can evaporate. Only the basic clothing is needed: singlet, shorts, and socks.

A loose, light-colored (to reflect the sun's rays) high-tech singlet is preferable to a cotton T-shirt unless you don't sweat much. Try this test. Go for a short run on a hot day in a cotton T-shirt. Then, go for a run wearing a moisture-transferring singlet. You may be amazed. The T-shirt will be heavy with moisture, but the high-tech top won't. In hot weather the key is coolness and comfort. Your tops should have excellent ventilation, dry quickly, and feel smooth against your skin. Some tops may, when wet, cause chafing of the nipples. Prevent this by applying lubricant to the area before you run. Or, select shirts or singlets that have a nonabrasive panel across the chest. Watch out: Lettering across the chest may be a source of friction. Sports bras made of a cool, wicking fabric covered by a singlet is the choice for many women runners. Sports bras have become so fashionable and popular that they are often worn as outerwear on hot days.

Shorts should also be soft, light, loose-fitting and quick-drying. The liners should let your body "breathe" and wick moisture away. The slits on the side should allow for a full stride. There is a difference between women's and men's shorts: They are made to fit their specific body builds. Most men prefer wearing shorts with built-in briefs. Others like a separate sports brief made from a soft, seamless, absorbent stretch fabric which is cool and moisture-wicking.

Socks are important even in warm weather. They provide shock absorption, increase comfort, and keep shoes from absorbing too much sweat. They should wick moisture away from the feet. Studies show that wet feet are more likely to blister. The worst fabric is cotton because it absorbs moisture; acrylic synthetics like polypropylene and Coolmax are best since they are good moisture wickers.

Adjust the training paces and speed workouts. On hot days start slowly and run a steady, slower pace in training. You may need to slow a minute per mile or more and be prepared to make further reductions along the way. Check your pulse frequently to see how your heart is responding to the heat. Be aware of the warning signs for heat illnesses and adjust pace accordingly. But don't run slow all summer or you'll lose leg speed. Keep up your normal intensity at least a few times a week, but cut the distance of runs.

Adjust speed training, too. After each interval, take longer recovery breaks than usual while walking instead of jogging (in the shade if possible), and drink plenty of fluids. Do fewer intervals or slow them. Don't compare times to those on cool days. In fact, it may be best to just run by perceived exertion and not look at a watch. If you need to get in some high-quality speed sessions during hot periods, try to do them early in the morning or later in the evening, or do them indoors on a track or treadmill.

Adjust training and racing distances. In hot weather shorten your distance. Since hot weather increases the rate at which glycogen is burned, a 6-miler in the heat can be the equivalent of a 10-miler on a cool day. Postpone a long run for a cooler day, or shift it to a cooler time of day. Emphasize shorter races of 2 miles to 10K during hot weather months.

Adjust race goals and strategy. If you properly adjust your starting pace and goal time, think "cool" while keeping relaxed, and pour plenty of fluids into and on yourself, you will outsmart and thus defeat competitors who stubbornly kept to their ideal weather race strategy. Starting too fast on a hot day may result in rapid increases in both body temperature and lactate, and thus a poor performance. Be prepared to run slower times. Adjust your starting and goal time by as much as a minute or more per mile. Be ready to make further pacing adjustments along the way. If you feel good after settling into a reasonably comfortable pace, gradually pick it up and pass all those runners that started too fast or didn't heat train as well as you did.

Hot weather racing strategy is risky. Sometimes you may get away with just minimizing the conditions in your mind and going out strong (but not too fast). If you are too conservative you may finish in good health, but realize that others put in a better effort and thus you underachieved. What to do? Always be very conservative if you are new to racing, when coming back after a layoff, or when racing the first time for the season in hot weather. Beyond that, let experience be your guide. If you do challenge the heat and attempt to race as fast as possible, be prepared to minimize the damage if your gamble isn't paying off. It is far safer and wiser to slow to a walk and, if necessary, drop out and seek medical help. Running beyond reasonable limits on a hot day may limit your ability to train and race well for weeks. Don't look at it as being a dropout, but rather as making an investment in your health and future performances.

Long races in hot weather are races of attrition. Runners cross the finish line in order of how well they adjust to the heat as much as by talent. It is essential that all levels of runners be realistic and cut back their starting pace. To deny the unpleasant truth that you will not run the race of your dreams is to invite a long, miserable struggle to the finish line, if you finish at all. Run for place, or just to finish, rather than time.

Days when the temperature isn't exceptionally high often cause the most trouble. When the temperature is in the 60s or 70s runners can be lured into thinking it isn't necessary to back off. An example was a New York City Marathon run in 68-degree heat and high humidity. It didn't seem too bad so lots of runners "went for it." The result: two fatal heart attacks, dozens of cases of heatstroke, and hundreds of cases of lesser heat illnesses.

When you've finished a hot weather race, compare your time with your peers. You can usually figure out what you *would have run* if the weather were cooler by seeing how you rank among those who usually run about the same times as you. At least it is a fun exercise to figure out what might have been! Some runners somehow manage to run just as fast in the heat as they do on a cool day. Unfair, but true.

Be in shape. The better your training and less your weight, the less the heat will affect you. But don't get too cocky: Even Elites have ended up in the hospital after racing hard on hot days.

Stock up on carbs. According to Dr. Costill, "Running at a given speed in the heat will require a greater use of muscle glycogen than the same run in cooler air. As a result, repeated days of training in the heat may cause a rapid depletion of muscle glycogen and the symptoms of chronic fatigue." A combination of eating plenty of carbs while drinking lots of fluids and heat training will greatly reduce (by as much as 50 to 60 percent) the rate of glycogen depletion on a hot day.

Avoid the heat. Run during the cool of the early morning or late evening. Besides not being as hot at these times, generally air pollution is less, too.

Run on cool surfaces. Hot pavement irritates the feet and reflects heat up. Try running on the dirt shoulders, or on trails or grass.

Run in the shade. If possible, select tree-lined paths to protect you from direct sunlight. Wherever you run, look for shaded areas even if it means crossing to the other side of the road or altering your course. When racing, look for shady spots.

Run into the wind. Look for breezy areas—like along the waterfront—to help keep you cool. The wind can help or hinder you when racing. In hot weather a headwind is cooler and a tail wind is warmer—that is, a headwind (blowing toward you) convects body heat away from you, but a tail wind (blowing against your back) wraps body heat around you like a blanket and therefore reduces convective heat loss. In training do the opposite of what you would do on a cold day for out-and-back courses: Begin runs with the wind at your back so you'll finish with a cooling headwind (rather than warming tail wind).

When racing, don't push the pace too hard if you have a tail wind or you may pay for it later by overheating. Pray for a slight headwind in hot races. Although it may slow your pace a bit, what you gain in "air-conditioning" is worth it. Don't draft unless the winds are very strong. Avoid the wind shadows of runners in front of you by either passing them or moving to the side to catch more of the helpful headwinds.

Acclimate. If you plan to race in hot weather, train in it. Otherwise try to avoid it. Ronald Maughan, Ph.D., states in *Sports Science Exchange*: "Regular exposure to hot, humid conditions causes physiologic adaptations that reduce the adverse affects on performance and lessen the risk of heat injury. Such responses include an increase in blood volume and an enhanced ability to sweat. The increase in blood volume helps assure that the body can meet the demand for blood supply by both muscles and skin. Acclimatization also results in a faster onset of sweating, a greater distribution of sweat over the body, and an increase in the sweat rate. In addition, the sodium content of sweat tends to be reduced." But don't think you'll need to drink less fluids once heat-trained. In fact, you'll need more since you'll lose more fluid with improved sweating.

Some adaptation occurs within the first few days, so even a little heat training helps. Most acclimatization takes at least ten days. Research by Larry Armstrong, Ph.D., indicates that 90 to 95 percent of adaptation takes place within two weeks of approximately 60 minutes per day of moderate-intensity training in hot conditions. It isn't necessary to train every day in the heat, but no more than two to three days should be skipped between hot weather training runs. To help acclimate, a few times a week I run at the hottest time of day, but at an easy pace.

If the weather suddenly turns hot, you have traveled to a hot climate, or you are purposely training in the heat, take it easy. Slow the pace; shorten runs. Most heat-related illnesses occur during the first few runs in the heat. During your first hot-weather workout, cut the intensity by a minute or more per mile. Start with runs of 30 minutes or less, gradually increasing to 60 to 90 minutes over a period of a few days. Once you can run fairly comfortably for this time period, work on picking up the intensity once or twice a week, starting with tempo runs. Do some interval training when it is hot to callous you for racing conditions.

If you plan to race in the heat, but must train in cool weather, you have three options: get into the best shape you can, and pray for clouds and rain; move into the climate zone of the race for one to two weeks to allow yourself to acclimatize; or, artificially simulate heat conditions. You can do the latter by heat training with extra clothing for a few days a week, or run indoors on a treadmill (with the room temperature set near what you expect to race in and a humidifier blasting away). To get ready for what is often a hot Boston Marathon in April coming off the winter in the Northeast, many of us veterans follow this rule: "The sweats don't come off until after Boston." We'll be out on the roads in our winter gear even on mild spring days when others are in shorts and singlets. Be fit before you try this and drink plenty of fluids.

Prepare mentally. Racing well in warm weather requires a strong mental attitude. If you think that the heat will beat you, it will. Work on staying relaxed and not getting mentally stressed by the heat. After all, everyone in the race has to face the same conditions. During hot weather races I think about how strong and fit I am and visualize that I am running slightly under control. But no matter how well you heat-train for races, remember you still can't run as fast on a hot day as on a cool day. Your best bet is to try to handle the heat better than your competitors and to improve your times for the distance in similar weather conditions. Run a few lead-up races in hot weather before a peak hot weather race to toughen you physically and mentally.

Take a break. Some runners insist they can't cope with the heat. They just stop running until it cools off. I agree; some days it's too miserable outside to really enjoy running. It's okay to take a break and skip a day or two. But don't quit for longer or it will be tough to regain lost fitness. A better choice if you prefer not to run in the heat is to exercise indoors on a bike, or go for a swim.

Run indoors. I usually head out for my favorite courses no matter how hot it gets. But after the second or third day of extremely muggy conditions I'll choose to run on my treadmill in front of the air conditioner with my water bottle right next to me. What a treat! You get no air resistance indoors to cool you, so use a fan.

Break it up. It becomes difficult reaching mileage goals when faced with a hot spell. A good way to cope is to break up some of your workouts into "two-a-days." For example: Instead of struggling for an hour in the heat, run for a half hour in the morning and another half hour in the evening. Two short runs are better than risking your health for a longer time. No matter how hot it is, you won't get too uncomfortable for the first 30 to 45 minutes. Another option is to go out for a short run, then finish the workout indoors, whether running on a treadmill or exercising on a bike.

Sleep cool. Some runners claim that avoiding air-conditioning helps them toughen up for racing in the heat. But getting quality sleep is difficult when you're uncomfortable. You're better off sleeping in a cool bedroom if that enhances sleep and thus recovery from hard training. Heat adaptation will not be affected.

Keep cool before and after racing. Keep out of the sun before and after races.

Warm up and cool down. Prepare the body for a training run even in hot weather. After a few minutes of limbering exercises, walk and then jog slowly to adjust to the heat. Then bring the pace up to a comfortable level that is adjusted for the weather. Minimize running before a hot weather race, especially a long one. Too long a warm-up will contribute to a buildup of body heat and dehydration. Studies show that a brisk warm-up may increase the body temperature by 1 to 2 degrees Fahrenheit which could increase the risk of overheating during the race. If possible, warm up in the shade. Keep the prerace run short and slow and then do a few quick pickups just prior to the start. Ease into your racing pace since the warm-up run was minimized.

After running in the heat, body temperature will remain high. Blood vessels are dilated in your skin, and arm and leg muscles. Stopping suddenly may stress your heart as it continues to pump blood through those dilated vessels. Walk slowly for 5 to 10 minutes as part of your cool-down to bring down both body temperature and heart rate. If you do a cool-down run after a hot weather race, be sure to drink plenty of fluids before starting, as well as during and after the run. Run in the shade if possible. You have just stressed your thermoregulatory system to the max, so don't go overboard on the cool-down run. Heat illnesses can hit you after a race, not just during one.

Use common sense. Don't train or race too hard in very hot or humid weather.

RAIN

I get calls all the time: "We don't have class in the rain, do we?" Only lightning stops us from going out. After all, what do you do when you return from a run? Get wet in the shower. Indeed, the hardest part about running in the rain is getting out the door. Running in a refreshing rain on a hot day is fun! A cold rain, however, is something else: I'll admit I sometimes wimp out and hop on my treadmill.

If dressed properly, rain usually has little effect once you are moving. Don't wear cotton (shirts, pants, or socks): It gets heavy, droops, and causes bunching and blistering. Choose wicking fabrics that don't hoard raindrops. Keep the legs warm if its not real warm out. Tights usually do the trick. Heavy rain may require a water-repellent jacket and pants. Save the waterproof outfits for cold, wet weather since you'll get quite warm in them. Wear reflective or bright clothing so motorists and other runners see you coming. A cap with a beak helps keep rain off your face. Alternate shoes in wet weather. Go out in an old pair of shoes if you don't want your good ones soaked, but make sure they have a fair amount of cushioning left in them.

When running in wet weather, beware of slippery surfaces. If you tense with fear of slipping, you cause muscle tightness. Stay relaxed and under control. Shorten stride slightly and slow the pace. If possible, don't share the road with vehicles. Drivers have less control on wet roads. Avoid the impulse to rush across streets to keep moving in the rain. Look both ways first.

No, they don't cancel races when it rains either, although lots of preregistered runners don't show up. That's okay. That'll just move you up that many more places! You may actually run faster in a light rain on a warm day since it'll keep you cool. But cold rains or heavy downpours will sabotage performance by weighing you down and tightening muscles. In these conditions, look to be mentally tougher than the competition. Run for place, not time. Two common mistakes made at rainy day races: wearing too much clothing and not warming up. If you're going for a fast time, skip the jacket and other extra clothing unless it's very cold. They'll restrict movement and build up heat once you're racing. Yes, you'll be uncomfortable at the start, but it's better than being uncomfortable a few miles down the road. If you'll be out in the rain for a while before the start, try wearing plastic bags over your shoes and a plastic bag over your body to keep dry. A thorough warm-up is still important. On wet days, I delay my warm-up run until 20 minutes or so before the start and keep running right up until the race.

LIGHTNING

Lightning is serious. My best friend and his eight-year-old son were hit by lightning while exercising. The boy was killed. Watch for lightning. "Sheet" lightning at a distance and increasingly loud thunder should make you very alert. If you hear thunder, lightning may be close enough to zap you. Use the "Flash-to-Bang" formula: Count the seconds between the flash and thunder and divide by 5 to determine how many miles away the lightning hit. But lightning can strike without thunder. Be aware of darkening clouds or sudden wind shifts.

Do not continue running in open areas when lightning threatens. A precaution is to run near tall buildings—like large apartment buildings—to minimize exposure. That's what we do with our classes if lightning is in the area. But we don't go out, or return immediately, if it's getting close. Don't get overconfident: Lightning goes to the best conductor, not the tallest object. Unfortunately, sometimes the best conductor is a runner.

Here are some tips from the Penn State Sports Medicine Newsletter. Nearby thunder or bolts of lightning should send you into a large, grounded building or vehicle. If one isn't available, look for a low spot like a ditch. Avoid large bodies of water, metal, and telephone poles. Don't seek shelter from rain under isolated trees (Large groups of trees minimize danger). If you're running in the open and lightning is close, or especially if you feel your hair standing on end, do not lie down or huddle with your running friends. That'll create too big a target. Create the smallest possible target and minimize ground contact. Drop into a tuck position by squatting low to the ground, hands on knees, head tucked between them, balls of feet on ground. Keep at least 15 feet between you and the next person.

Don't stubbornly continue running when lightning is in the immediate area. It isn't worth the risk. Wait out the storm and then continue your run. Give the storm at least 30 minutes to be sure it is out of the area. My friend didn't wait long enough; the lightning wasn't through doing its damage.

CHAPTER 37

Cold Weather Running

For every runner who loves hot weather, there is another who can't wait to see the temperature drop and the snow fly. Winter offers variety to your running program, and you get the added bonus of being in much better shape when spring arrives again. Cold weather, however, can be a burden to the runner. The cold can have a significant effect on your body's responses to exercise with increased health risk. Heavy snow and ice make training paths difficult to negotiate. You're often forced to share narrowed roads with cars that spray slush all over you. The footing is poor; you slip and slide and perhaps hurt yourself.

But, the biggest obstacle is just getting out the door. The dreariness of cold weather running is a significant psychological hurdle. It's dark both before and after work. The wind-whipped cold air burns your face and lungs. It is just too easy to say, "I'm not going out for a run today. It's too cold and dark and depressing." The excuses come easily and one lost run turns to several. Indeed, most runners cut back on their training when the weather turns cold and bleak.

But the cold truth is that fitness is a year-round endeavor. Maintaining a positive attitude is the key to success. Think of cold weather as a challenge to overcome rather than as an impossible obstacle. I look at the winter as a way to get an edge on my competitors: I'll force myself to keep training while many of them back off when the going gets tough. The weather often isn't as bad as it looks; you can run fairly comfortably in near-blizzard conditions. You don't have to be all that tough to run in the cold, you just have to be prepared and use common sense.

COLD AND PERFORMANCE

The effect of cold on performance depends upon the severity of the conditions. Running in cool or moderately cold weather (30 to 50 degrees Fahrenheit) yields fast race times since slowdown due to heat buildup and dehydration are greatly minimized. Less blood is needed to transport heat to the skin for cooling, and more blood is available to send needed energy to the working muscles in the legs. Record performances are usually achieved in cool conditions. But excessive cold is another story. Exposure to extreme cold reduces both the runner's core body temperature and maximal aerobic power, impairing performance. Further, the extra clothing you are forced to wear restricts movement. In extremely cold weather don't expect to run as fast as under ideal conditions. For the most part, your goal in cold weather is not fast personal records, but rather racing well enough to maintain some speed and strength so that you can run faster when the flowers bloom in the spring.

COLD-RELATED ILLNESSES

Even if you follow all the cold weather advice in this book, you may still run into trouble. Cold temperatures and strong winds can lead to a variety of problems:

Hypothermia. Cold weather pulls heat away from the runner's body. Cooling the body some is helpful, even in the winter. But pulling more heat away than running generates isn't good. Hypothermia is a condition of lower than normal body temperature. There are several ways cold weather can bring this about: In extreme cold, heat is pulled away from the body to an area of lesser concentration, similar to the action of a syphon; strong winds blow heat away from the body; wet skin and clothing—whether damp due to sweat, rain or snow—wick heat out of the body. Further, running slow creates less body heat than running fast under the same weather conditions. If you dress lightly to run a fast pace in your training run or race and fatigue so much that you end up at a slow pace or are forced to walk, the lower heat production and lack of insulation will leave you cold and primed for hypothermia.

When wet, you may get cold quite quickly. As body temperature falls, the body responds with shivering, which is the muscles' attempt to produce heat. If ignored, the runner could next become incoherent, lapse into a coma, and even die. Dressing properly to keep warm, dry, and to repel the wind is critical to preventing hypothermia. If, on a very cold day, you get wet and cold, keep moving and get inside quickly. Take off wet clothing immediately (a good practice even if you are only slightly wet from sweating). Take a hot bath or shower, and drink warm fluids. If a runner develops hypothermia, remove all wet clothing and warm his or her body with blankets. Get medical help quickly—but do not stop warming efforts.

Respiratory problems. First, freezing of the lungs is a myth. Even in sub-zero conditions, the air we inhale is sufficiently warmed by the body before it reaches the lungs. Runners with sensitive bronchials or asthma find that cold air irritates these conditions. Why? Inhaled air attracts moisture and heat from the body; significant amounts are then lost from the respiratory tract as we exhale. Running increases the volume of air inhaled and exhaled, and thus increases the amount of moisture and heat lost. Potential results: dehydration, dryness of the mouth, a burning sensation in the throat, irritation of respiratory passages, coughing, and an asthma attack.

How can runners with respiratory problems defend themselves? A protective cover helps most runners. Try a fleece face mask, polypro balaclava, wool scarf, or, my choice, a special air-warming mask (similar to air filter or surgical masks). Mouth and nose covers trap some of the exhaled moisture and warmth. It, in turn, warms and moistens the next inhalation. However, these covers sometimes capture too much heat and moisture and can become uncomfortable. I tend to overheat so I trim my mask to just cover my mouth. I slide it off my face when I get too warm, putting it back on when starting to feel symptoms of respiratory distress. I even use the mask when racing. I may look a little weird ("Who is that masked man?") but who cares if it helps stave off an asthma attack and improve performance.

I use a cromolyn sodium inhaler about 20 minutes prior to running in the cold since it works as an antihistamine to help prevent bronchial stress. Bring a bronchial dilator spray along on runs to give immediate relief if you develop a problem. Start training runs or races slowly and gradually pick up the pace once your body has adjusted to the shock of inhaling cold air. Indoor humidity is a factor to good health, too. Dry air may contribute to respiratory illnesses. The ideal indoor humidity is 40 to 50 percent. In the winter months when indoor heat drys out the air, I place a humidifier on each floor of our house as well as a hygrometer to monitor the dryness. Drinking plenty of fluids helps minimize respiratory illnesses when you are exposed to dry air.

Frostbite. This is a real danger to the fingers, toes, ears, face, and other exposed parts (and in a few embarrassing cases, your unexposed privates). Frostbitten skin is usually cold, pale, and firm-to-hard to the touch. The first step in treatment is to warm up rapidly without excessive heat. Use warm water. Do not massage or, in the case of the toes, walk on the injured area. Do not rub with snow (an old myth). Drink warm fluids. Immediately seek medical attention.

To prevent frostbite, keep exposed skin to a minimum. Cover your hands, ears and face. Keep dry. Keep moving. Avoid running into strong headwinds, especially if you've been perspiring or are otherwise wet. A mild form of cold injury called frostnip precedes frostbite. Be aware of warning signals: numbness, tingling, burning sensations, or whitening of the skin. Do not ignore these early signs.

THE WINDCHILL FACTOR

The air temperature plus the effect of any wind determines the "windchill factor." Figure 37.1 was designed by weather scientists to help people understand the dangers of frostbite. When running in cold weather, know what the windchill is as you start out the door. Another factor is your running pace. Running into the wind, the wind speed against your skin is increased by your velocity. If at rest the wind speed is 10 miles per hour and the temperature is 30 degrees Fahrenheit, the windchill factor would be 16 degrees Fahrenheit. But if you run into that wind at 10 miles per hour

(6 minutes per mile), then the wind speed would increase to 20 miles per hour, reducing the windchill factor to 4 degrees Fahrenheit. (At last! An advantage over those speedy Elites). Conversely, running with a tail wind of 10 miles per hour at a pace of 10 miles per hour would cancel out the wind speed felt against your skin. It would "feel" like a calm day with no wind at 30 degrees Fahrenheit.

Here's a rough guide to windchill:

- 10-mile-per-hour winds equal a temperature drop of about 15 degrees Fahrenheit.
- 15-mile-per-hour winds equal a temperature drop of about 20 degrees Fahrenheit.
- 20-miles-per-hour winds equal a temperature drop of about 25 degrees Fahrenheit.
- 25-miles-per-hour winds equal a temperature drop of about 30 degrees Fahrenheit.

FIGURE 37.1: WINDCHILL FACTOR

	Actual Thermometer Reading (F°)											
	50	**40**	**30**	**20**	**10**	**0**	**-10**	**-20**	**-30**	**-40**	**-50**	**-60**
EST. WIND SPEED (MPH)	EQUIVALENT TEMPERATURE (°F)											
CALM	50	40	30	20	10	0	-10	-20	-30	-40	-50	-60
5	48	37	27	16	6	-5	-15	-26	-36	-47	-57	-68
10	40	28	16	4	-9	-24	-33	-46	-58	-70	-83	-95
15	36	22	9	-5	-18	-32	-45	-58	-72	-85	-99	-112
20	32	18	4	-10	-25	-39	-53	-67	-82	-96	-110	-124
25	30	16	0	-15	-29	-44	-59	-74	-88	-104	-118	-133
30	28	13	-2	-18	-33	-48	-63	-79	-94	-109	-125	-140
(Wind speeds greater than 40 mph have little additional effect.)	LITTLE DANGER (for properly clothed person). Maximum danger of false sense of security.			INCREASING DANGER Danger from freezing of exposed flesh.			GREAT DANGER					

DRESSING FOR COLD WEATHER RUNNING

Fortunately, modern technology has replaced the layers of bulky, heavy, and uncomfortable clothing with sleek-looking, lightweight apparel offering freedom of movement. Nowadays runners can feel drier, warmer, and faster. But no matter how high-tech your outfits, you still need to use them correctly. The key is wearing the right clothes in the right combination. Here are some basic rules:

- Dress to stay warm, but not too warm. Overdressing may lead to overheating.
- Dress to keep dry. If your clothing lets excess heat escape as you run, it will minimize sweating and help you stay drier and warmer. Studies show that your body will lose heat thirty-two times faster in wet than in dry conditions.
- Dress to protect the extremities—toes, fingers, ears, and face—from discomfort and frostbite.
- Dress in layers to trap body heat.

Layering. This is the secret to maximum comfort: an inner wicking layer, an insulating middle layer, and an outer windbreaking layer. You may not always need three layers and some of the functions may be combined. Sometimes conditions will be so fierce you may need four layers. Adjust for comfort by unzipping or removing the outer layer, or more. If you cool off, zip it up or put the layer back on. Not only do layers of clothes effectively trap and allow you to regulate body heat, but they allow perspiration to move readily through the thin layers of clothing. Moisture is wicked away from the skin by the inner layer and transferred to the second or third layer for release into the environment. If one piece of clothing in the system fails in this function, you will not keep as dry. Wet clothing can't keep you warm.

The inner (wicking) layer. This is the one against your skin. It should consist of fabrics such as polypropylene or Coolmax, which are "breathable" and allow water vapor to pass through, wicking perspiration away from the skin and helping keep you dry. This layer should fit fairly snug to your skin. Don't wear an absorbent fabric like cotton next to your skin: It will get wet and soggy, and make you feel uncomfortable and cold. In mild weather, a lightweight wicking shirt may be the only layer needed. A heavier wicking shirt may be enough to wear in cool weather. The next step as it gets colder is to cover the wicking layer with a windbreaking layer. Another option is to wear a combination shirt, which has the qualities of a wicking and an insulating layer.

The middle (insulating) layer. This is generally used only on really cold days, although it is sometimes used instead of the outer windbreaking layer. It adds air space to trap heat—just like the insulation in your attic. It usually is heavier than the inner layer, but it also needs to be breathable. The middle layer has two functions: holding in body heat to keep you warm, and passing moisture to the outer layer to keep you dry. This layer should fit loosely and be easy to open or remove so you can make adjustments if you get too warm. Go with fabrics that keep you warm and dry, such as fleece, wool, Thermax, and Polartec.

What about the role of cotton as a middle layer? According to Andy Kimerling of the Westchester Road Runner, "Many runners wear a cotton T-shirt or sweatshirt as a middle layer because it will act like a diaper and soak up the moisture coming through an inner polypro shirt." Take your choice: a fancy, high-tech middle layer to keep you dry, or a diaper.

The outer (windbreaking) layer. This one protects from the wind, rain and snow. It should be "breathable" to allow moisture and excessive body heat to escape, at least repel water, fit loosely, and be zippered for easy adjustments. Waterproof jackets (which don't breathe as well) tend to be too warm if you are running hard or long. Gore-Tex is the industry standard in waterproof outerwear. Windproof and water-repellent clothing, which are breathable, often have exciting names like Windkiller and Windstopper. Nylon windbreakers—the old standby—will help protect against the wind, but are not breathable. Nylon may be too warm and it traps moisture. My recommendation is to wear waterproof clothes only in cold, wet weather; use water-repellent, windproof outerwear on windy days or in mild temperatures.

Here's a general guide for layering in cold weather:

- Extremely cold (10 degrees Fahrenheit and colder): three upper-body layers, two lower-body layers, gloves and mittens, headband, neck gaitor, and hat.

- Cold (10 degrees Fahrenheit to 40 degrees Fahrenheit): two upper-body layers, one or two lower-body layers, mittens and/or gloves, hat.
- Moderate (40 to 50 degrees Fahrenheit): one upper-body layer, one lower-body layer; hat and gloves are optional.

Dress a little warmer than the above guidelines on windy days; wear a little less if you tend to build up a lot of heat and when running at a faster pace than usual.

Upper body. Layering for the upper body is discussed earlier. Ideally, your jacket will have covered zippers, a hood, venting, and pockets for storing mittens and hat and other items. It should be cut long enough to cover below the waist, have drawstrings at the bottom, and a high collar you can close. Another good option is a vest, which adds some warmth but leaves your arms free. A turtleneck shirt (available in moisture-wicking fabrics), a gaiter, or a scarf will help keep cold away from your neck.

Legs. They generate a lot of heat and need less protection than your upper body. One layer is usually enough. The most common choice is a pair of tights. Lightweight Lycra-spandex tights are warm enough in most weather. For colder runs try heavier tights made of wicking fabrics. Other runners prefer to wear nylon, Coolmax, or Gore-Tex pants over a pair of shorts. On really cold or windy days, wear tights covered by windproof pants. These two layers are the most any runner needs.

Private parts. A word of caution: If a man gets wet down under and then catches a strong headwind, his private parts may get uncomfortably cold—or worse, frostbitten. Don't laugh, it has happened to more than one poor runner. Good protection is a special pair of windbriefs, which wick moisture and have a windproof panel in front. Women should also take precautions to keep warm and dry. Running briefs and sports bras are available in fabrics that wick moisture.

Feet. Running feet usually keep plenty warm as long as they stay dry and keep moving. Steer clear of puddles, wet snow, and slush! One layer of wicking socks made of fabrics such as acrylic, polypropylene, or that old standby, wool, is usually enough. In very cold weather you may choose to go with an inner, thin sock made of a wicking fabric covered by an insulating outer sock. Don't go with two thick pairs or you may impede circulation or cause blisters. Some veterans of the cold and wet wear plastic bags, or nylon or cyclists' booties over socks to stay warm and dry in nasty weather. But these choices don't breathe and you'll build up a lot of moisture from sweating. More high-tech choices are waterproof and breathable. Wear them over a light pair of wicking socks. If your feet get wet on a cold day, keep moving until you can get to a warm place, get wet shoes and socks off, and warm your feet.

Head. As much as 50 percent of your body's heat goes up the chimney and out your head. Use a hat as a chimney damper: Keep it on to keep heat from escaping. The hat is the first piece to remove if you need to open the damper and cool off. Put it back on if you cool too much. It is important to protect the ears from frostbite on very cold days—choose a hat or headband that covers them. In very cold weather, you might need a headband covered by a hat. In extreme cold protect the face too—either wear a face mask, balaclava, or slather exposed portions with petroleum jelly.

Shelly-lynn has streams of long hair and often wears just a headband to keep the frost off her ears. The less thatching up top, the more likely you are to need the supplemental coverage of a hat. What kind of hat depends on the weather and how much you heat up. I use a lightweight cotton cyclist cap in milder weather, switching to a polypro or Gore-Tex hat in more extreme cold. In weather that may change and bring the danger of frostbite, I'll carry along a headband or pack my polypro hat and trade back-and-forth with the cyclist's cap a few times during a run to keep comfortable. A simple baseball cap is popular with many runners. If the weather gets colder, I'll put on a Thermax cap or fleece hat. Cold, wet weather brings out my Gore-Tex hat; still colder and windier weather a jacket hood over the hat.

Hands. Mittens, or even socks worn as mittens, keep hands warmer than gloves because of the warmth shared by fingers. Being a Glover, I prefer gloves. I like light breathable ones. Polypro liners don't get too hot and can be covered by mittens on cold days. I often start runs with windproof mittens over lightweight gloves and then take the mittens off and on to adjust for comfort. Thermax gloves in heavier weights add a little more warmth.

When the going gets wet and cold, I'll cover them with Gore-Tex mittens.

OVERDRESS OR UNDERDRESS?

The underdressed runner on cold days is vulnerable to hypothermia and frostbite. Also, shivering can occur as you run, using up some of your fuel stores. Overdressing can cause overheating—which is more likely than getting too cold—resulting in excessive sweating which can ruin the insulation of your clothing. You could then start cooling quickly.

With experience you'll learn what works best for you. The key is knowing what to wear and wearing as little as possible. A good rule of thumb is to dress as though it were 20 degrees warmer out than it really is. You should feel a little chilly when first going outside but warm up within 5 minutes on the run. Be flexible. On a single run the conditions may change several times. Don't toss away any articles of clothing when running or racing unless you are positive you won't need them again. In cold weather always bring along a hat and gloves or mittens, even if you don't need them when you start. More than once I was happy to have them when the sun went down and the wind picked up late in a run. Be prepared to peel off layers as you warm up. Place small items into your jacket pocket or waistband. Larger items can be tied around your waist. The first item to remove is your hat, then your gloves. Unzip or remove your outer jacket if you start to overheat. As you cool, replace the clothing in reverse order.

DRESSING FOR COLD WEATHER RACING

Racing builds up more body heat than training. You won't need or want as many clothes. Overheating slows you down; too many clothes weigh you down and restrict movement. But if you underdress, you may also underperform: When cold, muscles might stiffen, and discomfort may cause you to lose your resolve. The trick is guessing how much is enough, but not too much, before the race goes off. You have limited flexibility in taking clothing on and off when racing compared to training.

Listen to the weather report before packing your bags race day. Include several options so that you can adjust your choice of clothing at the race site. Once there, check out the conditions: Is it sunny or cloudy, windy or calm, wet or dry? Start your warm-up run well dressed and gradually shed some of the clothing to get an idea of how your body is reacting to the elements. When you are down to your race clothing, run briskly for a few minutes. Adjust from there if it doesn't feel right. Remember, you should feel cold and uncomfortable at the start—but not by too much.

The shorter the race, the less clothing you will need. Race intensity will be high so you'll build up lots of body heat. Further, you won't be out in the cold for very long. The longer the race, the more clothing needed. Since pace will be slower, less heat is produced. However, exposure to the elements will be longer. Further, the weather is more likely to change by the time you reach the finish line. Be especially careful not to underdress in cold weather marathons. This is especially true if running at a slow, survival pace. If you intend to be out for a long time, bring along a lightweight jacket and other items to put on late in the race when you get tired and cold. Friends along the course with extra clothing may be a big help.

The more confident you feel and the harder you want to run, the less clothing you wear. I'll err on the underdressing side (except for hat and gloves) in order to challenge myself to go for it in cold weather. If I wimp out and dress more warmly, I'll be less likely to run a fast race. Once the fast pace is set, I'm challenged to keep up the effort—and the body heat.

For racing, I recommend a lightweight, wicking short-sleeved or long-sleeved shirt as an inner layer for the upper body. Cover this with a singlet or T-shirt on which you pin your number. In very cold weather, I'll go to a heavier wicking inner layer. If you are not going to be pushing the pace too fast or the wind is really bad, you may add a lightweight, breathable, windproof jacket or vest. But keep your number on the inside clothing in case you remove the outer jacket. Just unzip the jacket if you need to show your number to an official during the race and at the finish.

For the lower body, I'll choose shorts unless it gets very cold. Lightweight tights are my next choice to keep my hips and hamstrings from tightening as I get tired, especially in races over 10K in distance. Remember this: Legs sweat during races and getting hit with cold winds may cause problems. Tights are a good choice for longer races in the cold and wind. If it is cold enough to require heavier tights or running pants, don't expect to run a fast time. Go with comfort in these conditions.

Here's a tip to help you race faster: I always wear at least a pair of light gloves when I'm racing in cold or cool weather even if I line up at the start hatless in singlet and shorts. Why? That way my hands, which are often cold when the rest of my body has heated up, stay warm and my body won't pump blood to warm them up. By wearing gloves, my comfort level and my mental ability to concentrate on racing is improved, and more blood can be sent with needed energy to my fast-charging legs. So go with gloves on cool days and don't tell the ungloved competitors around you about Glover's tip. For cold days, at least a pair of lightweight gloves are recommended as you start.

The key to keeping your temperature controlled in a race—assuming you didn't overdress in the upper body—is with your hat. Keep it light. Again you can easily tuck it into your waistband if you overheat. The ears will be vulnerable to frostbite if they get wet with perspiration and then you catch a cold headwind, so it may be wise to bring along a headband if your hat doesn't cover your ears. I also wear a cold weather mask in winter races to allow me to get started without having an asthma attack.

It's important to have a towel to dry you off, and warm, dry clothing available to put on immediately when finishing your race. Either pack what you need in your bag and leave it with the baggage claim, or have a trusted friend or relative responsible for meeting you at the finish line.

TIPS FOR RUNNING IN COLD WEATHER

Since serious runners must train and race in the cold, they should make adjustments in order to maximize performance and safety on those cold, blustery days. Here are some tips to make cold weather runs more pleasurable, productive, and safer:

Avoid the bitter cold and the dreaded dark. Do the opposite of hot weather running: Schedule runs when the sun is the warmest. As much as possible, avoid running in the early morning and late evening when it's coolest and you'll face the perils of darkness. Beware of runs that start in the late afternoon when the sun is up and end as the sun is going down. You'll get colder and colder as you run along. If you run at this time, dress for the estimated temperature at the end of your run.

Check the wind. A cold headwind is a serious enemy. When running an out-and-back course, begin by running into the wind, when you are full of energy and prepared to face this obstacle. Starting out with the wind at your back allows you to build up a good sweat which will make you wet, cold, uncomfortable, and prone to frostbite on your return trip. Further, the bullying headwind will cause you to tire more and to go slower on the second half of the run. As a result, your body will be producing less heat when it needs it the most. Here's an idea I picked up from one of my students: She has her husband drive her down the road a few miles so she can run with a tail wind for the complete run. Why suffer more than necessary? If a course is sheltered from the wind, choose it on cold, blustery days even if it means running a few boring loops.

If racing on a cold day, check out the course in advance so you know where you may hit the winds. If you are likely to hit headwinds late in the race when sweaty and tired, make sure you are properly dressed. Don't get fooled by a sunny, calm starting area. The wind may be whipping across open fields a few miles down the road.

Warm up and cool down. A proper warm-up is even more important in winter because exposure to cold stiffens muscles and joints. Starting training runs or races too fast on cold days could result in muscle strain or respiratory problems. I warm up indoors for cold runs by walking on the treadmill for 5 to 10 minutes. If this isn't possible for you, start with a brisk walk and a slow jog to gradually adjust to cold conditions. Warming up before a speed workout or race is tricky. It's important to elevate the muscle temperature as well as your heart rate prior to taking off at a fast pace. I keep running right up until the start of the workout or race, gradually taking off the extra clothing. Then I pray that the race starts on time!

End runs with a slow jog or brisk walk. Don't stay outside for too long after you've slowed the pace or you'll soon be prone to cold injury. If you want to do a cool-down run after racing, first towel-off and change into dry, warm clothes. Make sure you have still more dry, warm clothes to put on after your cool-down run! I pack two bags when I race—one with items I may need for the race and one with clothing for afterwards. Instead of doing your cool-down stretching routine when you are wet and cold, shower and then stretch.

Group up. Winter can be a lonely time. Fewer runners appear on the road. To keep motivated, and make sure you get out the door, keep your date book busy. Believe me, I might skip some of those raw nasty days if I didn't have company! Don't run alone in very cold or slippery weather, especially off the beaten path. A partner can get help if you fall or are overcome by the cold. No partner? At least make sure someone knows your course and return time (a good practice in any weather).

Don't forget to drink. You can still dehydrate in cold weather. In fact, you may be even more vulnerable than in warm weather. Underneath all those layers of clothing, your body may produce plenty of sweat. Additional fluid is lost as your body humidifies incoming cold, dry air. Exposure to cold air may also increase urine production and decrease thirst. Drink plenty of fluids before and after runs—and along the course if running more than an hour.

Acclimate. Allow your body time to adjust to the cold. As it acclimates, it retains heat more effectively. Run outside for progressively longer periods over two or three weeks. However, when people exercise in cold weather, they demonstrate only a limited capacity for physiologic adaptation as compared to acclimatization to hot weather. We must do much of the adapting by dressing properly.

Adjust pace. Don't pay too much attention to your training pace on very cold days. With all the clothing, you have an excuse to run slowly. Just go fast enough to keep warm and concentrate more on your perceived exertion than pace per mile.

Adjust distances. Shorten runs on excessively cold days for comfort and safety. Postpone a long run (or long race) for a warmer day. Emphasize shorter races of 5K to 10K during cold months. The longer you are out there, the more exposure to the elements and risk of cold injury.

Adjust speed training. Think of winter speed training as an opportunity to keep reasonably sharp and in good position to increase the quality of your workouts when warmer weather arrives. You can keep in shape, or even improve your speed, over the winter months if you plan properly and are disciplined.

Don't run short, very fast speed workouts in very cold weather. Your muscles will be too tight to safely handle the intensity. If you run too hard, your lungs will feel scorched, your throat sore and raspy. While we do speed sessions throughout the winter with our New York Road Runners Club classes, we often don't time the workouts because it can be disheartening to run times that are slowed by the weather and heavy clothing. Instead, we emphasize plenty of strength-building hill running as well as continuous fartlek and tempo runs. If we do intervals on cold days, we run at race pace or slower and keep everybody moving during the recovery period so they can stay reasonably warm.

Having problems getting in your speed training in the snow and cold? Occasionally do some fartlek bursts when you find some bare patches; even in the worst conditions you can usually find a short hill to run up (especially since hills are often plowed and salted so cars can get up them). I may substitute hard snowshoe running or cross-country skiing for speed training runs. If it gets too cold or slippery, move speed sessions indoors to a treadmill. If you have access to indoor track training, be careful to ease into hard running. Indoor tracks have tight corners and slanted surfaces, which can cause injuries for some runners.

If you aren't able to do consistent speed training during the winter, practice "strides." Run quickly, but not all-out, for 50 to 150 yards, on the flats or up hills, at least once a week, or every other week. These short bursts keep speed and running form from disappearing over the winter.

Keep warm before and after races. If possible, do easy stretching in a warm building before cold weather races. Many races use a school gym for registration and this may be ideal. Otherwise, alternate jogging outside for short periods with staying indoors (or even in your car with the heat on) and relaxing. If there is no place to go to stay warm, try to get to the race near the starting time and keep moving. Here's a good time to make sure that you picked up your race number before race day. Again, get indoors where it is warm and get on dry clothes immediately after racing.

Adjust racing goals and strategy. You can outperform competitors of similar ability if you don't let the cold get to you psychologically and if you run a smart race under the conditions. I've run most of my fastest races, including my best marathon, in the winter. As long as it isn't so cold that you must wear excessive clothing, you can really push the pace without being concerned about overheating. Strong winds, however, will affect you more in the cold than in the heat because they not only brake you, they undermine your resolve by making you very uncomfortable due to windchill.

So if it isn't excessively cold or windy, dress as lightly as possible, start a little conservatively to warm up, and go for it. But don't try this unless you are in good shape and are adjusted to racing in the cold. If you intend to run conservatively, dress more for comfort and don't start too fast. Adjust your starting and goal time for bad weather rather than risk health. If you start too fast and must slow dramatically or drop out, you may be a long way from a warm shelter. If you drop out in the heat, you can walk to cool off. But in the cold, you will chill rapidly and be prone to frostbite and hypothermia. Know the course and potential places to seek help if you run into trouble. Stick money into your shoe or pin it to your number for emergencies. Don't be a hero. If you are struggling on a cold day and have a good place to drop out, drop out.

Don't cheat on your shoes. I used to save old shoes for running in the snow to avoid getting my new ones wet and caked with salt. Wrong choice! On snow you'll need the best snow tires possible, the less wear on the soles the better. Further, running on pavement in cold weather demands more midsole cushioning than you'll get out of shoes with too many miles on them.

COPING WITH WINTER

Here are some ideas for a compromise winter program—a runner's semihibernation, if you will. The goal is keeping in shape over the cold months with a minimum of discomfort.

Take a short break. I try to get outdoors to run every day no matter how bad the weather. But after several days in a row of arctic weather or slobbering through the snow, even I am ready for a break. It is okay to skip a day or two. But don't quit for any longer or it will be tough to regain lost fitness.

Take a long break. The body needs a rebuilding period, time to regenerate, and winter is a good time since races are scarce and competitive training is difficult. Cut back mileage substantially—up to 50 percent—for a month or more. Regenerate. But don't run less than these guidelines or you'll have trouble getting your legs out of mothballs when spring arrives. Also, eliminate long runs, hard speedwork, and racing for a few weeks or more. You might benefit from a few light speed sessions and low key races just to keep from getting too rusty or bored with your vacation from training.

Cross-train. Cut back running by 10 to 50 percent and replace those training minutes with cross-training. The most natural wintertime option is to head for snow-covered trails on cross-country skis. Try to run at least three times a week so your return to running is fairly comfortable.

Run indoors. When it gets too slippery out to run safely, or when the windchill count is dangerous, I'm real happy to have a treadmill at home. I'll look out the window at the wind whipping and the snow swirling and feel quite comfortable!

Break it up. Try "two-a-days." For example, instead of struggling for an hour in the cold or with sloppy footing, run for a half hour in the morning and another half hour later in the day. No matter how bad the weather, you won't get too uncomfortable for the first 30 to 45 minutes. Another option is to start indoors, whether running on a treadmill or exercising on a bike or other aerobic equipment, and then go out for a short run (after changing into dry clothes).

Take a runner's vacation. A week, or even a long weekend, in a warm-weather spot will give you a real boost. Even a brief period of running again in shorts and a singlet breaks up winter training and pumps up the motivation. Upon your return you face a shortened winter—a definite plus.

RUNNING IN SNOW, SLUSH, AND ICE

A light layer of snow provides good cushioning and reasonable traction. But after it gets packed down and becomes icy and crusty, it becomes treacherous. Slipping, sliding, and sloshing on snow or ice can sabotage your form and cause you to tense and use muscles abnormally. This puts you at more at risk of injury. Many runners have fallen on the ice while running, including Shelly-lynn's brother, and ended up with broken bones and bruised bodies that cost them weeks of running. Walk around icy areas. Be especially careful on downhills and turns, and when running after dark. If you find yourself running over slippery paths, slow the pace, shorten your stride, and try to run flat-footed with a low knee lift. Just shuffle along, maintaining good balance. Stay relaxed.

If it's snowing, your vision (and that of motorists) will be impaired. Run defensively. Better yet, don't share the road with cars under snowy or icy conditions. When the snow covers your favorite courses, switch runs to roads, sidewalks, or trails that are well-plowed and have minimal, or better yet, no car traffic. This may mean running loops around a parking lot or residential section. Another option is to try "ice joggers"—they are like old-fashioned galoshes but have small spikes on the bottom. Just slip them over running shoes for a good grip on snow and ice.

SNOWSHOE RUNNING

In my opinion, this is the best form of alternative training for runners. It's more specific than the other choices because it really is running—only more arduous and without much of the impact. The new breed of lightweight, flexible, snow-flotation devices are half the size of ordinary snowshoes, and one-third the weight. Just strap your running shoes into the bindings and take off running. The rubber decking keeps your foot from sinking into the snow. Since weight is distributed over a larger surface than running shoes there is more stability. You almost float over the snow with very little jarring. Steel cleats under the ball of the foot and heel provide excellent traction. No more slipping, sliding, and falling on the run for me! I can even run hard on slippery downhills with these devices.

Snowshoe running is a lot more efficient than running in snow and ice with running shoes. The ankles and quadriceps will get extra work, which will make them that much stronger for running when the snow melts. You can also really push the heart rate up, especially on uphills and in heavy snow. I find that I can get a higher-quality hard run at the upper limit of my training heart-rate range on snowshoes than I could possibly manage in the winter with regular running. I'll even use them for speed training by doing fartlek or hill repeats. Further, I can train harder more often due to the lower impact. Most important, it is an exhilarating experience that provides a great change of pace in my training routine. Running where few others are brave enough to tread is rewarding. So, too, are the beautiful winter scenes that I am able to enjoy.

But be warned! Snowshoe running is very tough. Your muscles and lungs will scream at you. Ease into it a few minutes at a time. Just shuffle along with short, quick strides and pump your arms. As you get in better shape, quicken the arm drive and stride rate. Your technique will improve with practice, so be patient at first if you feel somewhat awkward. Two tips: Concentrate on picking your feet up or you'll trip and fall, and keep your footsteps fairly wide or you'll clip your ankles with the shoes.

If you normally run at an 8-minute pace on bare roads, then you will probably run at about a 10-minute pace on snowshoes over packed trails (much slower over deeper or unpacked snow) for the same effort. I measure runs by time rather than distance. If I run for about 64 minutes at what felt like an 8-minute pace effort, I credit myself with 8 running miles in my diary. Even if the total distance covered was closer to 7 miles, believe me—it was worth an 8-mile run and then some.

PART X

SPECIFIC COMPETITORS

CHAPTER 38

The Masters Competitor

Surely, we all age, no matter how much we run. Although the various systems of the body slow down with age, running greatly reduces the rate of the aging process. Inactivity, not aging, causes us to rust. One of the most exciting trends in running is the continued growth of masters (age 40 plus) competition. America is getting older, consequently in most races masters comprise the majority of the field.

It's never too late to turn running into your fountain of youth. An inactive sixty-year-old who begins a running program can attain the same aerobic fitness level he or she had two decades earlier—as an inactive forty-year-old. Who wouldn't be interested in a twenty-year rejuvenation?

AGING AND PERFORMANCE

The bottom line is the declining capabilities of the heart, lungs, and muscles with aging gradually limit running performance. The trick is to slow the slowing! Aerobic capacity decreases by about 10 percent per decade in relatively sedentary individuals. But research at the Washington University School of Medicine in St. Louis determined that steady vigorous endurance training reduces the decline to only 5 percent per decade. That is, running can cut the loss of aerobic fitness due to aging in half! And runners who train intensely lose even less. Research by exercise physiologist Michael Pollock at the University of Florida with a group of highly fit masters runners showed only a minimal loss in aerobic capacity over a ten-year period for those who maintained regular quality training and raced frequently.

What about race times? Some runners will, like fine wine, actually improve with age. They might run faster times, for example, in their forties or fifties than when younger. This is merely because they didn't have the training background and experience to run faster before. If you are new to competitive training and racing, you may very well defy age and continue to run faster times. But eventually we all slow down, whether an Elite or back-of-the-pack runner. Theoretically, peak performance age for runners is somewhere between ages twenty and thirty-four. Various studies indicate that those runners who remain highly fit and avoid serious injury or illness will average at least a 0.5 percent decline in performance per year from age thirty-five to sixty (after age sixty performance dropoff tends to increase). But those who train less seriously as they age or are slowed by injury or illness experience performance losses averaging 1 to 2 percent per year or more. The message is clear: You can limit performance slowdown if you're willing to train hard. Pollock's research suggests that if we want to hold on to our performance longer as we age, we need to maintain quality work, not just run easy mileage.

Aging has a range of effects on competitive runners. Some seem to age much slower than others. For many, the slowdown is gradual until they notice an extreme performance drop, most often after a layoff due to injury. Don't get frustrated if other runners your age seem to be getting better as you are slowing down. Perhaps they peaked later in their running life or were blessed with better genes. Or maybe you need to adjust your training to compensate for the aging process.

AGE-ADJUSTED TRAINING

The following tips will help you age slower and run faster:

Adjust training mileage and pace. As a thirty-year-old I ran 10-mile training runs in 70 minutes; as a fifty-year-old the same effort took 80 minutes. At sixty it'll probably take me 90 minutes; when I'm seventy I might throw away the stopwatch. For me, a 60-mile week at fifty took as much training time and energy as a 70- or 80-mile week once did. You may not be able to handle the same number of miles as you age, but you may be able to run for the same number of minutes. Weekly mileage may also be less since at least one additional off day may be required for proper recovery.

Keep hard days hard. As we age it gets more difficult to maintain speed as muscle fibers decrease. The first to go are the fast-twitch muscle fibers (used for strength and speed), followed by slow-twitch fibers (used for endurance). Further, the motor nerve cells which coordinate fast running deteriorate with aging. Speed training (or at least brisk runs), racing on a regular basis, and weight training minimize the loss of precious fast-twitch fibers and maintain coordination. Tempo runs are beneficial since lactate threshold, according to some research, responds better to training for masters runners than other performance variables.

Research has shown that quality training is more important than quantity training to maintain race times with aging. Speed with caution. It carries an increased chance of injury for older runners. Many masters runners find that hard tracks contribute to injury so they shift to intervals or fartlek on dirt trails. Too many hard days will most likely be counterproductive. If you once did two speed workouts per week, by the time you reach your forties or fifties then one hard day a week may be best. If you take several weeks or more off from serious training, and you should, do some quick running so your speed doesn't go into permanent retirement. A few strides are sufficient to help maintain speed.

Keep easy days easy. The older we get, the more easy days we need. What is an easy day? Two minutes per mile slower than 10K race pace; a very comfortable conversation pace. A common mistake for masters runners is getting too enthused after a quality run and pushing the pace again the next day or the day after. Instead, ease back and savor the glory, lick your wounds, and slowly prepare to gallantly charge back to battle. My hard days are very hard, but my easy days are very easy. Few runners of any age can stay with me on hard days; even fewer have the patience to dawdle along with me on my pokey days (including Shelly-lynn).

Increase recovery time. The first thing masters notice is not losing speed or endurance, but longer recovery from hard or long runs. It may take twice as long or more to rejuvenate. At least into your forties you may run speed workouts almost as fast as when you were younger, but you'll probably be much sorer and slower for several days afterward. We just can't bounce back from hard training so we put in less high-quality runs. This is a key reason we can't maintain the times of our youth.

Improper recovery may result in injury or the loss of zip in your runs for several days or more. Adapt the hard day/easy day approach to hard day/easy days. This means fewer hard days and more easy days per week. Consider an added off day from running each week. Many older masters find success in training every other day, but running longer when they run.

Cross-train. As we need more time to recover from the impact of running, cross-training becomes more valuable. On days when you are too sore or stiff to run, or to prevent soreness and stiffness, substitute non-weight-bearing aerobic exercise.

Train on softer surfaces. As we get older—and I can attest to this—it takes longer to recover from running on hard surfaces. Running on dirt, grass, synthetic tracks, or treadmills, at least part of the time, will help your legs recover more quickly than when they're subjected to a daily pounding on hard roads.

Take more training breaks. More "vacations" in training are needed as we age. Rejuvenate up to two weeks or more, twice a year or more, by cutting running and racing way back.

Build slower to peak. With fewer intense workouts, it takes longer to sharpen for a competitive peak. Perhaps it will take twelve weeks or more of progressive speed training to peak compared to the six to eight weeks it took to whip yourself into shape in your youth.

Don't overrace. We don't recover as fast from races either. When you have a few good races, don't push your luck by extending the streak. Instead, back off for a recovery period and then go for it again.

Avoid injury. Injuries tend to develop more quickly and heal more slowly with age. The aging process makes ligaments, tendons, and joints stiffer and less distensible. Be careful. It is much harder to recapture fitness after a long layoff as we age. Take preventive steps, including strength and flexibility training.

Strength-train. Lean muscle mass is lost with aging. The number of muscle fibers decreases by 3 to 5 percent per decade after age thirty, resulting in a loss of as much as 30 percent of muscle power by age sixty. The size of fibers also decreases. Lost muscle is usually replaced by body fat. A less active lifestyle as we age causes muscles to atrophy faster. In short, use it or lose it. Running minimizes loss of muscle mass and bone density in the legs. But don't just work to improve leg strength. Upper-body strength training is important for good health and performance. Runners lose muscle mass and bone density (increasing the risk of osteoporosis) more quickly in their upper body.

Maintain stride. Research at the University of Northern Iowa by Dr. Nancy Hamilton indicates that stride rate decreases only minimally with aging, but stride length decreases significantly. Why? A combination of factors including decreased agility, coordination, power, and range of motion at the hips, knees, and ankles. Fast intervals, hill training, strength training, speed drills, and stretching for the hamstrings and quadriceps are all important factors in minimizing the loss of stride length with aging.

Keep flexible. The connective tissues between the muscles and bones become more rigid with aging. Maintain flexibility with a regular stretching program to minimize injury and keep an efficient, powerful running stride. Run a variety of paces so that you're not always moving through the same range of motion.

Eat well. One of the best weapons against aging is eating carefully. As we age we need fewer calories to maintain normal body weight, yet the need for essential nutrients is as great as it is for younger runners. There is less room for high-calorie, low-nutrient foods like sweets, alcohol, and fats. Eating plenty of fruits and vegetables, emphasizing carbohydrates, and eating foods rich in calcium and antioxidants will help you better handle the physical changes of aging and the demands of running.

Control weight. Most Americans get heavier as they get older. They become less active and eat more. Metabolic rate gradually slows with age resulting in a slowdown in the rate the body burns calories for normal daily functions. Lean muscle mass lost with aging is replaced with fat. To minimize weight gain with aging, taper caloric intake and maintain or increase both aerobic exercise and strength training.

Adjust your attitude. Due to aging all runners eventually have to adjust to life after the last personal record is set due to aging. The first step is to accept the inevitable. Sure, it takes a while to admit you can't run as fast in your forties, fifties, or beyond as you did in your youth. It's hard to keep the enthusiasm and desire burning, and easy to say "I'm getting too old for this" and give up. But if you train wisely you'll minimize performance loss with aging and race well compared to others in your age category. If you aren't able to train as seriously as you would like, due to lifestyle or injury, so what? Savor your accomplishments and set reasonable goals to motivate you. Look at the good side. Seasoned runners have more patience and mental strength than most younger competitors. Experience can compensate for some of the physical losses that come with aging. Masters runners tend to be better at pacing and adjusting to extremes of weather.

If you outtrain your age-group peers and stay healthy, you will gain an edge. You may even outrace some of them you couldn't beat when you were younger! By staying healthy and concentrating on the positive aspects of running, aging runners can enjoy training and competition even if we have run our last PR. Instead of feeling sorry for yourself when you can no longer run faster times, count your blessings. Compare yourself to other masters runners, not your youthful past. Competition can still be challenging and rewarding.

MASTERS COMPETITION

Running has created a new pride in aging. It is one of the few sports that rewards you for getting older. We all get a new competitive life every five years. Most races score according to 5- or 10-year masters age groups after age forty. Age-grouping is important to maintain motivation as Father Time cheats us on the finish line clock. Five-year breakdowns are fairer for aging runners. It's tough for a 49-year-old to compete with a 40-year-old, but even tougher for a 69-year-old to compete with a 60-year-old. As you age, look forward to moving into a new category. I've coached a lot of runners who celebrated their 40th, 50th, 60th, and even their 70th birthdays with a big party because they crossed into a new masters category and got to be the new "kid" in their age group. I retired from serious competition in my early thirties when

I was at my peak. I was lured back to competition by the age-group system as I approached age fifty. Soon I was winning awards again at races, which made me feel young and athletic again.

Be proud to look and feel good at your age. Stay motivated by recording personal records at each five-year mark. Compare yourself to competitors in your age group, not to what you used to be able to run. A great motivator is the following age-adjusted race time system. Join a team or group that encourages masters runners. Shelly-lynn formed the Mercury Masters, a women's only team for age fifty-plus runners. They support each other in all areas of their lives. We also formed the Greater New York Racing Team which includes several men and women in their forties and fifties. It sure is easier to keep training and racing as a masters runner when you have teammates to spur you on!

For more information on masters running refer to our *Masters Runner's Handbook*.

AGE-ADJUSTED AND AGE-GRADED RACE TIME CHARTS

Many runners, myself included, find it tough to accept slower times as they age. My best pace for a 5K as a fifty-year-old was slower than my marathon pace twenty years earlier. We can't dwell on what we used to do, but rather need to concentrate on what we can do now. To keep runners motivated as race times slow with age, the World Association of Veteran Athletes (WAVA) developed age-graded scoring tables. I used them as a goal when I made my comeback as a fifty-year-old. It was encouraging to be able to run times that were the age-adjusted equal to my prime twenty years earlier.

The program is keyed to the rate of decline based on age as compared to the approximate world record by single year age. With this system you can convert race performances to what you theoretically could have run in your prime years. Thus, as we age we can actually compete against our youthful times. The system also converts race times to a percentage of the standard for your age. This gives you a rating score for comparison with other race distances and to other runners, both male and female, of all ages. The complete charts for up to age 100 for road racing and track-and-field events can be ordered from National Masters News, P.O. Box 16597, North Hollywood, CA 91615-6597

The Age-Adjusted Chart (Figures 38.1–38.2)

The age factors in Figures 38.1–38.2 express the rate of decline based on age as compared with the world record by an open-class runner (age 20–34) when the charts were developed. To determine your age-adjusted time for a race:

1. Convert your race time to seconds by multiplying the minutes by 60 and adding this total to the leftover seconds:

   The sample is a 53-year-old woman with a 10K time of 45:18.
   45:18 = (45 minutes x 60) + (18 seconds)
   45:18 = 2,700 seconds + 18 seconds = 2,718 seconds

2. Multiply this time by the age factor for the specific race distance, age, and gender:

   The age factor for a 53-year-old woman for 10K is .8545
   2,718 seconds x .8545 = 2,323 seconds

3. Convert this time to minutes:seconds:

   2,323 seconds divided by 60 seconds = 38.72 minutes
   .72 minute x 60 seconds = 43 seconds
   2,323 seconds = 38:43 (38 minutes and 43 seconds)

This runner's time of 45:18 is equal to her potential prime-age time of 38:43.

I was thrilled to run 18:28 for 5K as I turned fifty. It doesn't sound good compared to my all-time best of 16:20 until I correct for age and get the adjusted time of 16:29. I achieved my goal of being as good at age fifty as I was at my peak at age thirty. Use this system to motivate you to get better with age!

The Age-Graded Chart (Figures 38.3–38.4)

The time standards in Figures 38.3–38.4 correspond approximately to world records for a person of that age and sex for each race distance when this table was compiled. The open class (age 20–34) times are the overall world records (100 percent). You can use your performance-level percentage as a rating to compare to your scores at various distances, your scores from years past, your progress over the racing season, and to other runners—regardless of age or sex. Some races now use this scoring system to award the top performances in the race, regardless of age.

To determine your age-graded score for a race:

FIGURE 38. 1: AGE-ADJUSTED RACE TIME FACTORS (MEN)

Age	5K	5 Mile/8K	10K	15K	10 Mile	20K	1/2 Mar	Mar
20–34	1.0000	1.0000	1.0000	1.0000	1.0000	1.0000	1.0000	1.0000
35	0.9963	1.0000	1.0000	1.0000	1.0000	1.0000	1.0000	1.0000
36	0.9895	0.9934	0.9953	0.9989	0.9996	1.0000	1.0000	1.0000
37	0.9827	0.9866	0.9884	0.9921	0.9928	0.9951	0.9957	1.0000
38	0.9760	0.9797	0.9816	0.9852	0.9859	0.9882	0.9888	0.9973
39	0.9692	0.9729	0.9747	0.9784	0.9791	0.9814	0.9820	0.9904
40	0.9624	0.9661	0.9679	0.9715	0.9722	0.9745	0.9751	0.9835
41	0.9555	0.9592	0.9610	0.9646	0.9653	0.9676	0.9682	0.9765
42	0.9487	0.9523	0.9541	0.9576	0.9583	0.9606	0.9612	0.9695
43	0.9418	0.9454	0.9471	0.9507	0.9514	0.9537	0.9543	0.9626
44	0.9350	0.9385	0.9402	0.9437	0.9444	0.9467	0.9473	0.9556
45	0.9281	0.9316	0.9333	0.9368	0.9375	0.9398	0.9404	0.9486
46	0.9211	0.9246	0.9262	0.9297	0.9304	0.9327	0.9333	0.9415
47	0.9141	0.9175	0.9192	0.9226	0.9233	0.9256	0.9262	0.9344
48	0.9071	0.9105	0.9121	0.9156	0.9163	0.9186	0.9192	0.9272
49	0.9001	0.9034	0.9051	0.9085	0.9092	0.9115	0.9121	0.9201
50	0.8931	0.8964	0.8980	0.9014	0.9021	0.9044	0.9050	0.9130
51	0.8859	0.8891	0.8907	0.8941	0.8948	0.8971	0.8977	0.9057
52	0.8787	0.8819	0.8834	0.8868	0.8875	0.8898	0.8904	0.8983
53	0.8714	0.8746	0.8762	0.8795	0.8802	0.8825	0.8831	0.8910
54	0.8642	0.8674	0.8689	0.8722	0.8729	0.8752	0.8758	0.8836
55	0.8570	0.8601	0.8616	0.8649	0.8656	0.8679	0.8685	0.8763
56	0.8495	0.8525	0.8540	0.8573	0.8580	0.8603	0.8609	0.8686
57	0.8419	0.8449	0.8464	0.8497	0.8504	0.8527	0.8533	0.8610
58	0.8344	0.8374	0.8388	0.8420	0.8427	0.8450	0.8456	0.8533
59	0.8268	0.8298	0.8312	0.8344	0.8351	0.8374	0.8380	0.8457
60	0.8193	0.8222	0.8236	0.8268	0.8275	0.8298	0.8304	0.8380
61	0.8113	0.8142	0.8156	0.8187	0.8194	0.8217	0.8223	0.8299
62	0.8033	0.8062	0.8075	0.8107	0.8114	0.8137	0.8143	0.8218
63	0.7954	0.7981	0.7995	0.8026	0.8033	0.8056	0.8062	0.8137
64	0.7874	0.7901	0.7914	0.7946	0.7953	0.7976	0.7982	0.8056
65	0.7794	0.7821	0.7834	0.7865	0.7872	0.7895	0.7901	0.7975
66	0.7708	0.7735	0.7748	0.7779	0.7786	0.7809	0.7815	0.7888
67	0.7623	0.7649	0.7662	0.7692	0.7699	0.7722	0.7728	0.7801
68	0.7537	0.7563	0.7575	0.7606	0.7613	0.7636	0.7642	0.7715
69	0.7452	0.7477	0.7489	0.7519	0.7526	0.7549	0.7555	0.7628
70	0.7366	0.7391	0.7403	0.7433	0.7440	0.7463	0.7469	0.7541
71	0.7273	0.7298	0.7309	0.7339	0.7346	0.7369	0.7375	0.7447
72	0.7180	0.7204	0.7216	0.7245	0.7252	0.7275	0.7281	0.7353
73	0.7087	0.7111	0.7122	0.7152	0.7159	0.7182	0.7188	0.7258
74	0.6994	0.7017	0.7029	0.7058	0.7065	0.7088	0.7094	0.7164
75	0.6901	0.6924	0.6935	0.6964	0.6971	0.6994	0.7000	0.7070
76	0.6798	0.6821	0.6832	0.6861	0.6868	0.6891	0.6897	0.6966
77	0.6696	0.6718	0.6729	0.6757	0.6764	0.6787	0.6793	0.6862
78	0.6593	0.6615	0.6625	0.6654	0.6661	0.6684	0.6690	0.6759
79	0.6491	0.6512	0.6522	0.6550	0.6557	0.6580	0.6586	0.6655
80	0.6388	0.6409	0.6419	0.6447	0.6454	0.6477	0.6483	0.6551

FIGURE 38.2: AGE-ADJUSTED RACE TIME FACTORS (WOMEN)								
Age	5K	5 Mile/8K	10K	15K	10 Mile	20K	½ Mar	Mar
20–34	1.0000	1.0000	1.0000	1.0000	1.0000	1.0000	1.0000	1.0000
35	0.9913	0.9954	0.9974	1.0000	1.0000	1.0000	1.0000	1.0000
36	0.9835	0.9876	0.9896	0.9934	0.9941	0.9963	0.9969	1.0000
37	0.9758	0.9798	0.9818	0.9856	0.9863	0.9885	0.9891	0.9979
38	0.9680	0.9721	0.9741	0.9779	0.9786	0.9807	0.9813	0.9901
39	0.9603	0.9643	0.9663	0.9701	0.9708	0.9729	0.9735	0.9823
40	0.9525	0.9565	0.9585	0.9623	0.9630	0.9651	0.9657	0.9745
41	0.9447	0.9486	0.9506	0.9544	0.9551	0.9572	0.9578	0.9666
42	0.9368	0.9408	0.9428	0.9466	0.9473	0.9493	0.9499	0.9587
43	0.9290	0.9329	0.9349	0.9387	0.9394	0.9415	0.9421	0.9509
44	0.9211	0.9251	0.9271	0.9309	0.9316	0.9336	0.9342	0.9430
45	0.9133	0.9172	0.9192	0.9230	0.9237	0.9257	0.9263	0.9351
46	0.9053	0.9092	0.9112	0.9150	0.9157	0.9177	0.9183	0.9271
47	0.8973	0.9012	0.9032	0.9070	0.9077	0.9097	0.9103	0.9191
48	0.8894	0.8932	0.8952	0.8990	0.8997	0.9016	0.9022	0.9110
49	0.8814	0.8852	0.8872	0.8910	0.8917	0.8936	0.8942	0.9030
50	0.8734	0.8772	0.8792	0.8830	0.8837	0.8856	0.8862	0.8950
51	0.8652	0.8690	0.8710	0.8748	0.8755	0.8774	0.8780	0.8868
52	0.8570	0.8608	0.8628	0.8666	0.8673	0.8691	0.8697	0.8785
53	0.8488	0.8525	0.8545	0.8583	0.8590	0.8609	0.8615	0.8703
54	0.8406	0.8443	0.8463	0.8501	0.8508	0.8526	0.8532	0.8620
55	0.8324	0.8361	0.8381	0.8419	0.8426	0.8444	0.8450	0.8538
56	0.8239	0.8276	0.8296	0.8334	0.8341	0.8358	0.8364	0.8452
57	0.8154	0.8190	0.8210	0.8248	0.8255	0.8273	0.8279	0.8367
58	0.8068	0.8105	0.8125	0.8163	0.8170	0.8187	0.8193	0.8281
59	0.7983	0.8019	0.8039	0.8077	0.8084	0.8102	0.8108	0.8196
60	0.7898	0.7934	0.7954	0.7992	0.7999	0.8016	0.8022	0.8110
61	0.7808	0.7844	0.7864	0.7902	0.7909	0.7926	0.7932	0.8020
62	0.7719	0.7754	0.7774	0.7812	0.7819	0.7836	0.7842	0.7930
63	0.7629	0.7665	0.7685	0.7723	0.7730	0.7746	0.7752	0.7840
64	0.7540	0.7575	0.7595	0.7633	0.7640	0.7656	0.7662	0.7750
65	0.7450	0.7485	0.7505	0.7543	0.7550	0.7566	0.7572	0.7660
66	0.7355	0.7389	0.7409	0.7447	0.7454	0.7470	0.7476	0.7564
67	0.7259	0.7294	0.7314	0.7352	0.7359	0.7374	0.7380	0.7468
68	0.7164	0.7198	0.7218	0.7256	0.7263	0.7279	0.7285	0.7373
69	0.7068	0.7103	0.7123	0.7161	0.7168	0.7183	0.7189	0.7277
70	0.6973	0.7007	0.7027	0.7065	0.7072	0.7087	0.7093	0.7181
71	0.6870	0.6904	0.6924	0.6962	0.6969	0.6984	0.6990	0.7078
72	0.6767	0.6801	0.6821	0.6859	0.6866	0.6881	0.6887	0.6975
73	0.6665	0.6698	0.6718	0.6756	0.6763	0.6777	0.6783	0.6871
74	0.6562	0.6595	0.6615	0.6653	0.6660	0.6674	0.6680	0.6768
75	0.6459	0.6492	0.6512	0.6550	0.6557	0.6571	0.6577	0.6665
76	0.6347	0.6379	0.6399	0.6437	0.6444	0.6458	0.6464	0.6552
77	0.6234	0.6267	0.6287	0.6325	0.6332	0.6345	0.6351	0.6439
78	0.6122	0.6154	0.6174	0.6212	0.6219	0.6233	0.6239	0.6327
79	0.6009	0.6042	0.6062	0.6100	0.6107	0.6120	0.6126	0.6214
80	0.5897	0.5929	0.5949	0.5987	0.5994	0.6007	0.6013	0.6101

FIGURE 38.3: AGE-GRADED RACE TIME STANDARDS (MEN)

Age	5K	5 Mile/8K	10K	15K	10 Mile	20K	½ Mar	Mar
20–34	12:58.4	21:18.9	26:58.4	41:26	44:40	56:20	59:03	2:06:50
35	13:01.3	21:18.9	26:58.4	41:26	44:40	56:20	59:39	2:06:50
36	13:06.6	21:27.4	27:06.1	41:29	44:41	56:20	59:39	2:06:50
37	13:12.1	21:36.3	27:17.3	41:46	44:59	56:37	0:59:55	2:06:50
38	13:17.6	21:45.3	27:28.7	42:03	45:18	57:00	1:00:19	2:07:11
39	13:23.1	21:54.5	27:40.3	42:21	45:37	57:24	1:00:45	2:08:04
40	13:28.8	22:03.7	27:52.1	42:39	45:57	57:48	1:01:10	2:08:58
41	13:34.6	22:13.3	28:04.1	42:57	46:16	58:13	1:01:37	2:09:53
42	13:40.5	22:22.9	28:16.3	43:16	46:37	58:39	1:02:03	2:10:49
43	13:46.5	22:32.7	28:28.7	43:35	46:57	59:04	1:02:30	2:11:46
44	13:52.5	22:42.7	28:41.3	43:54	47:18	59:30	1:02:58	2:12:44
45	13:58.7	22:52.8	28:54.0	44:14	47:39	59:57	1:03:26	2:13:42
46	14:05.1	23:03.2	29:07.3	44:34	48:00	1:00:24	1:03:55	2:14:43
47	14:11.5	23:13.8	29:20.7	44:54	48:23	1:00:52	1:04:24	2:15:45
48	14:18.1	23:24.6	29:34.3	45:15	48:45	1:01:20	1:04:54	2:16:47
49	14:24.8	23:35.6	29:48.1	45:36	49:08	1:01:48	1:05:24	2:17:51
50	14:31.6	23:46.7	30:02.2	45:58	49:31	1:02:17	1:05:55	2:18:55
51	14:38.7	23:58.3	30:16.9	46:20	49:55	1:02:48	1:06:27	2:20:03
52	14:45.9	24:10.2	30:31.9	46:43	50:20	1:03:19	1:06:60	2:21:11
53	14:53.2	24:22.2	30:47.1	47:07	50:45	1:03:50	1:07:33	2:22:21
54	15:00.7	24:34.4	31:02.6	47:30	51:10	1:04:22	1:08:07	2:23:32
55	15:08.3	24:46.9	31:18.3	47:54	51:36	1:04:54	1:08:41	2:24:44
56	15:16.3	25:00.1	31:35.1	48:20	52:04	1:05:29	1:09:17	2:26:01
57	15:24.5	25:13.6	31:52.1	48:46	52:32	1:06:04	1:09:55	2:27:19
58	15:32.9	25:27.3	32:09.4	49:12	53:00	1:06:40	1:10:32	2:28:38
59	15:41.4	25:41.2	32:27.0	49:39	53:29	1:07:16	1:11:11	2:29:59
60	15:50.1	25:55.4	32:45.0	50:07	53:59	1:07:53	1:11:50	2:31:21
61	15:59.4	26:10.7	33:04.4	50:36	54:31	1:08:33	1:12:32	2:32:50
62	16:08.9	26:26.4	33:24.1	51:07	55:03	1:09:14	1:13:15	2:34:20
63	16:18.7	26:42.3	33:44.3	51:37	55:36	1:09:56	1:13:69	2:35:52
64	16:28.6	26:58.6	34:04.9	52:09	56:10	1:10:38	1:14:44	2:37:26
65	16:38.7	27:15.2	34:25.8	52:41	56:44	1:11:21	1:15:30	2:39:02
66	16:49.8	27:33.4	34:48.8	53;16	57:22	1:12:09	1:16:20	2:40:47
67	17:01.1	27:51.9	35:12.3	53:52	58:01	1:12:57	1:17:11	2:42:35
68	17:12.7	28:11.0	35:36.4	54:29	58:40	1:13:47	1:18:03	2:44:24
69	17:24.6	28:30.4	36:01.0	55:06	59:21	1:14:37	1:18:57	2:46:17
70	17:36.7	28:50.3	36:26.1	55:45	1:00:02	1:15:29	1:19:52	2:48:11
71	17:50.2	29:12.5	36:45.1	56:27	1:00:48	1:16:27	1:20:53	2:50:19
72	18:04.1	29:35.2	37:22.8	57:11	1:01:35	1:17:26	1:21:55	2:52:30
73	18:18.3	29:58.5	37:52.3	57:56	1:02:24	1:18:26	1:22:59	2:54:44
74	18:32.9	30:22.4	38:22.6	58:42	1:03:13	1:19:29	1:24:05	2:57:02
75	18:47.9	30:47.0	38:53.6	59:30	1:04:04	1:20:33	1:25:13	2:59:24
76	19:05.0	31:14.9	39:28.9	1:00:24	1:05:02	1:21:45	1:26:30	3:02:04
77	19:22.5	31:43.6	40:05.2	1:01:19	1:06:02	1:22:60	1:27:49	3:04:49
78	19:40.6	32:13.3	40:42.7	1:02:16	1:07:04	1:24:17	1:29:10	3:07:40
79	19:59.3	32:43.9	41:21.3	1:03:15	1:08:07	1:25:36	1:30:34	3:10:35
80	20:18.5	33:15.4	42:01.2	1:04:16	1:09:12	1:26:58	1:32:01	3:13:37

FIGURE 38.4: AGE-GRADED RACE TIME STANDARDS (WOMEN)

Age	5K	5 Mile/8K	10K	15K	10 Mile	20K	½ Mar	Mar
20–34	14:23.7	23:39.0	29:55.0	45:51	49:23	1:02:10	1:05:48	2:18:51
35	14:31.3	23:45.6	29:59.7	45:51	49:23	1:02:10	1:05:48	2:18:51
36	14:38.1	23:56.8	30:13.8	46:09	49:41	1:02:24	1:06:00	2:18:51
37	14:45.1	24:08.2	30:28.2	46:31	50:04	1:02:53	1:06:32	2:19:09
38	14:52.2	24:19.8	30:42.8	46:53	50:28	1:03:23	1:07:03	2:20:14
39	14:59.4	24:31.6	30:57.6	47:16	50:52	1:03:54	1:07:35	2:21:21
40	15:06.8	24:43.5	31:12.7	47:39	51:17	1:04:25	1:08:08	2:22:29
41	15:14.3	24:55.8	31:28.2	48:02	51:42	1:04:57	1:08:42	2:23:39
42	15:21.9	25:08.3	31:43.9	48:26	52:08	1:05:29	1:09:16	2:24:50
43	15:29.7	25:21.0	31:60.0	48:51	52:34	1:06:02	1:09:51	2:26:02
44	15:37.6	25:34.0	32:16.2	49:15	53:01	1:06:35	1:10:26	2:27:15
45	15:45.7	25:47.1	32:32.8	49:40	53:28	1:07:09	1:11:02	2:28:29
46	15:54.0	26:00.7	32:49.9	50:07	53:56	1:07:45	1:11:39	2:29:46
47	16:02.5	26:14.6	33:07.4	50:33	54:24	1:08:20	1:12:17	2:31:05
48	16:11.1	26:28.7	33:25.1	51:00	54:53	1:08:57	1:12:56	2:32:24
49	16:19.9	26:43.0	33:43.2	51:28	55:23	1:09:34	1:13:35	2:33:46
50	16:28.9	26:57.6	34:01.6	51:56	55:53	1:10:12	1:14:15	2:35:08
51	16:38.3	27:12.9	34:20.9	52:25	56:24	1:10:51	1:14:57	2:36:35
52	16:47.8	27:28.5	34:40.5	52:55	56:57	1:11:32	1:15:39	2:38:03
53	16:57.5	27:44.4	35:00.5	53:25	57:29	1:12:13	1:16:23	2:39:33
54	17:07.5	28:00.6	35:20.9	53:56	58:03	1:12:55	1:17:07	2:41:04
55	17:17.6	28:17.2	35:41.7	54:28	58:36	1:13:37	1:17:52	2:42:38
56	17:28.3	28:34.7	36:03.8	55:01	59:13	1:14:23	1:18:40	2:44:16
57	17:39.3	28:52.6	36:26.3	55:35	59:49	1:15:09	1:19:29	2:45:57
58	17:50.5	29:10.8	36:49.3	56:10	1:00:27	1:15:56	1:20:19	2:47:40
59	18:01.9	29:29.5	37:12.8	56:46	1:01:05	1:16:44	1:21:10	2:49:25
60	18:13.6	29:48.5	37:36.7	57:22	1:01:44	1:17:33	1:22:01	2:51:13
61	18:26.1	30:09.0	38:02.5	58:01	1:02:26	1:18:26	1:22:57	2:53:06
62	18:38.9	30:29.9	38.28.9	58:41	1:03:09	1:19:20	1:23:54	2:55:06
63	18:52.1	30:51.4	38:55.8	59:22	1:03:53	1:20:15	1:24:53	2:57:06
64	19:05.5	31:13.3	39:23.5	1:00:04	1:04:38	1:21:12	1:25:53	2:59:10
65	19:19.3	31:35.8	39:51.7	1:00:47	1:05:25	1:22:10	1:26:50	3:01:16
66	19:34.4	32:00.3	40:22.6	1:01:34	1:06:15	1:23:13	1:28:01	3:03:24
67	19:49.8	32:25.5	40:54.3	1:02:22	1:07:06	1:24:18	1:29:09	3:05:55
68	20:05.6	32:51.3	41:26.8	1:03:11	1:07:59	1:25:25	1:30:20	3:08:20
69	20:21.9	33:17.9	42:00.1	1:04:02	1:08:54	1:26:33	1:31:32	3:10:49
70	20:38.6	33:45.1	42:34.4	1:04:54	1:09:50	1:27:43	1:32:46	3:13:21
71	20:57.2	34:15.3	43:12.4	1:05:51	1:10:52	1:29:01	1:34:08	3:16:11
72	21:16.3	34:46.5	43:51.6	1:06:51	1:11:55	1:30:21	1:35:33	3:19:05
73	21:35.9	35:18.5	44:31.9	1:07:52	1:13:01	1:31:44	1:37:00	3:22:04
74	21:56.2	35:51.6	45:13.5	1:08:55	1:14:09	1:33:09	1:38:30	3:25:09
75	22:17.2	36:25.8	45:56.4	1:10:00	1:15:19	1:34:36	1:40:03	3:28:20
76	22:40.9	37:04.3	46:45.0	1:11:13	1:16:38	1:36:16	1:41:47	3:31:55
77	23:05.4	37:44.3	47:35.2	1:12:30	1:17:60	1:37:58	1:43:36	3:35:38
78	23:30.8	38:25.7	48:27.3	1:13:48	1:19:24	1:39:45	1:45:28	3:39:28
79	23:57.2	39:08.7	49:21.3	1:15:10	1:20:52	1:41:35	1:47:25	3:43:27
80	24:24.6	39:53.3	50:17.3	1:16:35	1:22:23	1:43:29	1:49:26	3:47:35

THE FEMALE COMPETITIVE RUNNER

Physical characteristics make men runners different from women runners. For this reason, they are scored separately in races. Why are men faster runners? There are many reasons. The male sex hormone, testosterone, increases the concentration of red blood cells and promotes the production of hemoglobin, an oxygen-carrying protein found inside red blood cells. Estrogen, the female sex hormone, has no similar effect. As a result, each liter of a man's blood contains 150 to 160 grams of hemoglobin—20 grams more hemoglobin and 11 percent more oxygen than the average for women. Men also tend to have a larger heart and lung size, and greater heart volume than women even if their body size is similar. Thus, these men can more easily pump oxygen to the working muscles. Body fat is another factor. The average body fat percentage for thirty-year-old men is approximately 15 to 20 percent; for women it is approximately 23 to 26 percent. Elite male runners range from 4 to 8 percent body fat compared to 8 to 15 percent for women. The additional sex-specific fat which women carry cannot be eliminated by dieting or training. In fact, excessive attempts to lower weight and body fat percentage may lead to anorexia, weak bones, or other health problems. Body fat acts as dead weight; it increases the energy cost of running. Women also have less muscle than men to power them along in races. Approximately 45 percent of male body weight is muscle. In women, muscle amounts to only 35 percent (but they have nearly as much fast- and slow-twitch muscle fibers as men).

So the female runner has a distinct physiological disadvantage because, even after correcting for their smaller size, they have less hemoglobin, smaller heart size and heart volume, smaller lung size, lower percentage of muscle mass, and higher percentage of body fat. As a result, women differ sharply from men in their aerobic capacity, anaerobic capacity, and muscular strength. As a result, the average female is 10 to 12 percent slower than the average male at race distances up to the marathon. A highly trained woman, however, is faster than a moderately trained man.

While men and women are physically different, the basic physiological systems function in the same way. They can train and race in similar ways. In this book, and in my classes and teams, I coach women the same way as men. Women, however, may recover faster. Research from the University of Jyvaskyla in Finland indicates that women recover about 92 percent of their muscle strength within an hour following a rigorous workout; men only recover about 79 percent.

Women give men more of a run over longer distances. When we do short, fast workouts in our classes, most women cannot keep up with men who run similar 10K times. Men simply have more power for speed. Still, the same women fare much better on longer speed workouts and often beat the same men in the marathon. An analysis of world-record times in running, swimming, and speed skating, conducted by researchers at Northeastern University, found as distances increased, the performance gap between men and women lessened. Studies in South Africa show that a man would have to run the 10K about 3 percent faster than a woman to keep up with her for the marathon. The race comparison charts in Chapter 25 reflect these differences.

Women may have the physiological advantage over men in ultra-marathoning. The most popular theory is that women are more efficient than men at using fat as an energy source during moderate intensity, long-duration exercise (and have about 7 percent more body fat), thus they conserve critical glycogen stores. Some studies suggest the female sex hormone estrogen may help delay fatigue, prevent damage to muscles, and increase the delivery of oxygen to the working muscles.

NUTRITION AND WEIGHT MANAGEMENT

Shortages of calcium and iron in the diet can be of particular importance to the performance and health of women runners. Calcium helps maintain bone density and ward off stress fractures. Plenty of calcium in the diet along with weight-bearing exercise, including running (for the lower body) and weight training (for the upper body), helps prevent the bone-thinning disease osteoporosis, which many women develop in their later years. Young women who train heavily or develop irregular or loss of menstruation are prone. Estrogen therapy after menopause is often recommended as a prevention. Women are prone to anemia since they lose iron in blood during menstruation. Heavy training also contributes to iron loss. As many as half of menstruating runners have iron-poor blood. Many competitive runners take calcium and iron supplements. See Chapter 33 for more information on calcium shortage, iron deficiency, and "runner's anemia."

Many women runners diet excessively to lose weight. Excessive weight loss not only contributes to poor performances, but to increased health risks. What you eat doesn't just add fat to your body, it fuels your next workout. See Chapter 35 for more information on a healthy performance weight.

MENSTRUATION

For some women, running eases cramps, bloating, tension, fatigue, depression, irritability, and other bothersome symptoms related to their menstrual cycles. For others, running makes symptoms worse. A heavy blood flow during the first two days of their period makes running impractical for some runners; severe cramping may make it impossible. Running may be slower during this time. If necessary, adjust training for a few days. Accept a few sluggish runs, or just wait until the symptoms ease before running.

Women may experience food cravings when they are premenstrual. Some, in the belief they need to control weight, restrain their eating at this time. But that could be a mistake. The cravings may be a sign the body needs more fuel. According to sports nutritionist Nancy Clark, metabolic rate may increase during this time and you may need as much as 500 additional calories each day to accommodate body changes and the energy requirements for training. Women also may minimize fluid intake when premenstrual since they already feel bloated. But the opposite is necessary: Bloating is caused by retained sodium which can be counteracted with fluid intake. Denying yourself sufficient fuel and hydration will make running that much more difficult.

What about performance? One study of Olympic athletes found they won gold medals during all phases of their monthly cycle. Germany's Uta Pippig won the Boston Marathon in front of millions of viewers with an obvious trickling of menstrual blood going down her leg. The effects of menstruation on performance vary greatly from runner to runner. Various surveys show a range of 37 to 63 percent notice no difference in performance during menstruation, and between 13 and 29 percent report an improvement. Actually, the best performances were generally during the days immediately following menstruation.

Most women agree they sure don't think their periods help them much. This includes U.S. Olympic 10K runner Judi St. Hilaire who reported her negative experiences to *Women's Sports and Fitness*: "Usually the day before and definitely the first day of my period, I am worthless as far as competing. I can run and go through the motions, but I dread competing on the first day. My mind wants to do one thing but my legs—mostly I notice it in my quads—they just don't fire. It feels as if I have a short circuit." Training may be more of a problem: You may overcome discomfort in the excitement of a race but not in the drudgery of practice.

The most difficult time for women to run fast isn't during their period, but rather a week before menstruation begins (the mid-luteal phase). According to research by Tracy Williams, Ph.D., reported in *Medicine and Science in Sports and Exercise*, the female sex hormone progesterone is at very high levels at this time, causing a faster rate of breathing (an 8 percent increase), a perception that running fast feels more difficult, and a 3 percent decrease in running economy. Subjects in the study also reported an increase in feeling of fatigue and depression during this phase. Race times don't necessarily suffer during this stage, but a runner is more likely to have an occasional bad day. Williams emphasized: "If women start believing that it's impossible to perform well during the mid-luteal stage, then their pessimistic thinking may hurt their performances more than the physical changes do."

The time during and just after a woman's period is the best time for optimal performance according to research by Dr. Connie Lebrun at the University of Western Ontario. "During the first couple of days, there is a tendency to have menstrual cramps, which may have an adverse effect on training and competition," says Lebrun. "After the cramps go away, during the menses and into the follicular phase, estrogen and progesterone levels are at their lowest and are likely to have the least impact on athletic performance." It is believed that when these hormone levels are high that they interfere with the body's ability to use oxygen.

What about you? Pay attention to how well you run at various phases of your cycle. If you run very poorly at a certain phase, then it may be best to postpone your race to another day. If, however, you run very well at a certain part of your cycle, consider jumping into a race when the timing is right. Unless you experience significant problems, however, the best approach is to just accept your menstrual period, have confidence in your training, and stay focused on your race goals.

Delay of menarche. Young runners tend to experience their first menstrual cycle at a later date than less active girls. Some do not begin until they are seventeen or eighteen years old. If a girl doesn't start menstruating by sixteen, she should consult her physician.

Amenorrhea. Some women report that running regulates their periods. However, many report the cessation of menstruation. Amenorrhea occurs in only 2 to 3 percent of all women but in 25 percent or more of serious competitive runners. The cause is uncertain. Some studies indicate it's the result of high mileage and low body fat. Others that it's the sudden increase in mileage, not the high mileage itself that causes the problem. Still other research doesn't point to mileage at all but to the intensity of training, of not eating enough calories and the right foods to support the level of exercise, and/or emotional stresses.

This condition is generally not considered harmful. Regular menstrual cycles reoccur for most runners when they return to their original body fat levels or when they cut back training. However, Barbara Drinkwater, Ph.D, warns "Amenorrhea is a red flag that the female runner has gone too far in her training. For most women, it's a signal that estrogen production has dropped to a dangerously low level." Amenorrhea is not always easily reversed. Doctors suggest that any woman who has vaginal bleeding more often than every twenty-three days or less often than every twenty-five days should be examined. Although some women welcome not having to deal with menstruation, if the condition continues for a long time it's potentially harmful. Amenorrheic women have a decrease in bone mineral content. In a study of college women athletes, 9 percent of those with regular periods experienced stress fractures; of the women with irregular periods, however, 24 percent had stress fractures. There is another warning here: pregnancy. Irregular menstrual periods do not mean you will not get pregnant. You can—as some runners have discovered.

Menopause. Research now proves that running helps women cope with menopause, and race times demonstrate that postmenopausal women in their fifties and beyond are capable of awesome performances.

The cessation of menstrual periods occurs when hormone levels change and signals the end of childbearing years. The whole process of menopause takes approximately five to ten years. During this time, a woman may suffer from hot flashes, depression, irritability, and a host of other side effects. Most women begin to show changes in their menstrual cycle between the ages of forty-five and fifty, though a few may begin as early as forty. Most women have passed menopause by age sixty. Running will help with many of the side effects of menopause, including the depression that many women experience. After menopause, women have lower estrogen levels, which may make them more prone to osteoporosis and heart disease. Many women benefit from regular exercise combined with estrogen therapy.

Christine Wells, Ph.D., studied a group of women masters athletes at Arizona State University to look at the effect of menopause on fitness. She found that although aerobic capacity declines with age, menopause had little or no influence on fitness. Menopause, like menstruation, however, affects fitness less directly. I've coached several women who missed several days of training because of the side effects. Shifting hormone levels cause fluctuation in energy levels and performances. On the other hand, some women run through menopause with minimal problems. Those who are more strongly hindered may need to keep their racing low-key for a year or so.

BIRTH CONTROL PILLS

Although scientists don't know for sure, it appears that the pill may reduce running performance slightly. Studies indicate that aerobic capacity and muscular strength falls in athletes who use oral contraceptives. Many runners feel tired and sluggish once they start taking the pill. Most top women competitors prefer to use an alternative birth control measure.

PREGNANCY

Pregnant women have three key running-related concerns: Can they run during pregnancy, how soon can they come back, and how will it affect performance.

Is it safe to run? Not that many years ago doctors feared that vigorous exercise would endanger the health of both pregnant women and their babies. They assumed it could interfere with maternal and fetal weight gain, and harm the fetus due to decreased oxygen and blood flow to the uterus. Doctors advised women, including well-trained athletes, to dramatically cut back their running. The American College of Obstetricians and Gynecologists (ACOG) recommendations restricted pregnant women to no more than 15 minutes of exercise at a heart rate of less than 140.

Many women were furious with these limits. They listened to their bodies instead of the doctors and kept on running. Some ran marathons, even ultramarathons. As more and more of them produced normal, healthy babies despite mileage and intensity levels well above ACOG guidelines, scientists studied them. Researchers found that vigorous exercise, including running, during pregnancy can benefit both the mother and the baby. The fears of damage were unfounded. Studies demonstrate that the pregnant body compensates for decreased oxygen and blood flow to the uterus. According to the Melpomene Institute, a research organization for women, those who run throughout pregnancy are no more likely to have a miscarriage or stillbirth, require a cesarean, or have an underweight baby. Running may even help lessen the likelihood of such complications. And women who continue to exercise during pregnancy report having far fewer adverse symptoms of pregnancy—such as nausea, heartburn, leg cramps, and insomnia—than do nonexercisers. Further, those who exercise regularly return to their prepregnancy weight, strength, and flexibility levels faster than sedentary women.

ACOG now advises: "Women with uncomplicated pregnancies can let their own stamina and abilities be their guide for exercising. In such low-risk pregnancies there currently are no data to confirm that exercise during pregnancy has any deleterious effects on the fetus." ACOG cautions women not to assume they could exercise at their prepregnancy levels. But in the absence of complications, determined by their physicians, "Women who have achieved cardiovascular fitness prior to pregnancy should be able to safely maintain that level of fitness throughout pregnancy and the postpartum period."

Pregnancy greatly alters your body and you may have complications that would make running inadvisable. If your doctor tells you to stop running because you're pregnant, ask for a reason. If the answer isn't adequate (unfortunately, some doctors don't read the research), seek another opinion from a sports-minded doctor.

"Safety limits for total mileage and intensity haven't been determined for pregnant runners, and such limits probably differ among women of varying fitness levels and exercise routines." states Dr. Mona Shangold, director of The Center for Sports Gynecology and Women's Health in Philadelphia. There isn't scientific evidence showing a need for pregnant women to limit the duration and intensity of their runs. Some women have continued to do hard training and racing throughout their pregnancy with no apparent harm to them or their babies. In fact, studies by Dr. James Clapp at Case Western Reserve University show that performance in endurance athletic events may improve during the first twelve to fifteen weeks of pregnancy, before the increase in body weight and uterine size precludes involvement in competitive athletics. This improvement probably results from the increased blood volume and red blood cell mass, which function as a type of "blood doping" that can increase oxygen-carrying capacity. ACOG, however, cautions against exercising too strenuously. If you do decide to race it makes sense to focus on having fun rather than prepregnancy time goals.

Don't compare yourself to others. Every pregnant runner has different experiences, and each of your pregnancies could be different. And don't try to be a hero. At some point during even the healthiest of pregnancies and among the most fit athletes, running almost always becomes too uncomfortable to continue. The commonsense approach is listen to your body and be flexible. If you feel too uncomfortable to run at any point during your pregnancy, walk or swim instead. You don't have to run every day to maintain fitness. Transfer your passion for running to other activities. Cutting back to three days a week or less, combined with cross-training, will keep you fit. Most runners instinctively cut back on their running by one-third to one-half during the last eight to twelve weeks of their pregnancy. Work closely with a sports-minded physician for a personal program that will keep you and baby healthy and fit. Here are some general safety guidelines recommended by doctors:

- Adjust pace as your pregnancy advances. As weight is gained, the body works harder when you run. Since resting heart rate increases by about seven beats in the first weeks of pregnancy and plateaus at approximately sixteen beats per minute faster than the prepregnancy rate after thirty-two weeks, standard heart rate formulas are ineffective. Aim for the intensity that gives you the same perceived effort you expended before pregnancy rather than your normal pace per mile or training heart rate level.
- During pregnancy, fluid needs increase due to expanding blood volume. As you lose fluid in perspiration, blood volume is reduced, making it more difficult for the body to cool down. Drink at least twelve glasses of water a day; stay well-hydrated on runs.
- Shorten runs in hot weather. Consider swimming or working out indoors in air-conditioning during very hot, humid days. Research by Dr. Clapp shows that exercise does not cause the same level of increase in body temperature in pregnant women as it does in nonpregnant women. This may be because the work intensity achieved by pregnant women is not high enough to cause such a rise. Pregnant women may also be able to cool themselves with changes in regional blood flow. Use caution: Research isn't conclusive as to the dangers to the fetus when exercising in heat.
- Stretch carefully. During pregnancy, the body releases the hormone relaxin to loosen your joints and make room for the baby. At this time most pregnant women are more flexible. But this may also increase the risk of an injury from overstretch-

ing if you try to make the same effort as before you became pregnant.

- Run on a smooth track, paved road, or even trail. As your pregnancy advances, your center of gravity shifts. You are more likely to be unstable and to fall if you are running on uneven surfaces.
- If you experience pain, or bleeding while running, or if your water breaks, stop running and contact your physician immediately.
- Cool down properly after running. This helps maintain adequate blood flow to your baby after you have finished exercising.
- You need to gain weight, but not too much. One study found that inactive women gain 39 to 42 pounds during pregnancy compared to about 30 pounds for exercisers. ACOG recommends that most women gain about 25 to 35 pounds. Dr. Clapp's research found that adequate weight gain is achievable for active, pregnant runners. Pregnancy increases requirements by 150 calories a day in the first two trimesters, and by 300 calories per day in the third trimester. Running further increases caloric requirements since you will be exercising and feeding both yourself and baby. To ensure proper weight gain as you continue running, you may need as much as a 20 percent increase in calories compared to a sedentary pregnant woman. Eat according to your appetite, weight scale, and physician's advice. Vitamin, calcium, and iron supplements are generally recommended.

Postpartum running. How much and how fast you can run after the big moment differs from woman to woman. Many doctors recommend waiting about six weeks (longer after a C-section) before running again. Dr. Shangold issued more liberal advice in *Runner's World*: "You can safely resume running when you can do so comfortably. If your baby is born vaginally, this may be as soon as two or three days, depending on whether or not you have an episiotomy. If you have a cesarean birth, wait at least a week or two before returning to running. Regardless of the type of delivery, make sure all soreness and discomfort are gone before you resume running. Pain is usually an indication that healing is incomplete."

How quickly you'll be able to come back will vary according to your prebirth fitness and experiences during and immediately after delivery. Shortly after giving birth, do some stretching and other light exercises to help you recover. Especially concentrate on exercises such as the Pelvic Tilt (Chapter 43) for the abdominal muscles, which get stretched out of shape during pregnancy. Walk before you run. Most women can start walking within a few days following delivery. When you start running, alternate walking with running for the first few sessions. Baby can come along, too (See Chapter 40 for guidelines for baby stroller running). How quickly you regain quality training can vary from a few weeks to a few months or more.

What about breast-feeding? Research shows that moderate exercise has no effect on breast-milk volume, milk composition, or infant weight gain. Moderate exercise that doesn't cause dramatic weight loss may actually enhance nursing, boost energy levels, and reduce the fatigue of nursing mothers. Make sure to consume enough calories to meet the combined demands of running and nursing. You do not have to wait a certain amount of time before or after feeding to run at a moderate pace. If you are planning to run hard, try to schedule it after breast-feeding, or collect milk before a hard run for feeding afterward due to the lactic acid buildup (which causes a sour taste) during intense exercise. A sports bra with wide, nonelastic straps is a must.

Postbaby running performance. In the late 1970s, Dr. Ernst van Aaken theorized that motherhood may help athletic performance. He studied more than fifteen German runners who bore children during their careers. He found that five gave up sports after childbirth, but that of the remaining ten, two were able to maintain prepregnancy performance levels while eight improved measurably. All of the runners agreed that after childbirth they were "tougher" and had more strength and endurance. A study of Olympic athletes showed that half of those who continued training after pregnancy improved their times within a year following delivery.

Dr. Clapp studied women runners who exercised six times a

week for more than 30 minutes for two years. Then, half of them who had planned on conceiving became pregnant. Fifteen months later Dr. Clapp tested the aerobic capacity of all the runners once again. He found the fitness level of the women who had not become pregnant remained unchanged. But of the women who had babies, aerobic capacity had increased by 7 percent even though they had decreased their training. Dr. Clapp theorized that pregnancy has a similar effect on the body as training. Both pregnancy and exercise increase blood volume, bone mass, and metabolic rate. Perhaps running and walking with added weight contributed to fitness also, like exercising with a weighted vest. Other studies suggest that this added aerobic boost may continue for up to three years. All of these studies, however, were conducted with recreational runners rather than serious competitors. Reportedly, in the 1960s and 1970s East German athletes were ordered to become pregnant to boost their performance (then they aborted): It was considered a way of natural blood doping. There is no scientific proof that "pregnancy doping" will help competitive runners improve performance.

In any case, motherhood alone won't make you faster. You certainly will lose a fair amount of fitness while pregnant and while recovering from delivery. Lack of sleep, time constraints, day care, and breast-feeding are just some of the obstacles to overcome. There is also the guilt burden: When you're with your child, you may feel guilty about not being out training; and when you're out running, you may feel guilty about not being with the baby. For every runner that bounces back to run PRs within a year there is another that takes two years or more to regain her competitive fitness. To come back it takes a great deal of time management, cooperative family and friends—and hard work.

Many moms find their desire to train is much stronger after pregnancy. Nine months of greatly decreased running may leave you raring to go. Psychologists speculate that during pregnancy and labor women discover emotional and mental resources that carry over into their running. "No marathon has ever been as difficult as labor," says Joan Benoit Samuelson. Mary Decker Slaney, the U.S. record-holder for the mile, adds, "I've never experienced pain like I did during labor. Now I can push myself so much harder. I don't think women have pushed themselves as far as they can physically, which is why I believe women are going to run a sub-4-minute mile."

Cross-training during pregnancy is a good way to improve your chances of returning to competitive shape more quickly after giving birth. Swimming and deep-water running are good choices to allow for quality training that is more comfortable than running as pregnancy advances.

In sum, there is no reason for a mother (or father) not to run competitively after baby arrives. Even lack of time—the hardest obstacle—can be overcome. Mom and Dad can take turns running, or take the baby along in a running stroller. What about babies that keep you up all night? As I can attest, creative napping is the only solution.

SPORTS BRAS

To be more comfortable, and for reasons of modesty, most women wear a sports bra while running. Many women prefer to wear a fashionable sports bra made of a breathable, wicking fabric as outerwear (forgoing a singlet or T-shirt), particularly when training or racing in hot conditions. Sports bras are designed to minimize discomfort that may occur with breast motion during exercise, particularly just prior to a woman's period. The most important thing is that the sports bra fits comfortably. It should minimize breast motion but not be too constricting, provide for a full range of arm motion, and have seamless cups to prevent irritation. Sports bras utilize one of two basic support systems: compression or encapsulation. Women with small breasts often favor the compression style, which presses both breasts against the chest wall in a single mass. Most women with large breasts prefer the encapsulation style, in which each breast is held separately in a sturdy cup. Since breasts are composed mostly of fat, breast size often decreases with an increase in training. Thus, your sports bra size may change.

SAFETY

This is one of the most annoying issues that women runners must deal with. Running is a positive sport and all runners should feel free to run wherever they want, whenever they want. However, the reality is that many women have been attacked while running. Refer to the safety tips in Chapter 48.

For further information on women's running, refer to Shelly-lynn's *Women Runner's Handbook*.

CHAPTER 40

The Young Competitor

What about kids? If they wish to compete, it's best that they run primarily in events designed for boys and girls their age. Encourage them to experience the joys of running with their peers, as well as participating in a variety of sports. If young kids are gradually introduced to running for fun and later to age-appropriate competition, they are more likely to continue to enjoy running as adults. Following are my guidelines for kids ranging from preschoolers to teens.

PRESCHOOLERS

Kids should be exposed to running at an early age, but not forced into it. Running is a natural extension of play for children. Be sure that this experience is positive, successful, and enjoyable. Otherwise, they will quit, and may never go back to it. Young kids don't think like adults. They could care less about training or fitness. They just want to explore, have fun with friends and their parents, in bits and pieces, at their own pace. To keep them motivated, think like children. If you run with the kids, follow their lead, and when they want, chase them through fields, pick flowers, and play games along the way. Let them dash with you up and down hills playing hide-and-seek in the park. Encourage their erupting enthusiasm. Use your imagination to integrate running into your child's play. Don't force young children to run for long, as very few of them will enjoy nonstop running over any substantial distance. Even at this age parents can get too involved and push their kids to compete against their peers. Let the kids exercise for themselves, not you.

The New York Road Runners Club (NYRRC) pee wee program, which I founded, develops an awareness and joy of running for kids ages two to six. We also introduce them to low-key competition. Winning and losing, the thrills and disappointment of serious competition, can be learned later in life. The program attracts hundreds of kids to events held prior to adult races. The pee wees are divided into groups by age and run distances of one block to a quarter-mile. The kids all get cheered on by their parents and the adults waiting for their race. They develop a feeling that running is fun and something adults encourage. At the finish line everyone is a winner; each kid gets a brightly colored participation ribbon!

I've had several experiences that illustrate the lack of competitive instinct in preschoolers. My favorite was my first event. In 1973, I directed a youth track program in Rome, New York. One evening, we attracted hundreds of kids and adult spectators to a big meet. I had decided to add a new event—"the Pee Wee 440"—and anxiously awaited the results. This was my first experience with four- and five-year-old runners. About twenty kids fidgeted at the starting line of the one-lap race around the school track. They didn't understand the commotion, but they liked the excitement. When the race started, off the kids went with their nervous parents cheering madly. Less than 100 yards into the race, however, the lead runners caught sight of the long-jump pit beside the track. Naturally, they assumed it was a sandbox, and that pretty much ended the race. The kids veered off into the "sandbox" because it looked like more fun than continuing to run around the track.

If preschoolers want to run, encourage them to sprint short distances—maybe a few yards on the track to a sandbox. They may wish to build up to once around the local track or even around the block. Praise them for trying, no matter how fast or slow they run, how many times they stop. Run against them, letting them beat you to boost their self-esteem.

AGES 6 TO 12

Young children should let their bodies fly, but they must be harnessed so that growing bones and minds are not damaged. I do not encourage kids this age to compete in long-distance racing, or to compete in adult-oriented events. I prefer that kids under age twelve run youth-only races of a quarter-mile to 1½ miles—typical distances for competition on the track and for cross-country for kids this age. Research demonstrates that most active prepubescent kids naturally have high aerobic capacity levels. They can run an occasional race of a mile or so without formal training and not risk overexertion. Longer than that requires proper training. Up to 5K road races should be the limit for most kids this age, and they shouldn't overemphasize running competitively at these longer distances. Parents are cautioned: Don't push kids too soon; let your children choose to run and to compete—for themselves, not for you.

To encourage a healthy introduction to competition, I helped the NYRRC develop the age guidelines for their events: "In races of 10K distance or longer, runners must be twelve years of age or older to participate. Races under 10K distance are open to younger runners with their parents permission; however, awards will begin with the twelve- to fourteen-year-old age groups."

It is not appropriate, according to the American Academy of Pediatrics (AAP), for preadolescent children to compete for awards in adult-oriented events. Make the emphasis participating, having fun, and finishing. Kids may benefit from running along with adults if the event is basically a fun run, or if the parent and child run together in races less than 10K and treat it as fun. For reasons of safety, it may be wise in some events for young kids to be supervised by an adult running with them. However, adults should be there to provide support, not push the child to run faster. Run the pace the child chooses, staying a half-step behind. Take as many walk breaks and water stops as they wish. Emphasize fun and fellowship: When my nine-year-old son ran with me for a 4-mile race on Father's Day, we carried water pistols and kept it fun by squirting each other to keep cool. One additional rule: Participation should be the kid's idea of fun, not just the parent's.

Should kids this age train seriously? "Children are not miniature adults," says Greg Payne, P.E.D., professor of human performance at San Jose State University. "Physiologically and psychologically, the two differ dramatically." Various studies show conflicting results about the trainability of prepubescent children. A position statement by the AAP states that kids can improve their aerobic fitness by running; however, improvement is likely to be one-half to two-thirds that of an adult. It's hard to compare exactly because the aerobic capacity of a child's body changes as he or she grows. Payne responds to this position, "From a practical viewpoint, we shouldn't care what our children's max VO_2 values are, only that they are healthy and physically active. I suggest parents downplay intense training for their children and focus instead on correct technique and fun. Kids will still improve this way, only less stressfully."

Larry Greene, Ph.D., and Russ Pate, Ph.D., advise in *Training for Young Distance Runners*, "Considering the physical changes that occur during puberty, we recommend that youths wait until they are at least 12 to 14 years old before training on a regular basis. We define regular training as running 3 to 7 days a week for several months at a time. By 12 to 14 years, most girls and boys will have experienced key pubertal changes that will make them better able to handle the repetitive musculoskeletal stress of distance running."

As the pee wees in our NYRRC program grew up, we organized the Junior Road Runners Club Series. Kids ages seven to fourteen run ½-mile to 1-mile fun runs prior to adult races with all participants receiving finisher's ribbons. Another NYRRC program I founded is City-Sports-For-Kids, a track-and-field program for boys and girls ages five to thirteen. Each year 1,000 kids enjoy this unique program which consists of three 8-week sessions in the spring, summer, and fall. The kids are grouped by age and rotated through different events: sprints, hurdles, distance run, high jump, long jump, and relays. They are exposed to a variety of skills, not just long-distance running. After two weeks of practice, we have a competition each week in a different event. Although we award ribbons to the top finishers to acknowledge excellence, the emphasis is on fun and participation. All kids receive a colorful participation ribbon each week.

A few running clubs exist for kids this age. Some are good; some are bad. Don't allow your child to join one unless he or she really loves to run and wants to learn how to compete. Make sure the competition doesn't get out of hand and that the coaches emphasize sportsmanship and self-improvement, not just winning. Shelly-lynn started her running career as a competitor with the age-group track program in Hornell, New York.

Kids pick up most of their attitudes about fitness and competition during these years. Make sure their experiences are successful and fun. Look at this time as a foundation for a lifetime of running, whether for fitness or competition.

TEENS

I prefer that teens specialize in track and cross-country and save a limited amount of road racing for off-season fun. They run distances from a quarter-mile to 3 miles on their junior high or high school teams. We can only be young once, so enjoy your school races while you can. Besides, getting a good speed base while young will help at longer distances as an adult.

The best sport to build a love of running for teens is cross-country. Most school teams welcome kids of all abilities. Unlike sports like basketball or baseball, cuts aren't necessary and everyone gets to play. Teens may compete, in my opinion, on a low-key basis in road races up to 10K in distance. A select few may train wisely enough and be able to pace themselves appropriately in order to run half-marathons. A few road races can motivate teens to keep up the good work. But be careful of overdoing it. If you don't have a school team, or for whatever reason don't choose to participate, by all means enjoy road racing.

I do not recommend marathons until the late teenage years or older, when young men and women are better able to handle the training and the race distance physically and mentally. This is why the New York City Marathon and many others have a minimum age requirement of eighteen. You can run marathons when you are sixty years old, so why be in a rush?

Most thirteen- to fifteen-year-old runners should limit mileage to less than 30 miles per week. Most high school runners shouldn't go above 40 to 50 miles a week; many should run 20 to 40 miles a week depending upon their event, experience, and enthusiasm for the sport. Teens basically can follow the same training and racing advice as adults detailed in this book for 5K to 10K road races.

RUNNING FOR FITNESS

The earlier a child starts with regular physical activity, the better the foundation for a lifetime of good health and, if they choose, competitive running. The remarkably successful African distance runners started as youngsters by walking and running several miles to and from school as basic transportation. When Shellylynn and I were in grade school it was not unusual to walk or bike a mile or more to school and then go biking or play sports for hours after school. This is no longer the norm. Few kids exercise as a part of their lifestyle. Numerous studies indicate that the fitness level of our children—from preschoolers to teenagers—is poor and getting worse.

It's ideal for kids to run or do other vigorous exercise at least three times a week. *The Runner's Handbook* includes detailed information for helping kids get in shape with running. Here's a general guideline for various ages:

Grades K–3: Build gradually to 1 mile or 10 minutes of running.
Grades 4–6: Build gradually to 2 miles or 20 minutes of running.
Grades 7–12: Build gradually to 3 miles or 30 minutes or running.

The American Alliance for Health, Physical Education, Recreation, and Dance developed noncompetitive goal-times (Figure 40.1) for the 1-mile run-walk for kids ages five to eighteen. Encourage your child to achieve these goal times, which represent "the fitness level required to allow children to move into adulthood full of energy and free of degenerative diseases associated with low levels of fitness."

You might try the incentive system. For example, promise a fancy new pair of running shoes, a mountain bike, or a pair of inline skates if they achieve these goals. If they are way behind the standards at first, give them intermediate goals to gain some success.

FIGURE 40.1: YOUTH FITNESS GOALS

1-mile run/walk: minutes

Age	Girls	Boys
5	14:00	13:00
6	13:00	12:00
7	12:00	11:00
8	11:30	10:00
9	11:00	10:00
10	11:00	9:30
11	11:00	9:00
12	11:00	9:00
13	10:30	8:00
14	10:30	7:45
15–18	10:30	7:30

CAUTIONS FOR KIDS ON THE RUN

According to the AAP, youth are susceptible to the same injuries as adults, particularly those caused by overuse. The major difference is that "growth plate" injuries are a threat to children. According to Dr. Lyle Micheli, director of Sports Medicine at the Children's Hospital in Boston, "During growth, this cartilage is weaker than the rest of the long bones and is more easily injured than mature adult cartilage." Injuries to these growth plates, found at the end of bones, can have significant long-term consequences, including failure to achieve full height. If kids are running more than a few miles at a time a few times a week, it is important to have well-cushioned shoes to protect their growing bodies. Also, gradually build up the training. Too much too soon can be just as damaging to a young body as an old one.

The AAP warns that a child's body is not as efficient as an adult's in controlling its temperature. Kids don't generate as much heat in the cold weather and cool their bodies as well in the heat, so are at special risk for hypothermia and heat illness. Make sure your child learns the value of dressing properly in cold weather, and drinking plenty of fluids in hot weather. On hot days play it safe. Go swimming, not running.

The longest-lasting injury to kids is psychological. A California study by Dr. Harmon Brown found that after two years, half the children who started a running program had quit. After three years, 75 percent had stopped, and after four years, 85 percent weren't running at all. Why? Most of them had taken up long-distance running because of their parents. The impetus, of course, must come from the child, and support and direction from the parent. Never force kids to run or race.

Despite these many words of caution, the AAP recognizes that there is no medical proof why children should be precluded from long-distance running. Their official position stand: "If children enjoy the activity and are asymptomatic, there is no reason to preclude them from training for, and participating in, such events." The biggest danger to running kids according to the AAP: Pushy parents! Let the kids run for fun, for themselves, and they'll be more likely to be lifetime runners.

BABY STROLLER RUNNING

Parents often find that training time is restricted when baby comes along. I sure did! With baby stroller running you can keep fit while enjoying special time with your child. Also important: You get to show off your precious baby to all your running friends along your trails. Here are some tips for safety and training learned while pushing my youngster a few hundred miles:

- Run at any easy pace—about the heart rate level you would run at without the stroller. Once you are fit and ready for more of a challenge, push the baby and stroller up hills. You'll find the increased weight will make you work a lot harder.
- Think first of the safety of your child, not your workout. Running down hills or at high speeds lessens your ability to control the stroller. Walk down steep hills rather than risk losing control. Walk or stop if any sign of danger appears, such as bikers coming toward you at full speed. Run in parks at times when they are not congested. Do not run on roads with car traffic.

- *Do not* run in races pushing your child in a stroller. Show him or her off before or after your race. Consider the following guideline:

  "The Road Runners Club of America strongly recommends against the participation of baby strollers/joggers in road races and against race organizers creating baby stroller divisions. The reason for this recommendation is that the inclusion of strollers in races increases the potential for injury to race participants and the children. The RRCA has no objection to and does not discourage the safe and prudent use of strollers or baby joggers in training situations."
- Use only a well-made stroller with good shock absorption. Do not use lightweight, collapsible ones with small front wheels that pivot. They are made for walking the streets, not running. The front wheels may catch in a crack and catapult both baby and running parent. Standard, sturdy baby carriages may be used but are heavy and awkward for running. Specially designed running strollers are comfortable for both baby and parent. Choose one with a hand brake. It is a big help when you're trying to get your baby in and out, and it can help slow you down when you need to stop. A wrist tether is also recommended so that you and baby stay together. Look for a stroller with easily adjustable handles to fit the height of both Mom and Dad. This is important to your running comfort. Pick one that is easy to run with. It should be lightweight but sturdy and able to roll smoothly over roads as well as easily make it over curbs and rough terrain.
- Be prepared. Dress your child more warmly than yourself. Your body temperature will rise as you run, but the child is sitting still. Further, the wind resistance will cause the baby to be cooler as well. Be sure to bring extra clothing to keep you both

comfortable. Don't forget the diapers! Be especially careful in cold weather to protect the baby's skin from frostbite and in sunny weather to protect against the sun.

- The baby should be strapped in very securely. A full harness is best. Increase the baby's comfort by shifting the child to different positions during the run. Be prepared to take breaks and let the child out for his or her exercise.

PART XI

ILLNESS AND INJURY

CHAPTER 41

Illness

Running can help you fend off illness, or it can contribute to it. Whether the common cold or flu, or such maladies as allergies, asthma, air pollution, osteoarthritis, and gastrointestinal problems, illnesses affect training, race times, and good health.

IMMUNITY

The immune system is a complex defense that suppresses and eliminates infections. Among its challenges are a wide range of diseases. Some are viral; some are bacterial; and still others have other causes. These agents that invade your body live everywhere—in the air; on dust particles, food and plants; on and in animals and humans; in soil and water; and on virtually every other surface. They range from microscopic organisms to larger parasites. A healthy immune system usually controls these invading agents, but if that system becomes weakened or you encounter an organism to which you have not built up a resistance, illness follows. The following guidelines mostly pertain to colds and flus which are caused by viruses, but may also apply to many other illnesses that may affect your running.

Ninety percent of us come down with upper respiratory infections each year. Despite millions of dollars spent in research, a cure for the common cold and flu have yet to be discovered. Decongestants, cough suppressants, antihistamines, and other medicines only relieve some of the symptoms. Many runners have their own remedies that they swear by: chicken soup, peppermint tea, bee pollen. None of these will hurt you in moderation, and may even make you feel better. In fact, research demonstrates that vitamin C and zinc lozenges may reduce the duration of cold symptoms.

No matter what your mom said, running in the rain won't cause a cold or flu. Only a virus can do that. It can catch us two ways: by air or by touch. The virus can be passed on by people who sneeze or cough it into the air we breathe, or it can get into your body when you touch a virus-contaminated surface and then rub your nose, eyes, or mouth. Eluding these viruses requires a simple change of lifestyle—avoid all people! At least shun crowds and obviously sick people. Keep at least 3 feet away from coughers and sneezers. Avoid sharing water bottles, towels, or food with others who might be carrying a virus. Wash your hands frequently to prevent viruses from traveling from hand to face. The surest way to catch a cold or flu is to be exposed to lots of kids.

Running in cold, dry weather can dry out the lining of the nasal passages, which makes it easier for infectious agents to penetrate. Drink plenty of fluids all day, wear cold-air masks when running, and use humidifiers at home and the office to ensure that your nasal passages and mucous membranes stay well hydrated. Annual flu shots minimize risks. Get one if you have existing health conditions, such as sensitive bronchials. Various studies indicate supplements of up to 1,000 milligrams per day of vitamin C are associated with a significant reduction in colds.

Can you run away from the common cold, flu, and other illnesses by enhancing immunity with exercise? Yes, and no. Exercise physiologist David Nieman's research at Appalachian State University found moderate exercise, up to about 45 minutes per day or about 30 miles a week, appears to minimize illness. This may be because the number of white blood cells and antibodies circulating through the bloodstream increase during exercise, making it easier for those virus-fighting cells to do their job. High weekly mileage and extended intense exercise sessions, however, decrease some types of these virus-fighters, increasing the risk of illness. Runners averaging more than 60 miles a week experience twice as many illnesses as those training 20 miles a week or less. But it seems if you adjust to a mileage level—whether it be 20 miles per week or 60—that your body can tolerate, then you may continue to improve immunity. If you push the mileage and intensity up too much, however, you may overwhelm your defenses to illness. There is a fine line between training for peak performance and overtraining that leads to illness.

What about marathoners? Research shows that marathon runners may experience fewer illnesses in the early stages of their training. Nieman investigated runners averaging two marathons a year for twelve years. They had a far greater killer cell activity than nonexercisers. However, in a survey of runners who trained for the Los Angeles Marathon, more than 40 percent had at least one cold or flu episode during the two months prior to the race. You may be even more vulnerable after a marathon. These studies found that 12.9 percent of the marathoners suffered an upper respiratory infection the week after the marathon. Only 2.2 percent of runners who trained for the race but didn't run it got sick. The marathoners showed a drop of 30 to 40 percent in immune cell activity almost immediately after the race. A similar result takes place after shorter races or hard workouts, although it appears the marathon is significantly more taxing on the immune system. This depression is usually short-lived: The immune system remains suppressed for only six to eight hours. Take extra care to avoid people with colds and/or flu symptoms for the next few hours after hard running.

"The best advice for maintaining an effective immune system in heavy exercisers" states Nieman, "is to space vigorous workouts and races, avoid overtraining, eat a balanced, high-carbohydrate, low-fat diet, keep life stresses as low as possible, obtain adequate sleep, and avoid chronic fatigue." During an emotionally tough time, postpone hard training; sleep at consistent times and nap if necessary. Traveling across time zones also weakens the immune system.

SHOULD YOU RUN WHEN YOU'RE SICK?

That depends on the severity of your illness. Research by Thomas Weidner, Ph.D., at Ball State University suggests that exercising with a cold has no impact on the cold's severity or duration. Further, he found that the illness caused no significant impairment of pulmonary function, maximum oxygen consumption, maximum heart rate, or perceived exertion. These findings suggest that an "average" cold does not significantly impair performance even though many runners may believe it does.

Dr. Randy Eichner, chief of hematology at the University of Oklahoma, suggests using the neck test since the common cold is usually confined to the head. If symptoms are located above the neck, such as a runny nose, sneezing, a slight headache, or scratchy throat, it is probably okay for you to run, but with caution. He suggests running easy for a few minutes. If you feel okay, it should be all right to finish the run. "But if your head pounds with every step, go home and rest," he advises. If symptoms are below the neck, such as a fever, muscle ache, vomiting, diarrhea, loss of appetite, or a hacking cough deep within the chest, Dr. Eichner advises you not to run. Running when this sick may prolong illness. Further, a viral infection of the heart muscle has been linked to sudden death.

It is difficult and often unpleasant to run when feeling lousy. Rest, drink plenty of fluids, and come back when you're feeling better. If your temperature is more than 100 degrees Fahrenheit, wait until your fever breaks before running. The rule of thumb is to expect to feel terrible as long as a fever lasts, and then take twice that time to overcome the symptoms. If feeling ill, cut back mileage (or don't run at all), slow the pace, and run within the limitations of your energy.

COMING BACK FROM ILLNESS

You may be surprised how quickly you lose endurance to illness. Your comeback may even be slower than following an injury. When resuming running, if there's no daily improvement in your health and running, stop and rest some more. Do not train hard until completely recovered. Relapses are common, so be careful. If you don't take time off and care for that illness, the layoff may be longer. Sometimes an illness is actually a blessing: It may be a warning sign of overtraining and the layoff may actually prevent an injury.

When returning after significant illness, start first with 20 to 30 minutes of easy running, possibly even alternating with walking. Run every other day. Increase runs gradually to the distance you normally run. But continue to run one day and rest the next until you are back to full strength. Give yourself one or two days of building up for every day lost to illness. After training for at least a week at your normal training mileage, ease back into speed training by doing half of your normal workout at a reduced but brisk pace. If this goes well, you should be able to return to regular competitive training the following week. Don't race until you have trained without difficulty for at least two consecutive weeks.

ALLERGIES

As many as 40 million Americans are nagged by allergies, an exaggerated immune-system response to an ordinarily harmless substance (allergen). There is no evidence that running causes allergies, but running outdoors gives sufferers added trouble by exposing them to annoying allergens by contact or inhalation. Exposure can cause physical reactions in sensitive individuals—sneezing and coughing attacks; runny nose or itchy and watery eyes; bronchial, lung, and sinus infections; headaches; asthma; sore throat and mouth; skin irritation and rashes; fatigue; difficulty sleeping. Allergy symptoms interfere with the mechanics of breathing, reducing the amount of oxygen available to the working muscles. Additionally, there is the psychological factor: Fearing shortness of breath, runners may not push as hard. Needless to say, it's hard to train with these symptoms and race times suffer.

Shelly-lynn and I battle allergies year-round. Most suffer only seasonally—their symptoms appear at about the same time every year. You may be allergy-free for most of your life, like me, and then gradually find yourself more and more sensitive to more and more allergens.

Mother Nature challenges us with three types of allergens: pollen from weeds, grasses and trees; mold spores; and dust mites. It's hard to avoid these irritants because they are so small you can't see them. You may also be allergic to other sources, including certain foods.

Don't let allergies defeat you. Learn to prevent them before they interfere with your running, and general comfort. Search for the causes. You might figure this out yourself by judging how your body reacts to different irritants. An allergist can test to determine sensitivities and recommend a program to minimize problems. Also, limit your exposure. Here are some tips:

Regulate humidity. Mold spores and dust mites thrive in moist conditions; dryness contributes to bronchial problems. Keep humidity at 40 to 50 percent in your house and office by using dehumidifiers and humidifiers. Monitor with humidity gauges.

Clean regularly. Eliminate mold or mildew with a strong cleanser. Clean your heating system annually. Encase mattress and pillows in a washable cover designed to contain dust mites. Wash bedding in hot water regularly. Clean your home and office often to eliminate dust and mold buildup. Vacuum rugs regularly or eliminate them. Clean pets and their bedding frequently.

Run away from your problems. This may mean changing favorite routes during allergy season. Most allergens are seasonal. Find out what time of year you need to avoid which pollens. Many newspapers print a daily "allergy watch."

Schedule runs to minimize the problem. Run later in the day, when pollen levels are lower. Plants produce the most pollen between 5:00 and 10:00 A.M. Pollens are spread around more on windy days. Wait for the wind to die down before starting your run if your allergies are bothering you. A good time to run is after a rain since it clears pollens from the air and washes it away. Mold spores, however, may cause more of a problem when it is wet.

Protect yourself from pollens. Try a face mask that filters out pollen. Glasses or sunglasses provide protection from eye irritants. After running, shower immediately to eliminate allergens attached to your body and hair. If pollen counts are high and you are very sensitive, work out indoors. Air-conditioning and air filters clean pollens from the air. Keep windows closed all day during high pollen periods.

Consider medications. Try an over-the-counter (OTC) antihistamine or decongestant tablet a half hour before running. Choose one that doesn't cause drowsiness. Unfortunately, many OTC drugs may cause side effects that impair performance. Your doctor may prescribe inhalants, sprays, or tablets that don't have these problems. Alternatives to medicine that help some people include vitamin C, various herbs, and garlic. Allergy shots may be effective.

Learn to be flexible. Adjust your training and racing schedule according to allergy symptoms. I can continue to run for fun and fitness despite my allergies, but need to cut back on hard running and racing when my allergies are bothering me.

ASTHMA

Approximately a quarter of Americans have this respiratory disease. Symptoms may appear at any age. They may come on suddenly or gradually, and then they may disappear. Asthma strikes both the sedentary and the very fit. It is a condition in which the airways are constricted and/or obstructed as a result of sensitivity to allergens and other irritants such as cigarette smoke, auto exhaust, household dust, insects, pollens, molds, cold and dry air, certain foods, fatigue, respiratory infections, emotional stress—even exercise. These irritants can inflame the airways, or bronchi. The muscles surrounding the bronchi tighten or spasm, and the airways become narrower, causing an asthma attack. Symptoms include coughing, wheezing, chest tightness, and rapid breathing. For years I suffered from a chronic cough, sore throats, and periodic flulike symptoms. Then, while running hard up a hill on a cold, dry day, I suddenly felt as if I were trying to breathe through a straw. After a series of tests, doctors concluded that I was suffering from a mild asthma made worse by allergies, cold weather, and—oh my—exercise. By running regularly, using inhalants prior to running, and wearing a cold air mask, I am still able to run and race. In fact, running helps me cope with the asthma.

Asthma affects the exerciser in two ways: regular asthma and exercise-induced asthma (EIA). Many runners have both types. Approximately 10 percent of all exercisers suffer from EIA. Joseph Kolb, a sports medicine specialist, wrote in *Running Times*: "The exact causes of EIA are still unclear. The consensus is that it's caused by a cooling and drying of the respiratory tract from the increased air movement associated with exercise. This effect is heightened when the air is cool and dry, but EIA can also strike on warm, humid days when the atmosphere can be a storage tank for pollutants, pollen and mold. Whatever the weather, the ensuing inflammatory response results in a release of irritating chemicals, such as histamine, that cause bronchial spasms and fluid accumulation."

Asthmatic runners often have coughing, discomfort, or fatigue after 5 to 10 minutes of hard running, or after stopping the run. EIA affects various people differently. Some are irritated only during certain workouts, others may face EIA every time they run. Symptoms usually abate within an hour.

Here are some tips for asthmatic runners:

Get fit. The higher your fitness level, the more you can tolerate higher workloads and the less you will labor when breathing, thus decreasing irritation of the airways.

Eliminate triggers. Exercise indoors if pollens are high or it's very cold. When having a bad streak with asthma, back off the running and switch to swimming. This is the best exercise for asthmatics because of the warm, humid conditions of indoor pools. If you do go out under these conditions, wear a mask to warm and moisten the air and screen pollen. Find the time of day that minimizes problems. Since allergies contribute to asthma, follow previous guidelines for limiting allergen exposure.

Use inhalers. Three types, prescribed by a doctor, may minimize symptoms. Steroids prevent inflammation of the lungs. These are taken daily during periods of persistent problems. Cromolyn sodium is used 10 to 20 minutes prior to running to help prevent drying of the airways and decrease the sensitivity of cell membranes that store histamine in the lungs, preventing its release. This will offer protection for about two hours. A beta-adrenergic inhaler relaxes the muscles of the airways and opens them up. Take it 10 to 20 minutes prior to running, after any hard workout, and at any time you're experiencing difficulty breathing. This type of bronchodilator can be carried with you to be used in case of a flare-up during or after a run. A few puffs may allow you to regain control of your breathing and complete your run.

Warm up. EIA usually occurs about 5 to 10 minutes after you begin a steady, hard run, when your heart rate reaches about 80 percent of maximum. You can minimize EIA by warming up properly, thus dilating bronchial tubes and/or "tricking" the body into causing a minor asthma attack. This triggers a "refractory period" during which the symptoms diminish or disappear for two to four hours. Studies show you can minimize EIA by jogging slowly for 30 minutes, then resting for 20 minutes prior to an intense run.

Cool down gradually. A slow jog and then walk is recommended for 10 to 15 minutes. Sudden changes in the temperature of the air reaching your lungs can trigger an attack. If I suddenly stop after a hard run on a cold day I start coughing.

Breathe properly. Avoid fast, shallow breaths and practice "belly breathing." As you inhale, the stomach should go out. During workouts and races, I often sigh or hum, blowing out against pursed lips in cold weather.

Take caffeine. A cup or two of coffee, tea, or cola may help dilate bronchial tubes.

Drink up. Take in plenty of fluids before, during, and after running, especially in dry conditions, to inhibit bronchial drying.

AIR POLLUTION

Here is where man works with Mother Nature to create health problems. Air pollution levels can get so high public health warnings are issued. People are told to stay indoors, to not exercise outside.

Warm temperatures combined with air pollution increase the effect on lung function and running performance. If you run on hot, hazy days, you may have had an experience similar to mine. One summer New York City was in the middle of a terrible heat wave: three straight days with temperatures higher than 100 degrees Fahrenheit. Warnings were issued against exercising strenuously in the high-ozone levels. I didn't think much about going out and running for an hour at a fairly brisk pace. Near the end of my run I felt fatigued, lightheaded, and then nauseous. Later came a headache and diarrhea. That was one more reason to move my running gear to the country.

Our respiratory systems are exposed to more pollution when we run than people breathing at rest. The difference is 6 quarts of air per minute at rest compared to 80 to 100 quarts while running briskly. Not only can short-term exposure to air pollutants affect your running, but it can also cause coughing, wheezing, headaches, nausea, eye, nose and throat irritation, and other health problems. Chronic exposure may cause more serious pulmonary problems such as bronchitis and emphysema.

Pollution is at its worst in the United States from May to September. In warm weather areas like Southern California, it lasts almost year-round. Keep track of the air pollution levels through news reports. If the air quality in your area becomes "unacceptable," postpone your outdoor run to another day, or at least shorten the distance and cut back the pace. Some runners wear air filter masks for protection.

Two major enemies of runners today are ozone and carbon monoxide; other air contaminants include sulfur dioxide, lead, and nitrogen dioxide.

Ozone. Ground-level ozone is a colorless, toxic gas produced by sunlight reacting with vehicle exhaust and industry emissions. Urban areas in valleys and basins tend to trap the highest level of these pollutants. Research has found a 10 percent drop in aerobic capacity among exercisers breathing ozone at peak levels in smog-prone cities. That means you run 10 percent slower with the same effort! Ozone levels peak on hot, sunny, windless afternoons. The best time to run for minimum ozone exposure is morning or late evening.

Carbon monoxide. Odorless, colorless carbon monoxide spews from the exhaust pipes of internal-combustion vehicles. This very toxic pollutant is quickly absorbed by the body and attaches itself to hemoglobin, reducing the red blood cells' capacity to transport oxygen to your muscles. The worst place to run is along a highway or busy street. Studies indicate that it takes more than eight hours for hemoglobin to return to normal after a 60-minute exposure to peak rush-hour levels of carbon monoxide. A study at New York Hospital–Cornell University Medical Center found running for 30 minutes near heavy New York City traffic increased the blood's carbon monoxide levels as much as tenfold. This is the equivalent of smoking a pack of cigarettes! Unlike ozone, which is mostly a hot weather problem, carbon monoxide is still a danger in cool weather. The highest levels of vehicle exhaust are rush hours: from 6:30 to 9:30 A.M., and from 3:30 to 6:30 P.M. Run in open spaces, where wind currents help dissipate the exhausts, and as far from traffic as possible. Pollutants from vehicles dissipate quickly beyond 50 feet from roadways.

OSTEOARTHRITIS

Running does not cause osteoarthritis. In fact, it may prevent it from developing and help in the management of arthritic pain. Steven Blair, director of epidemiology at the Institute for Aerobic Research in Dallas, sorted through the data of nearly 5,000 exercisers and nonexercisers. He found no evidence of increased arthritis in knees or hips of runners, even those who competed at long distances. Exercise lubricates the various joint components and allows the connective tissue to function at the highest level possible. It can help arthritics retain maximum range of motion, and allow the person to move less stiffly and with less pain. Range of motion stretching exercises and weight training, combined with aerobic exercise, are recommended for most arthritics by the Arthritis Foundation.

Runners with arthritis should take a few days off when it becomes bothersome; instead, substitute swimming or biking. If arthritis exists in your joints, particularly hip or knees, a weight-bearing exercise may be harmful. Increased joint pain with running is a sign that exercise is doing more harm than good. Also, running is generally not advised for those suffering from rheumatoid arthritis.

GASTROINTESTINAL (GI) PROBLEMS

Exercise-related GI problems include nausea, vomiting, bloating, heartburn, acid redux, diarrhea, and GI bleeding. They strike not only the average runner, but Elites as well. Bob Kempainen gained considerable notoriety after he vomited several times on national television in the late stages of the U.S. Olympic Trials Marathon, and then again after crossing the finish line—in first place. The extreme effort of racing, whether the fast effort of a short race or the extensive endurance of a marathon, can cause exhaustion, dehydration, and hyperthermia, which can result in nausea, vomiting, and other problems. I sometimes experience annoying "dry heaves" as I near the finish of races. This is apparently caused by the physical and emotional stress associated with trying to push my body faster than it is capable (at least that was the diagnosis given by a doctor who tired of hearing me heave while chasing him in races). With better pacing, improved speed training, and attention to controlled breathing, I'm able to at least put off the heaves for when I've crossed the finish line.

Perhaps the most disturbing, and embarrassing, problem runners may face is "runner's trots." Various surveys show that as many as one-third of long distance racers have had diarrhea during or after their events. Uta Pippig visibly battled diarrhea but held on to win the 100th Boston Marathon.

GI conditions have a myriad of potential causes. Combining running and digesting can cause problems. The up-and-down pounding action jars the intestines. The body diverts blood needed for digestion to the working muscles. Blood flow to the GI tract is reduced by 60 to 70 percent for easy runs, as much as 80 percent for strenuous runs. So any prerun food that hasn't yet digested, or fuels consumed on the run, may hang around and cause trouble.

Train your stomach for racing along with the rest of your body. Learn what works for you, practice it, and stay with it. How well your body tolerates fueling is also affected by how well you handle emotional stress. Nervous racers tend to be more sensitive and should control stomach distress with stress management. Dehydration also sets you up for nausea or worse. In one study, 80 percent of runners who lost at least 4 percent of their body weight due to fluid losses during a marathon experienced GI symptoms. The solution to stomach distress for short races may be to skip food and drink. But for races an hour or longer this strategy will severely limit performance and risk heat illness.

Before and during runs, avoid foods high in dietary fiber, protein, or fat, as well as highly concentrated drinks such as fruit juices. Carbs are more easily digested on the run, when the stomach is operating at less than full efficiency. But carbs need to be taken in the proper concentration. Sports bars or gels provide needed fuel, but they'll also contribute to unneeded intestinal distress if they aren't taken with sufficient water to ensure proper absorption. I've experienced problems after consuming sports drinks during races that weren't properly diluted. In fact, my stomach still churns when I recall one such experience in the Boston Marathon that made Kempainen's spewing look tame by comparison. My lesson learned: If the drink tastes too strong, take water as soon as possible to dilute it.

Sudden changes in your daily diet, excessive amounts of vitamin C, sugary, or high-fiber foods may cause trouble, as well as dairy products (check for lactose intolerance). Gas-producing foods (such as beans, broccoli, and eggs) may cause bloating. A good way to determine why you have GI problems is to keep a daily food and running diary. Note when you ate and ran, what you ate, and how far and fast you ran. Especially note what and when you ate prior to running, and any stomach problems you had on the run. Look for trends that might solve the mystery, and adjust accordingly. Consult a sports nutritionist for guidance if problems persist.

Drugs of any kind may cause problems. Caffeine may stimulate performance, but it may also stimulate the intestines. Anti-inflammatories taken before running may help you cope with discomfort, but may also cause stomach distress. Some drugs may help you cope with GI problems. Over-the-counter antacids taken in limited quantity may be effective to treat heartburn, nausea, and acid reflux; antigas products may minimize bloating. Taking an antidiarrheal medication before running may help prevent diarrhea. Discuss potential side effects, such as interfering with heat dissipation, for any medications with your sports doctor.

Stomach distress is my most convincing warning sign of overtraining. An exceptionally hard run or race, a tiring long run, or sudden increases in training may cause an upset stomach or trigger the trots, especially under hot weather conditions where dehydration may also be a key factor. Try training at a different time of day if morning running tends to cause diarrhea. Another problem is bloody stools. This is reasonably common, in fact studies show that 23 percent of marathoners experience blood loss in their feces, although they often don't notice it. Excessive or persistent blood loss should be reported to your sports doctor.

Some medical problems, including lactose intolerance, glucose intolerance, and irritable bowel syndrome, may go undetected if not for the additional stress of running. The trots may have more serious causes including parasitic infection. So, see a doctor if problems don't clear up or worsen, especially if you have bloody stools, which could be a sign of serious bowel disease, including cancer.

Your best defense against GI distress is regularity. Eat, sleep, run, and have bowel movements on a regular schedule. Establish a prerun bowel movement routine. This might mean having a cup of coffee or going for a walk in order to trigger the urge for a bowel movement. I bring toilet paper (paper towels hold up best when wet with sweat or rain) with me on the run. If I forget, I'm sure to be cursed by the trots.

CHAPTER 42

Injury

There may be nothing worse than an injured runner! Fuss, fuss, fuss. Whine, whine, whine. Surveys indicate that 65 to 80 percent of competitive runners get an injury each year that results in significant loss of training time (more than three days). Fortunately, running injuries are rarely permanent. They will go away in time, but may come back if you don't learn from the experience.

Running injuries were labeled "diseases of excellence" by running guru, Dr. George Sheehan. While striving to improve race times, we are more prone to injury than those who don't train as hard. Like other athletes in other sports, accept the fact that this is a part of competitive training. Too much training may lead to injury, too little to underachievement. Learn to determine these outer limits for yourself and strive for the injury-free competitive area between. Often this is what makes the difference in reaching goals at all levels of competition. The runner who frequently loses training time won't be in as good shape as one who was able to train consistently.

The best predictors of injury are previous injuries, consecutive days run, and weekly mileage. Half of all injuries are recurrences of previous problems. Most runners benefit with one or more off days each week. Higher-mileage runners may actually have less risk per mile, but due to the volume their total risk is greater. One study estimates that runners experience injury, on the average, once per 150 to 200 hours of running. According to podiatrist Dr.

Murray Weisenfeld, author of *The Runner's Repair Manual*, most injuries appear after mileage creeps past 40 per week.

Most injuries are one of two types: acute or overuse. Acute injuries occur suddenly when stress is applied too abruptly for tissues to adapt. Examples include trauma, overstretching, and running fast without proper warm-up. Overuse injuries occur gradually when tissues are repeatedly stressed too much over a period of time. They usually give warning signs as they progress. What gets injured most? Knee injuries lead the way followed closely by the feet. Others ranking high: Achilles tendon/calf, hip/groin, ankle, shin splints, quadriceps, hamstrings, lower back.

Most running injuries are caused by training errors. Few overuse injuries are caused by a single factor, such as one particular run or race. Underlying the occurrence of shin splints, for example, may be several contributing factors, such as poor running form, a biomechanically weak foot, tight calf muscles, and worn-down running shoes. Most injuries do not occur suddenly, although you might think so. They are caused by a gradual and often predictable overstressing of a susceptible part of the body. Injuries may seem to happen for no reason at all, but there are reasons. You just have to ask yourself some questions. If you become injured, review the following checklist to see if you can determine the causes.

QUESTIONS TO ASK WHEN INJURED

- What have you done differently that may have caused the problem?
- Are you doing too much, too soon? Any sudden changes in mileage, speed, hills?
- Are you overtraining or overracing? Undertrained for the race distance?
- Are you recovering properly from races and hard workouts?
- Do you have unequal leg length, or biomechanically weak feet? Do you overpronate or oversupinate?
- Are opposing muscles (abdominals, quadriceps, shin area) relatively weak?

- Do you have sufficient flexibility? Do you stretch properly and regularly?
- Do you warm up and cool down properly?
- Do you have previous injuries? Did you return from an injury too quickly?
- Do you have good running form?
- Are you training on uneven or slanted terrain? Have you changed from one running surface to another? Have you been running in poor footing?
- Have you changed shoes? Are they in good repair?
- Are you overweight or underweight? Is your diet adequate for your training?
- Are you taking proper care of your feet?
- Have you changed any daily habits, such as driving, sitting or lifting more?
- Are you getting enough sleep? Are you under a lot of stress?
- Is playing other sports or doing other physical activity affecting your running?

WARNING SIGNS FOR INJURY

An important part of competitive training is learning to recognize warning signs early. Mild stiffness or tenderness that doesn't go away after a day of rest or after the first few minutes of a run is one of the first signals. The most obvious warning is pain. It's a sure signal that something's wrong. Pain should be heeded. Your body yells at you for a reason; without it you would continue to train, resulting in more serious injury. Runners can push through discomfort; pain is different.

Most early warning signals are mild. Don't panic; but don't ignore them. If they persist, cut back on the distance, frequency, and intensity of runs. Take a day or two off, or more. Too many runners think cutting back, resting, or taking time off makes them a wimp. Some worry they will lose valuable training time. Taking a few days or weeks off from running, over the long span of your career, will make very little difference.

Frank Shorter, the Olympic Marathon gold medalist, advises: "Staying healthy is a question of how quickly you can get beyond denial and deal with the reality. You then have an opportunity to back off that little bit you need to recover. And it doesn't take much adjustment, because what I've found is that you don't have to back off a lot if you can recognize the potential problem soon enough. My test is, any time you get to a point where something is truly interfering with your running gait, back off and let it heal. Don't keep going simply because you can keep going."

Listen to your body. Don't try to prove toughness by ignoring warning signs of injury. But, don't stop running at every little ache. When in doubt, back off. Watch for what troubles you or gives you pain. If the symptoms persist, see a sports doctor as a precaution. Don't be cheap here: You'll save on medical bills in the long run by seeking help early. A helpful aid is your diary. It may reveal the warning signs of previous injury. Rereading past experiences will help prevent future injury.

GRADING INJURIES

Most injuries come on gradually, allowing you time to listen to the warning signs and prevent more serious injury. Typically, injuries progress through the following four stages or grades, according to Tim Noakes, M.D., author of *The Lore of Running*:

Grade-one injuries. These minor aches and pains (such as hamstring tightness) often aren't noticed until a few hours after runs. They are early warning signs.

Grade-two injuries. They result in some discomfort, but not pain, during running. The hamstring tightness, for example, may now come on during a run. This stage doesn't interfere with performance, but it is only one step away from it.

Grade-three injuries. These may cause severe discomfort and pain, which limits training and racing performance. At this point that hamstring may hurt enough to throw off your stride. Back off your training and see a sports doctor.

Grade-four injuries. They are so bad you can't run. You waited too long to back off and now you have no choice. Medical treatment and rest are a must.

PSYCHOLOGICAL ASPECTS OF INJURY

Most runners experience psychological difficulty when injured and forced to stop running. They focus on the injury and become depressed from inactivity and lost training time. Yale psychiatry professor Dr. Victor Altshul notes that those who must temporarily give up running go through sequential emotional stages of loss similar to what one might experience with the death of a loved one. The five stages are:

1. ***Denial.*** Often runners will not accept their injuries and continue to run in pain until it forces them to stop.
2. ***Rage.*** Runners acknowledge they should stop running. However, they refuse and subject their bodies to more abuse. They may take out their frustrations on others.
3. ***Depression.*** After the anger subsides, runners become depressed and experience feelings of helplessness.
4. ***Acceptance.*** Runners accept injuries, and contain training within levels of tolerance. They may participate in alternative exercises to ease their depression. They develop an intelligent plan to return gradually to their preinjury fitness level.
5. ***Renewed neurotic disequilibrium.*** As runners begin to regain fitness, some forget the cause of injuries and neglect the warning signs of further injury. Too often they don't learn from experience and again attempt too much too soon, or train for goals that are beyond their present physical and psychological capacity.

Most runners, whether strongly or marginally addicted, will experience withdrawal symptoms after one to three days without running. These may include: insomnia, irritability, depression, tension, constipation, headaches, or muscle twinges. Here are some guidelines to help you get over the blues:

Accept your injury. Analyze why it happened, and determine the causes. Treat the injury properly; seek medical attention if necessary. You will be able to return to your training schedule if you allow the healing process the time it needs.

Stick to routines. If you usually run every morning, for example, at least go for morning walks if you can't run. Keeping close to your normal training rituals will help you continue to reap the psychological benefits of regular exercise.

Maintain your relationships and running friendships. Don't reject family, friends, or coworkers. Don't take out frustrations on them or withdraw from them during your inactivity. One of the worst aspects of being injured is not being able to run with training partners. Keep in touch, help time a few workouts, or go to races to cheer on your friends. It will minimize your sense of loss.

Think positively. Look at the injury as a scheduled rest period during your lifelong training program. Think of it as a time to improve strengthening and stretching programs, or enjoy cross-training options.

Take a break. Use the extra time to do things you couldn't while training, such as taking a trip with the family that isn't dependent on a big race.

Replace the habit. The sooner you bike or swim, for example, the easier it will be to defeat the depression and the better shape you'll be in when returning to running.

Return to running with realistic expectations. Be patient and conservative. You won't get it all back right away.

DETRAINING

Unfortunately, fitness is quickly lost when you stop all training. But how quickly? David Costill, Ph.D., answers in *Inside Running*: "In general, there is no loss for five to seven days. As a matter of fact, running performance may even be improved after two to five days of inactivity. Such rest periods allow the muscles and nervous system to recover and rebuild from the stress of training and provide the runner with improved energy reserves and tolerance of endurance exercise."

A few days off won't hurt. But beyond that deconditioning takes place quickly. The sad truth is you lose fitness much faster than you gain it. You'll lose approximately 2 to 3 percent of fitness per week of inactivity. At that rate, you could lose 3 to 5 minutes off your 10K time after a month or two off. Ed Coyle, Ph.D., studied detraining at the University of Texas. Two trends were observed: Highly trained athletes lost the most fitness; and the greatest loss happened at first and then fitness lessened more slowly but steadily. All the athletes were completely detrained by three months. Costill's studies show that even the most gifted runners are nearly indistinguishable from sedentary people after six to twelve months of inactivity.

If you experience a long layoff and become detrained, take heart in the knowledge that most researchers believe that former runners can regain fitness faster than their sedentary friends can gain it. "The muscles may have some memory," says Costill, "or maybe we are smarter with our training the second time." Further, the data above reflects total inactivity. The more active you are while off the running paths, the less you will decondition.

RUNNING THROUGH AND COMING BACK FROM INJURY

Don't give up in frustration if you develop a nagging injury. Learn to manage it properly and adjust workouts to keep in shape while recovering. Absolute rest from the stress of running for a few days or weeks may be required to allow some injuries to heal properly. This strategy may let you return sooner to quality training than if you had continued. Coming back takes patience, time, and common sense. Dr. Coyle estimates that two weeks of retraining is needed for every week lost. If you do no exercise for a month, it takes approximately two months to regain fitness.

Total rest beyond a few days, however, may not help many injuries. You may as well run, but within limits. The trick is to train enough to benefit while allowing the injured area to rest by doing relatively less work. Any injury requires good judgment by you and your doctor about whether or not you should continue running. Use the following rules as a guide when running through or coming back from an injury:

- If you can't walk briskly with little or no pain for a mile, don't run. You can run with slight pain, but if it worsens as you run, stop. If your injury is getting worse from day to day, take some time off. Don't run if pain makes you limp or otherwise alters form. It could cause another injury far worse than the one you already have. Bravely limping through a run is stupid! Never use pain-killing drugs to allow you to run. You must feel the pain to adjust to it. Pain protects you from overdoing.

- Develop a sense for your limits. For example, running up to 5 miles before the knee acts up and later, as it strengthens, increasing to 7 miles. Since you are the one experiencing the pain, only you can determine how much training is safe. If you challenge those limits you'll risk long-term setback. Try running twice a day with short runs in order to get in the miles with less continuous pounding. Reach the base your body can tolerate, and stay there until you feel strong. That might be 40 miles a week instead of the 50 miles that caused the breakdown. You may choose to make up the difference with cross-training.
- Losing a week or two may only require a week or two of gradually progressive training starting at one-half or so of the preinjury mileage. Longer layoffs require a more conservative comeback. Start slowly: You'll feel wobbly knees, muscle soreness, weakness. Veteran runners often find that their cardiorespiratory system can return much faster than their musculoskeletal systems. If necessary, alternate days of running with days off, or alternate running with walking for each exercise session. You may not be able to run more than a mile or two without having to walk. Try alternately running up to the edge of your capacity and then, before you feel pain, walking briskly. I used this system when coming back from a broken back: Walk 5 minutes at 60 percent of maximum heart rate, run 5 minutes at 70 to 80 percent. I did this over the same dirt trail courses I would have run, taking almost twice the time. Slowly increase the running period and decrease the walking time until you can run nonstop comfortably. Then slowly build back up to your normal training program.
- Avoid hills, speed training, races, long runs, slanted, or excessively soft or hard surfaces that aggravate injuries and intensify pain. After a layoff, don't at-

tempt hills and speedwork until you've run at least two weeks at your previous distance level with no problems. Run the first few speed sessions and races after a layoff only for "reexperience."

- If you lose a day or two to a minor injury, don't try to make them up. Proceed "at the rate of," and pick up your normal schedule as soon as it is safe. Making up may set you back instead of getting you back on schedule.
- If pain lessens when changing shoes, for example, or when switching sides (or slope) of the road, you have learned a contributing cause of your injury.
- Jogging very slowly may aggravate your injury or cause another. It may be better to run at a normal pace and take walk breaks to prevent continuous pounding. Unless you have a lower-leg injury, running uphill may be therapeutic because the body absorbs only about two-thirds the stress of running on flats. For this reason, many sports doctors advocate starting recovery training on a treadmill set at a slight grade.
- If you added or increased stretching and strengthening programs while not running, keep them up as you return to running. The added strength and flexibility will help prevent future injury and enhance performance.

CROSS-TRAINING FOR THE INJURED RUNNER

If you can't run or need to cut back your mileage, activities such as swimming and biking will help you keep in shape. But they do not use the leg muscles the same way running does; thus, some loss of training will occur. The exercises that come the closest to mimicking running are deep-water running, cross-country skiing, ellipse trainers, and stairclimbers. Including cross-training speed intervals helps minimize fitness loss. Chapter 45 details how to use cross-training when injured.

DEALING WITH INJURIES

When injured, runners respond in one of four ways:

1. Ignore the injury and run through it, often making it worse;
2. Quit running for a few days and pray that it will go away;
3. Attempt self-treatment;
4. Seek medical help. Most runners deal with an injury in that order.

Most injuries respond well to RICE—rest, ice, compression, and elevation. Follow this procedure immediately after the injury occurs and continue for a few days. Rest is the easiest answer for most injuries, but the hardest to accept by most runners. Icing is the most common treatment. It lessens pain, and decreases inflammation, blood flow, swelling, and fluid buildup in the injured area. It may also temporarily relieve muscle spasms by numbing and calming the irritated nerve fibers around the affected muscles. It can be combined with compression and elevation for immediate treatment of many injuries, such as ankle sprains. Icing is often used in combination with aspirin or ibuprofen, which also reduce pain and inflammation.

Icing should begin immediately after an injury to minimize inflammation. Keep icing frequently thereafter for at least twenty-four hours and throughout injury rehabilitation. Ice any injury that is bothering you immediately after each run. Apply for 10 to 20 minutes—longer than this may cause increased circulation in the area rather than the desired decrease. The area should become red and numb, not white. Then alternate 10 to 20 minutes on and off for the first three to four hours after an injury. Later, ice for 10 to 20 minutes, three times a day for up to a week. Ice after running until there is no further pain or tenderness. Be prepared to re-ice if the injury starts to come back.

You can use various types of ice packs: crushed ice between two towels, a plastic bag filled with ice, reusable frozen commercial gel packs, or chemical bags that mix to produce cold. Be careful not to apply these directly to the skin. Another method is to soak a towel in ice water and place it on the injured area. As it warms, resoak it. Continue that process for 15 to 20 minutes. An ice towel is good for large areas, such as the lower back and hamstrings. My favorite ice pack: a bag of frozen peas—it molds to the body! This allows you to ice both sides of the shin, Achilles tendon, or the entire knee. Frozen peas don't melt like ice, and stay cold longer than frozen gels.

Another good method to apply cold to an injured area is ice massage. Physical therapist Ted Corbitt, a 1952 U.S. Olympic marathoner, recommends this technique: Freeze ice in a paper cup for easy application, using a rubber glove or towel to protect hands while applying; and gently massage the area on and around the injury for 10 to 15 minutes. It is important to keep the ice moving to provide a massaging effect. Be very careful not to allow the ice to touch bare skin for too long at one time.

SPECIFIC TREATMENT FOR COMMON INJURIES

Following is a brief summary of the causes and treatment of the most common running injuries. Also included are recommended exercises to improve flexibility and strength that will help prevent the injury from happening again. Those exercises, as well as others that minimize injury, are detailed in the chapters on stretching and strength training. Massage is also recommended in the prevention and treatment of most injuries. When in serious training I consider my weekly massage, concentrating on the legs, as essential. I've also had success with chiropractory and acupuncture. Remember: Extended treatment of all ailments, and early treatment of serious injury, should be administered by a medical doctor.

Achilles tendinitis. This tendon connects the powerful lower leg muscles to the heel. If ignored in initial inflammation stages, a tear or rupture may result. Symptoms include stiffness or pain when arising in the morning and after sitting for long periods. You may experience pain as you start out, but it eases up as you run.

Causes: Trauma; heel deformity; poor calf flexibility; overstretching; overpronation or supination; improper, poor-fitting or worn-out shoes; running up on the toes or leaning too far forward; soft surfaces such as sand; high-heeled fashion shoes; overtraining—sudden changes in mileage, speed training, or hills.

Treatment: Correct causes above; completely rest or decrease mileage; avoid hills and speed until healed; anti-inflammatories,

ice after each run; avoid stretching area until pain and swelling is gone; elevate heels in walking and running shoes with lifts; orthotics may be prescribed; surgery as a last resort.
Stretching exercises: Wall Lean.

Ankle sprains. These result in torn ligaments, broken blood vessels, and inflammation, accompanied by pain and swelling. If you twist an ankle during a run, don't keep going if it hurts. Get off your feet and treat the injury. If you keep running, it may get far worse. Stay off the injured ankle until you can walk comfortably. Crutches may be needed the first forty-eight hours to decrease weight-bearing. Don't run until all pain and swelling are gone.
Causes: Trauma, running over uneven terrain, previous injury, improper shoes.
Treatment: Rest, ice, compression, elevation; anti-inflammatories; taping or using braces for support; use well-cushioned shoes in good condition; orthotics may be prescribed in some cases.
Strengthening exercises: Ankle Push, Ankle Walk, Towel Sweep.
Stretching exercises: Ankle Roll.

Back pain/sciatica. Lower-back problems are most frequent, but upper-back injuries also trouble many runners. The sciatic nerve begins in the lower back and extends all the way down the leg to the ankle. It has been called "the longest river of pain in the body." Pain may occur in the back, hip, leg, or even the ankle and the two lesser toes. It may be a numbing sensation or a severe pain shooting from the back down the leg. Back pain and sciatica can linger for months, or suddenly appear and disappear, only to reappear again.
Causes: Stress, inflexibility, muscle imbalances, leg-length discrepancy, overtraining, overstriding, slanted surfaces, misalignment of the spine, disk deterioration, trauma, biomechanically weak feet, overstretching, overweight, bad habits (lifting, sleeping, sitting).
Treatment: Treat causes above, relaxation exercises, massage, warm baths, anti-inflammatories, orthotics, surgery as a last resort.
Strengthening exercises: Crunches, Pelvic Tilt, Alternate Extensions.
Stretching exercises: Knee to Chest, Cat Back, Fold-up Stretch, Modified Hurdler Stretch, Lying Hamstring Stretch, Towel Hamstring Stretch.

Ball of foot pain. Sesamoiditis, pain under the head of the first metatarsal (the big knobby bone behind the big toe), is usually caused by trauma. Pain under the second, third, and fourth metatarsal heads are bone bruises. Neuroma, a burning or numbing sensation, occurs primarily around the area of the third and fourth metatarsals. This is caused by inflammation of the nerve, which may be squeezed by the metatarsals. Pain on the top of the forefoot over a specific area may be a sign of a stress fracture (although it may be caused by tying shoelaces too tightly).

Causes: Overtraining, especially too much speed or hills; running too high on the toes and leaning forward; shoes too inflexible in ball of the foot or too tight in the forefoot; structural weaknesses in the feet; downhill running.

Treatment: Correct causes above, ice after running, anti-inflammatories, rest for a few days if running form is affected, pad around (not over) the bruise, no speed or hills until recovered, cortisone injections, surgery as a last resort for neuroma.

Cramps. As Bryant Stamford, Ph.D., wrote in *The Physician and Sports Medicine*, "A cramp is a muscle contraction gone haywire, locking the muscle into a painful and sustained spasm. You have no control over when a cramp strikes, and if you don't intervene, it will continue." Fortunately, this is a temporary condition rather than a long-term injury. Running farther or faster than you are accustomed, especially in hot weather, will make you more prone. The calf muscles are the most frequent location, but any muscle may cramp. Some runners are more vulnerable than others. Recurrent cramps can be indicative of more serious medical problems.

Causes: Overworked muscles for conditioning; slight muscle strain; dehydration; tight hamstrings; too little potassium, sodium, calcium and magnesium in diet; exposure to extremes of temperature; inadequate warm-up; poor blood circulation; tight clothing; sudden change in shoes.

Treatment: Correct causes above; gently but firmly stretch the cramped muscle; massage it with your thumbs; ice.

Heel bruises and spurs. Bruises may result from stepping on sharp objects, such as rocks, or hitting too hard and too far back on the heel while running. Heel spurs have the same basic causes and symptoms as plantar fasciitis. They result from the plantar fascia pulling very hard at its attachment to the heel over time. Microscopic fibers of the fascia tear, leaving small droplets of blood, which eventually calcify. The spur irritates the soft tissue and a "bursal sac" forms, filling with fluid. Pressure on it from standing or running causes pain. Heel spurs sometimes show up on X rays.

Treatment: Same as for plantar fasciitis; also pad the bottom of the heel of both feet, cut a hole in the heel pad so the painful area will not be irritated, and have orthotics adjusted to take pressure off spurs.

Hip/piriformis. Muscle strains or stress fractures may develop in various parts of the hip. A common hip injury is "piriformis syndrome." This involves the hip rotating muscle deep in the buttock. The piriformis spasms, pressuring the sciatic nerve. Pain may radiate up into the lower back and down into the hamstrings.

Causes: Prolonged sitting, sitting on a wallet, overtraining, leg-length differences, muscle imbalances, tight hip flexors and low back, repeated rotations of the torso.

Treatment: Correct causes above, ice, rest, anti-inflammatories.

Strengthening exercises: Side Leg Raises, Chair Press, Squats, Lunges.

Stretching exercises: All hip stretches in Chapter 44.

Iliotibial band syndrome. The IT band is a broad connective tissue that extends from the outside portion of the hip over the lateral thigh, crossing over the knee and inserting into the tibia. It helps stabilize the knee during running. Pain occurs on the outside of the knee and up to the hip when the IT band becomes inflamed during running. Pain may disappear suddenly with the cessation of running.

Causes: Running on slanted surfaces, downhill running, improper shoes, overpronation, underpronation, inadequate warm-up or cool-down, too much too soon with mileage, a single excessive workout, bowlegs, excessive sitting, inflexibility, hills.

Treatment: Correct the causes above, stretching the IT Band, strengthening exercises for the structures that stabilize the hip, ice after running, anti-inflammatories, deep friction massage, decrease mileage, run on soft, level surfaces, reduction in mileage and intensity, rest.

Stretching exercises: Standing IT Band Stretch, Lateral Hip Stretch.

Runner's knee. Runner's knee (chondromalacia patella) involves the softening of the protective cartilage under the kneecap caused by improper tracking: the kneecap is forced out of its normal "groove" and irritates the cartilage. Pain usually occurs beneath or on both sides of the kneecap.

Causes: Overpronation, weak quads, inflexible hamstring and calf muscles, unequal leg length, knock-knees, running on slanted surfaces, improper or worn shoes, overstriding, overtraining.

Treatment: Correct potential causes above, well-cushioned shoes, ice after running, rest, anti-inflammatories, knee brace, possibly commercial arch supports or prescribed orthotics, surgery as a last resort.

Strengthening exercises: Sitting Leg Extensions, Squats, Lunges, Step-ups.

Stretching exercises: All hamstring exercises in Chapter 44.

Runner's nipple. This is one of those annoying problems that technically isn't an injury, but it is painful. Runners are more vulnerable in warm weather and when running long distances. Nipples chafe from friction between your skin and shirt. The result may be raw, painful, even bleeding nipples. To prevent this, choose loose, softer clothes. T-shirts or singlets with silk-screened designs across the chest can increase irritation. Singlets with a soft-fabric panel across the chest are ideal. Try covering the nipples with petroleum jelly or a patch (Band-Aid, corn cushion, etc.).

Plantar fasciitis. This is inflammation of the fibrous tissue that runs from the heel to the ball of the foot. It is caused by irritation of this fascia tissue and its separation from the heel bone. Characteristics include pain in the heel or arch when arising in the morning and after sitting for long periods. You also experience pain at the start of your run, but it eases as you loosen up. It may lead to heel spurs.

Causes: Flat or high-arched or rigid feet, overpronating, poor flexibility in the hamstrings and calf muscles, soft surfaces, inadequate shoes, running too high on the toes, overtraining—too much mileage on hard pavement and sudden increases in speed training and hills.

Treatment: Correct the causes above, avoid hills and speed until healed, ice after running, anti-inflammatories, rest, friction massage, night splints, taping, heel-lifts, orthotics, surgery as a last resort.

Strengthening exercises: Towel Exercise.

Stretching exercises: Plantar Fascia Stretch, Kneeling Arch Stretch.

Shin splints. A painful swelling of damaged muscles and tendons along the front of the lower leg at the fibula and tibia accompanies this injury. The pain occurs noticeably during running. Shin splints may signal that a stress fracture is lurking.

Causes: Tight calf and hamstring muscles; overpronation; muscle imbalance—weaknesses in the front of the leg compared to the back of the legs; running too high on toes; overstriding; leaning forward while running; running shoes that are inflexible or have heels that are not thick enough; sudden change from soft to hard surfaces; slanted surfaces; sudden change in mileage, speed training, or hill running.

Treatment: Correct causes above, well-cushioned shoes, anti-inflammatories, ice after runs, reduce mileage and pace or take off some time, avoid hills and hard running surfaces, elevate heels, taping, orthotics may be prescribed.

Strengthening exercises: Towel Sweep, Foot Press, Toe Lifts.

Stretching exercises: Wall Lean, Towel Calf Stretch.

Delayed Onset Muscle Soreness (DOMS). Most runners develop muscle soreness at one time or another due to overuse. Sore quads and hamstrings are especially common. Soreness doesn't necessarily mean you're injured, but it can make running uncomfortable, slow you down, and may increase the risk of injury. DOMS can make walking down stairs or sitting very difficult. It usually appears twelve to twenty-four hours after a workout and lasts from four to ten days. Peak soreness is usually twenty-four to forty-eight hours after the workout. There are many theories as to the cause of DOMS. A prevalent one is microscopic damage to muscle fibers. Ease back or stop running while sore. Damaged muscles need time to heal.

There are three types of runs that cause DOMS:

1. Unaccustomed exercise. Any run significantly longer or faster than normal makes you more vulnerable.
2. Eccentric exercise. This involves contracting the muscle while it is being lengthened, producing muscle fiber

damage. For example, downhill running. The Boston Marathon, with its many downhill stretches, is well known for producing DOMS.

3. Long runs. DOMS is common after long runs and races of a half-marathon and longer. These runs damage muscle fibers that have been depleted of glycogen.

Other causes: Improper warm-up or cool-down; inflexibility; improper recovery after hard runs; sudden increases in mileage, speed, or hills; shoes without adequate cushioning.
Treatment: Correct causes above; rest, or light exercise (walking or non-weight-bearing activity such as swimming or biking) to pump blood to the muscles may help you recover; ice, massage, and anti-inflammatories help.

Muscle strains (hamstring, quadriceps, calf, groin). These are a result of an actual tearing within the muscle group and are most often accompanied by inflammation. A muscle that is suddenly jerked by a sharp action (slipping on ice, sudden bursts of speed) or hasn't been properly warmed up may pull at its tendon or connection with the bone.
Causes: Trauma, muscle imbalance, inflexibility, improper warm-up, leg-length discrepancy, shoes with uneven wear or that are inflexible, slanted surfaces, overstriding, running too high on the toes, overstretching, overtraining.
Treatment: Correct causes above, rest (don't run if you favor the injury), ice, anti-inflammatories, massage, orthotics may be needed, do not stretch injured areas until all pain has disappeared.

Exercises for groin:
Strengthening: Chair press.
Stretching: All groin stretches in Chapter 44.
Exercises for quadriceps:
Strengthening: Leg Extensions, Squats, Lunges, Step-ups.
Stretching: Standing Quad Stretch.
Exercises for hamstrings:
Strengthening: Hamstring Curls, Squats, Lunges.
Stretching: All hamstring stretches in Chapter 44.
Exercises for calf muscles:
Strengthening: Toe Raises.
Stretching: Wall Lean, Towel Calf Stretch.

Stress fractures. Tiny breaks or cracks in a normal bone may be caused by repeated trauma or pounding. They usually occur in the metatarsals in the ball of the foot, or the lower leg bones. They may also occur in the upper leg, pelvis, and hip areas. Sometimes a runner can have a stress fracture and not be aware of it. Pain, if it exists, usually begins gradually and intensifies with running. If you can find a single spot on the bone that hurts intensely when you press down on it, you may have a stress fracture and should consult a doctor. Stress fractures come on slowly. At first it may seem to be a bad case of tendinitis, but if pain persists X rays should be taken. A stress fracture may not show up on X rays for the first two weeks or so. A bone scan may be necessary to confirm this injury.

Causes: Too much too soon—mileage, speedwork, hills; switching to harder surfaces; too little recovery after hard runs; improper shoes for foot type; running too high on the toes; biomechanical weaknesses in feet.

Treatment: Rest—sorry, that's the only option. You must stay off a stress fracture and stop running for four to eight weeks, depending upon the location and severity of the injury. If you don't, more serious and permanent injury may result. Switch to nonimpact exercise while recovering—swimming, biking, and the like.

The stitch. Although not really an injury, there may be no pain that strikes a runner with the suddenness and devastation of the dreaded side stitch. This sometimes sharp pain is usually located in the upper abdomen or at the base or between the ribs; it often occurs when you're running hard and ceases when you slow down or stop. The pain usually results from a spasm in the diaphragm—most often caused by faulty breathing or sudden, hard running that jars the organs and tugs on the ligaments that connect the gut to the diaphragm.

Other causes: Factors believed to contribute include: Stress, weak and tense abdominal muscles, running too soon after eating resulting in gas, intolerance to certain foods, running hard down hills, improper warm-up, starting too fast, dehydration, inadequate fitness for intensity of run, bad luck.

Treatment: Correct above causes and try the following techniques:

- Practice "belly breathing," not "shallow breathing." When you inhale, the diaphragm (the muscle that separates the chest cavity from the abdominal cavity) lowers. When you exhale, it moves up. If you take in a small volume of air with each breath, the diaphragm may not lower enough to allow connective tissue to the organs to relax, resulting in a spasm. If a stitch hits, by breathing even more deeply, forcing the belly to rise with each inhalation, the diaphragm lowers fully and is allowed to relax. If this doesn't solve the problem, try breathing in through your nose and then emptying the lungs by pursing your lips and blowing hard. This releases trapped air in the lungs. Breathe out against a slight resistance even if you groan a little or sound like you're playing the trumpet. Exhale deeply and noisily. Don't be shy. The clock is ticking at the finish line. Try Shelly-lynn's method: Breathe in like you are sucking air through a straw; noisily breathe out while pretending to blow up a balloon.
- A change in breathing pattern may help. Most runners breathe out as the same foot, usually the right, hits the ground. We usually breathe at the footstrike to breaths ratio of 4:1 (four steps per complete inhalation and exhalation). Try breathing off the other foot to break the pattern. Most runners develop a stitch on the right side. One theory is if you repeatedly exhale (causing the diaphragm to move up) when the right foot hits the ground (forcing the organs on the right side of the body—including the liver, the largest organ in the abdominal cavity—to move down) a stitch is more likely to occur. Try breathing out as the left foot hits. Some runners find that doubling their rate of breathing rids them of the dreaded stitch. Others raise their arms overhead, breathe deeply, expand their abdomen, and, as they lower their arms, exhale loudly and contract their abdomen. (This is not the time to worry about appearances!)

- Slow the pace until the pain subsides; resume speed once you feel comfortable. If that doesn't work, to relieve abdominal pressure, stop running, bend over and raise your knee on the stitch side while pressing your fingers deep into the painful area and tightening the abdominal muscles. Or, just walk while belly breathing and the stitch will gradually subside.
- A few runners get away with not thinking about the pain, and continue running. Try dissociation: thinking about something else or talking to another runner.
- You are always welcome to try my technique. When a stitch hits me in a race, I just pick up the pace and run harder and harder until the stitch goes away. It works for me—though everything else hurts! Then there is the technique developed by a former training partner. His rather bizarre method was to do a quick somersault when bothered by a stitch during a race. It worked—and really "psyched out" the opposition.

No one has ever died from a side stitch, although you may feel you are going to be the first. If you have tried everything and are still troubled by stitches, check with a sports doctor. You may have internal problems that should be handled medically.

BASIC FOOT CARE

Blisters. These are perhaps the most common and least respected injury for runners. They are caused by heat buildup from friction or pressure. As the skin heats up, the outer layers can separate, with fluid filling the gap. The fluid causes more pressure and pain. Infection may occur. Blisters take several days to go away on their own, but continuing to run on them may delay healing. If not properly treated, blisters cause just as much trouble as damaged muscles or joints. Favoring a blister may cause knee and other injuries. If you develop a painful blister during a run, stop. It may be better to take a few days off and give it time to heal properly.

Anything that intensifies rubbing contributes to blisters—that includes shoes that are too big or too small, abrasive or wet socks, faults in shoe or sock stitching, downhill running, foot abnormalities. You are more likely to blister in hot and wet weather and when running at fast paces or long distances. Keep feet dry, if possible (including being careful when pouring water on you in hot weather). Wear acrylic or polyester socks, not cotton or wool. Dual-layer socks designed to reduce rubbing against skin may help. Some runners wear their socks inside out so the seams don't rub against their feet. Friction-reducing insoles and moleskin applied to sensitive areas minimize blistering. Skin lubricants for athletes may help. Petroleum jelly and talcum powder have been rubbed on runners' feet for years to prevent blisters. Some studies, however, indicate that petroleum jelly works fine for the first hour, but then may contribute to blistering. Some blister problems may require orthotics to control excessive foot motion.

If a blister is small and not painful, leave it alone. Keep the area clean and protected, and the skin may heal itself. Try cutting a hole the size of the blister in a piece of moleskin, placing it over the blister and then covering it with gauze. If the blister gets bigger or is sore or painful, it must be opened to relieve the pressure. Use the following procedure:

Clean the area with a disinfectant such as alcohol or iodine. Sterilize a needle or razor blade by wiping it with alcohol, or heating it in a flame or boiling water. Prick the blister in several spots or make a small slit. Make the holes and slits large enough to prevent closure and fluid buildup again. Do not remove loose skin—it protects the sensitive underlayer of skin. Press lightly on the blister with sterile gauze to remove excess fluid. Most of the pain will go away when the fluid is released. Clean the area with antiseptic. Gentian violet can be used to dry it. After drying, use an antibiotic ointment to prevent infection. Cover the area. Use a square of gauze and tape it around the edges. Take it off at night or whenever able to let air at the injury. Try a protective dressing (such as Spenco 2nd Skin, or Compeed) available at most running stores. They cushion the area, keep it soft, and may allow you to run pain-free. If redness and pain persist, you have a badly infected blister and should see a doctor immediately.

Damaged nails. Keep toenails short; long nails jam into the front of your shoes, causing black or ingrown toenails. Cut the nails straight across, not in a curve, to prevent ingrown toenails. Black nails are caused by blistering under the nail after a toe becomes bruised from bumping against the end of your running shoe. It is most often caused by nails that are long combined with shoes that are tight or slide too much because they're big. Downhill running may cause the foot to slide forward, resulting in toenail trauma. If your nails turn black but don't hurt, leave them alone. Eventually these blisters may go away on their own. But if they are painful, take action or you'll mess up your running form favoring this injury, causing a different injury. Try cutting a slit in the shoe over the injured area to relieve pressure. "Sanding" thickened nails with an emery board or pumice stone may help to prevent and relieve this condition. You may need to release the pressure. If the blister is out to the end of the toe, slit it with a sterile blade, soak, and use antiseptic. If you can't reach it and are brave, heat a paper clip in a flame and push it through the nail. After draining the fluid, apply an antiseptic and bandage. If you aren't brave, you may need to have a podiatrist drill a hole in the nail to relieve pressure and drain blood. I once put off treatment for a blister under my big toenail until it throbbed so much I had to go to the emergency room in the wee hours of the morning. Usually an injured toenail will grow back normally. Most runners experience black toenails. Consider it a badge of honor!

Athlete's foot. This fungus occurs between toes or on the soles of feet. It can itch and burn and cause severe discomfort. It thrives in moist conditions—sweaty feet, socks, and shoes. To prevent it, wash feet daily in warm water, dry thoroughly, and sprinkle with antifungal powder. Fungus also feeds on dead skin tissue, so clean your feet regularly with a nail brush, emery board, or pumice stone. Wear dry, clean socks, especially in summer. This means both running footwear and "civilian" socks. Take out shoe insoles after running and allow the shoes to dry. In hot weather, alternate running shoes to allow them to dry out more thoroughly. Wearing sandals allows feet to ventilate and keep dry. If you get athlete's foot, treat it immediately with antifungal powder or cream.

Calluses. These develop from the constant rubbing of the foot in the shoe. They usually form on the bottom and back of heels, and under the ball of the foot. Calluses protect the foot, but can cause painful problems if they thicken and increase pressure on underlying tissues and bone. Blisters can form deep under the callus, which can be very painful. Rub calluses regularly with a pumice stone or emery board to keep them from building up and getting crusty. Moisturizing cream regularly applied prevents callus buildup. Have a podiatrist remove thick calluses. Orthotics or metatarsal pads are sometimes required to eliminate the pressure on the foot that can cause persistant callus buildup.

For basic foot care, apply moisturizing cream to your feet—especially the heels—in fall and winter to prevent drying and cracking, which can be quite painful. Also, corns, warts, slivers, ingrown toenails, and the like should be taken care of immediately by your podiatrist.

PART XII

SPECIAL TRAINING

CHAPTER 43

Strength Training

Whether your goal is total fitness or race performance, *muscular fitness* is important. It consists of muscular strength, power, and endurance. *Muscular strength* is the ability of a muscle or muscle group to generate force: how much weight, including that of your body, you can lift or move in one effort. *Muscular power* is the product of force and velocity: moving that weight through a given distance in a short period of time. It's a fast, explosive effort, such as bounding fast up a hill or sprinting to the finish line. *Muscular endurance* is the ability to sustain muscle action for an extended period; to avoid fatigue. This includes how many times you can lift a weight or do push-ups, and the ability to move your body weight over distance. Runners require a certain amount of muscular strength and power to generate speed and lots of muscular endurance to sustain a strong pace for long-distance racing. Runners don't need excessive muscular strength or power since they don't exert maximum force while running long distances and they don't sprint all-out.

Athletes, such as football players, that need to generate a lot of strength and power concentrate on a high-intensity, low-volume training program. The goal for runners should be to utilize low-intensity, high-volume training to gain substantial muscular endurance benefits as well as some muscular strength and power gains. Runners benefit most with a program of relatively light resistance loads performed with multiple repetitions (reps). Throughout this chapter I refer to "strength training" as exercises that improve all types of muscular fitness: strength, power, and endurance.

BENEFITS OF STRENGTH TRAINING

Race pace. The ability to hold pace throughout the race and to power up hills is enhanced with strength training. Lactate threshold can be improved by as much as 12 percent with circuit training according to studies at the University of Maryland. Why? The researchers believe improved strength of the slow-twitch muscle fibers delays recruitment of the fast-twitch fibers, thus delaying increased lactic acid production.

Running economy. Strength training allows for more efficient running. Running economy improved by 4 percent with a 10-week strength program for a group of experienced runners in a study at the University of New Hampshire. That translates to about a 4 percent performance boost—enough to knock a minute or two off 10K times.

Running form. Increased strength means decreased muscular fatigue and better form in races. Running itself does little to strengthen the upper body; fatigue here contributes to weakened arm drive. Strong postural muscles in the abdomen, hips, and back hold you erect and allow the powerful upper leg muscles to function smoothly and powerfully. Feet, ankles, and legs that fatigue affect footstrike, pushoff, and stride. Stride frequency and length may decrease late in races due to muscle fatigue. Strength training improves stride length by increasing power at pushoff.

Speed and finishing kick. According to research in Finland, maximal running speed is improved by up to 10 percent with strength training. The faster your all-out speed, the easier it is to hold a brisk pace and to change into a finishing kick. Stronger muscles require a smaller percentage of maximum force to generate speed.

Injury prevention. Strong muscles reduce injuries by supporting and protecting their respective joints. With greater strength, muscles are capable of withstanding greater forces without injury. They act as a shock absorber, protecting the skeleton from the pounding that comes with running. Running strengthens the pushing muscles (hamstrings, calves, and buttocks), but does little for the opposing muscles (quads, shin area, abs). Strength training minimizes these muscle imbalances which contribute to injury. Weakness in the core muscles of the back, abdominals, buttocks, quadriceps, and hamstring shift stress to vulnerable joints—ankles, knees, shins, hips—setting you up for injury. If vulnerable to certain injuries, include specific anti-injury strengthening exercises.

Aging. As we age, we lose muscle mass. Strength training minimizes this loss of strength—as well as lost time on the finish line clock.

Strong bones. Weight training helps to maintain bone density, minimizing the development of osteoporosis and stress fractures.

Weight loss and body fat. The amount runners should lift won't add body weight, but it will increase strength, decrease body fat percentages, and contribute to weight loss for those who need it. Moving quickly from one exercise to the next, as in circuit training, you'll burn off additional calories. Also, weight training adds muscle that is metabolically more active than fat: A pound of muscle burns 30 to 50 calories a day to maintain itself while at rest compared to only 2 calories per day for a pound of fat.

Appearance. Want to look lean and strong from top to bottom? Combined with running, strength training tones the whole body. Even if you don't lose weight you'll lose inches, since muscle weighs more than fat but takes up less space.

STRENGTH TRAINING OPTIONS

Runners can improve muscular fitness several ways. Basically, any exercise that provides resistance to the muscles is strength training. Whatever options you choose, emphasize the muscle groups used in running movement (legs and arms), and those that stabilize the body (abdomen, lower back, and hips). A key to keeping with a strengthening program is variety. You may choose to combine several of the following methods:

Weight training. This includes free weights (barbells and dumbbells) and weight-training machines (such as Nautilus).

Body weight for resistance (calesthenics). This includes exercises such as push-ups and crunches.

Circuit training. Circuits add spice to your training and provide both strength and aerobic gains. A circuit consists of a series of six to ten strength exercises (using body weight, free weights, or weight machines) arranged in a sequential pattern. Alternate muscle groups. Warm up properly before starting this vigorous routine. Do eight to twelve reps of each exercise, rest or jog for 20 to 30 seconds, then begin the next. You may choose to add brisk runs of a quarter-mile to half-mile, rope skipping, or other aerobic exercise to the routine. Each circuit should take 10 to 15 minutes. You may build up to three or more circuits. Make up your own circuit routines, have a coach or fitness specialist design one for you, or utilize parcourses available at many parks.

Cross-training. A well-balanced program (Chapter 45) promotes total-body fitness.

Strength-training runs. Running itself strengthens many muscles, especially those in the backs of the legs which push you along. Strengthen the quads by running hills (using gravity for resistance), and the ankles by running over rugged terrain. Speed training—fartlek, tempo, intervals, and especially hills—builds muscular fitness beyond that which you get with easy running; and beyond weight training since it strengthens muscles to meet the specific demands of running.

Sport-specific drills and exercises. Many college and club coaches have their athletes do a variety of specialized routines that specifically improve muscles important to fast racing. These include running with a weight vest or resistive rubber tubing, one-leg squats, step-ups, skipping drills, and plyometrics (bounding and jumping). It has been my experience that most of these fascinating-looking routines are best left for college-aged runners under the guidance of experienced coaches, since injuries may result if these exercises aren't performed properly.

RUNNING AND STRENGTH TRAINING

Can you save time by combining strength and running workouts? Strength gains are the same whether exercising before, after, or separate from your runs. If strength sessions are moderate and energizing, then it's okay to do it prior to running. When running directly after strength training, go short and easy because muscles will be fatigued. Running too long or hard prior to strength training will fatigue muscles and thus strength sessions won't be as effective. Do more intense strength workouts on an off day from running, after an easy run, or later in the day after recovering from a run. To maximize performance and minimize injury, don't strength-train for at least two days before or after races (a week for marathons), long runs, or very hard workouts.

Running with hand weights doesn't make sense. It makes the run less enjoyable and won't benefit you any more than if you strength-trained the same muscles before or after the run. Ankle weights are worse. I found out the hard way as a high schooler that running with them can result in injury by increasing force at footstrike. The best form of resistance on the run is gravity: Head for the hills!

GENERAL STRENGTH TRAINING GUIDELINES

Whether lifting weights or your own body weight, here are some guidelines:

- A set consists of a certain number of reps. Do one to three sets of an exercise with a rest period (about 1 minute) in between. You may exercise another muscle group or stretch between sets. Start with a few reps of an exercise and gradually increase the number. The goal is to improve muscular endurance, so for most exercises you will build to ten or more reps. To increase the work load you have two options: (1) do more reps or more sets; or (2) increase the resistance, for example by gradually adding weights. When increasing resistance reduce the number of reps, then gradually increase them again as you get stronger.
- Do the exercises with proper form and do them slowly in a controlled manner. This way you'll work the proper muscles through a full range of motion. If you do the exercises too quickly, momentum will minimize the resistance. Exhale as you lift the weight or go against resistance; inhale as you release. Don't hold your breath.
- Alternate muscle groups to avoid overstress. In general, start with large muscle groups and move on to

smaller ones. Don't work muscles that are sore or injured. That invites further injury. Push through mild discomfort, not pain. If you are slightly sore, go easy.

- Although it is ideal, you don't have to do all of your strength training during the same workout. If you don't have the time to keep with your scheduled strength workout, do at least a few of the exercises rather than follow the all-or-nothing philosophy.

STRENGTHENING EXERCISES USING BODY WEIGHT

You may do some of the following exercises on a daily basis along with your pre- or postrun stretches. Or, set aside two or three days per week for 15 to 30 minutes to focus only on strengthening.

Abdominals

* **Crunches (modified sit-ups):** Sit-ups have been a key exercise in fitness programs for decades. Can they flatten a protruding tummy or remove inches of fat from the waistline? No! There is no such thing as spot reduction. To remove body fat you must burn calories. Running a few miles will expend more calories than hundreds of sit-ups. Sit-ups are valuable, however, in toning muscles in the midsection, which can help protect your back from injury, improve your appearance, and help you maintain proper running posture. Full sit-ups, in which you raise all the way up to a sitting position, are no longer advised by fitness experts. This extra work does little to strengthen the abs and increases the chance of injury. Modified sit-ups, or crunches, are recommended because they are safer and do a better job of isolating the abs.

Proper form is essential. Lie on your back with knees bent about 90 degrees, feet flat on the floor, arms crossed on chest. Do not anchor the feet or the hip flexor muscles will take work away from the abs. Slowly raise the torso, shoulders, and head about 6 to 12 inches off the floor (about halfway to the upright position). Concentrate on using the abdominal muscles only. Tense the abs and hold for 2 seconds. Then slowly lower to the starting position. Touch the floor lightly with the upper back and head, keeping the abs tense, then gradually start back up. Exhale on the way up and inhale on the way down. Look at the ceiling as you sit up.

Concentrate on tilting the base of the ribs toward the hip bones. Don't jerk the upper body or arch the back in an attempt to come up. To increase the work, place your hands on the sides of your ears. Do not interlace your fingers behind your head or neck. This could cause you to pull on your head, which makes the abs work less and may stress the neck. Do two to three sets of ten to twenty crunches as long as good form is maintained. Gradually increase the number of reps you can do. To work the muscles on the side of the torso, turn one shoulder toward the opposite knee as you sit up; then repeat on the other side.

* **Reverse Sit-Ups:** Crunches work the upper abs; reverse sit-ups strengthen the lower abs (tranversus abdominis). Lie on your back with knees bent, feet flat on the floor, and arms at your side, palms down. Keeping the knees bent, bring your legs up until your knees are directly over your hips. This is the starting position. Keeping your lower back pressed against the floor, tilt the pelvis up toward the chest in a small, controlled movement while exhaling. Don't raise your hips off the ground or rock the body. The range of movement is only about 6 inches; any more will strain the back. Release. Do two or three sets of ten.

* **Pelvic Tilt:** Lie on your back, knees bent and feet flat on the floor. Tighten the butt muscles and abs at the same time while tilting the pelvis up and pressing the lower back into the floor. Concentrate on holding muscle contraction for 3 to 10 seconds while exhaling. Do three to five times.

Ankles

Strengthen the ankles to improve foot drive and prevent ankle sprains.

* **Ankle Push:** Provide resistance by pushing your hand (or use a bike inner tube or exercise band and pull) against the foot in four directions—inward, outward, downward, and upward—and holding each for 10 seconds. Do three to five times.

* **Ankle Walk:** Barefoot or in stocking feet, walk on the inside of the foot (inverted position), then walk on the outside of the foot (everted position). Start with ten steps of each and work up to 100 yards.

* **Towel Sweep:** Sit in a chair and place one foot on a towel with the heel on the edge of it. Grip the towel with the toes and push the

towel away from you to the inside in a sweeping motion while keeping the heel in contact with the ground. Do five times and then repeat while sweeping towel to the outside.

Arch

Strengthen the muscles in the arch to prevent plantar fasciitis.

* **Towel Exercise:** Sit or stand and place a towel under your foot. Curl your toes to pull the towel toward you (without moving your leg and keeping the heel on the floor). Release it and pull again. Keep going until the whole towel has been pulled under you. Then reverse the exercise by pushing the towel away. Do two or three times.

Back

Keeping upper- and lower-back muscles strong along with the abdominals improves posture and decreases propensity to back injury.

* **Alternate Extensions:** Lie on stomach with arms extended in front of you, forehead resting on a rolled-up towel. At the same time, slowly lift one arm and the opposite leg. Push the pubic region to the floor for stability. Hold for 3 seconds, then slowly lower to starting position. Repeat with opposite arm and leg. Do ten of each.

Buttocks

These muscles stabilize the hip and help leg drive.

* **Pelvic Tilt:** Described under abdominals.

* **Squats:** Described under quadriceps.

Calf Muscles

These muscles help power your runs. The following exercise helps minimize calf strains, Achilles tendinitis, and posterior shin splints.

* **Toe Raises:** Stand facing a wall or chair and place one hand against it for support. Slowly raise up on the toes and then slowly lower heels to the floor. Do two or three sets of ten to twenty toe raises. As you get stronger, gradually add weights you can hold in your hands (or place barbell over shoulders behind the neck) to increase resistance.

Hamstrings

The "hammies" help stabilize the hips and legs, extend the hip, and flex the knee. They provide much of the pushing action as you run.

* **Hamstring Curls:** Stand facing a table or other object that is thigh-high so that you can put your hands on it for support. Bend one foot toward the butt while keeping the thigh aligned with your upper body. Don't flex forward at the hip or bend backward. Slowly bring the foot up toward your buttock as far as you comfortably can and then slowly return to the starting position. Do two or three sets of 20 with each leg. Gradually add weight to the ankle to increase resistance.

Hips/Groin

These exercises strengthen the hip stabilizers, improving the power of pushoff, range of motion, and preventing hip- and groin-related injuries including iliotibial band syndrome and piriformis syndrome. The abductor muscles on the outside of the upper thigh get more work with running than the adductors on the inside of the leg, resulting in a potential imbalance.

* **Side Leg Raises (*for the abductors*):** Lie on your side. Align the upper leg with your body and bend the bottom leg. Lay your head on the outstretched bottom arm. Bring the opposite hand across and place it palm-down in front of your chest for support. Slowly lift the upper leg, leading with the heel, until you've reached as high as you can comfortably, then slowly lower it to the starting position. Don't allow your leg to move in front of your body, and keep your knee facing forward. Do two or three sets of ten to twenty with each leg.

* **Chair Press (*for the adductors*):** Sit in a chair with knees spread apart and feet flat on the floor shoulder-width apart. Place a beach ball between your knees. Slowly press the knees inward and hold for 10 to 20 seconds. Do ten to twenty times.

Quadriceps

The "quads" are the large muscle groups in the front of the upper thigh. They stabilize the knee joint, extend the lower leg, and lift the leg upward as you run. These exercises prevent knee injury (by balancing strength with the hamstrings) and improve your ability to run faster and to power up hills.

* **Sitting Leg Extensions:** Sit in a chair or on the edge of a table, straighten one leg to a position parallel to the floor. Tighten the muscles and hold for 2 or 3 seconds in an isometric contraction. Relax, and lower to start position. Do ten to twenty times. Then repeat with the other leg. As you get stronger, add a 2-pound ankle weight.

* **Squats:** Standing upright with feet flat on the ground shoulder-width apart, slowly squat about one-fourth to one-third of the way down and hold for 2 or 3 seconds before slowly returning to the standing position. Do ten to twenty times. Keep the back and head as straight as possible. Don't arch your back or squat lower than halfway down (thighs parallel with floor). A good precaution is to do chair squats: Lower buttocks over a chair.

* **Step-ups:** Start with the right foot on a step or sturdy box high enough that the thigh is parallel to the ground. Keeping the back straight, step up onto the step with the left foot, and then step down. Pump the arms as if you were performing your running stride. Do ten to twenty step-ups, then switch to the other side, stepping up with the right foot. As you get stronger, you may do two to three sets.

Shins

The anterior tibialis muscle in the front of the shin helps control foot and leg action as you strike the ground. Weaknesses here relative to strong and inflexible calf muscles on the back of the lower leg contribute to shin splints.

* **Toe Lifts:** Sit in a chair; extend your legs slightly with your heels resting on the ground about a foot beyond perpendicular. Then lower your toes until the feet are flat on the ground. Now, lift the toes slowly toward your knees while keeping the heels on the ground. When you feel the muscles in the front of the shins contract, hold that position for 3 to 10 seconds, then relax. Do ten times.

* **Towel Sweep:** See ankle exercises.

* **Foot press:** While sitting, place one foot on top of the other. Pull up with the lower foot and resist with the upper. Hold for 10 seconds, then switch feet. Do five sets.

Upper Body

Besides being important to good arm drive, upper-body muscle fitness is needed to safely lift objects during daily tasks.

* **Push-ups (for the arms and chest):** *For men:* This is the standard push-up. Lie on your stomach, placing hands, palms down, under the shoulders, fingers pointing straight ahead. Assume the starting position: Rest body weight on your hands with arms fully extended, and on your toes with your legs parallel to each other. Lower yourself to the floor until your chest lightly touches it. Then, push yourself back up to the starting position. Straighten your arms fully at the top of the push-up. Keep back and legs straight and knees off the ground throughout the push-up. Don't arch the back, or touch your knees or stomach to the floor. Only your chest should touch. Exhale as you push up, inhale coming down. Do two or three sets of five, gradually increasing to two or three sets of twenty reps or more with good form.

For women: Generally, women don't have as much upper-body muscle as men. Women usually do modified push-ups. (But go ahead and do the standard push-ups above if you are strong enough!) On a carpet or mat, get down on your hands and knees, ankles crossed, knees bent, palms down under your shoulders with fingers pointing straight ahead. Assume the starting position: Rest your weight on your hands with arms fully extended, and on your knees. Lower the upper body to the floor until your chest lightly touches it. Then, push yourself back up to the starting position. Keep your knees in contact with the floor while keeping your back straight and your head aligned with your spine. Straighten arms fully at the top of the push-up. Exhale as you push up and inhale as you come down. Do two or three sets of five, gradually increasing to two or three sets of twenty reps or more with good form.

* **Reverse Push-ups** (For the triceps at the back of the upper arm): Stand with your back to a well-anchored table or chair. Rest your hands on it and extend your legs out in front of you so that your weight is supported by your hands and your extended heels. Slowly lower your upper body toward the table, while keeping knees slightly flexed; return to starting position. Do two or three sets of ten to twenty. To make this more difficult, pick a lower object, such as a bench, for your support.

BASIC 6: SAMPLE STRENGTHENING WORKOUT USING BODY WEIGHT

Here is a sample strength routine using your body weight for resistance. These six exercises work important muscle groups for runners. You may add or subtract from the exercises described in this chapter. Emphasize exercises that relate to your specific injury vulnerabilities.

1. Squats (quads, hamstrings, buttocks)
2. Push-ups (upper body)
3. Crunches (abs)
4. Side Leg Raises (abductors)
5. Chair Press (adductors)
6. Foot Press (shins)

WEIGHT TRAINING

Which is best, free weights or machines? They both offer more resistance, and thus strength gain, than exercises using your body weight. Free weights require minimal equipment for a home gym: dumbbells, a barbell, a set of weight plates, and a bench. To use weight machines, you would need to go to a gym or purchase a multistation machine for home. Many experts favor free weights because along with lifting and lowering the weights, you must balance them. This works the major muscles as well as their assisting muscles. But injury is more of a risk using free weights, especially when using heavily weighted barbells. Free weights may be best if you know what you're doing and have a good training partner to spot you. On the other hand, machines offer an easier, safer exercise. You can quickly move from exercise to exercise in a room with machines (unless you have to wait in line to use them at a crowded club). They can better isolate the muscle groups you want to exercise without straining other muscles. Machines dictate the way your body can move, thus making it simpler and more efficient to do the exercises. The bottom line: For all-around strength gains, use free weights; for safety, convenience, and timesaving, use machines. For best results, if you have the time, use a combination of both options. Whether using free weights or machines, get qualified instruction on the proper and safe use of the equipment before starting.

GUIDELINES FOR WEIGHT TRAINING

In addition to the general strength training guidelines previously discussed, the following guidelines should be followed:

- When starting a weight training program, begin with a weight that is one-half your maximum strength (As you get stronger, exercise at up to 80 percent of your maximum strength). For example, if the heaviest weight you can bench-press is 100 pounds, begin your weight training program with 50 pounds. An easier, and safer, way to set the proper starting point is to determine how much weight you can lift eight to ten times with good form before having to stop. If you bench-press 50 pounds, for example, and have to quit before reaching eight reps, then start at a lower weight. If you were able to do more than ten reps, start at a higher weight. When weight training, the last rep should feel as if you couldn't do another.
- Do eight to twelve reps of each exercise. Multiple reps with low weights build muscular endurance without adding bulk. Do at least one set, but not more than three, of each exercise. You may not be able to do as many reps on the second and third set as you can on the first. For novice weight trainers, the American College of Sports Medicine recommends one set. It may also be enough for all but the more serious exercisers. Research at the University of Florida found that "one-set" lifters scored only 3 to 4 percent less on strength tests than "three-set" lifters. To maximize strength and running performance, I recommend two to three sets.
- Weight training is progressive, just like running. Start with low weights and gradually increase resistance as you become stronger. After you can handle twelve reps of a weight for each set for two consecutive workouts, slightly increase the weight (by no more than 5 percent) and restart with eight reps. You may cut back on the number of sets until you

adjust. Pay attention to how you feel. Decrease weight some days if you are feeling tired. It's better to lower the weight than decrease the number of reps.

- Lift at least two times per week, but not more than three. Studies show that you will get almost as much improvement (70 to 80 percent) by doing weight training two times a week as you would be doing it three times. Allow two or three days' rest between each lifting session to allow muscles to recover.
- Although even doing three or four different exercises would be of help, you ideally should do more so that each major muscle group is included. The ACSM recommends eight to ten different exercises. Concentrate on exercises that strengthen muscles neglected by running (such as the upper body and abdominals). The entire workout should take 20 to 40 minutes. That is enough to gain strength.
- Walk briskly or bike, for example, for 5 to 10 minutes to get the muscles warmed up before lifting. Stretch thoroughly afterward.
- Lift weights with a slow, controlled motion, pause for 1 or 2 seconds at the peak of the lift, and slowly return to the start position. If you work too fast you will build momentum, which lessens the work of your muscles. The negative, or return, part of an exercise may actually be the most important part for developing strength. The lift should take approximately 2 seconds and the return approximately 4 seconds.
- Concentrate on proper form and posture. Especially be careful to provide support for the lower back. No jerking or bouncing! Cheating by using other muscles to help lift means that the muscles you are trying to strengthen will do less work. If you can't hold form with each lift, you are lifting too much weight.

- Use a spotter to assist you on difficult exercises when using free weights.

WEIGHT TRAINING EXERCISES

The following exercises use free weights to strengthen key muscle groups. Do one to three sets of eight to twelve reps. Examples of exercises with machines are not included here since machines vary and keep changing. Get instruction with a trainer before using this equipment.

Abdominals

* **Weighted Crunches:** These are the same as crunches but with a weight plate held across the chest. Lie on back with knees bent, feet flat on the floor. Slowly curl up until shoulders are 6 inches off the ground, then slowly return to starting position. Keep lower back pushed against floor while sitting up.
* **Side Bends (obliques):** Stand with a dumbbell in your right hand. Keep feet flat on the floor, knees slightly bent, hips tucked. Slowly bend sideways to the left, pause, slowly return. After eight to twelve reps, switch weights to the left hand and repeat the exercise to the other side.

Back

* **Bent Over Row:** Place right knee and right hand on bench for support. Place left foot on floor and grasp dumbbell in left hand with knuckles facing forward. Keep back parallel to the floor. Slowly pull dumbbell to chest while turning hand so palm faces inward, pause, then slowly lower to elbow-extended position (but not to floor until set is completed). Repeat to other side.
* **Good Mornings:** Place barbell behind head on shoulders. Keep eyes forward, back straight, feet shoulder-width apart. Bend forward until back is nearly parallel to floor. Start with legs straight and as you bring weight forward, bend knees. Return to starting position.

Buttocks

Squats, lunges: See hamstrings.

Calf Muscles

* **Weighted Toe Raises:** Use a spotter. Stand with barbell resting on rear shoulders, gripping it with hands palms-up. Feet and hands are about shoulder-width apart, eyes straight ahead. Slowly rise up on toes until calf muscles are fully contracted, pause, then slowly lower heels to the ground.

Hamstrings

* **Squats:** Use a spotter. Stand with barbell resting on shoulders using palm-up grip. Feet and hands should be shoulder-width apart, eyes straight ahead. Keeping your chest high, slowly lower squat until thighs are one-fourth to one-third of the way to the floor, then slowly stand up. As you gain strength you may squat halfway or until thighs are parallel to floor. Don't go any farther or you may strain your knees.
* **Weighted Lunges:** Stand as in squats above with barbells resting on shoulders. Step forward with one foot (start with small steps and gradually lengthen with experience and strength). While inhaling, lower yourself until forward thigh is almost parallel to the floor and knee is directly over ankle. Keep your back straight and eyes looking ahead. Keep the bend of the rear leg to a minimum. Pause at peak of squat, exhale, and push back off the front foot to return to starting position. Repeat with other leg.
* **Weighted Step-ups:** Stand as in squats with barbells resting on shoulders. Step up to a step or bench with one foot, then the other. Pause, step down one foot at a time. Keep your back straight and eyes looking straight ahead.

Hips

* **Squats, Weighted Lunges, Weighted Step-ups:** See hamstrings.

Quadriceps

* **Leg Extension:** Use free-weight bench with extension. Sit with lower legs perpendicular to the floor and ankles behind the pad. Slowly lift until legs are fully extended and shins are parallel to the floor. Keep back straight. Pause, then slowly lower to starting position.
* **Squats, lunges:** See hamstrings.

Upper Body (Arms, Chest, Shoulders)

* **Bench Press:** Use a spotter. Lie flat on your back on a bench, face up, with feet flat on the floor (or bench). Place hands slightly more than shoulder-width apart on barbell and slowly lower it to chest. This is the starting position. Slowly press up until arms are fully extended, then slowly lower to starting position. Keep hips on bench and don't bounce bar off chest. Start at approximately 20 to 30 percent of body weight and build up to 50 to 60 percent.

* **Lateral Raises (for the shoulders):** Stand or sit, feet shoulder-width apart, knees slightly bent, holding dumbbell in each hand, arms at sides, palms inward. Slowly raise arms straight out to the side from body to about shoulder height while rotating palms to the front and keeping elbows slightly bent. Pause, then slowly lower.

* **Shoulder Shrugs:** Sit upright on a bench, but maintain a natural curve in your lower back. Keep chest lifted, shoulders down and relaxed. Hold a dumbbell in each hand, arms hanging down, palms in. Slowly pull shoulder blades up and together, keeping head up, eyes looking ahead. Then, slowly pull shoulder blades down and together, lifting chest slightly to help relax shoulders between repetitions. This completes one rep. Don't use too much weight; it's more important to have good form.

To use a barbell, stand erect with palms inward and grasp barbell with hands about shoulder-width apart. Let arms hang down with barbell in front of thighs. Without bending elbows, shrug your shoulders to your ears. Pause, then slowly lower.

* **Biceps Curls:** Stand erect holding barbell using an underhanded grip with arms extended downward, barbell against thighs. Hands and feet should be shoulder-width apart. Eyes should be straight ahead. Slowly curl barbell to chin while keeping elbows at the side (Do not lean back). Pause, then slowly lower to starting position. As an alternate, use dumbbells from standing or sitting position. Curl up and lower with one arm, then the other to complete one repetition.

* **Triceps Extension:** From either a sitting or standing position, hold a dumbbell with both hands behind the head. It should be vertical to the floor with palms against the top of the dumbbell head. Slowly raise overhead, elbows extended, then slowly lower behind the neck while pointing elbows toward the ceiling.

* **Bent Over Row:** See back exercises.

* **Dumbbell Arm Pumps:** Standing with one foot up on a bench or step for balance, pump the arms rapidly while holding light dumbbells in each hand. Use the same arm motion as in the running stride. Pump for about 30 seconds for each set.

BASIC 6: SAMPLE WEIGHT TRAINING WORKOUT

Here is an example of a strength training routine using weights for resistance. I've chosen six exercises using free weights that work important muscle groups for runners. You may choose to add or subtract from the exercises described above, particularly emphasizing exercises that relate to specific injuries to which you may be vulnerable. Running-specific exercises such as Dumbbell Arm Pumps, and Weighted Lunges, Step-ups, and Toe Raises which mimic what occurs in the running stride are particularly beneficial to improving running performance.

1. Squats, Weighted Lunges, or Weighted Step-ups (quads, hamstrings, buttocks)
2. Bent Over Row (back)
3. Weighted Crunches (abs)
4. Bench Press (chest, arms, shoulders)
5. Weighted Toe Raises
6. Dumbbell Arm Pumps

CHAPTER 44

Stretching

Flexibility, the ability of the muscles to move a joint through its full range of motion, is essential to total fitness and performance. Flexible runners are able to run efficiently with smooth form and long strides. But runners may become inflexible because running itself tightens muscles, and when extending stride during faster running, inflexible runners are more prone to muscle strains and tears.

The key to improving flexibility, and maintaining it as you get older, is to stretch muscles wisely and faithfully. Some runners maintain they don't need to stretch. Indeed, I've known many Elite runners who don't stretch at all. But these are mostly young, naturally gifted runners. As we accumulate mile after mile, year after year, and our muscles age, most of us would benefit from stretching. Most sports doctors encourage it. Though no scientific study has validated the injury prevention value of stretching, it makes sense that flexible muscles are less likely to injure. Many runners think of stretching as time that could have been spent running. Instead, think of it as time invested in better running.

WHEN TO STRETCH?

There are varying views as to when a runner should stretch. These include:

Stretch only after running. Running warms the muscles, making them more extensible which allows for greater gains in flexibility with stretching. A study at James Madison University found that stretching after a moderate paced run resulted in almost 10 percent greater flexibility than when stretching cold muscles. Research indicates that those who only stretch after a vigorous workout are less likely to be injured than those that stretch only before. Further, stretching muscles that aren't warmed up may cause injury. With this method be sure to warm up with 10 minutes or more of walking or easy jogging before settling into your training pace. Cool down with a 10-minute walk, then begin a thorough 10- to 20-minute stretching routine. This is the safest and most convenient method for most runners.

Stretch both before and after running. Here's the ideal program. Warm the muscles with a few minutes of walking, biking, or jogging, then stretch. Then, walk or jog slowly again to warm up before running, and stretch again after a cool-down walk following the run. This system may not be feasible or desirable for many runners. Since most of our students walk to class and thus are somewhat warmed up, we usually start with easy stretches before the workout and follow up with more stretching after running to help recover from the hard work and improve flexibility. If you stretch prior to running without a good prestretch warm-up, concentrate on mild stretches and save more extensive stretches for after running when muscles are warm. Prerun stretching is more important before races and hard workouts since you will be extending range of motion, thus further taxing the musculoskeletal system.

STRETCHING GUIDELINES:

- According to a study at the University of Cape Town in South Africa, you'll gain the most flexibility in the least amount of time by doing three reps of each exercise and holding the stretch for 30 seconds. According to the researchers, 60- to 90-second stretches showed the same gain as 30-second stretches, 2-minute stretches are less effective, and 10-second stretches were worthless. Also, two repeats of a stretch were better than one, but beyond three reps range of motion didn't improve any further.

- Breathe normally and in a relaxed manner. Do not hold your breath while stretching. Belly-breathe just like when you run. Take an abdominal breath (stomach extends as you inhale) and let it out slowly. Emphasize the exhalation as you stretch.
- Easy does it. Do not force stretches. Stretch easily to the point of mild sensation. This is called static stretching. Concentrate on proper form and smooth movement—both going into and coming out of each stretch. When a muscle is jerked into extension it tends to "fight back" and shorten. You can injure muscles by overstretching. It is better to under-stretch than to overstretch. Don't try to do more than your body is able to do. Leave a safety margin where you can stretch a little farther. Take your time. Do stretching step-by-step and thoroughly. When a muscle is slowly stretched and a comfortable position held, it relaxes and lengthens. You should feel the stretching sensation in the belly of the muscle. Think about the muscles being stretched; focus on feeling the stretch. Properly done, stretching feels good.
- Do not bounce or swing your body against a fixed joint. Avoid the following common stretches, determined to be high-risk exercises by the American College of Sports Medicine and other experts: Straight-Legged Standing Toe Touch, Standing One Leg Up Hamstring Stretch (as in foot up on a bench), Hurdler Stretch, The Plow, Full Neck Circles, Cobra (back extension). Don't do stretches where your head is lower than your heart while your heart rate is still elevated from exercising briskly; it could cause fainting or worse.
- Be especially careful about stretching in the early morning prior to running. Muscles will be stiff and vulnerable to injury. It may be better to skip stretching and walk briskly for 10 minutes prior to running, then stretch afterwards.

- A common error is to nervously or hurriedly rush through prerace stretches, causing more harm than good. Look around you at races; most likely the majority of runners will be stretching improperly. Don't overdo stretching after a long run, hard workout or race when you may be especially tight.
- Don't stretch injured or very sore muscles. This may aggravate them. Stick to easy limbering movements until the muscle is healed and ready to be stretched. Avoid exercises that aggravate preexisting conditions, especially knee or back pain.
- It is best to stretch on a firm but not too hard surface. If the surface is too hard, such as a bare floor or pavement, you won't be able to relax and stretch properly. If it is too soft, such as a very soft mattress, you won't get proper support and can strain muscles. I often stretch on my firm bed or the thick living room carpet, which are just right for comfort. You may choose to purchase an individual-sized exercise mat. Your environment for stretching is important. You can relax and thus stretch more thoroughly in a quiet, peaceful setting. Listening to music may be helpful.

Many use the same basic routine every day so they feel comfortable with it, know it, and stay with it. Others prefer variety. I'll give you a recommended daily routine as well as several options. Introduce new stretches gradually. Ease into more advanced stretches. Stretch all major muscles, especially areas prone to running injuries: hamstrings, calves, Achilles tendons, and lower back. If vulnerable to certain injuries, be sure to include specific anti-injury stretching exercises. Following are my recommended stretches.

Ankles

Ankle Roll: Sit cross-legged on the floor. Grasp your right foot with both hands and rotate the ankle with slight resistance from your hands for 10 seconds, then reverse direction. Repeat with the other ankle.

Arches

Plantar Fascia Stretch: Sit on the floor with right knee bent. Flex the right ankle by pulling the toes toward the shin with your hands. Keep the right heel on floor to stretch the Achilles tendon. Repeat with the left foot.

Back

Knee to Chest: Lie on your back with knees flexed, feet flat on the floor. Slide left leg out and slowly drop it to the floor. Raise right leg up toward your chest while keeping knee flexed and hands clasped behind the knee. Gently pull the leg toward your chest until feeling a mild stretch in the back, hips, and hamstrings. Keep head and low back flat against the floor. Repeat with other leg. This stretches both lower back and hamstrings. To emphasize lower back, pull one knee up to the chest and then the other to meet it. Hug both knees, lifting feet off the floor but keeping lower back flat. Return feet to floor one at a time.

Cat Back: Assume a kneeling position, resting on hands and knees. Arch your back like an angry cat, dropping your head at the same time. Then slowly reverse the arch by bringing up your head and forming a "U" with your spine.

Fold-up Stretch: In a kneeling position, lean forward and stretch hands forward, palms on floor. Reach forward while pressing chest into thighs until you feel a comfortable stretch. Rest forehead on floor between arms while keeping buttocks on your heels.

Calf Muscles and Achilles Tendon

Wall Lean: Stand 2 or 3 feet in front of a wall or tree with feet shoulder-width apart. Lean forward and place your palms chest-high against the wall. Place one foot 6 to 12 inches behind the other while keeping your back leg straight and toes pointed forward. Bend front knee and align over ankle. Lean hips forward. Keep both heels on floor and back straight until you feel a gentle stretch in the back of the rear leg. Repeat with other leg. You should feel this stretch in the upper calf. To reach the lower calf and Achilles tendon, assume the same position, but this time, when leaning into the wall, bend both knees slightly while keeping both heels on the floor.

Towel Calf Stretch: Sit with legs extended about a foot apart. Hold a towel or T-shirt at each end and loop it around the ball of one foot. Pull on the towel until you feel a gentle stretch in the calf muscles. Repeat with the other foot.

Groin (Adductors)

Sitting Groin Stretch: Sit with back straight, knees flexed and soles of feet together. Place elbows on the inside of your thighs and grasp ankles with hands. Gently pull feet toward the buttocks until feeling a gentle stretch in the groin.

Wide-V Stretch: Lie on the floor with your buttocks close to a wall and your feet up along the wall at a right angle. Let your legs slowly spread to form a "V." Spread until you feel a comfortable stretch and hold. You may wish to place towels under head and neck for comfort.

Hamstrings

Knee to Chest: See back exercises.

Sitting Toe Touch: Sit with legs extended and together. Slide fingertips of both hands forward on legs toward toes; keep knees slightly bent.

Towel Hamstring Stretch: Lie on your back with knees flexed and feet flat on the floor. Bring the right knee to your chest; grasp a towel, T-shirt, or rope at each end and loop under the ball of right foot. Slowly raise and straighten the right leg while keeping your shoulders flat on the floor. Repeat with left leg.

High Knee Stretch: Also stretches groin, front of hip, and calves. I do this while taking a break from the computer. Place ball of right foot on a raised surface such as a bench or table (knee- to hip-high). Keep hands on hips and left foot flat and pointed straight ahead. Bend right knee as you push hips forward. You should feel the stretch in the groin, hamstring, and front of hip. Repeat with other leg.

Hips

Standing Iliotibial Band Stretch: Stand with left side to a wall and support yourself against the wall with your left hand at shoulder height. Cross inside leg behind outside leg and place right hand on right hip. With most of your weight resting on the right leg and keeping the right knee bent slightly, lean your left hip toward the wall while keeping the left leg and left arm straight. You should feel the stretch along the outer thigh. Repeat with other leg.

Sitting Hip Abductor Stretch: Good for piriformis syndrome, back, neck, and torso. Sit on the floor with right leg extended; cross your left leg over the right leg and place the left foot on the floor even with right knee. Place left hand behind body for support and extend right arm outside left knee. Use the right elbow to push your left knee to the right while twisting your body to the left and turning head to look over left shoulder. Slowly twist until you feel a gentle stretch on the outside of the left hip. Keep the hips in place. Repeat to other side.

Chiropractor Stretch: Lie on your back with left leg extended and right knee flexed. Bring right knee toward your chest until at a 90 degree angle. Grasp it with left hand just above the knee and pull bent knee of right leg across the body and down toward the floor while keeping shoulders and back of head flat against floor. Gently push right knee across body until you feel a gentle stretch in the buttocks, lower back, and sides of the hip. Repeat on other side.

Lateral Hip Stretch: Cross left ankle to right knee, and grasp back of right leg with both hands interlocked. Gently pull both knees toward chest until you feel a comfortable stretch in outside of left hip. Repeat on other side.

Neck

Remember not to do full neck circles, which are considered high-risk exercises.

Lateral Neck Stretch: Standing or sitting, place hands behind your back and grasp the right wrist with the left hand. Tilt head gently toward the left ear while gently pulling right arm to the left. Reverse hand positions and repeat stretch to other side.

Side to Side: While standing, sitting, or lying, slowly turn head to the right, center, and then left.

Ear to Shoulder: While standing or sitting, slowly lower head to right shoulder, return to center, lower to left shoulder. Keep shoulders relaxed. To increase stretch, provide gentle pull to side with hand outstretched over top of head.

Forward and Return: While standing or sitting, slowly move head forward, looking down. Don't put chin on chest. To increase stretch, clasp hands behind top of head and apply gentle pressure. Slowly return to start.

Quadriceps

Standing Quad Stretch: Stand on your left leg next to a chair, table, or wall and grasp or touch it with left hand for balance. Bend right knee and lift leg. Grasp right ankle with right hand and push back with thigh until knee points straight down to floor. Do not move the pelvis or the small of the back. You should feel the stretch in the front of the thigh. Repeat with the other leg.

Upper Body: Chest, Upper Back, Shoulders

Chest and Shoulder Stretch: Stand with the right side of the body next to a wall. Extend your right arm backward with elbow at a 90 degree angle, and place the palm of right hand against the wall at shoulder height. While keeping shoulder close to the wall, slowly turn your head over your left shoulder until you feel a gentle stretch in chest, shoulder, and arms. Repeat on other side.

Side Reach: Stand with knees slightly bent. Place hands, palms inward, on outside of thighs. Reach straight up with left hand until arm is fully extended, palm facing away from body, and eyes looking up at outstretched hand. Lean to the right and brace body by pushing in with right hand against right thigh. Repeat on opposite side.

Posterior Shoulder Stretch: While standing or sitting, place right hand over left shoulder and left hand on outside of right elbow. Keep right elbow up and parallel to the floor. Pull right elbow toward left shoulder with left hand. Repeat on other side.

Anterior Shoulder Stretch: Grasp hands behind back. With elbows slightly bent, push arms upward until you feel a comfortable stretch in the back of the shoulders and in the chest. This also stretches the biceps.

Triceps Pull: While standing or sitting, extend one arm straight up above your head. Then bend at the elbow and bring hand to rest behind the neck. With the opposite hand, gently pull the elbow backward. Repeat on other side.

Pectoral Stretch: Rest on your hands and knees, then place lower arms and elbows on floor. Slide both hands forward while keeping your back and head straight, thighs perpendicular to the floor, hips up. Rest forehead on floor and hold position for a few seconds. Return to starting position.

PROGRESSIVE RELAXATION EXERCISES

Relaxation exercises are recommended by many fitness experts prior to prerun stretches to release tension from muscles and after postrun stretches to leave you feeling calm and energized. My mentor, Dr. Hans Kraus, was a leading proponent of the theory that muscles can't be properly stretched unless they are first relaxed. If you feel tense and tight, you should especially consider the relaxation exercises detailed below. Carrying tension with you often results in a lousy workout and invites injury.

Sample Progressive Relaxation Routine. The purpose of this series of exercises is to tense each muscle group and then release tension throughout the body. "Feel" the tension escape as you let go on each exercise.

- Lie on your back, knees flexed, feet flat on the floor, arms relaxed at your sides. Shut your eyes and take a deep breath in through the nose, letting your belly rise. Then, let go and breathe out through the mouth. Repeat two more times. Throughout the exercises below, continue to belly-breathe; don't hold your breath while holding a position.
- Tighten the muscles of your face for a few seconds. Really make a contortion, and then let go.
- Hunch your shoulders up toward the ears and tighten muscles in the neck and shoulders for a few seconds. Relax and let the shoulders drop to original position.
- To loosen and stretch neck, slowly drop head to one side, return to center, drop to other side. Repeat.

- Push small of your back into the floor and tighten muscles in back and buttocks for a few seconds. Let go.
- Raise one arm a few inches off the floor, tighten fist and arm muscles, hold for a few seconds, and let go. Drop arm gently to the floor and repeat with other arm.
- Slide one heel along the floor and drop leg gently to the floor. Raise leg a few inches while keeping lower back flat on the floor. Crunch your toes under and tighten all the muscles in that leg, hold for a few seconds, and let go. Slowly return to starting position. Repeat with the opposite leg.
- As the final exercise at the completion of your postrun stretching routine, lie on back with eyes closed and take several deep breaths. Then, allow your body to go completely limp. Think of something very relaxing, like floating in warm water in the Bahamas. Rest, float for 30 seconds to 1 minute or more. Slowly open your eyes and slowly get up, rising first to your hands, then knees, then one leg, then both legs but bent over, then slowly erect. You will feel very calm and refreshed.

BASIC 12: SAMPLE STRETCHING ROUTINE

Here is an example of a stretching routine to use after you are well warmed-up and/or after finishing running. I've chosen a variety of exercises that improve flexibility in many of the key muscle groups that are important to runners. Add or subtract from the stretching exercises detailed in this chapter to increase variety or to work on flexibility in an area where you may be vulnerable to injury. You may choose to follow the same routine each day for consistency. I've marked six of the exercises with an asterisk. At the least, do a basic series of these half-dozen stretching exercises daily if you feel you can't make time for more.

Do the routine in order from 1 to 12 prior to running; do in reverse order from 12 to 1 after running. This routine should take 10 to 20 minutes, depending on how long you hold each stretch and how many repetitions you do of each stretch.

1. Progressive Relaxation
2. Knee to Chest
3. *Chiropractor Stretch or Hip Roll
4. Lateral Hip Stretch
5. *Towel Hamstring Stretch
6. Ankle Roll
7. Plantar Fascia Stretch
8. *Sitting Groin Stretch
9. *High Knee Stretch
10. *Standing Quad Stretch
11. *Wall Lean
12. Posterior Shoulder, Anterior Shoulder Stretch, or Triceps Pull

FLEXIBILITY ENHANCERS

Stretching isn't the only way to improve and maintain flexibility. Speed training and drills put your body through a full range of motion, thus enhancing flexibility. Cross-training such as biking, cross-country skiing, swimming, and ellipse training benefit flexibility as does weight training. Regular sports massage prevents scar tissue buildup which limits flexibility.

CHAPTER 45

Cross-Training

Cross-training, the use of one or more sports to train for another, has become an important training method for competitive runners of all levels. The spread in popularity of the triathlon event and an increased emphasis on total fitness has fueled this approach. But is it necessary to performance? Many competitors maintain that only running will improve their running.

CROSS-TRAINING AND PERFORMANCE

If all you want to do is run, run, and run—then keep it up if you enjoy it, are injury-free, and are performing well in races. In fact, a study by Carl Foster, Ph.D., at the Sinai Samaritan Medical Center in Milwaukee demonstrated that cross-training improves running performance, but not as much as an increase in running. Adding cross-training on top of your running program may indeed improve your performance. You might improve as much or more if you just increased running mileage, but you would be more likely to break down due to increased pounding or slack off due to decreased motivation that comes with repetitive activity. So, for the average runner, cross-training offers many benefits that can't be provided solely by running.

BENEFITS OF CROSS-TRAINING

Aerobic fitness. To improve endurance most runners add more and more mileage, especially when marathon training. But you can only run so many miles in a week without risking injury. Swimmers and cyclists, however, can train longer and harder due to the nonimpact nature of these sports. So shouldn't runners adjust their training to take advantage of these and other cross-training sports?

Muscular fitness. Running strengthens the pushing muscles (hamstrings, calves, buttocks), but it does little to improve muscular fitness in other key parts of the body. Following are key muscle areas developed with some cross-training activities:

Ankles—Swimming, deep-water running, snowshoe running, cross-country skiing
Shins—Biking (with toe clips)
Quads—Biking, race walking, cross-country skiing, rowing, swimming, stair climbing, skating, deep-water running, snowshoe running
Upper body—Swimming, race walking, cross-country skiing, rowing, deep-water running, skating
Low back—Swimming, rowing, skating
Hip—Biking, swimming, race walking, cross-country skiing, skating
Buttocks—Race walking, cross-country skiing, rowing, swimming, skating
Abs—Race walking, cross-country skiing, rowing, swimming, deep-water running, skating

No one activity promotes fitness in all areas of the body—thus the value of combining activities. Here's an example of how cross-training can bring total fitness. Running does a great job of strengthening the muscles in the back of the legs, but does little for the muscles in the front of the legs. Biking does the exact opposite. Combine the sports and you get total fitness from the waist down. Add some upper-body weight training and you've achieved a total fitness program!

Flexibility. Running inhibits flexibility. Enhance it with such activities as swimming, elliptical training, and aerobic dance, which work the body through a full range of motion.

Injury prevention and recovery. Cross-training decreases risk of injury in two ways. First, muscle imbalance is a cause of injury and cross-training can strengthen key muscles not affected by running.

Second, non-weight-bearing activities can replace some running mileage, eliminating some of the injury-causing impact.

Speed training. Cross-training is a great way to add a second or third speed workout during the week without risking injury, or to speed-train when injured. Follow the same speed training principles as used with running. To do mile intervals, for example, swim or bike hard for as long as it would take to run a good mile. Take the appropriate rest interval and go again.

Recovery days. Follow hard days with a day or more of cross-training. Your tired body will welcome the opportunity to exercise without being pounded, and the increased supply of blood promotes recovery.

Change of pace. Training can become tiring. Give yourself some time off without guilt. Taking a day off, or even a week or two, for another aerobic exercise will give you a chance to rebuild, regenerate. Whatever exercise you select for a change of pace, continue to run a few times each week to keep your "running legs." For example, if you go for a two-week biking trip, try to run a couple of times each week for at least 30 minutes. This will ease the transition when you return to running.

Excuse buster. For many reasons, such as traveling or bad weather, you may not be able to get out the door to run. But you may still be able to cross-train. No obstacle needs to stop a determined exerciser. Rumor has it that the great Czech Olympic champion Emil Zatopek was on the way out the door for a run when his wife asked him to do the laundry. He reportedly placed the dirty clothes in the bathtub, filled the tub with water, added soap, and ran in place for two hours! How's that for cross-training!

Mental toughness. Cross-training can challenge you to hang in there. Some examples: keeping up with a computerized program on a bike, making it through a rugged mountain bike course, or completing an intense aerobics class.

Variety. By varying exercises, your running muscles won't get strained and your enthusiasm for running won't get drained.

RUNNING EQUIVALENT MILEAGE

Runners respect mileage—training mileage to record in diaries, to count and discuss and overestimate. Miles are the runner's language. How, then, to speak that language and still stop runners from overtraining? Or to make injured runners appreciate the value of sensible alternatives to running? I developed a system that I call the "running equivalent" (RE), and detailed its value originally in a feature article in *Runner's World*. RE is not running, but it is expressed in miles and goes into the training diary. Runners are comfortable with it.

In the RE system, any high-quality aerobic activity can be expressed in terms of running miles. Simply replace running minute for minute with cross-training. Approximate the distance you would have gone had you spent the exercise period running. If you normally run 4 miles in a half hour, then 30 minutes of cross-training earns you 4 RE miles. Log them in your diary as such: "RE—4 miles." RE training works because the heart and lungs don't differentiate. They benefit almost equally from equal amounts of aerobic activity, provided the heart rate is about the same. Fitness is improved when the heart rate stays in the training range for an extended period of time. It doesn't matter what form of exercise gets it there.

CROSS-TRAINING GUIDELINES

You can simulate the aerobic value of running and even the anaerobic value of running fast, but no alternative activity uses the same specific muscle fibers as running. Hour for hour, running is the best training for the runner. The ideal use of RE mileage would be to limit it to 10 to 25 percent of your total aerobic mileage. If using cross-training to supplement running, establish a minimum weekly running mileage goal and build cross-training around it. For example, if you want to run 40 miles a week but feel that 30 is the safe limit for your body, schedule in your 30 miles and space 10 or more RE miles around it.

Begin a cross-training program slowly, and do it every other day, alternating with running if possible. It's easy for a fit runner to zoom through a new activity full of energy. An hour may pass quite quickly. But it may be better to start with 20 to 30 minutes. Increase the length of workouts by no more than 10 to 20 minutes each week. Be conservative because different muscles will be used, or the same ones in different ways. Muscles will be vulnerable to soreness and injury if you don't start a new activity gradually. You may feel fine while exercising, but sore and stiff later from overtaxing your muscles. Training principles that apply to running also apply to cross-training, especially the principle of alternating hard and easy days. Train with moderation: Don't get carried away with the excitement of new activities and overstrain your body. A good warm-up and cool-down are also recommended. If new techniques are required, take lessons (for example, in cross-country skiing). Learn the basics of a new activity from those who are familiar with it. Wear appropriate safety equipment.

Exercise at a training heart rate or perceived exertion approximately equivalent to running. Keep the intensity level high enough to provide aerobic benefit. Don't cheat. Keep your heart rate in the training range. Since running is a weight-bearing exercise, heart rates are usually ten to fifteen beats per minute higher when running than with cross-training options. That is, a training heart rate of 150 while running may be equivalent to a THR of 140 while biking or swimming. A good guide: cross-train hard enough to keep your heart rate about ten beats per minute higher than during your runs. If your exercise is less demanding than running, do it longer. Examples may be walking or outdoor biking. An hour of outdoor biking (where you may coast down hills) may be equivalent to a half hour of running.

CROSS-TRAINING FOR THE INJURED RUNNER

When you can't run due to injury, or can only run on a limited basis, you most likely can still cross-train. Check with a sports doctor to make sure the cross-training options you choose will not aggravate existing injuries. When injured, lower running mileage to whatever level is safe and make up some or all the difference with RE miles. Perhaps start out alternating a day of running with a day of cross-training, or do 15 to 30 minutes of cross-training each day followed by 15 to 30 minutes of running. The goal is to return gradually to running full-time, but it's probably wise to reserve some training for RE miles to prevent further injury.

If unable to run at all, cross-train to minimize detraining. At least maintain minimal fitness by cross-training three to five times a week for 30 minutes at a time. If using this method, however, you may lose considerable fitness from your competitive level. So when running again, gradually ease back into hard training. To maintain near-normal fitness when forced off the running trails, replace running minute for minute with cross-training. This allows you to replace the running habit psychologically, and although you'll lose some fitness, you'll be able to return to running in good shape.

If you really *have* to be ready for a big race, then only a lack of imagination and discipline need stop you. Impersonate competitive training: Use cross-training for speed workouts and long runs. Ease into this program, follow the hard-easy system, and include training specific to your goal. To simulate a track workout of six times a half-mile in 3 minutes each with a 2-minute recovery, for example, bike or swim hard for 3 minutes, and then bike or swim easy for 2 minutes. A long run of 20 miles in three hours can be substituted on an indoor bike (or an outdoor bike if you keep the intensity up). Or, you can combine various types of equipment as long as you keep moving.

CROSS-TRAINING OPTIONS

Whatever your reasons for cross-training, many options exist. Two of the best aerobic alternatives to traditional running are treadmill running (Chapter 46) and snowshoe running (Chapter 37). Circuit training is detailed in Chapter 43. Choose one or more of the following activities to supplement running:

Aerobic dance. If you like to move to the beat of music, this may be your best bet for a fun cross-training exercise. Aerobic dance develops balance, coordination, flexibility, and muscular fitness along with aerobic fitness. Aerobic dance that involves jumping, hopping, and bouncing is an impact activity, just like running. Instead of high-impact aerobics, I recommend low-impact aerobic routines that avoid the jumping around and instead emphasize upper-body movement to raise heart rates. Step aerobics is another popular option. It consists of movements to music in which you step on and off platforms. Basically this is a low-impact, vigorous exercise that is especially good for the quads. Whatever program you use, wear shoes that are appropriate for the activity, not running shoes.

Biking. Running and biking complement each other since they strengthen opposing muscles in the legs—biking works the quads and muscles in the shin area (if toe clips are used) that are neglected with running. It also helps increase flexibility in the hip and knee joints. Regular, intense biking workouts used as a supplement to running have been proven in several studies to boost running performance.

Outdoor biking requires you to really push the pace since it is easy to coast down hills. Uphill climbs will push your heart rate much higher than if you ran the hill. It isn't easy to find areas to bike where you can push the pace fast enough to get a good workout without the interruptions of slowing for turns, traffic lights, cars, pedestrians, and more. Although biking produces its own cooling breeze, you will still dehydrate, so bring along a water bottle. You will need to bike vigorously outdoors for 3 or 4 miles to equal a mile of running. Mountain biking is popular for a good reason: It's fun. You can explore trails and rugged terrain while working the whole body. All that pushing and pulling to control the bike strengthens the upper body as well as the lower body. On tough trails, mountain biking is a very challenging a workout.

Biking on an indoor exercise bike is a safer, more consistent workout—just stay at a speed and resistance that puts you in your training range. Indoor biking can be approximately equivalent to running minute for minute. But it can be boring. To make it more enjoyable, put your bike in front of the television. Or, spend the time reading or listening to music while sweating. A good way to spice things up is to do intervals. Up the resistance and/or the pedaling rate for 1 to 3 minutes and then go easy for an equal time to recover. I enjoy the challenge of computerized bikes that automatically throw in hills and speed changes. Another challenging option is stationary bikes with arm levers. Try spin classes (rapid pedaling in low gears) if you want a really intense workout.

Biking simulates the leg motion of running, improving leg speed and the ability to run uphill. Try to pedal at a revolution per minute (rpm) similar to your running stride rate per minute. A faster rpm increases running leg speed. Periodically count your running stride rate per minute and compare it to your biking rpms. Most competitive bikers pedal at a rate of 90 rpms, which is the recommended stride rate for competitive runners. A 90-rpm cadence may be too fast for many runners, but at least strive for an 80-rpm pace. To keep this pace you may need to lower your gears or decrease the resistance on the bike. Working out in a high gear with too much resistance causes knee strain and slows turnover. Make sure the seat height is appropriate. You need a slight bend in the knee at the bottom of your stroke. Ease into biking to allow the shoulders and neck muscles, hands, and buttocks time to adjust to the work. Most runners find their legs fatigue quicker than they run out of breath when biking.

Cross-country skiing. Aerobics guru Dr. Ken Cooper ranks this as the number-one aerobic activity because it involves all the upper- and lower-body muscles in vigorous activity. Elite cross-country skiers are considered by many to be the most fit of all athletes. The gliding action of the legs strengthens and stretches the leg muscles, while driving the ski poles strengthens the shoulders, arms, and abdominals. In one invigorating workout you promote all the components of fitness. Another big plus: You skim along rather than pound the ground, thus minimizing the risk of injury. You can benefit from this total body workout all year by using a cross-country ski simulator.

Deep-water running. This activity mimics running well because you actually are running, but without the pounding. You run in deep water using a flotation device to keep you suspended. As you run, the resistance of the water makes your whole body work hard—even the upper body. While running in the water, heart rate will be 10 to 15 percent lower than for the same effort on land. Other than that, the same training principles apply. This can be an especially tiring workout when you first try it, so start off conservatively. Build gradually from a few minutes up to 30 minutes or more. If you don't have access to deep water or flotation devices, you can try shallow-water running. Just stand in water up to your waist and run widths of the shallow end of the pool (or parallel to shore) against the resistance of the water. You can also run in place in water up to your thighs, concentrating on raising the knees.

Elliptical trainers. With elliptical trainers you stand on pedals which cycle around in an elongated oval as you push. It's just like biking, but you're standing. Your legs go through a full range of motion so it's great for stretching out your muscles. You can get in more mileage with limited impact. Shock force is only half of that in treadmill running, yet it is a weight-bearing activity which helps keep bones strong. I find it helpful as a warmup prior to running and to add a few more miles to long runs without the pounding. I used mine to come back to running quickly after breaking my ribs and vertebrae in a fall. You can use arm levers to work the upper body and stride backward to relieve boredom and work different muscles. In some models you can increase elevation for hill running.

Racquet sports. Tennis, racquetball, and squash are excellent for developing muscle fitness and flexibility, and, if play is continuous and vigorous, aerobic fitness. Play singles, not doubles, at as high a level of intensity as you can, with minimal resting between volleys. The fast starts and stops and bursts of speed contribute to leg speed and can substitute to some degree for interval training.

Rowers/riders. Whether you use an indoor rowing machine or row on a lake or river, this is an excellent aerobic activity that places a minimum of strain on the bones and joints. It works the upper body as well as the lower body and can be a very rugged workout. Indoor rowing can get boring, so the use of intervals or computerized challenges make it more fun. Get tips for proper form to improve performance and minimize injury. Be sure to keep the back straight and avoid straining it by allowing your legs, arms, and shoulders to do the work. Canoeing and kayaking are two other similar and fun sports.

Riders are similar to rowing machines and also offer a tremendous total fitness workout. You sit on a bike seat and pull a bar toward you, using a variety of grips to work different muscles. The intensity of the workout can be adjusted by changing the position of the feet or adding more resistance. I use one of these machines as part of my weight training circuit to strengthen the upper body and improve range of motion while adding a few more RE miles.

Skating. There are many options for skating for fitness: roller-skating, inline-skating, and ice skating. If you swing your arms vigorously, skating works both the upper and lower body. Because of the lateral motion involved, skating strengthens muscles not used much in running: buttocks, abductors, adductors, and hip flexors. It particularly builds strong quads. You need to skate about twice as fast as you run to benefit aerobically. Further, you need to keep skating nonstop with your arms and legs always in motion. You lose fitness benefits while coasting along. If you choose to skate on the roads and sidewalks with runners, bikers, pedestrians, and cars—be careful! And *please*—don't weave in and out of traffic and buzz by us runners. It is wise to wear protective helmets and padding—knees, wrists, elbows. Skating is a nonimpact activity—until you fall.

Soccer and basketball. I've seen plenty of athletes with several years as soccer players develop into very good runners. Depending upon the length and intensity of play, a game of soccer may involve anywhere from 2 to 6 miles of stop-and-go running, including plenty of sprints. As a result it provides both a good aerobic and anaerobic workout. Basketball is also a great conditioner that involves lots of stop-and-go running. Full-court play at a fairly intense level gives plenty of aerobic work. You'll also get in some quality anaerobic action as you sprint up and down the court.

Lateral movement and stop-and-go activities such as soccer, basketball, and racquet sports may overstress your runner's legs and also increase the chance of ankle sprains. Further, these sports are weight-bearing activities that, combined with running, could result in overuse injuries. Don't wear running shoes while playing these sports or you'll risk turning an ankle. Wear shoes with good lateral support.

Stair climbers. These machines provide a similar aerobic benefit as running but without the impact. You don't go airborne, so the weight load is shared by both feet, and the platforms "give" as you step on them. Stair climbing is a very similar action to running because you are lifting your center of gravity by using your leg muscles. Since you need to lift your knees high while exercising, stair climbing really strengthens the quads, which don't get much work running on the flats. This improves your running stride length. Stride rate, however, isn't enhanced since leg turnover is slower on a stair climber. To get the most from your workout, pay attention to your posture. Don't lean forward or grip the rails. Pump the arms as in running to increase intensity, but be prepared to grab the rails or slow the machine if you are having trouble keeping up with the pace. Stair climbing may overstrain the Achilles tendons. To minimize this, don't drive down on the ball of the foot as you would with running; instead, keep your feet flat on the step—envision yourself running flat-footed.

To increase the fitness challenge and decrease boredom you can follow computerized programs of interval work. At my fitness club I take on the challenge of "the Gauntlet" machine, which throws speed bursts and hills at me at paces equivalent to sub-6-minute running miles. When I'm done with this hard session I'm soaked with sweat but my muscles aren't beaten-up like they would have been if I ran that fast on the roads or track.

A challenging option is a hill-climbing simulator that adds levers that you pull down with your arms while climbing. You feel like a monkey climbing a tree, but believe me, it is a total fitness workout deluxe.

Swimming. This is a full-body, no-impact workout. Swimming really strengthens the upper body, which is neglected with running, and the midsection and back, which are critical to good running posture. It stretches the hamstrings and hip flexor muscles, which are tightened with running. It also improves ankle, back, and shoulder flexibility. Further, the massaging action of the water helps tired muscles recover from the strain of exercise. Swimming is probably the least stressful cross-training choice, and therefore ideal after an injury. Water movement around the injured area has therapeutic benefits, and swimming seems to ensure more blood supply to injured areas and improve the possibility of quick recovery.

When swimming, you must really concentrate on breathing. The result is you learn to inhale and exhale more completely and more rhythmically. This control of your breathing carries over into your running and helps control the "panic breathing" that may occur in races. Since the body is completely surrounded by water there is a cooling effect. You can exercise without fear of overheating—no matter how hot it is outdoors. Thus, this is a great option when running in heat and humidity is getting you down. Doctors recommend swimming, because of the humidity at indoor pools, as the best option for runners suffering from asthma.

With swimming, your heart will beat slower for the given effort by ten or more beats per minute than with running. It's okay to let your heart rate fall off by that much, but not by much more. Swimming is such a relaxing exercise that it is easy to fall off your desired intensity. Just as in running, keep your arms and legs going. A good goal is to swim at a heart rate that is at least 60 percent of your maximum. Four or five miles of running is approximately equal to a mile of swimming. Unskilled swimmers may find their heart rates rising quickly, and it may be difficult for them to swim for long because of poor technique or unconditioned "swimming muscles." A few swimming lessons may be a good idea.

You have to be patient and disciplined to train in the limited atmosphere of swimming. For variety and to work different muscles, vary your speed and use different strokes. It may help to break up the swim with different strokes per lap, or to alternate a hard swim lap with a brief rest interval rather than swimming one monotonous lap after another.

Walking/race walking. The key to walking for fitness is to move along fast enough to produce a training effect. As you get fitter with running, the faster you will need to walk. This means really pumping the arms and striding along. To help keep the heart rate up to a recommended minimum of 60 percent of maximum, you can walk while using hand weights. By vigorously pumping weighted hands you will increase your heart rate quickly. Hiking over rugged trails and up hills, even mountains, is an activity that can be a lot of fun and provide fitness for the whole family.

While off running for nearly two months due to a bad fall that broke my ribs and a vertebra, I was determined to travel my running routes anyway to keep fit—both physically and mentally. So I walked them at a very fast pace, using my heart rate monitor to keep over 60 percent. My 8-mile loop that took an hour to run became, at first, a 2-hour walk. Instead of running 50 to 60 miles a week, I walked that distance. I included long walks of 2½ hours to prepare for my upcoming marathon. This program ate up a lot of time, but it also burned lots of calories and kept my legs in shape. I eased back to running by alternating 5 minutes of running at a quick pace with 5 minutes of very brisk walking, again over my normal courses. Within a few weeks I was able to run 20-milers continuously since my body was used to going long. Four months after my accident, I completed the New York City Marathon—running all the way! I still incorporate walks into my overall training schedule.

Race walking is the most intense form of this type of exercise. This Olympic sport is a combination of running and walking without the pounding of running. You race-walk faster than you walk, but slower than you run. A top race walker can walk sub-6-minute miles, but the average person will move along at paces ranging between 10 and 20 minutes per mile. Three miles of race walking will be approximately equal to 4 miles of running. Race walking involves vigorously driving the hips and pumping the arms to propel the body forward, but a part of one foot is always on the ground. You don't have to race to enjoy race walking, but you can compete if you choose. Race walking strengthens areas not affected by running or regular fitness walking—muscles in the front of the legs, abdominals, buttocks, upper body, arms. Because race walkers learn to drive their arms really powerfully, the runner who race-walks can also improve running form and gain an awareness of the value of arm action in increasing running speed. Race walking form involves an exaggerated motion causing your fanny to wiggle as you walk down the street. If you can ignore the stares and comments from onlookers, race walking is a great exercise.

CHAPTER 46

Treadmill Training

What, Bob Glover run on a treadmill? I would have been laughed out of town if I was caught running on one of those contraptions in the seventies. But now Shelly-lynn and I often take advantage of our treadmill. And we're certainly not alone: Treadmill sales exceed those of all other home exercise equipment.

Even Elites run on treadmills. Ingrid Kristiansen trained through tough Norwegian winters with two-a-day workouts on her treadmill. Once a week she ran 20 miles in about two hours. "I enjoy the time I spend on the treadmill," she said. "It helps me develop a good deal of concentration and mental toughness. When I am finally able to run the roads again, it's no problem to run long either in training or in races." She had no problem running long in the London Marathon in the spring of 1985. Coming off a winter of mostly treadmill running, she set a world record of 2:21:06.

BENEFITS OF TREADMILL TRAINING

I get questions all the time about the value of treadmill running. First, it's of equal aerobic value to running outside as long as your heart rate is in its training range. A 30-minute run is a 30-minute run. The treadmill eliminates worry about proper pacing. This allows you to concentrate on other things such as running form, breathing pattern, or visualization of an upcoming race. You can add the resistance of hills at the touch of a button. Just as important, you can make the hills go away! If you run on a treadmill at a gym you don't have to worry about finding a training partner—you may be surrounded by a roomful of exercisers. However, treadmills are so popular many clubs have 20-minute limits. You may need to move on to another aerobic machine to complete your workout. The better choice: Get a treadmill for your home. Here are additional benefits of treadmill training:

Takes bad weather out of the workout. Treadmilling provides a psychological break from either having to run in the heat, cold, or rain *again*, or feeling guilty about skipping a workout. An air-conditioned exercise room not only brings down the heat, but the humidity and pollution as well. This eliminates those slow, sluggish summertime runs when conditions are miserable and energy is low. Further, dehydration is controlled. Not only will you lose less fluids due to sweating, you can keep fluids nearby for easy hydration. Place a fan near the treadmill to keep you cool—you'll get warm in a hurry without a breeze.

Running inside where it is warm and the footing is good allows you to run faster than you can in the snow or while wearing several layers of clothing. This helps prevent your speed from slipping away over the winter. During the winter months, running indoors in a warm room will help you acclimate for upcoming races in warmer weather.

A good option is to split your runs in bad weather: Start with 30 to 60 minutes outdoors (or whatever time you can tolerate) and then head inside and jump on the treadmill to complete your workout. Finish split runs indoors to ensure comfort when most needed. Split running can be particularly helpful to survive long runs on hot or cold days. Try two-a-days a few times a week to lessen the effect of the weather: Run once outdoors and once indoors, for example in the morning and evening.

Safety. Shelly-lynn and I often run on our treadmill rather than go out after dark. When traveling, choose a hotel with a good treadmill in their fitness center.

Injury prevention and rehabilitation. If the treadmill has good shock-absorbing belts, it will produce less pounding than pavement. Treadmills eliminate slants encountered on most paved surfaces.

These factors reduce injury risk. Treadmill running on an incline is often prescribed as the safest way to ease back into running after injury.

Schedule conflicts. Sometimes a quick run on the treadmill is the only way to fit in a run. If you must be around to take an important call, just put the phone by the treadmill. Parents can work out while keeping track of the kids. You'll also please your spouse if at times you run at home instead of leaving them alone.

Extra or easy days. You can sneak in a few easy runs each week to increase mileage. Sometimes I'll hop on the treadmill while watching the news. Use treadmill runs to recover from hard training or to baby an injury. The machine offers less impact than the roads and eliminates tiring hills. Just set the speed at an easy pace and keep it there.

ADAPTING OUTDOOR TRAINING

You can do virtually any run on a treadmill that you can do outside:

Speed training. Want to run mile intervals in 6 minutes each? No problem. Turn on the treadmill, warm up with an easy mile or two, and then set the speed to 10 miles per hour (6-minute pace). When your 6 minutes are up, you've run a 6-minute mile. Slow the speed to an easy recovery period and go again. The treadmill makes sure you keep on pace. All you have to do is keep up! Tempo runs can be accomplished more precisely on a treadmill. Set the pace at, for example, 20 seconds per mile slower than 10K race pace and take off for 15 to 30 minutes. Fartlek runs can be yours with the touch of a button: Vary the speed and elevation to keep the run challenging. Treadmills are especially valuable for hill repeats. Just set the desired grade and complete the time period. Then level it and slow the pace for the recovery period. A special bonus here: You don't have the potentially dangerous downhills to get back to the start. "Running hills" on the treadmill is particularly valuable for runners lacking natural hills on their courses.

Long runs. Although running long outdoors is more specific to marathon racing, you can get in all or parts of your long runs on a treadmill. This is particularly helpful in extreme weather.

Practice racing. Some machines offer programs that vary the speed and elevation as you run along. They simulate the stresses of racing. You may also be able to program your own courses. You can even practice downhills: Put a block of wood under the rear support and take off running.

OUTRUNNING BOREDOM

Many runners think of treadmilling as going nowhere fast. To liven it up, vary the speed and elevation. Listen to music. Shellylynn prefers brisk marches and powerful classical music. Watch television. Tape track meets and road races and play them back to inspire your runs. I break my runs into halves—at halftime I take a short break, which allows me concentrate better on the second half of the run.

ADJUSTING TO TREADMILL TRAINING

Running on a treadmill is somewhat different from outdoor running. First, it feels like you're running much faster than the control panel indicates. The treadmill's belt pulls your foot beneath you, adding to your sense of increased speed. But not only do you feel like you're going faster, it requires less effort. About 7 percent less energy is required, equivalent to running a slight downhill, to run on a flat treadmill rather than a flat road. Why? You don't face any air resistance because your body is not moving forward, nor do you encounter headwinds. When your foot strikes the moving surface there is less braking action than on stationary surfaces. The treadmill does some of the work for you: You don't need to push off as hard as you would on a road surface.

Since you can run a given pace easier on a treadmill, you must run slightly faster to keep your effort consistent—about 15 to 30 seconds per mile on a flat treadmill compared to a flat road. As an option to running faster on the treadmill to equal outdoor effort, increase the incline 1 or 2 percent. Note that pace per mile as indicated on computerized machines may be inaccurate. As long as you are exercising at the same perceived exertion or heart rate, exact pace isn't important. Don't trust their mileage indicators either. Instead, estimate mileage by elapsed time.

Running form may change on a treadmill. To keep pace with the moving belt, runners tend to lean forward or run up too far on their toes. This combined with the slight pulling motion of the belts could cause lower leg and Achilles tendon problems. Concentrate on good form and be sure to warm up slowly before settling into your pace. The first few runs on a treadmill should be at a pace slower and a distance less than what's normal for you to allow adjustment to the feel of the machine. You want to get used to the rhythm and gain confidence that you aren't going to fly off the back.

If you are a dedicated treadmill runner and intend to run some races on the roads, it would be a good idea run on roads a few times a week to get used to the surface. Some runners actually marathon-train exclusively on treadmills. I advise them to ease into long runs on pavement to prepare for the stress of the marathon, but to stay on the treadmill for most of their runs if that's what they enjoy.

CHAPTER 47

Heart Rate Monitor Training

Heart rate is a good measure of how a runner's body responds physiologically during training. Heart rate, or pulse, is the number of times per minute your heart beats. It reflects the amount of work the heart must do to supply blood to the exercising body. Generally the faster it beats, the harder you are working out. The slower it beats in response to vigorous exercise, the better shape you are in. For example, perhaps your heart beat 140 times per minute at a pace of 8 minutes per mile for an easy 5-mile run. After perhaps two months of quality training, it may rise to only 130 to 135 beats per minute at the same speed and conditions.

Four levels of heart rates are important in developing a safe, effective training program: the resting, maximum, training, and recovery heart rates.

RESTING HEART RATE (RHR)

This is your heart rate at rest—either when first waking in the morning (before getting out of bed) or when you are very relaxed during the day. Your pre-exercise heart rate is not the same as RHR. Because your body anticipates getting called into action, pre-exercise heart rate will be higher than when you are relaxed. The average RHR for men is 60 to 80 beats-per-minute; for women, 70 to 90. RHR typically decreases with age. Sedentary individuals may have RHRs that exceed 100 beats per minute. As you get into better shape, RHR lowers. A well-conditioned adult's RHR may be around 60 or below. Serious endurance athletes often have RHRs in the 40- to 50-beats-per-minute range; some Elite athletes have been measured as low as 28 beats per minute. Record RHR each morning in your diary. This figure, over the course of a training season, is a good measure of fitness. RHR may serve as a warning signal of overtraining. A morning RHR 10 percent above average may indicate that you have not recovered sufficiently from training. Rest or cut back until it returns to normal. An elevated RHR may be a sign of illness. It may increase if you are not getting quality sleep, are overstressed or dehydrated, or consume too much caffeine. Significant increases may relate to extremes in temperature and altitude. It may also increase or decrease with various medications.

MAXIMUM HEART RATE (MHR)

When exercising, heart rate increases in direct response to the intensity of the work until you are at or near the point of exhaustion. At this point the heart "peaks out" and cannot beat faster. This level is referred to as maximum heart rate. MHR decreases with age by about 1 beat per year for adults, perhaps somewhat less for highly fit older runners. Knowing your MHR is essential to training programs based on heart rate monitoring. Accurate training heart rate ranges are dependent upon an accurate MHR.

There are three methods to determining MHR: laboratory testing, field testing, and estimates based on formulas. The most precise way to measure MHR is in a fitness laboratory with a maximal oxygen uptake test. Scientists monitor heart rate with an electrocardiogram while the work load is progressively increased on a treadmill. Very experienced, fit runners can estimate MHR fairly accurately by taking one of the following running tests. The highest heart rate you reach—usually toward the end of the test run—will be your MHR. For best results, use a heart rate monitor. If possible, get another runner to help push you at the end of these runs to get you as close as possible to your MHR. Since MHR will change slightly as you age, test it at least annually. Here are four examples of MHR tests:

Half-mile/mile test: Warm up for 30 minutes at an easy pace. Then, run a quarter-mile (or 400 meters) hard at about 95 percent effort. Run even harder for the second quarter-mile to complete the half-mile test. You may need to repeat this run after a very short recovery period of 2 minutes if you think you can reach a higher MHR figure. An alternative test is to run an all-out-effort mile.

Steep hill test: Warm up for 30 minutes at an easy pace. Then, run up a fairly steep hill for 1½ to 3 minutes at a hard pace. Run back down slowly to recover and then run the hill very hard again. This time run the last 100 yards at maximum speed. Run the hill three to five times if necessary to reach the highest possible MHR.

5K/10K race test: Run a 5K or 10K race at a hard, steady pace. You should reach within 5 to 10 beats of your MHR with about 1 mile to go in the race.

Treadmill test: This mimics the sophisticated lab tests. After warming up with 20 minutes of easy running on a flat treadmill, increase the speed to your tempo pace: about 85 percent of estimated MHR. This is about 15 to 30 seconds per mile slower than 10K race pace. Every minute, increase the elevation by 2 percent while keeping speed constant. When your heart rate reaches its highest level, you've come close to your MHR.

If you are able to push yourself, you will get within 5 to 10 beats of your actual MHR with these tests. If you don't want to take formal tests, just wear a heart rate monitor during hard speed workouts and races. You'll know that your MHR will be at least the highest heart rate ever recorded. These exhausting methods are not recommended for unfit runners. MHR is sport specific. You have to do a MHR test for each activity; bikers and swimmers, for example, may get an MHR 5 to 15 beats lower than that achieved with running.

Estimating with Formulas

Here are some formulas exercise scientists use to estimate MHR for runners not wanting to exhaust themselves with tests.

Subtract age from 220. This is the most common formula. It assumes you lose one beat from MHR each year as you age. At age fifty, for example, mine was 220 minus 50 for an estimated MHR of 170; Shelly-lynn's at age thirty-five was 185. Some studies indicate that women have a higher MHR than men and recommend that women subtract their age from 226 to determine MHR. Thus, Shelly-lynn's would be increased to 191. I recommend using the same formula for men and women. Very fit runners tend to have a slightly lower MHR (by about 5 to 10 beats per minute) than untrained individuals of the same age. Since the formulas were determined using the average unfit population, some experts suggest competitive runners add 5 or 10 points to modify the formula: 225 to 230 minus age. Otherwise, their training range may be slightly low.

Subtract one-half your age from 205. This formula may be best for masters athletes. It theorizes runners over age thirty who have remained "chronically fit" lose less than one beat per year from MHR. The 220-minus-age formula may result in a training range too easy for these athletes. Hence this formula is used: MHR = 205 minus ½ age. Thus for a fit fifty-year-old, MHR is increased from 170 to 180.

TRAINING HEART RATE (THR)

What should your heart rate be when training? You need to run at an intensity high enough to get a sufficient training effect, but not overstress the body. To safely increase endurance, run at a steady pace within your estimated THR. This range falls between two numbers—a minimum and a cutoff heart rate. Between 70 and 85 percent of MHR is where aerobic conditioning improves the most, although some easy runs in the 60 to 70 percent range will still be beneficial. How does this relate to pace per mile for highly trained competitive runners? A pace of 2 minutes per mile slower than your 10K race pace is approximately equal to 60 percent of your MHR; 1½ minutes slower than 10K pace equals about 70 percent; and a minute slower than 10K pace equals about 80 percent.

Above 85 percent of MHR you will spend a great deal of extra effort (and agony) with little additional aerobic fitness value. But to perform well in races you do need to train intensely. Somewhere between 80 to 90 percent of MHR is where aerobic training phases into anaerobic training. The area between aerobic and anaerobic training is called anaerobic or lactate threshold. Approximate pace for threshold is 10 to 30 seconds per mile slower than 10K race pace. If you push your heart rate above this threshold you are running anaerobically and you will begin to rapidly accumulate lactic acid, leading to fatigue. Most runners work at between 85 and 95 percent of their MHR during hard workouts and races.

Build a solid endurance base with plenty of training within the recommended THR range before adding harder runs and races. You can, and should, make adjustments during runs to keep within your THR. By slowing the pace you can lower your heart rate; by picking it up, you can raise it. If your THR is higher than normal for your effort, then search for the reasons. Extremes of heat and cold, headwind, and hills are obvious ones. Others include dehydration and diminishing glycogen stores. Overtraining, including lack of recovery from hard or long runs, may also be a reason. Slow the pace, shorten the run, or take off a day or more from running. Also, if RHR is elevated for any of the various reasons previously mentioned, THR may be affected.

THR based on a predicted MHR from formulas are only estimates. Some error is possible. You may find that you can exceed your cutoff without breathing hard. Or you may be tired at the minimum level of your range. This system is a general training target based on averages of many subjects. It works quite well for most runners. Some runners won't fit the averages. Let your body tell you what is best. When in doubt, rely on the talk test system: Run at a pace at which you can converse.

Determining THR

1. *Determine MHR*. Use the various methods detailed previously. For example, I'll use my estimated MHR of 170 at age fifty.
2. *Multiply MHR by 60 percent to determine the lower range of your training heart rate zone for easy runs* (60 percent of 170 is 102).
3. *Multiply MHR by 70 percent to determine the upper limit of easy runs and the lower limit of most aerobic training runs* (70 percent of 170 is 119).
4. *Multiply MHR by 85 percent to determine the upper range of your training heart rate zone* (85 percent of 170 is 145). In our example, I should do most of my runs between 119 and 145 beats per minute.

To save the math in determining THR, refer to Figure 47.1.

FIGURE 47.1: TRAINING HEART RATE RANGE*				
Age	**60 percent**	**70 percent**	**85 percent**	**Maximum**
15–19	123–121	144–141	174–171	205–201
20–24	120–118	140–137	170–167	200–196
25–29	117–115	136–134	166–162	195–191
30–34	114–112	133–130	161–158	190–186
35–39	111–109	129–127	157–154	185–181
40–44	108–106	126–123	153–150	180–176
45–49	105–103	122–120	148–145	175–171
50–54	102–100	119–116	144–141	170–166
55–59	99–97	115–113	140–137	165–161
60–64	96–94	112–109	136–133	160–156
65–69	93–91	108–106	132–128	155–151
70–74	90–88	105–102	127–124	150–146
75–79	87–85	101–99	123–120	145–141

**Beats per minute as percentage of estimated MHR based on the formula of 220 minus age. Heart rate ranges listed correlate with age range listed. Interpolate to estimate your training range if you are between the age ranges.*

FIGURE 47.2: RECOMMENDED TRAINING HEART RATE RANGES	
Percent of Maximum HR	**Recommended for**
60 to 70 percent	**Easy recovery days and easy long runs.**
70 to 85 percent	**Maximum aerobic fitness.**
85 to 90 percent	**Threshold between running aerobically and anaerobically; somewhere in this range you can't talk comfortably while running. For most runners, this is at about 85 percent. This is tempo run pace.**
85 to 98 percent	**Range for speed training at race pace and faster.**

RECOVERY HEART RATE

A proper cool-down is essential following all runs. This consists of an easy walk for 5 to 10 minutes followed by stretching. The goal of the cool-down is to get your heart rate down to within 20 beats of your pre-warm-up RHR. If it takes a long time for your heart rate to drop, you may be exercising too hard or haven't cooled down properly. It may take longer for your heart rate to recover when running in hot weather or at higher altitudes. The more fit you are, the sooner your heart rate will recover after exercise.

FINDING HEART RATE BY TOUCH

You can measure heart rate manually at several places on your body including the left side of the chest (directly over the heart) or at the upturned wrist (directly below the index finger). Use your fingers to take this measure—but not your thumb, which has its own pulse. The most common place to count heart rate is the carotid artery, which is just in front of the large vertical muscle along the sides of the neck beneath the jaw. Gently feel for a heartbeat there with the tips of your first two fingers. Don't press too hard, as this slows the heart rate.

Count the number of beats for 10 seconds and multiply by 6. That will give you your heart rate per minute. For example, if you count 20 beats in 10 seconds and multiply by six, your heart rate is approximately 120 beats per minute. It is more difficult to count exercise heart rate than RHR. You will need to stop briefly to do this. Count immediately after stopping or your heart rate drops too quickly for an accurate measure. It isn't necessary to jog in place while measuring. Move gently back into running as soon as you have checked your pulse. At first, you may want to monitor your heart rate three or four times during a run. Later, when you develop a feel for your pace, you may choose to monitor your heart rate halfway through your workout and immediately at the end of your run.

Monitoring heart rate by touch is inconvenient and inexact. It's hard to stop quickly and then count heartbeats when you are huffing, puffing, and sweating. Further, if you are not running, your heart rate is dropping quickly while you are counting.

HEART RATE MONITORS

By measuring heart rate accurately, runners can get more benefit from time spent training. The most efficient, simplest way to follow heart rate is to wear a monitor. They are very easy to use. A lightweight transmitter is strapped across the chest with an adjustable elastic belt. Electrodes sense the heart's electrical signals from the skin and transmit this information to a wrist monitor. This is just like a wristwatch except that besides time of day and running time, it also flashes your heart rate digitally—at rest, while running, while recovering, or anytime.

With a monitor you don't have to stop exercising to check heart rate—just read your watch. Further, you can see how your heart rate reacts to hills, heat, humidity, wind, change in pace, and so on. You get instant, accurate feedback. The fancier models set off alarms above or below a set training range. They give you all kinds of data including: average heart rate for the run, how many minutes you ran above and below your range, and the highest and lowest heart rate reached during the run. You can even get models that will download data to your computer.

I don't wear my monitor on each and every run. That to me is too stressful. It seems like I'm always being tested, taking the pure joy out of running. I find it motivating to use a few times a week as it provides something to think about. Many runners find monitors as valuable as their running shoes and bring them along on every workout. Most will benefit from wearing a monitor at least occasionally.

Here are a few miscellaneous tips for using monitors:

- Dampen the contact areas of the electrodes to make it easier for the transmitter to pick up accurate readings.
- If your monitor seems to be going haywire but soon goes back to normal, it may be due to electrical interference from various sources including power cables and electronic equipment (including your treadmill). If you run too close to another runner wearing a monitor your transmitter may pick up the wrong signal. In fact, Shelly-lynn and I have "crossed signals" a few times.
- Make sure the chest strap is properly placed in the center of the chest. For women, it should go just below the bra. Polar makes a special sports bra that includes insertion points for the chest strap. This may be more comfortable for many women.

BENEFITS OF HEART RATE MONITOR TRAINING

Prevents overtraining. Safe, effective training is enhanced with a monitor. Just keep within your training zone to keep from running too fast. This may require that you slow down. Check your monitor periodically to make sure you haven't increased the intensity. Monitors serve as a good brake.

Prevents undertraining. A few runners run too slow too often. The majority of runs should be in the 70 to 80 percent range; 85 to 95 percent range for speed training.

Tempo runs. The goal is to run at your lactate threshold: approximately 85 to 90 percent of MHR. You can estimate this intensity by your running pace (10 to 30 seconds slower than 10K pace), but heart rate is a much more effective monitor.

Intervals. Short intervals should be run in the 90 to 95 percent range; 85 to 90 percent for long intervals. The monitor can also help you judge your recovery period. The accepted standard is to wait until the recovery heart rate is below 120 before you go again. A good goal is to wait until your heart rate is below 65 percent of MHR before starting the next interval.

Monitor fitness. I periodically check my fitness on a familiar course. For example, I run 8-minute-per-mile pace for my regular 8-mile course and record my average heart rate for the run. I repeat this run several weeks later under similar weather conditions. If I notice an improvement in average heart rate, I have indication that I'm more fit.

Race pacing. Some runners, including Shelly-lynn, race with monitors so they can better judge the intensity of their effort. It keeps them from starting too fast, slowing too much during the race without realizing it (especially late in a race when running alone), or running hills too aggressively. Mile splits provide infrequent and sometimes inaccurate feedback as to effort. Rather than aiming to run an evenly paced race, try running an even effort race by holding at a steady heart rate level in the early going. Later you can pick up the pace if you feel good. With experience you'll find the heart rate you can sustain for each racing distance. Highly conditioned competitors may reach and sustain 95 percent of MHR or higher in their 5K and 10K races, and 90 percent or higher in their marathons. For most runners good goals are as follows:

> **5K:** 85 to 90 percent by the end of the first mile, and then gradually increase to 90 to 95 percent plus by the finish.

10K: 80 to 85 percent by the end of the first mile, and then gradually increase to 85 to 93 percent plus by the finish.

Half-marathon: 75 to 80 percent for the first 2 miles, and then gradually increase to 85 to 89 percent by the finish.

Marathon: 70 to 75 percent for the first 3 miles and then gradually increase to 80 to 85 percent by the finish. First-time marathoners may benefit from staying under 70 percent for the first 20 miles.

Due to "cardiac drift," heart rate tends to move upward (by 5 to 15 beats per minute) late in long training runs or races, especially under conditions of heat stress. This may be caused by a combination of glycogen depletion, muscle fatigue, and dehydration, which causes the heart to beat faster to keep blood supply constant. Thus you may be running the same pace, yet experience an increase in heart rate. In a marathon your heart rate may "drift" from 70 percent at the start to 80 percent by the finish while maintaining the same effort. Fueling and hydrating well can partially control, but not eliminate, cardiac drift. Studies show that heart rate increases about 7 beats per minute for every 1 percent loss in body weight due to dyhydration.

What to do when your heart rate drifts late in a race? Just let your HR increase slightly as long as you feel good enough to maintain that pace. Let fatigue, not imperfect technology be your guide.

Although many runners seem to benefit from using monitors to guide pacing, particularly in long races, a sensible goal pace based on build-up races is best. Heart rate during competition is not an accurate guide to running speed since it is affected by such factors as weather, the course, and race day excitement. In fact, some research indicates that heart rate during racing is higher than during training at the same running speeds. If you stay within the appropriate heart rate ranges in training, you'll be prepared to reach a peak performance without worrying about heart rate. Race more by your watch and breathing than by heart rate.

Long run pacing. It's a common mistake to start too fast on long runs. After all, the pace you go out at for daily runs seems easy.

But those 70 to 80 percent of MHR runs can't be held over longer distances without bringing on extreme fatigue. Thus, I recommend that you start off at 60 to 70 percent of MHR for long runs. After you have settled into a comfortable pace, try to keep your heart rate under 75 percent of MHR for the remainder of the run. Again, be prepared for your heart rate to "drift" upwards by 10 to 15 beats during long runs despite running a steady pace. If tired, slow down and keep your heart rate below 75 percent.

Easy, recovery runs. Let your monitor ensure that an easy day is really an easy day. Stay under 70 percent of MHR, but above 60 percent for maximum benefit.

Heart rate monitors are fun, motivational toys that can be used to improve the quality of your training. But don't be a slave to them. You don't have to run every day following an exact scientific approach. Some runners benefit from heart rate training more than others. As with any other training aid, including this book, it can only help if you use it properly.

PART XIII

BALANCE

CHAPTER 48

Balancing Running with Life

Running well requires being in balance with the rest of your life. You can't run, or live, in a vacuum. What goes on around you affects training and race performances, and your commitment to running affects other aspects of your life.

WELLNESS

Running 10 miles a day doesn't make you immune to heart disease, cancer, or other illnesses. A total wellness program is a marriage of fitness and good health practices. It's important to eat well, control weight, manage stress, avoid smoking, minimize alcohol, and schedule regular medical exams.

SLEEP

Almost half of us sleep an hour to 90 minutes less each night than needed. Without adequate sleep, the body's homeostasis—its internal equilibrium—malfunctions. Lack of sleep interrupts the hormonal and metabolic processes that take place during the nocturnal hours. In terms of race performance, it's the sleep over the final forty-eight hours that's critical, not just the night before. Adequate sleep is also necessary to fully recover from training and racing. If you're chronically short on sleep, you'll be short on energy for your running, too.

Common causes of long-term sleep deficit include too much caffeine, stress, and irregular sleep patterns. Switch to decaffeinated products, try relaxation exercises for stress management, and set a fixed bedtime and stick to it. If you get up extra-early to run, don't do so at the expense of your needed sleep. Go to bed an hour early if you'll be getting up an hour early. If you stay up late to work, party, or watch TV too often, you'll set yourself up for sleep deficit and sluggish runs.

Sleep affects your training and training affects your sleep. Moderate training generally contributes to better sleep. Running too close to bedtime (or eating late at night after an evening run) affects your ability to get to sleep—so does hard training and racing. But these are short-term problems. Overtraining causes poor sleep which can accumulate, resulting in both long-term sleep disorders and sluggish running.

Although some people can get by with less sleep than recommended, most runners won't and still get the most out of their training runs and races. Frequent naps, especially when training hard, are a wonderful benefit for those that can fit them in. I try to nap every day for at least 30 minutes. My runs are usually of much higher quality as a result. Ideally, nap to supplement regular sleep rather than to make up for lost sleep.

Occasional sleepless nights are normal. The Better Sleep Council reports that one in three people have difficulty falling or staying asleep any given night. What to do? Try reading or watching TV to relax.

SAFETY

Runners, slow and fast, are attacked in all sorts of settings—city parks, suburban streets, country roads—and run down by cars, bikers, and inline skaters. Don't let overconfidence make you take foolish risks. Use common sense. Run safe! Here are some important tips:

- Stay alert for cars, bikers, and skaters. Run defensively. When running the roads, face traffic, and stay as far away from cars as possible. If you're running in a group, don't fill the road and think you own it. The road belongs to vehicles, not runners. Wear bright, reflective clothing day and night. Keep off roads when driving conditions are slippery or visibility is poor. Avoid high-speed roads! Better yet, stick to running paths where you don't have to share the road with cars. Since my good friend and running partner Bill Coughlin was killed by a drunk driver while running in Jackson, Michigan, I refuse to run on roads with car traffic.

- Carry ID and money. In case of an accident, you will need to be identified. For several hours after my friend was killed no one knew who he was. Like too many runners, Bill didn't carry identification. Hey, he was just going out for a run. What could happen? He had run for decades with no problem. Bring change for pay phones and some cash for food, drink, or emergencies.
- Run with a friend, group, or large dog. If you have to run alone, do so in well-populated, well-lighted, familiar areas. Run in the daylight when possible. Tell a friend or family member where you will be running and your expected return time. Vary your schedule.
- Be alert at all times. Watch and know your surroundings. Run widely around places where attackers might hide. If you sense danger, turn around, cross the street, or run for assistance. Ignore verbal harassment. Project calmness, strength, and authority while on the run and if harassed. Be prepared; carry a noisemaker. Don't wear anything that might attract a mugger. Know the location of stores, gas stations, or buildings on your route you can go to for help. Think of possible escape routes in advance. Have car or house keys ready before you stop running.
- Tune into the environment, not out. Don't wear headphones unless you are running in a well-populated area free of traffic. Remain alert to the sounds of approaching cars or potential attackers. Be aware of who is behind and ahead of you.

- If you are unsure whether it is safe to run in a certain area, or you lack a running partner and aren't comfortable going alone, or the weather is bad, or it's dark—don't run. When in doubt about your safety, choose a different route or exercise indoors.

TRAVEL

No matter how carefully you schedule training, business trips and vacations can disrupt it. With proper planning, discipline, and a flexible attitude, you can continue to train at a reasonable level when your routine is broken by travel. Here are some suggestions:

- Write workouts into your daily calendar and make every effort to keep the commitment. Try running first thing in the morning before the day fills up with appointments or tours. Otherwise, you may end up out of time or energy for a run. But be flexible, too. You have to coordinate running with business, travel, and leisure plans. Don't expect to run at your usual time, pace, or distance. Skipping a day is okay, but try not to miss two in a row. Cut back mileage goals slightly if necessary. Strive for high-quality runs that enhance your trip, not for lots of miles to enter in your training diary. Better to coast through a 30-minute run and leave time for a relaxing shower and stretch, than to squeeze in an hour of running and arrive late or frazzled for an appointment.
- Cut the pace or distance for a few days if traveling to a warmer climate or high altitude. Don't overdo it if you're a flatlander and you suddenly find hills everywhere. You may not find measured courses. Don't panic. Take a break from logging miles and run for time. If you run for 40 minutes at a pace that feels like a 10-minute-per-mile pace, give yourself credit for a 4-miler. Don't give up on speed training. Fartlek and tempo runs can be done anywhere. You can find a good hill or track in most cities.

- Go into the trip with plenty of sleep. Run the day before, and maybe even the morning of your trip. Hey, get it in while you can! But don't squeeze in a hard workout or you'll get even more tight and tired while traveling. Don't forget to enjoy the trip!
- Prepare for time zone changes. Most people experience jet lag if they make a time zone change of two to three hours or more. Symptoms increase with the number of zones crossed. Traveling west to east causes more difficulty because it's harder to adjust to earlier bedtimes. A few days before your trip, change your schedule to coincide more closely with the time at your destination. That way the biological clock in your brain will gradually adapt the time it tells you to go to bed, eat, and wake up to that of your destination. Get up, go to bed, and eat an hour earlier (or later if going east to west) each day to gradually adjust. Match how many days you do this with time zones you will cross.
- Respect travel fatigue: jet lag, increased emotional stress, lost sleep. Adjust the pace and distance of runs according to your level of fatigue. Don't force yourself to run if tired. Try a short walk or swim instead. Or take a nap first, then run. But do run as soon as possible. Studies show that exercise minimizes jet lag. Don't expect to feel real peppy on your first few days after a long trip. It takes about one day to recover for every hour in time zone change. Get into a regular sleeping pattern as soon as possible.
- Arrive one day before races for each time zone crossed. You can minimize this if you trick your biological clock as detailed above. If it isn't possible to reset your clock or to arrive early, arrive the day of or day before the event and hope jet lag doesn't hit until after the race.
- Think of travel as a running opportunity gained, not lost. If you are convinced a trip will destroy your training, it will. Look at it as a chance to ex-

plore on the run—but add a dash of caution. Contact the hotel desk, local clubs, or running stores for safe running routes, group runs, and race schedules. Pick hotels near running trails and with a fitness center. If it is difficult or unsafe to run, particularly after dark, run indoors on a treadmill, swim, or bike.

- Pack wisely. I stuff running gear into my travel bag first. Then comes anything else that fits. Bring a small bag of running gear on the plane in case baggage is lost. I found that out the hard way on a book tour to San Francisco. Pack for the weather where you're going, not where you are. You want to be safe and comfortable.
- Drink plenty of fluids when flying. Low cabin humidity causes dehydration, which adds to travel fatigue. During the flight, get up and move around every 30 minutes or so. Try some gentle stretching and relaxation exercises. Wear loose clothes and remove your shoes. Your feet may swell considerably due to the pressure in the cabin. If driving more than an hour or two, stop regularly to get out, walk, and stretch. Share the driving.
- Drink only bottled water if the local water is of questionable quality. Carry it on the run. Beware of the local food. Eat only well-cooked food and fruits you can peel yourself. If you test local foods that you aren't familiar with, stomach stress may result.
- Find out in advance where to run if possible. One service available to the traveling runner is the Running Trails Network, provided by the American Running and Fitness Association (1-800-776-ARFA). They have maps showing the best places to run in several cities. Some runners like to follow a map and a route. I like to make up my own courses. Put me in a new city and the first thing I need to do is to go for a run to scout my way around.
- Here are some tips I've learned the hard way over the years on book tours. When running, bring with

you the name, address, and phone number of the hotel or home you are staying in. Before running too far, note a landmark—tall building, lake, mountain—to serve as a guide during your exploration. The best bet is to run in a large loop where you keep your return point to the left or right at all times. Or, run in one direction, keeping track of the time, and turn around at the halfway point (say after 30 minutes). Carry money for a taxi in case you get hopelessly lost. Have fun!

THE RUNNER'S TRIANGLE: BALANCING RUNNING, WORK, AND FAMILY

Commit to challenging goals, but keep running in perspective. Balance the triangle of life: the physical side of running (body), the intellectual and career side (mind), and the spiritual and emotional side (soul). I call this "the runner's triangle." All runners have to play this balancing game; some are more responsible about it than others. Competitive running requires sacrifices. Running takes priority at times, especially when training for a marathon. Other times work or family become increasingly important and training is sacrificed. Try to maintain a reasonable balance. Any time you put too much emphasis on any side of the triangle, the other sides are negatively affected, perhaps damaged.

Work. Don't think you're the only runner that often thinks of their running while at work. All of us do. The trick is to keep our jobs so we can afford to run! Look at it positively. Your running program can help you be more productive at work. Research shows regular vigorous exercise improves creativity and mood. The self-esteem gained with running success also results in more confidence in career decisions.

But it can work the other way, too. If you are late to work, leave early, or take too long a lunch break to get in your running, you may not be too popular with your boss and fellow workers. If you are overtired from getting up early to run before work, or "hungover" from a hard workout or race, or chronically overtired from overtraining, you won't be as sharp on the job. One mistake many runners make is to talk too much about their running. Your boss and fellow workers may be impressed with your accomplishments and think highly of you as a result. Or, they may think the time and energy you devote to running interferes with your dedication to the job. So, even if you would rather be running than working, don't let on.

Often runners are faced with a difficult dilemma. Their work hours and stress keep eating into their ability to train. What to do? First, structure a routine that minimizes conflict, such as running in the morning before work. Take a good look at your work hours. How much of the extra time you're voluntarily spending at work is really necessary? Consider discussing your need for more flexible work time with your boss.

Some runners make the ultimate decision. If running is a very rewarding part of your life and your job is seriously interfering with this pleasure, look for a different job. It's probably stressing your family and social life, too. You have a right to be happy. I know of many runners that made this decision. Most, but not all, of them never regretted it. But don't think I'm encouraging you to be a running bum. The best solution is to find happiness and success in both your running and your career. It can be done.

Family. Are competitive running and relationships compatible? One poll of runners found that half of them admitted that their partners felt neglected. I'm sure kids feel that way, too. Work as much to keep others happy as you do with your running. Try to make family and friends into allies, a support group. Bring them along as cheerleaders at races; take them on exciting trips. The best way to win at the game is to be flexible, sharing your running interest while still accommodating household duties, baby-sitting, romantic dinners, and the like into your schedule. If your mate or kids have their own passionate hobby, support that in exchange. Be fair.

Shelly-lynn and I are lucky. We can fully share our running experiences since we train and race at similar paces. But if your significant other, friend, or child runs slower than you, don't be a show-off. Run with them, not ahead of them. Sacrifice your workout occasionally. Encourage them even if their motivation and skill isn't up to your standard. You're both runners but you've got little ones at home? Now you're talking about real cooperation. Take turns baby-sitting so each of you can make the most of your running, but schedule some time to run together. That may mean getting someone else to watch junior, or try baby stroller running (Chapter 40).

Most runners have their running schedules well integrated into other aspects of their lives, even making a positive contribution to their nonrunning side. Being "hooked" on running can be a big asset. But the line between positive and negative addiction can be thin. Some runners lose perspective altogether. Running becomes an end, not a means. The final stage of this negative addiction occurs when running becomes your job, when friends and loved ones take second place in your life, or when you cannot stop running even when faced with serious injury. If you have reached any of these points, you need to reexamine why you run, and get your life back into balance. Don't let the "runner's triangle" collapse on you and your loved ones in exchange for more mileage and faster times.

APPENDIX

1M	5K	5M	10K	10M	½ Mar	Mar
0:05:00	0:15:32	0:25:00	0:31:05	0:50:00	1:05:30	2:11:06
0:05:05	0:15:48	0:25:25	0:31:36	0:50:50	1:06:35	2:13:17
0:05:10	0:16:03	0:25:50	0:32:07	0:51:40	1:07:41	2:15:28
0:05:15	0:16:19	0:26:15	0:32:38	0:52:30	1:08:46	2:17:39
0:05:16	0:16:22	0:26:20	0:32:44	0:52:40	1:09:00	2:18:06
0:05:17	0:16:25	0:26:25	0:32:50	0:52:50	1:09:13	2:18:32
0:05:18	0:16:28	0:26:30	0:32:56	0:53:00	1:09:26	2:18:58
0:05:19	0:16:31	0:26:35	0:33:03	0:53:10	1:09:39	2:19:24
0:05:20	0:16:34	0:26:40	0:33:09	0:53:20	1:09:52	2:19:50
0:05:21	0:16:38	0:26:45	0:33:15	0:53:30	1:10:05	2:20:17
0:05:22	0:16:41	0:26:50	0:33:21	0:53:40	1:10:18	2:20:43
0:05:23	0:16:44	0:26:55	0:33:27	0:53:50	1:10:31	2:21:09
0:05:24	0:16:47	0;27:00	0:33:34	0:54:00	1:10:44	2:21:35
0:05:25	0:16:50	0:27:05	0:33:40	0:54:10	1:10:57	2:22:01
0:05:26	0:16:53	0:27:10	0:33:46	0:54:20	1:11:11	2:22:28
0:05:27	0:16:56	0:27:15	0:33:52	0:54:30	1:11:24	2:22:54
0:05:28	0:16:59	0:27:20	0:33:59	0:54:40	1:11:37	2:23:20
0:05:29	0:17:02	0:27:25	0:34:05	0:54:50	1:11:50	2:23:46
0:05:30	0:17:05	0:27:30	0:34:11	0:55:00	1:12:03	2:24:13
0:05:31	0:17:09	0:27:35	0:34:17	0:55:10	1:12:16	2:24:39
0:05:32	0:17:12	0:27:40	0:34:23	0:55:20	1:12:29	2:25:05
0:05:33	0:17:15	0:27:45	0:34:30	0;55:30	1:12:42	2:25:31
0:05:34	0:17:18	0:27:50	0:34:36	0:55:40	1:12:55	2:25:57
0:05:35	0:17:21	0:27:55	0:34:42	0:55:50	1:13:08	2:26:24
0:05:36	0:17:24	0:28:00	0:34:48	0:56:00	1:13:22	2:26:50
0:05:37	0:17:27	0:28:05	0:34:54	0:56:10	1:13:35	2:27:16
0:05:38	0:17:30	0:28:10	0:35:01	0:56:20	1:13:48	2:27:42
0:05:39	0:17:33	0:28:15	0:35:07	0:56:30	1:14:01	2:28:09
0:05:40	0:17:37	0:28:20	0:35:13	0:56:40	1:14:14	2:28:35
0:05:41	0:17:40	0:28:25	0:35:19	0:56:50	1:14:27	2:29:01

1M	5K	5M	10K	10M	½ Mar	Mar
0:05:42	0:17:43	0:28:30	0:35:26	0:57:00	1:14:40	2:29:27
0:05:43	0:17:46	0:28:35	0:35:32	0:57:10	1:14:53	2:29:53
0:05:44	0:17:49	0:28:40	0:35:38	0:57:20	1:15:06	2:30:20
0:05:45	0:17:52	0:28:45	0:35:44	0:57:30	1:15:20	2:30:46
0:05:46	0:17:55	0:28:50	0:35:50	0:57:40	1:15:33	2:31:12
0:05:47	0:17:58	0:28:55	0:35:57	0:57:50	1:15:46	2:31:38
0:05:48	0:18:01	0:29:00	0:36:03	0:58:00	1:15:59	2:32:05
0:05:49	0:18:05	0;29:05	0:36:09	0:58:10	1:16:12	2:32:31
0:05:50	0:18:08	0:29:10	0:36:15	0:58:20	1:16:25	2:32:57
0:05:51	0:18:11	0:29:15	0:36:21	0:58:30	1:16:38	2:33:23
0:05:52	0:18:14	0:29:20	0:36:28	0:58:40	1:16:51	2:33:49
0:05:53	0:18:17	0:29:25	0:36:34	0:58:50	1:17:04	2:34:16
0:05:54	0:18:20	0:29:30	0:36:40	0:59:00	1:17:17	2:34:42
0:05:55	0:18:23	0:29:35	0:36:46	0:59:10	1:17:31	2:35:08
0:05:56	0:18:26	0:29:40	0:36:53	0:59:20	1:17:44	2:35:34
0:05:57	0:18:29	0:29:45	0:36:59	0:59:30	1:17:57	2:36:01
0:05:58	0:18:32	0:29:50	0:37:05	0:59:40	1:18:10	2:36:27
0:05:59	0:18:36	0:29:55	0:37:11	0:59:50	1:18:23	2:36:53
0:06:00	0:18:39	0:30:00	0:37:17	1:00:00	1:18:36	2:37:19
0:06:01	0:18:42	0:30:05	0:37:24	1:00:10	1:18:49	2:37:45
0:06:02	0:18:45	0:30:10	0:37:30	1:00:20	1:19:02	2:38:12
0:06:03	0:18:48	0:30:15	0:37:36	1:00:30	1:19:15	2:38:38
0:06:04	0:18:51	0:30:20	0:37:42	1:00:40	1:19:28	2:39:04
0:06:05	0:18:54	0:30:25	0:37:48	1:00:50	1:19:42	2:39:30
0:06:06	0:18:57	0:30:30	0:37:55	1:01:00	1:19:55	2:39:57
0:06:07	0:19:00	0:30:35	0:38:01	1:01:10	1:20:08	2:40:23
0:06:08	0:19:04	0:30:40	0:38:07	1:01:20	1:20:21	2:40:49
0:06:09	0:19:07	0:30:45	0:38:13	1:01:30	1:20:34	2:41:15
0:06:10	0:19:10	0:30:50	0:38:20	1:01:40	1:20:47	2:41:41
0:06:11	0:19:13	0:30:55	0:38:26	1:01:50	1:21:00	2:42:08

1M	5K	5M	10K	10M	½ Mar	Mar
0:06:12	0:19:16	0:31:00	0:38:32	1:02:00	1:21:13	2:42:34
0:06:13	0:19:19	0:31:05	0:38:38	1:02:10	1:21:26	2:43:00
0:06:14	0:19:22	0:31:10	0:38:44	1:02:20	1:21:39	2:43:26
0:06:15	0:19:25	0:31:15	0:38:51	1:02:30	1:21:53	2:43:53
0:06:16	0:19:28	0:31:20	0:38:57	1:02:40	1:22:06	2:44:19
0:06:17	0:19:32	0:31:25	0:39:03	1:02:50	1:22:19	2:44:45
0:06:18	0:19:35	0:31:30	0:39:09	1:03:00	1:22:32	2:45:11
0:06:19	0:19:38	0:31:35	0:39:16	1:03:10	1:22:45	2:45:37
0:06:20	0:19:41	0:31:40	0:39:22	1:03:20	1:22:58	2:46:04
0:06:21	0:19:44	0:31:45	0:39:28	1:03:30	1:23:11	2:46:30
0:06:22	0:19:47	0:31:50	0:39:34	1:03:40	1:23:24	2:46:56
0:06:23	0:19:50	0:31:55	0:39:40	1:03:50	1:23:37	2:47:22
0:06:24	0:19:53	0:32:00	0:39:47	1:04:00	1:23:50	2:47:48
0:06:25	0:19:56	0:32:05	0:39:53	1:04:10	1:24:04	2:48:15
0:06:26	0:20:00	0:32:10	0:39:59	1:04:20	1:24:17	2:48:41
0:06:27	0:20:03	0:32:15	0:40:05	1:04:30	1:24:30	2:49:07
0:06:28	0:20:06	0:32:20	0:40:11	1:04:40	1:24:43	2:49:33
0:06:29	0:20:09	0:32:25	0:40:18	1:04:50	1:24:56	2:50:00
0:06:30	0:20:12	0:32:30	0:40:24	1:05:00	1:25:09	2:50:26
0:06:31	0:20:15	0:32:35	0:40:30	1:05:10	1:25:22	2:50:52
0:06:32	0:20:18	0:32:40	0:40:36	1:05:20	1:25:35	2:51:18
0:06:33	0:20:21	0:32:45	0:40:43	1:05:30	1:25:48	2:51:44
0:06:34	0:20:24	0:32:50	0:40:49	1:05:40	1:26:01	2:52:11
0:06:35	0:20:27	0:32:55	0:40:55	1:05:50	1:26:15	2:52:37
0:06:36	0:20:31	0:33:00	0:41:01	1:06:00	1:26:28	2:53:03
0:06:37	0:20:34	0:33:05	0:41:07	1:06:10	1:26:41	2:53:29
0:06:38	0:20:37	0:33:10	0:41:14	1:06:20	1:26:54	2:53:56
0:06:39	0:20:40	0:33:15	0:41:20	1:06:30	1:27:07	2:54:22
0:06:40	0:20:43	0:33:20	0:41:26	1:06:40	1:27:20	2:54:48
0:06:41	0:20:46	0:33:25	0:41:32	1:06:50	1:27:33	2:55:14

1M	5K	5M	10K	10M	½ Mar	Mar
0:06:42	0:20:49	0:33:30	0:41:38	1:07:00	1:27:46	2:55:40
0:06:43	0:20:52	0:33:35	0:41:45	1:07:10	1:27:59	2:56:07
0:06:44	0:20:55	0:33:40	0:41:51	1:07:20	1:28:12	2:56:33
0:06:45	0:20:59	0:33:45	0:41:57	1:07:30	1:28:26	2:56:59
0:06:46	0:21:02	0:33:50	0:42:03	1:07:40	1:28:39	2:57:25
0:06:47	0:21:05	0:33:55	0:42:10	1:07:50	1:28:52	2:57:52
0:06:48	0:21:08	0:34:00	0:42:16	1:08:00	1:29:05	2:58:18
0:06:49	0:21:11	0:34:05	0:42:22	1:08:10	1:29:18	2:58:44
0:06:50	0:21:14	0:34:10	0:42:28	1:08:20	1:29:31	2:59:10
0:06:51	0:21:17	0:34:15	0:42:34	1:08:30	1:29:44	2:59:36
0:06:52	0:21:20	0:34:20	0:42:41	1:08:40	1:29:57	3:00:03
0:06:53	0:21:23	0:34:25	0:42:47	1:08:50	1:30:10	3:00:29
0:06:54	0:21:27	0:34:30	0:42:53	1:09:00	1:30:23	3:00:55
0:06:55	0:21:30	0:34:35	0:42:59	1:09:10	1:30:37	3:01:21
0:06:56	0:21:33	0:34:40	0:43:05	1:09:20	1:30:50	3:01:48
0:06:57	0:21:36	0:34:45	0:43:12	1:09:30	1:31:03	3:02:14
0:06:58	0:21:39	0:34:50	0:43:18	1:09:40	1:31:16	3:02:40
0:06:59	0:21:42	0:34:55	0:43:24	1:09:50	1:31:29	3:03:06
0:07:00	0:21:45	0:35:00	0:43:30	1:10:00	1:31:42	3:03:32
0:07:01	0:21:48	0:35:05	0:43:37	1:10:10	1:31:55	3:03:59
0:07:02	0:21:51	0:35:10	0:43:43	1:10:20	1:32:08	3:04:25
0:07:03	0:21:54	0:35:15	0:43:49	1:10:30	1:32:21	3:04:51
0:07:04	0:21:58	0:35:20	0:43:55	1:10:40	1:32:34	3:05:17
0:07:05	0:22:01	0:35:25	0:44:01	1:10:50	1:32:48	3:05:44
0:07:06	0:22:04	0:35:30	0:44:08	1:11:00	1:33:01	3:06:10
0:07:07	0:22:07	0:35:35	0:44:14	1:11:10	1:33:14	3:06:36
0:07:08	0:22:10	0:35:40	0:44:20	1:11:20	1:33:27	3:07:02
0:07:09	0:22:13	0:35:45	0:44:26	1:11:30	1:33:40	3:07:28
0:07:10	0:22:16	0:35:50	0:44:32	1:11:40	1:33:53	3:07:55
0:07:11	0:22:19	0:35:55	0:44:39	1:11:50	1:34:06	3:08:21

1M	5K	5M	10K	10M	½ Mar	Mar
0:07:12	0:22:22	0:36:00	0:44:45	1:12:00	1:34:19	3:08:47
0:07:13	0:22:26	0:36:05	0:44:51	1:12:10	1:34:32	3:09:13
0:07:14	0:22:29	0:36:10	0:44:57	1:12:20	1:34:45	3:09:39
0:07:15	0:22:32	0:36:15	0:45:04	1:12:30	1:34:59	3:10:06
0:07:16	0:22:35	0:36:20	0:45:10	1:12:40	1:35:12	3:10:32
0:07:17	0:22:38	0:36:25	0:45:16	1:12:50	1:35:25	3:10:58
0:07:18	0:22:41	0:36:30	0:45:22	1:13:00	1:35:38	3:11:24
0:07:19	0:22:44	0:36:35	0:45:28	1:13:10	1:35:51	3:11:51
0:07:20	0:22:47	0:36:40	0:45:35	1:13:20	1:36:04	3:12:17
0:07:21	0:22:50	0:36:45	0:45:41	1:13:30	1:36:17	3:12:43
0:07:22	0:22:54	0:36:50	0:45:47	1:13:40	1:36:30	3:13:09
0:07:23	0:22:57	0:36:55	0:45:53	1:13:50	1:36:43	3:13:35
0:07:24	0:23:00	0:37:00	0:45:59	1:14:00	1:36:56	3:14:02
0:07:25	0:23:03	0:37:05	0:46:06	1:14:10	1:37:10	3:14:28
0:07:26	0:23:06	0:37:10	0:46:12	1:14:20	1:37:23	3:14:54
0:07:27	0:23:09	0:37:15	0:46:18	1:14:30	1:37:36	3:15:20
0:07:28	0:23:12	0:37:20	0:46:24	1:14:40	1:37:49	3:15:47
0:07:29	0:23:15	0:37:25	0:46:31	1:14:50	1:38:02	3:16:13
0:07:30	0:23:18	0:37:30	0:46:37	1:15:00	1:38:15	3:16:39
0:07:31	0:23:21	0:37:35	0:46:43	1:15:10	1:38:28	3:17:05
0:07:32	0:23:25	0:37:40	0:46:49	1:15:20	1:38:41	3:17:31
0:07:33	0:23:28	0:37:45	0:46:55	1:15:30	1:38:54	3:17:58
0:07:34	0:23:31	0:37:50	0:47:02	1:15:40	1:39:07	3:18:24
0:07:35	0:23:34	0:37:55	0:47:08	1:15:50	1:39:21	3:18:50
0:07:36	0:23:37	0:38:00	0:47:14	1:16:00	1:39:34	3:19:16
0:07:37	0:23:40	0:38:05	0:47:20	1:16:10	1:39:47	3:19:43
0:07:38	0:23:43	0:38:10	0:47:26	1:16:20	1:40:00	3:20:09
0:07:39	0:23:46	0:38:15	0:47:33	1:16:30	1:40:13	3:20:35
0:07:40	0:23:49	0:38:20	0:47:39	1:16:40	1:40:26	3:21:01
0:07:41	0:23:53	0:38:25	0:47:45	1:16:50	1:40:39	3:21:27

1M	5K	5M	10K	10M	½ Mar	Mar
0:07:42	0:23:56	0:38:30	0:47:51	1:17:00	1:40:52	3:21:54
0:07:43	0:23:59	0:38:35	0:47:58	1:17:10	1:41:05	3:22:20
0:07:44	0:24:02	0:38:40	0:48:04	1:17:20	1:41:18	3:22:46
0:07:45	0:24:05	0:38:45	0:48:10	1:17:30	1:41:32	3:23:12
0:07:46	0:24:08	0:38:50	0:48:16	1:17:40	1:41:45	3:23:39
0:07:47	0:24:11	0:38:55	0:48:22	1:17:50	1:41:58	3:24:05
0:07:48	0:24:14	0:39:00	0:48:29	1:18:00	1:42:11	3:24:31
0:07:49	0:24:17	0:39:05	0:48:35	1:18:10	1:42:24	3:24:57
0:07:50	0:24:21	0:39:10	0:48:41	1:18:20	1:42:37	3:25:23
0:07:51	0:24:24	0:39:15	0:48:47	1:18:30	1:42:50	3:25:50
0:07:52	0:24:27	0:39:20	0:48:53	1:18:40	1:43:03	3:26:16
0:07:53	0:24:30	0:39:25	0:49:00	1:18:50	1:43:16	3:26:42
0:07:54	0:24:33	0:39:30	0:49:06	1:19:00	1:43:29	3:27:08
0:07:55	0:24:36	0:39:35	0:49:12	1:19:10	1:43:43	3:27:35
0:07:56	0:24:39	0:39:40	0:49:18	1:19:20	1:43:56	3:28:01
0:07:57	0:24:42	0:39:45	0:49:25	1:19:30	1:44:09	3:28:27
0:07:58	0:24:45	0:39:50	0:49:31	1:19:40	1:44:22	3:28:53
0:07:59	0:24:49	0:39:55	0:49:37	1:19:50	1:44:35	3:29:19
0:08:00	0:24:52	0:40:00	0:49:43	1:20:00	1:44:48	3:29:46
0:08:01	0:24:55	0:40:05	0:49:49	1:20:10	1:45:01	3:30:12
0:08:02	0:24:58	0:40:10	0:49:56	1:20:20	1:45:14	3:30:38
0:08:03	0:25:01	0:40:15	0:50:02	1:20:30	1:45:27	3:31:04
0:08:04	0:25:04	0:40:20	0:50:08	1:20:40	1:45:40	3:31:30
0:08:05	0:25:07	0:40:25	0:50:14	1:20:50	1:45:54	3:31:57
0:08:06	0:25:10	0:40:30	0:50:21	1:21:00	1:46:07	3:32:23
0:08:07	0:25:13	0:40:35	0:50:27	1:21:10	1:46:20	3:32:49
0:08:08	0:25:16	0:40:40	0:50:33	1:21:20	1:46:33	3:33:15
0:08:09	0:25:20	0:40:45	0:50:39	1:21:30	1:46:46	3:33:42
0:08:10	0:25:23	0:40:50	0:50:45	1:21:40	1:46:59	3:34:08
0:08:11	0:25:26	0:40:55	0:50:52	1:21:50	1:47:12	3:34:34

1M	5K	5M	10K	10M	½ Mar	Mar
0:08:12	0:25:29	0:41:00	0:50:58	1:22:00	1:47:25	3:35:00
0:08:13	0:25:32	0:41:05	0:51:04	1:22:10	1:47:38	3:35:26
0:08:14	0:25:35	0:41:10	0:51:10	1:22:20	1:47:51	3:35:53
0:08:15	0:25:38	0:41:15	0:51:16	1:22:30	1:48:05	3:36:19
0:08:16	0:25:41	0:41:20	0:51:23	1:22:40	1:48:18	3:36:45
0:08:17	0:25:44	0:41:25	0:51:29	1:22:50	1:48:31	3:37:11
0:08:18	0:25:48	0:41:30	0:51:35	1:23:00	1:48:44	3:37:38
0:08:19	0:25:51	0:41:35	0:51:41	1:23:10	1:48:57	3:38:04
0:08:20	0:25:54	0:41:40	0:51:48	1:23:20	1:49:10	3:38:30
0:08:21	0:25:57	0:41:45	0:51:54	1:23:30	1:49:23	3:38:56
0:08:22	0:26:00	0:41:50	0:52:00	1:23:40	1:49:36	3:39:22
0:08:23	0:26:03	0:41:55	0:52:06	1:23:50	1:49:49	3:39:49
0:08:24	0:26:06	0:42:00	0:52:12	1:24:00	1:50:02	3:40:15
0:08:25	0:26:09	0:42:05	0:52:19	1:24:10	1:50:16	3:40:41
0:08:26	0:26:12	0:42:10	0:52:25	1:24:20	1:50:29	3:41:07
0:08:27	0:26:16	0:42:15	0:52:31	1:24:30	1:50:42	3:41:34
0:08:28	0:26:19	0:42:20	0:52:37	1:24:40	1:50:55	3:42:00
0:08:29	0:26:22	0:42:25	0:52:43	1:24:50	1:51:08	3:42:26
0:08:30	0:26:25	0:42:30	0:52:50	1:25:00	1:51:21	3:42:52
0:08:31	0:26:28	0:42:35	0:52:56	1:25:10	1:51:34	3:43:18
0:08:32	0:26:31	0:42:40	0:53:02	1:25:20	1:51:47	3:43:45
0:08:33	0:26:34	0:42:45	0:53:08	1:25:30	1:52:00	3:44:11
0:08:34	0:26:37	0:42:50	0:53:15	1:25:40	1:52:13	3:44:37
0:08:35	0:26:40	0:42:55	0:53:21	1:25:50	1:52:27	3:45:03
0:08:36	0:26:43	0:43:00	0:53:27	1:26:00	1:52:40	3:45:30
0:08:37	0:26:47	0:43:05	0:53:33	1:26:10	1:52:53	3:45:56
0:08:38	0:26:50	0:43:10	0:53:39	1:26:20	1:53:06	3:46:22
0:08:39	0:26:53	0:43:15	0:53:46	1:26:30	1:53:19	3:46:48
0:08:40	0:26:56	0:43:20	0:53:52	1:26:40	1:53:32	3:47:14
0:08:41	0:26:59	0:43:25	0:53:58	1:26:50	1:53:45	3:47:41

1M	5K	5M	10K	10M	½ Mar	Mar
0:08:42	0:27:02	0:43:30	0:54:04	1:27:00	1:53:58	3:48:07
0:08:43	0:27:05	0:43:35	0:54:10	1:27:10	1:54:11	3:48:33
0:08:44	0:27:08	0:43:40	0:54:17	1:27:20	1:54:24	3:48:59
0:08:45	0:27:11	0:43:45	0:54:23	1:27:30	1:54:38	3:49:26
0:08:46	0:27:15	0:43:50	0:54:29	1:27:40	1:54:51	3:49:52
0:08:47	0:27:18	0:43:55	0:54:35	1:27:50	1:55:04	3:50:18
0:08:48	0:27:21	0:44:00	0:54:42	1:28:00	1:55:17	3:50:44
0:08:49	0:27:24	0:44:05	0:54:48	1:18:10	1:55:30	3:51:10
0:08:50	0:27:27	0:44:10	0:54:54	1:28:20	1:55:43	3:51:37
0:08:51	0:27:30	0:44:15	0:55:00	1:28:30	1:55:56	3:52:03
0:08:52	0:27:33	0:44:20	0:55:06	1:28:40	1:56:09	3:52:29
0:08:53	0:27:36	0:44:25	0:55:13	1:28:50	1:56:22	3:52:55
0:08:54	0:27:39	0:44:30	0:55:19	1:29:00	1:56:35	3:53:21
0:08:55	0:27:43	0:44:35	0:55:25	1:29:10	1:56:49	3:53:48
0:08:56	0:27:46	0:44:40	0:55:31	1:29:20	1:57:02	3:54:14
0:08:57	0:27:49	0:44:45	0:55:37	1:29:30	1:57:15	3:54:40
0:08:58	0:27:52	0:44:50	0:55:44	1:29:40	1:57:28	3:55:06
0:08:59	0:27:55	0:44:55	0:55:50	1:29:50	1:57:41	3:55:33
0:09:00	0:27:58	0:45:00	0:55:56	1:30:00	1:57:54	3:55:59
0:09:01	0:28:01	0:45:05	0:56:02	1:30:10	1:58:07	3:56:25
0:09:02	0:28:04	0:45:10	0:56:09	1:30:20	1:58:20	3:56:51
0:09:03	0:28:07	0:45:15	0:56:15	1:30:30	1:58:33	3:57:17
0:09:04	0:28:10	0:45:20	0:56:21	1:30:40	1:58:46	3:57:44
0:09:05	0:28:14	0:45:25	0:56:27	1:30:50	1:59:00	3:58:10
0:09:06	0:28:17	0:45:30	0:56:33	1:31:00	1:59:13	3:58:36
0:09:07	0:28:20	0:45:35	0:56:40	1:31:10	1:59:26	3:59:02
0:09:08	0:28:23	0:45:40	0:56:46	1:31:20	1:59:39	3:59:29
0:09:09	0:28:26	0:45:45	0:56:52	1:31:30	1:59:52	3:59:55
0:09:10	0:28:29	0:45:50	0:56:58	1:31:40	2:00:05	4:00:21
0:09:11	0:28:32	0:45:55	0:57:04	1:31:50	2:00:18	4:00:47

1M	5K	5M	10K	10M	½ Mar	Mar
0:09:12	0:28:35	0:46:00	0:57:11	1:32:00	2:00:31	4:01:13
0:09:13	0:28:38	0:46:05	0:57:17	1:32:10	2:00:44	4:01:40
0:09:14	0:28:42	0:46:10	0:57:23	1:32:20	2:00:57	4:02:06
0:09:15	0:28:45	0:46:15	0:57:29	1:32:30	2:01:11	4:02:32
0:09:16	0:28:48	0:46:20	0:57:36	1:32:40	2:01:24	4:02:58
0:09:17	0:28:51	0:46:25	0:57:42	1:32:50	2:01:37	4:03:25
0:09:18	0:28:54	0:46:30	0:57:48	1:33:00	2:01:50	4:03:51
0:09:19	0:28:57	0:46:35	0:57:54	1:33:10	2:02:03	4:04:17
0:09:20	0:29:00	0:46:40	0:58:00	1:33:20	2:02:16	4:04:43
0:09:21	0:29:03	0:46:45	0:58:07	1:33:30	2:02:29	4:05:09
0:09:22	0:29:06	0:46:50	0:58:13	1:33:40	2:02:42	4:05:36
0:09:23	0:29:10	0:46:55	0:58:19	1:33:50	2:02:55	4:06:02
0:09:24	0:29:13	0:47:00	0:58:25	1:34:00	2:03:08	4:06:28
0:09:25	0:29:16	0:47:05	0:58:31	1:34:10	2:03:22	4:06:54
0:09:26	0:29:19	0:47:10	0:58:38	1:34:20	2:03:35	4:07:21
0:09:27	0:29:22	0:47:15	0:58:44	1:34:30	2:03:48	4:07:47
0:09:28	0:29:25	0:47:20	0:58:50	1:34:40	2:04:01	4:08:13
0:09:29	0:29:28	0:47:25	0:58:56	1:34:50	2:04:14	4:08:39
0:09:30	0:29:31	0:47:30	0:59:03	1:35:00	2:04:27	4:09:05
0:09:31	0:29:34	0:47:35	0:59:09	1:35:10	2:04:40	4:09:32
0:09:32	0:29:38	0:47:40	0:59:15	1:35:20	2:04:53	4:09:58
0:09:33	0:29:41	0:47:45	0:59:21	1:35:30	2:05:06	4:10:24
0:09:34	0:29:44	0:47:50	0:59:27	1:35:40	2:05:19	4:10:50
0:09:35	0:29:47	0:47:55	0:59:34	1:35:50	2:05:33	4:11:17
0:09:36	0:29:50	0:48:00	0:59:40	1:36:00	2:05:46	4:11:43
0:09:37	0:29:53	0:48:05	0:59:46	1:36:10	2:05:59	4:12:09
0:09:38	0:29:56	0:48:10	0:59:52	1:36:20	2:06:12	4:12:35
0:09:39	0:29:59	0:48:15	0:59:59	1:36:30	2:06:25	4:13:01
0:09:40	0:30:02	0:48:20	1:00:05	1:36:40	2:06:38	4:13:28
0:09:41	0:30:05	0:48:25	1:00:11	1:36:50	2:06:51	4:13:54

1M	5K	5M	10K	10M	½ Mar	Mar
0:09:42	0:30:09	0:48:30	1:00:17	1:37:00	2:07:04	4:14:20
0:09:43	0:30:12	0:48:35	1:00:23	1:37:10	2:07:17	4:14:46
0:09:44	0:30:15	0:48:40	1:00:30	1:37:20	2:07:30	4:15:12
0:09:45	0:30:18	0:48:45	1:00:36	1:37:30	2:07:44	4:15:39
0:09:46	0:30:21	0:48:50	1:00:42	1:37:40	2:07:57	4:16:05
0:09:47	0:30:24	0:48:55	1:00:48	1:37:50	2:08:10	4:16:31
0:09:48	0:30:27	0:49:00	1:00:54	1:38:00	2:08:23	4:16:57
0:09:49	0:30:30	0:49:05	1:01:01	1:38:10	2:08:36	4:17:24
0:09:50	0:30:33	0:49:10	1:01:07	1:38:20	2:08:49	4:17:50
0:09:51	0:30:37	0:49:15	1:01:13	1:38:30	2:09:02	4:18:16
0:09:52	0:30:40	0:49:20	1:01:19	1:38:40	2:09:15	4:18:42
0:09:53	0:30:43	0:49:25	1:01:26	1:38:50	2:09:28	4:19:08
0:09:54	0:30:46	0:49:30	1:01:32	1:39:00	2:09:41	4:19:35
0:09:55	0:30:49	0:49:35	1:01:38	1:39:10	2:09:55	4:20:01
0:09:56	0:30;52	0:49:40	1:01:44	1:39:20	2:10:08	4:20:27
0:09:57	0:30:55	0:49:45	1:01:50	1:39:30	2:10:21	4:20:53
0:09:58	0:30:58	0:49:50	1:01:57	1:39:40	2:10:34	4:21:20
0:09:59	0:31:01	0:49:55	1:02:03	1:39:50	2:10:47	4:21:46
0:10:00	0:31:05	0:50:00	1:02:09	1:40:00	2:11:00	4:22:12
0:10:01	0:31:08	0:50:05	1:02:15	1:40:10	2:11:13	4:22:38
0:10:02	0:31:11	0:50:10	1:02:21	1:40:20	2:11:26	4:23:04
0:10:03	0:31:14	0:50:15	1:02:28	1:40:30	2:11:39	4:23:31
0:10:04	0:31:17	0:50:20	1:02;34	1:40:40	2:11:52	4:23:51
0:10:05	0:31:20	0:50:25	1:02:40	1:40:50	2:12:06	4:24:23
0:10:06	0:31:23	0:50:30	1:02:46	1:41:00	2:12:19	4:24:49
0:10:07	0:31:26	0:50:35	1:02:53	1:41:10	2:12:32	4:25:16
0:10:08	0:31:29	0:50:40	1:02:59	1:41:20	2:12:45	4:25:42
0:10:09	0:31:32	0:50:45	1:03:05	1:41:30	2:12:58	4:26:08
0:10:10	0:31:36	0:50:50	1:03:11	1:41:40	2:13:11	4:26:34
0:10:11	0:31:39	0:50:55	1:03:17	1:41:50	2:13:24	4:27:00

1M	5K	5M	10K	10M	½ Mar	Mar
0:10:12	0:31:42	0:51:00	1:03:24	1:42:00	2:13:37	4:27:27
0:10:13	0:31:45	0:51:05	1:03:30	1:42:10	2:13:50	4:27:53
0:10:14	0:31:48	0:51:10	1:03:36	1:42:20	2:14:03	4:28:19
0:10:15	0:31:51	0:51:15	1:03:42	1:42:30	2:14:17	4:28:45
0:10:16	0:31:54	0:51:20	1:03:48	1:42:40	2:14:30	4:29:12
0:10:17	0:31:57	0:51:25	1:03:55	1:42:50	2:14:43	4:29:38
0:10:18	0:32:00	0:51:30	1:04:01	1:43:00	2:14:56	4:30:04
0:10:19	0:32:04	0:51:35	1:04:07	1:43:10	2:15:09	4:30:30
0:10:20	0:32:07	0:51:40	1:04:13	1:43:20	2:15:22	4:30:56
0:10:21	0:32:10	0:51:45	1:04:20	1:43:30	2:15:35	4:31:23
0:10:22	0:32:13	0:51:50	1:04:26	1:43:40	2:15:48	4:31:49
0:10:23	0:32:16	0:51:55	1:04:32	1:43:50	2:16:01	4:32:15
0:10:24	0:32:19	0:52:00	1:04:38	1:44:00	2:16:14	4:32:41
0:10:25	0:32:22	0:52:05	1:04:44	1:44:10	2:16:28	4:33:08
0:10:26	0:32:25	0:52:10	1:04:51	1:44:20	2:16:41	4:33:34
0:10:27	0:32:28	0:52:15	1:04:57	1:44:30	2:16:54	4:34:00
0:10:28	0:32:32	0:52:20	1:05:03	1:44:40	2:17:07	4:34:26
0:10:29	0:32:35	0:52:25	1:05:09	1:44:50	2:17:20	4:34:52
0:10:30	0:32:38	0:52:30	1:05:15	1:45:00	2:17:33	4:35:19
0:10:31	0:32:41	0:52:35	1:05:22	1:45:10	2:17:46	4:35:45
0:10:32	0:32:44	0:52:40	1:05:28	1:45:20	2:17:59	4:36:11
0:10:33	0:32:47	0:52:45	1:05:34	1:45:30	2:18:12	4:36:37
0:10:34	0:32:50	0:52:50	1:05:40	1:45:40	2:18:25	4:37:03
0:10:35	0:32:53	0:52:55	1:05:47	1:45:50	2:18:39	4:37:30
0:10:36	0:32:56	0:53:00	1:05:53	1:46:00	2:18:52	4:37:56
0:10:37	0:32:59	0:53:05	1:05:59	1:46:10	2:19:05	4:38:22
0:10:38	0:33:03	0:53:10	1:06:05	1:46:20	2:19:18	4:38:48
0:10:39	0:33:06	0:53:15	1:06:11	1:46:30	2:19:31	4:39:15
0:10:40	0:33:09	0:53:20	1:06:18	1:46:40	2:19:44	4:39:41
0:10:41	0:33:12	0:53:25	1:06:24	1:46:50	2:19:57	4:40:07

1M	5K	5M	10K	10M	½ Mar	Mar
0:10:42	0:33:15	0:53:30	1:06:30	1:47:00	2:20:10	4:40:33
0:10:43	0:33:18	0:53:35	1:06:36	1:47:10	2:20:23	4:40:59
0:10:44	0:33:21	0:53:40	1:06:42	1:47:20	2:20:36	4:41:26
0:10:45	0:33:24	0:53:45	1:06:49	1:47:30	2:20:50	4:41:52
0:10:46	0:33:27	0:53:50	1:06:55	1:47:40	2:21:03	4:42:18
0:10:47	0:33:31	0:53:55	1:07:01	1:47:50	2:21:16	4:42:44
0:10:48	0:33:34	0:54:00	1:07:07	1:48:00	2:21:29	4:43:11
0:10:49	0:33:37	0:54:05	1:07:14	1:48:10	2:21:42	4:43:37
0:10:50	0:33:40	0:54:10	1:07:20	1:48:20	2:21:55	4:44:03
0:10:51	0:33:43	0:54:15	1:07:26	1:49:30	2:22:06	4:44:29
0:10:52	0:33:46	0:54:20	1:07:32	1:48:40	2:22:21	4:44:55
0:10:53	0:33:49	0:54:25	1:07:38	1:48:50	2:22:34	4:45:22
0:10:54	0:33:52	0:54:30	1:07:45	1:49:00	2:22:47	4:45:48
0:10:55	0:33:55	0:54:35	1:07:51	1:49:10	2:23:01	4:46:14
0:10:56	0:33:59	0:54:40	1:07:57	1:49:20	2:23:14	4:46:40
0:10:57	0:34:02	0:54:45	1:08:03	1:49:30	2:23:27	4:47:07
0:10:58	0:34:05	0:54:50	1:08:09	1:49:40	2:23:40	4:47:33
0:10:59	0:34:08	0:54:55	1:08:16	1:49:50	2:23:53	4:47:59
0:11:00	0:34:11	0:55:00	1:08:22	1:50:00	2:24:06	4:48:25

Index